SOURCES AND METHODS
LABOUR STATISTICS
VOLUME 3
ECONOMICALLY ACTIVE POPULATION, EMPLOYMENT, UNEMPLOYMENT AND HOURS OF WORK (HOUSEHOLD SURVEYS)

THIRD EDITION

SOURCES ET MÉTHODES
STATISTIQUES DU TRAVAIL
VOLUME 3
POPULATION ACTIVE, EMPLOI, CHÔMAGE ET DURÉE DU TRAVAIL (ENQUÊTES AUPRÈS DES MÉNAGES)

TROISIÈME ÉDITION

FUENTES Y METODOS
ESTADISTICAS DEL TRABAJO
VOLUMEN 3
POBLACION ECONOMICAMENTE ACTIVA, EMPLEO, DESEMPLEO Y HORAS DE TRABAJO (ENCUESTAS DE HOGARES)

TERCERA EDICION

SOURCES AND METHODS
LABOUR STATISTICS
VOLUME 3
ECONOMICALLY ACTIVE POPULATION, EMPLOYMENT, UNEMPLOYMENT AND HOURS OF WORK (HOUSEHOLD SURVEYS)

Companion to the *Yearbook of Labour Statistics*

THIRD EDITION

SOURCES ET MÉTHODES
STATISTIQUES DU TRAVAIL
VOLUME 3
POPULATION ACTIVE, EMPLOI, CHÔMAGE ET DURÉE DU TRAVAIL (ENQUÊTES AUPRÈS DES MÉNAGES)

Complément de l'*Annuaire des statistiques du travail*

TROISIÈME ÉDITION

FUENTES Y METODOS
ESTADISTICAS DEL TRABAJO
VOLUMEN 3
POBLACION ECONOMICAMENTE ACTIVA, EMPLEO, DESEMPLEO Y HORAS DE TRABAJO (ENCUESTAS DE HOGARES)

Complemento del *Anuario de Estadísticas del Trabajo*

TERCERA EDICION

INTERNATIONAL LABOUR OFFICE GENEVA
BUREAU INTERNATIONAL DU TRAVAIL GENÈVE
OFICINA INTERNACIONAL DEL TRABAJO GINEBRA

ISBN 92-2-011375-9
(the set of 2 volumes)
ISSN 0084-3857

This volume :
ISBN 92-2-012053-4
ISSN 1014-9856

Third edition 2004

ISBN 92-2-011375-9
(le jeu de 2 volumes)
ISSN 0084-3857

Ce volume :
ISBN 92-2-012053-4
ISSN 1014-9856

Troisième édition 2004

ISBN 92-2-011375-9
(el juego de 2 volúmenes)
ISSN 0084-3857

Este volumen :
ISBN 92-2-012053-4
ISSN 1014-9856

Tercera edición 2004

The designations employed in ILO publications, which are in conformity with United Nations practice, and the presentation of material therein do not imply the expression of any opinion whatsoever on the part of the International Labour Office concerning the legal status of any country, area or territory or of its authorities, or concerning the delimitation of its frontiers. The responsibility for opinions expressed in signed articles, studies and other contributions rests solely with their authors, and publication does not constitute an endorsement by the International Labour Office of the opinions expressed in them.

Reference to names of firms and commercial products and processes does not imply their endorsement by the International Labour Office, and any failure to mention a particular firm, commercial product or process is not a sign of disapproval.

ILO publications can be obtained through major booksellers or ILO local offices in many countries, or direct from ILO Publications, International Labour Office, CH-1211 Geneva 22, Switzerland. A catalogue or list of new publications will be sent free of charge from the above address.

Les désignations utilisées dans les publications du BIT, qui sont conformes à la pratique des Nations Unies, et la présentation des données qui y figurent n'impliquent de la part du Bureau international du Travail aucune prise de position quant au statut juridique de tel ou tel pays, zone ou territoire, ou de ses autorités, ni quant au tracé de ses frontières. Les articles, études et autres textes signés n'engagent que leurs auteurs et leur publication ne signifie pas que le Bureau international du Travail souscrit aux opinions qui y sont exprimées. La mention ou la non-mention de telle ou telle entreprise ou de tel ou tel produit ou procédé commercial n'implique de la part du Bureau international du Travail aucune appréciation favorable ou défavorable.

Les publications du Bureau international du Travail peuvent être obtenues dans les principales librairies ou auprès des bureaux locaux du BIT. On peut aussi se les procurer directement, de même qu'un catalogue ou une liste des nouvelles publications, à l'adresse suivante: Publications du BIT, Bureau international du Travail, CH-1211 Genève 22, Suisse.

Las denominaciones empleadas, en concordancia con la práctica seguida en las Naciones Unidas, y la forma en que aparecen presentados los datos en esta publicación no implican juicio alguno por parte de la Oficina Internacional del Trabajo sobre la condición jurídica de ninguno de los países, zonas o territorios citados o de sus autoridades, ni respecto de la delimitación de sus fronteras. La responsabilidad de las opiniones expresadas en los artículos, estudios y otras colaboraciones firmados incumbe exclusivamente a sus autores, y su publicación no significa que la OIT las sanciona.

Las referencias a firmas o a procesos o productos comerciales no implican aprobación alguna por la Oficina Internacional del Trabajo, y el hecho de que no se mencionen firmas o procesos o productos comerciales no implica desaprobación alguna.

Las publicaciones de la OIT pueden obtenerse en las principales librerías o en oficinas locales de la OIT en muchos países o pidiéndolas a: Publicaciones de la OIT, Oficina Internacional del Trabajo, CH-1211 Ginebra 22, Suiza, que también puede enviar a quienes lo soliciten un catálogo o una lista de nuevas publicaciones.

Printed in India

Imprimé en Inde

Impreso en India

AJA

Important

• In order to enhance the usefulness of the *Yearbook of Labour Statistics,* each issue is now accompanied by a methodological volume of the series *Sources and Methods: Labour Statistics* (formerly entitled *Statistical Sources and Methods*).

• This series provides methodological descriptions of the data published in the *Yearbook* and *Bulletin of Labour Statistics.* Each volume covers different subjects according to the source of the data; gradually, all the subjects in the *Yearbook* will be covered by a volume in this series.

• The methodological descriptions include information on the method of data collection, coverage, concepts and definitions, classifications, historical changes, technical references, etc. In each volume the information is presented by country under standard headings.

Important

• Afin de mettre en valeur l'utilité de l'*Annuaire des statistiques du travail,* chaque édition est maintenant accompagnée d'un volume méthodologique de la série *Sources et méthodes: statistiques du travail* (intitulée précédemment *Sources et méthodes statistiques*).

• Cette série fournit des descriptions méthodologiques des données publiées dans l'*Annuaire* et dans le *Bulletin des statistiques du travail.* Chaque volume traite de sujets différents suivant la source des données; progessivement, tous les sujets traités dans l'*Annuaire* seront couverts.

• Les descriptions méthodologiques contiennent des informations sur la méthode de collecte des données, la portée, les concepts et définitions, les classifications, les modifications apportées aux séries, les références techniques, etc. Dans chaque volume, les informations sont présentées par pays sous des rubriques standardisées.

Importante

• Con el fin de mejorar la utilidad del *Anuario de Estadísticas del Trabajo,* ahora cada edición va acompañada de un volumen metodológico de la serie *Fuentes y Métodos: Estadísticas del Trabajo* (titulada anteriormente *Fuentes y Métodos Estadísticos*).

• Esta serie proporciona las descripciones metodológicas de los datos que se publican en el *Anuario* y el *Boletín de Estadistícas del Trabajo.* Cada volumen abarca diferentes temas del *Anuario* de acuerdo con la fuente de los datos.

• Las descripciones metodológicas incluyen informaciones acerca del método de recolección de datos, el alcance, los conceptos y definiciones, las clasificaciones, los cambios históricos, las referencias técnicas, etc. En cada volumen, la información se presenta por país de acuerdo a encabezamientos estándar.

Preface

This new edition of Volume 3 of the series of Sources and Methods: Labour statistics is a revised and enlarged version of the second one published in 1990.

The other published volumes of the series are:

Volume 1: Consumer price indices (third edition, Geneva, 1992).

Volume 2: Employment, wages, hours of work and labour cost (establishment surveys) (second edition, Geneva, 1995).

Volume 4: Employment, unemployment, wages and hours of work (administrative records and related sources) (first edition, Geneva, 1989).

Volume 5: Total and economically active population, employment and unemployment (population censuses) (second edition, Geneva, 1996).

Volume 6: Household income and expenditure surveys (first edition, Geneva, 1994).

Volume 7: Strikes and lockouts (first edition, Geneva, 1993).

Volume 8: Occupational injuries (first edition, Geneva, 1999).

Volume 9: Transition countries (Geneva, 1999).

Volume 10: Estimates and projections of the economically active population 1950-2010 (first edition, Geneva, 2000).

The purpose of these volumes is to document national practices used in the collection of various types of labour statistics, in order to assist the users of these statistics in evaluating their quality and comparability, and their suitability for particular needs.

Sources and Methods: Labour statistics can consequently be seen as companion volumes to the various chapters of the ILO Yearbook of Labour Statistics and Bulletin of Labour Statistics.

The methodological descriptions presented in this volume cover labor force surveys and related household surveys (or individuals) from which statistics of the economically active population, employment, unemployment, underemployment, hours of work, employment-related income, informal sector employment, usual activity, etc. are collected. Methodological information relating to other countries will be made available on the dissemination website of the ILO Bureau of Statistics:
http://laborsta.ilo.org/.

Furthermore, due to other technical reasons some descriptions have not been translated in the other languages: descriptions relating to Belgium, France, Morocco and Switzerland and those relating to Brazil, Colombia, Chile, Mexico, Panama and Peru are not yet translated in English. Translations will be made available on this site in the near future.

This volume was produced by the ILO Bureau of Statistics.

Préface

Cette nouvelle édition du Volume 3 de la série Sources et Méthodes: statistiques du travail est la révision et l'actualisation de la deuxième édition publiée en 1991 sous forme de Document de travail.

Les autres volumes publiés dans cette série sont les suivants :

Volume 1: Indice des prix à la consommation (troisième édition, Genève 1992).

Volume 2: Emploi, salaires, durée du travail et coût de la main-d'œuvre (enquêtes auprès des établissements) (deuxième édition, Genève, 1995).

Volume 4: Emploi, chômage, salaires et durée du travail (documents administratifs et sources assimilées) (première édition, Genève, 1989).

Volume 5: Population totale et population active, emploi et chômage (recensements de population) (deuxième édition, Genève, 1996).

Volume 6: Enquêtes sur le revenu et les dépenses des ménages (première édition, Genève, 1994).

Volume 7: Grèves et lock-out (première édition, Genève, 1993).

Volume 8: Lésions professionnelles (première édition, Genève, 1999).

Volume 9: Pays en transition (Genève, 1999).

Volume 10: Evaluations et projections de la population active 1950-2010 (première édition, Genève, 2000).

Ces volumes ont pour but de renseigner sur les pratiques nationales appliquées pour établir différentes statistiques du travail, et d'aider ainsi les utilisateurs à en apprécier la qualité, la comparabilité et la valeur pour des besoins différents.

On peut donc voir dans les volumes de Sources et Méthodes: statistiques du travail un complément aux divers chapitres de l'Annuaire des statistiques du travail et du Bulletin des statistiques du travail du BIT.

Les descriptions méthodologiques présentées dans ce volume couvrent les enquêtes sur la main-d'œuvre et les enquêtes connexes réalisées auprès des ménages (ou des personnes), à partir desquelles sont établies les statistiques de la population active, de l'emploi, du chômage, du sous-emploi, de la durée du travail, du revenu lié à l'emploi, de l'emploi dans le secteur informel, de l'activité habituelle, etc. Les descriptions méthodologiques relatives à d'autres pays seront disséminées ultérieurement sur le site de diffusion de données du Bureau de statistique:
http://laborsta.ilo.org/.

En outre, pour des raisons techniques quelques descriptions n'ont pas été traduites dans les autres langues: les descriptions relatives au Brésil, à la Colombie, au Chili, Mexique, Panama et Pérou n'ont pas encore été traduites en français. Ces traductions seront disséminées prochainement sur ce site.

Ce volume a été réalisé par le Bureau de statistique du BIT.

Prefacio

Esta nueva edición del Volumen 3 de la serie Fuentes y Métodos: estadísticas del trabajo es la actualización y ampliación de la segunda edición publicada en 1992 como Documento de trabajo.

Los otros volúmenes de esta serie son:

Volumen 1: Indices de los precios del consumo (tercera edición, Ginebra, 1992).

Volumen 2: Empleo, salarios, horas de trabajo, y costo de la mano de obra (encuestas de establecimientos) (segunda edición, Ginebra, 1995).

Volumen 4: Empleo, desempleo, salarios y horas de trabajo (registros administrativos y fuentes conexas) (primera edición, Ginebra, 1989).

Volumen 5: Población total y población económicamente activa, empleo y desempleo (censos de población) (segunda edición, Ginebra, 1996).

Volumen 6: Encuestas de ingresos y gastos de los hogares ((primera edición, Ginebra, 1994).

Volumen 7: Huelgas y cierres patronales (primera edición, Ginebra, 1993).

Volumen 8: Lesiones profesionales (primera edición, Ginebra, 1999).

Volumen 9: Países en transición (Ginebra, 1999).

Volumen 10: Evaluaciones y proyecciones de la población económicamente activa 1950-2010 (primera edición, Ginebra, 2000).

El objetivo de estas publicaciones consiste en documentar las prácticas nacionales seguidas para recopilar los diferentes tipos de estadísticas del trabajo y ayudar a los usuarios a evaluar su calidad y comparabilidad, así como su adecuación a las necesidades diferentes.

Las Fuentes y Métodos: estadísticas del trabajo se pueden considerar por tanto volúmenes que acompañan a los diversos capítulos del Anuario de Estadísticas del Trabajo y del Boletín de Estadísticas del Trabajo de la OIT.

Las descripciones metodológicas que se presentan en este volumen abarcan las encuestas sobre la fuerza del trabajo y las encuestas de hogares (o individuos), a partir de las cuales se elaboran las estadísticas de la población económicamente activa, del empleo, del desempleo, del subempleo, de las horas de trabajo, de los ingresos relacionados con el empleo, del empleo en el sector informal, de la actividad habitual, etc. Las descripciones metodológicas relativas à otros países serán diseminadas ulteriormente en el sitio de difusión de datos de la Oficina de Estadística del Trabajo:
http://laborsta.ilo.org/.

La producción de este volumen estuvo a cargo de la Oficina de Estadística de la OIT.

CONTENTS

TABLE DES MATIERES

INDICE

Albania

Title of the survey: Household Living Conditions Survey, October 1998.
Organization responsible for the survey:
Planning and conduct of the survey: Albanian Institute of Statistics (INSTAT).
Analysis and publication of the results: Albanian Institute of Statistics (INSTAT).
Topics covered: Employment, unemployment, hours of work, wages, income, employment and unemployment duration, discouraged workers, occasional workers, industry, occupation, education.
Coverage of the survey:
Geographical: Whole country.
Population groups: All resident population.
Availability of estimates from other sources for the excluded areas/groups: Not applicable.
Groups covered by the survey but excluded from the published results: Not applicable.
Periodicity:
Conduct of the survey: First round in 1998.
Publication of results: In 2001.
Reference periods:
Employment: The week prior to the date of the interview.
Seeking work: The week prior to the date of the interview.
Availability for work: The week prior to the date of the interview.
Concepts and definitions:
Employment: All persons, aged 15 years and over who, during the survey week, did any work for at least one hour.
Are included in the employed:
a) persons with a job but temporarily absent due to illness or injury, annual leave, maternity/paternity leave, parental leave, educational or training leave, bad weather, mechanical breakdown, etc.;
b) full or part-time workers seeking other work during the reference period;
c) retired persons receiving a pension, persons registered as job-seekers and those receiving unemployment benefits who have worked for pay or profit during the reference week;
d) full-time and part-time students working full or part-time;
e) paid apprentices and trainees;
f) unpaid family workers at work during the survey week or temporarily absent from work.
Unemployment: All persons, aged 15 years and over, who have not worked during the last week, were seeking for a job and were available to work.
Underemployment
Time-related underemployment: Not covered.
Inadequate employment situations: Not covered.
Hours of work: No information.
Employment-related income
Income from paid employment: Average monthly wages of employees.
Income from self-employment: Income from private activity.
Informal sector: No information.
Usual activity: Economic status (employed, unemployed, inactive) during the last 12 months.
Classifications:
Branch of economic activity (industry):
Title of the classification: National classification based on European industrial classification NACE.
Population groups classified by industry: Employed and unemployed (industry of last job for the unemployed).
Number of groups used for coding: No information.
Links to ISIC: ISIC-Rev. 3.
Occupation:
Title of the classification: ISCO-88 at the 3rd digit level.
Population groups classified by occupation: Employed and unemployed (occupation of last job for the unemployed).
Number of groups used for coding: 116 minor groups.
Links to ISCO: ISCO-88.
Status in employment:
Title of the classification: National classification.
Population groups classified by status in employment: Employed.
Groups used for classification: Employees, employers and own-account workers.
Links to ICSE: No.
Education:
Title of the classification: National classification.
Population groups classified by education: Employed and unemployed.
Groups used for classification: 5 groups.
Links to ISCED: ISCED-1997.
Sample size and design:
Ultimate sampling unit: Household.
Sample size (ultimate sampling units): 11 826 households.
Overall sampling fraction: No information.
Sample frame: No information.
Updating of the sample: No information.
Rotation:
Scheme: Not applicable.
Percentage of units remaining in the sample for two consecutive survey rounds: Not applicable.
Maximum number of interviews per sample unit: Not applicable.
Length of time for complete renewal of the sample: Not applicable.
Field work:
Type of interview: Personal interviews.
Number of ultimate sampling units per sample area: No information.
Duration of field work:
Total: No information.
Per sample area: No information.
Survey organization: Ad hoc organization.
Number of field staff: No information.
Substitution of non-responding ultimate sampling units: No.
Estimation and adjustments:
Total non-response rate: No information.
Adjustment for total non-response: No information.
Imputation for item non-response: No information.
Adjustment for areas/population not covered: No information.
Adjustment for undercoverage: No information.
Adjustment for overcoverage: No information.
Adjustment for seasonal variations: No.
History of the survey:
Title and date of the first survey: Household Living Conditions Survey 1998.
Significant changes or revisions: Not applicable.
Documentation and dissemination:
Documentation:
Survey results: General Results of Household Living Conditions Survey 1998.
Survey methodology: General Results of Household Living Conditions Survey 1998.
Dissemination:
Time needed for initial release of survey results: About three years.
Advance information of public about date of initial release: Yes.
Availability of unpublished data upon request: No.
Availability of data in machine-readable form: No.
Website: http://www.instat.gov.al/.

Armenia

1.Title of the survey
Household Labour Force Survey (HLFS).
2.Organization responsible for the survey
The Department of Statistics of the Republic of Armenia (DSRA).
3.Coverage of the survey
(a) Geographical: Surveys conducted in November 1996 and December 1997 covered only the urban areas. Beginning 1999, it covers both urban and rural areas.
(b) Persons covered: Men aged 16-60 and women aged 16-55 years old present in the household at the moment of the interview. As from the 1997 round, all the population aged 16 years and above.
Excluded are:
1.students living in hostels and schoolchildren living in boarding schools;
2.inmates of penal and mental institutions;
3.military personnel (conscripts and career) living in barracks;
4.Periodicity of the survey
The survey, which was conducted annually in 1996 and 1997, has become biannual since 1999.
5.Reference period
The calendar week.
6.Topics covered
The survey provides information on the following topics: employment (main and secondary), unemployment, underemployment, duration of

unemployment, reasons for not being employed, occasional workers, industry, occupation, status in employment and level of education.

7.Concepts and definitions

(a) Employment: Employed persons are:

1.all persons who, during the reference week, did any work at all as paid employees, in their own business, profession, or on their own farm as well as persons who worked as unpaid family workers in an enterprise operated by a family member; and

2.all those who were not working but who had jobs or businesses from which they were temporarily absent because of illness, bad weather, vacation, labour-management disputes, or personal reasons, whether they were paid for the time off or were seeking other jobs.

Included in the totals are:

1.full- and part-time workers seeking other work during the reference period;

2.full- and part-time students working full- or part-time;

3.persons who performed some work during the reference week while being either retired and receiving a pension; or were registered as job seekers at an employment office or receiving unemployment benefits (beginning the 1997 round);

4.paid and unpaid family workers;

5.members of producers' co-operatives;

(b) Unemployment: Unemployed persons are all civilians who had no employment during the reference week, were available for work, except for temporary illness, and who had made specific steps to find employment.

Included in the unemployed are full- and part-time students seeking full- or part-time employment, provided they are currently available for work (if they are seeking work for some future date, such as for the summer months, they are considered inactive); as well as persons who found a job and made arrangements to start a new job on a date subsequent to the reference period.

8.Sample design

(a) The sample frame: The HLFS sample was built up on the basis of address lists which were used as a sample frame for the Household Family Budget Survey.

(b) The sample: The sample is based on a two-stage stratified random sampling design. At the first stage administrative regions are divided into strata on the basis of enumeration districts. At the second stage the ultimate sampling units/households are selected proportional to their size. In 1996, the sample size was about 1,500 households in urban areas which means that 0.3 per cent of all the households were interviewed. Beginning November 1999, the sample size is 1,200 households located in both urban and rural areas, which represent 0.1 per cent of all the households listed in Armenia.

(c) Rotation: The rotation pattern has not been established yet.

9.Documentation

Results of the HLFS will be published by the Department of Statistics of the Republic of Armenia in a special information bulletin and in the next issue of the Statistical Yearbook of the Armenian Republic.

Australia

Title of the survey: Labour Force Survey (LFS).

Organization responsible for the survey:

Planning and conduct of the survey: Australian Bureau of Statistics (ABS).

Analysis and publication of the results: ABS.

Topics covered: Persons currently economically active, employed and unemployed, hours of work, full-time/part-time status, job tenure, duration of unemployment, industry, occupation, status in employment. Sex, age, birthplace. Partial measure of time-related underemployment.

Topics covered by annual or less frequent supplements to the LFS include: persons currently in time-related underemployment; working arrangements; multiple jobholding; career experience; education and training experience; migrants; persons employed at home; retirement; job search experience; retrenchment and redundancy; persons currently inactive (outside the labour force: including the marginally attached and discouraged jobseekers).

Coverage of the survey:

Geographical: Excludes Jervis Bay Territory and External Territories.

Population groups: Australian usually resident civilian population of age 15 years and above.

Availability of estimates from other sources for the excluded areas/groups: National Population Census.

Groups covered by the survey but excluded from the published results: None.

Periodicity:

Conduct of the survey: Monthly.

Publication of results: Monthly.

Reference periods:

Employment: One week.

Seeking work: The last four weeks.

Availability for work: The reference week.

Concepts and definitions:

Employment: All persons aged 15 years and over who, during the reference week:

a) worked for one hour or more for pay, profit, commission or payment in kind in a job or business, or on a farm (comprising employees, employers and own account workers); or

b) worked for one hour or more without pay in a family business or on a farm (i.e. contributing family workers); or

c) were employees, who had a job, but were not at work and were:

i) away from work for less than four weeks up to the end of the reference week; or

ii) away from work for more than four weeks up to the end of the reference week and received pay for some or all of the four week period to the end of the reference week; or

iii) away from work as a standard work or shift arrangement; or

iv) on strike or locked out; or

v) on workers' compensation and expected to return to their job; or

d) were employers or own account workers, who had a job, business or farm, but were not at work.

Unemployment: Persons aged 15 years and over who were not employed during the reference week, and:

a) had actively looked for full-time or part-time work at any time in the four weeks up to the end of the reference week; and

b) were available for work in the reference week; or

c) were waiting to start a new job within four weeks from the end of the reference week and could have started in the reference week if the job had been available then.

Underemployment:

Time-related underemployment: Employed persons who want, and are available for, more hours of work than they currently have. They comprise:

a) full-time workers who worked part-time hours in the reference week for economic reasons (such as being stood down or insufficient work being available). It is assumed that these people wanted to work full-time and would have been available to do so in the reference week; and

b) part-time workers (usually work less than 35 hours a week and did so in the reference week) who want to work more hours, and are available to start work with more hours in the reference week. It is possible to distinguish between persons who have actively looked for work and those who have not.

This quarterly measure of time-related underemployment does not include part-time workers who want to work additional hours and who would be available to start work within the four weeks subsequent to the survey. The full measure of time-related underemployment is available from the results of the annual Survey of Underemployed Workers.

Inadequate employment situations: No information provided.

Hours of work: 'Actual hours worked' include both paid and unpaid hours worked. Actual hours worked in all jobs (and in main job) are collected. Full-time or part-time status is based on the number of hours worked. Full-time workers are defined as employed persons who usually worked 35 hours or more a week (in all jobs) and those who, although usually working less than 35 hours a week, worked 35 hours or more during the reference week.

The total number of hours usually worked (in all jobs) are also collected.

Employment-related income:

Income from paid employment: Estimates of employee earnings (average weekly earnings per employee) are available from an annual supplement survey: Employee Earnings, Benefits and Trade Union Membership Survey. Earnings measures in ABS household surveys relate to gross cash earnings received from either the main job or all jobs during the reference period and are not adjusted to exclude irregular bonuses, retrospective pay or pay in advance.

The ABS does not produce estimates of employment-related income as defined in the international guidelines. However, data are collected on the broader measure of income (income from various sources) in a number of household collections including: Survey of Income and Housing Costs, Household Expenditure Survey and Census of Population and Housing.

Income from self-employment: No information provided.

Informal sector: Not applicable.

Usual activity: No information provided.
Classifications:
Branch of economic activity (industry):
Title of the classification: Australian and New Zealand Standard Industrial Classification (ANZSIC) 1993.
Population groups classified by industry: Employed and unemployed persons (industry of last job for the unemployed).
Number of groups used for coding: 158.
Links to ISIC: ISIC-Rev. 3.
Occupation:
Title of the classification: Australian Standard Classification of Occupations, Second edition.
Population groups classified by occupation: Employed and unemployed persons (occupation of last job for the unemployed).
Number of groups used for coding: 340
Links to ISCO: ISCO-88 (the different treatment of armed forces has no practical consequences as they are not included in the LFS).
Status in employment:
Title of the classification: Employment Status.
Population groups classified by status in employment: Employed persons.
Number of groups used for coding: Employees; employers; own-account workers and contributing family workers (4 groups).
Links to ICSE: ICSE-1993.
Education:
Title of the classification: National classification, no title given.
Population groups classified education: All persons, in annual supplement.
Groups used for classification: No information provided.
Links to ISCED: ISCED-1976 and ISCED-1997.
Sample size and design:
Ultimate sampling unit: Dwellings.
Sample size (ultimate sampling units): 33 000 (monthly).
Overall sampling fraction: 0.005.
Sample frame: Deeply stratified multistage area frame. List frame of private dwellings in primary selection units (PSUs) based on the collection districts (CDs) used in the Australian Population Census.
Updating of the sample frame: Every five years on the basis of results from Population Census.
Rotation:
Scheme: Households in sample for 8 consecutive months. 1/8th of the sample is rotated out each month, and a new sample is introduced.
Percentage of units remaining in the sample for two consecutive survey rounds: 7/8ths common dwelling sample between consecutive surveys.
Maximum number of interviews per sample unit: No information provided.
Length of time for complete renewal of the sample: Eight months.
Field work:
Type of interview: Pen-and-paper; face-to-face in first interview, thereafter by phone if acceptable to respondent.
Number of ultimate sampling units per sample area: No information provided.
Duration of field work:
Total: 2 weeks.
Per sample area: No information provided.
Survey organization: Permanent.
Number of field staff: Approximately 600 interviewers.
Substitution of non-responding ultimate sampling units: No.
Estimation and adjustments:
Total non-response rate: 3.5 percent.
Adjustment for total non-response: Yes, by weighting against population benchmarks.
Imputation for item non-response: No, these questionnaires are excluded.
Adjustment for areas/population not covered: Yes, for armed forces: on basis of administrative count to estimate total labour force.
Adjustment for under-coverage: Yes, as for total non-response
Adjustment for over-coverage: Yes, as for total non-response
Adjustment for seasonal variations: Yes, for employment and unemployment by sex and main age groups, industry division (employed persons), long-term unemployed. Using X11-ARIMA variant, with annual review of seasonal adjustment factors.
History of the survey:
Title and date of the first survey: Labour Force Survey, February 1964.
Significant changes or revisions: August 1966: included Aboriginal and Torres Strait Islander population. May 1976: definition of unemployment revised to incorporate active job search and availability to start work in the reference week. February 1978: changed from quarterly to monthly survey. October 1982: changed basis for population benchmarks. April 1986: included in employment contributing family workers working less than 15 hours. August 1996: started introduction of telephone interviewing. April 2001: introduction of revised questionnaire and definitions. Persons absent from work on short-term unpaid leave initiated by the employer classed as employed (previously unemployed); persons without work, actively seeking work but unavailable to start work in reference week due to temporary illness classed as inactive (previously unemployed); contributing family workers away from work classed as either unemployed or inactive (previously employed).
Documentation and dissemination:
Documentation:
Survey results: Labour force Australia - Preliminary (Cat. no. 6202.0).
Survey methodology: Labour Statistics: Concepts Sources and Methods 2001 (Cat. No. 6102.0); Information Paper: Implementing the Redesigned Labour Force Survey Questionnaire (Cat. No. 6295.0); Information Paper: Questionnaire Used in the Labour Force Survey (Cat. No. 6232.0); Information Paper: Labour Force Survey Sample Design (Cat. No. 6269.0).
Dissemination:
Time needed for initial release of survey results: Within two weeks after month of reference week.
Advance information of public about date of initial release: Yes.
Availability of unpublished data upon request: Yes.
Availability of data in machine-readable form: Yes.
Website: http://www.abs.gov.au/.

Austria

Title of the survey: Up to 2002: Microcensus (Mikrozensus). Beginning 2003: Labour Force Survey LFS (Arbeitskräfteerhebung).
Organization responsible for the survey:
Planning and conduct of the survey: EUROSTAT and Statistik Austria (Bundesanstalt Statistik Austria).
Analysis and publication of the results: Statistik Austria (Bundesanstalt Statistik Austria) and EUROSTAT.
Topics covered: Employment, unemployment, underemployment, hours of work (normal hours of work, hours actually worked), duration of employment, duration of unemployment, discouraged workers, occasional workers (if working during the reference week), seasonal workers, industry, occupation, status in employment, education and qualification levels, main source of livelihood, second jobs; total questionnaire of Eurostat labor force surveys.
Coverage of the survey:
Geographical: Whole country.
Population groups: The survey covers the resident population of Austria, excluding unsettled persons. Persons living in institutions are covered by the quarterly Microcensus, but not by the annual Labour Force Survey.
Availability of estimates from other sources for the excluded areas/groups: Not applicable.
Groups covered by the survey but excluded from the published results: None.
Periodicity:
Conduct of the survey: Quarterly in March, June, September and December of each year (Microcensus with 15 core questions on economic activity); annually in March (all other questions of the European Union Labour Force Survey). Beginning 2003: continuous survey.
Publication of results: Quarterly (Microcensus); annually (whole Labour Force Survey).
Reference periods:
Employment: Moving reference period of one week prior to the interview date.
Seeking work: Moving reference period of four weeks prior to the interview date.
Availability for work: Moving reference period of two weeks following the interview date.
Concepts and definitions:
Employment: Persons aged 15 years or over who have a regular job of one or more hours per week, as well as persons with an irregular job if they worked for at least one hour during the reference week. Included are:
(a) contributing family workers at work during the reference week;
(b) full- or part-time workers seeking other work;
(c) persons who performed some work for pay or profit during the reference week but who were subject to compulsory schooling, or

retired and receiving a pension, or registered as job seekers at an employment office, or receiving unemployment benefits;
(d) full- time students working full- or part-time;
(e) part-time students working full- or part-time;
(f) paid or unpaid apprentices and trainees;
(g) participants in employment promotion schemes;
(h) persons engaged in the production of goods for own final use;
(i) members of the armed forces (career members, volunteers and conscripts and
(j) persons on civilian service equivalent to military service.

Also included are persons with a job or enterprise, who were temporarily absent from work during the reference week because of (a) illness or injury, (b) vacation or annual leave, (c) maternity or paternity leave, (d) parental leave, (e) educational or training leave of a duration of up to one year, (f) labour management dispute, or (g) bad weather, mechanical breakdown, etc.

This includes contributing family workers temporarily absent from work during the reference week.

Excluded are: (a) seasonal workers not at work during the off-season; (b) persons on educational or training leave of a duration of more than one year; (c) persons on temporary or indefinite lay-off without pay; (d) persons on unpaid leave initiated by the employer; (e) persons rendering unpaid or personal services to members of their own household; and (f) persons engaged in volunteer community or social service work.

Unemployment: Persons aged 15 years or over who were not employed during the reference week, had actively sought work during the last four weeks, and were available for work within two weeks.

Included are: (a) persons without work and currently available for work, who had made arrangements to start a new job on a date subsequent to the reference week; (b) persons without work and currently available for work, who were trying to establish their own enterprise; (c) persons on indefinite lay-off without pay, who were looking for a job; (d) persons seeking work and available for work who were subject to compulsory schooling or retired and receiving a pension; (e) full- time students seeking full- or part-time work; and (f) part-time students seeking full- or part-time work.

Excluded are persons without work and currently available for work, who were not actively seeking work for reasons other than (a) and (b) above, as well as persons without work who were not currently available for work.

Underemployment

Time-related underemployment: Employed persons willing to work additional hours, either in their current job, or in a new job, or in an additional job.

Inadequate employment situations: This topic is not covered by the survey.

Hours of work: Normal hours of work per week in the main job, hours actually worked during the reference week in the main job, hours actually worked during the reference week in the second job (if any).

Employment-related income:

Income from paid employment: Not covered by the survey.

Income from self-employment: Not covered by the survey.

Informal sector: Not covered by the survey.

Usual activity: Not covered by the survey.

Classifications:

Branch of economic activity (industry):

Title of the classification: National classification of branches of economic activity.

Population groups classified by industry: Employed persons; unemployed or economically inactive persons with previous work experience.

Number of groups used for coding: 31.

Links to ISIC: ISIC-Rev. 3.

Occupation:

Title of the classification: International Standard Classification of Occupations (ISCO-88).

Population groups classified by occupation: Employed persons; unemployed or economically inactive persons with previous work experience.

Number of groups used for coding: 78.

Links to ISCO: Not applicable.

Status in employment:

Title of the classification: National classification of status in employment.

Population groups classified by status in employment: Employed persons; unemployed or economically inactive persons with previous work experience.

Groups used for classification: (a) Employers in agriculture and forestry; (b) unpaid family workers in agriculture and forestry; (c) employers or self-employed persons in production, trade or tourism; (d) unpaid family workers in production, trade or tourism; (e) self-employed persons in other services (lawyers, doctors, etc.); (f) unpaid family workers working with self-employed persons in other services; (g) apprentices; (h) employees in blue-collar jobs; (i) employees in white-collar jobs (private sector); (j) employees in white-collar jobs (public sector).

There are 46 groups in total. Groups (a) to (d) are subdivided according to the size of the enterprise. Group (g) is subdivided into blue-collar jobs and white-collar jobs. Groups (h) to (j) are subdivided according to the skill level of the job.

Links to ICSE: ICSE-1993.

Education:

Title of the classification: National classification of levels of educational attainment.

Population groups classified by education: All persons aged 15 years or over.

Groups used for classification: (a) No compulsory schooling completed; (b) compulsory schooling; (c) apprenticeship (vocational school); (d) intermediate vocational school (excluding part-time vocational schooling); (e) general upper secondary school; (f) higher vocational school (normal type); (g) higher vocational school (course leading to qualifications for higher education); (h) institute of higher education; (i) university or equivalent.

Links to ISCED: ISCED-1976 and ISCED-1997.

Sample size and design:

Ultimate sampling unit: Dwelling.

Sample size (ultimate sampling units): 30 800 dwellings/addresses.

Overall sampling fraction: 0.9 percent of dwellings.

Sample frame: Area frame based on the address lists of the latest housing census, supplemented with information on new buildings.

Updating of the sample: The sample is updated once a year to include newly constructed buildings; these new addresses are a special stratum of the sample.

Rotation:

Scheme: Households in sample dwellings participate in the survey up to eight times during a period of two years. Every quarter, one eighth of the sample dwellings is rotated out of the sample and replaced by other addresses entering the sample.

Percentage of units remaining in the sample for two consecutive survey rounds: 87.5 percent.

Maximum number of interviews per sample unit: Eight.

Length of time for complete renewal of the sample: Two years.

All the above information on sample size and design is valid up to 2002.

Field work:

Type of interview: Information is obtained through personal interviews.

Number of ultimate sampling units per sample area: 25 addresses at maximum.

Duration of field work

Total: Three weeks for each quarterly round of the Microcensus; three weeks for the annual Labour Force Survey.

Per sample area: Three weeks at maximum.

Survey organization: A permanent survey organization exists for the survey.

Number of field staff: About 1,200 interviewers.

Substitution of non-responding ultimate sampling units: No replacement is made for cases of non-response.

Estimation and adjustments:

Total non-response rate: 4.1 percent of all sample addresses. 7.3 percent of the total sample are cases, in which no household member can be contacted, and 9.9 percent of the sample are cases of non-inhabited dwellings, secondary residences or incomplete addresses.

Adjustment for total non-response: Yes.

Imputation for item non-response: Missing values are imputed on the basis of information provided by persons with similar characteristics. However, such imputations are made only for data of the annual Labour Force Survey and quarterly Microcensus in March, and not for data of the Microcensus in June, September and December.

Adjustment for areas/population not covered: Not applicable.

Adjustment for under-coverage: Yes.

Adjustment for over-coverage: Yes.

Adjustment for seasonal variations: No.

History of the survey:

Title and date of the first survey: The first Microcensus was conducted in March 1968, and the first European Union Labour Force Survey (based on ILO guidelines) in March 1995.

Significant changes or revisions: Changes from national to international definitions were introduced to the Microcensus in March 1994. There has been no significant change in the Labour Force Survey since 1995.

Documentation and dissemination:

Documentation:

Survey results: Statistik Austria, Beiträge zur österreichischen Statistik, Heft 1.303: Arbeitskräfteerhebung (annually); Statistik Austria, Statistische Nachrichten (monthly). The first publication presents detailed survey results, while the second contains, on an ad-hoc basis, articles presenting an overview of the main results or analyzing data on specific topics.

Survey methodology: The above-mentioned publications include methodological information on the survey.

Dissemination:

Time needed for initial release of survey results: Six months for the annual Labour Force Survey.

Advance information of public about date of initial release: No.

Availability of unpublished data upon request: Yes, in the form of standardized tables.

Availability of data in machine-readable form: Standardized LFS tabulations are available in electronic form. Microcensus tables can also be made available in electronic form.

Website: http://www.statistik.at/.

Bahamas

Title of the survey: Labour Force and Household Survey.

Organization responsible for the survey:

Planning and conduct of the survey: Department of Statistics.

Analysis and publication of the results: Department of Statistics.

Topics covered: Employment, unemployment, hours of work, income, duration of unemployment, discouraged workers, industry, occupation, status in employment, education/qualification levels, usual activity, second jobs.

Coverage of the survey:

Geographical: Three main Islands: Grand Bahamas, New Providence and Abaco.

Population groups: Persons of 15 years and over, engaged in or willing and able to be engaged in the production of goods and services, with the exclusion of the institutional population.

Availability of estimates from other sources for the excluded areas/groups: NO.

Groups covered by the survey but excluded from the published results: NO.

Periodicity:

Conduct of the survey: Annual.

Publication of results: Annual.

Reference periods:

Employment: One week in April.

Seeking work: Four weeks in April.

Availability for work: Four weeks in April.

Concepts and definitions:

Employment: All persons of 15 years and over who, at any time during the reference period, worked for pay or without pay for at least one hour in a family operated enterprise.

It includes:

a) persons with a job but temporarily absent due to illness or injury, vacation or annual leave, maternity or paternity leave, educational or training leave, absence without leave, labour management dispute, bad weather, mechanical breakdown, etc.;

b) persons who performed some work for pay or profit during the reference period but were subject to compulsory schooling, retired and receiving a pension, registered as jobseekers at an employment office or receiving unemployment benefits;

c) full-time and part-time students working full or part time;

d) paid and unpaid apprentices and trainees;

e) unpaid family workers at work or temporarily absent from work;

f) persons engaged in production of goods for their own final uses;

g) seasonal workers not at work during the off-season.

It excludes members of the armed forces as well as persons on civilian service equivalent to military service and persons doing volunteer community or social service work.

Unemployment: All persons of 15 years and over who did not work or have a job from which they were temporarily absent during the reference week, but were actively looking for work in the four weeks prior to the survey week, and were able and willing to work.

Underemployment:

Time-related underemployment: Not covered by the survey.

Inadequate employment situations: Not covered by the survey.

Hours of work: Both hours worked during the reference week and usually worked are computed.

Employment-related income:

Income from paid employment: Gross income compensation from employment, including tips and commissions before any deductions and income from investment (dividends, rental income, royalties, alimony, etc.). It refers to primary and secondary jobs.

Income from self-employment: Income from all jobs, net of business expenses.

Informal sector: Not covered by the survey.

Usual activity: Not covered by the survey.

Classifications:

Branch of economic activity (industry):

Title of the classification: National classification, corresponding to ISIC Rev.2 at the major division level.

Population groups classified by industry: Employed and unemployed persons..

Number of groups used for coding: Nine branches.

Links to ISIC: ISIC Rev.2.

Occupation:

Title of the classification: National classification, corresponding to ISCO-1988.

Population groups classified by occupation: Employed and unemployed persons..

Number of groups used for coding: Nine major groups.

Links to ISCO: ISCO-1988.

Status in employment:

Title of the classification: National classification, corresponding to ISCE-1993.

Population groups classified by status in employment: Employed persons.

Groups used for classification: Employees (government and private employees separately), employers, self-employed, unpaid family workers.

Links to ICSE: ISCE-1993.

Education:

Title of the classification: National classification.

Population groups classified by education: Employed and unemployed persons.

Groups used for classification: Six groups: no school, primary school, secondary school, college, technical/vocational school, other.

Links to ISCED: NO.

Sample size and design:

Ultimate sampling unit: Household.

Sample size (ultimate sampling units): 2 700 households.

Sampling fraction: Varying according to the Island covered.

Sample frame: The 1990 Census of Housing and Population.

Updating of the sample: On the basis of the new Census.

Rotation

Scheme: Two-thirds (2/3) of the households remain in the sample during tree consecutive years while the remaining one-third (1/3) is sample for the first time.

Percentage of units remaining in the sample for two consecutive survey rounds: 66 per cent.

Maximum number of interviews per sample unit: Three times

Length of time for complete renewal of the sample: 10 years.

Field work:

Type of interview: Personal interviews.

Number of ultimate sampling units per sample area: No information provided.

Duration of field work

Total: Three weeks in May.

Per sample area: No information provided.

Survey organization: Enumerators are recruited for each survey.

Number of field staff: About 11 supervisors and 57 enumerators.

Substitution of non-responding ultimate sampling units: NO.

Estimation and adjustments

Total non-response rate: NO.

Adjustment for total non-response: NO.

Imputation for item non-response: NO.

Adjustment for areas/population not covered: NO.

Adjustment for undercoverage: NO.

Adjustment for overcoverage: NO.

Adjustment for seasonal variations: NO.

History of the survey:

Title and date of the first survey: Labour Force and Household Survey 19773.

Significant changes or revisions: Biannual surveys until 1979. No survey between 1979 and 1986.

Documentation and dissemination:
Documentation:
Survey results: Labour Force and Household Income Report (annual).
Survey methodology: Labour Force and Household Income Report (annual).
Dissemination:
Time needed for initial release of survey results: About one year.
Advance information of public about date of initial release: No.
Availability of unpublished data upon request: In some instances.
Availability of data in machine-readable form: Yes.

Bangladesh

Title of the survey: Labour Force Survey.
Organization responsible for the survey:
Planning and conduct of the survey: Bangladesh Bureau of Statistics.
Analysis and publication of the results: Bangladesh Bureau of Statistics.
Topics covered: Employment, unemployment, underemployment, hours actually worked, wages, income, informal sector employment, duration of employment, industry, occupation, status in employment, education/qualification levels, second jobs.
Coverage of the survey:
Geographical: Whole country.
Population groups: The survey covers usual members of private households in Bangladesh, whether they are present in the household at the time of the survey or temporarily absent from the household. Persons living in institutions, unsettled populations, members of the armed forces, non-residential citizens, foreigners and persons residing abroad are excluded.
Availability of estimates from other sources for the excluded areas/groups: Not applicable.
Groups covered by the survey but excluded from the published results: None.
Periodicity:
Conduct of the survey: Irregularly. So far, the survey has been conducted in 1983, 1984, 1985, 1989, 1990, 1995 and 1999.
Publication of results: Irregularly, depending upon the conduct of the survey.
Reference periods:
Employment: Moving reference period of one week prior to the interview date.
Seeking work: Fixed reference period of one week.
Availability for work: Fixed reference period of one week.
Concepts and definitions:
Employment: Persons aged 5 years or over who worked one or more hours during the reference week either for pay or profit, or without pay in a family farm or enterprise or organization.
Included are: (a) contributing family workers at work during the reference week; (b) full- or part-time workers seeking other work; (c) part-time students working full-time; (d) paid apprentices and trainees; and (e) persons engaged in the production of goods for own final use.
Also considered as employed are persons aged 5 years or over who were found not working, but who had a job or business from which they were temporarily absent during the reference week because of (a) illness or injury, (b) vacation or annual leave, (c) maternity or paternity leave, (d) parental leave, (e) educational or training leave, (f) absence without leave, (g) labour management dispute, (h) bad weather, mechanical breakdown, etc., or (i) temporary lay-off without pay.
Excluded are: (a) persons who performed some work for pay or profit during the reference week but who were subject to compulsory schooling, or retired and receiving a pension, or registered as job seekers at an employment office, or receiving unemployment benefits; (b) full-time students working full- or part-time; (c) unpaid apprentices and trainees; (d) persons on indefinite lay-off without pay; and (e) persons rendering unpaid or personal services to members of their own household.
Unemployment: Persons aged 5 years or over who were involuntarily out of gainful employment during the reference week, and who had been actively looking for work, or who were willing to work but not looking for work because of illness or the belief that no work was available.
Included are: (a) persons without work and available for work, who had made arrangements to start a new job on a date subsequent to the reference week; (b) persons without work and available for work, who were trying to establish their own enterprise; (c) persons without work and available for work, but not seeking work because they believe that no work is available at present; (d) persons on indefinite lay-off without pay; and (e) persons who performed some work for pay or profit during the reference week but who were registered as job seekers at an employment office or receiving unemployment benefits.
Excluded are: (a) persons without work who were seeking and/or available for work, but subject to compulsory schooling, or retired and receiving a pension; and (b) full- time students seeking full- or part-time work.
Underemployment:
Time-related underemployment: Employed persons, who were in employment considered inadequate in terms of time worked, income earned, productivity or use of their skills, and who were looking for additional work in conformity with their education or skills.
Inadequate employment situations: This topic is not covered by the survey.
Hours of work: Hours actually worked during the reference week. For persons holding more than one job, hours worked refers to the total number of hours worked in all jobs.
Employment-related income:
Income from paid employment: Gross regular earnings in cash or in kind during the reference period. For persons holding more than one job, gross earnings refers to the total of all jobs.
Income from self-employment: Gross income of self-employed persons during the reference period. For persons holding more than one job, gross income refers to the total of all jobs.
Informal sector: Unincorporated enterprises owned by households, including cottage industries.
Usual activity: This topic is not covered by the survey.
Classifications:
Branch of economic activity (industry):
Title of the classification: International Standard Industrial Classification of All Economic Activities (ISIC, Rev. 3).
Population groups classified by industry: Employed persons.
Number of groups used for coding: Two-digit level of ISIC, Rev. 3.
Links to ISIC: Not applicable.
Occupation:
Title of the classification: Bangladesh Standard Classification of Occupations.
Population groups classified by occupation: Employed persons.
Number of groups used for coding: Two-digit level.
Links to ISCO: ISCO-68.
Status in employment:
Title of the classification: National classification of status in employment.
Population groups classified by status in employment: Employed persons.
Groups used for classification: (a) Self-employed/own-account workers; (b) employers; (c) employees; (d) unpaid family helpers; (e) day labourers.
Links to ICSE: Partially.
Education
Title of the classification: National classification of levels of educational attainment.
Population groups classified by education: Employed persons and unemployed persons.
Groups used for classification: (a) No education; (b) Class I-V; (c) Class VI-VIII; (d) Class IX-X; (e) SSC, HSC or equivalent; (f) Diploma; (g) Degree; (h) Masters; (i) BAg and above; (j) MBBS and above; (k) BSc Engineering and above; (l) PhD.
Links to ISCED: No.
Sample size and design:
Ultimate sampling unit: Household.
Sample size (ultimate sampling units): 9 790 households.
Overall sampling fraction: No information provided.
Sample frame: Master frame of 442 primary sampling units based on the 1991 population census area frame.
Updating of the sample: Prior to the survey, a complete new listing of households in the sample areas is made.
Rotation:
Scheme: No sample rotation. Data collection is spread over a period of twelve months. To this end, the survey sample is divided into twelve independent monthly sub-samples.
Percentage of units remaining in the sample for two consecutive survey rounds: Not applicable.
Maximum number of interviews per sample unit: Not applicable.
Length of time for complete renewal of the sample: Not applicable.
Field work:
Type of interview: Information is obtained through personal interviews.

Number of ultimate sampling units per sample area: 25 households in urban areas; 20 households in rural areas.
Duration of field work:
Total: Twelve months (last survey: April 1999-March 2000).
Per sample area: One week.
Survey organization: A permanent survey organization exists for the survey.
Number of field staff: About 8 supervisors and 20 interviewers.
Substitution of non-responding ultimate sampling units: Non-responding households are replaced by other households.
Estimation and adjustments:
Total non-response rate: Not applicable.
Adjustment for total non-response: Not applicable.
Imputation for item non-response: No.
Adjustment for areas/population not covered: Not applicable.
Adjustment for under-coverage: No information provided.
Adjustment for over-coverage: No information provided.
Adjustment for seasonal variations: Not applicable.
History of the survey:
Title and date of the first survey: The first Labour Force Survey in Bangladesh was conducted in 1983.
Significant changes or revisions: Significant changes to the survey questionnaire were made in 1989. As from 1989, some production activities for own consumption (such as threshing, drying, parboiling, processing and preservation of food, care of livestock and poultry production, collection of firewood and making cow-dung cakes, fishing, production of vegetables, etc.) were considered as economic activities. As a result, female activity rates increased substantially.
Documentation and dissemination:
Documentation:
Survey results: Bangladesh Bureau of Statistics, Report on Labour Force Survey in Bangladesh (periodicity: irregular).
Survey methodology: The above-mentioned publication includes methodological information on the survey.
Dissemination:
Time needed for initial release of survey results: About 12 months after the completion of the survey.
Advance information of public about date of initial release: No.
Availability of unpublished data upon request: Yes.
Availability of data in machine-readable form: Yes.

Barbados

Title of the survey: Continuous Labour Force Sample Survey (CLFSS).
Organization responsible for the survey:
Planning and conduct of the survey: Barbados Statistical Service.
Analysis and publication of the results: Barbados Statistical Service.
Topics covered: Employment, unemployment, underemployment, hours of work, wages, income, years of work experience, duration of unemployment, industry, occupation, status in employment, education/qualification levels, second jobs.
Coverage of the survey:
Geographical: Whole country.
Population groups: Civilian non-institutional population of age 15 years and over, i.e. persons normally resident in private households. Excluded: persons living in institutions or group quarters such as hotels, prisons, hospitals, army barracks, etc.
Availability of estimates from other sources for the excluded areas/groups: No information provided.
Groups covered by the survey but excluded from the published results: None.
Periodicity:
Conduct of the survey: Quarterly.
Publication of results: Quarterly.
Reference periods:
Employment: One week prior to the date of the interview.
Seeking work: Three months prior to the date of interview.
Availability for work: Two weeks following the date of interview.
Concepts and definitions
Employment: Persons of age 15 years and over who:
a) performed some work for pay or profit during the reference week;
b) having already worked in their present job or business, were temporarily absent from work during the reference week because of illness, injury, industrial dispute, vacation or other leave, or temporary disorganization of work due to reasons such as bad weather or mechanical breakdown.
It includes:
a) full or part-time workers seeking other work during the reference week;
b) persons who performed some work for pay or profit during the reference week but were retired and receiving a pension, registered as job seekers at an employment office or receiving unemployment benefits;
c) full or part-time students working full or part-time;
d) members of the armed forces (career members, conscripts and volunteers).
e) paid and unpaid apprentices (persons who worked without pay as learners).
Excluded are:
a) unpaid family workers currently assisting in the operation of a business or farm who worked for less than 15 hours during the reference week
b) persons who performed some work for pay or profit during the reference week but were subject to compulsory schooling.
Unemployment: Persons of age 15 years and over who were:
a) currently available for work and whose contract of employment had been terminated or temporarily suspended and who were without a job and had been seeking work for pay or profit during the three-month period immediately preceding the date of the interview;
b) currently available for work (except for minor illness) and who had been seeking work for pay or profit during the three-month period preceding the date of the interview, including persons who were never previously employed or whose most recent status of employment was other than employee, i.e. former employers or persons who had been in retirement;
c) without a job and currently available for work provided that they had made arrangements to start a new job or establish their own enterprise at a date subsequent to the date of interview;
d) on temporary or indefinite lay-off without pay or on unpaid leave initiated by the employer;
e) without a job and had looked for work at some time during the three-month period preceding the reference week and were still available for and able to work during the reference week.
f) full- or part-time students seeking full- or part-time work and currently available for work.
Excluded are persons who performed some work for pay or profit during the reference week but were subject to compulsory schooling and those who were seeking and/or available for work but subject to compulsory schooling or retired and receiving a pension.
Underemployment:
Time-related underemployment: All employed persons, whether at work or not, who usually worked less than the normal duration of work determined for this specific activity for involuntary reasons, and who were seeking and available for additional work during the reference week.
Inadequate employment situations: Not applicable.
Hours of work: Actual and usual hours for all jobs during the reference week.
Employment-related income:
Income from paid employment: All earnings from all jobs during the reference week i.e. wages, salaries and other earnings in cash or kind; remuneration for time not worked and paid by the employer (excluding severance and termination pay); bonuses, gratuities, housing and family allowances paid by the employer; net current benefits from social security and insurance schemes for employees.
Income from self-employment: Not applicable.
Informal sector: Not applicable.
Usual activity: Not applicable.
Classifications:
Branch of economic activity (industry):
Title of the classification: Barbados Standard Industrial Classification.
Population groups classified by industry: Employed and unemployed persons (industry of last job for the unemployed).
Number of groups used for coding: 29 groups.
Links to ISIC: ISIC Rev. 2.
Occupation:
Title of the classification: Barbados Standard Occupational Classification (1989).
Population groups classified by occupation: Employed and unemployed persons (occupation of last job for the unemployed).
Number of groups used for coding: Eight groups.
Links to ISCO: ISCO-1968.
Status in employment:
Title of the classification: National classification.
Population groups classified by status in employment: Employed persons.

Groups used for classification: Employer, employee (further divided into government employees and private sector employee, self-employed, unpaid family worker, apprentice.
Links to ICSE: YES.
Education:
Title of the classification: National classification.
Population groups classified by education: Employed persons and unemployed.
Groups used for classification: No education, primary, secondary, university, technical or vocational, other, not stated.
Links to ISCED: ISCED-1976.
Sample size and design:
Ultimate sampling unit: Household.
Sample size (ultimate sampling units): 1 800 households per round (quarter).
Overall sampling fraction: 2 per cent of the total civilian non-institutional households.
Sample frame: The 2000 Population and Housing Census. The country is divided into 538 enumeration districts (ED) covering all eleven parishes. Each ED contains about 300 households.
Updating of the sample: Every 10 years on the basis of the population census results.
Rotation:
Scheme: No information provided.
Percentage of units remaining in the sample for two consecutive survey rounds: 50 per cent. The other 50 percent are interviewed four weeks later.
Maximum number of interviews per sample unit: Two.
Length of time for complete renewal of the sample: One year.
Field work:
Type of interview: Personal interviews.
Number of ultimate sampling units per sample area: 45.
Duration of field work
Total: Three months.
Per sample area: No information provided.
Survey organization: Permanent.
Number of field staff: 15 field officers and 3 supervisors.
Substitution of non-responding ultimate sampling units: No.
Estimation and adjustments:
Total non-response rate: No information provided.
Adjustment for total non-response: No.
Imputation for item non-response: For income received, hours of work, etc. on the basis of similar responding households.
Adjustment for areas/population not covered: No information provided.
Adjustment for under-coverage: No information provided.
Adjustment for over-coverage: No information provided.
Adjustment for seasonal variations: No.
History of the survey:
Title and date of the first survey: Barbados Continuous Labour Force Survey, October 1975.
Significant changes or revisions: No information provided.
Documentation and dissemination:
Documentation:
Survey results: Continuous Labour Force Sample Survey Report (annual); Labour Force Bulletin (quarterly).
Survey methodology: Continuous Labour Force Sample Survey Report (annual).
Dissemination:
Time needed for initial release of survey results: Two months.
Advance information of public about date of initial release: No..
Availability of unpublished data upon request: Yes.
Availability of data in machine-readable form: Yes and on national website.
Website: http://www.bgis.gov.bb/stats/.

Botswana

Title of the survey: Labour Force Survey (LFS).
Organization responsible for the survey:
Planning and conduct of the survey: Central Statistics Office (CSO).
Analysis and publication of the results: CSO.
Topics covered: Persons currently and usually economically active, employed and unemployed; persons currently underemployed, temporary absent from employment and outside the labour force; persons usually employed with and without some unemployment, persons with some employment and persons usually not economic active; training; income; institutional sector, industry, occupation, status in employment.
Coverage of the survey:
Geographical: Whole country.
Population groups: Non-institutional population of age 12 years and over, i.e. persons normally resident in private households. Visitors for less than 14 days and persons living in hotels, prisons, army barracks, etc. are excluded.
Availability of estimates from other sources for the excluded areas/groups: No information.
Groups covered by the survey but excluded from the published results: No information.
Periodicity:
Conduct of the survey: Occasional, i.e. 1995-96 and 1997-98.
Publication of results: Occasional.
Reference periods:
Employment: One week prior to the date of the interview.
Seeking work: One month search period for strict definition. No search needed for expanded definition.
Availability to work: No information.
Concepts and definitions:
Employment: Persons who a) performed some work for pay or profit during the reference week; or b) were temporarily absent from work during the reference week because of illness or leave, but were definitely going to return. Included are unpaid family workers in family business. Some work is defined as 1 hour or more during the reference week.
Unemployment: Strict definition: persons who were without work, currently available for work and who had searched for work during the last month. Expanded definition: persons who were without work and currently available for work.
Underemployment:
Time-related underemployment: Persons working less than 35 hours who said they were available to work more hours.
Inadequate employment situations: No information.
Hours of work: No information.
Employment-related income:
Income from paid employment: No information.
Income from self-employment: No information.
Informal sector: Excluded were all persons working on own or as paid employees in traditional agriculture, as well as those working for local or central government or for enterprises with 5 paid employees or more or which were a registered company or kept a complete set of records. Included, but identified separately, were domestics servants and others working for private households.
Usual activity: Economically active for 6 months or more of the 12 months reference.
Classifications:
Branch of economic activity (industry):
Title of the classification: Botswana Industrial Classification (BISIC).
Population groups classified by industry: No information.
Number of groups used for coding: No information.
Links to ISIC: ISIC-Rev.3 with extra codes to identify informal activities.
Occupation:
Title of the classification: Botswana Standard Classification of Occupations (BSCO).
Population groups classified by occupation: No information.
Number of groups used for coding: No information.
Links to ISCO: ISCO-88.
Status in employment:
Title of classification: National classification, no title given.
Population groups classified by status in employment: Employed population.
Groups used for classification: Paid employees; self-employed in traditional agriculture; self-employed outside traditional agriculture, sub-divided into those with paid employees, those without employees and the unpaid family workers.
Links to ICSE: Yes.
Education:
Title of the classification: National classification of subject of training.
Population groups classified by education: No information.
Groups used for classification: No information.
Links to ISCED: No information.
Sample size and design
Ultimate sampling unit: Household.
Sample size (ultimate sampling units): 11 000.
Overall sampling fraction: No information.
Sample frame: The 1991 Population Census, providing 5 urban and 9 rural strata, with a total of 420 sample blocks.

Updating of the sampling frame: None, but assumed 15 percent population growth.
Rotation:
Scheme: Not applicable.
Percentage of units remaining in the sample for two consecutive survey rounds: Not applicable.
Maximum number of interviews per sample unit: Not applicable.
Length of time for complete renewal of the sample: Not applicable.
Field work
Type of interview: Personal interviews.
Number of ultimate sampling units per sample area: No information.
Duration of field work:
Total: Thirteen months.
Per sample area: No information.
Survey organization: No information.
Number of field staff: No information.
Substitution of non-responding ultimate sampling units: No information.
Estimation and adjustments:
Total non-response rate: 2 percent.
Adjustment for total non-response: No.
Imputation for item non-response: No.
Adjustment for areas/population not covered: Not applicable.
Adjustment for undercoverage: Not applicable.
Adjustment for overcoverage: Not applicable.
Adjustment for seasonal variations: Not applicable.
History of the survey
Title and date of the first survey: Botswana Labour Force Survey, 1984/5.
Significant changes or revisions: No information.
Documentation and dissemination
Documentation:
Survey results: No information.
Survey methodology: 1995-96 Labour Force Survey: Technical & Operational Report (March 1998).
Dissemination:
Time needed for initial release of survey results: No information.
Advance information of public about date of initial release: No information.
Availability of unpublished data upon request: No information.
Availability of data in machine-readable form: No information.
Website: http://www.cso.gov.bw/cso/.

Bulgaria

Title of the survey: Labour Force Survey
Organization responsible for the survey:
Planning and conduct of the survey: National Statistical Institute
Analysis and publication of the results: National Statistical Institute
Topics covered: Employment, unemployment, underemployment, hours of work, duration of unemployment, discouraged workers, industry, occupation, status in employment and educational level.
Coverage of the survey:
Geographical: Whole country.
Population groups: All usual residents, aged 15 years and above living in non-institutional household, including those temporarily absent.
Availability of estimates from other sources for the excluded areas/groups: No.
Groups covered by the survey but excluded from the published results: None.
Periodicity:
Conduct of the survey: Since 2000, quarterly survey conducted in March, June, September and December. Previously, it was conducted three times a year.
Publication of results: Since 2000: quarterly. Previously: biannually.
Reference periods:
Employment: One week prior to the date of the interview.
Seeking work: Four weeks prior to the date of the interview.
Availability for work: Two weeks following the date of the interview.
Concepts and definitions:
Employment: employed are all persons aged 15 years and above who, during of reference period (a) performed some work for at least one hour for pay or profit (in cash or in kind); (b) did not work but had jobs or an enterprise from which they were temporarily absent due to leave, illness, bad weather, vocational training leave or other similar reason.

Considered as employed are persons who are in paid employment; operate their own enterprise, business or farm; performed independent work for profit and persons working without pay in an enterprise owned by a relative, member of the same household (for at least one hour) as well career members of the armed forces. Persons on maternity leave are considered as employed only during the fully-paid maternity leave (135 calendar days), otherwise they are considered as not in the labour force.
Unemployment: Unemployed are all persons of 15 years and above who did not work at all during the reference week, were actively looking for work during the four weeks previous to the interview and were available to start work within the two weeks following the survey week. Also included in the unemployed are persons who were not actively looking for work because they expected to return to their former job from which they were released or sent on an unpaid leave (if total duration of absence is more than one month), provided that they had the employer's promise and the concrete date of return to work as well as full- and part-time students seeking full- or part-time work.
Underemployment:
Time-related underemployment: Persons who usually worked part-time due to economic reasons.
Inadequate employment situations: Not applicable.
Hours of work: Usual hours worked in the main job and actual hours worked separately in the main and secondary job(s).
Employment-related income:
Income from paid employment: Not applicable.
Income from self-employment: Not applicable.
Informal sector: Not applicable.
Usual activity: Not applicable.
Classifications:
Branch of economic activity (industry):
Title of the classification: National classification.
Population groups classified by industry: Employed persons and not-employed persons with previous job experience during the last 8 years.
Number of groups used for coding: 503.
Links to ISIC: ISIC -Rev. 3 at the 3rd digit level.
Occupation:
Title of the classification: National classification.
Population groups classified by occupation: Employed persons and not-employed persons with previous work experience during the last 8 years.
Number of groups used for coding: 550.
Links to ISCO: ISCO-88 at the 3rd digit level.
Status in employment:
Title of the classification: National classification.
Population groups classified by status in employment: Employed persons and not-unemployed persons with previous work experience during the last 8 years.
Groups used for classification: 5 groups (employees, employers, own-account workers, members of productive co-operatives and unpaid family workers).
Links to ICSE: ICSE-1993.
Education:
Title of the classification: National classification.
Population groups classified by education: All population aged 15 years and over.
Groups used for classification: 8 groups (primary, secondary lower, vocational, secondary general, secondary vocational, secondary specialized, not completed higher (college), higher (university).
Links to ISCED: ISCED-97.
Sample size and design:
Ultimate sampling unit: Household.
Sample size (ultimate sampling units): About 24 000 households.
Overall sampling fraction: 0.8 per cent.
Sample frame: Population Census.
Updating of the sample: Annually.
Rotation:
Scheme: 2-2-2.
Percentage of units remaining in the sample for two consecutive survey rounds: 50 per cent
Maximum number of interviews per sample unit: Four.
Length of time for complete renewal of the sample: Four years.
Field work:
Type of interview: Paper and pencil.
Number of ultimate sampling units per sample area: 12 households per enumeration district.
Duration of field work:
Total: A calendar week (7 days).

Per sample area: A calendar week (7 days).
Survey organization: Permanent survey organization.
Number of field staff: Approximately 800 interviewers and 140 supervisors.
Substitution of non-responding ultimate sampling units: No.
Estimation and adjustments:
Total non-response rate: 12 to 15 per cent.
Adjustment for total non-response: No.
Imputation for item non-response: No.
Adjustment for areas/population not covered: No.
Adjustment for undercoverage: No.
Adjustment for overcoverage: No.
Adjustment for seasonal variations: No.
History of the survey:
Title and date of the first survey: Labour Force Survey, September 1993.
Significant changes or revisions: Two survey rounds, in June and October, in 1994. From 1995 to 2000, the survey has been conducted three times a year and the sample size decreased from 30 000 to 24 000 households. Quarterly survey since 2000. Since 2001 onwards, significant modifications of the questionnaire.
Documentation and dissemination:
Documentation
Survey results: Reference Book of the Republic of Bulgaria (annually); Employment and Unemployment (bi-annually).;Statistical Yearbook.
Survey methodology: Employment and Unemployment (bi-annually); Statistical Yearbook.
Dissemination
Time needed for initial release of survey results: 52 days after the survey reference period.
Advance information of public about date of initial release: Yes.
Availability of unpublished data upon request: Yes.
Availability of data in machine-readable form: Diskettes and internet (selected information).
Website: http://www.nsi.bg/.

Canada

Title of the survey: Labour Force Survey.
Organization responsible for the survey:
Planning and conduct of the survey: Statistics Canada.
Analysis and publication of the results: Statistics Canada.
Topics covered: Persons currently economically active, employed and unemployed; persons currently in time-related underemployment and persons currently outside the labour force; discouraged workers; hours of work; duration of employment and unemployment; wages; second jobs; industry; occupation; status in employment; education/training levels.
Coverage of the survey:
Geographical: Areas excluded are Yukon (collected, but not included in national estimates), Northwest Territories, Nunavut and Indian Reserves.
Population groups: Civilian non-institutional population of age 15 years and above, excluding the full-time members of the Canadian Armed Forces and inmates of institutions.
Availability of estimates from other sources for the excluded areas/groups: Estimates for Yukon as three months' moving averages.
Groups covered by the survey but excluded from the published results: Yukon, see above.
Periodicity:
Conduct of the survey: Monthly
Publication of results: Monthly, on first or second Friday of month following the month of the reference period.
Reference periods:
Employment: Week that includes the 15th day of month.
Seeking work: The last four weeks preceding the interview..
Availability for work: The reference week which includes the 15th of the month.
Concepts and definitions:
Employment: Employed persons are those aged 15 years and over who, during the reference week:
a) did any work at all at a job or business, that is, paid work in the context of an employer-employee relationship, or self-employed. It also includes unpaid family work, which is defined as unpaid work contributing directly to the operation of a farm, business or professional practice owned and operated by a related member of the same household; or,
b) had a job but were not at work due to factors such as own illness or disability, personal or family responsibilities, vacation, dispute or other reasons (excluding persons on layoff, between casual jobs, and those with a job to start at a future date).
Unemployment: Unemployed persons are those aged 15 years and over who, during the reference week:
a) were on temporary layoff during the reference week with an expectation of recall and were available for work, or
b) were without work, had actively looked for work in the past four weeks, and were available for work, or
c) had a new job to start within four weeks from reference weeks, and were available for work.
Underemployment:
Time-related underemployment: No information provided.
Inadequate employment situations: No information provided.
Hours of work: Actual hours worked include both paid and unpaid hours worked. Usual hours worked for paid employees refer to the normal paid or contract hours, not counting any overtime, but for self-employed it refers to the number of hours worked in a typical week.
Employment-related income:
Income from paid employment: Paid employees report wage/salary before taxes and other deductions, and include tips, commissions and bonuses, for main job.
Income from self-employment: No information provided.
Informal sector: Not applicable.
Usual activity: No information provided.
Classifications:
Branch of economic activity (industry):
Title of the classification: North American Industry Classification System (NAICS).
Population groups classified by industry: Employed and unemployed persons (if worked within last 12 months).
Number of groups used for coding: 312.
Links to ISIC: Indirect links to ISIC-Rev. 3.
Occupation:
Title of the classification: Standard Occupational Classification 1991 (SOC-91).
Population groups classified by occupation: Employed and unemployed persons (if worked within last 12 moths).
Number of groups used for coding: 514.
Links to ISCO: Indirect links to ISCO-88.
Status in employment:
Title of the classification: National classification, no title given.
Population groups classified by status in employment: Employed and unemployed persons (if worked within last 12 months).
Groups used for classification: Paid employees (distinguishing: private, public) and self-employed (distinguishing: incorporated, unincorporated and unpaid family worker).
Links to ICSE: ICSE-1993.
Education:
Title of the classification: National classification, no title given.
Population groups classified education: Employed and unemployed persons.
Groups used for classification: No information provided.
Links to ISCED: Indirect links to ISCED-1976.
Sample size and design:
Ultimate sampling unit: Dwelling and household.
Sample size (ultimate sampling units): 61 000 dwellings; 53 500 households.
Overall sampling fraction: 1/240.
Sample frame: Stratified multistage area frame. List frame of apartment buildings in large cities.
Updating of the sample frame: On-going to deal with growth. Major re-design every 10 years.
Rotation:
Scheme: Dwellings in sample for 6 consecutive months and then out.
Percentage of units remaining in the sample for two consecutive survey rounds: 83.3 percent.
Maximum number of interview per sample unit: No information provided.
Length of time for complete renewal of the sample: No information provided.
Field work:
Type of interview: Computer assisted interviewing, telephone and face-to-face.
Number of ultimate sampling units per sample area: No information provided.
Duration of field work:
Total: One week.
Per sample area: No information provided.

Survey organization: Permanent.
Number of field staff: 777 interviewers and 79 supervisors.
Substitution of non-responding ultimate sampling units: No.
Estimation and adjustments:
Total non-response rate: 5 percent.
Adjustment for total non-response: Yes.
Imputation for item non-response: Yes, by using previous month's response, if available, for maximum one month. Hot deck imputation.
Adjustment for areas/population not covered: No.
Adjustment for under-coverage: Yes.
Adjustment for over-coverage: Yes.
Adjustment for seasonal variations: Yes, using Statistics Canada version of X11-ARIMA.
History of the survey:
Title and date of the first survey: Labour Force Survey, November 1945.
Significant changes or revisions: (a) Usual hours of work definition for paid employees changed January 1997: Was previously the same as for self-employed and covered both paid and un-paid hours. (b) Estimates are re-calculated after census population estimates become available. LFS estimates are benchmarked to latest census population counts. Last revision with release of January 2000 results, for estimates back to 1976.
Documentation and dissemination:
Documentation:
Survey results: Labour force information (Catalogue number 71-001-PPB) (monthly).
Survey methodology: Guide to the Labour Force Survey (71-543-GIE); Methodology of the Canadian Labour Force Survey, December 1998 (71-526-XPB).
Dissemination:
Time needed for initial release of survey results: Within one month.
Advance information of public about date of initial release: Yes.
Availability of unpublished data upon request: Yes.
Availability of data in machine-readable form: CD-ROM: Labour Force Historical Review (Catalogue 71F0004XCB) (annually, usually in February).
Website: http://www.statcan.ca/.

China

Title of the survey: Urban Labour Force Sampling Survey
Organization responsible for the survey:
Planning and conduct of the survey: Department of Population, Social, Science and Technology Statistics
Analysis and publication of the results: Department of Population, Social, Science and Technology Statistics
Topics covered: Employment, unemployment, hours of work, nature of residence card, duration of unemployment, status in employment and educational level.
Coverage of the survey:
Geographical: Urban areas of the country.
Population groups: All persons 16 years and over, excluding armed forces and foreigners.
Availability of estimates from other sources for the excluded areas/groups: Only available for armed forces.
Groups covered by the survey but excluded from the published results: The unemployed.
Periodicity:
Conduct of the survey: Three times per year.
Publication of results: Annually, for certain variables.
Reference periods:
Employment: One week.
Seeking work: Three months prior to the date of the interview.
Availability for work: Two weeks following the date of the interview.
Concepts and definitions:
Employment: All persons living in urban areas above a specified age and receiving income from engagement in economic activities, i.e.: (1) those aged 16 years and above who worked for at least one hour during the reference week for income and (2) with a working unit or working site but not at work temporarily during the reference week because of holiday, vacation, study or suchlike.
It includes:
a) persons with a job but temporarily absent due to illness or injury, vacation or annual leave, maternity or paternity leave, parental leave, educational or training leave, bad weather, etc.;
b) persons without work, currently available for work who had made arrangements to start a new job on a date subsequent to the reference period;
c) persons who performed some work for pay or profit during the reference week but were retired and receiving a pension, were registered as jobseekers at an employment office or receiving unemployment benefits;
d) unpaid family workers at work during the reference week
e) all members of the armed forces.
Unemployment: All persons living in urban areas above a specified age, currently available for work, but without work during the reference week, and seeking a job by specific steps, i.e. aged 16 and above: (1) without work for income during the reference week and not belonging to the second group of the definition of employment, (2) seeking a job by specific steps within 3 months before the reference week and (3) available for work within two weeks.
It includes: persons without work and currently available for work who were trying to establish their own enterprise; persons who were seeking and/or available for work but were retired and receiving a pension.
Underemployment:
Time-related underemployment: Not applicable.
Inadequate employment situations: Not applicable.
Hours of work: Actual hours worked in all jobs; the time unit is the hour.
Employment-related income:
Income from paid employment: Not applicable.
Income from self-employment: Not applicable.
Informal sector: Not applicable.
Usual activity: Not applicable.
Classifications:
Branch of economic activity (industry):
Title of the classification: No information.
Population groups classified by industry: No information.
Number of groups used for coding: No information.
Occupation:
Title of the classification: No information.
Population groups classified by occupation: No information.
Number of groups used for coding: No information.
Status in employment:
Title of the classification: No information.
Population groups classified by status in employment: No information.
Groups used for classification: Seven groups: 1. Employment in urban units, 2. Employment in township enterprises, 3. Employment in agriculture, fishing, forestry and hunting, 4. Employees in private individual units, 5. Employers in private individual units, 6. Self-employed, 7. Other.
Links to ICSE: No.
Education:
Title of the classification: No information.
Population groups classified by education: No information.
Groups used for classification: Five groups: 1. Illiterate and semi-illiterate, 2. Primary school, 3. Junior middle school, 4. Senior middle school, 5. College and higher level.
Links to ISCED: No.
Sample size and design:
Ultimate sampling unit: Cluster of about 50 to 100 households.
Sample size (ultimate sampling units): (1.2 million households in the whole country) around 0.34 million in the urban areas.
Overall sampling fraction: 1 per cent; the sample design is combined with the annual Population Survey covering the whole country.
Sample frame: The frame is based on the latest Census data and the Register of the Public Security Ministry. For ultimate sampling units, the sample frame is made by the enumerators.
Updating of the sample: Usually each year; the ultimate sampling units are changed every year in each province.
Rotation: NO ROTATION SCHEME
Scheme: NOT APPLICABLE.
Percentage of units remaining in the sample for two consecutive survey rounds: NOT AVAILABLE.
Maximum number of interviews per sample unit: NOT AVAILABLE.
Length of time for complete renewal of the sample: NOT AVAILABLE.
Field work:
Type of interview: Personal interview using paper and pencil.
Number of ultimate sampling units per sample area: About 1400.
Duration of field work
Total: Twenty days
Per sample area: Not available.
Survey organization: In each province there exists a permanent survey organization. For each survey round, personnel are also recruited.

Number of field staff: Approximately 1500 field staff.
Substitution of non-responding ultimate sampling units: Yes.
Estimation and adjustments:
Total non-response rate: About 5 per cent.
Adjustment for total non-response: Yes.
Imputation for item non-response: No.
Adjustment for areas/population not covered: Yes.
Adjustment for under-coverage: Yes.
Adjustment for over-coverage: Yes.
Adjustment for seasonal variations: No.
History of the survey:
Title and date of the first survey: Urban Labour Force Survey System, October 1, 1996.
Significant changes or revisions: None.
Documentation and dissemination:
Documentation
Survey results: China Statistical Yearbook.
Survey methodology: China Statistical Yearbook.
Dissemination
Time needed for initial release of survey results: Not yet available.
Advance information of public about date of initial release: YES.
Availability of unpublished data upon request: Not up to now.
Availability of data in machine-readable form: Tabulations can be made available on diskette.
Website: http://www.stats.gov.cn/.

Croatia

Title of the survey: Labour Force Survey
Organization responsible for the survey:
Planning and conduct of the survey: Central Bureau of Statistics
Analysis and publication of the results: Central Bureau of Statistics
Topics covered: Employment, unemployment, underemployment, hours of work, duration of employment, duration of unemployment, discouraged workers, occasional workers, industry, occupation, status in employment, educational level and second jobs.
Coverage of the survey:
Geographical: Whole country with the exception of territories occupied during the war of 1995-1996.
Population groups: All usual residents, aged 15 years and above living in non-institutional household, including those temporarily absent. Excluded are persons residing abroad and non-resident citizens.
Availability of estimates from other sources for the excluded areas/groups: NO.
Groups covered by the survey but excluded from the published results: NONE
Periodicity:
Conduct of the survey: Continuous.
Publication of results: Bi-annually.
Reference periods:
Employment: Last week of each month, without public holidays or other non-working days.
Seeking work: Four weeks prior to the date of the interview.
Availability for work: Two weeks following the date of the interview.
Concepts and definitions:
Employment: employed are all persons aged 15 years and above who, during of reference period (a) performed some work for at least one hour for payment in cash or in kind; (b) did not work but had an assurance to return to the same job when the reason for absence holds no longer.
Also included in totals are persons who during the reference week were:
a)temporarily absent from work due to leave, illness, bad weather, vocational training leave or other similar reason.
b)full- and part-time workers seeking other work during the reference period;
c)full- and part-time students working full- or part-time;
d)persons who performed some work during the reference week while being either retired and receiving a pension; or were registered as job seekers at an employment office or receiving unemployment benefits;
f)paid and unpaid family workers (if they worked at least one hour);
g)private domestic servants;
h)career members of the armed forces living in households;
i)persons engage in production of goods for own final use.
Unemployment: Unemployed are all persons of 15 years and above who did not work at all during the reference week, were actively looking for work during the four weeks previous to the interview and were available to start work within the two weeks following the survey week. Also included in the unemployed are persons who were not actively looking for work because they have found a job to start in the future.
Underemployment:
Time-related underemployment: Persons who, during the reference week, worked less than statutory hours and were willing and available to work additional hours.
Inadequate employment situations: Persons who, during the reference week
a)were willing and available to change current job because they worked less than statutory hours against their will;
b) wished to change a job due to inappropriate use of their skill, unsatisfactory working conditions or personal/health reasons, etc.
Hours of work: Usual and actual hours worked during the reference week in the main job and actual hours worked during the reference week in the secondary job(s).
Employment-related income:
Income from paid employment: Net monthly income of each interviewed person.
Income from self-employment: Net monthly income of each interviewed person.
Informal sector: Not applicable.
Usual activity: Not applicable.
Classifications:
Branch of economic activity (industry):
Title of the classification: National classification.
Population groups classified by industry: Employed persons (in main and secondary jobs) and unemployed persons with previous job experience.
Number of groups used for coding: 571
Links to ISIC: ISIC-Rev. 3.
Occupation:
Title of the classification: National classification.
Population groups classified by occupation: Employed persons (in main and secondary jobs) and unemployed persons with previous work experience.
Number of groups used for coding: 402
Links to ISCO: ISCO-98.
Status in employment:
Title of the classification: National classification.
Population groups classified by status in employment: Employed persons and unemployed persons with previous work experience.
Groups used for classification: 4 groups (employees, employers, own-account worker, unpaid family workers).
Links to ICSE: ICSE-1993.
Education:
Title of the classification: National classification.
Population groups classified by education: All persons aged 15 years and over.
Groups used for classification: 9 groups (no schooling, 4-7 years of primary school, 1-2 years of secondary vocational schooling, 3rd year of secondary vocation schooling, 4th year of secondary vocational schooling, college, university, post-graduate, PhD).
Links to ISCED: Yes.
Sample size and design:
Ultimate sampling unit: Dwelling.
Sample size (ultimate sampling units): About 8 500 dwelling representing 6 900 household and covering some 20 000 persons.
Overall sampling fraction: 0.74 per cent.
Sample frame: From 2002 onwards, the sample frame is derived from the 2001 Population Census data base. If for the 1996-1999 period, the master sample frame is built up on the basis of the 1991 household census updated in 1996, it is based on the Croatian Electrical Utility Company data base for 2000 and 2001.
Updating of the sample: Updated for 2002 on the basis of the 2001 Population Census.
Rotation:
Scheme: From 2000 onwards, no rotation. For the 1996-1999 period, in every survey round (6 months), one third of sampled dwellings is dropped out and replaced by new dwellings, so that two thirds of units remain unchanged.
Percentage of units remaining in the sample for two consecutive survey rounds: Not applicable.
Maximum number of interviews per sample unit: No information provided.
Length of time for complete renewal of the sample: No information provided.
Field work:
Type of interview: Paper and pencil
Number of ultimate sampling units per sample area: 12 households per enumeration district.

Duration of field work:
Total: 14 days after each reference period.
Per sample area: 14 days after each reference period.
Survey organization: Permanent survey organization.
Number of field staff: Approximately 203 interviewers and 31 supervisors.
Substitution of non-responding ultimate sampling units: No.
Estimation and adjustments:
Total non-response rate: 10 per cent for the 2001 first semester survey. It is usually about 12 per cent.
Adjustment for total non-response: No.
Imputation for item non-response: No.
Adjustment for areas/population not covered: No.
Adjustment for undercoverage: No.
Adjustment for overcoverage: No.
Adjustment for seasonal variations: No.
History of the survey:
Title and date of the first survey: Labour Force Survey (Anketa o radno snazi), November 1996.
Significant changes or revisions: Regular improvements of the survey questionnaire; updating of the sample frame.
Documentation and dissemination:
Documentation:
Survey results: First Releases: LFS – Labour Force Survey in the Republic of Croatia (bi-annual); LFS Results: comparison with the European Union results (annually); Statistical Year Book; Monthly Statistical Report.
Survey methodology: Relevant methodological information is included in all the above-mentioned publication.
Dissemination
Time needed for initial release of survey results: Three months.
Advance information of public about date of initial release: Yes.
Availability of unpublished data upon request: Yes.
Availability of data in machine-readable form: Diskettes, CD-Rom and selected information on the internet.
Website: http://www.dzs.hr/.

Cyprus

Title of the survey: Labour force survey.
Organization responsible for the survey:
Planning and conduct of the survey: Statistical Service.
Analysis and publication of the results: Statistical Service.
Topics covered: Employment, unemployment, underemployment, hours of work, duration of employment and unemployment, industry, occupation, status in employment, education/qualification levels, second jobs.
Coverage of the survey:
Geographical: The Government-controlled area of Cyprus.
Population groups: Persons aged 15 years and over. Excluded: persons living in institutions, non-residents citizens, tourists, persons residing abroad and students studying abroad.
Availability of estimates from other sources for the excluded areas/groups: NOT APPLICABLE.
Groups covered by the survey but excluded from the published results: NOT APPLICABLE.
Periodicity:
Conduct of the survey: Annually.
Publication of results: Annually.
Reference periods:
Employment: One week within the second quarter.
Seeking work: Four weeks within the second quarter.
Availability for work: Two weeks within the second quarter.
Concepts and definitions:
Employment: Persons aged 15 years and over who, during the reference week, worked for at least one hour and persons who had a job from which they were temporarily absent.
It includes:
persons with a job but temporarily absent from work due to illness or injury, vacation or annual leave, maternity or paternity leave, educational or training leave if less than six months, absence without leave, labor management dispute, bad weather, mechanical breakdown, etc.
b) full or part-time workers seeking other work during the reference week;
c) persons who performed some work for pay or profit during the reference week but were subject to compulsory schooling, retired and receiving a pension, registered as job seekers at an employment office or receiving unemployment benefits;
d) full or part-time students working full or part-time;
e) paid apprentices and trainees;
f) unpaid family workers at work during the reference week or temporarily absent from work;
g) volunteers and career members of the armed forces and persons in paid civilian service equivalent to military service.
Unemployment: Persons aged 15 to 64 years who were currently without work and available for work during the reference week and had searched for work during the last four weeks or who are going to work or trying to establish their own enterprise within the next two weeks which follow the week interview. It also includes part-time students seeking full-time work and seasonal workers not at work during the off-season, if they are seeking work.
Underemployment:
Time-related underemployment: No information provided.
Inadequate employment situations: No information provided.
Hours of work: No information provided.
Employment-related income:
Income from paid employment: Not covered.
Income from self-employment: Not covered.
Informal sector: Not covered.
Usual activity: Not covered.
Classifications:
Branch of economic activity (industry):
Title of the classification: Nomenclature d'Activites de la Communauté Européenne (NACE).
Population groups classified by industry: Employed and unemployed persons.
Number of groups used for coding: No information provided.
Links to ISIC: ISIC Rev.3 at the two digits level (Division).
Occupation:
Title of the classification: ISCO-1988.
Population groups classified by occupation: Employed and unemployed persons.
Number of groups used for coding: 226 minor groups (three digits level).
Links to ISCO: ISCO-1988.
Status in employment:
Title of the classification: No information provided.
Population groups classified by status in employment: Employed and unemployed persons.
Groups used for classification: Four groups: self-employed with or without employees; employees; unpaid family workers.
Links to ICSE: ISCE-1993.
Education:
Title of the classification: ISCED-1997.
Population groups classified by education: Employed and unemployed persons.
Groups used for classification:
Links to ISCED: ISCED-1997.
Sample size and design:
Ultimate sampling unit: Dwelling.
Sample size (ultimate sampling units): 4 157 dwellings.
Overall sampling fraction: 1.6 per cent.
Sample frame: List of dwellings derived from the 1992 Population census.
Updating of the sample: Newly constructed dwellings are added, every year, to the frame.
Rotation:
Scheme: 25 per cent are replaced every year.
Percentage of units remaining in the sample for two consecutive survey rounds: 75 per cent.
Maximum number of interviews per sample unit: Four times.
Length of time for complete renewal of the sample: Four years.
Field work:
Type of interview: CAPI.
Number of ultimate sampling units per sample area: About 250 units.
Duration of field work:
Total: 13 weeks.
Per sample area: One week.
Survey organization: A core of three permanent persons.
Number of field staff: 22 persons.
Substitution of non-responding ultimate sampling units: YES.
Estimation and adjustments:
Total non-response rate: About one per cent.
Adjustment for total non-response: YES.
Imputation for item non-response: NO.
Adjustment for areas/population not covered: NO.
Adjustment for undercoverage: YES.
Adjustment for overcoverage: Not applicable.
Adjustment for seasonal variations: NO.

History of the survey:
Title and date of the first survey: Labour Force Survey 1999.
Significant changes or revisions: Not applicable.
Documentation and dissemination:
Documentation:
Survey results: No publication as yet; planned to be annually.
Survey methodology: No publication as yet; planned to be annually.
Dissemination
Time needed for initial release of survey results: No information provided.
Advance information of public about date of initial release: No.
Availability of unpublished data upon request: Yes.
Availability of data in machine-readable form: Yes.
Website: http://www.pio.gov.cy/dsr/.

Czech Republic

Title of the survey: Labour Force Sample Survey
Organization responsible for the survey:
Planning and conduct of the survey: Czech Statistical Office.
Analysis and publication of the results: Czech Statistical Office.
Topics covered: Employment, unemployment, underemployment, hours of work, duration of employment, duration of unemployment, discouraged workers, occasional workers, industry, occupation, status in employment, educational level, usual main status, second jobs.
Coverage of the survey:
Geographical: Whole country.
Population groups: All the population aged 15 and above living in households. More specifically, it covers all persons living in dwellings continuously for at least three months, disregarding the status of their staying there (permanent, temporary or non-registered). The exception are conscripts who are surveyed at their place of residences prior to their military service.
The survey does not cover persons living in collective accommodation establishments for a long period of time, which is why data on certain population groups (foreign nationals living and working in the CR in particular) are rather scarce.
Availability of estimates from other sources for the excluded areas/groups: No.
Groups covered by the survey but excluded from the published results: None.
Periodicity:
Conduct of the survey: Continuously.
Publication of results: Quarterly.
Reference periods:
Employment: One week (last seven days prior to the date of the interview).
Seeking work: Four weeks prior to the date of the interview.
Availability for work: Two weeks following the date of the interview.
Concepts and definitions:
Employment: All persons aged 15 years and over who, during the reference week, did any work for at least one hour, and were in the following categories:
a) paid employment:
At work: persons who executed any work during the reference week for wage salary, in cash or in kind. Work may be permanent, temporary, seasonal, occasional or referring to first or second jobs;
With a job but not at work: persons temporarily absent from their job, during the reference week, and have a formal link with their job, such as a working contract, etc.
b) employed in their own enterprise:
At work: persons who executed any work, during the reference week, for profit or family income, in cash or in kind;
With their enterprise but not at work: persons with an enterprise who were temporarily absent from work during the reference week for any specific reason.
Also included in the employed are the armed forces (career members and conscripts) as well as apprentices, students, domestic personnel, etc., who receive wage, salary or remuneration.
However, persons on additional child-care leave are not automatically classified as employed.
Excluded are persons engaged in the production of goods for their own household, such as housework, repairing, painting, etc.
Unemployment: All persons aged 15 years and over who met the following three conditions during the reference week:
(i) had no work;
(ii) were actively looking for work. The active form of seeking work includes registration with an employment office or private employment exchange, checking at work sites, farms, markets or other assembly places, placing or answering newspaper advertisements, taking own steps to establish own business, applying for work permit and license, or looking for a job in a different manner and
(iii) were currently available for work - i.e., were available during the reference period for paid employment or self-employment either immediately or within the two weeks following the date of the interview.
If persons fail to meet even one of the above conditions, they are classified as employed or inactive. The only exception refers to persons who do not seek work, because they have already found a job, but their commencement of work is fixed for a later date. According to Eurostat definition, these persons are classified as unemployed.
Underemployment:
Time-related underemployment: Persons who, during the reference week, involuntary worked less than the normal duration of working hours established for a given type of activity. Excluded are persons not working for more than four weeks.
Inadequate employment situations: Not applicable.
Hours of work: Usual and actual hours worked in the main job. Actual hours worked for in the secondary job(s).
Employment-related income:
Income from paid employment: Not applicable.
Income from self-employment: Not applicable.
Informal sector: Not applicable.
Usual activity: The following population groups are subject to questions about their usual economic status: apprentices, students at secondary schools, university students, persons on maternity and child-care leave (parental leave), housewives, retired persons, retired persons due to disability, retired persons due to partial disability, unemployed, conscripts, persons engaged in community service, children under 15 years.
Classifications:
Branch of economic activity (industry):
Title of the classification: CZ-NACE.
Population groups classified by industry: Employed persons and unemployed persons with previous job experience.
Number of groups used for coding: No information provided.
Links to ISIC: ISIC-Rev. 3 (4 digit level).
Occupation:
Title of the classification: CZ-ISCO-88.
Population groups classified by occupation: Employed persons and unemployed persons with previous work experience.
Number of groups used for coding: No information provided.
Links to ISCO: ISCO-88 (4 digit level).
Status in employment:
Title of the classification: CZ-ICSE.
Population groups classified by status in employment: Employed and unemployed persons.
Groups used for classification: 5 groups (employees, employers, own-account worker, members of producers' co-operatives, contributing family workers.
Links to ICSE: ICSE-1993.
Education:
Title of the classification: National Classification of Education Subjects (KKOV), 2nd edition, 1991 and ISCED-1997.
Population groups classified by education: all population groups.
Groups used for classification: No information provided.
Links to ISCED: ISCED-1997.
Sample size and design:
Ultimate sampling unit: Dwelling.
Sample size (ultimate sampling units): About 25 000 dwellings covering approximately 63 0000 persons.
Overall sampling fraction: 0.6 per cent of permanently occupied dwellings.
Sample frame: The sample frame is built on the basis of the Population Census conducted in 1991.
Updating of the sample: Quarterly.
Rotation:
Scheme: The panel of selected dwellings varied during the survey. One fifth of the panel is rotated every quarter.
Percentage of units remaining in the sample for two consecutive survey rounds: 80 per cent.
Maximum number of interviews per sample unit: five quarters.
Length of time for complete renewal of the sample: five quarters.
Field work:
Type of interview: Paper and pencil, telephone and CAPI/CATI where possible.
Number of ultimate sampling units per sample area: 300 dwellings per quarter.
Duration of field work:
Total: Continuously.

Per sample area: Each interviewer works 4 days per week plus one day for questionnaire supplements. **Survey organization:** Permanent survey organization.
Number of field staff: 113 interviewers and 14 supervisors.
Substitution of non-responding ultimate sampling units: No.
Estimation and adjustments:
Total non-response rate: 24 per cent.
Adjustment for total non-response: Yes.
Imputation for item non-response: No.
Adjustment for areas/population not covered: No.
Adjustment for undercoverage: No.
Adjustment for overcoverage: No.
Adjustment for seasonal variations: No.
History of the survey:
Title and date of the first survey: Czech Labour Force Sample Survey, December 1992.
Significant changes or revisions: Since 1993 the database has been corrected in the framework of the preparation of historical data. More specifically the following should be noted:
a) removal of differences in the reference periods: all data from 1993 to 1997, when the survey was conducted in seasonal quarters, were converted to calendar quarters;
b) inclusion of (i) conscripts and (ii) women on maternity and childcare leave into the 1992 and 1993 survey results;
c) re-weighting of 1993-1996 data retrospectively on the basis of the latest demographic data.
d) Full harmonization of the survey questionnaire with the Eurostat questionnaires for the survey rounds beginning in January 2002.
Documentation and dissemination:
Documentation:
Survey results: Employment and Unemployment in the Czech Republic as Measured by the Labour Force Survey (quarterly); Labour Market in the Czech Republic: Time series LFSS (1993-1999).
Survey methodology: Employment and Unemployment in the Czech Republic as Measured by the Labour Force Survey.
Dissemination:
Time needed for initial release of survey results: No information provided.
Advance information of public about date of initial release: Yes.
Availability of unpublished data upon request: Yes.
Availability of data in machine-readable form: Diskettes, internet and e-mail.
Website: http://www.czso.cz/.

Denmark

Title of the survey: Beskaeftigelsesundersökelsen (BU): Labour Force Survey (LFS).
Organization responsible for the survey:
Planning and conduct of the survey: Statistics Denmark (DS).
Analysis and publication of the results: Statistics Denmark DS.
Topics covered: Persons currently and usually economically active, employed and unemployed. Persons currently in time-related underemployment, persons in inadequate employment situations and persons currently outside the labour force. Discouraged workers. Hours of work. Duration of employment and unemployment. Second jobs. Industry, occupation, status in employment, education/training levels.
Coverage of the survey:
Geographical: Whole country, excluding the self-governing territories Greenland and the Faeroe Islands.
Population groups: Covers registered resident population of age 15-66 (-74 from 2001) years. Exclude non-residents and persons without fixed address.
Availability of estimates from other sources for the excluded areas/groups: None.
Groups covered by the survey but excluded from the published results: None.
Periodicity:
Conduct of the survey: Quarterly.
Publication of results: Quarterly.
Reference periods:
Employment: One week.
Seeking work: Within last four weeks.
Availability: Within two weeks.
Concepts and definitions:
Employment: Persons who a) performed some work for pay, profit or family gain during the reference week; and b) were temporarily absent from work during the reference week because of illness or leave, but were definitely going to return. Some work is defined as 1 hour or more during the reference week.
Unemployment: Persons who were currently without work and available for work within two weeks, and who had searched for work sometime during the last four weeks.
Underemployment:
Time-related underemployment: Employed persons who have searched for additional work during the reference period and/or were willing and available to engage in additional work.
Inadequate employment situations: Employed persons seeking another job or employment for reasons of getting better working conditions, better commuting situation and/or better use of skills.
Hours of work: Normal: according to agreement. Usual: in a typical week. Actual: hours actually worked during the reference week.
Employment-related income:
Income from paid employment: Not applicable.
Income from self-employment: Not applicable.
Informal sector: Not applicable.
Usual activity: No information.
Classifications:
Branch of economic activity (industry):
Title of the classification: Danish adaptation of NACE, rev. 1.
Population groups classified by industry: Employed and unemployed persons (last industry for the unemployed).
Number of groups used for coding: At the 3rd digit level.
Links to ISIC: ISIC-Rev2 and Rev.3.
Occupation:
Title of the classification: Dansk erhversnomenklatur (DISCO).
Population groups classified by occupation: Employed and unemployed persons (last occupation for the unemployed).
Number of groups used for coding: At the 4th digit level.
Links to ISCO: ISCO-68 and ISCO-88.
Status in employment:
Title of the classification: No information.
Population groups classified by status in employment: Employed and unemployed persons (last status for the unemployed).
Groups used for classification: Employees; self-employed with or without at least one employee; unpaid family workers.
Links to ICSE: ICSE-1993.
Education:
Title of the classification: National classification.
Population groups classified education: All persons.
Groups used for classification: No information.
Links to ISCED: ISCED-1997.
Sample size and design:
Ultimate sampling unit: Individuals.
Sample size (ultimate sampling units): 15 600.
Overall sampling fraction: 0.00428.
Sample frame: Central Population Register (CPR).
Updating of the sample frame: Weekly.
Rotation:
Scheme: No information. Every person is interviewed in two consecutive quarters and then one year after second interview, i.e. 66 percent of sample participated in the previous round.
Percentage of units remaining in the sample for two consecutive survey rounds: Every person is interviewed in two consecutive quarters and then one year after second interview, i.e. 66 percent of sample participated in the previous round.
Maximum number of interviews per sample unit: No information.
Length of time for complete renewal of the sample: No information.
Field work:
Type of interview: Computer assisted interviewing by telephone, and mail-out/mail-in for those that cannot be reached by phone.
Number of ultimate sampling units per sample area: No information.
Duration of field work:
Total: 6-7 weeks.
Per sample area: No information.
Survey organization: Permanent.
Number of field staff: 40 interviewers and supervisors.
Substitution of non-responding ultimate sampling units: No.
Estimation and adjustments:
Total non-response rate: 27 percent.
Adjustment for total non-response: Imputations, not described.
Imputation for item non-response: No.
Adjustment for areas/population not covered: No.
Adjustment for under-coverage: No.
Adjustment for over-coverage: No.
Adjustment for seasonal variations: No.
History of the survey:
Title and date of the first survey: Labour Force Survey (LFS), spring 1972.

Significant changes or revisions: Significant breaks in time series in 1984, 1987, 1992, 1994 and 2000
Documentation and dissemination:.
Documentation:
Survey results: Statistiske Efterretninger: Arbejdsmarked.
Survey methodology: Same.
Dissemination:
Time needed for initial release of survey results: 3 months.
Advance information of public about date of initial release: Yes.
Availability of unpublished data upon request: Yes.
Availability of data in machine-readable form: Diskettes or magnetic tapes.
Website: http://www.dst.dk/.

Egypt

Title of the survey: Labour force sample survey
Organization responsible for the survey
Planning and conduct of the survey: Central Agency for Public Mobilisation and Statistics, CAPMAS
Analysis and publication of the results: CAPMAS
Topics covered: Employment, unemployment, hours of work, duration of employment, duration of unemployment, occasional workers, industry, current and past occupation, status in employment, and education level.
Coverage of the survey:
Geographical: Whole country, including urban and rural areas.
Population groups: Armed forces, foreigners, unsettled populations, and Egyptian nationals residing abroad are excluded.
Availability of estimates from other sources for the excluded areas/groups: No information provided.
Groups covered by the survey but excluded from the published results: None.
Periodicity:
Conduct of the survey: Bi-annually.
Publication of results: Annual.
Reference periods:
Employment: Fixed reference week.
Seeking work: Reference week.
Availability for work: Reference week.
Concepts and definitions:
Employment: Persons, 6 years old and over, who were engaged in a production or service activity, for one hour or more during the reference week, or had a formal job attachment but were temporary absent from work during the reference week due to illness or injury, vacation or annual leave, maternity, paternity or parental leave, educational or training leave, absence without leave, labour management dispute, bad weather, mechanical breakdown.
It includes:
a) Persons who performed some work for pay or profit during the reference week but were subject to compulsory schooling, retired and receiving a pension, registered as jobseekers at an employment office, or receiving unemployment benefits.
b) Full or part-time students working full or part-time.
c) Paid apprentices and trainees, and participants in employment promotion schemes.
d) Persons engaged in production of goods for own final use.
Excluded are:
a) Unpaid apprentices and trainees, persons engaged in production of services for their household.
b) Unpaid family workers temporarily absent from work during the reference week and seasonal workers not at work during the off-season.
c) Persons on temporary or indefinite lay-off without pay and persons on unpaid leave initiated by the employer.
Unemployment: Persons, 15 years old and over, not employed during the reference week, who were able and willing to work, and were looking for work during the reference week.
It includes:
a) Persons without work and current available and looking for work who had made arrangements to start a new job on a date subsequent to the reference week.
b) Persons without work and currently available and looking for work, who were trying to establish their own enterprise.
c) Full or part-time students seeking full or part-time work.
d) Persons who were seeking or available for work but were subject to compulsory schooling or retired and receiving a pension.
Excluded are persons without work, available for work, but not seeking work during the reference week.

Classifications:
Branch of economic activity (industry):
Title of the classification: No information.
Population groups classified by industry: Employed and unemployed persons with previous work experience.
Number of groups used for coding: 18 categories.
Linked to ISIC: ISIC- Rev. 3.
Occupation:
Title of the classification: No information.
Population groups classified by occupation: Employed and unemployed persons with previous work experience.
Number of groups used for coding: 10 major groups.
Linked to ISCO: ISCO-88.
Status in employment:
Title of the classification: No information
Population groups classified by status in employment: Employed persons only.
Groups used for classification: Employee. Employer. Own-account worker. Unpaid family worker.
Linked to ICSE: ICSE-1993.
Education:
Title of the classification: No information.
Population groups classified by status in employment: Employed and unemployed persons.
Groups used for classification: Illiterate. Can read and write. Less than intermediate. Intermediate school completed. Above intermediate. University and higher.
Links to ISCED: Certain groups linked to ISCED.
Sample size and design:
Ultimate sampling unit: Housing unit (composed of one or more households).
Sample size (ultimate sampling units): 41'660 housing units divided equally between two yearly rounds (May and November).
Overall sampling fraction: 6%.
Sample frame: Master sample based on 1995 data. Two-stage sampling. In the first stage, primary sampling units covering about 1 500 households are selected systematically, 261 PSUs in urban areas and 185 PSUs in rural areas. In the second stage, 95 housing units are selected in each urban or rural sample PSU.
Updating of the sample: No updating has been carried out yet.
Rotation: None.
Field work:
Type of interview: Personal interview.
Number of ultimate sampling units per sample area: 95 housing units.
Duration of fieldwork:
Total: 28 days for the May round (1st to 28 June) and 28 days for the November round (1st to 28 December).
Per sample area: No information provided.
Survey organization: Permanent.
Number of field staff: About 210 interviewers and 70 supervisors.
Substitution of non-responding sampling units: No.
Estimation and adjustments
Total non-response rate: 1.7%.
Adjustment for total non-response: Yes.
Imputation for item non-response: No.
Adjustment for areas/population not covered: No.
Adjustment for under-coverage: No.
Adjustment for over-coverage: No.
Adjustment for seasonal variations: No.
History of the survey
Title and date of the first survey: Labour force sample survey, November 1957.
Significant changes or revisions: Surveys conducted between 1957 to 1964 totaled 24 rounds with different periodicities. From 1968 to 1985, the survey was conducted annually. From 1987 to 1992, quarterly. Since 1993, it is conducted bi-annually. In census years, the survey was not conducted. The surveys carried out between 1987 and 1992 covered two additional topics: usual activity and secondary jobs.
Documentation and dissemination
Documentation
Survey results: Annual Bulletin of Labour Force Sample Survey of the Arab Republic of Egypt.
Survey methodology: In Annual Bulletin.
Dissemination
Time needed for initial release of survey results: One year. Latest data for 1998, published on 30 December 1999.
Advance information of public about date of initial release: No.
Availability of unpublished data upon request: No information provided.

Availability of data in machine-readable form: Tabulated data available in diskettes on request. Internet dissemination envisaged for the future.
Website: http://www.capmas.gov.eg/.

Estonia

Title of the survey: Estonian Labour Force Survey 2001 (ELFS 2001)
Organization responsible for the survey:
Planning and conduct of the survey: Statistical Office of Estonia, Labour Force Statistics Division.
Analysis and publication of the results: Statistical Office of Estonia, Labour Force Statistics Division.
Topics covered: Employment, unemployment, underemployment, hours of work, wages, income, duration of employment, duration of unemployment, discouraged workers, occasional workers, industry, occupation, status in employment, educational level, usual activity, second jobs.
Coverage of the survey:
Geographical: Whole country.
Population groups: The target population of the ELFS 2001 were residents of Estonia of working age, i.e., persons who, as of 1 January 2001 had turned 15-74 years old (i.e., those born between 1926 and 1985). Career and voluntary military are included in the totals but separate data are not published.
Availability of estimates from other sources for the excluded areas/groups: No.
Groups covered by the survey but excluded from the published results: None.
Periodicity:
Conduct of the survey: Continuous survey.
Publication of results: Quarterly.
Reference periods:
Employment: One week (last seven days prior to the date of the interview).
Seeking work: Four weeks prior to the date of the interview.
Availability for work: Two weeks following the date of the interview.
Concepts and definitions:
Employment: Employed are all persons aged 15-74 years who, during the reference period, did any work for at least one hour and were in paid employment or self-employed. Persons on parental leave, granted to mother or father until the child is 3 years old are considered as not active. Conscripts are classified as not active, whereas volunteers and career military are included.
Included in the totals are persons who during the reference period were temporarily absent from work due to illness, injury, vacation or annual leave, educational leave, absence without leave, bad weather, labour management dispute, mechanical breakdown, other reduction in economic activity or temporary lay-off without pay provided that the period of such absence was less than 3months.
Also included are:
a) women on paid pre-natal and post-natal leave whose duration is 70 and 56 days respectively;
b) full- and part-time workers seeking other work during the reference period;
c) full- and part-time students working full- or part-time;
d) persons who performed some work during the reference week while being either retired and receiving a pension, or were registered as job seekers at an employment office or receiving unemployment benefits;
e) private domestic servants;
g) paid apprentices and trainees.
Excluded are persons engage in production of goods for their own household (painting, repairing, housework, etc.).
Unemployment: Unemployed are all persons aged 15-74 years who met the following three conditions during the reference week: (i) had no work; (ii) were actively looking for work; and (iii) were currently available for work - i.e., were available for paid employment or self-employment either immediately or within 14 days following the reference week.
Underemployment:
Time-related underemployment: Persons who, during the reference week, involuntary worked less than the normal duration of working hours established for a given type of activity and who were willing and available to work additional hours.
Inadequate employment situations: Persons who were seeking another job with better working conditions (salary, location, etc.).
Hours of work: Usual and actual hours worked in the main job.
Employment-related income:
Income from paid employment: Monthly income from main job, i.e. wages, salaries and other earnings in cash or in kind; remuneration for time not worked and paid by the employer; quarterly and annual bonuses, Christmas bonuses, etc.; all types of extra payments; compensation for temporary disability or caring for a sick person.
Income from self-employment: Entrepreneurs, farmers and freelancers are only asked about payments received in the form of their wage.
Informal sector: Not applicable.
Usual activity: The following population groups are subject to questions about their usual economic status: apprentices, students at secondary schools, university students, persons on maternity and child-care leave (parental leave), housewives, retired persons, retired persons due to disability, retired persons due to partial disability, unemployed, conscripts.
Classifications:
Branch of economic activity (industry):
Title of the classification: National classification.
Population groups classified by industry: Employed persons and unemployed persons with previous job experience.
Number of groups used for coding: 60 groups (codes 01-99).
Links to ISIC: ISIC- Rev.3.
Occupation:
Title of the classification: National classification.
Population groups classified by occupation: Employed persons and unemployed persons with previous work experience.
Number of groups used for coding: 400 groups (4-digit level groups).
Links to ISCO: ISCO-88 at the 4th digit level.
Status in employment:
Title of the classification: National classification.
Population groups classified by status in employment: Employed and unemployed persons.
Groups used for classification: 4 groups (employees, employers, own-account worker, unpaid family worker).
Links to ICSE: ICSE-1993.
Education:
Title of the classification: National classification.
Population groups classified by education: all population groups.
Groups used for classification: 10 groups (no primary education, primary education, basic education, secondary education, no vocational (specialized or professional) education, vocational/technical education, university diploma, bachelor's degree, master's degree, doctorate/PhD.)
Links to ISCED: ISCED-1997.
Sample size and design:
Ultimate sampling unit: Household.
Sample size (ultimate sampling units): 2 200 households per quarter.
Overall sampling fraction: 0.4 per cent of working age population per quarter.
Sample frame: The sample frame is built on the basis of the Population Database of the Andmevara Ltd.
Updating of the sample: Quarterly.
Rotation:
Scheme: 2-2-2. Every sampled household is interviewed four times; during two consecutive quarters and, after a two-quarters period, they are again interviewed twice in the corresponding quarters of the following year.
Percentage of units remaining in the sample for two consecutive survey rounds: 50 per cent.
Maximum number of interviews per sample unit: No information provided.
Length of time for complete renewal of the sample: 6 quarters.
Field work:
Type of interview: Paper and pencil.
Number of ultimate sampling units per sample area: No information provided.
Duration of field work:
Total: No information provided.
Per sample area: No information provided.
Survey organization: Permanent.
Number of field staff: 179 interviewers and 18 supervisors.
Substitution of non-responding ultimate sampling units: No.
Estimation and adjustments:
Total non-response rate: 9 per cent.
Adjustment for total non-response: Yes.
Imputation for item non-response: Yes.
Adjustment for areas/population not covered: No.
Adjustment for undercoverage: Yes.

Adjustment for overcoverage: No.
Adjustment for seasonal variations: No.
History of the survey:
Title and date of the first survey: Estonian Labour Force Survey, January-April 1995.
Significant changes or revisions: From 1997 to 1999, the survey was conducted during the second quarter. Continuous survey since 2000.
Documentation and dissemination:
Documentation
Survey results: "Estonian Labour Force Survey, 1995, 1997, 1998, 1999" (annually).
Survey methodology: "Estonian Labour Force Survey, 1995, 1997, 1998, 1999. Methodological report" (annually).
Dissemination
Time needed for initial release of survey results: Since 2000, two months for quarterly results and three months for annual results (end of March of following year). Data are made available to all interested users, on the same day, by issuing a news release 'Employment and Unemployment'.
Advance information of public about date of initial release: Yes.
Availability of unpublished data upon request: Yes.
Availability of data in machine-readable form: Diskettes and Emails.
Website: http://www.stat.ee/.

Ethiopia

Title of the survey: National Labor Force Survey.
Organization responsible for the survey:
Planning and conduct of the survey: Central Statistical Authority.
Analysis and publication of the results: Central Statistical Authority.
Topics covered: Employment, unemployment, underemployment, hours of work, informal sector employment, duration of unemployment, industry, occupation, status in employment, educational level, and usual activity. Other **Topics covered:** demographic variables on migration, ethnic group/religion, socio-economic and demographic characteristics of children aged 5-14 years, vocational/professional training.
Coverage of the survey:
Geographical: Whole country.
10 years and over are interviewed.
Population groups: All persons aged 10 years and over normally resident in the country. Excluded: unsettled populations, non-resident citizens, foreigners and persons residing abroad.
Availability of estimates from other sources for the excluded areas/groups: None.
Groups covered by the survey but excluded from the published results: NONE.
Periodicity:
Conduct of the survey: In 1981/82 and 1986/87.
Publication of results: Irregular.
Reference periods:
Employment: One week (the last seven days) prior to the date of the interview
Seeking work: Three months prior to the date of the interview.
Availability for work: One month following the date of the interview.
All periods are moving reference periods.
Concepts and definitions:
Employment: All persons aged 10 and over who were engaged in paid or self-employment during the last 7 days, performing some work (for at least 4 hours) for wages or salary, in cash or kind, or who were temporarily not at work but who had a formal job attachment.
It includes:
a) persons temporarily absent due to illness or injury, vacation or annual leave, maternity or paternity leave, parental leave, educational or training leave, labour management disputes, bad weather, etc.;
b) persons on unpaid leave initiated by the employer;
c) full or part-time workers seeking other work;
d) persons who performed some work for pay or profit during the reference week but were subject to compulsory schooling, were retired and receiving a pension, registered as job seekers at an employment office or receiving unemployment benefits;
e) full or part-time students working part- or full-time;
f) paid or unpaid apprentices and trainees;
g) participants in employment promotion schemes, if paid;
h) persons engaged in production of goods for own final use;
i) members of the armed forces (volunteers, career and conscripts and civilian service equivalent to military service);
j) unpaid family workers at work.
Unemployment: All persons aged 10 and over who were not engaged in paid or self-employment during the last7 days, who were available for a paid or self-employment job in a one month period from the date of interview, and who had been searching for a job by various steps (efforts) taken, in the last 3 months.
It includes:
a) persons on temporary or indefinite lay-off without pay;
b) persons who had made arrangements to start a new job or were trying to establish their own enterprise;
c) retired persons and those receiving a pension;
d) part-time students seeking full- or part-time work;
e) unpaid family workers temporarily absent from work and seasonal workers during the off-season, if available for other work;
f) persons not seeking work because no job was available on the market or suitable for their skills;
g) persons doing unpaid, volunteer community or social service work.
Underemployment:
Time-related underemployment: Persons who, during the reference week, were employed but willing and available to work for more hours (additional hours) in the current job, in another job, or another full-time job up to the chosen threshold.
Inadequate employment situations: Not applicable.
Hours of work: Only actual hours worked in each day in all jobs during the last 7 days.
Employment-related income:
Income from paid employment: Not applicable.
Income from self-employment: Not applicable.
Informal sector employment: 1. Whether their business enterprise (or enterprise they are working for) keeps a regular account of its transactions; 2. Whether the business enterprise has at least 10 workers; 3. Whether the enterprise has a licence or not. If persons fail to fit all 3 criteria with respect to the main job, they are classified in the informal sector.
Usual activity: The survey has two questions, one concerning engagement in economic activity during the last 12 months; the other concerning reasons for not working during the last 12 months, which serve to classify persons into either unemployment or inactivity.
Classifications:
Branch of economic activity (industry):
Title of the classification: Not available.
Population groups classified by industry: Employed persons.
Number of groups used for coding: 14
Links to ISIC Rev. 3 Yes.
Occupation:
Title of the classification: Not available.
Population groups classified by occupation: Employed persons.
Number of groups used for coding: 10
Links to ISCO-1988
Status in employment:
Title of the classification: Not available.
Population groups classified by status in employment: Employed persons.
Groups used for classification: Employers, employees (government, non-governmental, private, government developmental organization), own-account workers, unpaid family workers, apprentices, members of cooperative associations.
Links to ICSE-1993.
Education:
Title of the classification: Not available.
Population groups classified by education: Employed and unemployed persons.
Groups used for classification: a) Illiterate, b) Literate, c) Grade completed. The classification is expressed in terms of the highest grade completed and distinguishes the following levels:
1.Cannot read or write,
2.Non-formal education or grades 1 to 3,
3.Grades 4 to 6,
4.Grades 7 and 8,
5.Grades 9 to 11,
6.Grade 12,
7.Above grade 12.
Links to ISCED-1997: Yes.
Sample size and design:
Ultimate sampling unit: Household.
Sample size (ultimate sampling units): 35 households per enumeration area times 1448 rural enumeration areas plus 913 urban enumeration areas, resulting in 82 635 households.
Sampling fraction: not available.

Sample frame: List of enumeration areas prepared for the 1994 Census; for urban areas a fresh list of households was made, for rural areas, a list of households was prepared 6 months prior to the survey date.
Updating of the sample: none.
Rotation: No **Rotation** Scheme
Scheme: Not applicable.
Percentage of units remaining in the sample for two consecutive survey rounds: Not applicable.
Maximum number of interviews per sample unit: Not applicable.
Length of time for complete renewal of the sample: Not applicable.
Field work:
Type of interview: Personal interview.
Number of ultimate sampling units per sample area: Variable.
Duration of field work:
Total: 15 - 26 March 1999.
Per sample area:
Survey organization: Permanent survey organization.
Number of field staff: Interviewers are 1 654, Supervisors are 343, Trainers are 88. Total is 2 085 staff.
Substitution of non-responding ultimate sampling units: Yes.
Estimation and adjustments:
Total non-response rate: not available.
Adjustment for total non-response: none.
Imputation for item non-response: Non-response cases are assigned the code 9 or 99 or 999 based on their respective column digits.
Adjustment for areas/population not covered: none.
Adjustment for undercoverage: none.
Adjustment for overcoverage: none.
Adjustment for seasonal variations: none.
History of the survey:
Title and date of the first survey: The first Rural Labour Force Survey was conducted over the period April 1981 to April 1982. Another survey was conducted in 1987/88. This National Labour Force Survey was first conducted in March 1999.
Significant changes or revisions: The type of questions asked are very similar to those of the Rural Labour Force Surveys.
Documentation and dissemination:
Documentation
Survey results: No information.
Survey methodology: No information.
Dissemination
Time needed for initial release of survey results: No information.
Advance information of public about date of initial release: No information.
Availability of unpublished data upon request: No information.
Availability of data in machine-readable form: No information.

Finland

Title of the survey: Labour Force Survey
Organization responsible for the survey:
Planning and conduct of the survey: Statistics Finland.
Analysis and publication of the results: Statistics Finland.
Topics covered: Employment, unemployment, underemployment, hours of work, duration of employment, duration of unemployment, discouraged workers, industry, occupation, status in employment, educational level - from the Register of Completed Education and Degrees, (usual activity - see below) and second jobs.
Coverage of the survey:
Geographical: Whole country.
Population groups: All persons aged 15 to 74 residing in the country, including foreign workers, citizens who are temporarily abroad (less than one year), members of the armed forces, non-resident citizens, unsettled and institutional populations.
Availability of estimates from other sources for the excluded areas/groups: Not applicable.
Groups covered by the survey but excluded from the published results: Yes.
Periodicity:
Conduct of the survey: From 2000 onwards, continuous survey. Previously: monthly survey.
Publication of results: Monthly, quarterly and annually.
Reference periods:
Employment: One week. Prior to 2000, one fixed week (usually the week including the 15th of each month).
Seeking work: Four weeks (moving reference period).
Availability for work: Two weeks (moving reference period).

Concepts and definitions:
Employment: All persons who during the survey week did some work (for at least one hour),for pay or a fringe benefit, or to gain profit, or were temporarily absent from work due to being laid off for a certain period of time. The employed may be employees, self-employed persons or unpaid family workers.
It also includes:
a) persons with a job but temporarily absent from work due to illness, injury, vacation, annual leave, maternity or paternity leave, absence without leave, labour management dispute, bad weather, mechanical breakdown, etc. or on unpaid leave initiated by the employer;
b) full and part-time workers seeking other work during the reference week;
c) persons who performed some work for pay or profit during the reference week, while being subject to compulsory schooling, or were retired and receiving a pension, or were registered as job seekers at an employment office or receiving unemployment benefits;
d) full and part-time students working full or part-time;
e) paid apprentices and trainees;
f) paid and unpaid family workers, temporarily absent from work;
g) private domestic servants;
h) career members of the armed forces.
Unemployment: All persons who, for the whole survey week were without work, had been seeking a job actively during the past four weeks as an employee or a self-employed person and could accept a job within two weeks. Persons without a job and waiting to start a job within two weeks are also recorded as unemployed as are persons laid off for an indefinite period from their work who meet the job seeking and job acceptance criteria.
Only if available and seeking work, it also includes:
a) persons on unemployment pension;
a) persons trying to establish their own enterprise;
b) persons subject to compulsory schooling;
c) full and part-time students seeking full or part-time work;
d) participants in employment promotion schemes;
e) seasonal workers awaiting agricultural or other seasonal work.
Underemployment:
Time-related underemployment: Persons who were engaged in part-time work because full-time work was not available or whose employer has them work a reduced working week or who have had no work due to shortage of orders of customers or because of having been laid-off for a certain period of time.
Inadequate employment situations: Not applicable.
Hours of work: Actual hours and usual hours are collected. Hours actually worked during the reference week comprise all hours worked, both paid and unpaid, overtime and hours worked in secondary jobs. Usual hours refer to normal weekly hours of work of employed persons in the main job only. It is possible to present these two concepts separately when needed.
Employment-related income:
Income from paid employment: Not applicable.
Income from self-employment: Not applicable.
Informal sector employment: Not applicable.
Usual activity: (One question about the primary activity during the survey week is administered to non-employed persons. Employed persons are asked about their main activity but no special time-frame is given).
Classifications:
Branch of economic activity (industry):
Title of the classification: Standard Industrial Classification (SIC-1995).
Population groups classified by industry: Employed and unemployed persons.
Number of groups used for coding: About 95 groups at the 2-3 digit level.
Links to ISIC: ISIC-Rev. 3 at the 2-3 digit level.
Occupation:
Title of the classification: Statistics Finland's Classification of Occupations (CSO-2001), since 2002, at the four/five digit level.
Population groups classified by occupation: Employed and unemployed persons.
Number of groups used for coding: 489.
Links to ISCO: ISCO-88.
Status in employment:
Title of the classification: Industrial status groups.
Population groups classified by status in employment: Employed and unemployed persons.
Groups used for classification: Three groups: Employee, Employer/own-account worker, unpaid family worker.
Links to ICSE: ICSE-1993.

Education:
Title of the classification: Finnish Standard Classification of Education 1997 (FSCED-97).
Population groups classified by education: All persons aged 15 to 74 years.
Groups used for classification: Data are obtained from the Register of Complete Education and Degrees, at the 6-digit level.
Links to ISCED: ISCED-1997.
Sample size and design:
Ultimate sampling unit: Individual persons (15 - 74 years old).
Sample size (ultimate sampling units): 12 000 persons per month.
Overall sampling fraction: Approximately 1/311.
Sample frame: Drawn from the Population Register, maintained by Statistics Finland, which covers the whole population.
Updating of the sample: The sample data (addresses, etc.) are updated monthly using the changes which are received both from the CPR (which is continuously updated) and from interviewers.
Rotation:
Scheme: The rotation pattern is a five wave system - the first interview takes place at "t", the second at "t+3", the third at "t+6", the fourth at "t+12"and the fifth at "t+15".
Percentage of units remaining in the sample for two consecutive survey rounds: 0 per cent (the samples overlap by 3/5 from one quarter to the next and by 2/5 after a year).
Maximum number of interviews per sample unit: Five.
Length of time for complete renewal of the sample: Eighteen months.
Field work:
Type of interview: Computer assisted telephone interviewing (CATI) for 98 per cent and 2 per cent by computer assisted personal interview (CAPI).
Number of ultimate sampling units per sample area: Not applicable.
Duration of field work
Total: 10 to 15 days.
Per sample area: 10 to 15 days.
Survey organization: Permanent.
Number of field staff: About 160 interviewers.
Substitution of non-responding ultimate sampling units: No.
Estimation and adjustments:
Total non-response rate: 14 per cent.
Adjustment for total non-response: Yes.
Imputation for item non-response: Hours worked per week, if unknown.
Adjustment for areas/population not covered: Not applicable.
Adjustment for under-coverage: No.
Adjustment for over-coverage: Yes.
Adjustment for seasonal variations: Yes, using a slightly modified version of the Census X-11 Arima method for levels of employment, unemployment, labour force, employment rate and unemployment rate.
History of the survey:
Title and date of the first survey: The Finnish Labour Force Sample Survey, 1958.
Significant changes or revisions:
1983: The postal enquiry was revised to the interview survey. Data contents were expanded.
1997: New survey design more closely aligned to ILO recommendations.
2000: Continuous survey.
Documentation and dissemination:
Documentation
Survey results: Statistics Finland, Labour Market Series; Employment and Labour Force Bulletin. (**Periodicity:** monthly).
Survey methodology: Statistics Finland, Labour Market Series - Annual bulletin.
Dissemination
Time needed for initial release of survey results: Three weeks.
Advance information of public about date of initial release: Yes.
Availability of unpublished data upon request: Yes.
Availability of data in machine-readable form: Yes.
Website: http://tilastokeskus.fi/index_en.html/.

Gambia

Title of the survey: Labour Force Survey in Greater Banjul.
Organization responsible for the survey:
Planning and conduct of the survey: Central Statistics Department.
Analysis and publication of the results: Central Statistics Department.
Topics covered: Employment, unemployment, time-related underemployment, hours of work, income, informal sector employment, industry, occupation, status in employment, educational level, usual activity and training.
Coverage of the survey:
Geographical: Restricted to Banjul and Kombo St. Mary's.
Population groups: De facto population 10 years and above, i.e., including usual members and visitors who spent the night in the sample households.
Availability of estimates from other sources for the excluded areas/groups: Not available.
Groups covered by the survey but excluded from the published results: None.
Periodicity:
Conduct of the survey: Ad-hoc survey carried out in 1992.
Publication of results: August 1995.
Reference periods:
Employment: One week prior to the date of the interview.
Seeking work: One week prior to the date of the interview.
Availability for work: One week prior to the date of the interview.
Concepts and definitions:
Employment: Persons who worked for pay or profit or family gain in cash or in kind during the reference period, or who had a job or own enterprise from which they were absent due to illness or injury, vacation, maternity leave, education leave, labour management dispute, bad weather, mechanical breakdowns, etc. Persons temporarily laid off without pay are included but those on indefinite lay off are excluded. Probes were carried out to include marginal activities, most of which are intended for family consumption, such as work on the farm, fishing, repair activities, collection of firewood and manufacturing of baskets and clothes.
Unemployment: Persons who were not in employment but were available for work or preparing to start own work during the reference period. Included are persons who had made arrangements to start a new job on a date subsequent to the reference period, as well as full-time students who were available for work. Persons seeking work during the reference period can be separately identified.
Underemployment:
Time-related underemployment: Persons who, during the reference week, worked less than 35 hours, and were available to work more hours. It is possible to identify workers who sought to work additional hours.
Inadequate unemployment situations: No information.
Hours of work: Total number of hours actually worked on all jobs (excluding meal time and other time away from work) on each day during the reference period.
Employment-related income:
Income from paid employment: Usual monthly income from main paid job. Cash and non-cash income are separately identified.
Income from self-employment: No information.
Informal sector: No information.
Usual activity: Persons who worked for pay or family gain at any time during the last 12 months. Information on the number of weeks worked, as well as the number of weeks of availability for work during the last 12 months are obtained. For those usually employed, information on usual occupation, industry and status in employment is obtained, while for those usually unemployed, information on the last occupation, industry and status in employment were obtained. For those usually inactive, information on their status as student, homemaker, disabled or pensioner is obtained.
Classifications:
Branch of economic activity (industry):
Title of the classification: No information.
Population groups classified by industry: Employed persons and unemployed persons with previous work experience.
Number of groups used for coding: 10.
Links to ISIC: ISIC-Rev.2.
Occupation:
Title of the classification: No information.
Population groups classified by occupation: Employed persons and unemployed persons with previous work experience.
Number of groups used for coding: 7.
Links to ISCO-68: ISCO-68.
Status in employment:
Title of the classification: No information.
Population groups classified by status in employment: Employed persons and unemployed persons with previous work experience.
Groups used for classification: 6 groups (employer, own account worker, paid employee, unpaid family worker, apprentice, others).
Links to ICSE: ICSE-1993.

Education:
Title of the classification: No information.
Population groups classified by education: All persons of age 5 years and older.
Groups used for classification: 9 groups (no grade, grades 1 to 3, grades 4 to 6, grade 7, formal 1 to 4, 0 level, A Level, First Degree, Higher Degree and Others).
Links to ISCED: Yes.
Sample size and design:
Ultimate sampling unit: Households
Sample size (ultimate sampling units): 1280 household selected from 64 Enumeration Areas.
Overall sampling fraction: Not available.
Sample frame: Not available.
Updating of the sample: Not available.
Rotation:
Scheme: Not applicable.
Percentage of units remaining in the sample for two consecutive survey rounds: Not applicable.
Maximum number of interviews per sample unit: Not available.
Length of time for complete renewal of the sample: Not applicablc.
Field work:
Type of interview: Personal interview.
Number of ultimate sampling units per sample area: 1280 households.
Duration of field work
Total: One year.
Per sample area: One year.
Survey organization: Ad hoc organization.
Number of field staff: Eight enumerators and two supervisors.
Substitution of non-responding ultimate sampling units: Yes.
Estimation and adjustments:
Total non-response rate: Not available.
Adjustment for total non-response: Not available.
Imputation for item non-response: Not available.
Adjustment for areas/population not covered: Not available.
Adjustment for under-coverage: Not available.
Adjustment for over-coverage: Not available.
Adjustment for seasonal variations: Not available.
History of the survey:
Title and date of the first survey: The survey described is the first survey.
Significant changes or revisions: Not applicable.
Documentation and dissemination:
Documentation:
Survey results: Not available.
Survey methodology: Not available.
Dissemination:
Time needed for initial release of survey results: 3 years.
Advance information of public about date of initial release: No.
Availability of unpublished data upon request: Yes.
Availability of data in machine-readable form: Not available.

Georgia

1.Title of the survey
Labour force sample survey (LFSS).
2.Organization responsible for the survey
State Department for Statistics.
3.Coverage of the survey
(a) Geographical: The whole country with the exception of Apkhazeti and the South Osseti.
(b) Persons covered: All the population aged 15 years and over.
Excluded are:
1.persons absent from the household twelve months or more;
2.military personnel (conscripts and career) living in barracks
3.inmates of penal and mental institutions;
4.Periodicity of the survey
The survey, which has been conducted since January 1998, is quarterly.
5.Reference period
The calendar week.
6.Topics covered
Economically active and not economically active population, including main and secondary employment, classified by place of residence, age, sex, type of economic activity, level of education, status in employment, hours worked, reasons for seeking a new job; as well as registered and informal employment, and underemployment due to extended absences from work; duration and reasons of unemployment.
7.Concepts and definitions
(a) Employment: All persons of 15 years of age and over who, during the reference week:
1.did any work at all as paid employees during for at least one hour; and
2.all those who were not working but who had jobs or businesses from which they were temporarily absent
Included in the totals are:
1.full- and part-time workers seeking other work during the reference period;
2.full- and part-time students working full- or part-time;
3.persons who performed some work during the reference week while being either retired and receiving a pension; or were registered as job seekers at an employment office or receiving unemployment benefits;
4.paid and unpaid family workers (if they worked at least twelve hours);
5.private domestic servants;
6.members of producers' co-operatives;
7.members of the armed forces living in households.
Excluded are persons whose only activity consisted of work around the house (painting, repairing, or own housework) and on the family farming plots for their own consumption; as well as volunteer work for religious, charitable and similar organizations. They are considered as not economically active.
(b) Unemployment: All persons of 15 years and over who had no employment during the reference week, were available for work, except for temporary illness, and who had made specific steps to find employment during the four weeks previous to the interview. Also included are persons who found a job and made arrangements to start a new job on a date subsequent to the reference period.
Seeking work includes all steps taken by a person in order to find work or start entrepreneurship: registration with employment offices, placing and answering advertisements, seeking assistance of relatives and friends, arranging for financial resources, etc.
8.Sample design
(a) The sample frame: The LFSS sample was built up on the basis of the 1989 Population Census.
(b) The sample: The survey uses a stratified two-stage area sampling design in which probability of selection is proportional to the population size. At the first stage, 282 enumeration districts (EDs) are selected from the total of 12,000, using a random start. The selection is made so that each strata should have a number of EDs which can be divided by 3 without remainder (for the purpose of equal distribution among the months of the four quarters). Each urban strata has 7-12 sample addresses and each rural strata has 16-24 sample addresses. At the second stage 3,351 households are selected systematically using a random start, which represents 0.3% of the total number of households.
(c) Rotation: The sample has the following rotation pattern: selected EDs are equally divided into 12 rotation groups at the level of each strata. Each month the sample is renewed by 8.3%, which means that during a year the whole sample is renewed. Any household entering the sample is interviewed for a period of four consecutive quarters and then leaves the sample for ever.
9.Documentation
Preliminary results of LFSS were published in a press release prepared by the Department of Statistics. Final results are published in the Yearbook of Statistics.

Germany

Title of the survey: Micro-census (Mikrozensus)/European Union Labour Force Survey.
Organization responsible for the survey
Planning and conduct of the survey: Federal Statistical Office (Statistisches Bundesamt) and State Statistical Offices (Statistische Landesämter).
Analysis and publication of the results: Federal Statistical Office (Statistisches Bundesamt) and State Statistical Offices (Statistische Landesämter).
Topics covered: Employment, unemployment, underemployment, hours of work (usual hours of work, hours actually worked), income (net individual income, net household income, pensions, main sources of livelihood), informal sector employment, duration of employment (change of establishment during the last year, duration of fixed-term contracts, duration of employment with present employer), duration of unemployment, occasional workers (casual jobs, small

jobs), industry, occupation, status in employment, education and qualification levels, second jobs.

Coverage of the survey:

Geographical: Whole country.

Population groups: The survey covers the whole resident population of Germany, including the non-civilian population and persons living in institutions or
group living quarters. Excluded are foreign diplomats and members of foreign armed forces.

Availability of estimates from other sources for the excluded areas/groups: Not applicable.

Groups covered by the survey but excluded from the published results: As a matter of principle, estimates for population groups below a size of 5 000 persons are not published separately because the sampling error of such estimates is considered too high.

Periodicity:

Conduct of the survey: Annual.

Publication of results: Annual, plus advance reporting.

Reference periods:

Employment: One week, i.e. the last holiday-free week of April.

Seeking work: Four weeks prior to the date of the interview.

Availability for work: Two weeks following the date of the interview.

Concepts and definitions:

Employment: Persons aged 15 years or over who were employed during the reference week, irrespective of whether the employment was their main or a secondary activity, and of whether the job was undertaken regularly or occasionally. Included are: (a) contributing family workers at work during the reference week; (b) persons engaged in temporary work or subsidiary activities and employed in small jobs (i.e. jobs of less than 15 hours per week, or with an income below the threshold for social security contributions); (c) full- or part-time workers seeking other work during the reference period; (d) persons who performed some work for pay or profit during the reference week but who were subject to compulsory schooling, or retired and receiving a pension, or registered as job seekers at an employment office, or receiving unemployment benefits; (e) full- time students working full- or part-time; (f) part-time students working full- or part-time; (g) paid apprentices and trainees; (h) persons engaged in the production of goods for own final use; (i) members of the armed forces (career members, volunteers and conscripts); and (j) persons on civilian service equivalent to military service.

Also included are persons with a job or enterprise, who were temporarily absent from work during the reference week because of (a) illness or injury, (b) vacation or annual leave, (c) maternity or paternity leave, (d) parental leave, (e) absence without leave, (f) labour management dispute, or (g) bad weather, mechanical breakdown, etc. Contributing family workers temporarily absent from work during the reference week are considered employed if they usually work in the enterprise.

Excluded are: (a) unpaid apprentices and trainees; (b) participants in employment promotion schemes; (c) persons on educational or training leave, unless they worked during the reference week; (d) persons on unpaid leave initiated by the employer, if such leave corresponds to a dismissal; (e) persons rendering unpaid or personal services to members of their own household; and (f) persons engaged in volunteer community or social service work.

Unemployment: Persons aged 15 years or over who were without work during the reference week, and who are actively seeking work or had actively sought work during the four weeks prior to the date of the interview. A distinction is made between unemployed persons currently available for work (i.e. available to start work within the two weeks following the date of the interview) and other unemployed persons.

Included are: (a) persons who have already found work and who will start working soon; (b) persons trying to establish their own enterprise; (c) persons actively seeking work who were subject to compulsory schooling or retired and receiving a pension; (d) full- time students actively seeking full- or part-time work; (e) part-time students actively seeking full- or part-time work; (f) unpaid apprentices and trainees actively seeking work; (g) participants in employment promotion schemes actively seeking work; and (h) seasonal workers not employed during the off-season and actively seeking work.

Excluded are persons without work who are not actively seeking work, unless they have already found a new job.

Underemployment:

Time-related underemployment: Employed persons seeking a second job and employed persons seeking a job with more hours of work.

Inadequate employment situations: Employed persons seeking a job with better conditions of work.

Hours of work: Usual hours of work per week and hours actually worked during the reference week. Both are asked for the main job and the second job (if any).

Employment-related income:

Income from paid employment: Can only be derived approximately. Questions are asked on the: (a) main source of livelihood (one category is employment); (b) receipt of pensions and public transfers by type; (c) amount of net monthly individual income and of net monthly household income by income classes. Employees are identified through a question on status in employment (see 8.3).

Income from self-employment: Can only be derived approximately. Questions are asked on the: (a) main source of livelihood (one category is employment); (b) receipt of pensions and public transfers by type; (c) amount of net monthly individual income and of net monthly household income by income classes. Self-employed persons are identified through a question on status in employment (see 8.3).

Informal sector: Defined on the basis of questions on occupation and branch of economic activity of the main job and the second job.

Usual activity: The following is referring to main activity. Though this topic is not covered by the survey, three retrospective questions are asked regarding the situation one year before (activity status, status in employment, and branch of economic activity).

Classifications:

Branch of economic activity (industry):

Title of the classification: National Classification of Branches of Economic Activity 1993 (Klassifikation der Wirtschaftszweige - WZ93), micro-census version (three digits).

Population groups classified by industry: All employed persons, as well as unemployed or economically inactive persons.

Number of groups used for coding: Three-digit codes. Information on the number of groups not provided.

Links to ISIC: The classification corresponds to the Statistical Classification of Economic Activities in the European Community (NACE, Rev. 1).

Occupation:

Title of the classification: National Classification of Occupations (Klassifikation der Berufe), version derived for the micro-census 1992.

Population groups classified by occupation: All employed persons, as well as unemployed or economically inactive persons.

Number of groups used for coding: Information not provided.

Links to ISCO: ISCO-88, at the three-digit level.

Status in employment:

Title of the classification: National classification of status in employment (Gliederung nach der Stellung im Beruf).

Population groups classified by status in employment: All employed persons, as well as unemployed or economically inactive persons.

Groups used for classification: (a) self-employed persons in agriculture, forestry and fishing; (b) self-employed persons in other branches of economic activity; (c) contributing family workers; (d) civil servants; (e) salary earners; (f) wage earners; (g) apprentices in recognized commercial and technical occupations; (h) apprentices in recognized industrial occupations.

Links to ICSE: Information not provided.

Education:

Title of the classification: National classification of levels of educational attainment and vocational training (Gliederung nach dem allgemeinen und beruflichen Bildungsniveau).

Population groups classified by education: Employed and unemployed persons.

Groups used for classification: Information not provided.

Links to ISCED: ISCED-1997.

Sample size and design:

Ultimate sampling unit: Household, institution or group living quarter.

Sample size (ultimate sampling units): About 350 000 households or 820 000 persons (including those living in institutions or group living quarters).

Overall sampling fraction: 1.0 percent of the population.

Sample frame: Area frame based on the Population Census 1987 (for states of the former German Democratic Republic: based on the Population Register). Results are adjusted to current population benchmark data by sex and nationality (German/foreign).

Updating of the sample: The sample is updated every year in adding a sample of the newly constructed buildings to it.

Rotation:

Scheme: Sample households, institutions or group living quarters participate in the survey four times during four consecutive years. Every year, one fourth of the sample households, institutions or group living quarters is rotated out of the sample and replaced by new ones entering the sample.

Percentage of units remaining in the sample for two consecutive survey rounds: 75 percent.
Maximum number of interviews per sample unit: Four.
Length of time for complete renewal of the sample: Four years.
Field work:
Type of interview: Participation in the survey is compulsory. Respondents can choose between questionnaires to be completed by themselves or questionnaires completed by interviewers. Self-completed questionnaires are filled in using the paper-and-pencil method. Interviewers use computer-assisted personal interview (CAPI) or the paper-and-pencil method. For foreigners not speaking German, the self-completed questionnaire is available in several foreign languages.
Number of ultimate sampling units per sample area: Each sample area contains nine households in average.
Duration of field work:
Total: Three months (May-July) for personal interviews and six months (May-October) for self-completed questionnaires.
Per sample area: Information not provided. The duration of interviews depends on the size of the households. On average, the interviews take about 20 minutes per household.
Survey organization: A permanent survey organization exists with interviewers being mainly used for this survey.
Number of field staff: About 7 000 interviewers employed by the State Statistical Offices (Statistische Landesämter).
Substitution of non-responding ultimate sampling units: Ultimate sample units, which cannot be contacted or which are cases of total non-response for other reasons, are not replaced by others.
Estimation and adjustments:
Total non-response rate: About 4 percent.
Adjustment for total non-response: Yes, using the hot-deck method to impute missing records.
Imputation for item non-response: Yes, for a few variables, using the hot-deck method to impute missing values.
Adjustment for areas/population not covered: Not applicable.
Adjustment for under-coverage: Yes.
Adjustment for over-coverage: Yes.
Adjustment for seasonal variations: Not applicable.
History of the survey:
Title and date of the first survey: The first micro-census was conducted in 1957.
Significant changes or revisions: From 1957 to 1974, in addition to the 1 per cent annual sample, three small subsamples (0.1 per cent) were drawn. Since 1968, the European Labour Force Survey is integrated in the micro-census. Other major changes to the survey were made in 1990 after the 1987 Population Census and after the reunification of Germany. A new sample, based on the 1987 Population Census results was introduced.
Documentation and dissemination:
Documentation:
Survey results: (a) Statistisches Bundesamt, Fachserie 1: Bevölkerung und Erwerbstätigkeit, Reihe 3: Haushalte und Familien (annual); (b) Statistisches Bundesamt, Fachserie 1: Bevölkerung und Erwerbstätigkeit, Reihe 4.1.1: Stand und Entwicklung der Erwerbstätigkeit (annual); (c) Statistisches Bundesamt, Fachserie 1: Bevölkerung und Erwerbstätigkeit, Reihe 4.1.2: Beruf, Ausbildung und Arbeitsbedingungen der Erwerbstätigen (annual).
Survey methodology: The above-mentioned publications include methodological information on the survey.
Dissemination:
Time needed for initial release of survey results: There is a time-lack of nine months between the field work and the publication of results.
Advance information of public about date of initial release: There is no fixed date for release of the survey results. Usually, the release of the data is announced to the public by means of a press release which presents the first results of the survey.
Availability of unpublished data upon request: Yes, but not necessarily free of charge.
Availability of data in machine-readable form: Most of the data can be made available in electronic form.
Website: http://www.destatis.de/.

Greece

Title of the survey: Labour Force Survey
Organization responsible for the survey:
Planning and conduct of the survey: National Statistical Service of Greece.
Analysis and publication of the results: National Statistical Service of Greece.
Topics covered: Employment, unemployment, underemployment, hours of work, wages, income, duration of employment and unemployment, discouraged and occasional workers,, industry, occupation, status in employment, education/qualification levels, usual activity, second jobs, other topics such as demographic information, living conditions, social relationships, consumption and expenditures, etc..
Coverage of the survey:
Geographical: Whole country.
Population groups: All persons aged 15 years and over. Excluded are:
a) career members and conscripts even if they are living alone or with their family in a residence outside the camp;
b) permanent hotels clients;
c) members of collective households;
d) members of foreign households working in the embassies, consulates, in commercial, economic or military missions and members of foreign armed forces.
Availability of estimates from other sources for the excluded areas/groups: No information provided.
Groups covered by the survey but excluded from the published results: Some demographic data are collected for persons having left the household, such as conscripts, persons living in other collective households, etc. It is planned to estimate theses categories and publish the relevant data.
Periodicity:
Conduct of the survey: Quarterly.
Publication of results: Annually.
Reference periods:
Employment: One fixed week.
Seeking work: Four weeks preceding the survey interview (fixed period).
Availability for work: Within two weeks after the interview (fixed period).
Concepts and definitions:
Employment: Persons aged 15 years and over who, during the reference week preceding the survey, have worked for at least one hour or more or were temporarily absent from work due to illness, vacation, strikes, bad weather or machine breakdown etc. Paid apprentices and unpaid family members.
Are also included in the employed:
a) full or part-time workers seeking other job during the reference period;
b) persons who performed some work for pay or profit during the reference period but were subject to compulsory schooling, retired and receiving a pension, registered as jobseekers at en employment office or receiving unemployment benefits;
c) full and part-time students working full or part-time;
d) participants in employment promotion schemes if they work on a regular basis;
e) volunteer and career members of the armed forces.
Unemployment: All persons aged 15 years and over, without work, who were seeking work and have taken specific steps (such as registration g at a private or public employment office, placing or answering advertisements, applications to employers, seeking assistance of friends or relatives) during the last 4 weeks to find a job and are available to work within two weeks.
Underemployment:
Time-related underemployment: Persons who want to work more hours within the present job or in an additional job.
Inadequate employment situations: Persons who search another job to have a better use of current skills.
Hours of work: Usual and actual hours of work per week in the main job and actual hours in secondary job.
Employment-related income:
Income from paid employment: It comprises: a) the monthly payments in the main job, net of social security contributions and taxes, including extra payments made on a monthly basis such as overtime, tips, etc.; b) additional net payments (total yearly payments) such as bonuses or other benefits from the enterprise.
Income from self-employment: Not covered.
Informal sector: Not applicable.
Usual activity: Not covered.
Classifications:
Branch of economic activity (industry):
Title of the classification: National classification based on NACE Rev.1.
Population groups classified by industry: Employed and unemployed (industry of last job for the unemployed).

Number of groups used for coding: 17 and 60 groups at the 1st and 2nd digit levels respectively.
Links to ISIC: ISIC-Rev. 3.
Occupation:
Title of the classification: National classification based on ISCO-88 (COM).
Population groups classified by occupation: Employed and unemployed (occupation of last job for the unemployed).
Number of groups used for coding: 10, 46 and 210 at the 1st, 2nr and 3rd digit levels respectively.
Links to ISCO: ISCO-88.
Status in employment:
Title of the classification: National classification.
Population groups classified by status in employment: Employed and unemployed (status of the last job for the unemployed.
Groups used for classification: Employees, employers, own-account workers, unpaid family workers, paid apprentices.
Links to ICSE: ICSE-1993.
Education:
Title of the classification: National classification.
Population groups classified by education: Employed and unemployed.
Groups used for classification: 5 groups: pre-primary, primary, lower secondary, upper secondary and post tertiary education, first and second stages of tertiary education.
Links to ISCED: ISCED-1997.
Sample size and design:
Ultimate sampling unit: Household.
Sample size (ultimate sampling units): Approximately 31 000 households per quarter.
Overall sampling fraction: 8.698 per cent.
Sample frame: 1991 Population and Housing Census.
Updating of the sample: Every quarter.
Rotation:
Scheme: Every quarter 1/6 of the households sampled are rotated. By combining the following two ways: selection of a new sample of households from area units already in use and selection of new area units.
Percentage of units remaining in the sample for two consecutive survey rounds: 84 per cent.
Maximum number of interviews per sample unit: Six.
Length of time for complete renewal of the sample: 13 quarters.
Field work:
Type of interview: Door-to-door with paper and pencil.
Number of ultimate sampling units per sample area: No information.
Duration of field work:
Total: 13 weeks.
Per sample area: No information.
Survey organization: Permanent and ad-hoc staff.
Number of field staff: 200 interviewers and 10 supervisors.
Substitution of non-responding ultimate sampling units: No.
Estimation and adjustments:
Total non-response rate: 8 per cent.
Adjustment for total non-response: No.
Imputation for item non-response: Yes.
Adjustment for areas/population not covered: No.
Adjustment for undercoverage: No.
Adjustment for overcoverage: No.
Adjustment for seasonal variations: No.
History of the survey:
Title and date of the first survey: Labour Force Survey 1981.
Significant changes or revisions: From 1981 to 1997, the survey is conducted during the second quarter of each year. Quarterly survey from 1998 onwards. Revisions of the questionnaires in 1992 and 1998.
Documentation and dissemination:
Documentation:
Survey results: Labour Force Survey (Employment); Statistical Yearbook of Greece; Concise Statistical Yearbook of Greece.
Survey methodology: Statistical Yearbook of Greece.
Dissemination:
Time needed for initial release of survey results: About one year.
Advance information of public about date of initial release: Yes.
Availability of unpublished data upon request: Yes.
Availability of data in machine-readable form: Yes.
Website: http://www.statistics.gr/.

Hong Kong, China

Title of the survey: General Household Survey (GHS).
Organization responsible for the survey:
Planning and conduct of the survey: Census and Statistics Department (C&SD).
Analysis and publication of the results: C&SD.
Topics covered: Persons currently economically active, employed and unemployed; persons currently in time-related underemployment; persons currently outside the labour force; discouraged workers; hours of work; duration of unemployment; monthly employment earnings, etc., industry, occupation, status in employment, education levels.
Coverage of the survey:
Geographical: Whole territory, excluding marine regions.
Population groups: Civilian non-institutional population of age 15 years and above, excluding inmates of institutions and persons living on vessels.
Availability of estimates from other sources for the excluded areas/groups: None.
Groups covered by the survey but excluded from the published results: None.
Periodicity:
Conduct of the survey: Continuous.
Publication of results: Monthly publication of a three-months moving average centered on the middle month.
Reference periods:
Employment: Seven days before the enumeration.
Seeking work: Have sought work during the 30 days before enumeration.
Availability for work: The seven days before enumeration.
Concepts and definitions:
Employment: Persons who performed some work (at least one hour) for pay or profit during the seven days before enumeration or have had a formal job attachment during the seven days before enumeration.
Unemployment: Persons without a job and available for work during the seven days before the enumeration and who have sought work during the 30 days before enumeration.
Underemployment:
Time-related underemployment: Persons who have involuntary worked less than 35 hours during the seven days before the enumeration and have sought additional work during the 30 days before enumeration, or were available for additional work during the seven days before enumeration. Involuntary refers to slack work, shortage of materials, mechanical breakdowns and inability to find a full-time job.
Inadequate employment situations: No information provided.
Hours of work: Actual hours worked in all jobs during the seven days before enumeration include both paid and unpaid hours worked in both primary and secondary jobs.
Employment related income:
Income from paid employment: Monthly employment earnings: cash earnings from all jobs during the last month, and for paid employment jobs include wages and salaries, bonuses, commissions, housing allowances, as well as overtime and attendance allowance, but exclude back pays and payments in kind.
Income from self-employment: Cash earnings refer to amount drawn from own enterprise for personal and household use, but net earnings from business may be used as proxy.
Informal sector: Not applicable, but hawkers can be identified separately.
Usual activity: No information provided.
Classifications:
Branch of economic activity (industry):
Title of the classification: Hong Kong Standard Industrial Classification (HSIC).
Population groups classified by industry: Employed and unemployed persons
(industry of last job for the unemployed).
Number of groups used for coding: 96.
Links to ISIC: ISIC-Rev. 2.
Occupation:
Title of the classification: Occupation Index of Hong Kong Population Census (2001).
Population groups classified by occupation: Employed and unemployed persons (occupation of last job for the unemployed).
Number of groups used for coding: 45.
Links to ISCO: ISCO-88.
Status in employment:
Title of the classification: National classification, no title given.

Population groups classified by status in employment: Employed persons.
Groups used: Employees, excluding hawkers; outworkers; employers, excluding hawkers; self-employed, excluding hawkers; hawkers (distinguishing: employee, employer, self-employed); unpaid family worker.
Links to ICSE: ICSE-1993.
Education:
Title of the classification: National classification, no title given.
Population groups classified education: Employed and unemployed persons.
Groups used for classification: 25.
Links to ISCED: ISCED-1997.
Sample size and design:
Ultimate sampling unit: Permanent quarters in built-up areas and segments elsewhere.
Sample size (ultimate sampling units): 27 000 quarters per 3 months period.
Overall sampling fraction: 1.2 percent of the target population per 3 months period.
Sample frame: Register of Quarters (RQ) with addresses of all permanent quarters in built-up areas, and Register of Segments (RS) with segments delineated by landmarks such as footpaths and rivers, maintained by C&SD.
Updating of the sample frame: RQ is updated continuously upon notification of erection or demolition of buildings from various sources. RS is updated every 5 years before the conduct pf population censuses or by-censuses.
Rotation:
Scheme: Households in sample twice, with 3 months interval.
Number of ultimate sampling units per sample area: No information provided.
Maximum number of interviews per sample unit: No information provided.
Length of time for complete renewal of the sample: No information provided.
Field work:
Type of interview: Face-to-face and computer assisted telephone interviewing (CATI).
Number of ultimate sampling units per sample area: No information provided.
Duration of field work:
Total: One month.
Per sample area: No information provided.
Survey organization: Permanent.
Number of field staff: 76 interviewers, 14 supervisors and 3 fieldwork managers.
Substitution of non-responding ultimate sampling units: No.
Estimation and adjustments:
Total non-response rate: 10 percent.
Adjustment for total non-response: No.
Imputation for item non-response: No.
Adjustment for areas/population not covered: No.
Adjustment for under-coverage: Not applicable.
Adjustment for over-coverage: Not applicable.
Adjustment for seasonal variations: Unemployment rates only.
History of the survey:
Title and date of the first survey: Labour Force Survey (LFS), September 1975.
Significant changes or revisions: LFS was conducted at half-yearly intervals from September 1975 to September 1980. Replaced by continuous GHS in August 1981.
Documentation and dissemination:
Documentation:
Survey results: Quarterly Report on General Household Survey.
Survey methodology: Quarterly Report on General Household Survey.
Dissemination:
Time needed for initial release of survey results: 2 to 3 weeks after end of quarter.
Advance information of public about date of initial release: Yes.
Availability of unpublished data upon request: Yes.
Availability of data in machine-readable form: Yes, on C&SD website.
Website: http://www.info.gov.hk/censtatd/.

Hungary

Title of the survey: Labour Force Survey
Organization responsible for the survey:
Planning and conduct of the survey: Hungarian Central Statistical Office.
Analysis and publication of the results: Hungarian Central Statistical Office.
Topics covered: Employment, unemployment, underemployment, hours of work, duration of employment, duration of unemployment, discouraged workers, occasional workers, industry, occupation, status in employment, educational level, second jobs.
Coverage of the survey:
Geographical: Whole country.
Population groups: All the population aged 15-74 years living in private households during the reference week. Excluded is institutional and unsettled population as well as household members temporarily absent and those residing abroad provided they have common consumption with the surveyed household.
Availability of estimates from other sources for the excluded areas/groups: Yes, partially.
Groups covered by the survey but excluded from the published results: None.
Periodicity:
Conduct of the survey: Quarterly.
Publication of results: Quarterly.
Reference periods:
Employment: One week (last seven days prior to the date of the interview).
Seeking work: Four weeks prior to the date of the interview.
Availability for work: Two weeks following the date of the interview.
Concepts and definitions:
Employment: Persons aged 15-74 years who, during the reference week:
a) performed some work for at least one hour for pay in cash or in kind, or for profit;
b) worked at least for one hour without pay in a family business or on a farm ("unpaid/contributing family workers");
c) did not work, although having employment, as they were temporarily absent from their work because of illness, holidays, bad weather, labour-management dispute, etc.
Excluded from the employed are persons who during the survey week were engaged in the following activities:
a) work without remuneration for another household or institution (voluntary work);
b) construction or renovation of own house or apartment;
c) housework;
d) work in private garden or piece of land for own consumption.
Also included in the totals are:
a) members of the armed forces (career and conscripts), the number of conscripts being derived from administrative records and imputed at the end of data processing.
b) full- and part-time workers seeking other work during the reference period;
c) full- and part-time students working full- or part-time;
d) persons who performed some work during the reference week while being either retired and receiving a pension; or were registered as job seekers at an employment office or receiving unemployment benefits;
e) private domestic servants;
f) paid apprentices and trainees
Unemployment: Unemployed are all persons of 15-74 years of age who did not work at all during the reference week, were actively looking for work during the four weeks previous to the interview, were available to start work within the two weeks following the survey week and were waiting to start a new job within a period of 30 days.
The only exception are persons who did not look for work because they had already found work but it would start at a date subsequent to the reference period. These persons are classified as unemployed.
Underemployment:
Time-related underemployment: Persons who, during the reference week, involuntary worked less than 36 hours.
Inadequate employment situations: Persons who were seeking another job.
Hours of work: Usual and actual hours worked in the main job and in the second job(s).
Employment-related income:
Income from paid employment: Not applicable.
Income from self-employment: Not applicable.
Informal sector: Not applicable.
Usual activity: Not applicable.
Classifications:
Branch of economic activity (industry):
Title of the classification: National classification.

Population groups classified by industry: Employed persons and unemployed persons.
Number of groups used for coding: No information provided.
Links to ISIC: ISIC-Rev. 3.
Occupation:
Title of the classification: National classification.
Population groups classified by occupation: Employed persons and unemployed persons.
Number of groups used for coding: No information provided.
Links to ISCO: ISCO-88.
Status in employment:
Title of the classification: National classification.
Population groups classified by status in employment: Employed persons.
Groups used for classification: 5 groups (employees, employers, own-account workers, members of producers' co-operatives, unpaid family workers).
Links to ICSE: ICSE-1993.
Education:
Title of the classification: National classification is used.
Population groups classified by education: Employed and unemployed persons.
Groups used for classification: No information provided.
Links to ISCED: Yes.
Sample size and design:
Ultimate sampling unit: Dwelling.
Sample size (ultimate sampling units): About 32 000 households or some 65 000 persons
Overall sampling fraction: 0.8 per cent.
Sample frame: The sample frame consists of 12 775 sample units which cover 751 settlements of the country and comprise about 626 000 addresses.
Updating of the sample: Bi-annually.
Rotation:
Scheme: Any household entering the sample at some time is expected to provide labour market information at six consecutive quarters after which it leaves the sample forever.
Percentage of units remaining in the sample for two consecutive survey rounds: 83.
Maximum number of interviews per sample unit: Six.
Length of time for complete renewal of the sample: 18 months.
Field work:
Type of interview: Paper and pencil.
Number of ultimate sampling units per sample area: No information provided.
Duration of field work:
Total: One week.
Per sample area: No information provided.
Survey organization: Hungarian Central Statistical Office.
Number of field staff: About 700 interviewers and supervisors.
Substitution of non-responding ultimate sampling units: No..
Estimation and adjustments:
Total non-response rate: 12.2 per cent.
Adjustment for total non-response: No.
Imputation for item non-response: No.
Adjustment for areas/population not covered: No.
Adjustment for undercoverage: No.
Adjustment for overcoverage: No.
Adjustment for seasonal variations: No.
History of the survey:
Title and date of the first survey: Labour Force Survey, January 1992.
Significant changes or revisions: None..
Documentation and dissemination:
Documentation:
Survey results: Monthly Report, LFS Quarterly Bulletin and LFS Time-Series (annual).
Survey methodology: LFS Methodology (in Hungarian and partially in English)
Dissemination:
Time needed for initial release of survey results: No information provided.
Advance information of public about date of initial release: Yes.
Availability of unpublished data upon request: Yes.
Availability of data in machine-readable form: Yes.
Website: http://www.ksh.hu/.

India

Title of the survey: Employment and Unemployment Survey
Organization responsible for the survey:
Planning and conduct of the survey: National Sample Survey Organization (NSSO)
Analysis and publication of the results: SDRD, NSSO
Topics covered: Employment, unemployment, time-related underemployment, hours of work, wages, duration of employment and unemployment, occasional workers, industry, occupation, status in employment, educational level and usual activity.
Coverage of the survey:
Geographical: Whole country except certain interior areas of two states and one UT.
Population groups: Persons 5 years and above, except the non-household population.
Availability of estimates from other sources for the excluded areas/groups: no.
Groups covered by the survey but excluded from the published results: not available.
Periodicity:
Conduct of the survey: an annual survey is carried out on a small sample. The full sample is surveyed every five years, the last one from July 1993 to June 1994.
Publication of results: annually for "small" sample, every five years for the large sample.
Reference periods:
Employment: One week prior to the date of the interview.
Seeking work: One day and one week prior to the date of the interview.
Availability for work: One day and one week prior to the date of the interview.
Concepts and definitions:
Employment: Persons engaged in a gainful activity for at least one hour during the reference week. It includes persons in the armed forces, but excludes retired persons and persons receiving a pension who also worked.
Unemployment: Persons not engaged in a gainful activity but who had been seeking work or had been available for work (although not seeking) at any time during the reference period. Excluded are retired persons and persons receiving a pension.
Underemployment
Time-related underemployment: Employed persons who, during the reference week, were willing to work additional hours.
Inadequate employment situations: No information.
Hours of work: Not available.
Usual activity: Persons engaged in a gainful activity for a longer time during the last 365 days are considered usually employed. Persons either seeking or available for work for a longer time during the last 365 days are considered usually unemployed.
Classifications:
Branch of economic activity (industry):
Title of the classification: No information.
Population groups classified by industry: Employed persons.
Number of groups used for coding: 9
Links to ISIC: ISIC-Rev.3
Occupation:
Title of the classification: No information.
Population groups classified by occupation: Employed persons.
Number of groups used for coding: 31
Links to ISCO: ISCO-88.
Status in employment:
Title of the classification: No information.
Population groups classified by status in employment: Employed persons and unemployed persons with previous work experience.
Groups used for classification: 10 groups.
Links to ICSE: ICSE-1993.
Education:
Title of the classification: No information.
Population groups classified by education: Employed and unemployed persons.
Groups used for classification: 5 groups.
Links to ISCED: Yes.
Sample size and design:
Ultimate sampling unit: households
Sample size (ultimate sampling units): about 40 000 households for the annual survey, and about 125 000 households for five yearly survey.
Overall sampling fraction: 1/5000.
Sample frame: list of villages with hamlet formation in rural areas and urban blocks in urban areas.
Updating of the sample: once in ten years in the rural areas and every five years in the urban areas.

Rotation:
Scheme: half of the sample of the previous subround is rotated.
Percentage of units remaining in the sample for two consecutive survey rounds: 50%
Maximum number of interviews per sample unit: two.
Length of time for complete renewal of the sample: three years.
Field work:
Type of interview: personal interview.
Number of ultimate sampling units per sample area: 4 households for annual survey and ten for the five yearly survey.
Duration of field work
Total: One year.
Per sample area: One year.
Survey organization: permanent.
Number of field staff: about 1300 enumerators and 400 supervisors.
Substitution of non-responding ultimate sampling units: yes, of households.
Estimation and adjustments:
Total non-response rate: Not available.
Adjustment for total non-response: Yes.
Imputation for item non-response: Substitution.
Adjustment for areas/population not covered: No.
Adjustment for under-coverage: No.
Adjustment for over-coverage: No.
Adjustment for seasonal variations: No.
History of the survey:
Title and date of the first survey: Annual survey since May 1955-November 1955, Quinquennial survey since 1972-73.
Significant changes or revisions: In 1972-73 and in 1977-78 the usual status and the current status approaches were adopted. The latter quinquennial surveys are not comparable.
Documentation and dissemination:
Documentation:
Survey results: Government of India, Department of Statistics, national Sample Survey Organization: "NSSO Journal (Sarvekshana)" quarterly, New Dehli. Mimeographed NSS reports.
Survey methodology: idem.
Dissemination:
Time needed for initial release of survey results: 4 years.
Advance information of public about date of initial release: No.
Availability of unpublished data upon request: Yes.
Availability of data in machine-readable form: Yes.

Indonesia

Title of the survey: National Labor Force Survey (NLFS).
Organization responsible for the survey:
Planning and conduct of the survey: BPS-Statistics Indonesia.
Analysis and publication of the results: BPS-Statistics Indonesia.
Topics covered: Employment, unemployment, hours of work, wages, duration of unemployment, industry, occupation, status in employment, educational level, second jobs. (Informal sector employment may be derived from employment status.)
Coverage of the survey:
Geographical: Whole country.
Population groups: All persons 15 years and over, excluding institutional and unsettled populations and persons absent for more than 6 months.
Availability of estimates from other sources for the excluded areas/groups: Not available.
Groups covered by the survey but excluded from the published results: Not available.
Periodicity:
Conduct of the survey: Annually.
Publication of results: Annually.
Reference periods:
Employment: One week moving reference period.
Seeking work: No specific period.
Availability for work: No specific period.
Concepts and definitions:
Employment: Activity done at least one hour in the reference week by any person (aged 15 years and over) in order to earn or to help in obtaining income/profit or where the person holds a position but was temporarily not at work, for example on leave. This includes also activities done by unpaid family workers in helping their parents to obtain income/profit.
It also includes:
a) persons with a job but temporarily absent due to illness or injury, maternity or paternity leave, parental leave, educational or training leave, absence without leave, labour management dispute, bad weather, temporary and indefinite lay-off without pay;
b) full or part-time workers seeking other work during the reference period;
c) persons who performed some work for pay or profit during the reference week but were subject to compulsory schooling, and were registered as job seekers at an employment office;
d) full and part-time students working full or part-time;
e) unpaid family workers at work during the reference week;
f) all members of the armed forces.
Unemployment: All persons aged 15 years and over without work (did not have any job) during the reference week, who are still looking for a job.
It also includes:
a) persons without work and currently available for work who had made arrangements to start a new job subsequent to the reference week;
b) persons subject to compulsory schooling who were seeking and/or available for work; and full and part-time students seeking full or part-time work;
c) persons who were seeking and/or available for work but were retired and receiving a pension.
Underemployment:
Time-related underemployment: NOT APPLICABLE.
Inadequate employment situations: Persons who work less than 35 hours per week who are still looking for another job(s) or who have any willingness to change their current job(s) if there is any opportunity to do so.
Hours of work: Actual number of hours worked in the main job and any additional jobs per day during one (the reference) week.
Employment-related income:
Income from paid employment: All income received (including payment in kind and in services) after income taxes. This is measured for the currently active population.
Income from self-employment: NOT APPLICABLE.
Informal sector employment: This is derived from the employment status of workers; formal sector includes those who work as employers and employees. Informal sector includes those who work as self-employed without help of other people, self-employed assisted by family member(s)/temporary help and unpaid family workers.
Usual activity: NOT APPLICABLE.
Classifications:
Branch of economic activity (industry):
Title of the classification: Indonesian Standard Industrial Classification (Klui).
Population groups classified by industry: Employed persons.
Number of groups used for coding: Up to 1999, groups coded to the 2-digit level, from 2000, up to the 3-digit level.
Links to ISIC-68 up to 1999, and to ISIC Rev. 3 from 2000.
Occupation:
Title of the classification: Indonesian Standard Classification of Occupation (Kji).
Population groups classified by occupation: Employed persons.
Number of groups used for coding: Up to 1999, groups coded to the 2-digit level, from 2000, up to the 3-digit level.
Links to ISCO-68 up to 1999, and to ISCO-88 from 2000.
Status in employment:
Title of the classification: Not available.
Population groups classified by status in employment: Employed persons.
Groups used for classification: Five groups: 1. Self-employed, 2. Employers assisted by unpaid family workers, 3. Employers with paid (permanent) workers, 4. Employees, 5. Unpaid family workers.
Links to ICSE-1993: Yes.
Education:
Title of the classification: Not available.
Population groups classified by education: Employed and unemployed persons.
Groups used for classification: Ten groups: 1. No schooling, 2. Not finished primary school, 3. Primary school, 4. General junior high school, 5. Vocational junior high school, 6. General senior high school, 7. Vocational senior high school, 8. Diploma I/II, 9. Academy/Diploma III, 10. University.
Links to ISCED-76: Yes.
Sample size and design:
Ultimate sampling unit: Household.
Sample size (ultimate sampling units): 49 thousand households.
Overall sampling fraction: Varies between provinces and between urban and rural areas.

Sample frame: The frame is based on the Master file of village files, which consist of lists of the smallest area statistical units (which contain approximately 30 households) by urban and rural areas.
Updating of the sample: Not available.
Rotation: Not available.
Scheme: Not available.
Percentage of units remaining in the sample for two consecutive survey rounds: Not available.
Maximum number of interviews per sample unit: NOT AVAILABLE.
Length of time for complete renewal of the sample: NOT AVAILABLE.
Field work:
Type of interview: Personal interview.
Number of ultimate sampling units per sample area: Not available.
Duration of field work
Total: One month (every month of August).
Per sample area: Not available.
Survey organization: Permanent staff of Statistics Indonesia.
Number of field staff: Not available.
Substitution of non-responding ultimate sampling units: No.
Estimation and adjustments:
Total non-response rate: One per cent.
Adjustment for total non-response: Yes.
Imputation for item non-response: No.
Adjustment for areas/population not covered: No.
Adjustment for under-coverage: No.
Adjustment for over-coverage: No.
Adjustment for seasonal variations: No.
History of the survey:
Title and date of the first survey: National Labour Force Survey: Quarterly 1986 - 1993.
Significant changes or revisions: The Survey became annual from 1994.
Documentation and dissemination:
Documentation:
Survey results: Labour Force Situation in Indonesia; Labourers/Employees' Situation in Indonesia. (**Periodicity:** annual).
Survey methodology: Not available.
Dissemination:
Time needed for initial release of survey results: Six months (August 1998 results were released in February 1999.)
Advance information of public about date of initial release: No.
Availability of unpublished data upon request: Yes.
Availability of data in machine-readable form: The main tabulations are presented through the Internet: http://www.bps.go.id/.

Iran, Islamic Rep. of

Title of the survey: Survey of household employment and unemployment characteristics
Organization responsible for the survey:
Planning and conduct of the survey: Statistical Centre of Iran, Ministry of Planning.
Analysis and publication of the results: Statistical Centre of Iran, Ministry of Planning.
Topics covered: Employment, unemployment, hours of work, Duration of employment, duration of unemployment, occasional workers, industry, occupation, status in employment, education level, and secondary jobs.
Coverage of the survey
Geographical: All urban and rural areas of the country.
Population groups: All civilian population, excluding persons living in unsettled households and institutional households. Also excluded are guests and visitors and persons living abroad, for example, for work or education.
Availability of estimates from other sources for the excluded areas/groups: The survey results are limited to the population covered by the survey. When necessary, separate estimates are for the excluded population and these are added to the results of the survey.
Periodicity
Conduct of the survey: Annual.
Publication of results: Annual.
Reference period
Employment: Fixed reference week.
Seeking work: Fixed reference week.
Availability for work: Reference week.

Concepts and definitions
Employment: Persons, 10 years old and over, in regular settled households, who were engaged in a job at least for 2 days during the past seven days preceding the survey interview.
It includes:
a)Persons with a job but temporary absent for any reason, and persons on temporary lay-off without pay.
b)Full or part-time workers seeking other work during the reference period.
c)Persons who performed some work for pay or profit during the reference week but were subject to compulsory schooling, retired and receiving a pension, or unemployment benefits, or were registered as jobseekers at an employment office or were seeking other work during the reference week.
d)Full or part-time students working full or part-time.
e)Paid apprentices and trainees, and participants in employment promotion schemes.
f)Unpaid family workers at work or temporary absent from work.
g)Seasonal workers not at work during the off-season.
h)Members of the armed forces, including volunteers and career officers, conscripts and persons engaged in civilian service equivalent to military service.
Excluded are:
a) Unpaid apprentices and trainees.
b) Persons engaged in production of goods or services for own final use.
c) Persons doing volunteer community or social service work.
d) Persons with a job but absent without leave.
Unemployment: Persons, 10 years old and over, in regular settled households, who were not engaged in a job at least for 2 days and were seeking work during the last seven days preceding the survey interview.
It includes:
a) Persons on indefinite lay-off without pay or on unpaid leave initiated by the employer.
b) Persons without work and current available and looking for work who had made arrangements to start a new job on a date subsequent to the reference week.
c) Persons without work and currently available and looking for work who were trying to establish their own enterprise.
d) Full or part-time students seeking full or part-time work.
e) Persons who were seeking or available for work but were subject to compulsory schooling or retired and receiving a pension.
Excluded are persons without work but not seeking work during the reference period.
Underemployment:
Time-related underemployment: No information.
Inadequate employment situations: No information.
Hours of work: The total number of regular work hours and overtime work relating to the main job and other jobs of the employed.
Employment-related income:
Income from paid employment: No information.
Income from self-employment: No information.
Informal sector: No information.
Usual activity: No information.
Classifications:
Branch of economic activity (industry):
Title of the classification: Not known.
Population groups classified by industry: Employed and unemployed persons with previous work experience.
Number of groups used for coding: 4-digit codes, but published at alphabetical and 1-digit code.
Links to ISIC: ISIC- Rev. 3.
Occupation:
Title of the classification: Not known.
Population groups classified by occupation: Employed and unemployed persons with previous work experience.
Number of groups used for coding: 4-digit codes, but published at 1-digit level.
Links to ISCO: ISCO-88.
Status in employment:
Title of the classification: No information.
Population groups classified by status: Employed and unemployed persons with previous work experience.
Groups used for classification: Employer, Own-account worker, Public sector wage and salary earner, Private sector wage and salary earner, Cooperative sector wage and salary earner, Unpaid family worker.
Links to ICSE: ICSE-1986.
Education:
Title of the classification: No information.

Population groups classified by education: Employed and unemployed persons
Groups used for classification: No formal education, Literacy, Informal, Theological sciences, Primary school, Lower secondary level, Higher secondary school, High school diploma and pre-university, Higher education.
Links to ISCED: ISCED-1976.
Sample size and design:
Ultimate sampling unit: Person.
Sample size (ultimate sampling units): 56 753.
Overall sampling fraction: 0.95%.
Sample frame: The 1996 Nationwide Population and Housing Census.
Updating of the sample: Not available.
Rotation: None.
Field work:
Type of interview: Personal interview by enumerator.
Number of ultimate sampling units per sample area: 25 sample households per cluster. Each cluster requires on average 1.5 work-days for an enumerator. **Duration of fieldwork:** 15 days.
Survey organization: Permanent.
Number of field staff: Total personnel for executing the survey is 640 persons.
Substitution of non-responding sampling units: No.
Estimation and adjustments:
Total non-response rate: No information provided.
Adjustment for total non-response: No.
Imputation for item non-response: No.
Adjustment for areas/population not covered: No.
Adjustment for under-coverage: No.
Adjustment for over-coverage: No.
Adjustment for seasonal variations: No.
History of the survey:
Title and date of the first survey: Survey of household employment and unemployment characteristics (11-26 December 1977).
Significant changes or revisions: The first rounds of the survey (entitled "Labour force survey") were carried out by the Ministry of Labour and Social Affairs from 1969 to 1972.
The second round (entitled "Survey of the population and the labour force") was carried out by the Statistical Centre of Iran in February 1989.
The third round (entitled "Survey of household employment and unemployment characteristics") was carried out by the Statistical Centre of Iran in February 1994.
The fourth round (also entitled "Survey of household employment and unemployment characteristics") has been conducted by the Statistical Centre of Iran on an annual basis since December 1997.
There are plans to conduct the survey twice a year. There are also plans to add survey items to the questionnaire, in particular, "income", "citizenship", and "type of employment".
Documentation and dissemination:
Documentation:
Survey results: Iran Statistical Yearbook Results of the household employment and unemployment characteristics survey. Collection of statistical instruction manuals for each survey.
Survey methodology: Same as above.
Dissemination
Time needed for initial release of survey results: About 16 months. 1997 survey results released in June 1998.
Advance information of public about date of initial release: Yes.
Availability of unpublished data upon request: Yes through the Information **Dissemination** Unit and the domestic network of the Statistical Centre of Iran.
Availability of data in machine-readable form: Yes, diskettes and the SCI domestic network.
Website: http://www.sci.or.ir/.

Ireland

Title of the survey: Quarterly National Household Survey (QNHS).
Organization responsible for the survey:
Planning and conduct of the survey: Central Statistical Office (CSO).
Analysis and publication of the results: Central Statistical Office (CSO).
Topics covered: Persons currently and usually economically active, employed and unemployed; persons currently in time-related under-employment, persons in inadequate employment situations and persons currently outside the labour force; discouraged workers; hours of work; duration of employment and unemployment; second jobs; industry; occupation; status in employment; education/training levels.
Coverage of the survey:
Geographical: Whole country.
Population groups: Non-institutional population of age 15 years and above.
Availability of estimates from other sources for the excluded areas/groups: None.
Groups covered by the survey but excluded from the published results: None.
Periodicity:
Conduct of the survey: Continuous.
Publication of results: Quarterly.
Reference periods:
Employment: One week.
Seeking work: The four weeks preceding the interview..
Availability for work: The four weeks following the interview.
Concepts and definitions:
Employment: Persons aged 15 years and over, who a) performed some work in the week before the survey for one hour or more for pay or profit, including work on the family farm or business; and b) were temporarily absent from work during the reference week because of illness, holidays, etc. The armed forces are included in the employed.
Unemployment: Persons aged 15 years and over who were currently without work and available for work within four weeks, and who had searched for work sometime during the last four weeks.
Underemployment:
Time-related underemployment: Employed persons working in a part-time job with "too few hours", who have searched for and were available for another job.
Inadequate employment situations: Not currently published but additional analysis is possible.
Hours of work: Usual and actual (hours worked) during the reference week.
Employment-related income:
Income from paid employment: Not applicable.
Income from self-employment: Not applicable.
Informal sector: Not separately specified.
Usual activity: No information provided.
Classifications:
Branch of economic activity (industry):
Title of the classification: Irish adaptation of NACE, rev. 1.
Population groups classified by industry: Employed and unemployed persons (unemployed are only classified if they had a job in the past 10 years).
Number of groups used for coding: 3 digit level.
Links to ISIC: ISIC-Rev. 3 (2 digit level).
Occupation:
Title of the classification: Standard Occupations Classification 1990 (SOC 90).
Population groups classified by occupation: Employed and unemployed persons (unemployed are only classified if they had a job in the past 10 years).
Number of groups used for coding: 3 digit level.
Links to ISCO: ISCO-88 (3 digit level).
Status in employment:
Title of the classification: No information provided.
Population groups classified by status in employment: Employed persons.
Groups used for classification: Employees; self-employed with or without at least one employee; assisting relatives.
Links to ICSE: ICSE-1993.
Education:
Title of the classification: National classification.
Population groups classified education: All persons aged 15 years and over..
Groups used for classification: No formal education; pre-primary; primary; junior/group/intermediate certificate; transition year programme; leaving certificate applied; leaving certificate vocational programme; leaving certificate established; PLC; apprenticeship; certificate in farming; cadetship; national certificate/diploma; primary degree; postgraduate certificate/diploma; postgraduate degree; doctorate; other.
Links to ISCED: ISCED-1976 and ISCED-1997.
Sample size and design:
Ultimate sampling unit: Household.
Sample size (ultimate sampling units): 39 000 each quarter.
Overall sampling fraction: 1/32.
Sample frame: Based on 1996 population census. Two stage design: first stage sample of 2 600 blocks with about 75 dwellings each at

county level to represent 8 strata according to population density. 15 households surveyed in each block.
Updating of the sample frame: It was the intention to follow 2001 population census. However, due to foot and mouth precautions, the 2001 Census of Population was delayed until2002. The sample frame was updated using a combination of preliminary work done for the 2001 Census, the geo-directory and other sources, and updating will be done as Census of Population 2002 results become available.
Rotation:
Scheme: Households participate for 5 consecutive quarters and are then replaced by other households in the block.
Percentage of units remaining in the sample for two consecutive survey rounds: 80 percent.
Maximum number of interviews per sample unit: No information provided. **Length of time for complete renewal of the sample:** About 5 years.
Field work:
Type of interview: Computer assisted personal interviewing (CAPI).
Number of ultimate sampling units per sample area: No information.
Duration of field work:
Total: Continuous.
Per sample unit: No information.
Survey organization: Permanent.
Number of field staff: 150 interviewers and 10 field coordinators.
Substitution of non-responding ultimate sampling units: No.
Estimation and adjustments:
Total non-response rate: 6.3 percent.
Adjustment for total non-response: No.
Imputation for item non-response: No.
Adjustment for areas/population not covered: No.
Adjustment for undercoverage: No.
Adjustment for overcoverage: No.
Adjustment for seasonal variations: As the Quarterly National Household Survey is conducted since 1997, it has not yet been seasonally adjusted. However, background work is in progress.
History of the survey:
Title and date of the first survey: QNHS started in September-November 1997 and replaced the Annual Labour Force Survey conducted in April-May of each year.
Significant changes or revisions: None after 1997.
Documentation and dissemination
Documentation:
Survey results: Quarterly National Household Survey (ISSN 1393-6875).
Survey methodology: Quarterly National Household Survey (ISSN 1393-6875).
Dissemination:
Time needed for initial release of survey results: About 3 months.
Advance information of public about date of initial release: Yes.
Availability of unpublished data upon request: Yes.
Availability of data in machine-readable form: Yes, subject to charges.
Website: http://www.cso.ie/.

Italy

Title of the survey: Rilevazione Trimestrale sulle Forze di Lavoro.
Organization responsible for the survey:
Planning and conduct of the survey: Istituto Nazionale di Statistica (ISTAT).
Analysis and publication of the results: ISTAT.
Topics covered: Employment, unemployment, underemployment, hours of work,, duration of employment and unemployment, discouraged workers, industry, occupation, status in employment, education/qualification, second jobs.
Coverage of the survey:
Geographical: Whole country.
Population groups: Resident non-institutional persons aged 15 years and over, living in private households.
Availability of estimates from other sources for the excluded areas/groups: No information.
Groups covered by the survey but excluded from the published results: No information.
Periodicity:
Conduct of the survey: Quarterly.
Publication of results: Quarterly.
Reference periods:
Employment: One fixed week.
Seeking work: Fixed four weeks period.
Availability for work: Fixed two weeks period.
Concepts and definitions:
Employment: Persons aged 15 years and over who declare to be employed and those who declared not to be in employment but have worked at least one week during the reference week.
Also included in the employed are:
a) full or part-time workers seeking other work during the reference week;
b) persons who performed some work for pay or profit during the reference week but were subject to compulsory schooling, retired and receiving a pension, registered as jobseekers at an employment office, receiving unemployment benefits;
c) full and part-time students working full or part-time;
d) unpaid family workers at work during the reference week;
e) volunteers and career members of the armed forces.
Unemployment: Persons aged 15 years and over who have no employment during the reference week and who seeks a job, made at least one active search action during the reference week (4 weeks) and are available to start working within 2 weeks as well as persons who are not looking for a job because they have already found one which will start in the future.
Underemployment:
Time-related underemployment: Persons in employment who would have liked to work additional hours during the reference week and would have been available to work additional hours in the reference week.
Inadequate employment situations: No specific definition but the Italian labour force survey collects data on employed persons looking for another job or on reasons for looking for anther job (afraid to lose actual job; fixed-term job; looking for second activity; looking for better conditions, etc.).
Hours of work: Usual and actually worked hours in the main job during the reference week as well as hours actually worked in the second activity during the reference week.
Employment-related income:
Income from paid employment: Not applicable.
Income from self-employment: Not applicable.
Informal sector: Not applicable.
Usual activity: No information.
Classifications:
Branch of economic activity (industry):
Title of the classification: National classification.
Population groups classified by industry: Employed and unemployed persons with previous work experience.
Number of groups used for coding: 60 at the 2-digit level.
Links to ISIC: ISIC-Rev.3.
Occupation:
Title of the classification: National classification.
Population groups classified by occupation: Employed and unemployed persons with previous work experience.
Number of groups used for coding: 35.
Links to ISCO: ISCO-88.
Status in employment:
Title of the classification: National classification.
Population groups classified by status in employment: Employed and unemployed persons with previous work experience.
Groups used for classification: Employee, employer, own-account worker, family worker and member of a cooperative for the employed; employee, self-employed with employees, self-employed without employees and family worker for the unemployed.
Links to ICSE: ICSE-1993.
Education:
Title of the classification: ISCED-97.
Population groups classified by education: All persons.
Groups used for classification: No education attainment; primary education (level 1); lower secondary education (level 2); upper secondary education (level 3); post-secondary non-tertiary education (level 4); tertiary education (level 5); post-graduate education (level 6).
Links to ISCED: ISCED-97.
Sample size and design:
Ultimate sampling unit: Household.
Sample size (ultimate sampling units): 75 000 households each quarter.
Overall sampling fraction: 0.35 per cent of resident families each quarter.
Sample frame: Municipal registers.
Updating of the sample: In April of each year.
Rotation:
Scheme: 2-2-2.

Percentage of units remaining in the sample for two consecutive survey rounds: 50 per cent.
Maximum number of interviews per sample unit: 4.
Length of time for complete renewal of the sample: 15 quarters.
Field work:
Type of interview: Face to face basis: paper and pencil personal interview.
Number of ultimate sampling units per sample area:
Duration of field work:
Total: No information.
Per sample area: No information.
Survey organization: Permanent.
Number of field staff: 1 351 supervisors and 3 000 interviewers.
Substitution of non-responding ultimate sampling units: Yes.
Estimation and adjustments:
Total non-response rate: 5 per cent.
Adjustment for total non-response: Yes.
Imputation for item non-response: Yes
Adjustment for areas/population not covered: No.
Adjustment for undercoverage: Yes.
Adjustment for overcoverage: Yes.
Adjustment for seasonal variations: Yes for employment by geographical area and economic activity, for unemployment and unemployment rates by geographical area and for labor force by geographical area.
History of the survey:
Title and date of the first survey: Rilevazione Nazionale delle Forze di Lavoro 1959.
Significant changes or revisions: 1977; 1984: sample drawn from the 1981 Population Census; beginning second quarter of 1992: methodology revised and lower age limit refers to persons aged 15 years and over instead of 14 years previously.
Documentation and dissemination:
Documentation:
Survey results: Press releases (quarterly); Annual results.
Survey methodology: Idem.
Dissemination:
Time needed for initial release of survey results: About 3 months.
Advance information of public about date of initial release: Yes.
Availability of unpublished data upon request: Yes.
Availability of data in machine-readable form: Yes.
Website: http://www.istat.it/.

Jamaica

Title of the survey: Labour Force Survey.
Organization responsible for the survey:
Planning and conduct of the survey: Statistical Institute of Jamaica.
Analysis and publication of the results: Statistical Institute of Jamaica.
Topics covered: Employment, unemployment, hours of work, wages, income, duration of employment, industry, occupation, status in employment, education and second jobs.
Coverage of the survey:
Geographical: Whole country.
Population groups: All persons aged 14 years and over with the exception of persons living institutions, the non resident citizens and the diplomats.
Availability of estimates from other sources for the excluded areas/groups: No information.
Groups covered by the survey but excluded from the published results: No information.
Periodicity:
Conduct of the survey: Quarterly survey conducted in January, April, July and October.
Publication of results: Annually.
Reference periods:
Employment: One week.
Seeking work: Three months.
Availability for work: No information.
Concepts and definitions:
Employment: The employed comprises all those aged 14 years and over who, during the survey week, have worked for at least one hour and those who had jobs but were temporarily absent from work.
Persons working include those who:
a) worked for wages or salary, at time rates, at price rates, on commission, for tips, for board and lodgings, or for any other type of payment in kind;
b) worked as trainees or apprentices;
c) worked for profit or fees in his own business;
d) worked without money, wages or salary, at tasks (other than their own housework or household tasks) which contributed to the operation of a farm or business owned and operated for profit, in most cases by some member of his family;
e) spent some time in the operation of a business or profession even though no sales were made or professional services rendered, such as a doctor or lawyer spending time in his office waiting for clients.
Are also included all persons who had jobs but who, for some reasons did not work during the survey week. This comprises persons who:
a) had jobs, but worked for less than one hour during the survey week;
b) did not work because of illness or temporary disability, but whose jobs were being held for them until their return;
c) were unable to work because of bad weather;
d) did not work because they were on leave, including vacation leave, with or without pay, so long as their jobs were being held for them until their return;
e) did not work because of some labour dispute, such as strike or lockout;
f) were on short lay-off of not more than 30 days duration, with instructions to return to work at the end of the 30 days.
Unemployment: The unemployed comprise all those aged 14 years and over who were looking for work, wanting work and available for work. Persons looking for work must have made a positive attempt to seek a job such as:
a) registration at employment agency, whether government or private;
b) visiting job sites in search of a job;
c) applying in person to prospective employers;
d) putting advertisements in any public press or place;
e) writing letters of application;
f) asking someone to try to find a job;
g) making investigations with a view of starting own farm or business.
Underemployment:
Time-related underemployment: No information.
Inadequate employment situations: No information.
Hours of work: Usual hours worked per week in all jobs.
Employment-related income:
Income from paid employment: Gross average income, from employment and other sources, over the last past 12 months.
Income from self-employment: See above.
Informal sector: No information.
Usual activity: No information.
Classifications:
Branch of economic activity (industry):
Title of the classification: National classification.
Population groups classified by industry: Employed and unemployed (industry of last job for the unemployed).
Number of groups used for coding: Nine.
Links to ISIC: ISIC-Rev. 2.
Occupation:
Title of the classification: National classification.
Population groups classified by occupation: Employed and unemployed (occupation of last job for the unemployed).
Number of groups used for coding: Nine.
Links to ISCO: Partially linked to ISCO-88.
Status in employment:
Title of the classification: National classification.
Population groups classified by status in employment: Employed.
Groups used for classification: Five groups: paid government employees; private sector employees; unpaid family workers; employers; own-account workers.
Links to ICSE: ICSE-1993.
Education:
Title of the classification: Not applicable.
Population groups classified by education: Not applicable.
Groups used for classification: Not applicable.
Links to ISCED: Not applicable.
Sample size and design:
Ultimate sampling unit: Dwelling.
Sample size (ultimate sampling units): A two stage stratified sampling of 7 648 dwellings based on the 1997 listing.
Overall sampling fraction: 1.5 per cent.
Sample frame: The 1991 Population Census results.
Updating of the sample: Every 3 years on the basis of the new listings.
Rotation:
Scheme: Four panels are covered in each round of the survey.

Percentage of units remaining in the sample for two consecutive survey rounds: 50 per cent.
Maximum number of interviews per sample unit: No information.
Length of time for complete renewal of the sample: One year.
Field work:
Type of interview: Personal interview with paper and pencil.
Number of ultimate sampling units per sample area: No information.
Duration of field work:
Total: Tree to four weeks.
Per sample area: No information.
Survey organization: Permanent.
Number of field staff: 3 senior supervisors, 16 supervisors and 65 interviewers.
Substitution of non-responding ultimate sampling units: No.
Estimation and adjustments:
Total non-response rate: No information.
Adjustment for total non-response: Yes.
Imputation for item non-response: No.
Adjustment for areas/population not covered: Yes.
Adjustment for undercoverage: No.
Adjustment for overcoverage: No.
Adjustment for seasonal variations: No.
History of the survey:
Title and date of the first survey: The Labour Force 1968.
Significant changes or revisions: In 1991, new industrial classification.
Documentation and dissemination:
Documentation:
Survey results: The Labour Force (annually).
Survey methodology: The Labour Force (annually).
Dissemination:
Time needed for initial release of survey results: 6 months.
Advance information of public about date of initial release: No.
Availability of unpublished data upon request: Yes.
Availability of data in machine-readable form: Yes.
Website: http://www.stainja.com/.

Japan

Title of the survey: Labour Force Survey.
Organization responsible for the survey:
Planning and conduct of the survey: Statistics Bureau, Ministry of Public Management, Home Affairs, Posts and Telecommunications.
Analysis and publication of the results: Statistics Bureau, Ministry of Public Management, Home Affairs, Posts and Telecommunications.
Topics covered: Employment, unemployment, hours of work, wages, duration of unemployment, discouraged workers, industry, occupation, status in employment, education/qualification levels.
Coverage of the survey:
Geographical: Whole country, excluding the Northern Territories.
Population groups: All Japanese and foreigners aged 15 years and over who have lived (or will be living) in the country for more than three months, excluding foreign diplomatic corps, foreign military personnel and those who accompany them. The self-defense forces and inmates of reformatory institutions are separately enumerated and included in the results.
Persons who are temporarily absent from their household for traveling, working elsewhere or being hospitalized, are reported at their homes if the period of absence is less than three months. If they have been absent or are going to be absent from home for three months or more, they are enumerated at their destination.
Availability of estimates from other sources for the excluded areas/groups: No information provided.
Groups covered by the survey but excluded from the published results: No information provided.
Periodicity:
Conduct of the survey: Monthly.
Publication of results: Monthly and quarterly for the "Detailed Results" (previously the "Special Survey").
Reference periods:
Employment: One fixed week.
Seeking work: One fixed week, including for persons who were waiting for the results of past job search activity.
Availability for work: One fixed day.
Concepts and definitions:
Employment: The employed are:
1) "Employed persons at work", i.e. persons who worked for pay or profit for at least one hour during the reference week. Family workers who worked for at least one hour during the reference week are also included in this category.
2) "Employed persons with a job, but not at work, i.e. persons who had their job but did not work at all during the reference week.
Included are:
1) full- and part-time workers seeking other work during the reference week;
2) full- and part-time workers working full-or part-time;
3) persons who have performed some work for pay and profit during the reference week, while being retired and receiving a pension, or registered as jobseekers at an employment office;
4) paid and unpaid apprentices and trainees;
5) participants in employment promotion schemes;
6) paid and unpaid family workers, provided the latter are not absent from work during the reference week;
7) private domestic servants;
8) self-defence forces;
9) persons with a job but temporarily absent due to illness/injury, vacation/annual leave, maternity/paternity leave, education leave, absence without leave, bad weather or mechanical breakdown, labour-management dispute or other reduction in economic activity;
10) persons on temporary release from work (since they are not discharged and usually receive wage and salary). (Japan has no actual system of lay-off).
To be considered as employed when absent from work, employees must have received or expect to receive wage or salary, and self-employed workers' period of absence must not exceed 30 days.
Excluded from the employed and considered as out of the labour force are persons engaged in own housework and persons doing unpaid community or social work.
Unemployment: Unemployed are persons who did not work at all during the reference week, but were available for work and ready to take a job immediately, and were actively seeking a job or were waiting for the results of the past job search activity.
"Actively seeking a job" means having taken any of the following steps during the reference week: registered at an employment agency; placed or answered advertisements; applied for an examination; contacted friend or relatives; checked at work sites; preparing to start a business by procuring funds and materials, etc.
Included are full- and part-time students seeking full- and part-time work.
Unpaid family workers who were temporarily absent from work during the reference week are out of the labour force, unless they satisfy the above conditions.
Seasonal workers awaiting agricultural or other seasonal work are excluded from the unemployed and considered as out of the labour force.
Underemployment:
Time-related underemployment: Not covered by the survey.
Inadequate employment situations: Not covered by the survey.
Hours of work: "Hours worked during the survey week" refers to the actual number of hours worked, which include overtime and exclude hours spent for housework, voluntary work without pay, meal breaks, commuting, etc. If a person worked in more than one job during the survey week, all the hours of work for each job are summed up.
Employment-related income:
Income from paid employment: Not covered by the survey.
Income from self-employment: Not covered by the survey.
Informal sector: Not covered by the survey.
Usual activity: Not covered by the survey.
Classifications:
Branch of economic activity (industry):
Title of the classification: National classification.
Population groups classified by industry: Employed and unemployed persons (industry of last job for the unemployed).
Number of groups used for coding: 30 groups.
Links to ISIC: ISIC-Rev. 2 at the 3rd digit level (major groups).
Occupation:
Title of the classification: National classification.
Population groups classified by occupation: Employed and unemployed persons (occupation of last job for the unemployed).
Number of groups used for coding: 15 groups.
Links to ISCO: ISCO-68 at the 1st digit level (major groups).
Status in employment:
Title of the classification: National classification.
Population groups classified by status in employment: Employed and unemployed persons. Unemployed persons are classified according their last job, if any, only in "Detailed Results".
Groups used for classification: 4 groups; employees (regular employees, temporary employees and daily employees), self-employed workers, family workers and pieceworkers at home.

Links to ICSE: ICSE-1993.
Education:
Title of the classification: National classification.
Population groups classified by education: Employed and unemployed persons.
Groups used for classification: Only in the "Detailed Results". All persons are classified by 'school attendance' as of the survey date, into: attending school, graduated from school and never attending school. The 'attending school' and 'graduated from school' are further classified according to the level of education complete such as, primary school or junior school, senior school, junior school, college or university, including graduate school.
Links to ISCED: ISCED-1976.
Sample size and design:
Ultimate sampling unit: Dwelling.
Sample size (ultimate sampling units): About 2 900 enumeration districts (EDs) comprising 40 000 dwellings.
Overall sampling fraction: No information provided.
Sample frame: The quinquennial Population Census. The current sample is built up and updated on the basis of the 1995 Population Census.
Updating of the sample: Every year, a list of newly developed collective housing districts are prepared by the Prefectural Government to be added to the EDs.
Rotation:
Scheme: A sample of EDs remain in the sample for four consecutive months, leave the sample for the following eight months, and joins the sample again for the same four months in the following year.
For each ED, two sets of dwelling units are selected. In the first year of enumeration of a sample ED, the households in the sample dwellings units in the first set are surveyed for the first two consecutive moths, and then replaced by the households in the dwelling units of the other set. In the second year, the dwelling units of the first set enter the sample again and are replaced by those of the other set in the same way as in the first year.
Under this system, 1/4 of the sample EDs and half of the sample households are replaced every month. Three fourths of the sample Eds are common from month to month and half of them from year to year.
Percentage of units remaining in the sample for two consecutive survey rounds: 50 %.
Maximum number of interviews per sample unit: Four.
Length of time for complete renewal of the sample: 16 months.
Field work:
Type of interview: Paper and pencil.
Number of ultimate sampling units per sample area: No information provided.
Duration of field work:
Total: 13 days.
Per sample area: No information provided.
Survey organization: Permanent survey organization (Statistical Divisions of Prefectural Governments). Enumerators are temporarily recruited for each round.
Number of field staff: About 3 180 persons.
Substitution of non-responding ultimate sampling units: No.
Estimation and adjustments:
Total non-response rate: No.
Adjustment for total non-response: No.
Imputation for item non-response: No.
Adjustment for areas/population not covered: No.
Adjustment for undercoverage: No.
Adjustment for overcoverage: No.
Adjustment for seasonal variations: Yes. US Census Methods II (X-11).
History of the survey:
Title and date of the first survey: Labour Force Survey July 1947.
Significant changes or revisions: In year 1953.
Documentation and dissemination:
Documentation:
Survey results: Monthly Report on the Labour Force Survey; Annual Report on the Labour Force Survey (March of each year)
Survey methodology: No information provided.
Dissemination:
Time needed for initial release of survey results: One month.
Advance information of public about date of initial release: Yes.
Availability of unpublished data upon request: Yes.
Availability of data in machine-readable form: Internet.
Website: http://www.stat.go.jp/.

Jordan

Title of the survey: Employment and Unemployment Surveys, 2001.
Organization responsible for the survey:
Planning and conduct of the survey: Department of Statistics, Household Surveys Directorate.
Analysis and publication of the results: Department of Statistics, Household Surveys Directorate.
Topics covered: Current employment and unemployment. Actual hours worked at all jobs and reason for temporary absence from work. Desire for change of job and reason. Educational level, current industry, occupation and status in employment in main job. Monthly income from employment addressed to employees and self-employed persons. Past work experience, current availability for work, active job-search, channels used in seeking work, duration of job-search and timing of last job-search. Major activity of population not-in-labour-force.
Coverage of the survey:
Geographical: Entire nation expect nomadic areas.
Population groups: Total population, excluding population living in remote areas (mostly nomads) and those living in collective dwellings such as hotels, work camps, prisons, etc.
Availability of estimates from other sources for the excluded areas/groups: No.
Groups covered by the survey but excluded from the published results: Non-Jordanian. Survey results are limited to the Jordanian population. No separate estimates are available for Non-Jordanians.
Periodicity:
Conduct of the survey: Quarterly
Publication of results: Quarterly and Annual.
Reference periods:
Employment: Moving reference week. Seven days prior to date of interview.
Seeking work: Active job-search of the unemployed during the 4 weeks prior to the date of interview.
Availability for work: Seven days prior to the date of interview or in the next 15 days after the date of interview.
Concepts and definitions:
Employment: Persons, 15 years old and over, who worked at least one hour during the reference period in the government sector or in the private sector. Work includes any paid work, paid or unpaid activity in a business, completely or partially owned. Employed also include paid employees and self-employed persons who were temporary absent from work during the reference period for reasons such as own illness, vacation, holidays, reduction in economic activity (lack of customers, shortage of demand, etc.), temporary breakdown in the establishment (shutdown, shortage of raw materials, shortage of fuel, and electric or mechanical breakdown).
Unemployment: Persons, 15 years old and over, who were not employed, but able to work, available for work and actively looking for work. Availability for work means being ready or prepared to receive work immediately, during the seven days prior to the date of interview or within 15 days following the date of interview. Actively looking for work means having taken specific steps and spent some or all time in search for work during the four weeks prior to the date of interview. Specific steps include: registration and direct application for work to employers, search for work at special workers' gatherings or assembly places, placing or answering advertisements in newspapers, seeking assistance from friends and relatives, etc. The unemployed include persons without work, currently available for work, who did not search for work during the four weeks prior to the date of interview because they were waiting to return to their previous job or had found a job that starts later.
Underemployment: Refers to employed persons who want to obtain a replacement job or an additional job and were available for such work during the reference period. Three reasons for wanting a replacement or an additional job are: current work is insufficient in terms of salary and bonuses, current work does not suit the educational qualification of the person, and the hours of work in current job are too short.
Hours of work: Refers to the number of hours actually worked during the seven days prior to the date of interview. The number is the sum of five components: (1) hours actually worked during normal periods of work; (2) overtime hours; (3) time spent at the workplace not engaged in the business activity proper, but preparing, maintaining, and cleaning work tools and equipment, or preparing receipts, time-sheets and reports, etc.; (4) time spent at workplace waiting or standing by for the provision of work materials, or the repair of mechanical or electrical damages or breakdowns, etc.; and (5) time spent at the workplace on short breaks or rest periods.

It excludes hours paid but not worked such as paid annual vacations, paid official or public holidays, and paid sick leaves. It also excludes time designated for meal breaks which normally does not exceed three hours and time spent on travel from home to the workplace and vice versa.

Employment-related income:

Income from employment: Monthly income. The amount of money and other in-kind benefits received during the calendar month prior to the date of interview. It may be one of the following: (1) Wages or salaries, in cash or in-kind, received in return to work performed whether as a regular or temporary employee or a trainee. It includes overtime payments, whether in cash or in-kind. In cases of multiple jobholding, the total income from all jobs should be recorded. The in-kind payments include the market value of cloths, meals, transportation, housing, and similar subsidies provided by the employer; (2) Income from self-employment, in cash or in-kind revenue obtained as an employer or own-account worker, regardless of branch of economic activity.

Income from self-employment: No information.

Informal sector employment: No information.

Usual activity: No information.

Classifications:

Branch of economic activity (industry):

Title of the classification: No information.

Population groups classified by industry: Employed and unemployed persons with previous work experience.

Number of groups used for coding: 3-digit level. Results published at the 1-digit level with 17 categories.

Linked to ISIC: ISIC- Rev. 3.

Occupation:

Title of the classification: No information.

Population groups classified by occupation: Employed and unemployed persons with previous work experience.

Number of groups used for coding: 3-digit level. Results published at the 1-digit level with 9 categories..

Linked to ISCO: ISCO-88.

Status in employment:

Title of the classification: No information.

Population groups classified by status in employment: Employed and unemployed persons with work experience.

List of groups: Employees, employers, self-employed, unpaid family workers, unpaid workers.

Linked to ICSE: ICSE-1993.

Education:

Title of the classification: No information.

Population groups classified by educational level: Population 15 years old and above.

List of groups: Illiterate. Read & write. Elementary education. Preparatory. Basic education. Vocational apprenticeship. Secondary education. Intermediate diploma. B.S.C. Higher Diploma and above. Linked to ISCED: ISCED-1997.

Sample size and design:

Ultimate sampling unit: Households.

Quarterly sample size (ultimate sampling units): 8,800 households in 440 Primary Sampling Units (PSUs) that are area units or blocks.

Overall sampling fraction: 1%.

Sample frame: Based on the enumeration areas of the 1994 Population and housing census. Each of the 12 governorates in Jordan was considered as independent stratum. In each governorate, the localities were divided into urban and rural except for the five major cities: Amman, Wadi Essier, Zarqa, Russeifa and Irbid. The urban and rural localities were then further divided into categories according to the population size of the locality, and ordered according to their geographical succession.

The Primary Sampling Units (PSUs) within each stratum were divided into four categories (low, medium low, medium high, and high) according to scores calculated using socioeconomic information based on the results of the 1994 Population and Housing Census. The PSUs thus formed were ordered within each stratum according to a geographical procedure for urban and rural areas, and according to socio-economic characteristics for the major cities.

The sample was selected in two stages. In the first stage, a sample of 110 PSU's was then selected according to probabilities proportional to size with a systematic selection procedure. In the second stage, after updating the frame of selected PSUs, a constant number of ultimate sampling units (20 households) were selected from each PSU using a systematic procedure from the list of households.

Updating of the sample: The USUs are updated at the listing stage of the sampled PSUs in preparation of each new survey round.

Rotation:

Scheme: Beginning in 2000, a rotation sample scheme was introduced according to which a sample household initially selected is retained in the sample for two consecutive rounds, leaves the sample in the next two rounds, and returns in the sample for two more consecutive rounds before leaving the sample permanently.

Percentage of units remaining in the sample for two consecutive survey rounds: According to this design, there is an overlap of 75 percent of the sample units between consecutive quarters and 50 percent between quarters one-year apart.

Maximum number of interviews per sample unit: No information.

Length of time for complete renewal of the sample: One year and a half.

Field work:

Type of interview: Personal interview with paper and pencil recording.

Number of ultimate sampling units per sample area: 20 households.

Duration of fieldwork:

Total: One month including updating of PSUs, selection of sample households and interviewing

Per sample area: No information..

Survey organization: Permanent.

Number of field staff: Around 50 to 60 persons including interviewers and supervisors.

Substitution of non-responding sampling units: No.

Estimation and adjustments:

Total non-response rate: 2%. Number of successfully completed interviews after three callbacks, in the four quarters of 2001 was 32,540 corresponding to 92.4% of the total sample households. Among the reasons for non-interview were dwelling closed at time of visit (4.0%), dwelling vacant (2.5%), unavailability of eligible respondent and refusal (0.6%).

Adjustment for total non-response: Yes, by inverse of rate of response within strata.

Imputation for item non-response: No.

Adjustment for areas/population not covered: No.

Adjustment for under-coverage: Yes, by ratio-estimation to projected population figures.

Adjustment for over-coverage: No.

Adjustment for seasonal variations: No.

History of the survey:

Title and date of the first survey: Employment and unemployment survey, 1982.

Significant changes or revisions: Surveys of the labour force were conducted twice in 1982, once in both 1986 and 1987. Between 1991 and 1997, surveys were conducted once or twice a year, except for 1992 when the survey was not conducted. In 1998 and 1999, three survey rounds were conducted per year covering May-June, September-October and November-December. Since the beginning of 2000, the survey has been conducted on quarterly basis.

Documentation and dissemination:

Documentation:

Survey results: Annual Report of Employment and Unemployment Survey 2001, published in March 2002.

Survey methodology: Annual Report of Employment and Unemployment Survey 2001, published in March 2002.

Time needed for initial release of survey results: 2 months.

Advance information of public about date of initial release: No.

Availability of unpublished data upon request: Yes.

Availability of data in machine-readable form: Tabulated data available in machine readable format on request.

Website: http://www.dos.gov.jo/.

Korea, Republic of

Title of the survey: Economically Active Population Survey.

Organization responsible for the survey:

Planning and conduct of the survey: National Statistical Office.

Analysis and publication of the results: National Statistical Office.

Topics covered: Employment, unemployment, hours of work, duration of unemployment, industry, occupation, status in employment, education.

Coverage of the survey:

Geographical: Whole country.

Population groups: Persons aged 15 years and over who usually reside in private households within the territory at the time of the interview.

Excluded are members of the armed forces, prisoners, the institutional population, non-resident citizens, foreigners and persons residing abroad..
Availability of estimates from other sources for the excluded areas/groups: NO.
Groups covered by the survey but excluded from the published results: NO.
Periodicity:
Conduct of the survey: Monthly.
Publication of results: Monthly.
Reference periods:
Employment: The week which includes the 15th of the month.
Seeking work: The week which includes the 15th of the month.
Availability for work: The week which includes the 15th of the month.
Concepts and definitions:
Employment: All persons aged 15 years and over who worked for pay or profit for at least one hour during the reference week and unpaid family workers who worked 18 hours or more during the reference week.
It includes:
a) persons who have a job but were temporarily absent from work due to illness or injury, vacation or annual leave, maternity, paternity or parental leave, educational or training leave, labor management dispute, bad weather or mechanical breakdown;
b) full- or part-.time workers seeking other work during the reference week;
other family obligations, labor dispute, temporary disorganization during the reference week;
c) persons who performed some work for pay or profit during the reference week but were subject to compulsory schooling, retired and receiving a pension, registered as job seekers at an employment office, receiving unemployment benefits;
d) full- and part-time students working full- or part-time;
e) paid apprentices and trainees.
Members of the armed forces are excluded even if military duty is compulsory.
Unemployment: All persons aged 15 years and over who were not at work but were available for work and were actively looking for work during the reference week. In addition, since 1999, the National Statistical Office collects data on unemployed persons searching work during a four-months period which includes the survey week.
"Actively seeking work" means having taken one or more of the following steps during the reference week: registered at an employment office, sent curriculum vitae, placed or answered advertisements, checked at work sites, contacted friends or relatives, made arrangements to establish own business, etc.
"Availability for work" refers to the willingness of the person surveyed to take up a job immediately if reasonable work is available.
It also includes persons who were seeking and/or available for work but were subject to compulsory schooling, retired and receiving a pension and full- and part-time students seeking full- or part-time work if they are available during the reference week.
Excluded are seasonal workers awaiting agricultural or other seasonal work; further, they are considered as inactive.
Underemployment:
Time-related underemployment: Not applicable.
Inadequate employment situations: Not applicable.
Hours of work: Total hours actually worked in the main job during the reference week, including overtime and time spent on preparation such as making lecture notes, ordering commodities, etc.
Are excluded hours which are not linked to the job, such as hours corresponding to meal breaks, travel from to work and vice versa or to private affairs.
Employment-related income:
Income from paid employment: Not applicable.
Income from self-employment: Not applicable.
Informal sector: Not applicable.
Usual activity: Not applicable.
Classifications:
Branch of economic activity (industry):
Title of the classification: 1992 Korea Standard Industrial Classification (KSIC).
Population groups classified by industry: Employed and unemployed.
Number of groups used for coding: 60 divisions (2nd digit level).
Links to ISIC: ISIC- Rev. 3.
Occupation:
Title of the classification: 1993 Korea Standard Occupation Classification (KSOC).
Population groups classified by occupation: Employed and unemployed.
Number of groups used for coding: 27 divisions ("nd digit level).
Links to ISCO: ISCO-88.
Status in employment:
Title of the classification: No information.
Population groups classified by status in employment: Employed.
Groups used for classification: Regular employee, temporary employee, daily worker, employer, own-account worker and unpaid family worker (6 groups).
Links to ICSE: ICSE-1993.
Education:
Title of the classification: No information.
Population groups classified by education: Employed and unemployed.
Groups used for classification: Never attending school, primary school, middle school, high school, college, university (6 groups).
Links to ISCED: ISCED-1976.
Sample size and design:
Ultimate sampling unit: Household.
Sample size (ultimate sampling units): About 30 000 households.
Sampling fraction: About 1/430.
Sample frame: The 1995 Population and Housing Census.
Updating of the sample: Every 5 years, on the basis of the Census results.
Rotation:
Scheme: Not applicable.
Percentage of units remaining in the sample for two consecutive survey rounds: Not applicable.
Maximum number of interviews per sample unit: Not applicable.
Length of time for complete renewal of the sample: Not applicable.
Field work:
Type of interview: From 1999 onwards: CATI. Previously: CAPI.
Number of ultimate sampling units per sample area: About eight households.
Duration of field work:
Total: Two weeks, including the survey week.
Per sample area: Two weeks, including the survey week.
Survey organization: Permanent full-time enumerators working for the 47 regional offices.
Number of field staff: About 530 persons.
Substitution of non-responding ultimate sampling units: NO.
Estimation and adjustments:
Total non-response rate: 0.2 per cent.
Adjustment for total non-response: NO.
Imputation for item non-response: NO.
Adjustment for areas/population not covered: NO.
Adjustment for undercoverage: NO.
Adjustment for overcoverage: NO.
Adjustment for seasonal variations: Yes. From January 1999, the X12-12 ARIMA method is used.
History of the survey:
Title and date of the first survey: Economically Active Population Survey, 1963. From 1957 onwards, statistics on the labour force were collected through the local administrative network under the responsibility of the Ministry of Home Affairs.
Significant changes or revisions: In 1998, the survey questionnaire was revised to capture and reflect the social changes, the activity pattern of the labour force and to measure the four-weeks job-searching unemployed, in order to make comparisons with other countries. Furthermore, in June 1999, the estimates of the Economically Active Population Survey were revised, on the basis of the 1995 Population and Housing Census, since 1991 retrospectively.
Documentation and dissemination:
Documentation:
Survey results: "Monthly Report on the Economically Active Population" and "Annual Report on the Economically Active Population" (May of each year).
Survey methodology: "Monthly Report on the Economically Active Population" and "Annual Report on the Economically Active Population" (May of each year).
Dissemination:
Time needed for initial release of survey results: One month.
Advance information of public about date of initial release: YES.
Availability of unpublished data upon request: YES.
Availability of data in machine-readable form: Diskettes, magnetic tapes and internet website (http://www.nso.go.kr/).

Kosovo (Serbia and Montenegro)

Title of the survey: Labour Force Survey.
Organization responsible for the survey:
Planning and conduct of the survey: Statistical Office of Kosovo in cooperation with the Ministry of Labour and Social Welfare.
Analysis and publication of the results: Statistical Office of Kosovo in cooperation with the Ministry of Labour and Social Welfare.
Topics covered: Employment, unemployment, underemployment, hours of work (usual hours of work, hours actually worked), income from employment, informal sector employment, place of work, permanency of employment, duration of unemployment, discouraged workers, occasional workers, industry, occupation, status in employment, education and qualification levels, second jobs, sources of livelihood, household income.
Coverage of the survey:
Geographical: Whole territory.
Population groups: The survey covers the usual members of private households in Kosovo, irrespective of their ethnic origin (Albanian, Serbian, etc.). Persons living in institutions are not covered. Excluded are members of KFOR troops, international UNMIK staff and other foreigners temporarily living in Kosovo.
Availability of estimates from other sources for the excluded areas/groups: No.
Groups covered by the survey but excluded from the published results: None.
Periodicity:
Conduct of the survey: Annually (planned). The first survey was conducted in December 2001-January 2002.
Publication of results: Annually (planned).
Reference periods:
Employment: Moving reference period of one week prior to the interview date.
Seeking work: Moving reference period of four weeks prior to the interview date.
Availability for work: Moving reference period of one week prior to the interview date.
Concepts and definitions:
Employment: Persons aged 15-64 years who, during the reference week, worked in a job or own enterprise/activity, from which they or their household or family obtained an income in cash or in kind. Included are persons who worked as regular employees, casual employees, employers, own-account workers (self-employed persons), farmers, members of producers' co-operatives, unpaid family workers in a household- or family-owned enterprise or farm, or military service/policemen.

Also included are persons aged 15-64 years who, during the reference week, did any paid or unpaid work (excluding the production of goods for own final use and the provision of unpaid or personal services for their own household) for at least one hour, even if they were full- or part-time students, unemployed, housewives or retired persons and worked only part-time or occasionally. Examples are: paid employment as a part-time or temporary employee, help, substitute, casual worker, etc.; unpaid work in a household- or family-owned enterprise or farm; unpaid work as an apprentice; sale or exchange of agricultural products obtained from an individual plot, or the production of such products for sale; sale of foodstuffs, beverages, meals, clothes, books, office supplies, music disks, cigarettes, flowers, etc. on the street, in markets or at home; repair of houses, flats, cars or consumer durables for others for pay; transport of passengers or goods by car for pay; paid consultancies or private tuition (languages, computer training, etc.); house cleaning for others, car washing or taking care of others' children for pay.

Employed persons further include persons aged 15-64 years who had a job or an enterprise/activity to which they could return, but who did not work during the reference week for any of the following reasons: own illness, injury or temporary indisposition; maternity leave; standstill for personal reasons; caring for a member of their family; annual leave; other types of leave; bad weather conditions, technical and other stoppages; education or training; flexi-time or free days; lack of work, orders or clients; strike, labour dispute or lock-out; lay-off; other reason. This includes unpaid family workers temporarily absent from work during the reference week. Excluded are persons not at work during the reference week because their enterprise was shut due to natural disaster or the effects of war, or bankrupt, or closed down, as well as seasonal workers not at work during the off-season.

Persons aged 15-64 years, who reported that they were currently without work, are classified as employed persons if during the reference week they undertook one or more activities that provided them with some income, even if they themselves did not consider these activities as work.

Unemployment: Persons aged 15-64 years who were: (i) not employed during the reference week (including persons whose enterprise was shut due to natural disaster or the effects of war, bankrupt, or closed down); (ii) looking for a job or trying to establish their own enterprise or income-generating activity, and who during the last four weeks had taken one or more active steps to find a job or to establish their own enterprise or income-generating activity; and (iii) currently available for work, i.e. they would have been able and ready to start working during the reference week if there had been an opportunity for them to work (including persons temporarily sick during the reference week). This includes full-or part-time students, housewives or retired persons, who were seeking and available for work.

Unemployed persons also include persons aged 15-64 years who: (i) were not employed during the reference week; (ii) were looking for work or wanting to work, but had not undertaken any active step to find work during the last four weeks; (iii) were currently available for work; and (iv) had already found a job or arranged for an own enterprise to start later.

Underemployment:
Time-related underemployment: Employed persons whose total number of hours actually worked during the reference week in all of their jobs/activities was less than 40 hours, and who were willing and available to work more hours during the reference week.
Inadequate employment situations: Employed persons who would like to change their current work situation (i.e. persons who want a change in their current job/activity, to find an additional job/activity, or to switch to another job/activity) for any of the following reasons: they fear or know that they will be dismissed or that their enterprise will be closed down; they have a job of a limited duration as an employee for reasons other than being unable to take a permanent job or not wanting to have a permanent job, or a temporary, seasonal or occasional job as an employer, own-account worker (self-employed person), unpaid family worker or member of a producers' co-operative, and want to have a more stable employment; they want to work more hours; personal, family or health-related reasons; they earn a total income of less than 150 DM per month from all of their jobs/activities and want to have a better pay or remuneration per hour; they want to improve their working conditions (better working time arrangement, less strenuous job); their current work is below or above their qualifications and they want a job that is more in line with their qualifications or abilities; they want to work less hours with a corresponding reduction of their income; other reason.
Hours of work: Usual hours of work per week; overtime or extra hours during the reference week; hours not worked during the reference week; hours actually worked during the reference week. Information on usual hours of work and hours actually worked is collected separately for the main job/activity and for (the) other job(s)/activity(ies), if any.
Employment-related income:
Income from paid employment: Usual net wage or salary per month. The information is collected separately for the main job/activity and for (the) other job(s)/activity(ies), if any.
Income from self-employment: Usual net profit per month. The information is collected separately for the main job/activity and for (the) other job(s)/activity(ies), if any.
Informal sector: Informal sector enterprises are defined as businesses/activities operated by employers or own-account workers (self-employed persons) that have all of the following characteristics: the business/activity is an unincorporated enterprise (sole ownership or ordinary partnership); there are less than 10 persons working in the business/activity; and the business/activity is not registered with the municipality. Employment in the informal sector refers to the total number of persons employed in informal sector enterprises, including the operators of informal sector enterprises, business partners, unpaid family workers, and employees.
Usual activity: This topic is not covered by the survey.
Classifications:
Branch of economic activity (industry):
Title of the classification: General Industrial Classification of Economic Activities within the European Community (NACE, Rev. 1).
Population groups classified by industry: Employed persons; unemployed persons with work experience during the last 12 years; economically inactive persons with work experience during the last 12 years, if they wanted to work and were available for work during the reference week.
Number of groups used for coding: Groups at the 4-digit level.
Links to ISIC: ISIC, Rev. 3.
Occupation:
Title of the classification: International Standard Classification of Occupations (ISCO-88).

Population groups classified by occupation: Employed persons; unemployed persons with work experience during the last 12 years; economically inactive persons with work experience during the last 12 years, if they wanted to work and were available for work during the reference week.
Number of groups used for coding: ISCO-88 unit groups (4-digit level).
Links to ISCO: Not applicable.
Status in employment:
Title of the classification: National classification of status in employment.
Population groups classified by status in employment: Employed persons; unemployed persons with work experience during the last 12 years; economically inactive persons with work experience during the last 12 years, if they wanted to work and were available for work during the reference week.
Groups used for classification: (a) Employees (state firm, institution or organization); (b) employees (private sector); (c) employers; (d) own-account workers (self-employed persons) incl. free-lancers; (e) unpaid family workers; (f) members of producers' co-operatives.
Links to ICSE: ICSE-1993.
Education:
Title of the classification: National classification of levels of educational attainment.
Population groups classified by education: All persons aged 15-64 years.
Groups used for classification: (a) No school; (b) 1-4th grade of elementary school; (c) 5-7th grade of elementary school; (d) elementary school completed; (e) 1-3 years of secondary vocational school and school for skilled workers; (f) secondary vocational school lasting 4 years or more; (g) high school (gymnasium); (h) non-university college; (i) university or academy; (j) master of arts; (k) doctorate.
Links to ISCED: To be established.
Sample size and design:
Ultimate sampling unit: Household.
Sample size (ultimate sampling units): 3,239 households.
Overall sampling fraction: About 1.0 % of households.
Sample frame: Address lists for 180 urban enumeration areas and 180 rural villages or village segments. The address lists were prepared for the Living Standards Measurement Survey 2000. The enumeration areas and villages/village segments were selected from strata defined in terms of KFOR military zone (United States, United Kingdom, France, Germany, Italy), urban vs. rural character and ethnicity of their populations (Albanian vs. Serbian). For the Labour Force Survey, a new sample of households was selected from the address lists.
Updating of the sample: A new household sampling frame is being developed.
Rotation:
Scheme: To be determined.
Percentage of units remaining in the sample for two consecutive survey rounds: To be determined.
Maximum number of interviews per sample unit: To be determined.
Length of time for complete renewal of the sample: To be determined.
Field work:
Type of interview: Information is obtained through personal interviews.
Number of ultimate sampling units per sample area: 8-14 households per urban enumeration area; 8 households per rural village/village segment.
Duration of field work:
Total: About six weeks.
Per sample area: One day with four interviewers.
Survey organization: A permanent survey organization does not yet exist for the survey.
Number of field staff: 18 supervisors and 78 interviewers.
Substitution of non-responding ultimate sampling units: A reserve of households was selected for each enumeration area and village/village segment included in the sample. Non-responding households were replaced by households from the reserve lists.
Estimation and adjustments:
Total non-response rate: Not applicable.
Adjustment for total non-response: Not applicable.
Imputation for item non-response: Not applicable. Item non-response is identified during the data editing process. Sample households are re-contacted to obtain missing information.
Adjustment for areas/population not covered: Not applicable.
Adjustment for under-coverage: No.
Adjustment for over-coverage: No.
Adjustment for seasonal variations: Not applicable.
History of the survey:
Title and date of the first survey: The first Labour Force Survey was conducted in December 2001- January 2002.
Significant changes or revisions: Not applicable.
Documentation and dissemination:
Documentation:
Survey results: Statistical Office of Kosovo/Ministry of Labour and Social Welfare: Labour Force Survey 2001.
Survey methodology: The above-mentioned publication includes methodological information on the survey.
Dissemination:
Time needed for initial release of survey results: About four months.
Advance information of public about date of initial release: No.
Availability of unpublished data upon request: Yes.
Availability of data in machine-readable form: Yes.

Kuwait

Title of the survey: The Labour Force Sample Survey.
Organization responsible for the survey:
Planning and conduct of the survey: Central Statistical Office. Census & Population Statistics Department.
Analysis and publication of the results: Central Statistical Office. Census & Population Statistics Department.
Topics covered: Current employment and unemployment. Actual hours worked. Wages and salaries of employees. Educational level. Current industry, occupation and status in employment in main job. Number of months in current job. Duration of unemployment. Informal sector employment. Usual activity.
Coverage of the survey:
Geographical: Entire nation.
Population groups: Total population, both Kuwaiti and non-Kuwaiti nationals, and persons living in collective households.
Availability of estimates from other sources for the excluded areas/groups: NA.
Groups covered by the survey but excluded from the published results: NA.
Periodicity:
Conduct of the survey: Irregular, 1973, 1988.
Publication of results: Following after survey.
Reference periods:
Employment: Fixed reference week.
Seeking work: Same reference period as employment.
Availability for work: Same reference period as employment.
Concepts and definitions:
Employment: Persons, 15 years old and over, who formed the available manpower for the production of goods and services and who during the reference week were an employer, an own-account worker, an employee or an unpaid family worker. The Employed include persons with a job but temporary absent from work due to illness, injury, vacation, maternity leave, educational and training leave, labour management dispute, bad weather, mechanical breakdown, etc. It also includes persons on temporary or indefinite lay-off without pay and on unpaid leave initiated by the employer. Also included are full- and part-time workers seeking other work during the reference period as well as part-time students working full-time or part-time. Full-time students working part-time or full-time are excluded. Unpaid family workers temporary absent from work are included but apprentices and trainees, paid or unpaid, are excluded. Similarly, seasonal workers not at work during the off-season are excluded. Participants in employment promotion schemes and members of the armed forces are included. Persons engaged in production of goods or services for own final use are excluded. Excluded also were persons who performed some work during the reference week but were subject to compulsory schooling or were retired and receiving a pension.
Unemployment: Persons, 15 years old and over, who during the reference week were without work or worked less than 20 hours during the reference week, were currently available for work, and were seeking work during the reference week. The unemployed comprises of two groups: those who previously worked in the state of Kuwait, but were not employed and were looking for work during the reference week; and those who had never had a job before and were seeking work during the reference week. The Unemployed included persons without work and currently available for work who had made arrangements to start work at a date subsequent to the reference week as well as persons without work and currently available for work who were trying to establish their own enterprise. Also included were

part-time students seeking part-time or full-time work. Full-time students seeking part-time or full-time work were however excluded. Also excluded were persons seeking and available for work who were subject to compulsory schooling or were retired or receiving a pension. Also excluded were persons without work and available for work, who did not seek work during the reference week.

Underemployment:

Time-related underemployment: No information.

Inadequate employment situations: No information.

Hours of work: Refers to the number of hours actually worked at the place of work during the reference week. It includes the hours worked during the normal period of work as well as time worked in addition to normal hours of work (over time).

Employment-related income:

Income from paid employment: Wages and salaries: it include direct wages and salaries, total cash earnings, payments in kind and services, profit-related pay, employment-related social security benefits, overtime payments and other imputed values of goods and services offered from the place of work as in-kind payment for work done.

Income from self-employment: No information.

Informal sector employment: Employment in non-registered enterprises or in unorganized enterprises or businesses or in small and micro enterprises or businesses.

Usual activity: No information.

Classifications:

Branch of economic activity (industry):

Title of the classification: No information.

Population groups classified by industry: Employed and unemployed persons with previous work experience.

Number of groups used for coding: 2-digit level.

Links to ISIC: ISIC- Rev. 3.

Occupation:

Title of the classification: No information.

Population groups classified by occupation: Employed and unemployed persons with previous work experience.

Number of groups used for coding: 2-digit level.

Links to ISCO: ISCO-68.

Status in employment:

Title of the classification: No information.

Population groups classified by status in employment: Employed.

Groups used for classification: Employer. Self-employed. Employee. Unpaid family worker.

Links to ICSE: No.

Education:

Title of the classification: No information.

Population groups classified by educational level: Population 15 years old and above.

Groups used for classification: Illiterate. Can read & write. Primary education. Intermediate education. Secondary education. Above secondary but below university education. University education. Post-graduate studies.

Links to ISCED: ISCED 1976.

Sample size and design:

Ultimate sampling unit: Private households and individuals in collective households.

Sample size (ultimate sampling units): About 11,000 private households and 558 collective households.

Overall sampling fraction: 0.05%.

Sample frame: Based on the enumeration areas of the 1985 Population census of Kuwait, stratified into 54 strata for Kuwaiti private households and non-Kuwaiti private households, and 43 strata for non-Kuwaiti collective households.

The 1729 stratified census enumeration areas formed the primary sampling units (PSUs) of the survey. Some 345 PSUs were selected at the first-stage of the sample selection. These PSUs were updated by listing all buildings, dwellings and households. At the second stage some 11,000 private households were selected from the listed PSUs. In the case of the collective households, some 558 collective households were selected from the sampled PSUs and within the selected collective households about 11,000 individuals were sampled.

Updating of the sample: The PSUs were updated at the listing phase of the first stage of the sample selection.

Rotation: No rotation scheme.

Field work:

Type of interview: Personal interviews conducted by 60 interviewers and 5 field supervisors.

Number of ultimate sampling units per sample area: 20 households.

Duration of fieldwork: One month.

Survey organization: Permanent.

Number of field and office staff: About 60 interviewers, 5 field supervisors, 2 office clerks, 4 data entry operators, 1 statistical expert and 1 manager.

Substitution of non-responding sampling units: Yes.

Estimation and adjustments:

Total non-response rate: Not available.

Adjustment for total non-response: No.

Imputation for item non-response: No.

Adjustment for areas/population not covered: No.

Adjustment for undercoverage: No.

Adjustment for overcoverage: No.

Adjustment for seasonal variations: No.

History of the survey:

Title and date of the first survey: Labour force sample survey, 1973.

Significant changes or revisions: Not available.

Documentation and dissemination:

Documentation:

Survey results: Labour force sample survey, March 1988, First Part, June 1990. Ministry of Planning, State of Kuwait.

Survey methodology: Same as above.

Dissemination:

Time needed for initial release of survey results: No information.

Advance information of public about date of initial release: No.

Availability of unpublished data upon request: No information.

Availability of data in machine-readable form: No information.

Latvia

Title of the survey: Latvian Labour Force Survey

Organization responsible for the survey:

Planning and conduct of the survey: Central Statistical Bureau.

Analysis and publication of the results: Central Statistical Bureau.

Topics covered: Employment, unemployment, underemployment, hours of work, wages, source of income, duration of unemployment, discouraged workers, occasional workers, industry, occupation, status in employment, educational level, usual activity, second jobs and previous working experience.

Coverage of the survey:

Geographical: Whole country.

Population groups: All persons aged 15 years old and above living in private households during the reference week. Excluded are household members absent from a household for more than 3 months (such as conscripts, students living in hostels, sailors, etc.), as well as institutional population (inmates of penal and mental institutions, hospitals, prisons, etc.).

Availability of estimates from other sources for the excluded areas/groups: No.

Groups covered by the survey but excluded from the published results: None.

Periodicity:

Conduct of the survey: Bi-annually.

Publication of results: Bi-annually.

Reference periods:

Employment: One week (last seven days prior to the date of the interview).

Seeking work: Four weeks prior to the date of the interview.

Availability for work: Two weeks following the date of the interview.

Concepts and definitions:

Employment: employed are all persons aged 15 years and above who, during of reference period, (a) performed some work for at least one hour for pay or profit (in cash or in kind); (b) did not work but had jobs or an enterprise from which they were temporarily absent due to vacation/annual leave, illness, vocational training leave or other similar reason. In addition, considered as employed are persons who performed some paid or unpaid community and social work as well as women on child-care leave until the child's age of three months.

Also included in the totals are:

a)full- and part-time workers seeking other work during the reference period;

b)full- and part-time students working full- or part-time;

c)persons who performed some work during the reference week while being either retired and receiving a pension, or were registered as job seekers at an employment office or receiving unemployment benefits;

d)paid and unpaid family workers (if they worked at least one hour);

e)persons engaged in production of goods for own final use.

Unemployment: Unemployed are all persons of 15 years and above, whether or not registered with the State Employment Board, who:

a) did not work at all during the reference week nor were temporarily absent from work;
b) were actively looking for work during the four weeks previous to the interview;
c) were available to start work within the two weeks following the survey week.
Also included in the unemployed are persons who were not actively looking for work because they found a job and made arrangements to take up paid employment at a date subsequent to the reference period.
Underemployment:
Time-related underemployment: Persons who, during the reference week, worked less than established regular hours due to economic reasons (against their will).
Inadequate employment situations: Persons who were seeking another job with better working conditions (salary, location, professional background etc.).
Hours of work: Usual and actual hours worked in the main job. Hours actually worked for in secondary job(s).
Employment-related income:
Income from paid employment: Gross wages including taxes in the main job for the full calendar month.
Income from self-employment: Not applicable.
Informal sector: Not applicable.
Usual activity: Yes.
Classifications:
Branch of economic activity (industry):
Title of the classification: Statistical Classification of Economic Activities in European Community (NACE Rev. 1,).
Population groups classified by industry: Employed persons and unemployed persons with previous job experience (if they had a job during the last three years).
Number of groups used for coding: 33
Links to ISIC: ISIC-Rev. 3 (2 digit level).
Occupation:
Title of the classification: Latvian Classification of Occupations.
Population groups classified by occupation: Employed persons and unemployed persons with previous work experience (if they had a job during the last three years).
Number of groups used for coding: Numerous.
Links to ISCO: ISCO-88.
Status in employment:
Title of the classification: ICSE (International Classification by Status in Employment).
Population groups classified by status in employment: Employed persons and unemployed persons with previous work experience (if they had a job during the last three years).
Groups used for classification: 4 groups (employees, employers, own-account workers, unpaid family workers).
Links to ICSE: ICSE-1993.
Education:
Title of the classification: National classification is used.
Population groups classified by education: Total population, employed, unemployed and inactive persons.
Groups used for classification: 8 groups (no formal education, incomplete primary, primary, vocational, general secondary, technical secondary, specialized secondary, higher).
Links to ISCED: Not fully comparable with ISCED.
Sample size and design:
Ultimate sampling unit: For rural areas – household; for urban areas – individuals.
Sample size (ultimate sampling units): About 8 000 households.
Overall sampling fraction: Approximately 0.75 %.
Sample frame: The sample frame for urban areas is drawn from the Population Register. The sample frame for rural areas is built up on the complete list of households.
Updating of the sample: The last updating was made in 1998.
Rotation:
Scheme: Each household is retained in the survey for three consecutive rounds. This rotation scheme provides that one-third of households within each town selected for the sample are replaced in a new round. As for the rural areas, all households are replaced in one-third of primary sampling units ('pagasts').
Percentage of units remaining in the sample for two consecutive survey rounds: 66.7 per cent.
Maximum number of interviews per sample unit: 9.
Length of time for complete renewal of the sample: 18 months.
Field work:
Type of interview: Paper and pencil (face to face interview).
Number of ultimate sampling units per sample area: Seven in rural primary sampling units (PSUs); from 15 to 459 in urban PSUs.
Duration of field work:
Total: A calendar month.
Per sample area: A calendar month.
Survey organization: No information provided.
Number of field staff: Approximately 631 persons and 31 supervisors.
Substitution of non-responding ultimate sampling units: No.
Estimation and adjustments:
Total non-response rate: In May 1999: 9.46%; in May 2000: 10.12%.
Adjustment for total non-response: Yes.
Imputation for item non-response: No.
Adjustment for areas/population not covered: Yes.
Adjustment for undercoverage: Yes.
Adjustment for overcoverage: Yes.
Adjustment for seasonal variations: No.
History of the survey:
Title and date of the first survey: Latvian Labour Force Survey, November 1995.
Significant changes or revisions: Starting with May 1997, indicators such as activity rate, employment participation rate and unemployment rate are also calculated at regional level.
Documentation and dissemination:
Documentation:
Survey results: "Labour Force in Latvia" (bi-annually), "Monthly Bulletin of Latvian Statistics" (bi-annually).
Survey methodology: "Labour Force in Latvia" (bi-annually).
Dissemination:
Time needed for initial release of survey results: Four months.
Advance information of public about date of initial release: Yes.
Availability of unpublished data upon request: Yes.
Availability of data in machine-readable form: Diskettes.
Website: http://www.csb.lv/ (selected information).

Lithuania

Title of the survey: Labour Force Survey (LFS).
Organization responsible for the survey:
Planning and conduct of the survey: Statistics Lithuania.
Analysis and publication of the results: Employment Statistics Division of Statistics Lithuania.
Topics covered: Employment, unemployment, underemployment, hours of work, wages, income, informal sector employment, duration of employment and unemployment, discouraged and occasional workers, industry, occupation, status in employment, education/qualification skills, second jobs.
Coverage of the survey:
Geographical: Whole country.
Population groups: Population aged 15 years and over, living in private households (prior to 2000, civilian population aged 14 years and over), including persons absent for short periods for studies as well as household members temporarily absent.
Excluded are inmates of penal and mental institution, conscripts living in barracks and foreign citizens.
Availability of estimates from other sources for the excluded areas/groups: No.
Groups covered by the survey but excluded from the published results: None.
Periodicity:
Conduct of the survey: Twice a year, in May and November of each year.
Publication of results: Twice a year.
Reference periods:
Employment: One week.
Seeking work: The four weeks period prior to the interview week..
Availability for work: Within two weeks after the interview week.
Concepts and definitions:
Employment: Employed persons are all persons aged 15 years and over who, during the reference week, were in any of the following categories:
a) persons at work, either in paid or self-employment, who have worked one hour or more for wages or salaries in cash or in kind, or for profit or family income in cash or in kind;
b) persons with a job but not at work, i.e. persons who have already worked in their present job (either in paid or self-employment) but were absent from work during the reference week and had a formal job attachment.
Also included in the employed are:

a) persons with a job but temporarily absent from work because of illness or injury, maternity or parental leave, holidays, training or interruption of work due to economical or technical reasons, bad weather, breakdowns, etc.;
b) persons who performed some work for pay or profit during the reference week, while being subject to compulsory schooling, or retired and receiving a pension, or registered as job seekers at an employment office or receiving unemployment benefits;
c) full and part-time workers seeking work during the reference week;
d) full or part-time students working full or part-time;
e) paid apprentices and trainees;
f) paid and unpaid family workers;
g) private domestic servants;
h) participants in employment promotion schemes who receive payment or on-the-job training;
i) Career and paid volunteer members of the armed forces.
Excluded are unpaid apprentices and trainees, persons engaged in their own housework and those doing unpaid community or social work; these persons are classified as inactive.
Unemployment: All persons aged 15 years and over who were:
a) without work during the reference week;
b) available for work within four weeks;
c) actively seeking work, i.e. had taken specific steps (such a continued registration on the employment office records, contacts with private work agency, etc.) in the last four weeks, or had made arrangements to start a new job.
It also includes the full time and part time students seeking full time or part time work.
Persons without work, available for work but not looking for work and who report that no work is available, are excluded from the unemployed and classified as discouraged workers.
Underemployment:
Time-related underemployment: All employed persons who either work part time because they have not been able to find a full time job and are looking for another job or persons working less than 40 hours during the reference week and are looking for another job.
Inadequate employment situations: Not yet available.
Hours of work: Hours worked. They include overtime, but exclude hours paid for but not worked such as commuting time between home and workplace, hours lost due to illness, holidays, unemployment, etc.
Employment-related income:
Income from paid employment: Total cash earnings, including the employment-related social security contributions, etc. Payments in kind (foodstuffs) received for work in agriculture are excluded. It refers to all jobs.
Income from self-employment: Gross profits.
Informal sector: Theoretically covered by the survey.
Usual activity: Not applicable.
Classifications:
Branch of economic activity (industry):
Title of the classification: National classification.
Population groups classified by industry: Employed and unemployed persons (industry of last job for the unemployed).
Number of groups used for coding: 59 groups.
Links to ISIC: ISIC-Rev. 3.
Occupation:
Title of the classification: National classification.
Population groups classified by occupation: Employed and unemployed persons (occupation of last job for the unemployed).
Number of groups used for coding: 28 sub-major groups, 116 minor groups and 390 unit groups.
Links to ISCO: ISCO-88.
Status in employment:
Title of the classification: National classification.
Population groups classified by status in employment: Employed persons.
Groups used for classification: 5 groups: employers, employees, own-.account workers, contributing family workers, workers not classified by status.
Links to ICSE: ICSE-1993.
Education:
Title of the classification: National classification.
Population groups classified by education: Employed persons.
Groups used for classification: 6 groups: no schooling, primary, basic, secondary, college, higher.
Links to ISCED: ISCED-1997.
Sample size and design:
Ultimate sampling unit: Dwelling.
Sample size (ultimate sampling units): 8,500 persons living in 3,000 dwellings.
Overall sampling fraction: 0.3 per cent of total population.
Sample frame: The Population Register covering the resident population.
Updating of the sample: Continuously.
Rotation:
Scheme: Every sampled dwelling is interviewed three times. After having been retained in the sample for two consecutive surveys and excluded from the following third round, it came back in the sample and then is definitively excluded.
Percentage of units remaining in the sample for two consecutive survey rounds: 33 per cent.
Maximum number of interviews per sample unit: Three.
Length of time for complete renewal of the sample: Two years and a half.
Field work:
Type of interview: Pen-and-paper. Face-to-face for 75 per cent of respondents and phone interviews for the remaining 25 per cent.
Number of ultimate sampling units per sample area: No information.
Duration of field work:
Total: No information.
Per sample area: No information.
Survey organization: No information.
Number of field staff: 200 interviewers and 49 supervisors.
Substitution of non-responding ultimate sampling units: No.
Estimation and adjustments:
Total non-response rate: 15 per cent.
Adjustment for total non-response: Yes.
Imputation for item non-response: No.
Adjustment for areas/population not covered: No.
Adjustment for undercoverage: Yes.
Adjustment for overcoverage: Yes.
Adjustment for seasonal variations: No.
History of the survey:
Title and date of the first survey: Labour Force Survey 1994.
Significant changes or revisions: From 1994 to 1999, persons aged 14 years and over. Implemented survey questionnaires in 1998 and 1999.
Documentation and dissemination:
Documentation:
Survey results: Labour force, employment and unemployment (half-yearly); Economic and Social developments in Lithuania.
Survey methodology: Labour force, employment and unemployment (half-yearly); Economic and Social developments in Lithuania.
Dissemination:
Time needed for initial release of survey results: May results are published during the 4th quarter.
Advance information of public about date of initial release: No.
Availability of unpublished data upon request: No.
Availability of data in machine-readable form:
Website: http://www.std.lt/.

Macau, China

Title of the survey: Employment Survey (Inquérito ao Emprego).
Organization responsible for the survey:
Planning and conduct of the survey: Statistics and Census Service.
Analysis and publication of the results: Statistics and Census Service.
Topics covered: Employment, unemployment, underemployment, hours of work, wages, income, duration of unemployment, discouraged workers, industry, occupation, status in employment, education, second jobs.
Coverage of the survey:
Geographical: Whole territory of the Macau Special Administrative Region (MSAR).
Population groups: The non-institutional resident population, aged 14 years and over, with the exception of the armed forces.
Availability of estimates from other sources for the excluded areas/groups: No.
Groups covered by the survey but excluded from the published results: No.
Periodicity:
Conduct of the survey: Monthly.
Publication of results: Monthly/quarterly.
Reference periods:
Employment: Moving reference period of one week prior the date of the interview..

Seeking work: Moving reference period of one month prior the date of the interview..
Availability for work: Moving reference period of one week prior the date of the interview..
Concepts and definitions:
Employment: All persons aged 14 years and over who have worked for at least one hour during the reference week, for pay, profits or family earnings, in cash or in kind. Are also included persons who have a job but were temporarily absent from work, but maintaining a formal job attachment, for reasons such as illness, maternity, holidays, etc.
Also included are persons:
a) with a job but temporarily absent due to reasons such as illness or injury, vacation or annual leave, maternity/paternity leave, absence without pay or due to bad weather, mechanical breakdown, etc. as well as persons on lay-off without pay or on unpaid leave initiated by the employer within 30 day and workers seeking other work during the reference period.;
b) persons who performed some work for pay or profit during the reference period but were subject to compulsory school, retired and receiving a pension, registered at an employment office or receiving a pension.
c) full or part-time students working full or part-time, paid apprentices and trainees, participants in subsidized employment promotion schemes.
d) unpaid family workers.
Unemployment: All persons aged 14 years and over who, during the reference period, do not have a job or a formal job attachment, but are available to work for pay or running a business and have sought work during the last month. Seeking steps may be: seek assistance through relatives or friends, registration at an employment agency, place or answer newspapers advertisements, direct application to employers, checked at work places, look for factory equipment, finance or license to start own business.
Also included in the unemployed:
a) persons on lay-off with or without pay for more than 30 days;
b) full and part-time students, available for work, seeking full or part-time work.
Underemployment:
Time-related underemployment: Employed persons who, regardless of their employment situation, worked involuntary less than 35 hours during the reference period, and have sought or are available to take an additional work.
Inadequate employment situations: Not applicable.
Hours of work: Normal and actual working hours per week, referring to main and all jobs.
Employment-related income:
Income from paid employment: It refers to gross earnings (before any deduction), in cash or in kind, paid to the worker on a regular basis for time worked or job done, as well as for time not worked, such as holidays or other paid leave.
Income from self-employment: It is obtained by subtracting operating expenses and depreciation at replacement cost of productive assets from gross output. For each activity, gross output may be defined as the value of all goods and services produced, including any part which has been retained for own consumption or give free of charge or at reduced prices to hired labour. Operation expenses include payments to hired labour in cash and/or in kind, and other current expenses of the economic activity, such as the purchase of raw materials, fuel, tools and equipment, rent and interest payments, transport costs, and marketing.
Informal sector: Not applicable.
Usual activity: Not applicable.
Classifications:
Branch of economic activity (industry):
Title of the classification: National classification.
Population groups classified by industry: Employed and unemployed (industry of last job for the unemployed)..
Number of groups used for coding: 66 groups.
Links to ISIC: ISIC-Rev. 3.
Occupation:
Title of the classification: National classification.
Population groups classified by occupation: Employed and unemployed (occupation of last job for the unemployed).
Number of groups used for coding: 10 groups.
Links to ISCO: ISCO-88.
Status in employment:
Title of the classification: National classification.
Population groups classified by status in employment: Employed.
Groups used for classification: Four groups: employer; own-account worker; employee and unpaid family worker.
Links to ICSE: ICSE-1993.
Education:
Title of the classification: National classification.
Population groups classified by education: Employed and unemployed.
Groups used for classification: Six groups: no schooling/pre-school; primary; lower-secondary; upper-secondary; tertiary but not equivalent to a first university degree and tertiary equivalent to a first university degree.
Links to ISCED: ISCED-1997.
Sample size and design:
Ultimate sampling unit: Living quarter.
Sample size (ultimate sampling units): 3 600 living quarters per quarter.
Overall sampling fraction: 2.25 per cent.
Sample frame: "General File of Statistical Units" of the Statistics and Census Service, which contains the full record of living quarters (permanent and temporary structures) by geographical order.
Updating of the sample: Administrative records of new constructions and demolished buildings and feedback of the household surveys.
Rotation:
Scheme: 50 per cent of the sample in the current month will be enumerated three months later.
Percentage of units remaining in the sample for two consecutive survey rounds: 50 per cent.
Maximum number of interviews per sample unit: Two.
Length of time for complete renewal of the sample: Six months.
Field work:
Type of interview: Personal.
Number of ultimate sampling units per sample area: No information provided.
Duration of field work:
Total: 14 days.
Per sample area: No information provided.
Survey organization: Permanent.
Number of field staff: 20 persons.
Substitution of non-responding ultimate sampling units: No.
Estimation and adjustments:
Total non-response rate: About 8 per cent.
Adjustment for total non-response: No.
Imputation for item non-response: No.
Adjustment for areas/population not covered: No.
Adjustment for undercoverage: No.
Adjustment for overcoverage: No.
Adjustment for seasonal variations: No.
History of the survey:
Title and date of the first survey: Employment Survey May 1989.
Significant changes or revisions: May 1989- May 1991: biannual survey (May and November) with a sample of 2,100 living quarters per survey round. May 1992 - November 1995: quarterly survey (February, May, August and November) with a sample size of 1,290 living quarters per survey round. Since January 1996, monthly survey with a sample size of 1,200 living quarters per month.
Documentation and dissemination:
Documentation:
Survey results: "Employment Survey": Brief Report (monthly); Quarterly Report; Annual Report and Statistical Yearbook.
Survey methodology: Annex in the "Employment Survey".
Dissemination:
Time needed for initial release of survey results: One month after data collection.
Advance information of public about date of initial release: No.
Availability of unpublished data upon request: Yes.
Availability of data in machine-readable form: Yes and internet website (http://www.dsec.gov.mo/).

Macedonia, The former Yugoslav Rep. of

Title of the survey: Labour Force Sample Survey
Organization responsible for the survey:
Planning and conduct of the survey: Statistical Office.
Analysis and publication of the results: Statistical Office.
Topics covered: Employment, unemployment, hours of work, wages, income, informal sector employment, duration of unemployment, discouraged workers, occasional workers, industry, occupation, status in employment, educational level, usual activity, second jobs.

Coverage of the survey:
Geographical: Whole country.
Population groups: All permanent residents aged 15 years and above including those temporarily absent abroad for a period of less than one year.
Excluded are persons under 15 and above 80 years old as well as persons in the following categories:
a) persons on long-term missions abroad (over one year);
b) students living in hostels and unsettled population;
c) inmates of penal and mental institutions;
d) armed forces;
e) foreign citizens.
Availability of estimates from other sources for the excluded areas/groups: No.
Groups covered by the survey but excluded from the published results: None.
Periodicity:
Conduct of the survey: Annual.
Publication of results: Annual.
Reference periods:
Employment: One week prior to the date of the interview.
Seeking work: One week prior to the date of the interview.
Availability for work: One week following the date of the interview.
Concepts and definitions:
Employment: Persons aged 15 years and above who, during the reference week, did any work at all as paid employees, in their own business, profession, or on their own farm, or who worked at least one hour or more as unpaid family workers in an enterprise operated by a member of a family. Also included are all those who were not working but who had jobs or businesses from which they were temporarily absent because of illness, bad weather, vacation, advance qualification training, labour-management disputes, or personal reasons, as well as due to the end of activity of an enterprise.
Also included in the totals are:
a) full- and part-time workers seeking other work during the reference period;
b) full- and part-time students working full- or part-time
c) persons who performed some work during the reference week while being either retired and receiving a pension; or were registered as job seekers at an employment office or receiving unemployment benefits private domestic servants; paid apprentices and trainees
f) persons engaged in production of goods for own final use (e.g. subsistence farming).
Unemployment: Unemployed are all persons aged 15 years and over had no employment during the reference week, were available for work during the reference week or within one week following the reference week, and had made specific steps to find employment.
Underemployment:
Time-related underemployment: Persons working less hours than the regular hours and willing and available to work additional hours.
Inadequate employment situations: No information.
Hours of work: Usual and actual hours worked.
Employment-related income:
Income from paid employment: Usual monthly gains (net earnings) in the main job.
Income from self-employment: Usual monthly gains (net earnings) in the main job.
Informal sector: No information.
Usual activity: Situation during the past 12 months.
Classifications:
Branch of economic activity (industry):
Title of the classification: National classification.
Population groups classified by industry: Employed persons.
Number of groups used for coding: 14.
Links to ISIC: No.
Occupation:
Title of the classification: National classification.
Population groups classified by occupation: Employed persons.
Number of groups used for coding: 10.
Links to ISCO: No.
Status in employment:
Title of the classification: National classification.
Population groups classified by status in employment: Employed persons.
Groups used for classification: 4 groups (employees, employers, own-account workers, unpaid family workers).
Links to ICSE: Yes.
Education:
Title of the classification: National classification.
Population groups classified by education: Employed and unemployed persons.
Groups used for classification: 9 groups (without education, not completed primary education, primary education, three years of secondary education, four years of secondary education, higher, university level, master's degree and doctorate).
Links to ISCED: No.
Sample size and design:
Ultimate sampling unit: Household.
Sample size (ultimate sampling units): 7,200 households.
Overall sampling fraction: 1.3 per cent of the total number of households.
Sample frame: The sample frame is built on the basis of the 1994 Population Census and the Population Register.
Updating of the sample: Annually.
Rotation:
Scheme: No information provided.
Percentage of units remaining in the sample for two consecutive survey rounds: 34.5 per cent.
Maximum number of interviews per sample unit: 3.
Length of time for complete renewal of the sample: four years.
Field work:
Type of interview: Paper and pencil.
Number of ultimate sampling units per sample area: 8 households.
Duration of field work:
Total: No information provided.
Per sample area: No information provided.
Survey organization: Permanent.
Number of field staff: 117 interviewers.
Substitution of non-responding ultimate sampling units: No.
Estimation and adjustments:
Total non-response rate: No.
Adjustment for total non-response: No.
Imputation for item non-response: No.
Adjustment for areas/population not covered: No.
Adjustment for undercoverage: No.
Adjustment for overcoverage: No.
Adjustment for seasonal variations: No.
History of the survey:
Title and date of the first survey: Labour Force Survey, April 1996.
Significant changes or revisions: Since 1996 a number of changes have been introduced in 1997,1998 and 1999.
Documentation and dissemination:
Documentation:
Survey results: "Labour Force Survey: Basic definitions, methods and final results" (annually).
Survey methodology: "Labour Force Survey: Basic definitions, methods and final results".
Dissemination:
Time needed for initial release of survey results: No information provided.
Advance information of public about date of initial release: Yes.
Availability of unpublished data upon request: No.
Availability of data in machine-readable form: Diskettes, internet and e-mail.

Malaysia

Title of the survey: The Labour Force Survey.
Organization responsible for the survey:
Planning and conduct of the survey: Department of Statistics.
Analysis and publication of the results: Department of Statistics.
Topics covered: Employment, unemployment, underemployment, hours of work, informal sector employment (derived from employment status), industry, occupation, status in employment, educational level, usual activity.
Coverage of the survey:
Geographical: Whole country.
Population groups: All persons who are usual residents (3 months or more) in private living quarters. Excluding persons residing in "Institutional Living Quarters" (e.g. hotels, hostels, military barracks, prisons, etc.).
Availability of estimates from other sources for the excluded areas/groups: Not available.
Groups covered by the survey but excluded from the published results: Not available.
Periodicity:
Conduct of the survey: Quarterly.
Publication of results: Quarterly and annually.

Reference periods:
Employment: One week.
Seeking work: One fixed quarter.
Availability for work: Not available.
Concepts and definitions:
Employment: All persons aged 15-64 who at any time during the reference week did any work (at least for one hour) for pay, profit or family gain (as employer, employee, own-account worker or unpaid family worker). Also considered as employed were persons who did not work during the reference week because of illness, injury, disability, bad weather, vacation, labour dispute and social and religious reasons but had a job, farm, enterprise or other family enterprise to return to. Also included were those on temporary layoff with pay who would definitely be called back to work.
It also includes:
a) persons with a job but temporarily absent due to maternity or paternity leave, parental leave, educational or training leave, absence without leave, labour management dispute, bad weather;
b) full or part-time workers seeking other work during the reference period;
c) persons who performed some work for pay or profit during the reference week but were registered as job seekers at an employment office or receiving unemployment benefits;
d) part-time students working full or part-time;
e) paid apprentices and trainees;
f) unpaid family workers at work or temporarily absent from work, during the reference week;
g) persons engaged in subsistence farming
g) all members of the armed forces.
Unemployment: It includes both actively and inactively unemployed persons. The actively unemployed include all persons aged 15 to 64 who did not work during the reference week but were available for work and actively looking for work during the reference period.
The inactively unemployed include all persons aged 15 to 64 who were not looking for work because they believed no work was available or if available, they were not qualified, those who would have looked for work if they had not been temporarily ill or in confinement, or had it not been for bad weather, those waiting for answers to job applications and those who have looked for work prior to the reference week (i.e. in the last three months prior to the interview), and persons without a job and currently available for work who had made arrangements to start a new job within 30 days from the date of the interview.
Job seeking steps: registering at an employment office/labour exchange or on a professional register; visiting locations or meeting with prospective employers; placing or answering advertisements; writing application letters; checking with unions or similar; investigating professional or business possibilities; informing friends or relatives, etc. The job search period is classified into 5 groups: less than 3 months, 3-6 months, 6-12 months, 1-3 years, more than 3 years.
It also includes:
a) persons on temporary or indefinite lay-off without pay and unpaid leave initiated by the employer;
b) part-time students seeking full or part-time work;
c) persons who were seeking and/or available for work but were retired and receiving a pension;
d) unpaid apprentices and trainees and seasonal workers not at work during the off-season.
Underemployment:
Time-related underemployment: Those who worked less than 30 hours during the reference week for reasons such as insufficient work/nature of the job or others, but who were able and willing to work more hours if given a chance.
Inadequate employment situations: Not applicable.
Hours of work: Actual hours worked during the reference week for all jobs.
Employment-related income:
Income from paid employment: Not applicable.
Income from self-employment: Not applicable.
Informal sector employment: There is no specific question but it could be partially derived as a proxy from the employment status of workers as refers to the main job.
Usual activity: The occupation that the respondent usually performed during the last 12 months.
Classifications:
Branch of economic activity (industry):
Title of the classification: Malaysian Industrial Classification.
Population groups classified by industry: Employed persons.
Number of groups used for coding: 9.
Links to ISIC-68: Yes at all levels.
Occupation:
Title of the classification: Malaysian Occupational Classification.
Population groups classified by occupation: Employed persons.
Number of groups used for coding: 9.
Links to ISCO-68: Yes at all levels.
Status in employment:
Title of the classification: Not available.
Population groups classified by status in employment: Employed persons.
Groups used for classification: Four groups: 1. Employer, 2. Employee, 3. Own-account worker, 4. Unpaid family worker.
Links to ICSE-1993: Yes.
Education:
Title of the classification: Not available.
Population groups classified by education: All household members.
Groups used for classification: Four groups: 1. Primary school - from standard one up to standard six (age 6 to 12 years old), 2. Lower secondary (13 to 15 years old), 3. Upper secondary (16 to 17 years old), 4. Tertiary (17 years old +).
Links to ISCED: Yes, all levels adjusted to suit the local situation.
Sample size and design:
Ultimate sampling unit: Household.
Sample size (ultimate sampling units): 60 thousand households.
Overall sampling fraction: Not available.
Sample frame: The National Household Sampling Frame is made up of enumeration blocks (EBs) created for the 1991 Census of Population and Housing. EBs are geographically contiguous land areas with identifiable borders, each containing about 600 persons. EBs are formed within administrative boundaries.
Updating of the sample: Each year before enumeration starts, the second stage sample units or Living Quarters (LQs) within EBs are updated to include new LQs in the sample selection process. When the 2000 Census is implemented it will replace the current frame. EBs in growth areas (with overcrowded populations) will be sub-divided into smaller size EBs to retain the same population size of about 600 persons.
Rotation: Not available.
Scheme: Not available.
Percentage of units remaining in the sample for two consecutive survey rounds: Not available.
Maximum number of interviews per sample unit: NOT AVAILABLE.
Length of time for complete renewal of the sample: NOT AVAILABLE.
Field work:
Type of interview: Face to face interview. If respondents at LQs are not available after three visit attempts, the interview is done by telephone.
Number of ultimate sampling units per sample area: Not available.
Duration of field work
Total: Four weeks plus one week mapping period for each quarter of the year (each round).
Per sample area: Not available.
Survey organization: Permanent staff of the Department of Statistics (State branches).
Number of field staff: One enumerator covers one EB. About 10 enumerators for one supervisor.
Substitution of non-responding ultimate sampling units: Yes.
Estimation and adjustments:
Total non-response rate: Four per cent.
Adjustment for total non-response: Yes.
Imputation for item non-response: Yes. Information on persons from the nearest responding LQ is inserted for the non-response.
Adjustment for areas/population not covered: No.
Adjustment for under-coverage: No.
Adjustment for over-coverage: No.
Adjustment for seasonal variations: No.
History of the survey:
Title and date of the first survey: National Survey on Employment, Unemployment and Under-employment, 1962.
Significant changes or revisions:
1964-1965: covered only major urban centers in Peninsular Malaysia.
1967-1968: Malaysian Sample Survey of Households (three rounds).
1974-2000: Labour Force Survey conducted, except in 1991 and 1994.
Documentation and dissemination:
Documentation:
Survey results: The Labour Force Survey (year). (**Periodicity:** annual).

Survey methodology: idem.
Dissemination:
Time needed for initial release of survey results: 1999 results were released on December 1999.
Advance information of public about date of initial release: Yes.
Availability of unpublished data upon request: Yes.
Availability of data in machine-readable form: Yes.
Website: http://www.statistics.gov.my/.

Mauritius

Title of the survey: Labour Force Sample Survey.
Organization responsible for the survey:
Planning and conduct of the survey: Central Statistical Office, Ministry of Economic Planning and Development.
Analysis and publication of the results: Central Statistical Office, Ministry of Economic Planning and Development.
Topics covered: Employment, unemployment, underemployment, hours of work (normal/usual hours of work, hours actually worked), wages/salaries, duration of employment, duration of unemployment, industry, occupation, status in employment, education and qualification levels, usual activity, second jobs.
Coverage of the survey:
Geographical: Whole country (islands of Mauritius and Rodrigues).
Population groups: The survey covers the entire resident Mauritian population of the Republic of Mauritius living in private households. Persons living in institutions and foreign households (e.g., staff of embassies and foreigners working on contract in Mauritius) are not covered.
Availability of estimates from other sources for the excluded areas/groups: No information provided.
Groups covered by the survey but excluded from the published results: No information provided.
Periodicity:
Conduct of the survey: Every ten years during the mid-census years. The last survey was undertaken in June-July 1995.
Publication of results: Every ten years. The results of the last survey were published in January-March 1997.
Reference periods:
Employment: Fixed reference period of one week.
Seeking work: Moving reference period of two months prior to the interview date.
Availability for work: Moving reference period of one week prior to the interview date.
Concepts and definitions:
Employment: Persons aged 12 years or over, who had performed some work (i.e. for at least one hour) for pay, profit or family gain during the reference week. Also included are persons, who were temporarily absent from their work during the reference week because of illness, vacation, lack of work, industrial dispute, etc.
In the context of the survey, work implies the production of goods or services normally intended for sale on the market. However, certain types of non-market production are also included. In general, these are production of primary products for own consumption, own-account construction, and production of other fixed assets for own use.
Domestic activities and voluntary community services are excluded.
Unemployment: Persons aged 12 years or over, who were not employed during the reference week, available for work during the reference week, and had taken specific steps to seek work at any time during the two months preceding the interview date. Seeking work does not only imply looking for a paid employment job, but also covers steps taken to start a business of one's own (self-employment). Persons without work and available for work, but not seeking work because of arrangements already made to start work at a date subsequent to the reference week, are included among the unemployed.
Workers laid off by their employers, as well as self-employed persons out of work because of a shortage of work, are considered as being unemployed if they were available for work and had looked for work at any time during the two months preceding the interview date.
Underemployment:
Time-related underemployment: Employed persons, who during the reference week worked involuntarily less hours than the normal duration of work in their particular activity, and who were available for additional work.
Inadequate employment situations: This topic is not covered by the survey.
Hours of work: Hours actually worked during the reference week, and normal hours of work per week. For persons, to whom the concept of normal hours of work does not apply, the number of usual hours of work per week is recorded. Information on hours of work is collected for the main job and for the total of other jobs (if any).
Employment-related income:
Income from paid employment: Average gross wage or salary per month in Rupees (under 2000, 2001-4000, 4001-6000, 6001-8000, 8001-10000, 10001-15000, 15001-20000, 20001 or more) for the person's main job.
Income from self-employment: This topic is not covered by the survey.
Informal sector: This topic is not covered by the survey.
Usual activity: Usual activity refers to the main activity status of persons during a reference period of a whole year. The main activity status (usually active, not usually active) is determined from the number of weeks that persons report as having been employed, or looking and available for work, during the reference year. The usually active population comprises persons aged 12 years or over, who were economically active (employed or unemployed) for a total of 26 or more weeks during the last year. Usually active persons are categorized as employed or unemployed depending upon the number of weeks of employment and of unemployment during the last year.
Classifications:
Branch of economic activity (industry):
Title of the classification: International Standard Industrial Classification of All Economic Activities (ISIC, Rev. 3).
Population groups classified by industry: Employed persons; unemployed or economically inactive persons with previous work experience.
Number of groups used for coding: No information provided.
Links to ISIC: ISIC Rev. 3.
Occupation:
Title of the classification: International Standard Classification of Occupations (ISCO-88).
Population groups classified by occupation: Employed persons; unemployed or economically inactive persons with previous work experience.
Number of groups used for coding: No information provided.
Links to ISCO: ISCO-88.
Status in employment:
Title of the classification: National classification of status in employment.
Population groups classified by status in employment: Employed persons; unemployed or economically inactive persons with previous work experience.
Groups used for classification: (a) Self-employed persons; (a1) self-employed persons with employees; (a2) self-employed persons without employees; (b) employees; (b1) employees, time rate; (b2) employees, piece rate; (b3) outworkers; (b4) apprentices (paid or unpaid); (c) unpaid family workers; (d) others.
Links to ICSE: ICSE-1993.
Education:
Title of the classification: National classification of levels of educational attainment.
Population groups classified by education: All persons.
Groups used for classification: (a) Nil or pre-primary; (b) primary; (b1) primary, Std. I-V; (b2) primary, CPE or equivalent; (c) secondary; (c1) secondary, Forms I-IV; (c2) secondary, SC or equivalent; (c3) secondary, HSC or equivalent; (d) university degree or equivalent.
Links to ISCED: Yes.
Sample size and design:
Ultimate sampling unit: Household.
Sample size (ultimate sampling units): 9,900 households.
Overall sampling fraction: 4.1 percent of households.
Sample frame: On the basis of the latest Housing and Population Census, a sample of 495 enumeration areas is selected for the labour force survey. Prior to the survey, a complete new listing of households is made in the sample enumeration areas.
Updating of the sample: Not applicable.
Rotation:
Scheme: There is no sample rotation.
Percentage of units remaining in the sample for two consecutive survey rounds: Not applicable.
Maximum number of interviews per sample unit: Not applicable.
Length of time for complete renewal of the sample: Not applicable.
Field work:
Type of interview: Information is obtained through personal interviews.
Number of ultimate sampling units per sample area: 20 households.

Duration of field work:
Total: Two months.
Per sample area: No information provided.
Survey organization: Apart from the permanent staff of the Labour Statistics Section, no permanent survey organization exists for the survey. Field, editing and coding staff are recruited for the survey on a temporary basis.
Number of field staff: One chief supervisor, one assistant chief supervisor, 10 senior supervisors, 50 supervisors and 495 interviewers.
Substitution of non-responding ultimate sampling units: No information provided.
Estimation and adjustments:
Total non-response rate: No information provided.
Adjustment for total non-response: No information provided.
Imputation for item non-response: No information provided.
Adjustment for areas/population not covered: No information provided.
Adjustment for under-coverage: No information provided.
Adjustment for over-coverage: No information provided.
Adjustment for seasonal variations: Not applicable.
History of the survey:
Title and date of the first survey: The first Labour Force Sample Survey was conducted in June-July 1995.
Significant changes or revisions: Not applicable.
Documentation and dissemination:
Documentation:
Survey results: Central Statistical Office, Ministry of Economic Planning and Development: Labour Force Sample Survey (periodicity: every ten years). Prior to the publication, the main findings of the survey are released in a preliminary report.
Survey methodology: The above-mentioned publication includes methodological information on the survey.
Dissemination:
Time needed for initial release of survey results: 18 months.
Advance information of public about date of initial release: No information provided.
Availability of unpublished data upon request: No information provided.
Availability of data in machine-readable form: No information provided.

Moldova, Rep. of

Title of the survey: Labour Force Survey
Organization responsible for the survey:
Planning and conduct of the survey: Department for Statistics and Sociology.
Analysis and publication of the results: Department for Statistics and Sociology.
Topics covered: Employment, unemployment, underemployment, hours of work, duration of unemployment, discouraged workers, occasional workers, industry, occupation, status in employment, educational level, usual activity and second jobs.
Coverage of the survey:
Geographical: Whole country with the exception of the Transnistria region and the town of Tighina
Population groups: All permanent residents aged 15 and above living in households.
Excluded are:
a) students living in hostels and schoolchildren living in boarding schools;
b) old persons living in special boarding homes;
c) inmates of penal and mental institutions;
d) foreign citizens.
Availability of estimates from other sources for the excluded areas/groups: No.
Groups covered by the survey but excluded from the published results: None.
Periodicity:
Conduct of the survey: Continuously.
Publication of results: Quarterly.
Reference periods:
Employment: One week (last seven days prior to the date of the interview).
Seeking work: Four weeks prior to the date of the interview.
Availability for work: Two weeks following the date of the interview.
Concepts and definitions:
Employment: Employed are all persons aged 15 years and over who during the reference week performed some paid or unpaid some work for at least one hour, as well as unpaid family workers and persons who were not working but who had jobs or businesses from which they were temporarily absent because of illness, bad weather, holiday, labour-management dispute, etc.
Also included in the totals are:
a) full- and part-time workers seeking other work during the reference period;
b) full- and part-time students working full- or part-time;
c) persons who performed some work during the reference week while being either retired and receiving a pension; or were registered as job seekers at an employment office or receiving unemployment benefits;
d) private domestic servants;
e) paid apprentices and trainees
Excluded are persons engaged in production of goods for their own household (painting, repairing, housework, etc.).
Unemployment: Unemployed are considered to be persons aged 15 years and over who, during the reference week, did not work for pay or profit, were actively looking for work during the last four weeks prior to the survey and were available to start work in the two weeks following the survey.
Underemployment:
Time-related underemployment: Persons who, during the reference week, involuntary worked less than established duration of working and were both looking for and available to work more hours.
Inadequate employment situations: Not applicable.
Hours of work: Usual and actual hours worked in the main and secondary job(s).
Employment-related income:
Income from paid employment: Not applicable.
Income from self-employment: Not applicable.
Informal sector: Not applicable.
Usual activity: Not applicable.
Classifications:
Branch of economic activity (industry):
Title of the classification: National classification.
Population groups classified by industry: Employed persons and unemployed persons with previous job experience.
Number of groups used for coding: 55 groups.
Links to ISIC: ISIC-Rev.3 (4 digit level).
Occupation:
Title of the classification: National classification.
Population groups classified by occupation: Employed persons and unemployed persons with previous work experience.
Number of groups used for coding: 10 major groups.
Links to ISCO: ISCO-88 (3 digit level).
Status in employment:
Title of the classification: National classification.
Population groups classified by status in employment: Employed and unemployed persons.
Groups used for classification: 5 groups (employees, employers, own-account worker, members of producers' co-operatives, contributing family workers.
Links to ICSE: ICSE-1993.
Education:
Title of the classification: National classification is used.
Population groups classified by education: all population groups.
Groups used for classification: 7 groups (pre-primary education, primary, lower secondary, upper secondary, vocational school, college, higher education (university).
Links to ISCED: No.
Sample size and design:
Ultimate sampling unit: Dwelling address.
Sample size (ultimate sampling units): About 8 208.
Overall sampling fraction: 1/150.
Sample frame: The sample frame is built on the basis of the election lists used during the Presidential elections of 1996.
Updating of the sample: YES.
Rotation:
Scheme: Each sampled dwelling is interviewed two consecutive quarters then it drops out for two quarters, after which it is again interviewed for two consecutive quarters and leaves the sample for ever.
Percentage of units remaining in the sample for two consecutive survey rounds: 50 per cent.
Maximum number of interviews per sample unit: 4.
Length of time for complete renewal of the sample: About 7 years.
Field work:
Type of interview: Paper and pencil.

Number of ultimate sampling units per sample area: 72 dwellings per quarter.
Duration of field work:
Total: No information provided.
Per sample area: No information provided.
Survey organization: Department for Statistics and Sociology.
Number of field staff: 114 interviewers and 39 supervisors.
Substitution of non-responding ultimate sampling units: No.
Estimation and adjustments:
Total non-response rate: 11 per cent.
Adjustment for total non-response: Yes.
Imputation for item non-response: No.
Adjustment for areas/population not covered: No.
Adjustment for undercoverage: Yes.
Adjustment for overcoverage: Yes.
Adjustment for seasonal variations: No.
History of the survey:
Title and date of the first survey: Labour Force Survey, October 1998.
Significant changes or revisions: No significant changes.
Documentation and dissemination:
Documentation:
Survey results: "Economic active population, employment and unemployment" (annually).
Survey methodology: "Economic active population, employment and unemployment" (annually).
Dissemination:
Time needed for initial release of survey results: Two months.
Advance information of public about date of initial release: Yes.
Availability of unpublished data upon request: Yes.
Availability of data in machine-readable form: Diskettes, internet.
Website: http://www.moldova.md/.

Nepal

Title of the survey: Nepal Labour Force Survey.
Organization responsible for the survey:
Planning and conduct of the survey: Central Bureau of Statistics.
Analysis and publication of the results: Central Bureau of Statistics.
Topics covered: Employment, unemployment, underemployment, hours actually worked, wages, informal sector employment, duration of employment, duration of unemployment, industry, occupation, status in employment, education and qualification levels, usual activity, second jobs, past employment record.
Coverage of the survey:
Geographical: Whole country.
Population groups: The survey covers the permanent residents of Nepal, including foreign nationals. Homeless persons, persons living in institutions (such as school hostels, prisons, army camps or hospitals), and persons absent from their household for six months or more, are not covered. Households of diplomatic missions are excluded.
Availability of estimates from other sources for the excluded areas/groups: No information provided.
Groups covered by the survey but excluded from the published results: No information provided.
Periodicity:
Conduct of the survey: Irregularly. The first Nepal Labour Force Survey was conducted during the period May 1998-April 1999.
Publication of results: Irregularly, depending upon the conduct of the survey.
Reference periods:
Employment: Moving reference period of one week, i.e. the last seven days prior to the interview date.
Seeking work: Moving reference period of one month, i.e. the last 30 days prior to the interview date.
Availability for work: Moving reference period of one week, i.e. the last seven days prior to the interview date.
Concepts and definitions:
Employment: Persons aged 5 years or over who did some work (i.e. for at least one hour) for pay, profit or family gain during the reference week. Included are: (a) contributing family workers at work during the reference week; (b) full- or part-time workers seeking other work; (c) persons who performed some work during the reference week but who were subject to compulsory schooling, or retired and receiving a pension, or registered as job seekers at an employment office; (d) full-time students working full- or part-time; (e) part-time students working full- or part-time; (f) paid apprentices and trainees; (g) persons engaged in the production of goods for own final use; and (h) persons on civilian service equivalent to military service.
Persons, who were temporarily absent from work during the reference week because of illness or injury, vacation or annual leave, maternity or paternity leave, or educational or training leave, etc. are considered employed if (i) they had a job or own enterprise to return to, and (ii) either were receiving any pay (in cash or in kind) or other returns from a job or business while not at work, or had been absent from work without pay or returns for less than two months.
Excluded are: (a) contributing family workers not at work during the reference week; (b) unpaid apprentices and trainees; (c) persons absent from work due to labour management dispute; (d) persons absent from work due to bad weather, mechanical breakdown, etc.; (e) persons on temporary or indefinite lay-off without pay; (f) persons on unpaid leave initiated by the employer; (g) seasonal workers not at work during the off-season; (h) persons rendering unpaid or personal services to members of their own household; and (i) persons doing unpaid volunteer community or social service work.
Unemployment: Persons aged 5 years or over who (i) were not employed during the reference week (including persons who had a job or own enterprise to return to, but had been absent from it without pay or other returns for two months or more), (ii) were available for work during the reference week, and (iii) had been looking for work during the last 30 days, or had not been looking for work during the last 30 days for any of the following reasons: belief that no work is available; awaiting reply to earlier enquiries; waiting to start an arranged job or business; off-season for fishing or agriculture; other reason. The following are considered as methods of looking for work: applying to any employers; asking friends or relatives about finding work; taking action to start an own business; looking for work in other ways.
Included are: (a) persons without work and currently available for work, who had made arrangements to start a new job on a date subsequent to the reference week; (b) persons without work and currently available for work, who were trying to establish their own enterprise; (c) persons without work and currently available for work, but not seeking work for reasons other than (a) or (b) above; (d) persons seeking work and/or available for work who were subject to compulsory schooling, or retired and receiving a pension; (e) full-time students seeking and/or available for full- or part-time work; (f) part-time students seeking and/or available for full- or part-time work; and (g) participants in employment promotion schemes.
Excluded are persons without work who were not available for work during the reference week.
Separate estimates are available for unemployed persons, who had been looking for work during the last 30 days, and for unemployed persons, who had not been looking for work during the last 30 days.
Underemployment:
Time-related underemployment: Employed persons at work who worked less than 40 hours during the reference week for any of the following involuntary (i.e. economic) reasons: cannot find more work or lack of business; lack of finance or raw materials; machinery, electrical or other breakdown; off-season inactivity; strike or lay-off as the result of an industrial dispute; other involuntary reason. For persons with more than one job, the threshold of 40 hours refers to the total number of hours worked in all jobs during the reference week.
Inadequate employment situations: This topic is not covered by the survey.
Hours of work: Hours actually worked during the reference week. Information is collected on the total number of hours worked in all jobs and on the number of hours worked in the main job.
Employment-related income:
Income from paid employment: Gross wages or salaries received in cash or in kind during the last week or last month for the main paid employment job, before the deduction of tax, social security or pension payments. All additional benefits, such as bonuses, tips or incentives, are included. Other regular income from paid employment is also included, but converted to a weekly or monthly basis as appropriate (e.g., one twelfth of the 13th-month payment given to civil servants is added). Earnings in kind include the regular supply of food, clothing, housing, water, electricity, fuel, transport, etc. on a free or subsidized basis. Non-regular earnings, such as gifts in cash or in kind, are excluded.
Income from self-employment: This topic is not covered by the survey.
Informal sector: Employment in the informal sector includes the following groups: (a) paid employees working for private unregistered enterprises (or for other enterprises that are not government units, public corporations, NGOs/INGOs, or private registered companies) with less than 10 regular paid employees; (b) own-account workers

(i.e. persons operating their own business without regular paid employees); (c) employers (i.e. persons operating their own business with regular paid employees) employing less than 10 regular paid employees; and (d) contributing family members without pay and others working in businesses with less than 10 regular paid employees. Persons working in the agricultural sector are excluded. The information refers to the main job only; persons with a secondary job in the informal sector are not covered.
Usual activity: Usual economic activity refers to the work experience during a reference period of one year, i.e. the 12 full calendar months preceding the interview date. Persons aged 5 years or over are considered usually active if, during the 12 reference months, they worked or were available for work for a total of 180 or more days. Usually active persons can be sub-divided into usually employed persons and usually unemployed persons. Usually employed persons are those for whom the total length of employment periods during the 12 reference months was equal or larger than the total length of unemployment periods. Usually unemployed persons are those for whom the total length of unemployment periods during the 12 reference months was larger than the total length of employment periods.
Classifications:
Branch of oconomic activity (industry):
Title of the classification: International Standard Industrial Classification of All Economic Activities (ISIC, Rev. 3).
Population groups classified by industry: Employed persons.
Number of groups used for coding: Divisions (2-digit level).
Links to ISIC: ISIC Rev. 3.
Occupation:
Title of the classification: International Standard Classification of Occupations (ISCO-88).
Population groups classified by occupation: Employed persons.
Number of groups used for coding: Minor groups (3-digit level).
Links to ISCO: ISCO-88.
Status in employment:
Title of the classification: National classification of status in employment.
Population groups classified by status in employment: Employed persons
Groups used for classification: (a) Paid employees; (b) persons operating their own business or farm with regular paid employees; (c) persons operating their own business or farm without regular paid employees; (d) contributing family members without pay; (e) others.
Links to ICSE: ICSE-1993.
Education:
Title of the classification: National classification of levels of educational attainment.
Population groups classified by education: All persons aged 5 years or over.
Groups used for classification: (a) Never attended school; (b) preschool/kindergarten; (c) – (l) Classes 1-10; (m) intermediate if Class 11; (n) intermediate if Class 12; (o) B.A./B.Sc.; (p) M.A./M.Sc.; (q) Professional Degree; (r) other.
Links to ISCED: ISCED-1976, 3-digit level.
Sample size and design:
Ultimate sampling unit: Household.
Sample size (ultimate sampling units): 14,400 households (7,200 in urban areas and 7,200 in rural areas).
Overall sampling fraction: About 0.4 percent of households (1.5 percent in urban areas and 0.2 percent in rural areas).
Sample frame: Area sample frame based on the list of enumeration areas from the Population Census 1991. Enumeration areas in new municipalities created since 1991 were transferred from the rural frame to the urban frame. Prior to the survey, a complete new listing of households was made in all the 720 enumeration areas included in the sample.
Updating of the sample: Not applicable.
Rotation:
Scheme: No sample rotation. Data collection is spread over a period of one year in dividing the survey sample into three independent subsamples, each one representing four months in the Nepalese calendar (rainy season, winter season, dry season).
Percentage of units remaining in the sample for two consecutive survey rounds: Not applicable.
Maximum number of interviews per sample unit: Not applicable.
Length of time for complete renewal of the sample: Not applicable.
Field work:
Type of interview: Information is obtained through personal interviews.
Number of ultimate sampling units per sample area: 20 households per sample enumeration area.
Duration of field work: One year.
Per sample area: Five days per sample enumeration area.
Survey organization: A permanent survey organization is used for the survey.
Number of field staff: 15 supervisors and 46 interviewers.
Substitution of non-responding ultimate sampling units: No replacement is made for non-responding households.
Estimation and adjustments:
Total non-response rate: 0.3 percent of sample households.
Adjustment for total non-response: Yes.
Imputation for item non-response: No.
Adjustment for areas/population not covered: No.
Adjustment for under-coverage: No.
Adjustment for over-coverage: Not applicable.
Adjustment for seasonal variations: Not applicable.
History of the survey:
Title and date of the first survey: The first Nepal Labour Force Survey was conducted in 1998/1999.
Significant changes or revisions: Not applicable.
Documentation and dissemination:
Documentation:
Survey results: Central Bureau of Statistics, Report on the Nepal Labour Force Survey 1998/99, December 1999.
Survey methodology: The above publication also contains methodological information on the survey.
Dissemination:
Time needed for initial release of survey results: About eight months.
Advance information of public about date of initial release: No.
Availability of unpublished data upon request: Yes, in the form of additional tables.
Availability of data in machine-readable form: Yes, on diskettes.

Netherlands

Title of the survey: The Labour Force Survey.
Organization responsible for the survey:
Planning and conduct of the survey: Central Bureau of Statistics.
Analysis and publication of the results: Central Bureau of Statistics.
Topics covered: Employment, unemployment, hours of work, informal sector employment, duration of unemployment, industry, occupation, status in employment, education/qualification skills, usual activity, other subjects such as, for example, working conditions and parental leave.
Coverage of the survey:
Geographical: Whole country.
Population groups: Persons aged 15 to 64 years, living in the Netherlands, except persons living in institutions.
Availability of estimates from other sources for the excluded areas/groups: No.
Groups covered by the survey but excluded from the published results: Children below 15 years.
Periodicity:
Conduct of the survey: Continuous survey.
Publication of results: Annually.
Reference periods:
Employment: When interviewed.
Seeking work: When interviewed.
Availability for work: When interviewed.
Concepts and definitions:
Employment: All persons aged 15 to 64 years living in private households surveyed during the reference week, with the exclusion of the institutional population.
From 1992 onwards, national data are based on a definition of employment which includes only persons who worked 12 hours or more per week. For international purposes, the one hour criterion is applied.
Also included in the employed are:
a) persons with a job but temporarily absent from work due to illness or injury, vacation or annual leave, maternity/paternity or parental leave, educational or training leave, absence without leave, labor management dispute, bad weather or mechanical breakdown, etc, as well as persons on temporary or indefinite lay-off without pay or on unpaid leave initiated by the employer and full or part-time workers seeking work during the reference period;
b) persons who performed some work for pay or profit during the reference period but were subject to compulsory schooling, retired

and receiving a pension, registered as jobseekers at an employment office or those receiving unemployment benefits;
c) full or part-time students working full or part-time;
d) paid apprentices and trainees and participants in employment promotion schemes;
e) unpaid family workers at work during the reference period or temporarily absent from work;
f) volunteers and career members of the armed forces and persons in civilian service equivalent to military service.
Unemployment: National unemployment data include persons looking for work for 12 hours or more per week. Persons working less than 12 hours are no longer classified in the labor force, except if they are seeking to work 12 hours or more per week; in this case, they are classified as unemployed.
Also included in the unemployed are:
a) persons without work and currently available for work who had made arrangements to start a new job on a date subsequent to the reference period or who were trying to establish their own enterprise;
b) persons who were seeking work and/or available for work but were subject to compulsory schooling or retired and receiving a pension;
c) full or part-time students seeking full or part-time work;
d) unpaid apprentices and trainees.
Underemployment:
Time-related underemployment: Not applicable.
Inadequate employment situations: Not applicable.
Hours of work: Not available.
Employment-related income:
Income from paid employment: Not applicable.
Income from self-employment: Not applicable.
Informal sector: No information provided.
Usual activity: No information provided.
Classifications:
Branch of economic activity (industry):
Title of the classification: ISIC-Rev. 3.
Population groups classified by industry: Employed persons.
Number of groups used for coding: 18 groups.
Links to ISIC: ISIC-Rev. 2 and Rev. 3.
Occupation:
Title of the classification: ISCO-88.
Population groups classified by occupation: Employed persons.
Number of groups used for coding: 11 groups.
Links to ISCO: ISCO-88.
Status in employment:
Title of the classification: No information.
Population groups classified by status in employment: Employed.
Groups used for classification: Employees, employers and family workers.
Links to ICSE: Indirect links to ICSE-1993.
Education:
Title of the classification: ISCED-1997.
Population groups classified by education: Employed and unemployed persons.
Groups used for classification: 5 groups.
Links to ISCED: ISCED-1997.
Sample size and design:
Ultimate sampling unit: Household.
Sample size (ultimate sampling units) 8 000 household each month:
Overall sampling fraction: 1 per cent.
Sample frame: The survey is based on a stratified two stage sample. The Geographic Basic Register (GBR) constitutes the sample frame. The GBR is a list of all addresses in the Netherlands established by the Post office of the Netherlands. For the labour force survey, a sample of about 11 000 addresses is drawn each month.
Updating of the sample: No information provided.
Rotation:
Scheme: No information provided.
Percentage of units remaining in the sample for two consecutive survey rounds: No information provided.
Maximum number of interviews per sample unit: Five times.
Length of time for complete renewal of the sample: One year.
Field work:
Type of interview: CAPI and CATI: personal interviews during the first wave and by telephone during the second, third, fourth and fifth waves. The time between each wave is three months.
Number of ultimate sampling units per sample area: No information provided.
Duration of field work:
Total: Continuous.
Per sample area: Continuous.
Survey organization: Permanent.
Number of field staff: About 300 persons.
Substitution of non-responding ultimate sampling units: No.
Estimation and adjustments:
Total non-response rate: 45 per cent.
Adjustment for total non-response: No.
Imputation for item non-response: No.
Adjustment for areas/population not covered: No.
Adjustment for undercoverage: Yes.
Adjustment for overcoverage: Yes.
Adjustment for seasonal variations: No.
History of the survey:
Title and date of the first survey: 1987 Labour force survey.
Significant changes or revisions: 1992 and 2000.
Documentation and dissemination:
Documentation:
Survey results: No information provided.
Survey methodology: No information provided.
Dissemination:
Time needed for initial release of survey results: One year.
Advance information of public about date of initial release: No.
Availability of unpublished data upon request: Yes.
Availability of data in machine-readable form: Excel spreadsheets on request and internet website (http://www.cbs.nl).

New Zealand

Title of the survey: Household Labour Force Survey (HLFS).
Organization responsible for the survey:
Planning and conduct of the survey: Statistics New Zealand (SNZ).
Analysis and publication of the results: SNZ.
Topics covered: Persons currently economically active, employed and unemployed; persons currently in time-related underemployment and persons currently outside the labour force; discouraged workers; actual and usual hours of work; duration of unemployment; ethnicity; industry; occupation; status in employment; education/training levels.
Coverage of the survey:
Geographical: Whole country, excluding External Territories.
Population groups: Civilian non-institutional population of age 15 years and above.
Availability of estimates from other sources for the excluded areas/groups: No.
Groups covered by the survey but excluded from the published results: None.
Periodicity:
Conduct of the survey: Continuous.
Publication of results: Quarterly.
Reference periods:
Employment: One week.
Unemployed: The last four weeks.
Availability for work: During the reference week.
Concepts and definitions:
Employment: Persons who a) performed some work for pay or profit during the reference week; and b) were temporarily absent from work during the reference week because of illness or paid leave, or had business to which they were definitely going to return. Some work is defined as 1 hour or more during the reference week.
Unemployment: Persons who were currently without work and available for work during the reference week, and who had actively searched for work sometime during the last four weeks.
Underemployment:
Time-related underemployment: Employed persons who work part time and have been looking for full time work in the last four weeks and/or wanting to work more hours.
Inadequate employment situations: No information provided.
Hours of work: Both 'actual' and 'usual' hours worked include both paid and unpaid hours worked, in main job and in second job(s).
Employment-related income:
Income from employment: No information provided.
Income from self-employment: No information provided.
Informal sector: Not applicable.
Usual activity: No information provided.
Classifications:
Branch of economic activity (industry):
Title of the classification: Australian and New Zealand Standard Industrial Classification (ANZSIC).
Population groups classified by industry: Employed and unemployed (industry of last job for the unemployed).
Number of groups used for coding: 158.
Links to ISIC: ISIC-Rev. 3.

Occupation:
Title of the classification: New Zealand Standard Classification of Occupations (NZSCO).
Population groups classified by occupation: Employed and unemployed (occupation of last job for the unemployed).
Number of groups used for coding: 96.
Links to ISCO: ISCO-88.
Status in employment:
Title of the classification: Status in Employment-Standard Classification 1998.
Population groups classified by status in employment: Employed and unemployed (status of the last job for the unemployed).
Groups used for classification: Working for wages or salary; employer of others in own business; self-employed and not employing others; working without pay in a family business.
Links to ICSE: ICSE-1993.
Education:
Title of the classification: Household Labour Force Survey Qualification Type Classification (HLF.QUALHIG)
Population groups classified education: All persons.
Groups used for classification: 17.
Links to ISCED: ISCED-1997.
Sample size and design:
Ultimate sampling unit: Households.
Sample size (ultimate sampling units): 18 000.
Overall sampling fraction: 0.01.
Sample frame: Quinquennial censuses. Small geographic areas are the primary sampling units (PSU).
Updating of the sample frame: Every five years.
Rotation scheme:
Scheme: Households in sample for 8 consecutive months and then out.
Percentage of units remaining in the sample for two consecutive survey rounds: 87.5 percent remains in sample for two consecutive months. Each PSU is allocated to one of the eight rotation groups, and one rotation group is replaced every quarter with new dwellings from the same PSU.
Maximum number of interviews per sample unit: No information provided.
Length of time for complete renewal of the sample: No information provided.
Field work:
Type of interview: Pen-and-paper; face-to-face (for the first interview) and by phone (for remaining interviews).
Number of ultimate sampling units per sample area: No information provided.
Duration of field work:
Total: 1 week.
Per sample area: No information provided.
Survey organization: Permanent.
Number of field staff: 135 interviewers and 5 regional supervisors.
Substitution of non-responding ultimate sampling units: No.
Estimation and adjustments:
Total non-response rate: 10 percent.
Adjustment for total non-response: Yes.
Imputation for item non-response: Yes.
Adjustment for areas/population not covered: Yes.
Adjustment for under-coverage: Yes.
Adjustment for over-coverage: Not applicable.
Adjustment for seasonal variations: Yes, for employment and unemployment by sex, total hours worked and persons working full and part time. Using X-12 concurrent seasonal adjustment.
History of the survey:
Title and date of the first survey: Household Labour Force Survey, December 1985 quarter.
Significant changes or revisions: June 1990: New questionnaire with new variables: underemployment, qualification, occupation (to three digit level), industry (to three digit level).
Documentation and dissemination:
Documentation:
Survey results: Hot off the press - Household Labour Force Survey (Cat. no. 05-500); Labour Market (yearly) Catalogue no. 01.029.0098 ISSN 1171-283X
Survey methodology: Survey Information Manager - Household Labour Force Survey on website.
Dissemination:
Time needed for initial release of survey results: Within six weeks after end of survey reference period.
Advance information of public about date of initial release: Yes.
Availability of unpublished data upon request: Yes.
Availability of data in machine-readable form: Yes.
Website: http://www.stats.govt.nz/.

Norway

Title of the survey: Labour Force Survey.
Organization responsible for the survey:
Planning and conduct of the survey: Statistics Norway.
Analysis and publication of the results: Statistics Norway.
Topics covered: Employment, unemployment, underemployment, hours of work, duration of employment and unemployment, discouraged workers, occasional workers, industry, occupation, status in employment, education/qualification levels, usual activity, second jobs, temporary employment, as well as other topics, corresponding to EUROSTAT's labour force surveys program.
Coverage of the survey:
Geographical: Whole country.
Population groups: All persons aged 16 to 74 years residing in the country.
Availability of estimates from other sources for the excluded areas/groups: Not applicable.
Groups covered by the survey but excluded from the published results: None.
Periodicity:
Conduct of the survey: Continuous survey.
Publication of results: Quarterly.
Reference periods:
Employment: One fixed week.
Seeking work: Four weeks.
Availability for work: Two weeks.
Concepts and definitions:
Employment: All persons aged 16 to 74 who performed work for pay or profit for at least one hour in the reference week, or who were temporarily absent from work because of illness, holidays, etc. Included are persons on paid leave, or unpaid leave until one year, if they still have a job to return to, unpaid family workers, conscripts, as well as persons engaged by Government measures to promote employment, if they receive pay.
It includes:
a) persons with a job but temporarily absent from work due to illness or injury, vacation or annual leave, maternity, paternity or parental leave until one year (unless it is still paid), educational or training leave until one year (unless it is still paid), absence without leave if this person has a job and a date of return, labour management dispute, bad weather or mechanical breakdown, etc.;
b) full- or part-time workers seeking other work during the reference week;
c) persons who performed some work for pay or profit during the reference week while subject to compulsory schooling, retired and receiving a pension, registered as jobseekers at an employment office or receiving unemployment benefits;
d) full-time or part-time students working full-time or part-time;
e) paid apprentices and trainees;
f) participants in employment promotion schemes receiving pay by their employers;
g) unpaid family workers at work during the reference week or temporarily absent from work, if not seasonal work.
h) volunteers and career members of the armed forces, conscripts and persons in civilian service equivalent to military service.
Unemployment: All persons aged 16 to 74 years who were not employed during the survey week, who have been seeking work during the last four weeks and were available within the next two weeks. Prior to 1996, they have to be available during the survey week.
Also included are:
a) persons on temporary lay-off without pay;
b) persons without work and currently available for work who have made arrangements to start a new job on a date subsequent to the reference week or who were trying to establish their own enterprise;
c) persons without work, available for work, but not seeking work during the reference week but awaiting answer from the employer, if seeking work five to eight weeks ago;
d) persons who were seeking work and available to work but were subject to compulsory schooling, retired and receiving a pension, if they were seeking work one to four weeks ago and were available to work within the next two weeks;
e) part- and full-time students seeking full- or part-time work, is they were seeking work one to four weeks ago and available to work within the next two weeks.

Underemployment:

Time-related underemployment: Part-time workers seeking longer regular (or usual) working hours of work per week and who were able to start with increased working hours within a month.

Inadequate employment situations: Persons looking for another job because of:

a) risk or certainty of loss or termination of present job;

b) actual job is considered as a transitional job;

c) seeking a second job;

d) wish to have better working conditions (working or travel time, quality of work);

e) wish higher pay;

f) other reasons.

Hours of work: They refer both to hours actually worked and regular (or usual) hours per week. Main and secondary jobs are covered separately. The distinction between part- and full-time work is done on the basis of total regular working hours in the main and secondary employment.

Employment-related income:

Income from paid employment: Not covered by the survey.

Income from self-employment: Not covered by the survey.

Informal sector: Not covered by the survey.

Usual activity: Not covered by the survey.

Classifications:

Branch of economic activity (industry):

Title of the classification: National classification.

Population groups classified by industry: Employed and unemployed persons (industry of the last job for the unemployed).

Number of groups used for coding: 60 groups.

Links to ISIC: ISIC Rev. 3 at the 2-digit level.

Occupation:

Title of the classification: National classification.

Population groups classified by occupation: Employed and unemployed persons (occupation of the last job for the unemployed).

Number of groups used for coding: 353 groups.

Links to ISCO: ISCO-88.

Status in employment:

Title of the classification: National classification

Population groups classified by status in employment: Employed and unemployment persons (status of the last job for the unemployed).

Groups used for classification: Four groups: employees, employers, self-employed and unpaid family members.

Links to ICSE: ICSE-1993.

Education:

Title of the classification: National classification.

Population groups classified by education: Employed and unemployed persons.

Groups used for classification: Five levels: primary school, level 1 of secondary school, level 2 of secondary school, university levels of one to four years and five years and more respectively. In addition, there are nine fields (programs) of study.

Links to ISCED: ISCED-1976.

Sample size and design:

Ultimate sampling unit: Family unit.

Sample size (ultimate sampling units): 24 000 persons per quarter.

Overall sampling fraction: 0.8 per cent.

Sample frame: Central Population Register, which is updated on a continuous basis by the local population registration offices.

Updating of the sample: Each quarter, 1/8 of the sample is renewed.

Rotation:

Scheme: Each household participates in the survey eight times over a period of eight consecutive quarters.

Percentage of units remaining in the sample for two consecutive survey rounds: 87.5 per cent.

Maximum number of interviews per sample unit: Eight.

Length of time for complete renewal of the sample: Eight quarters.

Field work:

Type of interview: Mostly by telephone and for a few by personal interview (CAPI).

Number of ultimate sampling units per sample area: From about 800 to 2,500 per county, and there are 19 counties.

Duration of field work:

Total: Two or three weeks after the survey week.

Per sample area: No information provided.

Survey organization: A permanent organization.

Number of field staff: About 160 persons.

Substitution of non-responding ultimate sampling units: No.

Estimation and adjustments:

Total non-response rate: About 10 per cent.

Adjustment for total non-response: Yes (in the estimating procedure).

Imputation for item non-response: Yes.

Adjustment for areas/population not covered: Not applicable.

Adjustment for undercoverage: Not applicable.

Adjustment for overcoverage: Not applicable.

Adjustment for seasonal variations: Yes. (X12-ARIMA method).

History of the survey:

Title and date of the first survey: Labour Force Survey, 1st quarter 1972.

Significant changes or revisions: New questionnaires introduced in 1988 and in 1996.

Documentation and dissemination:

Documentation:

Survey results: Labour Market Statistics (annual).

Survey methodology: Labour Market Statistics (annual).

Dissemination:

Time needed for initial release of survey results: Beginning of the month following the quarter surveyed.

Advance information of public about date of initial release: Yes.

Availability of unpublished data upon request: Yes.

Availability of data in machine-readable form: Diskettes, Internet.

Website: http://www.ssb.no/.

Pakistan

Title of the survey: Labour force survey.

Organization responsible for the survey.

Planning and conduct of the survey: Federal Bureau of Statistics, Statistics Division, Ministry of Finance and Economic Affairs

Analysis and publication of the results: Federal Bureau of Statistics

Topics covered: Employment, unemployment, underemployment, hours of work, wages, informal sector employment, duration of unemployment, industry, occupation, status in employment, education level, and secondary jobs.

Coverage of the survey:

Geographical: All urban and rural areas of the four provinces of Pakistan and Azad Jammu and Kashmir as defined by the 1981 Population Census excluding FATA % Military restricted areas, the districts of Kohistan, Malakand and the protected areas of the North West Frontier Province.

Population groups: Un-settled population, Defense personnel, Foreigners, and Nationals residing abroad are excluded.

Availability of estimates from other sources for the excluded areas/groups: The population excluded from the geographical coverage constitutes about 4% of the total population.

Groups covered by the survey but excluded from the published results: Not applicable.

Periodicity:

Conduct of the survey: Annual.

Publication of results: Annual.

Reference periods:

Employment: Moving reference week.

Seeking work: Reference week.

Availability for work: Reference week.

Concepts and definitions:

Employment: Persons, 10 years old and over, who worked at least one hour during the reference week and were either "paid employed" or "self-employed". Persons, employed on permanent footing, who had not worked for any reason during the reference week are treated as employed.

It includes:

a) Persons reporting housekeeping or other related activities, but having spent time on specified agricultural and non-agricultural activities.

b) Persons with a job but temporary absent for any reason, and persons on temporary or indefinite lay-off without pay.

c) Persons who performed some work for pay or profit during the reference week but were subject to compulsory schooling, retired and receiving a pension, or unemployment benefits, or were registered as jobseekers at an employment office or were seeking other work during the reference week.

d) Full or part-time students working full or part-time.

e) Paid apprentices and trainees, and participants in employment promotion schemes.

f) Unpaid family workers at work or temporary absent from work.

g) Persons engaged in production of goods for own final use.

h) Seasonal workers not at work during the off-season.
Excluded are:
a) Unpaid apprentices and trainees.
b) Persons engaged in production of services for their household.
c) Persons engaged in immoral pursuits such as prostitution, begging, stealing and smuggling.
d) Voluntary social workers doing work outside the family enterprise.

Unemployment: Persons, 10 years old and over, who during the reference week were: i) "without work" i.e. were not in paid employment or self-employment; ii) "currently available for work" i.e. were available for paid employment or self-employment during the reference week; and iii) "seeking work" i.e. had taken specific steps in a specified recent period to seek paid employment or self-employment.
It includes:
a) Persons without work and current available and looking for work who had made arrangements to start a new job on a date subsequent to the reference week.
b) Persons without work and currently available and looking for work who were trying to establish their own enterprise.
c) Persons without work, available for work, but not seeking work during the a recent period due to specific reasons.
d) Full or part-time students seeking full or part-time work.
e) Persons who were seeking or available for work but were subject to compulsory schooling or retired and receiving a pension.
Excluded are:
a) Persons on temporary or indefinite lay-off without pay.

Underemployment:
Time-related underemployment: Employed persons who during the reference period satisfied simultaneously the following three criteria: i) were working less than normal duration (i.e. less than 35 hours per week), ii) were doing so on an involuntary basis, and iii) were seeking or being available for additional work.
Inadequate employment situations: See above.
Hours of work: The number of hours worked in the last week subsequent to the date of interview at the main and subsidiary occupations.
Employment related income:
Income from paid employment: Gross income of employees at their main and subsidiary occupations.
Income from self-employment: No information.
Informal sector: All household enterprises owned and operated by own-account workers, irrespective of the size of the enterprise (informal own-account enterprises) and household enterprises owned and operated by employers with less than 10 persons engaged. Excluded are all household enterprises engaged in agricultural activities or wholly engaged in non-market production.
Usual activity: No information.
Classifications:
Branch of economic activity (industry):
Title of the classification: Pakistan Standard Industrial Classification PSIC-1970.
Population groups classified by industry: Employed and unemployed persons with previous work experience.
Number of groups used for coding: 2-digit level codes, but published at 1-digit level.
Links to ISIC: ISIC Rev. 2.
Occupation:
Title of the classification: Pakistan Standard Classification of Occupations
PSCO-1994.
Population groups classified by occupation: Employed and unemployed persons with previous work experience.
Number of groups used for coding: 2-digit level codes, but published at 1-digit level.
Links to ISCO: ISCO-68.
Status in employment:
Title of the classification: No information.
Population groups classified by status: Employed and unemployed persons with previous work experience.
Groups used for classification: Employer, Self-employed, Unpaid family helper, and Employee.
Links to ICSE: ICSE-1993.
Education:
Title of the classification: No information.
Population groups classified by education: Employed and unemployed persons.
Groups used for classification: No formal education. Below Matric. Matric but less than intermediate. Intermediate but less than degree. Degree and above.
Links to ISCED: Not specified.

Sample size and design:
Ultimate sampling unit: Household.
Sample size (ultimate sampling units): 22,272 households (10,368 in urban areas and 11,904 in rural areas).
Overall sampling fraction: 1/465 in urban areas and 1/1,119 in rural areas.
Sample frame: Two types of frame are used: list frame and area frame. The 1981 Population Census enumeration blocks and villages are used as primary sampling units.
Updating of the sample: The list of enumeration blocks has been updated in 1995. The urban area frame was developed by a Quick Count Record Survey in 1972 and is being updated every five years.
Rotation: None.
Scheme: Not applicable.
Percentage of units remaining in the sample: Not applicable.
Maximum number of interviews per sample unit: Not applicable.
Length of time for completed renewal of the sample: Not applicable.
Field work:
Type of interview: Personal interview.
Number of ultimate sampling units per sample area: No information provided. **Duration of fieldwork:**
Total: From 1st July 1996 to 30th June 1997.
Per sample area: No information provided..
Survey organization: Permanent.
Number of field staff: About 68 enumerators and 34 supervisors.
Substitution of non-responding sampling units: No.
Estimation and adjustments:
Total non-response rate: No information provided.
Adjustment for total non-response: No.
Imputation for item non-response: No.
Adjustment for areas/population not covered: No.
Adjustment for under-coverage: No.
Adjustment for over-coverage: No.
Adjustment for seasonal variations: No.
History of the survey:
Title and date of the first survey: Labour Force Survey (July 1963 to June 1964).
Significant changes or revisions: From 1967-68, households located in institutions (jails, asylums, hotels, messes, etc.) are included. Also, beggar households with a member working for pay or profit are also included.
Since 1978-79, unpaid family helpers working less than 15 hours a week are treated as employed. To improve the measurement of employment and unemployment, several probing questions were incorporated in the questionnaire on a) willingness to work if a job is provided, b) reason for not looking for work, and c) any work for pay or profit addressed to persons reporting as "housekeeper" or "student".
In 1990-91, more probing questions were incorporated in the questionnaire in line with the requirements of the ILO 1982 resolution. In particular, a special probing section on economic activity was designed for persons 10 years of age and above who reported housekeeping and other related activities.
In 1995, questions on migration and formal & informal sector characteristics were introduced..
Documentation and dissemination:
Documentation:
Survey results: Report of the Labour Force Survey.
Survey methodology: Report of the Labour Force Survey.
Dissemination:
Time needed for initial release of survey results: About 16 months. Data from survey conducted 1st July 1996 to 30th June 1997 released in October 1998.
Advance information of public about date of initial release: No.
Availability of unpublished data upon request: Yes
Availability of data in machine-readable form: Yes.

Philippines

Title of the survey: The Labour Force Survey
Organization responsible for the survey:
Planning and conduct of the survey: National Statistics Office.
Analysis and publication of the results: National Statistics Office.
Topics covered: Employment, unemployment, underemployment, hours of work, duration of employment, discouraged workers, occasional workers, industry, occupation (primary and other jobs), status in employment, educational level, usual activity and other topics such as new entrants, basis of payment and basic pay per day, etc.

Coverage of the survey:

Geographical: Whole country - national, regional, provincial/key cities, urban and rural areas.

Population groups: All persons living in private households. Not considered as members of a household are:

a) Persons or family members who are inmates of institutions, such as penal colonies/farms, detention camps, homes for the aged, orphanages, mental institutions, tuberculosis sanitaria, leprosaria, etc. and who are not expected to return within 30 days;

b) Members of the Armed Forces of the Philippines if they have been away from their usual place of residence for more than 30 days;

c) Filipino/as whose usual place of residence is in a foreign country, who have been /will be in the Philippines for less than one year from date of arrival;

d) citizens of foreign countries and members of their families who are in the country as tourists, students, on business or for employment provided they expect to stay in the country for one year or less from date of arrival;

e) Foreign ambassadors, ministers, consuls, or other diplomatic representatives and members of their families, regardless of their length of stay in the country;

f) citizens of foreign countries who are chiefs or officials of international organizations such as United Nations etc. and members of their families, regardless of their length of stay in the country.

Availability of estimates from other sources for the excluded areas/groups: Not available.

Groups covered by the survey but excluded from the published results: Overseas Contract Workers.

Periodicity:

Conduct of the survey: Quarterly.

Publication of results: Quarterly.

Reference periods:

Employment: Past week (moving reference period).

Seeking work: Past week (moving reference period).

Availability for work: Past week (moving reference period).

Concepts and definitions:

Employment: All persons aged 15 years and over as of their last birthday who, during the reference week, did any work for pay or profit, or unpaid work on a farm or business enterprise operated by a related member of the same household for at least one hour, resulting in the production of goods or services, as well as those who had a job or business but were absent from work due to temporary illness, vacation or leave, temporary lay-off without pay and unpaid leave initiated by the employer, strike, reduction in economic activity, etc., and those who are expected to report for work or to start operation of a farm or business enterprise within two weeks from the date of interview.

It also includes:

a) full and part-time workers seeking other work during the reference week;

b) persons who performed some work for pay or profit during the reference week, but were subject to compulsory schooling, were retired and receiving a pension; were full or part-time students working full or part-time, were registered as job seekers at an employment office or receiving unemployment benefits;

c) pre-employment arrangement apprentices or paid trainees;

d) unpaid family workers at work and temporarily absent from work;

e) private domestic servants;

f) members of producers' co-operatives;

g) persons doing civilian service equivalent to military service;

h) persons engaged in production of goods for sale or for family consumption (gardening in at least 100 square meters of solid patches);

Unemployment: All persons 15 years and over as of their last birthday who did not work at all for pay or profit or as unpaid family workers during the reference period, but were reported wanting and looking for work. Also included are persons without a job or business who reported not seeking work because of the belief that no work was available, or due to bad weather, minor illness, pending job applications/job recall, waiting for job interviews, etc. Persons on indefinite lay-off without pay, seasonal workers awaiting seasonal work, and the following categories of people are also included:

a) persons making an effort to start a business or private practice;

b) persons seeking and/or available for work but who were retired and receiving a pension;

c) full and part-time students seeking full or part-time work;

d) unpaid apprentices and trainees;

e) participants in employment promotion schemes.

Underemployment:

Time-related underemployment: Employed persons who expressed the desire to have additional hours of work in their present job or an additional job, or to have a new job with longer working hours.

Inadequate employment situations: Not applicable.

Hours of work: Actual number of hours worked in all jobs by a person during the reference week.

Employment-related income:

Income from paid employment: From January 2001 onwards, following the introduction of the new survey questionnaire: basic pay per day.

Income from self-employment: Not applicable.

Informal sector employment: This is not clearly segregated. Employed persons are classified by "class of worker" (see under Status in Employment below), including the informal sector, with reference to main job/occupation only.

Usual activity: The main activity/usual occupation refers to the kind of job or business which persons were engaged in most of the time (more than 6 months or that which had the longest duration) during the last 12 months.

Classifications:

Branch of economic activity (industry):

Title of the classification: 1994 Philippine Standard Industrial Classification (PSIC).

Population groups classified by industry: Employed persons.

Number of groups used for coding: 9 major divisions and one code for activities not adequately defined.

Links to ISIC: ISIC-Rev. 2, at major division level only, except for Division 6 which excludes restaurants and hotels. These are included in Division 9 (code 98).

Occupation:

Title of the classification: 1992 Philippine Standard Occupational Classification (PSOC).

Population groups classified by occupation: Employed persons.

Number of groups used for coding: 9 major groups.

Links to ISCO: ISCO-68, at 2-digit level, except for major group 3. (ISCO code 3.1 - government executive officials are included in PSOC code 2.0 - legislative officials, government administrators and government executives.)

Status in employment:

Title of the classification: Class of Workers.

Population groups classified by status in employment: Employed persons.

Groups used for classification: Seven groups: 0. Worked for private household, 1. Worked for private establishments, 2. Worked for Government /Government corporation, 3. Self-employed without any employee, 4. Employer in own family-operated farm or business, 5. Worked with pay on own family-operated farm or business, 6. Worked without pay on own family-operated farm or business.

Links to ICSE: ICSE-1993. Codes 0, 1 and 2 above, refer to ICSE code 1.

Education:

Title of the classification: Philippine Standard Classification of Education (PSCED).

Population groups classified by education: Employed and unemployed persons.

Groups used for classification: Seven groups: 00.No grade completed, 01.Elementary undergraduate, 02.Elementary graduate, 03. High school undergraduate, 04.High school graduate, 05.College undergraduate, 06.College graduate (specification of highest degree completed and field of study).

Links to ISCED: Not available.

Sample size and design:

Ultimate sampling unit: Household.

Sample size (ultimate sampling units): Expanded sample size is 3 416 barangays/enumeration areas (EA) or 40 992 households, for reliable provincial level estimates; Core sample size is 2 247 EAs or26 964 households, at the regional/national level. Use of expanded or core samples depends on budget.

Overall sampling fraction: Approximately 1/250 for urban and 1/400 for rural.

Sample frame: Constructed basically from the results of the 1995 Population Census (POPCEN). The list of barangays serves as the frame for the first stage. The list of EAs in each selected barangays serves as the frame for the second stage, while the list of households in each selected EA serves as the third stage sampling frame.

Updating of the sample: The master sample of EAs is divided into 4 systematic 25 per cent subsamples, identified as subsamples 1, 2, 3, and 4. Listing of households (ideally done yearly or one subsample each quarter) was done in subsample 4 only due to budget limitations. New listings gather information on name of household head, nickname of household head and address.

Rotation:

Scheme: About 25 per cent (one subsample) of the sample households are dropped in each sample EA every quarter and replaced by a new set of sample households from the respective sample areas.

Percentage of units remaining in the sample for two consecutive survey rounds: 75 per cent.
Maximum number of interviews per sample unit: As designed it should be 4 times, but to accommodate all household-based survey requirements, it can be higher than 4.
Length of time for complete renewal of the sample: Generally one year.
Field work:
Type of interview: Personal interview.
Number of ultimate sampling units per sample area: Twelve households per sample barangay.
Duration of field work
Total: Three weeks (for October 2001, from 8-31 October).
Per sample area: Not available.
Survey organization: The regular Statistical Coordination Office, with additional statistical researchers.
Number of field staff: For October 2001: 569 field staff and 285 hired statistical researchers.
Substitution of non-responding ultimate sampling units: Yes, replacement is done for newly rotated panel where dwelling unit/household cannot be located.
Estimation and adjustments:
Total non-response rate: 4.6 per cent for October 2001.
Adjustment for total non-response: Yes.
Imputation for item non-response: No.
Adjustment for areas/population not covered: Not available.
Adjustment for under-coverage: Yes.
Adjustment for over-coverage: Not available.
Adjustment for seasonal variations: Yes, using the X-II Arima method for levels of employment, unemployment and labour force by sex only.
History of the survey:
Title and date of the first survey: Philippine Statistical Survey of Households, 1956.
Significant changes or revisions:
1962: New sampling design adopted, based on the 1960 (POPCEN) results, enabling publication of urban and rural classification at the national level, up to 1969.
1971 (March): New design providing estimates of employment and population characteristics at the regional level. Frequency of the survey increased to quarterly.
1975: New survey, revised sampling design and concepts used for labour force data. Biggest change is the reference period goes from past week to past quarter.
1976: The integration of the Agricultural Survey and the Labour Force Survey with the first survey of the integrated scheme conducted in November. All estimates from the household surveys conducted used the projected population to control fluctuations in the levels of estimates.
1987: The reference period for employment statistics reverts back to the "past week". The first quarter round of 1987 was the last series to use the "past quarter" reference period.
1996: From July 1996, new sample design based on the 1995 Census of Population results.
2000: From October 2000, estimates are based on the 1995 Census Population Projection.
2001: From January, revisions of the survey questionnaire, with the inclusion of questions on other jobs, new entrants, basis of payment and basic pay per day, and implementation of 1994 industrial and 1992 occupational classifications.
Documentation and dissemination:
Documentation:
Survey results: ISH Bulletin (quarterly).
Survey methodology: ISH Bulletin (quarterly).
Dissemination:
Time needed for initial release of survey results: About two months (October 2001 results were released on 15 December 2001).
Advance information of public about date of initial release: Yes.
Availability of unpublished data upon request: Yes.
Availability of data in machine-readable form: Yes.
Website: http://www.census.gov.ph/.

Poland

Title of the survey: The Labour Force Survey.
Organization responsible for the survey:
Planning and conduct of the survey: Central Statistical Office, Labour Statistics Division.
Analysis and publication of the results: Central Statistical Office, Labour Statistics Division.
Topics covered: Employment, unemployment, underemployment, hours of work, wages, duration of employment, duration of unemployment, discouraged workers, occasional workers, industry, occupation, status in employment, educational level, second jobs.
Coverage of the survey:
Geographical: Whole country.
Population groups: All persons aged 15 years and over, who are members of private households selected for the survey, including members absent from the household for less than two months abroad for such reasons as traveling for business, etc. and those absent for more than two months such as sailors, fishermen, etc.
Excluded are:
1. persons living in collective households (e.g., workers' and students' hostels, boarding schools, army barracks, old age pensioners homes, etc.);
2. inmates of penal and mental institutions;
3. member of private households staying for more than two months abroad;
4. temporary guests staying for less than two month in a given household;
5. foreigners.
Availability of estimates from other sources for the excluded areas/groups: Not available.
Groups covered by the survey but excluded from the published results: Not available.
Periodicity:
Conduct of the survey: Continuous.
Publication of results: Quarterly.
Reference periods:
Employment: One week (moving reference period).
Seeking work: Four weeks (the reference week being the 4th week).
Availability for work: Two weeks (the reference period plus the following week).
Concepts and definitions:
Employment: Persons aged 15 years and over who during the reference week:
- performed some work for at least one hour for pay or profit as hired employees, worked on their own farm or ran their own business outside agriculture, helped without pay (contributing family workers) in running a family business outside agriculture;
- did not perform any work for reasons such as sickness, vacation, leave, stoppages in the enterprise, strike, bad weather conditions, etc. but had a formal job
attachment as employee or self-employed (employer or own-account worker).
Also considered as employed are apprentices in paid occupational training or preparation contracts paid by their future employer (whether private
or public) during the contractual training period.
It also includes:
a) persons on temporary lay-off without pay and on unpaid leave initiated by the employer;
b) full and part-time workers seeking other work during the reference week;
c) persons who performed some work for pay or profit during the reference week, but were subject to compulsory schooling or were full or part-time students working full or part-time; were retired and receiving a pension; registered as job seekers at an employment office or receiving unemployment benefits;
d) participants in employment promotion schemes;
e) persons engaged in production of goods for own final use;
f) all members of the armed forces, including persons doing civilian service equivalent to military service.
Unemployment: Persons aged 15 years and over who were not employed by the above criteria during the reference week, were available for work during the reference week or the week which followed, and had actively looked for work for four weeks (the reference period being the fourth week) and been involved in concrete action directed towards finding work. Persons who did not look for work because they had already found it and were waiting to start a new job within a 30-day period are included.
It also includes:
a) persons who were making an effort to establish their own business or private practice;
b) seasonal workers awaiting seasonal work;
c) persons retired and receiving a pension;
d) persons subject to compulsory schooling;
e) full and part-time students seeking full or part-time work.

Underemployment:

Time-related underemployment: Persons working part-time because of economic reasons (e.g. work stoppages, compulsory leave, impossibility to find a full-time job. (Currently work is being carried out to change the definition according to the new ILO Definition.)

Inadequate employment situations: Not applicable.

Hours of work: Actual number of hours worked in all (main and additional) jobs by a person during the reference week.

Employment-related income:

Income from paid employment: Net monthly earnings from full-time paid employment, referring to the main job and relating to the month preceding the reference week.

Income from self-employment: Not applicable.

Informal sector employment: Not applicable.

Usual activity: Not applicable.

Classifications:

Branch of economic activity (industry):

Title of the classification: Not available.

Population groups classified by industry: Employed and unemployed persons.

Number of groups used for coding: 35 groups.

Links to ISIC: ISIC- Rev.3.

Occupation:

Title of the classification: Not available.

Population groups classified by occupation: Employed and unemployed persons.

Number of groups used for coding: 371 groups.

Links to ISCO: ISCO-88.

Status in employment:

Title of the classification: Not available.

Population groups classified by status in employment: Employed and unemployed persons.

Groups used for classification: Four groups: Employee, Employer, Own-account workers, Unpaid family worker.

Links to ICSE: ICSE-1993.

Education:

Title of the classification: Not available.

Population groups classified by education: Employed and unemployed persons.

Groups used for classification: Six groups: Primary school and incomplete primary, basic vocational, general secondary, vocational secondary, post secondary, tertiary.

Links to ISCED: ISCED-76 and ISCED-1997.

Sample size and design:

Ultimate sampling unit: Dwelling.

Sample size (ultimate sampling units): 24,400 dwellings. The total quarterly elementary sample consists of four independent e-samples (for short).

Overall sampling fraction: Differentiated territorial allocation, approximately 1/2,000 registered dwellings for urban areas and 1/1,818 for rural areas.

Sample frame: The sample is derived from the CSO Register of geographical statistical units, enumeration districts (EDs), groups of EDs or census clusters and housing units from the national census. This register is updated annually, taking into consideration information about dwellings newly built, demolished or converted into non-residential one as at the 1st of January.

Updating of the sample: is a consequence of the yearly updating of the frame.

Rotation:

Scheme: Four rotation groups called elementary samples (e-samples for short): in a given quarter, the sample comprises two e-samples surveyed in the previous quarter, one new e-sample introduced into the survey for the first time and one e-sample introduced in the corresponding quarter of the previous year. The quarterly four e-samples rotate according to the 2-(2)-2 scheme, i.e. a housing unit remains two consecutive quarters in a sample, leaves it for two quarters and returns again for another two consecutive quarters before leaving the sample definitively.

Percentage of units remaining in the sample for two consecutive survey rounds: 50 per cent.

Maximum number of interviews per sample unit: 4 times.

Length of time for complete renewal of the sample: 5 quarters.

Field work:

Type of interview: Personal or telephone interviews using paper and pencil.

Number of ultimate sampling units per sample area: 1880 dwellings.

Duration of field work

Total: Not available.

Per sample area: One calendar week.

Survey organization: A permanent survey staff has been created in order to implement the new continuous survey methodology.

Number of field staff: About 300.

Substitution of non-responding ultimate sampling units: No.

Estimation and adjustments:

Total non-response rate: 11.6 per cent.

Adjustment for total non-response: Yes.

Imputation for item non-response: No.

Adjustment for areas/population not covered: Yes.

Adjustment for under-coverage: No.

Adjustment for over-coverage: No.

Adjustment for seasonal variations: No.

History of the survey:

Title and date of the first survey: Labour Force Survey, 1992.

Significant changes or revisions:

The quarterly survey was suspended in 2nd and 3rd quarters 1999. The survey changed from the periodical to a continuous observation as of the 4th quarter 1999.

In May 1994, application of the economic classifications was linked to the international ones.

Documentation and dissemination:

Documentation:

Survey results: Statistical Yearbook of the Republic of Poland. The following publications: Labour Force Survey in Poland, (Information and statistical papers) (in English); Quarterly Information on the Labour Market Developments (in Polish/English); Quarterly Economic Activity of the Population (in Polish); and Economic Activity and Unemployment in Poland (in Polish). (**Periodicity:** quarterly).

Survey methodology: Labour Force Survey in Poland.

Dissemination:

Time needed for initial release of survey results: Same quarter.

Advance information of public about date of initial release: Yes.

Availability of unpublished data upon request: Yes.

Availability of data in machine-readable form: Yes on diskette and by email.

Website: http://www.stat.gov.pl/.

Portugal

Title of the survey: Inquérito ao emprego.

Organization responsible for the survey:

Planning and conduct of the survey: Instituto Nacional de Estatística (INE).

Analysis and publication of the results: Instituto Nacional de Estatística (INE).

Topics covered: Employment, unemployment, underemployment, hours of work, income, duration of employment and unemployment, discouraged workers, occasional workers, second jobs, industry, occupation, status in employment, education.

Coverage of the survey:

Geographical: Whole country.

Population groups: Resident non-institutional population aged 15 years and over living in private dwellings. Excluded are persons living in collective houses if they have not family links with the private households and those living in mobile homes.

Availability of estimates from other sources for the excluded areas/groups: Not applicable.

Groups covered by the survey but excluded from the published results: Not covered.

Periodicity:

Conduct of the survey: Continuous survey.

Publication of results: Quarterly.

Reference periods:

Employment: The week preceding the interview.

Seeking work: Four weeks preceding the interview.

Availability for work: Two weeks after the interview.

Concepts and definitions:

Employment: Employed are all those, aged 15 years and over who, during the reference week:

a) had worked for earnings or benefits (in cash or in kind) for at least one hour;

b) while not working, they had a job and maintain a formal link with it;

c) owned a business but were absent from work for a certain reason;

d) were pre-retired but were working during the reference week.

Also included in the employed are:

a) persons with a job but temporarily absent due to illness or injury, during 3 months maximum, annual leave, maternity/paternity or parental leave, education or training leave, labour management dispute, bad weather, mechanical breakdown;

b) on unpaid leave initiated by the employer or on lay-off with or without pay during 3 months maximum;
c) full or part-time workers seeking other work during the reference period;
d) persons who performed some work for pay or profit during the reference week while subject to compulsory schooling, retired and receiving a pension, registered as jobseekers at an employment office or receiving unemployment benefits;
e) full and part-time students working full or part-time;
f) paid apprentices and trainees;
g) participants in employment promotion schemes;
h) unpaid family workers;
i) seasonal workers, if the season is starting within 3 months;
j) volunteers and career members of the armed forces.
Unemployment: Persons aged 15 years and over who were not working during the reference week, were available for work within two weeks, were seeking work (i.e. had taken specific steps to seek employment) during the last four weeks or were not working nor searching but have found a job to start within 3 months.
Are also included in the unemployed:
a) persons who were seeking and/or available for work while being subject to compulsory schooling or retired and receiving a pension;
b) full and part-time students seeking full or part-time work and immediately available for work.
Specific steps to find a job are as following: contacts with public employment office or private agency (temporary work agency, firm specialized in recruitment, etc.); applications to employers; seeking assistance from friends, relatives, unions, etc.; placing, answering or studying job advertisements; taking a recruitment test or examination or being interviewed; looking for land, premises or equipment; applying for permits, licences or financial resources.
Underemployment:
Time-related underemployment: Employed persons aged 15 years and over who, during the reference week, were willing to work additional hours (looking for additional job to current job(s), another job with more hours than in current job(s) or more hours in current job(s)) and were available to work additional hours.
Inadequate employment situations: Working conditions such as education level, remuneration, that, compared to others, may lead to a reduction of competence or productivity of workers.
Hours of work: Actual hours in main and second jobs: number of hours actually worked during the reference week, including overtime but excluding absences. Usual hours in main job: number of hours usually worked per week, including usual overtime.
Employment-related income:
Income from paid employment: Net earnings of employees: monthly earnings for regular payments and annual amounts for others.
Income from self-employment: Not applicable.
Informal sector: Not applicable.
Usual activity: No information.
Classifications:
Branch of economic activity (industry):
Title of the classification: NACE.
Population groups classified by industry: Employed and unemployed (industry of last job for the unemployed).
Number of groups used for coding: No information.
Links to ISIC: ISIC-Rev. 3.
Occupation:
Title of the classification: National Classification of Occupations (CNP 1994).
Population groups classified by occupation: Employed and unemployed (occupation of last job for the unemployed).
Number of groups used for coding: No information.
Links to ISCO: ISCO-88.
Status in employment:
Title of the classification: No information.
Population groups classified by status in employment: Employed and unemployed (status of last job for the unemployed).
Groups used for classification: Employees; employers with employees; own-account without employees; unpaid family workers; others.
Links to ICSE: ICSE-1993.
Education:
Title of the classification: No information.
Population groups classified by education: Employed and unemployed.
Groups used for classification: 10 groups.
Links to ISCED: No information.

Sample size and design:
Ultimate sampling unit: Dwellings.
Sample size (ultimate sampling units): 20,747 dwellings.
Overall sampling fraction: 0.68 per cent.
Sample frame: Results of the 1989 Electoral Census and the "Geographical Spatial Reference Framework" used for the 1991 Census of Population and Housing.
Updating of the sample: No information.
Rotation:
Scheme: Dwellings remain in the sample for six consecutive quarters. Each quarter one-sixth of the sample is replaced.
Percentage of units remaining in the sample for two consecutive survey rounds: 83.3 per cent.
Maximum number of interviews per sample unit: Six.
Length of time for complete renewal of the sample: Six quarters.
Field work:
Type of interview: Computer assisted personal interviews (CAPI).
Number of ultimate sampling units per sample area: No information.
Duration of field work:
Total: Continuous survey.
Per sample area: No information.
Survey organization: Interviewers are recruited for each survey.
Number of field staff: No information.
Substitution of non-responding ultimate sampling units: No.
Estimation and adjustments:
Total non-response rate: 10 per cent.
Adjustment for total non-response: No.
Imputation for item non-response: No.
Adjustment for areas/population not covered: No.
Adjustment for undercoverage: No.
Adjustment for overcoverage: No.
Adjustment for seasonal variations: No.
History of the survey:
Title and date of the first survey: Inquérito ao emprego 1974.
Significant changes or revisions: 1983-1997: quarterly survey. Beginning 1998: continuous survey, sample design revised and modifications of the survey questionnaire.
Documentation and dissemination:
Documentation
Survey results: Boletim Mensal de Estatística (monthly); Estatísticas de Emprego (quarterly).
Survey methodology: Estatísticas de Emprego (quarterly).
Dissemination
Time needed for initial release of survey results: About 2 months after the end of the quarter.
Advance information of public about date of initial release: Yes.
Availability of unpublished data upon request: Yes.
Availability of data in machine-readable form: Yes.
Website: http://www.ine.pt/.

Qatar

Title of the survey: Labour force sample survey, April 2001.
Organization responsible for the survey:
Planning and conduct of the survey: Department of Statistics, Planning Council
Analysis and publication of the results: Department of Statistics, and Department of Social Planning, Planning Council.
Topics covered: Current employment and unemployment status of the working age Qatari and non-Qatari population. Earnings, hours and pattern of work of the employed population. Educational level, current or last occupation, branch of economic activity, status in employment, sector of employment, and duration of job tenure of the currently employed and the unemployed with past work experience. Duration and methods of job search currently used by the unemployed to seek work, and previously used by the employed to obtain their current jobs. Participation in training programmes and reason for not seeking work in the private and mixed sectors by the Qatari unemployed.
Reason for economic inactivity of the population not currently in the labour force.
Coverage of the survey:
Geographical: Entire nation.
Population groups: All resident Qatari and non-Qatari persons living in non-institutional households. Also included are non-Qatari persons living in compounds and collective households.
Availability of estimates from other sources for the excluded areas/groups: NA.

Groups covered by the survey but excluded from the published results: Labour force measurement addresses population 12 years old and over, but due to the insignificant size of the reported labour force between the ages of 12 and 14, the published results are limited to the population 15 years old and over. Data on the omitted youth population are however available.
Periodicity:
Conduct of the survey: Occasional
Publication of results: Not yet published.
Reference periods:
Employment: Fixed reference week. From 24 to 30 March 2001.
Seeking work: Active job search of the unemployed during previous month. The information is, however, not used for classification of the respondent as unemployed. **Availability for work:** Availability for work is not explicitly tested in the questionnaire.
Concepts and definitions:
Employment: Persons, 12 years old and over, who were engaged in any work, at least for one hour on any day during the survey week, or had a formal job attachment but were temporarily absent from work, with or without leave, for any reason during the survey week. Work is defined broadly in terms of work for pay, profit or family gain.
Unemployment: Persons, 12 years old and over, who did not work even for one hour during the survey week, nor were temporary absence from work with a formal job attachment, and who reported to not find a job during the survey week.
Underemployment:
Time-related underemployment: Not explicitly defined, but time-related underemployment may be derived on the basis of two questions: Employed persons who worked less than 6 days during the survey week because of lack of job opportunities in the other days of the week.
Inadequate employment situations: Not applicable.
Hours of work: Three concepts: Number of days actually worked during the survey week. Number of actual hours worked during the survey week including overtime. Normal weekly hours of work. Actual hours worked covers total hours spent at work including overtime, time spent for maintenance, waiting time, and short break periods. It excludes hours paid but not worked, mealtime, and commuting time.
Employment-related income:
Income from paid employment: Total earnings of employees during the last payment period. The payment period may be daily, weekly, or monthly. Earning is defined as gross total take-home pay, including basic salaries overtime pay, bonuses, special compensation in relation to nature of work, housing allowances, family allowances, transportation cost, food, and other in-kind subsidies.
Income from self-employment: Not applicable.
Informal sector: No information.
Usual activity: No information.
Classifications:
The classifications used in the 2001 Qatar labour force survey are those developed for the March 1997 population and housing census.
Branch of economic activity (industry):
Title of the classification: The National Standard Classification of Economic Activities (May 1996).
Population groups classified by industry: Employed and unemployed persons with previous work experience.
Number of groups used for coding: 4-digit level. Results published at the 1-digit level.18 categories.
Linked to ISIC: ISIC- Rev. 3.
Occupation:
Title of the classification: The Standard Classification of Occupations (May 1996).
Population groups classified by occupation: Employed and unemployed persons with previous work experience.
Number of groups used for coding: 4-digit level, and the results are to be published at the 1-digit level.
Linked to ISCO: ISCO-88.
Status in employment:
Title of the classification: No information.
Population groups classified by status in employment: Employed persons only.
List of groups: Employer. Own-account worker. Employee. Unpaid family worker. Other.
Linked to ICSE: ICSE-1966.
Education:
Title of the classification: No information.
Population groups classified by educational level: Population 10 years old and above.
List of groups: Coding at the 5-digit level, and the results to be published at the 1-digit level for educational level. Also, 5-digit details on specialization for the population with secondary education or higher.
Linked to ISCED: ISCED 1977.
Sample size and design:
Ultimate sampling unit: Households.
Sample size (ultimate sampling units): 1'956 Qatari households, 1'892 Non-Qatari households and 4'287 Collective households.
Overall sampling fraction: 5%.
Sample frame: Enumeration areas of the 1997 Population and housing census 1997. Two-stage sampling. Primary Sampling Units (PSUs) are formed by grouping contiguous census blocks (enumeration areas) such that each PSU contains at least 25 Ultimate Sampling Units (households in the case of Qatari and Non-Qatari households, and individuals in the case of collective households). In order to respect to the extent possible the administrative structure of Qatar, the number of PSUs that cut across administrative zones is minimized and those cutting municipality boundaries are avoided altogether. For practical purposes, very large PSUs of the collective households strata were divided into parts.
The PSUs are sampled in proportion to their size, measured in terms of number households in the case of the first two strata and in terms of individual persons in the case of the third strata. The size measures are determined according to the 1997 census In the second stage, 20 households are selected in each sample PSU. In the case of collective households: primary sampling units are urban or rural sample PSU.
At the second stage, in each PSU a sample of 20 households are selected in the two strata of Qatari and Non-Qatari households, according to a systematic sampling scheme. In the case of the Collective households, 50 persons were systematically selected in each listing of the sampled PSUs.
Updating of the sample: Updating at listing stage of the sampled PSUs.
Rotation: None.
Field work:
Type of interview: Personal interview.
Number of ultimate sampling units per sample area: About 20 households in the case of Qatari and Non-Qatari households, and 50 individuals in the case of Collective households.
Duration of fieldwork:
Total: Listing of PSUs during February 2001. Interviewing during April 2001.
Per sample area: 3 to 4 households per day in the case of Qatari and Non-Qatari households, and about 20 to 24 persons per day in the case of Collective households.
Survey organization: Ad-hoc.
Number of field staff: About 64 interviewers and 15 supervisors.
Substitution of non-responding sampling units: No.
Estimation and adjustments:
Total non-response rate: 3.6% in Qatari households and 1.3% in On-Qatari households.
Adjustment for total non-response: Yes, by inverse of rate of response within strata.
Imputation for item non-response: Yes, Group means.
Adjustment for areas/population not covered: No.
Adjustment for under-coverage: Yes, by ratio-estimation to projected populations of Qataris and Non-Qataris. Also, by Generalized Least Squares to sex and age distribution of 1997 Census results for Qatari population.
Adjustment for over-coverage: Not available.
Adjustment for seasonal variations: No.
History of the survey:
Title and date of the first survey: Labour force sample survey, 1993.
Significant changes or revisions: The 2001 Qatar labour force survey follows a series of limited household surveys conducted in 1984, 1989 and 1993. The 1984 and 1989 surveys were household income and expenditure surveys with limited information on the employment characteristics of the population. The 1993 survey was a labour force survey, but the results were not published.
Documentation and dissemination:
Documentation:
Survey results: Forthcoming. December 2001.
Survey methodology: Forthcoming. December 2001.
Dissemination:
Time needed for initial release of survey results: 8 months.
Advance information of public about date of initial release: No.
Availability of unpublished data upon request: Yes.
Availability of data in machine-readable form: Tabulated data available in diskettes on request.

Romania

Title of the survey: Household Labour Force Survey (AMIGO).
Organization responsible for the survey:
Planning and conduct of the survey: National Institute for Statistics (NIS).
Analysis and publication of the results: National Institute for Statistics (NIS).
Topics covered: Employment, unemployment, underemployment, hours of work, duration of unemployment, discouraged workers, industry, occupation, status in employment, educational level, second jobs.
Coverage of the survey:
Geographical: Whole country.
Population groups: All permanent residents living in households selected for the survey, including those temporarily absent for a period longer than six months if they are permanently in touch with their family, such as conscripts, students and school children who study away from their place of permanent residence, persons working in localities other than their permanent residence, temporary inmates of penal and mental institutions and persons in hospital as well as those undergoing rehabilitation treatment. Persons living permanently in common units, such as specialized institutions, old-age pensioners' homes, establishments for handicapped persons, sanatoriums, etc. are excluded.
Availability of estimates from other sources for the excluded areas/groups: Not available.
Groups covered by the survey but excluded from the published results: Not available.
Periodicity:
Conduct of the survey: Quarterly continuous survey.
Publication of results: Quarterly and annual.
Reference periods:
Employment: One week (moving reference period):
Seeking work: Past four weeks.
Availability for work: Next fifteen days.
Concepts and definitions:
Employment: Comprises all people aged 15 years and over who have carried out an economic or social activity producing goods or services with a duration of one hour at least during the reference period (one week), with a view to achieve certain incomes in the form of salaries, in kind remuneration or other benefits. Also considered as employed are persons temporarily absent from work preserving their formal relations with the working place, and members of the armed forces (active staff and conscripts). For the self-employed and unpaid family workers in agriculture, the minimum duration of work during the reference week is 15 hours.
It includes:
a) persons with a job but temporarily absent due to illness/injury, vacation/ annual leave, statutory maternity leave, parental leave, study leave, professional training and vocational courses, strike or dispute, temporary stoppages due to bad weather conditions, mechanical breakdown, shortage of raw materials or energy, technical incidents, etc.;
b) persons on lay-off who continue to receive at least 50 per cent of their wage or salary from their employer or have an assurance of return to work within a period of three months;
c) persons on long-term absence from work (three months and over) if they continue to receive at least 50 per cent of their wage or salary from their employer;
d) full or part-time workers seeking another job;
e) persons who performed some work for pay or profit during the reference week, while being subject to compulsory schooling, or retired and receiving a pension, even if registered as job-seekers at an employment office or receiving unemployment benefits;
f) full and part-time students working full or part-time;
g) paid apprentices and trainees;
h) unpaid family workers temporarily absent during the reference week and seasonal workers not at work during the off-season (unless they are actively seeking and available for work in which case they are considered as unemployed).
Unemployment: Persons aged 15 years and over who during the reference period were without work (did not have a job and were not carrying out an activity with a view to achieving an income), available to start work within 15 days and were actively seeking work by various methods during the last four weeks.
It includes:
a) persons who found a job staring within a period of at most three months;
b) persons on lay-off who do not receive any significant wage and salary (less than 50 per cent) from their employer and who are currently available for work and actively seeking work;
c) seasonal workers during the off-season if they are currently available for work and actively seeking work.
Underemployment:
Time-related underemployment: Persons with a job who have worked less than the usual working duration irrespective of their willingness, and are wishing a full-time activity or a complementary job and are available to work more hours in the next 15 days.
Inadequate employment situations: Not applicable.
Hours of work:
Usual hours of work is the duration of a typical working week including overtime hours, if worked systematically, in contrast to the hours set by collective working contract or by other conventions or agreements.
Hours actually worked are hours in the main job only during the reference week, including overtime hours not systematically worked and may be higher, equal or less than usual hours.
Employment-related income:
Income from paid employment: Not applicable.
Income from self-employment: Not applicable.
Informal sector employment: Not applicable.
Usual activity: Main activity status refers the self-appreciation of each person on her/his activity status during the last three months.
Classifications:
Branch of economic activity (industry):
Title of the classification: CANE (Classification of All Activities of National Economy).
Population groups classified by industry: Employed and unemployed persons (industry of last job for the unemployed).
Number of groups used for coding: 17 groups.
Links to ISIC: ISIC-Rev. 3.
Occupation:
Title of the classification: CORE (Classification of Occupations in Romania).
Population groups classified by occupation: Employed and unemployed persons (occupation of last job for the unemployed).
Number of groups used for coding: 10 groups.
Links to ISCO: ISCO-88.
Status in employment:
Title of the classification: Not available.
Population groups classified by status in employment: Employed and unemployed persons (status of last job for the unemployed).
Groups used for classification: Five groups: Employee, Self-employed with employees (Employer), Self-employed without employees (Own-account worker), Unpaid family worker, Member of an agricultural holding or co-operative.
Links to ICSE: ICSE-1993.
Education:
Title of the classification: Not available.
Population groups classified by education: Employed and unemployed persons.
Groups used for classification: Five groups: With no education, Primary education (2 sub-groups), Vocational education (2 sub-groups), High-school education (2 sub-groups), University education (2 sub-groups).
Links to ISCED: ISCED-1997.
Sample size and design:
Ultimate sampling unit: Dwelling (with all component households).
Sample size (ultimate sampling units): 18 036 dwellings located in the selected geographic areas.
Overall sampling fraction: At the first sampling stage, 0.0331 for rural areas and 0.0325 for urban areas.
Sample frame: Designed during 1992-1993, based on the January 1992 Population and Housing Census results as a master sample (EMZOT) of 501 geographical areas (about 250 000 dwellings). These areas are considered the Primary sampling units (PSUs) in the 1st stage of the sampling design for all the household surveys; 259 PSUs in urban areas and 242 in rural areas. In the second stage Housing units were systematically selected within each PSU.
Updating of the sample: The EMZOT master sample is regularly updated.
Rotation:
Scheme: The rotation sample is designed on the 2-(2)-2 pattern. Thus four rotation groups or sub-samples are identified. A dwelling is included in the sample for two consecutive quarters, leaves it for two quarters and returns again for another two consecutive quarters before leaving the sample forever.

Percentage of units remaining in the sample for two consecutive survey rounds: 50 per cent.
Maximum number of interviews per sample unit: Four per ultimate sampling unit.
Length of time for complete renewal of the sample: A dwelling is managed for 6 quarters.
Field work:
Type of interview: Face to face, using paper and pencil.
Number of ultimate sampling units per sample area: 36 dwellings per quarter.
Duration of field work:
Total: The reference weeks are evenly spread throughout the whole year (52 weeks). Interviewing is the week following the reference week.
Per sample area: One calendar week.
Survey organization: A permanent survey organization.
Number of field staff: 501 interviewers, 140 supervisors and 47 responsible officers.
Substitution of non-responding ultimate sampling units: No..
Estimation and adjustments:
Total non-response rate: 6.2 per cent (in the third quarter 2001 for example).
Adjustment for total non-response: Yes.
Imputation for item non-response: Yes, using the Hot-deck, Cold-deck method.
Adjustment for areas/population not covered: Not available.
Adjustment for under-coverage: Yes.
Adjustment for over-coverage: Yes.
Adjustment for seasonal variations: No.
History of the survey:
Title and date of the first survey: Household Labour Force Survey (AMIGO) - March 1992.
Significant changes or revisions: Up to 1996, the survey was annual and covered persons aged 14 years old and over. Beginning with the first quarter of 1999, the underemployment concept complies with the provisions of the 16th International Conference of Labour Statisticians (1998). Beginning with the first quarter of 2002, the employment, unemployment and main activity status concepts comply with the provisions agreed by the Commission Regulation (EC) N° 1897/2000 and N° 1575/2000.
Documentation and dissemination:
Documentation:
Survey results: Household Labour Force Survey (AMIGO) - detailed report; - quick report; Statistical Yearbook (NIS); Quarterly Bulletin (NIS).
Survey methodology: idem.
Dissemination:
Time needed for initial release of survey results: Approximately one quarter.
Advance information of public about date of initial release: No.
Availability of unpublished data upon request: Yes.
Availability of data in machine-readable form: Yes on diskette.
Website: http://www.insse.ro/.

Russian Federation

Title of the survey: Population Sample Survey of Employment
Organization responsible for the survey:
Planning and conduct of the survey: State Committee of the Russian Federation on Statistics.
Analysis and publication of the results: State Committee of the Russian Federation on Statistics.
Topics covered: Employment, unemployment, underemployment, hours of work, employment in the informal sector, duration of unemployment, discouraged workers, occasional workers, industry, occupation, status in employment, educational level, second jobs and persons involved in production of products and goods in individual subsidiary farming plots.
Coverage of the survey:
Geographical: Whole country with the exception of the Chechen Republic (during military actions).
Population groups: All the population aged 15-72 years living in households. Excluded is institutional population and persons absent from households for six months and longer.
Availability of estimates from other sources for the excluded areas/groups: None.
Groups covered by the survey but excluded from the published results: None.
Periodicity:
Conduct of the survey: Quarterly.
Publication of results: Quarterly.
Reference periods:
Employment: One week (fixed week - last week of the second month of each quarter, i.e. that of February, May, August and November).
Seeking work: Four weeks prior to the reference week.
Availability for work: Two weeks following the reference week.
Concepts and definitions:
Employment: Persons aged 15-72 years who, during the reference week, did any work at all as paid employees, in their own business, profession, or on their own farm, or who worked at least one hour or more as unpaid family workers in an enterprise operated by a family member, as well as all those who were not working but who had jobs or businesses from which they were temporarily absent because of illness, bad weather, vacation, advance qualification training, labour-management disputes, or personal reasons, whether they were paid for the time off or were seeking other jobs.
Also included in the totals are:
a)full- and part-time workers seeking other work during the reference period;
b)full- and part-time students working full- or part-time;
c)persons who performed some work during the reference week while being either retired and receiving a pension; or were registered as job seekers at an employment office or receiving unemployment benefits;
d)paid and unpaid family workers (if they worked at least one hour);
e)private domestic servants;
f)members of producers' co-operatives;
g)members of the armed forces living in households.
Each employed person is counted only once. Those who held more than one job are counted in the job which they consider to be the major one.
Excluded are persons whose only activity consisted of work around the house (painting, repairing, or own housework); volunteer work for religious, charitable and similar organizations and unpaid apprentices and trainees. They are considered as unemployed or not economically active.
Unemployment: Unemployed persons are all civilians who had no employment during the reference week, were available for work, except for temporary illness, and who had made specific steps to find employment.
Note: Temporarily not working paid/unpaid family workers are considered to be unemployed or not economically active depending on whether or not they were seeking work during the reference week.
Also included in the unemployed are full- and part-time students, pensioners and invalids provided they are seeking work and are currently available for work (if they are seeking work for some future date, such as for the summer months, they are considered inactive). Persons staying on unpaid administrative leave for 6 months and more are classified as unemployed or not economically active.
Underemployment:
Time-related underemployment: Persons who, during the reference week, worked less number of hours than established for a given category of occupation or job, provided they were looking for and available to perform some additional work.
Inadequate employment situations: Not applicable.
Hours of work: Usual and actual hours worked in the main and secondary job(s).
Employment-related income:
Income from paid employment: Not applicable.
Income from self-employment: Not applicable.
Informal sector: Information on the informal sector is provided to the extent that survey respondents report on their activities.
Usual activity: Not applicable.
Classifications:
Branch of economic activity (industry):
Title of the classification: National ISIC Rev. 3 compatible classification.
Population groups classified by industry: Employed persons and unemployed persons with previous job experience.
Number of groups used for coding: 17.
Links to ISIC: ISIC-Rev. 3 (4 digit level).
Occupation:
Title of the classification: National ISCO-88 compatible classification.
Population groups classified by occupation: Employed persons and unemployed persons with previous work experience.
Number of groups used for coding: 31 (first and second levels).
Links to ISCO: ISCO-88 (4 digit level).
Status in employment:
Title of the classification: ICSE-1993 is used.

Population groups classified by status in employment: Employed persons (main and secondary jobs).
Groups used for classification: 5 groups (employees, employers, own-account worker, members of producers co-operatives, unpaid family workers).
Links to ICSE: ICSE-1993.
Education:
Title of the classification: National Classification.
Population groups classified by education: all population groups.
Groups used for classification: 8 groups (without primary general, primary general, secondary, secondary general, primary vocational, secondary vocational; not completed higher; higher (university).
Links to ISCED: No.
Sample size and design:
Ultimate sampling unit: Household.
Sample size (ultimate sampling units): About 65 000 persons per quarter and some 240 000 persons annually.
Overall sampling fraction: 0.24 per cent.
Sample frame: The sample is built up automatically at the Federal level on the basis of the 1994 micro-census list of households.
Updating of the sample: Annually.
Rotation:
Scheme: 100 per cent rotation from one quarter to another.
A household can return to the sample and be interviewed for the second time after two years.
Field work:
Type of interview: Paper and pencil.
Number of ultimate sampling units per sample area: 60 persons per enumeration district.
Duration of field work:
Total: Two calendar weeks following the reference week (14 days).
Per sample area: No information provided.
Survey organization: The survey is organized as a face-to-face interview. The interviewers are temporarily employed for the duration of the survey. Data entry and logical control are carried out at the Regional (oblast) level, after which the primary data are transferred to the Federal Level (State Statistics Committee). It is at the Federal level that the micro-data base is constructed, data processing takes place, weights are adjusted and relevant variable produced to classify the population by economic activity status.
Number of field staff: Approximately 1 100 interviewers and 130 supervisors.
Substitution of non-responding ultimate sampling units: Yes.
Estimation and adjustments:
Total non-response rate: 4.5 per cent.
Adjustment for total non-response: No.
Imputation for item non-response: No.
Adjustment for areas/population not covered: No.
Adjustment for undercoverage: No.
Adjustment for overcoverage: No.
Adjustment for seasonal variations: Yes.
History of the survey:
Title and date of the first survey: Population Sample Survey of Employment, October 1992.
Significant changes or revisions: Since 1999 the survey has been conducted quarterly.
Documentation and dissemination:
Documentation:
Survey results: "Obsliedovaniye naseleniya po problemam zaniytosty" (Population Sample Survey of Employment) - quarterly, "Rossijsky statistichesky yezhegodnik" (Statistical Yearbook of Russia) – annual, "Trud I zanis tost v Rossijskoj Federatsii" (Labour and Employment in the Russian Federation) – every 2 years, "Statisticheskoye obozrieniye" (Statistical Review) – quarterly.
Survey methodology: "Obsliedovaniye naseleniya po problemam zaniytosty" (Population Sample Survey of Employment) - quarterly, "Metodologichskiye poplozheniya, No. 3" (Methodological descriptions).
Dissemination:
Time needed for initial release of survey results: 3 months following the reference week.
Advance information of public about date of initial release: YES.
Availability of unpublished data upon request: YES.
Availability of data in machine-readable form: Diskettes and internet (selected).
Website: http://www.gks.ru/.

Saudi Arabia

Title of the survey: Labour force survey.
Organization responsible for the survey:
Planning and conduct of the survey: Central Department of Statistics, Ministry of Planning
Analysis and publication of the results: Central Department of Statistics, Ministry of Planning
Topics covered: Employment, unemployment, hours of work, industry, occupation, status in employment, education level, secondary jobs, and work experience.
Coverage of the survey:
Geographical: Whole country.
Population groups: Nomads and persons living in collective quarters are excluded.
Availability of estimates from other sources for the excluded areas/groups: No information is provided.
Groups covered by the survey but excluded from the published results: None.
Periodicity:
Conduct of the survey: Annual.
Publication of results: Annual.
Reference periods:
Employment: Fixed reference week.
Seeking work: Four weeks.
Availability for work: Reference week.
Concepts and definitions:
Employment: Persons, 12 years old and over, who worked for pay or profit or without pay or profit on family farm or business during most of the week (Saturday through Friday) preceding enumeration, or who had a job but were sick or on vacation during the reference week. Such persons must be on the payroll and expecting to report back to work after the vacation or sickness.
It includes:
a) Persons who performed some work for pay or profit during the reference week but were subject to compulsory schooling, retired and receiving a pension, or were registered as jobseekers at an employment office or were seeking other work during the reference week.
b) Part-time students working full or part-time.
c) Paid apprentices and trainees.
d) Unpaid family workers, unpaid apprentices, and persons doing volunteer community or social service work who worked more than 15 hours during the reference week.
e) Persons engaged in production of goods for own final use.
f) Volunteer and career members of the armed forces as well as persons engaged in civil service equivalent to military service.
Excluded are:
a) Full-time students working full or part-time.
b) Unpaid apprentices and trainees, persons engaged in production of services for their household.
c) Unpaid family workers temporarily absent from work during the reference week and seasonal workers not at work during the off-season.
d) Persons on educational or training leave.
Unemployment: Persons, 12 years old and over, not employed during the reference week, who were actively looking for work during the previous four weeks, and were available for work during the reference week. [Active job search appears to be tested after determining the unemployment status of the persons.]
It includes:
a) Persons without work and current available and looking for work who had made arrangements to start a new job on a date subsequent to the reference week.
b) Persons without work and currently available and looking for work who were trying to establish their own enterprise.
c) Full or part-time students seeking full or part-time work.
d) Persons who were seeking or available for work but were subject to compulsory schooling or retired and receiving a pension.
Excluded are:
a) Persons on temporary or indefinite lay-off without pay if they had not been seeking work or available for work.
b) Persons who were seeking and/or available for work but were subject to compulsory schooling or were retired and receiving a pension.
c) Full or part-time students seeking full or part-time work..
Underemployment:
Time-related underemployment: No information.
Inadequate employment situations: No information.
Hours of work: No information
Employment-related income:
Income from paid employment: No information.
Income from self-employment: No information.
Informal sector: No information.

Usual activity: No information.
Classifications:
Branch of economic activity (industry):
Title of the classification: No information.
Population groups classified by industry: Employed only.
Number of groups used for coding: 16 categories.
Linked to ISIC: At the fourth level.
Occupation:
Title of the classification: No information.
Population groups classified by occupation: Employed only.
Number of groups used for coding: 9 major groups.
Linked to ISCO: At the third level.
Status in employment:
Title of the classification: Not applicable.
Population groups classified by status in employment: Not applicable.
Groups used for classification: Not applicable.
Links to ICSE: Not applicable.
Education:
Title of classification used: No information.
Population groups classified by education: Employed and unemployed persons.
Groups used for classification: Illiterate. Can read and write. Elementary. Intermediate. Secondary. Pre-University Diploma. BA or BSc MA. And Ph.D.
Linked to ISCED: At the first level.
Sample size and design:
Ultimate sampling unit: Household.
Sample size (ultimate sampling units): 750 Primary sampling units (PSUs).
Overall sampling fraction: 4%.
Sample frame: Population Census 1993 excluding nomads and persons living in collective quarters.
Updating of the sample: Updating of the main sample in 1998.
Rotation:
Scheme: The main sample is divided into four panels. Each survey sample covers 3 panels.
Percentage of units (PSUs) remaining in the sample for two consecutive survey rounds: 50%.
Maximum number of interviews per sample unit: 5.
Length of time for complete renewal of the sample: 5 years.
Field work:
Type of interview: Personal interview.
Number of ultimate sampling units per sample area: 20 households per PSU. **Duration of fieldwork:**
Total: 20 days for 24 May to 13 June 1999.
Per sample area: 4 days in urban areas; 5 days in rural areas.
Survey organization: Permanent.
Number of field staff: About 320 interviewers, 80 crew leaders and 13 supervisors.
Substitution of non-responding sampling units: No.
Estimation and adjustments:
Total non-response rate: 9%.
Adjustment for total non-response: Yes.
Imputation for item non-response: No.
Adjustment for areas/population not covered: Yes.
Adjustment for under-coverage: No information provided.
Adjustment for over-coverage: No information provided.
Adjustment for seasonal variations: No.
History of the survey:
Title and date of the first survey: Labour Force Survey, 1981.
Significant changes or revisions: The survey programme breaks from 1987 to 1999.
Documentation and dissemination:
Documentation:
Survey results: Labour Force in the Kingdom of Saudi Arabia.
Survey methodology: Labour Force in the Kingdom of Saudi Arabia.
Dissemination:
Time needed for initial release of survey results: May 1987.
Advance information of public about date of initial release: Yes.
Availability of unpublished data upon request: Yes
Availability of data in machine-readable form: Yes.

Seychelles

Title of the survey: Labour Force Survey (LFS).
Organization responsible for the survey:
Planning and conduct of the survey: Management and Information Systems Division (MISD), Ministry of Information Technology & Communication.
Analysis and publication of the results: MISD.
Topics covered: Persons currently and usually economically active, employed and unemployed; persons currently in time-related underemployment or in inadequate employment situations and persons currently outside the labour force. Persons usually employed with and without some unemployment, persons usually unemployed with some employment and persons usually not economic active (distinguishing students, home duties, too old, sick and disabled). Hours of work. Informal sector employment. Duration of employment and unemployment. Discouraged workers. Second jobs. Industry, occupation, status in employment, education/training levels.
Coverage of the survey:
Geographical: Three principal islands: Mahé, Praslin and La Digue.
Population groups: Population of age 15 years resident in households.
Availability of estimates from other sources for the excluded areas/groups: Not applicable.
Groups covered by the survey but excluded from the published results: None.
Periodicity:
Conduct of the survey: Occasional, i.e. 18.8-17.9 1992.
Publication of results: Occasional, no information about release date for first results.
Reference periods:
Employment: One week prior to the date of the interview.
Seeking work: Four weeks.
Availability for work: Four weeks.
Concepts and definitions:
Employment: Persons who a) performed some work for pay or profit during the reference week; b) were temporarily absent from work during the reference week because of illness or leave, but were definitely going to return (including to seasonal work after off-season ended), or c) were engaged in production of goods for own final use. Excluded are unpaid family workers in family business. Some work is defined as 1 hour or more during the reference week.
Unemployment: Persons who were currently without work and available for work, and who had searched for work during the last four weeks, as well as persons who had not looked for work because they thought no work was available or were waiting for reply to previous inquiries or were waiting to start work.
Underemployment:
Time-related underemployment: Persons working less than 35 hours who said they were available to work more hours and did not for economic reasons.
Inadequate employment situations: No information provided.
Hours of work: No information provided.
Employment-related income:
Income from paid employment: Not applicable.
Income from self-employment: Not applicable.
Informal sector: Those unregistered enterprises (determined by name of enterprise) in the private sector (cooperatives included) with less than five persons employed and which operate from the home of the respondent, a market stall or from some temporary location.
Usual activity: Economically active for 6 months or more during the 12 months reference period and employed for most of that time.
Classifications:
Branch of economic activity (industry):
Title of the classification: No name given.
Population groups classified by industry: Employed and unemployed persons (industry of last job for the unemployed).
Number of groups used for coding: 26.
Links to ISIC: ISIC- Rev. 3.
Occupation:
Title of the classification: No name given.
Population groups classified by occupation: Employed and unemployed persons (occupation of last job for the unemployed).
Number of groups used for coding: 35.
Links to ISCO: ISCO-88.
Status in employment:
Title of the classification: National classification.
Population groups classified by status in employment: Employed and unemployed persons (status of last job for the unemployed)..
Groups used for classification: Government employees; para-statal employees; private sector employees; co-operative employees; self-employed; employers and the unpaid family workers.
Links to ICSE: ICSE-1993.
Education:
Title of the classification: National classification.
Population groups classified education: Employed and unemployed persons.

Groups used for classification: No schooling; P1-P6; FI-FII, P7-P8, S1-S2; FIII, P9, S3; FIV, S4, NYS; Vocational; Poly1-2, TTC; Poly3-4, FVI; Pre-university; University.
Links to ISCED: ISCED-1976.
Sample size and design:
Ultimate sampling unit: Household.
Sample size (ultimate sampling units): 800.
Overall sampling fraction: 6 percent.
Sample frame: The 1987 Population Census.
Updating of the sample frame: 1991.
Rotation scheme:
Scheme: Not applicable.
Percentage of units remaining in the sample for two consecutive survey rounds: Not applicable.
Maximum number of interviews per sample unit: Not applicable.
Length of time for complete renewal of the sample: Not applicable.
Field work:
Type of interview: Personal interviews, paper and pencil.
Number of ultimate sampling units per sample area: No information.
Duration of field work:
Total: One month, with two extra weeks for replacements.
Per sample area: No information.
Survey organization: Permanent.
Number of field staff: 6 interviewers and 3 supervisors.
Substitution of non-responding ultimate sampling units: Some refusals, non-respondents and movers were replaced.
Estimation and adjustments:
Total non-response rate: 15 percent.
Adjustment for total non-response: Yes.
Imputation for item non-response: No.
Adjustment for areas/population not covered: No.
Adjustment for undercoverage: No.
Adjustment for overcoverage: No.
Adjustment for seasonal variations: Not applicable.
History of the survey:
Title and date of the first survey: Labour Force Survey, 1979/80.
Significant changes or revisions: No information.
Documentation and dissemination:
Documentation:
Survey results: No information.
Survey methodology: No information.
Dissemination:
Time needed for initial release of survey results: No information.
Advance information of public about date of initial release: No.
Availability of unpublished data upon request: Yes.
Availability of data in machine-readable form: Yes.
Website: http://www.seychelles.net/misd/.

Singapore

Title of the survey: Labour Force Survey (LFS).
Organization responsible for the survey:
Planning and conduct of the survey: Manpower Research and Statistics Department (MRSD), Ministry of Manpower.
Analysis and publication of the results: Manpower Research and Statistics Department (MRSD), Ministry of Manpower.
Topics covered: Persons currently economically active, employed and unemployed; persons currently in time-related underemployment and persons currently outside the labour force; discouraged workers; hours of work and whether full- or part-time; duration of employment and unemployment; wages and income; second jobs; industry; occupation; status in employment; education/training levels.
Coverage of the survey:
Geographical: Main island of Singapore, excluding off-shore islands.
Population groups: Population of age 15 years and above living in private households. Excludes wayfarers and transients living on land, in hotels or on ships, boats and ocean-going vessels, as well as construction workers living on work-sites and commuters to Singapore from abroad.
Availability of estimates from other sources for the excluded areas/groups: None
Groups covered by the survey but excluded from the published results: None
Periodicity:
Conduct of the survey: Quarterly
Publication of results: Quarterly
Reference periods:
Employment: One week
Seeking work: Last four weeks.
Availability for work: Within two weeks.
Concepts and definitions:
Employment: Persons who a) performed some work for pay, profit or family gain during the reference week; and b) were temporarily absent from work during the reference week because of illness or leave, but were definitely going to return. Some work is defined as 1 hour or more during the reference week.
Unemployment: Persons who were currently without work and available for work within two weeks, and who had searched for work sometime during the last four weeks.
Underemployment:
Time-related underemployment: Persons who worked less than 30 hours during the reference period and were willing and available to engage in additional work.
Inadequate employment situations: No information provided.
Hours of work: Usual hours worked in a typical week.
Employment-related income:
Income from paid employment: Total amount of income from employment during the previous full month. For paid employment jobs include wages and salaries, bonuses, allowances, commissions, overtime pay, tips and bonuses as well as the employee's Central Provident Fund contribution but not that of the employer.
Income from self-employment: Total receipts from sales and services less the business expenses.
Informal sector: Not applicable.
Usual activity: No information provided.
Classifications:
Branch of economic activity (industry):
Title of the classification: Singapore Standard Industrial Classification, 1996.
Population groups classified by industry: Employed and unemployed persons.
Number of groups used for coding: 9.
Links to ISIC: ISIC-Rev. 3 at the first digit level (tabulation categories).
Occupation:
Title of the classification: Singapore Standard Occupational Classification, 1990.
Population groups classified by occupation: Employed and unemployed persons.
Number of groups used for coding: 8.
Links to ISCO: ISCO-88.
Status in employment:
title of the classification: No information provided.
Population groups classified by status in employment: Employed persons.
Groups used for classification: Employees; employers; own account workers; contributing family workers.
Links to ICSE: ICSE-1993.
Education:
Title of the classification: Singapore Standard Educational Classification.
Population groups classified by education: Employed and unemployed persons.
Groups used for classification: Never attended school/lower primary; primary; lower secondary; secondary; post secondary; polytechnic diploma; degree.
Links to ISCED: ISCED-1997
Sample size and design:
Ultimate sampling unit: Housing units.
Sample size (ultimate sampling units): 25 000 housing units for the major June survey.
Overall sampling fraction: 3 percent for the major June survey.
Sample frame: National Database of Dwellings, maintained by Department of Statistics, Singapore.
Updating of the sample frame: No information provided.
Rotation scheme:
Scheme: Not applicable.
Percentage of units remaining in the sample for two consecutive surveys rounds: Not applicable.
Maximum number of interviews per sample unit: Not applicable.
Length of time for complete renewal of the sample: Not applicable.
Field work:
Type of interview: Computer assisted telephone interviewing (CATI) and face-to-face.
Number of ultimate sampling units per sample area: No information provided.

Duration of field work:
Total: 7-8 weeks.
Per sample unit: No information provided.
Survey organization: Permanent.
Number of field staff: About 140 interviewers and supervisors.
Substitution of non-responding ultimate sampling units: No.
Estimation and adjustments:
Total non-response rate: 2 per cent.
Adjustment for total non-response: No.
Imputation for item non-response: No.
Adjustment for areas/population not covered: No.
Adjustment for under-coverage: No.
Adjustment for over-coverage: No.
Adjustment for seasonal variations: For quarterly unemployment rate, using X-11 ARIMA.
History of the survey:
Title and date of the first survey: Labour Force Survey (LFS), June 1974.
Significant changes or revisions: None.
Documentation and dissemination:
Documentation:
Survey results: "Quarterly Labour Market Reports" for unemployment figures.
Survey methodology: Report on the Labour Force Survey of Singapore (annually), except in census and mid-census years.
Dissemination:
Time needed for initial release of survey results: Less than six months after end of field work.
Advance information of public about date of initial release: Yes.
Availability of unpublished data upon request: Yes.
Availability of data in machine-readable form: Yes.
Website: http://www.singstat.gov.sg/.

Slovakia

Title of the survey: Labour Force Sample Survey
Organization responsible for the survey:
Planning and conduct of the survey: Statistical Office of the Slovak Republic.
Analysis and publication of the results: Statistical Office of the Slovak Republic.
Topics covered: Employment, unemployment, underemployment, hours of work, duration of employment, duration of unemployment, discouraged workers, occasional workers, industry, occupation, status in employment, educational level, second jobs and atypical work.
Coverage of the survey:
Geographical: Whole country.
Population groups: All permanent residents aged 15 and above living in households.
Excluded are:
a) students living in hostels and schoolchildren living in boarding schools;
b) inmates of penal and mental institutions;
c) foreign citizens on short-term stays up to 6 months..
Availability of estimates from other sources for the excluded areas/groups: No.
Groups covered by the survey but excluded from the published results: None.
Periodicity:
Conduct of the survey: Continuously.
Publication of results: Quarterly.
Reference periods:
Employment: One week (last seven days prior to the date of the interview).
Seeking work: Four weeks prior to the date of the interview.
Availability for work: Two weeks following the date of the interview.
Concepts and definitions:
Employment: Employed are all persons aged 15 years and over who during the reference week did some work at least for one hour, as well as unpaid family workers and persons who were not working but who had jobs or businesses from which they were temporarily absent because of illness, bad weather, holiday, labour-management dispute, etc. Excluded are persons on extended maternity (parental) leave.
Also included in the totals are:
a)full- and part-time workers seeking other work during the reference period;
b)full- and part-time students working full- or part-time;
c)persons who performed some work during the reference week while being either retired and receiving a pension; or were registered as job seekers at an employment office or receiving unemployment benefits;
d)private domestic servants;
e)paid apprentices and trainees
Excluded are persons engaged in production of goods for their own household (painting, repairing, housework, etc.).
Unemployment: Unemployed are considered to be persons aged 15 years and over who, during the reference week, did not work for pay or profit, were actively looking for work during the last four weeks prior to the survey and were available to start work in the two weeks following the survey.
Underemployment:
Time-related underemployment: Persons who, during the reference week, involuntary worked part-time but would like to work full-time.
Inadequate employment situations: Persons who were seeking another job in order to improve working conditions (higher income, professional background, better work, etc.).
Hours of work: Actual and usual hours worked for in the main job.
Employment-related income:
Income from paid employment: Not applicable.
Income from self-employment: Not applicable.
Informal sector: Not applicable.
Usual activity: Not applicable.
Classifications:
Branch of economic activity (industry):
Title of the classification: National classification.
Population groups classified by industry: Employed persons and unemployed persons with previous job experience.
Number of groups used for coding: 16 major groups.
Links to ISIC: ISIC-Rev. 3 (2 digit level).
Occupation:
Title of the classification: National classification.
Population groups classified by occupation: Employed persons and unemployed persons with previous work experience.
Number of groups used for coding: 10 main groups.
Links to ISCO: ISCO-88 (3 digit).
Status in employment:
Title of the classification: National classification.
Population groups classified by status in employment: Employed and unemployed persons.
Groups used for classification: 6 groups (employees, employers, own-account worker, members of producers' co-operatives, contributing family workers, workers not classified by status.
Links to ICSE: ICSE-1993.
Education:
Title of the classification: National classification is used.
Population groups classified by education: all population groups.
Groups used for classification: 12 groups (without school education, primary (1st and 2nd stages), apprenticeship, secondary (without examination), apprenticeship with exam, full secondary general, full secondary vocational, higher, bachelor, university, research qualification.
Links to ISCED: ISCED-1976.
Sample size and design:
Ultimate sampling unit: Dwelling.
Sample size (ultimate sampling units): About 10 250.
Overall sampling fraction: 0.6 per cent.
Sample frame: The sample frame is built on the basis of the municipal population registers and the Population Census conducted in 1991.
Updating of the sample: Annually.
Rotation:
Scheme: 20 per cent of sampled dwellings are replaced every quarter. One fifth of the panel is rotated every quarter.
Percentage of units remaining in the sample for two consecutive survey rounds: 75 per cent.
Maximum number of interviews per sample unit: No information provided.
Length of time for complete renewal of the sample: Five quarters.
Field work:
Type of interview: Paper and pencil, telephone and CAPI/CATI where possible.
Number of ultimate sampling units per sample area: 250 dwellings continuously per quarter.
Duration of field work:
Total: 30 minutes per household.
Per sample area: No information provided.
Survey organization: Statistical Office of the Slovak Republic.
Number of field staff: 45 interviewers and 8 supervisors.

Substitution of non-responding ultimate sampling units: No.
Estimation and adjustments:
Total non-response rate: 6 per cent.
Adjustment for total non-response: No.
Imputation for item non-response: No.
Adjustment for areas/population not covered: No.
Adjustment for undercoverage: No.
Adjustment for overcoverage: No.
Adjustment for seasonal variations: Yes.
History of the survey:
Title and date of the first survey: Labour Force Sample Survey, December 1992.
Significant changes or revisions: Beginning the first quarter of 1997, conscripts are included in the sample. Since the first quarter of 1999, a new sample design has been used. Since the first quarter of 2000, transition from seasonal to calendar processing quarters.
Documentation and dissemination:
Documentation:
Survey results: " Labour Force Sample Survey Results" (quarterly).
Survey methodology: " Labour Force Sample Survey Results" (quarterly).
Dissemination:
Time needed for initial release of survey results: 80 days.
Advance information of public about date of initial release: Yes.
Availability of unpublished data upon request: Yes.
Availability of data in machine-readable form: Diskettes, e-mails.
Website: http://www.statistics.sk/.

Slovenia

Title of the survey: Labour Force Survey.
Organization responsible for the survey:
Planning and conduct of the survey: Statistical Office of the Republic of Slovenia.
Analysis and publication of the results: Statistical Office of the Republic of Slovenia.
Topics covered: Employment, underemployment, unemployment, hours of work, informal sector, duration of unemployment, discouraged workers, occasional workers, industry, occupation, status in employment, educational level, second jobs.
Coverage of the survey:
Geographical: Whole country.
Population groups: All persons living in private households whose usual place of residence is in the territory of Slovenia, including persons temporarily absent (for less than six months). Excluded are the institutional population (e.g. military living in barracks) and persons temporarily or permanently living abroad. Children up to 15 years of age are asked only a few basic questions (name, sex, age, nationality).
Availability of estimates from other sources for the excluded areas/groups: Not available.
Groups covered by the survey but excluded from the published results: Not available.
Periodicity:
Conduct of the survey: Quarterly continuous survey.
Publication of results: Quarterly and annual.
Reference periods:
Employment: Last week (moving reference period) Monday to Sunday.
Seeking work: Past four weeks.
Availability for work: Two weeks.
Concepts and definitions:
Employment: All persons aged 15 years and over who during the reference week performed any work for payment (in cash or kind) or profit, including unpaid family workers and persons who were not working but had a job from which they were temporarily absent. The same applies to workers on lay-off (temporary or indefinite) and persons on maternity leave (12 months).
It includes:
a) persons with a job but temporarily absent due to illness/injury, vacation/ annual leave, parental leave, unpaid leave initiated by the employer, educational or training leave, absence without leave, strike or dispute, temporary stoppages due to bad weather conditions, mechanical breakdown, shortage of raw materials or energy, etc.;
b) full or part-time workers seeking other work;
e) persons who performed some work for pay or profit during the reference week, while being subject to compulsory schooling, or retired and receiving a pension, or registered as job-seekers at an employment office or receiving unemployment benefits;
f) full and part-time students working at least one hour in the reference week;
g) paid apprentices and trainees;
h) participants in employment promotion schemes;
i) persons engaged in the production of goods or services for own consumption;
j) volunteer and career members of the armed forces
Unemployment: All persons aged 15 years and over who, during the reference week, did not work for payment, profit or family gain and were actively seeking work during the past four weeks, and were currently available for work within two weeks.
It includes:
a) persons who took specific steps to set up their own business to begin within two weeks;
b) persons who had made arrangements to start a new job within two weeks;
c) full and part-time students seeking full or part-time work, compulsory school children and retired persons.
Underemployment:
Time-related underemployment: Persons who work less than 36 hours a week, wish to work more hours a week (through an additional job or through the present job or through another job working more hours than the present job) and are willing to start working more hours within the next two weeks.
Inadequate employment situations: Not applicable.
Hours of work: Hours usually worked (per week) including regular overtime. Hours actually worked (per week) relate to the main job performed during the reference week.
Employment-related income:
Income from paid employment: Not applicable.
Income from self-employment: Not applicable.
Informal sector employment: Those workers who receive "cash in hand" for their economic activity.
Usual activity: Not applicable.
Classifications:
Branch of economic activity (industry):
Title of the classification: Not available.
Population groups classified by industry: Employed persons.
Number of groups used for coding: 16 groups; coding at the 2-digit level.
Links to ISIC: ISIC-Rev. 3.
Occupation:
Title of the classification: Not available.
Population groups classified by occupation: Employed persons.
Number of groups used for coding: Not available.
Links to ISCO: ISCO-88.
Status in employment:
Title of the classification: Not available.
Population groups classified by status in employment: Employed persons.
Groups used for classification: Twelve groups: Employee in an enterprise or organization, Employee - artisan, Employee - freelance, Employee - farmer, Works in own enterprise (self-employed), Artisan, Farmer, Freelance, Unpaid family worker, Contract workers - Type 1 and 2, Cash-in-hand worker (informal).
Links to ICSE: ICSE-1993.
Education:
Title of the classification: Not available.
Population groups classified by education: Employed and unemployed persons.
Groups used for classification: Nine groups: Did not attend any school, Uncompleted Primary school, Primary school, One-two year Secondary (abridged curriculum), Two-three year Secondary, Four-five year Secondary, Non-University degree, University degree, Postgraduate.
Links to ISCED: ISCED-1997 with cross tables.
Sample size and design:
Ultimate sampling unit: Household.
Sample size (ultimate sampling units): Approximately 7 000 households (and 19 000 responding individuals).
Overall sampling fraction: Approximately one per cent of the population.
Sample frame: The LFS sample is built on the basis of the population register., from which each quarter a list of adult persons is created. Members of the household living at the address of the selected persons are interviewed.
Updating of the sample: Each quarter approximately 2 000 new households are selected.
Rotation: Rotating panel survey conducted continuously throughout the whole calendar year.

Scheme: The rotation sample is designed on the 3-(1)-2 pattern. Thus households are interviewed for three consecutive quarters, excluded for one quarter then return for another two consecutive quarters before falling out of the sample definitively.
Percentage of units remaining in the sample for two consecutive survey rounds: 60 per cent.
Maximum number of interviews per sample unit: Five times.
Length of time for complete renewal of the sample: Eighteen months.
Field work:
Type of interviews: A mixture of face to face using paper and pencil, computer-assisted personal interviews (CAPI) using laptops and telephone interviews.
Number of ultimate sampling units per sample area: Approximately 28 000 households per year.
Duration of field work
Total: The whole year.
Per sample area: Not applicable.
Survey organization: A permanent survey organization exists.
Number of field staff: Approximately 55.
Substitution of non-responding ultimate sampling units: No.
Estimation and adjustments:
Total non-response rate: 11.2 per cent (refusal rate is 7.4%). In the panel part of the sample, the overall non-response rate is 8.9%; among households interviewed by telephone 9.4%, face-to-face 5%.
Adjustment for total non-response: Yes.
Imputation for item non-response: Yes, using the Hot-deck method - use data from previous interview; if not available, data from a similar person (by sex, age and education).
Adjustment for areas/population not covered: Yes.
Adjustment for under-coverage: Yes.
Adjustment for over-coverage: Yes.
Adjustment for seasonal variations: No.
History of the survey:
Title and date of the first survey: Labour Force Survey, 1993.
Significant changes or revisions: None. The questionnaire was changed in 1995 and in 1997 with no significant breaks in time series.
Documentation and dissemination:
Documentation:
Survey results: Labour Force Survey: Results; Labour Force Survey: Rapid Results; Statistical Yearbook of the Republic of Slovenia, Monthly Statistical Review; CESTAT Bulletin. (monthly, quarterly and annual).
Survey methodology: idem.
Dissemination:
Time needed for initial release of survey results: Approximately one quarter.
Advance information of public about date of initial release: Yes.
Availability of unpublished data upon request: Yes.
Availability of data in machine-readable form: Yes on diskette and by email.
Website: http://www.sigov.si/zrs/.

South Africa

Title of the survey: Labour Force Survey.
Organization responsible for the survey:
Planning and conduct of the survey: Statistics South Africa (Stats SA).
Analysis and publication of the results: Statistics South Africa (Stats SA).
Topics covered: Employment, unemployment, underemployment, hours of work, wages, income, informal sector employment, duration of employment and unemployment, discouraged workers, industry, occupation, status in employment, education/qualification levels.
Coverage of the survey:
Geographical: Whole country.
Population groups: The survey includes all population groups (private households and resident in workers hostels), but the employment and unemployment questions are only asked to persons aged 15 years and above. Persons living in institutions (student hostels, old age homes, hospitals, prisons and military barracks) are excluded.
Availability of estimates from other sources for the excluded areas/groups: None.
Groups covered by the survey but excluded from the published results: None.
Periodicity:
Conduct of the survey: Bi-annually.
Publication of results: Bi-annually.

Reference periods:
Employment: The week prior to the interview, in February and September of each year.
Seeking work: Four weeks prior to the interview, in February and September of each year.
Availability for work: One week after the interview, in February and September of each year.
Concepts and definitions:
Employment: All persons aged 15 to 65 years who have done any of the following activities, except begging;
a) run or do any kind of business, big or small, for himself/herself or with one or more partners;
b) do any work for a wage, salary, commission or any payment in kind (excl. Domestic work);
c) do any work as a domestic worker for a wage, salary, or any payment in kind;
d) help unpaid in a household business of any kind;
e) do any work on his/her own or the household's plot, farm, food garden, cattle post or kraal, or help in growing farm produce or in looking after animals for the household;
f) do any construction or major repair work on his/her own home, plot, cattle post or business or those of the household; catch any fish, prawns, shells, wild animals or other food for sale or household food.
Persons who did not work during the reference week but, who have a job to return to, are also classified as employed. The off-season agriculture is not a temporary absence.
Are also considered as employed full-time and part-time students working full time and those working part-time in the seven days prior to the interview, as well as paid and unpaid apprentices and trainees.
Unemployment: Two definitions, the "official" and the "expanded", of unemployment are used.
The "official definition" refers to people, aged 15 to 65 years, who:
a) did not work during the seven days prior to the interview;
b) want to work and are available to start work within a week after the interview;
c) have taken steps to look to work or start some forms of self-employment in the four weeks prior to the interview.
The "expanded definition" excludes criterion (c).
Underemployment
Time-related underemployment: It covers persons who:
a) are working less hours than the normal hours worked in a specific activity;
b) have no choice to work less hours (number of hours of work are not voluntary);
c) are willing to work longer hours;
d) have taken steps to look for extra work in the four weeks prior to the survey.
Inadequate employment situations: Not covered.
Hours of work: Hours actually worked and usual hours are covered in the survey. In both these instances, data are presented for the main job, other work activities and total hours, separately.
Employment-related income:
Income from paid employment: It refers to regular or total cash earnings including overtime, allowances and bonuses before any tax or deductions. It refers only to main job.
Income from self-employment: Same as above if it is the main activity.
Informal sector: Respondents are asked about their place of work, whether it is in the formal or informal sector. Informal sector employment is where the employer (institution, business or private employer) is not registered to perform its activity.
Usual activity: Not covered.
Classifications:
Branch of economic activity (industry):
Title of the classification: International classification.
Population groups classified by industry: Employed and unemployed (industry of last job for the unemployed:
Number of groups used for coding: 190.
Links to ISIC: ISIC Rev. 3 (1988).
Occupation:
Title of the classification: International classification.
Population groups classified by occupation: Employed and the unemployed (occupation of last job for the unemployed).
Number of groups used for coding: 369.
Links to ISCO: ISCO-88.
Status in employment:
Title of the classification: National classification.
Population groups classified by status in employment: Employed.
Groups used for classification: Employees and self-employed.

Links to ICSE: No information.
Education:
Title of the classification: National classification.
Population groups classified by education: Employed and unemployed persons as well as inactive population (all ages).
Groups used for classification: No schooling; grade 0 to grade 12; NTC I to NTC III; diploma/certificate with less than grade 12; diploma/certificate with grade 12; degree, postgraduate degree or diploma.
Links to ISCED: ISCED-1997.
Sample size and design:
Ultimate sampling unit: Dwelling.
Sample size (ultimate sampling units): 30 000 dwellings.
Overall sampling fraction: No information.
Sample frame: The database of enumerator areas(EAs), as established during the demarcation phase of Census 1996, constituted the sample frame for selecting EAs for the Labour Force Survey.
Updating of the sample: Yearly.
Rotation:
Scheme: The same dwellings are visited on, at most, five different occasions. This means a rotation of 20 per cent of dwelling units at each time.
Percentage of units remaining in the sample for two consecutive survey rounds: 80 per cent.
Maximum number of interviews per sample unit: Five.
Length of time for complete renewal of the sample: Five rounds.
Field work:
Type of interview: Personal interviews.
Number of ultimate sampling units per sample area: Ten.
Duration of field work:
Total: 21 days (for example, from 2 to 22 September 2001).
Per sample area: About 14 hours.
Survey organization: Permanent and ad-hoc organizations.
Number of field staff: About 936 persons (both permanent and contractual staff members).
Substitution of non-responding ultimate sampling units: No.
Estimation and adjustments:
Total non-response rate: About 10 per cent.
Adjustment for total non-response: Yes.
Imputation for item non-response: No.
Adjustment for areas/population not covered: No.
Adjustment for undercoverage: Yes.
Adjustment for overcoverage: Yes.
Adjustment for seasonal variations: No.
History of the survey:
Title and date of the first survey: Labour Force Survey 2000.
Significant changes or revisions: Not applicable.
Documentation and dissemination:
Documentation:
Survey results: Labour Force Survey (bi-annually); Statistical Releases (P0210).
Survey methodology: Labour Force Survey (bi-annually).
Dissemination
Time needed for initial release of survey results: About 6 months after fieldwork (26 March 2002 for the September 2001 results).
Advance information of public about date of initial release: Yes.
Availability of unpublished data upon request: No.
Availability of data in machine-readable form: Yes.
Website: http://www.statssa.gov.za/.

Sri Lanka

Title of the survey: Sri Lanka Labour Force Survey.
Organization responsible for the survey:
Planning and conduct of the survey: Department of Census and Statistics
Analysis and publication of the results: Department of Census and Statistics
Topics covered: Employment, unemployment, time-related underemployment, hours of work, income, duration of employment and unemployment, reasons for not seeking work, type of work sought, industry, occupation, status in employment, shift work, educational level, vocational training, usual activity and secondary jobs.
Coverage of the survey:
Geographical: Whole country except Northern and Eastern provinces.
Population groups: Persons 10 years and above, except the institutional population, the armed forces and family members who live away from their home.
Availability of estimates from other sources for the excluded areas/groups: NO.
Groups covered by the survey but excluded from the published results: None.
Periodicity:
Conduct of the survey: Quarterly.
Publication of results: Quarterly.
Reference periods:
Employment: Past week (fixed).
Seeking work: Past week (fixed).
Availability for work: Past week (fixed).
Concepts and definitions:
Employment: Household members who during the reference period worked for at least one hour as paid employees, employers, own account workers (self-employed) or unpaid family workers, in family enterprises. Also included are persons who had a job but were temporarily absent from work because of such reasons as vacation, illness, bad weather, and labour management disputes, etc. It includes paid apprentices and trainees.
Unemployment: Persons who during the reference period were available and/or looking for paid or self-employment work, and had no employment.
Underemployment:
Time-related underemployment: Employed persons who during the reference period did not have a secondary job and were available for additional work. Those who looked for such work can be identified separately.
Inadequate employment situations: No information provided.
Hours of work: Hours actually worked during the week.
Employment related income:
Income from paid employment: Cash earnings only.
Income from self-employment: No information provided.
Informal sector: No information provided.
Usual activity: Persons who during the past 12 months were employed and/or unemployed for 26 weeks or more.
Classifications:
Branch of economic activity (industry):
Title of the classification: National classification.
Population groups classified by industry: Employed persons.
Number of groups used for coding: 10
Links to ISIC: ISIC-Rev. 2.
Occupation:
Title of the classification: National classification.
Population groups classified by occupation: Employed persons.
Number of groups used for coding: 10
Links to ISCO: ISCO-88.
Status in employment:
Title of the classification: National classification.
Population groups classified by status in employment: Employed persons.
Groups used for classification: employee, employer, own account worker, unpaid family worker.
Links to ICSE: ICSE-1993.
Education:
Title of the classification: National classification.
Population groups classified by education: Employed and unemployed persons.
Groups used for classification: no schooling, grade 1-5, 6-10, GCE (O/L), GCE (A/L) and above.
Links to ISCED: No.
Sample size and design:
Ultimate sampling unit: Housing unit.
Sample size (ultimate sampling units): Annual sample size of 16,000 housing units.
Overall sampling fraction: Not available.
Sample frame: The master sampling frame (list of housing units) was created for the Demographic Survey of 1994. From 2002 onwards, the 2001 Census of Population and Housing is used as the sample frame.
Updating of the sample: Up to 2001, the list of housing units in the selected PSUs are updated prior to the survey enumeration; from 2002 onwards, the list of the Census blocks is updated prior to the survey enumeration..
Rotation: Not applicable.
Scheme: Not applicable.
Percentage of units remaining in the sample for two consecutive survey rounds: Not applicable.
Maximum number of interviews per sample unit: No information provided.

Length of time for the complete renewal of the sample: No information provided.
Field work:
Type of interview: Personal interview.
Number of ultimate sampling units per sample area: Not available.
Duration of field work
Total: Two weeks.
Per sample area: One week.
Survey organization: Permanent survey staff.
Number of field staff: About 300 enumerators and supervisors.
Substitution of non-responding ultimate sampling units: No.
Estimation and adjustments:
Total non-response rate: 5 %.
Adjustment for total non-response: Yes.
Imputation for item non-response: No.
Adjustment for areas/population not covered: No.
Adjustment for under-coverage: Yes.
Adjustment for over-coverage: Yes.
Adjustment for seasonal variations: No.
History of the survey:
Title and date of the first survey: Sri Lanka Labour Force Survey - 1990.
Significant changes or revisions: New questions were added from the first quarter of 1996.
Documentation and dissemination:
Documentation:
Survey results: Quarterly Report of the Sri Lanka Labour force Survey; Bulletin of Labour Force (quarterly); Annual Bulletin of Labour Force-Provincial Profile.
Survey methodology: Idem.
Dissemination:
Time needed for initial release of survey results: About three months.
Advance information of public about date of initial release: No.
Availability of unpublished data upon request: Yes.
Availability of data in machine-readable form: Diskettes and magnetic tapes.
Website: http://www.statistics.gov.lk/.

Sudan

Title of the survey: Household Survey.
Organization responsible for the survey
Planning and conduct of the survey: Ministry of Manpower.
Analysis and publication of the results: Ministry of Manpower.
Topics covered: Current employment and unemployment. Hours of work. Wages. Household income. Informal sector employment. Duration of unemployment. Educational level. Current industry, occupation and status in employment in main job. Secondary jobs. Usual activity.
Coverage of the survey
Geographical: Urban and rural areas in 16 states in Northern Sudan. Excluded were 9 states in Southern Sudan.
Population groups: All permanent household residents including foreign nationals and persons absent for less than 3 months.
Availability of estimates from other sources for the excluded areas/groups: Estimates based on population census results are available for the excluded areas and population groups.
Groups covered by the survey but excluded from the published results: Children less than 10 years of age.
Periodicity
Conduct of the survey: Three household surveys since 1990 (1990, 1994, and 1996).
Publication of results: Following each survey.
Reference period
Employment: Fixed reference week for current activity and reference year for usual activity.
Seeking work: Same reference periods as employment.
Availability for work: NA.
Concepts and definitions
Current employment: Persons, 10 years old and over, who worked for at least 2 days in the week preceding the survey. [Usual employment: Persons, 10 years old and over, who worked for three months or more during the reference year.] The Employed include persons with a job but temporary absent from work due to illness, injury, vacation, maternity leave, educational and training leave, labour management dispute, bad weather, mechanical breakdown, etc. It also includes persons on indefinite lay-off without pay and persons without work and currently available for work who had made arrangements to start work at a date subsequent to the reference period. Persons absent without leave are excluded. Paid apprentices and participants of employment promotion schemes are included. Full-time and part-time students working full-time are included but students working part-time are excluded. Unpaid apprentices and trainees, and unpaid family workers temporary absent from work are excluded. Persons engaged in own-account production of goods are included, but persons engaged in unpaid or personal services for their own household are excluded. Conscripts and persons engaged in civilian service equivalent to military service are included, but persons doing volunteer community or social service work are excluded. Also excluded were persons who performed some work for pay or profit during the reference period but were subject to compulsory schooling, or retired and receiving a pension, or registered as jobseeker at an employment office or receiving unemployment benefits.
Unemployment: Persons, 10 years old and over, who during the reference week did not work or worked less than 2 days, but were able to work, desired and searched for work, whether or not they had ever worked before. [Usual unemployment: Persons, 10 years old and over, who worked for less than 3 months during the reference year, but were able to work and desired and searched for work during the year.] The Unemployed included persons on temporary lay-off without pay, persons on unpaid leave initiated by the employer. Also included were unpaid family workers temporarily absent from work as well as unpaid apprentices and trainees. It excluded full-time and part-time students seeking part-time work, but included part-time students seeking full-time work. Persons who were seeking work but who subject to compulsory schooling or retired and receiving a pension were excluded. Persons without work, available for work, but not seeking work during the reference period were also excluded.
Hours of work: Refers to the number of hours actually worked in the main activity and hours spent in secondary job.
Wages and salaries: Include regular wages and salaries, in cash and in kind, after deduction of social security contributions, for the main job and all other jobs carried out during the reference period. Income from self-employment was also measured in terms of value of production from agriculture and livestock activities and hired land and capital from all jobs over the one-year reference period.
Informal sector employment: Employment in an economic unit that has no fixed place of operation, or is not registered with the commercial registration system, or does not pay taxes on its activities.
Classifications
Branch of economic activity (industry)
Population groups classified by industry: NA.
Number of groups used for coding: NA.
Linked to ISIC Rev. 3, 1988.
Occupation
Population groups classified by occupation: NA.
Number of groups used for coding: NA.
Linked to ISCO-1988.
Status in employment
Population groups classified by status in employment: NA.
List of groups: Employee. Employer. Own-account worker. Family worker and trainee.
Not linked to ICSE-1993.
Education
Population groups classified by educational level: NA.
List of groups: Illiterate. Can read & write. Primary education. Intermediate education. Secondary education. University education. Post university studies.
Sample size and design
Ultimate sampling unit: Private households and individuals in collective households.
Sample size (ultimate sampling units): Some 3,390 private households in urban and rural areas.
Overall sampling fraction: 0.1% of total population.
Sample frame: Based on the enumeration areas of the 1993 Population census and 1996 Agricultural Census of Sudan. The sample selection was based on a multi-phase stratified design.
Updating of the sample: Re-listing of the sample PSUs.
Rotation: Households were interviewed three times, each quarter during the survey year.
Field work
Type of interview: Personal interviews using paper and pencil.
Duration of fieldwork per sample area: 2 days.
Duration of fieldwork: 15 days.
Survey organization: Personnel recruited for each survey round.
Number of field staff: A total of 155 interviewers, supervisors, and other field staff.
Substitution of non-responding sampling units: No.

Estimation and adjustments
Total non-response rate: NA.
Adjustments: No adjustments were made for possible under-coverage or over-coverage and survey non-responses.
Imputation for item non-response: No.
History of the survey
Title and date of the first survey: Migration and Labour force survey, 1990.
Significant changes or revisions: NA.
Documentation and dissemination
Documentation
Results published in separate volumes on: 1 Population characteristics; 2 Economic participation rates; 3 Unemployment rates; Marital status; 5 Internal migration; 6 International migration; and 7 Return migration.
Time needed for initial release of survey results: 12 months. Survey period April 1995. Initial release of survey results April 1996..
Advance information of public about date of initial release: Yes.
Availability of unpublished data upon request: Upon request in database and diskettes.

Sweden

Title of the survey: Labour Force Survey (LFS).
Organization responsible for the survey:
Planning and conduct of the survey: Statistics Sweden.
Analysis and publication of the results: Statistics Sweden.
Topics covered: Employment, unemployment, underemployment, hours of work, duration of unemployment, discouraged workers, occasional workers, industry, occupation, status in employment, education/qualification levels, usual activity, second jobs and family.
Coverage of the survey:
Geographical: Whole country.
Population groups: All inhabitants aged 15 to 74 years covered by civil registration, including volunteer and career members of the armed forces.
Availability of estimates from other sources for the excluded areas/groups: No information provided.
Groups covered by the survey but excluded from the published results: Separate estimates are available for persons aged 15 years and those aged 65 to 74 years.
Periodicity:
Conduct of the survey: Monthly.
Publication of results: Monthly.
Reference periods:
Employment: One week..
Seeking work: One week.
Availability for work: One week.
Concepts and definitions:
Employment: All persons aged 16 to 64 years who:
1) during the measurement week, were gainfully employed for at least one hour either as paid employees or as entrepreneurs or self-employed and persons working as unpaid helpers in a business belonging to spouse or other family member in the same household (employed and at work);
2) who did not carry out any work according to the above definition, but who had employment or work as unpaid family workers or as entrepreneurs or self-employed and who were temporarily absent during the entire measurement week because of illness, vacation, other leave (care of children, studies, military service, other leave or industrial dispute), irrespective of whether or not the absence was paid (= employed, temporarily absent).
Also included are:
a) full- and part-time workers seeking other work during the measurement week;.
b) full- and part-time students working full- or part-time;
c) persons on temporary lay-off with pay (lay-off without pay does not exist in Sweden);
d) persons who performed some work for pay or profit during the measurement week while being subject to compulsory schooling or retired and receiving a pension or registered as jobseekers at an employment office or receiving unemployment benefits;
e) paid apprentices and trainees;
f) participants in employment promotion schemes (sheltered workshops, relief work, youth teams or employed on special public grants or subsidies);
g) paid and unpaid family workers, including those who were temporarily absent from work during the measurement week;
h) private domestic servants;
i) members of producers´ co-operatives;
j) volunteer and career members of the armed forces;
k) conscripts and persons doing civilian service equivalent to military service and provided they were employed prior to and on leave (i.e. temporarily absent) from a civil job during their military or civilian service.
Persons on education or training leave with pay from employer (during paid working hours or as paid leave of absence) are classified as employed and "at work". Persons on education leave without pay (leave granted for studies) are classified as employed and "not at work".
Excluded from the Swedish labour force are persons who work abroad and have no work in Sweden, whether commuting across a border or both living and working in a foreign country.
Unemployment: Persons aged 16 to 64 years who, during the measurement week, were not employed, but who wanted and could have accepted work and had looked for work, or would have looked for work if they had not been temporarily prevented from doing so, or who were waiting for the outcome of some measure they had instituted during the preceding four weeks to get work. Also included are persons who are waiting to begin a new job starting within four weeks. Part-time students looking for full- or part-time work are also classified as unemployed.
Full-time students looking for full- or part-time work are excluded from the unemployed and considered as inactive; however, data about the size of this group are collected.
Seasonal workers awaiting agricultural or other kind of seasonal work are classified as unemployed provided they fulfill the criteria of the unemployment definition; otherwise, they are classified as out of the labour force.
"Having looked for work" is interpreted as having taken one or more of the following actions during the four weeks preceding the interview: contacted the employment office or employers directly; read and/or placed advertisements; contacted friends or relatives, etc.
Underemployment:
Time-related underemployment: the underemployed are those persons who work less than they want to due to labour market reasons.
Inadequate employment situations: Not applicable.
Hours of work: Both hours actually worked (including overtime) during the measurement week and usual (contractual) hours of work are collected. Both variables are measured separately for the main and secondary jobs.
Employment-related income:
Income from paid employment: Not covered by the survey.
Income from self-employment: Not covered by the survey.
Informal sector: Not covered by the survey.
Usual activity: Persons without gainful employment and occasional workers are asked about their usual main activity.
Classifications:
Branch of economic activity (industry):
Title of the classification: Swedish Standard Industrial Classification 1992 (SE-SIC 92).
Population groups classified by industry: Employed and unemployed (industry of last job for the unemployed).
Number of groups used for coding: Data are collected and classified according to 64 groups but presented according to 48 groups.
Links to ISIC: ISIC-Rev. 3 at the 2-digit level.
Occupation:
Title of the classification: Swedish Standard Classification of Occupations 1996 (SSYK 96).
Population groups classified by occupation: Employed and unemployed (occupation of last job for the unemployed).
Number of groups used for coding: Data are collected and classified according to 381 groups (4-digit level) but presented according to 68 groups.
Links to ISCO: ISCO-88.
Status in employment:
Title of the classification: National classification.
Population groups classified by status in employment: Employed and unemployed (status of last job for the unemployed).
Groups used for classification: Employers, entrepreneurs/self-employed (with and without employees), family workers.
Links to ICSE: ICSE-1993.
Education:
Title of the classification: Swedish Standard Classification of Education (SUN 2000).
Population groups classified by education: All respondents are classified according to the highest level of education and the highest complete field of education. This information is not asked for in the survey, but taken from the Swedish Register of Education.

Groups used for classification: The 'level-code' consists of 47 codes (3 digits) but data are presented according to 7 groups. The 'field-code' consists of a 4-digit code but data are presented according to 9 groups.
Links to ISCED: ISCED-1997.
Sample size and design:
Ultimate sampling unit: The persons.
Sample size (ultimate sampling units): 22 000 individuals from a population of about 6.5 millions (aged 15 to 74 years) and 21 000 from a 5.6 millions (aged 16 to 64 years)..
Overall sampling fraction: No information.
Sample frame: The SCB (Statistics Sweden) register of population which is more or less continuously updated.
Updating of the sample: The sample is drawn at each turn of the year to cover the requirements of the coming year (April-March). It is then updated each month with respect to migrations, deaths and changes in marital status. The sample is supplemented by immigrants once a quarter.
Rotation:
Scheme: Persons in the sample are interviewed once a quarter on a total of 8 occasions during a two-year period before being replaced. Each month, 1/8 of the sample is renewed.
Percentage of units remaining in the sample for two consecutive survey rounds: 87.5 per cent remain in the same sample in two consecutive quarters.
Maximum number of interviews per sample unit: No information.
Length of time for complete renewal of the sample: Two years.
Field work:
Type of interview: Telephone interviews (CATI) completed by a personal visit (about 0.2 per cent of the interviews) when the sample person can not be reached.
Number of ultimate sampling units per sample area: No information.
Duration of field work:
Total: 5-6 weeks.
Per sample area: No information.
Survey organization: Permanent.
Number of field staff: About 200.
Substitution of non-responding ultimate sampling units: No.
Estimation and adjustments:
Total non-response rate: About 15 per cent in February 2002.
Adjustment for total non-response: Yes.
Imputation for item non-response: No.
Adjustment for areas/population not covered: No information.
Adjustment for undercoverage: No.
Adjustment for overcoverage: No.
Adjustment for seasonal variations: Yes.
History of the survey:
Title and date of the first survey: The first Swedish Labour Force Survey was carried out in May 1959 by the National Market Board.
Significant changes or revisions: Quarterly from August 1961 to 1970 and then monthly.
1987: revised concepts and definitions. 1981: introduction of CATI. 1995: new industrial classification. 1997: new occupational classification. 2000: new educational classification. 2003: major changes are planned according to EU regulations.
Documentation and dissemination:
Documentation:
Survey results: Statistical Messages (SM): SM Am 10 (monthly), SM Am 11 (quarterly), SM Am 12 (annually).
Survey methodology: 2001:5 Urvals- och estimationsförfarandet i de svenska arbetskraftsundersökningarna (AKU (Design and estimations in LFS9. This will be translated in English.
Dissemination:
Time needed for initial release of survey results: 2 weeks after the end of the month.
Advance information of public about date of initial release: Yes.
Availability of unpublished data upon request: Yes.
Availability of data in machine-readable form: Yes.
Website: http://www.scb.se/.

Tanzania, United Rep. of

Title of the survey: Labour Force Survey.
Organization responsible for the survey:
Planning and conduct of the survey: National Bureau of Statistics in cooperation with the Labour Department.
Analysis and publication of the results: National Bureau of Statistics in cooperation with the Labour Department.
Topics covered: Employment, unemployment, underemployment, hours of work (usual hours of work, hours actually worked), income from employment, informal sector employment, type of work place, duration of employment, duration of unemployment, discouraged workers, industry, occupation, status in employment, education and qualification levels, usual activity, second jobs.
Coverage of the survey:
Geographical: Tanzania Mainland. The islands of Zanzibar are not covered.
Population groups: The survey covers the usual residents of private dwellings in Tanzania Mainland, irrespective of their citizenship. Persons living in institutions are not covered. Excluded are foreign diplomats resident in Tanzania.
Availability of estimates from other sources for the excluded areas/groups: Yes, from similar surveys conducted in Zanzibar and from population censuses.
Groups covered by the survey but excluded from the published results: None.
Periodicity:
Conduct of the survey: Every ten years. Data are collected during a period of 12 months divided into four quarters. The last survey was undertaken during the period April 2000-March 2001. The present description refers to the Labour Force Survey 1990/1991 which was conducted during the period October 1990-September 1991.
Publication of results: Every ten years.
Reference periods:
Employment: Moving reference period of one week, i.e. the last full calendar week (Monday to Sunday) prior to the interview date.
Seeking work: Moving reference period of four weeks prior to the interview date.
Availability for work: Moving reference period of one week, i.e. the last full calendar week (Monday to Sunday) prior to the interview date.
Concepts and definitions:
Employment: Persons aged 10 years or over who did some work (i.e. for at least one hour) during the reference week, either as employees for payment in cash or in kind, or as self-employed persons (including farmers) for profit or family gain. Included are: (a) contributing family workers at work during the reference week; (b) full- or part-time workers seeking other work; (c) persons who performed some work for pay or profit during the reference week but who were subject to compulsory schooling, or retired and receiving a pension; (d) full-time students working part-time; (e) part-time students working full- or part-time; (f) paid or unpaid apprentices and trainees; and (g) persons engaged in the production of goods for own final use.
Also included are persons with a job or enterprise who were temporarily absent from work during the reference week, but definitely going to return to it, because of: (a) illness or injury, (b) vacation or annual leave, (c) maternity or paternity leave, (d) educational or training leave, (e) labour management dispute, (f) bad weather, mechanical breakdown, etc, or (g) temporary lay-off without pay. The duration of absence is limited to four months for employees and to one month for self-employed persons.
Excluded are: (a) contributing family workers not at work during the reference week; (b) casual workers not at work during the reference week; (c) employees absent from work for more than four months; (d) self-employed persons absent from work for more than one month; (e) persons on indefinite lay-off without pay; and (f) persons rendering unpaid or personal services to members of their own household.
Unemployment: Two definitions are used: (1) persons aged 10 years or over who were not employed during the reference week, were available for work during the reference week, and had taken active steps to find work during the last four weeks; and (2) persons aged 10 years or over who were not employed during the reference week, and who were available for work during the reference week. The following are considered as active steps to find work: applied to prospective employers; checked at farms, factories or work sites; asked friends and relatives; took action to start business; took action to start agriculture; other.
Included are: (a) persons without work and available for work, who had made arrangements to start a new job on a date subsequent to the reference week (definitions 1 and 2); (b) persons without work and available for work, who were trying to establish their own enterprise (definitions 1 and 2); (c) persons without work and available for work, but not seeking work for reasons other than (a) or (b) above (definition 2); (d) persons seeking work and/or available for work who were subject to compulsory schooling, or retired and receiving a pension (definitions 1 and 2); (e) full-time students seeking and/or available for full- or part-time work (definitions 1 and 2); and (f) part-time students seeking and/or available for full- or part-time work (definitions 1 and 2).

Excluded are persons without work and available for work, who were not seeking work for reasons other than (a) and (b) above (definition 1), or persons without work who were not available for work (definitions 1 and 2).

Underemployment:

Time-related underemployment: Employed persons who worked less than 40 hours during the reference week for an economic reason, and who were available to work more hours.

Inadequate employment situations: This topic is not covered by the survey.

Hours of work: Usual hours of work per week and hours actually worked during the reference week. For both usual hours of work and hours actually worked, information is collected separately for the main economic activity and any other economic activity.

Employment-related income:

Income from paid employment: Gross wages or salaries received in cash during the last month for the total of all paid employment jobs. Wages or salaries in kind are excluded.

Income from self-employment: Net profit obtained from the business or businesses during the last week or month. For self-employed persons engaged in non-agricultural activities, the net profit is derived from questions on gross income and operating expenses; for self-employed persons engaged in agriculture, the information on net profit is obtained directly.

Informal sector: Persons working in enterprises that (i) are not government units, parastatals, CCM party organizations or formally established co-operatives, (ii) employ less than six paid employees, and (iii) are located in a temporary structure, on a footpath or street, or have no fixed location. Traditional agriculture, livestock and fishing, as well as professional or business services and other enterprises with distinct formal characteristics, are excluded. Households employing paid domestic workers are included.

Usual activity: Usual economic activity refers to the main activity status during a reference period of one year, i.e. the 12 full calendar months preceding the interview date. Persons aged 10 years or over are considered usually active if they worked or were available for work during six or more of the 12 reference months. Usually active persons are sub-divided into usually employed persons and usually unemployed persons. Usually employed persons are those who worked during half or more of the economically active months. Usually unemployed persons are those who spent more than half of the economically active months not working and available for work.

Classifications:

Branch of economic activity (industry):

Title of the classification: Tanzanian adaptation of the International Standard Industrial Classification of All Economic Activities (ISIC, Rev. 2); additional codes are created to describe informal sector activities.

Population groups classified by industry: Employed persons.

Number of groups used for coding: Groups at the 4-digit level.

Links to ISIC: ISIC, Rev. 2.

Occupation:

Title of the classification: Tanzania Standard Classification of Occupations (TASCO).

Population groups classified by occupation: Employed persons and unemployed persons.

Number of groups used for coding: Groups at the 4-digit level.

Links to ISCO: ISCO-88.

Status in employment:

Title of the classification: National classification of status in employment.

Population groups classified by status in employment: Employed persons.

Groups used for classification: (a) Paid employees; (b) self-employed persons (non-agricultural activities) with employees; (c) self-employed persons (non-agricultural activities) without employees; (d) unpaid family helpers (non-agricultural activities); (e) persons working on their own or family farm or shamba.

Links to ICSE: Partially.

Education:

Title of the classification: National classification of levels of educational attainment.

Population groups classified by education: All persons aged 10 years or over.

Groups used for classification: (a) None; (b) primary not completed; (c) primary completed; (d) secondary up to Form 2; (e) secondary up to Form 4; (f) secondary up to Form 6; (g) university.

Links to ISCED: No information provided.

Sample size and design:

Ultimate sampling unit: Household.

Sample size (ultimate sampling units): 7,762 households.

Overall sampling fraction: About 0.2 percent of households.

Sample frame: A National Master Sample (NMS) comprising 122 urban enumeration areas and 50 rural villages was used as area sample frame for the survey. Prior to the survey, households were listed in all the enumeration areas and villages included in the NMS.

Updating of the sample: The sample will be updated after the cartographic work for the Population Census 2002 has been completed.

Rotation:

Scheme: No sample rotation. The survey sample is divided into four independent quarterly sub-samples.

Percentage of units remaining in the sample for two consecutive survey rounds: Not applicable.

Maximum number of interviews per sample unit: Not applicable.

Length of time for complete renewal of the sample: Not applicable.

Field work:

Type of interview: Information is obtained through personal interviews.

Number of ultimate sampling units per sample area: 30-35 households per urban enumeration area; 80 households per rural village.

Duration of field work

Total: One year.

Per sample area: 14 days for urban enumeration areas and 27 days for rural villages.

Survey organization: Field staff is recruited for every survey round.

Number of field staff: No information provided.

Substitution of non-responding ultimate sampling units: No replacement is made for non-responding households.

Estimation and adjustments:

Total non-response rate: 2.4 percent of sample households.

Adjustment for total non-response: Yes.

Imputation for item non-response: No.

Adjustment for areas/population not covered: Not applicable.

Adjustment for under-coverage: Yes.

Adjustment for over-coverage: Not applicable.

Adjustment for seasonal variations: Not applicable.

History of the survey:

Title and date of the first survey: The first Labour Force Survey of Tanzania was conducted in 1965.

Significant changes or revisions: No labour force survey was undertaken during the period 1966-1989. The Labour Force Surveys 1990/91 and 2000/01 were based on the recommendations adopted by the 13th International Conference of Labour Statisticians. Modules on child labour and on the informal sector were added to the Labour Force Survey 2000/01.

Documentation and dissemination:

Documentation:

Survey results: Bureau of Statistics and Labour Department, Tanzania (Mainland), The Labour Force Survey 1990/91, June 1993.

Survey methodology: Bureau of Statistics and Labour Department, Tanzania (Mainland), The Labour Force Survey 1990/91, Technical Report, June 1993.

Dissemination:

Time needed for initial release of survey results: About 21 months.

Advance information of public about date of initial release: Yes.

Availability of unpublished data upon request: Yes.

Availability of data in machine-readable form: Tabulations of the survey data can be made available on diskettes.

Thailand

Title of the survey: Labour Force Survey.

Organization responsible for the survey:

Planning and conduct of the survey: National Statistical Office (NSO).

Analysis and publication of the results: National Statistical Office (NSO).

Topics covered: Employment, unemployment, underemployment, hours of work, wages, income, informal sector employment, duration of unemployment, industry, occupation, status in employment, educational level, usual activity.

Coverage of the survey:

Geographical: Whole country.

Population groups: Persons 13 years and above except those living in institutional households (including the army).

Availability of estimates from other sources for the excluded areas/groups: Not applicable.

Groups covered by the survey but excluded from the published results: None.
Periodicity:
Conduct of the survey: Quarterly.
Publication of results: Quarterly.
Reference periods:
Employment: One week (fixed).
Seeking work: One month (fixed).
Availability for work: One week (fixed).
Concepts and definitions:
Employment: Persons aged 13 years or over who, during the reference week (a) worked for at least one hour for wages, profit, dividends or any kind of payment in kind; (b) did not work at all but had regular jobs, business enterprises or farms from which they were temporarily absent because of illness or injury, vacation or holiday, strike or lockout, bad weather, off-season or other reasons, such as temporary closure of the workplace, whether or not they were paid by their employers during their period of absence, provided that in the case of a temporary closure of the workplace, the expected it to be reopened within 30 days from the date of closure and to be recalled to their former job; or (c) persons who worked for at least one hour without pay in business enterprises or on farms owned or operated by household heads or members.
Unemployment: Persons aged 13 years or over who, during the reference week, did not work even for one hour, had no jobs, business enterprises, or farms of their own, from which they were temporarily absent, but were available for work. It includes persons who had been looking for work during the preceding 30 days and those who had not been looking for work because of illness or belief that no suitable work was available, waiting to take up a new job, waiting for the agricultural season or another reason. Persons on temporary or indefinite lay off without pay are included.
Underemployment:
Time-related underemployment: Persons 13 years of age and over who work less than 35 hours per week, are available and willing to work additional hour.
Inadequate employment situations: No information.
Hours of work: Hours actually worked during the reference week in all jobs. For persons absent from work during the reference week, it is the normal hours of work.
Employment-related income:
Income from paid employment: It refers to the main job in the reference week and includes payments in cash, in kind or services.
Income from self-employment: It refers to the output minus the operation expenses of own account workers and unpaid family workers.
Informal sector: Own account workers, employers of private employees and unpaid family workers in business establishments with less than 10 persons.
Usual activity: Measured with a reference period of one year.
Classifications:
Branch of economic activity (industry):
Title of the classification: Thailand Standard Industrial Classification (TSIC).
Population groups classified by industry: Employed persons and unemployed persons with previous work experience.
Number of groups used for coding: 10 major groups.
Links to ISIC: ISIC Rev- 2.
Occupation:
Title of the classification: No information.
Population groups classified by occupation: Employed persons and unemployed persons with previous work experience.
Number of groups used for coding: 10 major groups.
Links to ISCO: ISCO-68.
Status in employment:
Title of the classification: No information.
Population groups classified by status in employment: Employed persons and unemployed persons with previous work experience.
Groups used for classification: Employer, Government employee, Private employee.
Links to ICSE: ICSE-93, except for members of producer cooperatives which does not exist in the national classification.
Education:
Title of the classification: No information.
Population groups classified by education: Employed and unemployed persons.
Groups used for classification: no education, less than lower elementary, lower elementary.
Links to ISCED: ISCED-76 and ISCED-97.
Sample size and design:
Ultimate sampling unit: Household.
Sample size (ultimate sampling units): About 60,500 households.
Overall sampling fraction: About 6 per cent (5 610/94 955 blocks and villages).
Sample frame: Blocks and village listing based on the 1990 Population and Housing Census.
Updating of the sample: Annually.
Rotation:
Scheme: Not applicable.
Percentage of units remaining in the sample for two consecutive surveys: Not applicable.
Maximum number of interviews per sample unit: Not applicable.
Length of time for complete renewal of the sample: Not applicable.
Field work:
Type of interview: Personal interview.
Number of ultimate sampling units per sample area: 12 households for municipal areas, 9 household for non-municipal areas.
Duration of field work:
Total: One month.
Per sample area: Not available.
Survey organization: not available.
Number of field staff: 800 persons.
Substitution of non-responding ultimate sampling units: No.
Estimation and adjustments:
Total non-response rate: 10 per cent.
Adjustment for total non-response: No.
Imputation for item non-response: No.
Adjustment for areas/population not covered: No.
Adjustment for under-coverage: No.
Adjustment for over-coverage: No.
Adjustment for seasonal variations: No.
History of the survey:
Title and date of the first survey: Labour Force Survey 1963.
Significant changes or revisions: The current concepts and definitions have been used since 1983, and the minimum age limit from 13 years has been used since 1989.
Documentation and dissemination:
Documentation:
Survey results: Report of the Labour Force survey (quarterly)
Survey methodology: idem.
Dissemination:
Time needed for initial release of survey results: About 5 months.
Advance information of public about date of Initial release: No.
Availability of unpublished data upon request: Yes.
Availability of data in machine-readable form: Diskettes, internet.
Website: http://www.nso.go.th/.

Turkey

Title of the survey: Household Labour Force Survey.
Organization responsible for the survey:
Planning and conduct of the survey: State Institute of Statistics.
Analysis and publication of the results: State Institute of Statistics.
Topics covered: Employment, unemployment, underemployment, hours of work, place of work, informal sector employment, duration of unemployment, discouraged workers, industry, occupation, status in employment, educational level and second jobs.
Coverage of the survey:
Geographical: Whole country.
Population groups: Persons in private households whose members are Turkish nationals, excluding residents of schools, dormitories, kindergartens, homes for elderly persons, special hospitals, military barracks and recreation quarters for officers. As from 2000, the economically active population refers to persons aged 15 years or over.
Availability of estimates from other sources for the excluded areas/groups: Not applicable.
Groups covered by the survey but excluded from the published results: None.
Periodicity:
Conduct of the survey: Monthly.
Publication of results: Quarterly.
Reference periods:
Employment: One week (last seven days prior to the date of the interview).
Seeking work: Three months prior to the date of the interview.
Availability for work: 15 days following the date of the interview.
Concepts and definitions:
Employment: Persons aged 15 years or over who, during the reference week, worked for at least one hour as regular or casual employees, employers, self-employed persons or unpaid family workers

(persons at work), and persons with a job who did not work, during the reference week, for various reasons but had a job attachment (persons not at work).

It includes:

a) persons with a job but temporarily absent from it due to illness or injury, vacation or annual leave, maternity or paternity leave, parental leave, educational or training leave, absence without leave, labour management dispute, bad weather, etc.;

b) full or part-time workers seeking other work;

c) persons who performed some work for pay or profit during the reference week but were subject to compulsory schooling, were retired and receiving a pension, or were registered as jobseekers at an employment office;

d) full or part-time students working part- or full-time;

e) paid or unpaid apprentices and trainees;

f) participants in employment promotion schemes;

g) persons engaged in production of goods for own final use;

h) persons in civilian service equivalent to military service.

Members of the armed forces (volunteers, career members, conscripts) are excluded.

Unemployment: Persons aged 15 years or over (including persons subject to compulsory schooling or retired and receiving a pension) who, during the reference week, were not employed, had taken specific steps to obtain a job during the last three months and were available to start work within 15 days.

Also considered as unemployed are persons who had already found a job or established their own enterprise but were waiting for documents to be completed in order to start work and were available to work within 15 days, as well as full- or part-time students seeking full- or part-time work and available to work within 15 days.

Underemployment:

Time-related underemployment: Persons who, during the reference week, worked less than 40 hours due to economic reasons and were able to work more hours in their present job or in another one at their current wage rate. Reasons may be slack work for technical or economic reasons, no work, impossibility to find a full-time job, or that the job has just started and/or ended during the reference week.

Inadequate employment situations: Persons (excluding those in time-related underemployment) who were seeking other work because of insufficient income or inadequate occupation.

Hours of work: Usual and actual hours worked in the main and secondary job(s). Actual hours are asked for each day of the reference week.

Employment-related income:

Income from paid employment: Not applicable.

Income from self-employment: Not applicable.

Informal sector: All non-agricultural economic units which are unincorporated (legal status: individual ownership or simple partnership), paying lump sum tax or no tax at all, and working with less than 10 persons engaged.

Usual activity: Not applicable.

Classifications:

Branch of economic activity (industry):

Title of the classification: International Standard Industrial Classification (ISIC Rev.3).

Population groups classified by industry: Employed persons and unemployed persons with previous work experience.

Number of groups used for coding: All the 292 ISIC classes (4 digit level)

Links to ISIC: ISIC- Rev. 3.

Occupation:

Title of the classification: International Standard Classification of Occupations (ISCO-88).

Population groups classified by occupation: Employed persons and unemployed persons with previous work experience.

Number of groups used for coding: All the 390 ISCO unit groups (4 digit level).

Links to ISCO: ISCO-88.

Status in employment:

Title of the classification: No information.

Population groups classified by status in employment: Employed persons and unemployed persons with previous work experience.

Groups used for classification: 6 groups (regular employees, casual employees, paid domestic workers, employers, self employed persons and unpaid family workers.

Links to ICSE: ICSE-1993.

Education:

Title of the classification: No information.

Population groups classified by education: All persons of age 6 years and older.

Groups used for classification: 11 groups (no school, primary school, primary education, general junior high school, vocational junior high school, general high school, national high school, two year vocational training school, three year vocational training school, university, master or post graduate, etc.).

Links to ISCED: Yes.

Sample size and design:

Ultimate sampling unit: Household.

Sample size (ultimate sampling units): About 23 000 households per quarter

(18 000 from urban and 5 000 from rural areas).

Overall sampling fraction: 0.388 per cent.

Sample frame: Starting with the 2000 survey, the frame is based on the 1997 Population Count. Previously, it was based on the results of the 1980, 1985 and 1990 General Population Censuses.

Updating of the sample: Annually.

Rotation: None.

Scheme: Not applicable.

Percentage of units remaining in the sample for two consecutive survey rounds: Not applicable.

Maximum number of interviews per sample unit: Not applicable.

Length of time for complete renewal of the sample: Not applicable.

Field work:

Type of interview: CAPI (Computer-assisted personal interview).

Number of ultimate sampling units per sample area: Variable.

Duration of field work:

Total: Two weeks.

Per sample area: Two weeks.

Survey organization: Permanent survey organization.

Number of field staff: Approximately 150 interviewers, 30 supervisors and 23 persons responsible for organizing the survey.

Substitution of non-responding ultimate sampling units: No.

Estimation and adjustments:

Total non-response rate: About 10 per cent.

Adjustment for total non-response: Yes.

Imputation for item non-response: No.

Adjustment for areas/population not covered: No.

Adjustment for under-coverage: No.

Adjustment for over-coverage: No.

Adjustment for seasonal variations: No.

History of the survey:

Title and date of the first survey: Household Labour Force Survey 1966.

Significant changes or revisions: Various modifications have been introduced, either in the questionnaire design (in particular in 1988, 1990 and 2000), geographical coverage, sample size or sample design.

Documentation and dissemination:

Documentation:

Survey results: Household Labour Force Results (bi-annual).

Survey methodology: Household Labour Force Survey Results (bi-annual).

Dissemination:

Time needed for initial release of survey results: About 4 months.

Advance information of public about date of initial release: No.

Availability of unpublished data upon request: Yes.

Availability of data in machine-readable form: Diskettes, internet.

Website: http://www.die.gov.tr/.

Uganda

Title of the survey: Uganda National Household Survey 1996-97: Pilot Labour Force Survey.

Organization responsible for the survey:

Planning and conduct of the survey: Uganda Bureau of Statistics.

Analysis and publication of the results: Uganda Bureau of Statistics.

Topics covered: Persons currently and usually economically active, employed and unemployed. Persons currently in time-related underemployment and persons currently outside the labour force. Persons usually employed, persons usually unemployed and persons usually not economic active (distinguishing students, home duties, too old, sick and disabled). Hours of work (for currently employed). Days worked (for usually employed). Duration of unemployment. Second jobs. Industry, occupation, status in employment, education/training levels.

Coverage of the survey:

Geographical: 36 out of 39 districts in country covered. The 3 excluded for security reasons.

Population groups: Population of age 7 years and above who were the usual residents in the selected households. Excluded where irregular members present or absent as well as visitors.
Availability of estimates from other sources for the excluded areas/groups: Not available.
Groups covered by the survey but excluded from the published results: None.
Periodicity:
Conduct of the survey: Occasional, i.e. March-November 1997.
Publication of results: Occasional, first results published December 1998.
Reference periods:
Employment: One week prior to the date of the interview for the currently employed and during the last 12 months, by own assessment, for the usually employed.
Seeking work: The survey week for the current unemployed and during the last 12 months, by own assessment, for the usually unemployed.
Availability for work: The survey week for the current unemployed and during the last 12 months, by own assessment, for the usually unemployed.
Concepts and definitions:
Employment: Persons who a) performed some work for pay or profit during the reference week; b) were temporarily absent from work during the reference week because of illness or leave, but were definitely going to return; and c) were engaged in production of goods for on use.
Excluded are persons subject to compulsory schooling and persons who were retired and were receiving a pension. Some work is defined as 1 hour or more during the reference week.
Unemployment: Persons who were currently without work and available for work, and who had searched for work.
Underemployment:
Time related underemployment: No information.
Inadequate employment situations: No information.
Hours of work: Actual hours worked, measured separately for each of 7 days used for measuring current employment.
Employment related income:
Income from paid employment: Not applicable.
Income from self-employment: Not applicable.
Informal sector: Not applicable.
Usual activity: No information.
Classifications:
Branch of economic activity (industry):
Title of the classification: No information.
Population groups classified by industry: Employed persons.
Number of groups used for coding: 58.
Links to ISIC: ISIC-Rev. 3.
Occupation:
Title of the classification: No information.
Population groups classified by occupation: Employed persons.
Number of groups used for coding: 87.
Links to ISCO: ISCO-88.
Status in employment:
Title of classification: National classification.
Population groups classified by status in employment: Employed persons.
Groups used for classification: Paid employees (distinguishing: government permanent, government temporary, government casual, private permanent, private temporary and private casual) and self-employed (distinguishing: employer, own-account worker and unpaid family worker).
Links to ICSE: ICSE-1993.
Education:
Title of the classification: National classification.
Population groups classified education: All persons.
Groups used for classification: 24.
Links to ISCED: ISCED-1976.
Sample size and design:
Ultimate sampling unit: Household.
Sample size (ultimate sampling units): 6 656.
Overall sampling fraction: 0.0017
Sample frame: The 1991 Population Census.
Updating of the sample: Each survey has a new sample.
Rotation:
Scheme: Not applicable.
Percentage of units remaining in the sample for two consecutive survey rounds: Not applicable.
Maximum number of interviews per sample unit: Not applicable.
Length of time for complete renewal of the sample: Not applicable.
Field work:
Type of interview: Personal interviews, paper and pencil.
Number of ultimate sampling units per sample area: No information.
Duration of field work:
Total: March-November, 1997.
Per sample area: No information.
Survey organization: Permanent.
Number of field staff: 48 interviewers and 12 supervisors.
Substitution of non-responding ultimate sampling units: Yes.
Estimation and adjustments:
Total non-response rate: 0.0006.
Adjustment for total non-response: Yes.
Imputation for item non-response: Yes, by use of multipliers for ten interviewed households in each sampled enumeration area to adjust according to the number of households interviewed.
Adjustment for areas/population not covered: No.
Adjustment for under-coverage: No.
Adjustment for over-coverage: No.
Adjustment for seasonal variations: No.
History of the survey:
Title and date of the first survey: Uganda National Household Survey 1996-97.
Significant changes or revisions: Not applicable.
Documentation and dissemination:
Documentation:
Survey results: 1997 Pilot Labour Force Survey No further bibliographical information.
Survey methodology: As for results.
Dissemination:
Time needed for initial release of survey results: No information.
Advance information of public about date of initial release: No.
Availability of unpublished data upon request: Yes.
Availability of data in machine-readable form: Yes.

Ukraine

Title of the survey: Population Economic Activity Sample Survey (PEASS).
Organization responsible for the survey:
Planning and conduct of the survey: State Statistics Committee of Ukraine.
Analysis and publication of the results: State Statistics Committee of Ukraine.
Topics covered: Employment (main and secondary), unemployment, hours of work, duration of employment, duration of unemployment, discouraged workers, occasional workers, industry, occupation, status in employment, educational level, as well as employment in the informal economy.
Coverage of the survey:
Geographical: Whole country, excluding the first and the second zones of nuclear contamination by the Chernobyl nuclear power plant accident (forced relocation zone).
Population groups: All the population aged 15-70 years living in private households during the reference week. Excluded is institutional and unsettled population, members of the armed force (conscripts and career) living in barracks, students living in hostels and schoolchildren living in boarding schools, as well as household members on long-time missions (six months and longer) and those residing abroad.
Availability of estimates from other sources for the excluded areas/groups: Yes.
Groups covered by the survey but excluded from the published results: NONE.
Periodicity:
Conduct of the survey: Quarterly.
Publication of results: Quarterly.
Reference periods:
Employment: One week (last seven days prior to the date of the interview).
Seeking work: Four weeks prior to the date of the interview.
Availability for work: Two weeks following the date of the interview.
Concepts and definitions:
Employment: Persons aged 15-70 years who, during the reference week:
a) performed some work for at least one hour for pay in cash or in kind, or for profit;

b) worked at least for 30 hours on individual subsidiary farming plots or in a family business or on a farm without pay ("unpaid/contributing family workers");
c) did not work, although having employment, as they were temporarily absent from their work because of illness, holidays, bad weather, labour-management dispute, etc.
Excluded from the employed are persons who during the survey week were engaged in the following activities:
a) work on individual subsidiary farming plots for own consumption;
b) voluntary work in religious, charitable or public institutions;
c) construction or renovation of own house or apartment;
d) housework.
Also included in the totals are:
a) career members of the armed forces living in households;
b) full- and part-time workers;
c) full- and part-time students working full- or part-time;
d) persons who performed some work during the reference week while being either retired and receiving a pension; or were registered as job seekers at an employment office or receiving unemployment benefits;
e) private domestic servants;
f) paid apprentices and trainees;
g) members of producers' cooperatives.
Unemployment: Unemployed are all persons of 15-70 years of age who did not work at all during the reference week, were actively looking for work during the four weeks previous to the interview, were available to start work within the two weeks following the survey week and were waiting to start a new job within a period of 30 days.
The only exception are persons who did not look for work because they had already found work but it would start at a date subsequent to the reference period. These persons are classified as unemployed.
Underemployment:
Time-related underemployment: Persons who, during the reference week, worked less number of hours than established for a given category of occupation or job, provided they were looking for and available to perform some additional work.
Inadequate employment situations: Not applicable.
Hours of work: Usual and actual hours worked in the main job and in the second job(s).
Employment-related income:
Income from paid employment: Not applicable.
Income from self-employment: Not applicable.
Informal sector: Persons engaged in any (main or secondary) non-registered economic activity with pay in cash or in kind.
Usual activity: Not applicable.
Classifications:
Branch of economic activity (industry):
Title of the classification: National ISIC Rev. 3 compatible classification.
Population groups classified by industry: Employed persons and unemployed persons with previous job experience.
Number of groups used for coding: 159 groups.
Links to ISIC: ISIC-Rev. 3 at the third digit level.
Occupation:
Title of the classification: National ISCO-88 compatible classification.
Population groups classified by occupation: Employed persons and unemployed persons with previous work experience.
Number of groups used for coding: 390 groups.
Links to ISCO: ISCO-88 at the fourth digit level.
Status in employment:
Title of the classification: ICSE-1993.
Population groups classified by status in employment: Employed persons (main and secondary jobs).
Groups used for classification: 5 groups (employees, employers, own-account worker, members of producers co-operatives, unpaid family workers).
Links to ICSE: ICSE-1993.
Education:
Title of the classification: National Classification.
Population groups classified by education: all population groups.
Groups used for classification: 8 groups (without primary general, primary general, secondary, secondary general, primary vocational, secondary vocational; not completed higher; higher (university).
Links to ISCED: No.
Sample size and design:
Ultimate sampling unit: Household.
Sample size (ultimate sampling units): About 31.000 households per quarter or some 150.000 persons annually.
Overall sampling fraction: 0.12 per cent.
Sample frame: The sample is built up automatically at the national level on the basis of the 1992 master sample (5%) drawn up for a series of special sample surveys, such as socio-demographic survey, etc. As of 2004, a new sample will be used built up on the basis of the 2001 Population Census.
Updating of the sample: Annually.
Rotation:
Scheme: Any household entering the sample at some time is expected to provide labour market information at four consecutive quarters after which it leaves the sample forever. As of 2004, a new rotation scheme will be introduced: the 2-(2)-2 pattern. Thus, a household will be included in the sample for two consecutive quarters, leave it for two quarters and return again for another two consecutive quarters before leaving the sample for ever.
Percentage of units remaining in the sample for four consecutive survey rounds: 75 per cent.
Maximum number of interviews per sample unit Four.
Length of time for complete renewal of the sample: 18 months.
Field work:
Type of interview: Paper and pencil.
Number of ultimate sampling units per sample area: No information provided.
Duration of field work:
Total: One month.
Per sample area: No information provided.
Survey organization: State Statistics Committee of Ukraine.
Number of field staff: About 510 interviewers and supervisors.
Substitution of non-responding ultimate sampling units: No.
Estimation and adjustments:
Total non-response rate:12% per cent.
Adjustment for total non-response: No.
Imputation for item non-response: Partial.
Adjustment for areas/population not covered: No.
Adjustment for undercoverage: No.
Adjustment for overcoverage: No.
Adjustment for seasonal variations: No.
History of the survey:
Title and date of the first survey: Population Economic Activity Sample Survey, October 1995 (annual).
Significant changes or revisions: Since 1999, the survey has been conducted quarterly.
Documentation and dissemination:
Documentation:
Survey results: "Economic Activity of the Population" (annual), "Economic Activity of the Population: quarterly report", "Labour in Ukraine, 2002 (year)".
Survey methodology: "LFS Methodology" (in Ukrainian and partially in English).
Dissemination:
Time needed for initial release of survey results: No information provided.
Advance information of public about date of initial release: Yes.
Availability of unpublished data upon request: Yes.
Availability of data in machine-readable form: Yes.
Website: http://www.ukrstat.gov.ua/.

United Kingdom

Title of the survey: Labour Force Survey.
Organization responsible for the survey:
Planning and conduct of the survey: Office for National Statistics.
Analysis and publication of the results: Office for National Statistics.
Topics covered: Employment, unemployment, underemployment, hours of work, wages, duration of employment, duration of unemployment, discouraged workers, industry, occupation, status in employment, educational level, second jobs.
Other topics included: earnings, disability, education and training, travel to work, sickness, union representation, benefits and health.
Coverage of the survey:
Geographical: Whole country.
Population groups: All persons aged 16 years and over living in private households and including career armed forces personnel, plus students in residence halls (enumerated at parents' address), plus National Health Service (NHS) and hospital staff living in NHS/hospital trust accommodations. Other institutional populations and communal army bases are excluded. For those aged under 16 years, only demographic details are collected. The UK working age population is 16-59 for women and 16-64 for men.

Availability of estimates from other sources for the excluded areas/groups: Not available.
Groups covered by the survey but excluded from the published results: All groups included in the sample are included in the results.
Periodicity:
Conduct of the survey: The survey is continuous, providing quarterly results.
Publication of results: Three-month rolling averages are published on a monthly basis; quarterly and annually.
Reference periods:
Employment: One moving week.
Seeking work: Last four weeks (moving reference period).
Availability for work: Two weeks (moving reference period).
Concepts and definitions:
Employment: Work for pay or profit for at least one hour per week, including unpaid family workers. Persons temporarily absent from work are employed if the temporary absence is less than six months or the person continues to be paid and has a guarantee of a return to work.
It includes:
a) persons absent due to illness, injury, vacation, annual leave, maternity or paternity leave, educational or training leave, absence without leave, labour management dispute, bad weather, mechanical breakdown, temporary or indefinite (6 months) lay-off without pay and unpaid leave initiated by the employer;
b) full and part-time workers seeking other work during the reference week;
c) persons who performed some work for pay or profit during the reference week, who were retired and receiving a pension, registered as job seekers at an employment office or receiving unemployment benefits;
d) full and part-time students working full or part-time;
e) paid apprentices and trainees;
f) participants in employment promotion schemes;
g) volunteer and career members of the armed forces.
Unemployment: Without work during the reference week, available to start work within two weeks and either has looked for work in the previous four weeks or has already found a job to start in the future.
It includes:
a) persons trying to establish their own enterprise;
b) persons retired and receiving a pension, unpaid family workers temporarily absent from work and seasonal workers not at work -if available and seeking work;
c) full and part-time students seeking full or part-time work.
Underemployment:
Time-related underemployment: ONS collects data on people who want to work additional hours and will soon begin an evaluation of the data; estimates of time-related underemployment are not published. In future a definition of underemployment in line with a Eurostat 'operationalized' interpretation of the international recommendations will be implemented.
Inadequate employment situations: Not applicable.
Hours of work: Hours usually worked in main job, actual number of hours worked in the reference week in the main job and in the second job, including paid and unpaid overtime, excluding time spent for meal breaks.
Employment-related income:
Income from paid employment: All cash earnings, payments in kind, profit-related pay and certain benefits (Income Support, Job Seekers Allowance) if quoted by the respondent. Pay can be identified by both gross and net, for both main and second jobs. The reference period is that stated in the last pay packet.
Income from self-employment: Not applicable.
Informal sector employment: Not applicable.
Usual activity: Not applicable.
Classifications:
Branch of economic activity (industry):
Title of the classification: Standard Industrial Classification 1992 (SIC92).
Population groups classified by industry: Employed and unemployed persons.
Number of groups used for coding: 458.
Links to ISIC: ISIC-Rev. 3 at the 4-digit level; SIC92 is identical.
Occupation:
Title of the classification: Standard Occupational Classification (SOC).
Population groups classified by occupation: Employed and unemployed persons.
Number of groups used for coding: 374.
Links to ISCO: SOC is as close as possible at the aggregate level. ONS and the Institute of Employment Research are revising SOC which will improve harmonization with ISCO.
Status in employment:
Title of the classification: Not available.
Population groups classified by status in employment: Employed and unemployed persons.
Groups used for classification: Four groups: Employees, Self-employed, People on Government Training Schemes, Unpaid family workers.
Links to ICSE: ICSE-1993.
Education:
Title of the classification: Not available.
Population groups classified by education: Employed and unemployed persons.
Groups used for classification: All ISCED groups.
Links to ISCED: From 1999 onwards, ISCED97 can be derived from the UK LFS data.
Sample size and design:
Ultimate sampling unit: Address.
Sample size (ultimate sampling units): 88 740 addresses.
Overall sampling fraction: Just under 0.04 per cent.
Sample frame: The "small users" subfile from the Postal Address File (PAF) plus the NHS/hospital accommodation list. The PAF is a computer list prepared by the Post Office of all the addresses (delivery points) to which mail is delivered. "Small users" are delivery points which receive fewer than 25 articles of mail per day (known to include the majority of private households).
Updating of the sample: The PAF is updated every six months by the Post Office and the NHS/hospital accommodation list is updated around once every 5 years.
Rotation:
Scheme: The sample is divided equally into five waves - one wave enters and one leaves each quarter. Sample units are interviewed once per quarter.
Percentage of units remaining in the sample for two consecutive survey rounds: 80 per cent.
Maximum number of interviews per sample unit: Five.
Length of time for complete renewal of the sample: Five quarters.
Field work:
Type of interview: Computer-assisted personal interviewing (CAPI) and Computer-assisted telephone interviewing (CATI).
Number of ultimate sampling units per sample area: (68 250 ultimate sampling units.)
Duration of field work
Total: Continuous over the year.
Per sample area: Not available.
Survey organization: Permanent.
Number of field staff: 420.
Substitution of non-responding ultimate sampling units: No.
Estimation and adjustments:
Total non-response rate: 22.3 per cent (for wave one and 5.5 per cent for waves 2-5).
Adjustment for total non-response: Yes.
Imputation for item non-response: Yes, for non-respondents and circumstantial refusals, data from the previous interview are carried forward for one period only.
Adjustment for areas/population not covered: No.
Adjustment for under-coverage: Yes.
Adjustment for over-coverage: Yes.
Adjustment for seasonal variations: Yes, using the Census X-11 Arima package. A single, standard model is used across series. Item non-response imputation improves the additivity of the seasonally adjusted series. Additivity is imposed for most seasonally adjusted series.
History of the survey:
Title and date of the first survey: The Labour Force Survey, 1973.
Significant changes or revisions:
1973 - 1983: The survey was conducted in the spring quarter every other year. (Results for 1973, 1975, and 1977 are not published due to the survey being experimental in those years.)
1984 - 1991: The survey was conducted in the spring quarter every year; various changes in the classification of specific groups in economic activity (e.g. students, training scheme participants etc. from inactivity to employment) in line with the international recommendations.
Spring 1992 onwards: The survey is continuous; updating/revision of the major economic classifications applied in the survey.
Documentation and dissemination:

Documentation:
Survey results: Labour Force Survey (year) (annual); LFS User Guide, Volume 1 (from page 130). (**Periodicity:** annual).
Survey methodology: LFS User Guide, Volume 1.
Dissemination:
Time needed for initial release of survey results: One-two months.
Advance information of public about date of initial release: Yes.
Availability of unpublished data upon request: ONS makes simple non-published tabulations available to government users and international institutions. Other tabulations can be provided by a marketing agent who will charge a fee.
Availability of data in machine-readable form: Yes.
Website: http://www.statistics.gov.uk/.

United States

Title of the survey: Current Population Survey (CPS).
Organization responsible for the survey:
Planning and conducting the survey: U.S. Bureau of the Census.
Analyzing and publishing the results: U.S. Bureau of Labor Statistics.
Topics covered:
Economically active population, employment, unemployment, underemployment (involuntary part-time), hours of work, median weekly earnings, annual income (March supplement), duration of employment and unemployment, discouraged and occasional workers, industry, occupation, status in employment, education level, usual activity (March supplement) and second jobs.
Coverage of the survey:
Geographical: Whole country.
Population groups: The civilian non-institutional population aged 16 years and over.
Excluded are: the armed forces, the institutionalized population, citizens of other countries living in embassy and US citizens living abroad.
Availability of estimates from other sources for the excluded areas/groups: Not applicable.
Groups covered by the survey but excluded from the published results: None.
Periodicity:
Conduct of the survey: Monthly.
Publication of the results: Monthly.
Reference periods:
Employment: Calendar week (Sunday through Saturday) which includes the 12th day of the month.
Seeking work: Four weeks.
Availability for work: One week.
Concepts and definitions:
Employment: Employed are all those, who during the reference week:
a) did any work at all (at least one hour) as paid employees, worked in their own business, profession, or on their own farm, or who worked 15 hours or more as unpaid workers in an enterprise operated by a member of the family;
b) all those who were not working but who had jobs or businesses from which they were temporarily absent because of vacation, illness, bad weather, childcare problems, maternity or paternity leave, labor-management dispute, job training, or other family or personal reasons, whether or not they were paid for the time off or were seeking other jobs.
Also included in the employed are:
a) persons without wage and salary work who were trying to establish their own enterprise;
b) full or part-time workers seeking other work during the reference week;
c) persons who performed some work for pay or profit during the reference week but were subject to compulsory schooling, retired and receiving a pension, registered as job seekers at an employment office or receiving unemployment benefits;
d) full or part-time students working full-time or part-time;
e) paid apprentices and trainees;
f) citizens of other countries who reside in the United Sates but not on the premises of an embassy;
g) persons residing in the United States but working in Mexico or Canada.
Excluded are persons whose only activity consisted of work around their own house (painting, repairing, or own home housework) or volunteer work for religious, charitable, and other organizations.
Unemployment: Unemployed persons are all those who had no employment during the reference week, were available for work, except for temporarily illness, and had made specific efforts to find employment some time during the 4-week-period ending with the reference week. Persons who were waiting to be recalled to a job from which they had been laid off need not have been looking for work to be classified as unemployed.
Also included in the unemployed are:
a) persons on temporary lay-off without pay;
b) persons who were seeking and available for work but were subject to compulsory schooling or were retired and receiving a pension;
c) full or part-time students seeking full or part-time work.
Underemployment:
Time-related underemployment: It covers persons working part-time for an economic reason.
Inadequate employment situations: Not applicable.
Hours of work: Actual and usual hours worked per week. Hours refer to all jobs combined.
Employment-related income: Income is not collected as part of the monthly survey, but is collected in the March supplement that is the responsibility of the Bureau of the Census.
Income from paid employment: March supplement.
Income from self-employment: March supplement.
Informal sector: No official estimates are derived directly from the survey.
Usual activity: Questions on usual activity are asked only of those not in the labor force, and only in the annual income supplement.
Classifications:
Branch of economic activity (industry):
Title of the classification: U. S. Census Bureau' s 1990 Industrial Classification System.
Population groups classified by industry: Employed and unemployed (industry of last job for the unemployed).
Number of groups used for coding: 13 major groups and 236 categories.
Links to ISIC: Indirect links to ISIC Rev.2.
Occupation:
Title of the classification: U. S. Census Bureau' s 1990 Occupational Classification System.
Population groups classified by occupation: Employed and unemployed (occupation of the last job held for the unemployed).
Number of groups used for coding: 6 summary groups, 13 major groups and 501 categories.
Links to ISCO: Indirect links to ISCO-1968.
Status in employment:
Title of the classification: U. S. Census Bureau' s Class of Worker Categories.
Population groups classified by status in employment: Employed and unemployed (status of the last job held for the unemployed).
Number of groups classified by status in employment: Three major categories: wage and salary workers in the private sector and government; self-employed and unpaid family workers.
Links to ICSE: Indirect links to ICSE-1993 with some categories comparable.
Education:
Title of the classification: U. S. Census Bureau' s education categories.
Population groups classified by education: Employed and unemployed.
Groups used for classification: Four major groups: less than a high school diploma; high school graduates, no college; less than a bachelor's degree; college graduates.
Links to ISCED: Indirect links to ISCED-1976 with some categories comparable.
Sample size and design:
Ultimate sample unit: Household.
Sample size (ultimate sampling units): About 60 000 households.
Sampling fraction: One in 2 000.
Sample frame: Decennial Censuses. Actually, the 1990 Census; beginning 2003, the 2000 Census.
Updating of the sample: Throughout the decade, updating of the sample with new construction housing units identified by building permits and periodic listing of eligible units.
Rotation:
Scheme: Rotation pattern is 4-8-4, that is households are in the sample for 4 consecutive months, then drop out of the sample for the next 8 months, finally returning to the sample for 4 final months.
Percentage of units remaining in the sample for two consecutive survey rounds: 75 per cent.
Maximum number of interviews per sample unit: Eight.
Length of time for complete renewal of the sample: 17 months.

Field work:
Type of interview: Combination of personal and telephone interviews, using CAPI (about 90 per cent) and CATI (10 per cent).
Number of ultimate sampling units per sample area: Varying.
Duration of field work:
Total: Sunday of the reference week through Wednesday of the following week.
Per sample area: No information provided.
Survey organization: Permanent.
Number of field staff: 2 000 interviewers and 100 supervisors.
Substitution of non-responding ultimate sampling units: No.
Estimations and adjustments:
Total non-response rate: 7 per cent.
Adjustment for total non-response rate: Yes.
Imputation for item non-response: Yes.
Adjustment for areas/population not covered: No.
Adjustment for undercoverage: Yes.
Adjustment for overcoverage: No.
Adjustment for seasonal variations: Yes.
History of the survey:
Title and date of the first survey: Sample Survey of Unemployment 1940.
Significant changes and revisions: In 1994, major changes to the CPS were introduced, which included a complete redesign of the questionnaire and the use of computer-assisted interviewing for the entire survey. In addition, there were revisions to some of the labor force concepts and definitions, including the implementation of some changes recommended in 1979 by the National Commission on Employment and Unemployment. In addition to the introduction of a redesigned and automated questionnaire, some of the major changes concern the criteria to define discouraged workers and persons employed part-time for economic reasons, and the addition of direct questions on layoff and multiple jobholding.
Documentation and dissemination:
Documentation:
Survey results: Employment and Earnings (monthly); The Employment Situation news release (monthly).
Survey methodology: Employment and Earnings (monthly); BLS Handbook of Methods 1997 and Current Population Survey: Design and Methodology (Technical Paper 63).
Dissemination:
Time needed for initial release of survey results: About two weeks.
Advance information of public about date of initial release: Yes.
Availability of unpublished data upon request: Yes.
Availability of data in machine-readable form: Diskettes and magnetic tapes.
Website: http://www.bls.gov/.

West Bank and Gaza strip

Title of the survey: Labour Force Survey.
Organization responsible for the survey:
Planning and conduct of the survey: Palestinian Central Bureau of Statistics (PCBS).
Analysis and publication of the results: Palestinian Central Bureau of Statistics (PCBS).
Topics covered: Employment, unemployment, underemployment, hours of work, wages, duration of employment and unemployment, discouraged workers, industry, occupation, status in employment, education, second jobs, outside the labor force, monthly working days.
Coverage of the survey:
Geographical: Whole territory.
Population groups: All persons aged 10 years and over, excluding persons living in institutions and those residing abroad for more than one year.
Availability of estimates from other sources for the excluded areas/groups: No information.
Groups covered by the survey but excluded from the published results: Persons aged 10 to 14 years.
Periodicity:
Conduct of the survey: Continuous survey.
Publication of results: Quarterly and annual.
Reference periods:
Employment: Moving reference week. The week ending on the Friday preceding the interviewer's visit to the household.
Seeking work: Moving reference week. The week ending on the Friday preceding the interviewer's visit to the household.
Availability for work: Moving reference week. The week ending on the Friday preceding the interviewer's visit to the household.
Concepts and definitions:
Employment: Persons aged 15 years old and over who worked at least one hour during the reference period, or who were not at work during the reference week, but held a job or owned a business from which they were temporarily absent (because of illness, vacation, temporary stoppage,maternity, parental or educational/training leave, or any other reason).
Are also considered as employed:
a) persons on temporary lay-off without pay;
b) full or part-time workers seeking other work during the reference week;
c) full or part-time students working part or full-time;
d) paid and unpaid apprentices and trainees;
e) unpaid family workers (at work or temporarily absent from work during the reference week);
f) members of the armed forces (volunteers, career members and conscripts).
Unemployment: Persons aged 15 years and over, who did not work during the reference week, who were not absent from a job and were available for work and actively seeking a job during the reference week. Seeking work is defined as having taken specific steps, during the reference week, to find paid employment or self-employment. Job seekers are classified into:
i) available for work: a person ready to work if he/she is offered any job, and there is no reason preventing him/her from accepting such a job although he/she did nothing to obtain one;
ii) actively seeking work: a person who is willing to work and is actively seeking work trough reading newspapers advertisements, asking friends, registration at the labour exchange offices, or asking employers.
Are also considered as unemployed:
a) persons who work in Israel and were absent from work due to closures;
b) persons on indefinite lay-off without pay or on unpaid leave initiated by the employer;
c) persons without work and currently available for work who had made arrangements to start a new job on a date subsequent to the reference week or who were trying to establish their own enterprise;
d) full or part-time students, available for work, seeking full or part-time work.
Underemployment:
Time related underemployment: Persons who worked less than 35 hours during the reference week or worked less than the normal hours of work in their occupation.
Inadequate employment situations: Misapplication of labour resources or fundamental imbalance as between labour and other factors, such as insufficient income, underutilization, bad conditions of the current work, or other economic reasons.
Hours of work: Total number of hours actually worked during the reference week as well as overtime and time spent at the place of work on activities such as preparation of the workplace. Leaves, meal breaks and time spent on travel from home to work and vice versa are excluded from worked hours.
Employment-related income:
Income from paid employment: Not covered by the survey.
Income from self-employment: Not covered by the survey.
Informal sector: Not covered by the survey.
Usual activity: Not covered by the survey.
Classifications:
Branch of economic activity (industry):
Title of the classification: National classification based on ISIC-Rev.3.
Population groups classified by industry: Employed and unemployed persons with previous work experience during the last 12 months.
Number of groups used for coding: 4-digit level.
Linked to ISIC: ISIC- Rev. 3.
Occupation:
Title of the classification: National classification based on ISCO-88.
Population groups classified by occupation: Employed and unemployed persons with previous work experience during the last 12 months.
Number of groups used for coding: 3-digit level.
Linked to ISCO: ISCO-88.
Status in employment:
Title of the classification: National classification.

Population groups classified by status in employment: Employed and unemployed persons with work experience during the last 12 months.
Groups used for classification: Employers, employees, self-employed persons, unpaid family workers, others.
Linked to ICSE: ICSE-1993.
Education:
Title of the classification: National classification.
Population groups classified by educational level: All persons aged 10 years and above.
Groups used for classification: Illiterate; can read and write; elementary education; preparatory education; secondary education; associate diploma; BA/BS; higher diploma; master degree; Ph. D.
Linked to ISCED: ISCED-76.
Sample size and design:
Ultimate sampling unit: Households.
Sample size (ultimate sampling units): About 7 600 households covering approximately 22 000 persons of working age.
Overall sampling fraction: 1.7 %.
Sample frame: Master Sample based on the 1997 Housing and Establishments Census. The survey is based on a two-stage stratified cluster random sample.
Updating of the sample: December 1999, on the basis of households listings.
Rotation:
Scheme: Households are retained in the sample for two consecutive rounds, then leaves the sample in the next two rounds, and returns in the sample for two more consecutive rounds before leaving the sample.
Percentage of units remaining in the sample for two consecutive survey rounds: 50 %.
Maximum number of interviews per sample unit: 4.
Length of time for complete renewal of the sample: 5 years.
Field work:
Type of interview: Personal interview with paper and pencil recording.
Number of ultimate sampling units per sample area: 16 households.
Duration of fieldwork:
Total: 3 months (continuous field work).
Per sample unit: Two days.
Survey organization: Permanent.
Number of field staff: 12 interviewers, 4 supervisors, 2 coders, 2 editors and 1 coordinator.
Substitution of non-responding sampling units: No.
Estimation and adjustments:
Total non-response rate: 9 %.
Adjustment for total non-response: Yes.
Imputation for item non-response: No.
Adjustment for areas/population not covered: Not applicable.
Adjustment for undercoverage: Yes.
Adjustment for overcoverage: Yes.
Adjustment for seasonal variations: No.
History of the survey:
Title and date of the first survey: Labor Force Survey 1995.
Significant changes or revisions: Not applicable.
Documentation and dissemination:
Documentation:
Survey results: Labour Force Survey: Main Findings (quarterly); Labour Force Survey: Annual Report.
Survey methodology: Same as above.
Dissemination:
Time needed for initial release of survey results: About 2 months.
Advance information of public about date of initial release: Yes.
Availability of unpublished data upon request: Yes.
Availability of data in machine-readable form: Tabulated data available in machine readable format on request.
Website: http://www.pcbs.org/.

Yemen, Rep. of

Title of the survey: Labour force sample survey for the year 1999.
Organization responsible for the survey:
Planning and conduct of the survey: Central Statistical Organization & Ministry of Labour and Vocational Training.
Analysis and publication of the results: Central Statistical Organization.
Topics covered: Employment, unemployment, hours of work, wages, duration of employment, duration of unemployment, discouraged workers, occasional workers, industry, current and past occupation, status in employment, and education level.
Coverage of the survey:
Geographical: Whole country except islands of Soqotra and Kamaran and remote desert areas in Hadhramout and Al-Jouf. The cost of conducting the survey in these areas is high and the proportion of population insignificant.
Population groups: Excluded are persons living in hospitals, camps, hotels, motels, dormitories and other institutional compounds, nomads, and persons living abroad during survey period and homeless persons without permanent place of living.
Availability of estimates from other sources for the excluded areas/groups: Estimates based on the 1994 census exist for population in islands and remote areas (Muderias), nomadic population and population living in institutions.
Groups covered by the survey but excluded from the published results: Foreigners.
Periodicity:
Conduct of the survey: Occasional.
Publication of results: Following each survey.
Reference periods:
Employment: Fixed reference week.
Seeking work: One month.
Availability for work: Two weeks.
Concepts and definitions
Employment: Persons, 15 years old and over, who were worked even for one hour during the reference week in return for reward, wage or family earning, or who were temporarily away from work because of leave or sickness. [Questions on economic characteristics are however addressed to all persons 6 years of age and older.]
It includes:
a) Persons who performed some work for pay or profit during the reference week but were subject to compulsory schooling, retired and receiving a pension, registered as jobseekers at an employment office, or receiving unemployment benefits.
b) Full or part-time students working full or part-time.
c) Paid and unpaid apprentices and trainees if associated with work.
d) Persons engaged in production of goods for own final use.
e) Unpaid family workers at work or temporarily absent from work during the reference week.
f) Members of the armed forces including conscripts, volunteers and career officers, and persons engaged in civilian service equivalent to military service.
Excluded are:
a) Persons engaged in production of services for their household.
b) Persons on temporary or indefinite lay-off without pay and persons on unpaid leave initiated by the employer.
Unemployment: Persons, 15 years old and over, not employed during the reference week, who were capable and ready to work within two weeks of the date of the interview, and have taken steps to search for work during the month prior the survey period.
It includes:
a) Persons on temporary or indefinite lay off without pay.
b) Persons without work and current available and looking for work who had made arrangements to start a new job on a date subsequent to the reference week.
c) Persons without work and currently available and looking for work trying to establish their own enterprise.
d) Persons without work, available for work, but not seeking work during the month prior to the survey period for specific reasons.
e) Full or part-time students seeking full or part-time work.
f) Persons who were seeking or available for work but were subject to compulsory schooling or retired and receiving a pension.
Underemployment:
Time-related underemployment: No information.
Inadequate employment situations: No information.
Hours of work: Total number of hours actually worked in the main job in each working day of the reference week. Total number of hours actually worked in the secondary job during the reference week.
Employment related income:
Income from paid employment: Total wages and salaries of paid employees before income taxes and other fees, whether in cash or in kind, received on daily, weekly, fortnightly or monthly basis, including vacation allowances and incentives, and similar payments. Wages refer to the last payment received. Data are collected for the main job and secondary jobs separately.
Income from self-employment: No information.
Classifications:
Branch of economic activity (industry):
Title of the classification: No information.

Population groups classified by industry: Employed and unemployed persons with previous work experience.
Number of groups used for coding: At third level of the classification.
Linked to ISIC: ISIC-Re. 3 at the third digit.
Occupation:
Title of the classification: No information.
Population groups classified by occupation: Employed and unemployed persons with previous work experience.
Number of groups used for coding: At the fourth level of the classification.
Linked to ISCO: ISCO-1988 at the fourth digit.
Status in employment:
Title of the classification: No information.
Population groups classified by status in employment: Employed persons only.
Groups used for classification: Paid employee. Work owner. Working on his or her own. Working for family without wage. Working for others without wage.
Linked to ICSE: ICSE-1993.
Education:
Title of the classification: No information.
Population groups classified by education: All persons 10 years of age and over.
Groups used for classification: Illiterate. Can read and write; primary; unified. Elementary/basic; institute and vocational training center; technical and vocational secondary school; general secondary school; diploma after secondary school; university; higher studies (post graduate).
Links to ISCED: Certain groups linked to ISCED-1997.
Sample size and design:
Ultimate sampling unit: Household.
Sample size (ultimate sampling units): 19 955 households.
Overall sampling fraction: 0.92%.
Sample frame: Master sample frame constructed for the 1999 National Poverty Survey based on the list of Enumeration Areas of the 1994 Population Census. The Master Sample Frame was stratified into 20 Governorates and within each Governorate into urban and rural areas. A sub-sample of the 1999 National Poverty Survey was selected for the 1999 Labour Force Survey.
Updating of the sample: Updating of the sample was carried through the household listing process in each selected enumeration area.
Rotation: None.
Field work:
Type of interview: Personal interview.
Number of ultimate sampling units per sample area: 15 households in rural areas and 20 households in rural areas.
Duration of fieldwork:
Total: 20 days from 13th November to 2nd December 1999.
Per sample area: One day per team of three interviewers covering 15 rural households or 20 urban households.
Survey organization: Ad-hoc.
Number of field staff: About 253 interviewers, 81 team leaders and 20 supervisors.
Substitution of non-responding sampling units: No information provided.
Estimation and adjustments:
Total non-response rate: 4.4%.
Adjustment for total non-response: No information provided.
Imputation for item non-response: No.
Adjustment for areas/population not covered: Yes.
Adjustment for under-coverage: No information provided.
Adjustment for over-coverage: No information provided.
Adjustment for seasonal variations: No.
History of the survey:
Title and date of the first survey: Labour force sample survey, 6th December 1991.
Significant changes or revisions: Not applicable.
Documentation and dissemination:
Documentation:
Survey results: Final Report. 1999 Labour Force Survey Results
Survey methodology: In Final Report.
Dissemination:
Time needed for initial release of survey results: One year. Data for 1999 published in November 2000.
Advance information of public about date of initial release: No information provided.
Availability of unpublished data upon request: No information provided.
Availability of data in machine-readable form: Tabulated data available in diskettes on request, and through the Labour Market Information System.

Zimbabwe

Title of the survey: Indicator Monitoring - Labour Force Survey.
Organization responsible for the survey:
Planning and conduct of the survey: Central Statistical Office.
Analysis and publication of the results: Central Statistical Office.
Topics covered: Employment, unemployment, hours of work, income from employment, informal sector employment, occasional workers, industry, occupation, status in employment, education and qualification (skill) levels, main and secondary activities during the last twelve months.
Coverage of the survey:
Geographical: Whole country.
Population groups: No information provided.
Availability of estimates from other sources for the excluded areas/groups: Not applicable.
Groups covered by the survey but excluded from the published results: None.
Periodicity:
Conduct of the survey: Every five years. The last survey was conducted in June 1999.
Publication of results: Every five years.
Reference periods:
Employment: Moving reference period of seven days prior to the interview date.
Seeking work: Moving reference period of seven days prior to the interview date.
Availability for work: Moving reference period of seven days prior to the interview date.
Concepts and definitions:
Employment: Persons aged 15 years or over whose main activity during the reference week was employment, and who worked for at least one hour during the reference week. Included are: (a) contributing family workers at work during the reference week; (b) full- or part-time workers seeking other work; (c) persons who performed some work for pay or profit during the reference week but who were registered as job seekers at an employment office or receiving unemployment benefits; (d) full-time students working full- or part-time; (e) part-time students working full- or part-time; (f) paid or unpaid apprentices and trainees; (g) participants in employment promotion schemes; and (h) persons engaged in the production of goods for own final use.
Also included are persons in paid employment or self-employment, who were temporarily absent from work during the reference week because of (a) illness or injury, (b) vacation or annual leave, (c) maternity or paternity leave, (d) parental leave, (e) educational or training leave, (f) absence without leave, (g) labour management dispute, (h) bad weather, mechanical breakdown, etc., (i) temporary lay-off without pay, or (j) unpaid leave initiated by the employer.
This includes contributing family workers temporarily absent from work during the reference week, as well as seasonal workers not at work during the off-season.
Excluded are: (a) persons who performed some work for pay or profit during the reference week but who were subject to compulsory schooling, or retired and receiving a pension; (b) persons on indefinite lay-off without pay; and (c) persons rendering unpaid or personal services to members of their own household.
Unemployment: Persons aged 15 years or over whose main activity during the reference week was unemployment, who were available for work during the reference week, and who had actively looked for work during the reference week. Included are: (a) persons without work and currently available for work, who had made arrangements to start a new job on a date subsequent to the reference week; (b) persons without work and currently available for work, who were trying to establish their own enterprise; (c) persons seeking work and available for work, who were subject to compulsory schooling or retired and receiving a pension; and (d) part-time students seeking full- or part-time work.
Excluded are full-time students seeking full- or part-time work, unless their main activity during the reference week was unemployment.
Persons without work and available for work during the reference week, who were not seeking work, are excluded from the unemployed defined strictly. However, such persons are including under a broad definition of unemployment.
Underemployment
Time-related underemployment: This topic is not covered by the survey. However, questions are asked to employed persons on

whether or not they would have liked to work more hours during the reference week without being paid overtime, and on the number of additional hours which they would have preferred to work during the reference week without being paid overtime.
Inadequate employment situations: This topic is not covered by the survey.
Hours of work: Hours worked during the reference week, including overtime and approved time away from work. The information refers to the main job.
Employment-related income:
Income from paid employment: Cash income received for work in the last month (under $500, $500-$749, $750-$999, $1000-$1499, $1500-$1999, $2000-$2499, $2500-$2999, $3000 or more).
Income from self-employment: Cash income received for work in the last month (under $500, $500-$749, $750-$999, $1000-$1499, $1500-$1999, $2000-$2499, $2500-$2999, $3000 or more).
Informal sector: Questions are asked about the sector of the establishment (private, central government, local government, parastatal, cooperative, other), the number of persons working in the establishment (less than 10, 10 or more), and the registration/licensing of the establishment (registered only, licensed only with premises, licensed only without premises, registered and licensed, none).
Usual activity: This topic is not covered by the survey. However, questions are asked about the main and secondary activities of persons during the last twelve months.
Classifications:
Branch of economic activity (industry):
Title of the classification: No information provided.
Population groups classified by industry: Employed persons.
Number of groups used for coding: 13.
Links to ISIC: ISIC- Rev. 2.
Occupation:
Title of the classification: No information provided.
Population groups classified by occupation: Employed persons.
Number of groups used for coding: 23.
Links to ISCO: ISCO-88.
Status in employment:
Title of the classification: National classification of status in employment.
Population groups classified by status in employment: Employed persons.
Groups used for classification: (a) Paid employees – permanent; (b) paid employees – casual, temporary, contract or seasonal; (c) employers; (d) own-account workers – communal and resettlement farmers; (e) own-account workers – others; (f) unpaid family workers.
Links to ICSE: Partially to ICSE-1993..
Education:
Title of the classification used: National classification of levels of education.
Population groups classified by education: All persons aged 5 years or over.
Groups used for classification: (a) Grade 1 not completed; (b) Grade 1; (c) Grade 2; (d) Grade 3; (e) Grade 4; (f) Grade 5; (g) Grade 6; (h) Grade 7; (i) Form 1; (j) Form 2; (k) Form 3; (l) Form 4; (m) Form 5; (n) Form 6; (o) Diploma/Certificate after primary; (p) Diploma/Certificate after secondary; (q) graduate or postgraduate.
Links to ISCED: No information provided.
Sample size and design:
Ultimate sampling unit: Household.
Sample size (ultimate sampling units): 14,000 households.
Overall sampling fraction: No information provided. The sampling rate varies among provinces.
Sample frame: The Zimbabwe Master Sample 1992 (ZMS 92) is used as area sampling frame for the survey. It was developed following the Population Census 1992.
Updating of the sample: Prior to the survey, households in the sample enumeration areas (EA) are re-listed. This is done together with the updating of EA maps.
Rotation:
Scheme: Households included in the master sample are rotated about every three years.
Percentage of units remaining in the sample for two consecutive survey rounds: 0 percent.
Maximum number of interviews per sample unit: One.
Length of time for complete renewal of the sample: Three years.
Field work:
Type of interview: Information is obtained through personal interviews.
Number of ultimate sampling units per sample area: No information provided.
Duration of field work:
Total: Two weeks.
Per sample area: No information provided.
Survey organization: A permanent survey organization exists for the survey.
Number of field staff: 160.
Substitution of non-responding ultimate sampling units: No replacement is made for non-responding households. However, based on past experience the initial sample size is increased in order to account for non-response. For urban areas, the over-sampling is higher than for rural areas.
Estimation and adjustments:
Total non-response rate: 25 percent.
Adjustment for total non-response: Yes.
Imputation for item non-response: No.
Adjustment for areas/population not covered: No.
Adjustment for under-coverage: No.
Adjustment for over-coverage: No.
Adjustment for seasonal variations: Not applicable.
History of the survey
Title and date of the first survey: The first Labour Force Survey was conducted in February 1986.
Significant changes or revisions: No information provided.
Documentation and dissemination
Documentation:
Survey results: Central Statistical Office, Indicator Monitoring – Labour Force Survey Report (periodicity: every five years).
Survey methodology: The above-mentioned publication includes methodological information on the survey.
Dissemination:
Time needed for initial release of survey results: About two years.
Advance information of public about date of initial release: No information provided.
Availability of unpublished data upon request: Unpublished data can be released upon a written request to the Director of the Central Statistical Office.
Availability of data in machine-readable form: Yes.

Afrique du Sud

Titre de l'enquête: Labour Force Survey.
Organisme responsable de l'enquête:
Organisation et déroulement de l'enquête: Statistics South Africa (Stats SA).
Analyse et Publication des résultats: Statistics South Africa (Stats SA).
Sujets couverts par l'enquête: Emploi, chômage, sous-emploi, durée du travail, salaires, revenu, emploi dans le secteur informel, durée de l'emploi et du chômage, travailleurs découragés, industrie, profession, situation dans la profession, niveau d'instruction/de qualification.
Champ de l'enquête:
Territoire: L'ensemble du pays.
Groupes de population: L'enquête inclut tous les groupes de population (ménages ordinaires et résidents de foyers de travailleurs), mais les questions relatives à l'emploi et au chômage ne sont posées qu'aux personnes âgées de 15 ans et plus. Les personnes vivant en établissement (cités universitaires, homes pour personnes âgées, hôpitaux, prisons et casernes) sont exclues.
Disponibilité d'estimations selon d'autres sources pour les régions ou groupes exclus: Néant.
Groupes couverts par l'enquête mais exclus des résultats publiés: Néant.
Périodicité:
Réalisation de l'enquête: Deux fois par an.
Publication des résultats: Deux fois par an.
Période de référence:
Emploi: La semaine précédant l'entretien, en février et en septembre de chaque année.
Recherche d'un emploi: Quatre semaines avant l'entretien, en février et en septembre de chaque année.
Disponibilité pour travailler: Une semaine après l'entretien, en février et en septembre de chaque année.
Concepts et définitions:
Emploi: Toutes les personnes âgées de 15 à 65 ans qui ont exercé l'une des activités ci-après, sauf la mendicité:
a)dirigé n'importe quel type d'entreprise, grande ou petite, ou fait n'importe quel type de transactions, pour leur propre compte ou avec un ou plusieurs associés;
b)effectué un travail quelconque pour un salaire, un traitement, une commission ou un quelconque paiement en nature (sauf le travail ménager);
c)effectué un travail quelconque en tant qu'employé de maison pour un salaire, un traitement ou un quelconque paiement en nature;
d)effectué un travail quelconque, seules ou dans la parcelle, la ferme, le jardin potager, le ranch ou le kraal (enclos à bétail) du ménage, ou aidé à faire pousser des produits agricoles ou à s'occuper d'animaux pour le ménage;
e)effectué un quelconque travail de construction ou un travail de réparation important à son domicile, dans sa parcelle, son ranch ou son entreprise ou dans ceux du ménage; ont attrapé des poissons, des crevettes, des coquillages, des animaux sauvages ou se sont procuré toute autre denrée alimentaire destinée à la vente ou à l'alimentation du ménage.
Les personnes qui n'ont pas travaillé pendant la semaine de référence mais qui ont un emploi auquel elles peuvent retourner sont également classées comme ayant un emploi. La morte-saison agricole n'est pas une absence temporaire.
Sont également considérées comme ayant un emploi les étudiants à plein temps ou à temps partiel ayant travaillé à plein temps et ceux qui ont travaillé à temps partiel au cours des sept jours précédant l'entretien, ainsi que les apprentis et stagiaires rémunérés ou non.
Chômage: Deux définitions du chômage sont utilisées: l'« officielle » et l'« élargie ».
La « définition officielle » se réfère aux personnes âgées de 15 à 65 ans qui:
a)n'ont pas travaillé au cours des sept jours précédant l'entretien;
b)veulent travailler et sont disponibles pour commencer à travailler dans un délai d'une semaine après l'entretien;
c)ont effectué des démarches pour chercher du travail ou commencer à exercer certaines formes de travail indépendant au cours des quatre semaines précédant l'entretien.
La « définition élargie » exclut le critère c).
Sous-emploi:
Sous-emploi lié à la durée du travail: Cette catégorie couvre les personnes qui:
a)travaillent moins d'heures que la durée normale du travail dans une activité donnée;
b)n'ont pas choisi de travailler moins d'heures (le nombre d'heures de travail n'est pas le fait de leur volonté);
c)sont disposées à faire davantage d'heures de travail;
d)ont effectué des démarches pour chercher du travail supplémentaire au cours des quatre semaines précédant l'enquête.
Situations d'emploi inadéquat: Non couvert par l'enquête.
Durée du travail: Les heures de travail réellement effectuées et les heures habituelles sont couvertes par l'enquête. Dans les deux cas, les données sont présentées séparément pour l'activité principale, les autres activités exercées et le nombre total d'heures.
Revenu lié à l'emploi:
Revenu lié à l'emploi salarié: Se réfère aux gains réguliers ou totaux en espèces, y compris la rémunération des heures supplémentaires, les indemnités et les primes avant impôts ou déductions quelconques. Ne se réfère qu'à l'activité principale.
Revenu lié à l'emploi indépendant: Même chose s'il s'agit de l'activité principale.
Secteur informel: Les enquêtés sont interrogés sur leur lieu de travail, qu'il se trouve dans le secteur formel ou informel. Il y a emploi dans le secteur informel lorsque l'employeur (institution, entreprise ou employeur privé) n'est pas enregistré pour exercer son activité.
Activité habituelle: Non couvert par l'enquête.
Classifications:
Branche d'activité économique (industrie)
Titre de la classification: Classification internationale.
Groupes de population classifiés selon l'industrie: Les personnes ayant un emploi et les chômeurs (industrie du dernier emploi occupé pour ces derniers).
Nombre de groupes de codage: 190.
Convertibilité avec la CITI: CITI-Rév.3 (1988).
Profession
Titre de la classification: Classification internationale.
Groupes de population classifiés selon la profession: Les personnes ayant un emploi et les chômeurs (profession exercée dans le dernier emploi pour ces derniers).
Nombre de groupes de codage: 369.
Convertibilité avec la CITP: CITP-1988.
Situation dans la profession
Titre de la classification: Classification nationale.
Groupes de population classifiés par situation dans la profession: Les personnes ayant un emploi.
Catégories de codage: Salariés et travailleurs indépendants.
Convertibilité avec la CISP: Non disponible.
Education
Titre de la classification: Classification nationale.
Groupes de population classifiés selon l'éducation: Les personnes ayant un emploi et les chômeurs ainsi que les inactifs (de tout âge).
Catégories de codage: Pas de scolarité; années d'études 0 à 12; NTC I à NTC III; diplôme/certificat au niveau inférieur à l'année d'études 12; diplôme/certificat au niveau d'année d'études 12; diplôme universitaire, diplôme ou titre universitaire de troisième cycle.
Convertibilité avec la CITE: CITE-1997.
Taille de l'échantillon et plan de sondage:
Unité finale d'échantillonnage: Logement.
Taille de l'échantillon (unités finales d'échantillonnage): 30 000 logements.
Taux de sondage: Non disponible.
Base de sondage: La base de données des secteurs de recensement, telle qu'elle a été établie pendant la phase de démarcation du recensement de 1996, a constitué la base de sondage à partir de laquelle ont été sélectionnés les secteurs de recensement utilisés pour l'Enquête sur la main-d'œuvre.
Renouvellement de l'échantillon: Annuel.
Rotation:
Schéma: Les mêmes logements sont visités à cinq reprises différentes au maximum, ce qui signifie une rotation de 20 pour cent des unités de logement à chaque fois.
Pourcentage d'unités restant dans l'échantillon durant deux enquêtes successives: 80 pour cent.
Nombre maximum d'interrogatoires par unité de sondage: Cinq.
Durée nécessaire au renouvellement complet de l'échantillon: Cinq enquêtes.
Déroulement de l'enquête:
Type d'entretien: Entretiens personnels.
Nombre d'unités finales d'échantillonnage par zone de sondage: Dix.
Durée de déroulement de l'enquête:
Totale: 21 jours (par exemple du 2 au 22 septembre 2001).

Par zone de sondage: Environ 14 heures.
Organisation: Structures d'enquête permanente et ad hoc.
Nombre de personnes employées: Environ 936 personnes (personnel permanent et contractuel).
Substitution des unités finales en cas de non-réponse: Non.
Estimations et redressements:
Taux de non-réponse: Environ 10%.
Redressement pour non-réponse: Oui.
Imputation en cas de non-réponse à une question spécifique: Non.
Redressement pour les régions/populations non couvertes: Non.
Redressement en cas de sous-représentation: Oui.
Redressement en cas de sur-représentation: Oui.
Corrections des variations saisonnières: Non.
Historique de l'enquête:
Titre et date de la première enquête: Labour Force Survey 2000.
Modifications et révisions significatives: Ne s'applique pas.
Documentation et dissémination:
Documentation
Titre des publications publiant les résultats (deux fois par an):Statistical Releases (P0210).
Titre des publications méthodologiques: Labour Force Survey (deux fois par an).
Dissémination
Délai de publication des premiers résultats: Environ 6 mois après le déroulement de l'enquête (le 26 mars 2002 pour les résultats de septembre 2001).
Information à l'avance du public des dates de publication initiale des résultats: Oui.
Mise à disposition, sur demande, des données non publiées: Non.
Mise à disposition des données sur support informatique: Oui.
Site web: http://www.statssa.gov.za/.

Albanie

Titre de l'enquête: Household Living Conditions Survey, octobre 1998.
Organisme responsable de l'enquête:
Organisation et déroulement de l'enquête: Albanian Institute of Statistics (INSTAT).
Analyse et Publication des résultats: Albanian Institute of Statistics (INSTAT).
Sujets couverts par l'enquête: Emploi, chômage, durée du travail, salaires, revenu, durée de l'emploi et du chômage, travailleurs découragés, travailleurs occasionnels, industrie, profession, éducation.
Champ de l'enquête:
Territoire: L'ensemble du pays.
Groupes de population: La totalité de la population résidente.
Disponibilité d'estimations selon d'autres sources pour les régions ou groupes exclus: Ne s'applique pas.
Groupes couverts par l'enquête mais exclus des résultats publiés: Ne s'applique pas.
Périodicité:
Réalisation de l'enquête: Première enquête en 1998.
Publication des résultats: En 2001.
Période de référence:
Emploi: La semaine précédant la date de l'entretien.
Recherche d'un emploi: La semaine précédant la date de l'entretien.
Disponibilité pour travailler: La semaine précédant la date de l'entretien.
Concepts et définitions:
Emploi: Toutes les personnes âgées de 15 ans et plus qui, au cours de la semaine de l'enquête, ont effectué un travaillé quelconque pendant au moins une heure.
Sont inclus dans les personnes ayant un emploi:
a) les personnes ayant un emploi mais temporairement absentes pour cause de maladie ou d'accident, de vacances annuelles, de congé de maternité ou de paternité, de congé parental, de congé d'éducation ou de formation, d'intempéries, de panne mécanique, etc.;
b) les travailleurs occupés à plein temps ou à temps partiel et en quête d'un autre travail durant la période de référence;
c) les personnes à la retraite et au bénéfice d'une pension, les personnes inscrites en tant que demandeurs d'emploi et celles percevant des allocations de chômage, qui ont travaillé en vue d'une rémunération ou d'un bénéfice pendant la semaine de référence;
d) les étudiants à plein temps ou à temps partiel travaillant à plein temps ou à temps partiel;
e) les apprentis et stagiaires rémunérés;
f) les travailleurs familiaux non rémunérés travaillant pendant la semaine de l'enquête ou temporairement absents de leur travail.
Chômage: Toutes les personnes âgées de 15 ans et plus qui n'ont pas travaillé au cours de la dernière semaine, qui cherchaient un emploi et étaient disponibles pour travailler.
Sous-emploi
Sous-emploi lié à la durée du travail: Non couvert par l'enquête.
Situations d'emploi inadéquat: Non couvert par l'enquête.
Durée du travail: Non disponible.
Revenu lié à l'emploi
Revenu lié à l'emploi salarié: Salaire mensuel moyen des salariés.
Revenu lié à l'emploi indépendant: Revenu lié à une activité privée.
Secteur informel: Non disponible.
Activité habituelle: Situation économique (personnes ayant un emploi, chômeurs, inactifs) au cours des 12 derniers mois.
Classifications:
Branche d'activité économique (industrie):
Titre de la classification: Classification nationale fondée sur la nomenclature européenne NACE.
Groupes de population classifiés selon l'industrie: Les personnes ayant un emploi et les chômeurs (industrie du dernier emploi occupé pour ces derniers).
Nombre de groupes de codage: Non disponible.
Convertibilité avec la CITI: CITI-Rév.3.
Profession:
Titre de la classification: CITP-1988 au niveau à trois chiffres.
Groupes de population classifiés selon la profession: Les personnes ayant un emploi et les chômeurs (profession exercée dans le dernier emploi pour ces derniers).
Nombre de groupes de codage: 116 sous-groupes.
Convertibilité avec la CITP: CITP-1988.
Situation dans la profession:
Titre de la classification: Classification nationale.
Groupes de population classifiés par situation dans la profession: Les personnes ayant un emploi.
Catégories de codage: Salariés, employeurs et travailleurs indépendants.
Convertibilité avec la CISP: Non.
Education:
Titre de la classification: Classification nationale.
Groupes de population classifiés selon l'éducation: Les personnes ayant un emploi et les chômeurs.
Catégories de codage: 5 groupes.
Convertibilité avec la CITE: CITE-1997.
Taille de l'échantillon et plan de sondage:
Unité finale d'échantillonnage: Ménage.
Taille de l'échantillon (unités finales d'échantillonnage): 11 826 ménages.
Taux de sondage: Non disponible.
Base de sondage: Non disponible.
Renouvellement de l'échantillon: Non disponible.
Rotation:
Schéma: Ne s'applique pas.
Pourcentage d'unités restant dans l'échantillon durant deux enquêtes successives: Ne s'applique pas.
Nombre maximum de fois que peut être interrogée une unité de sondage: Ne s'applique pas.
Temps nécessaire au renouvellement complet de l'échantillon: Ne s'applique pas.
Déroulement de l'enquête:
Type d'entretien: Entretiens personnels.
Nombre d'unités finales de sondage par zone de sondage: Non disponible.
Durée de déroulement de l'enquête:
Totale: Non disponible.
Par zone de sondage: Non disponible.
Organisation: Ad hoc.
Nombre de personnes employées pour la réalisation de l'enquête: Non disponible.
Substitution des unités finales en cas de non-réponse: Non.
Estimations et redressements:
Taux de non-réponse: Non disponible.
Redressement pour non-réponse: Non disponible.
Imputation en cas de non-réponse à une question spécifique: Non disponible.
Redressement pour les régions/populations non couvertes: Non disponible.
Redressement en cas de sous-représentation: Non disponible.
Redressement en cas de sur-représentation: Non disponible.

Corrections des variations saisonnières: Non.
Historique de l'enquête:
Titre et date de la première enquête: Household Living Conditions Survey 1998.
Modifications et révisions significatives: Ne s'applique pas.
Documentation et dissémination:
Documentation:
Titre des publications publiant les résultats: General Results of Household Living Conditions Survey 1998.
Titre des publications méthodologiques: General Results of Household Living Conditions Survey 1998.
Dissémination:
Délai de publication des premiers résultats: Environ trois ans.
Information à l'avance du public des dates de publication initiale des résultats: Oui.
Mise à disposition, sur demande, des données non publiées: Non.
Mise à disposition des données sur support informatique: Non.
Site web: http://www.instat.gov.al.

Allemagne

Titre de l'enquête: Micro-census (Mikrozensus)/ European Union Labour Force Survey
Organisme responsable de l'enquête:
Organisation et déroulement de l'enquête: Federal Statistical Office (Statistisches Bundesamt) et State Statistical Offices (Statistiche Landesämter).
Analyse et Publication des résultats: Federal Statistical Office (Statistisches Bundesamt) et State Statistical Offices (Statistiche Landesämter).
Sujets couverts par l'enquête: Emploi, chômage, sous-emploi, durée du travail (heures de travail habituelles, heures de travail réellement effectuées), revenu (revenu net des particuliers, revenu net des ménages, pensions, principales sources de subsistance), emploi dans le secteur informel, durée de l'emploi (changement d'établissement au cours de la dernière année, durée des contrats à durée déterminée, durée de l'emploi occupé auprès de l'employeur actuel), durée du chômage, travailleurs occasionnels (emplois occasionnels, petits emplois), industrie, profession, situation dans la profession, niveau d'instruction et de qualification, exercice d'autres emplois.
Champ de l'enquête:
Territoire: L'ensemble du pays.
Groupes de population: L'enquête couvre l'ensemble de la population résidente d'Allemagne, y compris la population non civile et les personnes vivant en institution ou en collectivité. Sont exclus les diplomates étrangers et les membres des forces armées étrangères.
Disponibilité d'estimations selon d'autres sources pour les régions ou groupes exclus: Ne s'applique pas.
Groupes couverts par l'enquête mais exclus des résultats publiés: Par principe, les estimations relatives aux groupes de population d'une taille inférieure à 5 000 personnes ne sont pas publiées séparément, car l'erreur d'échantillonnage de telles estimations est jugée trop élevée.
Périodicité:
Réalisation de l'enquête: Annuelle.
Publication des résultats: Annuelle, plus notification préliminaire.
Période de référence:
Emploi: Une semaine: la dernière semaine d'avril sans jours de congé.
Recherche d'un emploi: Quatre semaines avant la date de l'entretien.
Disponibilité pour travailler: Deux semaines après la date de l'entretien.
Concepts et définitions:
Emploi: Les personnes âgées de 15 ans et plus ayant un emploi durant la semaine de référence, que cet emploi soit leur activité principale ou une activité secondaire et qu'il soit occupé régulièrement ou occasionnellement. Sont inclus: a) les travailleurs familiaux non rémunérés travaillant durant la période de référence; b) les personnes occupant un emploi temporaire ou exerçant des activités subsidiaires et occupant de petits emplois (c'est-à-dire des emplois de moins de 15 heures par semaine, ou ayant un revenu inférieur au seuil des cotisations de sécurité sociale); c) les travailleurs occupés à plein temps ou à temps partiel et en quête d'un autre travail pendant la période de référence; d) les personnes ayant effectué un travail quelconque, rémunéré ou en vue d'un bénéfice, pendant la semaine de référence, mais qui étaient alors assujetties à la scolarité obligatoire ou à la retraite et au bénéfice d'une pension, ou inscrites en tant que demandeurs d'emploi auprès d'un bureau de placement ou qui percevaient des allocations de chômage; e) les étudiants à plein temps travaillant à plein temps ou à temps partiel; f) les étudiants à temps partiel travaillant à plein temps ou à temps partiel; g) les apprentis et stagiaires rémunérés; h) les personnes occupées dans la production de biens pour leur usage final personnel; i) les membres des forces armées (militaires de carrière, volontaires et conscrits); et j) les personnes effectuant un service civil équivalent au service militaire.
Sont également incluses les personnes ayant un emploi ou une entreprise temporairement absentes de leur travail pendant la période de référence pour cause a) de maladie ou d'accident, b) de congés ou de vacances annuelles, c) de congé de maternité ou de paternité, d) de congé parental, e) d'absence non autorisée, f) de conflit du travail ou g) d'intempéries, de panne mécanique, etc. Les travailleurs familiaux non rémunérés temporairement absents de leur travail durant la semaine de référence sont considérés comme ayant un emploi s'ils travaillent habituellement dans l'entreprise.
Sont exclus: a) les apprentis et stagiaires non rémunérés; b) les bénéficiaires de mesures de promotion de l'emploi; c) les personnes en congé d'éducation ou de formation, à moins qu'elles n'aient travaillé pendant la semaine de référence; d) les personnes en mise en congé non rémunéré à l'initiative de l'employeur, si ce congé correspond à un renvoi; e) les personnes rendant des services non rémunérés ou personnels à des membres de leur propre ménage; et f) les personnes effectuant un travail communautaire ou des activités sociales.
Chômage: Les personnes âgées de 15 ans et plus n'ayant pas d'emploi pendant la semaine de référence et qui cherchaient activement du travail ou en avaient cherché activement au cours des quatre semaines précédant la date de l'entretien. Une distinction est faite entre les personnes sans emploi immédiatement disponibles pour travailler (c'est-à-dire disponibles pour commencer à travailler dans les deux semaines suivant la date de l'entretien) et les autres personnes sans emploi.
Sont inclus: a) les personnes ayant déjà trouvé du travail et qui commenceront prochainement à travailler; b) les personnes essayant de créer leur propre entreprise; c) les personnes cherchant activement un emploi tout en étant assujetties à la scolarité obligatoire ou à la retraite et au bénéfice d'une pension; d) les étudiants à plein temps cherchant activement un emploi à plein temps ou à temps partiel; e) les étudiants à temps partiel cherchant activement un emploi à plein temps ou à temps partiel; f) les apprentis et stagiaires non rémunérés cherchant activement un emploi; g) les bénéficiaires de mesures de promotion de l'emploi cherchant activement un emploi; et h) les travailleurs saisonniers sans emploi pendant la morte-saison et cherchant activement un emploi.
Sont exclues les personnes sans emploi ne cherchant pas activement du travail, à moins qu'elles n'aient déjà trouvé un emploi.
Sous-emploi:
Sous-emploi lié à la durée du travail: Les personnes ayant un emploi et en cherchant un second et les personnes ayant un emploi et en cherchant un qui comporte davantage d'heures de travail.
Situations d'emploi inadéquat: Les personnes ayant un emploi et en cherchant un qui offre de meilleures conditions de travail.
Durée du travail: Les heures de travail hebdomadaires habituelles et les heures de travail réellement effectuées durant la semaine de référence. Les deux sont demandées pour l'activité principale et l'exercice d'un autre emploi, le cas échéant.
Revenu lié à l'emploi:
Revenu lié à l'emploi salarié: Ne peut être dérivé qu'approximativement.
Des questions sont posées sur: a) la principale source de subsistance (une catégorie est l'emploi); b) la jouissance de pensions et de transferts publics par type; c) le montant du revenu mensuel net des particuliers et des ménages par tranches de revenu. Les salariés sont identifiés par une question sur la situation dans la profession (voir 8.3).
Revenu lié à l'emploi indépendant: Ne peut être dérivé qu'approximativement.
Des questions sont posées sur: a) la principale source de subsistance (une catégorie est l'emploi); b) la jouissance de pensions et de transferts publics par type; c) le montant du revenu mensuel net des particuliers et des ménages par tranches de revenu. Les travailleurs indépendants sont identifiés par une question sur la situation dans la profession (voir 8.3).
Secteur informel: Défini sur la base des questions sur la profession et la branche d'activité économique de l'activité principale et de la deuxième activité.
Activité habituelle: Ce qui suit se réfère à l'activité principale. Bien que ce sujet ne soit pas couvert par l'enquête, trois questions rétros-

pectives sont posées sur la situation un an auparavant (situation au regard de l'activité, situation dans la profession et branche d'activité économique).

Classifications:

Branche d'activité économique (industrie)

Titre de la classification: Classification nationale des branches d'activité économique 1993 (Klassifikation der Wirtschaftszweige – WZ93), version du Micro-recensement (trois chiffres).

Groupes de population classifiés selon l'industrie: Toutes les personnes ayant un emploi ainsi que les chômeurs et les inactifs.

Nombre de groupes de codage: codes à trois chiffres. Aucune information sur le nombre de groupes n'est disponible.

Convertibilité avec la CITI: Cette classification correspond à la Nomenclature statistique des activités économiques dans la Communauté européenne (NACE Rév.1).

Profession

Titre de la classification: Classification nationale des professions (Klassifikation der Berufe), version dérivée pour le Micro-recensement de 1992.

Groupes de population classifiés selon la profession: Toutes les personnes ayant un emploi ainsi que les chômeurs et les inactifs.

Nombre de groupes de codage: Non disponible.

Convertibilité avec la CITP: CITP-1988 au niveau à trois chiffres.

Situation dans la profession

Titre de la classification: Classification nationale d'après la situation dans la profession (Gliederung nach der Stellung im Beruf).

Groupes de population classifiés par situation dans la profession: Toutes les personnes ayant un emploi ainsi que les chômeurs et les inactifs.

Catégories de codage: a) travailleurs indépendants occupés dans l'agriculture, la sylviculture et la pêche; b) travailleurs indépendants occupés dans d'autres branches d'activité économique; c) travailleurs familiaux non rémunérés; d) fonctionnaires; e) salariés touchant un traitement; f) salariés; g) apprentis dans des professions commerciales et techniques reconnues; h) apprentis dans des professions industrielles reconnues.

Convertibilité avec la CISP: Non disponible.

Education

Titre de la classification: Classification nationale des degrés d'instruction et de formation professionnelle (Gliederung nach dem allgemeinen und beruflichen Bildungsniveau).

Groupes de population classifiés selon l'éducation: Les personnes ayant un emploi et les chômeurs.

Catégories de codage: Non disponible.

Convertibilité avec la CITE: CITE-1997.

Taille de l'échantillon et plan de sondage:

Unité finale d'échantillonnage: Ménage, institution ou collectivité.

Taille de l'échantillon (unités finales d'échantillonnage): Environ 350 000 ménages ou 820 000 personnes (y compris celles vivant en institution ou en collectivité).

Taux de sondage: 1,0 pour cent de la population.

Base de sondage: Base aréolaire fondée sur le recensement de la population de 1987 (pour les Etats de l'ex-République démocratique allemande, sur le registre de la population). Les résultats sont corrigés en fonction des données de calage actuelles par sexe et nationalité (Allemand/étranger).

Renouvellement de l'échantillon: L'échantillon est renouvelé chaque année par l'ajout d'un échantillon des nouvelles constructions.

Rotation:

Schéma: Les ménages, institutions ou collectivités de l'échantillon participent à l'enquête quatre fois au cours de quatre années successives. Chaque année, un quart des ménages, institutions ou collectivités de l'échantillon sont remplacés par d'autres qui l'intègrent à leur tour.

Pourcentage d'unités restant dans l'échantillon durant deux enquêtes successives: 75 pour cent.

Nombre maximum d'interrogatoires par unité de sondage: Quatre.

Durée nécessaire au renouvellement complet de l'échantillon: Quatre ans.

Déroulement de l'enquête:

Type d'entretien: La participation à l'enquête est obligatoire. Les enquêtés peuvent choisir entre des questionnaires à remplir eux-mêmes et des questionnaires à remplir par les enquêteurs. Les questionnaires remplis par eux-mêmes le sont sur papier avec écriture manuelle. Les enquêteurs ont recours à l'entretien par téléphone assisté par ordinateur ou au questionnaire sur papier avec écriture manuelle. Pour les étrangers qui ne parlent pas allemand, le questionnaire à remplir soi-même est disponible en plusieurs langues étrangères.

Nombre d'unités finales d'échantillonnage par zone de sondage: Chaque zone de sondage compte neuf ménages en moyenne.

Durée de déroulement de l'enquête:

Totale: Trois mois (mai à juillet) pour les entretiens personnels et six mois (mai à octobre) pour les questionnaires à remplir soi-même.

Par zone de sondage: Non disponible. La durée des entretiens dépend de la taille des ménages. En moyenne, l'entretien prend environ 20 minutes par ménage.

Organisation: Il existe une structure d'enquête permanente avec des enquêteurs mobilisés essentiellement pour l'enquête.

Nombre de personnes employées: Environ 7 000 enquêteurs employés par les Offices nationaux de statistique (Statistische Landesämter).

Substitution des unités finales en cas de non-réponse: Les unités finales impossibles à joindre ou qui constituent des cas de non-réponse pour d'autres raisons ne sont pas remplacées.

Estimations et redressements:

Taux de non-réponse: Environ 4%.

Redressement pour non-réponse: Oui, en utilisant l'imputation "hot-deck" pour imputer les relevés manquants.

Imputation en cas de non-réponse à une question spécifique: Oui, pour quelques variables, en utilisant l'imputation "hot-deck" pour imputer les valeurs manquantes.

Redressement pour les régions/populations non couvertes: Ne s'applique pas.

Redressement en cas de sous-représentation: Oui.

Redressement en cas de sur-représentation: Oui.

Corrections des variations saisonnières: Ne s'applique pas.

Historique de l'enquête:

Titre et date de la première enquête: Le premier micro-recensement a été réalisé en 1957.

Modifications et révisions significatives: De 1957 à 1974, en plus de l'échantillon annuel de 1 pour cent, trois petits sous-échantillons (0,1 pour cent) ont été tirés. Depuis 1968, l'Enquête européenne sur les forces de travail est intégrée dans le Micro-recensement. D'autres modifications importantes ont été apportées à l'enquête en 1990, après le recensement de la population de 1987 et la réunification de l'Allemagne. Un nouvel échantillon, basé sur les résultats du recensement de la population de 1987, a été introduit.

Documentation et dissémination:

Documentation

Titre des publications publiant les résultats: a) Statistisches Bundesamt, Fachserie 1: Bevölkerung und Erwerbstätigkeit, Reihe 3: Haushalte und Familien (annuel); b) Statistisches Bundesamt, Fachserie 1: Bevölkerung und Erwerbstätigkeit, Reihe 4.1.1: Stand und Entwicklung der Erwerbstätigkeit (annuel); c) Statistisches Bundesamt, Fachserie 1: Bevölkerung und Erwerbstätigkeit, Reihe 4.1.2: Beruf, Ausbildung und Arbeitsbedingungen der Erwerbstätigen (annuel).

Titre des publications méthodologiques: Les publications susmentionnées incluent les informations méthodologiques relatives à l'enquête.

Dissémination

Délai de publication des premiers résultats: Il y a un décalage de neuf mois entre le déroulement de l'enquête et la publication des résultats.

Information à l'avance du public des dates de publication initiale des résultats: Il n'y a pas de date fixée pour la publication des résultats. Habituellement, la publication des données est annoncée au public par un communiqué de presse présentant les premiers résultats de l'enquête.

Mise à disposition, sur demande, des données non publiées: Oui, mais pas forcément gratuitement.

Mise à disposition des données sur support informatique: La plupart des données peuvent être mises à disposition sous forme électronique.

Site web: http://www.destatis.de/.

Arabie saoudite

Titre de l'enquête: Labour force survey.

Organisme responsable de l'enquête:

Organisation et déroulement de l'enquête: Central Department of Statistics, Ministry of Planning

Analyse et Publication des résultats: Central Department of Statistics, Ministry of Planning

Sujets couverts par l'enquête: Emploi, chômage, durée du travail, industrie, profession, situation dans la profession, niveau d'instruction, activités secondaires et expérience professionnelle.

Champ de l'enquête:
Territoire: L'ensemble du pays.
Groupes de population: Les nomades et les personnes vivant en logements collectifs sont exclus.
Disponibilité d'estimations selon d'autres sources pour les régions ou groupes exclus: Non disponible.
Groupes couverts par l'enquête mais exclus des résultats publiés: Néant.
Périodicité:
Réalisation de l'enquête: Annuelle.
Publication des résultats: Annuelle.
Période de référence:
Emploi: Semaine de référence fixe.
Recherche d'un emploi: Quatre semaines.
Disponibilité pour travailler: Semaine de référence.
Concepts et définitions:
Emploi: Les personnes âgées de 12 ans et plus qui ont effectué un travail, rémunéré ou en vue d'un bénéfice ou non rémunéré et sans attendre de bénéfice, dans une ferme familiale ou une entreprise pendant la plus grande partie de la semaine (de samedi à vendredi) précédant le recensement, ou qui avaient un emploi mais étaient malades ou en vacances pendant la semaine de référence. Ces personnes doivent figurer sur les états de paie et compter se représenter au travail après leurs vacances ou leur maladie.
Cette catégorie inclut:
a)les personnes ayant effectué un travail quelconque, rémunéré ou en vue d'un bénéfice, durant la semaine de référence, mais qui étaient alors assujetties à la scolarité obligatoire, à la retraite et au bénéfice d'une pension ou inscrites en tant que demandeurs d'emploi auprès d'un bureau de placement, ou qui cherchaient un autre emploi pendant la semaine de référence;
b)les étudiants à temps partiel travaillant à plein temps ou à temps partiel;
c)les apprentis et stagiaires rémunérés;
d)les travailleurs familiaux non rémunérés, les apprentis non rémunérés et les personnes effectuant un travail communautaire ou des activités sociales qui ont travaillé plus de 15 heures au cours de la semaine de référence;
e)les personnes occupées dans la production de biens pour leur usage final personnel;
f)les volontaires et les militaires de carrière ainsi que les personnes effectuant un service civil équivalent au service militaire.
Sont exclus:
a)les étudiants à plein temps travaillant à plein temps ou à temps partiel;
b)les apprentis et stagiaires non rémunérés, les personnes engagées dans la prestation de services dans leur ménage;
c)les travailleurs familiaux non rémunérés temporairement absents de leur travail pendant la semaine de référence et les travailleurs saisonniers ne travaillant pas durant la morte-saison;
d)les personnes en congé d'éducation ou de formation.
Chômage: Les personnes âgées de 12 ans et plus sans emploi pendant la semaine de référence, qui ont cherché activement du travail au cours des quatre semaines précédentes et étaient disponibles pour travailler pendant la semaine de référence. [La recherche active d'un emploi est vérifiée après avoir déterminé le statut de la personne au regard du chômage.]
Cette catégorie inclut:
a)les personnes sans emploi, immédiatement disponibles pour travailler et en quête d'un emploi qui ont pris des dispositions pour commencer à travailler dans un nouvel emploi à une date postérieure à la semaine de référence;
b)les personnes sans emploi, immédiatement disponibles pour travailler et en quête d'un emploi qui ont essayé de créer leur propre entreprise;
c)les étudiants à plein temps ou à temps partiel à la recherche d'un emploi à plein temps ou à temps partiel;
d)les personnes en quête d'un emploi ou immédiatement disponibles pour travailler mais assujetties à la scolarité obligatoire ou à la retraite et au bénéfice d'une pension.
Sont exclus:
a)les personnes en mise à pied temporaire ou de durée indéterminée sans rémunération, si elles n'ont pas cherché de travail ou n'étaient pas disponibles pour travailler;
b)les personnes en quête d'un emploi et/ou immédiatement disponibles pour travailler mais assujetties à la scolarité obligatoire ou à la retraite et au bénéfice d'une pension;
c)les étudiants à plein temps ou à temps partiel en quête d'un emploi à plein temps ou à temps partiel.
Sous-emploi:
Sous-emploi lié à la durée du travail: Non disponible.
Situations d'emploi inadéquat: Non disponible.
Durée du travail: Non disponible.
Revenu lié à l'emploi:
Revenu lié à l'emploi salarié: Non disponible.
Revenu lié à l'emploi indépendant: Non disponible.
Secteur informel: Non disponible.
Activité habituelle: Non disponible.
Classifications:
Branche d'activité économique (industrie)
Titre de la classification: Non disponible.
Groupes de population classifiés selon l'industrie: Les personnes ayant un emploi uniquement.
Nombre de groupes de codage: 16 catégories.
Convertibilité avec la CITI: Au niveau à quatre chiffres.
Profession
Titre de la classification: Non disponible.
Groupes de population classifiés selon la profession: Les personnes ayant un emploi uniquement.
Nombre de groupes de codage: 9 grands groupes.
Convertibilité avec la CITP: Au niveau à trois chiffres.
Situation dans la profession
Titre de la classification: Ne s'applique pas.
Groupes de population classifiés par situation dans la profession: Ne s'applique pas.
Catégories de codage: Ne s'applique pas.
Convertibilité avec la CISP: Ne s'applique pas.
Education
Titre de la classification: Non disponible.
Groupes de population classifiés selon l'éducation: Les personnes ayant un emploi et les chômeurs.
Catégories de codage: Analphabète. Sait lire et écrire. Niveau élémentaire. Niveau intermédiaire. Niveau secondaire. Diplôme préuniversitaire. BA ou BSc. MA et Ph.D.
Convertibilité avec la CITE: Au niveau à un chiffre.
Taille de l'échantillon et plan de sondage:
Unité finale d'échantillonnage: Ménage.
Taille de l'échantillon (unités finales d'échantillonnage): 750 unités primaires d'échantillonnage.
Taux de sondage: 4 pour cent.
Base de sondage: Le recensement de la population de 1993, à l'exclusion des nomades et des personnes vivant en logements collectifs.
Renouvellement de l'échantillon: Renouvellement de l'échantillon principal en 1998.
Rotation:
Schéma: L'échantillon principal est divisé en quatre groupes-témoins. Chaque échantillon de l'enquête couvre 3 groupes-témoins.
Pourcentage d'unités restant dans l'échantillon durant deux enquêtes successives: 50 pour cent.
Nombre maximum d'interrogatoires par unité de sondage: 5.
Durée nécessaire au renouvellement complet de l'échantillon: 5 ans.
Déroulement de l'enquête:
Type d'entretien: Entretien personnel.
Nombre d'unités finales d'échantillonnage par zone de sondage: 20 ménages par unité primaire d'échantillonnage.
Durée de déroulement de l'enquête:
Totale: 20 jours (du 24 mai au 13 juin 1999).
Par zone de sondage: 4 jours dans les zones urbaines, 5 jours dans les zones rurales.
Organisation: Permanente.
Nombre de personnes employées: Environ 320 enquêteurs, 80 chefs d'équipe et 13 cadres.
Substitution des unités finales en cas de non-réponse: Non.
Estimations et redressements:
Taux de non-réponse: 9%.
Redressement pour non-réponse: Oui.
Imputation en cas de non-réponse à une question spécifique: Non.
Redressement pour les régions/populations non couvertes: Oui.
Redressement en cas de sous-représentation: Non disponible.
Redressement en cas de sur-représentation: Non disponible.
Corrections des variations saisonnières: Non.
Historique de l'enquête:
Titre et date de la première enquête: Labour Force Survey, 1981.
Modifications et révisions significatives: Le programme d'enquête a été interrompu de 1987 à 1999.
Documentation et dissémination:
Documentation
Titre des publications publiant les résultats: Labour Force in the Kingdom of Saudi Arabia.

Titre des publications méthodologiques: Labour Force in the Kingdom of Saudi Arabia.

Dissémination

Délai de publication des premiers résultats: Mai 1987.

Information à l'avance du public des dates de publication initiale des résultats: Oui.

Mise à disposition, sur demande, des données non publiées: Oui.

Mise à disposition des données sur support informatique: Oui.

Arménie

1.Titre de l'enquête

Enquête sur la main-d'oeuvre des ménages (HLFS).

2.Organisation responsable de l'enquête

The Department of Statistics of the Republic of Armenia (DSRA) (Département des statistiques de la République d'Arménie (DSRA)).

3.Champ d'application

(a) Géographie

Les enquêtes effectuées en novembre 1996 et décembre 1997 n'ont englobé que les zones urbaines. A partir de 1999, elles prennent en compte les régions urbaines et rurales.

(b) Personnes prises en compte

Les hommes âgés de 16 à 60 ans et les femmes de 16 à 55 ans, présents dans le ménage au moment de l'interview. A partir de 1997, toute la population âgée de 16 ans et plus.

Sont exclus: les étudiants vivant en foyer et les écoliers en pensionnat; les occupants d'institutions pénitentiaires ou psychiatriques; le personnel militaire (conscrit ou de carrière) vivant en caserne.

4.Périodicité de l'enquête

L'enquête, réalisée annuellement en 1996 et 1997, est devenue semestrielle à partir de 1999.

5.Période de référence

La semaine civile.

6.Sujets traités

L'enquête donne des informations sur les sujets suivants: emploi (principal et secondaire), chômage, sous-emploi, durée d'emploi, durée du chômage et raisons, travailleurs occasionnels, branche d'activité, profession, situation dans la profession, et niveau d'instruction.

7.Concepts et définitions

(a) Emploi

Les personnes titulaires d'un emploi sont:

a) toutes les personnes qui, durant la semaine de référence, ont effectué un travail, quel qu'il soit, en échange d'une rémunération, dans leur entreprise, profession ou exploitation agricole personnelles, ainsi que les travailleurs familiaux non rémunérés, ayant collaboré dans une entreprise gérée par un membre de la famille; et

b) toutes personnes n'ayant pas travaillé, mais ayant un emploi ou une activité dont ils se sont temporairement absentés pour maladie, intempérie, vacances, conflits d'organisation du travail, ou pour raisons personnelles, qu'elles aient été payées pour les heures d'absence, ou aient été à la recherche d'un autre emploi.

Sont inclus dans les chiffres totaux:

a) les travailleurs à plein temps ou à temps partiel à la recherche d'une autre situation pendant la période de référence;

b) les étudiants à plein temps ou à temps partiel, travaillant à temps partiel ou à temps plein;

c) les personnes ayant travaillé pendant la semaine de référence tout en étant, soit retraités et titulaires d'une pension, soit inscrites comme étant à la recherche d'un emploi dans une agence pour l'emploi, ou encore percevant des allocations de chômage (à compter de l'enquête de 1997);

d) les travailleurs familiaux rémunérés ou non;

e) les membres de coopératives de producteurs;

(b) Chômage

Les chômeurs sont tous les civils n'ayant occupé aucun emploi pendant la semaine de référence, et disponibles en vue d'un emploi, sauf maladie passagère, et qui avaient pris des mesures concrètes afin de trouver un emploi.

Font partie des chômeurs, les étudiants à temps partiel ou à temps plein recherchant un emploi à temps partiel ou à temps plein, pourvu qu'ils soient actuellement disponibles en vue d'un travail (s'ils sont à la recherche d'un travail pour une date future, tel que durant les mois d'été, ils sont considérés comme inactifs); de même, les personnes ayant trouvé un emploi et pris des dispositions pour commencer un nouveau travail à une date postérieure à la période de référence.

8.Méthode d'échantillonnage

(a) Le cadre d'échantillonnage

L'échantillon de l'enquête HLFS a été développé sur la base de listes d'adresses, qui ont servi de cadre d'échantillonnage à l'enquête sur le budget des familles.

(b) L'échantillon

Un plan de sondage aléatoire, stratifié et à deux degrés est utilisé. Au premier degré, les régions administratives sont divisées en strates, sur la base des districts de dénombrement. Au second degré, les unités/ménages finales de sondage sont sélectionnés proportionnellement à leur tailles. En 1996, la taille de l'échantillon était d'environ 1500 ménages situés dans les zones urbaines; en d'autres termes, 0,3% de tous les ménages étaient interviewés. Au début de novembre 1999, la taille de l'échantillon est passée à 1200 ménages, situés à la fois dans les régions urbaines et rurales, et représentant 0,1% de tous les ménages dont on possède la liste en Arménie.

(c) La rotation

Le schéma de rotation n'a pas encore été défini.

9.La documentation

Les résultats des enquêtes sur la main-d'oeuvre et les ménages (HLFS) seront publiés par le Département des Statistiques de la République d'Arménie dans un bulletin d'informations spéciales, ainsi que dans la prochaine édition de *l'Annuaire des Statistiques de la République d'Arménie*.

Australie

Titre de l'enquête: Labour Force Survey (LFS).

Organisme responsable de l'enquête:

Organisation et déroulement de l'enquête: Australian Bureau of Statistics (ABS).

Analyse et Publication des résultats: ABS.

Sujets couverts par l'enquête: Personnes actuellement actives, personnes ayant un emploi et chômeurs, durée du travail, plein temps/temps partiel, ancienneté dans l'emploi, durée du chômage, industrie, profession, situation dans la profession. Sexe, âge, lieu de naissance. Mesure partielle du sous-emploi lié à la durée du travail.

Sujets couverts par des suppléments annuels ou moins fréquents du LFS: personnes se trouvant actuellement en situation de sous-emploi lié à la durée du travail; conditions de travail; cumul d'emplois; expérience professionnelle; expérience en matière d'éducation et de formation; migrants; personnes travaillant à domicile; retraite; expérience de recherche d'emploi; suppression d'emplois et licenciement; personnes actuellement inactives (en dehors de la population active: y compris les personnes ayant un lien marginal avec l'emploi et les demandeurs d'emploi découragés).

Champ de l'enquête:

Territoire: Exclut le Territoire de Jervis Bay et les Territoires extérieurs.

Groupes de population: La population civile australienne habituellement résidente âgée de 15 ans et plus.

Disponibilité d'estimations selon d'autres sources pour les régions ou groupes exclus: National Population Census.

Groupes couverts par l'enquête mais exclus des résultats publiés: Néant.

Périodicité:

Réalisation de l'enquête: Mensuelle.

Publication des résultats: Mensuelle.

Période de référence:

Emploi: Une semaine.

Recherche d'un emploi: Les quatre dernières semaines.

Disponibilité pour travailler: La semaine de référence.

Concepts et définitions:

Emploi: Toutes les personnes âgées de 15 ans et plus qui, au cours de la semaine de référence:

a) ont travaillé pendant au moins une heure contre une rémunération, un bénéfice, une commission ou un paiement en nature dans une activité ou une entreprise ou dans une exploitation agricole (y compris les salariés, les employeurs et les travailleurs indépendants); ou

b) ont travaillé pendant au moins une heure sans rémunération dans une entreprise familiale ou une exploitation agricole (travailleurs familiaux non rémunérés); ou

c) étaient salariées, avaient un emploi mais n'étaient pas au travail et:

i) ont été absentes de leur travail pendant moins de quatre semaines jusqu'à la fin de la semaine de référence; ou

ii) ont été absentes de leur travail pendant plus de quatre semaines jusqu'à la fin de la semaine de référence et ont perçu une rémunération pour tout ou partie de la période de quatre semaines allant jusqu'à la fin de la semaine de référence; ou

iii) étaient absentes de leur travail dans le cadre d'un régime de travail ou d'un travail posté standard; ou
iv) étaient en grève ou en lock-out; ou
v) étaient au bénéfice d'une indemnité pour accident du travail et censées retourner au travail; ou
d) étaient employeurs ou travailleurs indépendants, avaient un emploi, une entreprise ou une exploitation agricole mais n'étaient pas au travail.
Chômage: les personnes âgées de 15 ans et plus n'ayant pas d'emploi pendant la semaine de référence et qui:
a) ont activement cherché du travail à plein temps ou à temps partiel à un moment quelconque au cours des quatre semaines allant jusqu'à la fin de la semaine de référence; et
b) étaient disponibles pour travailler durant la semaine de référence; ou
c) attendaient de commencer à travailler dans un nouvel emploi dans les quatre semaines suivant la fin de la semaine de référence et auraient pu commencer pendant la semaine de référence si l'emploi avait été disponible à ce moment-là.
Sous-emploi:
Sous-emploi lié à la durée du travail: Les personnes ayant un emploi qui souhaitent faire davantage d'heures de travail que ce qu'elles font actuellement et qui sont disponibles pour ce faire. Cette catégorie comprend:
a) les travailleurs occupés à plein temps ayant travaillé à temps partiel durant la semaine de référence pour des motifs économiques (tels que chômage technique ou charge de travail insuffisante). On présume que ces personnes voulaient travailler à plein temps et qu'elles auraient été disponibles pour ce faire pendant la semaine de référence; et
b) les travailleurs occupés à temps partiel (qui travaillent habituellement moins de 35 heures par semaine, ce qui a été le cas pendant la semaine de référence) qui veulent travailler davantage et sont disponibles pour commencer à faire davantage d'heures de travail pendant la semaine de référence. On peut distinguer les personnes ayant activement cherché du travail de celles qui ne l'ont pas fait.
Cette mesure trimestrielle du sous-emploi lié à la durée du travail n'inclut pas les travailleurs occupés à temps partiel désireux de faire davantage d'heures de travail et qui seraient disponibles pour commencer à travailler dans les quatre semaines suivant l'enquête. On trouvera la mesure complète du sous-emploi lié à la durée du travail dans les résultats de l'enquête annuelle intitulée Survey of Underemployed Workers.
Situations d'emploi inadéquat: Non disponible.
Durée du travail: Les "heures réellement effectuées" recouvrent les heures effectuées, rémunérées ou non. Sont recueillies les heures réellement effectuées dans toutes les activités (et dans l'activité principale). Le plein temps ou le temps partiel est fonction du nombre d'heures effectuées. Sont définis comme travailleurs occupés à plein temps les personnes pourvues d'un emploi qui travaillent habituellement 35 heures par semaine ou plus (dans toutes les activités) et celles qui, bien que travaillant habituellement moins de 35 heures par semaine, ont travaillé 35 heures ou plus durant la semaine de référence.
Est également recueilli le nombre total d'heures de travail habituelles (dans toutes les activités).
Revenu lié à l'emploi:
Revenu lié à l'emploi salarié: Les estimations des gains des salariés (gains hebdomadaires moyens par salarié) se trouvent dans une enquête annuelle supplémentaire intitulée: Employee Earnings, Benefits and Trade Union Membership Survey. Les mesures des gains qui figurent dans les enquêtes sur les ménages réalisées par l'ABS se réfèrent aux gains bruts en espèces perçus soit au titre de l'activité principale, soit au titre de l'ensemble des activités pendant la période de référence, et ne sont pas corrigées pour exclure les primes irrégulières, les rappels ou les avances sur salaire.
L'ABS ne produit pas d'estimations du revenu lié à l'emploi tel qu'il est défini dans les directives internationales. En revanche, des données sont recueillies sur la mesure du revenu au sens large (revenu provenant de diverses sources) dans plusieurs collections d'enquêtes auprès des ménages dont: Survey of Income and Housing Costs, Household Expenditure Survey et Census of Population and Housing.
Revenu lié à l'emploi indépendant: Non disponible.
Secteur informel: Ne s'applique pas.
Activité habituelle: Non disponible.
Classifications:
Branche d'activité économique (industrie):
Titre de la classification: Australian and New Zealand Standard Industrial Classification (ANZSIC) 1993.
Groupes de population classifiés selon l'industrie: Les personnes ayant un emploi et les chômeurs (industrie du dernier emploi occupé pour ces derniers).
Nombre de groupes de codage: 158.
Convertibilité avec la CITI: CITI-Rév.3.
Profession:
Titre de la classification: Australian Standard Classification of Occupations, Second edition.
Groupes de population classifiés selon la profession: Les personnes ayant un emploi et les chômeurs (profession exercée dans le dernier emploi pour ces derniers).
Nombre de groupes de codage: 340
Convertibilité avec la CIPT: CITP-1988 (le traitement différent réservé aux forces armées n'a pas de conséquences pratiques, puisqu'elles ne sont pas incluses dans le LFS).
Situation dans la profession:
Titre de la classification: Employment Status.
Groupes de population classifiés par situation dans la profession: Les personnes ayant un emploi.
Catégories de codage: Salariés; employeurs; travailleurs indépendants et travailleurs familiaux non rémunérés (4 groupes).
Convertibilité avec la CISP: CISP-1993.
Education:
Titre de la classification: Classification nationale, sans titre.
Groupes de population classifiés selon l'éducation: Toutes les personnes, dans le supplément annuel.
Catégories de codage: Non disponible.
Convertibilité avec la CITE: CITE-1976 et CITE-1997.
Taille de l'échantillon et plan de sondage:
Unité finale d'échantillonnage: Ménages.
Taille de l'échantillon (unités finales d'échantillonnage): 33 000 (mensuel).
Taux de sondage: 0,005.
Base de sondage: Base aréolaire à plusieurs degrés avec stratification en profondeur. Liste des logements individuels figurant dans les unités primaires de sélection fondée sur les zones de collecte utilisées dans le recensement (Australian Population Census).
Renouvellement de la base de sondage: Tous les cinq ans, sur la base des résultats du recensement.
Rotation:
Schéma: Ménages restant dans l'échantillon durant 8 mois consécutifs. 1/8ème de l'échantillon est supprimé par renouvellement chaque mois, et un nouvel échantillon est introduit.
Pourcentage d'unités de sondage restant dans l'échantillon durant deux enquêtes successives: 7/8èmes de l'échantillon de logements collectifs entre deux enquêtes successives.
Nombre maximum d'interrogatoires par unité de sondage: Non disponible.
Durée nécessaire au renouvellement complet de l'échantillon: Huit mois.
Déroulement de l'enquête:
Type d'entretien: Sur papier avec écriture manuelle; face à face pour le premier entretien, puis par téléphone si cela est acceptable pour l'enquêté.
Nombre d'unités finales d'échantillonnage par zone de sondage: Non disponible.
Durée de déroulement de l'enquête:
Totale: 2 semaines.
Par zone de sondage: Non disponible.
Organisation: Permanente.
Nombre de personnes employées: Environ 600 enquêteurs.
Substitution des unités finales en cas de non-réponse: Non.
Estimations et redressements:
Taux de non-réponse: 3,5%.
Redressement pour non-réponse: Oui, par pondération par les données de calage.
Imputation en cas de non-réponse à une question spécifique: Non: ces questionnaires sont exclus.
Redressement pour les régions/populations non couvertes: Oui, pour les forces armées: sur la base d'un décompte administratif servant à estimer la population active totale.
Redressement en cas de sous-représentation: Oui, comme en cas de non-réponse.
Redressement en cas de sur-représentation: Oui, comme en cas de non-réponse.
Corrections des variations saisonnières: Oui, pour l'emploi et le chômage par sexe et par principaux groupes d'âge, pour l'industrie (personnes ayant un emploi) et les chômeurs de longue durée. Utilisation d'une variante de la méthode X11-ARIMA, avec vérification annuelle des facteurs de correction des variations saisonnières.

Historique de l'enquête:
Titre et date de la première enquête: Labour Force Survey, février 1964.
Modifications et révisions significatives: Août 1966: inclusion de la population aborigène et des insulaires du détroit de Torres. Mai 1976: définition du chômage révisée pour y incorporer la recherche active d'un emploi et la disponibilité pour commencer à travailler pendant la semaine de référence. Février 1978: passage d'une enquête trimestrielle à une enquête mensuelle. Octobre 1982: modification de la base des données de calage. Avril 1986: inclusion dans l'emploi des travailleurs familiaux non rémunérés travaillant moins de 15 heures. Août 1996: début de l'introduction des entretiens par téléphone. Avril 2001: introduction du questionnaire et des définitions révisés. Les personnes absentes de leur travail en mise en congé non rémunéré de courte durée à l'initiative de l'employeur sont classées comme ayant un emploi (auparavant, comme chômeurs); les personnes sans emploi, cherchant activement un emploi mais non disponibles pour commencer à travailler pendant la semaine de référence pour cause de maladie temporaire sont classées comme inactifs (auparavant, comme chômeurs); les travaillleurs familiaux non rémunérés absents de leur travail sont classés soit comme chômeurs soit comme inactifs (auparavant, comme personnes ayant un emploi).
Documentation et dissémination:
Documentation:
Titre des publications publiant les résultats: Labour force Australia - Preliminary (Cat. n° 6202.0).
Titre des publications méthodologiques: Labour Statistics: Concepts Sources and Methods 2001 (Cat. n° 6102.0); Information Paper: Implementing the Redesigned Labour Force Survey Questionnaire (Cat. No. 6295.0); Information Paper: Questionnaire Used in the Labour Force Survey (Cat. No. 6232.0); Information Paper: Labour Force Survey Sample Design (Cat. No. 6269.0).
Dissémination:
Délai de publication des résultats: Dans les deux semaines suivant le mois de la semaine de référence.
Information à l'avance du public des dates de publication initiale des résultats: Oui.
Mise à disposition, sur demande, des données non publiées: Oui.
Mise à disposition des données sur support informatique: Oui.
Site web: http://www.abs.gov.au.

Autriche

Titre de l'enquête: Jusqu'en 2002: Microcensus (Mikrozensus). Début 2003: Labour Force Survey LFS (Arbeitskräfteerhebung).
Organisme responsable de l'enquête:
Organisation et déroulement de l'enquête: Statistik Austria (Bundesanstalt Statistik Austria) et EUROSTAT.
Analyse et Publication des résultats: Statistik Austria (Bundesanstalt Statistik Austria) et EUROSTAT.
Sujets couverts par l'enquête: Emploi, chômage, sous-emploi, durée du travail (heures de travail normales, heures réellement effectuées), durée de l'emploi, durée du chômage, travailleurs découragés, travailleurs occasionnels (s'ils ont travaillé durant la semaine de référence), travailleurs saisonniers, industrie, profession, situation dans la profession, niveau d'instruction et de qualification, principale source de subsistance, exercice d'autres emplois; totalité du questionnaire des enquêtes sur les forces de travail d'Eurostat.
Champ de l'enquête:
Territoire: L'ensemble du pays.
Groupes de population: L'enquête couvre la population résidente de l'Autriche à l'exception des nomades. Les personnes vivant en institution sont couvertes par le Microcensus trimestriel, mais non par l'enquête annuelle sur la main-d'œuvre (Annual Labour Force Survey).
Disponibilité d'estimations selon d'autres sources pour les régions ou groupes exclus: Ne s'applique pas.
Groupes couverts par l'enquête mais exclus des résultats publiés: Néant.
Périodicité:
Réalisation de l'enquête: Trimestrielle, en mars, juin, septembre et décembre de chaque année (Microcensus avec 15 questions de base sur l'activité économique); annuelle, en mars (toutes les autres questions de l'Enquête sur les forces de travail de l'Union européenne). Début 2003: enquête en continu.
Publication des résultats: Trimestrielle (Microcensus); annuelle (intégralité de l'enquête (Labour Force Survey).

Période de référence:
Emploi: Période de référence variable d'une semaine avant la date de l'entretien.
Recherche d'un emploi: Période de référence variable de quatre semaines avant la date de l'entretien.
Disponibilité pour travailler: Période de référence variable de deux semaines après la date de l'entretien.
Concepts et définitions:
Emploi: Les personnes âgées de 15 ans et plus ayant un emploi permanent d'une heure ou plus par semaine, ainsi que les personnes ayant un emploi irrégulier si elles ont travaillé au moins une heure pendant la semaine de référence. Sont inclus:
a) les travailleurs familiaux non rémunérés travaillant durant la semaine de référence;
b) les travailleurs occupés à plein temps ou à temps partiel et en quête d'un autre travail;
c) les personnes ayant effectué un travail quelconque, rémunéré ou en vue d'un bénéfice, pendant la semaine de référence, mais qui étaient alors assujetties à la scolarité obligatoire, ou à la retraite et au bénéfice d'une pension, ou inscrites en tant que demandeurs d'emploi auprès d'un bureau de placement, ou qui percevaient des allocations de chômage;
d) les étudiants à plein temps travaillant à plein temps ou à temps partiel;
e) les étudiants à temps partiel travaillant à plein temps ou à temps partiel;
f) les apprentis et stagiaires rémunérés ou non;
g) les bénéficiaires de mesures de promotion de l'emploi;
h) les personnes occupées dans la production de biens pour leur usage final personnel;
i) les membres des forces armées (militaires de carrière, volontaires et conscrits) et
j) les personnes effectuant un service civil équivalent au service militaire.
Sont également incluses les personnes ayant un emploi ou une entreprise qui étaient temporairement absentes de leur travail durant la semaine de référence pour cause de: a) maladie ou accident, b) congés ou vacances annuelles, c) congé de maternité ou de paternité, d) congé parental, e) congé d'éducation ou de formation d'une durée d'un an maximum, f) conflit du travail, ou g) intempéries, panne mécanique, etc.
Cela inclut les travailleurs familiaux non rémunérés temporairement absents de leur travail durant la semaine de référence.
Sont exclus: a) les travailleurs saisonniers ne travaillant pas durant la morte-saison; b) les personnes en congé d'éducation ou de formation pendant plus d'un an; c) les personnes en mise à pied temporaire ou de durée indéterminée sans rémunération; d) les personnes en mise en congé non rémunéré à l'initiative de l'employeur; e) les personnes rendant des services non rémunérés ou personnels à des membres de leur propre ménage; et f) les personnes effectuant un travail communautaire ou des activités sociales.
Chômage: Les personnes âgées de 15 ans et plus sans emploi durant la semaine de référence, ayant activement cherché un emploi au cours des quatre dernières semaines et disponibles pour travailler dans les deux semaines. Sont inclus: a) les personnes sans emploi et immédiatement disponibles pour travailler, qui ont pris des dispositions pour commencer à travailler dans un nouvel emploi à une date postérieure à la semaine de référence; b) les personnes sans emploi et immédiatement disponibles pour travailler, qui ont essayé de créer leur propre entreprise; c) les personnes en mise à pied de durée indéterminée sans rémunération à la recherche d'un emploi; d) les personnes à la recherche d'un emploi et disponibles pour travailler qui étaient assujetties à la scolarité obligatoire ou à la retraite et au bénéfice d'une pension; e) les étudiants à plein temps à la recherche d'un emploi à plein temps ou à temps partiel; et f) les étudiants à temps partiel à la recherche d'un emploi à plein temps ou à temps partiel.
Sont exclues les personnes sans emploi et immédiatement disponibles pour travailler n'ayant pas cherché activement un emploi pour des raisons autres que a) et b) ci-dessus, ainsi que les personnes sans emploi non immédiatement disponibles pour travailler.
Sous-emploi:
Sous-emploi lié à la durée du travail: Les personnes ayant un emploi et disposées à faire davantage d'heures de travail, soit dans leur emploi actuel soit dans un nouvel emploi, ou dans un emploi supplémentaire.
Situations d'emploi inadéquat: Ce sujet n'est pas couvert par l'enquête.
Durée du travail: Les heures de travail hebdomadaires normales effectuées dans l'activité principale, les heures réellement effectuées dans l'activité principale durant la semaine de référence, les heures réellement effectuées dans l'exercice d'un autre emploi (le cas échéant) durant la semaine de référence.

Revenu lié à l'emploi:
Revenu lié à l'emploi salarié: Non couvert par l'enquête.
Revenu lié à l'emploi indépendant: Non couvert par l'enquête.
Secteur informel: Non couvert par l'enquête.
Activité habituelle: Non couvert par l'enquête.
Classifications:
Branche d'activité économique (industrie):
Titre de la classification: Classification nationale des branches d'activité économique.
Groupes de population classifiés selon l'industrie: Les personnes ayant un emploi; les chômeurs ou les inactifs ayant une expérience professionnelle préalable.
Nombre de groupes de codage: 31.
Convertibilité avec la CITI: CITI-Rév.3.
Profession:
Titre de la classification: Classification internationale type des professions (CITP-1988).
Groupes de population classifiés selon la profession: Les personnes ayant un emploi; les chômeurs ou les inactifs ayant une expérience professionnelle préalable.
Nombre de groupes de codage: 78.
Convertibilité avec la CITP: Ne s'applique pas.
Situation dans la profession:
Titre de la classification: Classification nationale d'après la situation dans la profession.
Groupes de population classifiés par situation dans la profession: Les personnes ayant un emploi; les chômeurs ou les inactifs ayant une expérience professionnelle préalable.
Catégories de codage: a) employeurs dans l'agriculture et la sylviculture; b) travailleurs familiaux non rémunérés dans l'agriculture et la sylviculture; c) employeurs ou travailleurs indépendants occupés dans la production, le commerce ou le tourisme; d) travailleurs familiaux non rémunérés occupés dans la production, le commerce ou le tourisme; e) travailleurs indépendants actifs dans d'autres services (avocats, médecins, etc.); f) travailleurs familiaux non rémunérés travaillant avec des travailleurs indépendants dans d'autres services; g) apprentis; h) salariés occupant des emplois de travailleur manuel; i) salariés occupant des emplois de travailleur non manuel (secteur privé); j) salariés occupant des emplois de travailleur non manuel (secteur public).
Il y a 46 groupes en tout. Les groupes a) à d) sont subdivisés selon la taille de l'entreprise. Le groupe g) est subdivisé en emplois de travailleur manuel et de travailleur non manuel. Les groupes h) à j) sont subdivisés selon le niveau de qualification de l'emploi.
Convertibilité avec la CISP: CISP-1993.
Education:
Titre de la classification: Classification nationale des degrés d'instruction.
Groupes de population classifiés selon l'éducation: Toutes les personnes âgées de 15 ans et plus.
Catégories de codage: a) pas de scolarité obligatoire, ou scolarité obligatoire non terminée; b) scolarité obligatoire; c) apprentissage (école professionnelle); d) école professionnelle intermédiaire (sauf enseignement professionnel à temps partiel); e) deuxième cycle de l'enseignement secondaire général; f) haute école professionnelle (de type normal); g) haute école professionnelle (filière sanctionnée par des qualifications ouvrant droit à l'enseignement supérieur); h) institut d'enseignement supérieur; i) université ou équivalent.
Convertibilité avec la CITE: CITE-1976 et CITE-1997.
Taille de l'échantillon et plan de sondage:
Unité finale d'échantillonnage: Logement.
Taille de l'échantillon (unités finales d'échantillonnage): 30 800 logements/adresses.
Taux de sondage: 0,9 pour cent des logements.
Base de sondage: Base aréolaire fondée sur les listes d'adresses du dernier recensement des logements, complétée par des informations sur les nouvelles constructions.
Renouvellement de l'échantillon: L'échantillon est renouvelé une fois par an pour inclure des bâtiments nouvellement construits; ces nouvelles adresses constituent une strate spéciale de l'échantillon.
Rotation:
Schéma: Les ménages vivant dans les logements de l'échantillon participent à l'enquête jusqu'à huit fois sur une période de deux ans. Chaque trimestre, un huitième des logements de l'échantillon en est supprimé par renouvellement et remplacé par d'autres adresses.
Pourcentage d'unités restant dans l'échantillon durant deux enquêtes successives: 87,5 pour cent.
Nombre maximum d'interrogatoires par unité de sondage: Huit.
Durée nécessaire au renouvellement complet de l'échantillon: Deux ans.

Toutes les informations qui précèdent sur la taille de l'échantillon et le plan de sondage sont valables jusqu'en 2002.
Déroulement de l'enquête:
Type d'entretien: Les informations sont obtenues au cours d'entretiens personnels.
Nombre d'unités finales d'échantillonnage par zone de sondage: 25 adresses au maximum.
Durée de déroulement de l'enquête
Totale: Trois semaines pour chaque enquête trimestrielle du Microcensus; trois semaines pour l'enquête annuelle (Annual Labour Force Survey).
Par zone de sondage: Trois semaines au maximum.
Organisation: Il existe une structure d'enquête permanente.
Nombre de personnes employées: Environ 1 200 enquêteurs.
Substitution des unités finales en cas de non-réponse: Aucun remplacement n'est effectué en cas de non-réponse.
Estimations et redressements:
Taux de non-réponse: 4,1% de la totalité des adresses de l'échantillon. Pour 7,3% de l'échantillon total, aucun membre du ménage n'a pu être contacté et pour 9,9% de l'échantillon, il s'agit de logements non habités, de résidences secondaires ou d'adresses incomplètes.
Redressement pour non-réponse: Oui.
Imputation en cas de non-réponse à une question spécifique: Les valeurs manquantes sont imputées sur la base d'informations fournies par des personnes présentant des caractéristiques similaires. De telles imputations ne sont toutefois faites que pour les données de l'Enquête annuelle et du Microcensus trimestriel de mars, non pour celles du Microcensus de juin, de septembre et de décembre.
Redressement pour les régions/populations non couvertes: Ne s'applique pas.
Redressement en cas de sous-représentation: Oui.
Redressement en cas de sur-représentation: Oui.
Corrections des variations saisonnières: Non.
Historique de l'enquête:
Titre et date de la première enquête: Le premier Microcensus a été réalisé en mars 1968 et la première Enquête sur les forces de travail de l'Union européenne (basée sur les directives du BIT) en mars 1995.
Modifications et révisions significatives: Des modifications accompagnant le passage de définitions nationales à des définitions internationales ont été apportées au Microcensus en mars 1994. Aucune modification significative n'a été apportée à l'enquête sur la main-d'œuvre depuis 1995.
Documentation et dissémination:
Documentation:
Titre des publications publiant les résultats: Statistik Austria, Beiträge zur österreichischen Statistik, Heft 1.303: Arbeitskräfteerhebung (annuel); Statistik Austria, Statistische Nachrichten (mensuel). La première publication présente le détail des résultats de l'enquête, alors que la seconde contient des articles spécifiques qui présentent une vue d'ensemble des principaux résultats ou analysent des données relatives à des sujets précis.
Titre des publications méthodologiques: Les publications précitées contiennent des informations méthodologiques sur l'enquête.
Dissémination:
Délai de publication des premiers résultats: Six mois pour l'Enquête annuelle.
Information à l'avance du public de la date de publication initiale des résultats: Non.
Mise à disposition, sur demande, des données non publiées: Oui, sous forme de tableaux standardisés.
Mise à disposition des données sur support informatique: Les tableaux standardisés du LFS sont disponibles sous forme électronique. Les tableaux du Microcensus peuvent également être mis à disposition sous cette forme.
Site web: http://www.statistik.at/.

Bahamas

Titre de l'enquête: Labour Force and Household Survey.
Organisme responsable de l'enquête:
Organisation et déroulement de l'enquête: Department of Statistics.
Analyse et Publication des résultats: Department of Statistics.
Sujets couverts par l'enquête: Emploi, chômage, durée du travail, revenu, durée du chômage, travailleurs découragés, industrie, profession, situation dans la profession, niveau d'instruction/de qualification, activité habituelle, exercice d'autres emplois.

Champ de l'enquête:
Territoire: Trois îles principales: Grand Bahama, New Providence et Abaco.
Groupes de population: Les personnes âgées de 15 ans et plus, occupées dans la production de biens et la prestation de services ou disposées à l'être et capables de l'être, à l'exception de la population institutionnelle.
Disponibilité d'estimations selon d'autres sources pour les régions ou groupes exclus: NON.
Groupes couverts par l'enquête mais exclus des résultats publiés: NON.
Périodicité:
Réalisation de l'enquête: Annuelle.
Publication des résultats: Annuelle.
Périodes de référence:
Emploi: Une semaine en avril.
Recherche d'emploi: Quatre semaines en avril.
Disponibilité pour travail: Quatre semaines en avril.
Concepts et définitions:
Emploi: Toutes les personnes âgées de 15 ans et plus qui, à un moment quelconque de la période de référence, ont travaillé pour une rémunération ou sans rémunération pendant au moins une heure dans une entreprise familiale.
Cette catégorie inclut:
a) les personnes ayant un emploi mais temporairement absentes pour cause de maladie ou d'accident, de congés ou de vacances annuelles, de congé de maternité ou de congé de paternité, de congé d'éducation ou de formation, d'absence non autorisée, de conflit du travail, d'intempéries, de panne mécanique, etc.;
b) les personnes ayant effectué un travail quelconque, rémunéré ou en vue d'un bénéfice, pendant la période de référence, mais qui étaient alors assujetties à la scolarité obligatoire, à la retraite et au bénéfice d'une pension, inscrites en tant que demandeurs d'emploi auprès d'un bureau de placement ou qui percevaient des allocations de chômage;
c) les étudiants à plein temps ou à temps partiel travaillant à plein temps ou à temps partiel;
d) les apprentis et stagiaires rémunérés ou non;
e) les travailleurs familiaux non rémunérés au travail ou temporairement absents de leur travail;
f) les personnes occupées dans la production de biens pour leur usage final personnel;
g) les travailleurs saisonniers ne travaillant pas durant la morte-saison.
Elle exclut les membres des forces armées ainsi que les personnes effectuant un service civil équivalent au service militaire et les personnes effectuant un travail communautaire ou des activités sociales.
Chômage: Toutes les personnes âgées de 15 ans et plus n'ayant pas travaillé ou n'ayant pas un emploi dont elles étaient temporairement absentes pendant la semaine de référence, mais qui ont cherché activement du travail au cours des quatre semaines précédant la semaine de l'enquête, étaient capables de travailler et disposées à le faire.
Sous-emploi:
Sous-emploi lié à la durée du travail: Non couvert par l'enquête.
Situations d'emploi inadéquat: Non couvert par l'enquête.
Durée du travail: Sont comptabilisées aussi bien les heures de travail effectuées pendant la semaine de référence que les heures de travail effectuées habituellement.
Revenu lié à l'emploi:
Revenu lié à l'emploi salarié: Revenu brut lié à l'emploi, y compris les pourboires et commissions avant toute déduction et le revenu de placement (dividendes, revenu locatif, redevances, aliments, etc.). Il se réfère aux activités primaires et secondaires.
Revenu lié à l'emploi indépendant: Revenu lié à l'ensemble des activités, net des frais professionnels.
Secteur informel: Non couvert par l'enquête.
Activité habituelle: Non couvert par l'enquête.
Classifications:
Branche d'activité économique (industrie):
Titre de la classification: Classification nationale correspondant à la CITI Rév.2 au niveau des branches.
Groupes de population classifiés selon l'industrie: Les personnes ayant un emploi et les chômeurs.
Nombre de groupes de codage: Neuf branches.
Convertibilité avec la CITI: CITI Rév.2.
Profession:
Titre de la classification: Classification nationale correspondant à la CITP-1988.
Groupes de population classifiés selon la profession: Les personnes ayant un emploi et les chômeurs.
Nombre de groupes de codage: Neuf grands groupes.
Convertibilité avec la CITP: CITP-1988.
Situation dans la profession:
Titre de la classification: Classification nationale correspondant à la CISP-1993.
Groupes de population classifiés par situation dans la profession: Les personnes ayant un emploi.
Catégories de codage: Salariés (salariés du secteur public et du secteur privé séparément), employeurs, travailleurs indépendants, travailleurs familiaux non rémunérés.
Convertibilité avec la CISP: CISP-1993.
Education:
Titre de la classification: Classification nationale.
Groupes de population classifiés selon l'éducation: Les personnes ayant un emploi et les chômeurs.
Catégories de codage: Six groupes: pas de scolarité, enseignement primaire, enseignement secondaire, collège, enseignement technique/professionnel, autres.
Convertibilité avec la CITE: NON.
Taille de l'échantillon et plan de sondage:
Unité finale d'échantillonnage: Ménage.
Taille de l'échantillon (unités finales d'échantillonnage): 2 700 ménages.
Taux de sondage: Variable selon l'île couverte.
Base de sondage: Le Census of Housing and Population de 1990.
Renouvellement de l'échantillon: Sur la base du nouveau recensement.
Rotation
Schéma: Deux tiers (2/3) des ménages restent dans l'échantillon durant trois années successives, le tiers (1/3) restant étant sondé pour la première fois.
Pourcentage d'unités restant dans l'échantillon durant deux enquêtes successives: 66 pour cent.
Nombre maximum d'interrogatoires par unité de sondage: Trois fois.
Durée nécessaire au renouvellement complet de l'échantillon: 10 ans.
Déroulement de l'enquête:
Type d'entretien: Entretiens personnels.
Nombre d'unités finales d'échantillonnage par zone de sondage: Non disponible.
Durée de déroulement de l'enquête:
Totale: Trois semaines en mai.
Par zone de sondage: Non disponible.
Organisation: Des enquêteurs sont recrutés pour chaque enquête.
Nombre de personnes employées: Environ 11 cadres et 57 enquêteurs.
Substitution des unités finales en cas de non-réponse: NON.
Estimations et redressements
Taux de non-réponse: NON.
Redressement pour non-réponse: NON.
Imputation en cas de non-réponse à une question spécifique: NON.
Redressement pour les régions/populations non couvertes: NON.
Redressement en cas de sous-représentation: NON.
Redressement en cas de sur-représentation: NON.
Corrections des variations saisonnières: NON.
Historique de l'enquête:
Titre et date de la première enquête: Labour Force and Household Survey 1973.
Modifications et révisions significatives: Enquêtes réalisées deux fois par an jusqu'en 1979. Aucune entre 1979 et 1986.
Documentation et dissémination:
Documentation:
Titre des publications publiant les résultats: Labour Force and Household Income Report (annuel).
Titre des publications méthodologiques: Labour Force and Household Income Report (annuel).
Dissémination:
Délai de publication des premiers résultats: Environ un an.
Information à l'avance du public des dates de publication initiale des résultats: Non.
Mise à disposition, sur demande, des données non publiées: Dans certains cas.
Mise à disposition des données sur support informatique: Oui.

Bangladesh

Titre de l'enquête: Labour Force Survey.

Organisme responsable de l'enquête:

Organisation et déroulement de l'enquête: Bangladesh Bureau of Statistics.

Analyse et Publication des résultats: Bangladesh Bureau of Statistics.

Sujets couverts par l'enquête: Emploi, chômage, sous-emploi, heures de travail réellement effectuées, salaires, revenu, emploi dans le secteur informel, durée de l'emploi, industrie, profession, situation dans la profession, niveau d'instruction/de qualification, exercice d'autres emplois.

Champ de l'enquête:

Territoire: L'ensemble du pays.

Groupes de population: L'enquête couvre les membres habituels des ménages ordinaires du Bangladesh, qu'ils y soient présents au moment de l'enquête ou qu'ils en soient temporairement absents. Les personnes vivant en institution, les nomades, les membres des forces armées, les citoyens non-résidents, les étrangers et les personnes résidant à l'étranger sont exclus.

Disponibilité d'estimations selon d'autres sources pour les régions ou groupes exclus: Ne s'applique pas.

Groupes couverts par l'enquête mais exclus des résultats publiés: Néant.

Périodicité:

Réalisation de l'enquête: Irrégulière. Jusqu'à présent, l'enquête a été réalisée en 1983, 1984, 1985, 1989, 1990, 1995 et 1999.

Publication des résultats: Irrégulière, en fonction de la réalisation de l'enquête.

Période de référence:

Emploi: Période de référence variable d'une semaine avant la date de l'entretien.

Recherche d'emploi: Période de référence fixe d'une semaine.

Disponibilité pour travailler: Période de référence fixe d'une semaine.

Concepts et définitions:

Emploi: Les personnes âgées de 5 ans ou plus ayant effectué au moins une heure de travail durant la semaine de référence, soit contre rémunération ou en vue d'un bénéfice, soit sans rémunération, dans une exploitation agricole familiale, une entreprise ou une organisation.

Sont inclus: a) les travailleurs familiaux non rémunérés travaillant durant la semaine de référence; b) les travailleurs occupés à plein temps ou à temps partiel et en quête d'un autre travail; c) les étudiants à temps partiel travaillant à plein temps; d) les apprentis et stagiaires rémunérés; et e) les personnes occupées dans la production de biens pour leur usage final personnel.

Sont également considérées comme ayant un emploi les personnes âgées de 5 ans et plus qui, bien que ne travaillant pas au moment de l'enquête, avaient un emploi ou une entreprise dont elles étaient temporairement absentes durant la semaine de référence pour cause de a) maladie ou accident, b) congés ou vacances annuelles, c) congé de maternité ou congé de paternité, d) congé parental, e) congé d'éducation ou de formation, f) absence non autorisée, g) conflit du travail, h) intempéries, panne mécanique, etc., ou i) mise à pied temporaire sans rémunération.

Sont exclues: a) les personnes ayant effectué un travail quelconque, rémunéré ou en vue d'un bénéfice, pendant la semaine de référence, mais qui étaient alors assujetties à la scolarité obligatoire, ou à la retraite et au bénéfice d'une pension, ou inscrites en tant que demandeurs d'emploi auprès d'un bureau de placement, ou qui percevaient des allocations de chômage; b) les étudiants à plein temps travaillant à plein temps ou à temps partiel; c) les apprentis et stagiaires non rémunérés; d) les personnes en mise à pied de durée indéterminée sans rémunération; et e) les personnes rendant des services non rémunérés ou personnels à des membres de leur propre ménage.

Chômage: Les personnes âgées de 5 ans et plus se trouvant involontairement sans emploi lucratif durant la semaine de référence et ayant activement cherché un emploi, ou disposées à travailler mais ne cherchant pas de travail pour cause de maladie ou parce qu'elles pensaient qu'il n'y en avait pas.

Sont incluses: a) les personnes sans emploi et disponibles pour travailler qui ont pris des dispositions pour commencer à travailler dans un nouvel emploi à une date postérieure à la semaine de référence; b) les personnes sans emploi et disponibles pour travailler qui ont essayé de créer leur propre entreprise; c) les personnes sans emploi et disponibles pour travailler mais ne cherchant pas de travail parce qu'elles pensent qu'il n'y en a pas pour le moment; d) les personnes en mise à pied de durée indéterminée sans rémunération; et e) les personnes ayant effectué un travail quelconque, rémunéré ou en vue d'un bénéfice, pendant la semaine de référence, mais qui étaient inscrites en tant que demandeurs d'emploi auprès d'un bureau de placement ou qui percevaient des allocations de chômage.

Sont exclues: a) les personnes sans emploi en quête d'un emploi et/ou immédiatement disponibles pour travailler, mais assujetties à la scolarité obligatoire ou à la retraite et au bénéfice d'une pension; et b) les étudiants à plein temps à la recherche d'un emploi à plein temps ou à temps partiel.

Sous-emploi:

Sous-emploi lié à la durée du travail: Les personnes ayant un emploi jugé inadéquat du point de vue du temps de travail effectué, du revenu perçu, de la productivité ou de l'utilisation de leurs qualifications, et à la recherche d'un emploi supplémentaire conforme à leur niveau d'instruction ou à leurs qualifications.

Situations d'emploi inadéquat: Ce sujet n'est pas couvert par l'enquête.

Durée du travail: Les heures de travail réellement effectuées durant la semaine de référence. Pour les personnes occupant plus d'un emploi, les heures de travail effectuées se réfèrent au nombre total d'heures effectuées dans l'ensemble des activités.

Revenu lié à l'emploi:

Revenu lié à l'emploi salarié: Gains réguliers bruts en espèces ou en nature durant la période de référence. Pour les personnes occupant plus d'un emploi, les gains bruts se réfèrent au total de l'ensemble des activités.

Revenu lié à l'emploi indépendant: Revenu brut des travailleurs indépendants durant la période de référence. Pour les personnes occupant plus d'un emploi, le revenu brut se réfère au total de l'ensemble des activités.

Secteur informel: Les entreprises individuelles appartenant à des ménages, y compris les industries familiales.

Activité habituelle: Ce sujet n'est pas couvert par l'enquête.

Classifications:

Branche d'activité économique (industrie):

Titre de la classification: Classification internationale type, par industrie, de toutes les branches d'activité économique (CITI Rév.3).

Groupes de population classifiés selon l'industrie: Les personnes ayant un emploi.

Nombre de groupes de codage: Niveau à deux chiffres de la CITI Rév.3.

Convertibilité avec la CITI: Ne s'applique pas.

Profession:

Titre de la classification: Bangladesh Standard Classification of Occupations.

Groupes de population classifiés selon la profession: Les personnes ayant un emploi.

Nombre de groupes de codage: Niveau à deux chiffres.

Convertibilité avec la CITP: CITP-1968.

Situation dans la profession:

Titre de la classification: Classification nationale d'après la situation dans la profession.

Groupes de population classifiés par situation dans la profession: Les personnes ayant un emploi.

Catégories de codage: a) travailleurs à leur compte/indépendants; b) employeurs; c) salariés; d) aides familiales non rémunérées; e) journaliers.

Convertibilité avec la CISP: Partielle.

Education

Titre de la classification: Classification nationale des degrés d'instruction.

Groupes de population classifiés selon l'éducation: Les personnes ayant un emploi et les chômeurs.

Catégories de codage: a) Sans instruction; b) Classes I-V; c) Classes VI-VIII; d) Classes IX-X; e) SSC, HSC ou équivalent; f) Diplôme; g) Diplôme universitaire; h) Mastères; i) BAg et au-delà; j) MBBS et au-delà; k) BSc en ingénierie et au-delà; l) PhD (doctorat).

Convertibilité avec la CITE: Non.

Taille de l'échantillon et plan de sondage:

Unité finale d'échantillonnage: Ménage.

Taille de l'échantillon (unités finales d'échantillonnage): 9 790 ménages.

Taux de sondage: Non disponible.

Base de sondage: Base principale de 442 unités primaires d'échantillonnage fondée sur la base aréolaire du recensement de la population de 1991.

Renouvellement de l'échantillon: Avant l'enquête, une nouvelle liste complète des ménages figurant dans les zones sélectionnées est établie.

Rotation:

Schéma: Pas de renouvellement de l'échantillon. La collecte des données est étalée sur douze mois. A cette fin, l'échantillon de l'enquête est divisé en douze sous-échantillons mensuels indépendants.

Pourcentage d'unités restant dans l'échantillon durant deux enquêtes successives: Ne s'applique pas.

Nombre maximum d'interrogatoires par unité de sondage: Ne s'applique pas.

Durée nécessaire au renouvellement complet de l'échantillon: Ne s'applique pas.

Déroulement de l'enquête:

Type d'entretien: Les informations sont obtenues au cours d'entretiens personnels.

Nombre d'unités finales d'échantillonnage par zone de sondage: 25 ménages dans les zones urbaines; 20 dans les zones rurales.

Durée de déroulement de l'enquête:

Totale: Douze mois (dernière enquête: avril 1999-mars 2000).

Par zone de sondage: Une semaine.

Organisation: Il existe une structure d'enquête permanente.

Nombre de personnes employées: Environ 8 cadres et 20 enquêteurs.

Substitution des unités finales en cas de non-réponse: Les ménages défaillants sont remplacés par d'autres.

Estimations et redressements:

Taux de non-réponse: Ne s'applique pas.

Redressement pour non-réponse: Ne s'applique pas.

Imputation en cas de non-réponse à une question spécifique: Non.

Redressement pour les régions/population non couvertes: Ne s'applique pas.

Redressement en cas de sous-représentation: Non disponible.

Redressement en cas de sur-représentation: Non disponible.

Corrections des variations saisonnières: Ne s'applique pas.

Historique de l'enquête:

Titre et date de la première enquête: 1983 Labour Force Survey in Bangladesh.

Modifications et révisions significatives: Des modifications significatives ont été apportées au questionnaire en 1989. A partir de 1989, certaines activités de production destinées à la consommation personnelle (telles que battage, séchage, étuvage, transformation et conservation des aliments, élevage de bétail et production de volailles, collecte de bois de chauffage et fabrication de tourteaux de bouse de vache, pêche, production de légumes, etc.) ont été considérées comme des activité économiques. Cela s'est traduit par une augmentation importante des taux d'activité féminins.

Documentation et dissémination:

Documentation:

Titre des publications publiant les résultats: Bangladesh Bureau of Statistics, Report on Labour Force Survey in Bangladesh (**Périodicité:** irrégulière).

Titre des publications méthodologiques: La publication précitée contient des informations méthodologiques sur l'enquête.

Dissémination:

Délai de publication des premiers résultats: Environ 12 mois après la fin de l'enquête.

Information à l'avance du public des dates de publication initiale des résultats: Non.

Mise à disposition, sur demande, des données non publiées: Oui.

Mise à disposition des données sur support informatique: Oui.

Barbade

Titre de l'enquête: Continuous Labour Force Sample Survey (CLFSS).

Organisme responsable de l'enquête:

Organisation et déroulement de l'enquête: Barbados Statistical Service.

Analyse et Publication des résultats: Barbados Statistical Service.

Sujets couverts par l'enquête: Emploi, chômage, sous-emploi, durée du travail, salaires, revenu, années d'expérience professionnelle, durée du chômage, industrie, profession, situation dans la profession, niveau d'instruction/de qualification, exercice d'autres emplois.

Champ de l'enquête:

Territoire: L'ensemble du pays.

Groupes de population: La population civile non institutionnelle âgée de 15 ans et plus, c'est-à-dire les personnes résidant normalement dans des ménages ordinaires.

Sont exclues: les personnes vivant en institution ou dans des collectivités telles qu'hôtels, prisons, hôpitaux, casernes, etc.

Disponibilité d'estimations selon d'autres sources pour les régions ou groupes exclus: Non disponible.

Groupes couverts par l'enquête mais exclus des résultats publiés: Néant.

Périodicité:

Réalisation de l'enquête: Trimestrielle.

Publication des résultats: Trimestrielle.

Périodes de référence:

Emploi: Une semaine avant la date de l'entretien.

Recherche d'un emploi: Trois mois avant la date de l'entretien.

Disponibilité pour travailler: Deux semaines après la date de l'entretien.

Concepts et définitions

Emploi: Les personnes âgées de 15 ans et plus qui:

a) ont effectué un travail quelconque, rémunéré ou en vue d'un bénéfice, pendant la semaine de référence;

b) ont déjà travaillé dans leur emploi ou leur entreprise actuels mais étaient temporairement absentes de leur travail pendant la semaine de référence pour cause de maladie, d'accident, de conflit du travail, de vacances ou autres congés, ou de désorganisation temporaire du travail pour des raisons telles qu'intempéries ou panne mécanique.

Cette catégorie inclut:

a) les travailleurs occupés à plein temps ou à temps partiel et en quête d'un autre travail pendant la semaine de référence;

b) les personnes ayant effectué un travail quelconque, rémunéré ou en vue d'un bénéfice, pendant la semaine de référence, mais qui étaient alors à la retraite et au bénéfice d'une pension, inscrites en tant que demandeurs d'emploi auprès d'un bureau de placement ou qui percevaient des allocations de chômage;

c) les étudiants à plein temps ou à temps partiel travaillant à plein temps ou à temps partiel;

d) les membres des forces armées (militaires de carrière, conscrits et volontaires);

e) les apprentis, rémunérés ou non (les personnes ayant travaillé sans rémunération en tant qu'apprenants).

Sont exclus:

a) les travailleurs familiaux non rémunérés aidant actuellement à exploiter une entreprise ou une ferme qui ont travaillé moins de 15 heures pendant la semaine de référence;

b) les personnes ayant effectué un travail quelconque, rémunéré ou en vue d'un bénéfice, pendant la semaine de référence, mais qui étaient alors assujetties à la scolarité obligatoire.

Chômage: Les personnes âgées de 15 ans et plus et qui étaient:

a) immédiatement disponibles pour travailler et dont le contrat de travail a été résilié ou temporairement suspendu, sans emploi et ayant cherché du travail rémunéré ou en vue d'un bénéfice pendant les trois mois précédant immédiatement la date de l'entretien;

b) immédiatement disponibles pour travailler (sauf pour cause de maladie bénigne) et ayant cherché du travail rémunéré ou en vue d'un bénéfice pendant les trois mois précédant la date de l'entretien, y compris les personnes n'ayant jamais eu d'emploi auparavant ou dont le statut professionnel le plus récent était autre que celui de salarié, c'est-à-dire d'anciens employeurs ou des personnes ayant été à la retraite;

c) sans emploi et immédiatement disponibles pour travailler, à condition qu'elles aient pris des dispositions pour commencer à travailler dans un nouvel emploi ou pour créer leur propre entreprise à une date postérieure à la date de l'entretien;

d) en mise à pied temporaire ou de durée indéterminée sans rémunération ou en mise en congé non rémunéré à l'initiative de l'employeur;

e) sans emploi et ayant cherché du travail à un moment quelconque au cours des trois mois précédant la semaine de référence et qui étaient encore disponibles pour travailler et capables de le faire pendant la semaine de référence;

f) les étudiants à plein temps ou à temps partiel à la recherche d'un emploi à plein temps ou à temps partiel et immédiatement disponibles pour travailler.

Sont exclues les personnes ayant effectué un travail quelconque, rémunéré ou en vue d'un bénéfice, pendant la semaine de référence, mais qui étaient alors assujetties à la scolarité obligatoire et celles en quête d'un emploi et/ou immédiatement disponibles pour travailler mais qui étaient assujetties à la scolarité obligatoire, ou à la retraite et au bénéfice d'une pension.

Sous-emploi:

Sous-emploi lié à la durée du travail: Toutes les personnes ayant un emploi, qu'elles soient au travail ou non, qui travaillent habituellement moins que la durée normale du travail fixée pour cette activité particulière pour des raisons indépendantes de leur volonté, sont en

quête d'un emploi supplémentaire et immédiatement disponibles pour travailler davantage pendant la semaine de référence.
Situations d'emploi inadéquat: Ne s'applique pas.
Durée du travail: Les heures de travail réellement effectuées et les heures de travail habituelles pour l'ensemble des activités pendant la semaine de référence.
Revenu lié à l'emploi:
Revenu lié à l'emploi salarié: Tous les gains liés à l'ensemble des activités pendant la semaine de référence, à savoir les salaires, traitements et autres gains en espèces ou en nature; la rémunération perçue pour le temps non travaillé payé par l'employeur (sauf les indemnités de départ et de cessation de fonctions); les primes, gratifications, allocations de logement et allocations familiales versées par l'employeur; les prestations courantes nettes de sécurité sociale et les régimes d'assurance en faveur des salariés.
Revenu lié à l'emploi indépendant: Ne s'applique pas.
Secteur informel: Ne s'applique pas.
Activité habituelle: Ne s'applique pas.
Classifications:
Branche d'activité économique (industrie):
Titre de la classification: Barbados Standard Industrial Classification.
Groupes de population classifiés selon l'industrie: Les personnes ayant un emploi et les chômeurs (industrie du dernier emploi occupé pour ces derniers).
Nombre de groupes de codage: 29 groupes.
Convertibilité avec la CITI: CITI Rév.2.
Profession:
Titre de la classification: Barbados Standard Occupational Classification (1989).
Groupes de population classifiés selon la profession: Les personnes ayant un emploi et les chômeurs (profession exercée dans le dernier emploi pour ces derniers).
Nombre de groupes de codage: Huit groupes.
Convertibilité avec la CITP: CITP-1968.
Situation dans la profession:
Titre de la classification: Classification nationale.
Groupes de population classifiés par situation dans la profession: Les personnes ayant un emploi.
Catégories de codage: Employeur, salarié (subdivisé en salariés du secteur public et salariés du secteur privé), travailleur indépendant, travailleur familial non rémunéré, apprenti.
Convertibilité avec la CISP: OUI.
Education:
Titre de la classification: Classification nationale.
Groupes de population classifiés selon l'éducation: Les personnes ayant un emploi et les chômeurs.
Catégories de codage: Sans instruction, enseignement primaire, enseignement secondaire, enseignement universitaire, enseignement technique ou professionnel, autres, non spécifié.
Convertibilité avec la CITE: CITE-1976.
Taille de l'échantillon et plan de sondage:
Unité finale d'échantillonnage: Ménage.
Taille de l'échantillon (unités finales d'échantillonnage): 1 800 ménages par enquête (trimestre).
Taux de sondage: 2 pour cent du total des ménages civils non institutionnels.
Base de sondage: 2000 Population and Housing Census. Le pays est divisé en 538 districts de recensement couvrant la totalité des onze paroisses. Chaque district de recensement contient environ 300 ménages.
Renouvellement de l'échantillon: Tous les 10 ans, sur la base des résultats du recensement de la population.
Rotation:
Schéma: Non disponible.
Pourcentage d'unités restant dans l'échantillon durant deux enquêtes successives: 50 pour cent. Les 50 pour cent restants sont interrogés quatre semaines plus tard.
Nombre maximum d'interrogatoires par unité de sondage: Deux.
Durée nécessaire au renouvellement complet de l'échantillon: Une année.
Déroulement de l'enquête:
Type d'entretien: Entretiens personnels.
Nombre d'unités finales d'échantillonnage par zone de sondage: 45.
Durée de déroulement de l'enquête:
Totale: Trois mois.
Par zone de sondage: Non disponible.
Organisation: Permanente.
Nombre de personnes employées: 15 agents itinérants et 3 cadres.
Substitution des unités finales en cas de non-réponse: Non.
Estimations et redressements:
Taux de non-réponse: Non disponible.
Redressement pour non-réponse: Non.
Imputation en cas de non-réponse à une question spécifique: Pour le revenu perçu, la durée du travail, etc., sur la base de ménages répondants similaires.
Redressement pour les régions/populations non couvertes: Non disponible.
Redressement en cas de sous-représentation: Non disponible.
Redressement en cas de sur-représentation: Non disponible.
Corrections des variations saisonnières: Non.
Historique de l'enquête:
Titre et date de la première enquête: Barbados Continuous Labour Force Survey, octobre 1975.
Modifications et révisions significatives: Non disponible.
Documentation et dissémination:
Documentation:
Titre des publications publiant les résultats: Continuous Labour Force Sample Survey Report (annuel); Labour Force Bulletin (trimestriel).
Titre des publications méthodologiques: Continuous Labour Force Sample Survey Report (annuel).
Dissémination:
Délai de publication des premiers résultats: Deux mois.
Information à l'avance du public des dates de publication initiale des résultats: Non.
Mise à disposition, sur demande, des données non publiées: Oui.
Mise à disposition des données sur support informatique: Oui, ainsi que sur le site web national: http://www.bgis.gov.bb/stats/.

Belgique

Titre de l'enquête: Enquête sur les Forces du Travail.
Organisme responsable de l'enquête:
Organisation et déroulement de l'enquête: Institut National de Statistique.
Analyse et Publication des résultats: Institut National de Statistique.
Sujets couverts par l'enquête: Emploi, chômage, sous-emploi, durée du travail, salaires, revenu, durée de l'emploi et du chômage, travailleurs découragés et occasionnels, industrie, profession, situation dans l'emploi, niveau d'éducation ou de qualification, autres emplois, lieu de travail, motifs du temps partiel, horaires atypiques, dernier emploi occupé, formations suivies, etc.
Champ de l'enquête:
Territoire: Ensemble du pays.
Groupes de population: Personnes âgées de 15 ans ou plus. Sont exclues les populations institutionnelles et les personnes résidant à l'étranger.
Disponibilité d'estimations selon d'autres sources pour les régions ou groupes exclus: Ne s'applique pas.
Groupes couverts par l'enquête mais exclus des résultats publiés: Ne s'applique pas.
Périodicité:
Réalisation de l'enquête: Enquête continue.
Publication des résultats: Annuellement.
Période de référence:
Emploi: Une semaine (variable).
Recherche d'un emploi: Quatre semaines (variable).
Disponibilité pour travailler: Deux semaines (variable).
Concepts et définitions:
Emploi: Personnes âgées de 15 ans ou plus qui se trouvaient, durant la semaine de référence, dans l'une des catégories suivantes:
1) Emploi salarié:
a) personnes au travail: personnes qui, durant la période de semaine de référence, ont effectué un travail (avec ou sans contrat formel) moyennant un salaire ou un traitement en espèces ou en nature;
b) personnes qui ont un travail mais qui sont pas au travail: personnes qui, ayant déjà travaillé dans leur emploi actuel, en étaient absentes durant la semaine de référence (pour cause de vacances, maladie, maternité, conflit social, intempéries ou autre) et avaient un lien formel avec leur emploi. Les apprentis ayant reçu une rémunération en espèces ou en nature sont considérés comme travailleurs salariés.
2) Emploi non salarié:
a) personnes au travail: personnes qui, durant la semaine de référence, ont effectué un travail en vue d'un bénéfice ou d'un gain familial, en espèces ou en nature, (les aides familiaux non rémunérés sont considérés comme travailleurs non salariés);

b) personnes ayant une entreprise mais n'étant pas au travail: personnes qui, durant la semaine de référence, avaient une entreprise (industrielle, commerciale, agricole ou de services) mais n'étaient temporairement pas au travail pour tout raison spécifique.
Dans la pratique, on interprète la notion de travail effectué au cours de la semaine de référence comme un travail d'une heure au moins. De ce fait, un travailleur à temps très partiel est ainsi considéré comme ayant un emploi.
Sont considérées comme ayant un emploi:
a) les personnes temporairement absentes de leur travail, pour une durée inférieure à trois mois, pour cause de maladie ou d'accident, congé parental, d'éducation ou de formation, d'absence non autorisée, de conflit du travail, intempéries ou panne, ainsi que celles qui sont en congés annuels on en congé de maternité ou paternité;
b) les personnes mises à pied, pour une durée inférieure à trois mois;
c) les personnes ayant effectué un travail quelconque, rémunéré ou en vue d'un bénéfice, pendant la semaine de référence mais qui étaient assujetties à la scolarité obligatoire, à la retraite et au bénéfice d'une pension, inscrites en tant que demandeurs d'emploi auprès d'un bureau de placement ou percevant des allocations de chômage;
d) les étudiants à plein temps ou à temps partiel travaillant à plein temps ou à temps partiel;
e) les apprentis et stagiaires rémunérés;
f) les travailleurs familiaux non rémunérés ayant travaillé durant la semaine de référence;
g) les militaires de carrière et les volontaires.
Chômage: Personnes âgées de 15 ans ou plus qui, au cours de la semaine de référence, étaient sans travail, disponibles pour travailler et à la recherche d'un emploi.
Sous-emploi:
Sous-emploi lié à la durée du travail: Personnes souhaitant travailler plus ans leur emploi actuel ou dans un autre.
Situations d'emploi inadéquat: Personnes à la recherche d'autres conditions de travail telles que salaires, horaires, trajets, etc.
Durée du travail: Heures effectives et habituelles.
Revenu lié à l'emploi:
Revenu lié à l'emploi salarié: Salaire net mensuel et les autres gains, payés sur une base annuelle, tels que primes de fin d'année, de vacances, participation aux bénéfices, etc.
Revenu lié à l'emploi indépendant: Non couvert par l'enquête.
Secteur informel: Ne s'applique pas.
Activité habituelle: Ne s'applique pas.
Classifications:
Branche d'activité économique (industrie)
Titre de la classification: Nomenclature d'Activités dans la Communauté Européenne (NACE).
Groupes de population classifiés selon l'industrie: Personnes ayant un emploi ainsi que celles qui ont quitté leur activité depuis huit ans au plus.
Nombre de groupes de codage: 60 groupes.
Convertibilité avec la CITI: CITI- Rév.3.
Profession
Titre de la classification: Codification nationale basée sur la CITP.
Groupes de population classifiés selon la profession: Personnes ayant un emploi ainsi que celles qui ont quitté leur activité depuis huit ans au plus.
Nombre de groupes de codage: Environ 300 groupes.
Convertibilité avec la CITP: CITP-88.
Situation dans la profession
Titre de la classification: Classification nationale.
Groupes de population classifiés par situation dans la profession: Personnes ayant un emploi ainsi que celles qui ont quitté leur activité depuis huit ans au plus.
Catégories de codage: Salariés (ouvriers, employés et fonctionnaires) et travailleurs non salariés (travailleurs indépendants, employeurs et aides familiaux).
Convertibilité avec la CISP: Pas d'information.
Education
Titre de la classification: Pas d'information.
Groupes de population classifiés selon l'éducation: Personnes âgées de 15 ans et plus.
Catégories de codage: 13 catégories: primaire (ou sans diplôme); secondaire inférieur général; secondaire inférieur technique, artistique ou professionnel; secondaire supérieur général; secondaire supérieur technique; secondaire supérieur artistique; secondaire supérieur professionnel; post-secondaire non supérieur; supérieur non universitaire court ou long; universitaire ou ingénieur; deuxième degré universitaire; doctorat.
Convertibilité avec la CITE: CITE-1976.
Taille de l'échantillon et plan de sondage:
Unité finale d'échantillonnage: Ménage.
Taille de l'échantillon (unités finales d'échantillonnage): Environ 47 000 ménages (soit 11 960 ménages par trimestre).
Taux de sondage: Environ 1.1 pour cent.
Base de sondage: Registre national des personnes physiques, dérivé des registres de population des communes.
Renouvellement de l'échantillon: Pas d'information.
Rotation:
Schéma: Un premier entretien est suivi, 13 semaines plus tard, d'un second entretien.
Pourcentage d'unités restant dans l'échantillon durant deux enquêtes successives: 50 pur cent.
Nombre maximum d'interrogatoires par unité de sondage: Pas d'information.
Durée nécessaire au renouvellement complet de l'échantillon: Treize semaines.
Déroulement de l'enquête:
Type d'entretien: Les ménages sont interrogés à deux reprises: premier entretien, par enquêteurs, en face-à-face et seconde interrogation, trois mois plus tard, sur la base d'un questionnaire simplifié soit par courrier soit par téléphone.
Nombre d'unités finales d'échantillonnage par zone de sondage: Environ 2 390 groupes de 20 ménages.
Durée de déroulement de l'enquête:
Totale: Un an.
Par zone de sondage: Pas d'information.
Organisation: Structure permanente.
Nombre de personnes employées: Environ 10 personnes pour l'encadrement et 300 enquêteurs.
Substitution des unités finales en cas de non-réponse: Oui.
Estimations et redressements:
Taux de non-réponse: Environ 17 pour cent.
Redressement pour non-réponse: Oui.
Imputation en cas de non réponse à une question spécifique: Non.
Redressement pour les régions/populations non couvertes: Non.
Redressement en cas de sous-représentation: Oui.
Redressement en cas de sur-représentation: Oui.
Corrections des variations saisonnières: Non.
Historique de l'enquête:
Titre et date de la première enquête: Enquête sur la population active 1968.
Modifications et révisions significatives: A partir de janvier 1999, passage à un système d'enquête continue et adoption du critère d'une heure de travail dans le nouveau questionnaire.
Documentation et dissémination:
Documentation
Titre des publications publiant les résultats: Emploi et chômage: enquête sur les forces de travail et Statistiques sociales (annuellement).
Titre des publications méthodologiques: Emploi et chômage: enquête sur les forces de travail et Statistiques sociales (annuellement).
Dissémination
Délai de publication des premiers résultats: Environ quatre mois après l'année de référence pour les premiers résultats et dix mois pour les résultats détaillés.
Information à l'avance du public des dates de publication initiale des résultats: Non.
Mise à disposition, sur demande, des données non publiées: Oui.
Mise à disposition des données sur support informatique: Website: http://www.statbel.fgov.be.

Botswana

Titre de l'enquête: Labour Force Survey (LFS).
Organisme responsable de l'enquête:
Organisation et déroulement de l'enquête: Central Statistics Office (CSO).
Analyse et Publication des résultats: CSO.
Sujets couverts par l'enquête: Les personnes actuellement et habituellement actives, les personnes ayant un emploi et les chômeurs; les personnes actuellement sous-employées, temporairement absentes de leur emploi et en dehors de la population active; les personnes ayant habituellement un emploi avec ou sans périodes de chômage, les personnes connaissant des périodes d'emploi et les personnes habituellement inactives; formation; revenu; secteur institutionnel, industrie, profession, situation dans la profession.
Champ de l'enquête:
Territoire: L'ensemble du pays.

Groupes de population: La population non institutionnelle âgée de 12 ans et plus, c'est-à-dire les personnes résidant normalement dans des ménage ordinaires. Les hôtes de passage restant moins de 14 jours et les personnes vivant à l'hôtel, en prison, en caserne, etc. sont exclues.
Disponibilité d'estimations selon d'autres sources pour les régions ou groupes exclus: Non disponible.
Groupes couverts par l'enquête mais exclus des résultats publiés: Non disponible.
Périodicité:
Réalisation de l'enquête: Occasionnelle: en 1995-1996 et en 1997-1998.
Publication des résultats: Occasionnelle.
Période de référence:
Emploi: Une semaine avant la date de l'entretien.
Recherche d'un emploi: Un mois de recherche d'après la définition au sens strict. Aucune recherche n'est nécessaire d'après la définition au sens large.
Disponibilité pour travailler: Non disponible.
Concepts et définitions:
Emploi: Les personnes qui a) ont effectué un travail quelconque, rémunéré ou en vue d'un bénéfice, pendant la semaine de référence; ou b) étaient temporairement absentes de leur travail pendant la semaine de référence pour cause de maladie ou de congés, mais allaient assurément y retourner. Sont inclus les travailleurs familiaux non rémunérés occupés dans une entreprise familiale. Par "un travail quelconque", on entend 1 heure de travail ou plus effectuée pendant la semaine de référence.
Chômage: Définition au sens strict: les personnes sans travail, immédiatement disponibles pour travailler et ayant cherché du travail au cours du dernier mois. Définition au sens large: les personnes sans travail et immédiatement disponibles pour travailler.
Sous-emploi:
Sous-emploi lié à la durée du travail: Les personnes travaillant moins de 35 heures et ayant déclaré qu'elles étaient disponibles pour faire davantage d'heures.
Situations d'emploi inadéquat: Non disponible.
Durée du travail: Non disponible.
Revenu lié à l'emploi:
Revenu lié à l'emploi salarié: Non disponible.
Revenu lié à l'emploi indépendant: Non disponible.
Secteur informel: Ont été exclues toutes les personnes travaillant à leur compte ou comme salariés dans l'agriculture traditionnelle, ainsi que celles qui travaillent pour une collectivité locale ou l'administration centrale ou pour des entreprises employant 5 salariés ou plus ou qui sont des sociétés enregistrées conformément à la loi ou qui ont des documents comptables complets. Sont inclus, mais désignés séparément, les domestiques et autres personnes travaillant pour des ménages privés.
Activité habituelle: Actif pendant 6 mois ou plus sur les 12 mois de référence.
Classifications:
Branche d'activité économique (industrie):
Titre de la classification: Botswana Industrial Classification (BISIC).
Groupes de population classifiés selon l'industrie: Non disponible.
Nombre de groupes de codage: Non disponible.
Convertibilité avec la CITI: CITI-Rév.3 avec des codes supplémentaires pour désigner les activités informelles.
Profession:
Titre de la classification: Botswana Standard Classification of Occupations (BSCO).
Groupes de population classifiés selon la profession: Non disponible.
Nombre de groupes de codage: Non disponible.
Convertibilité avec la CITP: CITP-1988.
Situation dans la profession:
Titre de la classification: Classification nationale, sans titre.
Groupes de population classifiés par situation dans la profession: La population ayant un emploi.
Catégories de codage: Salariés; travailleurs indépendants occupés dans l'agriculture traditionnelle; travailleurs indépendants occupés en dehors de l'agriculture traditionnelle, divisés à leur tour entre ceux qui ont des salariés, ceux qui n'en ont pas et les travailleurs familiaux non rémunérés.
Convertibilité avec la CISP: Oui.
Education:
Titre de la classification: Classification nationale des domaines de formation.
Groupes de population classifiés selon l'éducation: Non disponible.
Catégories de codage: Non disponible.
Convertibilité avec la CITE: Non disponible.
Taille de l'échantillon et plan de sondage
Unité finale d'échantillonnage: Ménage.
Taille de l'échantillon (unités finales d'échantillonnage): 11 000.
Taux de sondage: Non disponible.
Base de sondage: 1991 Population Census, qui donne 5 strates urbaines et 9 strates rurales, avec un total de 420 blocs-échantillons.
Renouvellement de la base de sondage: Néant, mais croissance présumée de la population de 15 pour cent.
Rotation:
Schéma: Ne s'applique pas.
Pourcentage d'unités restant dans l'échantillon durant deux enquêtes successives: Ne s'applique pas.
Nombre maximum d'interrogatoires par unité de sondage: Ne s'applique pas.
Durée nécessaire au renouvellement complet de l'échantillon: ne s'applique pas.
Déroulement de l'enquête
Type d'entretien: Entretiens personnels.
Nombre d'unités finales d'échantillonnage par zone de sondage: Non disponible.
Durée de déroulement de l'enquête:
Totale: Treize mois.
Par zone de sondage: Non disponible.
Organisation: Non disponible.
Nombre de personnes employées: Non disponible.
Substitution des unités finales en cas de non-réponse: Non disponible.
Estimations et redressements:
Taux de non-réponse: 2%.
Redressement pour non-réponse: Non.
Imputation en cas de non-réponse à une question spécifique: Non.
Redressement pour les régions/populations non couvertes: Ne s'applique pas.
Redressement en cas de sous-représentation: Ne s'applique pas.
Redressement en cas de sur-représentation: Ne s'applique pas.
Corrections des variations saisonnières: Ne s'applique pas.
Historique de l'enquête
Titre et date de la première enquête: Botswana Labour Force Survey, 1984-85.
Modifications et révisions significatives: Non disponible.
Documentation et dissémination
Documentation:
Titre des publications publiant les résultats: Non disponible.
Titre des publications méthodologiques: 1995-96 Labour Force Survey: Technical & Operational Report (mars 1998).
Dissémination:
Délai de publication des premiers résultats: Non disponible.
Information à l'avance du public des dates de publication initiale des résultats: Non disponible.
Mise à disposition, sur demande, des données non publiées: Non disponible.
Mise à disposition des données sur support informatique: Non disponible.
Site web: http://www.cso.gov.bw/cso/.

Bulgarie

Titre de l'enquête: Labour Force Survey
Organisme responsable de l'enquête:
Organisation et déroulement de l'enquête: National Statistical Institute
Analyse et Publication des résultats: National Statistical Institute
Sujets couverts par l'enquête: Emploi, chômage, sous-emploi, durée du travail, durée du chômage, travailleurs découragés, industrie, profession, situation dans la profession et niveau d'instruction.
Champ de l'enquête:
Territoire: L'ensemble du pays.
Groupes de population: La totalité des résidents habituels âgés de 15 ans et plus vivant dans un ménage non institutionnel, y compris ceux qui sont temporairement absents.
Disponibilité d'estimations selon d'autres sources pour les régions ou groupes exclus: Non.
Groupes couverts par l'enquête mais exclus des résultats publiés: Néant.

Périodicité:
Réalisation de l'enquête: Depuis 2000, enquête trimestrielle réalisée en mars, juin, septembre et décembre. Auparavant, elle était réalisée trois fois par an.
Publication des résultats: Depuis 2000: trimestrielle. Auparavant, deux fois par an.
Périodes de référence:
Emploi: Une semaine avant la date de l'entretien.
Recherche d'un emploi: Quatre semaines avant la date de l'entretien.
Disponibilité pour travailler: Deux semaines après la date de l'entretien.
Concepts et définitions:
Emploi: On entend par personnes ayant un emploi toutes les personnes âgées de 15 ans et plus qui, pendant la période de référence a) ont effectué un travail quelconque pendant au moins une heure, rémunéré ou en vue d'un bénéfice (en espèces ou en nature); b) ne travaillaient pas mais avaient un emploi ou une entreprise d'où elles étaient temporairement absentes pour cause de congé, de maladie, d'intempéries, de congé de formation professionnelle ou autre motif similaire.
Sont considérées comme ayant un emploi les personnes occupant un emploi salarié; exploitant leur propre entreprise, activité ou exploitation agricole; ayant effectué un travail indépendant en vue d'un bénéfice et les personnes travaillant sans rémunération dans une entreprise appartenant à un parent ou à un membre du même ménage (pendant au moins une heure), ainsi que les militaires de carrière. Les personnes en congé de maternité sont considérées comme ayant un emploi uniquement pendant la durée du congé de maternité rémunéré à taux plein (135 jours civils); autrement, elles sont considérées comme en dehors de la population active.
Chômage: Sont sans emploi toutes les personnes ayant un emploi âgées de 15 ans et plus qui n'ont pas travaillé du tout pendant la semaine de référence, ont cherché activement un emploi durant les quatre semaines précédant l'entretien et étaient disponibles pour commencer à travailler dans les deux semaines suivant la semaine de l'enquête. Sont également incluses dans les sans emploi les personnes n'ayant pas cherché activement un travail parce qu'elles comptaient retourner à leur emploi précédent, d'où elles avaient été libérées ou mises en congé non rémunéré (si la durée totale de l'absence dépasse un mois), à condition qu'elles aient la promesse de l'employeur et la date précise de retour au travail, ainsi que les étudiants à plein temps ou à temps partiel à la recherche d'un emploi à plein temps ou à temps partiel.
Sous-emploi:
Sous-emploi lié à la durée du travail: Les personnes travaillant habituellement à temps partiel pour des motifs économiques.
Situations d'emploi inadéquat: Ne s'applique pas.
Durée du travail: Les heures de travail habituelles effectuées dans l'activité principale et les heures réellement effectuées dans l'activité principale et la ou les activités secondaires séparément.
Revenu lié à l'emploi:
Revenu lié à l'emploi salarié: Ne s'applique pas.
Revenu lié à l'emploi indépendant: Ne s'applique pas.
Secteur informel: Ne s'applique pas.
Activité habituelle: Ne s'applique pas.
Classifications:
Branche d'activité économique (industrie):
Titre de la classification: Classification nationale.
Groupes de population classifiés selon l'industrie: Les personnes ayant un emploi et les chômeurs ayant eu une expérience professionnelle au cours des 8 dernières années.
Nombre de groupes de codage: 503.
Convertibilité avec la CITI: CITI-Rév.3 au niveau à trois chiffres.
Profession:
Titre de la classification: Classification nationale.
Groupes de population classifiés selon la profession: Les personnes ayant un emploi et les chômeurs ayant eu une expérience professionnelle au cours des 8 dernières années.
Nombre de groupes de codage: 550.
Convertibilité avec la CITP: CITP-1988 au niveau à trois chiffres.
Situation dans la profession:
Titre de la classification: Classification nationale.
Groupes de population classifiés par situation dans la profession: Les personnes ayant un emploi et les chômeurs ayant eu une expérience professionnelle au cours des 8 dernières années.
Catégories de codage: 5 groupes (salariés, employeurs, travailleurs indépendants, membres de coopératives de production et travailleurs familiaux non rémunérés).
Convertibilité avec la CISP: CISP-1993.
Education:
Titre de la classification: Classification nationale.
Groupes de population classifiés selon l'éducation: L'ensemble de la population âgée de 15 ans et plus.
Catégories de codage: 8 groupes (enseignement primaire, premier cycle du secondaire, enseignement professionnel, enseignement secondaire général, enseignement secondaire professionnel, enseignement secondaire spécialisé, enseignement supérieur inachevé (collège), enseignement supérieur (université).
Convertibilité avec la CITE: CITE-1997.
Taille de l'échantillon et plan de sondage:
Unité finale d'échantillonnage: Ménage.
Taille de l'échantillon (unités finales d'échantillonnage): Environ 24 000 ménages.
Taux de sondage: 0,8 pour cent.
Base de sondage: Population Census.
Renouvellement de l'échantillon: Annuel.
Rotation:
Schéma: 2-2-2.
Pourcentage d'unités restant dans l'échantillon durant deux enquêtes successives: 50 pour cent.
Nombre maximum d'interrogatoires par unité de sondage: Quatre.
Durée nécessaire au renouvellement complet de l'échantillon: Quatre ans.
Déroulement de l'enquête:
Type d'entretien: Sur papier avec écriture manuelle.
Nombre d'unités finales d'échantillonnage par zone de sondage: 12 ménages par district de recensement.
Durée de déroulement de l'enquête:
Totale: Une semaine civile (7 jours).
Par zone de sondage: Une semaine civile (7 jours).
Organisation: Structure d'enquête permanente.
Nombre de personnes employées: Environ 800 enquêteurs et 140 cadres.
Substitution des unités finales en cas de non-réponse: Non.
Estimations et redressements:
Taux de non-réponse: 12% à 15%.
Redressement pour non-réponse: Non.
Imputation en cas de non-réponse à une question spécifique: Non.
Redressement pour les régions/populations non couvertes: Non.
Redressement en cas de sous-représentation: Non.
Redressement en cas de sur-représentation: Non.
Corrections des variations saisonnières: Non.
Historique de l'enquête:
Titre et date de la première enquête: Labour Force Survey, septembre 1993.
Modifications et révisions significatives: Deux enquêtes, en juin et en octobre, en 1994. De 1995 à 2000, l'enquête a été réalisée trois fois par an et la taille de l'échantillon a diminué pour passer de 30 000 à 24 000 ménages. Enquête trimestrielle depuis 2000. Depuis 2001, des modifications significatives ont été apportées au questionnaire.
Documentation et dissémination:
Documentation
Titre des publications publiant les résultats: Reference Book of the Republic of Bulgaria (annuel); Employment and Unemployment (deux fois par an); Statistical Yearbook.
Titre des publications méthodologiques: Employment and Unemployment (deux fois par an); Statistical Yearbook.
Dissémination
Délai de publication des premiers résultats: 52 jours après la période de référence de l'enquête.
Information à l'avance du public des dates de publication initiale des résultas: Oui.
Mise à disposition, sur demande, des données non publiées: Oui.
Mise à disposition des données sur support informatique: Disquettes et Internet (informations sélectionnées).
Site web: http://www.nsi.bg.

Canada

Titre de l'enquête: Enquête sur la population active.
Organisme responsable de l'enquête:
Organisation et déroulement de l'enquête: Statistique Canada.
Analyse et Publication des résultats: Statistique Canada.
Sujets couverts par l'enquête: Les personnes actuellement actives, ayant un emploi ou sans emploi; les personnes se trouvant actuellement en situation de sous-emploi lié à la durée du travail et les per-

sonnes se trouvant actuellement en dehors de la population active; les travailleurs découragés; la durée du travail; la durée de l'emploi et du chômage; les salaires; l'exercice d'autres emplois; l'industrie; la profession; la situation dans la profession; le niveau d'instruction/de qualification.

Champ de l'enquête:

Territoire: Les régions exclues sont le Yukon (données recueillies mais non incluses dans les estimations nationales), les Territoires du Nord-Ouest, le Nunavut et les réserves indiennes.

Groupes de population: La population civile non institutionnelle âgée de 15 ans et plus, à l'exception des membres à plein temps des Forces armées canadiennes et des personnes vivant en institution.

Disponibilité d'autres estimations selon d'autres sources pour les régions ou groupes exclus: Estimations pour le Yukon sous forme de moyennes mobiles sur trois mois.

Groupes couverts par l'enquête mais exclus des résultats publiés: Yukon, voir supra.

Périodicité:

Réalisation de l'enquête: Mensuelle

Publication des résultats: Mensuelle, le premier ou le deuxième vendredi du mois suivant celui de la période de référence.

Période de référence:

Emploi: La semaine qui comporte le 15ème jour du mois.

Recherche d'un emploi: Les quatre dernières semaines précédant l'entretien.

Disponibilité pour travailler: La semaine de référence qui comporte le 15ème jour du mois.

Concepts et définitions:

Emploi: Les personnes ayant un emploi sont celles âgées de 15 ans et plus qui, durant la semaine de référence:

a) ont effectué un travail quelconque dans un emploi ou une entreprise, c'est-à-dire un travail rémunéré dans le cadre d'une relation employeur-salarié ou en tant que travailleur indépendant. Cette catégorie inclut aussi le travail familial non rémunéré, défini comme un travail non rémunéré contribuant directement à l'exploitation d'une ferme, d'une entreprise ou d'un cabinet professionnel appartenant à un membre du même ménage apparenté qui y exerce ses activités; ou

b) avaient un emploi mais n'étaient pas au travail en raison de facteurs tels que maladie ou handicap, responsabilités personnelles ou familiales, vacances, conflit ou autres motifs (à l'exception des personnes mises à pied, entre deux emplois occasionnels, et de celles qui ont un emploi dans lequel elles commenceront à travailler à une date ultérieure).

Chômage: Les personnes sans emploi sont celles âgées de 15 ans et plus qui, durant la semaine de référence:

a) étaient en mise à pied temporaire, attendant d'être rappelées et disponibles pour travailler, ou

b) étaient sans emploi, avaient activement cherché du travail au cours des quatre dernières semaines et étaient disponibles pour travailler, ou

c) devaient commencer à travailler dans un nouvel emploi dans les quatre semaines à compter des semaines de référence et étaient disponibles pour travailler.

Sous-emploi:

Sous-emploi lié à la durée du travail: Non disponible.

Situations d'emploi inadéquat: Non disponible.

Durée du travail: Les heures de travail réellement effectuées recouvrent aussi bien les heures de travail rémunérées que non rémunérées. Les heures de travail habituelles, pour les salariés, se réfèrent aux heures de travail normales rémunérées ou horaire contractuel, sans tenir compte des heures supplémentaires; pour les travailleurs indépendants, en revanche, elles se réfèrent au nombre d'heures effectuées pendant une semaine normale.

Revenu lié à l'emploi:

Revenu lié à l'emploi salarié: Les salariés déclarent leur salaire/traitement avant impôts et autres déductions, en y incluant les pourboires, commissions et primes perçus au titre de leur activité principale.

Revenu lié à l'emploi indépendant: Non disponible.

Secteur informel: Ne s'applique pas.

Activité habituelle: Non disponible.

Classifications:

Branche d'activité économique (industrie):

Titre de la classification: Système de classification des industries de l'Amérique du Nord (SCIAN).

Groupes de population classifiés selon l'industrie: Les personnes ayant un emploi et les chômeurs (s'ils ont travaillé au cours des 12 derniers mois).

Nombre de groupes de codage: 312.

Convertibilité avec la CITI: Convertibilité indirecte avec la CITI-Rév.3.

Profession:

Titre de la classification: Classification type des professions 1991 (CTP-91).

Groupes de population classifiés selon la profession: Les personnes ayant un emploi et les chômeurs (s'ils ont travaillé au cours des 12 derniers mois).

Nombre de groupes de codage: 514.

Convertibilité avec la CITP: Convertibilité indirecte avec la CITP-1988.

Situation dans la profession:

Titre de la classification: Classification nationale, sans titre.

Groupes de population classifiés par situation dans la profession: Les personnes ayant un emploi et les chômeurs (s'ils ont travaillé au cours des 12 derniers mois).

Catégories de codage: Salariés (distinction entre privé et public) et travailleurs indépendants (distinction entre constitués en société, non constitués en société et travailleurs familiaux non rémunérés).

Convertibilité avec la CISP: CISP-1993.

Education:

Titre de la classification: Classification nationale, sans titre.

Groupes de population classifiés selon l'éducation: Les personnes ayant un emploi et les chômeurs.

Catégories de codage: Non disponible.

Convertibilité avec la CITE: Convertibilité indirecte avec la CITE-1976.

Taille de l'échantillon et plan de sondage:

Unité finale d'échantillonnage: Logement et ménage.

Taille de l'échantillon (unités finales d'échantillonnage): 61 000 logements; 53 500 ménages.

Taux de sondage: 1/240.

Base de sondage: Base de sondage aréolaire stratifiée à plusieurs degrés. Liste d'immeubles d'habitation dans les grandes villes.

Renouvellement de la base de sondage: En continu pour tenir compte de la croissance. Grande refonte tous les 10 ans.

Rotation:

Schéma: Les logements restent dans l'échantillon pendant 6 mois consécutifs avant d'être renouvelés.

Pourcentage d'unités restant dans l'échantillon pendant deux enquêtes successives: 83,3 pour cent.

Nombre maximum d'interrogatoires par unité de sondage: Non disponible.

Durée nécessaire au renouvellement complet de l'échantillon: Non disponible.

Déroulement de l'enquête:

Type d'entretien: Entretien assisté par ordinateur, par téléphone et face à face.

Nombre d'unités finales d'échantillonnage par zone de sondage: Non disponible.

Durée de déroulement de l'enquête:

Totale: Une semaine.

Par zone de sondage: Non disponible.

Organisation: Permanente.

Nombre de personnes employées: 777 enquêteurs et 79 cadres.

Substitution des unités finales en cas de non-réponse: Non.

Estimations et redressements:

Taux de non-réponse: 5%.

Redressement pour non-réponse: Oui.

Imputation en cas de non-réponse à une question spécifique: Oui, en utilisant la réponse du mois précédent, le cas échéant, pendant un mois maximum. Imputation hot-deck.

Redressement pour les régions/populations non couvertes: Non.

Redressement en cas de sous-représentation: Oui.

Redressement en cas de sur-représentation: Oui.

Corrections des variations saisonnières: Oui, en utilisant la version de X11-ARIMA de Statistique Canada.

Historique de l'enquête:

Titre et date de la première enquête: Enquête sur la population active, novembre 1945.

Modifications et révisions significatives: a) la définition des heures de travail habituelles pour les salariés a été modifiée en janvier 1997. C'était auparavant la même que pour les travailleurs indépendants et elle recouvrait aussi bien les heures rémunérées que les heures non rémunérées. b) Les estimations sont recalculées après communication des estimations du recensement de la population. Les estimations de l'EPA sont calées sur les décomptes du dernier recensement de la population. La dernière révision a eu lieu au moment de la publication des résultats de janvier 2000 pour les estimations remontant à 1976.

Documentation et dissémination:
Documentation:
Titre des publications publiant les résultats: Information population active (numéro de catalogue 71-001-PPB) (mensuel).
Titre des publications méthodologiques: Guide de l'Enquête sur la population active (71-543-GIE); Méthodologie de l'Enquête sur la population active du Canada, décembre 1998 (71-526-XPB).
Dissémination:
Délai de publication des premiers résultats: Dans un délai d'un mois.
Information à l'avance du public des dates de publication initiale des résultats: Oui.
Mise à disposition, sur demande, des données non publiées: Oui.
Mise à disposition des données sur support informatique: CD-ROM: Revue chronologique de la population active (Catalogue 71F0004XCB) (annuelle, habituellement en février).
Site web: http://www.statcan.ca/.

Chine

Titre de l'enquête: Urban Labour Force Sampling Survey
Organisme responsable de l'enquête:
Organisation et déroulement de l'enquête: Department of Population, Social, Science and Technology Statistics
Analyse et Publication des résultats: Department of Population, Social, Science and Technology Statistics
Sujets couverts par l'enquête: Emploi, chômage, durée du travail, nature de la carte de séjour, durée du chômage, situation dans la profession et niveau d'instruction.
Champ de l'enquête:
Territoire: Les zones urbaines du pays.
Groupes de population: Toutes les personnes âgées de 16 ans et plus, à l'exception des forces armées et des étrangers.
Disponibilité d'estimations selon d'autres sources pour les régions ou groupes exclus: Disponibles uniquement pour les forces armées.
Groupes couverts par l'enquête mais exclus des résultats publiés: Les chômeurs.
Périodicité:
Réalisation de l'enquête: Trois fois par an.
Publication des résultats: Annuelle pour certaines variables.
Période de référence:
Emploi: Une semaine.
Recherche d'un emploi: Trois mois avant la date de l'entretien.
Disponibilité pour travailler: Deux semaines après la date de l'entretien.
Concepts et définitions:
Emploi: Toutes les personnes au-delà d'un âge spécifié vivant en zones urbaines et percevant un revenu lié à l'exercice d'une activité économique, à savoir: 1) les personnes âgées de 16 ans et plus ayant effectué un travail rémunéré pendant au moins une heure durant la semaine de référence et 2) celles qui sont rattachées à une unité ou à un lieu de travail mais qui ne travaillent pas, temporairement, pendant la semaine de référence pour cause de vacances, de congés, d'études ou assimilés.
Cette catégorie inclut:
a)les personnes ayant un emploi mais temporairement absentes pour cause de maladie ou d'accident, de congés ou de vacances annuelles, de congé de maternité ou de congé de paternité, de congé parental, de congé d'éducation ou de formation, d'intempéries, etc.
b)les personnes sans emploi, immédiatement disponibles pour travailler, qui ont pris des dispositions pour commencer à travailler dans un nouvel emploi à une date postérieure à la période de référence;
c)les personnes ayant effectué un travail quelconque, rémunéré ou en vue d'un bénéfice, pendant la semaine de référence, mais qui étaient alors à la retraite et au bénéfice d'une pension, inscrites en tant que demandeurs d'emploi auprès d'un bureau de placement ou qui percevaient des allocations de chômage;
d)les travailleurs familiaux non rémunérés travaillant durant la période de référence;
e)tous les membres des forces armées.
Chômage: Toutes les personnes au-delà d'un âge spécifié vivant en zones urbaines, immédiatement disponibles pour travailler mais sans emploi pendant la période de référence et qui cherchent un emploi en faisant des démarches concrètes, à savoir les personnes âgées de 16 ans et plus: 1) sans emploi rémunéré pendant la semaine de référence et qui ne font pas partie du deuxième groupe de la définition de l'emploi, 2) qui ont cherché un emploi en faisant des démarches concrètes au cours des 3 mois précédant la semaine de référence et 3) disponibles pour travailler dans les deux semaines.
Cette catégorie inclut: les personnes sans emploi et immédiatement disponibles pour travailler qui ont essayé de créer leur propre entreprise; les personnes en quête d'un emploi et/ou immédiatement disponibles pour travailler mais qui étaient à la retraite et au bénéfice d'une pension.
Sous-emploi:
Sous-emploi lié à la durée du travail: Ne s'applique pas.
Situations d'emploi inadéquat: Ne s'applique pas.
Durée du travail: Les heures de travail réellement effectuées dans toutes les activités, l'unité de temps étant l'heure.
Revenu lié à l'emploi:
Revenu lié à l'emploi salarié: Ne s'applique pas.
Revenu lié à l'emploi indépendant: Ne s'applique pas.
Secteur informel: Ne s'applique pas.
Activité habituelle: Ne s'applique pas.
Classifications:
Branche d'activité économique (industrie)
Titre de la classification: Non disponible.
Groupes de population classifiés selon l'industrie: Non disponible.
Nombre de groupes de codage: Non disponible.
Profession
Titre de la classification: Non disponible.
Groupes de population classifiés selon la profession: Non disponible.
Nombre de groupes de codage: Non disponible.
Situation dans la profession
Titre de la classification: Non disponible.
Groupes de population classifiés par situation dans la profession: Non disponible.
Nombre de groupes de codage: Sept groupes: 1. emploi dans les unités urbaines, 2. emploi dans des entreprises municipales, 3. emploi dans l'agriculture, la pêche, la sylviculture et la chasse, 4. salariés dans des unités gérées par des particuliers, 5. employeurs dans des unités gérées par des particuliers, 6. travailleurs indépendants, 7. autres.
Convertibilité avec la CISP: Non.
Education
Titre de la classification: Non disponible.
Groupes de population classifiés selon l'éducation: Non disponible.
Catégories de codage: Cinq groupes: 1. analphabète et semi-analphabète, 2. enseignement primaire, 3. premier cycle de l'enseignement secondaire, 4. deuxième cycle de l'enseignement secondaire, 5. collège et enseignement supérieur.
Convertibilité avec la CITE: Non.
Taille de l'échantillon et plan de sondage:
Unité finale d'échantillonnage: Grappe d'environ 50 à 100 ménages.
Taille de l'échantillon (unités finales d'échantillonnage): (1,2 million de ménages dans l'ensemble du pays); environ 0,34 million dans les zones urbaines.
Taux de sondage: 1 pour cent; le plan de sondage va de pair avec l'enquête annuelle sur la population, qui couvre l'ensemble du pays.
Base de sondage: La base est fondée sur les données du dernier recensement et sur le registre du Ministère de la sécurité publique. Pour les unités finales d'échantillonnage, la base de sondage est faite par les enquêteurs.
Renouvellement de l'échantillon: Habituellement, chaque année; les unités finales d'échantillonnage sont changées chaque année dans chaque province.
Rotation: PAS DE SCHEMA DE ROTATION.
Schéma: NE S'APPLIQUE PAS.
Pourcentage d'unités restant dans l'échantillon durant deux enquêtes successives: NON DISPONIBLE.
Nombre maximum d'interrogatoires par unité de sondage: NON DISPONIBLE.
Durée nécessaire au renouvellement complet de l'échantillon: NON DISPONIBLE.
Déroulement de l'enquête:
Type d'entretien: Entretien personnel reproduit sur papier avec écriture manuelle.
Nombre d'unités finales d'échantillonnage par zone de sondage: Environ 1400.
Durée de déroulement de l'enquête:
Totale: Vingt jours.
Par zone de sondage: Non disponible.

Organisation: Il existe une structure d'enquête permanente dans chaque province. Du personnel est également recruté pour chaque enquête.
Nombre de personnes employées: Environ 1500.
Substitution des unités finales en cas de non-réponse: Oui.
Estimations et redressements:
Taux de non-réponse: Environ 5%.
Redressement pour non-réponse: Oui.
Imputation en cas de non-réponse à une question spécifique: Non.
Redressement pour les régions/populations non couvertes: Oui.
Redressement en cas de sous-représentation: Oui.
Redressement en cas de sur-représentation: Oui.
Corrections des variations saisonnières: Non.
Historique de l'enquête:
Titre et date de la première enquête: Urban Labour Force Survey System, 1er octobre 1996.
Modifications et révisions significatives: Néant.
Documentation et dissémination:
Documentation
Titre des publications publiant les résultats: China Statistical Yearbook.
Titre des publications méthodologiques: China Statistical Yearbook.
Dissémination
Délai de publication des premiers résultats: Pas encore disponible.
Information à l'avance du public des dates de publication initiale des résultats: OUI.
Mise à disposition, sur demande, des données non publiées: Pas jusqu'à présent.
Mise à disposition des données sur support informatique: Les tableaux peuvent être mis à disposition sur disquette.
Site web: http://www.stats.gov.cn/.

Chypre

Titre de l'enquête: Labour force survey.
Organisme responsable de l'enquête:
Organisation et déroulement de l'enquête: Statistical Service.
Analyse et Publication des résultats: Statistical Service.
Sujets couverts par l'enquête: Emploi, chômage, sous-emploi, durée du travail, durée de l'emploi et du chômage, industrie, profession, situation dans la profession, niveau d'instruction/de qualification, exercice d'autres emplois.
Champ de l'enquête:
Territoire: La zone de Chypre sous contrôle du Gouvernement.
Groupes de population: Les personnes âgées de 15 ans et plus. Sont exclus: les personnes vivant en institution, les citoyens non résidents, les touristes, les personnes résidant à l'étranger et les étudiants faisant leurs études à l'étranger.
Disponibilité d'estimations selon d'autres sources pour les régions ou groupes exclus: NE S'APPLIQUE PAS.
Groupes couverts par l'enquête mais exclus des résultats publiés: NE S'APPLIQUE PAS.
Périodicité:
Réalisation de l'enquête: Annuelle.
Publication des résultats: Annuelle.
Période de référence:
Emploi: Une semaine au cours du deuxième trimestre.
Recherche d'un emploi: Quatre semaines au cours du deuxième trimestre.
Disponibilité pour travailler: Deux semaines au cours du deuxième trimestre.
Concepts et définitions:
Emploi: Les personnes âgées de 15 ans et plus qui, pendant la semaine de référence, ont travaillé pendant au moins une heure et celles ayant un emploi d'où elles étaient temporairement absentes.
Cette catégorie inclut:
a)les personnes ayant un emploi mais temporairement absentes de leur travail pour cause de maladie ou d'accident, de congés ou de vacances annuelles, de congé de maternité ou de congé de paternité, de congé d'éducation ou de formation si celui-ci est de moins de six mois, d'absence non autorisée, de conflit du travail, d'intempéries, de panne mécanique, etc.
b)les travailleurs occupés à plein temps ou à temps partiel et en quête d'un autre travail pendant la période de référence;
c)les personnes ayant effectué un travail quelconque, rémunéré ou en vue d'un bénéfice, pendant la semaine de référence, mais qui étaient alors assujetties à la scolarité obligatoire, à la retraite et au bénéfice d'une pension, inscrites en tant que demandeurs d'emploi auprès d'un bureau de placement ou qui percevaient des allocations de chômage;
d)les étudiants à plein temps ou à temps partiel travaillant à plein temps ou à temps partiel;
e)les apprentis et stagiaires rémunérés;
f)les travailleurs familiaux non rémunérés travaillant durant la période de référence ou temporairement absents de leur travail;
g)les volontaires et les militaires de carrière ainsi que les personnes effectuant un service civil rémunéré équivalent au service militaire.
Chômage: Les personnes âgées de 15 à 64 ans actuellement sans emploi et disponibles pour travailler pendant la semaine de référence, qui ont cherché un emploi au cours des quatre dernières semaines, ou qui vont travailler ou tenter de créer leur propre entreprise dans les deux semaines suivant celle de l'entretien. Cette catégorie inclut également les étudiants à temps partiel à la recherche d'un emploi à plein temps et les travailleurs saisonniers ne travaillant pas durant la morte-saison, s'ils cherchent du travail.
Sous-emploi:
Sous-emploi lié à la durée du travail: Non disponible.
Situations d'emploi inadéquat: Non disponible.
Durée du travail: Non disponible.
Revenu lié à l'emploi:
Revenu lié à l'emploi salarié: Non couvert par l'enquête.
Revenu lié à l'emploi indépendant: Non couvert par l'enquête.
Secteur informel: Non couvert par l'enquête.
Activité habituelle: Non couvert par l'enquête.
Classifications:
Branche d'activité économique (industrie)
Titre de la classification: Nomenclature d'Activités de la Communauté Européenne (NACE).
Groupes de population classifiés selon l'industrie: Les personnes ayant un emploi et les chômeurs.
Nombre de groupes de codage: Non disponible.
Convertibilité avec la CITI: CITI-Rév.3 au niveau à deux chiffres (division).
Profession
Titre de la classification: CITP-1988.
Groupes de population classifiés selon la profession: Les personnes ayant un emploi et les chômeurs.
Nombre de groupes de codage: 226 sous-groupes (au niveau à trois chiffres).
Convertibilité avec la CITP: CITP-1988
Situation dans la profession
Titre de la classification: Non disponible.
Groupes de population classifiés par situation dans la profession: Les personnes ayant un emploi et les chômeurs.
Catégories de codage: Quatre groupes: travailleurs indépendants avec ou sans salariés; salariés; employeurs; travailleurs familiaux non rémunérés.
Convertibilité avec la CISP: CISP-1993.
Education
Titre de la classification: CITE-1997.
Groupes de population classifiés selon l'éducation: Les personnes ayant un emploi et les chômeurs.
Catégories de codage:
Convertibilité avec la CITE: CITE-1997.
Taille de l'échantillon et plan de sondage:
Unité finale d'échantillonnage: Logement.
Taille de l'échantillon (unités finales d'échantillonnage): 4 157 logements.
Taux de sondage: 1,6 pour cent.
Base de sondage: La liste de logements tirée du recensement de la population de 1992.
Renouvellement de l'échantillon: Les logements nouvellement construits sont ajoutés chaque année à la base.
Rotation:
Schéma: 25 pour cent sont remplacés chaque année.
Pourcentage d'unités restant dans l'échantillon durant deux enquêtes successives: 75 pour cent.
Nombre maximum d'interrogatoires par unité de sondage: Quatre fois.
Durée nécessaire au renouvellement complet de l'échantillon: Quatre ans.
Déroulement de l'enquête:
Type d'entretien: Entretien personnel assisté par ordinateur.
Nombre d'unités finales d'échantillonnage par zone de sondage: Environ 250 unités.
Durée de déroulement de l'enquête:
Totale: 13 semaines

Par zone de sondage: Une semaine.
Organisation: Il existe un noyau dur de trois personnes permanentes.
Nombre de personnes employées: 22.
Substitution des unités finales en cas de non-réponse: OUI.
Estimations et redressements:
Taux de non-réponse: Environ 1%.
Redressement pour non-réponse: OUI.
Imputation en cas de non-réponse à une question spécifique: NON.
Redressement pour les régions/populations non couvertes: NON.
Redressement en cas de sous-représentation: OUI.
Redressement en cas de sur-représentation: Ne s'applique pas.
Corrections des variations saisonnières: NON.
Historique de l'enquête:
Titre et date de la première enquête: Labour Force Survey 1999.
Modifications et révisions significatives: Ne s'applique pas.
Documentation et dissémination:
Documentation
Titre des publications publiant les résultats: Aucune publication à ce jour; une publication annuelle est prévue.
Titre des publications méthodologiques: Aucune publication à ce jour; une publication annuelle est prévue.
Dissémination
Délai de publication des premiers résultats: Non disponible.
Information à l'avance du public des dates de publication initiale des résultats: Non.
Mise à disposition, sur demande, des données non publiées: Oui.
Mise à disposition des données sur support informatique: Oui.
Site web: http://www.pio.gov.cy/dsr/

République de Corée

Titre de l'enquête: Economically Active Population Survey (EAPS).
Organisme responsable de l'enquête:
Organisation et déroulement de l'enquête: National Statistical Office.
Analyse et Publication des résultats: National Statistical Office.
Sujets couverts par l'enquête: Emploi, chômage, durée du travail, durée du chômage, industrie, profession, situation dans la profession, éducation.
Champ de l'enquête:
Territoire: L'ensemble du pays.
Groupes de population: Les personnes âgées de 15 ans et plus résidant habituellement dans des ménages ordinaires situés dans les limites du territoire au moment de l'entretien.
Sont exclus les membres des forces armées, les prisonniers, les personnes placées en établissement, les citoyens non résidents, les étrangers et les personnes résidant à l'étranger.
Disponibilité d'estimations selon d'autres sources pour les régions ou groupes exclus: NON.
Groupes couverts par l'enquête mais exclus des résultats publiés: NON.
Périodicité:
Réalisation de l'enquête: Mensuelle.
Publication des résultats: Mensuelle.
Période de référence:
Emploi: La semaine comportant le 15 du mois.
Recherche d'un emploi: La semaine comportant le 15 du mois.
Disponibilité pour travailler: La semaine comportant le 15 du mois.
Concepts et définitions:
Emploi: Toutes les personnes âgées de 15 ans et plus ayant effectué un travail, rémunéré ou en vue d'un bénéfice, pendant au moins une heure au cours de la semaine de référence et les travailleurs familiaux non rémunérés ayant travaillé 18 heures ou plus durant la semaine de référence.
Cette catégorie inclut:
a)les personnes ayant un emploi mais qui étaient temporairement absentes de leur travail pour cause de maladie ou d'accident, de congés ou de vacances annuelles, de congé de maternité, de paternité ou de congé parental, de congé d'éducation ou de formation, de conflit du travail, d'intempéries ou de panne mécanique;
b)les travailleurs occupés à plein temps ou à temps partiel et en quête d'un autre travail durant la semaine de référence; autres obligations familiales, conflit du travail, désorganisation temporaire durant la semaine de référence;
c)les personnes ayant effectué un travail quelconque, rémunéré ou en vue d'un bénéfice, durant la semaine de référence, mais qui étaient alors assujetties à la scolarité obligatoire, à la retraite et au bénéfice d'une pension, inscrites en tant que demandeurs d'emploi auprès d'un bureau de placement ou qui percevaient des allocations de chômage;
d)les étudiants à plein temps ou à temps partiel travaillant à plein temps ou à temps partiel;
e)les apprentis et stagiaires rémunérés.
Les membres des forces armées sont exclus, même si le service militaire est obligatoire.
Chômage: Toutes les personnes âgées de 15 ans et plus qui n'étaient pas au travail mais disponibles pour travailler et qui ont cherché activement du travail pendant la semaine de référence. En outre, depuis 1999, l'Office National de Statistiques (National Statistical Office) recueille des données sur les chômeurs cherchant du travail sur une période de quatre mois incluant la semaine de l'enquête.
Par « cherchant activement un emploi », on entend le fait d'avoir effectué une ou plusieurs des démarches ci-après au cours de la semaine de référence: s'être inscrit auprès d'un bureau de placement, avoir envoyé des curriculums vitae, avoir fait paraître des petites annonces ou y avoir répondu, s'être enquis d'éventuels emplois auprès de lieux de travail, avoir pris contact avec des amis ou des parents, avoir pris des dispositions pour créer sa propre entreprise, etc.
Par « disponibilité pour travailler », on entend la disposition de l'enquêté à prendre un emploi immédiatement si un travail raisonnable est disponible.
Cette catégorie inclut également les personnes en quête d'un emploi et/ou immédiatement disponibles pour travailler mais qui étaient assujetties à la scolarité obligatoire, à la retraite et au bénéfice d'une pension, et les étudiants à plein temps ou à temps partiel à la recherche d'un emploi à plein temps ou à temps partiel s'ils sont disponibles durant la semaine de référence.
Sont exclus les travailleurs saisonniers attendant un travail agricole ou un autre emploi saisonnier, qui sont par ailleurs considérés comme inactifs.
Sous-emploi:
Sous-emploi lié à la durée du travail: Ne s'applique pas.
Situations d'emploi inadéquat: Ne s'applique pas.
Durée du travail: Le nombre total d'heures de travail réellement effectuées dans l'activité principale pendant la semaine de référence, y compris les heures supplémentaires et le temps passé en préparatifs tels que faire des résumés de conférences, commander des marchandises, etc.
Sont exclues les heures n'ayant pas de lien avec l'emploi, telles que les heures correspondant aux pauses-repas, aux déplacements du domicile au lieu de travail et vice versa ou au règlement d'affaires privées.
Revenu lié à l'emploi:
Revenu lié à l'emploi salarié: Ne s'applique pas.
Revenu lié à l'emploi indépendant: Ne s'applique pas.
Secteur informel: Ne s'applique pas.
Activité habituelle: Ne s'applique pas.
Classifications:
Branche d'activité économique (industrie)
Titre de la classification: 1992 Korea Standard Industrial Classification (KSIC).
Groupes de population classifiés selon l'industrie: Les personnes ayant un emploi et les chômeurs.
Nombre de groupes de codage: 60 divisions (au niveau à 2 chiffres).
Convertibilité avec la CITI: CITI-Rév.3.
Profession
Titre de la classification: 1993 Korea Standard Occupation Classification (KSOC).
Groupes de population classifiés selon la profession: Les personnes ayant un emploi et les chômeurs.
Nombre de groupes de codage: 27 divisions (au niveau à 2 chiffres).
Convertibilité avec la CITP: CITP-1988.
Situation dans la profession
Titre de la classification: Non disponible.
Groupes de population classifiés par situation dans la profession: Les personnes ayant un emploi.
Catégories de codage: Salarié permanent, salarié temporaire, journalier, employeur, travailleur indépendant et travailleur familial non rémunéré (6 groupes).
Convertibilité avec la CISP: CISP-1993.
Education
Titre de la classification: Non disponible.

Groupes de population classifiés selon l'éducation: Les personnes ayant un emploi et les chômeurs.
Catégories de codage: Jamais scolarisé, enseignement primaire, enseignement primaire du premier degré, enseignement secondaire, collège, université (6 groupes).
Convertibilité avec la CITE: CITE-1976.
Taille de l'échantillon et plan de sondage:
Unité finale d'échantillonnage: Ménage.
Taille de l'échantillon (unités finales d'échantillonnage): Environ 30 000 ménages.
Taux de sondage: Environ 1/430.
Base de sondage: Recensement de la Population et du Logement de 1995 (1995 Population and Housing Census).
Renouvellement de l'échantillon: Tous les 5 ans, sur la base des résultats du recensement.
Rotation:
Schéma: Ne s'applique pas.
Pourcentage d'unités restant dans l'échantillon durant deux enquêtes successives: Ne s'applique pas.
Nombre maximum d'interrogatoires par unité de sondage: Ne s'applique pas.
Durée nécessaire au renouvellement complet de l'échantillon: Ne s'applique pas.
Déroulement de l'enquête:
Type d'entretien: Depuis 1999, entretien par téléphone assisté par ordinateur. Auparavant, entretien personnel assisté par ordinateur.
Nombre d'unités finales d'échantillonnage par zone de sondage: Environ huit ménages.
Durée de déroulement de l'enquête:
Totale: Deux semaines, dont la semaine de l'enquête.
Par zone de sondage: Deux semaines, dont la semaine de l'enquête.
Organisation: Recenseurs permanents travaillant à plein temps pour les 47 bureaux régionaux.
Nombre de personnes employées: Environ 530 personnes.
Substitution des unités finales en cas de non-réponse: NON.
Estimations et redressements:
Taux de non-réponse: 0,2%.
Redressement pour non-réponse: NON.
Imputation en cas de non-réponse à une question spécifique: NON.
Redressement pour les régions/populations non couvertes: NON.
Redressement en cas de sous-représentation: NON.
Redressement en cas de sur-représentation: NON.
Corrections des variations saisonnières: Oui. Depuis janvier 1999, la méthode ARIMA X12-12 est utilisée.
Historique de l'enquête:
Titre et date de la première enquête: Economically Active Population Survey, 1963. Depuis 1957, des statistiques sur la population active ont été recueillies par le réseau administratif local sous la responsabilité du Ministry of Home Affairs.
Modifications et révisions significatives: En 1998, le questionnaire de l'enquête a été révisé pour recueillir et refléter les changements sociaux, la forme d'activité de la population active et mesurer le nombre de chômeurs ayant cherché un emploi pendant quatre semaines afin d'établir des comparaisons avec d'autres pays. En outre, en 1999, les estimations de l'Enquête (EAPS) ont été révisées rétrospectivement depuis 1991 sur la base du Recensement de 1995 (1995 Population and Housing Census).
Documentation et dissémination:
Documentation
Titre des publications publiant les résultats: « Monthly Report on the Economically Active Population" et "Annual Report on the Economically Active Population" (en mai de chaque année).
Titre des publications méthodologiques: « Monthly Report on the Economically Active Population" et "Annual Report on the Economically Active Population" (en mai de chaque année).
Dissémination
Délai de publication des premiers résultats: Un mois.
Information à l'avance du public des dates de publication initiale des résultats: OUI.
Mise à disposition, sur demande, des données non publiées: OUI.
Mise à disposition des données sur support informatique: Disquettes, bandes magnétiques et site web Internet (http://www.nso.go.kr/).

Croatie

Titre de l'enquête: Labour Force Survey
Organisme responsable de l'enquête:
Organisation et déroulement de l'enquête: Central Bureau of Statistics
Analyse et Publication des résultats: Central Bureau of Statistics
Sujets couverts par l'enquête: Emploi, chômage, sous-emploi, durée du travail, durée de l'emploi, durée du chômage, travailleurs découragés, travailleurs occasionnels, industrie, profession, situation dans la profession, niveau d'instruction et exercice d'autres emplois.
Champ de l'enquête:
Territoire: L'ensemble du pays, à l'exception des territoires occupés pendant la guerre de 1995-1996.
Groupes de population: Tous les résidents habituels âgés de 15 ans et plus vivant dans des ménages non institutionnels, y compris ceux temporairement absents. Sont exclus les personnes résidant à l'étranger et les citoyens non résidents.
Disponibilité d'estimations selon d'autres sources pour les régions ou groupes exclus: NON.
Groupes couverts par l'enquête mais exclus des résultats publiés: NEANT.
Périodicité:
Réalisation de l'enquête: En continu.
Publication des résultats: Deux fois par an.
Période de référence:
Emploi: La dernière semaine de chaque mois, sans jours fériés ou autres jours non ouvrables.
Recherche d'un emploi: Quatre semaines avant la date de l'entretien.
Disponibilité pour travailler: Deux semaines après la date de l'entretien.
Concepts et définitions:
Emploi: Sont considérées comme ayant un emploi toutes les personnes âgées de 15 ans et plus qui, pendant la période de référence, a) ont effectué un travail quelconque pendant au moins une heure, rémunéré en espèces ou en nature; b) n'ont pas travaillé mais étaient assurées de réintégrer le même emploi lorsque leur absence ne se justifierait plus.
Sont également incluses dans les totaux les personnes qui, pendant la semaine de référence:
a)étaient temporairement absentes de leur travail pour cause de congé, de maladie, d'intempéries, de congé de formation professionnelle ou autre motif similaire;
b)les travailleurs occupés à plein temps ou à temps partiel et en quête d'un autre travail;
c)les étudiants à plein temps ou à temps partiel travaillant à plein temps ou à temps partiel;
d)les personnes ayant effectué un travail quelconque tout en étant soit à la retraite et au bénéfice d'une pension, soit inscrites en tant que demandeurs d'emploi auprès d'un bureau de placement, soit en percevant des allocations de chômage;
e)les travailleurs familiaux rémunérés ou non (s'ils ont travaillé au moins une heure);
f)les domestiques privés;
g)les militaires de carrière vivant dans des ménages;
h)les personnes occupées dans la production de biens pour leur usage final personnel.
Chômage: Sont considérées comme sans emploi toutes les personnes âgées de 15 ans et plus n'ayant pas du tout travaillé pendant la semaine de référence, qui ont activement cherché un emploi au cours des quatre semaines précédant l'entretien et qui étaient disponibles pour commencer à travailler dans les deux semaines suivant la semaine de l'enquête. Sont également incluses dans cette catégorie les personnes n'ayant pas cherché activement du travail parce qu'elles avaient trouvé un emploi dans lequel elles devaient commencer à travailler ultérieurement.
Sous-emploi:
Sous-emploi lié à la durée du travail: Les personnes qui, pendant la semaine de référence, ont travaillé moins que la durée légale du travail, étaient disposées à faire davantage d'heures et disponibles pour ce faire.
Situations d'emploi inadéquat: Les personnes qui, pendant la semaine de référence:
a)étaient disposées à changer leur emploi actuel et disponibles pour ce faire, parce qu'elles travaillaient moins que la durée légale du travail, et ce contre leur volonté;
b)souhaitaient changer d'emploi pour cause de mauvaise utilisation de leurs qualifications, de conditions de travail insatisfaisantes ou pour des raisons personnelles ou de santé, etc.

Durée du travail: Les heures de travail habituelles et les heures réellement effectuées pendant la semaine de référence dans l'activité principale, ainsi que les heures réellement effectuées pendant la semaine de référence dans la ou les activités secondaires.

Revenu lié à l'emploi:

Revenu lié à l'emploi salarié: Revenu mensuel net de chacune des personnes interrogées.

Revenu lié à l'emploi indépendant: Revenu mensuel net de chacune des personnes interrogées.

Secteur informel: Ne s'applique pas.

Activité habituelle: Ne s'applique pas.

Classifications:

Branche d'activité économique (industrie)

Titre de la classification: Classification nationale.

Groupes de population classifiés selon l'industrie: Les personnes ayant un emploi (dans une activité principale et une ou plusieurs activités secondaires) et les personnes sans emploi ayant une expérience professionnelle préalable.

Nombre de groupes de codage: 571

Convertibilité avec la CITI: CITI-Rév.3

Profession

Titre de la classification: Classification nationale

Groupes de population classifiés selon la profession: Les personnes ayant un emploi (dans une activité principale et une ou plusieurs activités secondaires) et les personnes sans emploi ayant une expérience professionnelle préalable.

Nombre de groupes de codage: 402

Convertibilité avec la CITP: CITP-1998

Situation dans la profession

Titre de la classification: Classification nationale

Groupes de population classifiés par situation dans la profession: Les personnes ayant un emploi et les personnes sans emploi ayant une expérience professionnelle préalable.

Catégories de codage: 4 groupes (salariés, employeurs, travailleurs indépendants, travailleurs familiaux non rémunérés).

Convertibilité avec la CISP: CISP-1993

Education

Titre de la classification: Classification nationale.

Groupes de population classifiés selon l'éducation: Toutes les personnes âgées de 15 ans et plus.

Catégories de codage: 9 groupes (non scolarisé, 4 à 7 ans d'école primaire, 1 à 2 ans d'enseignement secondaire professionnel, 3ème année d'enseignement secondaire professionnel, 4ème année d'enseignement secondaire professionnel, collège, université, troisième cycle, doctorat).

Convertibilité avec la CITE: Oui.

Taille de l'échantillon et plan de sondage:

Unité finale d'échantillonnage: Logement.

Taille de l'échantillon (unités finales d'échantillonnage): Environ 8 500 logements représentant 6 900 ménages et couvrant quelque 20 000 personnes.

Taux de sondage: 0,74 pour cent.

Base de sondage: Depuis 2002, la base de sondage est dérivée de la base de données du recensement de la population de 2001. Si, pour la période 1996-1999, la base de sondage principale était construite à partir du recensement des ménages de 1991 mis à jour en 1996, elle se fonde sur la base de données de la société nationale d'électricité (Croatian Electrical Utility Company) pour 2000 et 2001.

Renouvellement de l'échantillon: Renouvelé, pour 2002, sur la base du recensement de la population de 2001.

Rotation:

Schéma: Depuis 2000, aucune rotation. Pour la période 1996-1999, à chaque enquête (6 mois), un tiers des logements sondés était renouvelé et remplacé par de nouveaux logements, de sorte que les deux tiers des unités restaient inchangées.

Pourcentage d'unités restant dans l'échantillon durant deux enquêtes successives: Ne s'applique pas.

Nombre maximum d'interrogatoires par unité de sondage: Non disponible.

Durée nécessaire au renouvellement complet de l'échantillon: Non disponible.

Déroulement de l'enquête:

Type d'entretien: Sur papier avec écriture manuelle.

Nombre d'unités finales d'échantillonnage par zone de sondage: 12 ménages par district de recensement.

Durée de déroulement de l'enquête:

Totale: 14 jours après chaque période de référence.

Par zone de sondage: 14 jours après chaque période de référence.

Organisation: Structure d'enquête permanente.

Nombre de personnes employées: Environ 203 enquêteurs et 31 cadres.

Substitution des unités finales en cas de non-réponse: Non.

Estimations et redressements:

Taux de non-réponse: 10% pour l'enquête du premier semestre 2001. Il est habituellement d'environ 12%.

Redressement pour non-réponse: Non.

Imputation en cas de non-réponse à une question spécifique: Non.

Redressement pour les régions/populations non couvertes: Non.

Redressement en cas de sous-représentation: Non.

Redressement en cas de sur-représentation: Non.

Corrections des variations saisonnières: Non.

Historique de l'enquête:

Titre et date de la première enquête: Labour Force Survey (Anketa o radno snazi), novembre 1996.

Modifications et révisions significatives: Améliorations régulières apportées au questionnaire; renouvellement de la base de sondage.

Documentation et dissémination:

Documentation

Titre des publications publiant les résultats: First Releases: LFS – Labour Force Survey in the Republic of Croatia (deux fois par an); LFS Results: comparison with the European Union results (annuel); Statistical Year Book; Monthly Statistical Report.

Titre des publications méthodologiques: Les informations méthodologiques pertinentes figurent dans toutes les publications précitées.

Dissémination

Délai de publication des premiers résultats: Trois mois.

Information à l'avance du public des dates de publication initiale des résultats: Oui.

Mise à disposition, sur demande, des données non publiées: Oui.

Mise à disposition des données sur support informatique: Disquettes, CD-ROM et informations sélectionnées sur le site web: http://www.dzs.hr/

Danemark

Titre de l'enquête: Beskaeftigelsesundersökelsen (BU): Labour Force Survey (LFS).

Organisme responsable de l'enquête:

Organisation et déroulement de l'enquête: Statistics Denmark (DS).

Analyse et Publication des résultats: Statistics Denmark (DS).

Sujets couverts par l'enquête: Les personnes actuellement et habituellement actives, ayant un emploi ou sans emploi. Les personnes se trouvant actuellement en situation de sous-emploi lié à la durée du travail, les personnes en situation d'emploi inadéquat et les personnes se trouvant actuellement en dehors de la population active. Travailleurs découragés. Durée du travail. Durée de l'emploi et du chômage. Exercice d'autres emplois. Industrie, profession, situation dans la profession, niveau d'instruction/de formation.

Champ de l'enquête:

Territoire: L'ensemble du pays, sauf les territoires autonomes du Groenland et des îles Féroé.

Groupes de population: Couvre la population résidente enregistrée âgée de 15 à 66 ans (à 74 ans à partir de 2001). Sont exclus les non-résidents et les personnes sans adresse fixe.

Disponibilité d'estimations selon d'autres sources pour les régions ou groupes exclus: Néant.

Groupes couverts par l'enquête mais exclus des résultats publiés: Néant.

Périodicité:

Réalisation de l'enquête: Trimestrielle.

Publication des résultats: Trimestrielle.

Période de référence:

Emploi: Une semaine.

Recherche d'un emploi: Au cours des quatre dernières semaines.

Disponibilité pour travailler: Dans les deux semaines.

Concepts et définitions:

Emploi: Les personnes qui a) ont effectué un travail quelconque, rémunéré ou en vue d'un bénéfice ou d'un gain familial pendant la semaine de référence; et b) étaient temporairement absentes de leur travail pendant la semaine de référence pour cause de maladie ou de congé mais allaient assurément y retourner. On entend par "un travail quelconque" une heure ou plus effectuée pendant la semaine de référence.

Chômage: Les personnes actuellement sans emploi et disponibles pour travailler dans les deux semaines, qui ont cherché du travail à un moment quelconque au cours des quatre dernières semaines.

Sous-emploi:
Sous-emploi lié à la durée du travail: Les personnes ayant un emploi qui ont cherché du travail supplémentaire pendant la période de référence et/ou qui étaient disposées à effectuer un travail supplémentaire et disponibles pour ce faire.
Situations d'emploi inadéquat: Les personnes ayant un emploi et cherchant un autre travail ou un autre emploi pour avoir de meilleures conditions de travail, de meilleures conditions de déplacement entre leur domicile et leur lieu de travail et/ou obtenir une meilleure utilisation de leurs qualifications.
Durée du travail: Normale: selon convention. Habituelle: au cours d'une semaine normale. Réelle: les heures de travail réellement effectuées pendant la semaine de référence.
Revenu lié à l'emploi:
Revenu lié à l'emploi salarié: Ne s'applique pas.
Revenu lié à l'emploi indépendant: Ne s'applique pas.
Secteur informel: Ne s'applique pas.
Activité habituelle: Non disponible.
Classifications:
Branche d'activité économique (industrie)
Titre de la classification: Adaptation danoise de la NACE, rév.1.
Groupes de population classifiés selon l'industrie: Les personnes ayant un emploi et les chômeurs (dernière industrie pour ces derniers).
Nombre de groupes de codage: Au niveau à 3 chiffres.
Convertibilité avec la CITI: CITI-Rév.2 et Rév.3.
Profession
Titre de la classification: Dansk erhversnomenklatur (DISCO).
Groupes de population classifiés selon la profession: Les personnes ayant un emploi et les chômeurs (dernière profession exercée pour ces derniers).
Nombre de groupes de codage: Au niveau à 4 chiffres.
Convertibilité avec la CITP: CITP-1968 et CITP-1988.
Situation dans la profession
Titre de la classification: Non disponible.
Groupes de population classifiés par situation dans la profession: Les personnes ayant un emploi et les chômeurs (dernière situation occupée pour ces derniers).
Catégories de codage: Salariés; travailleurs indépendants avec ou sans au moins un salarié; travailleurs familiaux non rémunérés.
Convertibilité avec la CISP: CISP-1993.
Education
Titre de la classification: Classification nationale.
Groupes de population classifiés selon l'éducation: Toutes les personnes.
Catégories de codage: Non disponible.
Convertibilité avec la CITE: CITE-1997.
Taille de l'échantillon et plan de sondage:
Unité finale d'échantillonnage: Personnes.
Taille de l'échantillon (unités finales d'échantillonnage): 15 600.
Taux de sondage: 0,00428
Base de sondage: Central Population Register (CPR).
Renouvellement de l'échantillon: Hebdomadaire.
Rotation:
Schéma: Non disponible. Chaque personne est interrogée au cours de deux trimestres successifs puis une année après le second entretien, de sorte que 66 pour cent de l'échantillon a participé à la précédente enquête.
Pourcentage d'unités restant dans l'échantillon durant deux enquêtes successives: Chaque personne est interrogée au cours de deux trimestres successifs puis une année après le second entretien, de sorte que 66 pour cent de l'échantillon a participé à la précédente enquête.
Nombre maximum d'interrogatoires par unité de sondage: Non disponible.
Durée nécessaire au renouvellement complet de l'échantillon: Non disponible.
Déroulement de l'enquête:
Type d'entretien: Entretien par téléphone assisté par ordinateur et coupon-réponse envoyé par la poste pour ceux qui ne peuvent pas être joints par téléphone.
Nombre d'unités finales d'échantillonnage par zone de sondage: Non disponible.
Durée de déroulement de l'enquête:
Totale: 6 à 7 semaines.
Par zone de sondage: Non disponible.
Organisation: Permanente.
Nombre de personnes employées: 40 enquêteurs et cadres.
Substitution des unités finales en cas de non-réponse: Non.
Estimations et redressements:
Taux de non-réponse: 27%.
Redressement pour non-réponse: Imputations, non décrites.
Imputation en cas de non-réponse à une question spécifique: Non.
Redressement pour les régions/populations non couvertes: Non.
Redressement en cas de sous-représentation: Non.
Redressement en cas de sur-représentation: Non.
Corrections des variations saisonnières: Non.
Historique de l'enquête:
Titre et date de la première enquête: Labour Force Survey (LFS), printemps 1972.
Modifications et révisions significatives: Rupture importante dans la série chronologique en 1984, 1987, 1992, 1994 et 2000.
Documentation et dissémination:
Documentation
Titre des publications publiant les résultats: Statistiske Efterretninger: Arbejdsmarked.
Titre des publications méthodologiques: Idem.
Dissémination
Délai de publication des premiers résultats: 3 mois.
Information à l'avance du public des dates de publication initiale des résultats: Oui.
Mise à disposition, sur demande, des données non publiées: Oui.
Mise à disposition des données sur support informatique: Disquettes ou bandes magnétiques.
Site web: http://www.dst.dk/

Egypte

Titre de l'enquête: Labour force sample survey.
Organisme responsable de l'enquête:
Organisation et déroulement de l'enquête: Central Agency for Public Mobilisation and Statistics, CAPMAS.
Analyse et Publication des résultats: CAPMAS.
Sujets couverts par l'enquête: Emploi, chômage, durée du travail, durée de l'emploi, durée du chômage, travailleurs occasionnels, industrie, profession actuelle et passée, situation dans la profession et niveau d'instruction.
Champ de l'enquête:
Territoire: L'ensemble du pays, y compris les zones urbaines et rurales.
Groupes de population: L'armée, les étrangers, les nomades et les ressortissants égyptiens résidant à l'étranger sont exclus.
Disponibilité d'autres estimations selon d'autres sources pour les régions ou groupes exclus: Non disponible.
Groupes couverts par l'enquête mais exclus des résultats publiés: Néant.
Périodicité:
Réalisation de l'enquête: Deux fois par an.
Publication des résultats: Annuelle.
Périodes de référence:
Emploi: Semaine de référence fixe.
Recherche d'un emploi: Semaine de référence.
Disponibilité pour travailler: Semaine de référence.
Concepts et définitions:
Emploi: Les personnes âgées de 6 ans et plus, occupées dans une activité de production ou de service pendant une heure ou plus durant la semaine de référence ou qui avaient un lien formel avec l'emploi mais étaient temporairement absentes de leur travail durant la semaine de référence pour cause de maladie ou d'accident, de congés ou de vacances annuelles, de congé de maternité, de paternité ou de congé parental, de congé d'éducation ou de formation, d'absence non autorisée, de conflit du travail, d'intempéries ou de panne mécanique.
Cette catégorie inclut:
a)les personnes ayant effectué un travail quelconque, rémunéré ou en vue d'un bénéfice, pendant la semaine de référence, mais qui étaient alors assujetties à la scolarité obligatoire, à la retraite et au bénéfice d'une pension, inscrites en tant que demandeurs d'emploi auprès d'un bureau de placement ou qui percevaient des allocations de chômage;
b)les étudiants à plein temps ou à temps partiel travaillant à plein temps ou à temps partiel;
c)les apprentis et stagiaires rémunérés et les bénéficiaires de mesures de promotion de l'emploi;
d)les personnes occupées dans la production de biens pour leur usage final personnel.
Sont exclus:
a)les apprentis et stagiaires non rémunérés, les personnes occupées dans la prestation de services dans leur ménage;

b)les travailleurs familiaux non rémunérés temporairement absents de leur travail pendant la semaine de référence et les travailleurs saisonniers ne travaillant pas durant la morte-saison;
c)les personnes en mise à pied temporaire ou de durée indéterminée sans rémunération et les personnes en mise en congé non rémunéré à l'initiative de l'employeur.
Chômage: Les personnes âgées de 15 ans et plus, sans emploi durant la semaine de référence, disposées à travailler et disponibles pour ce faire et qui ont cherché du travail pendant la semaine de référence.
Cette catégorie inclut:
a)les personnes sans emploi et immédiatement disponibles pour travailler, en quête d'un emploi et qui ont pris des dispositions pour commencer à travailler dans un nouvel emploi à une date postérieure à la semaine de référence;
b)les personnes sans emploi et immédiatement disponibles pour travailler, en quête d'un emploi et qui ont essayé de créer leur propre entreprise;
c)les étudiants à plein temps ou à temps partiel à la recherche d'un emploi à plein temps ou à temps partiel;
d)les personnes en quête d'un emploi ou immédiatement disponibles pour travailler mais qui étaient assujetties à la scolarité obligatoire ou à la retraite et au bénéfice d'une pension.
Sont exclues les personnes sans emploi, disponibles pour travailler, mais n'ayant pas cherché un travail durant la semaine de référence.
Classifications:
Branche d'activité économique (industrie):
Titre de la classification: Non disponible.
Groupes de population classifiés selon l'industrie: Les personnes ayant un emploi et les chômeurs ayant une expérience professionnelle préalable.
Nombre de groupes de codage: 18 catégories.
Convertibilité avec la CITI: CITI-Rév.3.
Profession:
Titre de la classification: Non disponible.
Groupes de population classifiés selon la profession: Les personnes ayant un emploi et les chômeurs ayant une expérience professionnelle préalable.
Nombre de groupes de codage: 10 grands groupes.
Convertibilité avec la CITP: CITP-1988.
Situation dans la profession:
Titre de la classification: Non disponible.
Groupes de population classifiés par situation dans la profession: Les personnes ayant un emploi uniquement.
Catégories de codage: Salarié; employeur; travailleur indépendant; travailleur familial non rémunéré.
Convertibilité avec la CISP: CISP-1993.
Education:
Titre de la classification: Non disponible.
Groupes de population classifiés selon l'éducation: Les personnes ayant un emploi et les chômeurs.
Catégories de codage: Analphabète. Sait lire et écrire. N'a pas atteint le niveau de l'école secondaire. A terminé le premier cycle de l'école secondaire. A dépassé le niveau de l'école secondaire. Université et au-delà.
Convertibilité avec la CITE: Certains groupes sont convertibles avec la CITE.
Taille de l'échantillon et plan de sondage:
Unité finale d'échantillonnage: Unité de logement (composée d'un ou de plusieurs ménages).
Taille de l'échantillon (unités finales d'échantillonnage): 41 660 unités de logement divisées à parts égales entre deux enquêtes annuelles (mai et novembre).
Taux de sondage: 6 pour cent.
Base de sondage: Echantillon principal basé sur les données de 1995. Echantillonnage à deux degrés. Au cours du premier degré, les unités primaires d'échantillonnage couvrant environ 1 500 ménages sont sélectionnées de manière systématique, 261 unités primaires dans les zones urbaines et 185 dans les zones rurales. Au cours du second degré, 95 unités de logement sont sélectionnées dans chaque unité primaire d'échantillonnage urbaine ou rurale.
Renouvellement de l'échantillon: Aucun renouvellement n'a encore eu lieu.
Rotation: Néant.
Déroulement de l'enquête:
Type d'entretien: Entretien personnel.
Nombre d'unités finales d'échantillonnage par zone de sondage: 95 unités de logement.
Durée de déroulement de l'enquête:
Totale: 28 jours pour l'enquête de mai (du 1er au 28 juin) et 28 jours pour l'enquête de novembre (du 1er au 28 décembre).
Par zone de sondage: Non disponible.
Organisation: Permanente.
Nombre de personnes employées: Environ 210 enquêteurs et 70 cadres.
Substitution des unités finales en cas de non-réponse: Non.
Estimations et redressements:
Taux de non-réponse: 1,7%.
Redressement pour non-réponse: Oui.
Imputation en cas de non-réponse à une question spécifique: Non.
Redressement pour les régions/populations non couvertes: Non.
Redressement en cas de sous-représentation: Non.
Redressement en cas de sur-représentation: Non.
Corrections des variations saisonnières: Non.
Historique de l'enquête:
Titre et date de la première enquête: Labour force sample survey, novembre 1957.
Modifications et révisions significatives: Il y a eu au total 24 enquêtes réalisées entre 1957 et 1964 avec des périodicités différentes. De 1968 à 1985, l'enquête a été réalisée tous les ans. De 1987 à 1992, tous les trimestres. Depuis 1993, deux fois par an. Les années de recensement, l'enquête n'a pas été réalisée. Les enquêtes effectuées entre 1987 et 1992 couvraient deux sujets supplémentaires: l'activité habituelle et les activités secondaires.
Documentation et dissémination:
Documentation:
Titre des publications publiant les résultats: Annual Bulletin of Labour Force Sample Survey of the Arab Republic of Egypt.
Titre des publications méthodologiques: Annual Bulletin of Labour Force Sample Survey of the Arab Republic of Egypt.
Dissémination:
Délai de publication des premiers résultats: Une année. Les dernières données pour 1998 ont été publiées le 30 décembre 1999.
Information à l'avance du public des dates de publication initiale des résultats: Non.
Mise à disposition, sur demande, des données non publiées: Non disponible.
Mise à disposition des données sur support informatique: Les données totalisées sont disponibles, sur demande, sur disquettes. A l'avenir, il est envisagé de procéder à une dissémination par Internet.
Site web: http://www.capmas.gov.eg/.

Estonie

Titre de l'enquête: Estonian Labour Force Survey 2001 (ELFS 2001)
Organisme responsable de l'enquête:
Organisation et déroulement de l'enquête: Statistical Office of Estonia, Labour Force Statistics Division.
Analyse et Publication des résultats: Statistical Office of Estonia, Labour Force Statistics Division.
Sujets couverts par l'enquête: Emploi, chômage, sous-emploi, durée du travail, salaires, revenu, durée de l'emploi, durée du chômage, travailleurs découragés, travailleurs occasionnels, industrie, profession, situation dans la profession, niveau d'instruction, activité habituelle, exercice d'autres emplois.
Champ de l'enquête:
Territoire: L'ensemble du pays.
Groupes de population: La population cible de l'ELFS 2001 était constituée des résidents estoniens en âge de travailler, c'est-à-dire des personnes qui, au 1er janvier 2001, avaient entre 15 et 74 ans révolus (nées entre 1926 et 1985). Les militaires de carrière et les volontaires sont inclus dans les totaux mais aucune donnée séparée n'est publiée.
Disponibilité d'estimations selon d'autres sources pour les régions ou groupes exclus: Non.
Groupes couverts par l'enquête mais exclus des résultats publiés: Néant.
Périodicité:
Réalisation de l'enquête: Enquête en continu.
Publication des résultats: Trimestrielle.
Période de référence:
Emploi: Une semaine (les sept derniers jours avant la date de l'entretien).
Recherche d'un emploi: Quatre semaines avant la date de l'entretien.
Disponibilité pour travailler: Deux semaines après la date de l'entretien.
Concepts et définitions:
Emploi: Sont considérées comme ayant un emploi toutes les personnes âgées de 15 à 74 ans qui, pendant la période de référence,

ont effectué un travail quelconque pendant au moins une heure dans le cadre d'un emploi salarié ou à titre de travailleur indépendant. Les personnes en congé parental, accordé à la mère ou au père jusqu'à ce que l'enfant ait 3 ans, sont considérées comme inactifs. Les conscrits sont classifiés comme inactifs alors que les volontaires et les militaires de carrière sont inclus.
Sont incluses dans les totaux les personnes qui, pendant la période de référence, étaient temporairement absentes de leur travail pour cause de maladie, d'accident, de congés ou de vacances annuelles, de congé d'éducation, d'absence non autorisée, d'intempéries, de conflit du travail, de panne mécanique, d'autres formes de réduction de l'activité économique ou de mise à pied temporaire sans rémunération, à condition que cette absence soit d'une durée inférieure à 3 mois.
Sont également inclus:
a)les femmes en congé prénatal ou post-natal rémunéré, dont la durée respective est de 70 et 56 jours;
b)les travailleurs occupés à plein temps ou à temps partiel et en quête d'un autre travail durant la période de référence;
c)les étudiants à plein temps ou à temps partiel travaillant à plein temps ou à temps partiel;
d)les personnes ayant effectué un travail quelconque pendant la semaine de référence tout en étant soit à la retraite et au bénéfice d'une pension, soit inscrites en tant que demandeurs d'emploi auprès d'un bureau de placement, soit tout en percevant des allocations de chômage;
e)les domestiques privés;
f)les apprentis et stagiaires rémunérés.
Sont exclues les personnes occupées dans la production de biens pour leur
propre ménage (peinture, réparations, travaux ménagers, etc.).
Chômage: Sont considérées comme sans emploi toutes les personnes âgées de 15 à 74 ans qui remplissaient les trois conditions ci-après durant la semaine de référence: i) n'avaient pas de travail; ii) cherchaient activement un emploi; et iii) étaient immédiatement disponibles pour travailler, c'est-à-dire disponibles pour occuper un emploi salarié ou pour travailler comme travailleur indépendant, soit immédiatement, soit dans les 14 jours suivant la semaine de référence.
Sous-emploi:
Sous-emploi lié à la durée du travail: Les personnes qui, pendant la semaine de référence, ont travaillé, contre leur gré, moins que la durée normale du travail fixée pour un type donné d'activité et qui étaient disposés à faire davantage d'heures de travail et disponibles pour ce faire.
Situations d'emploi inadéquat: Les personnes à la recherche d'un autre emploi offrant de meilleures conditions de travail (salaire, situation géographique, etc.).
Durée du travail: Les heures de travail habituelles et les heures réellement effectuées dans l'activité principale.
Revenu lié à l'emploi:
Revenu lié à l'emploi salarié: Revenu mensuel lié à l'activité principale, c'est-à-dire salaires, traitements et autres gains en espèces ou en nature; rémunération du temps non travaillé et payé par l'employeur; primes trimestrielles et annuelles, primes de Noël, etc.; tous les types de paiements supplémentaires; indemnités pour invalidité temporaire ou pour s'occuper d'un malade.
Revenu lié à l'emploi indépendant: Les entrepreneurs, les agriculteurs et les travailleurs free-lance ne sont interrogés que sur les paiements reçus sous forme de salaire.
Secteur informel: Ne s'applique pas.
Activité habituelle: Les groupes de population ci-après sont questionnés sur leur situation économique habituelle: apprentis, élèves d'écoles secondaires, étudiants à l'université, personnes en congé de maternité ou d'éducation (congé parental), femmes au foyer, retraités pour cause d'invalidité, retraités pour cause d'invalidité partielle, chômeurs, conscrits.
Classifications:
Branche d'activité économique (industrie)
Titre de la classification: Classification nationale.
Groupes de population classifiés selon l'industrie: Les personnes ayant un emploi et les chômeurs ayant une expérience professionnelle préalable.
Nombre de groupes de codage: 60 groupes (codes 01-99).
Convertibilité avec la CITI: CITI-Rév.3.
Profession
Titre de la classification: Classification nationale.
Groupes de population classifiés selon la profession: Les personnes ayant un emploi et les chômeurs ayant une expérience professionnelle préalable.
Nombre de groupes de codage: 400 groupes (groupes au niveau à 4 chiffres).
Convertibilité avec la CITP: CITP-1988 au niveau à 4 chiffres.
Situation dans la profession
Titre de la classification: Classification nationale.
Groupes de population classifiés par situation dans la profession: Les personnes ayant un emploi et les chômeurs.
Catégories de codage: 4 groupes (salariés, employeurs, travailleurs indépendants, travailleurs familiaux non rémunérés).
Convertibilité avec la CISP: CISP-1993.
Education
Titre de la classification: Classification nationale.
Groupes de population classifiés selon l'éducation: Tous les groupes de population.
Catégories de codage: 10 groupes (pas d'enseignement primaire, enseignement primaire, enseignement de base, enseignement secondaire, pas d'enseignement professionnel (spécialisé ou professionnel), enseignement professionnel/technique, diplôme universitaire, licence, maîtrise, doctorat/PhD.).
Convertibilité avec la CITE: CITE-1997.
Taille de l'échantillon et plan de sondage:
Unité finale d'échantillonnage: Ménage.
Taille de l'échantillon (unités finales d'échantillonnage): 2 200 ménages par trimestre.
Taux de sondage: 0,4 pour cent de la population en âge de travailler par trimestre.
Base de sondage: La base de sondage est construite à partir de la base de données sur la population de la société Andmevara Ltd.
Renouvellement de l'échantillon: Trimestriel.
Rotation:
Schéma: 2-2-2. Chaque ménage est interrogé quatre fois, durant deux trimestres successifs et, après deux trimestres, il est de nouveau interrogé deux fois lors des trimestres correspondants de l'année suivante.
Pourcentage d'unités restant dans l'échantillon durant deux enquêtes successives: 50 pour cent.
Nombre maximum d'interrogatoires par unité de sondage: Non disponible.
Durée nécessaire au renouvellement complet de l'échantillon: 6 trimestres.
Déroulement de l'enquête:
Type d'entretien: Sur papier avec écriture manuelle.
Nombre d'unités finales d'échantillonnage par zone de sondage: Non disponible.
Durée de déroulement de l'enquête:
Totale: Non disponible.
Par zone de sondage: Non disponible.
Organisation: Permanente.
Nombre de personnes employées: 179 enquêteurs et 18 cadres.
Substitution des unités finales en cas de non-réponse: Non.
Estimations et redressements:
Taux de non-réponse: 9%.
Redressement pour non-réponse: Oui.
Imputation en cas de non-réponse à une question spécifique: Oui.
Redressement pour les régions/populations non couvertes: Non.
Redressement en cas de sous-représentation: Oui.
Redressement en cas de sur-représentation: Non.
Corrections des variations saisonnières: Non.
Historique de l'enquête:
Titre et date de la première enquête: Estonian Labour Force Survey, janvier-avril 1995.
Modifications et révisions significatives: De 1997 à 1999, l'enquête a été réalisée au cours du deuxième trimestre. Elle l'est en continu depuis 2000.
Documentation et dissémination:
Documentation
Titre des publications publiant les résultats: "Estonian Labour Force Survey, 1995, 1997, 1998, 1999" (annuel).
Titre des publications méthodologiques: "Estonian Labour Force Survey, 1995, 1997, 1998, 1999. Methodological report" (annuel).
Dissémination
Délai de publication des premiers résultats: Depuis 2000, deux mois pour les résultats trimestriels et trois mois pour les résultats annuels (fin mars de l'année suivante). Les données sont mises à la disposition de tous les utilisateurs intéressés, le jour même, par la publication d'un communiqué de presse intitulé 'Employment and Unemployment'.
Information à l'avance du public des dates de publication initiale des résultats: Oui.

Mise à disposition, sur demande, des données non publiées: Oui.
Mise à disposition des données sur support informatique: Disquettes et courrier électronique.
Site web: http://www.stat.ee.

Etats-Unis

Titre de l'enquête: Current Population Survey (CPS).
Organisme responsable de l'enquête:
Organisation et déroulement de l'enquête: U.S. Bureau of the Census.
Analyse et Publication des résultats: U.S. Bureau of Labor Statistics.
Sujets couverts par l'enquête: Population active, emploi, chômage, sous-emploi (temps partiel non choisi), durée du travail, gains hebdomadaires moyens, revenu annuel (supplément de mars), durée de l'emploi et du chômage, travailleurs découragés et occasionnels, industrie, profession, situation dans la profession, niveau d'instruction, activité habituelle (supplément de mars) et exercice d'autres emplois.
Champ de l'enquête:
Territoire: L'ensemble du pays.
Groupes de population: La population civile non institutionnelle âgée de 16 ans et plus. Sont exclus: l'armée, la population vivant en établissement, les citoyens d'autres pays vivant dans des ambassades et les citoyens des Etats-Unis vivant à l'étranger.
Disponibilité d'estimations selon d'autres sources pour les régions ou groupes exclus: Ne s'applique pas.
Groupes couverts par l'enquête mais exclus des résultats publiés: Néant.
Périodicité:
Réalisation de l'enquête: Mensuelle.
Publication des résultats: Mensuelle.
Période de référence:
Emploi: La semaine civile (de dimanche à samedi) qui comporte le 12ème jour du mois.
Recherche d'un emploi: Quatre semaines.
Disponibilité pour travailler: Une semaine.
Concepts et définitions:
Emploi: Ont un emploi tous ceux qui, pendant la semaine de référence:
a)ont effectué un travail quelconque (au moins une heure) en tant que salariés, ont travaillé dans leur propre entreprise, profession ou dans leur propre exploitation agricole, ou ont travaillé 15 heures ou plus en tant que travailleurs non rémunérés dans une entreprise exploitée par un membre de leur famille;
b)n'ont pas travaillé mais avaient un emploi ou une entreprise d'où ils étaient temporairement absents pour cause de vacances, de maladie, d'intempéries, de problèmes de garde d'enfants, de congé de maternité ou de paternité, de conflit du travail, de formation professionnelle ou pour d'autres raisons familiales ou personnelles, qu'ils aient été ou non rémunérés pendant le temps où ils étaient absents ou qu'ils aient ou non cherché d'autres emplois.
Sont également inclus dans la catégorie des personnes ayant un emploi:
a)les personnes sans travail salarié essayant de créer leur propre entreprise;
b)les travailleurs occupés à plein temps ou à temps partiel et en quête d'un autre travail pendant la semaine de référence;
c)les personnes ayant effectué un travail quelconque, rémunéré ou en vue d'un bénéfice, pendant la semaine de référence, mais qui étaient alors assujetties à la scolarité obligatoire, à la retraite et au bénéfice d'une pension, inscrites en tant que demandeurs d'emploi auprès d'un bureau de placement ou qui percevaient des allocations de chômage;
d)les étudiants à plein temps ou à temps partiel travaillant à plein temps ou à temps partiel;
e)les apprentis et stagiaires rémunérés;
f)les citoyens d'autres pays résidant aux Etats-Unis mais non dans les locaux d'une ambassade;
g)les personnes résidant aux Etats-Unis mais travaillant au Mexique ou au Canada.
Sont exclues les personnes dont l'activité a consisté à travailler à leur domicile (à faire de la peinture, des réparations ou des travaux ménagers chez elles) ou à faire du bénévolat pour des organisations religieuses, caritatives et autres.
Chômage: Sont chômeurs tous ceux qui n'avaient pas d'emploi pendant la semaine de référence, étaient disponibles pour travailler, sauf en cas de maladie temporaire, et avaient entrepris des démarches concrètes pour trouver un emploi à un moment quelconque au cours de la période de 4 semaines prenant fin avec la semaine de référence. Les personnes attendant d'être rappelées à un travail dont elles avaient été mises à pied n'ont pas besoin d'avoir cherché du travail pour être classées comme chômeurs.
Sont également inclus dans les chômeurs:
a)les personnes en mise à pied temporaire sans rémunération;
b)les personnes en quête d'un emploi et immédiatement disponibles pour travailler mais assujetties à la scolarité obligatoire ou à la retraite et au bénéfice d'une pension;
c)les étudiants à plein temps ou à temps partiel à la recherche d'un emploi à plein temps ou à temps partiel.
Sous-emploi:
Sous-emploi lié à la durée du travail: Cette catégorie recouvre les personnes travaillant à temps partiel pour des motifs économiques.
Situations d'emploi inadéquat: Ne s'applique pas.
Durée du travail: Les heures de travail hebdomadaires réellement effectuées et habituelles. Les heures se réfèrent à l'ensemble des activités combinées.
Revenu lié à l'emploi: Le revenu n'est pas collecté dans le cadre de l'enquête mensuelle mais dans celui du supplément de mars, lequel est du ressort du Bureau du recensement (Bureau of the Census).
Revenu lié à l'emploi salarié: Supplément de mars.
Revenu lié à l'emploi indépendant: Supplément de mars.
Secteur informel: Aucune estimation officielle n'est directement dérivée de l'enquête.
Activité habituelle: Les questions relatives à l'activité habituelle ne sont posées qu'aux personnes en dehors de la population active, et uniquement dans le supplément annuel sur le revenu.
Classifications:
Branche d'activité économique (industrie)
Titre de la classification: U. S. Census Bureau's 1990 Industrial Classification System.
Groupes de population classifiés selon l'industrie: Les personnes ayant un emploi et les chômeurs (industrie du dernier emploi occupé pour ces derniers).
Nombre de groupes de codage: 13 grands groupes et 236 catégories.
Convertibilité avec la CITI: Convertibilité indirecte avec la CITI Rév.2.
Profession
Titre de la classification: Census Bureau's 1990 Occupational Classification System.
Groupes de population classifiés selon la profession: Les personnes ayant un emploi et les chômeurs (profession exercée dans le dernier emploi occupé pour ces derniers).
Nombre de groupes de codage: 6 groupes sommaires, 13 grands groupes et 501 catégories.
Convertibilité avec la CITP: Convertibilité indirecte avec la CITP-1968.
Situation dans la profession
Titre de la classification: U. S. Census Bureau's Class of Worker Categories.
Groupes de population classifiés par situation dans la profession: Les personnes ayant un emploi et les chômeurs (situation occupée dans le dernier emploi pour ces derniers).
Catégories de codage: Trois grandes catégories: les salariés du secteur privé et du secteur public; les indépendants et les travailleurs familiaux non rémunérés.
Convertibilité avec la CISP: Convertibilité indirecte avec la CISP-1993, avec quelques catégories comparables.
Education
Titre de la classification: U. S. Census Bureau's education categories.
Groupes de population classifiés selon l'éducation: Les personnes ayant un emploi et les chômeurs.
Catégories de codage: Quatre grands groupes: inférieur à un diplôme de fin d'études secondaires; diplôme de fin d'études secondaires sans collège; inférieur à une licence; diplômé de l'enseignement supérieur.
Convertibilité avec la CITE: Convertibilité indirecte avec la CITE-1976, avec quelques catégories comparables.
Taille de l'échantillon et plan de sondage:
Unité finale d'échantillonnage: Ménage.
Taille de l'échantillon (unités finales d'échantillonnage): Environ 60 000 ménages.
Taux de sondage: Un sur 2 000.
Base de sondage: Recensements décennaux. Actuellement, Recensement de 1990; début 2003, Recensement de 2000.
Renouvellement de l'échantillon: Pendant toute la décennie, le renouvellement de l'échantillon s'est fait à l'aide des logements nou-

vellement construits identifiés par des permis de construire et l'établissement périodique de listes des logements désignés.

Rotation:

Schéma: Le schéma de rotation est de 4-8-4, ce qui signifie que les ménages restent dans l'échantillon pendant 4 mois successifs, le quittent pendant les 8 mois suivants et le réintègrent pendant les 4 derniers mois.

Pourcentage d'unités restant dans l'échantillon durant deux enquêtes successives: 75 pour cent.

Nombre maximum d'interrogatoires par unité de sondage: Huit.

Durée nécessaire au renouvellement complet de l'échantillon: 17 mois.

Déroulement de l'enquête:

Type d'entretien: Mélange d'entretiens personnels et par téléphone: environ 90 pour cent d'entretiens personnels assistés par ordinateur et 10 pour cent d'entretiens par téléphone assistés par ordinateur.

Nombre d'unités finales d'échantillonnage par zone de sondage: Variable.

Durée de déroulement de l'enquête:

Totale: Du dimanche de la semaine de référence jusqu'au mercredi de la semaine suivante.

Par zone de sondage: Non disponible.

Organisation: Permanente.

Nombre de personnes employées: 2 000 enquêteurs et 100 cadres.

Substitution des unités finales en cas de non-réponse: Non.

Estimations et redressements:

Taux de non-réponse: 7%.

Redressement pour non-réponse: Oui.

Imputation en cas de non-réponse à une question spécifique: Oui.

Redressement pour les régions/populations non couvertes: Non.

Redressement en cas de sous-représentation: Oui.

Redressement en cas de sur-représentation: Non.

Corrections des variations saisonnières: Oui.

Historique de l'enquête:

Titre et date de la première enquête: Sample Survey of Unemployment 1940.

Modifications et révisions significatives: En 1994, des modifications importantes ont été apportées au CPS, parmi lesquelles une refonte complète du questionnaire et le recours à des entretiens assistés par ordinateur pour l'intégralité de l'enquête. De plus, certains des concepts et définitions relatifs à la population active ont fait l'objet de révisions, dont l'application de certaines modifications recommandées en 1979 par la Commission nationale sur l'emploi et le chômage (National Commission on Employment and Unemployment). Outre l'introduction d'un questionnaire remanié et informatisé, certains des principaux changements touchent aux critères d'après lesquels définir les travailleurs découragés et les personnes ayant un emploi à temps partiel pour des motifs économiques, ainsi qu'à l'ajout de questions directes sur la mise à pied et le cumul d'emplois.

Documentation et dissémination:

Documentation

Titre des publications publiant les résultats: Employment and Earnings (mensuel); The Employment Situation news release (mensuel).

Titre des publications méthodologiques: Employment and Earnings (mensuel); BLS Handbook of Methods 1997 et Current Population Survey: Design and Methodology (Technical Paper 63).

Dissémination

Délai de publication des premiers résultats: Environ deux semaines.

Information à l'avance du public des dates de publication initiale des résultats: Oui.

Mise à disposition, sur demande, des données non publiées: Oui.

Mise à disposition des données sur support informatique: Disquettes et bandes magnétiques.

Site web: http://www.bls.gov/.

Ethiopie

Titre de l'enquête: National Labor Force Survey.

Organisme responsable de l'enquête:

Organisation et déroulement de l'enquête: Central Statistical Authority.

Analyse et Publication des résultats: Central Statistical Authority.

Sujets couverts par l'enquête: Emploi, chômage, sous-emploi, durée du travail, emploi dans le secteur informel, durée du chômage, industrie, profession, situation dans la profession, niveau d'instruction et activité habituelle. Autres sujets couverts: variables démographiques sur les migrations, groupe ethnique/religion, caractéristiques socioéconomiques et démographiques des enfants âgés de 5 à 14 ans, formation professionnelle.

Champ de l'enquête:

Territoire: L'ensemble du pays.

Les personnes âgées de 10 ans et plus sont interrogées.

Groupes de population: Toutes les personnes âgées de 10 ans et plus résidant normalement dans le pays. Sont exclus: les nomades, les citoyens non résidents, les étrangers et les personnes résidant à l'étranger.

Disponibilité d'estimations selon d'autres sources pour les régions ou groupes exclus: Néant.

Groupes couverts par l'enquête mais exclus des résultats publiés: NEANT.

Périodicité:

Réalisation de l'enquête: En 1981-82 et en 1986-87.

Publication des résultats: Irrégulière.

Période de référence:

Emploi: Une semaine (les sept derniers jours) avant la date de l'entretien.

Recherche d'un emploi: Trois mois avant la date de l'entretien.

Disponibilité pour travailler: Un mois apres la date de l'entretien.

Toutes les périodes de référence sont variables.

Concepts et définitions:

Emploi: Toutes les personnes âgées de 10 ans et plus qui occupaient un emploi salarié ou étaient travailleurs indépendants au cours des sept derniers jours, effectuant un travail quelconque (pendant au moins 4 heures) pour un salaire ou un traitement, en espèces ou en nature, ou qui n'étaient temporairement pas au travail mais avaient un lien formel avec l'emploi.

Cette catégorie inclut:

a)les personnes temporairement absentes pour cause de maladie ou d'accident, de congés ou de vacances annuelles, de congé de maternité ou de congé de paternité, de congé parental, de congé d'éducation ou de formation, de conflits du travail, d'intempéries, etc.;

b)les personnes en mise en congé non rémunéré à l'initiative de l'employeur;

c)les travailleurs occupés à plein temps ou à temps partiel et en quête d'un autre travail;

d)les personnes ayant effectué un travail quelconque, rémunéré ou en vue d'un bénéfice, pendant la semaine de référence, mais qui étaient alors assujetties à la scolarité obligatoire, à la retraite et au bénéfice d'une pension, inscrites en tant que demandeurs d'emploi auprès d'un bureau de placement ou qui percevaient des allocations de chômage;

e)les étudiants à plein temps ou à temps partiel travaillant à temps partiel ou à plein temps;

f)les apprentis et stagiaires rémunérés ou non;

g)les bénéficiaires de mesures de promotion de l'emploi, s'ils sont rémunérés;

h)les personnes occupées dans la production de biens pour leur usage final personnel;

i)les membres des forces armées (volontaires, militaires de carrière et conscrits ainsi que les personnes effectuant un service civil équivalent au service militaire);

j)les travailleurs familiaux non rémunérés au travail.

Chômage: Toutes les personnes âgées de 10 ans et plus qui n'occupaient pas un emploi salarié ou n'étaient pas travailleurs indépendants au cours des sept derniers jours, étaient disponibles pour occuper un emploi salarié ou indépendant dans un délai d'un mois à compter de la date de l'entretien et avaient fait diverses démarches (efforts) pour chercher un emploi au cours des 3 derniers mois.

Cette catégorie inclut:

a)les personnes en mise à pied temporaire ou de durée indéterminée sans rémunération;

b)les personnes qui ont pris des dispositions pour commencer à travailler dans un nouvel emploi ou qui ont essayé de créer leur propre entreprise;

c)les retraités et les personnes au bénéfice d'une pension;

d)les étudiants à temps partiel à la recherche d'un emploi à plein temps ou à temps partiel;

e)les travailleurs familiaux non rémunérés temporairement absents de leur travail et les travailleurs saisonniers pendant la morte-saison, s'ils sont disponibles pour un autre travail;

f)les personnes n'ayant pas cherché un emploi parce qu'il n'y en avait pas sur le marché ou parce qu'aucun n'était adapté à leurs qualifications;

g)les personnes effectuant un travail communautaire ou des activités sociales non rémunérées.

Sous-emploi:
Sous-emploi lié à la durée du travail: Les personnes qui, durant la semaine de référence, avaient un emploi mais étaient disposées à faire davantage d'heures de travail (heures complémentaires) dans leur emploi actuel, dans un autre emploi ou dans un autre emploi à plein temps jusqu'au seuil choisi, et qui étaient disponibles pour ce faire.
Situations d'emploi inadéquat: Ne s'applique pas.
Durée du travail: Uniquement les heures de travail réellement effectuées chaque jour, dans toutes les activités, au cours des sept derniers jours.
Revenu lié à l'emploi:
Revenu lié à l'emploi salarié: Ne s'applique pas.
Revenu lié à l'emploi indépendant: Ne s'applique pas.
Emploi dans le secteur informel: 1. L'entreprise des personnes concernées (ou l'entreprise pour laquelle elles travaillent) tient-elle un compte systématique de ses opérations? 2. L'entreprise compte-t-elle au moins 10 travailleurs? 3. L'entreprise a-t-elle un agrément? Si l'activité principale de ces personnes ne satisfait pas à ces trois critères, celles-ci sont classées comme travaillant dans le secteur informel.
Activité habituelle: L'enquête comporte deux questions, l'une sur la participation à l'activité économique au cours des 12 derniers mois, l'autre sur les raisons pour lesquelles la personne n'a pas travaillé pendant les 12 derniers mois, qui servent à classer les personnes soit comme chômeurs soit comme inactifs.
Classifications:
Branche d'activité économique (industrie)
Titre de la classification: Non disponible.
Groupes de population classifiés selon l'industrie: Les personnes ayant un emploi.
Nombre de groupes de codage: 14
Convertibilité avec la CITI Rév.3: Oui.
Profession
Titre de la classification: Non disponible
Groupes de population classifiés selon la profession: Les personnes ayant un emploi.
Nombre de groupes de codage: 10
Convertibilité avec la CITP-1988.
Situation dans la profession
Titre de la classification: Non disponible.
Groupes de population classifiés par situation dans la profession: Les personnes ayant un emploi.
Catégories de codage: Employeurs, salariés (de l'Etat, autres que de l'Etat, du secteur privé, d'une organisation publique de développement), travailleurs indépendants, travailleurs familiaux non rémunérés, apprentis, membres d'associations coopératives.
Convertibilité avec la CISP-1993.
Education
Titre de la classification: Non disponible.
Groupes de population classifiés selon l'éducation: Les personnes ayant un emploi et les chômeurs.
Catégories de codage: a) analphabète; b) alphabétisé, c) année d'études achevée. La classification est fonction de la plus haute d'année d'études achevée et distingue les niveaux ci-après:
1.ne sait ni lire ni écrire;
2.éducation non scolaire ou années d'études 1 à 3;
3.années d'études 4 à 6;
4.années d'études 7 et 8;
5.années d'études 9 à 11;
6.année d'études 12;
7.au-delà.
Convertibilité avec la CITE: CITE-1997.
Taille de l'échantillon et plan de sondage:
Unité finale d'échantillonnage: Ménage.
Taille de l'échantillon (unités finales d'échantillonnage): 35 ménages par secteur de recensement, multiplié par 1 448 secteurs de recensement ruraux, plus 913 secteurs de recensement urbains, soit 82 635 ménages.
Taux de sondage: Non disponible.
Base de sondage: Liste des secteurs de recensement établie pour le recensement de 1994; pour les zones urbaines, une nouvelle liste des ménages a été faite; pour les zones rurales, une liste des ménages a été établie 6 mois avant la date de l'enquête.
Renouvellement de l'échantillon: Néant.
Rotation: Pas de schéma de rotation.
Schéma: Ne s'applique pas.
Pourcentage d'unités restant dans l'échantillon durant deux enquêtes successives: Ne s'applique pas.
Nombre maximum d'interrogatoires par unité de sondage: Ne s'applique pas.
Durée nécessaire au renouvellement complet de l'échantillon: Ne s'applique pas.
Déroulement de l'enquête:
Type d'entretien: Entretien personnel.
Nombre d'unités finales d'échantillonnage par zone de sondage: Variable.
Durée de déroulement de l'enquête:
Totale: 15 au 26 mars 1999.
Par zone de sondage:
Organisation: Structure d'enquête permanente.
Nombre de personnes employées: 1654 enquêteurs, 343 cadres, 88 formateurs. Total: 2 085 employés.
Substitution des unités finales en cas de non-réponse: Oui.
Estimations et redressements:
Taux de non-réponse: Non disponible.
Redressement pour non-réponse: Néant.
Imputation en cas de non-réponse à une question spécifique: Les cas de non-réponse se voient attribuer le code 9 ou 99 ou 999 en fonction de leurs codages respectifs.
Redressement pour les régions/populations non couvertes: Néant.
Redressement en cas de sous-représentation: Néant.
Redressement en cas de sur-représentation: Néant.
Corrections des variations saisonnières: Néant.
Historique de l'enquête:
Titre et date de la première enquête: La première Enquête sur la main-d'œuvre dans les zones rurales (Rural Labour Force Survey) a été réalisée d'avril 1981 à avril 1982. Une autre enquête a été réalisée en 1987-88. La présente Enquête Nationale (National Labour Force Survey) a été réalisée pour la première fois en mars 1999.
Modifications et révisions significatives: Le type de questions posées est très similaire à celui des Enquêtes sur la main-d'œuvre dans les zones rurales.
Documentation et dissémination:
Documentation
Titre des publications publiant les résultats: Non disponible.
Titre des publications méthodologiques: Non disponible.
Dissémination
Délai de publication des premiers résultats: Non disponible.
Information à l'avance du public des dates de publication initiale des résultats: Non disponible.
Mise à disposition, sur demande, des données non publiées: Non disponible.
Mise à disposition des données sur support informatique: Non disponible.

Finlande

Titre de l'enquête: Labour Force Survey
Organisme responsable de l'enquête:
Organisation et déroulement de l'enquête: Statistics Finland.
Analyse et Publication des résultats: Statistics Finland.
Sujets couverts par l'enquête: Emploi, chômage, sous-emploi, durée du travail, durée de l'emploi, durée du chômage, travailleurs découragés, industrie, profession, situation dans la profession, niveau d'instruction (Register of Completed Education and Degrees), activité habituelle (voir ci-après) et exercice d'autres emplois.
Champ de l'enquête:
Territoire: L'ensemble du pays.
Groupes de population: Toutes les personnes âgées de 15 à 74 ans résidant dans le pays, y compris les travailleurs étrangers, les citoyens se trouvant temporairement à l'étranger (pendant moins d'un an), l'armée, les citoyens non résidents, les nomades et les populations institutionnelles.
Disponibilité d'estimations selon d'autres sources pour les régions ou groupes exclus: Ne s'applique pas.
Groupes couverts par l'enquête mais exclus des résultats publiés: Oui.
Périodicité:
Réalisation de l'enquête: A partir de 2000, enquête en continu. Auparavant, enquête mensuelle.
Publication des résultats: Mensuelle, trimestrielle et annuelle.
Période de référence:
Emploi: Une semaine. Avant 2000, une semaine fixe (souvent la semaine comprenant le 15 de chaque mois).
Recherche d'un emploi: Quatre semaines (période de référence variable).

Disponibilité pour travailler: Deux semaines (période de référence variable).

Concepts et définitions:

Emploi: Toutes les personnes ayant effectué un travail quelconque pendant la semaine de référence (pendant au moins une heure), rémunéré ou en vue d'un avantage complémentaire ou pour en retirer un bénéfice, ou qui étaient temporairement absentes de leur travail parce que mises à pied pendant un certain temps. Les personnes ayant un emploi peuvent être des salariés, des travailleurs indépendants ou des travailleurs familiaux non rémunérés.

Cette catégorie inclut également:

a)les personnes ayant un emploi mais temporairement absentes de leur travail pour cause de maladie, d'accident, de congés, de vacances annuelles, de congé de maternité ou de paternité, d'absence non autorisée, de conflit du travail, d'intempéries, de panne mécanique, etc. ou en mise en congé non rémunéré à l'initiative de l'employeur;

b)les travailleurs occupés à plein temps ou à temps partiel et en quête d'un autre travail pendant la période de référence;

c)les personnes ayant effectué un travail quelconque, rémunéré ou en vue d'un bénéfice, pendant la semaine de référence, tout en étant assujetties à la scolarité obligatoire, à la retraite et au bénéfice d'une pension ou inscrites en tant que demandeurs d'emploi auprès d'un bureau de placement, ou tout en percevant des allocations de chômage;

d)les étudiants à plein temps ou à temps partiel travaillant à plein temps ou à temps partiel;

e)les apprentis et stagiaires rémunérés;

f)les travailleurs familiaux, rémunérés ou non, temporairement absents de leur travail;

g)les domestiques privés;

h)les militaires de carrière.

Chômage: Toutes les personnes sans emploi durant toute la semaine de l'enquête, ayant cherché activement un emploi comme salarié ou comme travailleur indépendant au cours des quatre dernières semaines et pouvant accepter un emploi dans les deux semaines. Les personnes sans emploi attendant de commencer à travailler dans un nouvel emploi dans les deux semaines sont également déclarées comme étant sans emploi, de même que celles mises à pied pour une durée indéterminée remplissant les critères de recherche et d'acceptation d'emploi.

Cette catégorie inclut également, uniquement s'ils sont disponibles pour travailler et à la **Recherche d'un emploi:**

a)les personnes au bénéfice d'une pension de préretraite-chômage;

b)les personnes qui essaient de créer leur propre entreprise;

c)les personnes assujetties à la scolarité obligatoire;

d)les étudiants à plein temps ou à temps partiel à la recherche d'un emploi à plein temps ou à temps partiel;

e)les bénéficiaires de mesures de promotion de l'emploi;

f)les travailleurs saisonniers en attente d'un travail agricole ou d'un autre travail saisonnier.

Sous-emploi:

Sous-emploi lié à la durée du travail: Les personnes occupant un emploi à temps partiel faute d'avoir trouvé un emploi à plein temps, ou dont l'employeur les fait effectuer une semaine de travail réduite ou qui n'ont pas de travail pour cause de manque de commandes ou de mise à pied pendant un certain temps.

Situations d'emploi inadéquat: Ne s'applique pas.

Durée du travail: Sont collectées les heures réellement effectuées et les heures habituelles. Les heures de travail réellement effectuées pendant la semaine de référence comprennent toutes les heures travaillées, rémunérées ou non, les heures supplémentaires et les heures effectuées dans des activités secondaires. Les heures habituelles se réfèrent aux heures de travail hebdomadaires normales effectuées par les personnes ayant un emploi dans leur activité principale uniquement. Si besoin est, ces deux concepts peuvent être présentés séparément.

Revenu lié à l'emploi:

Revenu lié à l'emploi salarié: Ne s'applique pas.

Revenu lié à l'emploi indépendant: Ne s'applique pas.

Emploi dans le secteur informel: Ne s'applique pas.

Activité habituelle: (Une question sur l'activité primaire exercée pendant la semaine de l'enquête est posée aux personnes n'ayant pas d'emploi. Les personnes ayant un emploi sont interrogées sur leur activité principale mais aucune période de référence particulière n'est indiquée).

Classifications:

Branche d'activité économique (industrie)

Titre de la classification: Classification type des industries (CTI-1995).

Groupes de population classifiés selon l'industrie: Les personnes ayant un emploi et les chômeurs.

Nombre de groupes de codage: Environ 95 groupes au niveau à 2-3 chiffres.

Convertibilité avec la CITI: CITI-Rév.3 au niveau à 2-3 chiffres.

Profession

Titre de la classification: Statistics Finland's Classification of Occupations (CSO-2001); depuis 2002, au niveau à 4-5 chiffres.

Groupes de population classifiés selon la profession: Les personnes ayant un emploi et les chômeurs.

Nombre de groupes de codage: 489

Convertibilité avec la CITP: CITP-1988.

Situation dans la profession

Titre de la classification: Industrial status groups.

Groupes de population classifiés par situation dans la profession: Les personnes ayant un emploi et les chômeurs.

Catégories de codage: Trois groupes: salarié, employeur/travailleur indépendant, travailleur familial non rémunéré.

Convertibilité avec la CISP: CISP-1993

Education

Titre de la classification: Finnish Standard Classification of **Education** 1997 (FSCED-97).

Groupes de population classifiés selon l'éducation: Toutes les personnes âgées de 15 à 74 ans.

Catégories de codage: Les données proviennent du Registre de l'éducation et des diplômes (Register of Completed **Education** and Degrees), au niveau à 6 chiffres.

Convertibilité avec la CITE: CITE-1997.

Taille de l'échantillon et plan de sondage:

Unité finale d'échantillonnage: Personnes (15 à 74 ans).

Taille de l'échantillon (unités finales d'échantillonnage): 12 000 personnes par mois.

Taux de sondage: Environ 1/311.

Base de sondage: Tirée du registre de la population tenu par Statistics Finland et qui couvre l'ensemble de la population.

Renouvellement de l'échantillon: Les données-échantillons (adresses, etc.) sont mises à jour tous les mois à l'aide des modifications reçues du RCP (registre central de la population, mis à jour en continu) et des enquêteurs.

Rotation:

Schéma: Le schéma de rotation est un système à cinq vagues – le premier entretien a lieu au temps "t", le deuxième à "t+3", le troisième à "t+6", le quatrième à "t+12" et le cinquième à "t+15".

Pourcentage d'unités restant dans l'échantillon durant deux enquêtes successives: 0 pour cent (les échantillons se chevauchent de 3/5 d'un trimestre à l'autre et de 2/5 au bout d'un an).

Nombre maximum d'interrogatoires par unité de sondage: Cinq.

Durée nécessaire au renouvellement complet de l'échantillon: Dix-huit mois.

Déroulement de l'enquête:

Type d'entretien: Entretien par téléphone assisté par ordinateur (98 pour cent) et entretien personnel assisté par ordinateur (2 pour cent).

Nombre d'unités finales d'échantillonnage par zone de sondage: Ne s'applique pas.

Durée de déroulement de l'enquête:

Totale: 10 à 15 jours.

Par zone de sondage: 10 à 15 jours.

Organisation: Permanente.

Nombre de personnes employées: Environ 160 enquêteurs.

Substitution des unités finales en cas de non-réponse: Non.

Estimations et redressements:

Taux de non-réponse: 14%.

Redressement pour non-réponse: Oui.

Imputation en cas de non-réponse à une question spécifique: Les heures de travail effectuées par semaine si le nombre n'en est pas connu.

Redressement pour les régions/populations non couvertes: Ne s'applique pas.

Redressement en cas de sous-représentation: Non.

Redressement en cas de sur-représentation: Oui.

Corrections des variations saisonnières: Oui, en utilisant une version légèrement modifiée de la méthode X-11 Arima du recensement pour les niveaux d'emploi, de chômage, de main-d'oeuvre, de taux d'emploi et de taux de chômage.

Historique de l'enquête:

Titre et date de la première enquête: The Finnish Labour Force Sample Survey, 1958.

Modifications et révisions significatives:

1983: l'enquête par correspondance a été remplacée par l'enquête par entretien. Le contenu des données a été élargi.

1997: nouveau plan d'enquête suivant plus strictement les recommandations de l'OIT.
2000: enquête en continu.
Documentation et dissémination:
Documentation
Titre des publications publiant les résultats: Statistics Finland, Labour Market Series; Employment and Labour Force Bulletin. (**Périodicité:** mensuelle).
Titre des publications méthodologiques: Statistics Finland, Labour Market Series - Annual bulletin.
Dissémination
Délai de publication des premiers résultats: Trois semaines.
Information à l'avance du public des dates de publication initiale des résultats: Oui.
Mise à disposition, sur demande, des données non publiées: Oui.
Mise à disposition des données sur support informatique: Oui.
Site web: http://tilastokeskus.fi/index_en.html.

France

Titre de l'enquête: Enquête annuelle Emploi
Organisme responsable de l'enquête:
Organisation et déroulement de l'enquête: Institut National de la Statistique et des Etudes économiques (INSEE).
Analyse et Publication des résultats: INSEE.
Sujets couverts par l'enquête: Emploi, chômage, sous-emploi, durée du travail, salaires, durée de l'emploi et du chômage (ancienneté), travailleurs découragés, industrie, profession, situation dans la profession, éducation/qualification, autres emplois.
Champ de l'enquête:
Territoire: France métropolitaine.
Groupes de population: Personnes âgées de 15 ans ou plus vivant dans des résidences principales. Sont exclues les personnes vivant dans des communautés, à l'exception toutefois de celles qui sont rattachées à un ménage ordinaire parce qu'elles y reviennent régulièrement (élèves en internat, résidence universitaire, etc.)
Disponibilité d'estimations selon d'autres sources pour les régions ou groupes exclus: Ne s'applique pas.
Groupes couverts par l'enquête mais exclus des résultats publiés: Ne s'applique pas.
Périodicité:
Réalisation de l'enquête: Annuelle.
Publication des résultats: Annuelle.
Période de référence:
Emploi: Une semaine (variable).
Recherche d'un emploi: Un mois (variable).
Disponibilité pour travailler: 15 jours (variable).
Concepts et définitions:
Emploi: Personnes de 15 ans et plus se déclarant active ou ayant travaillé au moins une heure durant la semaine de référence (semaine précédant l'enquête), sous réserve qu'elles aient bien une activité effective, ou n'ayant pas travaillé durant la semaine de référence mais ayant conservé un lien formel avec l'emploi (vacances, congé maternité, etc.), sans faire intervenir le critère de rémunération.
Sont considérées comme ayant un emploi:
a) les personnes temporairement absentes de leur travail pour cause de maladie ou d'accident pour une durée inférieure à un an, de congés annuels, congés de maternité ou paternité, d'absence non autorisée, de conflit du travail, d'intempéries ou de panne mécanique, etc.;
b) les travailleurs occupés à plein temps ou à temps partiel et en quête d'un autre travail durant la période de référence;
c) les personnes ayant effectué un travail quelconque, rémunéré ou en vue d'un bénéfice, pendant la période de référence, mais qui étaient assujetties à la scolarité obligatoire, à la retraite et au bénéfice d'une pension, inscrites en tant que demandeur d'emploi auprès d'un bureau de placement, ou percevant des allocations de chômage;
d) les étudiants à plein temps ou à temps partiel travaillant à plein temps ou temps partiel;
e) les apprentis et stagiaires rémunérés ou non, s'ils participent effectivement à la production de l'entreprise;
f) les travailleurs familiaux non rémunérés travaillant durant la période de référence;
g) les forces armées (volontaires, militaires de carrière et conscrits) ainsi que les personnes effectuant un service civil équivalent au service militaire.
Chômage: Personnes de 15 ans et plus sans emploi durant la semaine de référence, ayant effectué depuis un mois des démarches de recherche d'emploi et disponibles pour travailler dans un délai inférieur à 15 jours.
Sous-emploi:
Sous-emploi lié à la durée du travail: Deux catégories sont distinguées:
a) personnes à temps partiel recherchant un emploi pour travailler davantage (à temps complet ou à temps partiel plus important) ou ne recherchant pas un autre emploi mais souhaitant travailler plus et disponibles;
b) Personnes à temps complet ayant involontairement travaillé moins que d'habitude (chômage partiel, etc.).
Aucun seuil de durée du travail n'est pris en compte dans la détermination du sous-emploi.
Situations d'emploi inadéquat: Pour les personnes ayant un emploi, il y a dans l'enquête une question sur la raison principale de recherche d'un autre emploi (rémunération, qualification, désir de travailler plus, etc.).
Durée du travail: Heures de travail réellement effectuées durant la semaine de référence et nombre d'heures habituel par semaine uniquement pour l'activité principale.
Revenu lié à l'emploi:
Revenu lié à l'emploi salarié: Pas mesuré.
Revenu lié à l'emploi indépendant: Pas mesuré.
Secteur informel: Ne s'applique pas.
Activité habituelle: Ne s'applique pas.
Classifications:
Branche d'activité économique (industrie)
Titre de la classification: Nomenclature d'Activités Française (NAF).
Groupes de population classifiés selon l'industrie: Personnes pourvues d'un emploi.
Nombre de groupes de codage: 696 postes dont 334 pour l'industrie.
Convertibilité avec la CITI: Table de passage entre NAF, NACE (Nomenclature d'Activités de la Communauté Européenne) et CITI.
Profession
Titre de la classification: Professions et Catégories Socioprofessionnelles (PCS).
Groupes de population classifiés selon la profession: Personnes pourvues d'un emploi.
Nombre de groupes de codage: 455 postes.
Convertibilité avec la CITP: CITP-1988.
Situation dans la profession
Titre de la classification: Classification nationale.
Groupes de population classifiés par situation dans la profession: Personnes pourvues d'un emploi.
Catégories de codage: A son compte; salarié mais chef de son entreprise; salarié de l'Etat ou des collectivités locales; autre salarié.
Convertibilité avec la CISP: Non.
Education
Titre de la classification: Classification nationale.
Groupes de population classifiés selon l'éducation: Pas d'information.
Catégories de codage: Niveau atteint dans: l'enseignement général (12 modalités), l'enseignement technique (13 modalités) et l'enseignement supérieur (10 modalités).
Convertibilité avec la CITE: Non.
Taille de l'échantillon et plan de sondage:
Unité finale d'échantillonnage: Logement.
Taille de l'échantillon (unités finales d'échantillonnage): 105 000 logements.
Taux de sondage: 1/300 des logements.
Base de sondage: Dernier recensement disponible ainsi que les fichiers SITADEL du Ministère de l'Equipement pour constitution de l'échantillon des "Grappes Spéciales Emploi" (GSE) représentant les logements construits, depuis le dernier recensement de population, sur permis de 10 logements et plus.
Renouvellement de l'échantillon: Par tiers à chaque enquête.
Rotation:
Schéma: Pas d'information.
Pourcentage d'unités restant dans l'échantillon durant deux enquêtes successives: Pas d'information.
Nombre maximum d'interrogatoires par unité de sondage: Pas d'information.
Durée nécessaire au renouvellement complet de l'échantillon: Trois ans.
Déroulement de l'enquête:
Type d'entretien: Enquête en face à face réalisée par saisie portable.
Nombre d'unités finales d'échantillonnage par zone de sondage: Pas d'information

Durée de déroulement de l'enquête:
Totale: Cinq semaines à partir du début mars.
Par zone de sondage: Pas d'information.
Organisation: Gestion de l'enquête par la Direction générale et les Directions régionales de l'INSEE.
Nombre de personnes employées: Environ 250 personnes à l'INSEE (mais pas à temps plein) et environ 750 enquêteurs.
Substitution des unités finales en cas de non-réponse: Non.
Estimations et redressements:
Taux de non-réponse: 11 % des logements.
Redressement pour non-réponse: Oui.
Imputation en cas de non réponse à une question spécifique: Pas d'information.
Redressement pour les régions/populations non couvertes: Pas d'information.
Redressement en cas de sous-représentation: Oui.
Redressement en cas de sur-représentation: Oui.
Corrections des variations saisonnières: Non.
Historique de l'enquête:
Titre et date de la première enquête: Enquête sur l'Emploi 1950.
Modifications et révisions significatives: 1982: passage à la nomenclature PCS (**Professions** et Catégories socio-professionnelles) pour le chiffrement des professions.
1990: classification des militaires du contingent parmi les actifs occupés.
Documentation et dissémination:
Documentation
Titre des publications publiant les résultats: INSEE Première et INSEE-Résultats (annuellement)
Titre des publications méthodologiques: INSEE-Résultats (annuellement)
Dissémination
Délai de publication des premiers résultats: Environ trois mois: les résultats de l'Enquête de mars 2000 ont été publiés en juin 2000.
Information à l'avance du public des dates de publication initiale des résultats: Non.
Mise à disposition, sur demande, des données non publiées: Oui.
Mise à disposition des données sur support informatique: CD Rom.
Site web: http://www.insee.fr/.

Gambie

Titre de l'enquête: Labour Force Survey in Greater Banjul.
Organisme responsable de l'enquête:
Organisation et déroulement de l'enquête: Central Statistics Department.
Analyse et Publication des résultats: Central Statistics Department.
Sujets couverts par l'enquête: Emploi, chômage, sous-emploi lié à la durée du travail, durée du travail, revenu, emploi dans le secteur informel, industrie, profession, situation dans la profession, niveau d'instruction, activité habituelle et formation.
Champ de l'enquête:
Territoire: Limité à Banjul et à Kombo St. Mary's.
Groupes de population: La population de facto âgée de 10 ans et plus, c'est-à-dire y compris les membres habituels des ménages-échantillons et les visiteurs qui y ont passé la nuit.
Disponibilité d'estimations selon d'autres sources pour les régions ou groupes exclus: Non disponible.
Groupes couverts par l'enquête mais exclus des résultats publiés: Néant.
Périodicité:
Réalisation de l'enquête: Enquête ad hoc réalisée en 1992.
Publication des résultats: Août 1995.
Période de référence:
Emploi: Une semaine avant la date de l'entretien.
Recherche d'un emploi: Une semaine avant la date de l'entretien.
Disponibilité pour travailler: Une semaine avant la date de l'entretien.
Concepts et définitions:
Emploi: Les personnes ayant effectué un travail rémunéré ou en vue d'un bénéfice ou d'un gain familial, en espèces ou en nature, pendant la période de référence, ou ayant un emploi ou leur propre entreprise dont elles étaient absentes pour cause de maladie ou d'accident, de vacances, de congé de maternité, de congé d'éducation, de conflit du travail, d'intempéries, de pannes mécaniques, etc. Les personnes en mise à pied temporaire sans rémunération sont incluses mais celles en mise à pied de durée indéterminée sont exclues. Des essais ont été faits pour inclure les activités marginales, dont la plupart sont destinées à la consommation familiale, telles que travaux à la ferme, pêche, réparations, collecte de bois de chauffage et confection de paniers et de vêtements.
Chômage: Les personnes n'ayant pas d'emploi mais disponibles pour travailler ou qui se préparaient à commencer à travailler à leur compte durant la période de référence. Sont incluses les personnes ayant pris des dispositions pour commencer à travailler dans un nouvel emploi à une date postérieure à la période de référence ainsi que les étudiants à plein temps disponibles pour travailler. Les personnes à la recherche d'un emploi pendant la période de référence peuvent être désignées séparément.
Sous-emploi:
Sous-emploi lié à la durée du travail: Les personnes qui, durant la semaine de référence, ont travaillé moins de 35 heures et étaient disponibles pour faire davantage d'heures. Il est possible d'indiquer les travailleurs ayant cherché à faire davantage d'heures.
Situations d'emploi inadéquat: Non disponible.
Durée du travail: Le nombre total d'heures de travail réellement effectuées dans toutes les activités (sauf les heure des repas et autres moments d'absence du travail) pendant chaque jour de la période de référence.
Revenu lié à l'emploi:
Revenu lié à l'emploi salarié: Revenu mensuel habituel lié à l'activité principale rémunérée. Le revenu en espèces et le revenu autre qu'en espèces sont désignés séparément.
Revenu lié à l'emploi indépendant: Non disponible.
Secteur informel: Non disponible.
Activité habituelle: Les personnes ayant effectué un travail rémunéré ou en vue d'un gain familial à un moment quelconque au cours des 12 derniers mois. Des informations sont recueillies sur le nombre de semaines travaillées ainsi que sur le nombre de semaines de disponibilité pour travailler au cours des 12 derniers mois. Pour les personnes ayant habituellement un emploi, des informations ont été recueillies sur la profession habituelle, l'industrie et la situation dans l'emploi; pour celles qui sont habituellement sans emploi, des informations ont été recueillies sur la dernière profession exercée, l'industrie et la situation dans l'emploi. Pour les personnes habituellement inactives, des informations sont recueillies sur leur statut d'étudiant, de personne au foyer, d'handicapé ou de retraité.
Classifications:
Branche d'activité économique (industrie)
Titre de la classification: Non disponible.
Groupes de population classifiés selon l'industrie: Les personnes ayant un emploi et les chômeurs ayant une expérience professionnelle préalable.
Nombre de groupes de codage: 10.
Convertibilité avec la CITI: CITI-Rév.2.
Profession
Titre de la classification: Non disponible.
Groupes de population classifiés selon la profession: Les personnes ayant un emploi et les chômeurs ayant une expérience professionnelle préalable.
Nombre de groupes de codage: 7.
Convertibilité avec la CITP-1968: CITP-1968.
Situation dans la profession
Titre de la classification: Non disponible.
Groupes de population classifiés par situation dans la profession: Les personnes ayant un emploi et les chômeurs ayant une expérience professionnelle préalable.
Catégories de codage: 6 groupes (employeur, travailleur indépendant, salarié, travailleur familial non rémunéré, apprenti, autres).
Convertibilité avec la CISP: CISP-1993.
Education
Titre de la classification: Non disponible.
Groupes de population classifiés selon l'éducation: Toutes les personnes âgées de 5 ans et plus.
Catégories de codage: 9 groupes (aucune année d'études, années d'études 1 à 3, années d'études 4 à 6, année d'études 7, éducation formelle 1 à 4, "O-Level", "A-Level", diplôme de premier cycle, diplôme de troisième cycle et autres).
Convertibilité avec la CITE: Oui.
Taille de l'échantillon et plan de sondage:
Unité finale d'échantillonnage: Ménages.
Taille de l'échantillon (unités finales d'échantillonnage): 1280 ménages sélectionnés dans 64 secteurs de recensement.
Taux de sondage: Non disponible.
Base de sondage: Non disponible.
Renouvellement de l'échantillon: Non disponible.

Rotation:
Schéma: Ne s'applique pas.
Pourcentage d'unités restant dans l'échantillon durant deux enquêtes successives: Ne s'applique pas.
Nombre maximum d'interrogatoires par unité de sondage: Non disponible.
Durée nécessaire au renouvellement complet de l'échantillon: Ne s'applique pas.
Déroulement de l'enquête:
Type d'entretien: Entretien personnel.
Nombre d'unités finales d'échantillonnage par zone de sondage: 1280 ménages.
Durée de déroulement de l'enquête:
Totale: Une année.
Par zone de sondage: Une année.
Organisation: Organisation ad hoc.
Nombre de personnes employées: Huit enquêteurs et deux cadres.
Substitution des unités finales en cas de non-réponse: Oui.
Estimations et redressements:
Taux de non-réponse: Non disponible.
Redressement pour non-réponse: Non disponible.
Imputation en cas de non-réponse à une question spécifique: Non disponible.
Redressement pour les régions/populations non couvertes: Non disponible.
Redressement en cas de sous-représentation: Non disponible.
Redressement en cas de sur-représentation: Non disponible.
Corrections des variations saisonnières: Non disponible.
Historique de l'enquête:
Titre et date de la première enquête: L'enquête décrite est la première.
Modifications et révisions significatives: Ne s'applique pas.
Documentation et dissémination:
Documentation
Titre des publications publiant les résultats: Non disponible.
Titre des publications méthodologiques: Non disponible.
Dissémination
Délai de publication des premiers résultats: 3 ans.
Information à l'avance du public des dates de publication initiale des résultats: Non.
Mise à disposition, sur demande, des données non publiées: Oui.
Mise à disposition des données sur support informatique: Non disponible.

Géorgie

1.Titre de l'enquête
Labour Force Sample Survey (LFSS) (Enquête par sondage sur la main-d'oeuvre (LFSS)).
2.Organisation responsable de l'enquête
State Department for Statistics (Département d'Etat des Statistiques)
3.Champ d'application
(a) Géographie
Ensemble du pays, à l'exception d'Apkhazeti et d'Osseti Sud.
(b) Personnes prises en compte
Toutes celles âgées de 15 ans et plus.
Sont exclues:
a) les personnes absentes du ménage pendant douze mois et plus;
b) le personnel militaire de carrière et les conscrits vivant en casernes
c) les pensionnaires d'institutions pénales et psychiatriques;
4.Périodicité de l'enquête
L'enquête, menée depuis janvier 1998, est trimestrielle.
5.Période de référence
La semaine civile.
6.Sujets traités
Population active et non active; emploi (principal et secondaire), chômage, classés selon le lieu de résidence, l'âge, le sexe, la branche d'activité économique, le niveau d'instruction, la situation dans la profession, la durée du travail, ainsi que l'emploi déclaré et informel et le sous-emploi liés à des absences prolongées au travail, durée et raisons du chômage. service; durée et raisons de chômage.
7.Concepts et définitions
(a) Emploi
Toutes les personnes âgées de 15 ans et plus qui, pendant la semaine de référence:
a) ont travaillé comme salariés rémunérés au moins une heure;
b) toutes les personnes qui, ayant un emploi ou une entreprise, n'ont pas travaillé car elles étaient momentanément absentes de leur travail,

Sont inclus dans les chiffres totaux:
a) les travailleurs à plein temps et à temps partiel qui ont recherché un autre travail pendant la **Période de référence:**
b) les étudiants à plein temps et à temps partiel travaillant à plein temps ou à temps partiel.
c) les personnes ayant réalisé certains travaux pendant la semaine de référence, tout en étant, soit retraités - et percevant une pension - soit inscrits comme demandeurs d'emploi dans un bureau de placement et bénéficiant d'indemnités de chômage;
d) les travailleurs familiaux rémunérés ou non (sous réserve d'avoir travaillé au moins douze heures);
e) le personnel domestique privé;
f) les membres de coopératives de producteurs;
g) les membres des forces armées ne vivant pas dans les casernes.
Sont exclues les personnes dont la seule activité a consisté à travailler à la maison (travaux de peinture, de réparation, de ménage), ainsi que dans leurs exploitations agricoles, en vue de l'autoconsommation. Sont également exclus les personnes travaillant bénévolement en faveur d'organisations religieuses, charitables et similaires. Elles sont considérées comme inactives.
(b) Chômage
Toutes les personnes de 15 ans et plus, qui n'avaient pas d'emploi pendant la période de référence, étaient disponibles en vue d'un travail, sauf maladie momentanée, et qui avaient pris des dispositions spécifiques pour trouver un emploi pendant les quatre semaines précédant l'entretien. Sont également incluses les personnes ayant trouvé un emploi et pris des mesures de nature à leur permettre de commencer un nouveau travail, à une date postérieure à la période de référence.
La recherche de travail comprend toutes les initiatives prises par une personne pour trouver un emploi ou entreprendre une activité indépendante telles que: s'inscrire dans les bureaux de placement, faire paraître des annonces et y répondre, rechercher de l'aide auprès de parents ou d'amis, entreprendre des démarches pour se procurer des ressources financières, etc.
8.Méthode d'échantillonnage
(a) Le cadre d'échantillonnage
L'échantillon a été développé sur la base des résultats du recensement de la population effectué en 1989.
(b) L'échantillon
Un plan de sondage aréolaire stratifié à deux degrés, avec probabilité de sélection proportionnelle à la population est sélectionné. Au premier degré, 282 circonscriptions de dénombrement (CD) sont sélectionnées, sur un total de 12000, de manière aléatoire. La sélection est effectuée de telle manière que chaque strate doit avoir un nombre de CD divisible par 3, sans reste (dans un but de répartition égale entre les mois des quatre trimestres). Chaque strate urbaine comporte 7 à 12 adresses échantillons, et chaque strate rurale en a 16 à 24. Au deuxième degré, on sélectionne 3351 ménages de manière aléatoire, ce qui représente 0,3% du nombre total de ménages.
(c) La rotation
L'échantillon est caractérisé par le schéma de rotation suivant: les CD sélectionnés sont divisés en 12 groupes égaux au niveau de chaque strate. On renouvelle chaque mois l'échantillon à hauteur de 8,3%: autrement dit, sur une année, la totalité de l'échantillon se trouve renouvelé. Tout ménage faisant son entrée dans l'échantillon est interrogé sur une période de quatre trimestres consécutifs, puis le quitte définitivement.
9.La documentation
Les résultats préliminaires de l'enquête par sondage sur la main-d'oeuvre (LFSS) ont fait l'objet d'un communiqué de presse, préparé par le Service Statistiques. Les résultats définitifs sont publiés dans *l'Annuaire des Statistiques.*

Grèce

Titre de l'enquête: Labour Force Survey
Organisme responsable de l'enquête:
Organisation et déroulement de l'enquête: National Statistical Service of Greece.
Analyse et Publication des résultats: National Statistical Service of Greece.
Sujets couverts par l'enquête: Emploi, chômage, sous-emploi, durée du travail, salaires, revenu, durée de l'emploi et du chômage, travailleurs occasionnels et découragés, industrie, profession, situation dans la profession, niveau d'instruction/de qualification, activité habituelle, exercice d'autres emplois, autres sujets tels qu'informations démographiques, conditions de vie, relations sociales, consommation et dépenses, etc.

Champ de l'enquête:
Territoire: L'ensemble du pays.
Groupes de population: Toutes les personnes âgées de 15 ans et plus. Sont exclus:
a)les militaires de carrière et les conscrits, même s'ils vivent seuls ou avec leur famille dans une résidence en dehors du camp;
b)les clients permanents des hôtels;
c)les membres de ménages collectifs;
d)les membres de ménages étrangers travaillant dans des ambassades, consulats, missions commerciales, économiques ou militaires et les membres des forces armées.
Disponibilité d'estimations selon d'autres sources pour les régions ou groupes exclus: Non disponible.
Groupes couverts par l'enquête mais exclus des résultats publiés: Des données démographiques sont recueillies pour les personnes ayant quitté le ménage, telles que les conscrits, les personnes vivant dans d'autres ménages collectifs, etc. Il est prévu d'estimer ces catégories et de publier les données les concernant.
Périodicité:
Réalisation de l'enquête: Trimestrielle.
Publication des résultats: Annuelle.
Période de référence:
Emploi: Une semaine fixe.
Recherche d'un emploi: Quatre semaines avant l'entretien (période fixe).
Disponibilité pour travailler: Dans les deux semaines suivant l'entretien (période fixe).
Concepts et définitions:
Emploi: Les personnes âgées de 15 ans et plus qui, pendant la semaine de référence précédant l'enquête, ont travaillé pendant au moins une heure ou étaient temporairement absentes de leur travail pour cause de maladie, de vacances, de grèves, d'intempéries ou de panne mécanique, etc. Les apprentis rémunérés et les membres de la famille non rémunérés.
Sont également incluses dans les personnes ayant un emploi:
a)les travailleurs occupés à plein temps ou à temps partiel et en quête d'un autre travail durant la période de référence;
b)les personnes ayant effectué un travail quelconque, rémunéré ou en vue d'un bénéfice, pendant la période de référence, mais qui étaient alors assujetties à la scolarité obligatoire, à la retraite et au bénéfice d'une pension, inscrites en tant que demandeurs d'emploi auprès d'un bureau de placement ou qui percevaient des allocations de chômage;
c)les étudiants à plein temps ou à temps partiel travaillant à plein temps ou à temps partiel;
d)les bénéficiaires de mesures de promotion de l'emploi s'ils travaillent régulièrement;
e)les volontaires et les militaires de carrière.
Chômage: Toutes les personnes âgées de 15 ans et plus, sans emploi, qui cherchaient du travail et ont effectué des démarches concrètes (telles que s'inscrire auprès d'un bureau de placement privé ou public, faire passer des petites annonces ou y répondre, postuler auprès d'employeurs, demander de l'aide à des amis ou à des parents) au cours des quatre dernières semaines pour trouver un emploi, et qui sont disponibles pour travailler dans les deux semaines.
Sous-emploi:
Sous-emploi lié à la durée du travail: Les personnes qui veulent faire davantage d'heures de travail dans leur emploi actuel ou dans un emploi supplémentaire.
Situations d'emploi inadéquat: Les personnes en quête d'un autre emploi pour faire un meilleur usage de leurs qualifications actuelles.
Durée du travail: Les heures de travail hebdomadaires, habituelles et réellement effectuées, dans l'activité principale et les heures réellement effectuées dans l'activité secondaire.
Revenu lié à l'emploi:
Revenu lié à l'emploi salarié: Cela comprend: a) les paiements mensuels perçus dans l'activité principale, nets de cotisations de sécurité sociale et d'impôts, y compris les paiements supplémentaires perçus tous les mois tels que les heures supplémentaires, les pourboires, etc.; b) les paiements supplémentaires nets (paiements totaux annuels) tels que primes ou autres prestations versées par l'entreprise.
Revenu lié à l'emploi indépendant: Non couvert par l'enquête.
Secteur informel: Ne s'applique pas.
Activité habituelle: Non couvert par l'enquête.
Classifications:
Branche d'activité économique (industrie)
Titre de la classification: Classification nationale fondée sur la NACE Rév.1.
Groupes de population classifiés selon l'industrie: Les personnes ayant un emploi et les chômeurs (industrie du dernier emploi occupé pour ces derniers).
Nombre de groupes de codage: 17 et 60 groupes aux niveaux à un chiffre et à deux chiffres respectivement.
Convertibilité avec la CITI: CITI-Rév.3.
Profession
Titre de la classification: Classification nationale fondée sur la CITP-1988 (COM).
Groupes de population classifiés selon la profession: Les personnes ayant un emploi et les chômeurs (profession exercée dans le dernier emploi pour ces derniers).
Nombre de groupes de codage: 10, 46 et 210 aux niveaux à un chiffre, à deux chiffres et à trois chiffres respectivement.
Convertibilité avec la CITP: CITP-1988.
Situation dans la profession
Titre de la classification: Classification nationale.
Groupes de population classifiés par situation dans la profession: Les personnes ayant un emploi et les chômeurs (situation occupée dans le dernier emploi pour ces derniers).
Catégories de codage: Salariés, employeurs, travailleurs indépendants, travailleurs familiaux non rémunérés, apprentis rémunérés.
Convertibilité avec la CISP: CISP-1993.
Education
Titre de la classification: Classification nationale.
Groupes de population classifiés selon l'éducation: Les personnes ayant un emploi et les chômeurs.
Catégories de codage: 5 groupes: pré-primaire, primaire, premier cycle de l'enseignement secondaire, deuxième cycle de l'enseignement secondaire et enseignement post-tertiaire, premier et second cycles de l'enseignement tertiaire.
Convertibilité avec la CITE: CITE-1997.
Taille de l'échantillon et plan de sondage:
Unité finale d'échantillonnage: Ménage.
Taille de l'échantillon (unités finales d'échantillonnage): Environ 31 000 ménages par trimestre.
Taux de sondage: 8,698 pour cent.
Base de sondage: Population and Housing Census de 1991.
Renouvellement de l'échantillon: Tous les trimestres.
Rotation:
Schéma: Tous les trimestres, 1/6 des ménages sondés sont renouvelés par rotation, par association des deux méthodes ci-après: sélection d'un nouvel échantillon de ménages provenant d'unités aréolaires déjà utilisées et sélection de nouvelles unités aréolaires.
Pourcentage d'unités restant dans l'échantillon durant deux enquêtes successives: 84 pour cent.
Nombre maximum d'interrogatoires par unité de sondage: Six.
Durée nécessaire au renouvellement complet de l'échantillon: 13 trimestres.
Déroulement de l'enquête:
Type d'entretien: Porte à porte avec écriture manuelle sur papier.
Nombre d'unités finales d'échantillonnage par zone de sondage: Non disponible.
Durée de déroulement de l'enquête:
Totale: 13 semaines.
Par zone de sondage: Non disponible.
Organisation: Personnel permanent et ad hoc.
Nombre de personnes employées: 200 enquêteurs et 10 cadres.
Substitution des unités finales en cas de non-réponse: Non.
Estimations et redressements:
Taux de non-réponse: 8%.
Redressement pour non-réponse: Non.
Imputation en cas de non-réponse à une question spécifique: Oui.
Redressement pour les régions/populations non couvertes: Non.
Redressement en cas de sous-représentation: Non.
Redressement en cas de sur-représentation: Non.
Corrections des variations saisonnières: Non.
Historique de l'enquête:
Titre et date de la première enquête: Labour Force Survey 1981.
Modifications et révisions significatives: De 1981 à 1997, l'enquête a été réalisée au cours du deuxième trimestre de chaque année. A partir de 1998, enquête trimestrielle. Révision des questionnaires en 1992 et 1998.
Documentation et dissémination:
Documentation
Titre des publications publiant les résultats: Labour Force Survey (Employment); Statistical Yearbook of Greece; Concise Statistical Yearbook of Greece.

Titre des publications méthodologiques: Statistical Yearbook of Greece.
Dissémination
Délai de publication des premiers résultats: Environ une année.
Information à l'avance du public des dates de publication initiale des résultats: Oui.
Mise à disposition, sur demande, des données non publiées: Oui.
Mise à disposition des données sur support informatique: Oui.
Site web: http://www.statistics.gr/.

Hong-kong, Chine

Titre de l'enquête: General Household Survey (GHS).
Organisme responsable de l'enquête:
Organisation et déroulement de l'enquête: Census and Statistics Department (C&SD).
Analyse et Publication des résultats: C&SD.
Sujets couverts par l'enquête: Personnes actuellement actives, ayant un emploi ou sans emploi; personnes actuellement en situation de sous-emploi lié à la durée du travail; personnes actuellement en dehors de la population active; travailleurs découragés; durée du travail; durée du chômage; gains mensuels provenant d'un emploi, etc., industrie, profession, situation dans la profession, niveaux d'instruction.
Champ de l'enquête:
Territoire: L'ensemble du territoire à l'exception des régions marines.
Groupes de population: La population civile non institutionnelle âgée de 15 ans et plus, à l'exception des personnes vivant en institution et des personnes vivant sur des navires.
Disponibilité d'estimations selon d'autres sources pour les régions ou groupes exclus: Néant.
Groupes couverts par l'enquête mais exclus des résultats publiés: Néant.
Périodicité:
Réalisation de l'enquête: En continu.
Publication des résultats: Publication mensuelle d'une moyenne mobile sur trois mois centrée sur le mois intermédiaire.
Période de référence:
Emploi: Sept jours avant le recensement.
Recherche d'un emploi: Avoir cherché un emploi au cours des 30 jours précédant le recensement.
Disponibilité pour travailler: Sept jours avant le recensement.
Concepts et définitions:
Emploi: Les personnes ayant effectué un travail quelconque (pendant au moins une heure), rémunéré ou en vue d'un bénéfice, au cours des sept jours précédant le recensement ou ayant eu un lien formel avec l'emploi pendant les sept jours précédant le recensement.
Chômage: Les personnes sans emploi et disponibles pour travailler au cours des sept jours précédant le recensement et qui ont cherché du travail au cours des 30 jours précédant le recensement.
Sous-emploi:
Sous-emploi lié à la durée du travail: Les personnes ayant travaillé contre leur gré moins de 35 heures au cours des sept jours précédant le recensement et ayant cherché à travailler davantage au cours des sept jours précédant le recensement, ou qui étaient disponibles pour travailler davantage au cours des sept jours précédant le recensement. Le terme "contre leur gré" se réfère à un ralentissement de l'activité, à un manque de matériaux, à des pannes mécaniques et à l'incapacité de trouver un emploi à plein temps.
Situations d'emploi inadéquat: Non disponible.
Durée du travail: Les heures de travail réellement effectuées dans toutes les activités au cours des sept jours précédant le recensement comprennent les heures de travail, rémunérées ou non, effectuées dans les emplois primaires et secondaires.
Revenu lié à l'emploi:
Revenu lié à l'emploi salarié: Gains mensuels provenant d'un emploi: gains en espèces provenant de toutes les activités au cours du dernier mois; pour les emplois salariés, cela inclut les salaires et traitements, primes, commissions, allocations de logement ainsi que les indemnités pour heures supplémentaires et les indemnités de présence, mais exclut les rappels et paiements en nature.
Revenu lié à l'emploi indépendant: Les gains en espèces se réfèrent aux montants provenant de sa propre entreprise utilisés à des fins personnelles ou domestiques, mais les gains industriels ou commerciaux nets peuvent être utilisés comme variable de remplacement.
Secteur informel: Ne s'applique pas, mais les colporteurs peuvent être désignés séparément.
Activité habituelle: Non disponible.

Classifications:
Branche d'activité économique (industrie)
Titre de la classification: Hong Kong Standard Industrial Classification (HSIC).
Groupes de population classifiés selon l'industrie: Les personnes ayant un emploi et les chômeurs (industrie du dernier emploi occupé pour ces derniers).
Nombre de groupes de codage: 96
Convertibilité avec la CITI: CITI-Rév.2.
Profession
Titre de la classification: Occupation Index of Hong Kong Population Census (2001).
Groupes de population classifiés selon la profession: Les personnes ayant un emploi et les chômeurs (profession du dernier emploi occupé pour ces derniers).
Nombre de groupes de codage: 45
Convertibilité avec la CITP: CITP-1988.
Situation dans la profession
Titre de la classification: Classification nationale, sans titre.
Groupes de population classifiés par situation dans la profession: Les personnes ayant un emploi.
Catégories de codage: Salariés, à l'exception des colporteurs; travailleurs extérieurs à l'entreprise; employeurs, à l'exception des colporteurs; travailleurs indépendants, à l'exception des colporteurs; colporteurs (distinction entre salarié, employeur et travailleur indépendant); travailleur familial non rémunéré.
Convertibilité avec la CISP: CISP-1993.
Education
Titre de la classification: Classification nationale, sans titre.
Groupes de population classifiés selon l'éducation: Les personnes ayant un emploi et les chômeurs.
Catégories de codage: 25
Convertibilité avec la CITE: CITE-1997.
Taille de l'échantillon et plan de sondage:
Unité finale d'échantillonnage: Logements permanents dans les zones bâties et segments ailleurs.
Taille de l'échantillon (unités finales d'échantillonnage): 27 000 logements par période de trois mois.
Taux de sondage: 1,2 pour cent de la population cible par période de trois mois.
Base de sondage: Le Registre des quartiers (Register of Quarters, RQ), qui contient les adresses de tous les logements permanents dans les zones bâties, et le Registre des segments (Register of Segments, RS), qui recense les segments délimités par des points de repère tels que sentiers et cours d'eau et est tenu par le C&SD.
Renouvellement de l'échantillon: Le RQ est renouvelé en continu, sur avis de construction ou de démolition de bâtiments émanant de diverses sources. Le RS est renouvelé tous les cinq ans, avant la tenue des recensements ou des recensements intermédiaires de la population.
Rotation:
Schéma: Les ménages figurent deux fois dans l'échantillon, à trois mois d'intervalle.
Pourcentage d'unités restant dans l'échantillon durant deux enquêtes successives: Non disponible.
Nombre maximum d'interrogatoires par unité de sondage: Non disponible.
Durée nécessaire au renouvellement complet de l'échantillon: Non disponible.
Déroulement de l'enquête:
Type d'entretien: Entretien direct et entretien par téléphone assisté par ordinateur.
Nombre d'unités finales d'échantillonnage par zone de sondage: Non disponible.
Durée de déroulement de l'enquête:
Totale: Un mois.
Par zone de sondage: Non disponible.
Organisation: Permanente.
Nombre de personnes employées: 76 enquêteurs, 14 cadres et 3 responsables sur le terrain.
Substitution des unités finales en cas de non-réponse: Non.
Estimations et redressements:
Taux de non-réponse: 10%.
Redressement pour non-réponse: Non.
Imputation en cas de non-réponse à une question spécifique: Non.
Redressement pour les régions/populations non couvertes: Non.
Redressement en cas de sous-représentation: Ne s'applique pas.
Redressement en cas de sur-représentation: Ne s'applique pas.

Corrections des variations saisonnières: Taux de chômage uniquement.
Historique de l'enquête:
Titre et date de la première enquête: Labour Force Survey (LFS), septembre 1975.
Modifications et révisions significatives: Le LFS a été réalisé tous les semestres, de septembre 1975 à septembre 1980. A été remplacé par l'enquête GHS en continu en août 1981.
Documentation et dissémination:
Documentation
Titre des publications publiant les résultats: Quaterly Report on General Household Survey.
Titre des publications méthodologiques: Quaterly Report on General Household Survey.
Dissémination
Délai de publication des premiers résultats: Deux à trois semaines après la fin du trimestre.
Information à l'avance du public des dates de publication initiale des résultats: Oui.
Mise à disposition, sur demande, des données non publiées: Oui.
Mise à disposition des données sur support informatique: Oui, sur le site web du C&SD: http://www.info.gov.hk/censtatd.

Hongrie

Titre de l'enquête: Labour Force Survey
Organisme responsable de l'enquête:
Organisation et déroulement de l'enquête: Hungarian Central Statistical Office.
Analyse et Publication des résultats: Hungarian Central Statistical Office.
Sujets couverts par l'enquête: Emploi, chômage, sous-emploi, durée du travail, durée du chômage, travailleurs découragés, travailleurs occasionnels, industrie, profession, situation dans la profession, niveau d'instruction, exercice d'autres emplois.
Champ de l'enquête:
Territoire: L'ensemble du pays.
Groupes de population: Toute la population âgée de 15 à 74 ans vivant dans des ménages ordinaires pendant la semaine de référence. Sont exclus la population institutionnelle et les nomades ainsi que les membres des ménages temporairement absents et ceux résidant à l'étranger, à condition qu'ils aient une consommation commune avec le ménage inclus dans l'enquête.
Disponibilité d'estimations selon d'autres sources pour les régions ou groupes exclus: Oui, partiellement.
Groupes couverts par l'enquête mais exclus des résultats publiés: Néant.
Périodicité:
Réalisation de l'enquête: Trimestrielle.
Publication des résultats: Trimestrielle.
Période de référence:
Emploi: Une semaine (les sept derniers jours avant la date de l'entretien).
Recherche d'un emploi: Quatre semaines avant la date de l'entretien.
Disponibilité pour travailler: Deux semaines après la date de l'entretien.
Concepts et définitions:
Emploi: Les personnes âgées de 15 à 74 ans qui, pendant la semaine de référence:
a)ont effectué un travail quelconque pendant au moins une heure, rémunéré en espèces ou en nature, ou en vue d'un bénéfice;
b)ont travaillé au moins une heure sans rémunération dans une entreprise familiale ou une exploitation agricole ("travailleurs familiaux non rémunérés");
c)n'ont pas travaillé, bien qu'elles aient un emploi, car elles étaient temporairement absentes de leur travail pour cause de maladie, de vacances, d'intempéries, de conflit du travail, etc.
Sont exclues des personnes ayant un emploi les personnes qui, pendant la semaine de l'enquête, exerçaient les activités ci-après:
a)travail non rémunéré pour un autre ménage ou une institution (bénévolat);
b)construction ou rénovation de leur propre maison ou appartement;
c)travail ménager;
d)travail dans un jardin ou une parcelle privés destinés à leur consommation personnelle.
Sont également inclus dans les totaux:
a)les membres des forces armées (militaires de carrière et conscrits), le nombre de conscrits étant tiré de dossiers administratifs et imputé à la fin du traitement des données;
b)les travailleurs occupés à plein temps ou à temps partiel et en quête d'un autre travail durant la période de référence;
c)les étudiants à plein temps ou à temps partiel travaillant à plein temps ou à temps partiel;
d)les personnes ayant effectué un travail quelconque pendant la semaine de référence, tout en étant soit à la retraite et au bénéfice d'une pension, soit inscrites en tant que demandeurs d'emploi auprès d'un bureau de placement, ou tout en percevant des allocations de chômage;
e)les domestiques privés;
f)les apprentis et stagiaires rémunérés.
Chômage: Sont sans emploi toutes les personnes âgées de 15 à 74 ans n'ayant pas travaillé du tout pendant la semaine de référence, qui ont cherché activement du travail pendant les quatre semaines précédant l'entretien, étaient disponibles pour commencer à travailler dans les deux semaines suivant la semaine de l'enquête et attendaient de commencer à travailler dans un nouvel emploi dans les 30 jours.
La seule exception est constituée par les personnes n'ayant pas cherché de travail parce qu'elles en avaient déjà trouvé un, celui-ci devant commencer à une date postérieure à la période de référence. Ces personnes sont classées comme sans emploi.
Sous-emploi:
Sous-emploi lié à la durée du travail: Les personnes qui, durant la semaine de référence, ont travaillé moins de 36 heures sans l'avoir choisi.
Situations d'emploi inadéquat: Les personnes cherchant un autre emploi.
Durée du travail: Les heures de travail habituelles et réellement effectuées dans l'activité principale et dans l'exercice d'un ou de plusieurs autres emplois.
Revenu lié à l'emploi:
Revenu lié à l'emploi salarié: Ne s'applique pas.
Revenu lié à l'emploi indépendant: Ne s'applique pas.
Secteur informel: Ne s'applique pas.
Activité habituelle: Ne s'applique pas.
Classifications:
Branche d'activité économique (industrie)
Titre de la classification: Classification nationale.
Groupes de population classifiés selon l'industrie: Les personnes ayant un emploi et les chômeurs.
Nombre de groupes de codage: Non disponible.
Convertibilité avec la CITI: CITI-Rév.3.
Profession
Titre de la classification: Classification nationale.
Groupes de population classifiés selon la profession: Les personnes ayant un emploi et les chômeurs.
Nombre de groupes de codage: Non disponible.
Convertibilité avec la CITP: CITP-1988.
Situation dans la profession
Titre de la classification: Classification nationale.
Groupes de population classifiés par situation dans la profession: Les personnes ayant un emploi.
Catégories de codage: 5 groupes (salariés, employeurs, travailleurs indépendants, membres de coopératives de producteurs, travailleurs familiaux non rémunérés).
Convertibilité avec la CISP: CISP-1993.
Education
Titre de la classification: Classification nationale.
Groupes de population classifiés selon l'éducation: Les personnes ayant un emploi et les chômeurs.
Catégories de codage: Non disponible.
Convertibilité avec la CITE: Oui.
Taille de l'échantillon et plan de sondage:
Unité finale d'échantillonnage: Logement.
Taille de l'échantillon (unités finales d'échantillonnage): Environ 32 000 ménages, soit quelque 65 000 personnes.
Taux de sondage: 0,8 pour cent.
Base de sondage: La base de sondage est constituée de 12 775 unités d'échantillonnage recouvrant 751 ensembles résidentiels dans le pays et comprenant environ 626 000 adresses.
Renouvellement de l'échantillon: Deux fois par an.
Rotation:
Schéma: Tout ménage qui intègre l'échantillon à un moment quelconque est censé fournir des informations sur le marché de l'emploi pendant six trimestres successifs avant de quitter définitivement l'échantillon.

Pourcentage d'unités restant dans l'échantillon durant deux enquêtes successives: 83 pour cent.
Nombre maximum d'interrogatoires par unité de sondage: Six.
Durée nécessaire au renouvellement complet de l'échantillon: 18 mois.
Déroulement de l'enquête:
Type d'entretien: Sur papier avec écriture manuelle.
Nombre d'unités finales d'échantillonnage par zone de sondage: Non disponible.
Durée de déroulement de l'enquête:
Totale: Une semaine.
Par zone de sondage: Non disponible.
Organisation: Hungarian Central Statistical Office.
Nombre de personnes employées: Environ 700 enquêteurs et cadres.
Substitution des unités finales en cas de non-réponse: Non.
Estimations et redressements:
Taux de non-réponse: 12,2%.
Redressement pour non-réponse: Non.
Imputation en cas de non-réponse à une question spécifique: Non.
Redressement pour les régions/populations non couvertes: Non.
Redressement en cas de sous-représentation: Non.
Redressement en cas de sur-représentation: Non.
Corrections des variations saisonnières: Non.
Historique de l'enquête:
Titre et date de la première enquête: Labour Force Survey, janvier 1992.
Modifications et révisions significatives: Néant.
Documentation et dissémination:
Documentation
Titre des publications publiant les résultats: Monthly Report, LFS Quaterly Bulletin et LFS Time-Series (annuel).
Titre des publications méthodologiques: LFS Methodology (en hongrois et en partie en anglais).
Dissémination
Délai de publication des premiers résultats: Non disponible.
Information à l'avance du public des dates de publication initiale des résultats: Oui.
Mise à disposition, sur demande, des données non publiées: Oui.
Mise à disposition des données sur support informatique: Oui.
Site web: http://www.ksh.hu.

Inde

Titre de l'enquête: Employment and Unemployment Survey
Organisme responsable de l'enquête:
Organisation et déroulement de l'enquête: National Sample Survey Organisation (NSSO)
Analyse et Publication des résultats: SDRD, NSSO
Sujets couverts par l'enquête: Emploi, chômage, sous-emploi lié à la durée du travail, durée du travail, salaires, durée de l'emploi et du chômage, travailleurs occasionnels, industrie, profession, situation dans la profession, niveau d'instruction et activité habituelle.
Champ de l'enquête:
Territoire: L'ensemble du pays, à l'exception de certaines zones intérieures de deux Etats et d'un C.N.O. (canton non organisé).
Groupes de population: Les personnes âgées de 5 ans et plus, à l'exception des populations comptées à part.
Disponibilité d'estimations selon d'autres sources pour les régions ou groupes exclus: Non.
Groupes couverts par l'enquête mais exclus des résultats publiés: Non disponible.
Périodicité:
Réalisation de l'enquête: Une enquête annuelle est réalisée sur un petit échantillon. L'échantillon complet est inclus dans l'enquête tous les cinq ans, la dernière en date de juillet 1993 à juin 1994.
Publication des résultats: Annuelle pour le "petit" échantillon, tous les cinq ans pour le grand.
Période de référence:
Emploi: Une semaine avant la date de l'entretien.
Recherche d'un emploi: Une semaine et un jour avant la date de l'entretien.
Disponibilité pour travailler: Une semaine et un jour avant la date de l'entretien.
Concepts et définitions:
Emploi: les personnes ayant exercé une activité lucrative pendant au moins une heure au cours de la semaine de référence. Cette catégorie inclut les personnes servant dans l'armée mais exclut les retraités et les personnes au bénéfice d'une pension ayant aussi travaillé.
Chômage: Les personnes n'exerçant aucune activité lucrative mais ayant cherché du travail ou disponibles pour travailler (même si elles n'en cherchaient pas) à un moment quelconque de la période de référence. Sont exclus les retraités et les personnes au bénéfice d'une pension.
Sous-emploi:
Sous-emploi lié à la durée du travail: les personnes ayant un emploi qui, pendant la semaine de référence, étaient disposées à faire davantage d'heures de travail.
Situations d'emploi inadéquat: Non disponible.
Durée du travail: Non disponible.
Activité habituelle: Les personnes ayant exercé une activité lucrative pendant une longue période au cours des 365 derniers jours sont considérées comme ayant habituellement un emploi. Les personnes ayant cherché à travailler plus longtemps ou qui étaient disponibles pour ce faire au cours des 365 derniers jours sont considérées comme habituellement sans emploi.
Classifications:
Branche d'activité économique (industrie)
Titre de la classification: Non disponible.
Groupes de population classifiés selon l'industrie: Les personnes ayant un emploi.
Nombre de groupes de codage: 9
Convertibilité avec la CITI: CITI-Rév.3.
Profession
Titre de la classification: Non disponible.
Groupes de population classifiés selon la profession: Les personnes ayant un emploi.
Nombre de groupes de codage: 31
Convertibilité avec la CITP: CITP-1988.
Situation dans la profession
Titre de la classification: Non disponible.
Groupes de population classifiés par situation dans la profession: Les personnes ayant un emploi et les chômeurs ayant une expérience professionnelle préalable.
Catégories de codage: 10 groupes.
Convertibilité avec la CISP: CISP-1993.
Education
Titre de la classification: Non disponible.
Groupes de population classifiés selon l'éducation: Les personnes ayant un emploi et les chômeurs.
Catégories de codage: 5 groupes.
Convertibilité avec la CITE: Oui.
Taille de l'échantillon et plan de sondage:
Unité finale d'échantillonnage: Ménages.
Taille de l'échantillon (unités finales d'échantillonnage): Environ 40 000 ménages pour l'enquête annuelle et environ 125 000 pour l'enquête quinquennale.
Taux de sondage: 1/5000.
Base de sondage: Liste des villages comptant des hameaux dans les zones rurales et îlots urbains dans les zones urbaines.
Renouvellement de l'échantillon: Une fois tous les dix ans dans les zones rurales et une fois tous les cinq ans dans les zones urbaines.
Rotation:
Schéma: La moitié de l'échantillon de la sous-enquête précédente est renouvelée.
Pourcentage d'unités restant dans l'échantillon durant deux enquêtes successives: 50 pour cent.
Nombre maximum d'interrogatoires par unité de sondage: Deux.
Durée nécessaire au renouvellement complet de l'échantillon: Trois ans.
Déroulement de l'enquête:
Type d'entretien: Entretien personnel.
Nombre d'unités finales d'échantillonnage par zone de sondage: Quatre ménages pour l'enquête annuelle et dix pour l'enquête quinquennale.
Durée de déroulement de l'enquête:
Totale: Une année.
Par zone de sondage: Une année.
Organisation: Permanente.
Nombre de personnes employées: Environ 1 300 enquêteurs et 400 cadres.
Substitution des unités finales en cas de non-réponse: Oui, des ménages.
Estimations et redressements:
Taux de non-réponse: Non disponible.
Redressement pour non-réponse: Oui.

Imputation en cas de non-réponse à une question spécifique: Substitution.
Redressement pour les régions/populations non couvertes: Non.
Redressement en cas de sous-représentation: Non.
Redressement en cas de sur-représentation: Non.
Corrections des variations saisonnières: Non.
Historique de l'enquête:
Titre et date de la première enquête: Annual survey depuis mai 1955-novembre 1955, Quinquennial survey depuis 1972-1973.
Modifications et révisions significatives: En 1972-73 et 1977-78, adoption de l'approche par la situation habituelle et la situation actuelle. Les enquêtes quinquennales récentes ne sont pas comparables.
Documentation et dissémination:
Documentation
Titre des publications publiant les résultats: Government of India, Department of Statistics, national Sample Survey Organisation: "NSSO Journal (Sarvekshana)" trimestriel, New Dehli. Rapports ronéotypés du NSS.
Titre des publications méthodologiques: Idem.
Dissémination
Délai de publication des premiers résultats: Quatre ans.
Information à l'avance du public des dates de publication initiale des résultats: Non.
Mise à disposition, sur demande, des données non publiées: Oui.
Mise à disposition des données sur support informatique: Oui.

Indonésie

Titre de l'enquête: National Labor Force Survey (NLFS).
Organisme responsable de l'enquête:
Organisation et déroulement de l'enquête: BPS-Statistics Indonesia
Analyse et Publication des résultats: BPS-Statistics Indonesia
Sujets couverts par l'enquête: Emploi, chômage, durée du travail, salaires, durée du chômage, industrie, profession, situation dans la profession, niveau d'instruction, exercice d'autres emplois. (L'emploi dans le secteur informel peut être dérivé de la situation dans la profession).
Champ de l'enquête:
Territoire: L'ensemble du pays.
Groupes de population: Toutes les personnes âgées de 15 ans et plus, à l'exception de la population institutionnelle, des nomades et des personnes absentes pendant plus de 6 mois.
Disponibilité d'estimations selon d'autres sources pour les régions ou groupes exclus: Non disponible.
Groupes couverts par l'enquête mais exclus des résultats publiés: Non disponible.
Périodicité:
Réalisation de l'enquête: Annuelle.
Publication des résultats: Annuelle.
Période de référence:
Emploi: Période de référence variable d'une semaine.
Recherche d'un emploi: Pas de période déterminée.
Disponibilité pour travailler: Pas de période déterminée.
Concepts et définitions:
Emploi: Activité exercée pendant au moins une heure pendant la semaine de référence par toute personne (âgée de 15 ans et plus) dans le but de gagner ou de contribuer à obtenir un revenu/bénéfice, ou cas dans lesquels la personne occupe un poste mais n'était temporairement pas au travail, par exemple pour cause de congé. Cette catégorie inclut également les activités exercées par les travailleurs familiaux non rémunérés pour aider leurs parents à obtenir un revenu/bénéfice.
Elle inclut également:
a)les personnes ayant un emploi mais temporairement absentes pour cause de maladie ou d'accident, de congé de maternité ou de congé de paternité, de congé parental, de congé d'éducation ou de formation, d'absence non autorisée, de conflit du travail, d'intempéries, de mise à pied temporaire ou de durée indéterminée sans rémunération;
b)les travailleurs occupés à plein temps ou à temps partiel et en quête d'un autre travail durant la période de référence;
c)les personnes ayant effectué un travail quelconque, rémunéré ou en vue d'un bénéfice, pendant la semaine de référence, mais qui étaient alors assujetties à la scolarité obligatoire ou inscrites en tant que demandeurs d'emploi auprès d'un bureau de placement;
d)les étudiants à plein temps ou à temps partiel travaillant à plein temps ou à temps partiel;
e)les travailleurs familiaux non rémunérés travaillant durant la période de référence;
f)tous les membres des forces armées.
Chômage: Toutes les personnes âgées de 15 ans et plus sans emploi (qui n'avaient aucun emploi) pendant la semaine de référence et cherchant encore du travail.
Cette catégorie inclut également:
a)les personnes sans emploi et immédiatement disponibles pour travailler, qui ont pris des dispositions pour commencer à travailler dans un nouvel emploi à une date postérieure à la semaine de référence;
b)les personnes assujetties à la scolarité obligatoire, en quête d'un emploi et/ou immédiatement disponibles pour travailler; et les étudiants à plein temps ou à temps partiel à la recherche d'un emploi à plein temps ou à temps partiel;
c)les personnes en quête d'un emploi et/ou immédiatement disponibles pour travailler mais à la retraite et au bénéfice d'une pension.
Sous-emploi:
Sous-emploi lié à la durée du travail: NE S'APPLIQUE PAS.
Situations d'emploi inadéquat: Les personnes travaillant moins de 35 heures par semaine et cherchant encore un ou plusieurs autres emplois ou disposées à changer leur(s) emploi(s) actuel(s) si elles en ont la possibilité.
Durée du travail: Le nombre quotidien d'heures de travail réellement effectuées dans l'activité principale et dans toute activité supplémentaire pendant une semaine (la semaine de référence).
Revenu lié à l'emploi:
Revenu lié à l'emploi salarié: Tout revenu perçu (y compris les paiements en nature et sous forme de services) après impôts sur le revenu. Mesuré pour la population actuellement active.
Revenu lié à l'emploi indépendant: NE S'APPLIQUE PAS.
Emploi dans le secteur informel: Tiré de la situation dans la profession des travailleurs; le secteur structuré inclut ceux qui travaillent en tant qu'employeurs ou que salariés. Le secteur informel inclut ceux qui travaillent en tant que travailleurs indépendants sans l'aide de tiers, les travailleurs indépendants aidés d'un ou de plusieurs membres de la famille ou assistés d'une aide temporaire et les travailleurs familiaux non rémunérés.
Activité habituelle: NE S'APPLIQUE PAS.
Classifications:
Branche d'activité économique (industrie)
Titre de la classification: Indonesian Standard Industrial Classification (Klui).
Groupes de population classifiés selon l'industrie: Les personnes ayant un emploi.
Nombre de groupes de codage: Jusqu'en 1999, groupes codés au niveau à 2 chiffres; à partir de 2000, jusqu'au niveau à 3 chiffres.
Convertibilité avec la CITI-1968 jusqu'en 1999 et avec la CITI Rév.3 à partir de 2000.
Profession
Titre de la classification: Indonesian Standard Classification of Occupation (Kji).
Groupes de population classifiés selon la profession: Les personnes ayant un emploi.
Nombre de groupes de codage: Jusqu'en 1999, groupes codés au niveau à 2 chiffres; à partir de 2000, jusqu'au niveau à 3 chiffres.
Convertibilité avec la CITP-1968 jusqu'en 1999 et avec la CITP-1988 à partir de 2000.
Situation dans la profession
Titre de la classification: Non disponible.
Groupes de population classifiés par situation dans la profession: Les personnes ayant un emploi.
Catégories de codage: Cinq groupes: 1. travailleurs indépendants, 2. employeurs assistés de travailleurs familiaux non rémunérés, 3. employeurs ayant des travailleurs rémunérés (permanents), 4. salariés, 5. travailleurs familiaux non rémunérés.
Convertibilité avec la CISP-1993: Oui.
Education
Titre de la classification: Non disponible.
Groupes de population classifiés selon l'éducation: Les personnes ayant un emploi et les chômeurs.
Catégories de codage: Dix groupes: 1. non scolarisé, 2. école primaire inachevée, 3. école primaire, 4. école secondaire de premier cycle d'enseignement général, 5. école secondaire de premier cycle d'enseignement professionnel, 6. école secondaire de deuxième cycle d'enseignement général, 7. école secondaire de deuxième cycle d'enseignement professionnel, 8. diplôme I/II, 9. école supérieure/diplôme III, 10. université.
Convertibilité avec la CITE-1976: Oui.

Taille de l'échantillon et plan de sondage:
Unité finale d'échantillonnage: Ménage.
Taille de l'échantillon (unités finales d'échantillonnage): 49 000 ménages.
Taux de sondage: Variable d'une province à l'autre et entre zones urbaines et zones rurales.
Base de sondage: La base est fondée sur le fichier principal du fichier des villages, constitué de listes des unités statistiques géographiques les plus petites (qui contiennent environ 30 ménages) par zones urbaines et zones rurales.
Renouvellement de l'échantillon: Non disponible.
Rotation: Non disponible.
Schéma: Non disponible.
Pourcentage d'unités restant dans l'échantillon durant deux enquêtes successives: Non disponible.
Nombre maximum d'interrogatoires par unité de sondage: NON DISPONIBLE.
Durée nécessaire au renouvellement complet de l'échantillon: NON DISPONIBLE.
Déroulement de l'enquête:
Type d'entretien: Entretien personnel.
Nombre d'unités finales d'échantillonnage par zone de sondage: Non disponible.
Durée de déroulement de l'enquête:
Totale: Un mois (tous les mois d'août).
Par zone de sondage: Non disponible.
Organisation: Personnel permanent de Statistics Indonesia.
Nombre de personnes employées: Non disponible.
Substitution des unités finales en cas de non-réponse: Non.
Estimations et redressements:
Taux de non-réponse: 1%.
Redressement pour non-réponse: Oui.
Imputation en cas de non-réponse à une question spécifique: Non.
Redressement pour les régions/populations non couvertes: Non.
Redressement en cas de sous-représentation: Non.
Redressement en cas de sur-représentation: Non.
Corrections des variations saisonnières: Non.
Historique de l'enquête:
Titre et date de la première enquête: National Labour Force Survey: trimestrielle de 1986 à 1993.
Modifications et révisions significatives: L'enquête est devenue annuelle à partir de 1994.
Documentation et dissémination:
Documentation
Titre des publications publiant les résultats: Labour Force Situation in Indonesia; Labourers/Employees' Situation in Indonesia (**Périodicité:** annuelle).
Titre des publications méthodologiques: Non disponible.
Dissémination
Délai de publication des premiers résultats: Six mois (les résultats d'août 1998 ont été publiés en février 1999).
Information à l'avance du public des dates de publication initiale des résultats: Non.
Mise à disposition, sur demande, des données non publiées: Oui.
Mise à disposition des données sur support informatique: Les principaux tableaux sont présentés sur Internet: http://www.bps.go.id.

Iran, Rép. islamique d'

Titre de l'enquête: Survey of household employment and unemployment characteristics
Organisme responsable de l'enquête:
Organisation et déroulement de l'enquête: Statistical Centre of Iran, Ministry of Planning.
Analyse et publication des résultats Statistical Centre of Iran, Ministry of Planning.
Sujets couverts par l'enquête: Emploi, chômage, durée du travail, durée de l'emploi, durée du chômage, travailleurs occasionnels, industrie, profession, situation dans la profession, niveau d'instruction et emplois secondaires.
Champ de l'enquête:
Territoire: Toutes les zones urbaines et rurales du pays.
Groupes de population: Toute la population civile, à l'exception des personnes vivant dans des ménages nomades ou collectifs. Sont également exclus les hôtes de passage et les visiteurs ainsi que les personnes vivant à l'étranger pour leur travail ou leurs études, par exemple.

Disponibilité d'estimations selon d'autres sources pour les régions ou groupes exclus: Les résultats de l'enquête se limitent à la population couverte par l'enquête. Si nécessaire, des estimations séparées sont faites pour la population exclue et sont ajoutées aux résultats de l'enquête.
Périodicité:
Réalisation de l'enquête: Annuelle.
Publication des résultats: Annuelle.
Période de référence:
Emploi: Semaine de référence fixe.
Recherche d'un emploi: Semaine de référence fixe.
Disponibilité pour travailler: Semaine de référence.
Concepts et définitions:
Emploi: Les personnes âgées de 10 ans et plus vivant dans des ménages ordinaires sédentaires et ayant occupé un emploi pendant au moins deux jours au cours des sept derniers jours précédant l'entretien.
Cette catégorie inclut:
a)les personnes ayant un emploi mais temporairement absentes pour une raison quelconque, ainsi que les personnes en mise à pied temporaire sans rémunération;
b)les travailleurs occupés à plein temps ou à temps partiel et en quête d'un autre travail pendant la période de référence;
c)les personnes ayant effectué un travail quelconque, rémunéré ou en vue d'un bénéfice, pendant la semaine de référence, mais qui étaient alors assujetties à la scolarité obligatoire, à la retraite et au bénéfice d'une pension ou qui percevaient des allocations de chômage, étaient inscrites en tant que demandeurs d'emploi auprès d'un bureau de placement ou cherchaient un autre travail pendant la semaine de référence;
d)les étudiants à plein temps ou à temps partiel travaillant à plein temps ou à temps partiel;
e)les apprentis et stagiaires rémunérés ainsi que les bénéficiaires de mesures de promotion de l'emploi;
f)les travailleurs familiaux non rémunérés au travail ou temporairement absents de leur travail;
g)les travailleurs saisonniers ne travaillant pas durant la morte-saison;
h)les membres des forces armées, y compris les volontaires et les militaires de carrière, les conscrits et les personnes effectuant un service civil équivalent au service militaire.
Sont exclus:
a)les apprentis et stagiaires non rémunérés;
b)les personnes occupées dans la production de biens ou la prestation de services pour leur usage final personnel;
c)les personnes effectuant un travail communautaire ou des activités sociales;
d)les personnes ayant un emploi mais absentes sans autorisation.
Chômage: les personnes âgées de 10 ans et plus vivant dans des ménages ordinaires sédentaire, n'ayant occupé aucun emploi pendant ne serait-ce que deux jours et ayant cherché du travail pendant les sept jours précédant l'entretien.
Cette catégorie inclut:
a)les personnes en mise à pied de durée indéterminée sans rémunération ou en mise en congé non rémunéré à l'initiative de l'employeur;
b)les personnes sans emploi et immédiatement disponibles pour travailler qui cherchent du travail et ont pris des dispositions pour commencer à travailler dans un nouvel emploi à une date postérieure à la semaine de référence;
c)les personnes sans emploi et immédiatement disponibles pour travailler qui cherchent du travail et ont essayé de créer leur propre entreprise;
d)les étudiants à plein temps ou à temps partiel à la recherche d'un emploi à plein temps ou à temps partiel;
e)les personnes en quête d'un emploi ou immédiatement disponibles pour travailler mais qui étaient assujetties à la scolarité obligatoire ou à la retraite et au bénéfice d'une pension.
Sont exclues les personnes sans emploi n'ayant pas cherché de travail pendant la période de référence.
Sous-emploi:
Sous-emploi lié à la durée du travail: Non disponible.
Situations d'emploi inadéquat: Non disponible.
Durée du travail: Le nombre total d'heures de travail normales et d'heures supplémentaires liées à l'activité principale et aux autres activités des personnes ayant un emploi.
Revenu lié à l'emploi:
Revenu lié à l'emploi salarié: Non disponible.
Revenu lié à l'emploi indépendant: Non disponible.
Secteur informel: Non disponible.
Activité habituelle: Non disponible.

Classifications:
Branche d'activité économique (industrie)
Titre de la classification: Inconnu.
Groupes de population classifiés selon l'industrie: Les personnes ayant un emploi et les chômeurs ayant une expérience professionnelle préalable.
Nombre de groupes de codage: Codes à quatre chiffres mais publiés sous forme de code alphabétique et à un chiffre.
Convertibilité avec la CITI: CITI-Rév.3.
Profession
Titre de la classification: Inconnu.
Groupes de population classifiés selon la profession: Les personnes ayant un emploi et les chômeurs ayant une expérience professionnelle préalable.
Nombre de groupes de codage: Codes à quatre chiffres mais publiés au niveau à un chiffre.
Convertibilité avec la CITP: CITP-1988.
Situation dans la profession:
Titre de la classification: Non disponible.
Groupes de population classifiés par situation dans la profession: Les personnes ayant un emploi et les chômeurs ayant une expérience professionnelle préalable.
Catégories de codage: Employeur, travailleur indépendant, salarié du secteur public, salarié du secteur privé, salarié du secteur coopératif, travailleur familial non rémunéré.
Convertibilité avec la CISP: CISP-1986.
Education
Titre de la classification: Non disponible.
Groupes de population classifiés selon l'éducation: Les personnes ayant un emploi et les chômeurs.
Catégories de codage: Non scolarisé, alphabétisé, enseignement non scolaire, sciences théologiques, école primaire, école secondaire du premier cycle, école secondaire du deuxième cycle, diplôme de fin d'études secondaires et pré-universitaire, enseignement supérieur.
Convertibilité avec la CITE: CITE-1976.
Taille de l'échantillon et plan de sondage:
Unité finale d'échantillonnage: Personne.
Taille de l'échantillon (unités finales d'échantillonnage): 56 753.
Taux de sondage: 0,95 pour cent.
Base de sondage: Nationwide Population and Housing Census de 1996.
Renouvellement de l'échantillon: Non disponible.
Rotation: Néant.
Déroulement de l'enquête:
Type d'entretien: Entretien personnel mené par l'enquêteur.
Nombre d'unités finales d'échantillonnage par zone de sondage: 25 ménages-échantillons par grappe. Chaque grappe demande en moyenne 1,5 journée de travail par enquêteur. **Durée de déroulement de l'enquête:** 15 jours.
Organisation: Permanente.
Nombre de personnes employées: Le nombre total de personnes employées pour réaliser l'enquête est de 640.
Substitution des unités finales en cas de non-réponse: Non.
Estimations et redressements:
Taux de non-réponse: Non disponible.
Redressement pour non-réponse: Non.
Imputation en cas de non-réponse à une question spécifique: Non.
Redressement pour les régions/populations non couvertes: Non.
Redressement en cas de sous-représentation: Non.
Redressement en cas de sur-représentation: Non.
Corrections des variations saisonnières: Non.
Historique de l'enquête:
Titre et date de la première enquête: Survey of household employment and unemployment characteristics (11-26 décembre 1977).
Modifications et révisions significatives: La première enquête (intitulée "Labour force survey") a été réalisée par le Ministère du Travail et des Affaires Sociales (Ministry of Labour and Social Affairs) de 1969 à 1972.
La deuxième enquête (intitulée "Survey of the population and the labour force") a été réalisée par le Bureau de statistique (Statistical Centre of Iran) en février 1989.
La troisième enquête (intitulée "Survey of household employment and unemployment characteristics") a été réalisée par le Bureau de statistique (Statistical Centre of Iran) en février 1994.
La quatrième enquête (également intitulée "Survey of household employment and unemployment characteristics") est réalisée par le Bureau de statistique (Statistical Centre of Iran) tous les ans depuis décembre 1997.
Il est prévu d'effectuer cette enquête deux fois par an. Il est aussi prévu d'ajouter de nouveaux points au questionnaire, notamment les rubriques "revenu", "citoyenneté" et "type d'emploi".
Documentation et dissémination:
Documentation
Titre des publications publiant les résultats: Iran Statistical Yearbook Results of the household employment and unemployment characteristics survey. Collection des manuels d'instruction relatifs à chaque enquête.
Titre des publications méthodologiques: Idem.
Dissémination
Délai de publication des premiers résultats: Environ 16 mois. Les résultats de l'enquête de 1997 ont été publiés en juin 1998.
Information à l'avance du public des dates de publication initiale des résultats: Oui.
Mise à disposition, sur demande, des données non publiées: Oui, via l'Information Dissemination Unit et le réseau intérieur du Statistical Centre of Iran.
Mise à disposition des données sur support informatique: Oui, sur disquette et via le réseau intérieur du Statistical Centre of Iran; site web: http://www.sci.or.ir/.

Irlande

Titre de l'enquête: Quarterly National Household Survey (QNHS).
Organisme responsable de l'enquête:
Organisation et déroulement de l'enquête: Central Statistical Office (CSO).
Analyse et Publication des résultats: Central Statistical Office (CSO).
Sujets couverts par l'enquête: Personnes actuellement ou habituellement actives, ayant un emploi ou sans emploi; personnes actuellement en situation de sous-emploi lié à la durée du travail, personnes en situation d'emploi inadéquat et personnes actuellement en dehors de la population active; travailleurs découragés; durée du travail; durée de l'emploi et du chômage; exercice d'autres emplois; industrie; profession; situation dans la profession; niveau d'instruction/de formation.
Champ de l'enquête:
Territoire: L'ensemble du pays.
Groupes de population: La population hors institutions âgée de 15 ans et plus.
Disponibilité d'estimations selon d'autres sources pour les régions ou groupes exclus: Néant.
Groupes couverts par l'enquête mais exclus des résultats publiés: Néant.
Périodicité:
Réalisation de l'enquête: En continu.
Publication des résultats: Trimestrielle.
Période de référence:
Emploi: Une semaine.
Recherche d'un emploi: Les quatre semaines précédant l'entretien.
Disponibilité pour travailler: Les quatre semaines suivant l'entretien.
Concepts et définitions:
Emploi: Les personnes âgées de 15 ans et plus qui a) ont effectué, pendant la semaine précédant l'enquête, un travail quelconque pendant une heure ou plus, rémunéré ou en vue d'un bénéfice, y compris dans l'exploitation agricole ou l'entreprise familiales; et b) étaient temporairement absentes de leur travail pendant la semaine de référence pour cause de maladie, de vacances, etc. Les forces armées sont incluses dans les personnes ayant un emploi.
Chômage: Les personnes âgées de 15 ans et plus, actuellement sans emploi et disponibles pour travailler dans les quatre semaines et ayant cherché du travail à un moment quelconque au cours des quatre dernières semaines.
Sous-emploi:
Sous-emploi lié à la durée du travail: Les personnes ayant un emploi à temps partiel comportant "trop peu d'heures", ayant cherché un autre emploi et disponibles pour l'occuper.
Situations d'emploi inadéquat: Non publié actuellement, mais une analyse supplémentaire est possible.
Durée du travail: Les heures (de travail) habituelles et réellement effectuées au cours de la semaine de référence.
Revenu lié à l'emploi:
Revenu lié à l'emploi salarié: Ne s'applique pas.
Revenu lié à l'emploi indépendant: Ne s'applique pas.
Secteur informel: Pas indiqué séparément.
Activité habituelle: Non disponible.

Classifications:

Branche d'activité économique (industrie)

Titre de la classification: Adaptation irlandaise de la NACE Rév.1.

Groupes de population classifiés selon l'industrie: Les personnes ayant un emploi et les chômeurs (les chômeurs ne sont répertoriés que s'ils ont eu un emploi au cours des dix dernières années).

Nombre de groupes de codage: Niveau à trois chiffres.

Convertibilité avec la CITI: CITI-Rév.3 (niveau à deux chiffres).

Profession

Titre de la classification: Classification type des professions 1990 (CTP 90)

Groupes de population classifiés selon la profession: Les personnes ayant un emploi et les chômeurs (les chômeurs ne sont répertoriés que s'ils ont eu un emploi au cours des dix dernières années).

Nombre de groupes de codage: Niveau à trois chiffres.

Convertibilité avec la CITP: CITP-1988 (niveau à trois chiffres).

Situation dans la profession

Titre de la classification: Non disponible.

Groupes de population classifiés par situation dans la profession: Les personnes ayant un emploi.

Catégories de codage: Salariés; travailleurs indépendants avec ou sans au moins un salarié; parents offrant leur aide.

Convertibilité avec la CISP: CISP-1993.

Education

Titre de la classification: Classification nationale.

Groupes de population classifiés selon l'éducation: Toutes les personnes âgées de 15 ans et plus.

Catégories de codage: Non scolarisé; enseignement pré-primaire; enseignement primaire; certificat d'études primaires/d'enseignement professionnel/d'enseignement secondaire du premier cycle; programme d'année de transition; certificat de fin d'études passé; programme de formation professionnelle de certificat de fin d'études; certificat de fin d'études obtenu; contrat d'apprentissage personnel (PLC); apprentissage; certificat en agriculture; stage de découverte professionnelle (cadetship); certificat/diplôme national; diplôme universitaire de premier cycle; certificat/diplôme universitaire d'études supérieures; diplôme universitaire de troisième cycle; doctorat; autres.

Convertibilité avec la CITE: CITE-1976 et CITE-1997.

Taille de l'échantillon et plan de sondage:

Unité finale d'échantillonnage: Ménage.

Taille de l'échantillon (unités finales d'échantillonnage): 39 000 chaque trimestre.

Taux de sondage: 1/32.

Base de sondage: Fondée sur le recensement de la population de 1996. Plan de sondage à deux degrés: échantillon du premier degré composé de 2 600 blocs d'environ 75 logements chacun au niveau du comté, ce qui représente 8 strates en fonction de la densité de population. Quinze ménages sont retenus pour l'enquête dans chaque bloc.

Renouvellement de la base de sondage: Censé suivre le recensement de la population de 2001 mais, en raison des précautions entourant la fièvre aphteuse, le recensement de la population de 2001 a été reporté à 2002. La base de sondage a été renouvelée en associant les travaux préparatoires faits pour le recensement en 2001, le Geo Directory et d'autres sources, et le renouvellement aura lieu dès que les résultats du recensement de la population de 2002 seront disponibles.

Rotation:

Schéma: Les ménages participent à l'enquête pendant 5 trimestres successifs avant d'être remplacés par d'autres ménages du bloc.

Pourcentage d'unités restant dans l'échantillon durant deux enquêtes successives: 80 pour cent.

Nombre maximum d'interrogatoires par unité de sondage: Non disponible.

Durée nécessaire au renouvellement complet de l'échantillon: Environ 5 ans.

Déroulement de l'enquête:

Type d'entretien: Entretien personnel assisté par ordinateur.

Nombre d'unités finales d'échantillonnage par zone de sondage: Non disponible.

Durée de déroulement de l'enquête:

Totale: En continu.

Par zone de sondage: Non disponible.

Organisation: Permanente.

Nombre de personnes employées: 150 enquêteurs et 10 coordinateurs.

Substitution des unités finales en cas de non-réponse: Non.

Estimations et redressements:

Taux de non-réponse: 6,3%.

Redressement pour non-réponse: Non.

Imputation en cas de non-réponse à une question spécifique: Non.

Redressement pour les régions/populations non couvertes: Non.

Redressement en cas de sous-représentation: Non.

Redressement en cas de sur-représentation: Non.

Corrections des variations saisonnières: L'enquête QN H étant réalisée depuis 1997, elle n'a pas encore été corrigée des variations saisonnières, mais des travaux préparatoires sont en cours.

Historique de l'enquête:

Titre et date de la première enquête: Le QNHS a débuté en septembre-novembre 1997, remplaçant l'Enquête annuelle (Annual Labour Force Survey) réalisée en avril-mai de chaque année.

Modifications et révisions significatives: Aucune après 1997.

Documentation et dissémination:

Documentation

Titre des publications publiant les résultats: Quarterly National Household Survey (ISSN 1393-6875).

Titre des publications méthodologiques: Quarterly National Household Survey (ISSN 1393-6875).

Dissémination

Délai de publication des premiers résultats: Environ 3 mois.

Information à l'avance du public des dates de publication initiale des résultats: Oui.

Mise à disposition, sur demande, des données non publiées: Oui.

Mise à disposition des données sur support informatique: Oui, contre paiement.

Site web: http://www.cso.ie

Italie

Titre de l'enquête: Rilevazione Trimestrale sulle Forze di Lavoro.

Organisme responsable de l'enquête:

Organisation et déroulement de l'enquête: Instituto Nazionale di Statistica (ISTAT).

Analyse et Publication des résultats: ISTAT.

Sujets couverts par l'enquête: Emploi, chômage, sous-emploi, durée du travail, durée de l'emploi et du chômage, travailleurs découragés, industrie, profession, situation dans la profession, instruction/qualification, exercice d'autres emplois.

Champ de l'enquête:

Territoire: L'ensemble du pays.

Groupes de population: Les personnes résidentes non placées en établissement, âgées de 15 ans et plus et vivant dans des ménages ordinaires.

Disponibilité d'estimations selon d'autres sources pour les régions ou groupes exclus: Non disponible.

Groupes couverts par l'enquête mais exclus des résultats publiés: Non disponible.

Périodicité:

Réalisation de l'enquête: Trimestrielle.

Publication des résultats: Trimestrielle.

Période de référence:

Emploi: Une semaine fixe.

Recherche d'un emploi: Période fixe de quatre semaines.

Disponibilité pour travailler: Période fixe de deux semaines.

Concepts et définitions:

Emploi: Les personnes âgées de 15 ans et plus qui déclarent avoir un emploi et celles ayant déclaré ne pas avoir d'emploi mais qui ont travaillé au moins une semaine durant la période de référence.

Sont également inclus dans les personnes ayant un emploi:

a)les travailleurs occupés à plein temps ou à temps partiel et en quête d'un autre travail pendant la semaine de référence;

b)les personnes ayant effectué un travail quelconque, rémunéré ou en vue d'un bénéfice, pendant la semaine de référence, mais qui étaient alors assujetties à la scolarité obligatoire, à la retraite et au bénéfice d'une pension, inscrites en tant que demandeurs d'emploi auprès d'un bureau de placement ou qui percevaient des allocations de chômage;

c)les étudiants à plein temps ou à temps partiel travaillant à plein temps ou à temps partiel;

d)les travailleurs familiaux non rémunérés au travail pendant la semaine de référence;

e)les volontaires et les militaires de carrière.

Chômage: Les personnes âgées de 15 ans et plus n'ayant pas d'emploi pendant la semaine de référence et qui cherchent un emploi, ont fait au moins une démarche active de recherche d'emploi au cours de la période de référence (4 semaines) et sont disponibles pour commencer à travailler dans les deux semaines, ainsi que les personnes ne cherchant pas d'emploi parce qu'elles en ont déjà trouvé un qui commencera ultérieurement.

Sous-emploi:

Sous-emploi lié à la durée du travail: Les personnes ayant un emploi qui auraient aimé faire davantage d'heures de travail pendant la semaine de référence et auraient été disponibles pour ce faire.

Situations d'emploi inadéquat: Pas de définition précise, mais l'enquête sur la population active italienne collecte des données sur les personnes ayant un emploi et à la recherche d'un autre emploi ou sur les raisons de rechercher un autre emploi (peur de perdre son emploi actuel; emploi à durée déterminée; recherche d'une seconde activité; recherche de meilleures conditions, etc.).

Durée du travail: Les heures de travail habituelles et réellement effectuées dans l'activité principale pendant la semaine de référence ainsi que les heures de travail réellement effectuées dans la seconde activité pendant la semaine de référence.

Revenu lié à l'emploi:

Revenu lié à l'emploi salarié: Ne s'applique pas.

Revenu lié à l'emploi indépendant: Ne s'applique pas.

Secteur informel: Ne s'applique pas.

Activité habituelle: Non disponible.

Classifications:

Branche d'activité économique (industrie)

Titre de la classification: Classification nationale.

Groupes de population classifiés selon l'industrie: Les personnes ayant un emploi et les chômeurs ayant une expérience professionnelle préalable.

Nombre de groupes de codage: 60, au niveau à deux chiffres.

Convertibilité avec la CITI: CITI-Rév.3.

Profession

Titre de la classification: Classification nationale.

Groupes de population classifiés selon la profession: Les personnes ayant un emploi et les chômeurs ayant une expérience professionnelle préalable.

Nombre de groupes de codage: 35

Convertibilité avec la CITP: CITP-1988.

Situation dans la profession

Titre de la classification: Classification nationale.

Groupes de population classifiés par situation dans la profession: Les personnes ayant un emploi et les chômeurs ayant une expérience professionnelle préalable.

Catégories de codage: Salarié, employeur, travailleur indépendant, travailleur familial et membre d'une coopérative, pour les personnes ayant un emploi; salarié, travailleur indépendant ayant des salariés, travailleur indépendant sans salariés et travailleur familial, pour les chômeurs.

Convertibilité avec la CISP: CISP-1993.

Education

Titre de la classification: CITE-1997.

Groupes de population classifiés selon l'éducation: Toutes les personnes.

Catégories de codage: Aucune instruction; enseignement primaire (niveau 1); enseignement secondaire du premier cycle (niveau 2); enseignement secondaire du deuxième cycle (niveau 3); enseignement post-secondaire non tertiaire (niveau 4); enseignement tertiaire (niveau 5); enseignement universitaire supérieur (niveau 6).

Convertibilité avec la CITE: CITE-1997.

Taille de l'échantillon et plan de sondage:

Unité finale d'échantillonnage: Ménage.

Taille de l'échantillon (unités finales d'échantillonnage): 75 000 ménages par trimestre.

Taux de sondage: 0,35 pour cent des familles résidentes par trimestre.

Base de sondage: Registres municipaux.

Renouvellement de l'échantillon: En avril de chaque année.

Rotation:

Schéma: 2-2-2.

Pourcentage d'unités restant dans l'échantillon durant deux enquêtes successives: 50 pour cent.

Nombre maximum d'interrogatoires par unité de sondage: 4.

Durée nécessaire au renouvellement complet de l'échantillon: 15 trimestres.

Déroulement de l'enquête:

Type d'entretien: Entretien personnel direct: sur papier avec écriture manuelle.

Nombre d'unités finales d'échantillonnage par zone de sondage:

Durée de déroulement de l'enquête:

Totale: Non disponible.

Par zone de sondage: Non disponible.

Organisation: Permanente.

Nombre de personnes employées: 1 351 cadres et 3 000 enquêteurs.

Substitution des unités finales en cas de non-réponse: Oui.

Estimations et redressements:

Taux de non-réponse: 5%.

Redressement pour non-réponse: Oui.

Imputation en cas de non-réponse à une question spécifique: Oui.

Redressement pour les régions/populations non couvertes: Non.

Redressement en cas de sous-représentation: Oui.

Redressement en cas de sur-représentation: Oui.

Corrections des variations saisonnières: Oui, pour l'emploi par zone géographique et activité économique, pour le chômage et les taux de chômage par zone géographique, et pour la population active par zone géographique.

Historique de l'enquête:

Titre et date de la première enquête: Rilevazione Nazionale delle Forze di Lavoro 1959.

Modifications et révisions significatives: 1977; 1984: échantillon tiré du recensement de la population de 1981; à partir du deuxième trimestre de 1992: la méthodologie est revue et la modification de la limite d'âge se réfère à des personnes âgées de 15 ans et plus au lieu de 14 ans précédemment.

Documentation et dissémination:

Documentation

Titre des publications publiant les résultats: Communiqués de presse (trimestriels); résultats annuels.

Titre des publications méthodologiques: Idem.

Dissémination

Délai de publication des premiers résultats: Environ 3 mois.

Information à l'avance du public des dates de publication initiale des résultats: Oui.

Mise à disposition, sur demande, des données non publiées: Oui.

Mise à disposition des données sur support informatique: Oui.

Site web: http://www.istat.it/.

Jamaïque

Titre de l'enquête: Labour Force Survey.

Organisme responsable de l'enquête:

Organisation et déroulement de l'enquête: Statistical Institute of Jamaica.

Analyse et Publication des résultats: Statistical Institute of Jamaica.

Sujets couverts par l'enquête: Emploi, chômage, durée du travail, salaires, revenu, durée de l'emploi, industrie, profession, situation dans la profession, éducation et exercice d'autres emplois.

Champ de l'enquête:

Territoire: L'ensemble du pays.

Groupes de population: Toutes les personnes âgées de 14 ans et plus, à l'exception des personnes vivant en établissement, des citoyens non résidents et des diplomates.

Disponibilité d'estimations selon d'autres sources pour les régions ou groupes exclus: Non disponible.

Groupes couverts par l'enquête mais exclus des résultats publiés: Non disponible.

Périodicité:

Réalisation de l'enquête: Enquête trimestrielle réalisée en janvier, avril, juillet et octobre.

Publication des résultats: Annuelle.

Période de référence:

Emploi: Une semaine.

Recherche d'un emploi: Trois mois.

Disponibilité pour travailler: Non disponible.

Concepts et définitions:

Emploi: Les personnes ayant un emploi comprennent toutes celles âgées de 14 ans et plus qui, pendant la semaine de l'enquête, ont travaillé pendant au moins une heure et celles qui avaient un emploi mais étaient temporairement absentes de leur travail.

La catégorie des personnes qui travaillent inclut celles qui:

a)ont travaillé pour un salaire ou un traitement, pour un salaire à l'heure, une rémunération aux pièces, à la commission, pour des pourboires, pour le vivre et le couvert ou pour tout autre type de paiement en nature;

b)ont travaillé comme stagiaires ou comme apprentis;

c)ont travaillé en vue d'un bénéfice ou pour des honoraires dans leur propre entreprise;

d)ont travaillé sans rémunération, salaire ou traitement, à des tâches (autres que leur propre travail ménager ou que des tâches ménagè-

res) ayant contribué à l'exploitation d'une ferme ou d'une entreprise à but lucratif appartenant, dans la plupart des cas, à un membre de la famille qui l'exploite en vue d'un bénéfice;
e)ont consacré du temps à l'exploitation d'une entreprise ou à l'exercice d'une profession, même en l'absence de toute vente ou de toute prestation de service professionnel, comme un médecin ou un avocat qui passe du temps à son cabinet ou à son étude à attendre les clients.
Sont également incluses toutes les personnes ayant un emploi mais qui, pour une raison quelconque, n'ont pas travaillé durant la semaine de l'enquête. Cela inclut les personnes qui:
a)avaient un emploi mais ont travaillé pendant moins d'une heure au cours de la semaine de l'enquête;
b)n'ont pas travaillé pour cause de maladie ou d'invalidité temporaire mais dont l'emploi leur a été conservé jusqu'à leur retour;
c)n'ont pas pu travailler pour cause d'intempéries;
d)n'ont pas travaillé pour cause de congé, y compris de vacances, rémunéré ou non, à condition que leur emploi leur ait été conservé jusqu'à leur retour;
e)n'ont pas travaillé pour cause de conflit du travail, tel que grève ou lock-out;
f)étaient en mise à pied de courte durée (pas plus de 30 jours) avec pour ordre de retourner travailler à la fin des 30 jours.
Chômage: Les chômeurs comprennent toutes les personnes âgées de 14 ans et plus qui cherchaient du travail, voulaient travailler et étaient disponibles pour ce faire. Les personnes cherchant du travail doivent avoir fait des démarches concrètes de recherche d'emploi, telles que:
a)s'être inscrites auprès d'un bureau de placement public ou privé;
b)avoir visité des lieux de travail à la recherche d'un emploi;
c)s'être présentées en personne à des employeurs potentiels;
d)avoir fait paraître des petites annonces dans un organe de presse public ou en avoir affiché dans un lieu public;
e)avoir rédigé des lettres de candidature;
f)avoir demandé à quelqu'un de lui trouver du travail;
g)s'être renseignées sur les possibilités de créer sa propre exploitation agricole ou sa propre entreprise.
Sous-emploi:
Sous-emploi lié à la durée du travail: Non disponible.
Situations d'emploi inadéquat: Non disponible.
Durée du travail: Les heures de travail hebdomadaires réellement effectuées dans toutes les activités.
Revenu lié à l'emploi:
Revenu lié à l'emploi salarié: Revenu moyen brut lié à l'emploi et à d'autres sources au cours des 12 derniers mois écoulés.
Revenu lié à l'emploi indépendant: Voir ci-dessus.
Secteur informel: Non disponible.
Activité habituelle: Non disponible.
Classifications:
Branche d'activité économique (industrie)
Titre de la classification: Classification nationale.
Groupes de population classifiés selon l'industrie: Les personnes ayant un emploi et les chômeurs (industrie du dernier emploi occupé pour ces derniers).
Nombre de groupes de codage: Neuf.
Convertibilité avec la CITI: CITI-Rév.2.
Profession
Titre de la classification: Classification nationale.
Groupes de population classifiés selon la profession: Les personnes ayant un emploi et les chômeurs (profession exercée dans le dernier emploi occupé pour ces derniers).
Nombre de groupes de codage: Neuf.
Convertibilité avec la CITP: Convertibilité partielle avec la CITP-1988.
Situation dans la profession
Titre de la classification: Classification nationale.
Groupes de population classifiés par situation dans la profession: Les personnes ayant un emploi.
Catégories de codage: Cinq groupes: salariés du secteur public; salariés du secteur privé; travailleurs familiaux non rémunérés; employeurs; travailleurs indépendants.
Convertibilité avec la CISP: CISP-1993.
Education
Titre de la classification: Ne s'applique pas.
Groupes de population classifiés selon l'éducation: Ne s'applique pas.
Catégories de codage: Ne s'applique pas.
Convertibilité avec la CITE: Ne s'applique pas.
Taille de l'échantillon et plan de sondage:
Unité finale d'échantillonnage: Logement.
Taille de l'échantillon (unités finales d'échantillonnage): Echantillonnage stratifié à deux degrés de 7 648 logements, basé sur la liste de 1997.
Taux de sondage: 1,5 pour cent.
Base de sondage: Les résultats du recensement de la population de 1991.
Renouvellement de l'échantillon: Tous les 3 ans, sur la base des nouvelles listes.
Rotation:
Schéma: Quatre groupes-témoins sont couverts par chaque enquête.
Pourcentage d'unités restant dans l'échantillon durant deux enquêtes successives: 50 pour cent.
Nombre maximum d'interrogatoires par unité de sondage: Non disponible.
Durée nécessaire au renouvellement complet de l'échantillon: Une année.
Déroulement de l'enquête:
Type d'entretien: Entretien personnel avec écriture manuelle sur papier.
Nombre d'unités finales d'échantillonnage par zone de sondage: Non disponible.
Durée de déroulement de l'enquête:
Totale: Trois à quatre semaines.
Par zone de sondage: Non disponible.
Organisation: Permanente.
Nombre de personnes employées: 3 surveillants-chefs, 16 cadres et 65 enquêteurs.
Substitution des unités finales en cas de non-réponse: Non.
Estimations et redressements:
Taux de non-réponse: Non disponible.
Redressement pour non-réponse: Oui.
Imputation en cas de non-réponse à une question spécifique: Non.
Redressement pour les régions/populations non couvertes: Oui.
Redressement en cas de sous-représentation: Non.
Redressement en cas de sur-représentation: Non.
Corrections des variations saisonnières: Non.
Historique de l'enquête:
Titre et date de la première enquête: The Labour Force 1968.
Modifications et révisions significatives: En 1991, nouvelle classification des industries.
Documentation et dissémination:
Documentation
Titre des publications publiant les résultats: The Labour Force (annuel).
Titre des publications méthodologiques: The Labour Force (annuel).
Dissémination
Délai de publication des premiers résultats: 6 mois.
Information à l'avance du public des dates de publication initiale des résultats: Non.
Mise à disposition, sur demande, des données non publiées: Oui.
Mise à disposition des données sur support informatique: Oui.
Site web: http://www.stainja.com.

Japon

Titre de l'enquête: Labour Force Survey.
Organisme responsable de l'enquête:
Organisation et déroulement de l'enquête: Statistics Bureau, Ministry of Public Management, Home Affairs, Posts and Telecommunications.
Analyse et Publication des résultats: Statistics Bureau, Ministry of Public Management, Home Affairs, Posts and Telecommunications.
Sujets couverts par l'enquête: Emploi, chômage, durée du travail, salaires, durée du chômage, travailleurs découragés, industrie, profession, situation dans la profession, niveau d'instruction/de qualification.
Champ de l'enquête:
Territoire: L'ensemble du pays à l'exception des Territoires du Nord.
Groupes de population: Tous les Japonais et les étrangers âgés de 15 ans et plus ayant vécu (ou qui vivront) dans le pays pendant plus de trois mois, à l'exception des corps diplomatiques étrangers, du personnel militaire étranger et des personnes qui les accompagnent. Les forces d'autodéfense et les personnes vivant dans des centres de redressement sont recensées séparément et incluses dans les résultats.
Les personnes temporairement absentes de leur ménage pour cause de déplacement, parce qu'elles travaillent autre part ou qu'elles sont

hospitalisées sont déclarées comme étant à leur domicile si leur absence est d'une durée inférieure à trois mois. Si elles ont été absentes de leur domicile ou en seront absentes pendant trois mois ou plus, elles sont recensées sur leur lieu de destination.

Disponibilité d'estimations selon d'autres sources pour les régions ou groupes exclus: Non disponible.

Groupes couverts par l'enquête mais exclus des résultats publiés: Non disponible.

Périodicité:

Réalisation de l'enquête: Mensuelle.

Publication des résultats: Mensuelle et trimestrielle pour les Résultats détaillés (Detailed Results) (auparavant « Spécial Survey »).

Période de référence:

Emploi: Une semaine fixe.

Recherche d'un emploi: Une semaine fixe, y compris pour les personnes attendant l'issue d'une démarche de recherche d'emploi.

Disponibilité pour travailler: Un jour fixe.

Concepts et définitions:

Emploi: Les personnes ayant un emploi sont les suivantes:

1)» Les personnes ayant un emploi qui travaillent »: c'est-à-dire les personnes ayant effectué un travail, rémunéré ou en vue d'un bénéfice, pendant au moins une heure durant la semaine de référence. Sont également inclus dans cette catégorie les travailleurs familiaux ayant travaillé pendant au moins une heure pendant la semaine de référence.

2)» Les personnes ayant un emploi mais qui ne travaillent pas»: c'est-à-dire les personnes ayant un emploi mais qui n'ont pas travaillé du tout pendant la semaine de référence.

Sont inclus:

1)les travailleurs occupés à plein temps ou à temps partiel et en quête d'un autre travail durant la semaine de référence;

2)les étudiants à plein temps ou à temps partiel travaillant à plein temps ou à temps partiel;

3)les personnes ayant effectué un travail quelconque, rémunéré ou en vue d'un bénéfice, durant la semaine de référence, alors qu'elles étaient à la retraite et au bénéfice d'une pension ou inscrites en tant que demandeurs d'emploi auprès d'un bureau de placement;

4)les apprentis et stagiaires rémunérés ou non;

5)les bénéficiaires de mesures de promotion de l'emploi;

6)les travailleurs familiaux rémunérés ou non, à condition que ces derniers ne soient pas absents de leur travail durant la semaine de référence;

7)les domestiques privés;

8)les forces d'autodéfense;

9)les personnes ayant un emploi mais temporairement absentes pour cause de maladie/d'accident, de congés/de vacances annuelles, de congé de maternité/de paternité, de congé d'éducation, d'absence non autorisée, d'intempéries ou de panne mécanique, de conflit du travail ou autre réduction de l'activité économique;

10)les personnes temporairement libérées de leur travail (puisqu'elles ne sont pas licenciées et qu'elles perçoivent habituellement un salaire ou un traitement). (Le Japon n'a pas de système de mise à pied proprement dit).

Pour être considérés comme ayant un emploi tout en étant absents de leur travail, les salariés doivent avoir perçu ou s'attendre à percevoir un salaire ou un traitement, et la durée de l'absence des travailleurs indépendants ne doit pas dépasser 30 jours.

Sont exclues des personnes ayant un emploi et considérées comme en dehors de la population active les personnes effectuant des travaux ménagers pour leur propre compte et les personnes effectuant un travail communautaire ou des activités sociales non rémunérées.

Chômage: Sont sans emploi les personnes n'ayant pas travaillé du tout pendant la semaine de référence mais disponibles pour travailler et prêtes à prendre un emploi immédiatement, et qui ont cherché activement du travail ou attendaient l'issue d'une démarche de recherche d'emploi.

« Chercher activement un emploi » signifie avoir effectué une des démarches ci-après au cours de la semaine de référence: s'être inscrit auprès d'un bureau de placement; avoir fait paraître des petites annonces ou y avoir répondu; s'être présenté à un examen; avoir pris contact avec des amis ou des parents; avoir contacté des lieux de travail pour s'enquérir d'éventuels emplois; se préparer à créer une entreprise en se procurant des fonds et des matériaux, etc.

Sont inclus les étudiants à plein temps ou à temps partiel à la recherche d'un emploi à plein temps ou à temps partiel.

Les travailleurs familiaux non rémunérés qui étaient temporairement absents de leur travail durant la semaine de référence sont en dehors de la population active, à moins de remplir les conditions ci-dessus.

Les travailleurs saisonniers dans l'attente d'un travail agricole ou d'un autre emploi saisonnier sont exclus des sans emploi et considérés comme en dehors de la population active.

Sous-emploi:

Sous-emploi lié à la durée du travail: Non couvert par l'enquête.

Situations d'emploi inadéquat: Non couvert par l'enquête.

Durée du travail: « Les heures de travail réellement effectuées pendant la semaine de l'enquête » se réfèrent au nombre d'heures réellement effectuées, qui comprend les heures supplémentaires et exclut les heures passées à faire des travaux ménagers ou du bénévolat, les pauses-repas, les heures passées dans les transports, etc. Si une personne a travaillé dans plus d'un emploi au cours de la semaine de l'enquête, toutes les heures de travail effectuées dans chaque activité sont additionnées.

Revenu lié à l'emploi:

Revenu lié à l'emploi salarié: Non couvert par l'enquête.

Revenu lié à l'emploi indépendant: Non couvert par l'enquête.

Secteur informel: Non couvert par l'enquête.

Activité habituelle: Non couvert par l'enquête.

Classifications:

Branche d'activité économique (industrie)

Titre de la classification: Classification nationale.

Groupes de population classifiés selon l'industrie: Les personnes ayant un emploi et les chômeurs (industrie du dernier emploi occupé pour ces derniers).

Nombre de groupes de codage: 30 groupes.

Convertibilité avec la CITI: CITI-Rév.2 au niveau à 3 chiffres (grands groupes).

Profession

Titre de la classification: Classification nationale.

Groupes de population classifiés selon la profession: Les personnes ayant un emploi et les chômeurs (profession exercée dans le dernier emploi occupé pour ces derniers).

Nombre de groupes de codage: 15 groupes.

Convertibilité avec la CITP: CITP-1968 au niveau à 1 chiffre (grands groupes).

Situation dans la profession

Titre de la classification: Classification nationale.

Groupes de population classifiés par situation dans la profession: Les personnes ayant un emploi et les chômeurs. Ces derniers sont classifiés selon leur dernier emploi, le cas échéant, dans « Detailed Results» uniquement.

Catégories de codage: 4 groupes: salariés (salariés permanents, salariés temporaires et journaliers), travailleurs indépendants, travailleurs familiaux et ouvriers à la tâche travaillant à domicile.

Convertibilité avec la CISP: CISP-1993.

Education

Titre de la classification: Classification nationale.

Groupes de population classifiés selon l'éducation: Les personnes ayant un emploi et les chômeurs.

Catégories de codage: Dans « Detailed Results » uniquement. Toutes les personnes sont classées en fonction de leur « fréquentation scolaire» à la date de l'enquête, en: scolarisé, diplômé de l'enseignement scolaire et jamais scolarisé. Les catégories « scolarisé » et « diplômé de l'enseignement scolaire» sont ensuite classifiées en fonction du niveau d'instruction auquel la personne est parvenue, tel qu'école primaire ou élémentaire, deuxième cycle de l'enseignement secondaire, collège ou université, y compris les institutions d'enseignement supérieur.

Convertibilité avec la CITE: CITE-1976.

Taille de l'échantillon et plan de sondage:

Unité finale d'échantillonnage: Logement.

Taille de l'échantillon (unités finales d'échantillonnage): Environ 2 900 districts de recensement comprenant 40 000 logements.

Taux de sondage: Non disponible.

Base de sondage: Le recensement quinquennal de la population. L'échantillon actuel est construit et renouvelé sur la base du recensement de la population de 1995.

Renouvellement de l'échantillon: Chaque année, une liste de districts de logements collectifs nouvellement construits est établie par le gouvernement préfectoral pour être ajoutée aux districts de recensement.

Rotation:

Schéma: Un échantillon de districts de recensement reste dans l'échantillon pendant quatre mois successifs, le quitte pendant les huit mois suivants et le réintègre pendant les quatre mêmes mois de l'année suivante.

Pour chaque district, deux ensembles d'unités de logement sont sélectionnés. La première année de recensement d'un district-échantillon, les ménages qui se trouvent dans les unités de logement de l'échantillon du premier ensemble sont inclus dans l'enquête pendant les deux premiers mois avant d'être remplacés par les ménages des unités de logement de l'autre ensemble. La deuxième année, les unités de logement du premier ensemble réintègrent l'échantillon et sont remplacées par celles de l'autre ensemble, de la même façon que la première année.

En vertu de ce système, un quart des districts de recensement de l'échantillon et la moitié des ménages de l'échantillon sont remplacés chaque mois. Les trois quarts des districts de l'échantillon sont communs de mois en mois et la moitié d'entre eux d'année en année.

Pourcentage d'unités restant dans l'échantillon durant deux enquêtes successives: 50 pour cent.

Nombre maximum d'interrogatoires par unité de sondage: Quatre.

Durée nécessaire au renouvellement complet de l'échantillon: 16 mois.

Déroulement de l'enquête:

Type d'entretien: Sur papier avec écriture manuelle.

Nombre d'unités finales d'échantillonnage par zone de sondage: Non disponible.

Durée de déroulement de l'enquête:

Totale: 13 jours.

Par zone de sondage: Non disponible.

Organisation: Structure d'enquête permanente (services statistiques des gouvernements préfectoraux). Les enquêteurs sont recrutés temporairement pour chaque enquête.

Nombre de personnes employées: Environ 3 180 personnes.

Substitution des unités finales en cas de non-réponse: Non.

Estimations et redressements:

Taux de non-réponse: Non.

Redressement pour non-réponse: Non.

Imputation en cas de non-réponse à une question spécifique: Non.

Redressement pour les régions/populations non couvertes: Non.

Redressement en cas de sous-représentation: Non.

Redressement en cas de sur-représentation: Non.

Corrections des variations saisonnières: Oui. US Census Methods II (X-11).

Historique de l'enquête:

Titre et date de la première enquête: Labour Force Survey, juillet 1947.

Modifications et révisions significatives: En 1953.

Documentation et dissémination:

Documentation

Titre des publications publiant les résultats: Monthly Report on the Labour Force Survey; Annual Report on the Labour Force Survey (en mars de chaque année).

Titre des publications méthodologiques: Non disponible.

Dissémination

Délai de publication des premiers résultats: Un mois.

Information à l'avance du public des dates de publication initiale des résultats: Oui.

Mise à disposition, sur demande, des données non publiées: Oui.

Mise à disposition des données sur support informatique: Internet.

Site web: http://www.stat.go.jp.

Jordanie

Titre de l'enquête: Employment and Unemployment Surveys, 2001.

Organisme responsable de l'enquête:

Organisation et déroulement de l'enquête: Department of Statistics, Household Surveys Directorate.

Analyse et Publication des résultats: Department of Statistics, Household Surveys Directorate.

Sujets couverts par l'enquête: Emploi et chômage actuels; heures de travail réellement effectuées dans toutes les activités et motif de l'absence temporaire du travail; désir de changer d'emploi et raison de ce désir; niveau d'instruction, industrie actuelle, profession et situation dans la profession dans l'emploi principal; revenu mensuel provenant d'un emploi pour les salariés et les travailleurs indépendants; expérience professionnelle préalable, disponibilité actuelle pour travailler, recherche active d'un emploi, moyens utilisés pour rechercher un emploi, durée de la recherche d'emploi et moment de la dernière recherche d'emploi; activité principale de la population en dehors de la population active.

Champ de l'enquête:

Territoire: Toute la nation, à l'exception des régions nomades.

Groupes de population: La totalité de la population, à l'exception de la population vivant dans des zones reculées (nomade pour la plupart) ou dans des logements collectifs tels qu'hôtels, camps de travail, prisons, etc.

Disponibilité d'estimations selon d'autres sources pour les régions ou groupes exclus: Non.

Groupes couverts par l'enquête mais exclus des résultats publiés: Les non-Jordaniens. Les résultats de l'enquête sont limités à la population jordanienne. Il n'y a pas d'estimations séparées pour les non-Jordaniens.

Périodicité:

Réalisation de l'enquête: Trimestrielle.

Publication des résultats: Trimestrielle et annuelle.

Période de référence:

Emploi: Semaine de référence variable. Sept jours avant la date de l'entretien.

Recherche d'un emploi: Recherche active d'un emploi de la part des chômeurs au cours des quatre semaines précédant la date de l'entretien.

Disponibilité pour travailler: Sept jours avant la date de l'entretien ou dans les 15 jours suivant cette date.

Concepts et définitions:

Emploi: Les personnes âgées de 15 ans et plus ayant travaillé au moins une heure pendant la période de référence dans le secteur public ou le secteur privé. Par « travail », on entend tout travail rémunéré, toute activité rémunérée ou non dans une entreprise que l'on possède en tout ou en partie. Par « personnes ayant un emploi », on entend les salariés et les travailleurs indépendants temporairement absents de leur travail durant la période de référence pour des raisons telles que maladie de l'enquêté, congés, vacances, réduction de l'activité économique (manque de clients, pénurie de demande, etc.), rupture temporaire d'activité de l'établissement (fermeture, pénurie de matières premières, pénurie de carburant et panne électrique ou mécanique).

Chômage: Les personnes âgées de 15 ans et plus, sans emploi mais capables de travailler, disponibles pour ce faire et recherchant activement un emploi. Par « disponibilité pour travailler », on entend être prêt ou disposé à prendre un emploi immédiatement, au cours des sept jours précédant la date de l'entretien ou dans les 15 jours suivant celle-ci. Par « recherchant activement un emploi », on entend avoir effectué des démarches concrètes et avoir passé un certain temps ou tout son temps, pendant les quatre semaines précédant la date de l'entretien, à rechercher un emploi. Par « démarches concrètes », on entend: s'être inscrit et avoir postulé directement auprès d'employeurs, avoir cherché du travail lors de réunions spécialement destinées aux travailleurs ou sur des lieux de rassemblement, avoir fait paraître des petites annonces dans les journaux ou y avoir répondu, avoir cherché de l'aide auprès d'amis et de parents, etc. Les chômeurs incluent les personnes sans emploi, immédiatement disponibles pour travailler et n'ayant pas cherché de travail pendant les quatre semaines précédant la date de l'entretien parce qu'elles attendaient de retourner à leur emploi précédant ou qu'elles avaient trouvé un emploi commençant à une date ultérieure.

Sous-emploi:

Sous-emploi lié à la durée du travail: Se réfère aux personnes ayant un emploi qui veulent trouver un autre emploi ou un emploi supplémentaire et disponibles pour travailler dans un tel emploi durant la période de référence. Les raisons de vouloir trouver un autre emploi ou un emploi supplémentaire sont au nombre de trois: emploi actuel insuffisant en termes de salaire et de primes; emploi actuel non conforme aux qualifications de la personne du point de vue du niveau d'instruction ou emploi actuel ne comportant pas suffisamment d'heures de travail.

Durée du travail: Se réfère au nombre d'heures de travail réellement effectuées durant les sept jours précédant la date de l'entretien. Ce chiffre est la somme de cinq composantes: 1) les heures de travail réellement effectuées durant les périodes de travail normales; 2) les heures supplémentaires; 3) le temps passé sur le lieu de travail à faire autre chose que l'activité professionnelle proprement dite, soit à préparer, à entretenir et à nettoyer les outils de travail et le matériel, soit à rédiger des reçus, des feuilles de présence et des rapports, etc.; 4) le temps passé sur le lieu de travail à attendre ou à être en disponibilité en attendant la fourniture de matériaux ou la réparation d'avaries ou de pannes mécaniques ou électriques, etc.; et 5) le temps passé sur le lieu de travail à prendre de courtes pauses ou des moments de repos.

Cela exclut les heures rémunérées mais non travaillées telles que les vacances annuelles, les jours fériés non ouvrés rémunérés et les congés de maladie payés. Cela exclut également le temps réservé aux pauses-repas, qui ne dépasse normalement pas trois heures, et le temps passé à effectuer le trajet du domicile au lieu de travail et vice versa.

Revenu lié à l'emploi:

Revenu lié à l'emploi salarié: Revenu mensuel. La somme d'argent et les autres bénéfices en nature perçus au cours du mois civil précédant la date de l'entretien. Il peut s'agir de l'un des éléments ci-après: 1) salaires ou traitements, en espèces ou en nature, perçus en contrepartie d'un travail effectué soit en tant qu'employé permanent ou temporaire, soit en tant que stagiaire. Cela inclut le paiement des heures supplémentaires en espèces ou en nature. En cas de cumul d'emplois, le revenu total provenant de toutes les activités doit être déclaré. Les paiements en nature incluent la valeur marchande des vêtements, repas, transports, logements et indemnités analogues fournies par l'employeur; 2) revenu lié à l'emploi indépendant, revenu en espèces ou en nature perçu soit en tant qu'employeur soit en tant que travailleur indépendant quelle que soit la branche d'activité économique.

Revenu lié à l'emploi indépendant: Non disponible.

Secteur informel: Non disponible.

Activité habituelle: Non disponible.

Classifications:

Branche d'activité économique (industrie)

Titre de la classification: Non disponible.

Groupes de population classifiés selon l'industrie: Les personnes ayant un emploi et les chômeurs ayant une expérience professionnelle préalable.

Nombre de groupes de codage: Niveau à 3 chiffres. Les résultats sont publiés au niveau à 1 chiffre avec 17 catégories.

Convertibilité avec la CITI: CITI-Rév.3.

Profession

Titre de la classification: Non disponible.

Groupes de population classifiés selon la profession: Les personnes ayant un emploi et les chômeurs ayant une expérience professionnelle préalable.

Nombre de groupes de codage: Niveau à 3 chiffres. Les résultats sont publiés au niveau à 1 chiffre avec 9 catégories.

Convertibilité avec la CITP: CITP-1988.

Situation dans la profession

Titre de la classification: Non disponible.

Groupes de population classifiés par situation dans la profession: Les personnes ayant un emploi et les chômeurs ayant une expérience professionnelle préalable.

Catégories de codage: Salariés, employeurs, travailleurs indépendants, travailleurs familiaux non rémunérés, travailleurs non rémunérés.

Convertibilité avec la CISP: CISP-1993.

Education

Titre de la classification: Non disponible.

Groupes de population classifiés selon l'éducation: La population âgée de 15 ans et plus.

Catégories de codage: Analphabète; sait lire et écrire; études primaires; niveau préparatoire; enseignement de base; apprentissage professionnel; enseignement secondaire; diplôme d'enseignement secondaire; B.S.C.; diplôme d'études supérieures et au-delà.

Convertibilité avec la CITE: CITE-1997.

Taille de l'échantillon et plan de sondage:

Unité finale d'échantillonnage: Ménages.

Taille de l'échantillon (unités finales d'échantillonnage): 8 800 ménages répartis en 440 unités primaires d'échantillonnage constituant des unités aréolaires ou blocs.

Taux de sondage: 1 pour cent.

Base de sondage: Fondée sur les secteurs du Recensement de 1994 (1994 Population and Housing Census). Chacun des 12 gouvernorats jordaniens a été considéré comme une strate indépendante. Dans chaque gouvernorat, les localités ont été divisées en localités urbaines et localités rurales, sauf pour les cinq plus grandes villes: Amman, Wadi Essier, Zarqa, Russeifa et Irbid. Les localités urbaines et rurales ont ensuite été de nouveau divisées en catégories en fonction de la taille de la population et classées dans l'ordre de leur succession géographique.

Les unités primaires d'échantillonnage de chaque strate ont été divisées en quatre catégories (basse, moyenne, moyenne à haute et haute) selon des scores calculés à l'aide d'informations socioéconomiques basées sur les résultats du Recensement de 1994 (1994 Population and Housing Census). Les unités primaires ainsi constituées ont été ordonnées au sein de chaque strate selon une procédure géographique pour les zones urbaines et rurales et selon des caractéristiques socioéconomiques pour les grandes villes.

L'échantillon a été sélectionné en deux étapes. Au cours de la première étape, un échantillon de 110 unités primaires a été sélectionné avec une probabilité proportionnelle à la taille à l'aide d'une procédure systématique de sélection. Au cours de la deuxième étape, après renouvellement de la base des unités primaires sélectionnées, un nombre constant d'unités finales d'échantillonnage (20 ménages) a été sélectionné dans chaque unité primaire à l'aide d'une procédure systématique à partir de la liste des ménages.

Renouvellement de l'échantillon: les unités finales d'échantillonnage sont renouvelées au stade de l'établissement des listes d'unités primaires retenues dans l'échantillon en préparation de chaque nouvelle enquête.

Rotation:

Schéma: A partir de 2000 a été introduit un échantillon renouvelé selon lequel un ménage-échantillon sélectionné au départ est retenu dans l'échantillon pendant deux enquêtes successives, le quitte pendant deux enquêtes successives et le réintègre pendant deux autres enquêtes successives avant de le quitter définitivement.

Pourcentage d'unités restant dans l'échantillon durant deux enquêtes successives: Selon ce plan, il y a un chevauchement de 75 pour cent des unités d'échantillonnage entre deux trimestres successifs et de 50 pour cent entre deux trimestres séparés par une année.

Nombre maximum d'interrogatoires par unité de sondage: Non disponible.

Durée nécessaire au renouvellement complet de l'échantillon: Une année et demie.

Déroulement de l'enquête:

Type d'entretien: Entretien personnel avec écriture manuelle sur papier.

Nombre d'unités finales d'échantillonnage par zone de sondage: 20 ménages.

Durée de déroulement de l'enquête:

Totale: Un mois, en comptant le renouvellement des unités primaires d'échantillonnage, la sélection des ménages-échantillons et les entretiens.

Par zone de sondage: Non disponible.

Organisation: Permanente.

Nombre de personnes employées: Environ 50 à 60 personnes en comptant les enquêteurs et les cadres.

Substitution des unités finales en cas de non-réponse: Non.

Estimations et redressements:

Taux de non-réponse: 2%. Le nombre d'entretiens achevés après trois rappels, au cours des quatre trimestres de 2001, était de 32 540, ce qui correspond à 92,4 pour cent du nombre total de ménages de l'échantillon. Parmi les raisons pour lesquelles l'entretien n'a pas eu lieu, figurent la fermeture du logement au moment de la visite (4,0 pour cent), la vacuité du logement (2,5 pour cent), l'indisponibilité du répondant désigné et le refus de répondre (0,6 pour cent).

Redressement pour non-réponse: Oui, par l'inverse du taux de réponse par strate.

Imputation en cas de non-réponse à une question spécifique: Non.

Redressement pour les régions/populations non couvertes: Non.

Redressement en cas de sous-représentation: Oui, par estimation par le quotient des données de projection de la population.

Redressement en cas de sur-représentation: Non.

Corrections des variations saisonnières: Non.

Historique de l'enquête:

Titre et date de la première enquête: Employment and unemployment survey, 1982.

Modifications et révisions significatives: Des enquêtes sur la population active ont été réalisées deux fois en 1982, une fois en 1986 et une fois en 1987. Entre 1991 et 1997, des enquêtes ont eu lieu une ou deux fois par an, sauf en 1992 où il n'y en a pas eu. En 1998 et 1999, trois enquêtes ont été réalisées par an, couvrant mai-juin, septembre-octobre et novembre-décembre. Depuis début 2000, l'enquête est réalisée tous les trimestres.

Documentation et dissémination:

Documentation

Titre des publications publiant les résultats: Annual Report of Employment and Unemployment Survey 2001, publié en mars 2002.

Titre des publications méthodologiques: Annual Report of Employment and Unemployment Survey 2001, publié en mars 2002.

Délai de publication des premiers résultats: 2 mois.

Information à l'avance du public des dates de publication initiale des résultats: Non.

Mise à disposition, sur demande, des données non publiées: Oui.

Mise à disposition des données sur support informatique: Les données totalisées sont disponibles sur support informatique à la demande.

Site web: http://www.dos.gov.jo.

Kosovo (Serbie-et-Monténégro)

Titre de l'enquête: Labour Force Survey.

Organisme responsable de l'enquête:

Organisation et déroulement de l'enquête: Office Statistique du Kosovo (Statistical Office of Kosovo), en collaboration avec le Ministère du Travail (Ministry of Labour and Social Welfare).

Analyse et Publication des résultats: Idem.

Sujets couverts par l'enquête: Emploi, chômage, sous-emploi, durée du travail (heures de travail habituelles, heures de travail réellement effectuées), revenu lié à l'emploi, emploi dans le secteur informel, lieu de travail, permanence de l'emploi, durée du chômage, travailleurs découragés, travailleurs occasionnels, industrie, profession, situation dans la profession, niveau d'instruction et de qualification, exercice d'autres emplois, sources de subsistance, revenu des ménages.

Champ de l'enquête:

Territoire: L'ensemble du territoire.

Groupes de population: L'enquête couvre les membres habituels des ménages ordinaires du Kosovo quelle que soit leur origine ethnique (Albanais, Serbes, etc.). Les personnes vivant dans des établissements ne sont pas couvertes. Sont exclus les membres des troupes de la KFOR, le personnel international de la MINUK et les autres étrangers vivant temporairement au Kosovo.

Disponibilité d'estimations selon d'autres sources pour les régions ou groupes exclus: Non.

Groupes couverts par l'enquête mais exclus des résultats publiés: Néant.

Périodicité:

Réalisation de l'enquête: Annuelle (projet). La première enquête a été réalisée en décembre 2001-janvier 2002.

Publication des résultats: Annuelle (projet).

Période de référence:

Emploi: Période de référence variable d'une semaine avant la date de l'entretien.

Recherche d'un emploi: Période de référence variable de quatre semaines avant la date de l'entretien.

Disponibilité pour travailler: Période de référence variable d'une semaine avant la date de l'entretien.

Concepts et définitions:

Emploi: Les personnes âgées de 15 à 64 ans qui, durant la semaine de référence, ont exercé un emploi ou travaillé dans leur propre entreprise/activité, dont elles, leur ménage ou leur famille ont tiré un revenu en espèces ou en nature. Sont inclus les personnes ayant travaillé comme salariés permanents, salariés occasionnels, employeurs, travailleurs indépendants (personnes travaillant à leur compte), exploitants agricoles, membres de coopératives de producteurs, travailleurs familiaux non rémunérés dans une entreprise ou une exploitation agricole appartenant à un ménage ou à une famille, ou les personnes effectuant leur service militaire et les agents de police.

Sont également incluses les personnes âgées de 15 à 64 ans qui, durant la semaine de référence, ont effectué un travail quelconque, rémunéré ou non (sauf la production de biens pour leur usage final personnel et la prestation de services non rémunérés ou personnels dans leur propre ménage), pendant au moins une heure, même s'il s'agissait d'étudiants à plein temps ou à temps complet, de chômeurs, de femmes au foyer ou de retraités et même s'ils ne travaillaient qu'à temps partiel ou occasionnellement. En voici quelques exemples: emploi salarié exercé en tant que salarié à temps partiel ou temporaire, en tant qu'aide, en tant que remplaçant, en tant que travailleur occasionnel, etc.; le travail non rémunéré dans une entreprise ou une exploitation agricole appartenant à un ménage ou à une famille; le travail non rémunéré effectué en tant qu'apprenti; la vente ou l'échange de produits agricoles obtenus dans une parcelle individuelle ou la production de tels produits destinés à la vente; la vente de denrées alimentaires, de boissons, de repas, de vêtements, de livres, de fournitures de bureau, de disques, de cigarettes, de fleurs, etc. dans la rue, sur des marchés ou à domicile; les travaux de réparation de maisons, d'appartements, de voitures ou de biens de consommation durables contre rémunération par des tiers; le transport de passagers ou de marchandises en voiture contre rémunération; les consultations ou cours particuliers payants (de langues, de formation en informatique, etc.); le nettoyage de maisons pour le compte de tiers, le lavage de voitures ou la garde d'enfants contre rémunération.

Au nombre des personnes ayant un emploi figurent également les personnes âgées de 15 à 64 ans ayant un emploi ou une entreprise/activité auxquels elles pouvaient retourner mais qui n'ont pas travaillé pendant la semaine de référence pour l'une quelconque des raisons ci-après: maladie de l'enquêté, accident ou indisposition temporaire; congé de maternité; période d'arrêt pour raisons personnelles; soins apportés à un membre de la famille; congés annuels; autres types de congés; intempéries, incidents techniques ou autres; éducation ou formation; horaire flexible ou jours de liberté; manque de travail, de commandes ou de clients; grève, conflit du travail ou lock-out; mise à pied; autres motifs. Cette catégorie inclut les travailleurs familiaux non rémunérés temporairement absents de leur travail durant la semaine de référence. Sont exclues les personnes ne travaillant pas pendant la semaine de référence parce que leur entreprise a été fermée pour cause de catastrophe naturelle ou du fait des conséquences de la guerre ou pour cause de faillite ou de fermeture, ainsi que les travailleurs saisonniers ne travaillant pas durant la morte-saison.

Les personnes âgées de 15 à 64 ans ayant déclaré être actuellement sans emploi sont classifiées comme ayant un emploi si, pendant la semaine de référence, elles ont exercé une ou plusieurs activités leur ayant rapporté un revenu quelconque, même si elles-mêmes ne considéraient pas ces activités comme du travail.

Chômage: Les personnes âgées de 15 à 64 ans qui: i) n'avaient pas d'emploi pendant la semaine de référence (y compris les personnes dont l'entreprise a été fermée pour cause de catastrophe naturelle ou du fait des conséquences de la guerre, pour cause de faillite ou de fermeture); ii) ont cherché un emploi ou tenté de créer leur propre entreprise ou activité rémunératrice et qui, au cours des quatre dernières semaines, ont effectué une ou plusieurs démarches concrètes pour trouver un emploi ou créer leur propre entreprise ou activité rémunératrice; et iii) étaient immédiatement disponibles pour travailler, c'est-à-dire qu'elles auraient été capables de commencer à travailler et prêtes à le faire durant la semaine de référence si elles en avaient eu la possibilité (y compris les personnes en maladie temporaire pendant la semaine de référence). Cette catégorie inclut les étudiants à plein temps ou à temps partiel, les femmes au foyer ou les retraités cherchant du travail et disponibles pour travailler.

Au nombre des sans emploi figurent aussi les personnes âgées de 15 à 64 ans qui: i) étaient sans emploi pendant la semaine de référence; ii) cherchaient du travail ou voulaient travailler mais n'avaient effectué aucune démarche concrète pour trouver un emploi au cours des quatre dernières semaines; iii) étaient immédiatement disponibles pour travailler; et iv) avaient déjà trouvé un emploi ou pris des dispositions pour commencer à travailler dans leur propre entreprise à une date ultérieure.

Sous-emploi:

Sous-emploi lié à la durée du travail: Les personnes ayant un emploi, dont le nombre total d'heures de travail réellement effectuées pendant la semaine de référence dans l'ensemble des emplois/activités était inférieur à 40 et qui étaient disposées à faire davantage d'heures pendant la semaine de référence et disponibles pour ce faire.

Situations d'emploi inadéquat: Les personnes ayant un emploi et désireuses de changer leur situation d'emploi actuelle (c'est-à-dire les personnes souhaitant voir un changement dans leur emploi/activité actuels, trouver un emploi/une activité supplémentaires ou changer d'emploi/d'activité) pour l'un quelconque des motifs ci-après: par crainte d'être licenciées ou que leur entreprise ne ferme ou parce qu'elles savent que cela va être le cas; parce qu'elles ont un emploi salarié de durée déterminée pour des raisons autres que l'incapacité ou le refus d'occuper un emploi permanent, ou parce qu'elles occupent un emploi temporaire, saisonnier ou occasionnel en tant qu'employeur, que travailleur indépendant (personne travaillant à son compte), que travailleur familial non rémunéré ou que membre d'une coopérative de producteurs et qu'elles souhaitent avoir un emploi plus stable; parce qu'elles veulent faire plus d'heures; pour des raisons personnelles, familiales ou de santé; parce que le revenu total qu'elles perçoivent, provenant de l'ensemble de leurs emplois et activités, est inférieur à 150 DM par mois et qu'elles veulent une meilleure paie ou une meilleure rémunération horaire; parce qu'elles veulent améliorer leurs conditions de travail (modalités horaires de travail plus favorables, emploi moins fatigant); parce que leur emploi actuel est inférieur ou supérieur à leurs qualifications et qu'elles veulent un emploi plus adapté à leurs qualifications ou à leurs capacités; parce qu'elles veulent travailler moins d'heures avec une réduction correspondante de leur revenu; pour d'autres raisons.

Durée du travail: Heures de travail hebdomadaires habituelles; heures supplémentaires effectuées durant la semaine de référence; heures non travaillées pendant la semaine de référence; heures de travail réellement effectuées pendant la semaine de référence. Des informations sur les heures de travail habituelles et les heures de travail réellement effectuées sont recueillies séparément pour l'emploi ou l'activité principale et pour le ou les autres emplois ou activités, le cas échéant.

Revenu lié à l'emploi:
Revenu lié à l'emploi salarié: Salaire ou traitement habituel net par mois. Les informations sont recueillies séparément pour l'emploi ou l'activité principale et pour le ou les autres emplois ou activités, le cas échéant.
Revenu lié à l'emploi indépendant: Bénéfice habituel net par mois. Les informations sont recueillies séparément pour l'emploi ou l'activité principale et pour le ou les autres emplois ou activités, le cas échéant.
Secteur informel: Les entreprises du secteur informel sont définies comme des entreprises ou activités exploitées par des employeurs ou des travailleurs indépendants (personnes travaillant à leur compte) et présentant la totalité des caractéristiques ci-après: l'entreprise/l'activité est une entreprise non constituée en société (entreprise individuelle ou société simple); l'entreprise/l'activité emploie moins de 10 personnes; et l'entreprise/l'activité n'est pas enregistrée auprès de la municipalité. L'emploi dans le secteur informel se réfère au nombre total de personnes employées dans les entreprises du secteur informel, y compris les exploitants d'entreprises de ce secteur, les partenaires commerciaux, les travailleurs familiaux non rémunérés et les salariés.
Activité habituelle: Ce sujet n'est pas couvert par l'enquête.
Classifications:
Branche d'activité économique (industrie)
Titre de la classification: Nomenclature générale des activités économiques dans les Communautés européennes (NACE Rév.1).
Groupes de population classifiés selon l'industrie: Les personnes ayant un emploi; les chômeurs ayant eu une expérience professionnelle au cours des 12 derniers mois; les inactifs ayant eu une expérience professionnelle au cours des 12 derniers mois s'ils voulaient travailler et étaient disponibles pour ce faire pendant la semaine de référence.
Nombre de groupes de codage: Groupes au niveau à 4 chiffres.
Convertibilité avec la CITI: CITI-Rév.3.
Profession
Titre de la classification: Classification internationale type des professions (CITP-1988).
Groupes de population classifiés selon la profession: Les personnes ayant un emploi; les chômeurs ayant eu une expérience professionnelle au cours des 12 derniers mois; les inactifs ayant eu une expérience professionnelle au cours des 12 derniers mois s'ils voulaient travailler et étaient disponibles pour ce faire pendant la semaine de référence.
Nombre de groupes de codage: Groupes de base de la CITP-1988 (niveau à 4 chiffres).
Convertibilité avec la CITP: Ne s'applique pas.
Situation dans la profession
Titre de la classification: Classification nationale d'après la situation dans la profession.
Groupes de population classifiés par situation dans la profession: Les personnes ayant un emploi; les chômeurs ayant eu une expérience professionnelle au cours des 12 derniers mois; les inactifs ayant eu une expérience professionnelle au cours des 12 derniers mois s'ils voulaient travailler et étaient disponibles pour ce faire pendant la semaine de référence.
Catégories de codage: a) Salariés (entreprise d'Etat, institution ou organisation); b) salariés (secteur privé); c) employeurs; d) travailleurs indépendants (personnes travaillant à leur compte) y compris les free-lance; e) travailleurs familiaux non rémunérés; f) membres de coopératives de producteurs.
Convertibilité avec la CISP: CISP-1993.
Education
Titre de la classification: Classification nationale des degrés d'instruction.
Groupes de population classifiés selon l'éducation: Toutes les personnes âgées de 15 à 64 ans.
Catégories de codage: a) Non scolarisé; b) de la première année à la quatrième année d'école élémentaire; c) de la 5ème à la 7ème année d'école élémentaire; d) école élémentaire achevée; e) 1 à 3 ans d'enseignement secondaire professionnel et école pour travailleurs qualifiés; f) enseignement secondaire professionnel durant au moins 4 ans; g) enseignement secondaire du second degré (lycée); h) collège non universitaire; i) université ou école supérieure; j) maîtrise; k) doctorat.
Convertibilité avec la CITE: A établir.
Taille de l'échantillon et plan de sondage:
Unité finale d'échantillonnage: Ménage.
Taille de l'échantillon (unités finales d'échantillonnage): 3 239 ménages.
Taux de sondage: Environ 1,0 pour cent des ménages.
Base de sondage: Listes d'adresses pour 180 secteurs de recensement urbains et 180 villages ou segments de villages. Les listes d'adresses ont été élaborées pour le Living Standards Measurement Survey de 2000. Les secteurs de recensement et les villages et segments de village ont été sélectionnés à partir de strates définies d'après les zones militaires de la KFOR (Etats-Unis, Royaume-Uni, France, Allemagne, Italie), le caractère urbain ou, au contraire, rural, de leurs populations et l'origine ethnique de celles-ci (Albanais par opposition à Serbes, etc.). Pour l'Enquête sur la main-d'œuvre (Labour Force Survey), un nouvel échantillon de ménages a été sélectionné à partir des listes d'adresses.
Renouvellement de l'échantillon: Une nouvelle base de sondage des ménages est en cours d'élaboration.
Rotation:
Schéma: A déterminer.
Pourcentage d'unités restant dans l'échantillon durant deux enquêtes successives: A déterminer.
Nombre maximum d'interrogatoires par unité de sondage: A déterminer.
Durée nécessaire au renouvellement complet de l'échantillon: A déterminer.
Déroulement de l'enquête:
Type d'entretien: Les informations sont obtenues au cours d'entretiens personnels.
Nombre d'unités finales d'échantillonnage par zone de sondage: 8 à 14 ménages par secteur de recensement urbain; 8 ménages par village/segment de village.
Durée de déroulement de l'enquête:
Totale: Environ six semaines.
Par zone de sondage: Une journée, avec quatre enquêteurs.
Organisation: Il n'existe pas encore de structure d'enquête permanente pour cette enquête.
Nombre de personnes employées: 18 cadres et 78 enquêteurs.
Substitution des unités finales en cas de non-réponse: Une réserve de ménages a été sélectionnée pour chaque secteur de recensement et chaque village/segment de village compris dans l'échantillon. Les ménages défaillants ont été remplacés par des ménages pris dans les listes de réserve.
Estimations et redressements:
Taux de non-réponse: Ne s'applique pas.
Redressement pour non-réponse: Ne s'applique pas.
Imputation en cas de non-réponse à une question spécifique: Ne s'applique pas. La non-réponse à une question spécifique est identifiée au cours du processus de mise en forme des données. Les ménages-échantillons sont recontactés pour obtenir les informations manquantes.
Redressement pour les régions/populations non couvertes: Ne s'applique pas.
Redressement en cas de sous-représentation: Non.
Redressement en cas de sur-représentation: Non.
Corrections des variations saisonnières: Ne s'applique pas.
Historique de l'enquête:
Titre et date de la première enquête: La première enquête a été réalisée en décembre 2001-janvier 2002.
Modifications et révisions significatives: Ne s'applique pas.
Documentation et dissémination:
Documentation
Titre des publications publiant les résultats: Statistical Office of Kosovo/Ministry of Labour and Social Welfare: Labour Force Survey 2001.
Titre des publications méthodologiques: La publication susmentionnée inclut les informations méthodologiques concernant l'enquête.
Dissémination
Délai de publication des premiers résultats: Environ quatre mois.
Information à l'avance du public des dates de publication initiale des résultats: Non.
Mise à disposition, sur demande, des données non publiées: Oui.
Mise à disposition des données sur support informatique: Oui.

Koweït

Titre de l'enquête: The Labour Force Sample Survey.
Organisme responsable de l'enquête:
Organisation et déroulement de l'enquête: Central Statistical Office; Census & Population Statistics Department.
Analyse et Publication des résultats: Central Statistical Office; Census & Population Statistics Department.
Sujets couverts par l'enquête: Emploi et chômage actuels; heures de travail réellement effectuées; salaires et traitement des salariés;

niveau d'instruction; industrie, profession et situation dans la profession actuelles dans l'activité principale; nombre de mois passés dans l'emploi actuel; durée du chômage; emploi dans le secteur informel; activité habituelle.

Champ de l'enquête:

Territoire: Le pays tout entier.

Groupes de population: La population totale, aussi bien les Koweitiens que les non-Koweitiens, et les personnes vivant dans des ménages collectifs.

Disponibilité d'estimations selon d'autres sources pour les régions ou groupes exclus: Non disponible.

Groupes couverts par l'enquête mais exclus des résultats publiés: Non disponible.

Périodicité:

Réalisation de l'enquête: Irrégulière: 1973, 1988.

Publication des résultats: A la suite de l'enquête.

Période de référence:

Emploi: Semaine de référence fixe.

Recherche d'un emploi: Même période de référence que pour l'emploi.

Disponibilité pour travailler: Même période de référence que pour l'emploi.

Concepts et définitions:

Emploi: Les personnes âgées de 15 ans et plus constituant la main-d'œuvre disponible pour la production de biens et la prestation de services et qui, pendant la semaine de référence, travaillaient en tant qu'employeur, que travailleur indépendant, que salarié ou que travailleur familial non rémunéré. Au nombre des personnes ayant un emploi figurent les personnes ayant un emploi mais temporairement absentes de leur travail pour cause de maladie, d'accident, de vacances, de congé de maternité, de congé d'éducation ou de formation, de conflit du travail, d'intempéries, de panne mécanique, etc. Cette catégorie inclut aussi les personnes en mise à pied temporaire ou de durée indéterminée sans rémunération et les personnes en congé non rémunéré à l'initiative de l'employeur. Sont également inclus les travailleurs occupés à plein temps ou à temps partiel et en quête d'un autre travail pendant la période de référence ainsi que les étudiants à temps partiel travaillant à plein temps ou à temps partiel. Les étudiants à plein temps travaillant à plein temps ou à temps partiel sont exclus. Les travailleurs familiaux non rémunérés temporairement absents de leur travail sont inclus mais les apprentis et stagiaires rémunérés ou non sont exclus, de même que les travailleurs saisonniers ne travaillant pas durant la morte-saison. Les bénéficiaires de mesures de promotion de l'emploi et les membres des forces armées sont inclus. Les personnes occupées dans la production de biens ou la prestation de services pour leur usage final personnel sont exclues. Sont également exclues les personnes ayant effectué un travail quelconque pendant la semaine de référence mais qui étaient alors assujetties à la scolarité obligatoire ou à la retraite et au bénéfice d'une pension.

Chômage: Les personnes de 15 ans et plus qui, durant la semaine de référence, étaient sans emploi ou ont travaillé moins de 20 heures, étaient immédiatement disponibles pour travailler et cherchaient du travail. Les sans emploi se composent de deux groupes: ceux qui ont travaillé auparavant dans l'Etat du Koweït mais n'avaient pas d'emploi et cherchaient du travail pendant la semaine de référence; et ceux qui n'avaient jamais eu d'emploi auparavant et cherchaient du travail pendant la semaine de référence. Au nombre des sans emploi figurent les personnes sans emploi et immédiatement disponibles pour travailler qui ont pris des dispositions pour commencer à travailler à une date postérieure à la semaine de référence et les personnes sans emploi et immédiatement disponibles pour travailler qui ont essayé de créer leur propre entreprise. Sont également inclus les étudiants à temps partiel en quête d'un emploi à temps partiel ou à plein temps. Les étudiants à plein temps en quête d'un emploi à temps partiel ou à plein temps sont par contre exclus. Sont également exclues les personnes cherchant un emploi et disponibles pour travailler qui étaient assujetties à la scolarité obligatoire ou à la retraite ou au bénéfice d'une pension ainsi que les personnes sans travail et disponibles pour travailler n'ayant pas cherché d'emploi pendant la semaine de référence.

Sous-emploi:

Sous-emploi lié à la durée du travail: Non disponible.

Situations d'emploi inadéquat: Non disponible.

Durée du travail: Se réfère au nombre d'heures de travail réellement effectuées sur le lieu de travail pendant la semaine de référence. Cela inclut les heures de travail effectuées pendant la durée normale du travail ainsi que le temps de travail effectué en plus de la durée normale du travail (heures supplémentaires).

Revenu lié à l'emploi:

Revenu lié à l'emploi salarié: Salaires et traitements: inclut les salaires et traitements directs, les gains totaux en espèces, les paiements en nature ou sous forme de services, la rémunération liée aux bénéfices, les prestations de sécurité sociale liées à l'emploi, le paiement des heures supplémentaires et autres valeurs imputées des biens et des services offerts par le lieu de travail sous forme de paiement en nature du travail effectué.

Revenu lié à l'emploi indépendant: Non disponible.

Emploi dans le secteur informel: Emploi dans des entreprises non enregistrées ou dans des entreprises ou activités non organisées ou dans des micro-entreprises ou micro-activités.

Activité habituelle: Non disponible.

Classifications:

Branche d'activité économique (industrie)

Titre de la classification: Non disponible.

Groupes de population classifiés selon l'industrie: Les personnes ayant un emploi et les chômeurs ayant une expérience professionnelle préalable.

Nombre de groupes de codage: Niveau à 2 chiffres.

Convertibilité avec la CITI: CITI-Rév.3.

Profession

Titre de la classification: Non disponible.

Groupes de population classifiés selon la profession: Les personnes ayant un emploi et les chômeurs ayant une expérience professionnelle préalable.

Nombre de groupes de codage: Niveau à 2 chiffres.

Convertibilité avec la CITP: CITP-1968.

Situation dans la profession

Titre de la classification: Non disponible.

Groupes de population classifiés par situation dans la profession: Les personnes ayant un emploi.

Catégories de codage: Employeur, travailleur indépendant, salarié, travailleur familial non rémunéré.

Convertibilité avec la CISP: Non.

Education

Titre de la classification: Non disponible.

Groupes de population classifiés selon l'éducation: La population âgée de 15 ans et plus.

Catégories de codage: Analphabète, sait lire et écrire, enseignement primaire, enseignement intermédiaire, enseignement secondaire, au-delà de l'enseignement secondaire mais en deçà de l'enseignement universitaire, enseignement universitaire, études de troisième cycle.

Convertibilité avec la CITE: CITE-1976.

Taille de l'échantillon et plan de sondage:

Unité finale d'échantillonnage: Ménages ordinaires et particuliers vivant dans des ménages collectifs.

Taille de l'échantillon (unités finales d'échantillonnage): Environ 11 000 ménages ordinaires et 558 ménages collectifs.

Taux de sondage: 0,05 pour cent.

Base de sondage: Fondée sur les secteurs de recensement du recensement de la population koweïtienne de 1985, stratifiés en 54 strates pour les ménages ordinaires koweïtiens et non koweïtiens et en 43 strates pour les ménages collectifs non koweïtiens.

Les 1729 secteurs de recensement stratifiés ont constitué les unités primaires d'échantillonnage de l'enquête. Quelque 345 unités primaires ont été sélectionnées lors de la première étape de la sélection de l'échantillon. Ces unités ont été renouvelées en faisant la liste de tous les bâtiments, logements et ménages.

Au cours de la deuxième étape, quelque 11 000 ménages ordinaires ont été sélectionnés parmi les unités primaires d'échantillonnage figurant sur les listes. Dans le cas des ménages collectifs, quelque 558 d'entre eux ont été sélectionnés dans les unités primaires retenues dans l'échantillon et environ 11 000 particuliers ont été retenus dans l'échantillon parmi les ménages collectifs sélectionnés.

Renouvellement de l'échantillon: Les unités primaires d'échantillonnage ont été renouvelées lors de l'établissement des listes de la première étape de la sélection de l'échantillon.

Rotation: Pas de schéma de rotation.

Déroulement de l'enquête:

Type d'entretien: Entretiens personnels réalisés par 60 enquêteurs et 5 responsables de secteur.

Nombre d'unités finales d'échantillonnage par zone de sondage: 20 ménages.

Durée de déroulement de l'enquête: Un mois.

Organisation: Permanente.

Nombre de personnes employées sur le terrain et dans les bureaux: Environ 60 enquêteurs, 5 responsables de secteur, 2 employés de bureau, 4 opérateurs préposés à l'entrée des données, 1 expert en statistiques et 1 cadre.

Substitution des unités finales en cas de non-réponse: Oui.
Estimations et redressements:
Taux de non-réponse: Non disponible.
Redressement pour non-réponse: Non.
Imputation en cas de non-réponse à une question spécifique: Non.
Redressement pour les régions/populations non couvertes: Non.
Redressement en cas de sous-représentation: Non.
Redressement en cas de sur-représentation: Non.
Corrections des variations saisonnières: Non.
Historique de l'enquête:
Titre et date de la première enquête: Labour force sample survey, 1973.
Modifications et révisions significatives: Non disponible.
Documentation et dissémination:
Documentation
Titre des publications publiant les résultats: Labour Force Sample Survey, mars 1988, First Part, juin 1990. Ministry of Planning, State of Kuwait.
Titre des publications méthodologiques: Idem.
Dissémination
Délai de publication des premiers résultats: Non disponible.
Information à l'avance du public des dates de publication initiale des résultats: Non.
Mise à disposition, sur demande, des données non publiées: Non disponible.
Mise à disposition des données sur support informatique: Non disponible.

Lettonie

Titre de l'enquête: Latvian Labour Force Survey.
Organisme responsable de l'enquête:
Organisation et déroulement de l'enquête: Central Statistical Bureau.
Analyse et Publication des résultats: Central Statistical Bureau.
Sujets couverts par l'enquête: Emploi, chômage, sous-emploi, durée du travail, salaires, source de revenu, durée du chômage, travailleurs découragés, travailleurs occasionnels, industrie, profession, situation dans la profession, niveau d'instruction, activité habituelle, exercice d'autres emplois et expérience professionnelle préalable.
Champ de l'enquête:
Territoire: L'ensemble du pays.
Groupes de population: Toutes les personnes âgées de 15 ans et plus vivant dans des ménages ordinaires durant la semaine de référence. Sont exclus les membres des ménages absents pendant plus de 3 mois (tels que conscrits, étudiants vivant en résidence, marins, etc.) ainsi que la population institutionnelle (personnes vivant en établissement pénitentiaire ou psychiatrique, à l'hôpital, en prison, etc.).
Disponibilité d'estimations selon d'autres sources pour les régions ou groupes exclus: Non.
Groupes couverts par l'enquête mais exclus des résultats publiés: Néant.
Périodicité:
Réalisation de l'enquête: Deux fois par an.
Publication des résultats: Deux fois par an.
Période de référence:
Emploi: Une semaine (les sept derniers jours précédant la date de l'entretien).
Recherche d'un emploi: Quatre semaines avant la date de l'entretien.
Disponibilité pour travailler: Deux semaines après la date de l'entretien.
Concepts et définitions:
Emploi: Sont considérées comme ayant un emploi toutes les personnes âgées de 15 ans et plus qui, durant la période de référence, a) ont effectué un travail quelconque, rémunéré ou en vue d'un bénéfice (en espèces ou en nature), pendant au moins une heure; b) n'ont pas travaillé mais avaient un emploi ou une entreprise d'où elles étaient temporairement absentes pour cause de vacances/congés annuels, de maladie, de congé de formation professionnelle ou autre motif similaire. De plus, sont considérées comme ayant un emploi les personnes ayant effectué un travail communautaire ou des activités sociales quelconques, rémunérés ou non, ainsi que les femmes en congé parental jusqu'à ce que l'enfant atteigne l'âge de trois mois.
Sont également inclus dans les totaux:
a)les travailleurs occupés à plein temps ou à temps partiel et en quête d'un autre travail durant la période de référence;
b)les étudiants à plein temps ou à temps partiel travaillant à plein temps ou à temps partiel;
c)les personnes ayant effectué un travail quelconque pendant la semaine de référence tout en étant soit à la retraite et au bénéfice d'une pension, soit inscrites en tant que demandeurs d'emploi auprès d'un bureau de placement, ou tout en percevant des allocations de chômage;
d)les travailleurs familiaux, rémunérés ou non (s'ils ont travaillé pendant au moins une heure);
e)les personnes occupées dans la production de biens pour leur usage final personnel.
Chômage: Sont sans emploi toutes les personnes âgées de 15 ans et plus, qu'elles soient inscrites ou non auprès du State Employment Board, qui:
a)n'ont pas travaillé du tout pendant la semaine de référence ou étaient temporairement absentes de leur travail;
b)ont activement cherché un emploi au cours des quatre semaines précédant l'entretien;
c)étaient disponibles pour commencer à travailler dans les deux semaines suivant la semaine de l'enquête.
Sont également incluses dans les chômeurs les personnes n'ayant pas cherché activement du travail parce qu'elles avaient trouvé un emploi et pris des dispositions pour occuper un emploi rémunéré à une date postérieure à la période de référence.
Sous-emploi:
Sous-emploi lié à la durée du travail: Les personnes qui, durant la semaine de référence, ont travaillé (contre leur gré) moins que les heures normales fixées pour des motifs économiques.
Situations d'emploi inadéquat: Les personnes cherchant un autre emploi offrant de meilleures conditions de travail (salaire, situation géographique, antécédents professionnels, etc.).
Durée du travail: Les heures de travail habituelles et réellement effectuées dans l'activité principale. Les heures de travail réellement effectuées dans l'activité ou les activités secondaires.
Revenu lié à l'emploi:
Revenu lié à l'emploi salarié: Salaire brut, impôts compris, perçu dans l'activité principale pour le mois civil complet.
Revenu lié à l'emploi indépendant: Ne s'applique pas.
Secteur informel: Ne s'applique pas.
Activité habituelle: Oui.
Classifications:
Branche d'activité économique (industrie)
Titre de la classification: Nomenclature statistique des activités économiques dans la Communauté européenne (NACE Rév.1).
Groupes de population classifiés selon l'industrie: Les personnes ayant un emploi et les chômeurs ayant une expérience professionnelle préalable (s'ils avaient un emploi au cours des trois dernières années).
Nombre de groupes de codage: 33
Convertibilité avec la CITI: CITI-Rév.3 (au niveau à 2 chiffres).
Profession
Titre de la classification: Classification lettone des professions.
Groupes de population classifiés selon la profession: Les personnes ayant un emploi et les chômeurs ayant une expérience professionnelle préalable (s'ils avaient un emploi au cours des trois dernières années).
Nombre de groupes de codage: Un grand nombre.
Convertibilité avec la CITP: CITP-1988.
Situation dans la profession
Titre de la classification: CISP (Classification internationale d'après la situation dans la profession).
Groupes de population classifiés par situation dans la profession: Les personnes ayant un emploi et les chômeurs ayant une expérience professionnelle préalable (s'ils avaient un emploi au cours des trois dernières années).
Catégories de codage: 4 groupes (salariés, employeurs, travailleurs indépendants, travailleurs familiaux non rémunérés).
Convertibilité avec la CISP: CISP-1993.
Education
Titre de la classification: Classification nationale.
Groupes de population classifiés selon l'éducation: Population totale, personnes ayant un emploi, chômeurs et inactifs.
Catégories de codage: 8 groupes (pas d'enseignement scolaire, enseignement primaire inachevé, enseignement primaire, enseignement professionnel, enseignement secondaire général, enseignement secondaire technique, enseignement secondaire spécialisé, enseignement supérieur).
Convertibilité avec la CITE: Pas l'équivalent intégral de la CITE.
Taille de l'échantillon et plan de sondage:
Unité finale d'échantillonnage: Ménages pour les zones rurales; personnes pour les zones urbaines.

Taille de l'échantillon (unités finales d'échantillonnage): Environ 8 000 ménages.
Taux de sondage: Environ 0,75 pour cent.
Base de sondage: La base de sondage pour les zones urbaines est tirée du registre de la population. La base de sondage pour les zones rurales est construite à partir de la liste complète des ménages.
Renouvellement de l'échantillon: Le dernier renouvellement remonte à 1998.
Rotation:
Schéma: Chaque ménage est retenu dans l'enquête pendant trois enquêtes successives. Ce schéma de rotation fait qu'un tiers des ménages de chaque ville sélectionnée pour figurer dans l'échantillon est remplacé lors d'une nouvelle enquête. Quant aux zones rurales, tous les ménages sont remplacés dans un tiers des unités primaires d'échantillonnage (« pagasts »).
Pourcentage d'unités restant dans l'échantillon durant deux enquêtes successives: 66,7 pour cent.
Nombre maximum d'interrogatoires par unité de sondage: 9.
Durée nécessaire au renouvellement complet de l'échantillon: 18 mois.
Déroulement de l'enquête:
Type d'entretien: Ecriture manuelle sur papier (entretien direct).
Nombre d'unités finales d'échantillonnage par zone de sondage: Sept dans les unités primaires d'échantillonnage rurales; de 15 à 459 dans les unités primaires d'échantillonnage urbaines.
Durée de déroulement de l'enquête:
Totale: Un mois civil.
Par zone de sondage: Un mois civil.
Organisation: Non disponible.
Nombre de personnes employées: Environ 631 personnes et 31 cadres.
Substitution des unités finales en cas de non-réponse: Non.
Estimations et redressements:
Taux de non-réponse: En mai 1999: 9,46%; en mai 2000: 10,12%.
Redressement pour non-réponse: Oui.
Imputation en cas de non-réponse à une question spécifique: Non.
Redressement pour les régions/populations non couvertes: Oui.
Redressement en cas de sous-représentation: Oui.
Redressement en cas de sur-représentation: Oui.
Corrections des variations saisonnières: Non.
Historique de l'enquête:
Titre et date de la première enquête: Latvian Labour Force Survey, novembre 1995.
Modifications et révisions significatives: Depuis mai 1997, des indicateurs tels que le taux d'activité, le taux de participation à la vie active et le taux de chômage sont également calculés au niveau régional.
Documentation et dissémination:
Documentation
Titre des publications publiant les résultats: « Labour Force in Latvia » (deux fois par an), « Monthly Bulletin of Latvian Statistics » (deux fois par an).
Titre des publications méthodologiques: « Labour Force in Latvia » (deux fois par an).
Dissémination
Délai de publication des premiers résultats: Quatre mois.
Information à l'avance du public des dates de publication initiale des résultats: Oui.
Mise à disposition, sur demande, des données non publiées: Oui.
Mise à disposition des données sur support informatique: Disquettes.
Site web: http://www.csb.lv (informations sélectionnées).

Lituanie

Titre de l'enquête: Labour Force Survey (LFS).
Organisme responsable de l'enquête:
Organisation et déroulement de l'enquête: Statistics Lithuania.
Analyse et Publication des résultats: Employment Statistics Division of Statistics Lithuania.
Sujets couverts par l'enquête: Emploi, chômage, sous-emploi, durée du travail, salaires, revenu, emploi dans le secteur informel, durée de l'emploi et du chômage, travailleurs découragés et occasionnels, industrie, profession, situation dans la profession, niveau d'instruction/de qualification, exercice d'autres emplois.
Champ de l'enquête:
Territoire: L'ensemble du pays.
Groupes de population: La population âgée de 15 ans et plus, vivant dans des ménages ordinaires (avant 2000, la population civile âgée de 14 ans et plus), y compris les personnes absentes pour de courtes périodes pour leurs études ainsi que les membres des ménages temporairement absents.
Sont exclus les pensionnaires d'établissements pénitentiaires ou psychiatriques, les conscrits vivant en caserne et les citoyens étrangers.
Disponibilité d'estimations selon d'autres sources pour les régions ou groupes exclus: Non.
Groupes couverts par l'enquête mais exclus des résultats publiés: Néant.
Périodicité:
Réalisation de l'enquête: Deux fois par an, en mai et en novembre de chaque année.
Publication des résultats: Deux fois par an.
Période de référence:
Emploi: Une semaine.
Recherche d'un emploi: Les quatre semaines précédant la semaine de l'entretien.
Disponibilité pour travailler: Dans les deux semaines suivant la semaine de l'entretien.
Concepts et définitions:
Emploi: Sont considérées comme personnes ayant un emploi toutes les personnes âgées de 15 ans et plus qui, durant la semaine de référence, figuraient dans l'une des catégories ci-après:
a)les personnes au travail, soit en tant que salariés soit en tant que travailleurs indépendants, ayant travaillé une heure ou plus contre un salaire ou un traitement en espèces ou en nature, ou en vue d'un bénéfice ou d'un revenu familial en espèces ou en nature;
b)les personnes ayant un emploi mais non au travail, c'est-à-dire les personnes ayant déjà travaillé dans leur emploi actuel (soit en tant que salariés soit en tant que travailleurs indépendants) mais qui étaient absentes de leur travail pendant la semaine de référence et qui avaient un lien formel avec l'emploi.
Sont également inclus dans les personnes ayant un emploi:
a)les personnes ayant un emploi mais temporairement absentes de leur travail pour cause de maladie ou d'accident, de congé de maternité ou de congé parental, de vacances, de formation ou d'interruption du travail pour des raisons économiques ou techniques, d'intempéries, de pannes, etc.;
b)les personnes ayant effectué un travail quelconque, rémunéré ou en vue d'un bénéfice, durant la semaine de référence, tout en étant assujetties à la scolarité obligatoire, ou à la retraite et au bénéfice d'une pension, ou inscrites en tant que demandeurs d'emploi auprès d'un bureau de placement, ou tout en percevant des allocations de chômage;
c)les travailleurs occupés à plein temps ou à temps partiel et en quête d'un travail pendant la semaine de référence;
d)les étudiants à plein temps ou à temps partiel travaillant à plein temps ou à temps partiel;
e)les apprentis et stagiaires rémunérés;
f)les travailleurs familiaux rémunérés ou non;
g)les domestiques privés;
h)les bénéficiaires de mesures de promotion de l'emploi percevant un paiement ou recevant une formation en entreprise;
i)les militaires de carrière et les volontaires rémunérés.
Sont exclus les apprentis et stagiaires non rémunérés, les personnes occupées à leurs propres travaux ménagers et celles effectuant un travail communautaire ou des activités sociales non rémunérés; ces personnes sont classifiées comme inactifs.
Chômage: Toutes les personnes âgées de 15 ans et plus qui:
a)étaient sans emploi durant la semaine de référence;
b)étaient disponibles pour travailler dans les quatre semaines;
c)cherchaient activement un emploi, c'est-à-dire qui avaient effectué des démarches concrètes (telles qu'être inscrit en permanence sur les listes du bureau de placement, avoir pris des contacts avec une agence de placement privée, etc.) au cours des quatre dernières semaines ou qui avaient pris des dispositions pour commencer à travailler dans un nouvel emploi.
Cette catégorie inclut également les étudiants à plein temps ou à temps partiel à la recherche d'un emploi à plein temps ou à temps partiel.
Les personnes sans emploi, disponibles pour travailler mais ne cherchant pas de travail et qui déclarent qu'il n'y a pas d'emploi disponible sont exclues de la catégorie des chômeurs et classifiées parmi les travailleurs découragés.
Sous-emploi:
Sous-emploi lié à la durée du travail: Toutes les personnes ayant un emploi qui soit travaillent à temps partiel parce qu'elles n'ont pas

pu trouver un emploi à plein temps et cherchent un autre emploi, soit ont travaillé moins de 40 heures pendant la semaine de référence et cherchent un autre emploi.
Situations d'emploi inadéquat: Pas encore disponible.
Durée du travail: Les heures de travail effectuées. Celles-ci incluent les heures supplémentaires mais excluent les heures payées mais non travaillées telles que le temps de trajet entre le domicile et le lieu de travail, les heures perdues pour cause de maladie, de vacances, de chômage, etc.
Revenu lié à l'emploi:
Revenu lié à l'emploi salarié: Gains totaux en espèces, y compris les cotisations de sécurité sociale liées à l'emploi, etc. Les paiements en nature (denrées alimentaires) perçus pour un travail dans l'agriculture sont exclus. Cette catégorie se réfère à toutes les activités.
Revenu lié à l'emploi indépendant: Bénéfices bruts.
Secteur informel: Sujet théoriquement couvert par l'enquête.
Activité habituelle: Ne s'applique pas.
Classifications:
Branche d'activité économique (industrie)
Titre de la classification: Classification nationale.
Groupes de population classifiés selon l'industrie: Les personnes ayant un emploi et les chômeurs (industrie du dernier emploi occupé pour ces derniers).
Nombre de groupes de codage: 59 groupes.
Convertibilité avec la CITI: CITI-Rév.3.
Profession
Titre de la classification: Classification nationale.
Groupes de population classifiés selon la profession: Les personnes ayant un emploi et les chômeurs (profession exercée dans le dernier emploi pour ces derniers).
Nombre de groupes de codage: 28 sous-grands groupes, 116 sous-groupes et 390 groupes de base.
Convertibilité avec la CITP: CITP-1988.
Situation dans la profession
Titre de la classification: Classification nationale.
Groupes de population classifiés par situation dans la profession: Les personnes ayant un emploi.
Catégories de codage: 5 groupes: employeurs, salariés, travailleurs indépendants, travailleurs familiaux non rémunérés, travailleurs non classifiés d'après leur situation.
Convertibilité avec la CISP: CISP-1993.
Education
Titre de la classification: Classification nationale.
Groupes de population classifiés selon l'éducation: Les personnes ayant un emploi.
Catégories de codage: 6 groupes: non scolarisé, enseignement primaire, enseignement de base, enseignement secondaire, collège, enseignement supérieur.
Convertibilité avec la CITE: CITE-1997.
Taille de l'échantillon et plan de sondage:
Unité finale d'échantillonnage: Logement.
Taille de l'échantillon (unités finales d'échantillonnage): 8 500 personnes vivant dans 3 000 logements.
Taux de sondage: 0,3 pour cent de la population totale.
Base de sondage: Le registre de la population, qui couvre la population résidente.
Renouvellement de l'échantillon: En continu.
Rotation:
Schéma: Chaque logement retenu dans l'échantillon est interrogé trois fois. Après avoir été conservé dans l'échantillon pendant deux enquêtes successives et exclu de la troisième enquête, il réintègre l'échantillon avant d'en être définitivement exclu.
Pourcentage d'unités restant dans l'échantillon durant deux enquêtes successives: 33 pour cent.
Nombre maximum d'interrogatoires par unité de sondage: Trois.
Durée nécessaire au renouvellement complet de l'échantillon: Deux ans et demi.
Déroulement de l'enquête:
Type d'entretien: Sur papier avec écriture manuelle. Entretiens directs pour 75 pour cent des enquêtés et par téléphone pour les 25 pour cent restants.
Nombre d'unités finales d'échantillonnage par zone de sondage: Non disponible.
Durée de déroulement de l'enquête:
Totale: Non disponible.
Par zone de sondage: Non disponible.
Organisation: Non disponible.
Nombre de personnes employées: 200 enquêteurs et 49 cadres.
Substitution des unités finales en cas de non-réponse: Non.
Estimations et redressements:
Taux de non-réponse: 15%.
Redressement pour non-réponse: Oui.
Imputation en cas de non-réponse à une question spécifique: Non.
Redressement pour les régions/populations non couvertes: Non.
Redressement en cas de sous-représentation: Oui.
Redressement en cas de sur-représentation: Oui.
Corrections des variations saisonnières: Non.
Historique de l'enquête:
Titre et date de la première enquête: Labour Force Survey 1994.
Modifications et révisions significatives: De 1994 à 1999, les personnes âgées de 14 ans et plus. Les questionnaires de l'enquête ont été mis en service en 1998 et 1999.
Documentation et dissémination:
Documentation
Titre des publications publiant les résultats: Labour force, employment and unemployment (semestriel); Economic and Social developments in Lithuania.
Titre des publications méthodologiques: Labour force, employment and unemployment (semestriel); Economic and Social developments in Lithuania.
Dissémination
Délai de publication des premiers résultats: Les résultats de mai sont publiés au cours du 4ème trimestre.
Information à l'avance du public des dates de publication initiale des résultats: Non.
Mise à disposition, sur demande, des données non publiées: Non.
Mise à disposition des données sur support informatique: Site web: http://www.std.lt.

Macao, Chine

Titre de l'enquête: Employment Survey (Inquérito ao Emprego).
Organisme responsable de l'enquête:
Organisation et déroulement de l'enquête: Statistics and Census Service.
Analyse et Publication des résultats: Statistics and Census Service.
Sujets couverts par l'enquête: Emploi, chômage, sous-emploi, durée du travail, salaires, revenu, durée du chômage, travailleurs découragés, industrie, profession, situation dans la profession, éducation, exercice d'autres emplois.
Champ de l'enquête:
Territoire: L'ensemble du territoire de la Région administrative spéciale de Macao.
Groupes de population: La population résidente hors institutions âgée de 14 ans et plus, à l'exception de l'armée.
Disponibilité d'estimations selon d'autres sources pour les régions ou groupes exclus: Non.
Groupes couverts par l'enquête mais exclus des résultats publiés: Non.
Périodicité:
Réalisation de l'enquête: Mensuelle.
Publication des résultats: Mensuelle/trimestrielle.
Période de référence:
Emploi: Période de référence variable d'une semaine avant la date de l'entretien.
Recherche d'un emploi: Période de référence variable d'un mois avant la date de l'entretien.
Disponibilité pour travailler: Période de référence variable d'une semaine avant la date de l'entretien.
Concepts et définitions:
Emploi: Toutes les personnes âgées de 14 ans et plus ayant travaillé au moins une heure durant la semaine de référence en vue d'une rémunération, de bénéfices ou de gains familiaux en espèces ou en nature. Sont également incluses les personnes ayant un emploi mais qui, tout en étant temporairement absentes de leur travail, conservent un lien formel avec l'emploi pour des motifs tels que maladie, maternité, vacances, etc.
Sont également incluses les personnes:
a)ayant un emploi mais temporairement absentes pour des motifs tels que maladie ou accident, congés ou vacances annuelles, congés de maternité/de paternité, absence non rémunérée, ou pour cause d'intempéries, de panne mécanique, etc., ainsi que les personnes en mise à pied sans rémunération ou en mise en congé non rémunéré à l'initiative de l'employeur d'une durée inférieure ou égale à 30 jours et les travailleurs à la recherche d'un autre emploi durant la période de référence;

b)les personnes ayant effectué un travail quelconque, rémunéré ou en vue d'un bénéfice, durant la période de référence, mais qui étaient alors assujetties à la scolarité obligatoire, à la retraite et au bénéfice d'une pension, inscrites en tant que demandeurs d'emploi auprès d'un bureau de placement ou au bénéfice d'une pension;
c)les étudiants à plein temps ou à temps partiel travaillant à plein temps ou à temps partiel, les apprentis et stagiaires rémunérés, les bénéficiaires de mesures subventionnées de promotion de l'emploi;
d)les travailleurs familiaux non rémunérés.
Chômage: Toutes les personnes âgées de 14 ans et plus qui, durant la période de référence, n'avaient ni emploi ni lien formel avec l'emploi, mais qui sont disponibles pour travailler contre rémunération ou pour diriger une entreprise et qui ont cherché du travail au cours du dernier mois. Les démarches de recherche d'emploi peuvent être les suivantes: chercher de l'aide par l'entremise de parents ou d'amis, s'inscrire auprès d'un bureau de placement, faire paraître des petites annonces dans les journaux ou y répondre, postuler directement auprès d'employeurs, s'enquérir d'éventuels emplois auprès de lieux de travail, chercher à se procurer du matériel d'usine, un financement ou un agrément pour créer sa propre entreprise.
Sous-emploi:
Sous-emploi lié à la durée du travail: Les personnes ayant un emploi qui, quelle que soit leur situation par rapport à l'emploi, ont travaillé contre leur gré moins de 35 heures durant la période de référence et ont cherché à prendre un emploi supplémentaire ou sont disponibles pour ce faire.
Situations d'emploi inadéquat: Ne s'applique pas.
Durée du travail: Les heures de travail hebdomadaires normales et réellement effectuées, par référence à l'activité principale et à toutes les activités.
Revenu lié à l'emploi:
Revenu lié à l'emploi salarié: Se réfère aux gains bruts (avant toute déduction), en espèces ou en nature, régulièrement versés au travailleur en échange du temps travaillé ou du travail effectué, ainsi que du temps non travaillé tel que vacances ou autres congés payés.
Revenu lié à l'emploi indépendant: S'obtient en déduisant de la valeur brute de la production les frais d'exploitation et l'amortissement aux prix de remplacement des avoirs productifs. Pour chaque activité, la valeur brute de la production peut se définir comme la valeur de tous les biens et services produits, y compris toute partie retenue pour sa consommation personnelle ou donnée gratuitement ou à des prix réduits aux salariés. Les frais d'exploitation comprennent les versements effectués aux salariés en espèces et/ou en nature et autres dépenses courantes entraînées par l'activité économique, telles que l'achat de matières premières, de carburant, d'outils et de matériel, le paiement des loyers et des intérêts, les coûts de transport et la commercialisation.
Secteur informel: Ne s'applique pas.
Activité habituelle: Ne s'applique pas.
Classifications:
Branche d'activité économique (industrie)
Titre de la classification: Classification nationale.
Groupes de population classifiés selon l'industrie: Les personnes ayant un emploi et les chômeurs (industrie du dernier emploi occupé pour ces derniers).
Nombre de groupes de codage: 66 groupes.
Convertibilité avec la CITI: CITI-Rév.3.
Profession
Titre de la classification: Classification nationale.
Groupes de population classifiés selon la profession: Les personnes ayant un emploi et les chômeurs (profession exercée dans le dernier emploi pour ces derniers).
Nombre de groupes de codage: 10 groupes.
Convertibilité avec la CITP: CITP-1988.
Situation dans la profession
Titre de la classification: Classification nationale.
Groupes de population classifiés par situation dans la profession: Les personnes ayant un emploi.
Catégories de codage: Quatre groupes: employeur, travailleur indépendant, salarié et travailleur familial non rémunéré.
Convertibilité avec la CISP: CISP-1993.
Education
Titre de la classification: Classification nationale.
Groupes de population classifiés selon l'éducation: Les personnes ayant un emploi et les chômeurs.
Catégories de codage: Six groupes: non scolarisé/enseignement préscolaire; enseignement primaire; premier cycle de l'enseignement secondaire; deuxième cycle de l'enseignement secondaire; enseignement tertiaire mais non équivalent à un diplôme universitaire de premier cycle et enseignement tertiaire équivalent à un diplôme universitaire de premier cycle.

Convertibilité avec la CITE: CITE-1997.
Taille de l'échantillon et plan de sondage:
Unité finale d'échantillonnage: Logement.
Taille de l'échantillon (unités finales d'échantillonnage): 3 600 logements par trimestre.
Taux de sondage: 2,25 pour cent.
Base de sondage: Le "Fichier général des unités statistiques" (General File of Statistical Units) du "Service de statistique et du recensement" (Statistics and Census Service), qui contient la liste complète des logements (structures permanentes et temporaires) par ordre géographique.
Renouvellement de l'échantillon: Dossiers administratifs des nouvelles constructions et des immeubles démolis et retour d'information des enquêtes sur les ménages.
Rotation:
Schéma: 50 pour cent de l'échantillon du mois en cours sera recensé trois mois plus tard.
Pourcentage d'unités restant dans l'échantillon durant deux enquêtes successives: 50 pour cent.
Nombre maximum d'interrogatoires par unité de sondage: Deux.
Durée nécessaire au renouvellement complet de l'échantillon: Six mois.
Déroulement de l'enquête:
Type d'entretien: Personnel.
Nombre d'unités finales d'échantillonnage par zone de sondage: Non disponible.
Durée de déroulement de l'enquête:
Totale: 14 jours.
Par zone de sondage: Non disponible.
Organisation: Permanente.
Nombre de personnes employées: 20.
Substitution des unités finales en cas de non-réponse: Non.
Estimations et redressements:
Taux de non-réponse: Environ 8%.
Redressement pour non-réponse: Non.
Imputation en cas de non-réponse à une question spécifique: Non.
Redressement pour les régions/populations non couvertes: Non.
Redressement en cas de sous-représentation: Non.
Redressement en cas de sur-représentation: Non.
Corrections des variations saisonnières: Non.
Historique de l'enquête:
Titre et date de la première enquête: Employment Survey, mai 1989.
Modifications et révisions significatives: Mai 1989-mai 1991: enquête semestrielle (en mai et en novembre) réalisée sur un échantillon de 2 100 logements par enquête. Mai 1992-novembre 1995: enquête trimestrielle (en février, mai, août et novembre) avec une taille d'échantillon de 1 290 logements par enquête. Depuis janvier 1996, enquête mensuelle avec une taille d'échantillon de 1 200 logements par mois.
Documentation et dissémination:
Documentation
Titre des publications publiant les résultats: « Employment Survey »: Brief Report (mensuel); Quaterly Report; Annual Report et Statistical Yearbook.
Titre des publications méthodologiques: Annexe du « Employment Survey ».
Dissémination
Délai de publication des premiers résultats: Un mois après la collecte des données.
Information à l'avance du public des dates de publication initiale des résultats: Non.
Mise à disposition, sur demande, des données non publiées: Oui.
Mise à disposition des données sur support informatique: Oui, et site Web sur Internet: (http://www.dsec.gov.mo/).

Macédoine, Ex-Rép. yougoslave de

Titre de l'enquête: Labour Force Sample Survey
Organisme responsable de l'enquête:
Organisation et déroulement de l'enquête: Statistical Office.
Analyse et Publication des résultats: Statistical Office.
Sujets couverts par l'enquête: Emploi, chômage, durée du travail, salaires, revenu, emploi dans le secteur informel, durée du chômage, travailleurs découragés, travailleurs occasionnels, industrie, profession, situation dans la profession, niveau d'instruction, activité habituelle, exercice d'autres emplois.

Champ de l'enquête:
Territoire: L'ensemble du pays.
Groupes de population: Tous les résidents permanents âgés de 15 ans et plus, y compris ceux qui sont temporairement absents pour une durée inférieure à une année.
Sont exclues les personnes âgées de moins de 15 ans ou de plus de 80 ans ainsi que les personnes se trouvant dans les catégories ci-après:
a)les personnes en mission de longue durée à l'étranger (plus d'une année);
b)les étudiants vivant en résidence et les nomades;
c)les personnes vivant dans des établissements pénitentiaires ou psychiatriques;
d)l'armée;
e)les citoyens étrangers.
Disponibilité d'estimations selon d'autres sources pour les régions ou groupes exclus: Non.
Groupes couverts par l'enquête mais exclus des résultats publiés: Néant.
Périodicité:
Réalisation de l'enquête: Annuelle.
Publication des résultats: Annuelle.
Période de référence:
Emploi: Une semaine avant la date de l'entretien.
Recherche d'un emploi: Une semaine avant la date de l'entretien.
Disponibilité pour travailler: Une semaine après la date de l'entretien.
Concepts et définitions:
Emploi: Les personnes âgées de 15 ans et plus qui, durant la semaine de référence, ont effectué un travail quelconque en tant que salariés, dans leur propre entreprise, leur profession ou dans leur propre exploitation agricole, ou qui ont travaillé au moins une heure en tant que travailleurs familiaux non rémunérés dans une entreprise exploitée par un membre de leur famille. Sont également inclus tous ceux qui ne travaillaient pas mais qui avaient un emploi ou une entreprise d'où ils étaient temporairement absents pour cause de maladie, d'intempéries, de vacances, de formation de qualification avancée, de conflits du travail ou pour des raisons personnelles, ainsi que pour cause de cessation d'activité de l'entreprise.
Sont également inclus dans les totaux:
a)les travailleurs occupés à plein temps ou à temps partiel et en quête d'un autre travail durant la période de référence;
b)les étudiants à plein temps ou à temps partiel travaillant à plein temps ou à temps partiel;
c)les personnes ayant effectué un travail quelconque pendant la semaine de référence tout en étant soit à la retraite et au bénéfice d'une pension, soit inscrites en tant que demandeurs d'emploi auprès d'un bureau de placement ou tout en percevant des allocations de chômage;
d)les domestiques privés;
e)les apprentis et stagiaires rémunérés;
f)les personnes occupées dans la production de biens pour leur usage final personnel (agriculture vivrière, par exemple).
Chômage: Sont sans emploi toutes les personnes âgées de 15 ans et plus qui n'avaient pas d'emploi durant la semaine de référence, étaient disponibles pour travailler pendant la semaine de référence ou dans la semaine qui suivait et qui avaient effectué des démarches concrètes pour trouver un emploi.
Sous-emploi:
Sous-emploi lié à la durée du travail: Les personnes travaillant moins d'heures que la durée normale du travail, disposées à faire davantage d'heures et disponibles pour ce faire.
Situations d'emploi inadéquat: Non disponible.
Durée du travail: Les heures de travail habituelles et réellement effectuées.
Revenu lié à l'emploi:
Revenu lié à l'emploi salarié: Les gains mensuels habituels (gains nets) perçus dans l'activité principale.
Revenu lié à l'emploi indépendant: Les gains mensuels habituels (gains nets) perçus dans l'activité principale.
Secteur informel: Non disponible.
Activité habituelle: Situation au cours des 12 derniers mois.
Classifications:
Branche d'activité économique (industrie)
Titre de la classification: Classification nationale.
Groupes de population classifiés selon l'industrie: Les personnes ayant un emploi.
Nombre de groupes de codage: 14.
Convertibilité avec la CITI: Non.
Profession
Titre de la classification: Classification nationale.
Groupes de population classifiés selon la profession: Les personnes ayant un emploi.
Nombre de groupes de codage: 10.
Convertibilité avec la CITP: Non.
Situation dans la profession
Titre de la classification: Classification nationale.
Groupes de population classifiés par situation dans la profession: Les personnes ayant un emploi.
Catégories de codage: 4 groupes (salariés, employeurs, travailleurs indépendants, travailleurs familiaux non rémunérés).
Convertibilité avec la CISP: Oui.
Education
Titre de la classification: Classification nationale.
Groupes de population classifiés selon l'éducation: Les personnes ayant un emploi et les chômeurs.
Catégories de codage: 9 groupes (sans instruction, enseignement primaire inachevé, enseignement primaire, trois ans d'enseignement secondaire, quatre ans d'enseignement secondaire, enseignement supérieur, niveau universitaire, maîtrise et doctorat).
Convertibilité avec la CITE: Non.
Taille de l'échantillon et plan de sondage:
Unité finale d'échantillonnage: Ménage.
Taille de l'échantillon (unités finales d'échantillonnage): 7 200 ménages.
Taux de sondage: 1,3 pour cent du nombre total de ménages.
Base de sondage: La base de sondage est construite à partir du recensement de la population de 1994 et du registre de la population.
Renouvellement de l'échantillon: Annuel.
Rotation:
Schéma: Non disponible.
Pourcentage d'unités restant dans l'échantillon durant deux enquêtes successives: 34, 5 pour cent.
Nombre maximum d'interrogatoires par unité de sondage: 3.
Durée nécessaire au renouvellement complet de l'échantillon: Quatre ans.
Déroulement de l'enquête:
Type d'entretien: Ecriture manuelle sur papier.
Nombre d'unités finales d'échantillonnage par zone de sondage: 8 ménages.
Durée de déroulement de l'enquête:
Totale: Non disponible.
Par zone de sondage: Non disponible.
Organisation: Permanente.
Nombre de personnes employées: 117 enquêteurs.
Substitution des unités finales en cas de non-réponse: Non.
Estimations et redressements:
Taux de non-réponse: Non.
Redressement pour non-réponse: Non.
Imputation en cas de non-réponse à une question spécifique: Non.
Redressement pour les régions/populations non couvertes: Non.
Redressement en cas de sous-représentation: Non.
Redressement en cas de sur-représentation: Non.
Corrections des variations saisonnières: Non.
Historique de l'enquête:
Titre et date de la première enquête: Labour Force Survey, avril 1996.
Modifications et révisions significatives: Depuis 1996, un certain nombre de modifications ont été introduites en 1997, 1998 et 1999.
Documentation et dissémination:
Documentation
Titre des publications publiant les résultats: « Labour Force Survey: Basic definitions, methods and final results » (annuel).
Titre des publications méthodologiques: « Labour Force Survey: Basic definitions, methods and final results ».
Dissémination
Délai de publication des premiers résultats: Non disponible.
Information à l'avance du public des dates de publication initiale des résultats: Oui.
Mise à disposition, sur demande, des données non publiées: Non.
Mise à disposition des données sur support informatique: Disquettes, Internet et courrier électronique.

Malaisie

Titre de l'enquête: The Labour Force Survey.
Organisme responsable de l'enquête:
Organisation et déroulement de l'enquête: Department of Statistics.

Analyse et Publication des résultats: Department of Statistics.
Sujets couverts par l'enquête: Emploi, chômage, sous-emploi, durée du travail, emploi dans le secteur informel (tiré de la situation dans la profession), industrie, profession, situation dans la profession, niveau d'instruction, activité habituelle.
Champ de l'enquête:
Territoire: L'ensemble du pays.
Groupes de population: Tous les résidents habituels (3 mois ou plus) de logements privés. Sont exclues les personnes résidant dans des « logements collectifs » (tels qu'hôtels, résidences, casernes, prisons, etc.).
Disponibilité d'estimations selon d'autres sources pour les régions ou groupes exclus: Non disponible.
Groupes couverts par l'enquête mais exclus des résultats publiés: Non disponible.
Périodicité:
Réalisation de l'enquête: Trimestrielle.
Publication des résultats: Trimestrielle et annuelle.
Période de référence:
Emploi: Une semaine.
Recherche d'un emploi: Un trimestre fixe.
Disponibilité pour travailler: Non disponible.
Concepts et définitions:
Emploi: Toutes les personnes âgées de 15 à 64 ans qui, à un moment quelconque durant la semaine de référence, ont effectué un travail quelconque (pendant au moins une heure), rémunéré, en vue d'un bénéfice ou d'un gain familial (en tant qu'employeur, salarié, travailleur indépendant ou travailleur familial non rémunéré). Sont également considérées comme ayant un emploi les personnes qui, tout en n'ayant pas travaillé pendant la semaine de référence pour cause de maladie, d'accident, d'invalidité, d'intempéries, de vacances, de conflit du travail ou pour des motifs sociaux et religieux, avaient un emploi, une exploitation agricole, une entreprise ou autre entreprise familiale auxquels retourner. Sont également incluses les personnes en mise à pied temporaire rémunérée dont il était certain qu'elles seraient rappelées au travail.
Cette catégorie inclut également:
a)les personnes ayant un emploi mais temporairement absentes pour cause de congé de maternité ou de paternité, de congé parental, de congé d'éducation ou de formation, d'absence non autorisée, de conflit du travail ou d'intempéries;
b)les travailleurs occupés à plein temps ou à temps partiel et en quête d'un autre travail pendant la période de référence;
c)les personnes ayant effectué un travail quelconque, rémunéré ou en vue d'un bénéfice, pendant la période de référence, mais qui étaient alors inscrites en tant que demandeurs d'emploi auprès d'un bureau de placement ou qui percevaient des allocations de chômage;
d)les étudiants à temps partiel travaillant à plein temps ou à temps partiel;
e)les apprentis et stagiaires rémunérés;
f)les travailleurs familiaux non rémunérés, au travail ou temporairement absents de leur travail pendant la semaine de référence;
g)les personnes occupées dans l'agriculture vivrière;
h)tous les membres des forces armées.
Chômage: Cette catégorie inclut aussi bien les chômeurs recherchant activement un emploi que les chômeurs ne recherchant pas activement un emploi. Les premiers incluent toutes les personnes âgées de 15 à 64 ans n'ayant pas travaillé pendant la semaine de référence mais disponibles pour travailler et qui ont cherché activement du travail durant la période de référence.
Les seconds incluent toutes les personnes âgées de 15 à 64 ans n'ayant pas cherché de travail parce qu'elles pensaient qu'il n'y en avait pas ou que s'il y en avait, elles n'étaient pas qualifiées pour l'effectuer, celles qui auraient cherché du travail si elles n'avaient pas été temporairement malades ou obligées de garder la chambre, ou s'il n'y avait pas eu d'intempéries, celles qui attendaient une réponse aux candidatures qu'elles avaient présentées et celles qui avaient cherché du travail avant la semaine de référence (c'est-à-dire au cours des trois derniers mois précédant l'entretien), ainsi que les personnes sans emploi et actuellement disponibles pour travailler ayant pris des dispositions pour commencer à travailler dans un nouvel emploi dans les 30 jours à compter de la date de l'entretien.
Démarches de recherche d'emploi: S'inscrire auprès d'un bureau de placement/d'une bourse du travail ou à un registre professionnel; visiter des lieux de travail ou rencontrer des employeurs potentiels; faire paraître des petites annonces ou y répondre; rédiger des lettres de candidature; prendre contact avec des syndicats ou assimilés; s'enquérir des possibilités professionnelles ou industrielles et commerciales; informer ses amis ou parents, etc.
La période de recherche d'emploi est classifiée en 5 groupes: moins de 3 mois, de 3 à 6 mois, de 6 à 12 mois, de 1 à 3 ans, plus de 3 ans.
Cette catégorie inclut également:
a)les personnes en mise à pied temporaire ou de durée indéterminée sans rémunération, ou en congé non rémunéré à l'initiative de l'employeur;
b)les étudiants à temps partiel à la recherche d'un emploi à plein temps ou à temps partiel;
c)les personnes en quête d'un emploi et/ou immédiatement disponibles pour travailler, mais à la retraite et au bénéfice d'une pension;
d)les apprentis et stagiaires non rémunérés et les travailleurs saisonniers ne travaillant pas durant la morte-saison.
Sous-emploi:
Sous-emploi lié à la durée du travail: Les personnes ayant travaillé moins de 30 heures durant la semaine de référence, pour des motifs tels que charge de travail insuffisante, nature de l'emploi ou autres, mais capables de faire davantage d'heures si elles en avaient eu la possibilité et disposées à le faire.
Situations d'emploi inadéquat: Ne s'applique pas.
Durée du travail: Les heures de travail réellement effectuées pendant la semaine de référence dans toutes les activités.
Revenu lié à l'emploi:
Revenu lié à l'emploi salarié: Ne s'applique pas.
Revenu lié à l'emploi indépendant: Ne s'applique pas.
Emploi dans le secteur informel: Pas de question spécifique, mais pourrait être partiellement dérivé, comme variable de remplacement, de la situation dans l'emploi des travailleurs par référence à l'activité principale.
Activité habituelle: La profession que l'enquêté a exercée habituellement au cours des 12 derniers mois.
Classifications:
Branche d'activité économique (industrie)
Titre de la classification: Malaysian Industrial Classification.
Groupes de population classifiés selon l'industrie: Les personnes ayant un emploi.
Nombre de groupes de codage: 9.
Convertibilité avec la CITI: Oui, à tous les niveaux.
Profession
Titre de la classification: Malaysian Occupational Classification.
Groupes de population classifiés selon la profession: Les personnes ayant un emploi.
Nombre de groupes de codage: 9.
Convertibilité avec la CITP: Oui, à tous les niveaux.
Situation dans la profession
Titre de la classification: Non disponible.
Groupes de population classifiés par situation dans la profession: Les personnes ayant un emploi.
Catégories de codage: Quatre groupes: 1. employeur; 2. salarié; 3. travailleur indépendant; 4. travailleur familial non rémunéré.
Convertibilité avec la CISP: Oui.
Education
Titre de la classification: Non disponible.
Groupes de population classifiés selon l'éducation: Tous les membres des ménages.
Catégories de codage: Quatre groupes: 1. école primaire – de la première à la sixième années (de 6 à 12 ans); 2. premier cycle de l'enseignement secondaire (de 13 à 15 ans); 3. deuxième cycle de l'enseignement secondaire (de 16 à 17 ans); 4. enseignement tertiaire (17 ans et plus).
Convertibilité avec la CITE: Oui, à tous les niveaux, corrigés pour tenir compte de la situation locale.
Taille de l'échantillon et plan de sondage:
Unité finale d'échantillonnage: Ménage.
Taille de l'échantillon (unités finales d'échantillonnage): 60 000 ménages.
Taux de sondage: Non disponible.
Base de sondage: La base de sondage (National Household Sampling Frame) se compose d'îlots de recensement créés pour le Recensement de la population et du logement de 1991 (1991 Census of Population and Housing). Les îlots de recensement sont des superficies de terrain contiguës géographiquement avec des limites repérables contenant chacun environ 600 personnes. Ces îlots sont constitués dans des limites administratives.
Renouvellement de l'échantillon: Chaque année, avant le début du recensement, les unités secondaires d'échantillonnage ou logements au sein des îlots de recensement sont renouvelés pour inclure les nouveaux logements dans le processus de sélection de l'échantillon. Lorsque le recensement de 2000 sera en vigueur, il remplacera la base actuelle. Les îlots de recensement situés dans des secteurs de croissance (avec des populations marquées par le surpeuplement)

seront subdivisés en îlots plus petits pour conserver la même taille de population d'environ 600 personnes.
Rotation: Non disponible.
Schéma: Non disponible.
Pourcentage d'unités restant dans l'échantillon durant deux enquêtes successives: Non disponible.
Nombre maximum d'interrogatoires par unité de sondage: NON DISPONIBLE.
Durée nécessaire au renouvellement complet de l'échantillon: NON DISPONIBLE.
Déroulement de l'enquête:
Type d'entretien: Entretien direct. Si les enquêtés des logements ne sont pas disponibles après trois tentatives, l'entretien a lieu par téléphone.
Nombre d'unités finales d'échantillonnage par zone de sondage: Non disponible.
Durée de déroulement de l'enquête:
Totale: Quatre semaines, plus une semaine de cartographie à chaque trimestre de l'année (à chaque enquête).
Par zone de sondage: Non disponible.
Organisation: Le personnel permanent du Département de statistiques (Department of Statistics).
Nombre de personnes employées: Un enquêteur couvre un îlot de recensement. Environ 10 enquêteurs pour un cadre.
Substitution des unités finales en cas de non-réponse: Oui.
Estimations et redressements:
Taux de non-réponse: 4%.
Redressement pour non-réponse: Oui.
Imputation en cas de non-réponse à une question spécifique: Oui. En cas de non-réponse, des informations relatives aux personnes venant du logement répondant le plus proche sont insérées.
Redressement pour les régions/populations non couvertes: Non.
Redressement en cas de sous-représentation: Non.
Redressement en cas de sur-représentation: Non.
Corrections des variations saisonnières: Non.
Historique de l'enquête:
Titre et date de la première enquête: National Survey on Employment, Unemployment and Under-employment, 1962.
Modifications et révisions significatives:
1964-1965: ne couvrait que les grands centres urbains de la Malaisie péninsulaire.
1967-1968: Malaysian Sample Survey of Households (trois enquêtes).
1974-2000: réalisation du Labour Force Survey, sauf en 1991 et 1994.
Documentation et dissémination:
Documentation
Titre des publications publiant les résultats: The Labour Force Survey (annuel). **(Périodicité:** annuelle).
Titre des publications méthodologiques: Idem.
Dissémination
Délai de publication des premiers résultats: Les résultats de 1999 ont été publiés en décembre 1999.
Information à l'avance du public des dates de publication initiale des résultats: Oui.
Mise à disposition, sur demande, des données non publiées: Oui.
Mise à disposition des données sur support informatique: Oui.
Site web: http://www.statistics.gov.my/.

Maroc

Titre de l'enquête: Enquête nationale sur l'emploi.
Organisme responsable de l'enquête:
Organisation et déroulement de l'enquête: Direction de la Statistique.
Analyse et Publication des résultats: Direction de la Statistique.
Sujets couverts par l'enquête: Emploi, chômage, sous-emploi, durée du travail, salaires, emploi dans le secteur informel, durée de l'emploi et du chômage, travailleurs occasionnels, industrie, profession, situation dans la profession, niveau d'éducation, autres emplois.
Champ de l'enquête:
Territoire: Ensemble du pays.
Groupes de population: Personnes âgées de 15 ans et plus. Sont exclues du champ de l'enquête les personnes faisant partie de la population vivant dans des ménages collectifs tels que casernes, prisons, chantiers de travaux publics, etc.
Disponibilité d'estimations selon d'autres sources pour les régions ou groupes exclus: Pas d'information.
Groupes couverts par l'enquête mais exclus des résultats publiés: Aucun.
Périodicité:
Réalisation de l'enquête: Continue.
Publication des résultats: Trimestriellement et annuellement.
Période de référence:
Emploi: Un jour.
Recherche d'un emploi: Un jour.
Disponibilité pour travailler: Quatre semaines.
Concepts et définitions:
Emploi: La population active occupée comprend toutes les personnes de 15 ans et plus participant à la production de biens et services, ne serait ce que pour une heure, pendant les 24 heures qui précèdent l'entretien, ainsi que toutes les personnes pourvues normalement d'un emploi, mais temporairement absentes de leur travail.
Sont considérés comme ayant un emploi:
a) les personnes temporairement absentes pour cause de maladie ou accident, congés ou vacances annuelles, congé de maternité ou paternité ou parental, congé d'éducation ou de formation dans le cadre de l'entreprise et pour une durée inférieure à deux mois avec assurance de retravailler, conflits du travail de moins de deux mois, intempéries, panne mécanique, etc.
b) les personnes mises à pied temporairement sans rémunération mais ayant gardé un lien formel avec l'emploi;
c) les travailleurs à plein temps ou à temps partiel à la recherche d'un autre emploi durant la période de référence;
d) les personnes assujetties à la scolarité obligatoire, en retraite ou bénéficiant d'une pension, inscrites comme demandeurs d'emploi ou percevant des allocations de chômage, qui ont effectué un travail quelconque (rémunéré ou en vue d'un bénéfice) pendant la période de référence;
e) les étudiants à plein temps ou à temps partiel travaillant à plein temps ou à temps partiel;
f) les apprentis et stagiaires rémunérés et, s'ils participent à la production, les apprentis et stagiaires non rémunérés;
g) les travailleurs familiaux non rémunérés travaillant durant la période de référence ou temporairement absents pour une période inférieure à deux mois et ayant gardé un lien formel avec l'emploi;
h) les personnes occupées dans la production de biens pour leur usage final personnel;
i) les volontaires et militaires de carrière, les conscrits ainsi que les personnes effectuant un service civil équivalent au service militaire.
Chômage: Personnes de 15 ans et plus, sans activité professionnelle, disponibles pour travailler et à la recherche d'un emploi, y compris les travailleurs découragés.
Sont également considérées comme chômeurs:
a) les personnes temporairement absentes de leur travail pour cause de mise à pied de durée indéterminée sans rémunération ou mise en congés non rémunérés à l'initiative de l'employeur;
b) les personnes sans emploi et immédiatement disponibles pour travailler qui ont pris des dispositions pour travailler dans un nouvel emploi à une date ultérieure ou qui ont essayé de créer leur propre entreprise;
c) les personnes en quête d'un emploi et/ou immédiatement disponibles pour travailler mais qui étaient soumises à la scolarité obligatoire, en retraite ou au bénéfice d'une pension;
d) les étudiants à plein ou à temps partiel à la recherche d'un emploi à plein ou à temps partiel;
e) les travailleurs saisonniers ne travaillant pas durant la saison morte et non payés durant cette période.
Sous-emploi:
Sous-emploi lié à la durée du travail: Personnes de 15 ans et plus ayant travaillé moins de 48 heures au cours de la semaine de référence, disposées à faire des heures complémentaires et disponibles pour les faire.
Situations d'emploi inadéquat: Personnes de 15 ans et plus ayant travaillé plus que 48 heures durant la semaine de référence et qui déclarent être à la recherche d'un autre emploi ou disposées à changer d'emploi pour l'une des deux raisons suivantes:
a) inadéquation de leur emploi actuel avec leur formation ou leur qualification;
b) insuffisance du revenu procuré par leur travail actuel.
Durée du travail: Heures effectivement travaillées durant la semaine.
Revenu lié à l'emploi:
Revenu lié à l'emploi salarié: Salaires en espèces et/ou en nature, y compris les prestations de la sécurité sociale et les autres avantages liés à l'emploi.
Revenu lié à l'emploi indépendant: Exclu du champ de l'enquête.
Secteur informel: Exclu du champ de l'enquête.
Activité habituelle: Pas d'information.

Classifications:
Branche d'activité économique (industrie)
Titre de la classification: Classification nationale.
Groupes de population classifiés selon l'industrie: Personnes ayant un emploi et chômeurs (industrie du dernier emploi pour les chômeurs).
Nombre de groupes de codage: 17 grands groupes.
Convertibilité avec la CITI: CITI-Rév.3.
Profession
Titre de la classification: Classification nationale.
Groupes de population classifiés selon la profession: Personnes ayant un emploi et chômeurs (profession du dernier emploi pour les chômeurs).
Nombre de groupes de codage: 11 grand groupes.
Convertibilité avec la CITP: CITP-88.
Situation dans la profession
Titre de la classification: Classification nationale.
Groupes de population classifiés par situation dans la profession: Personnes ayant un emploi et chômeurs (situation dans la profession du dernier emploi pour les chômeurs).
Catégories de codage: Salariés, travailleurs indépendants, employeurs, aides familiaux, apprentis, associées ou membres de coopératives, personnes en formation-insertion, autres.
Convertibilité avec la CISP: CISP-1993.
Education
Titre de la classification: Classification nationale.
Groupes de population classifiés selon l'éducation: Personnes ayant un emploi et chômeurs.
Catégories de codage: Préscolaire, école coranique, fondamental 1, fondamental 2, secondaire, supérieur, autre.
Convertibilité avec la CITE: CITE-1976 et CITE-1997.
Taille de l'échantillon et plan de sondage:
Unité finale d'échantillonnage: Ménage.
Taille de l'échantillon (unités finales d'échantillonnage): 48 000 ménages dont 17 000 en zone rurale.
Taux de sondage: 1/100.
Base de sondage: Recensement Général de la Population et de l'Habitat de 1994 (RGPH 1994). Echantillon aréolaire à deux degrés: les unités primaires (UP) sont constituées de zones aréolaires de 600 ménages en moyenne constituées sur la base des travaux cartographiques du RGPH; les UP sont découpées en segments de 25 ménages.
Renouvellement de l'échantillon: Chaque année par moitié.
Rotation:
Schéma: Renouvellement partiel de l'échantillon.
Pourcentage d'unités restant dans l'échantillon durant deux enquêtes successives: 50 %.
Nombre maximum d'interrogatoires par unité de sondage: Deux.
Durée nécessaire au renouvellement complet de l'échantillon: Deux ans.
Déroulement de l'enquête:
Type d'entretien: Entrevues directes; questionnaire papier.
Nombre d'unités finales d'échantillonnage par zone de sondage: Pas d'information.
Durée de déroulement de l'enquête:
Totale: Une année.
Par zone de sondage: 45 minutes par ménage.
Organisation: Pas d'information.
Nombre de personnes employées: 15 superviseurs.
Substitution des unités finales en cas de non-réponse: Pas d'information.
Estimations et redressements:
Taux de non-réponse: 12 %.
Redressement pour non-réponse: Oui.
Imputation en cas de non réponse à une question spécifique: Oui.
Redressement pour les régions/populations non couvertes: Oui.
Redressement en cas de sous-représentation: Oui.
Redressement en cas de sur-représentation: Oui.
Corrections des variations saisonnières: Non.
Historique de l'enquête:
Titre et date de la première enquête: Enquête permanente sur l'emploi en milieu urbain 1976.
Modifications et révisions significatives: Révisions opérées à l'occasion des recensements de la population de 1982 et 1994: changement de la base de sondage, révision des questionnaires à la lumière de l'expérience, etc. Ces révisions n'ont pas provoqué de ruptures importantes dans les séries historiques.
Documentation et dissémination:
Documentation
Titre des publications publiant les résultats: Activité, emploi et chômage (trimestriel); Activité, emploi et chômage: rapport de synthèse (annuel); Activité, emploi et chômage: rapport des résultats détaillés (annuel); Annuaire Statistique du Maroc.
Titre des publications méthodologiques: Activité, emploi et chômage: rapport des résultats détaillés (annuel).
Dissémination
Délai de publication des premiers résultats: Avant la fin du 2ème mois du trimestre suivant, pour les résultats trimestriels. Rapport de synthèse: mai de l'année suivante.
Information à l'avance du public des dates de publication initiale des résultats: Pas d'information.
Mise à disposition, sur demande, des données non publiées: Oui, après étude de faisabilité.
Mise à disposition des données sur support informatique: En fonction du type de renseignements demandés.
Site web: http://www.statistic.gov.ma.

Maurice

Titre de l'enquête: Labour Force Sample Survey.
Organisme responsable de l'enquête:
Organisation et déroulement de l'enquête: Central Statistical Office, Ministry of Economic Planning and Development.
Analyse et Publication des résultats: Central Statistical Office, Ministry of Economic Planning and Development.
Sujets couverts par l'enquête: Emploi, chômage, sous-emploi, durée du travail (heures de travail normales/habituelles, heures de travail réellement effectuées), salaires/traitements, durée de l'emploi, durée du chômage, industrie, profession, situation dans la profession, niveau d'instruction et de qualification, activité habituelle, exercice d'autres emplois.
Champ de l'enquête:
Territoire: L'ensemble du pays (îles de Maurice et de Rodrigues).
Groupes de population: L'enquête couvre toute la population mauricienne résidente de la République de Maurice vivant dans des ménages ordinaires. Les personnes vivant en institution et les ménages étrangers (par exemple le personnel des ambassades et les étrangers travaillant à façon à Maurice) ne sont pas couverts.
Disponibilité d'estimations selon d'autres sources pour les régions ou groupes exclus: Non disponible.
Groupes couverts par l'enquête mais exclus des résultats publiés: Non disponible.
Périodicité:
Réalisation de l'enquête: Tous les dix ans, au milieu de la période séparant deux recensements. La dernière enquête a été réalisée en juin-juillet 1995.
Publication des résultats: Les résultats de la dernière enquête ont été publiés en janvier-mars 1997.
Période de référence:
Emploi: Période de référence fixe d'une semaine.
Recherche d'un emploi: Période de référence variable de deux mois avant la date de l'entretien.
Disponibilité pour travailler: Période de référence variable d'une semaine avant la date de l'entretien.
Concepts et définitions:
Emploi: Les personnes âgées de 12 ans et plus ayant effectué un travail quelconque (pendant au moins une heure), rémunéré, en vue d'un bénéfice ou d'un gain familial au cours de la semaine de référence. Sont également incluses les personnes qui étaient temporairement absentes de leur travail pendant la semaine de référence pour cause de maladie, de vacances, de manque de travail, de conflit du travail, etc.
Dans le cadre de l'enquête, le travail implique la production de biens ou la prestation de services normalement destinés à la mise à la vente sur le marché, mais certains types de production non marchande sont aussi inclus. En règle générale, il s'agit de la production de produits primaires destinés à la consommation personnelle, de travaux de construction pour son propre compte et de production d'autres actifs immobilisés pour son usage personnel.
Les activités domestiques et les travaux communautaires sont exclus.
Chômage: Les personnes âgées de 12 ans et plus qui n'avaient pas d'emploi pendant la semaine de référence, étaient disponibles pour travailler pendant cette semaine-là et avaient effectué des démarches concrètes pour chercher du travail à un moment quelconque au cours des deux mois précédant la date de l'entretien. La recherche d'un emploi n'implique pas seulement le fait de chercher un emploi salarié mais couvre également les démarches effectuées pour créer sa

propre entreprise (emploi indépendant). Les personnes sans emploi et disponibles pour travailler mais qui ne cherchent pas d'emploi parce qu'elles ont déjà pris des dispositions pour commencer à travailler à une date postérieure à la semaine de référence sont incluses dans les chômeurs.
Les travailleurs mis à pied par leur employeur ainsi que les travailleurs indépendants sans emploi pour cause de manque de travail sont considérés comme sans emploi s'ils sont disponibles pour travailler et ont cherché du travail à un moment quelconque au cours des deux mois précédant la date de l'entretien.
Sous-emploi:
Sous-emploi lié à la durée du travail: Les personnes ayant un emploi qui, durant la semaine de référence, ont travaillé moins d'heures, contre leur gré, que la durée normale du travail dans leur activité particulière et qui étaient disponibles pour travailler davantage.
Situations d'emploi inadéquat: Ce sujet n'est pas couvert par l'enquête.
Durée du travail: Les heures de travail réellement effectuées pendant la semaine de référence ainsi que les heures normales de travail hebdomadaires. Pour les personnes auxquelles le concept d'heures normales de travail ne s'applique pas, c'est le nombre d'heures de travail hebdomadaires habituelles qui est déclaré. Les informations sur la durée du travail sont recueillies pour l'activité principale et pour le total des autres activités (le cas échéant).
Revenu lié à l'emploi:
Revenu lié à l'emploi salarié: Salaire brut moyen ou traitement mensuel en roupies (moins de 2 000, de 2 001 à 4 000, de 4 001 à 6 000, de 6 001 à 8 000, de 8 001 à 10 000, de 10 001 à 15 000, de 15 001 à 20 000, 20 001 ou plus) perçu au titre de l'activité principale.
Revenu lié à l'emploi indépendant: Ce sujet n'est pas couvert par l'enquête.
Secteur informel: Ce sujet n'est pas couvert par l'enquête.
Activité habituelle: L'activité habituelle se réfère à la situation principale au regard de l'activité pendant une période de référence d'une année entière. La situation principale au regard de l'activité (habituellement actif, habituellement inactif) est déterminée en fonction du nombre de semaines que les personnes déclarent avoir passé en ayant eu un emploi ou à chercher du travail.
Classifications:
Branche d'activité économique (industrie)
Titre de la classification: Classification internationale type, par industrie, de toutes les branches d'activité économique (CITI-Rév.3).
Groupes de population classifiés selon l'industrie: Les personnes ayant un emploi; les chômeurs ou les inactifs ayant une expérience professionnelle préalable.
Nombre de groupes de codage: Non disponible.
Convertibilité avec la CITI: CITI-Rév.3.
Profession
Titre de la classification: Classification internationale type des professions (CITP-1988).
Groupes de population classifiés selon la profession: Les personnes ayant un emploi; les chômeurs ou les inactifs ayant une expérience professionnelle préalable.
Nombre de groupes de codage: Non disponible.
Convertibilité avec la CITP: CITP-1988.
Situation dans la profession
Titre de la classification: Classification nationale d'après la situation dans la profession.
Groupes de population classifiés par situation dans la profession: Les personnes ayant un emploi; les chômeurs ou les inactifs ayant une expérience professionnelle préalable.
Catégories de codage: a) travailleurs indépendants; a1) travailleurs indépendants ayant des salariés; a2) travailleurs indépendants sans salariés; b) salariés; b1) salariés rémunérés à l'heure; b2) salariés rémunérés aux pièces; b3) travailleurs extérieurs à l'établissement; b4) apprentis (rémunérés ou non); c) travailleurs familiaux non rémunérés; d) autres.
Convertibilité avec la CISP: CISP-1993.
Education
Titre de la classification: Classification nationale des niveaux d'instruction.
Groupes de population classifiés selon l'éducation: Toutes les personnes.
Catégories de codage: a) néant ou enseignement préscolaire; b) enseignement primaire; b1) enseignement primaire, années I à V; b2) enseignement primaire, "CPE" ou équivalent; c) enseignement secondaire; c1) enseignement secondaire, années I à IV; c2) enseignement secondaire, "SC" ou équivalent; c3)) enseignement secondaire, "HSC" ou équivalent; d) diplôme universitaire ou équivalent.
Convertibilité avec la CITE: Oui.
Taille de l'échantillon et plan de sondage:
Unité finale d'échantillonnage: Ménages.
Taille de l'échantillon (unités finales d'échantillonnage): 9 900 ménages.
Taux de sondage: 4,1 pour cent des ménages.
Base de sondage: Un échantillon de 495 secteurs de recensement est sélectionné pour l'enquête sur la population active à partir du dernier Recensement de la population et du logement (Housing and Population Census). Avant l'enquête, une nouvelle liste complète des ménages est établie dans les secteurs de recensement de l'échantillon.
Renouvellement de l'échantillon: Ne s'applique pas.
Rotation:
Schéma: Pas de rotation de l'échantillon.
Pourcentage d'unités restant dans l'échantillon durant deux enquêtes successives: Ne s'applique pas.
Nombre maximum d'interrogatoires par unité de sondage: Ne s'applique pas.
Durée nécessaire au renouvellement complet de l'échantillon: Ne s'applique pas.
Déroulement de l'enquête:
Type d'entretien: Les informations sont obtenues au cours d'entretiens personnels.
Nombre d'unités finales d'échantillonnage par zone de sondage: 20 ménages.
Durée de déroulement de l'enquête:
Totale: Deux mois.
Par zone de sondage: Non disponible.
Organisation: A part le personnel permanent de la Section des statistiques du travail (Labour Statistics Section), il n'existe aucune structure permanente pour l'enquête. Le personnel de terrain, de mise en forme et de codage des données est recruté temporairement pour l'enquête.
Nombre de personnes employées: Un surveillant-chef, un assistant du surveillant-chef, 10 surveillants principaux, 50 cadres et 495 enquêteurs.
Substitution des unités finales en cas de non-réponse: Non disponible.
Estimations et redressements:
Taux de non-réponse: Non disponible.
Redressement pour non-réponse: Non disponible.
Imputation en cas de non-réponse à une question spécifique: Non disponible.
Redressement pour les régions/populations non couvertes: Non disponible.
Redressement en cas de sous-représentation: Non disponible.
Redressement en cas de sur-représentation: Non disponible.
Corrections des variations saisonnières: Ne s'applique pas.
Historique de l'enquête:
Titre et date de la première enquête: La première enquête (Labour Force Sample Survey) a été réalisée en juin-juillet 1995.
Modifications et révisions significatives: Ne s'applique pas.
Documentation et dissémination:
Documentation
Titre des publications publiant les résultats: Central Statistical Office, Ministry of Economic Planning and Development: Labour Force Sample Survey (périodicité: tous les dix ans). Avant publication, les principaux résultats de l'enquête sont publiés dans un rapport préliminaire.
Titre des publications méthodologiques: La publication précitée comporte des informations méthodologiques sur l'enquête.
Dissémination
Délai de publication des premiers résultats: 18 mois.
Information à l'avance du public des dates de publication initiale des résultats: Non disponible.
Mise à disposition, sur demande, des données non publiées: Non disponible.
Mise à disposition des données sur support informatique: Non disponible.

Moldavie, Rép. de

Titre de l'enquête: Labour Force Survey
Organisme responsable de l'enquête:
Organisation et déroulement de l'enquête: Department for Statistics and Sociology.
Analyse et Publication des résultats: Department for Statistics and Sociology.

Sujets couverts par l'enquête: Emploi, chômage, sous-emploi, durée du travail, durée du chômage, travailleurs découragés, travailleurs occasionnels, industrie, profession, situation dans la profession, niveau d'instruction, activité habituelle et exercice d'autres emplois.
Champ de l'enquête:
Territoire: L'ensemble du pays, à l'exception de la région de la Transnistrie et de la ville de Tighina.
Groupes de population: Tous les résidents permanents âgés de 15 ans et plus et vivant dans des ménages.
Sont exclus:
a)les étudiants vivant en résidence et les écoliers vivant en pension;
b)les personnes âgées vivant en résidence spécialisée;
c)les pensionnaires d'établissements pénitentiaires ou psychiatriques;
d)les citoyens étrangers.
Disponibilité d'estimations selon d'autres sources pour les régions ou groupes exclus: Non.
Groupes couverts par l'enquête mais exclus des résultats publiés: Néant.
Périodicité:
Réalisation de l'enquête: En continu.
Publication des résultats: Trimestrielle.
Période de référence:
Emploi: Une semaine (les sept derniers jours avant la date de l'entretien).
Recherche d'un emploi: Quatre semaines avant la date de l'entretien.
Disponibilité pour travailler: Deux semaines après la date de l'entretien.
Concepts et définitions:
Emploi: Sont considérées comme ayant un emploi toutes les personnes âgées de 15 ans et plus qui, pendant la semaine de référence, ont effectué un travail quelconque, rémunéré ou non, pendant au moins une heure, ainsi que les travailleurs familiaux non rémunérés et les personnes qui ne travaillaient pas mais qui avaient un emploi ou une entreprise d'où elles étaient temporairement absentes pour cause de maladie, d'intempéries, de vacances, de conflit du travail, etc.
Sont également inclus dans les totaux:
a)les travailleurs occupés à plein temps ou à temps partiel et en quête d'un autre travail pendant la période de référence;
b)les étudiants à plein temps ou à temps partiel travaillant à plein temps ou à temps partiel;
c)les personnes ayant effectué un travail quelconque, pendant la semaine de référence, tout en étant soit à la retraite et au bénéfice d'une pension, soit inscrites en tant que demandeurs d'emploi auprès d'un bureau de placement, ou tout en percevant des allocations de chômage;
d)les domestiques privés;
e)les apprentis et stagiaires rémunérés.
Sont exclues les personnes occupées dans la production de biens pour leur propre ménage (travaux de peinture, de réparation, travaux ménagers, etc.).
Chômage: Sont considérées comme sans emploi les personnes âgées de 15 ans et plus qui, pendant la semaine de référence, n'ont pas travaillé pour une rémunération ou en vue d'un bénéfice, ont activement cherché du travail au cours des quatre semaines précédant l'enquête et étaient disponibles pour commencer à travailler dans les deux semaines suivant l'enquête.
Sous-emploi:
Sous-emploi lié à la durée du travail: Les personnes qui, durant la semaine de référence, ont travaillé moins, contre leur gré, que la durée du travail fixée, ont cherché à faire davantage d'heures et étaient disponibles pour ce faire.
Situations d'emploi inadéquat: Ne s'applique pas.
Durée du travail: Les heures de travail habituelles et réellement effectuées dans l'activité principale et la ou les activités secondaires.
Revenu lié à l'emploi:
Revenu lié à l'emploi salarié: Ne s'applique pas.
Revenu lié à l'emploi indépendant: Ne s'applique pas.
Secteur informel: Ne s'applique pas.
Activité habituelle: Ne s'applique pas.
Classifications:
Branche d'activité économique (industrie)
Titre de la classification: Classification nationale.
Groupes de population classifiés selon l'industrie: Les personnes ayant un emploi et les chômeurs ayant une expérience professionnelle préalable.
Nombre de groupes de codage: 55 groupes.
Convertibilité avec la CITI: CITI-Rév.3 (au niveau à quatre chiffres).
Profession
Titre de la classification: Classification nationale.
Groupes de population classifiés selon la profession: Les personnes ayant un emploi et les chômeurs ayant une expérience professionnelle préalable.
Nombre de groupes de codage: 10 grands groupes.
Convertibilité avec la CITP: CITP-1988 (au niveau à trois chiffres).
Situation dans la profession
Titre de la classification: Classification nationale.
Groupes de population classifiés par situation dans la profession: Les personnes ayant un emploi et les chômeurs.
Catégories de codage: 5 groupes (salariés, employeurs, travailleurs indépendants, membres de coopératives de producteurs, travailleurs familiaux non rémunérés).
Convertibilité avec la CISP: CISP-1993.
Education
Titre de la classification: Classification nationale.
Groupes de population classifiés selon l'éducation: Tous les groupes de population.
Catégories de codage: 7 groupes (enseignement préscolaire, enseignement primaire, premier cycle de l'enseignement secondaire, deuxième cycle de l'enseignement secondaire, enseignement professionnel, collège, enseignement supérieur (universitaire)).
Convertibilité avec la CITE: Non.
Taille de l'échantillon et plan de sondage:
Unité finale d'échantillonnage: Adresse.
Taille de l'échantillon (unités finales d'échantillonnage): Environ 8 208.
Taux de sondage: 1/150.
Base de sondage: La base de sondage est construite à partir des listes électorales utilisées pour les élections présidentielles de 1996.
Renouvellement de l'échantillon: OUI.
Rotation:
Schéma: Chaque logement employé retenu dans l'échantillon est interrogé pendant deux trimestres successifs, puis écarté pendant deux trimestres avant d'être interrogé de nouveau pendant deux trimestres successifs puis de quitter l'échantillon définitivement.
Pourcentage d'unités restant dans l'échantillon durant deux enquêtes successives: 50 pour cent.
Nombre maximum d'interrogatoires par unité de sondage: 4.
Durée nécessaire au renouvellement complet de l'échantillon: Environ 7 ans.
Déroulement de l'enquête:
Type d'entretien: Sur papier avec écriture manuelle.
Nombre d'unités finales d'échantillonnage par zone de sondage: 72 logements par trimestre.
Durée de déroulement de l'enquête:
Totale: Non disponible.
Par zone de sondage: Non disponible.
Organisation: Department for Statistics and Sociology.
Nombre de personnes employées: 114 enquêteurs et 39 cadres.
Substitution des unités finales en cas de non-réponse: Non.
Estimations et redressements:
Taux de non-réponse: 11%.
Redressement pour non-réponse: Oui.
Imputation en cas de non-réponse à une question spécifique: Non.
Redressement pour les régions/populations non couvertes: Non.
Redressement en cas de sous-représentation: Oui.
Redressement en cas de sur-représentation: Oui.
Corrections des variations saisonnières: Non.
Historique de l'enquête:
Titre et date de la première enquête: Labour Force Survey, octobre 1998.
Modifications et révisions significatives: Aucune modification significative.
Documentation et dissémination:
Documentation
Titre des publications publiant les résultats: "Economic active population, employment and unemployment" (annuel).
Titre des publications méthodologiques: "Economic active population, employment and unemployment" (annuel).
Dissémination
Délai de publication des premiers résultats: Deux mois.
Information à l'avance du public des dates de publication initiale des résultats: Oui.
Mise à disposition, sur demande, des données non publiées: Oui.
Mise à disposition des données sur support informatique: Disquettes et Internet.
Site web: http://www.moldova.md.

Népal

Titre de l'enquête: Nepal Labour Force Survey.

Organisme responsable de l'enquête:

Organisation et déroulement de l'enquête: Central Bureau of Statistics.

Analyse et Publication des résultats: Central Bureau of Statistics.

Sujets couverts par l'enquête: Emploi, chômage, sous-emploi, heures de travail réellement effectuées, salaires, emploi dans le secteur informel, durée de l'emploi, durée du chômage, industrie, profession, situation dans la profession, niveau d'instruction et de qualification, activité habituelle, exercice d'autres emplois, expérience professionnelle antérieure.

Champ de l'enquête:

Territoire: L'ensemble du pays.

Groupes de population: L'enquête couvre les résidents permanents du Népal, y compris les ressortissants étrangers. Les sans-abri, les personnes vivant en institution (telles que résidences scolaires, prisons, casernes ou hôpitaux) et les personnes absentes de leur ménage pendant six mois ou plus ne sont pas couverts par l'enquête. Les ménages des missions diplomatiques sont exclus.

Disponibilité d'estimations selon d'autres sources pour les régions ou groupes exclus: Non disponible.

Groupes couverts par l'enquête mais exclus des résultats publiés: Non disponible.

Périodicité:

Réalisation de l'enquête: Irrégulière. La première enquête a été réalisée pendant la période comprise entre mai 1998 et avril 1999.

Publication des résultats: Irrégulière, en fonction de la réalisation de l'enquête.

Période de référence:

Emploi: Période de référence variable d'une semaine, à savoir les sept derniers jours avant la date de l'entretien.

Recherche d'un emploi: Période de référence variable d'un mois, à savoir les 30 derniers jours avant la date de l'entretien.

Disponibilité pour travailler: Période de référence variable d'une semaine, à savoir les sept derniers jours avant la date de l'entretien.

Concepts et définitions:

Emploi: Les personnes âgées de 5 ans et plus ayant effectué un travail quelconque (pendant au moins une heure), rémunéré ou en vue d'un bénéfice ou d'un gain familial, pendant la semaine de référence. Sont inclus: a) les travailleurs familiaux non rémunérés au travail durant la semaine de référence; b) les travailleurs occupés à plein temps ou à temps partiel et en quête d'un autre emploi; c) les personnes ayant effectué un travail quelconque pendant la semaine de référence mais qui étaient alors assujetties à la scolarité obligatoire, ou à la retraite et au bénéfice d'une pension, ou inscrites en tant que demandeurs d'emploi auprès d'un bureau de placement; d) les étudiants à plein temps travaillant à plein temps ou à temps partiel; e) les étudiants à temps partiel travaillant à plein temps ou à temps partiel; f) les apprentis et stagiaires rémunérés; g) les personnes occupées dans la production de biens pour leur usage final personnel; et h) les personnes effectuant un service civil équivalent au service militaire.

Les personnes qui étaient temporairement absentes de leur travail durant la semaine de référence pour cause de maladie ou d'accident, de congés ou de vacances annuelles, de congé de maternité ou de paternité ou de congé d'éducation ou de formation, etc. sont considérées comme ayant un emploi si i) elles avaient un emploi ou leur propre entreprise auxquels retourner et ii) elles percevaient soit une rémunération quelconque (en espèces ou en nature) soit d'autres revenus liés à un emploi ou à une entreprise alors qu'elles n'étaient pas au travail, ou si elles avaient été absentes de leur travail sans rémunération ni revenus pendant moins de deux mois.

Sont exclus: a) les travailleurs familiaux non rémunérés non au travail durant la semaine de référence; b) les apprentis et stagiaires non rémunérés; c) les personnes absentes de leur travail pour cause de conflit du travail; d) les personnes absentes de leur travail pour cause d'intempéries, de panne mécanique, etc.; e) les personnes en mise à pied temporaire ou de durée indéterminée sans rémunération; f) les personnes en mise en congé non rémunéré à l'initiative de l'employeur; g) les travailleurs saisonniers ne travaillant pas durant la morte-saison; h) les personnes rendant des services non rémunérées ou personnels à des membres de leur propre ménage; et i) les personnes effectuant un travail communautaire ou des activités sociales non rémunérés.

Chômage: Les personnes âgées de 5 ans et plus qui i) n'avaient pas d'emploi durant la semaine de référence (y compris les personnes qui avaient un emploi ou leur propre entreprise auxquels retourner mais qui en avaient été absentes sans rémunération ou autres revenus pendant deux mois ou plus), ii) étaient disponibles pour travailler pendant la semaine de référence et iii) avaient cherché du travail au cours des 30 derniers jours, ou n'avaient pas cherché de travail au cours des 30 derniers jours pour les raisons ci-après: conviction qu'il n'y a pas de travail; attente d'une réponse à des démarches préalables; attente de commencer à travailler dans un emploi arrangé ou dans une entreprise; morte-saison pour la pêche ou l'agriculture; autres. Les méthodes ci-après sont considérées comme des démarches de recherche d'emploi: présenter sa candidature à des employeurs; demander à des amis ou à des parents s'ils savent comment trouver du travail; faire des démarches en vue de créer sa propre entreprise; chercher du travail d'autres manières.

Sont inclus: a) les personnes sans emploi et immédiatement disponibles pour travailler qui ont pris des dispositions pour commencer à travailler dans un nouvel emploi à une date postérieure à la semaine de référence; b) les personnes sans emploi et immédiatement disponibles pour travailler qui ont essayé de créer leur propre entreprise; c) les personnes sans emploi et immédiatement disponibles pour travailler mais n'ayant pas cherché de travail pour des raisons autres que a) ou b) ci-dessus; d) les personnes en quête d'un emploi et/ou immédiatement disponibles pour travailler mais assujetties à la scolarité obligatoire ou à la retraite et au bénéfice d'une pension; e) les étudiants à plein temps à la recherche d'un emploi et/ou immédiatement disponibles pour travailler à plein temps ou à temps partiel; f) les étudiants à temps partiel à la recherche d'un emploi et/ou immédiatement disponibles pour travailler à plein temps ou à temps partiel; et g) les bénéficiaires de mesures de promotion de l'emploi.

Sont exclues les personnes sans emploi qui n'étaient pas disponibles pour travailler pendant la semaine de référence.

Des estimations séparées sont disponibles pour les personnes sans emploi ayant cherché du travail au cours des 30 derniers jours et pour les personnes sans emploi n'ayant pas cherché de travail au cours des 30 derniers jours.

Sous-emploi:

Sous-emploi lié à la durée du travail: Les personnes ayant un emploi et au travail qui ont travaillé moins de 40 heures au cours de la semaine de référence pour l'une des raisons indépendantes de leur volonté (c'est-à-dire économiques) ci-après: incapacité de trouver davantage de travail par manque d'activité; manque de financement ou de matières premières; panne de machines, panne électrique ou autre; inactivité durant la morte-saison; grève ou mise à pied résultant d'un conflit du travail; autre raison indépendante de leur volonté. Pour les personnes occupant plus d'un emploi, le seuil de 40 heures se réfère au nombre total d'heures de travail effectuées dans toutes les activités durant la semaine de référence.

Situations d'emploi inadéquat: Ce sujet n'est pas couvert par l'enquête.

Durée du travail: Les heures de travail réellement effectuées pendant la semaine de référence. Des informations sont recueillies sur le nombre total d'heures de travail effectuées dans toutes les activités et sur le nombre d'heures effectuées dans l'activité principale.

Revenu lié à l'emploi:

Revenu lié à l'emploi salarié: Salaires ou traitements bruts perçus en espèces ou en nature pendant la dernière semaine ou le dernier mois pour le principal emploi salarié, avant impôts, versements au titre de la sécurité sociale ou versements de pensions. Tous les avantages complémentaires tels que primes, pourboires ou incitations sont inclus. Tout autre revenu régulier lié à l'emploi salarié est également inclus mais converti en montant hebdomadaire ou mensuel selon que de besoin (ajout, par exemple, d'un douzième du 13ème mois accordé aux fonctionnaires). Les gains en nature incluent la fourniture régulière de nourriture, de vêtements, de logements, d'eau, d'électricité, de carburant, de transport, etc., gratuitement ou sous forme d'indemnités. Les gains non réguliers, tels que les cadeaux en espèces ou en nature, sont exclus.

Revenu lié à l'emploi indépendant: Ce sujet n'est pas couvert par l'enquête.

Secteur informel: L'emploi dans le secteur informel inclut les groupes ci-après: a) les salariés travaillant pour des entreprises privées non enregistrées (ou pour d'autres entreprises autres que des entreprises d'Etat, des organismes parapublics, des ONG/ONGI ou des entreprises privées enregistrées) employant moins de 10 salariés permanents; b) les travailleurs indépendants (c'est-à-dire les personnes exploitant leur propre entreprise sans salariés permanents); c) les employeurs (c'est-à-dire les personnes exploitant leur propre entreprise avec des salariés permanents) employant moins de 10 salariés permanents; et d) les membres de la famille non rémunérés et autres personnes travaillant dans des entreprises employant moins de 10 salariés permanents. Les personnes travaillant dans le secteur agricole sont exclues. Les informations se réfèrent à la seule activité principale; les personnes ayant une activité secondaire dans le secteur informel ne sont pas couvertes par l'enquête.

Activité habituelle: L'activité habituelle se réfère à l'expérience professionnelle au cours d'une période de référence d'une année, c'est-à-dire des 12 mois civils pleins précédant la date de l'entretien. Les personnes âgées de 5 ans et plus sont considérées comme habituellement actives si, au cours des 12 mois de référence, elles ont travaillé ou ont été disponibles pour travailler pendant un total de 180 jours ou plus. Les personnes habituellement actives peuvent être subdivisées entre les personnes ayant habituellement un emploi et les personnes habituellement sans emploi. Les personnes ayant habituellement un emploi sont celles pour lesquelles la durée totale des périodes d'emploi au cours des 12 mois de référence a été égale ou supérieure à la durée totale des périodes de chômage. Les personnes habituellement sans emploi sont celles pour lesquelles la durée totale des périodes de chômage au cours des 12 mois de référence a été égale ou supérieure à la durée totale des périodes d'emploi.

Classifications:

Branche d'activité économique (industrie)

Titre de la classification: Classification internationale type, par industrie, de toutes les branches d'activité économique (CITI Rév.3).

Groupes de population classifiés selon l'industrie: Les personnes ayant un emploi.

Nombre de groupes de codage: Divisions (au niveau à deux chiffres).

Convertibilité avec la CITI: CITI Rév.3.

Profession

Titre de la classification: Classification internationale type des professions (CITP-1988).

Groupes de population classifiés selon la profession: Les personnes ayant un emploi.

Nombre de groupes de codage: Sous-groupes (au niveau à trois chiffres).

Convertibilité avec la CITP: CITP-1988.

Situation dans la profession

Titre de la classification: Classification nationale d'après la situation dans la profession.

Groupes de population classifiés par situation dans la profession: Les personnes ayant un emploi.

Catégories de codage: a) Salariés; b) personnes exploitant leur propre entreprise ou exploitation agricole avec des salariés permanents; c) personnes exploitant leur propre entreprise ou exploitation agricole sans salariés permanents; d) membres de la famille non rémunérés; e) autres.

Convertibilité avec la CISP: CISP-1993.

Education

Titre de la classification: Classification nationale des niveaux d'instruction.

Groupes de population classifiés selon l'éducation: Toutes les personnes âgées de 5 ans et plus.

Catégories de codage: a) Jamais scolarisé; b) enseignement préscolaire/maternelle; c) classes 1 à 10; m) premier cycle de l'enseignement secondaire si classe 11; n) premier cycle de l'enseignement secondaire si classe 12; o) B.A./B.Sc.; p) M.A./M.Sc., q) diplôme professionnel; r) autres.

Convertibilité avec la CITE: CITE-1976, au niveau à trois chiffres.

Taille de l'échantillon et plan de sondage:

Unité finale d'échantillonnage: Ménage.

Taille de l'échantillon (unités finales d'échantillonnage): 14 400 ménages (7 200 en zones urbaines et 7 200 en zones rurales).

Taux de sondage: Environ 0,4 pour cent des ménages (1,5 pour cent en zones urbaines et 0,2 pour cent en zones rurales).

Base de sondage: Base de sondage aréolaire fondée sur la liste des secteurs de recensement du recensement de la population de 1991. Les secteurs de recensement situés dans les nouvelles municipalités créées depuis 1991 ont été transférés de la base rurale à la base urbaine. Avant l'enquête, une nouvelle liste complète des ménages a été établie dans la totalité des 720 secteurs de recensement inclus dans l'échantillon.

Renouvellement de l'échantillon: Ne s'applique pas.

Rotation:

Schéma: Pas de rotation de l'échantillon. La collecte des données est répartie sur un an, en divisant l'échantillon sur lequel porte l'enquête en trois sous-échantillons indépendants dont chacun représente quatre mois du calendrier népalais (saison des pluies, saison d'hiver, saison sèche).

Pourcentage d'unités restant dans l'échantillon durant deux enquêtes successives: Ne s'applique pas.

Nombre maximum d'interrogatoires par unité de sondage: Ne s'applique pas.

Durée nécessaire au renouvellement complet de l'échantillon: Ne s'applique pas.

Déroulement de l'enquête:

Type d'entretien: Les informations sont obtenues au cours d'entretiens personnels.

Nombre d'unités finales d'échantillonnage par zone de sondage: 20 ménages par secteur de recensement de l'échantillon.

Durée de déroulement de l'enquête:

Totale: Une année.

Par zone de sondage: Cinq jours par secteur de recensement de l'échantillon.

Organisation: Une structure d'enquête permanente est utilisée pour l'enquête.

Nombre de personnes employées: 15 cadres et 46 enquêteurs.

Substitution des unités finales en cas de non-réponse: Aucun remplacement n'est fait pour les ménages défaillants.

Estimations et redressements:

Taux de non-réponse: 0,3% des ménages-échantillons.

Redressement pour non-réponse: Oui.

Imputation en cas de non-réponse à une question spécifique: Non.

Redressement pour les régions/populations non couvertes: Non.

Redressement en cas de sous-représentation: Non.

Redressement en cas de sur-représentation: Ne s'applique pas.

Corrections des variations saisonnières: Ne s'applique pas.

Historique de l'enquête:

Titre et date de la première enquête: Nepal Labour Force Survey 1998-1999.

Modifications et révisions significatives: Ne s'applique pas.

Documentation et dissémination:

Documentation

Titre des publications publiant les résultats: Central Bureau of Statistics, Report on the Nepal Labour Force Survey 1998/99, décembre 1999.

Titre des publications méthodologiques: La publication susmentionnée contient également des informations méthodologiques sur l'enquête.

Dissémination

Délai de publication des premiers résultats: Environ huit mois.

Information à l'avance du public des dates de publication initiale des résultats: Non.

Mise à disposition, sur demande, des données non publiées: Oui, sous forme de tableaux supplémentaires.

Mise à disposition des données sur support informatique: Oui, sur disquettes.

Norvège

Titre de l'enquête: Labour Force Survey.

Organisme responsable de l'enquête:

Organisation et déroulement de l'enquête: Statistics Norway.

Analyse et Publication des résultats: Statistics Norway.

Sujets couverts par l'enquête: Emploi, chômage, sous-emploi, durée du travail, durée de l'emploi et du chômage, travailleurs découragés, travailleurs occasionnels, industrie, profession, situation dans la profession, niveau d'instruction/de qualification, activité habituelle, exercice d'autres emplois, emploi temporaire ainsi que d'autres sujets correspondant au programme d'enquêtes sur les forces de travail d'EUROSTAT.

Champ de l'enquête:

Territoire: L'ensemble du pays.

Groupes de population: Toutes les personnes âgées de 16 à 74 ans résidant dans le pays.

Disponibilité d'estimations selon d'autres sources pour les régions ou groupes exclus: Ne s'applique pas.

Groupes couverts par l'enquête mais exclus des résultats publiés: Néant.

Périodicité:

Réalisation de l'enquête: En continu.

Publication des résultats: Trimestrielle.

Période de référence:

Emploi: Une semaine fixe.

Recherche d'un emploi: Quatre semaines.

Disponibilité pour travailler: Deux semaines.

Concepts et définitions:

Emploi: Toutes les personnes âgées de 16 à 74 ans ayant effectué un travail quelconque, rémunéré ou en vue d'un bénéfice, pendant au moins une heure durant la semaine de référence, ou qui étaient

temporairement absentes de leur travail pour cause de maladie, de vacances, etc. Sont inclus les personnes en congé rémunéré ou en congé non rémunéré jusqu'à une année si elles ont encore un emploi auquel retourner, les travailleurs familiaux non rémunérés, les conscrits ainsi que les personnes engagées au titre de mesures gouvernementales de promotion de l'emploi si elles perçoivent une rémunération.
Cette catégorie inclut:
a)les personnes ayant un emploi mais temporairement absentes de leur travail pour cause de maladie ou d'accident, de congés ou de vacances annuelles, de congé de maternité, de paternité ou de congé parental jusqu'à un an (à moins qu'il ne soit toujours rémunéré), de congé d'éducation ou de formation jusqu'à un an (à moins qu'il ne soit toujours rémunéré), d'absence non autorisée si cette personne a un emploi auquel retourner et une date de retour, de conflit du travail, d'intempéries ou de panne mécanique, etc.;
b)les travailleurs occupés à plein temps ou à temps partiel et en quête d'un autre emploi durant la semaine de référence;
c)les personnes ayant effectué un travail quelconque, rémunéré ou en vue d'un bénéfice, durant la semaine de référence, tout en étant assujetties à la scolarité obligatoire, à la retraite et au bénéfice d'une pension, inscrites en tant que demandeurs d'emploi auprès d'un bureau de placement ou tout en percevant des allocations de chômage;
d)les étudiants à plein temps ou à temps partiel travaillant à plein temps ou à temps partiel;
e)les apprentis et stagiaires rémunérés;
f)les bénéficiaires de mesures de promotion de l'emploi percevant une rémunération de la part de leur employeur;
g)les travailleurs familiaux non rémunérés au travail pendant la semaine de référence ou temporairement absents de leur travail, s'il ne s'agit pas d'un travail saisonnier;
h)les volontaires et les militaires de carrière, les conscrits et les personnes effectuant un service civil équivalent au service militaire.
Chômage: Toutes les personnes âgées de 16 à 74 ans qui n'avaient pas d'emploi pendant la semaine de l'enquête, ont cherché du travail au cours des quatre dernières semaines et étaient disponibles dans les deux semaines suivantes. Avant 1996, il fallait qu'elles soient disponibles au cours de la semaine de l'enquête.
Sont également inclus:
a)les personnes en mise à pied temporaire sans rémunération;
b)les personnes sans emploi et immédiatement disponibles pour travailler qui ont pris des dispositions pour commencer à travailler dans un nouvel emploi à une date postérieure à la semaine de référence ou qui ont essayé de créer leur propre entreprise;
c)les personnes sans emploi, disponibles pour travailler mais n'ayant pas cherché de travail au cours de la semaine de référence car elles attendaient une réponse d'un employeur, si elles ont cherché du travail cinq à huit semaines auparavant;
d)les personnes cherchant du travail et disponibles pour travailler, mais assujetties à la scolarité obligatoire ou à la retraite et au bénéfice d'une pension, si elles ont cherché du travail une à quatre semaines auparavant et si elles étaient disponibles pour travailler dans les deux semaines suivantes;
e)les étudiants à temps partiel ou à plein temps en quête d'un emploi à plein temps ou à temps partiel, s'ils ont cherché du travail une à quatre semaines auparavant et sont disponibles pour travailler dans les deux semaines suivantes.
Sous-emploi:
Sous-emploi lié à la durée du travail: Les travailleurs occupés à temps partiel cherchant à faire davantage d'heures de travail normales (ou habituelles) par semaine et pouvant commencer à faire davantage d'heures dans un délai d'un mois.
Situations d'emploi inadéquat: Les personnes en quête d'un autre emploi pour cause de:
a)risque ou certitude de perdre leur emploi actuel ou qu'il y soit mis fin;
b)vision de l'emploi actuel comme d'un emploi de transition;
c)recherche d'un second emploi;
d)désir d'avoir de meilleures conditions de travail (temps de travail ou de trajet, qualité du travail);
e)désir d'avoir une meilleure rémunération;
f)autres raisons.
Durée du travail: Se réfère aussi bien aux heures de travail hebdomadaires réellement effectuées qu'aux heures hebdomadaires normales (ou habituelles). Les activités principale et secondaires sont couvertes séparément. La distinction entre travail à temps partiel et travail à plein temps est faite sur la base du nombre total d'heures de travail normales dans l'emploi principal et dans l'emploi secondaire.
Revenu lié à l'emploi:
Revenu lié à l'emploi salarié: Sujet non couvert par l'enquête.
Revenu lié à l'emploi indépendant: Sujet non couvert par l'enquête.
Secteur informel: Sujet non couvert par l'enquête.
Activité habituelle: Sujet non couvert par l'enquête.
Classifications:
Branche d'activité économique (industrie)
Titre de la classification: Classification nationale.
Groupes de population classifiés selon l'industrie: Les personnes ayant un emploi et les chômeurs (industrie du dernier emploi occupé pour ces derniers).
Nombre de groupes de codage: 60 groupes.
Convertibilité avec la CITI: CITI-Rév.3 au niveau à deux chiffres.
Profession
Titre de la classification: Classification nationale.
Groupes de population classifiés selon la profession: Les personnes ayant un emploi et les chômeurs (profession exercée dans le dernier emploi pour ces derniers).
Nombre de groupes de codage: 353 groupes.
Convertibilité avec la CITP: CITP-1988.
Situation dans la profession
Titre de la classification: Classification nationale.
Groupes de population classifiés par situation dans la profession: Les personnes ayant un emploi et les chômeurs (situation dans le dernier emploi pour ces derniers).
Catégories de codage: Quatre groupes: salariés, employeurs, travailleurs indépendants et membres de la famille non rémunérés.
Convertibilité avec la CISP: CISP-1993.
Education
Titre de la classification: Classification nationale.
Groupes de population classifiés selon l'éducation: Les personnes ayant un emploi et les chômeurs.
Catégories de codage: Cinq niveaux: école primaire, niveau 1 de l'école secondaire, niveau 2 de l'école secondaire, cycles universitaires de un à quatre ans et de cinq ans et plus respectivement. Il y a en outre neuf domaines (programmes) d'étude.
Convertibilité avec la CITE: CITE-1976.
Taille de l'échantillon et plan de sondage:
Unité finale d'échantillonnage: Cellule familiale.
Taille de l'échantillon (unités finales d'échantillonnage): 24 000 personnes par trimestre.
Taux de sondage: 0,8 pour cent.
Base de sondage: Le Central Population Register, mis à jour en continu par les services locaux de l'état civil.
Renouvellement de l'échantillon: Chaque trimestre, 1/8 de l'échantillon est renouvelé.
Rotation:
Schéma: Chaque ménage participe huit fois à l'enquête au cours de huit trimestres successifs.
Pourcentage d'unités restant dans l'échantillon durant deux enquêtes successives: 87,5 pour cent.
Nombre maximum d'interrogatoires par unité de sondage: Huit.
Durée nécessaire au renouvellement complet de l'échantillon: Huit trimestres.
Déroulement de l'enquête:
Type d'entretien: La plupart par téléphone et quelques-uns sous forme d'entretien personnel (entretien personnel assisté par ordinateur).
Nombre d'unités finales d'échantillonnage par zone de sondage: D'environ 800 à 2 500 par comté, qui sont au nombre de 19.
Durée de déroulement de l'enquête:
Totale: Deux ou trois semaines après la semaine de l'enquête.
Par zone de sondage: Non disponible.
Organisation: Permanente.
Nombre de personnes employées: Environ 160 personnes.
Substitution des unités finales en cas de non-réponse: Non.
Estimations et redressements:
Taux de non-réponse: Environ 10%.
Redressement pour non-réponse: Oui (lors de la procédure d'estimation).
Imputation en cas de non-réponse à une question spécifique: Oui.
Redressement pour les régions/populations non couvertes: Ne s'applique pas.
Redressement en cas de sous-représentation: Ne s'applique pas.
Redressement en cas de sur-représentation: Ne s'applique pas.
Corrections des variations saisonnières: Oui (méthode X12-ARIMA).
Historique de l'enquête:
Titre et date de la première enquête: Labour Force Survey, 1er trimestre 1972.

Modifications et révisions significatives: Introduction de nouveaux questionnaires en 1988 et 1996.

Documentation et dissémination:

Documentation

Titre des publications publiant les résultats: Labour Market Statistics (annuel).

Titre des publications méthodologiques: Labour Market Statistics (annuel).

Dissémination

Délai de publication des premiers résultats: Au début du mois suivant le trimestre sur lequel a porté l'enquête.

Information à l'avance du public des dates de publication initiale des résultats: Oui.

Mise à disposition, sur demande, des données non publiées: Oui.

Mise à disposition des données sur support informatique: Disquettes et Internet.

Site web: http://www.ssb.no/

Nouvelle-Zélande

Titre de l'enquête: Household Labour Force Survey (HLFS).

Organisme responsable de l'enquête:

Organisation et déroulement de l'enquête: Statistics New Zealand (SNZ).

Analyse et Publication des résultats: SNZ.

Sujets couverts par l'enquête: Personnes actuellement actives, ayant un emploi ou sans emploi; personnes actuellement en situation de sous-emploi lié à la durée du travail et personnes actuellement en dehors de la population active; travailleurs découragés; heures de travail réellement effectuées et habituelles; durée du chômage; origine ethnique; industrie; profession; situation dans la profession; niveau d'instruction/de formation.

Champ de l'enquête:

Territoire: L'ensemble du pays, à l'exception des Territoires extérieurs.

Groupes de population: La population civile non institutionnelle âgée de 15 ans et plus.

Disponibilité d'estimations selon d'autres sources pour les régions ou groupes exclus: Non.

Groupes couverts par l'enquête mais exclus des résultats publiés: Néant.

Périodicité:

Réalisation de l'enquête: En continu.

Publication des résultats: Trimestrielle.

Période de référence:

Emploi: Une semaine.

Recherche d'un emploi: Les quatre dernières semaines.

Disponibilité pour travailler: Au cours de la semaine de référence.

Concepts et définitions:

Emploi: Les personnes qui a) ont effectué un travail quelconque, rémunéré ou en vue d'un bénéfice, durant la semaine de référence; et b) étaient temporairement absentes de leur travail pendant la semaine de référence pour cause de maladie ou de congé payé, ou qui avaient une entreprise à laquelle elles allaient retourner avec certitude. Par "un travail quelconque", on entend une heure de travail ou plus effectuée au cours de la semaine de référence.

Chômage: Les personnes actuellement sans emploi, disponibles pour travailler pendant la semaine de référence et ayant activement cherché du travail à un moment quelconque au cours des quatre dernières semaines.

Sous-emploi:

Sous-emploi lié à la durée du travail: Les personnes ayant un emploi travaillant à temps partiel qui ont cherché un emploi à plein temps au cours des quatre dernières semaines et/ou qui veulent faire davantage d'heures.

Situations d'emploi inadéquat: Non disponible.

Durée du travail: Les heures de travail "réellement effectuées" et "habituelles" incluent les heures de travail rémunérées ou non, dans l'activité principale et dans l'exercice d'un ou de plusieurs autres emplois.

Revenu lié à l'emploi:

Revenu lié à l'emploi salarié: Non disponible.

Revenu lié à l'emploi indépendant: Non disponible.

Secteur informel: Ne s'applique pas.

Activité habituelle: Non disponible.

Classifications:

Branche d'activité économique (industrie)

Titre de la classification: Australian and New Zealand Standard Industrial Classification (ANZSIC).

Groupes de population classifiés selon l'industrie: Les personnes ayant un emploi et les chômeurs (industrie du dernier emploi occupé pour ces derniers).

Nombre de groupes de codage: 158.

Convertibilité avec la CITI: CITI-Rév.3.

Profession

Titre de la classification: New Zealand Standard Classification of Occupations (NZSCO).

Groupes de population classifiés selon la profession: Les personnes ayant un emploi et les chômeurs (profession exercée dans le dernier emploi pour ces derniers).

Nombre de groupes de codage: 96.

Convertibilité avec la CITP: CITP-1988.

Situation dans la profession

Titre de la classification: Status in Employment-Standard Classification 1998.

Groupes de population classifiés par situation dans la profession: Les personnes ayant un emploi et les chômeurs (situation du dernier emploi pour ces derniers).

Catégories de codage: Travaille pour un salaire ou un traitement; employeur d'autres personnes dans sa propre entreprise; travailleur indépendant n'employant pas d'autres personnes; travaille sans rémunération dans une entreprise familiale.

Convertibilité avec la CISP: CISP-1993.

Education

Titre de la classification: Household Labour Force Survey Qualification Type Classification (HLF.QUALHIG)

Groupes de population classifiés selon l'éducation: Toutes les personnes.

Catégories de codage: 17.

Convertibilité avec la CITE: CITE-1997.

Taille de l'échantillon et plan de sondage:

Unité finale d'échantillonnage: Ménages.

Taille de l'échantillon (unités finales d'échantillonnage): 18 000.

Taux de sondage: 0,01.

Base de sondage: Recensements quinquennaux. Des zones géographiques restreintes constituent les unités primaires d'échantillonnage.

Renouvellement de l'échantillon: Tous les cinq ans.

Rotation:

Schéma: Les ménages restent dans l'échantillon pendant huit mois successifs avant de le quitter.

Pourcentage d'unités restant dans l'échantillon durant deux enquêtes successives: 87,5 pour cent restent dans l'échantillon pendant deux mois successifs. Chaque unité primaire d'échantillonnage est affectée à l'un des huit groupes de rotation, dont un est remplacé chaque trimestre par de nouveaux logements de la même unité primaire.

Nombre maximum d'interrogatoires par unité de sondage: Non disponible.

Durée nécessaire au renouvellement complet de l'échantillon: Non disponible.

Déroulement de l'enquête:

Type d'entretien: Sur papier avec écriture manuelle; direct (pour le premier entretien) et par téléphone (pour les autres).

Nombre d'unités finales d'échantillonnage par zone de sondage: Non disponible.

Durée de déroulement de l'enquête:

Totale: Une semaine.

Par zone de sondage: Non disponible.

Organisation: Permanente.

Nombre de personnes employées: 135 enquêteurs et 5 cadres régionaux.

Substitution des unités finales en cas de non-réponse: Non.

Estimations et redressements:

Taux de non-réponse: 10%.

Redressement pour non-réponse: Oui.

Imputation en cas de non-réponse à une question spécifique: Oui.

Redressement pour les régions/populations non couvertes: Oui.

Redressement en cas de sous-représentation: Oui.

Redressement en cas de sur-représentation: Ne s'applique pas.

Corrections des variations saisonnières: Oui, pour l'emploi et le chômage par sexe, le nombre total d'heures de travail et les personnes travaillant à plein temps et à temps partiel. Méthode de désaisonnalisation comparable à la méthode X-12.

Historique de l'enquête:

Titre et date de la première enquête: Household Labour Force Survey, trimestre de décembre 1985.

Modifications et révisions significatives: Juin 1990: nouveau questionnaire avec de nouvelles variables: sous-emploi, qualification, profession (au niveau à trois chiffres), industrie (au niveau à trois chiffres).
Documentation et dissémination:
Documentation
Titre des publications publiant les résultats: Hot off the press - Household Labour Force Survey (Cat. no. 05-500); Labour Market (annuel) Catalogue no. 01.029.0098 ISSN 1171-283X
Titre des publications méthodologiques: Survey Information Manager - Household Labour Force Survey sur site web.
Dissémination
Délai de publication des premiers résultats: Dans les six semaines après la fin de la période de référence de l'enquête.
Information à l'avance du public des dates de publication initiale des résultats: Oui.
Mise à disposition, sur demande, des données non publiées: Oui.
Mise à disposition des données sur support informatique: Oui.
Site web: http://www.stats.govt.nz

Ouganda

Titre de l'enquête: Uganda National Household Survey 1996-97: Pilot Labour Force Survey.
Organisme responsable de l'enquête:
Organisation et déroulement de l'enquête: Uganda Bureau of Statistics.
Analyse et Publication des résultats: Uganda Bureau of Statistics.
Sujets couverts par l'enquête: Les personnes actuellement et habituellement actives ayant un emploi ou chômeurs. Les personnes actuellement en situation de sous-emploi lié à la durée du travail et les personnes actuellement en dehors de la population active. Les personnes ayant habituellement un emploi, les personnes habituellement sans emploi et les personnes habituellement inactives (en distinguant les étudiants, les personnes se consacrant aux activités ménagères, trop âgées, malades ou handicapées). Durée du travail (pour les personnes ayant actuellement un emploi). Jours travaillés (pour les personnes ayant habituellement un emploi). Durée du chômage. Exercice d'autres emplois. Industrie, profession, situation dans la profession, niveau d'instruction/de formation.
Champ de l'enquête:
Territoire: 36 districts couverts sur les 39 que compte le pays. Les 3 districts exclus le sont pour des raisons de sécurité.
Groupes de population: La population âgée de 7 ans et plus constituée des résidents habituels des ménages sélectionnés. Ont été exclus les membres irréguliers du ménage, présents ou absents, ainsi que les visiteurs.
Disponibilité d'estimations selon d'autres sources pour les régions ou groupes exclus: Non disponible.
Groupes couverts par l'enquête mais exclus des résultats publiés: Néant.
Périodicité:
Réalisation de l'enquête: Occasionnelle: de mars à novembre 1997.
Publication des résultats: Occasionnelle: premiers résultats publiés en décembre 1998.
Période de référence:
Emploi: Une semaine avant la date de l'entretien pour les personnes ayant actuellement un emploi et au cours des 12 derniers mois, d'après leur propre estimation, pour les personnes ayant habituellement un emploi.
Recherche d'un emploi: La semaine de l'enquête pour les personnes actuellement sans emploi et au cours des 12 derniers mois, d'après leur propre estimation, pour les personnes habituellement sans emploi.
Disponibilité pour travailler: La semaine de l'enquête pour les personnes actuellement sans emploi et au cours des 12 derniers mois, d'après leur propre estimation, pour les personnes habituellement sans emploi.
Concepts et définitions:
Emploi: Les personnes qui a) ont effectué un travail quelconque, rémunéré ou en vue d'un bénéfice, pendant la semaine de référence; b) étaient temporairement absentes de leur travail pendant la semaine de référence pour cause de maladie ou de congés mais allaient y retourner avec certitude; et c) étaient occupées dans la production de biens pour leur usage personnel.
Sont exclues les personnes assujetties à la scolarité obligatoire et les personnes à la retraite et au bénéfice d'une pension. Par "un travail quelconque", on entend une heure ou plus effectuée pendant la semaine de référence.
Chômage: Les personnes actuellement sans emploi, disponibles pour travailler et ayant cherché du travail.
Sous-emploi:
Sous-emploi lié à la durée du travail: Non disponible.
Situations d'emploi inadéquat: Non disponible.
Durée du travail: Heures de travail réellement effectuées, mesurées séparément pour chacun des 7 jours utilisés pour mesurer l'emploi actuel.
Revenu lié à l'emploi:
Revenu lié à l'emploi salarié: Ne s'applique pas.
Revenu lié à l'emploi indépendant: Ne s'applique pas.
Secteur informel: Ne s'applique pas.
Activité habituelle: Non disponible.
Classifications:
Branche d'activité économique (industrie)
Titre de la classification: Non disponible.
Groupes de population classifiés selon l'industrie: Les personnes ayant un emploi.
Nombre de groupes de codage: 58.
Convertibilité avec la CITI: CITI-Rév.3.
Profession
Titre de la classification: Non disponible.
Groupes de population classifiés selon la profession: Les personnes ayant un emploi.
Nombre de groupes de codage: 87.
Convertibilité avec la CITP: CITP-1988.
Situation dans la profession
Titre de la classification: Classification nationale.
Groupes de population classifiés par situation dans la profession: Les personnes ayant un emploi.
Catégories de codage: Salariés (en distinguant les fonctionnaires permanents, les fonctionnaires temporaires, les employés occasionnels de l'Etat, les employés permanents du secteur privé, les employés temporaires du secteur privé et les employés occasionnels du secteur privé) et travailleurs indépendants (en distinguant les employeurs, les travailleurs à leur compte et les travailleurs familiaux non rémunérés).
Convertibilité avec la CISP: CISP-1993.
Education
Titre de la classification: Classification nationale.
Groupes de population classifiés selon l'éducation: Toutes les personnes.
Catégories de codage: 24.
Convertibilité avec la CITE: CITE-1976.
Taille de l'échantillon et plan de sondage:
Unité finale d'échantillonnage: Ménage.
Taille de l'échantillon (unités finales d'échantillonnage): 6 656.
Taux de sondage: 0,0017.
Base de sondage: Le Recensement de 1991.
Renouvellement de l'échantillon: Chaque enquête a un nouvel échantillon.
Rotation:
Schéma: Ne s'applique pas.
Pourcentage d'unités restant dans l'échantillon durant deux enquêtes successives: Ne s'applique pas.
Nombre maximum d'interrogatoires par unité de sondage: Ne s'applique pas.
Durée nécessaire au renouvellement complet de l'échantillon: Ne s'applique pas.
Déroulement de l'enquête:
Type d'entretien: Entretiens personnels avec écriture manuelle sur papier.
Nombre d'unités finales d'échantillonnage par zone de sondage: Non disponible.
Durée de déroulement de l'enquête:
Totale: De mars à novembre 1997.
Par zone de sondage: Non disponible.
Organisation: Permanente.
Nombre de personnes employées: 48 enquêteurs et 12 cadres.
Substitution des unités finales en cas de non-réponse: Oui.
Estimations et redressements:
Taux de non-réponse: 0,0006.
Redressement pour non-réponse: Oui.
Imputation en cas de non-réponse à une question spécifique: Oui, en utilisant des multiplicateurs pour dix ménages interrogés dans chaque secteur de recensement de l'échantillon afin d'opérer un redressement en fonction du nombre de ménages interrogés.
Redressement pour les régions/populations non couvertes: Non.
Redressement en cas de sous-représentation: Non.
Redressement en cas de sur-représentation: Non.

Corrections des variations saisonnières: Non.
Historique de l'enquête:
Titre et date de la première enquête: Uganda National Household Survey 1996-97.
Modifications et révisions significatives: Ne s'applique pas.
Documentation et dissémination:
Documentation
Titre des publications publiant les résultats: 1997 Pilot Labour Force Survey. Aucune autre information bibliographique.
Titre des publications méthodologiques: Même chose que pour les résultats.
Dissémination
Délai de publication des premiers résultats: Non disponible.
Information à l'avance du public des dates de publication initiale des résultats: Non.
Mise à disposition, sur demande, des données non publiées: Oui.
Mise à disposition des données sur support informatique: Oui.

Pakistan

Titre de l'enquête: Labour force survey.
Organisme responsable de l'enquête:
Organisation et déroulement de l'enquête: Federal Bureau of Statistics, Statistics Division, Ministry of Finance and Economic Affairs
Analyse et Publication des résultats: Federal Bureau of Statistics
Sujets couverts par l'enquête: Emploi; chômage, sous-emploi, durée du travail, salaires, emploi dans le secteur informel, durée du chômage, industrie, profession, situation dans la profession, niveau d'instruction et emplois secondaires.
Champ de l'enquête:
Territoire: Toutes les zones urbaines et rurales des quatre provinces du Pakistan ainsi que l'Azad Jammu et le Cachemire tels qu'ils sont définis par le recensement de la population de 1981, à l'exception des zones militaires réservées des FATA, des districts du Kohistan, de Malakand et des zones protégées de la Province de la Frontière du Nord-Ouest.
Groupes de population: Les nomades, le personnel de défense, les étrangers et les ressortissants pakistanais résidant à l'étranger sont exclus.
Disponibilité d'estimations selon d'autres sources pour les régions ou groupes exclus: La population exclue du champ géographique constitue environ 4 pour cent de la population totale.
Groupes couverts par l'enquête mais exclus des résultats publiés: Ne s'applique pas.
Périodicité:
Réalisation de l'enquête: Annuelle.
Publication des résultats: Annuelle.
Période de référence:
Emploi: Semaine de référence variable.
Recherche d'un emploi: Semaine de référence.
Disponibilité pour travailler: Semaine de référence.
Concepts et définitions:
Emploi: Les personnes âgées de 10 ans et plus ayant travaillé au moins une heure pendant la semaine de référence, soit en tant que "salariés", soit en tant que "travailleurs indépendants". Les personnes ayant un emploi permanent qui n'ont pas travaillé pour une raison quelconque pendant la semaine de référence sont considérées comme ayant un emploi.
Cette catégorie inclut:
a)les personnes déclarant effectuer des travaux ménagers ou d'autres activités connexes mais qui ont passé du temps à exercer des activités agricoles ou non agricoles spécifiées;
b)les personnes ayant un emploi mais temporairement absentes pour une raison quelconque, ainsi que les personnes en mise à pied temporaire ou de durée indéterminée sans rémunération;
c)les personnes ayant effectué un travail quelconque, rémunéré ou en vue d'un bénéfice, durant la semaine de référence, mais qui étaient alors assujetties à la scolarité obligatoire, à la retraite et au bénéfice d'une pension, au bénéfice d'allocations de chômage ou qui étaient inscrites en tant que demandeurs d'emploi auprès d'un bureau de placement ou en quête d'un autre travail durant la semaine de référence;
d)les étudiants à plein temps ou à temps partiel travaillant à plein temps ou à temps partiel;
e)les apprentis et stagiaires rémunérés, ainsi que les bénéficiaires de mesures de promotion de l'emploi;
f)les travailleurs familiaux non rémunérés au travail ou temporairement absents de leur travail;
g)les personnes occupées dans la production de biens pour leur usage final personnel;
h)les travailleurs saisonniers ne travaillant pas durant la morte-saison.
Sont exclus:
a)les apprentis et stagiaires non rémunérés;
b)les personnes occupées dans la prestation de services dans leur ménage;
c)les personnes exerçant des activités immorales telles que la prostitution, la mendicité, le vol et la contrebande;
d)les travailleurs sociaux bénévoles travaillant hors de l'entreprise familiale.
Chômage: Les personnes âgées de 10 ans et plus qui, pendant la semaine de référence, étaient i) "sans emploi", c'est-à-dire qui n'exerçaient ni emploi salarié ni emploi indépendant; ii) "immédiatement disponibles pour travailler", c'est-à-dire qui étaient disponibles pour occuper un emploi salarié ou indépendant au cours de la semaine de référence; et iii) "à la recherche d'un emploi", c'est-à-dire qui avaient effectué des démarches concrètes au cours d'une période récente précise pour chercher un emploi salarié ou indépendant.
Cette catégorie inclut:
a)les personnes sans emploi, immédiatement disponibles et à la recherche d'un emploi, qui ont pris des dispositions pour commencer à travailler dans un nouvel emploi à une date postérieure à la semaine de référence;
b)les personnes sans emploi, immédiatement disponibles et à la recherche d'un emploi qui ont essayé de créer leur propre entreprise;
c)les personnes sans emploi, disponibles pour travailler mais n'ayant pas cherché de travail au cours d'une période récente pour des raisons précises;
d)les étudiants à plein temps ou à temps partiel en quête d'un emploi à plein temps ou à temps partiel;
e)les personnes en quête d'un emploi ou immédiatement disponibles pour travailler mais assujetties à la scolarité obligatoire ou à la retraite et au bénéfice d'une pension.
Sont exclues:
a)les personnes en mise à pied temporaire ou de durée indéterminée sans rémunération.
Sous-emploi:
Sous-emploi lié à la durée du travail: Les personnes ayant un emploi qui, durant la période de référence, remplissaient simultanément les trois critères ci-après: i) travaillaient moins que la durée normale du travail (c'est-à-dire moins de 35 heures par semaine), ii) le faisaient contre leur gré et iii) cherchaient à travailler davantage ou étaient disponibles pour ce faire.
Situations d'emploi inadéquat: Voir ci-dessus.
Durée du travail: Le nombre d'heures de travail effectuées dans la profession principale et les occupations secondaires pendant la dernière semaine suivant la date de l'entretien.
Revenu lié à l'emploi:
Revenu lié à l'emploi salarié: Revenu brut des salariés dans leur profession principale et leurs occupations secondaires.
Revenu lié à l'emploi indépendant: Non disponible.
Secteur informel: Toutes les entreprises familiales appartenant à des travailleurs indépendants, qui les exploitent, quelle que soit la taille de l'entreprise (entreprises indépendantes du secteur informel), et les entreprises familiales appartenant à des employeurs qui les exploitent avec moins de 10 employés. Sont exclues toutes les entreprises familiales exerçant des activités agricoles ou n'exerçant que des activités de production non marchande.
Activité habituelle: Non disponible.
Classifications:
Branche d'activité économique (industrie)
Titre de la classification: Pakistan Standard Industrial Classification PSIC-1970.
Groupes de population classifiés selon l'industrie: Les personnes ayant un emploi et les chômeurs ayant une expérience professionnelle préalable.
Nombre de groupes de codage: Codes au niveau à deux chiffres mais publiés au niveau à un chiffre.
Convertibilité avec la CITI: CITI-Rév.2.
Profession
Titre de la classification: Pakistan Standard Classification of Occupations
PSCO-1994.
Groupes de population classifiés selon la profession: Les personnes ayant un emploi et les chômeurs ayant une expérience professionnelle préalable.
Nombre de groupes de codage: Codes au niveau à deux chiffres mais publiés au niveau à un chiffre.
Convertibilité avec la CITP: CITP-1968.

Situation dans la profession
Titre de la classification: Non disponible.
Groupes de population classifiés par situation dans la profession: Les personnes ayant un emploi et les chômeurs ayant une expérience professionnelle préalable.
Catégories de codage: Employeur, travailleur indépendant, travailleur familial non rémunéré et salarié.
Convertibilité avec la CISP: CISP-1993.
Education
Titre de la classification: Non disponible.
Groupes de population classifiés selon l'éducation: Les personnes ayant un emploi et les chômeurs.
Catégories de codage: Non scolarisé. Niveau inférieur à l'immatriculation ("matric"). Immatriculation ("matric") mais niveau inférieur au premier cycle de l'enseignement secondaire. Premier cycle de l'enseignement secondaire mais niveau inférieur à un diplôme universitaire. Diplôme universitaire et au-delà.
Convertibilité avec la CITE: Non précisée.
Taille de l'échantillon et plan de sondage:
Unité finale d'échantillonnage: Ménage.
Taille de l'échantillon (unités finales d'échantillonnage): 22 272 ménages (10 368 en zones urbaines et 11 904 en zones rurales).
Taux de sondage: 1/465 en zones urbaines et 1/1119 en zones rurales.
Base de sondage: Deux types de bases de sondage sont utilisés: la liste et la base de sondage aréolaire. Les îlots de recensement et les villages du recensement de la population de 1981 servent d'unités primaires d'échantillonnage.
Renouvellement de l'échantillon: La liste des îlots de recensement a été renouvelée en 1995. La base de sondage aréolaire urbaine, mise au point par un Quick Count Record Survey en 1972, est renouvelée tous les cinq ans.
Rotation: Néant.
Schéma: Ne s'applique pas.
Pourcentage d'unités restant dans l'échantillon durant deux enquêtes successives: Ne s'applique pas.
Nombre maximum d'interrogatoires par unité de sondage: Ne s'applique pas.
Durée nécessaire au renouvellement complet de l'échantillon: Ne s'applique pas.
Déroulement de l'enquête:
Type d'entretien: Entretien personnel.
Nombre d'unités finales d'échantillonnage par zone de sondage: Non disponible.
Durée de déroulement de l'enquête:
Totale: Du 1er juillet 1996 au 30 juin 1997.
Par zone de sondage: Non disponible.
Organisation: Permanente.
Nombre de personnes employées: Environ 68 enquêteurs et 34 cadres.
Substitution des unités finales en cas de non-réponse: Non.
Estimations et redressements:
Taux de non-réponse: Non disponible.
Redressement pour non-réponse: Non.
Imputation en cas de non-réponse à une question spécifique: Non.
Redressement pour les régions/populations non couvertes: Non.
Redressement en cas de sous-représentation: Non.
Redressement en cas de sur-représentation: Non.
Corrections des variations saisonnières: Non.
Historique de l'enquête:
Titre et date de la première enquête: Labour Force Survey (juillet 1963 à juin 1964).
Modifications et révisions significatives: Depuis 1967-68, les ménages situés dans des établissements (prisons, asiles, hôtels, mess, etc.) sont inclus. En outre, les ménages de mendiants dont un membre travaille pour une rémunération ou un bénéfice sont également inclus.
Depuis 1978-79, les travailleurs familiaux non rémunérés travaillant moins de 15 heures par semaine sont considérés comme ayant un emploi. Afin d'améliorer la mesure de l'emploi et du chômage, plusieurs questions d'approfondissement ont été incorporées au questionnaire sur a) la disposition à travailler si un emploi est fourni, b) le motif de non-recherche d'emploi et c) l'existence d'un travail quelconque, rémunéré ou en vue d'un bénéfice, questions posées aux personnes se déclarant « ménagère » ou « étudiant ».
En 1990-91, d'autres questions d'approfondissement ont été incorporées au questionnaire, conformément aux prescriptions de la résolution du BIT de 1982. Une section d'approfondissement particulière sur l'activité économique a notamment été conçue pour les personnes âgées de 10 ans et plus qui ont déclaré exercer des activités relatives aux soins du ménage et autres activités connexes.
En 1995, des questions sur la migration et les caractéristiques du secteur formel et informel ont été introduites.
Documentation et dissémination:
Documentation
Titre des publications publiant les résultats: Report of the Labour Force Survey.
Titre des publications méthodologiques: Report of the Labour Force Survey.
Dissémination
Délai de publication des premiers résultats: Environ 16 mois. Les données tirées de l'enquête réalisée du 1er juillet 1996 au 30 juin 1997 ont été publiées en octobre 1998.
Information à l'avance du public des dates de publication initiale des résultats: Non.
Mise à disposition, sur demande, des données non publiées: Oui.
Mise à disposition des données sur support informatique: Oui.

Pays-Bas

Titre de l'enquête: The Labour Force Survey.
Organisme responsable de l'enquête:
Organisation et déroulement de l'enquête: Central Bureau of Statistics.
Analyse et Publication des résultats: Central Bureau of Statistics.
Sujets couverts par l'enquête: Emploi, chômage, durée du travail, emploi dans le secteur informel, durée du chômage, industrie, profession, situation dans la profession, niveau d'instruction/de qualification, activité habituelle, autres sujets tels que, par exemple, conditions de travail et congé parental.
Champ de l'enquête:
Territoire: L'ensemble du pays.
Groupes de population: Les personnes âgées de 15 à 64 ans vivant aux Pays-Bas, à l'exception des personnes vivant en institutions.
Disponibilité d'estimations selon d'autres sources pour les régions ou groupes exclus: Non.
Groupes couverts par l'enquête mais exclus des résultats publiés: Les enfants de moins de 15 ans.
Périodicité:
Réalisation de l'enquête: En continu.
Publication des résultats: Annuelle.
Période de référence:
Emploi: Lors de l'entretien.
Recherche d'un emploi: Lors de l'entretien.
Disponibilité pour travailler: Lors de l'entretien.
Concepts et définitions:
Emploi: Toutes les personnes âgées de 15 à 64 ans vivant dans des ménages ordinaires et retenues pour l'enquête pendant la semaine de référence, à l'exception de la population institutionnelle.
Depuis 1992, les données nationales sont basées sur une définition de l'emploi qui n'inclut que les personnes ayant travaillé 12 heures ou plus par semaine. Dans un contexte international, c'est le critère d'une heure de travail qui est appliqué.
Sont également inclus dans les personnes ayant un emploi:
a)les personnes ayant un emploi mais temporairement absentes de leur travail pour cause de maladie ou d'accident, de congés ou de vacances annuelles, de congé de maternité/de paternité ou de congé parental, de congé d'éducation ou de formation, d'absence non autorisée, de conflit du travail, d'intempéries ou de panne mécanique, etc., ainsi que les personnes en mise à pied temporaire ou de durée indéterminée sans rémunération ou en mise en congé non rémunéré à l'initiative de l'employeur et les travailleurs occupés à plein temps ou à temps partiel et en quête d'un travail pendant la période de référence;
b)les personnes ayant effectué un travail quelconque, rémunéré ou en vue d'un bénéfice, durant la période de référence, mais qui étaient alors assujetties à la scolarité obligatoire, à la retraite et au bénéfice d'une pension, inscrites en tant que demandeurs d'emploi auprès d'un bureau de placement ou qui percevaient des allocations de chômage;
c)les étudiants à plein temps ou à temps partiel travaillant à plein temps ou à temps partiel;
d)les apprentis et stagiaires rémunérés ainsi que les bénéficiaires de mesures de promotion de l'emploi;
e)les travailleurs familiaux non rémunérés au travail pendant la période de référence ou temporairement absents de leur travail;
f)les volontaires et les militaires de carrière ainsi que les personnes effectuant un service civil équivalent au service militaire.

Chômage: Les données nationales relatives au chômage incluent les personnes cherchant du travail 12 heures ou plus par semaine. Les personnes travaillant moins de 12 heures ne sont plus classées dans la population active sauf si elles cherchent à travailler 12 heures ou plus par semaine, auquel cas elles sont classées comme sans emploi.

Sont également inclus dans les sans emploi:

a)les personnes sans emploi et immédiatement disponibles pour travailler qui ont pris des dispositions pour commencer à travailler dans un nouvel emploi à une date postérieure à la période de référence, ou qui ont essayé de créer leur propre entreprise;

b)les personnes en quête d'un emploi et/ou immédiatement disponibles pour travailler mais assujetties à la scolarité obligatoire ou à la retraite et au bénéfice d'une pension;

c)les étudiants à plein temps ou à temps partiel en quête d'un emploi à plein temps ou à temps partiel;

d)les apprentis et stagiaires non rémunérés.

Sous-emploi:

Sous-emploi lié à la durée du travail: Ne s'applique pas.

Situations d'emploi inadéquat: Ne s'applique pas.

Durée du travail: Non disponible.

Revenu lié à l'emploi:

Revenu lié à l'emploi salarié: Ne s'applique pas.

Revenu lié à l'emploi indépendant: Ne s'applique pas.

Secteur informel: Non disponible.

Activité habituelle: Non disponible.

Classifications:

Branche d'activité économique (industrie)

Titre de la classification: CITI-Rév.3.

Groupes de population classifiés selon l'industrie: Les personnes ayant un emploi.

Nombre de groupes de codage: 18 groupes.

Convertibilité avec la CITI: CITI-Rév.2 et Rév.3

Profession

Titre de la classification: CITP-1988.

Groupes de population classifiés selon la profession: Les personnes ayant un emploi.

Nombre de groupes de codage: 11 groupes.

Convertibilité avec la CITP: CITP-1988.

Situation dans la profession

Titre de la classification: Non disponible.

Groupes de population classifiés par situation dans la profession: Les personnes ayant un emploi.

Catégories de codage: Salariés, employeurs et travailleurs familiaux.

Convertibilité avec la CISP: Convertibilité indirecte avec la CISP-1993.

Education

Titre de la classification: CITE-1997.

Groupes de population classifiés selon l'éducation: Les personnes ayant un emploi et les chômeurs.

Catégories de codage: 5 groupes.

Convertibilité avec la CITE: CITE-1997.

Taille de l'échantillon et plan de sondage:

Unité finale d'échantillonnage: Ménage.

Taille de l'échantillon (unités finales d'échantillonnage): 8 000 ménages chaque mois.

Taux de sondage: 1 pour cent.

Base de sondage: L'enquête est basée sur un échantillon stratifié à deux degrés. Le Geographic Basic Register (GBR) constitue la base de sondage. Le GBR est une liste de toutes les adresses des Pays-Bas établie par la Poste néerlandaise. Pour l'enquête sur la population active, un échantillon d'environ 11 000 adresses est tiré chaque mois.

Renouvellement de l'échantillon: Non disponible.

Rotation:

Schéma: Non disponible.

Pourcentage d'unités restant dans l'échantillon durant deux enquêtes successives: Non disponible.

Nombre maximum d'interrogatoires par unité de sondage: Cinq fois.

Durée nécessaire au renouvellement complet de l'échantillon: Une année.

Déroulement de l'enquête:

Type d'entretien: Entretien personnel assisté par ordinateur et entretien par téléphone assisté par ordinateur: entretiens personnels au cours de la première vague et par téléphone au cours des deuxième, troisième, quatrième et cinquième vagues. Le temps écoulé entre deux vagues est de trois mois.

Nombre d'unités finales d'échantillonnage par zone de sondage: Non disponible.

Durée de déroulement de l'enquête:

Totale: En continu.

Par zone de sondage: En continu.

Organisation: Permanente.

Nombre de personnes employées: Environ 300 personnes.

Substitution des unités finales en cas de non-réponse: Non.

Estimations et redressements:

Taux de non-réponse: 45%.

Redressement pour non-réponse: Non.

Imputation en cas de non-réponse à une question spécifique: Non.

Redressement pour les régions/populations non couvertes: Non.

Redressement en cas de sous-représentation: Oui.

Redressement en cas de sur-représentation: Oui.

Corrections des variations saisonnières: Non.

Historique de l'enquête:

Titre et date de la première enquête: 1987 Labour force survey.

Modifications et révisions significatives: En 1999 et 2000.

Documentation et dissémination:

Documentation

Titre des publications publiant les résultats: Non disponible.

Titre des publications méthodologiques: Non disponible.

Dissémination

Délai de publication des premiers résultats: Un an.

Information à l'avance du public des dates de publication initiale des résultats: Non.

Mise à disposition, sur demande, des données non publiées: Oui.

Mise à disposition des données sur support informatique: Tableurs Excel sur demande et site Web sur Internet (http://www.cbs.nl).

Philippines

Titre de l'enquête: The Labour Force Survey

Organisme responsable de l'enquête:

Organisation et déroulement de l'enquête: National Statistics Office.

Analyse et Publication des résultats: National Statistics Office.

Sujets couverts par l'enquête: Emploi, chômage, sous-emploi, durée du travail, durée de l'emploi, travailleurs découragés, travailleurs occasionnels, industrie, profession (emploi primaire et autres emplois), situation dans la profession, niveau d'instruction, activité habituelle et autres sujets tels que nouveaux arrivants, base de rémunération et salaire journalier de base, etc.

Champ de l'enquête:

Territoire: L'ensemble du pays – villes au niveau national, régional, provincial/villes principales, zones urbaines et rurales.

Groupes de population: Toutes les personnes vivant dans des ménages ordinaires. Ne sont pas considérés comme membres d'un ménage:

a)les personnes ou membres de la famille vivant dans des établissements tels que colonies/fermes pénitentiaires, camps de détention, homes pour personnes âgées, orphelinats, établissements psychiatriques, sanatoriums pour tuberculeux, léproseries, etc. et qui ne sont pas censés revenir dans les 30 jours;

b)les membres des forces armées des Philippines s'ils ont été absents de leur lieu de résidence habituel pendant plus de 30 jours;

c)les Philippins, dans la mesure où leur lieu de résidence habituel se trouve dans un pays étranger, qui sont arrivés aux Philippines depuis moins d'un an ou seront aux Philippines pendant moins d'un an à compter de la date de leur arrivée;

d)les citoyens de pays étrangers et les membres de leur famille se trouvant dans le pays en tant que touristes, qu'étudiants, pour affaires ou pour leur travail, à condition qu'ils comptent rester dans le pays pendant une année ou moins à compter de la date de leur arrivée;

e)les ambassadeurs, ministres, consuls étrangers ou autres représentants diplomatiques ainsi que les membres de leur famille, quelle que soit la durée de leur séjour dans le pays;

f)les citoyens de pays étrangers dirigeants ou fonctionnaires d'organisations internationales telles que les Nations Unies, etc., ainsi que les membres de leur famille, quelle que soit la durée de leur séjour dans le pays.

Disponibilité d'estimations selon d'autres sources pour les régions ou groupes exclus: Non disponible.

Groupes couverts par l'enquête mais exclus des résultats publiés: Les travailleurs étrangers occupés en sous-traitance.

Périodicité:

Réalisation de l'enquête: Trimestrielle.

Publication des résultats: Trimestrielle.
Période de référence:
Emploi: La semaine précédente (période de référence variable).
Recherche d'un emploi: La semaine précédente (période de référence variable).
Disponibilité pour travailler: La semaine précédente (période de référence variable).
Concepts et définitions:
Emploi: Toutes les personnes âgées de 15 ans et plus à la date de leur dernier anniversaire, qui, pendant la semaine de référence, ont effectué un travail quelconque, rémunéré ou en vue d'un bénéfice, ou un travail non rémunéré dans une exploitation agricole ou une entreprise exploitée par un membre apparenté du même ménage pendant au moins une heure, ayant pour résultat la production de biens ou la prestation de services, ainsi que celles qui avaient un emploi ou une entreprise mais étaient absentes de leur travail pour cause de maladie temporaire, de vacances ou de congés, de mise à pied temporaire sans rémunération ou de mise en congé non rémunéré à l'initiative de l'employeur, de grève, de réduction de l'activité économique, etc., et que celles qui doivent se présenter au travail ou commencer à exploiter une ferme ou une entreprise dans les deux semaines à compter de la date de l'entretien.
Cette catégorie inclut également:
a)les travailleurs occupés à plein temps ou à temps partiel et en quête d'un autre travail pendant la semaine de référence;
b)les personnes ayant effectué un travail quelconque, rémunéré ou en vue d'un bénéfice, pendant la semaine de référence, mais qui étaient alors assujetties à la scolarité obligatoire, à la retraite et au bénéfice d'une pension, étudiants à plein temps ou à temps partiel travaillant à plein temps ou à temps partiel, inscrites en tant que demandeurs d'emploi auprès d'un bureau de placement ou qui percevaient des allocations de chômage;
c)les apprentis en pré-emploi ou les stagiaires rémunérés;
d)les travailleurs familiaux non rémunérés au travail ou temporairement absents de leur travail;
e)les domestiques privés;
f)les membres de coopératives de producteurs;
g)les personnes effectuant un service civil équivalent au service militaire;
h)les personnes occupées dans la production de biens destinés à la vente ou à la consommation familiale (travaux de jardinage dans une parcelle d'au moins 100 m2).
Chômage: Toutes les personnes âgées de 15 ans et plus à la date de leur dernier anniversaire, n'ayant pas travaillé du tout pour une rémunération ou en vue d'un bénéfice ou en tant que travailleurs familiaux non rémunérés pendant la période de référence mais déclarées comme voulant travailler et cherchant du travail. Sont également incluses les personnes sans emploi ou entreprise ayant déclaré ne pas chercher d'emploi par conviction qu'il n'y a pas de travail ou pour cause d'intempéries, de maladie bénigne, d'attente de réponses à des dossiers de candidature ou de rappel au travail, d'entretiens d'embauche, etc. Sont également inclus les personnes en mise à pied de durée indéterminée sans rémunération, les travailleurs saisonniers attendant un emploi saisonnier et les catégories de personnes ci-après:
a)les personnes qui s'efforcent de créer une entreprise ou un cabinet privé;
b)les personnes en quête d'un emploi et/ou immédiatement disponibles pour travailler mais à la retraite et au bénéfice d'une pension;
c)les étudiants à plein temps ou à temps partiel en quête d'un emploi à plein temps ou à temps partiel;
d)les apprentis et stagiaires non rémunérés;
e)les bénéficiaires de mesures de promotion de l'emploi.
Sous-emploi:
Sous-emploi lié à la durée du travail: Les personnes ayant un emploi qui ont exprimé le souhait de faire davantage d'heures de travail dans leur emploi actuel ou d'exercer un emploi supplémentaire, ou encore d'avoir un nouvel emploi comportant davantage d'heures de travail.
Situations d'emploi inadéquat: Ne s'applique pas.
Durée du travail: Le nombre d'heures de travail réellement effectuées par une personne dans toutes les activités au cours de la semaine de référence.
Revenu lié à l'emploi:
Revenu lié à l'emploi salarié: A partir de janvier 2001, à la suite de l'introduction du nouveau questionnaire de l'enquête: salaire journalier de base.
Revenu lié à l'emploi indépendant: Ne s'applique pas.
Emploi dans le secteur informel: Cette catégorie n'est pas nettement séparée. Les personnes ayant un emploi sont classifiées par « classe de travailleurs » (voir au point « **Situation dans la profession** » ci-après), y compris dans le secteur informel, par référence à l'emploi principal ou à la profession principale uniquement.
Activité habituelle: L'activité principale/la profession habituelle se réfère au genre d'emploi ou d'entreprise dans lequel les personnes ont été occupées la plupart du temps (plus de 6 mois ou celui qui a eu la plus longue durée) au cours des 12 derniers mois.
Classifications:
Branche d'activité économique (industrie)
Titre de la classification: 1994 Philippine Standard Industrial Classification (PSIC).
Groupes de population classifiés selon l'industrie: Les personnes ayant un emploi.
Nombre de groupes de codage: 9 grandes divisions et un code pour les activités définies sans suffisamment de précision.
Convertibilité avec la CITI: CITI-Rév.2, au niveau des grandes divisions uniquement, sauf la division 6 qui exclut les restaurants et les hôtels, inclus dans la division 9 (code 98).
Profession
Titre de la classification: 1992 Philippine Standard Occupational Classification (PSOC).
Groupes de population classifiés selon la profession: Les personnes ayant un emploi.
Nombre de groupes de codage: 9 grands groupes.
Convertibilité avec la CITP: CITP-1968 au niveau à deux chiffres, sauf pour le grand groupe 3. (Les cadres supérieurs de l'administration publique - code 3.1 de la CITP – sont inclus dans le code 2.0 de la PSOC – membres des corps législatifs, membres de l'administration publique et cadres supérieurs de l'administration publique).
Situation dans la profession
Titre de la classification: Class of Workers.
Groupes de population classifiés par situation dans la profession: Les personnes ayant un emploi.
Catégories de codage: Sept groupes: 0. A travaillé pour un ménage privé, 1. A travaillé pour des établissements privés, 2. A travaillé pour l'administration publique/un établissement parapublic, 3. Travailleur indépendant sans salariés, 4. Employeur occupé dans sa propre exploitation agricole ou sa propre entreprise familiales, 5. A travaillé pour une rémunération dans sa propre exploitation agricole ou sa propre entreprise familiales, 6. A travaillé sans rémunération dans sa propre exploitation agricole ou sa propre entreprise familiales.
Convertibilité avec la CISP: CISP-1993. Les codes 0, 1 et 2 ci-dessus se réfèrent au code 1 de la CISP.
Education
Titre de la classification: Philippine Standard Classification of **Education** (PSCED).
Groupes de population classifiés selon l'éducation: Les personnes ayant un emploi et les chômeurs.
Catégories de codage: Sept groupes: 00. Aucune année d'étude terminée, 01. Elève de l'enseignement élémentaire, 02. Diplômé de l'enseignement élémentaire, 03. Lycéen, 04. Diplômé de l'enseignement secondaire, 05. Etudiant dans l'enseignement supérieur, 06. Diplômé de l'enseignement supérieur (mention du diplôme le plus élevé obtenu et du domaine d'étude).
Convertibilité avec la CITE: Non disponible.
Taille de l'échantillon et plan de sondage:
Unité finale d'échantillonnage: Ménage.
Taille de l'échantillon (unités finales d'échantillonnage): La taille de l'échantillon élargi est de 3 416 barangays/secteurs de recensement ou 40 992 ménages, pour des estimations fiables au niveau provincial; la taille de l'échantillon de base est de 2 247 secteurs de recensement ou 26 964 ménages, au niveau régional/national. L'utilisation d'échantillons de base ou élargis dépend du budget.
Taux de sondage: Environ 1/250 pour les zones urbaines et 1/400 pour les zones rurales.
Base de sondage: Construite essentiellement d'après les résultats du Population Census (POPCEN) de 1995. La liste des barangays sert de base pour le premier degré. La liste des secteurs de recensement situés dans chaque barangay sélectionné sert de base pour le deuxième degré, et la liste des ménages situés dans chaque secteur de recensement sélectionné sert de base de sondage pour le troisième degré.
Renouvellement de l'échantillon: L'échantillon principal des secteurs de recensement est divisé en 4 sous-échantillons systématiques de 25 pour cent, désignés comme sous-échantillons 1, 2, 3 et 4. La liste des ménages (en théorie, établie annuellement, c'est-à-dire à raison d'un sous-échantillon par trimestre) n'a été établie que pour le sous-échantillon 4 pour cause de restrictions budgétaires. De nouvelles listes recueillent des informations sur le nom du chef de ménage, son surnom et son adresse.

Rotation:

Schéma: Environ 25 pour cent (un sous-échantillon) des ménages-échantillons sont renouvelés dans chaque secteur de recensement de l'échantillon chaque trimestre et remplacés par un nouvel ensemble de ménages-échantillons issus des surfaces-échantillons respectives.

Pourcentage d'unités restant dans l'échantillon durant deux enquêtes successives: 75 pour cent.

Nombre maximum d'interrogatoires par unité de sondage: Théoriquement quatre, mais pour tenir compte de toutes les exigences de l'enquête sur les ménages, ce nombre peut être supérieur.

Durée nécessaire au renouvellement complet de l'échantillon: En règle générale, une année.

Déroulement de l'enquête:

Type d'entretien: Entretien personnel.

Nombre d'unités finales d'échantillonnage par zone de sondage: Douze ménages par barangay-échantillon.

Durée de déroulement de l'enquête:

Totale: Trois semaines (pour octobre 2001, du 8 au 31 octobre).

Par zone de sondage: Non disponible.

Organisation: Le Statistical Coordination Office, permanent, assisté de chercheurs en statistique supplémentaires.

Nombre de personnes employées: Pour octobre 2001, 569 personnes employées sur le terrain et 285 chercheurs en statistique recrutés.

Substitution des unités finales en cas de non-réponse: Oui, un remplacement est effectué pour l'échantillon renouvelé dans les cas où le logement/le ménage ne peut pas être localisé.

Estimations et redressements:

Taux de non-réponse: 4,6% pour octobre 2001.

Redressement pour non-réponse: Oui.

Imputation en cas de non-réponse à une question spécifique: Non.

Redressement pour les régions/populations non couvertes: Non disponible.

Redressement en cas de sous-représentation: Oui.

Redressement en cas de sur-représentation: Non disponible.

Corrections des variations saisonnières: Oui, à l'aide de la méthode X-II Arima pour les niveaux d'emploi, de chômage et de la population active par sexe uniquement.

Historique de l'enquête:

Titre et date de la première enquête: Philippine Statistical Survey of Households, 1956.

Modifications et révisions significatives:

1962: adoption d'un nouveau plan de sondage basé sur les résultats du POPCEN de 1960, ce qui permet la publication d'une classification urbaine et rurale au niveau national jusqu'en 1969.

1971 (mars): nouveau plan qui donne des estimations des caractéristiques de l'emploi et de la population au niveau régional. La fréquence de l'enquête a augmenté pour devenir trimestrielle.

1975: nouvelle enquête, révision du plan de sondage et des concepts utilisés pour décrire les données relatives à la population active. La modification la plus importante est le passage de la semaine précédente au trimestre précédent pour la période de référence.

1976: intégration de l'Enquête sur l'agriculture (Agricultural Survey) et de l'Enquête sur la main-d'œuvre (Labour Force Survey) à la première enquête du plan général réalisée en novembre. Toutes les estimations découlant des enquêtes sur les ménages qui ont été réalisées ont utilisé les projections de population pour vérifier les fluctuations des estimations.

1987: la période de référence utilisée pour les statistiques de l'emploi revient à la « semaine précédente ». L'enquête du premier trimestre 1987 a été la dernière série à utiliser la période de référence du « trimestre précédent ».

1996: depuis juillet 1996, nouveau plan de sondage basé sur les résultats du recensement de la population de 1995.

2000: depuis octobre 2000, les estimations sont basées sur les Projections du Recensement de la population de 1995 (1995 Census Population Projection).

2001: depuis janvier, révisions du questionnaire de l'enquête, avec l'inclusion de questions relatives à l'exercice d'autres emplois, aux nouveaux arrivants, à la base de rémunération et au salaire journalier de base, et mise en œuvre des classifications par industrie de 1994 et des professions de 1992.

Documentation et dissémination:

Documentation

Titre des publications publiant les résultats: ISH Bulletin (trimestriel).

Titre des publications méthodologiques: ISH Bulletin (trimestriel).

Dissémination

Délai de publication des premiers résultats: Environ deux mois (les résultats d'octobre 2001 ont été publiés le 15 décembre 2001).

Information à l'avance du public des dates de publication initiale des résultats: Oui.

Mise à disposition, sur demande, des données non publiées: Oui.

Mise à disposition des données sur support informatique: Oui.

Site web: http://www.census.gov.ph.

Pologne

Titre de l'enquête: The Labour Force Survey.

Organisme responsable de l'enquête:

Organisation et déroulement de l'enquête: Central Statistical Office, Labour Statistics Division.

Analyse et Publication des résultats: Central Statistical Office, Labour Statistics Division.

Sujets couverts par l'enquête: Emploi, chômage, sous-emploi, durée du travail, salaires, durée de l'emploi, durée du chômage, travailleurs découragés, travailleurs occasionnels, industrie, profession, profession, situation dans la profession, niveau d'instruction, exercice d'autres emplois.

Champ de l'enquête:

Territoire: L'ensemble du pays.

Groupes de population: Toutes les personnes âgées de 15 ans et plus membres de ménages ordinaires sélectionnés pour l'enquête, y compris les membres absents du ménage pendant moins de deux mois car se trouvant à l'étranger pour des motifs tels que voyages d'affaires, etc., et ceux absents pendant plus de deux mois tels que marins, pêcheurs, etc.

Sont exclus:

1.les personnes vivant dans des ménages collectifs (par exemple, foyers de travailleurs, résidences universitaires, pensionnats, casernes, résidences pour personnes âgées, etc.);

2.les pensionnaires d'établissements pénitentiaires ou psychiatriques;

3.les membres de ménages ordinaires séjournant plus de deux mois à l'étranger;

4.les visiteurs temporaires séjournant moins de deux mois dans un ménage donné;

5.les étrangers.

Disponibilité d'estimations selon d'autres sources pour les régions ou groupes exclus: Non disponible.

Groupes couverts par l'enquête mais exclus des résultats publiés: Non disponible.

Périodicité:

Réalisation de l'enquête: En continu.

Publication des résultats: Trimestrielle.

Période de référence:

Emploi: Une semaine (période de référence variable).

Recherche d'un emploi: Quatre semaines (la semaine de référence étant la 4ème).

Disponibilité pour travailler: Deux semaines (la période de référence plus la semaine suivante).

Concepts et définitions:

Emploi: Les personnes âgées de 15 ans et plus qui, pendant la semaine de référence:

-ont effectué un travail quelconque pendant au moins une heure, rémunéré ou en vue d'un bénéfice, en tant que travailleurs salariés, ont travaillé dans leur propre exploitation agricole ou dirigé leur propre entreprise, active dans un secteur autre que l'agriculture, ont aidé, sans rémunération (travailleurs familiaux non rémunérés), à diriger une entreprise familiale active dans un secteur autre que l'agriculture;

-n'ont effectué aucun travail, pour des motifs tels que maladie, vacances, congés, débrayages dans l'entreprise, grève, intempéries, etc., tout en ayant un lien formel avec l'emploi en tant que salarié ou que travailleur indépendant (employeur ou personne travaillant à son compte).

Sont également considérés comme ayant un emploi les apprentis en formation professionnelle rémunérée payés par leur futur employeur (public ou privé) pendant la période de formation contractuelle.

Cette catégorie inclut également:

a)les personnes en mise à pied temporaire sans rémunération ou en mise en congé sans rémunération à l'initiative de l'employeur;

b)les travailleurs occupés à plein temps ou à temps partiel et en quête d'un autre travail durant la semaine de référence;

c)les personnes ayant effectué un travail quelconque, rémunéré ou en vue d'un bénéfice, pendant la semaine de référence, mais qui étaient alors assujetties à la scolarité obligatoire ou étudiants à plein temps ou à temps partiel travaillant à plein temps ou à temps partiel;

à la retraite et au bénéfice d'une pension; inscrites en tant que demandeurs d'emploi auprès d'un bureau de placement, ou qui percevaient des allocations de chômage;
d)les bénéficiaires de mesures de promotion de l'emploi;
e)les personnes occupées dans la production de biens pour leur usage final personnel;
f)tous les membres des forces armées, y compris les personnes effectuant un service civil équivalent au service militaire.
Chômage: Les personnes âgées de 15 ans et plus qui n'avaient pas d'emploi au sens des critères définis ci-dessus au cours de la semaine de référence, étaient disponibles pour travailler pendant cette semaine-là ou la semaine suivante et avaient activement cherché du travail pendant quatre semaines (la période de référence étant la quatrième) et effectué des démarches concrètes visant à trouver un emploi. Sont incluses les personnes n'ayant pas cherché de travail parce qu'elles en avaient déjà trouvé et attendaient de commencer à travailler dans un nouvel emploi dans les 30 jours.
Cette catégorie inclut également:
a)les personnes essayant de créer leur propre entreprise ou leur cabinet privé;
b)les travailleurs saisonniers dans l'attente d'un emploi saisonnier;
c)les personnes assujetties à la scolarité obligatoire;
d)les étudiants à plein temps ou à temps partiel à la recherche d'un emploi à plein temps ou à temps partiel.
Sous-emploi:
Sous-emploi lié à la durée du travail: Les personnes travaillant à temps partiel pour des motifs économiques (débrayages, absence obligatoire, impossibilité de trouver un emploi à plein temps, par exemple). (Actuellement, des travaux sont en cours pour modifier la définition dans le sens de la nouvelle définition du BIT).
Situations d'emploi inadéquat: Ne s'applique pas.
Durée du travail: Le nombre d'heures de travail réellement effectuées par une personne dans toutes les activités (principale et supplémentaires) au cours de la semaine de référence.
Revenu lié à l'emploi:
Revenu lié à l'emploi salarié: Gains mensuels nets liés à l'emploi salarié à plein temps se référant à l'activité principale et au mois précédant la semaine de référence.
Revenu lié à l'emploi indépendant: Ne s'applique pas.
Secteur informel: Ne s'applique pas.
Activité habituelle: Ne s'applique pas.
Classifications:
Branche d'activité économique (industrie)
Titre de la classification: Non disponible.
Groupes de population classifiés selon l'industrie: Les personnes ayant un emploi et les chômeurs.
Nombre de groupes de codage: 35 groupes.
Convertibilité avec la CITI: CITI-Rév.3
Profession
Titre de la classification: Non disponible.
Groupes de population classifiés selon la profession: Les personnes ayant un emploi et les chômeurs.
Nombre de groupes de codage: 371 groupes.
Convertibilité avec la CITP: CITP-1988.
Situation dans la profession
Titre de la classification: Non disponible.
Groupes de population classifiés par situation dans la profession: Les personnes ayant un emploi et les chômeurs.
Catégories de codage: Quatre groupes: salarié, employeur, travailleur indépendant, travailleur familial non rémunéré.
Convertibilité avec la CISP: CISP-1993.
Education
Titre de la classification: Non disponible.
Groupes de population classifiés selon l'éducation: Les personnes ayant un emploi et les chômeurs.
Catégories de codage: Six groupes: école primaire, achevée ou non, enseignement professionnel de base, enseignement secondaire général, enseignement secondaire professionnel, enseignement post-secondaire et enseignement tertiaire.
Convertibilité avec la CITE: CITE-1976 et CITE-1997.
Taille de l'échantillon et plan de sondage:
Unité finale d'échantillonnage: Logement.
Taille de l'échantillon (unités finales d'échantillonnage): 24 400 logements. L'échantillon élémentaire trimestriel total consiste en quatre échantillons élémentaires indépendants.
Taux de sondage: Allocation territoriale différenciée: environ 1/2000 logements enregistrés pour les zones urbaines et 1/1818 pour les zones rurales.
Base de sondage: L'échantillon est tiré du registre des unités statistiques géographiques du CSO, des districts de recensement, des groupes de districts de recensement ou groupes de recensement et des logements du recensement national. Ce registre est mis à jour chaque année en prenant en compte les informations relatives aux logements nouvellement construits, démolis ou transformés en surfaces non résidentielles au 1er janvier.
Renouvellement de l'échantillon: Conséquence du renouvellement annuel de la base.
Rotation:
Schéma: Quatre groupes de rotation appelés échantillons élémentaires: au cours d'un trimestre donné, l'échantillon comprend deux échantillons élémentaires inclus dans l'enquête au cours du trimestre précédent, un nouvel échantillon élémentaire introduit dans l'enquête pour la première fois et un autre, introduit dans l'enquête au cours du trimestre correspondant de l'année précédente. Les quatre échantillons élémentaires trimestriels sont renouvelés par rotation selon le schéma 2-(2)-2, c'est-à-dire qu'une unité de logement reste pendant deux trimestres successifs dans un échantillon, le quitte pendant deux trimestres et le réintègre pendant deux autres trimestres successifs avant de le quitter définitivement.
Pourcentage d'unités restant dans l'échantillon durant deux enquêtes successives: 50 pour cent.
Nombre maximum d'interrogatoires par unité de sondage: 4.
Durée nécessaire au renouvellement complet de l'échantillon: 5 trimestres.
Déroulement de l'enquête:
Type d'entretien: Entretiens personnels ou par téléphone avec écriture manuelle sur papier.
Nombre d'unités finales d'échantillonnage par zone de sondage: 1 880 logements.
Durée de déroulement de l'enquête:
Totale: Non disponible.
Par zone de sondage: Une semaine civile.
Organisation: Une équipe d'enquête permanente a été créee pour appliquer la nouvelle méthodologie de l'enquête en continu.
Nombre de personnes employées: Environ 300.
Substitution des unités finales en cas de non-réponse: Non.
Estimations et redressements:
Taux de non-réponse: 11,6%.
Redressement pour non-réponse: Oui.
Imputation en cas de non-réponse à une question spécifique: Non.
Redressement pour les régions/populations non couvertes: Oui.
Redressement en cas de sous-représentation: Non.
Redressement en cas de sur-représentation: Non.
Corrections des variations saisonnières: Non.
Historique de l'enquête:
Titre et date de la première enquête: Labour Force Survey, 1992.
Modifications et révisions significatives:
L'enquête trimestrielle a été interrompue pendant les 2ème et 3ème trimestres 1999. L'enquête est passée d'une observation périodique à une observation continue à compter du 4ème trimestre 1999.
En mai 1994, l'application des classifications économiques a été liée aux classifications internationales.
Documentation et dissémination:
Documentation
Titre des publications publiant les résultats: Statistical Yearbook of the Republic of Poland. Les publications ci-après: Labour Force Survey in Poland (Information and statistical papers) (en anglais); Quarterly Information on the Labour Market Developments (en polonais/anglais); Quarterly Economic Activity of the Population (en polonais); et Economic Activity and Unemployment in Poland (en polonais). (**Périodicité:** trimestrielle).
Titre des publications méthodologiques: Labour Force Survey in Poland.
Dissémination
Délai de publication des premiers résultats: Le même trimestre.
Information à l'avance du public des dates de publication initiale des résultats: Oui.
Mise à disposition, sur demande, des données non publiées: Oui.
Mise à disposition des données sur support informatique: Oui, sur disquette et par courrier électronique.
Site web: http://www.stat.gov.pl

Portugal

Titre de l'enquête: Inquérito ao emprego.
Organisme responsable de l'enquête:
Organisation et déroulement de l'enquête: Instituto Nacional de Estatística (INE).

Analyse et Publication des résultats: Instituto Nacional de Estatística (INE).

Sujets couverts par l'enquête: Emploi, chômage, sous-emploi, durée du travail, revenu, durée de l'emploi et du chômage, travailleurs découragés, travailleurs occasionnels, exercice d'autres emplois, industrie, profession, situation dans la profession, éducation.

Champ de l'enquête:

Territoire: L'ensemble du pays.

Groupes de population: La population résidente non institutionnelle âgée de 15 ans et plus vivant dans des logements privés. Sont exclues les personnes vivant dans des ménages collectifs si elles n'ont pas de liens familiaux avec des ménages ordinaires et les personnes vivant dans des caravanes résidentielles.

Disponibilité d'estimations selon d'autres sources pour les régions ou groupes exclus: Ne s'applique pas.

Groupes couverts par l'enquête mais exclus des résultats publiés: Non couvert par l'enquête.

Périodicité:

Réalisation de l'enquête: En continu.

Publication des résultats: Trimestrielle.

Période de référence:

Emploi: La semaine précédant l'entretien.

Recherche d'un emploi: Les quatre semaines précédant l'entretien.

Disponibilité pour travailler: Deux semaines après l'entretien.

Concepts et définitions:

Emploi: Ont un emploi toutes les personnes âgées de 15 ans et plus qui, durant la semaine de référence:

a) ont travaillé au moins une heure en vue d'un gain ou d'un bénéfice (en espèces ou en nature);

b) tout en ne travaillant pas, avaient un emploi avec lequel elles conservaient un lien formel;

c) possédaient une entreprise mais étaient absentes de leur travail pour une raison donnée;

d) étaient en préretraite mais travaillaient.

Sont également inclus dans les personnes ayant un emploi: a) les personnes ayant un emploi mais temporairement absentes pour cause de maladie ou d'accident pendant une durée maximum de 3 mois, de vacances annuelles, de congé de maternité/de paternité ou de congé parental, de congé d'éducation ou de formation, de conflit du travail, d'intempéries, de panne mécanique;

b) les personnes en mise en congé non rémunéré à l'initiative de l'employeur ou en mise à pied avec ou sans rémunération pendant 3 mois maximum;

c) les travailleurs occupés à plein temps ou à temps partiel et en quête d'un autre travail pendant la période de référence;

d) les personnes ayant effectué un travail quelconque, rémunéré ou en vue d'un bénéfice, durant la semaine de référence, tout en étant assujetties à la scolarité obligatoire, à la retraite et au bénéfice d'une pension, inscrites en tant que demandeurs d'emploi auprès d'un bureau de placement ou tout en percevant des allocations de chômage;

e) les étudiants à plein temps ou à temps partiel travaillant à plein temps ou à temps partiel;

f) les apprentis et stagiaires rémunérés;

g) les bénéficiaires de mesures de promotion de l'emploi;

h) les travailleurs familiaux non rémunérés;

i) les travailleurs saisonniers si la saison commence dans les 3 mois;

j) les volontaires et les militaires de carrière.

Chômage: Les personnes âgées de 15 ans et plus n'ayant pas travaillé pendant la semaine de référence, disponibles pour travailler dans les deux semaines, qui ont cherché du travail (c'est-à-dire effectué des démarches concrètes pour chercher un emploi) au cours des quatre dernières semaines ou qui n'ont ni travaillé ni cherché du travail mais ont trouvé un emploi censé commencer dans les 3 mois.

Sont également inclus dans les chômeurs:

a) les personnes à la recherche d'un emploi et/ou disponibles pour travailler tout en étant assujetties à la scolarité obligatoire ou à la retraite et au bénéfice d'une pension;

b) les étudiants à plein temps ou à temps partiel à la recherche d'un emploi à plein temps ou à temps partiel et immédiatement disponibles pour travailler.

Par "démarches concrètes pour trouver un emploi", on entend ce qui suit: avoir pris contact avec un bureau de placement public ou une agence de placement privée (agence de travail temporaire, cabinet de recrutement, etc.); avoir envoyé sa candidature à des employeurs; avoir cherché de l'aide auprès d'amis, de parents, de syndicats, etc.; avoir fait paraître ou consulté des petites annonces d'offres d'emploi ou y avoir répondu; avoir passé un test ou un examen de recrutement ou un entretien d'embauche; avoir cherché un terrain, des locaux ou du matériel; avoir demandé un permis, un agrément ou un financement.

Sous-emploi:

Sous-emploi lié à la durée du travail: Les personnes ayant un emploi âgées de 15 ans et plus qui, durant la semaine de référence, étaient disposées à faire davantage d'heures (en cherchant un emploi en plus de leur(s) emploi(s) actuel(s), un autre emploi comportant plus d'heures que leur(s) emploi(s) actuel(s) ou à faire plus d'heures dans leur(s) emploi(s) actuel(s)) et étaient disponibles pour ce faire.

Situations d'emploi inadéquat: On entend par là des conditions de travail, telles que le niveau d'instruction ou de rémunération, qui, comparées à d'autres, peuvent entraîner une diminution de la compétence ou de la productivité des travailleurs.

Durée du travail: Heures réellement effectuées dans l'emploi principal et dans l'exercice d'autres emplois: le nombre d'heures de travail réellement effectuées pendant la semaine de référence, y compris les heures supplémentaires mais non compris les absences. Heures habituelles effectuées dans l'emploi principal: le nombre d'heures de travail hebdomadaires habituellement effectuées, y compris les heures supplémentaires habituelles.

Revenu lié à l'emploi:

Revenu lié à l'emploi salarié: Gains nets des salariés: gain mensuel pour les paiements réguliers et montants annuels pour les autres.

Revenu lié à l'emploi indépendant: Ne s'applique pas.

Secteur informel: Ne s'applique pas.

Activité habituelle: Non disponible.

Classifications:

Branche d'activité économique (industrie)

Titre de la classification: NACE.

Groupes de population classifiés selon l'industrie: Les personnes ayant un emploi et les chômeurs (industrie du dernier emploi occupé pour ces derniers).

Nombre de groupes de codage: Non disponible.

Convertibilité avec la CITI: CITI-Rév.3.

Profession

Titre de la classification: National Classification of Occupations (CNP 1994).

Groupes de population classifiés selon la profession: Les personnes ayant un emploi et les chômeurs (profession exercée dans le dernier emploi occupé pour ces derniers).

Nombre de groupes de codage: Non disponible.

Convertibilité avec la CITP: CITP-1988.

Situation dans la profession

Titre de la classification: Non disponible.

Groupes de population classifiés par situation dans la profession: Les personnes ayant un emploi et les chômeurs (situation dans le dernier emploi occupé pour ces derniers).

Catégories de codage: Salariés; employeurs ayant des salariés; travailleurs indépendants sans salariés; travailleurs familiaux non rémunérés; autres.

Convertibilité avec la CISP: CISP-1993.

Education

Titre de la classification: Non disponible.

Groupes de population classifiés selon l'éducation: Les personnes ayant un emploi et les chômeurs.

Catégories de codage: 10 groupes.

Convertibilité avec la CITE: Non disponible.

Taille de l'échantillon et plan de sondage:

Unité finale d'échantillonnage: Logements.

Taille de l'échantillon (unités finales d'échantillonnage): 20 747 logements.

Taux de sondage: 0,68 pour cent.

Base de sondage: Les résultats du Recensement électoral de 1989 et le "Geographical Spatial Reference Framework" utilisé pour le Recensement de la population et des logements de 1991.

Renouvellement de l'échantillon: Non disponible.

Rotation:

Schéma: Les logements restent dans l'échantillon pendant six trimestres successifs. Chaque trimestre, un sixième de l'échantillon est remplacé.

Pourcentage d'unités restant dans l'échantillon durant deux enquêtes successives: 83,3 pour cent.

Nombre maximum d'interrogatoires par unité de sondage: Six.

Durée nécessaire au renouvellement complet de l'échantillon: Six trimestres.

Déroulement de l'enquête:

Type d'entretien: Entretiens personnels assistés par ordinateur.

Nombre d'unités finales d'échantillonnage par zone de sondage: Non disponible.

Durée de déroulement de l'enquête:
Totale: En continu.
Par zone de sondage: Non disponible.
Organisation: Des enquêteurs sont recrutés pour chaque enquête.
Nombre de personnes employées: Non disponible.
Substitution des unités finales en cas de non-réponse: Non.
Estimations et redressements:
Taux de non-réponse: 10%.
Redressement pour non-réponse: Non.
Imputation en cas de non-réponse à une question spécifique: Non.
Redressement pour les régions/populations non couvertes: Non.
Redressement en cas de sous-représentation: Non.
Redressement en cas de sur-représentation: Non.
Corrections des variations saisonnières: Non.
Historique de l'enquête:
Titre et date de la première enquête: Inquérito ao emprego 1974.
Modifications et révisions significatives: 1983-1997: enquête trimestrielle. Début 1998: enquête en continu, révision du plan de sondage et modifications apportées au questionnaire d'enquête.
Documentation et dissémination:
Documentation
Titre des publications publiant les résultats: Boletim Mensal de Estatística (mensuel); Estatísticas de Emprego (trimestriel).
Titre des publications méthodologiques: Estatísticas de Emprego (trimestriel).
Dissémination
Délai de publication des premiers résultats: Environ 2 mois après la fin du trimestre.
Information à l'avance du public des dates de publication initiale des résultats: Oui.
Mise à disposition, sur demande, des données non publiées: Oui.
Mise à disposition des données sur support informatique: Oui.
Site web: http://www.ine.pt.

Qatar

Titre de l'enquête: Labour force sample survey, avril 2001.
Organisme responsable de l'enquête:
Organisation et déroulement de l'enquête: Department of Statistics, Planning Council.
Analyse et Publication des résultats: Department of Statistics et Department of Social Planning, Planning Council.
Sujets couverts par l'enquête: Situation actuelle au regard de l'emploi et du chômage de la population qatarie et non qatarie en âge de travailler. Gains, durée et caractéristiques du travail des personnes ayant un emploi. Niveau d'instruction, profession actuelle ou exercée en dernier, branche d'activité économique, situation dans la profession, secteur d'emploi et ancienneté dans l'emploi des personnes ayant actuellement un emploi et des chômeurs ayant une expérience professionnelle préalable. Durée de la recherche d'emploi et méthodes utilisées actuellement par les chômeurs pour chercher du travail et auparavant par les personnes ayant un emploi pour trouver leur emploi actuel. Participation à des programmes de formation et motif de non-recherche d'emploi par les chômeurs qataris dans les secteurs privé et de l'économie mixte. Raison de l'inactivité des personnes actuellement en dehors de la population active.
Champ de l'enquête:
Territoire: Le pays tout entier.
Groupes de population: Tous les Qataris résidents et tous les non-Qataris ne vivant pas en collectivité. Sont également inclus les non-Qataris vivant dans des complexes d'habitation et dans des ménages collectifs.
Disponibilité d'estimations selon d'autres sources pour les régions ou groupes exclus: Non disponible.
Groupes couverts par l'enquête mais exclus des résultats publiés: La mesure de la population active concerne la population âgée de 12 ans et plus, mais en raison de la taille insignifiante de la population active déclarée âgée de 12 à 14 ans, les résultats publiés se limitent à la population âgée de 15 ans et plus. Les données relatives à la population jeune omise sont toutefois disponibles.
Périodicité:
Réalisation de l'enquête: Occasionnelle.
Publication des résultats: Pas encore publiés.
Période de référence:
Emploi: Semaine de référence fixe. Du 24 au 30 mars 2001.
Recherche d'un emploi: Recherche active d'un emploi par les chômeurs au cours du mois précédent. Ces informations ne sont toutefois pas utilisées pour classer l'enquêté dans la catégorie des chômeurs.
Disponibilité pour travailler: La disponibilité pour travailler n'est pas explicitement contrôlée dans le questionnaire.
Concepts et définitions:
Emploi: Les personnes âgées de 12 ans et plus qui ont été occupées à un travail quelconque pendant au moins une heure de n'importe quel jour de la semaine de l'enquête, ou qui avaient un lien formel avec l'emploi mais étaient temporairement absentes de leur travail, avec ou sans autorisation, pour une raison quelconque au cours de la semaine de l'enquête. Le travail est défini au sens large comme un travail rémunéré, en vue d'un bénéfice ou d'un gain familial.
Chômage: Les personnes âgées de 12 ans et plus qui n'ont pas travaillé, ne serait-ce qu'une heure, au cours de la semaine de l'enquête, n'étaient pas non plus temporairement absentes de leur travail tout en ayant un lien formel avec l'emploi et qui ont déclaré ne pas avoir trouvé d'emploi pendant la semaine de l'enquête.
Sous-emploi:
Sous-emploi lié à la durée du travail: Cette catégorie n'est pas définie explicitement mais le sous-emploi lié à la durée du travail peut être dérivé de deux questions: les personnes ayant un emploi qui ont travaillé moins de 6 jours pendant la semaine de l'enquête par manque de perspectives d'emploi pendant les autres jours de la semaine.
Situations d'emploi inadéquat: Ne s'applique pas.
Durée du travail: Trois concepts: le nombre de jours de travail réellement effectués pendant la semaine de l'enquête, le nombre d'heures de travail réellement effectuées pendant la semaine de l'enquête, y compris les heures supplémentaires, et la durée normale du travail hebdomadaire. Les heures de travail réellement effectuées couvrent le total des heures passées au travail, y compris les heures supplémentaires, le temps passé à effectuer des travaux d'entretien ou à attendre, et les pauses de courte durée. Cela exclut les heures rémunérées mais non travaillées, les pauses-repas et le temps de trajet travail-domicile.
Revenu lié à l'emploi:
Revenu lié à l'emploi salarié: Les gains totaux des salariés au cours de la dernière période de paie, qui peut être journalière, hebdomadaire ou mensuelle. Par gain, on entend la rémunération brute totale effectivement perçue, y compris la rémunération des heures supplémentaires en plus du traitement de base, les primes, la compensation spéciale en fonction de la nature du travail, les allocations de logement, les allocations familiales, les frais de transport, la nourriture et autres indemnités en nature.
Revenu lié à l'emploi indépendant: Ne s'applique pas.
Secteur informel: Non disponible.
Activité habituelle: Non disponible.
Classifications:
Les classifications utilisées dans l'enquête sur la population active qatarie de 2001 sont celles qui ont été mises au point pour le recensement de la population et des logements de mars 1997.
Branche d'activité économique (industrie)
Titre de la classification: Classification nationale type des activités économiques (mai 1996).
Groupes de population classifiés selon l'industrie: Les personnes ayant un emploi et les chômeurs ayant une expérience professionnelle préalable.
Nombre de groupes de codage: Niveau à quatre chiffres. Résultats publiés au niveau à un chiffre. 18 catégories.
Convertibilité avec la CITI: CITI-Rév.3.
Profession
Titre de la classification: Classification type des professions (mai 1996).
Groupes de population classifiés selon la profession: Les personnes ayant un emploi et les chômeurs ayant une expérience professionnelle préalable.
Nombre de groupes de codage: Niveau à quatre chiffres. Les résultats doivent être publiés au niveau à un chiffre.
Convertibilité avec la CITP: CITP-1988.
Situation dans la profession
Titre de la classification: Non disponible.
Groupes de population classifiés par situation dans la profession: Les personnes ayant un emploi uniquement.
Catégories de codage: Employeur. Travailleur indépendant. Salarié. Travailleur familial non rémunéré. Autres.
Convertibilité avec la CISP: CISP-1996.
Education
Titre de la classification: Non disponible.
Groupes de population classifiés selon l'éducation: La population âgée de 10 ans et plus.

Catégories de codage: Codage au niveau à cinq chiffres. Les résultats doivent être publiés au niveau à un chiffre pour le niveau d'instruction. Il existe également un codage au cinquième niveau de détail pour la spécialisation de la population ayant suivi l'enseignement secondaire ou supérieur.
Convertibilité avec la CITE: CITE-1977.
Taille de l'échantillon et plan de sondage:
Unité finale d'échantillonnage: Ménages.
Taille de l'échantillon (unités finales d'échantillonnage): 1 956 ménages qataris, 1 892 ménages non qataris et 4 287 ménages collectifs.
Taux de sondage: 5 pour cent.
Base de sondage: Les secteurs de recensement du recensement de la population et des logements de 1997. Echantillonnage à deux degrés. Les unités primaires d'échantillonnage sont formées en regroupant des îlots de recensement (secteurs de recensement) contigus, de telle sorte que chaque unité primaire contienne au moins 25 unités finales d'échantillonnage (ménages pour les ménages qataris et non qataris, personnes pour les ménages collectifs). Afin de respecter, dans la mesure du possible, la structure administrative du Qatar, le nombre d'unités primaires à cheval sur plusieurs zones administratives est réduit au minimum et celles à cheval sur des limites municipales sont totalement évitées. Pour des raisons pratiques, les très grandes unités primaires des strates des ménages collectifs ont été divisées en plusieurs parties.
Les unités primaires sont échantillonnées en proportion de leur taille, mesurée en nombre de ménages pour les deux premières strates et en nombre de personnes pour la troisième. Les mesures de la taille sont déterminées en fonction du recensement de 1997. Au cours de la deuxième phase, 20 ménages sont sélectionnés dans chaque unité primaire d'échantillonnage. Pour les ménages collectifs, les unités primaires sont les unités primaires d'échantillonnage urbaines ou rurales.
Au cours de la deuxième phase, un échantillon de 20 ménages dans chaque unité primaire est sélectionné dans les deux strates formées par les ménages qataris et non qataris selon un plan d'échantillonnage systématique. Dans le cas des ménages collectifs, 50 personnes ont été systématiquement sélectionnées sur chaque liste d'unités primaires d'échantillonnage.
Renouvellement de l'échantillon: Le renouvellement se fait au stade de l'établissement des listes d'unités primaires d'échantillonnage.
Rotation: Néant.
Déroulement de l'enquête:
Type d'entretien: Entretien personnel.
Nombre d'unités finales d'échantillonnage par zone de sondage: Environ 20 ménages pour les ménages qataris et non qataris, et 50 personnes pour les ménages collectifs.
Durée de déroulement de l'enquête:
Totale: Etablissement des listes d'unités primaires d'échantillonnage au cours du mois de février 2001. Conduite des entretiens au cours du mois d'avril 2001.
Par zone de sondage: 3 à 4 ménages par jour pour les ménages qataris et non qataris et 20 à 24 personnes par jour pour les ménages collectifs.
Organisation: Ad hoc.
Nombre de personnes employées: Environ 64 enquêteurs et 15 cadres.
Substitution des unités finales en cas de non-réponse: Non.
Estimations et redressements:
Taux de non-réponse: 3,6% chez les ménages qataris et 1,3% chez les ménages non qataris.
Redressement pour non-réponse: Oui, par l'inverse du taux de réponse par strate.
Imputation en cas de non-réponse à une question spécifique: Oui, en faisant la moyenne du groupe.
Redressement pour les régions/populations non couvertes: Non.
Redressement en cas de sous-représentation: Oui, par estimations par le quotient des données de projection de la population qatarie et non qatarie. Aussi par la méthode généralisée des moindres carrés appliquée à la répartition par sexe et âge des résultats du recensement de 1997 pour la population qatarie.
Redressement en cas de sur-représentation: Non disponible.
Corrections des variations saisonnières: Non.
Historique de l'enquête:
Titre et date de la première enquête: Labour force sample survey, 1993.
Modifications et révisions significatives: L'enquête sur la population active qatarie de 2001 fait suite à une série d'enquêtes limitées sur les ménages réalisées en 1984, 1989 et 1993. Les enquêtes de 1984 et 1989 étaient des enquêtes sur le revenu et les dépenses des ménages contenant des informations limitées sur les caractéristiques de l'emploi de la population. L'enquête de 1993 était une enquête sur la population active mais les résultats n'en ont pas été publiés.
Documentation et dissémination:
Documentation
Titre des publications publiant les résultats: A paraître. Décembre 2001.
Titre des publications méthodologiques: A paraître. Décembre 2001.
Dissémination
Délai de publication des premiers résultats: 8 mois.
Information à l'avance du public des dates de publication initiale des résultats: Non.
Mise à disposition, sur demande, des données non publiées: Oui.
Mise à disposition des données sur support informatique: Les données totalisées sont disponibles sur disquettes, sur demande.

Rive occidentale et Bande de Gaza

Titre de l'enquête: Labour Force Survey
Organisme responsable de l'enquête:
Organisation et déroulement de l'enquête: Palestinian Central Bureau of Statistics (PCBS).
Analyse et publication des résultats: Palestinian Central Bureau of Statistics (PCBS).
Sujets couverts par l'enquête: Emploi, chômage, sous-emploi, durée du travail, salaires, durée de l'emploi et du chômage, travailleurs découragés, industrie, profession, situation dans la profession, niveau d'instruction, exercice d'autres emplois, situation des personnes en dehors de la population active, nombre de jours de travail mensuels.
Champ de l'enquête:
Territoire: L'ensemble du territoire.
Groupes de population: Toutes les personnes âgées de 10 ans et plus, à l'exception de celles vivant en institution et de celles qui résident à l'étranger pendant plus d'un an.
Disponibilité d'estimations selon d'autres sources pour les régions ou groupes exclus: Non disponible.
Groupes couverts par l'enquête mais exclus des résultats publiés: Les personnes âgées de 10 à 14 ans.
Périodicité:
Réalisation de l'enquête: En continu.
Publication des résultats: Trimestrielle et annuelle.
Période de référence:
Emploi: Semaine de référence variable. La semaine qui se termine le vendredi précédant la visite de l'enquêteur au ménage.
Recherche d'un emploi: Semaine de référence variable. La semaine qui se termine le vendredi précédant la visite de l'enquêteur au ménage.
Disponibilité pour travailler: Semaine de référence variable. La semaine qui se termine le vendredi précédant la visite de l'enquêteur au ménage.
Concepts et définitions:
Emploi: Les personnes âgées de 15 ans et plus qui ont travaillé au moins une heure pendant la période de référence ou qui ne travaillaient pas pendant la semaine de référence mais avaient un emploi ou possédaient une entreprise d'où elles étaient temporairement absentes (pour cause de maladie, de vacances, d'arrêt de travail temporaire, de maternité, de congé parental ou d'éducation, de congé de formation ou pour toute autre raison).
Sont également considérées comme ayant un emploi:
a) les personnes en mise à pied temporaire sans rémunération;
b) les travailleurs à temps complet ou à temps partiel à la recherche d'un autre travail pendant la semaine de référence;
c) les étudiants à temps complet ou à temps partiel travaillant à temps complet ou à temps partiel;
d) les apprentis et stagiaires rémunérés ou non;
e) les travailleurs familiaux non rémunérés (au travail ou temporairement absents de leur travail pendant la semaine de référence);
f) les membres des forces armées (volontaires, militaires de carrière et conscrits).
Chômage: Les personnes âgées de 15 ans et plus qui n'ont pas travaillé pendant la semaine de référence, n'étaient pas absentes de leur emploi, étaient disponibles pour travailler et cherchaient activement du travail pendant la semaine de référence. Par "recherche d'emploi", on entend avoir entrepris des démarches concrètes, pendant la semaine de référence, pour trouver un emploi salarié ou

indépendant. Les personnes à la recherche d'un emploi sont classés selon qu'elles sont :

i) disponibles pour travailler: toute personne disposée à travailler si on lui offre un emploi et si aucune raison ne l'empêche de l'accepter, même si elle n'a rien fait pour en trouver un;

ii) à la recherche active d'un emploi: toute personne désireuse de travailler et qui recherche activement un emploi, par la lecture des petites annonces parues dans la presse, en interrogeant ses amis, en s'inscrivant aux bureaux de placement ou en sollicitant des employeurs.

Sont également considérés comme chômeurs:

a) les personnes travaillant en Israël et qui étaient absentes de leur travail en raison des bouclages;

b) les personnes en mise en congé non rémunéré pour une durée indéterminée ou en congé non rémunéré à l'initiative de l'employeur;

c) les personnes sans emploi et immédiatement disponibles pour travailler, qui ont pris des dispositions pour commencer à travailler dans un nouvel emploi à une date ultérieure à la semaine de référence ou qui ont tenté de créer leur propre entreprise;

d) les étudiants à temps complet ou à temps partiel, disponibles pour travailler et qui cherchent un emploi à temps complet ou à temps partiel.

Sous-emploi:

Sous-emploi lié à la durée du travail: Les personnes ayant travaillé moins de 35 heures au cours de la semaine de référence ou qui ont travaillé moins de la durée normale du travail dans leur profession.

Situations d'emploi inadéquat: Mauvaise affectation des ressources humaines ou déséquilibre fondamental entre main-d'œuvre et d'autres facteurs, tel que revenu insuffisant, sous-utilisation, mauvaises conditions de travail dans l'emploi actuel ou d'autres motifs d'ordre économique.

Durée du travail: Le nombre d'heures réellement effectuées au cours de la semaine de référence ainsi que les heures supplémentaires et le temps passé sur le lieu de travail à faire des activités telles que la préparation de celui-ci. Les congés, les pauses repas et le temps passé en transport du domicile au lieu de travail et vice versa sont exclus des heures travaillées.

Revenu lié à l'emploi:

Revenu lié à l'emploi salarié: Non couvert par l'enquête.

Revenu lié à l'emploi indépendant: Non couvert par l'enquête.

Secteur informel: Non couvert par l'enquête.

Activité habituelle: Non couvert par l'enquête.

Classifications:

Branche d'activité économique (industrie):

Titre de la classification: Classification nationale fondée sur la CITI Rév.3.

Groupes de population classifiés selon l'industrie: Les personnes ayant un emploi et les chômeurs ayant eu une expérience professionnelle au cours des 12 derniers mois.

Nombre de groupes de codage: Au niveau à 4 chiffres.

Convertibilité avec la CITI: CITI-Rév. 3.

Profession:

Titre de la classification: Classification nationale fondée sur la CITP-1988.

Groupes de population classifiés selon la profession: Les personnes ayant un emploi et les chômeurs ayant eu une expérience professionnelle au cours des 12 derniers mois.

Nombre de groupes de codage: Au niveau à 3 chiffres.

Convertibilité avec la CITP: CITP-1988.

Situation dans la profession:

Titre de la classification: Classification nationale.

Groupes de population classifiés par situation dans la profession: Les personnes ayant un emploi et les chômeurs ayant eu une expérience professionnelle au cours des 12 derniers mois.

Catégories de codage: Employeurs, salariés, travailleurs indépendants, travailleurs familiaux non rémunérés, autres.

Convertibilité avec la CISP: CISP-1993.

Education:

Titre de la classification: Classification nationale.

Groupes de population classifiés selon l'éducation: Toutes les personnes âgées de 10 ans et plus.

Catégories de codage: Analphabète; sait lire et écrire; enseignement élémentaire; enseignement préparatoire; enseignement secondaire; diplôme associé; diplôme de premier cycle en lettres ou en sciences; diplôme de deuxième cycle ; mastère ; doctorat.

Convertibilité avec la CITE: CITE-76.

Taille de l'échantillon et plan de sondage:

Unité finale d'échantillonnage: Ménages.

Taille de l'échantillon (unités finales d'échantillonnage): Environ 7 600 ménages représentant approximativement 22 000 personnes en âge de travailler.

Taux de sondage: 1,7 pour cent.

Base de sondage: Echantillon maître basé sur le Housing and Establishments Census de 1997. L'enquête est basée sur un échantillon aléatoire en grappes stratifié à deux degrés.

Renouvellement de l'échantillon: En décembre 1999, à partir des listes des ménages.

Rotation:

Schéma: Les ménages sont conservés dans l'échantillon pendant deux enquêtes successives, le quittent pendant les deux enquêtes suivantes et le réintègrent pendant deux autres enquêtes successives avant de le quitter définitivement.

Pourcentage d'unités restant dans l'échantillon durant deux enquêtes successives: 50 pour cent.

Nombre maximum d'interrogatoires par unité de sondage: 4.

Durée nécessaire au renouvellement complet de l'échantillon: 5 ans.

Déroulement de l'enquête:

Type d'entretien: Entretien personnel avec enregistrement manuel sur papier.

Nombre d'unites finales d'echantillonnage par zone de sondage: 16 ménages.

Durée de déroulement de l'enquête:

Totale: 3 mois (déroulement en continu).

Par zone de sondage: 2 jours.

Organisation: Permanente.

Nombre de personnes employées: 12 enquêteurs, 4 cadres, 2 codeurs, 2 responsables de la mise en forme des données et 1 coordinateur.

Substitution des unités de sondage en cas de non-réponse: Non.

Estimations et redressements:

Taux de non-réponse: 9%.

Redressement pour non-réponse: Oui.

Imputation en cas de non-réponse à une question spécifique: Non.

Redressement pour les régions/populations non couvertes: Ne s'applique pas.

Redressement en cas de sous-représentation: Oui.

Redressement en cas de sur-représentation: Oui.

Corrections des variations saisonnières: Non.

Historique de l'enquête:

Titre et date de la première enquête: Labor Force Survey 1995.

Modifications et révisions significatives: Ne s'applique pas.

Documentation et dissémination:

Documentation:

Titre des publications publiant les résultats: Labour Force Survey: Main Findings (trimestriel); Labour Force Survey: Annual Report.

Titre des publications méthodologiques: Idem.

Dissémination:

Délai de publication des premiers résultats: Environ 2 mois.

Information à l'avance du public des dates de publication initiale des résultats: Oui.

Mise à disposition, sur demande, des données non publiées: Oui.

Mise à disposition des données sur support informatique: Les données totalisées sont disponibles sur support informatique sur demande.

Site web: http://www.pcbs.org.

Roumanie

Titre de l'enquête: Household Labour Force Survey (AMIGO).

Organisme responsable de l'enquête:

Organisation et déroulement de l'enquête: National Institute for Statistics (NIS).

Analyse et Publication des résultats: National Institute for Statistics (NIS).

Sujets couverts par l'enquête: Emploi, chômage, sous-emploi, durée du travail, durée du chômage, travailleurs découragés, industrie, profession, situation dans la profession, niveau d'instruction, exercice d'autres emplois.

Champ de l'enquête:

Territoire: L'ensemble du pays.

Groupes de population: Tous les résidents permanents vivant dans des ménages sélectionnés pour l'enquête, y compris ceux qui sont temporairement absents pendant plus de six mois s'ils sont en contact permanent avec leur famille, tels que conscrits, étudiants et écoliers étudiant loin de leur lieu de résidence permanent, les personnes travaillant dans d'autres localités que leur lieu de résidence permanent, les pensionnaires temporaires d'établissements pénitentiaires ou psychiatriques et les personnes hospitalisées ainsi que celles qui suivent un traitement de rééducation. Les personnes vivant en permanence dans des établissements communs tels qu'institutions spécialisées, homes pour personnes âgées, établissements pour handicapés, sanatoriums, etc. sont exclues.

Disponibilité d'estimations selon d'autres sources pour les régions ou groupes exclus: Non disponible.

Groupes couverts par l'enquête mais exclus des résultats publiés: Non disponible.

Périodicité:

Réalisation de l'enquête: Enquête trimestrielle en continu.

Publication des résultats: Trimestrielle et annuelle.

Période de référence:

Emploi: Une semaine (période de référence variable).

Recherche d'un emploi: Les quatre dernières semaines.

Disponibilité pour travailler: Les quinze prochains jours.

Concepts et définitions:

Emploi: Cette catégorie comprend toutes les personnes âgées de 15 ans et plus ayant exercé une activité économique ou sociale de production de biens ou de prestation de services pendant au moins une heure au cours de la période de référence (une semaine), dans le but de gagner un certain revenu sous forme de salaire, de rémunération en nature ou d'autres avantages. Sont également considérées comme ayant un emploi les personnes temporairement absentes de leur travail qui ont conservé des liens formels avec leur lieu de travail et les membres des forces armées (personnel d'active et conscrits). Pour les travailleurs indépendants et les travailleurs familiaux non rémunérés occupés dans l'agriculture, la durée minimum du travail effectué pendant la semaine de référence est de 15 heures.

Cette catégorie inclut:

a)les personnes ayant un emploi mais temporairement absentes pour cause de maladie/d'accident, de congés/de vacances annuelles, de congé de maternité légal, de congé parental, de congé pour études, de stages de formation professionnelle et de cours professionnels, de grève ou de conflit, d'arrêts temporaires du travail pour cause d'intempéries, de panne mécanique, de pénurie de matières premières ou d'énergie, d'incidents techniques, etc.

b)les personnes en mise à pied qui continuent de percevoir au moins 50 pour cent de leur salaire ou traitement de la part de leur employeur ou qui ont l'assurance de retourner au travail dans les trois mois;

c)les personnes absentes de leur travail pour une longue durée (trois mois et plus), si elles continuent de percevoir au moins 50 pour cent de leur salaire ou traitement de la part de leur employeur;

d)les travailleurs occupés à plein temps ou à temps partiel et en quête d'un autre emploi;

e)les personnes ayant effectué un travail quelconque, rémunéré ou en vue d'un bénéfice, durant la semaine de référence, tout en étant assujetties à la scolarité obligatoire ou à la retraite et au bénéfice d'une pension, même si elles étaient inscrites en tant que demandeurs d'emploi auprès d'un bureau de placement ou même si elles percevaient des allocations de chômage;

f)les étudiants à plein temps ou à temps partiel travaillant à plein temps ou à temps partiel;

g)les apprentis et stagiaires rémunérés;

h)les travailleurs familiaux non rémunérés temporairement absents pendant la semaine de référence et les travailleurs saisonniers ne travaillant pas pendant la morte-saison (à moins qu'ils ne cherchent activement un emploi et qu'ils ne soient disponibles pour travailler, auquel cas ils sont considérés comme chômeurs).

Chômage: Les personnes âgées de 15 ans et plus qui, durant la période de référence, étaient sans emploi (n'avaient pas d'emploi et n'exerçaient pas d'activité dans le but de s'assurer un revenu), disponibles pour commencer à travailler dans les 15 jours et ayant cherché activement du travail par des moyens divers au cours des quatre dernières semaines.

Cette catégorie inclut:

a)les personnes ayant trouvé un emploi commençant dans un délai maximum de trois mois;

b)les personnes en mise à pied qui ne perçoivent ni salaire ni traitement significatif (moins de 50 pour cent) de leur employeur, sont immédiatement disponibles pour travailler et recherchent activement un emploi;

c)les travailleurs saisonniers durant la morte-saison, s'ils sont immédiatement disponibles pour travailler et recherchent activement un emploi.

Sous-emploi:

Sous-emploi lié à la durée du travail: Les personnes ayant un emploi qui ont travaillé moins que la durée habituelle du travail dans des circonstances indépendantes de leur volonté, souhaitent exercer une activité à temps complet ou exercer un emploi complémentaire et sont disponibles pour faire davantage d'heures au cours des 15 prochains jours.

Situations d'emploi inadéquat: Ne s'applique pas.

Durée du travail:

Les heures de travail habituelles correspondent à la durée d'une semaine de travail normale, y compris les heures supplémentaires, si elles ont été systématiquement travaillées, par opposition aux heures fixées par convention collective ou par d'autres conventions ou accords.

Les heures de travail réellement effectuées sont les heures effectuées pendant la semaine de référence dans l'activité principale uniquement, y compris les heures supplémentaires non systématiquement travaillées; leur nombre peut être supérieur, égal ou inférieur au nombre d'heures habituelles.

Revenu lié à l'emploi:

Revenu lié à l'emploi salarié: Ne s'applique pas.

Revenu lié à l'emploi indépendant: Ne s'applique pas.

Secteur informel: Ne s'applique pas.

Activité habituelle: La situation au regard de l'activité principale se réfère à l'appréciation que porte chaque personne sur sa situation au regard de l'activité au cours des trois derniers mois.

Classifications:

Branche d'activité économique (industrie)

Titre de la classification: CANE (Classification de toutes les activités de l'économie nationale).

Groupes de population classifiés selon l'industrie: Les personnes ayant un emploi et les chômeurs (industrie du dernier emploi occupé pour ces derniers).

Nombre de groupes de codage: 17 groupes.

Convertibilité avec la CITI: CITI-Rév.3

Profession

Titre de la classification: CORE (Classification des professions en Roumanie).

Groupes de population classifiés selon la profession: Les personnes ayant un emploi et les chômeurs (profession exercée dans le dernier emploi pour ces derniers).

Nombre de groupes de codage: 10 groupes.

Convertibilité avec la CITP: CITP-1988.

Situation dans la profession

Titre de la classification: Non disponible.

Groupes de population classifiés par situation dans la profession: Les personnes ayant un emploi et les chômeurs (situation du dernier emploi pour ces derniers).

Catégories de codage: Cinq groupes: salarié, travailleur indépendant ayant des salariés (employeur), travailleur indépendant sans salariés (travailleur à son compte), travailleur familial non rémunéré, membre d'une entreprise ou d'une coopérative agricoles.

Convertibilité avec la CISP: CISP-1993.

Education

Titre de la classification: Non disponible.

Groupes de population classifiés selon l'éducation: Les personnes ayant un emploi et les chômeurs.

Catégories de codage: Cinq groupes: sans instruction, enseignement primaire (2 sous-groupes), enseignement professionnel (2 sous-groupes), enseignement secondaire (2 sous-groupes), enseignement universitaire (2 sous-groupes).

Convertibilité avec la CITE: CITE-1997.

Taille de l'échantillon et plan de sondage:

Unité finale d'échantillonnage: Logement (avec tous les ménages).

Taille de l'échantillon (unités finales d'échantillonnage): 18 036 logements situés dans les zones géographiques sélectionnées.

Taux de sondage: Au premier degré de sondage, 0,0331 pour les zones rurales et 0,0325 pour les zones urbaines.

Base de sondage: Conçue en 1992-1993, basée sur les résultats du Recensement de la population et du logement de janvier 1992 (January 1992 Population and Housing Census) en tant qu'échantillon principal (EMZOT) de 501 zones géographiques (environ 250 000 logements). Ces zones sont considérées comme les unités primaires d'échantillonnage au premier degré du plan de sondage pour toutes les enquêtes sur les ménages; 259 unités primaires dans les zones urbaines et 242 dans les zones rurales. Au deuxième degré, les unités de logement de chaque unité primaire ont été systématiquement sélectionnées.

Renouvellement de l'échantillon: L'échantillon principal EMZOT est régulièrement renouvelé.

Rotation:

Schéma: L'échantillon renouvelé est conçu selon le modèle 2-(2)-2. Ainsi, quatre groupes de rotation ou sous-échantillons sont désignés.

Un logement est inclus dans l'échantillon pendant deux trimestres successifs, le quitte pendant deux trimestres, puis le réintègre pendant deux autres trimestres successifs avant de le quitter définitivement.

Pourcentage d'unités restant dans l'échantillon durant deux enquêtes successives: 50 pour cent.

Nombre maximum d'interrogatoires par unité de sondage: Quatre par unité finale d'échantillonnage.

Durée nécessaire au renouvellement complet de l'échantillon: Un logement est traité pendant six trimestres.

Déroulement de l'enquête:

Type d'entretien: Entretien direct avec écriture manuelle sur papier.

Nombre d'unités finales d'échantillonnage par zone de sondage: 36 logements par trimestre.

Durée de déroulement de l'enquête:

Totale: Les semaines de référence sont réparties également sur toute l'année (52 semaines). L'entretien a lieu dans la semaine suivant la semaine de référence.

Par zone de sondage: Une semaine civile.

Organisation: Structure d'enquête permanente.

Nombre de personnes employées: 501 enquêteurs, 140 cadres et 47 responsables.

Substitution des unités finales en cas de non-réponse: Non.

Estimations et redressements:

Taux de non-réponse: 6,2 % (au cours du troisième trimestre de 2001, par exemple).

Redressement pour non-réponse: Oui.

Imputation en cas de non-réponse à une question spécifique: Oui, à l'aide de l'imputation « hot-deck », imputation «cold-deck ».

Redressement pour les régions/populations non couvertes: Non disponible.

Redressement en cas de sous-représentation: Oui.

Redressement en cas de sur-représentation: Oui.

Corrections des variations saisonnières: Non.

Historique de l'enquête:

Titre et date de la première enquête: Household Labour Force Survey (AMIGO), mars 1992.

Modifications et révisions significatives: Jusqu'en 1996, l'enquête était annuelle et couvrait les personnes âgées de 14 ans et plus. A partir du premier trimestre 1999, le concept de sous-emploi est conforme aux prescriptions de la 16ème Conférence internationale des statisticiens du travail (1998). A partir du premier trimestre 2002, les concepts d'emploi, de chômage et de situation au regard de l'activité principale sont conformes aux dispositions du Règlement (CE) n°1897/2000 de la Commission et du Règlement (CE) n°1575/2000 de la Commission.

Documentation et dissémination:

Documentation

Titre des publications publiant les résultats: Household Labour Force Survey (AMIGO) – rapport détaillé - communiqué de presse; Statistical Yearbook (NIS); Quarterly Bulletin (NIS).

Titre des publications méthodologiques: Idem.

Dissémination

Délai de publication des premiers résultats: Environ un trimestre.

Information à l'avance du public des dates de publication initiale des résultats: Non.

Mise à disposition, sur demande, des données non publiées: Oui.

Mise à disposition des données sur support informatique: Oui, sur disquette.

Site web: http://www.insse.ro/.

Royaume-Uni

Titre de l'enquête: Labour Force Survey.

Organisme responsable de l'enquête:

Organisation et déroulement de l'enquête: Office for National Statistics.

Analyse et Publication des résultats: Office for National Statistics.

Sujets couverts par l'enquête: Emploi, chômage, sous-emploi, durée du travail, salaires, durée de l'emploi, durée du chômage, travailleurs découragés, industrie, profession, situation dans la profession, niveau d'instruction, exercice d'autres emplois.

Autres sujets couverts: gains, invalidité, éducation et formation, trajet pour se rendre au travail, maladie, représentation syndicale, prestations et santé.

Champ de l'enquête:

Territoire: L'ensemble du pays.

Groupes de population: Toutes les personnes âgées de 16 ans et plus vivant dans des ménages ordinaires, y compris les militaires de carrière, les étudiants vivant en résidence universitaire (recensés à l'adresse de leurs parents), le personnel du Service national de la santé (National Health Service NHS) et le personnel hospitalier vivant dans des logements administrés par le NHS ou des hôpitaux. Les autres populations institutionnelles et les bases militaires communales sont exclues. Pour les personnes âgées de moins de 16 ans, seuls les détails démographiques sont recueillis. La population britannique en âge de travailler est de 16 à 59 ans pour les femmes et de 16 à 64 ans pour les hommes.

Disponibilité d'estimations selon d'autres sources pour les régions ou groupes exclus: Non disponible.

Groupes couverts par l'enquête mais exclus des résultats publiés: Tous les groupes inclus dans l'échantillon le sont dans les résultats.

Périodicité:

Réalisation de l'enquête: L'enquête a lieu en continu et donne des résultats trimestriels.

Publication des résultats: Des moyennes mobiles sur trois mois sont publiées tous les mois, tous les trimestres et tous les ans.

Période de référence:

Emploi: Une semaine variable.

Recherche d'un emploi: Les quatre dernières semaines (période de référence variable).

Disponibilité pour travailler: Deux semaines (période de référence variable).

Concepts et définitions:

Emploi: Travail rémunéré ou en vue d'un bénéfice effectué pendant au moins une heure par semaine, y compris par les travailleurs familiaux non rémunérés. Les personnes temporairement absentes de leur travail ont un emploi si cette absence temporaire est de moins de six mois ou si la personne continue d'être rémunérée et a l'assurance de retourner au travail.

Cette catégorie inclut:

a)les personnes absentes pour cause de maladie, d'accident, de vacances, de congés annuels, de congé de maternité ou de paternité, de congé d'éducation ou de formation, d'absence non autorisée, de conflit du travail, d'intempéries, de panne mécanique, de mise à pied temporaire ou de durée indéterminée (6 mois) sans rémunération et de mise en congé non rémunéré à l'initiative de l'employeur;

b)les travailleurs occupés à plein temps ou à temps partiel et en quête d'un autre travail pendant la semaine de référence;

c)les personnes ayant effectué un travail quelconque, rémunéré ou en vue d'un bénéfice, pendant la semaine de référence, à la retraite et au bénéfice d'une pension, inscrites en tant que demandeurs d'emploi auprès d'un bureau de placement ou percevant des allocations de chômage;

d)les étudiants à plein temps ou à temps partiel travaillant à plein temps ou à temps partiel;

e)les apprentis et stagiaires rémunérés;

f)les bénéficiaires de mesures de promotion de l'emploi;

g)les volontaires et les militaires de carrière.

Chômage: Sans emploi durant la semaine de référence, disponibles pour commencer à travailler dans les deux semaines et ayant soit cherché du travail au cours des quatre semaines précédentes soit déjà trouvé un emploi devant commencer ultérieurement.

Cette catégorie inclut:

a)les personnes qui essayent de créer leur propre entreprise;

b)les personnes à la retraite et au bénéfice d'une pension, les travailleurs familiaux non rémunérés temporairement absents de leur travail et les travailleurs saisonniers non au travail, s'ils sont disponibles et cherchent du travail;

c)les étudiants à plein temps ou à temps partiel à la recherche d'un emploi à plein temps ou à temps partiel.

Sous-emploi:

Sous-emploi lié à la durée du travail: L'ONS recueille des données sur les personnes souhaitant effectuer davantage d'heures de travail et entamera sous peu une évaluation de ces données; les estimations relatives au sous-emploi lié à la durée du travail ne sont pas publiées. A l'avenir, une définition du sous-emploi conforme à l'interprétation "opérationnalisée" des recommandations internationales par Eurostat sera appliquée.

Situations d'emploi inadéquat: Ne s'applique pas.

Durée du travail: Les heures de travail habituellement effectuées dans l'activité principale, le nombre réel d'heures de travail effectuées au cours de la semaine de référence dans l'activité principale et dans l'exercice d'un autre emploi, y compris les heures supplémentaires rémunérées ou non, et non compris le temps consacré aux pauses-repas.

Revenu lié à l'emploi:

Revenu lié à l'emploi salarié: Tous les gains en espèces, paiements en nature, la rémunération liée aux bénéfices et certaines prestations

(soutien du revenu, allocations chômage), s'ils sont cités par l'enquêté. La paie peut être exprimée en chiffres bruts ou nets, tant pour l'activité principale que pour l'exercice d'autres emplois. La période de référence est celle indiquée dans la dernière enveloppe de paie.
Revenu lié à l'emploi indépendant: Ne s'applique pas.
Secteur informel: Ne s'applique pas.
Activité habituelle: Ne s'applique pas.
Classifications:
Branche d'activité économique (industrie)
Titre de la classification: Standard Industrial Classification 1992 (SIC92).
Groupes de population classifiés selon l'industrie: Les personnes ayant un emploi et les chômeurs.
Nombre de groupes de codage: 458.
Convertibilité avec la CITI: CITI-Rév.3 au niveau à quatre chiffres; le SIC92 est identique.
Profession
Titre de la classification: Standard Occupational Classification (SOC).
Groupes de population classifiés selon la profession: Les personnes ayant un emploi et les chômeurs.
Nombre de groupes de codage: 374.
Convertibilité avec la CITP: Le SOC en est aussi proche que possible au niveau agrégé. L'ONS et l'Institute of Employment Research révisent le SOC dans le sens d'une meilleure harmonisation avec la CITP.
Situation dans la profession
Titre de la classification: Non disponible.
Groupes de population classifiés par situation dans la profession: Les personnes ayant un emploi et les chômeurs.
Catégories de codage: Quatre groupes: salariés, travailleurs indépendants, bénéficiaires des programmes de formation de l'Etat, travailleurs familiaux non rémunérés.
Convertibilité avec la CISP: CISP-1993.
Education
Titre de la classification: Non disponible.
Groupes de population classifiés selon l'éducation: Les personnes ayant un emploi et les chômeurs.
Catégories de codage: Tous les groupes de la CITE.
Convertibilité avec la CITE: A partir de 1999, la CITE-1997 peut être dérivée des données du LFS britannique.
Taille de l'échantillon et plan de sondage:
Unité finale d'échantillonnage: Adresse.
Taille de l'échantillon (unités finales d'échantillonnage): 88 740 adresses.
Taux de sondage: Juste en dessous de 0,04 pour cent.
Base de sondage: Le sous-fichier des "petits utilisateurs" du fichier des adresses postales (PAF), plus la liste des logements gérés par le NHS et les hôpitaux. Le PAF est une liste informatique, établie par la Poste, de toutes les adresses (points de remise) auxquelles le courrier est distribué. Les "petits utilisateurs" sont les points de remise recevant moins de 25 unités de courrier par jour (ce qui est le cas de la majorité des ménages ordinaires).
Renouvellement de l'échantillon: Le PAF est mis à jour tous les six mois par la Poste et la liste des logements gérés par le NHS et les hôpitaux l'est environ une fois tous les cinq ans.
Rotation:
Schéma: L'échantillon est divisé également en cinq vagues, une vague entrant dans l'échantillon et une autre le quittant chaque trimestre. Les unités d'échantillonnage sont interrogées une fois par trimestre.
Pourcentage d'unités restant dans l'échantillon durant deux enquêtes successives: 80 pour cent.
Nombre maximum d'interrogatoires par unité de sondage: Cinq.
Durée nécessaire au renouvellement complet de l'échantillon: Cinq trimestres.
Déroulement de l'enquête:
Type d'entretien: Entretien personnel assisté par ordinateur et entretien par téléphone assisté par ordinateur.
Nombre d'unités finales d'échantillonnage par zone de sondage: 68 250 unités finales d'échantillonnage.
Durée de déroulement de l'enquête:
Totale: Toute l'année en continu.
Par zone de sondage: Non disponible.
Organisation: Permanente.
Nombre de personnes employées: 420.
Substitution des unités finales en cas de non-réponse: Non.
Estimations et redressements:
Taux de non-réponse: 22,3% (pour la vague 1 et 5,5% pour les vagues 2 à 5).
Redressement pour non-réponse: Oui.
Imputation en cas de non-réponse à une question spécifique: Oui; pour les adresses défaillantes et les refus circonstanciés, les données de l'entretien précédent sont reprises pour une seule période.
Redressement pour les régions/populations non couvertes: Non.
Redressement en cas de sous-représentation: Oui.
Redressement en cas de sur-représentation: Oui.
Corrections des variations saisonnières: Oui, à l'aide du programme X-11 ARIMA de recensement. Un modèle type unique est utilisé pour toutes les séries. L'imputation en cas de non-réponse à une question spécifique améliore l'additivité des séries corrigées des variations saisonnières. L'additivité est imposée pour la plupart des séries corrigées des variations saisonnières.
Historique de l'enquête:
Titre et date de la première enquête: The Labour Force Survey, 1973.
Modifications et révisions significatives:
1973-1983: L'enquête était réalisée tous les deux ans au cours du trimestre de printemps. (Les résultats pour 1973, 1975 et 1977 ne sont pas publiés, car l'enquête, ces années-là, était expérimentale).
1984-1991: L'enquête était réalisée tous les ans au cours du trimestre de printemps; diverses modifications ont été apportées à la classification de groupes spécifiques par rapport à l'activité (par exemple les étudiants, les bénéficiaires de mesures de promotion de l'emploi, etc., qui sont passés des inactifs aux personnes ayant un emploi), conformément aux recommandations internationales.
A partir du printemps 1992: enquête continue; mise à jour/révision des grandes classifications économiques utilisées ans l'enquête.
Documentation et dissémination:
Documentation
Titre des publications publiant les résultats: Labour Force Survey (année) (annuel); LFS User Guide, Volume 1 (à partir de la page 130). (**Périodicité:** annuelle).
Titre des publications méthodologiques: LFS User Guide, Volume 1.
Dissémination
Délai de publication des premiers résultats: De un à deux mois.
Information à l'avance du public des dates de publication initiale des résultats: Oui.
Mise à disposition, sur demande, des données non publiées: L'ONS met à la disposition des utilisateurs gouvernementaux et des institutions internationales des tableaux simples non publiés. D'autres résultats peuvent être fournis par un agent de commercialisation contre une commission.
Mise à disposition des données sur support informatique: Oui.
Site web: http://www.statistics.gov.uk/.

Russie, Fédération de

Titre de l'enquête: Population Sample Survey of Employment
Organisme responsable de l'enquête:
Organisation et déroulement de l'enquête: State Committee of the Russian Federation on Statistics.
Analyse et Publication des résultats: State Committee of the Russian Federation on Statistics.
Sujets couverts par l'enquête: Emploi, chômage, sous-emploi, durée du travail, emploi dans le secteur informel, durée du chômage, travailleurs découragés, travailleurs occasionnels, industrie, profession, situation dans la profession, niveau d'instruction, exercice d'autres emplois et personnes occupées dans la production de biens dans des parcelles agricoles exploitées à titre accessoire.
Champ de l'enquête:
Territoire: L'ensemble du pays, à l'exception de la République tchétchène (pendant les opérations militaires).
Groupes de population: Toute la population âgée de 15 à 72 ans vivant dans des ménages. Sont exclues la population institutionnelle et les personnes absentes des ménages pendant six mois ou plus.
Disponibilité d'estimations selon d'autres sources pour les régions ou groupes exclus: Néant.
Groupes couverts par l'enquête mais exclus des résultats publiés: Néant.
Périodicité:
Réalisation de l'enquête: Trimestrielle.
Publication des résultats: Trimestrielle.
Période de référence:
Emploi: Une semaine (semaine fixe, la dernière du deuxième mois de chaque trimestre, c'est-à-dire de février, mai, août et novembre).
Recherche d'un emploi: Quatre semaines avant la semaine de référence.

Disponibilité pour travailler: Deux semaines après la semaine de référence

Concepts et définitions:

Emploi: Les personnes âgées de 15 à 72 ans qui, durant la semaine de référence, ont effectué un travail quelconque en tant que salariés, dans leur propre entreprise, profession ou dans leur propre exploitation agricole, ou qui ont travaillé pendant au moins une heure en tant que travailleurs familiaux non rémunérés dans une entreprise exploitée par un membre de leur famille, ainsi que celles qui ne travaillaient pas mais qui avaient un emploi ou une entreprise d'où elles étaient temporairement absentes pour cause de maladie, d'intempéries, de vacances, de formation professionnelle avancée, de conflits du travail ou pour des raisons personnelles, qu'elles aient été payées pour le temps passé sans travailler ou qu'elles aient cherché un autre emploi.

Sont également inclus dans les totaux:

a)les travailleurs occupés à plein temps ou à temps partiel et en quête d'un autre travail durant la période de référence;

b)les étudiants à plein temps ou à temps partiel travaillant à plein temps ou à temps partiel;

c)les personnes ayant effectué un travail quelconque durant la semaine de référence tout en étant soit à la retraite et au bénéfice d'une pension, soit inscrites en tant que demandeurs d'emploi auprès d'un bureau de placement, soit en percevant des allocations de chômage;

d)les travailleurs familiaux rémunérés ou non (s'ils ont travaillé au moins une heure);

e)les domestiques privés;

f)les membres de coopératives de producteurs;

g)les membres des forces armées vivant dans des ménages.

Chaque personne ayant un emploi n'est comptée qu'une seule fois. Celles qui occupent plus d'un emploi sont comptées dans l'activité qu'elles considèrent comme la principale.

Sont exclus les personnes dont la seule activité a consisté à travailler dans la maison (peinture, réparation ou travail ménager); à faire du bénévolat pour des organisations religieuses, caritatives ou assimilées, ainsi que les apprentis et stagiaires non rémunérés. Ces personnes sont considérées comme chômeurs ou inactifs.

Chômage: Sont chômeurs tous les civils qui n'avaient pas d'emploi pendant la semaine de référence, étaient immédiatement disponibles pour travailler, sauf pour cause de maladie temporaire, et avaient effectué des démarches concrètes pour trouver un emploi.

Note: Les travailleurs familiaux rémunérés ou non ne travaillant pas temporairement sont considérés comme chômeurs ou inactifs suivant s'ils ont cherché du travail ou non pendant la semaine de référence.

Sont également inclus dans les chômeurs les étudiants à plein temps ou à temps partiel, les retraités et les invalides, à condition qu'ils cherchent du travail et qu'ils soient immédiatement disponibles pour travailler (s'ils cherchent du travail pour une date ultérieure, comme pour les mois d'été, ils sont considérés comme inactifs). Les personnes en congé administratif non rémunéré pendant 6 mois ou plus sont classifiées comme chômeurs ou inactifs.

Sous-emploi:

Sous-emploi lié à la durée du travail: Les personnes qui, pendant la semaine de référence, ont effectué un nombre d'heures de travail inférieur à celui fixé pour une certaine catégorie de profession ou d'emploi, à condition qu'elles aient cherché à travailler davantage et qu'elles soient disponibles pour ce faire.

Situations d'emploi inadéquat: Ne s'applique pas.

Durée du travail: Les heures de travail habituelles et réellement effectuées dans l'activité principale et la ou les activités secondaires.

Revenu lié à l'emploi:

Revenu lié à l'emploi salarié: Ne s'applique pas.

Revenu lié à l'emploi indépendant: Ne s'applique pas.

Secteur informel: Des informations sur le secteur informel sont fournies dans la mesure où les enquêtés déclarent leurs activités.

Activité habituelle: Ne s'applique pas.

Classifications:

Branche d'activité économique (industrie)

Titre de la classification: Classification nationale compatible avec la CITI Rév.3.

Groupes de population classifiés selon l'industrie: Les personnes ayant un emploi et les chômeurs ayant une expérience professionnelle préalable.

Nombre de groupes de codage: 17.

Convertibilité avec la CITI: CITI-Rév.3 (niveau à quatre chiffres).

Profession

Titre de la classification: Classification nationale compatible avec la CITP-1988.

Groupes de population classifiés selon la profession: Les personnes ayant un emploi et les chômeurs ayant une expérience professionnelle préalable.

Nombre de groupes de codage: 31 (niveaux à un et à deux chiffres).

Convertibilité avec la CITP: CITP-1988 (niveau à quatre chiffres).

Situation dans la profession

Titre de la classification: CISP-1993.

Groupes de population classifiés par situation dans la profession: Les personnes ayant un emploi (activité principale et activités secondaires).

Catégories de codage: 5 groupes (salariés, employeurs, travailleurs indépendants, membres de coopératives de producteurs, travailleurs familiaux non rémunérés).

Convertibilité avec la CISP: CISP-1993.

Education

Titre de la classification: Classification nationale.

Groupes de population classifiés selon l'éducation: Tous les groupes de population.

Catégories de codage: 8 groupes (pas d'enseignement primaire général, enseignement primaire général, enseignement secondaire, enseignement secondaire général, enseignement primaire professionnel, enseignement secondaire professionnel; enseignement supérieur inachevé; enseignement supérieur (université)).

Convertibilité avec la CITE: Non.

Taille de l'échantillon et plan de sondage:

Unité finale d'échantillonnage: Ménage.

Taille de l'échantillon (unités finales d'échantillonnage): Environ 65 000 personnes par trimestre et quelque 240 000 personnes par an.

Taux de sondage: 0,24 pour cent.

Base de sondage: L'échantillon est construit automatiquement au niveau fédéral, sur la base de la liste des ménages du microrecensement de 1994.

Renouvellement de l'échantillon: Annuel.

Rotation:

Schéma: Rotation de 100 pour cent d'un trimestre à l'autre.

Un ménage peut réintégrer l'échantillon et être interrogé pour la deuxième fois au bout de deux ans.

Déroulement de l'enquête:

Type d'entretien: Sur papier avec écriture manuelle.

Nombre d'unités finales d'échantillonnage par zone de sondage: 60 personnes par district de recensement.

Durée de déroulement de l'enquête:

Totale: Deux semaines civiles après la semaine de référence (14 jours).

Par zone de sondage: Non disponible.

Organisation: L'enquête est organisée sous forme d'entretien direct. Les enquêteurs sont employés temporairement pour la durée de l'enquête. La saisie des données et le contrôle logique se font au niveau régional (oblast) avant le transfert des données primaires au niveau fédéral (State Statistics Committee). C'est au niveau fédéral que la base de micro-données est construite, que le traitement des données a lieu, que les pondérations sont ajustées et que la variable pertinente est produite pour classer la population d'après sa situation au regard de l'activité économique.

Nombre de personnes employées: Environ 1 100 enquêteurs et 130 cadres.

Substitution des unités finales en cas de non-réponse: Oui.

Estimations et redressements:

Taux de non-réponse: 4,5%.

Redressement pour non-réponse: Non.

Imputation en cas de non-réponse à une question spécifique: Non.

Redressement pour les régions/populations non couvertes: Non.

Redressement en cas de sous-représentation: Non.

Redressement en cas de sur-représentation: Non.

Corrections des variations saisonnières: Oui.

Historique de l'enquête:

Titre et date de la première enquête: Population Sample Survey of Employment, octobre 1992.

Modifications et révisions significatives: Depuis 1999, l'enquête est réalisée tous les trimestres.

Documentation et dissémination:

Documentation

Titre des publications publiant les résultats: "Obsliedovaniye naseleniya po problemam zaniytosty" (Population Sample Survey of Employment) - trimestriel, "Rossijsky statistichesky yezhegodnik" (Statistical Yearbook of Russia) – annuel, "Trud I zanis tost v Rossijskoj Federatsii" (Labour and Employment in the Russian Federation) – tous les 2 ans, "Statisticheskoye obozrieniye" (Statistical Review) – trimestriel.

Titre des publications méthodologiques: ("Obsliedovaniye naseleniya po problemam zaniytosty" (Population Sample Survey of Employment) - trimestriel, "Metodologichskiye poplozheniya, No. 3" (Methodological descriptions).
Dissémination
Délai de publication des premiers résultats: 3 mois après la semaine de référence.
Information à l'avance du public des dates de publication initiale des résultats: OUI.
Mise à disposition, sur demande, des données non publiées: OUI.
Mise à disposition des données sur support informatique: Disquettes et Internet (sélection).
Site web: http://www.gks.ru.

Seychelles

Titre de l'enquête: Labour Force Survey (LFS).
Organisme responsable de l'enquête:
Organisation et déroulement de l'enquête: Management and Information Systems Division (MISD), Ministry of Information Technology & Communication.
Analyse et Publication des résultats: MISD.
Sujets couverts par l'enquête: Personnes actuellement et habituellement actives, ayant un emploi ou chômeurs; personnes actuellement en situation de sous-emploi lié à la durée du travail ou en situations d'emploi inadéquat et personnes actuellement en dehors de la population active. Personnes ayant habituellement un emploi avec ou sans périodes de chômage, personnes habituellement sans emploi avec des périodes d'emploi, et personnes habituellement inactives (en distinguant les étudiants, les personnes se consacrant aux tâches ménagères, trop âgées, malades ou invalides). Durée du travail. Emploi dans le secteur informel. Durée de l'emploi et du chômage. Travailleurs découragés. Exercice d'autres emplois. Industrie, profession, situation dans la profession, niveau d'instruction/de formation.
Champ de l'enquête:
Territoire: Les trois îles principales: Mahé, Praslin et La Digue.
Groupes de population: La population âgée de 15 ans résidant dans des ménages.
Disponibilité d'estimations selon d'autres sources pour les régions ou groupes exclus: Ne s'applique pas.
Groupes couverts par l'enquête mais exclus des résultats publiés: Néant.
Périodicité:
Réalisation de l'enquête: Occasionnelle (18 août au 17 septembre 1992).
Publication des résultats: Occasionnelle: aucune information disponible sur la date de publication des premiers résultats.
Période de référence:
Emploi: Une semaine avant la date de l'entretien.
Recherche d'un emploi: Quatre semaines.
Disponibilité pour travailler: Quatre semaines.
Concepts et définitions:
Emploi: Les personnes qui a) ont effectué un travail quelconque, rémunéré ou en vue d'un bénéfice, pendant la semaine de référence; b) étaient temporairement absentes de leur travail durant la semaine de référence pour cause de maladie ou de congés mais allaient assurément y retourner (y compris à un emploi saisonnier après la fin de la morte-saison), ou c) étaient occupées dans la production de biens pour leur usage final personnel. Sont exclus les travailleurs familiaux non rémunérés occupés dans une entreprise familiale. Par « un travail quelconque », on entend une heure ou plus de travail effectuée pendant la semaine de référence.
Chômage: Les personnes actuellement sans emploi et immédiatement disponibles pour travailler ayant cherché du travail au cours des quatre dernières semaines, ainsi que les personnes n'ayant pas cherché d'emploi parce qu'elles pensaient qu'il n'y en avait pas, qu'elles attendaient la réponse à des démarches antérieures ou qu'elles attendaient de commencer à travailler.
Sous-emploi:
Sous-emploi lié à la durée du travail: Les personnes travaillant moins de 35 heures qui ont déclaré être disponibles pour faire davantage d'heures et ne pas le faire pour des motifs économiques.
Situations d'emploi inadéquat: Non disponible.
Durée du travail: Non disponible.
Revenu lié à l'emploi:
Revenu lié à l'emploi salarié: Ne s'applique pas.
Revenu lié à l'emploi indépendant: Ne s'applique pas.
Secteur informel: Les entreprises non constituées en société (déterminé par le nom de l'entreprise), dans le secteur privé (y compris les coopératives), employant moins de cinq personnes et qui opèrent depuis le domicile de l'enquêté, un étal de marché ou un emplacement temporaire.
Activité habituelle: Actifs pendant 6 mois ou plus au cours de la période de référence de 12 mois et ayant eu un emploi pendant la plus grande partie de cette période.
Classifications:
Branche d'activité économique (industrie)
Titre de la classification: Pas de nom.
Groupes de population classifiés selon l'industrie: Les personnes ayant un emploi et les chômeurs (industrie du dernier emploi occupé pour ces derniers).
Nombre de groupes de codage: 26.
Convertibilité avec la CITI: CITI-Rév.3.
Profession
Titre de la classification: Pas de nom.
Groupes de population classifiés selon la profession: Les personnes ayant un emploi et les chômeurs (profession exercée dans le dernier emploi occupé pour ces derniers).
Nombre de groupes de codage: 35.
Convertibilité avec la CITP: CITP-1988.
Situation dans la profession
Titre de la classification: Classification nationale.
Groupes de population classifiés par situation dans la profession: Les personnes ayant un emploi et les chômeurs (situation du dernier emploi occupé pour ces derniers).
Catégories de codage: Fonctionnaires; salariés d'organismes parapublics; salariés du secteur privé; salariés de coopératives; travailleurs indépendants; employeurs et travailleurs familiaux non rémunérés.
Convertibilité avec la CISP: CISP-1993.
Education
Titre de la classification: Classification nationale.
Groupes de population classifiés selon l'éducation: Les personnes ayant un emploi et les chômeurs.
Catégories de codage: Non scolarisé; P1-P6; FI-FII, P7-P8, S1-S2; FIII, P9, S3; FIV, S4, NYS; enseignement professionnel; Poly1-2, TTC; Poly3-4, FVI; enseignement pré-universitaire; enseignement universitaire.
Convertibilité avec la CITE: CITE-1976.
Taille de l'échantillon et plan de sondage:
Unité finale d'échantillonnage: Ménage.
Taille de l'échantillon (unités finales d'échantillonnage): 800.
Taux de sondage: 6 pour cent.
Base de sondage: Le recensement de la population de 1987.
Renouvellement de l'échantillon: 1991.
Rotation:
Schéma: Ne s'applique pas.
Pourcentage d'unités restant dans l'échantillon durant deux enquêtes successives: Ne s'applique pas.
Nombre maximum d'interrogatoires par unité de sondage: Ne s'applique pas.
Durée nécessaire au renouvellement complet de l'échantillon: Ne s'applique pas.
Déroulement de l'enquête:
Type d'entretien: Entretiens personnels avec écriture manuelle sur papier.
Nombre d'unités finales d'échantillonnage par zone de sondage: Non disponible.
Durée de déroulement de l'enquête:
Totale: Un mois, plus deux semaines supplémentaires pour les remplacements.
Par zone de sondage: Non disponible.
Organisation: Permanente.
Nombre de personnes employées: 6 enquêteurs et 3 cadres.
Substitution des unités finales en cas de non-réponse: Certains refus, les enquêtés défaillants ou ayant déménagé ont été remplacés.
Estimations et redressements:
Taux de non-réponse: 15%.
Redressement pour non-réponse: Oui.
Imputation en cas de non-réponse à une question spécifique: Non.
Redressement pour les régions/populations non couvertes: Non.
Redressement en cas de sous-représentation: Non.
Redressement en cas de sur-représentation: Non.
Corrections des variations saisonnières: Ne s'applique pas.
Historique de l'enquête:
Titre et date de la première enquête: Labour Force Survey, 1979-80.
Modifications et révisions significatives: Non disponible.

Documentation et dissémination:
Documentation
Titre des publications publiant les résultats: Non disponible.
Titre des publications méthodologiques: Non disponible.
Dissémination
Délai de publication des premiers résultats: Non disponible.
Information à l'avance du public des dates de publication initiale des résultats: Non.
Mise à disposition, sur demande, des données non publiées: Oui.
Mise à disposition des données sur support informatique: Oui.
Site web: http://www.seychelles.net/misd/.

Singapour

Titre de l'enquête: Labour Force Survey (LFS).
Organisme responsable de l'enquête:
Organisation et déroulement de l'enquête: Manpower Research and Statistics Department (MRSD), Ministry of Manpower.
Analyse et Publication des résultats: Manpower Research and Statistics Department (MRSD), Ministry of Manpower.
Sujets couverts par l'enquête: Personnes actuellement actives, ayant un emploi ou chômeurs; personnes se trouvant actuellement en situation de sous-emploi lié à la durée du travail et personnes se trouvant actuellement en dehors de la population active; travailleurs découragés; durée du travail, à plein temps ou à temps partiel; durée de l'emploi et du chômage; salaires et revenu; exercice d'autres emplois; industrie; profession; situation dans la profession; niveau d'instruction/de formation.
Champ de l'enquête:
Territoire: L'île principale de Singapour, à l'exclusion des îles côtières.
Groupes de population: La population âgée de 15 ans et plus vivant dans des ménages ordinaires. Cela exclut les voyageurs et les personnes de passage vivant à terre, dans des hôtels ou sur des navires, bateaux et navires de haute mer, ainsi que les ouvriers du bâtiment vivant sur les chantiers et les personnes venant tous les jours de l'étranger pour travailler à Singapour.
Disponibilité d'estimations selon d'autres sources pour les régions ou groupes exclus: Néant.
Groupes couverts par l'enquête mais exclus des résultats publiés: Néant.
Périodicité:
Réalisation de l'enquête: Trimestrielle.
Publication des résultats: Trimestrielle.
Période de référence:
Emploi: Une semaine.
Recherche d'un emploi: Les quatre dernières semaines.
Disponibilité pour travailler: Dans les deux semaines.
Concepts et définitions:
Emploi: Les personnes qui a) ont effectué un travail quelconque, rémunéré, en vue d'un bénéfice ou d'un gain familial, pendant la semaine de référence et b) étaient temporairement absentes de leur travail pendant la semaine de référence pour cause de maladie ou de congés mais allaient assurément y retourner. Par « un travail quelconque », on entend une heure ou plus effectuée pendant la semaine de référence.
Chômage: Les personnes actuellement sans emploi et disponibles pour travailler dans les deux semaines, ayant cherché du travail à un moment quelconque au cours des quatre dernières semaines.
Sous-emploi:
Sous-emploi lié à la durée du travail: Les personnes ayant travaillé moins de 30 heures pendant la période de référence, disposées à travailler davantage et disponibles pour ce faire.
Situations d'emploi inadéquat: Non disponible.
Durée du travail: Les heures de travail habituelles au cours d'une semaine normale.
Revenu lié à l'emploi:
Revenu lié à l'emploi salarié: Le montant total du revenu lié à l'emploi au cours du précédent mois plein. Pour les emplois salariés, cela inclut les salaires et traitements, primes, indemnités, commissions, rémunération des heures supplémentaires, pourboires ainsi que la cotisation du salarié au « Central Provident Fund », mais non celle de l'employeur.
Revenu lié à l'emploi indépendant: Les recettes totales tirées des ventes et des services, déduction faite des frais d'exploitation.
Secteur informel: Ne s'applique pas.
Activité habituelle: Non disponible.

Classifications:
Branche d'activité économique (industrie)
Titre de la classification: Singapore Standard Industrial Classification, 1996.
Groupes de population classifiés selon l'industrie: Les personnes ayant un emploi et les chômeurs.
Nombre de groupes de codage: 9.
Convertibilité avec la CITI: CITI-Rév.3, au niveau des catégories de classement (indicatif à une lettre).
Profession
Titre de la classification: Singapore Standard Occupational Classification, 1990.
Groupes de population classifiés selon la profession: Les personnes ayant un emploi et les chômeurs.
Nombre de groupes de codage: 8.
Convertibilité avec la CITP: CITP-1988.
Situation dans la profession
Titre de la classification: Non disponible.
Groupes de population classifiés par situation dans la profession: Les personnes ayant un emploi.
Catégories de codage: Salariés; employeurs; travailleurs indépendants; travailleurs familiaux non rémunérés.
Convertibilité avec la CISP: CISP-1993.
Education
Titre de la classification: Singapore Standard Educational Classification.
Groupes de population classifiés selon l'éducation: Les personnes ayant un emploi et les chômeurs.
Catégories de codage: Jamais scolarisé/premier cycle de l'enseignement primaire; enseignement primaire; premier cycle de l'enseignement secondaire; enseignement secondaire; post-enseignement secondaire; diplôme d'une école polytechnique; diplôme universitaire.
Convertibilité avec la CITE: CITE-1997.
Taille de l'échantillon et plan de sondage:
Unité finale d'échantillonnage: Unités de logement.
Taille de l'échantillon (unités finales d'échantillonnage): 25 000 unités de logement pour la grande enquête de juin.
Taux de sondage: 3 pour cent pour la grande enquête de juin.
Base de sondage: La Base de données nationale sur les logements (National Database of Dwellings), gérée par le Département de statistiques (Department of Statistics).
Renouvellement de l'échantillon: Non disponible.
Rotation:
Schéma: Ne s'applique pas.
Pourcentage d'unités restant dans l'échantillon durant deux enquêtes successives: Ne s'applique pas.
Nombre maximum d'interrogatoires par unité de sondage: Ne s'applique pas.
Durée nécessaire au renouvellement complet de l'échantillon: Ne s'applique pas.
Déroulement de l'enquête:
Type d'entretien: Entretien par téléphone assisté par ordinateur et entretien direct.
Nombre d'unités finales d'échantillonnage par zone de sondage: Non disponible.
Durée de déroulement de l'enquête:
Totale: 7 à 8 semaines.
Par zone de sondage: Non disponible.
Organisation: Permanente.
Nombre de personnes employées: Environ 140 enquêteurs et cadres.
Substitution des unités finales en cas de non-réponse: Non.
Estimations et redressements:
Taux de non-réponse: 2%.
Redressement pour non-réponse: Non.
Imputation en cas de non-réponse à une question spécifique: Non.
Redressement pour les régions/populations non couvertes: Non.
Redressement en cas de sous-représentation: Non.
Redressement en cas de sur-représentation: Non.
Corrections des variations saisonnières: Pour le taux de chômage trimestriel, utilisation de la méthode X-11 ARIMA.
Historique de l'enquête:
Titre et date de la première enquête: Labour Force Survey (LFS), juin 1974.
Modifications et révisions significatives: Néant.

Documentation et dissémination:
Documentation
Titre des publications publiant les résultats: "Quarterly Labour Market Reports" pour les chiffres du chômage.
Titre des publications méthodologiques: Report on the Labour Force Survey of Singapore (annuel), sauf les années de recensement et les années se trouvant au milieu de la période séparant deux recensements.
Dissémination
Délai de publication des premiers résultats: Moins de six mois après la fin du déroulement de l'enquête.
Information à l'avance du public des dates de publication initiale des résultats: Oui.
Mise à disposition, sur demande, des données non publiées: Oui.
Mise à disposition des données sur support informatique: Oui.
Site web: http://www.singstat.gov.sg.

Slovaquie

Titre de l'enquête: Labour Force Sample Survey.
Organisme responsable de l'enquête:
Organisation et déroulement de l'enquête: Statistical Office of the Slovak Republic.
Analyse et Publication des résultats: Statistical Office of the Slovak Republic.
Sujets couverts par l'enquête: Emploi, chômage, sous-emploi, durée du travail, durée de l'emploi, durée du chômage, travailleurs découragés, travailleurs occasionnels, industrie, profession, situation dans la profession, niveau d'instruction, exercice d'autres emplois et travail atypique.
Champ de l'enquête:
Territoire: L'ensemble du pays.
Groupes de population: Tous les résidents permanents âgés de 15 ans et plus vivant dans des ménages.
Sont exclus:
a)les étudiants vivant en résidence et les écoliers vivant en pensionnat;
b)les pensionnaires des établissements pénitentiaires et psychiatriques;
c)les citoyens étrangers en court séjour d'une durée maximum de six mois.
Disponibilité d'estimations selon d'autres sources pour les régions ou groupes exclus: Non.
Groupes couverts par l'enquête mais exclus des résultats publiés: Néant.
Périodicité:
Réalisation de l'enquête: En continu.
Publication des résultats: Trimestrielle.
Période de référence:
Emploi: Une semaine (les sept derniers jours avant la date de l'entretien).
Recherche d'un emploi: Quatre semaines avant la date de l'entretien.
Disponibilité pour travailler: Deux semaines après la date de l'entretien.
Concepts et définitions:
Emploi: Sont considérées comme ayant un emploi toutes les personnes âgées de 15 ans et plus qui, durant la semaine de référence, ont effectué un travail quelconque pendant au moins une heure, ainsi que les travailleurs familiaux non rémunérés et les personnes qui ne travaillaient pas mais qui avaient un emploi ou une entreprise dont elles étaient temporairement absentes pour cause de maladie, d'intempéries, de vacances, de conflit du travail, etc. Sont exclues les personnes en congé de maternité (congé parental) prolongé.
Sont également inclus dans les totaux:
a)les travailleurs occupés à plein temps ou à temps partiel et en quête d'un autre travail pendant la période de référence;
b)les étudiants à plein temps ou à temps partiel travaillant à plein temps ou à temps partiel;
c)les personnes ayant effectué un travail quelconque, durant la semaine de référence, tout en étant soit à la retraite et au bénéfice d'une pension, soit inscrites en tant que demandeurs d'emploi auprès d'un bureau de placement, soit tout en percevant des allocations de chômage;
d)les domestiques privés;
e)les apprentis et stagiaires rémunérés.
Sont exclues les personnes occupées dans la production de biens pour leur propre ménage (travaux de peinture, réparations, travail ménager, etc.).

Chômage: Sont considérées comme chômeurs les personnes âgées de 15 ans et plus qui, au cours de la semaine de référence, n'ont pas effectué de travail rémunéré ou en vue d'un bénéfice, ont cherché activement du travail pendant les quatre semaines précédant l'enquête et étaient disponibles pour commencer à travailler dans les deux semaines suivant l'enquête.
Sous-emploi:
Sous-emploi lié à la durée du travail: Les personnes qui, pendant la semaine de référence, ont travaillé à temps partiel contre leur gré mais aimeraient travailler à plein temps.
Situations d'emploi inadéquat: Les personnes cherchant un autre emploi pour améliorer leurs conditions de travail (revenu plus élevé, meilleur environnement professionnel, meilleur emploi, etc.).
Durée du travail: Les heures de travail réellement effectuées et les heures de travail habituelles effectuées dans l'activité principale.
Revenu lié à l'emploi:
Revenu lié à l'emploi salarié: Ne s'applique pas.
Revenu lié à l'emploi indépendant: Ne s'applique pas.
Secteur informel: Ne s'applique pas.
Activité habituelle: Ne s'applique pas.
Classifications:
Branche d'activité économique (industrie)
Titre de la classification: Classification nationale.
Groupes de population classifiés selon l'industrie: Les personnes ayant un emploi et les chômeurs ayant une expérience professionnelle préalable.
Nombre de groupes de codage: 16 grands groupes.
Convertibilité avec la CITI: CITI-Rév.3 (niveau à deux chiffres).
Profession
Titre de la classification: Classification nationale.
Groupes de population classifiés selon la profession: Les personnes ayant un emploi et les chômeurs ayant une expérience professionnelle préalable.
Nombre de groupes de codage: 10 grands groupes.
Convertibilité avec la CITP: CITP-1988 (niveau à trois chiffres).
Situation dans la profession
Titre de la classification: Classification nationale.
Groupes de population classifiés par situation dans la profession: Les personnes ayant un emploi et les chômeurs.
Catégories de codage: 6 groupes (salariés, employeurs, travailleurs indépendants, membres de coopératives de producteurs, travailleurs familiaux non rémunérés, travailleurs non classés d'après leur situation).
Convertibilité avec la CISP: CISP-1993.
Education
Titre de la classification: Classification nationale.
Groupes de population classifiés selon l'éducation: Tous les groupes de population.
Catégories de codage: 12 groupes (non scolarisé, école primaire (1er et 2ème cycles), apprentissage, enseignement secondaire (sans examen), apprentissage sanctionné par un examen, enseignement secondaire général complet, enseignement secondaire professionnel complet, enseignement supérieur, licence, enseignement universitaire, aptitude à faire de la recherche.
Convertibilité avec la CITE: CITE-1976.
Taille de l'échantillon et plan de sondage:
Unité finale d'échantillonnage: Logement.
Taille de l'échantillon (unités finales d'échantillonnage): Environ 10 250.
Taux de sondage: 0,6 pour cent.
Base de sondage: La base de sondage est construite à partir des registres municipaux de la population et du recensement de la population réalisé en 1991.
Renouvellement de l'échantillon: Annuel.
Rotation:
Schéma: 20 pour cent des logements de l'échantillon sont remplacés chaque trimestre. Un cinquième du groupe-témoin est renouvelé par rotation chaque trimestre.
Pourcentage d'unités restant dans l'échantillon durant deux enquêtes successives: 75 pour cent.
Nombre maximum d'interrogatoires par unité de sondage: Non disponible.
Durée nécessaire au renouvellement complet de l'échantillon: Cinq trimestres.
Déroulement de l'enquête:
Type d'entretien: Sur papier avec écriture manuelle, par téléphone, et entretien personnel/par téléphone assisté par ordinateur lorsque c'est possible.
Nombre d'unités finales d'échantillonnage par zone de sondage: 250 logements en continu par trimestre.

Durée de déroulement de l'enquête:
Totale: 30 minutes par ménage.
Par zone de sondage: Non disponible.
Organisation: Statistical Office of the Slovak Republic.
Nombre de personnes employées: 45 enquêteurs et 8 cadres.
Substitution des unités finales en cas de non-réponse: Non.
Estimations et redressements:
Taux de non-réponse: 6%.
Redressement pour non-réponse: Non.
Imputation en cas de non-réponse à une question spécifique: Non.
Redressement pour les régions/populations non couvertes: Non.
Redressement en cas de sous-représentation: Non.
Redressement en cas de sur-représentation: Non.
Corrections des variations saisonnières: Oui.
Historique de l'enquête:
Titre et date de la première enquête: Labour Force Sample Survey, décembre 1992.
Modifications et révisions significatives: A partir du premier trimestre 1997, les conscrits sont inclus dans l'échantillon. Depuis le premier trimestre 1999, un nouveau plan de sondage est utilisé. Depuis le premier trimestre 2000, passage de trimestres saisonniers à des trimestres civils.
Documentation et dissémination:
Documentation
Titre des publications publiant les résultats: « Labour Force Sample Survey Results » (trimestriel).
Titre des publications méthodologiques: « Labour Force Sample Survey Results » (trimestriel).
Dissémination
Délai de publication des premiers résultats: 80 jours.
Information à l'avance du public des dates de publication initiale des résultats: Oui.
Mise à disposition, sur demande, des données non publiées: Oui.
Mise à disposition des données sur support informatique: Disquettes et courrier électronique.
Site web: http://www.statistics.sk

Slovénie

Titre de l'enquête: Labour Force Survey.
Organisme responsable de l'enquête:
Organisation et déroulement de l'enquête: Statistical Office of the Republic of Slovenia.
Analyse et Publication des résultats: Statistical Office of the Republic of Slovenia.
Sujets couverts par l'enquête: Emploi, sous-emploi, chômage, durée du travail, secteur informel, durée du chômage, travailleurs découragés, travailleurs occasionnels, industrie, profession, situation dans la profession, niveau d'instruction, exercice d'autres emplois.
Champ de l'enquête:
Territoire: L'ensemble du pays.
Groupes de population: Toutes les personnes vivant dans des ménages ordinaires et dont le lieu de résidence habituel se trouve sur le territoire slovène, y compris les personnes temporairement absentes (pendant moins de six mois). Sont exclues la population institutionnelle (telle que les militaires vivant en caserne) et les personnes vivant temporairement ou en permanence à l'étranger. Seules quelques questions de base (nom, sexe, âge, nationalité) sont posées aux enfants jusqu'à 15 ans.
Disponibilité d'estimations selon d'autres sources pour les régions ou groupes exclus: Non disponible.
Groupes couverts par l'enquête mais exclus des résultats publiés: Non disponible.
Périodicité:
Réalisation de l'enquête: Enquête trimestrielle en continu.
Publication des résultats: Trimestrielle et annuelle.
Période de référence:
Emploi: Lundi à dimanche de la semaine précédente (période de référence variable).
Recherche d'un emploi: Les quatre dernières semaines.
Disponibilité pour travailler: Deux semaines.
Concepts et définitions:
Emploi: Toutes les personnes âgées de 15 ans et plus qui, pendant la semaine de référence, ont effectué un travail quelconque, rémunéré (en espèces ou en nature) ou en vue d'un bénéfice, y compris les travailleurs familiaux non rémunérés et les personnes qui ne travaillaient pas mais avaient un emploi d'où elles étaient temporairement absentes. Il en va de même pour les travailleurs en mise à pied (temporaire ou de durée indéterminée) et les personnes en congé de maternité (12 mois).
Cette catégorie inclut:
a)les personnes ayant un emploi mais temporairement absentes pour cause de maladie/accident, de congés/vacances annuelles, de congé parental, de congé sans rémunération à l'initiative de l'employeur, de congé d'éducation ou de formation, d'absence non autorisée, de grève ou de conflit, d'arrêts temporaires dus à des intempéries, de panne mécanique, de pénurie de matières premières ou d'énergie, etc.;
b)les travailleurs occupés à plein temps ou à temps partiel et en quête d'un autre emploi;
c)les personnes ayant effectué un travail quelconque, rémunéré ou en vue d'un bénéfice, pendant la semaine de référence, alors qu'elles étaient assujetties à la scolarité obligatoire, à la retraite et au bénéfice d'une pension ou inscrites en tant que demandeurs d'emploi auprès d'un bureau de placement, ou qu'elles percevaient des allocations de chômage;
d)les étudiants à plein temps ou à temps partiel ayant travaillé au moins une heure pendant la semaine de référence;
e)les apprentis et stagiaires rémunérés;
f)les bénéficiaires de mesures de promotion de l'emploi;
g)les personnes occupées dans la production de biens ou la prestation de services pour leur consommation personnelle;
h)les volontaires et les militaires de carrière.
Chômage: Toutes les personnes âgées de 15 ans et plus qui, durant la semaine de référence, n'ont pas travaillé pour une rémunération, en vue d'un profit ou d'un gain familial, ont cherché activement un emploi au cours des quatre dernières semaines et étaient immédiatement disponibles pour commencer à travailler dans les deux semaines.
Cette catégorie inclut:
a)les personnes ayant effectué des démarches concrètes pour créer leur propre entreprise, dans laquelle elles doivent commencer à travailler dans les deux semaines;
b)les personnes ayant pris des dispositions pour commencer à travailler dans un nouvel emploi dans les deux semaines;
c)les étudiants à plein temps ou à temps partiel à la recherche d'un emploi à plein temps ou à temps partiel, les enfants assujettis à la scolarité obligatoire et les retraités.
Sous-emploi:
Sous-emploi lié à la durée du travail: Les personnes qui travaillent moins de 36 heures par semaine, souhaitent faire davantage d'heures de travail dans la semaine (grâce à un emploi supplémentaire, à leur emploi actuel ou à un autre emploi comportant plus d'heures de travail que l'actuel) et sont disposées à commencer à faire davantage d'heures dans les deux prochaines semaines.
Situations d'emploi inadéquat: Ne s'applique pas.
Durée du travail: Les heures de travail (hebdomadaires) habituelles, y compris les heures supplémentaires normales. Les heures de travail (hebdomadaires) réellement effectuées se réfèrent à l'activité principale exercée pendant la semaine de référence.
Revenu lié à l'emploi:
Revenu lié à l'emploi salarié: Ne s'applique pas.
Revenu lié à l'emploi indépendant: Ne s'applique pas.
Secteur informel: Les travailleurs rémunérés en espèces « de la main à la main » en contrepartie de leur activité économique.
Activité habituelle: Ne s'applique pas.
Classifications:
Branche d'activité économique (industrie)
Titre de la classification: Non disponible.
Groupes de population classifiés selon l'industrie: Les personnes ayant un emploi.
Nombre de groupes de codage: 16 groupes; codage au niveau à deux chiffres.
Convertibilité avec la CITI: CITI-Rév.3.
Profession
Titre de la classification: Non disponible.
Groupes de population classifiés selon la profession: Les personnes ayant un emploi.
Nombre de groupes de codage: Non disponible.
Convertibilité avec la CITP: CITP-1988.
Situation dans la profession
Titre de la classification: Non disponible.
Groupes de population classifiés par situation dans la profession: Les personnes ayant un emploi.
Catégories de codage: Douze groupes: salarié dans une entreprise ou une organisation, salarié artisan, salarié free-lance, salarié exploitant agricole, travaille dans sa propre entreprise (travailleur indépendant), artisan, exploitant agricole, free-lance, travailleur familial non

rémunéré, travailleur occupé en sous-traitance – type 1 et 2, travailleur rémunéré en espèces de la main à la main (informel).
Convertibilité avec la CISP: CISP-1993.
Education
Titre de la classification: Non disponible.
Groupes de population classifiés selon l'éducation: Les personnes ayant un emploi et les chômeurs.
Catégories de codage: Neuf groupes: non scolarisé, école primaire inachevée, école primaire, un à deux ans d'école secondaire (programme abrégé), deux à trois ans d'école secondaire, quatre à cinq ans d'école secondaire, diplôme non universitaire, diplôme universitaire, diplôme de troisième cycle.
Convertibilité avec la CITE: CITE-1997 avec tableaux croisés.
Taille de l'échantillon et plan de sondage:
Unité finale d'échantillonnage: Ménage.
Taille de l'échantillon (unités finales d'échantillonnage): Environ 7 000 ménages (et 19 000 répondants).
Taux de sondage: Environ un pour cent de la population.
Base de sondage: L'échantillon du LSF est construit sur la base du registre de la population, à partir duquel une liste de personnes adultes est créée chaque trimestre. Les membres du ménage vivant à l'adresse des personnes sélectionnées sont interrogés.
Renouvellement de l'échantillon: Chaque trimestre, environ 2 000 nouveaux ménages sont sélectionnés.
Rotation: Enquête avec renouvellement de panel réalisée en continu toute l'année civile.
Schéma: L'échantillon renouvelé est conçu sur le modèle 3-(1)-2. Les ménages sont donc interrogés pendant trois trimestres successifs, exclus pendant un trimestre, puis réintégrés pendant deux autres trimestres successifs avant de quitter définitivement l'échantillon.
Pourcentage d'unités restant dans l'échantillon durant deux enquêtes successives: 60 pour cent.
Nombre maximum d'interrogatoires par unité de sondage: Cinq.
Durée nécessaire au renouvellement complet de l'échantillon: Dix-huit mois.
Déroulement de l'enquête:
Type d'entretien: Mélange d'entretiens directs avec écriture manuelle sur papier, d'entretiens personnels assistés par ordinateur (portables) et d'entretiens par téléphone.
Nombre d'unités finales d'échantillonnage par zone de sondage: Environ 28 000 ménages par an.
Durée de déroulement de l'enquête:
Totale: Toute l'année.
Par zone de sondage: Ne s'applique pas.
Organisation: Structure d'enquête permanente.
Nombre de personnes employées: Environ 55.
Substitution des unités finales en cas de non-réponse: Non.
Estimations et redressements:
Taux de non-réponse: 11,2% (le taux de refus est de 7,4%). Dans la partie de l'échantillon constituée par le groupe-témoin, le taux de non-réponse est de 8,9%; parmi les ménages interrogés par téléphone, de 9,4%; au cours d'un entretien direct, de 5%.
Redressement pour non-réponse: Oui.
Imputation en cas de non-réponse à une question spécifique: Oui, à l'aide de l'imputation « hot-deck » - utilisation des données de l'entretien précédent; s'il n'y en a pas, on utilise les données d'une personne similaire (par le sexe, l'âge et l'éducation).
Redressement pour les régions/populations non couvertes: Oui.
Redressement en cas de sous-représentation: Oui.
Redressement en cas de sur-représentation: Oui.
Corrections des variations saisonnières: Non.
Historique de l'enquête:
Titre et date de la première enquête: Labour Force Survey, 1993.
Modifications et révisions significatives: Néant. Le questionnaire a été modifié en 1995 et 1997 sans rupture importante dans la série chronologique.
Documentation et dissémination:
Documentation
Titre des publications publiant les résultats: Labour Force Survey: Results; Labour Force Survey: Rapid Results; Statistical Yearbook of the Republic of Slovenia, Monthly Statistical Review; CESTAT Bulletin. (mensuel, trimestriel et annuel).
Titre des publications méthodologiques: Idem.
Dissémination
Délai de publication des premiers résultats: Environ un trimestre.
Information à l'avance du public des dates de publication initiale des résultats: Oui.
Mise à disposition, sur demande, des données non publiées: Oui.
Mise à disposition des données sur support informatique: Oui, sur disquette et par courrier électronique.
Site web: http://www.sigov.si/zrs/.

Soudan

Titre de l'enquête: Household Survey.
Organisme responsable de l'enquête:
Organisation et déroulement de l'enquête: Ministry of Manpower.
Analyse et Publication des résultats: Ministry of Manpower.
Sujets couverts par l'enquête: Emploi et chômage actuels; durée du travail; salaires; revenu des ménages; emploi dans le secteur informel; durée du chômage; niveau d'instruction; industrie, profession et situation dans la profession actuelles dans l'activité principale; activités secondaires; activité habituelle.
Champ de l'enquête:
Territoire: Les zones urbaines et rurales dans 16 Etats du Nord-Soudan. Ont été exclus 9 Etats du Sud-Soudan.
Groupes de population: Tous les résidents permanents d'un ménage, y compris les ressortissants étrangers et les personnes absentes pendant moins de 3 mois.
Disponibilité d'estimations selon d'autres sources pour les régions ou groupes exclus: Des estimations basées sur les résultats du recensement de la population sont disponibles pour les régions et groupes de population exclus.
Groupes couverts par l'enquête mais exclus des résultats publiés: Les enfants âgés de moins de 10 ans.
Périodicité:
Réalisation de l'enquête: Trois enquêtes sur les ménages depuis 1990 (1990, 1994 et 1996).
Publication des résultats: Après chaque enquête.
Période de référence:
Emploi: Semaine de référence fixe pour l'activité actuelle et année de référence pour l'activité habituelle.
Recherche d'un emploi: Mêmes périodes de référence que pour l'emploi.
Disponibilité pour travailler: Non disponible.
Concepts et définitions:
Emploi: Les personnes âgées de 10 ans et plus ayant travaillé au moins 2 jours pendant la semaine précédant l'enquête. [Emploi habituel: les personnes âgées de 10 ans et plus ayant travaillé trois mois ou plus au cours de l'année de référence]. Les personnes ayant un emploi incluent les personnes ayant un emploi mais temporairement absentes de leur travail pour cause de maladie, d'accident, de vacances, de congé de maternité, de congé d'éducation ou de formation, de conflit du travail, d'intempéries, de panne mécanique, etc. Cette catégorie inclut également les personnes en mise à pied de durée indéterminée sans rémunération et les personnes sans emploi et immédiatement disponibles pour travailler qui ont pris des dispositions pour commencer à travailler à une date postérieure à la période de référence. Les personnes absentes sans autorisation sont exclues. Les apprentis rémunérés et les bénéficiaires de mesures de promotion de l'emploi sont inclus. Les étudiants à plein temps ou à temps partiel travaillant à plein temps sont inclus mais les étudiants travaillant à temps partiel sont exclus. Les apprentis et stagiaires non rémunérés ainsi que les travailleurs familiaux non rémunérés temporairement absents de leur travail sont exclus. Les personnes occupées dans la production de biens pour leur propre compte sont incluses mais les personnes occupées dans la prestation de services non rémunérés ou personnels dans leur propre ménage sont exclues. Les conscrits et les personnes effectuant un service civil équivalent au service militaire sont inclus mais les personnes effectuant un travail communautaire ou des activités sociales sont exclues. Sont également exclues les personnes ayant effectué un travail quelconque, rémunéré ou en vue d'un bénéfice, durant la période de référence, mais qui étaient alors assujetties à la scolarité obligatoire, ou à la retraite et au bénéfice d'une pension ou inscrites en tant que demandeurs d'emploi auprès d'un bureau de placement, ou qui percevaient des allocations de chômage.
Chômage: Les personnes âgées de 10 ans et plus qui, pendant la semaine de référence, n'ont pas travaillé ou ont travaillé moins de 2 jours, alors qu'elles étaient capables de travailler, voulaient travailler et cherchaient du travail, qu'elles aient ou non travaillé auparavant. [Chômage habituel: les personnes âgées de 10 ans et plus ayant travaillé moins de 3 mois au cours de l'année de référence alors qu'elles étaient capables de travailler, voulaient travailler et avaient cherché du travail pendant l'année]. Les chômeurs incluent les personnes en mise à pied temporaire sans rémunération et les personnes en mise en congé sans rémunération à l'initiative de l'employeur. Sont également inclus les travailleurs familiaux non rémunérés tem-

porairement absents de leur travail ainsi que les apprentis et stagiaires non rémunérés. Cette catégorie exclut les étudiants à plein temps ou à temps partiel en quête d'un travail à temps partiel mais inclut les étudiants à temps partiel à la recherche d'un emploi à plein temps. Les personnes cherchant un emploi mais assujetties à la scolarité obligatoire ou à la retraite et au bénéfice d'une pension sont exclues, ainsi que les personnes sans emploi, disponibles pour travailler mais n'ayant pas cherché de travail durant la période de référence.
Durée du travail: Se réfère au nombre d'heures de travail réellement effectuées dans l'activité principale et aux heures passées dans l'exercice de l'activité secondaire.
Salaires et traitements: Cela inclut les salaires et traitements réguliers, en espèces ou en nature, après déduction des cotisations de sécurité sociale, perçus au titre de l'activité principale et de toutes les autres activités exercées durant la période de référence. Le revenu lié à l'emploi indépendant a aussi été mesuré en termes de valeur de la production provenant des activités liées à l'agriculture et à l'élevage, de la location des terres et du capital dans toutes les activités au cours de la période de référence d'une année.
Emploi dans le secteur informel: L'emploi dans une unité économique dépourvue d'établissement stable ou non inscrite au registre du commerce ou qui ne paie pas d'impôts sur ses activités.
Classifications:
Branche d'activité économique (industrie)
Groupes de population classifiés selon l'industrie: Non disponible.
Nombre de groupes de codage: Non disponible.
Convertibilité avec la CITI Rév.3 de 1988.
Profession
Groupes de population classifiés selon la profession: Non disponible.
Nombre de groupes de codage: Non disponible.
Convertibilité avec la CITP-1988.
Situation dans la profession
Groupes de population classifiés par situation dans la profession: Non disponible.
Catégories de codage: Salarié, employeur, travailleur indépendant, travailleur familial et stagiaire.
Non-convertibilité avec la CISP-1993.
Education
Groupes de population classifiés selon l'éducation: Non disponible.
Catégories de codage: Analphabète. Sait lire et écrire. Enseignement primaire. Enseignement intermédiaire. Enseignement secondaire. Enseignement universitaire. Etudes de troisième cycle universitaire.
Taille de l'échantillon et plan de sondage:
Unité finale d'échantillonnage: Ménages ordinaires et personnes vivant dans des ménages collectifs.
Taille de l'échantillon (unités finales d'échantillonnage): Quelque 3 390 ménages ordinaires en zones urbaines et rurales.
Taux de sondage: 0,1 pour cent de la population totale.
Base de sondage: Fondée sur les secteurs de recensement du Recensement de 1993 et du Recensement de l'agriculture de 1996 (1996 Agricultural Census of Sudan). La sélection de l'échantillon est basée sur un plan stratifié à deux degrés ou plus.
Renouvellement de l'échantillon: Etablissement d'une nouvelle liste des unités primaires d'échantillonnage.
Rotation: Les ménages ont été interrogés trois fois chaque trimestre pendant l'année de l'enquête.
Déroulement de l'enquête:
Type d'entretien: Entretiens personnels avec écriture manuelle sur papier.
Durée de déroulement de l'enquête par zone de sondage: 2 jours.
Durée de déroulement de l'enquête: 15 jours.
Organisation: Personnel recruté pour chaque enquête.
Nombre de personnes employées: Au total, 155 enquêteurs, cadres et autre personnel sur le terrain.
Substitution des unités finales en cas de non-réponse: Non.
Estimations et redressements:
Taux de non-réponse: Non disponible.
Redressements: Aucun redressement n'a été effectué en cas d'éventuelle sous-représentation ou sur-représentation ou de non-réponse à l'enquête.
Imputation en cas de non-réponse à une question spécifique: Non.
Historique de l'enquête:
Titre et date de la première enquête: Migration and Labour force survey, 1990.
Modifications et révisions significatives: Non disponible.

Documentation et dissémination:
Documentation
Résultats publiés en volumes distincts consacrés: 1 aux caractéristiques de la population; 2 aux taux de participation économique; 3 aux taux de chômage; 4 à la situation matrimoniale; 5 aux migrations internes; 6 aux migrations internationales; et 7 aux migrations de retour.
Délai de publication des premiers résultats: 12 mois. Période couverte par l'enquête: avril 1995. Publication des premiers résultats en avril 1996.
Information à l'avance du public des dates de publication initiale des résultats: Oui.
Mise à disposition, sur demande, des données non publiées: Sur demande, sous forme de base de données et de disquettes.

Sri Lanka

Titre de l'enquête: Sri Lanka Labour Force Survey.
Organisme responsable de l'enquête:
Organisation et déroulement de l'enquête: Department of Census and Statistics
Analyse et Publication des résultats: Department of Census and Statistics
Sujets couverts par l'enquête: Emploi, chômage, sous-emploi lié à la durée du travail, durée du travail, revenu, durée de l'emploi et du chômage, motifs de non-recherche d'emploi, type d'emploi recherché, industrie, profession, situation dans la profession, travail posté, niveau d'instruction, formation professionnelle, activité habituelle et emplois secondaires.
Champ de l'enquête:
Territoire: L'ensemble du pays, à l'exception des provinces du Nord et de l'Est.
Groupes de population: Les personnes âgées de 10 ans et plus, à l'exception de la population institutionnelle, de l'armée et des membres de la famille vivant loin du foyer.
Disponibilité d'estimations selon d'autres sources pour les régions ou groupes exclus: NON.
Groupes couverts par l'enquête mais exclus des résultats publiés: Néant.
Périodicité:
Réalisation de l'enquête: Trimestrielle.
Publication des résultats: Trimestrielle.
Période de référence:
Emploi: La semaine précédente (fixe).
Recherche d'un emploi: La semaine précédente (fixe).
Disponibilité pour travailler: La semaine précédente (fixe).
Concepts et définitions:
Emploi: Les membres du ménage qui, au cours de la période de référence, ont travaillé au moins une heure en tant que salariés, employeurs, travailleurs à leur compte (indépendants) ou travailleurs familiaux non rémunérés dans des entreprises familiales. Sont également incluses les personnes ayant un emploi mais temporairement absentes de leur travail pour des motifs tels que vacances, maladie, intempéries, conflits du travail, etc. Cela inclut les apprentis et stagiaires rémunérés.
Chômage: Les personnes qui, pendant la période de référence, étaient disponibles et/ou en quête d'un emploi salarié ou indépendant et n'avaient pas d'emploi.
Sous-emploi:
Sous-emploi lié à la durée du travail: Les personnes ayant un emploi qui, pendant la période de référence, n'avaient pas d'activité secondaire et étaient disponibles pour travailler davantage. Les personnes à la recherche de ce type d'emploi peuvent être désignées séparément.
Situations d'emploi inadéquat: Non disponible.
Durée du travail: Les heures de travail réellement effectuées pendant la semaine.
Revenu lié à l'emploi:
Revenu lié à l'emploi salarié: Gains en espèces uniquement.
Revenu lié à l'emploi indépendant: Non disponible.
Secteur informel: Non disponible.
Activité habituelle: Les personnes qui, au cours des 12 derniers mois, ont eu un emploi et/ou ont été sans emploi pendant 26 semaines ou plus.
Classifications:
Branche d'activité économique (industrie)
Titre de la classification: Classification nationale.
Groupes de population classifiés selon l'industrie: Les personnes ayant un emploi.
Nombre de groupes de codage: 10.

Convertibilité avec la CITI: CITI-Rév.2.
Profession
Titre de la classification: Classification nationale.
Groupes de population classifiés selon la profession: Les personnes ayant un emploi.
Nombre de groupes de codage: 10.
Convertibilité avec la CITP: CITP-1988.
Situation dans la profession
Titre de la classification: Classification nationale.
Groupes de population classifiés par situation dans la profession: Les personnes ayant un emploi.
Catégories de codage: Salarié, employeur, travailleur indépendant, travailleur familial non rémunéré.
Convertibilité avec la CISP: CISP-1993.
Education
Titre de la classification: Classification nationale.
Groupes de population classifiés selon l'éducation: Les personnes ayant un emploi et les chômeurs.
Catégories de codage: Pas de scolarité, années d'études 1 à 5, 6 à 10, GCE (O/L), GCE (A/L) et au-delà.
Convertibilité avec la CITE: Non.
Taille de l'échantillon et plan de sondage:
Unité finale d'échantillonnage: Unité de logement.
Taille de l'échantillon (unités finales d'échantillonnage): La taille de l'échantillon annuel est de 16 000 unités de logement.
Taux de sondage: Non disponible.
Base de sondage: La base de sondage principale (liste des unités de logement) a été créée pour l'Enquête démographique de 1994 (1994 Demographic Survey). Depuis 2002, c'est le Recensement de population et du logement de 2001 (2001 Census of Population and Housing) qui est utilisé comme base de sondage.
Renouvellement de l'échantillon: Jusqu'en 2001, la liste des unités de logement dans les unités primaires d'échantillonnage sélectionnées était renouvelée avant le recensement fait pour l'enquête; depuis 2002, c'est la liste des îlots de recensement qui est renouvelée avant le recensement fait pour l'enquête.
Rotation: Ne s'applique pas.
Schéma: Ne s'applique pas.
Pourcentage d'unités restant dans l'échantillon durant deux enquêtes successives: Ne s'applique pas.
Nombre maximum d'interrogatoires par unité de sondage: Non disponible.
Durée nécessaire au renouvellement complet de l'échantillon: Non disponible.
Déroulement de l'enquête:
Type d'entretien: Entretien personnel.
Nombre d'unités finales d'échantillonnage par zone de sondage: Non disponible.
Durée de déroulement de l'enquête:
Totale: Deux semaines.
Par zone de sondage: Une semaine.
Organisation: Personnel d'enquête permanent.
Nombre de personnes employées: Environ 300 enquêteurs et cadres.
Substitution des unités finales en cas de non-réponse: Non.
Estimations et redressements:
Taux de non-réponse: 5%.
Redressement pour non-réponse: Oui.
Imputation en cas de non-réponse à une question spécifique: Non.
Redressement pour les régions/populations non couvertes: Non.
Redressement en cas de sous-représentation: Oui.
Redressement en cas de sur-représentation: Oui.
Corrections des variations saisonnières: Non.
Historique de l'enquête:
Titre et date de la première enquête: Sri Lanka Labour Force Survey - 1990.
Modifications et révisions significatives: De nouvelles questions ont été ajoutées à partir du premier trimestre 1996.
Documentation et dissémination:
Documentation
Titre des publications publiant les résultats: Quarterly Report of the Sri Lanka Labour force Survey; Bulletin of Labour Force (trimestriel); Annual Bulletin of Labour Force-Provincial Profile.
Titre des publications méthodologiques: Idem.
Dissémination
Délai de publication des premiers résultats: Environ trois mois.
Information à l'avance du public des dates de publication initiale des résultats: Non.
Mise à disposition, sur demande, des données non publiées: Oui.
Mise à disposition des données sur support informatique: Disquettes et bandes magnétiques.
Site web: http://www.statistics.gov.lk/.

Suède

Titre de l'enquête: Labour Force Survey (LFS).
Organisme responsable de l'enquête:
Organisation et déroulement de l'enquête: Statistics Sweden.
Analyse et Publication des résultats: Statistics Sweden.
Sujets couverts par l'enquête: Emploi, chômage, sous-emploi, durée du travail, durée du chômage, travailleurs découragés, travailleurs occasionnels, industrie, profession, situation dans la profession, niveau d'instruction/de qualification, activité habituelle, exercice d'autres emplois et famille.
Champ de l'enquête:
Territoire: L'ensemble du pays.
Groupes de population: Tous les habitants âgés de 15 à 74 ans enregistrés auprès de l'état civil, y compris les volontaires et les militaires de carrière.
Disponibilité d'estimations selon d'autres sources pour les régions ou groupes exclus: Non disponible.
Groupes couverts par l'enquête mais exclus des résultats publiés: Des estimations séparées sont disponibles pour les personnes âgées de 15 ans et pour celles âgées de 65 à 74 ans.
Périodicité:
Réalisation de l'enquête: Mensuelle.
Publication des résultats: Mensuelle.
Période de référence:
Emploi: Une semaine.
Recherche d'un emploi: Une semaine.
Disponibilité pour travailler: Une semaine.
Concepts et définitions:
Emploi: Toutes les personnes âgées de 16 à 64 ans qui:
1)ont exercé, au cours de la semaine pendant laquelle a eu lieu la mesure, une activité lucrative pendant au moins une heure, soit en tant que salariés, soit en tant qu'entrepreneurs, soit en tant que travailleurs indépendants, et les personnes travaillant comme aides non rémunérées dans une entreprise appartenant à un conjoint ou à un autre membre de la famille du même ménage (ayant un emploi et au travail);
2)n'ont pas effectué de travail au sens de la définition ci-dessus mais avaient un emploi ou un travail en qualité de travailleurs familiaux non rémunérés, d'entrepreneurs ou de travailleurs indépendants et étaient temporairement absentes durant toute la semaine où a été faite la mesure pour cause de maladie, de vacances, d'autres congés (pour s'occuper d'enfants, pour études, service militaire, autre congé ou conflit du travail), que leur absence ait été rémunérée ou non (= ayant un emploi, temporairement absentes).
Sont également inclus:
a)les travailleurs occupés à plein temps ou à temps partiel et en quête d'un autre emploi pendant la semaine où a eu lieu la mesure;
b)les étudiants à plein temps ou à temps partiel travaillant à plein temps ou à temps partiel;
c)les personnes en mise à pied temporaire rémunérée (la mise à pied sans rémunération n'existe pas en Suède);
d)les personnes ayant effectué un travail quelconque, rémunéré ou en vue d'un bénéfice, pendant la semaine au cours de laquelle a eu lieu la mesure, tout en étant assujetties à la scolarité obligatoire ou à la retraite et au bénéfice d'une pension ou inscrites en tant que demandeurs d'emploi auprès d'un bureau de placement, ou tout en percevant des allocations de chômage;
e)les apprentis et stagiaires rémunérés;
f)les bénéficiaires de mesures de promotion de l'emploi (ateliers protégés, travail de relève, équipes de jeunes ou employés grâce à des aides publiques ou à des subventions gouvernementales spéciales);
g)les travailleurs familiaux rémunérés ou non, y compris ceux qui étaient temporairement absents de leur travail pendant la semaine au cours de laquelle la mesure a été effectuée;
h)les domestiques privés;
i)les membres de coopératives de producteurs;
j)les volontaires et les militaires de carrière;
k)les conscrits et les personnes effectuant un service civil équivalent au service militaire, sous réserve qu'ils aient eu un emploi auparavant et qu'ils soient en congé (c'est-à-dire temporairement absents) d'un emploi civil pendant leur service militaire ou civil.

Les personnes en congé d'éducation ou de formation rémunéré par l'employeur (pendant les heures de travail rémunérées ou sous forme de congé autorisé payé) sont classées comme ayant un emploi et « au travail ». Les personnes en congé d'éducation non rémunéré (congé accordé pour faire des études) sont classées comme ayant un emploi et «non au travail».
Sont exclues de la population active suédoise les personnes travaillant à l'étranger et n'ayant pas d'emploi en Suède, qu'elles traversent la frontière tous les jours pour venir travailler ou qu'elles vivent et travaillent dans un pays étranger.
Chômage: Les personnes âgées de 15 à 64 ans qui, au cours de la semaine où a eu lieu la mesure, n'avaient pas d'emploi mais voulaient travailler, auraient pu accepter un emploi et avaient cherché du travail, ou qui en auraient cherché si elles n'en avaient pas été temporairement empêchées, ou qui attendaient l'issue d'une démarche de recherche d'emploi effectuée au cours des quatre semaines précédentes. Sont également incluses les personnes attendant de commencer dans un nouvel emploi dans les quatre semaines.
Les étudiants à temps partiel à la recherche d'un emploi à plein temps ou à temps partiel sont également classés comme chômeurs.
Les étudiants à plein temps à la recherche d'un emploi à plein temps ou à temps partiel sont exclus de la catégorie des chômeurs et considérés comme inactifs; les données relatives à la taille de ce groupe sont toutefois recueillies.
Les travailleurs saisonniers attendant un travail agricole ou un autre genre de travail saisonnier sont classés comme chômeurs à condition qu'ils remplissent les critères utilisés dans la définition du chômage; autrement, ils sont classés comme en dehors de la population active.
Par « ayant cherché du travail », on entend avoir entrepris une ou plusieurs des démarches ci-après au cours des quatre semaines précédant l'entretien: avoir pris contact avec le bureau de placement ou directement avec des employeurs; avoir consulté et/ou fait paraître des petites annonces; avoir pris contact avec des amis ou des parents, etc.
Sous-emploi:
Sous-emploi lié à la durée du travail: Les personnes sous-employées sont les personnes travaillant moins que ce qu'elles voudraient pour des raisons liées au marché de l'emploi.
Situations d'emploi inadéquat: Ne s'applique pas.
Durée du travail: Sont recueillies les heures de travail aussi bien réellement effectuées (y compris les heures supplémentaires) pendant la semaine au cours de laquelle a eu lieu la mesure que les heures de travail habituelles (contractuelles). Ces deux variables sont mesurées séparément pour l'activité principale et la ou les activités secondaires.
Revenu lié à l'emploi:
Revenu lié à l'emploi salarié: Non couvert par l'enquête.
Revenu lié à l'emploi indépendant: Non couvert par l'enquête.
Secteur informel: Non couvert par l'enquête.
Activité habituelle: Les personnes sans activité lucrative et les travailleurs occasionnels sont interrogés sur leur activité principale habituelle.
Classifications:
Branche d'activité économique (industrie)
Titre de la classification: Swedish Standard Industrial Classification 1992 (SE-SIC 92).
Groupes de population classifiés selon l'industrie: Les personnes ayant un emploi et les chômeurs (industrie du dernier emploi occupé pour ces derniers).
Nombre de groupes de codage: Les données sont recueillies et classées en 64 groupes mais présentées selon 48 groupes.
Convertibilité avec la CITI: CITI-Rév.3 au niveau à deux chiffres.
Profession
Titre de la classification: Swedish Standard Classification of Occupations 1996 (SSYK 96).
Groupes de population classifiés selon la profession: Les personnes ayant un emploi et les chômeurs (profession exercée dans le dernier emploi occupé pour ces derniers).
Nombre de groupes de codage: Les données sont recueillies et classées en 381 groupes (niveau à quatre chiffres) mais présentées selon 68 groupes.
Convertibilité avec la CITP: CITP-1988.
Situation dans la profession
Titre de la classification: Classification nationale.
Groupes de population classifiés par situation dans la profession: Les personnes ayant un emploi et les chômeurs (situation occupée dans le dernier emploi pour ces derniers).
Catégories de codage: Employeurs, entrepreneurs/travailleurs indépendants (avec ou sans salariés), travailleurs familiaux.
Convertibilité avec la CISP: CISP-1993.

Education
Titre de la classification: Swedish Standard Classification of **Education** (SUN 2000).
Groupes de population classifiés selon l'éducation: Groupes de population classés selon l'éducation: tous les enquêtés sont classés en fonction du plus haut niveau d'instruction et du domaine du savoir le plus complet qu'ils aient atteint. Ces informations ne sont pas demandées au cours de l'enquête mais prises dans le Registre suédois de l'éducation (Swedish Register of **Education**).
Catégories de codage: Le « code de niveau » est composé de 47 codes (à 3 chiffres) mais les données sont présentées selon 7 groupes. Le « code de rubrique » est composé d'un code à 4 chiffres mais les données sont présentées selon 9 groupes.
Convertibilité avec la CITE: CITE-1997.
Taille de l'échantillon et plan de sondage:
Unité finale d'échantillonnage: Les personnes.
Taille de l'échantillon (unités finales d'échantillonnage): 22 000 personnes sur une population d'environ 6,5 millions (âgée de 15 à 74 ans), et 21 000 sur 5,6 millions (âgée de 16 à 64 ans).
Taux de sondage: Non disponible.
Base de sondage: Le registre de la population du SCB (Statistics Sweden), plus ou moins mis à jour en continu.
Renouvellement de l'échantillon: L'échantillon est tiré à chaque changement d'année pour répondre aux besoins de l'année suivante (avril-mars). Il est ensuite renouvelé chaque mois pour tenir compte des migrations, des décès et des changements de situation maritale. L'échantillon est complété par les immigrants une fois par trimestre.
Rotation:
Schéma: Les personnes retenues dans l'échantillon sont interrogées une fois par trimestre à 8 reprises au total sur une période de deux ans avant d'être remplacées. Chaque mois, 1/8 de l'échantillon est renouvelé.
Pourcentage d'unités restant dans l'échantillon durant deux enquêtes successives: 87,5 pour cent restent dans le même échantillon durant deux trimestres successifs.
Nombre maximum d'interrogatoires par unité de sondage: Non disponible.
Durée nécessaire au renouvellement complet de l'échantillon: Deux ans.
Déroulement de l'enquête:
Type d'entretien: Entretiens par téléphone complétés par une visite personnelle (environ 0,2 pour cent des entretiens) quand la personne de l'échantillon ne peut pas être atteinte.
Nombre d'unités finales d'échantillonnage par zone de sondage: Non disponible.
Durée de déroulement de l'enquête:
Totale: 5 à 6 semaines.
Par zone de sondage: Non disponible.
Organisation: Permanente.
Nombre de personnes employées: Environ 200.
Substitution des unités finales en cas de non-réponse: Non.
Estimations et redressements:
Taux de non-réponse: Environ 15% en février 2002.
Redressement pour non-réponse: Oui.
Imputation en cas de non-réponse à une question spécifique: Non.
Redressement pour les régions/populations non couvertes: Non disponible.
Redressement en cas de sous-représentation: Non.
Redressement en cas de sur-représentation: Non.
Corrections des variations saisonnières: Oui.
Historique de l'enquête:
Titre et date de la première enquête: Swedish Labour Force Survey-May 1959 (National Market Board).
Modifications et révisions significatives: Enquête trimestrielle d'août 1961 à 1970, puis mensuelle.
1987: révision des concepts et définitions. 1981: introduction de l'entretien par téléphone assisté par ordinateur. 1995: nouvelle classification des industries. 1997: nouvelle classification des professions. 2000: nouvelle classification selon l'éducation. 2003: des modifications importantes sont prévues pour s'aligner sur les règlements de l'UE.
Documentation et dissémination:
Documentation
Titre des publications publiant les résultats: Statistical Messages (SM): SM Am 10 (mensuel), SM Am 11 (trimestriel), SM Am 12 (annuel).
Titre des publications méthodologiques: 2001:5 Urvals- och estimationsförfarandet i de svenska arbetskraftsundersökningarna (AKU (Design and estimations in LFS)).

Dissémination
Délai de publication des premiers résultats: 2 semaines après la fin du mois.
Information à l'avance du public des dates de publication initiale des résultats: Oui.
Mise à disposition, sur demande, des données non publiées: Oui.
Mise à disposition des données sur support informatique: Oui.
Site web: http://www.scb.se/.

Suisse

Titre de l'enquête: Enquête suisse sur la population active.
Organisme responsable de l'enquête:
Organisation et déroulement de l'enquête: Office fédéral de statistique.
Analyse et Publication des résultats: Office fédéral de statistique.
Sujets couverts par l'enquête: Emploi, chômage, sous-emploi, durée du travail, salaires, revenu, durée de l'emploi et du chômage, travailleurs occasionnels, industrie, profession, situation dans l'emploi, autres emplois.
Champ de l'enquête:
Territoire: Ensemble du pays.
Groupes de population: Personnes âgées de 15 ans et plus. Sont exclues les personnes qui n'y sont pas domiciliées durant toute l'année, tels que les saisonniers, frontaliers, requérants d'asile ainsi que les personnes qui y résident brièvement.
Disponibilité d'estimations selon d'autres sources pour les régions ou groupes exclus: Ne s'applique pas.
Groupes couverts par l'enquête mais exclus des résultats publiés: Ne s'applique pas.
Périodicité:
Réalisation de l'enquête: Annuellement.
Publication des résultats: Annuellement.
Période de référence:
Emploi: Une semaine au cours du 2ème trimestre.
Recherche d'un emploi: Quatre semaines au cours du 2ème trimestre.
Disponibilité pour travailler: Deux semaines au cours du 2ème trimestre.
Concepts et définitions:
Emploi: Personnes âgées de 15 ans ou plus, salariées ou indépendantes, ayant travaillé au moins une heure, contre rémunération, durant la semaine de référence (semaine précédant l'entretien), ainsi que les personnes momentanément absentes de leur travail, et celles qui ont travaillé durant la semaine de référence, sans rémunération, dans l'entreprise familiale.
Sont considérées comme ayant un emploi:
a) les personnes absentes de leur travail, durant une période inférieure à trois mois, pour cause de maladie ou accident, congés annuels, congé de maternité ou paternité, congé d'éducation ou de formation, absence non autorisée, conflit du travail, intempéries ou panne mécanique, etc., ainsi que les personnes mises à pied temporairement sans rémunération (moins de trois mois);
b) les personnes ayant effectué un travail quelconque, rémunéré ou en vue d'un bénéfice, pendant la semaine de référence, mais qui étaient assujetties à la scolarité obligatoire, en retraite et au bénéfice d'une pension, inscrites en tant que demandeurs d'emploi auprès d'un bureau de placement ou percevant des allocations de chômage.
c) les étudiants à plein temps ou à temps partiel, travaillant à plein temps ou à temps partiel;
d) les apprentis et stagiaires rémunérés ou non, les bénéficiaires de mesures de promotion de l'emploi tels que programmes d'emploi temporaire, stages professionnels, etc.
e) les travailleurs familiaux non rémunérés travaillant durant la période de référence;
f) les forces armées: militaires de carrière ainsi que les conscrits et les personnes effectuant un service civil équivalent au service militaire de 12 semaines ou occupant un emploi durant leur service militaire.
Chômage: Personnes âgées de 15 ans et plus qui n'ont exercé aucune activité rémunérée durant la semaine précédant l'entretien, qui ont cherché un emploi au cours des quatre dernières semaines et ont entrepris durant cette période une ou plusieurs démarches spécifiques pour trouver un emploi et qui pourraient commencer à travailler au cours des quatre semaines suivantes.
Les personnes qui ont déjà trouvé un emploi sont considérées comme étant en chômage si leur entrée en fonction doit intervenir dans les trois mois.
Sont également considérés comme chômeurs:
a) les personnes sans emploi et immédiatement disponibles pour travailler, qui ont essayé de créer leur propre entreprise;
b) les personnes en quête d'un emploi et/ou immédiatement disponibles pour travailler, mais qui étaient assujetties à la scolarité obligatoire ou en retraite et au bénéfice d'une pension;
c) les étudiants à plein temps ou à temps partiel à la recherche d'un emploi à plein temps ou à temps partiel.
Sous-emploi:
Sous-emploi lié à la durée du travail: Trois critères sont retenus: disposition à faire d'avantage d'heures, disponibilité pour travailler plus et durée du travail inférieur à un seuil spécifique, à définir.
Situations d'emploi inadéquat: Exclu du champ de l'enquête.
Durée du travail: Heures réellement effectuées et heures habituelles par semaine pour toutes les activités. Les heures réellement effectuées se réfèrent à l'activité principale et à la dernière activité.
Revenu lié à l'emploi:
Revenu lié à l'emploi salarié: Revenu professionnel (brut et net) pour toutes les activités.
Revenu lié à l'emploi indépendant: Exclu du champ de l'enquête.
Secteur informel: Exclu du champ de l'enquête.
Activité habituelle: Exclu du champ de l'enquête.
Classifications:
Branche d'activité économique (industrie)
Titre de la classification: Classification nationale.
Groupes de population classifiés selon l'industrie: Personnes ayant un emploi et chômeurs (industrie du dernier emploi pour les chômeurs).
Nombre de groupes de codage: 222 groupes.
Convertibilité avec la CITI: CITI-Rév.3.
Profession
Titre de la classification: Classification nationale.
Groupes de population classifiés selon la profession: Personnes ayant un emploi et chômeurs (profession du dernier emploi pour les chômeurs).
Nombre de groupes de codage: 87 groupes, 388 genres et environ 16 000 professions.
Convertibilité avec la CITP: CITP-88.
Situation dans la profession
Titre de la classification: Classification nationale.
Groupes de population classifiés par situation dans la profession: Personnes ayant un emploi et chômeurs (situation dans l'emploi du dernier emploi pour les chômeurs).
Catégories de codage: Indépendants, salariés, collaborateurs familiaux. Les deux premières catégories sont subdivisées en sous groupes.
Convertibilité avec la CISP: CISP-1993.
Education
Titre de la classification: Classification nationale.
Groupes de population classifiés selon l'éducation: Personnes ayant un emploi et chômeurs.
Catégories de codage: Scolarité obligatoire; formation professionnelle élémentaire; école ménagère; école de culture générale; apprentissage; école professionnelle à plein temps; maturité; formation professionnelle supérieure; école technique ou professionnelle; école professionnelle supérieure; université ou haute école; pas de formation achevée.
Convertibilité avec la CITE: ISCED-1997.
Taille de l'échantillon et plan de sondage:
Unité finale d'échantillonnage: Personnes.
Taille de l'échantillon (unités finales d'échantillonnage): Entre 16 000 et 18 000 personnes. A partir de 2002, environ 35 000 personnes.
Taux de sondage: 0.3 pour cent de la population résidante permanente.
Base de sondage: Annuaires téléphoniques: y sont répertoriées toutes les personnes disposant d'un raccordement téléphonique. Le plan de sélection des adresses est basé sur le principe de l'échantillon aléatoire, stratifié par canton. Le nombre des adresses tirées au sort est proportionnel à celui des habitants et au taux de réponse des différents cantons.
Renouvellement de l'échantillon: Pas d'information.
Rotation:
Schéma: L'échantillon se compose d'environ un cinquième de personnes interrogées pour la première fois et de quatre cinquièmes environ de personnes ayant déjà été interrogées au moins une fois.
Pourcentage d'unités restant dans l'échantillon durant deux enquêtes successives: 80 pour cent.
Nombre maximum d'interrogatoires par unité de sondage: Cinq fois.

Durée nécessaire au renouvellement complet de l'échantillon: Cinq ans.
Déroulement de l'enquête:
Type d'entretien: Entretien par téléphone assisté par ordinateur (CATI).
Nombre d'unités finales d'échantillonnage par zone de sondage: Pas d'information.
Durée de déroulement de l'enquête:
Totale: 3 mois.
Par zone de sondage: Pas d'information.
Organisation: Structure plutôt permanente.
Nombre de personnes employées: Cinq personnes au niveau fédéral et environ 250 enquêteurs d'une entreprise privée.
Substitution des unités finales en cas de non-réponse: Non.
Estimations et redressements:
Taux de non-réponse: 20 pur cent.
Redressement pour non-réponse: Non.
Imputation en cas de non réponse à une question spécifique: Non.
Redressement pour les régions/populations non couvertes: Non.
Redressement en cas de sous-représentation: Oui.
Redressement en cas de sur-représentation: Oui.
Corrections des variations saisonnières: Non.
Historique de l'enquête:
Titre et date de la première enquête: Enquête suisse sur la population active 1991.
Modifications et révisions significatives: 1996: questions concernant le volume du travail. 2001: adaptation aux recommandation internationales et nouvelles questions concernant le travail atypique.
Documentation et dissémination:
Documentation
Titre des publications publiant les résultats: Enquête suisse sur la population active (ESPA): résultats commentés et tableaux (Publication annuelle).
Titre des publications méthodologiques: Enquête suisse sur la population active (ESPA): concepts, bases méthodologiques, considérations pratiques (1996).
Dissémination
Délai de publication des premiers résultats: Novembre de l'année de référence de l'enquête.
Information à l'avance du public des dates de publication initiale des résultats: Oui.
Mise à disposition, sur demande, des données non publiées: Oui.
Mise à disposition des données sur support informatique: Oui.
Site web: http://www.statistik.admin.ch.

Tanzanie, Rép.-Unie de

Titre de l'enquête: Labour Force Survey.
Organisme responsable de l'enquête:
Organisation et déroulement de l'enquête: National Bureau of Statistics en collaboration avec le Département du Travail (Labour Department).
Analyse et Publication des résultats: National Bureau of Statistics en collaboration avec le Département du Travail (Labour Department).
Sujets couverts par l'enquête: Emploi, chômage, sous-emploi, durée du travail (heures de travail habituelles, heures de travail réellement effectuées), revenu lié à l'emploi, emploi dans le secteur informel, type de lieu de travail, durée de l'emploi, durée du chômage, travailleurs découragés, industrie, profession, situation dans la profession, niveau d'instruction et de qualification, activité habituelle, exercice d'autres emplois.
Champ de l'enquête:
Territoire: La Tanzanie continentale. Les îles de Zanzibar ne sont pas couvertes.
Groupes de population: L'enquête couvre les résidents habituels de logements privés en Tanzanie continentale, quelle que soit leur nationalité. Les personnes vivant en institution ne sont pas couvertes. Sont exclus les diplomates étrangers résidant en Tanzanie.
Disponibilité d'estimations selon d'autres sources pour les régions ou groupes exclus: Oui, selon des enquêtes similaires réalisées à Zanzibar et des recensements.
Groupes couverts par l'enquête mais exclus des résultats publiés: Néant.
Périodicité:
Réalisation de l'enquête: Tous les dix ans. Les données sont recueillies sur une période de 12 mois divisée en quatre trimestres. La dernière enquête a été réalisée pendant la période comprise entre avril 2000 et mars 2001. La présente description se réfère à l'Enquête de 1990-1991, réalisée d'octobre 1990 à septembre 1991.
Publication des résultats: Tous les dix ans.
Période de référence:
Emploi: Période de référence variable d'une semaine, la dernière semaine civile pleine (de lundi à dimanche) avant la date de l'entretien.
Recherche d'un emploi: Période de référence variable de quatre semaines avant la date de l'entretien.
Disponibilité pour travailler: Période de référence variable d'une semaine, la dernière semaine civile pleine (de lundi à dimanche) avant la date de l'entretien.
Concepts et définitions:
Emploi: Les personnes âgées de 10 ans et plus ayant effectué un travail quelconque (pendant au moins une heure) au cours de la semaine de référence, soit comme salariés contre rémunération en espèces ou en nature, soit comme travailleurs indépendants (y compris les exploitants agricoles) en vue d'un bénéfice ou d'un gain familial. Sont inclus: a) les travailleurs familiaux non rémunérés au travail pendant la semaine de référence; b) les travailleurs occupés à plein temps ou à temps partiel et en quête d'un autre travail; c) les personnes ayant effectué un travail quelconque, rémunéré ou en vuo d'un bénéfice, pendant la période de référence, mais qui étaient alors assujetties à la scolarité obligatoire ou à la retraite et au bénéfice d'une pension; d) les étudiants à plein temps travaillant à temps partiel; e) les étudiants à temps partiel travaillant à plein temps ou à temps partiel; f) les apprentis et stagiaires rémunérés ou non; et g) les personnes occupées dans la production de biens pour leur usage final personnel.
Sont également incluses les personnes ayant un emploi ou une entreprise qui étaient temporairement absentes de leur travail au cours de la semaine de référence mais allaient assurément y retourner, pour cause de a) maladie ou accident, b) congés ou vacances annuelles; c) congé de maternité ou de paternité; d) congé d'éducation ou de formation; e) conflit du travail, f) intempéries, panne mécanique, etc., ou g) mise à pied temporaire sans rémunération. La durée de l'absence est limitée à quatre mois pour les salariés et à un mois pour les travailleurs indépendants.
Sont exclus: a) les travailleurs familiaux non rémunérés non au travail durant la semaine de référence; b) les travailleurs occasionnels non au travail durant la semaine de référence; c) les salariés absents de leur travail pendant plus de quatre mois; d) les travailleurs indépendants absents de leurs travail pendant plus d'un mois; e) les personnes en mise à pied de durée indéterminée sans rémunération; et f) les personnes rendant des services non rémunérés ou personnels à des membres de leur propre ménage.
Chômage: Deux définitions sont utilisées: 1) les personnes âgées de 10 ans et plus sans emploi pendant la semaine de référence, disponibles pour travailler cette semaine-là et qui avaient effectué des démarches concrètes pour trouver du travail au cours des quatre dernières semaines; et 2) les personnes âgées de 10 ans et plus sans emploi pendant la semaine de référence et disponibles pour travailler cette semaine-là. Ce qui suit est considéré comme démarches concrètes visant à trouver du travail: avoir présenté sa candidature à des employeurs potentiels; s'être enquis d'éventuels emplois auprès d'exploitations agricoles, d'usines ou sur des chantiers; avoir interrogé des amis et des parents; avoir pris des dispositions pour créer une entreprise; avoir pris des dispositions pour créer une exploitation agricole; autres.
Sont incluses: a) les personnes sans emploi et immédiatement disponibles pour travailler qui ont pris des dispositions pour commencer à travailler dans un nouvel emploi à une date postérieure à la semaine de référence (définitions 1 et 2); b) les personnes sans emploi et immédiatement disponibles pour travailler qui ont essayé de créer leur propre entreprise (définitions 1 et 2); c) les personnes sans emploi, disponibles pour travailler mais n'ayant pas cherché de travail pour des raisons autres que a) ou b) ci-dessus (définition 2); d) les personnes en quête d'un emploi et/ou immédiatement disponibles pour travailler mais assujetties à la scolarité obligatoire ou à la retraite et au bénéfice d'une pension (définitions 1 et 2); e) les étudiants à plein temps en quête d'un emploi à plein temps ou à temps partiel et/ou immédiatement disponibles pour occuper un tel emploi (définitions 1 et 2); et f) les étudiants à temps partiel en quête d'un emploi à plein temps ou à temps partiel et/ou immédiatement disponibles pour occuper un tel emploi (définitions 1 et 2).
Sont exclues les personnes sans emploi et immédiatement disponibles pour travailler mais n'ayant pas cherché de travail pour des raisons autres que a) et b) ci-dessus (définition 1), ou les personnes sans emploi qui n'étaient pas disponibles pour travailler (définitions 1 et 2).

Sous-emploi:

Sous-emploi lié à la durée du travail: Les personnes ayant un emploi qui ont travaillé moins de 40 heures pendant la semaine de référence pour des motifs économiques et étaient disponibles pour faire davantage d'heures.

Situations d'emploi inadéquat: Ce sujet n'est pas couvert par l'enquête.

Durée du travail: Les heures de travail hebdomadaires habituelles et les heures de travail réellement effectuées pendant la semaine de référence. Pour les heures de travail habituelles et les heures de travail réellement effectuées, les informations sont recueillies séparément pour l'activité principale et les autres activités.

Revenu lié à l'emploi:

Revenu lié à l'emploi salarié: Les salaires ou traitements bruts perçus en espèces au cours du dernier mois au titre de la totalité des emplois salariés. Les salaires ou traitements en nature sont exclus.

Revenu lié à l'emploi indépendant: Le bénéfice net tiré de la ou des activités au cours de la dernière semaine ou du dernier mois. Pour les travailleurs indépendants occupés dans des activités non agricoles, le bénéfice net est dérivé de questions relatives au revenu brut et aux frais d'exploitation; pour les travailleurs indépendants occupés dans l'agriculture, les informations relatives au bénéfice net sont obtenues directement.

Secteur informel: Les personnes travaillant dans des entreprises i) autres que des entreprises d'Etat, des organismes parapublics, des organisations appartenant au parti du CCM ou des coopératives préexistantes, ii) employant moins de six salariés et iii) situées dans une structure temporaire, sur un chemin ou dans une rue, ou sans établissements fixes. L'agriculture traditionnelle, l'élevage et la pêche, ainsi que les services professionnels ou les services aux entreprises et autres entreprises présentant des caractéristiques formelles distinctes sont exclus. Les ménages employant des domestiques rémunérés sont inclus.

Activité habituelle: L'activité habituelle se réfère à la situation au regard de l'activité principale pendant une période de référence d'une année, à savoir les 12 mois civils pleins précédant la date de l'entretien. Les personnes âgées de 10 ans et plus sont considérées comme habituellement actives si elles ont travaillé ou étaient disponibles pour travailler pendant six mois ou plus des 12 mois de référence. Les personnes habituellement actives sont subdivisées en personnes ayant habituellement un emploi et en personnes habituellement sans emploi. Les personnes ayant habituellement un emploi sont celles qui ont travaillé pendant la moitié ou plus de la moitié des mois d'activité économique. Les personnes habituellement sans emploi sont celles qui ont passé plus de la moitié des mois d'activité économique à ne pas travailler alors qu'elles étaient disponibles pour ce faire.

Classifications:

Branche d'activité économique (industrie)

Titre de la classification: Adaptation tanzanienne de la Classification internationale type, par industrie, de toutes les branches d'activité économique (CITI Rév.2); des codes supplémentaires ont été créés pour décrire les activités du secteur informel.

Groupes de population classifiés selon l'industrie: Les personnes ayant un emploi.

Nombre de groupes de codage: Groupes au niveau à 4 chiffres.

Convertibilité avec la CITI: CITI Rév.2

Profession

Titre de la classification: Tanzania Standard Classification of Occupations (TASCO).

Groupes de population classifiés selon la profession: Les personnes ayant un emploi et les chômeurs.

Nombre de groupes de codage: Groupes au niveau à 4 chiffres.

Convertibilité avec la CITP: CITP-1988.

Situation dans la profession

Titre de la classification: Classification nationale d'après la situation dans la profession.

Groupes de population classifiés par situation dans la profession: Les personnes ayant un emploi.

Catégories de codage: a) Salariés; b) travailleurs indépendants (activités non agricoles) ayant des salariés; c) travailleurs indépendants (activités non agricoles) sans salariés; d) aides familiales non rémunérées (activités non agricoles); e) personnes travaillant dans leur propre exploitation agricole ou dans celle de leur famille ou shamba.

Convertibilité avec la CISP: Partielle.

Education

Titre de la classification: Classification nationale des niveaux d'instruction.

Groupes de population classifiés selon l'éducation: Toutes les personnes âgées de 10 ans et plus.

Catégories de codage: a) Néant; b) enseignement primaire inachevé; c) enseignement primaire achevé; d) enseignement secondaire jusqu'à la classe 2; e) enseignement secondaire jusqu'à la classe 4); f) enseignement secondaire jusqu'à la classe 6); g) enseignement universitaire.

Convertibilité avec la CITE: Non disponible.

Taille de l'échantillon et plan de sondage:

Unité finale d'échantillonnage: Ménage.

Taille de l'échantillon (unités finales d'échantillonnage): 7 762 ménages.

Taux de sondage: Environ 0,2 pour cent des ménages.

Base de sondage: Un National Master Sample (NMS) comprenant 122 secteurs de recensement urbains et 50 villages a servi de base de sondage aréolaire pour l'enquête. Avant l'enquête, une liste des ménages a été établie dans tous les secteurs de recensement et villages compris dans le NMS.

Renouvellement de l'échantillon: L'échantillon sera renouvelé après l'achèvement du travail cartographique effectué pour le Recensement de 2002.

Rotation:

Schéma: Pas de schéma de rotation. L'échantillon sur lequel porte l'enquête est divisé en quatre sous-échantillons trimestriels indépendants.

Pourcentage d'unités restant dans l'échantillon durant deux enquêtes successives: Ne s'applique pas.

Nombre maximum d'interrogatoires par unité de sondage: Ne s'applique pas.

Durée nécessaire au renouvellement complet de l'échantillon: Ne s'applique pas.

Déroulement de l'enquête:

Type d'entretien: Les informations sont obtenues au cours d'entretiens personnels.

Nombre d'unités finales d'échantillonnage par zone de sondage: 30 à 35 ménages par secteur de recensement urbain; 80 ménages par village.

Durée de déroulement de l'enquête:

Totale: Une année.

Par zone de sondage: 14 jours pour les secteurs de recensement urbains et 27 jours pour les villages.

Organisation: Le personnel sur le terrain est recruté pour chaque enquête.

Nombre de personnes employées: Non disponible.

Substitution des unités finales en cas de non-réponse: Aucun remplacement des ménages défaillants n'a lieu.

Estimations et redressements:

Taux de non-réponse: 2,4% des ménages-échantillons.

Redressement pour non-réponse: Oui.

Imputation en cas de non-réponse à une question spécifique: Non.

Redressement pour les régions/populations non couvertes: Ne s'applique pas.

Redressement en cas de sous-représentation: Oui.

Redressement en cas de sur-représentation: Ne s'applique pas.

Corrections des variations saisonnières: Ne s'applique pas.

Historique de l'enquête:

Titre et date de la première enquête: 1965 Labour Force Survey.

Modifications et révisions significatives: Aucune enquête sur la population active n'a été réalisée pendant la période comprise entre 1966 et 1989. Les Enquêtes de 1990-1991 et 2000-2001 (1990-91 and 2000-01 Labour Force Surveys) étaient basées sur les recommandations adoptées par la 13ème Conférence internationale des statisticiens du travail. Des modules portant sur le travail des enfants et le secteur informel ont été ajoutés à l'Enquête 2000-2001 (Labour Force Survey 2000-2001).

Documentation et dissémination:

Documentation

Titre des publications publiant les résultats: Bureau of Statistics and Labour Department, Tanzania (Mainland), The Labour Force Survey 1990/91, juin 1993.

Titre des publications méthodologiques: Bureau of Statistics and Labour Department, Tanzania (Mainland), The Labour Force Survey 1990/91, Technical Report, juin 1993.

Dissémination

Délai de publication des premiers résultats: Environ 21 mois.

Information à l'avance du public des dates de publication initiale des résultats: Oui.

Mise à disposition, sur demande, des données non publiées: Oui.

Mise à disposition des données sur support informatique: Les tableaux des résultats de l'enquête peuvent être mis à disposition sur disquette.

République tchèque

Titre de l'enquête: Labour Force Sample Survey
Organisme responsable de l'enquête:
Organisation et déroulement de l'enquête: Czech Statistical Office/Office Tchèque des Statistiques.
Analyse et Publication des résultats: Czech Statistical Office/Office Tchèque des Statistiques.
Sujets couverts par l'enquête: Emploi, chômage, sous-emploi, durée du travail, durée de l'emploi, durée du chômage, travailleurs découragés, travailleurs occasionnels, industrie, profession, situation dans la profession, niveau d'instruction, statut principal habituel, exercice d'autres emplois.
Champ de l'enquête:
Territoire: L'ensemble du pays.
Groupes de population: Toute la population âgée de 15 ans et plus vivant dans des ménages. Plus précisément, toutes les personnes vivant dans un logement de manière continue pendant au moins trois mois, indépendamment du statut de leur séjour (permanent, temporaire ou non inscrit). L'exception est constituée par les conscrits interrogés sur leur lieu de résidence avant leur service militaire.
L'enquête ne couvre pas les personnes vivant en collectivité pendant une longue période, raison pour laquelle les données relatives à certains groupes de population (ressortissants étrangers vivant et travaillant en République tchèque en particulier) sont assez rares.
Disponibilité d'estimations selon d'autres sources pour les régions ou groupes exclus: Non.
Groupes couverts par l'enquête mais exclus des résultats publiés: Néant.
Périodicité:
Réalisation de l'enquête: En continu.
Publication des résultats: Trimestrielle.
Période de référence:
Emploi: Une semaine (les sept derniers jours avant la date de l'entretien).
Recherche d'un emploi: Quatre semaines avant la date de l'entretien.
Disponibilité pour travailler: Deux semaines après la date de l'entretien.
Concepts et définitions:
Emploi: Toutes les personnes âgées de 15 ans et plus qui, pendant la semaine de référence, ont effectué un travail quelconque pendant au moins une heure et figuraient dans les catégories ci-après:
a)emploi salarié:
Au travail: les personnes ayant effectué un travail quelconque au cours de la semaine de référence contre un salaire en espèces ou en nature. Le travail peut être permanent, temporaire, saisonnier, occasionnel ou se référer à l'activité principale ou à des activités secondaires.
Ayant un emploi mais ne travaillant pas: les personnes temporairement absentes de leur travail au cours de la semaine de référence et ayant un lien formel avec leur emploi tel qu'un contrat de travail, etc.
b)emploi dans sa propre entreprise:
Au travail: les personnes ayant effectué un travail quelconque, au cours de la semaine de référence, en vue d'obtenir un bénéfice ou un revenu familial en espèces ou en nature.
Ayant leur entreprise mais ne travaillant pas: les personnes ayant une entreprise et temporairement absentes de leur travail pendant la semaine de référence pour une raison particulière.
Sont également inclus dans les personnes ayant un emploi les membres des forces armées (militaires de carrière et conscrits) ainsi que les apprentis, les étudiants, le personnel de maison, etc. percevant un salaire, un traitement ou une rémunération.
Par contre, les personnes en congé parental prolongé ne sont pas automatiquement classifiées comme ayant un emploi.
Sont exclues les personnes occupées dans la production de biens pour leur propre ménage, tels que travaux ménagers, réparations, travaux de peinture, etc.
Chômage: Toutes les personnes âgées de 15 ans et plus ayant rempli les trois conditions ci-après pendant la semaine de référence:
i)ne pas avoir d'emploi;
ii)avoir cherché activement du travail. Au nombre des manières actives de chercher du travail figurent le fait de s'être inscrit auprès d'un bureau de placement ou d'une agence de placement privée, de s'être enquis d'éventuels emplois auprès de lieux de travail, d'exploitations agricoles, sur des marchés ou dans d'autres lieux de rassemblement, de faire paraître des petites annonces de recherche d'emploi ou d'y répondre, d'entreprendre des démarches personnelles pour créer sa propre entreprise, de demander un permis de travail ou un agrément ou de chercher un emploi d'une autre façon, et;
iii)être immédiatement disponible pour travailler, c'est-à-dire être disponible, pendant la période de référence, pour occuper un emploi salarié ou de travailleur indépendant, soit immédiatement soit dans les deux semaines suivant la date de l'entretien.
Si les personnes ne remplissent pas ne serait-ce qu'une des conditions précitées, elles sont classifiées comme ayant un emploi ou comme inactifs. La seule exception concerne les personnes ne cherchant pas de travail parce qu'elles ont déjà trouvé un emploi mais qui ne commenceront à travailler qu'à une date ultérieure. Selon la définition d'Eurostat, ces personnes sont classifiées comme étant sans emploi.
Sous-emploi:
Sous-emploi lié à la durée du travail: Les personnes qui, pendant la semaine de référence, ont travaillé contre leur gré moins que la durée normale du travail fixée pour un type donné d'activité. Sont exclues les personnes n'ayant pas travaillé pendant plus de quatre semaines.
Situations d'emploi inadéquat: Ne s'applique pas.
Durée du travail: Les heures de travail habituelles et réellement effectuées dans l'activité principale. Les heures de travail réellement effectuées dans la ou les activités secondaires.
Revenu lié à l'emploi:
Revenu lié à l'emploi salarié: Ne s'applique pas.
Revenu lié à l'emploi indépendant: Ne s'applique pas.
Secteur informel: Ne s'applique pas.
Activité habituelle: Les groupes de population ci-après sont interrogés sur leur statut économique habituel: apprentis, élèves dans une école secondaire, étudiants à l'université, personnes en congé de maternité ou d'éducation (congé parental), femmes au foyer, retraités, personnes mises à la retraite pour invalidité, personnes mises à la retraite pour invalidité partielle, chômeurs, conscrits, personnes effectuant un travail communautaire, enfants de moins de 15 ans.
Classifications:
Branche d'activité économique (industrie)
Titre de la classification: CZ-NACE.
Groupes de population classifiés selon l'industrie: Les personnes ayant un emploi et les chômeurs ayant une expérience professionnelle préalable.
Nombre de groupes de codage: Non disponible.
Convertibilité avec la CITI: CITI-Rév.3 (au niveau à quatre chiffres).
Profession
Titre de la classification: CZ-CITP-1988.
Groupes de population classifiés selon la profession: Les personnes ayant un emploi et les chômeurs ayant une expérience professionnelle préalable.
Nombre de groupes de codage: Non disponible.
Convertibilité avec la CITP: CITP-1988 (au niveau à quatre chiffres).
Situation dans la profession
Titre de la classification: CZ-CISP.
Groupes de population classifiés par situation dans la profession: Les personnes ayant un emploi et les chômeurs.
Catégories de codage: 5 groupes (salariés, employeurs, travailleurs indépendants, membres de coopératives de producteurs; travailleurs familiaux non rémunérés).
Convertibilité avec la CISP: CISP-1993.
Education
Titre de la classification: Classification nationale des sujets relatifs à l'éducation (KKOV), 2ème édition, 1991 et CITE-1997.
Groupes de population classifiés selon l'éducation: Tous les groupes de population.
Catégories de codage: Non disponible.
Convertibilité avec la CITE: CITE-1997.
Taille de l'échantillon et plan de sondage:
Unité finale d'échantillonnage: Logement.
Taille de l'échantillon (unités finales d'échantillonnage): Environ 25 000 logements couvrant quelque 63 000 personnes.
Taux de sondage: 0,6 pour cent des logements occupés en permanence.
Base de sondage: La base de sondage est construite à partir du recensement de la population réalisé en 1991.
Renouvellement de l'échantillon: Trimestriel.
Rotation:
Schéma: Le groupe-témoin de logements sélectionnés varie au cours de l'enquête. Un cinquième du groupe-témoin est renouvelé chaque trimestre.

Pourcentage d'unités restant dans l'échantillon durant deux enquêtes successives: 80 pour cent.
Nombre maximum d'interrogatoires par unité de sondage: Cinq: cela correspond à un taux de rotation de 20%.
Durée nécessaire au renouvellement complet de l'échantillon: Cinq trimestres.
Déroulement de l'enquête:
Type d'entretien: Sur papier avec écriture manuelle, par téléphone et entretien personnel/par téléphone assisté par ordinateur lorsque c'est possible.
Nombre d'unités finales d'échantillonnage par zone de sondage: 300 logements par trimestre.
Durée de déroulement de l'enquête:
Totale: En continu.
Par zone de sondage: Chaque enquêteur travaille 4 jours par semaine plus un jour pour les suppléments aux questionnaires.
Organisation: Structure d'enquête permanente.
Nombre de personnes employées: 113 enquêteurs et 14 cadres.
Substitution des unités finales en cas de non-réponse: Non.
Estimations et redressements:
Taux de non-réponse: 24%.
Redressement pour non-réponse: Oui.
Imputation en cas de non-réponse à une question spécifique: Non.
Redressement pour les régions/populations non couvertes: Non.
Redressement en cas de sous-représentation: Non.
Redressement en cas de sur-représentation: Non.
Corrections des variations saisonnières: Non.
Historique de l'enquête:
Titre et date de la première enquête: Czech Labour Force Sample Survey, décembre 1992.
Modifications et révisions significatives: Depuis 1993, la base de données a été corrigée dans le cadre de l'élaboration de données historiques. Plus précisément, il convient de noter ce qui suit:
a)la suppression des différences entre les périodes de référence: toutes les données de 1993 à 1997, quand l'enquête était réalisée au cours de trimestres saisonniers, ont été converties en trimestres civils;
b)inclusion i) des conscrits et ii) des femmes en congé de maternité et d'éducation dans les résultats des enquêtes de 1992 et 1993;
c)redressement rétrospectif des données de 1993 à 1996 sur la base des données démographiques les plus récentes;
d)harmonisation intégrale du questionnaire de l'enquête avec les questionnaires d'Eurostat pour les enquêtes commençant en janvier 2002.
Documentation et dissémination:
Documentation
Titre des publications publiant les résultats: Employment and Unemployment in the Czech Republic as Measured by the Labour Force Survey (trimestriel); Labour Market in the Czech Republic: Time series LFSS (1993-1999).
Titre des publications méthodologiques: Employment and Unemployment in the Czech Republic as Measured by the Labour Force Survey.
Dissémination
Délai de publication des premiers résultats: Non disponible.
Information à l'avance du public des dates de publication initiale des résultats: Oui.
Mise à disposition, sur demande, des données non publiées: Oui.
Mise à disposition des données sur support informatique: Disquettes, Internet et courrier électronique.
Site web: http://www.czso.cz/

Thaïlande

Titre de l'enquête: Labour Force Survey.
Organisme responsable de l'enquête:
Organisation et déroulement de l'enquête: National Statistical Office (NSO).
Analyse et Publication des résultats: National Statistical Office (NSO).
Sujets couverts par l'enquête: Emploi, chômage, sous-emploi, durée du travail, salaires, revenu, emploi dans le secteur informel, durée du chômage, industrie, profession, situation dans la profession, niveau d'instruction, activité habituelle.
Champ de l'enquête:
Territoire: L'ensemble du pays.
Groupes de population: Les personnes âgées de 13 ans et plus, sauf celles qui vivent dans des ménages collectifs (y compris l'armée).
Disponibilité d'estimations selon d'autres sources pour les régions ou groupes exclus: Ne s'applique pas.
Groupes couverts par l'enquête mais exclus des résultats publiés: Néant.
Périodicité:
Réalisation de l'enquête: Trimestrielle.
Publication des résultats: Trimestrielle.
Période de référence:
Emploi: Une semaine (fixe).
Recherche d'un emploi: Un mois (fixe).
Disponibilité pour travailler: Une semaine (fixe).
Concepts et définitions:
Emploi: Les personnes âgées de 13 ans et plus qui, pendant la semaine de référence, a) ont travaillé au moins une heure pour un salaire, un bénéfice, des dividendes ou n'importe quel type de paiement en nature; b) n'ont pas travaillé du tout mais avaient un emploi régulier, une entreprise ou une exploitation agricole d'où elles étaient temporairement absentes pour cause de maladie ou d'accident, de congés ou de vacances, de grève ou de lock-out, d'intempéries, de morte-saison ou pour d'autres motifs tels que fermeture temporaire de leur lieu de travail; qu'elles soient rémunérées ou non par leur employeur pendant leur absence, sous réserve qu'en cas de fermeture temporaire du lieu de travail elles comptent le voir rouvrir dans les 30 jours à compter de la date de fermeture et être rappelées à leur ancien emploi; ou c) les personnes ayant travaillé au moins une heure sans rémunération dans une entreprise ou une exploitation agricole appartenant à un chef de ménage ou à des membres du ménage ou exploitées par eux.
Chômage: Les personnes âgées de 13 ans et plus qui, durant la semaine de référence, n'ont pas travaillé, ne serait-ce qu'une heure, n'avaient ni emploi, ni leur propre entreprise ou exploitation agricole d'où elles étaient temporairement absentes, mais qui étaient disponibles pour travailler. Cette catégorie inclut les personnes ayant cherché du travail au cours des 30 jours précédents et celles qui n'en avaient pas cherché pour cause de maladie ou parce qu'elles pensaient qu'il n'y avait pas de travail convenable, qu'elles attendaient de prendre un nouvel emploi, qu'elles attendaient la saison agricole ou pour une autre raison. Les personnes en mise à pied temporaire ou de durée indéterminée sans rémunération sont incluses.
Sous-emploi:
Sous-emploi lié à la durée du travail: Les personnes âgées de 13 ans et plus travaillant moins de 35 heures par semaine, disponibles pour faire davantage d'heures et disposées à le faire.
Situations d'emploi inadéquat: Non disponible.
Durée du travail: Les heures de travail réellement effectuées pendant la semaine de référence dans toutes les activités. Pour les personnes absentes de leur travail pendant la semaine de référence, les heures de travail normales.
Revenu lié à l'emploi:
Revenu lié à l'emploi salarié: Se réfère à l'activité principale exercée au cours de la semaine de référence et inclut les paiements en espèces, en nature ou sous forme de services.
Revenu lié à l'emploi indépendant: Se réfère à la valeur de la production moins les frais d'exploitation des travailleurs indépendants et des travailleurs familiaux non rémunérés.
Secteur informel: Les travailleurs indépendants, les employeurs de salariés privés et les travailleurs familiaux non rémunérés travaillant dans des établissements industriels ou commerciaux employant moins de 10 personnes.
Activité habituelle: Celle-ci est mesurée sur une période de référence d'une année.
Classifications:
Branche d'activité économique (industrie)
Titre de la classification: Thailand Standard Industrial Classification (TSIC).
Groupes de population classifiés selon l'industrie: Les personnes ayant un emploi et les chômeurs ayant une expérience professionnelle préalable.
Nombre de groupes de codage: 10 grands groupes.
Convertibilité avec la CITI: CITI Rév.-2.
Profession
Titre de la classification: Non disponible.
Groupes de population classifiés selon la profession: Les personnes ayant un emploi et les chômeurs ayant une expérience professionnelle préalable.
Nombre de groupes de codage: 10 grands groupes.
Convertibilité avec la CITP: CITP-1968.

Situation dans la profession
Titre de la classification: Non disponible.
Groupes de population classifiés par situation dans la profession: Les personnes ayant un emploi et les chômeurs ayant une expérience professionnelle préalable.
Catégories de codage: Employeur, agent de l'Etat, salarié privé.
Convertibilité avec la CISP: CISP-1993, sauf pour les membres de coopératives de producteurs, catégorie qui n'existe pas dans la classification nationale.
Education
Titre de la classification: Non disponible.
Groupes de population classifiés selon l'éducation: Les personnes ayant un emploi et les chômeurs.
Catégories de codage: Sans instruction, niveau inférieur au premier cycle de l'enseignement élémentaire, premier cycle de l'enseignement élémentaire.
Convertibilité avec la CITE: CITE-1976 et CITE-1997.
Taille de l'échantillon et plan de sondage:
Unité finale d'échantillonnage: Ménage.
Taille de l'échantillon (unités finales d'échantillonnage): Environ 60 500 ménages.
Taux de sondage: Environ 6 pour cent (5 160 / 94 955 îlots et villages).
Base de sondage: Liste des îlots et villages basée sur le Recensement de la population et du logement de 1990 (1990 Population and Housing Census).
Renouvellement de l'échantillon: Annuel.
Rotation:
Schéma: Ne s'applique pas.
Pourcentage d'unités restant dans l'échantillon durant deux enquêtes successives: Ne s'applique pas.
Nombre maximum d'interrogatoires par unité de sondage: Ne s'applique pas.
Durée nécessaire au renouvellement complet de l'échantillon: Ne s'applique pas.
Déroulement de l'enquête:
Type d'entretien: Entretien personnel.
Nombre d'unités finales d'échantillonnage par zone de sondage: 12 ménages pour les communes, 9 pour les zones non organisées en commune.
Durée de déroulement de l'enquête:
Totale: Un mois.
Par zone de sondage: Non disponible.
Organisation: Non disponible.
Nombre de personnes employées: 800.
Substitution des unités finales en cas de non-réponse: Non.
Estimations et redressements:
Taux de non-réponse: 10%.
Redressement pour non-réponse: Non.
Imputation en cas de non-réponse à une question spécifique: Non.
Redressement pour les régions/populations non couvertes: Non.
Redressement en cas de sous-représentation: Non.
Redressement en cas de sur-représentation: Non.
Corrections des variations saisonnières: Non.
Historique de l'enquête:
Titre et date de la première enquête: Labour Force Survey 1963.
Modifications et révisions significatives: Les concepts et définitions actuels sont utilisés depuis 1983 et la limite d'âge minimum de 13 ans depuis 1989.
Documentation et dissémination:
Documentation
Titre des publications publiant les résultats: Report of the Labour Force survey (trimestriel).
Titre des publications méthodologiques: Idem.
Dissémination
Délai de publication des premiers résultats: Environ 5 mois.
Information à l'avance du public des dates de publication initiale des résultats: Non.
Mise à disposition, sur demande, des données non publiées: Oui.
Mise à disposition des données sur support informatique: Disquettes et Internet.
Site web: http://www.nso.go.th/.

Turquie

Titre de l'enquête: Household Labour Force Survey.
Organisme responsable de l'enquête:
Organisation et déroulement de l'enquête: State Institute of Statistics.
Analyse et Publication des résultats: State Institute of Statistics.
Sujets couverts par l'enquête: Emploi, chômage, sous-emploi, durée du travail, lieu de travail, emploi dans le secteur informel, durée du chômage, travailleurs découragés, industrie, profession, situation dans la profession, niveau d'instruction et exercice d'autres emplois.
Champ de l'enquête:
Territoire: L'ensemble du pays.
Groupes de population: Les personnes vivant dans des ménages ordinaires dont les membres sont des ressortissants turcs, à l'exception des résidents d'écoles, de dortoirs, d'écoles maternelles, de homes pour personnes âgées, d'hôpitaux spécialisés, de casernes et de locaux récréatifs destinés aux officiers. Depuis 2000, la population active se réfère aux personnes âgées de 15 ans et plus.
Disponibilité d'estimations selon d'autres sources pour les régions ou groupes exclus: Ne s'applique pas.
Groupes couverts par l'enquête mais exclus des résultats publiés: Néant.
Périodicité:
Réalisation de l'enquête: Mensuelle.
Publication des résultats: Trimestrielle.
Période de référence:
Emploi: Une semaine (les sept derniers jours avant la date de l'entretien).
Recherche d'un emploi: Trois mois avant la date de l'entretien.
Disponibilité pour travailler: 15 jours après la date de l'entretien.
Concepts et définitions:
Emploi: Les personnes âgées de 15 ans et plus qui, pendant la semaine de référence, ont travaillé au moins une heure en tant qu'employés permanents ou occasionnels, employeurs, travailleurs indépendants ou travailleurs familiaux non rémunérés (personnes au travail), et les personnes ayant un emploi qui n'ont pas travaillé pendant la semaine de référence pour diverses raisons mais qui avaient un lien avec l'emploi (personnes non au travail).
Cette catégorie inclut:
a)les personnes ayant un emploi mais qui en sont temporairement absentes pour cause de maladie ou d'accident, de congés ou de vacances annuelles, de congé de maternité ou de paternité, de congé parental, de congé d'éducation ou de formation, d'absence non autorisée, de conflit du travail, d'intempéries, etc.;
b)les travailleurs occupés à plein temps ou à temps partiel et en quête d'un autre travail;
c)les personnes ayant effectué un travail quelconque, rémunéré ou en vue d'un bénéfice, pendant la semaine de référence, mais qui étaient alors assujetties à la scolarité obligatoire, à la retraite et au bénéfice d'une pension ou inscrites en tant que demandeurs d'emploi auprès d'un bureau de placement;
d)les étudiants à plein temps ou à temps partiel travaillant à plein temps ou à temps partiel;
e)les apprentis et stagiaires rémunérés ou non;
f)les bénéficiaires de mesures de promotion de l'emploi;
g)les personnes occupées dans la production de biens pour leur usage final personnel;
h)les personnes effectuant un service civil équivalent au service militaire.
Les membres des forces armées (volontaires, militaires de carrière, conscrits) sont exclus.
Chômage: Les personnes âgées de 15 ans et plus (y compris les personnes assujetties à la scolarité obligatoire ou à la retraite et au bénéfice d'une pension) qui, durant la semaine de référence, étaient sans emploi, avaient effectué des démarches concrètes pour trouver un emploi au cours des trois derniers mois et étaient disponibles pour commencer à travailler dans les 15 jours.
Sont également considérées comme chômeurs les personnes ayant déjà trouvé un emploi ou créé leur propre entreprise mais attendant que les documents soient prêts pour commencer à travailler et disponibles pour travailler dans les 15 jours, ainsi que les étudiants à plein temps ou à temps partiel en quête d'un travail à plein temps ou à temps partiel et disponibles pour travailler dans les 15 jours.
Sous-emploi:
Sous-emploi lié à la durée du travail: Les personnes qui, au cours de la semaine de référence, ont travaillé moins de 40 heures pour des motifs économiques et qui pouvaient faire davantage d'heures de travail dans leur emploi actuel ou dans un autre à leur taux de salaire actuel. Les raisons peuvent en être le ralentissement de l'activité pour des motifs techniques ou économiques, l'absence de travail, l'impossibilité de trouver un emploi à temps complet ou le fait que l'emploi vient de commencer ou de prendre fin au cours de la semaine de référence.

Situations d'emploi inadéquat: Les personnes (à l'exception de celles en situation de sous-emploi lié à la durée du travail) cherchant un autre emploi pour cause de revenu insuffisant ou d'occupation inadéquate.
Durée du travail: Les heures de travail habituelles et réellement effectuées dans l'activité principale et la ou les activités secondaires. Le nombre d'heures réellement effectuées est demandé pour chaque jour de la semaine de référence.
Revenu lié à l'emploi:
Revenu lié à l'emploi salarié: Ne s'applique pas.
Revenu lié à l'emploi indépendant: Ne s'applique pas.
Secteur informel: Toutes les unités économiques non agricoles non constituées en société (statut juridique: société individuelle ou société simple) qui paient un impôt forfaitaire ou pas d'impôt du tout et ont un effectif de moins de 10 personnes.
Activité habituelle: Ne s'applique pas.
Classifications:
Branche d'activité économique (industrie)
Titre de la classification: Classification internationale type des industries (CITI Rév.3).
Groupes de population classifiés selon l'industrie: Les personnes ayant un emploi et les chômeurs ayant une expérience professionnelle préalable.
Nombre de groupes de codage: La totalité des 292 classes de la CITI (au niveau à quatre chiffres).
Convertibilité avec la CITI: CITI-Rév.3.
Profession
Titre de la classification: Classification internationale type des professions (CITP-1988).
Groupes de population classifiés selon la profession: Les personnes ayant un emploi et les chômeurs ayant une expérience professionnelle préalable.
Nombre de groupes de codage: La totalité des 390 groupes de base de la CITP (au niveau à quatre chiffres).
Convertibilité avec la CITP: CITP-1988.
Situation dans la profession
Titre de la classification: Non disponible.
Groupes de population classifiés par situation dans la profession: Les personnes ayant un emploi et les chômeurs ayant une expérience professionnelle préalable.
Catégories de codage: 6 groupes (employés permanents, employés occasionnels, employés de maison rémunérés, employeurs, travailleurs indépendants et travailleurs familiaux non rémunérés).
Convertibilité avec la CISP: CISP-1993.
Education
Titre de la classification: Non disponible.
Groupes de population classifiés selon l'éducation: Toutes les personnes âgées de 6 ans et plus.
Catégories de codage: 11 groupes (pas de scolarité, école primaire, enseignement primaire, premier cycle de l'enseignement secondaire général, premier cycle de l'enseignement secondaire professionnel, école secondaire générale, école secondaire nationale, deux ans d'école de formation professionnelle, trois ans d'école de formation professionnelle, enseignement universitaire, maîtrise ou troisième cycle, etc.).
Convertibilité avec la CITE: Oui.
Taille de l'échantillon et plan de sondage:
Unité finale d'échantillonnage: Ménage.
Taille de l'échantillon (unités finales d'échantillonnage): Environ 23 000 ménages par trimestre (18 000 dans les zones urbaines et 5 000 dans les zones rurales).
Taux de sondage: 0,388 pour cent.
Base de sondage: Depuis l'enquête de 2000, la base se fonde sur le chiffre de population de 1997. Elle se fondait auparavant sur les résultats des Recensements généraux de 1980, 1985 et 1990.
Renouvellement de l'échantillon: Annuel.
Rotation: Néant.
Schéma: Ne s'applique pas.
Pourcentage d'unités restant dans l'échantillon durant deux enquêtes successives: Ne s'applique pas.
Nombre maximum d'interrogatoires par unité de sondage: Ne s'applique pas.
Durée nécessaire au renouvellement complet de l'échantillon: Ne s'applique pas.
Déroulement de l'enquête:
Type d'entretien: Entretien personnel assisté par ordinateur.
Nombre d'unités finales d'échantillonnage par zone de sondage: Variable.
Durée de déroulement de l'enquête:
Totale: Deux semaines.
Par zone de sondage: Deux semaines.
Organisation: Structure d'enquête permanente.
Nombre de personnes employées: Environ 150 enquêteurs, 30 cadres et 23 responsables de l'organisation.
Substitution des unités finales en cas de non-réponse: Non.
Estimations et redressements:
Taux de non-réponse: Environ 10%.
Redressement pour non-réponse: Oui.
Imputation en cas de non-réponse à une question spécifique: Non.
Redressement pour les régions/populations non couvertes: Non.
Redressement en cas de sous-représentation: Non.
Redressement en cas de sur-représentation: Non.
Corrections des variations saisonnières: Non.
Historique de l'enquête:
Titre et date de la première enquête: Household Labour Force Survey 1966.
Modifications et révisions significatives: Diverses modifications ont été apportées, que ce soit dans le plan des questionnaires (notamment en 1988, 1990 et 2000), la couverture géographique, la taille de l'échantillon ou le plan de sondage.
Documentation et dissémination:
Documentation:
Titre des publications publiant les résultats: Household Labour Force Results (deux fois par an).
Titre des publications méthodologiques: Household Labour Force Survey Results (deux fois par an).
Dissémination:
Délai de publication des premiers résultats: Environ 4 mois.
Information à l'avance du public des dates de publication initiale des résultats: Non.
Mise à disposition, sur demande, des données non publiées: Oui.
Mise à disposition des données sur support informatique: Disquettes et Internet.
Site web: http://www.die.gov.tr/.

Ukraine

Titre de l'enquête: Population Economic Activity Sample Survey (PEASS).
Organisme responsable de l'enquête:
Organisation et déroulement de l'enquête: State Statistics Committee of Ukraine.
Analyse et Publication des résultats: State Statistics Committee of Ukraine.
Sujets couverts par l'enquête: Emploi (principal et secondaire), chômage, durée du travail, durée de l'emploi, durée du chômage, travailleurs découragés, travailleurs occasionnels, industrie, profession, situation dans la profession, niveau d'instruction et emploi dans le secteur informel.
Champ de l'enquête:
Territoire: L'ensemble du territoire, à l'exclusion des première et deuxième zones de contamination nucléaire due à l'accident de la centrale nucléaire de Tchernobyl (zone de déplacement forcé).
Groupes de population: Toute la population âgée de 15 à 70 ans vivant dans des ménages ordinaires durant la semaine de référence. Sont exclus la population institutionnelle et les nomades, les membres des forces armées (conscrits et militaires de carrière) vivant en caserne, les étudiants vivant en résidence universitaire et les écoliers vivant en pensionnat, ainsi que les membres des ménages en mission de longue durée (six mois et plus) et ceux résidant à l'étranger.
Disponibilité d'estimations selon d'autres sources pour les régions ou groupes exclus: Oui.
Groupes couverts par l'enquête mais exclus des résultats publiés: NEANT.
Périodicité:
Réalisation de l'enquête: Trimestrielle.
Publication des résultats: Trimestrielle.
Période de référence:
Emploi: Une semaine (les sept derniers jours avant la date de l'entretien).
Recherche d'un emploi: Quatre semaines avant la date de l'entretien.
Disponibilité pour travailler: Deux semaines après la date de l'entretien.
Concepts et définitions:
Emploi: Les personnes âgées de 15 à 70 ans qui, au cours de la semaine de référence:

a)ont effectué un travail quelconque pendant au moins une heure contre une rémunération en espèces ou en nature ou en vue d'un bénéfice;
b)ont travaillé au moins 30 heures sur des parcelles individuelles d'exploitation agricole à titre accessoire ou dans une entreprise familiale ou une exploitation agricole sans rémunération ("travailleurs familiaux non rémunérés");
c)n'ont pas travaillé, bien qu'ayant un emploi, pour cause d'absence temporaire du travail due à la maladie, aux vacances, aux intempéries, à un conflit du travail, etc.
Sont exclues des personnes ayant un emploi celles qui, pendant la semaine de référence, étaient occupées aux activités ci-après:
a)travail sur des parcelles individuelles d'exploitation agricole à titre accessoire pour leur consommation personnelle;
b)bénévolat pour des institutions religieuses, caritatives ou publiques;
c)construction ou rénovation de leur propre maison ou appartement;
d)travail ménager.
Sont également inclus dans les totaux:
a)les militaires de carrière vivant dans des ménages;
b)les travailleurs occupés à plein temps ou à temps partiel;
c)les étudiants à plein temps ou à temps partiel travaillant à plein temps ou à temps partiel;
d)les personnes ayant effectué un travail quelconque pendant la semaine de référence tout en étant à la retraite et au bénéfice d'une pension ou inscrites en tant que demandeurs d'emploi auprès d'un bureau de placement, ou tout en percevant des allocations de chômage;
e)les domestiques privés;
f)les apprentis et stagiaires rémunérés;
g)les membres de coopératives de producteurs.

Chômage: Par "chômeurs", on entend toutes les personnes âgées de 15 à 70 ans n'ayant pas travaillé du tout pendant la semaine de référence, ayant cherché activement un emploi au cours des quatre semaines précédant l'entretien, disponibles pour commencer à travailler dans les deux semaines suivant la semaine de l'enquête et attendant de commencer un nouveau travail dans les 30 jours.
La seule exception est constituée par les personnes n'ayant pas cherché de travail parce qu'elles en avaient déjà trouvé mais qu'il commençait à une date postérieure à la période de référence. Ces personnes sont classées comme chômeurs.

Sous-emploi:

Sous-emploi lié à la durée du travail: Les personnes qui, pendant la semaine de référence, ont effectué un nombre d'heures de travail inférieur à celui fixé pour une certaine catégorie de profession ou d'emploi, à condition qu'elles cherchent du travail et qu'elles soient disponibles pour travailler davantage.

Situations d'emploi inadéquat: Ne s'applique pas.

Durée du travail: Les heures de travail habituelles et réellement effectuées dans l'activité principale et la ou les activités secondaires.

Revenu lié à l'emploi:

Revenu lié à l'emploi salarié: Ne s'applique pas.

Revenu lié à l'emploi indépendant: Ne s'applique pas.

Secteur informel: Les personnes occupées dans une activité (principale ou secondaire) quelconque, non enregistrée et rémunérée en espèces ou en nature.

Activité habituelle: Ne s'applique pas.

Classifications:

Branche d'activité économique (industrie)

Titre de la classification: Classification nationale compatible avec la CITI Rév.3.

Groupes de population classifiés selon l'industrie: Les personnes ayant un emploi et les chômeurs ayant une expérience professionnelle préalable.

Nombre de groupes de codage: 159 groupes.

Convertibilité avec la CITI: CITI-Rév.3 au niveau à trois chiffres.

Profession

Titre de la classification: Classification nationale compatible avec la CITP-1988.

Groupes de population classifiés selon la profession: Les personnes ayant un emploi et les chômeurs ayant une expérience professionnelle préalable.

Nombre de groupes de codage: 390 groupes.

Convertibilité avec la CITP: CITP-1988 au niveau à quatre chiffres.

Situation dans la profession

Titre de la classification: CISP-1993.

Groupes de population classifiés par situation dans la profession: Les personnes ayant un emploi (activité principale et activités secondaires).

Catégories de codage: 5 groupes (salariés, employeurs, travailleurs indépendants, membres de coopératives de producteurs, travailleurs familiaux non rémunérés).

Convertibilité avec la CISP: CISP-1993.

Education

Titre de la classification: Classification nationale.

Groupes de population classifiés selon l'éducation: Tous les groupes de population.

Catégories de codage: 8 groupes (pas d'enseignement primaire général, enseignement primaire général, enseignement secondaire, enseignement secondaire général, enseignement primaire professionnel, enseignement secondaire professionnel, enseignement supérieur inachevé, enseignement supérieur (universitaire)).

Convertibilité avec la CITE: Non.

Taille de l'échantillon et plan de sondage:

Unité finale d'échantillonnage: Ménage.

Taille de l'échantillon (unités finales d'échantillonnage): Environ 31 000 ménages par trimestre ou quelque 150 000 personnes par an.

Taux de sondage: 0,12 pour cent.

Base de sondage: L'échantillon est construit automatiquement au niveau national sur la base de l'échantillon principal de 1992 (5%) tiré d'une série d'enquêtes par sondage spéciales telles qu'enquêtes socio-démographiques, etc. A partir de 2004, un nouvel échantillon, construit sur la base du Recensement de 2001, sera utilisé.

Renouvellement de l'échantillon: Annuel.

Rotation:

Schéma: Tout ménage entrant dans l'échantillon à un moment quelconque est censé fournir des informations sur le marché de l'emploi pendant quatre trimestres successifs avant de quitter définitivement l'échantillon. En 2004, un nouveau schéma de rotation, le schéma 2-(2)-2, sera introduit. Ainsi, un ménage sera inclus dans l'échantillon pendant deux trimestres successifs, le quittera pendant deux trimestres puis le réintègrera pendant deux autres trimestres successifs avant de le quitter définitivement.

Pourcentage d'unités restant dans l'échantillon durant deux enquêtes successives: 75 pour cent.

Nombre maximum d'interrogatoires par unité de sondage: Quatre.

Durée nécessaire au renouvellement complet de l'échantillon: 18 mois.

Déroulement de l'enquête:

Type d'entretien: Ecriture manuelle sur papier.

Nombre d'unités finales d'échantillonnage par zone de sondage: Non disponible.

Durée de déroulement de l'enquête:

Totale: Un mois.

Par zone de sondage: Non disponible.

Organisation: State Statistics Committee of Ukraine.

Nombre de personnes employées: Environ 510 enquêteurs et cadres.

Substitution des unités finales en cas de non-réponse: Non.

Estimations et redressements:

Taux de non-réponse: 12%.

Redressement pour non-réponse: Non.

Imputation en cas de non-réponse à une question spécifique: Partielle.

Redressement pour les régions/populations non couvertes: Non.

Redressement en cas de sous-représentation: Non.

Redressement en cas de sur-représentation: Non.

Corrections des variations saisonnières: Non.

Historique de l'enquête:

Titre et date de la première enquête: Population Economic Activity Sample Survey, octobre 1995 (annuelle).

Modifications et révisions significatives: Depuis 1999, l'enquête est réalisée tous les trimestres.

Documentation et dissémination:

Documentation

Titre des publications publiant les résultats: "Economic Activity of the Population" (annuel), "Economic Activity of the Population: quarterly report", "Labour in Ukraine, 2002 (année)".

Titre des publications méthodologiques: LFS Methodology" (en ukrainien et en partie en anglais).

Dissémination

Délai de publication des premiers résultats: Non disponible.

Information à l'avance du public des dates de publication initiale des résultats: Oui.

Mise à disposition, sur demande, des données non publiées: Oui.

Mise à disposition des données sur support informatique: Oui.

Site web: http://www.ukrstat.gov.ua.

Yémen, Rép. du

Titre de l'enquête: Labour force sample survey for the year 1999.
Organisme responsable de l'enquête:
Organisation et déroulement de l'enquête: Central Statistical Organization & Ministry of Labour and Vocational Training.
Analyse et Publication des résultats: Central Statistical Organization.
Sujets couverts par l'enquête: Emploi, chômage, durée du travail, salaires, durée de l'emploi, durée du chômage, travailleurs découragés, travailleurs occasionnels, industrie, profession actuelle et passée, situation dans la profession et niveau d'instruction.
Champ de l'enquête:
Territoire: L'ensemble du pays à l'exception des îles de Soqotra et de Kamaran et des zones désertiques reculées de Hadhramout et d'Al-Jouf. Le coût de réalisation de l'enquête dans ces régions est élevé et la proportion de la population insignifiante.
Groupes de population: Sont exclues les personnes vivant en hôpital, dans des camps, à l'hôtel, en motel, en dortoirs et autres établissements collectifs, les nomades et les personnes vivant à l'étranger pendant la période de l'enquête ainsi que les sans-abri sans domicile fixe.
Disponibilité d'estimations selon d'autres sources pour les régions ou groupes exclus: Il existe des estimations fondées sur le Recensement de 1994 pour la population des îles et des zones reculées (Muderias), les nomades et la population vivant en institution.
Groupes couverts par l'enquête mais exclus des résultats publiés: Les étrangers.
Périodicité:
Réalisation de l'enquête: Occasionnelle.
Publication des résultats: Après chaque enquête
Période de référence:
Emploi: Semaine de référence fixe.
Recherche d'un emploi: Un mois.
Disponibilité pour travailler: Deux semaines.
Concepts et définitions:
Emploi: Les personnes âgées de 15 ans et plus ayant travaillé ne serait-ce qu'une heure pendant la semaine de référence contre une récompense, un salaire ou un gain familial, ou qui étaient temporairement absentes de leur travail pour cause de congés ou de maladie. [Les questions relatives aux caractéristiques économiques sont toutefois posées à toutes les personnes âgées de 6 ans et plus].
Cette catégorie inclut:
a)les personnes ayant effectué un travail quelconque, rémunéré ou en vue d'un bénéfice, pendant la semaine de référence, mais qui étaient alors assujetties à la scolarité obligatoire, à la retraite et au bénéfice d'une pension, inscrites en tant que demandeurs d'emploi auprès d'un bureau de placement ou qui percevaient des allocations de chômage;
b)les étudiants à plein temps ou à temps partiel travaillant à plein temps ou à temps partiel;
c)les apprentis et stagiaires rémunérés ou non s'ils ont un lien avec l'emploi;
d)les personnes occupées dans la production de biens pour leur usage final personnel;
e)les travailleurs familiaux non rémunérés au travail ou temporairement absents de leur travail pendant la semaine de référence;
f)les membres des forces armées, y compris les conscrits, les volontaires et les militaires de carrière, ainsi que les personnes effectuant un service civil équivalent au service militaire.
Sont exclues:
a)les personnes occupées dans la prestation de services dans leur ménage;
b)les personnes en mise à pied temporaire ou de durée indéterminée sans rémunération et les personnes en mise en congé non rémunéré à l'initiative de l'employeur.
Chômage: Les personnes âgées de 15 ans et plus sans emploi durant la semaine de référence, capables de travailler dans les deux semaines à compter de la date de l'entretien et disposées à le faire, et ayant entrepris des démarches pour chercher du travail au cours du mois précédant la période de l'enquête.
Cette catégorie inclut:
a)les personnes en mise à pied temporaire ou de durée indéterminée sans rémunération;
b)les personnes sans emploi, immédiatement disponibles pour travailler et à la recherche d'un emploi qui ont pris des dispositions pour commencer à travailler dans un nouvel emploi à une date postérieure à la semaine de référence;
c)les personnes sans emploi, immédiatement disponibles pour travailler et à la recherche d'un emploi qui essayent de créer leur propre entreprise;
d)les personnes sans emploi, disponibles pour travailler mais n'ayant pas cherché de travail durant le mois précédant la période de l'enquête pour des raisons particulières;
e)les étudiants à plein temps ou à temps partiel en quête d'un emploi à plein temps ou à temps partiel;
f)les personnes en quête d'un emploi ou immédiatement disponibles pour travailler, mais assujetties à la scolarité obligatoire ou à la retraite et au bénéfice d'une pension.
Sous-emploi:
Sous-emploi lié à la durée du travail: Non disponible.
Situations d'emploi inadéquat: Non disponible.
Durée du travail: Le nombre total d'heures de travail réellement effectuées dans l'activité principale chaque jour ouvré de la semaine de référence. Le nombre total d'heures de travail réellement effectuées dans l'activité secondaire au cours de la semaine de référence.
Revenu lié à l'emploi:
Revenu lié à l'emploi salarié: Salaires et traitements totaux des salariés avant impôt sur le revenu et autres taxes, en espèces ou en nature, perçus par jour, par semaine, par quinzaine ou par mois, y compris les indemnités de congé annuel et les incitations et autres versements analogues. Le salaire se réfère au dernier paiement perçu. Les données sont recueillies séparément pour l'activité principale et les activités secondaires.
Revenu lié à l'emploi indépendant: Non disponible.
Classifications:
Branche d'activité économique (industrie)
Titre de la classification: Non disponible.
Groupes de population classifiés selon l'industrie: Les personnes ayant un emploi et les chômeurs ayant une expérience professionnelle préalable.
Nombre de groupes de codage: Au niveau à trois chiffres de la classification.
Convertibilité avec la CITI: CITI-Rév.3 au niveau à trois chiffres.
Profession
Titre de la classification: Non disponible.
Groupes de population classifiés selon la profession: Les personnes ayant un emploi et les chômeurs ayant une expérience professionnelle préalable.
Nombre de groupes de codage: Au niveau à quatre chiffres de la classification.
Convertibilité avec la CITP: CITP-1988 au niveau à quatre chiffres.
Situation dans la profession
Titre de la classification: Non disponible.
Groupes de population classifiés par situation dans la profession: Les personnes ayant un emploi uniquement.
Catégories de codage: Salarié, propriétaire exploitant, travailleur indépendant, travailleur familial non rémunéré, travailleur non rémunéré.
Convertibilité avec la CISP: CISP-1993.
Education
Titre de la classification: Non disponible.
Groupes de population classifiés selon l'éducation: Toutes les personnes âgées de 10 ans et plus.
Catégories de codage: Analphabète. Sait lire et écrire. Enseignement primaire. Enseignement unifié. Enseignement élémentaire/fondamental. Institut ou centre de formation professionnelle. Enseignement secondaire technique et professionnel. Enseignement secondaire général. Diplôme de fin d'études secondaires. Enseignement universitaire. Etudes supérieures (troisième cycle).
Convertibilité avec la CITE: Certains groupes sont convertibles avec la CITE-1997.
Taille de l'échantillon et plan de sondage:
Unité finale d'échantillonnage: Ménage.
Taille de l'échantillon (unités finales d'échantillonnage): 19 955 ménages.
Taux de sondage: 0,92 pour cent.
Base de sondage: La base de sondage principale a été construite pour l'Enquête nationale sur la pauvreté de 1999 (1999 National Poverty Survey) à partir de la liste des secteurs de recensement du Recensement de 1994. La base de sondage principale a été stratifiée en 20 gouvernorats et, au sein de chaque gouvernorat, en zones urbaines et zones rurales. Un sous-échantillon du National Poverty Survey de 1999 a été sélectionné pour le Labour Force Survey de 1999.
Renouvellement de l'échantillon: Le renouvellement de l'échantillon a été effectué grâce au listage des ménages dans chaque secteur de recensement sélectionné.

Rotation: Néant.
Déroulement de l'enquête:
Type d'entretien: Entretien personnel.
Nombre d'unités finales d'échantillonnage par zone de sondage: 15 ménages en zones rurales et 20 ménages en zones urbaines.
Durée de déroulement de l'enquête:
Totale: 20 jours, du 13 novembre au 2 décembre 1999.
Par zone de sondage: Une journée par équipe de trois enquêteurs couvrant 15 ménages ruraux ou 20 ménages urbains.
Organisation: Ad hoc.
Nombre de personnes employées: Environ 253 enquêteurs, 81 chefs d'équipe et 20 cadres.
Substitution des unités finales en cas de non-réponse: Non disponible.
Estimations et redressements:
Taux de non-réponse: 4,4%.
Redressement pour non-réponse: Non disponible.
Imputation en cas de non-réponse à une question spécifique: Non.
Redressement pour les régions/populations non couvertes: Oui.
Redressement en cas de sous-représentation: Non disponible.
Redressement en cas de sur-représentation: Non disponible.
Corrections des variations saisonnières: Non.
Historique de l'enquête:
Titre et date de la première enquête: Labour force sample survey, 6 décembre 1991.
Modifications et révisions significatives: Ne s'applique pas.
Documentation et dissémination:
Documentation
Titre des publications publiant les résultats: Final Report. 1999 Labour Force Survey Results.
Titre des publications méthodologiques: In Final Report.
Dissémination
Délai de publication des premiers résultats: Une année. Les données pour 1999 ont été publiées en novembre 2000.
Information à l'avance du public des dates de publication initiale des résultats: Non disponible.
Mise à disposition, sur demande, des données non publiées: Non disponible.
Mise à disposition des données sur support informatique: Les données totalisées sont disponibles sur demande, sur disquette et via le système d'information sur le marché du travail.

Zimbabwe

Titre de l'enquête: Indicator Monitoring - Labour Force Survey.
Organisme responsable de l'enquête:
Organisation et déroulement de l'enquête: Central Statistical Office.
Analyse et Publication des résultats: Central Statistical Office.
Sujets couverts par l'enquête: Emploi, chômage, durée du travail, revenu lié à l'emploi, emploi dans le secteur informel, travailleurs occasionnels, industrie, profession, situation dans la profession, niveau d'instruction et de qualification (compétence), activités principale et secondaires au cours des douze derniers mois.
Champ de l'enquête:
Territoire: L'ensemble du pays.
Groupes de population: Non disponible.
Disponibilité d'estimations selon d'autres sources pour les régions ou groupes exclus: Ne s'applique pas.
Groupes couverts par l'enquête mais exclus des résultats publiés: Néant.
Périodicité:
Réalisation de l'enquête: Tous les cinq ans. La dernière enquête a été réalisée en juin 1999.
Publication des résultats: Tous les cinq ans.
Période de référence:
Emploi: Période de référence variable de sept jours avant la date de l'entretien.
Recherche d'un emploi: Période de référence variable de sept jours avant la date de l'entretien.
Disponibilité pour travailler: Période de référence variable de sept jours avant la date de l'entretien.
Concepts et définitions:
Emploi: Les personnes âgées de 15 ans et plus dont l'emploi a constitué l'activité principale au cours de la semaine de référence et ayant travaillé au moins une heure durant la semaine de référence.
Sont inclus: a) les travailleurs familiaux non rémunérés au travail pendant la semaine de référence; b) les travailleurs occupés à plein temps ou à temps partiel et en quête d'un autre travail; c) les personnes ayant effectué un travail quelconque, rémunéré ou en vue d'un bénéfice, durant la semaine de référence, mais qui étaient alors inscrites en tant que demandeurs d'emploi auprès d'un bureau de placement ou qui percevaient des allocations de chômage; d) les étudiants à plein temps travaillant à plein temps ou à temps partiel; e) les étudiants à temps partiel travaillant à plein temps ou à temps partiel; f) les apprentis et stagiaires rémunérés ou non; g) les bénéficiaires de mesures de promotion de l'emploi; et h) les personnes occupées dans la production de biens pour leur usage final personnel.
Sont également incluses les personnes occupant un emploi salarié ou indépendant qui étaient temporairement absentes de leur travail pendant la semaine de référence pour cause de a) maladie ou accident, b) congés ou vacances annuelles, c) congé de maternité ou de paternité, d) congé parental, e) congé d'éducation ou de formation, f) absence non autorisée, g) conflit du travail, h) intempéries, panne mécanique, etc., i) mise à pied temporaire sans rémunération ou j) mise en congé non rémunéré à l'initiative de l'employeur.
Cela inclut les travailleurs familiaux non rémunérés temporairement absents de leur travail pendant la semaine de référence ainsi que les travailleurs saisonniers ne travaillant pas durant la morte-saison.
Sont exclus: a) les personnes ayant effectué un travail quelconque, rémunéré ou en vue d'un bénéfice, pendant la semaine de référence, mais qui étaient alors assujetties à la scolarité obligatoire ou à la retraite et au bénéfice d'une pension; b) les personnes en mise à pied de durée indéterminée sans rémunération; et c) les personnes rendant des services non rémunérés ou personnels à des membres de leur propre ménage.
Chômage: Les personnes âgées de 15 ans et plus dont le chômage a constitué l'activité principale pendant la semaine de référence, disponibles pour travailler pendant la semaine de référence et ayant activement cherché du travail pendant cette période. Sont inclus: a) les personnes sans emploi, immédiatement disponibles pour travailler et qui ont pris des dispositions pour commencer à travailler dans un nouvel emploi à une date postérieure à la semaine de référence; b) les personnes sans emploi, immédiatement disponibles pour travailler et qui ont essayé de créer leur propre entreprise; c) les personnes en quête d'un emploi et disponibles pour travailler qui étaient assujetties à la scolarité obligatoire ou à la retraite et au bénéfice d'une pension; et d) les étudiants à temps partiel à la recherche d'un emploi à plein temps ou à temps partiel.
Sont exclus les étudiants à plein temps à la recherche d'un emploi à plein temps ou à temps partiel à moins que le chômage n'ait constitué leur activité principale au cours de la semaine de référence.
Les personnes sans emploi et disponibles pour travailler pendant la semaine de référence mais n'ayant pas cherché de travail sont exclues de la catégorie des chômeurs définie stricto sensu. Ces personnes sont par contre incluses dans la définition du chômage au sens large.
Sous-emploi:
Sous-emploi lié à la durée du travail: Ce sujet n'est pas couvert par l'enquête.
Des questions sont toutefois posées aux personnes ayant un emploi pour savoir si elles auraient aimé effectuer davantage d'heures de travail pendant la semaine de référence sans être rémunérées en heures supplémentaires, ainsi que sur le nombre d'heures de travail supplémentaires qu'elles auraient aimé faire, de préférence, pendant la semaine de référence sans être rémunérées en heures supplémentaires.
Situations d'emploi inadéquat: Ce sujet n'est pas couvert par l'enquête.
Durée du travail: Les heures de travail effectuées pendant la semaine de référence, y compris les heures supplémentaires et le temps autorisé d'absence du travail. Ces informations se réfèrent à l'activité principale.
Revenu lié à l'emploi:
Revenu lié à l'emploi salarié: Le revenu en espèces perçu en contrepartie du travail effectué au cours du dernier mois (inférieur à \$500, \$500-\$749, \$750-\$999, \$1000-\$1499, \$1500-\$1999, \$2000-\$2499, \$2500-\$2999, \$3000 ou plus).
Revenu lié à l'emploi indépendant: Le revenu en espèces perçu en contrepartie du travail effectué au cours du dernier mois (inférieur à \$500, \$500-\$749, \$750-\$999, \$1000-\$1499, \$1500-\$1999, \$2000-\$2499, \$2500-\$2999, \$3000 ou plus).
Secteur informel: Des questions sont posées sur le secteur de l'établissement (privé, administration centrale, collectivité locale, parapublic, coopérative, autres), le nombre de personnes travaillant dans l'établissement (moins de 10, 10 ou plus) et l'enregistrement/l'agrément de l'établissement (enregistré uniquement, agréé

uniquement avec locaux, agréé uniquement sans locaux, enregistré et agréé, néant).

Activité habituelle: Ce sujet n'est pas couvert par l'enquête mais des questions sont posées sur les activités principale et secondaires exercées par les personnes au cours des douze derniers mois.

Classifications:

Branche d'activité économique (industrie)

Titre de la classification: Non disponible.

Groupes de population classifiés selon l'industrie: Les personnes ayant un emploi.

Nombre de groupes de codage: 13.

Convertibilité avec la CITI: CITI-Rév.2.

Profession

Titre de la classification: Non disponible.

Groupes de population classifiés selon la profession: Les personnes ayant un emploi.

Nombre de groupes de codage: 23.

Convertibilité avec la CITP: CITP-1988.

Situation dans la profession

Titre de la classification: Classification nationale d'après la situation dans la profession.

Groupes de population classifiés par situation dans la profession: Les personnes ayant un emploi.

Catégories de codage: a) Salariés permanents; b) salariés occasionnels, temporaires, contractuels ou saisonniers; c) employeurs; d) travailleurs indépendants – exploitants de fermes collectives et dans le cadre du recasement agricole; e) travailleurs indépendants – autres; f) travailleurs familiaux non rémunérés.

Convertibilité avec la CISP: Convertibilité partielle avec la CISP-1993.

Education

Titre de la classification: Classification nationale des niveaux d'instruction.

Groupes de population classifiés selon l'éducation: Toutes les personnes âgées de 5 ans et plus.

Catégories de codage: a) Année d'études 1 inachevée; b) année d'études 1; c) année d'études 2; d) année d'études 3; e) année d'études 4; f) année d'études 5; g) année d'études 6; h) année d'études 7; i) classe 1; j) classe 2; k) classe 3; l) classe 4; m) classe 5; n) classe 6; o) diplôme/certificat de fin d'études primaires; p) diplôme/certificat de fin d'études secondaires; q) diplôme universitaire ou diplôme de troisième cycle.

Convertibilité avec la CITE: Non disponible.

Taille de l'échantillon et plan de sondage:

Unité finale d'échantillonnage: Ménage.

Taille de l'échantillon (unités finales d'échantillonnage): 14 000 ménages.

Taux de sondage: Non disponible. Le taux de sondage varie d'une province à l'autre.

Base de sondage: Le Zimbabwe Master Sample 1992 (ZMS 92) sert de base de sondage aréolaire pour l'enquête. Il a été mis au point à la suite du Recensement de 1992.

Renouvellement de l'échantillon: Avant l'enquête, une nouvelle liste des ménages figurant dans les secteurs de recensement de l'échantillon est établie, en même temps que sont mises à jour les cartes des secteurs de recensement.

Rotation:

Schéma: Les ménages inclus dans l'échantillon principal sont renouvelés par rotation environ tous les trois ans.

Pourcentage d'unités restant dans l'échantillon durant deux enquêtes successives: 0 pour cent.

Nombre maximum d'interrogatoires par unité de sondage: Un.

Durée nécessaire au renouvellement complet de l'échantillon: Trois ans.

Déroulement de l'enquête:

Type d'entretien: Les informations sont obtenues au cours d'entretiens personnels.

Nombre d'unités finales d'échantillonnage par zone de sondage: Non disponible.

Durée de déroulement de l'enquête:

Totale: Deux semaines.

Par zone de sondage: Non disponible.

Organisation: Structure d'enquête permanente.

Nombre de personnes employées: 160.

Substitution des unités finales en cas de non-réponse: Aucun remplacement n'est effectué pour les ménages défaillants mais la taille de l'échantillon initial est augmentée, comme l'expérience en a démontré l'utilité, pour tenir compte des non-réponses. Le suréchantillonnage est plus important pour les zones urbaines que pour les zones rurales.

Estimations et redressements:

Taux de non-réponse: 25%.

Redressement pour non-réponse: Oui.

Imputation en cas de non-réponse à une question spécifique: Non.

Redressement pour les régions/populations non couvertes: Non.

Redressement en cas de sous-représentation: Non.

Redressement en cas de sur-représentation: Non.

Corrections des variations saisonnières: Ne s'applique pas.

Historique de l'enquête:

Titre et date de la première enquête: La première enquête a été réalisée en février 1986 (February 1986 Labour Force Survey).

Modifications et révisions significatives: Non disponible.

Documentation et dissémination:

Documentation

Titre des publications publiant les résultats: Central Statistical Office, Indicator Monitoring – Labour Force Survey Report (**Périodicité:** tous les cinq ans).

Titre des publications méthodologiques: La publication susmentionnée inclut les informations méthodologiques concernant l'enquête.

Dissémination:

Délai de publication des premiers résultats: Environ deux ans.

Information à l'avance du public des dates de publication initiale des résultats: Non disponible.

Mise à disposition, sur demande, des données non publiées: Les données non publiées peuvent être communiquées sur demande écrite adressée au Directeur de l'Office central de statistique (Director of the Central Statistical Office).

Mise à disposition des données sur support informatique: Oui.

Albania

Título de la encuesta: Encuesta sobre las condiciones de vida en los hogares (Household Living Conditions Survey), octubre de 1998.

Organismo responsable de la encuesta:

Planificar y realizar la encuesta: Instituto de Estadísticas de Albania (Albanian Institute of Statistics (INSTAT)).

Analizar y publicar los resultados: Instituto de Estadísticas de Albania (Albanian Institute of Statistics (INSTAT)).

Temas abarcados: Empleo, desempleo, horas de trabajo, salarios, ingresos, duración del empleo y el desempleo, trabajadores desalentados, trabajadores ocasionales, rama de actividad económica (industria), ocupación, educación.

Alcance de la encuesta:

Ámbito geográfico: Todo el país.

Grupos de población: Toda la población residente.

Disponibilidad de estimaciones de otras fuentes para las áreas/grupos excluidos: No corresponde.

Grupos abarcados por la encuesta pero excluidos de los resultados publicados: No corresponde.

Periodicidad:

Recolección de datos: Primera ronda en 1998.

Publicación de los resultados: En 2001.

Períodos de referencia:

Empleo: La semana anterior a la fecha de la entrevista.

Búsqueda de trabajo: La semana anterior a la fecha de la entrevista.

Disponibilidad para trabajo: La semana anterior a la fecha de la entrevista.

Conceptos y definiciones:

Empleo: Todas las personas de 15 años y más de edad que realizaron algún trabajo por lo menos una hora durante la semana de la encuesta.

Se incluyen en el empleo:

a) personas con un empleo pero temporalmente ausentes debido a enfermedad o lesión, licencia anual, licencia de maternidad/paternidad, licencia parental, licencia para estudios o capacitación, mal tiempo, desperfectos mecánicos, etc.;

b) trabajadores a tiempo completo o parcial que buscaban otro empleo durante el período de referencia;

c) personas jubiladas que percibían una pensión, personas inscritas como desempleados en busca de trabajo y personas que percibían indemnizaciones por desempleo que realizaron un trabajo remunerado o por un beneficio durante la semana de referencia;

d) estudiantes de dedicación completa y parcial que trabajaban a tiempo completo o parcial;

e) aprendices y personas en formación remunerados;

f) trabajadores familiares no remunerados que trabajaban durante la semana de la encuesta o que estaban temporalmente ausentes del trabajo.

Desempleo: Todas las personas, de 15 años y más de edad, que no habían trabajado durante la última semana, buscaban trabajo y estaban disponibles para trabajar.

Subempleo:

Subempleo por insuficiencia de horas: No está cubierto.

Situaciones de empleo inadecuado: No está cubierto.

Horas de trabajo: No se dispone de información.

Ingresos relacionados con el empleo:

Ingresos relacionados con el empleo asalariado: Promedio mensual de salarios de los empleados.

Ingresos relacionados con el empleo independiente: Ingresos procedentes de actividades privadas.

Sector informal: No se dispone de información.

Actividad habitual: Situación económica (empleado, desempleado, inactivo) durante los últimos 12 meses.

Clasificaciones:

Rama de actividad económica (industria):

Título de la clasificación utilizada: Clasificación nacional basada en la Clasificación Industrial Europea NACE.

Grupos de población clasificados por industria: Empleados y desempleados (rama de actividad económica del último trabajo para el desempleado).

Número de Grupos utilizados para la codificación: No se dispone de información.

Vínculos con la CIIU: CIIU-Rev.3.

Ocupación:

Título de la clasificación utilizada: ISCO-88 a nivel de 3 dígitos.

Grupos de población clasificados por ocupación: Empleados y desempleados (ocupación en el último trabajo para el desempleado).

Número de Grupos utilizados para la codificación: 116 grupos menores.

Vínculos con la CIUO: CIUO-88.

Situación en el empleo:

Título de la clasificación utilizada: Clasificación nacional.

Grupos de población clasificados por situación en el empleo: Empleados.

Grupos utilizados para la codificación: Empleados, empleadores y trabajadores por cuenta propia.

Vínculos con la CISE: No.

Educación:

Título de la clasificación utilizada: Clasificación nacional.

Grupos de población clasificados por educación: Empleados y desempleados.

Grupos utilizados para la codificación: 5 grupos.

Vínculos con la CINE: CINE-1997.

Tamaño y diseño de la muestra:

Unidad final de muestreo: Hogar.

Tamaño de la muestra (unidades finales de muestreo): 11 826 hogares.

Fracción de muestreo: No se dispone de información.

Marco de la muestra: No se dispone de información.

Actualización de la muestra: No se dispone de información.

Rotación:

Esquema: No corresponde.

Porcentaje de unidades que permanecen en la muestra durante dos encuestas consecutivas: No corresponde.

Número máximo de entrevistas por unidad de muestreo: No corresponde.

Tiempo necesario para renovar completamente la muestra: No corresponde.

Levantamiento da la encuesta:

Tipo de entrevista: Entrevistas personales.

Número de unidades finales de muestreo por área de muestra: No se dispone de información.

Duración del trabajo de campo:

Total: No se dispone de información.

Por área de muestra: No se dispone de información.

Organización de la encuesta: Organización ad hoc.

Número de personas que trabajan en el campo: No se dispone de información.

Substitución de las unidades finales de muestreo que no responden: No.

Estimaciones y ajustes:

Tasa de no-respuesta total: No se dispone de información.

Ajuste por no-respuesta total: No se dispone de información.

Imputación por no respuesta de ítemes: No se dispone de información.

Ajuste por áreas/poblaciones no abarcadas: No se dispone de información.

Ajuste por falta de cobertura: No se dispone de información.

Ajuste por exceso de cobertura: No se dispone de información.

Ajuste por exceso de cobertura: No.

Historia de la encuesta:

Título y fecha de la primera encuesta: Encuesta sobre las condiciones de vida en los hogares (Household Living Conditions Survey) 1998.

Modificaciones y revisiones significativas: No corresponde.

Documentación y difusión:

Documentación:

Título de las publicaciones con los resultados de la encuesta: Resultados generales de la encuesta sobre las condiciones de vida en los hogares (General Results of Household Living Conditions Survey) de 1998.

Título de las publicaciones con la metodología de la encuesta: Resultados generales de la encuesta sobre las condiciones de vida en los hogares (General Results of Household Living Conditions Survey) de 1998.

Difusión:

Tiempo necesario para difundir los primeros datos: Unos tres años.

Información adelantada acerca de la fecha de la primera difusión pública: Sí.

Disponibilidad de datos no publicados si se solicitan: No.

Disponibilidad de datos por medios informáticos: No.

Sitio web: http://www.instat.gov.al.

Alemania

Título de la encuesta: Microcenso (Mikrozensus)/Encuesta sobre la Fuerza de Trabajo de la Unión Europea.

Organismo responsable de la encuesta:

Planificar y realizar la encuesta: Oficina Federal de Estadísticas (Statistisches Bundesamt) y Oficinas Estadísticas de los Laender (Statistische Landesämter).

Analizar y publicar los resultados: Oficina Federal de Estadísticas (Statistisches Bundesamt) y Oficinas Estadísticas de los Laender (Statistische Landesämter).

Temas abarcados: Empleo, desempleo, subempleo, horas de trabajo (horas habituales de trabajo, horas realmente trabajadas), ingresos (ingresos netos individuales, ingresos netos del hogar, pensiones, principales fuentes de subsistencia), empleo en el sector informal, duración del empleo (cambio de establecimiento durante el último año, duración de contratos de plazo fijo, duración del empleo con el empleador actual), duración del desempleo, trabajadores ocasionales (empleos ocasionales, pequeños trabajos), rama de actividad económica (industria), ocupación, situación en el empleo, nivel de educación/calificación, empleos secundarios.

Alcance de la encuesta:

Ámbito geográfico: Todo el país.

Grupos de población: La encuesta abarca toda la población que reside en el país, incluida la población no civil y las personas que viven en instituciones o en hogares colectivos. Se excluyen los diplomáticos extranjeros y miembros de fuerzas armadas extranjeras.

Disponibilidad de estimaciones de otras fuentes para las áreas/grupos excluidos: No corresponde.

Grupos abarcados por la encuesta pero excluidos de los resultados publicados: Como cuestión de principio, las estimaciones para grupos de población de menos de 5 000 personas no se publican por separado porque se considera que en esas estimaciones el error de muestreo es demasiado alto.

Periodicidad:

Recolección de datos: Anual.

Publicación de los resultados: Anual, más informes adelantados.

Períodos de referencia:

Empleo: Una semana, es decir la última semana sin día de fiesta de abril.

Búsqueda de trabajo: Cuatro semanas antes de la fecha de la entrevista.

Disponibilidad para trabajo: Dos semanas antes de la fecha de la entrevista.

Conceptos y definiciones:

Empleo: Personas de 15 años y más de edad que tuvieron un empleo durante la semana de referencia, independientemente de si el empleo era su actividad principal o secundaria, y de si el trabajo se realizaba periódica o esporádicamente. Se incluyen: a) trabajadores familiares que estaban en el trabajo durante la semana de referencia; b) personas ocupadas en un trabajo temporal o actividades subsidiarias y empleadas en pequeños empleos (es decir, trabajos de menos de 15 horas por semana, o con ingresos inferiores al nivel mínimo de cotizaciones a la seguridad social); c) trabajadores a tiempo completo o parcial que buscaban otro empleo durante el período de referencia; d) personas que realizaron algún trabajo remunerado o por un beneficio durante la semana de referencia pero que estaban sometidas a escolaridad obligatoria, jubiladas y percibían una pensión, inscritas como desempleadas en busca de trabajo en una oficina de empleo o percibiendo indemnizaciones de desempleo; e) estudiantes de dedicación completa que trabajan a tiempo completo o parcial; f) estudiantes de dedicación parcial que trabajan a tiempo completo o parcial; g) aprendices y personas en formación remunerados; h) personas ocupadas en la producción de bienes para su propio uso final; (i) miembros de las fuerzas armadas (miembros de carrera, voluntarios y reclutas); y j) miembros del servicio civil equivalente al servicio militar.

Se incluyen también personas con un empleo o una empresa, que estaban temporalmente ausentes del trabajo durante la semana de referencia por: a) enfermedad o lesión, b) vacaciones o licencia anual, c) licencia de maternidad o paternidad, d) licencia parental, e) ausencia sin autorización, f) conflictos laborales, o g) mal tiempo, desperfectos mecánicos, etc. Los trabajadores familiares temporalmente ausentes del trabajo durante la semana de referencia se consideran empleados si habitualmente trabajan en la empresa.

Se excluyen: a) aprendices y personas en formación no remunerados; b) personas que participan en planes de promoción del empleo; c) personas con licencia para estudios o capacitación, a menos que hayan trabajado durante la semana de referencia; d) personas con licencia sin goce de sueldo por iniciativa del empleador, si esa licencia corresponde a una destitución; e) personas ocupadas en servicios no remunerados o personales para los miembros de su propio hogar, y f) personas que realizan un trabajo social para la comunidad.

Desempleo: Personas de 15 años o más que estaban sin empleo durante la semana de referencia, y que buscaban activamente un empleo o lo habían hecho durante las cuatro semanas anteriores a la fecha de la entrevista. Se hace una diferencia entre personas desempleadas corrientemente disponibles para trabajar (es decir, disponibles para comenzar a trabajar dos semanas después de la fecha de la entrevista) y otras personas desempleadas.

Se incluyen: a) personas que ya han encontrado un trabajo y que comenzarán a trabajar pronto; b) personas que tratan de establecer su propia empresa; c) personas que buscan activamente trabajo pero que estaban sometidas a escolaridad obligatoria o jubiladas y percibían una pensión; d) estudiantes de dedicación completa que buscan trabajo a tiempo completo o parcial; e) estudiantes de dedicación parcial que buscan trabajo a tiempo completo o parcial; f) aprendices y personas en formación no remunerados que buscan activamente trabajo; g) personas que participan en planes de promoción del empleo y que buscan activamente trabajo; y h) trabajadores estacionales que no trabajan durante la temporada inactiva y buscan activamente trabajo.

Se excluyen personas sin empleo que no buscan activamente trabajo, a menos que ya hayan encontrado un nuevo empleo.

Subempleo:

Subempleo por insuficiencia de horas: Personas empleadas que buscan un segundo empleo y personas empleadas que buscan un empleo con más horas de trabajo.

Situaciones de empleo inadecuado: Personas empleadas que buscan un empleo con mejores condiciones de trabajo.

Horas de trabajo: Horas de trabajo habituales por semana y horas realmente trabajadas durante la semana de referencia. Al respecto, se pide información tanto sobre el empleo principal como el secundario (si lo hay).

Ingresos relacionados con el empleo:

Ingresos relacionados con el empleo asalariado: Sólo se pueden calcular de manera aproximada. Se hacen preguntas sobre: a) principal fuente de subsistencia (una posibilidad es el empleo); b) ingresos por concepto de pensiones y transferencias públicas por tipo; c) monto de los ingresos netos mensuales de particulares y de los ingresos netos mensuales del hogar por clase de ingresos. Los empleados se identifican mediante una cuestión sobre la situación en el empleo (véase el punto 8.3).

Ingresos relacionados con el empleo independiente: Sólo se pueden calcular de manera aproximada. Se hacen preguntas sobre: a) principal fuente de subsistencia (una posibilidad es el empleo); b) ingresos por concepto de pensiones y transferencias públicas por tipo; c) monto de los ingresos netos mensuales de particulares y de los ingresos netos mensuales del hogar por clase de ingresos. Los empleados independientes se identifican mediante una cuestión sobre la situación en el empleo (véase el punto 8.3).

Sector informal: Se define en base a las cuestiones sobre ocupación y rama de actividad económica del empleo principal y el empleo secundario.

Actividad habitual: Se refiere a la actividad principal. Si bien la encuesta no abarca este tema, se hacen tres preguntas retrospectivas relativas a la situación un año antes (situación en la actividad, situación en el empleo y rama de actividad económica).

Clasificaciones:

Rama de actividad económica (industria):

Título de la clasificación utilizada: Clasificación Nacional de Ramas de Actividad Económica de 1993 (Klassifikation der Wirtschaftszweige - WZ93), versión del microcenso (tres dígitos).

Grupos de población clasificados por industria: Todas las personas empleadas, así como desempleadas o económicamente inactivas.

Número de Grupos utilizados para la codificación: Códigos de tres dígitos. No se proporcionó información sobre el número de grupos.

Vínculos con la CIIU: La clasificación corresponde a la Clasificación Industrial General de Actividades Económicas de las Comunidades Europeas (NACE, Rev.1).

Ocupación:

Título de la clasificación utilizada: Clasificación Nacional de Ocupaciones (Klassifikation der Berufe), versión derivada del microcenso de 1992.

Grupos de población clasificados por ocupación: Todas las personas empleadas, así como desempleadas o económicamente inactivas.
Número de Grupos utilizados para la codificación: No se proporcionó información.
Vínculos con la CIUO: CIUO-88, a nivel de tres dígitos.
Situación en el empleo:
Título de la clasificación utilizada: Clasificación nacional de la situación en el empleo (Gliederung nach der Stellung im Beruf).
Grupos de población clasificados por situación en el empleo: Todas las personas empleadas, así como desempleados y personas económicamte inactivas.
Grupos utilizados para la codificación: a) trabajadores independientes en el sector de la agricultura, la silvicultura y la pesca; b) trabajadores independientes en otras ramas de actividad económica; c) trabajadores familiares; d) funcionarios públicos; e) trabajadores asalariados; f) trabajadores remunerados; g) aprendices en ocupaciones comerciales y técnicas reconocidas; h) aprendices en ocupaciones industriales reconocidas.
Vínculos con la CISE: No se proporcionó información.
Educación:
Título de la clasificación utilizada: Clasificación nacional de niveles de educación y capacitación profesional (Gliederung nach dem allgemeinen und beruflichen Bildungsniveau).
Grupos de población clasificados por educación: Personas empleadas y desempleadas.
Grupos utilizados para la codificación: No se proporcionó información.
Vínculos con la CINE: CINE-1997.
Tamaño y diseño de la muestra:
Unidad final de muestreo: Hogar, institución u hogar colectivo.
Tamaño de la muestra (unidades finales de muestreo): Unos 350 000 hogares o 820 000 personas (incluidas las que viven en instituciones o en hogares colectivos).
Fracción de muestreo: 1,0 por ciento de la población.
Marco de la muestra: El marco de la muestra se basa en el Censo de Población de 1987 (para los Estados de la Ex República Democrática de Alemania: basado en el Registro de la Población). Los resultados se ajustan a los datos de referencia de la población actual por sexo y nacionalidad (alemán/extranjero).
Actualización de la muestra: La muestra se actualiza cada año al añadirse una muestra de edificios recientemente construidos.
Rotación:
Esquema: Muestras de hogares, instituciones u hogares colectivos participan en la encuesta cuatro veces durante cuatro años consecutivos. Cada año, un cuarto de la muestra de hogares, instituciones u hogares colectivos se saca de la muestra y se sustituye por otros nuevos que entran en la muestra.
Porcentaje de unidades que permanecen en la muestra durante dos encuestas consecutivas: 75 por ciento.
Número máximo de entrevistas por unidad de muestreo: Cuatro.
Tiempo necesario para renovar completamente la muestra: Cuatro años.
Levantamiento da la encuesta:
Tipo de entrevista: La participación en la encuesta es obligatoria. Los entrevistados pueden escoger entre cuestionarios que deben completar por si mismos o cuestionarios que completan los entrevistadores. Los cuestionarios que completan los entrevistados se llenan según el método de papel y lápiz. Los entrevistadores utilizan el método de entrevistas personales asistidas por computadora (CAPI) o el método de papel y lápiz. Para los extranjeros que no hablan alemán, los cuestionarios que completan los entrevistados están disponibles en varios idiomas.
Número de unidades finales de muestreo por área de muestra: Cada área de muestra contiene una media de nueve hogares.
Duración del trabajo de campo:
Total: Tres meses (mayo a julio) para entrevistas personales y seis meses (mayo a octubre) para los cuestionarios que llenan los entrevistados.
Por área de muestra: No se proporcionó información. La duración de la entrevista depende del tamaño de los hogares. En promedio, las entrevistas toman unos 20 minutos por hogar.
Organización de la encuesta: Existe una encuesta permanente y los entrevistadores se utilizan principalmente para esta encuesta.
Número de personas que trabajan en el campo: Unos 7 000 entrevistadores que emplean las Oficinas Estadísticas de los Laender (Statistische Landesämter).
Substitución de las unidades finales de muestreo que no responden: Las unidades finales de muestreo, con los que no se puede entrar en contacto o casos de no respuesta total por otras razones, no se sustituyen por otras.
Estimaciones y ajustes:
Tasa de no-respuesta total: Un 4 por ciento.
Ajuste por no-respuesta total: Sí, se utiliza el método de imputación por asignación dinámica ("hot-deck") para atribuir registros faltantes.
Imputación por no respuesta de ítemes: Sí, para unas cuantas variables, se utiliza el método "hot-deck" para atribuir valores faltantes.
Ajuste por áreas/poblaciones no abarcadas: No corresponde.
Ajuste por falta de cobertura: Sí.
Ajuste por exceso de cobertura: Sí.
Ajuste por variaciones estacionales: No corresponde.
Historia de la encuesta:
Título y fecha de la primera encuesta: El primer microcenso se realizó en 1957.
Modificaciones y revisiones significativas: De 1957 a 1974, se prepararon, además del 1 por ciento de la muestra anual, tres pequeñas submuestras (0,1 por ciento). Desde 1968, la Encuesta sobre la Fuerza de Trabajo Europea está integrada en el microcenso. En 1990, se hicieron otros cambios importantes en la encuesta después del Censo de Población de 1987 y tras la reunificación alemana. Se introdujó una nueva muestra, basada en los resultados del Censo de Población de 1987.
Documentación y difusión:
Documentación:
Título de las publicaciones con los resultados de la encuesta: (periodicidad)
a) Statistisches Bundesamt, Fachserie 1: Bevölkerung und Erwerbstätigkeit, Reihe 3: Haushalte und Familien (anual); b) Statistisches Bundesamt, Fachserie 1: Bevölkerung und Erwerbstätigkeit, Reihe 4.1.1: Stand und Entwicklung der Erwerbstätigkeit (anual); c) Statistisches Bundesamt, Fachserie 1: Bevölkerung und Erwerbstätigkeit, Reihe 4.1.2: Beruf, Ausbildung und Arbeitsbedingungen der Erwerbstätigen (anual).
Título de las publicaciones con la metodología de la encuesta: Las publicaciones antes mencionadas incluyen información metodológica sobre la encuesta.
Difusión:
Tiempo necesario para difundir los primeros datos: Existe un retraso de nueves meses entre el trabajo sobre el terreno y la publicación de los resultados.
Información adelantada acerca de la fecha de la primera difusión pública: No existe una fecha fija para la publicación de los resultados de la encuesta. En general, la publicación de los datos se anuncia al público mediante un comunicado de prensa en el que figuran los primeros resultados de la encuesta.
Disponibilidad de datos no publicados si se solicitan: Sí, pero no necesariamente gratis.
Disponibilidad de datos por medios informáticos: La mayoría de los datos se pueden obtener en medios electrónicos. Sitio web: http://www.destatis.de/ .

Arabia Saudita

Título de la encuesta: Encuesta sobre la Fuerza de Trabajo (Labour force survey).
Organismo responsable de la encuesta:
Planificar y realizar la encuesta: Departamento Central de Estadísticas, Ministerio de Planificación (Central Department of Statistics, Ministry of Planning).
Analizar y publicar los resultados: Departamento Central de Estadísticas, Ministerio de Planificación (Central Department of Statistics, Ministry of Planning).
Temas abarcados: Empleo, desempleo, horas de trabajo, rama de actividad industrial (industria), ocupación, situación en el empleo, nivel de educación, empleo secundario y experiencia laboral.
Alcance de la encuesta:
Ámbito geográfico: Todo el país.
Grupos de población: Se excluyen nómadas y personas que viven en hogares colectivos.
Disponibilidad de estimaciones de otras fuentes para las áreas/grupos excluidos: No se proporcionó información.
Grupos abarcados por la encuesta pero excluidos de los resultados publicados: Ninguno.
Periodicidad:
Recolección de datos: Anual.
Publicación de los resultados: Anual.

Periodo de referencia:
Empleo: Semana de referencia fija.
Búsqueda de trabajo: Cuatro semanas.
Disponibilidad para trabajo: Semana de referencia.
Conceptos y definiciones:
Empleo: Personas de 12 años y más de edad que realizaron algún trabajo remunerado o por un beneficio, trabajaron sin remuneración en una explotación agrícola o negocio familiar durante la mayor parte de la semana (sábado a viernes) antes de realizarse la encuesta, o que tenían un empleo pero estaban enfermos o en vacaciones durante la semana de referencia. Esas personas deben figurar en la nómina de empleados y se debe prever su reintegro al trabajo después de las vacaciones o la enfermedad.
Se incluyen las siguientes categorías:
a)personas que realizaron algún trabajo remunerado o por un beneficio durante la semana de referencia pero estaban sometidas a escolaridad obligatoria, jubiladas y percibían una pensión, inscritas como desempleados en busca de trabajo en una oficina de empleo o buscaban otro trabajo durante la semana de referencia;
b)estudiantes de dedicación parcial que trabajaban a tiempo completo o parcial;
c)aprendices y personas en formación remunerados;
d)trabajadores familiares no remunerados, aprendices no remunerados y personas que realizaban un trabajo voluntario para la comunidad o un servicio social y que trabajaron más de 15 horas durante la semana de referencia;
e)personas ocupadas en la producción de bienes para su propio uso final;
f)voluntarios y miembros de carrera de las fuerzas armadas, así como miembros del servicio civil equivalente al servicio militar.
Se excluyen:
a)estudiantes de dedicación completa que trabajan a tiempo completo o parcial;
b)aprendices y personas en formación no remunerados, personas ocupadas en la producción de servicios para su propio hogar;
c)trabajadores familiares no remunerados temporalmente ausentes del trabajo durante la semana de referencia y trabajadores estacionales que no trabajan durante la temporada inactiva;
d)personas con licencia para estudios o capacitación.
Desempleo: Personas de 12 años y más de edad que no estaban empleadas durante la semana de referencia, estaban buscando activamente un empleo durante las cuatro semanas anteriores y estaban disponibles para trabajar durante la semana de referencia. [La búsqueda activa de trabajo se comprobó después de determinar la situación de desempleo de las personas.]
Se incluyen:
a)personas sin trabajo y corrientemente disponibles para trabajar, que buscaban un empleo y que habían tomado disposiciones para comenzar un nuevo empleo en una fecha ulterior a la semana de referencia;
b)personas sin trabajo y corrientemente disponibles para trabajar, que buscaban un trabajo y estaban tratando de establecer su propio negocio;
c)estudiantes de dedicación completa o parcial que buscaban un empleo a tiempo completo o parcial;
d)personas que estaban buscando un trabajo y estaban disponibles para trabajar pero estaban sometidas a escolaridad obligatoria o jubiladas y percibían una pensión.
Se excluyen:
a)personas suspendidas de su trabajo temporalmente o por tiempo indeterminado sin remuneración, si no buscaban un trabajo ni estaban disponibles para trabajar;
b)personas que estaban buscando un trabajo y/o estaban disponibles para trabajar pero estaban sometidas a escolaridad obligatoria o jubiladas y recibían una pensión;
c)estudiantes de dedicación completa o parcial que buscaban un empleo a tiempo completo o parcial.
Subempleo:
Subempleo por insuficiencia de horas: No se dispone de información.
Situaciones de empleo inadecuado: No se dispone de información.
Horas de trabajo: No se dispone de información.
Ingresos relacionados con el empleo:
Ingresos relacionados con el empleo asalariado: No se dispone de información.
Ingresos relacionados con el empleo independiente: No se dispone de información.
Sector informal: No se dispone de información.
Actividad habitual: No se dispone de información.

Clasificaciones:
Rama de actividad económica (industria):
Título de la clasificación utilizada: No se dispone de información.
Grupos de población clasificados por industria: Empleados únicamente.
Número de Grupos utilizados para la codificación: 16 categorías.
Vínculos con la CIIU: Al cuarto nivel.
Ocupación:
Título de la clasificación utilizada: No se dispone de información.
Grupos de población clasificados por ocupación: Empleados únicamente.
Número de Grupos utilizados para la codificación: 9 grupos principales.
Vínculos con la CIUO: Al tercer nivel.
Situación en el empleo:
Título de la clasificación utilizada: No corresponde.
Grupos de población clasificados por situación en el empleo: No corresponde.
Grupos utilizados para la codificación: No corresponde.
Vínculos con la CISE: No corresponde.
Educación:
Título de la clasificación utilizada: No se dispone de información.
Grupos de población clasificados por educación: Personas empleadas y desempleadas.
Grupos utilizados para la codificación: Analfabetos. Pueden leer y escribir. Escuela elemental. Escuela intermedia. Escuela secundaria. Diploma preuniversitario. Licenciatura. Doctorado
Vínculos con la CINE: Al primer nivel.
Tamaño y diseño de la muestra:
Unidad final de muestreo: Hogares.
Tamaño de la muestra (unidades finales de muestreo): 750 unidades primarias de muestreo (UPM).
Fracción de muestreo: 4 por ciento.
Marco de la muestra: En el Censo de población de 1993 se excluyen nómadas y personas que viven en hogares colectivos.
Actualización de la muestra: La actualización de la muestra principal se realizó en 1998.
Rotación:
Esquema: La muestra principal se divide en cuatro grupos. Cada muestra de la encuesta abarca 3 grupos.
Porcentaje de unidades que permanecen en la muestra durante dos encuestas consecutivas: 50 por ciento
Número máximo de entrevistas por unidad de muestreo: 5.
Tiempo necesario para renovar completamente la muestra: 5 años.
Levantamiento da la encuesta:
Tipo de entrevista: Entrevistas personales.
Número de unidades finales de muestreo por área de muestra: 20 hogares por UPM.
Duración del trabajo de campo:
Total: 20 días, del 24 de mayo al 13 de junio de 1999.
Por área de muestra: 4 días en zonas urbanas; 5 días en zonas rurales.
Organización de la encuesta: Permanente.
Número de personas que trabajan en el campo: 320 entrevistadores, 80 jefes de equipo y 13 supervisores.
Substitución de las unidades finales de muestreo que no responden: No.
Estimaciones y ajustes:
Tasa de no-respuesta total: 9 por ciento.
Ajuste por no-respuesta total: Sí.
Imputación por no respuesta de ítemes: No.
Ajuste por áreas/poblaciones no abarcadas: Sí.
Ajuste por falta de cobertura: No se proporcionó información.
Ajuste por exceso de cobertura: No se proporcionó información.
Ajuste por variaciones estacionales: No.
Historia de la encuesta:
Título y fecha de la primera encuesta: Encuesta sobre la Fuerza de Trabajo (Labour Force Survey), 1981.
Modificaciones y revisiones significativas: El programa de la encuesta se interrumpió de 1987 a 1999.
Modificaciones y revisiones significativas:
Documentación:
Título de las publicaciones con los resultados de la encuesta: Labour Force in the Kingdom of Saudi Arabia.
Título de las publicaciones con la metodología de la encuesta: Labour Force in the Kingdom of Saudi Arabia.

Difusión:
Tiempo necesario para difundir los primeros datos: mayo de 1987.
Información adelantada acerca de la fecha de la primera difusión pública: Sí.
Disponibilidad de datos no publicados si se solicitan: Sí
Disponibilidad de datos por medios informáticos: Sí.

Armenia

1.Título de la encuesta
Household Labour Force Survey (HLFS) (Encuesta sobre la Mano de Obra por Hogares).
2.Organización responsable de la encuesta
The Department of Statistics of the Republic of Armenia (DSRA) (Departamento de Estadísticas de la República de Armenia).
3.Alcance de la encuesta
(a) Ambito geográfico
Las encuestas realizadas en noviembre de 1996 y diciembre de 1997 sólo abarcan las zonas urbanas. A partir de 1999, abarcan las zonas urbanas y rurales.
(b) Personas comprendidas
Los hombres de 16 a 60 años y las mujeres de 16 a 55 años presentes en el hogar en el momento de la entrevista. Desde 1997, toda la población a partir de 16 años de edad.
Están excluidos:
•los estudiantes que viven en residencias estudiantiles y los escolares en pensionado;
•las personas internadas en establecimientos penales y psiquiátricos;
•el personal militar (reclutas y de carrera) que viven en cuarteles;
4.Periodicidad de la encuesta
La encuesta, realizada anualmente en 1996 y 1997, pasó a ser bianual desde 1999.
5.Período de referencia
La semana civil.
6.Temas abarcados
La encuesta proporciona información sobre los siguientes temas: empleo (principal y secundario), desempleo, subempleo, duración del desempleo, razones del desempleo, trabajadores ocasionales, rama de actividad, ocupación, condición en el empleo y nivel de educación.
7.Conceptos y definiciones:
(a) Empleo
Son personas empleadas:
•todas las que, durante la semana de referencia, efectuaron algún trabajo como asalariados, en su propio negocio, profesión o explotación agrícola, así como las personas que han trabajado como trabajadores familiares no remunerados en una empresa explotada por un miembro de la familia; y
•todas las que no trabajaban pero tenían empleos o negocios de los que se encontraban temporalmente ausentes por enfermedad, mal tiempo, vacaciones, conflictos de organización del trabajo, o motivos personales, remunerados por el tiempo de ausencia o bien en busca de otros empleos.
Están incluidos en los totales:
•los trabajadores a tiempo completo y parcial que buscan otro trabajo durante el período de referencia;
•los estudiantes a tiempo completo y parcial que trabajan a tiempo completo o parcial;
•las personas que realizaron algún trabajo durante la semana de referencia siendo jubilados o pensionistas; o bien inscritas como personas en busca de empleo en una oficina del trabajo o que perciben indemnizaciones de paro (a partir de la encuesta de 1997);
•trabajadores familiares remunerados y no remunerados;
•miembros de cooperativas de productores;
(b) Desempleo
Son personas desempleadas todos civiles que no tenían empleo durante la semana de referencia y estaban disponibles para trabajar, excepto por enfermedad temporal, y que habían tomado disposiciones específicas para encontrar trabajo.
Se incluyen entre los desempleados los estudiantes a tiempo completo y parcial en busca de un empleo a tiempo completo o parcial, a condición de estar disponibles para trabajar (si buscan trabajo para una fecha ulterior, como los meses de verano, se consideran inactivos); así como las personas que encontraron un empleo y tomaron disposiciones para incorporarse al nuevo trabajo en una fecha posterior al período de referencia.

8.Diseño de la muestra
(a) Marco de la muestra
La muestra de la encuesta HLFS se preparó sobre la base de listas de direcciones utilizadas como marco de muestra para la encuesta del presupuesto familiar.
(b) La muestra
La muestra se basa en un diseño de muestreo aleatorio estratificado en dos fases. En la primera fase administrativa las regiones se dividen en estratos sobre la base de distritos enumerados. En la segunda fase se seleccionan las unidades/hogares de muestreo definitivo en proporción a su tamaño. En 1996, el tamaño de la muestra era de unos 1 500 hogares en las zonas urbanas, es decir que se había entrevistado al 0.3 por ciento de todos los hogares. A partir de noviembre de 1999, la muestra abarca 1 200 hogares ubicados en zonas urbanas y rurales, que representan el 0.1 por ciento de todos los hogares consignados en Armenia.
(c) Rotación
Todavía no se ha establecido el modelo de rotación.
9.Documentación
El departamento de Estadísticas de la República de Armenia publicará los resultados de la encuesta HLFS en un boletín de información especial y en el próximo número del Statistical Yearbook of the Armenian Republic.

Australia

Título de la encuesta: Encuesta sobre la Fuerza de Trabajo (Labour Force Survey - LFS).
Organismo responsable de la encuesta:
Planificar y realizar la encuesta: Servicio Australiano de Estadísticas (Australian Bureau of Statistics - ABS).
Analizar y publicar los resultados: ABS.
Temas abarcados: Personas corriente y económicamente activas, empleadas y desempleadas, horas de trabajo, situación a tiempo completo/parcial, permanencia en el empleo, duración del desempleo, rama de actividad económica (industria), ocupación, situación en el empleo. Sexo, edad, lugar de nacimiento. Medición parcial del tiempo de subempleo por insuficiencia de horas.
En suplementos anuales o menos frecuentes de la LFS se abarcan los siguientes temas: personas corrientemente subempleadas por insuficiencia de horas; acuerdos laborales; múltiples empleos; experiencia profesional; educación y capacitación; migrantes; personas empleadas en el hogar; jubilación; experiencia en la búsqueda de trabajo; reducción de puestos y despidos; personas corrientemente inactivas (fuera de la población activa: incluidas las personas inscritas como desempleadas que buscan empleo y desalentadas).
Alcance de la encuesta:
Ámbito geográfico: Se excluyen el territorio de la Bahía de Jervis y los territorios externos.
Grupos de población: Población civil que habitualmente reside en Australia de 15 años y más de edad.
Disponibilidad de estimaciones de otras fuentes para las áreas/grupos excluidos: Censo Nacional de la Población.
Grupos abarcados por la encuesta pero excluidos de los resultados publicados: Ninguno.
Periodicidad:
Recolección de datos: Mensualmente.
Publicación de los resultados: Mensualmente.
Períodos de referencia:
Empleo: Una semana.
Búsqueda de trabajo: Las últimas cuatro semanas.
Disponibilidad para trabajo: La semana de referencia.
Conceptos y definiciones:
Empleo: Todas las personas de 15 años y más de edad que, durante la semana de referencia:
a)trabajaron una hora o más por una remuneración, beneficio, comisión o pago en especie en un empleo, negocio o explotación agrícola (incluidos empleados, empleadores y trabajadores por cuenta propia); o
b)trabajaron una hora o más sin remuneración en un negocio o una explotación agrícola familiar (es decir, trabajadores que contribuyen con la familia); o
c)personas con un empleo del que estaban:
i) ausentes menos de cuatro semanas hasta el fin de la semana de referencia; o
ii) ausentes durante más de cuatro semanas hasta el fin de la semana de referencia y fueron remunerados por parte o todo el período de cuatro semanas hasta el fin de la semana de referencia;

iii) ausentes de conformidad con normas de trabajo o arreglos de turnos; o

iv) en huelga o cierre patronal; o

v) en período de compensación y esperaban reintegrarse a su empleo; o

d) eran empleadores o trabajadores por cuenta propia, con un empleo, negocio o explotación agrícola pero estaban ausentes.

Desempleo: Personas de 15 años y más de edad que no tenían empleo durante la semana de referencia; y:

a) habían buscado activamente trabajo, de tiempo completo o parcial, en cualquier momento de las cuatro semanas precedentes al fin de la semana de referencia; y

b) estaban disponibles para trabajar en la semana de referencia; o

c) esperaban comenzar un nuevo empleo dentro de las cuatro semanas siguientes al fin de la semana de referencia y hubiesen podido hacerlo durante esta semana de haber tenido la oportunidad.

Subempleo:

Subempleo por insuficiencia de horas: Personas que quieren y están disponibles para trabajar más horas de las que actualmente hacen. En esta categoría se incluyen:

a) trabajadores a tiempo completo que durante la semana de referencia trabajaron a tiempo parcial por razones económicas (tales como interrupciones del trabajo o actividad económica insuficiente). Se supone que esas personas querían trabajar a tiempo completo y estaban disponibles para hacerlo durante la semana de referencia, y

b) trabajadores a tiempo parcial (en general trabajaban menos de 35 horas semanales y así lo hicieron en la semana de referencia) que querían trabajar más horas y estaban disponibles para comenzar a trabajar más horas en la semana de referencia. Es posible hacer una diferencia entre las personas que buscaban activamente o no un empleo.

En esta medición trimestral del subempleo por insuficiencia de horas no se incluyen los trabajadores a tiempo parcial que querían trabajar horas adicionales y que hubiesen estado disponibles para comenzar a trabajar dentro de las cuatro semanas siguientes a la encuesta. Los datos completos del subempleo por insuficiencia de horas se obtienen de los resultados de la encuesta anual Survey of Underemployed Workers.

Situaciones de empleo inadecuado: No se proporcionó información.

Horas de trabajo: En las horas reales trabajadas se incluyen tanto las horas remuneradas como no remuneradas. Se recopilaron las horas reales trabajadas en todos los empleos (y en el empleo principal). La situación de tiempo completo o parcial se determina a partir del número de horas trabajadas. Los trabajadores a tiempo completo se definen como las personas empleadas que generalmente trabajaron 35 horas o más semanales (en todos los empleos) y las que, aunque por lo general trabajaron menos de 35 semanales, trabajaron 35 horas o más durante la semana de referencia.

Se recopiló también el número total de horas habitualmente trabajadas (en todos los empleos).

Ingresos relacionados con el empleo:

Ingresos relacionados con el empleo asalariado: Las estimaciones de los ingresos de los empleados (promedio de ingresos semanales por empleado) se obtienen del suplemento anual de la encuesta Employee Earnings, Benefits and Trade Union Membership Survey. Los datos de ingresos obtenidos en las encuestas de hogares realizadas por el ABS se refieren a los ingresos brutos en efectivo percibidos del empleo principal o de todos los trabajos realizados durante el período de referencia y no se ajustan para excluir irregularidades por concepto de bonificaciones, pagos retrospectivos o adelantados.

El ABS no prepara estimaciones de ingresos relacionados con el empleo como se determina en las directrices internacionales. Sin embargo, los datos se recopilan según criterios más amplios de ingresos (ingreso de varias fuentes) en algunas recopilaciones de datos de los hogares como, por ejemplo, la encuesta de ingresos y gastos del hogar, la encuesta de gastos de los hogares y el censo de la población y los hogares.

Ingresos relacionados con el empleo independiente: No se proporcionó información.

Sector informal: No corresponde.

Actividad habitual: No se proporcionó información.

Clasificaciones:

Rama de actividad económica (industria)

Título de la clasificación utilizada: Australian and New Zealand Standard Industrial Classification (ANZSIC) 1993.

Grupos de población clasificados por industria: Personas empleadas y desempleadas (rama de actividad económica en el último empleo para los desempleados).

Número de Grupos utilizados para la codificación:158.

Vínculos con la CIIU: CIIU-Rev.3.

Ocupación:

Título de la clasificación utilizada: Clasificación Australiana Uniforme de Ocupaciones (Australian Standard Classification of Occupations), segunda edición.

Grupos de población clasificados por ocupación: Personas empleadas y desempleadas (ocupación en el último empleo para los desempleados).

Número de Grupos utilizados para la codificación: 340

Vínculos con la CIUO: CIUO-88 (el tratamiento diferente que se da a las fuerzas armadas no tiene repercusiones prácticas porque no se incluyen en la LFS).

Situación en el empleo:

Título de la clasificación utilizada: Situación de empleo.

Grupos de población clasificados por situación en el empleo: Personas empleadas.

Grupos utilizados para la codificación: Empleados, empleadores, trabajadores por cuenta propia y trabajadores que contribuyen con la familia (4 grupos).

Vínculos con la CISE: CISE-1993.

Educación:

Título de la clasificación utilizada: Clasificación nacional, no se dan títulos.

Grupos de población clasificados por educación: Todas las personas, en suplemento anual.

Grupos utilizados para la codificación: No se proporcionó información.

Vínculos con la CINE: CINE-1976 y CINE-1997.

Tamaño y diseño de la muestra:

Unidad final de muestreo: Viviendas.

Tamaño de la muestra (unidades finales de muestreo): 33 000 (mensualmente)

Fracción de muestreo: 0,005.

Marco de la muestra: Marco de área muy estratificado en varias etapas. La lista marco de viviendas privadas en unidades de selección primaria (USP) se basa en los distritos de recopilación (DR) utilizados en el Censo de la Población de Australia.

Actualización de la muestra: Cada cinco años según los resultados del Censo de la Población.

Rotación:

Esquema: Hogares en la muestra durante 8 meses consecutivos. Cada mes se hace la rotación de 1/8 de la muestra y se introduce una nueva muestra.

Porcentaje de unidades que permanecen en la muestra durante dos encuestas consecutivas: 7/8 de muestras de viviendas comunes entre dos encuestas consecutivas.

Número máximo de entrevistas por unidad de muestreo: No se proporcionó información.

Tiempo necesario para renovar completamente la muestra: Ocho meses.

Levantamiento de la encuesta:

Tipo de entrevista: La primera entrevista es directa y la información se recopila en papel, posteriormente se hace por teléfono si el entrevistado está de acuerdo.

Número de unidades finales de muestreo por área de muestra: No se proporcionó información.

Duración del trabajo de campo:

Total: 2 semanas.

Por área de muestra: No se proporcionó información.

Organización de la encuesta: Permanente.

Número de personas que trabajan en el campo: Unos 600 entrevistadores.

Substitución de las unidades finales de muestreo que no responden: No.

Estimaciones y ajustes:

Tasa de no-respuesta total: 3,5 por ciento.

Ajuste por no-respuesta total: Sí, por ponderación con respecto a la población de referencia.

Imputación por no respuesta de ítemes: No, esos cuestionarios se excluyeron.

Ajuste por áreas/poblaciones no abarcadas: Sí, para las fuerzas armadas: en base a cálculos administrativos para estimar la fuerza de trabajo total.

Ajuste por falta de cobertura: Sí, igual que para el ajuste por no-respuesta total.

Ajuste por exceso de cobertura: Sí, igual que para el ajuste por no-respuesta total.

Ajuste por variaciones estacionales: Sí, para empleados y desempleados por sexo y principales grupos de edad, división de la actividad económica (personas empleadas), desempleados a largo plazo. Se utiliza la variante X11-ARIMA, con una revisión anual de los factores de ajuste estacional.

Historia de la encuesta:

Título y fecha de la primera encuesta: Encuesta sobre la Fuerza de Trabajo (Labour Force Survey), febrero de 1964.

Modificaciones y revisiones significativas: agosto de 1966: se incluyó la población de aborígenes e isleños de Torres Strait. Mayo de 1976: revisión de la definición de desempleo para incorporar la búsqueda activa de trabajo y la disponibilidad para comenzar a trabajar en la semana de referencia. Febrero de 1978: la encuesta trimestral pasó a ser mensual. Octubre de 1982: se cambió la base para la población de referencia. Abril de 1986: se incluyeron en el desempleo los trabajadores que contribuían con la familia y que trabajaban menos de 15 horas. Agosto de 1996: se iniciaron las entrevistas por teléfono. Abril de 2001: introducción de cuestionarios y definiciones revisadas. Las personas ausentes del trabajo a corto plazo con permiso no remunerado por iniciativa del empleador se clasificaron como empleados (antes desempleados); las personas sin trabajo, que buscaban trabajo activamente pero que no estaban disponibles para trabajar en la semana de referencia debido a una enfermedad temporal se clasificaron como inactivos (antes desempleados); los trabajadores que contribuían con la familia, pero que no estaban en el trabajo se clasificaron como desempleados o inactivos (antes empleados).

Documentación y difusión:

Documentación

Título de las publicaciones con los resultados de la encuesta: Labour force Australia - Preliminary (Catálogo No. 6202.0).

Título de las publicaciones con la metodología de la encuesta: Labour Statistics: Concepts Sources and Methods 2001 (Catálogo No. 6102.0); Documento de información: Implementing the Redesigned Labour Force Survey Questionnaire (Catálogo No. 6295.0); Documento de información: Questionnaire Used in the Labour Force Survey (Catálogo No. 6232.0); Documento de información: Labour Force Survey Sample Design (Catálogo No. 6269.0).

Difusión:

Tiempo necesario para difundir los primeros datos: Dos semanas después del mes de la semana de referencia.

Información adelantada acerca de la fecha de la primera difusión pública: Sí.

Disponibilidad de datos no publicados si se solicitan: Sí.

Disponibilidad de datos por medios informáticos: Sí. Sitio web: http://www.abs.gov.au.

Austria

Título de la encuesta: Hasta 2002: Microcenso (Mikrozensus). A comienzos de 2003: Encuesta sobre la Fuerza de Trabajo (Labour Force Survey LFS (Arbeitskräfteerhebung)).

Organismo responsable de la encuesta:

Planificar y realizar la encuesta: EUROSTAT y Oficina de Estadísticas de Austria (Bundesanstalt Statistik Austria).

Analizar y publicar los resultados: Oficina de Estadísticas de Austria (Bundesanstalt Statistik Austria) y EUROSTAT.

Temas abarcados: Empleo, desempleo, subempleo, horas de trabajo (horas de trabajo normales, horas realmente trabajadas), duración del empleo, duración del subempleo, trabajadores desalentados, trabajadores ocasionales (si trabajaron durante la semana de referencia), trabajadores estacionales, rama de actividad económica (industria), ocupación, situación en el empleo, nivel de educación y calificación, principal fuente de subsistencia, empleos secundarios; cuestionario total de encuestas sobre la fuerza del trabajo de Eurostat.

Alcance de la encuesta:

Ámbito geográfico: Todo el país.

Grupos de población: La encuesta abarca la población residente de Austria, excluidas personas no asentadas. Las personas que viven en instituciones están incluidas en el Microcenso trimestral, pero no en la Encuesta anual sobre la Fuerza de Trabajo.

Disponibilidad de estimaciones de otras fuentes para las áreas/grupos excluidos: No corresponde.

Grupos abarcados por la encuesta pero excluidos de los resultados publicados: Ninguno.

Periodicidad:

Recolección de datos: Trimestralmente en marzo, junio, septiembre y diciembre de cada año (Microcenso con 15 cuestiones básicas sobre la actividad económica); anualmente en marzo (todas las demás cuestiones de la Encuesta de la Unión Europea sobre la Fuerza de Trabajo). Comienzos de 2003: encuesta continua.

Publicación de los resultados: Trimestralmente (Microcenso); anualmente (toda la Encuesta sobre la Fuerza de Trabajo).

Períodos de referencia:

Empleo: El período de referencia se adelanta una semana antes de la fecha de la entrevista.

Búsqueda de trabajo: El período de referencia se adelanta cuatro semanas antes de la fecha de la entrevista.

Disponibilidad para trabajo: El período de referencia se adelanta dos semana después de la fecha de la entrevista.

Conceptos y definiciones:

Empleo: Personas de 15 años o más de edad que tienen un trabajo regular de una o más horas por semana, así como personas con un trabajo irregular si trabajaron por lo menos una hora durante la semana de referencia. En ellas se incluyen:

(a) trabajadores familiares que trabajaron durante la semana de referencia;

(b) trabajadores a tiempo completo o parcial que buscan otro empleo;

(c) personas que realizaron algún trabajo remunerado o por un beneficio durante la semana de referencia pero que estaban sometidas a escolaridad obligatoria, o jubiladas y percibían una pensión, o inscritas como desempleadas en busca de trabajo en una oficina de empleo, o percibiendo indemnizaciones de desempleo;

(d) estudiantes de dedicación completa que trabajaban a tiempo completo o parcial;

(e) estudiantes de dedicación parcial que trabajaban a tiempo completo o parcial;

(f) aprendices y personas en formación remunerados o no;

(g) participantes en planes de promoción de empleo;

(h) personas ocupadas en la producción de bienes para su propio uso final;

(i) miembros de las fuerzas armadas (miembros de carrera, voluntarios y reclutas) y

(j) miembros del servicio civil equivalente al servicio militar.

Se incluyen también las personas con un empleo o una empresa, que estaban temporalmente ausentes del trabajo durante la semana de referencia debido a: a) enfermedad o lesión, b) vacaciones o licencia anual, c) licencia por maternidad/paternidad, d) licencia parental, e) licencia para estudios o capacitación hasta de un año de duración, f) conflictos laborales, o g) mal tiempo, desperfectos mecánicos, etc.

Se incluyen en esta definición los trabajadores familiares temporalmente ausentes del trabajo durante la semana de referencia.

Se excluyen: a) trabajadores estacionales que no trabajan durante la temporada inactiva; b) personas con licencia para estudios o capacitación durante más de un año; c) personas suspendidas de su trabajo temporalmente o por tiempo indeterminado sin remuneración; d) personas con licencia sin goce de sueldo por iniciativa del empleador; e) personas ocupadas en servicios no remunerados o personales para miembros de su propio hogar; y f) personas que realizan un trabajo voluntario o social para la comunidad.

Desempleo: Personas de 15 años o más de edad que no estaban empleadas durante la semana de referencia, habían buscado activamente trabajo durante las últimas cuatro semanas y estaban disponibles para trabajar dentro de dos semanas. Se incluyen: a) personas sin empleo y corrientemente disponibles para trabajar, que habían tomado disposiciones para comenzar un nuevo empleo en una fecha subsiguiente a la semana de referencia; b) personas sin empleo y corrientemente disponibles para trabajar, que estaban procurando establecer su propia empresa; c) personas suspendidas de su trabajo por tiempo indeterminado sin remuneración, que estaban buscando un empleo; d) personas que buscaban trabajo y estaban disponibles para trabajar, pero estaban sometidas a escolaridad obligatoria o jubiladas y percibían una pensión; e) estudiantes de dedicación completa que buscaban trabajo a tiempo completo o parcial; y f) estudiantes de dedicación parcial que buscaban trabajo a tiempo completo o parcial.

Se excluyen las personas sin empleo y corrientemente disponibles para trabajar, pero que no buscaban trabajo de manera activa por otras razones a las expuestas en los apartados a) y b) antes mencionados, así como las personas sin empleo que no estaban corrientemente disponibles para trabajar.

Subempleo:

Subempleo por insuficiencia de horas: Personas empleadas que deseaban trabajar horas adicionales, en el empleo habitual, en un nuevo empleo o en un empleo adicional.

Situaciones de empleo inadecuado: La encuesta no abarca este punto.

Horas de trabajo: Horas de trabajo normales por semana en el empleo principal, horas realmente trabajadas durante la semana de referencia en el empleo principal, horas realmente trabajadas durante la semana de referencia en el empleo secundario (si procede).

Ingresos relacionados con el empleo:

Ingresos relacionados con el empleo asalariado: La encuesta no abarca este punto.

Ingresos relacionados con el empleo independiente: La encuesta no abarca este punto.

Sector informal: La encuesta no abarca este punto.

Actividad habitual: La encuesta no abarca este punto.

Clasificaciones:

Rama de actividad económica (industria):

Título de la clasificación utilizada: Clasificación nacional de los sectores de la actividad económica.

Grupos de población clasificados por industria: Personas empleadas; desempleadas o económicamente inactivas con experiencia previa de trabajo.

Número de Grupos utilizados para la codificación: 31.

Vínculos con la CIIU: CIIU-Rev.3.

Ocupación:

Título de la clasificación utilizada: Clasificación Internacional Uniforme de Ocupaciones (CIUO-88).

Grupos de población clasificados por ocupación: Personas empleadas; desempleadas o económicamente inactivas con experiencia previa de trabajo.

Número de Grupos utilizados para la codificación: 78.

Vínculos con la CIUO: No corresponde.

Situación en el empleo:

Título de la clasificación utilizada: Clasificación nacional de la situación en el empleo.

Grupos de población clasificados por situación en el empleo: Personas empleadas; desempleadas o económicamente inactivas con experiencia previa de trabajo.

Grupos utilizados para la codificación: (a) Empleadores en el sector de la agricultura y la silvicultura; b) trabajadores familiares sin remuneración en el sector de la agricultura y la silvicultura; c) empleadores o trabajadores independientes en el sector de la producción, el comercio o el turismo; d) trabajadores familiares sin remuneración en el sector de la producción, el comercio o el turismo; e) trabajadores independientes en otros servicios (abogados, médicos, etc.); f) trabajadores familiares sin remuneración que trabajan con trabajadores independientes en otros servicios; g) aprendices; h) obreros; (i) empleados de oficina (sector privado); (j) empleados de oficina (sector público).

En total hay 46 grupos. Los grupos a) a d) se subdividen de acuerdo con el tamaño de la empresa. El grupo g) se subdivide en obreros y empleados de oficina. Los grupos h) a j) se subdividen de acuerdo con el nivel de conocimientos que se requiere para el empleo.

Vínculos con la CISE: CISE-1993.

Educación:

Título de la clasificación utilizada: Clasificación nacional de niveles de instrucción.

Grupos de población clasificados por educación: Todas las personas de 15 años o más de edad.

Grupos utilizados para la codificación: a) Escolaridad no obligatoria completa; b) escolaridad obligatoria; c) aprendizaje (formación profesional); d) formación profesional intermedia (excluida escolaridad profesional a tiempo parcial); e) escuela secundaria general superior; f) escuela profesional superior (tipo normal); g) escuela profesional superior (cursos que permiten seguir estudios superiores); h) instituto de educación superior; i) universidad o equivalente.

Vínculos con la CINE: CINE -1976 y CINE -1997.

Tamaño y diseño de la muestra:

Unidad final de muestreo: Vivienda.

Tamaño de la muestra (unidades finales de muestreo): 30 800 viviendas/direcciones.

Fracción de muestreo: 0,9 por ciento de viviendas.

Marco de la muestra: El marco de área se basa en la lista de direcciones del último censo de habitaciones, complementado con información sobre nuevas construcciones.

Actualización de la muestra: La muestra se actualiza una vez al año para incluir viviendas recientemente construidas; esas nuevas direcciones representan un estrato especial de la muestra.

Rotación:

Esquema: Los hogares en la muestra de viviendas permanecen en la encuesta hasta ocho veces durante un periodo de dos años. Cada trimestre se hace la rotación de 1/8 de la muestra de viviendas y se sustituye por otras direcciones que entran en la muestra.

Porcentaje de unidades que permanecen en la muestra durante dos encuestas consecutivas: 87,5 por ciento.

Número máximo de entrevistas por unidad de muestreo: Ocho.

Tiempo necesario para renovar completamente la muestra: Dos años.

Toda la información que figura más arriba sobre el tamaño y el diseño de la muestra es válida hasta el 2002.

Levantamiento de la encuesta:

Tipo de entrevista: La información se obtiene mediante entrevistas personales.

Número de unidades finales de muestreo por área de muestra: 25 direcciones como máximo.

Duración del trabajo de campo

Total: Tres semanas para cada trimestre del Microcenso; tres semanas para la Encuesta anual sobre la Fuerza de Trabajo.

Por área de muestra: Tres semanas como máximo.

Organización de la encuesta: La organización de la encuesta es permanente.

Número de personas que trabajan en el campo: Unos 1 200 entrevistadores.

Substitución de las unidades finales de muestreo que no responden: No se hacen sustituciones para los casos de no respuesta.

Estimaciones y ajustes:

Tasa de no-respuesta total: 4,1 por ciento de toda la muestra de direcciones. El 7,3 por ciento del total de la muestra son casos en los que no se ha podido entrar en contacto con ningún miembro del hogar, y el 9,9 por ciento de la muestra son casos de viviendas no habitadas, residencias secundarias o direcciones incompletas.

Ajuste por no-respuesta total: Sí.

Imputación por no respuesta de ítemes: Los valores faltantes se atribuyen sobre la base de la información proporcionada por personas con características similares. Sin embargo, esas imputaciones sólo se hacen para los datos de la Encuesta anual sobre la Fuerza de Trabajo y el Microcenso de marzo, y no para los datos del Microcenso de junio, septiembre y diciembre.

Ajuste por áreas/poblaciones no abarcadas: No corresponde

Ajuste por falta de cobertura: Sí.

Ajuste por exceso de cobertura: Sí.

Ajuste por variaciones estacionales: No.

Historia de la encuesta:

Título y fecha de la primera encuesta: El primer Microcenso se realizó en marzo de 1968, y la primera Encuesta de la Unión Europea sobre la Fuerza de Trabajo (basada en directrices de la OIT) en marzo de 1995.

Modificaciones y revisiones significativas: Los cambios de definiciones nacionales a internacionales se introdujeron para el Microcenso en marzo de 1994. No se han hecho cambios importantes en la Encuesta sobre la Fuerza de Trabajo desde 1995.

Documentación y difusión:

Documentación:

Título de las publicaciones con los resultados de la encuesta (periodicidad): Statistik Austria, Beiträge zur österreichischen Statistik, Heft 1.303: Arbeitskräfteerhebung (annually); Statistik Austria, Statistische Nachrichten (mensualmente). La primera publicación tiene detalles sobre los resultados de la encuesta, mientras que la segunda contiene, según el caso, artículos que presentan una visión general de los principales resultados o análisis de datos sobre temas específicos.

Título de las publicaciones con la metodología de la encuesta: (periodicidad) Las publicaciones antes mencionadas incluyen información metodológica sobre la encuesta.

Difusión:

Tiempo necesario para difundir los primeros datos: Seis meses para la Encuesta anual sobre la Fuerza de Trabajo.

Información adelantada acerca de la fecha de la primera difusión pública: No.

Disponibilidad de datos no publicados si se solicitan: Sí, en forma de cuadros normalizados.

Disponibilidad de datos por medios informáticos: Las tabulaciones normalizadas de la Encuesta sobre la Fuerza de Trabajo se pueden obtener en formato electrónico. Los cuadros del Microcenso también se pueden obtener en formato electrónico a partir del sitio web: http://www.statistik.at/ .

Bahamas

Título de la encuesta: Encuesta sobre la Fuerza de Trabajo y de Hogares (Labour Force and Household Survey).

Organismo responsable de la encuesta:

Planificar y realizar la encuesta: Departamento de Estadísticas.

Analizar y publicar los resultados: Departamento de Estadísticas.

Temas abarcados: Empleo, desempleo, horas de trabajo, ingresos, duración del desempleo, trabajadores desalentados, rama de actividad económica (industria), ocupación, situación en el empleo, nivel de educación/calificación, actividad habitual, empleos secundarios.

Alcance de la encuesta:

Ámbito geográfico: Las tres islas principales: Grand Bahamas, New Providence y Abaco.

Grupos de población: Personas de 15 años y más de edad, ocupadas o que desean ocuparse y están disponibles para trabajar en la producción de bienes y servicios, excluidas las personas que viven en hogares colectivos.

Disponibilidad de estimaciones de otras fuentes para las áreas/grupos excluidos: No.

Grupos abarcados por la encuesta pero excluidos de los resultados publicados: No.

Periodicidad:

Recolección de datos: Anual.

Publicación de los resultados: Anual.

Períodos de referencia:

Empleo: Una semana en abril.

Búsqueda de trabajo: Cuatro semanas en abril.

Disponibilidad para trabajo: Cuatro semanas en abril.

Conceptos y definiciones:

Empleo: Todas las personas de 15 años y más de edad que, en cualquier momento durante el periodo de referencia, trabajaron por una remuneración o no por lo menos una hora en una empresa familiar.

Se incluyen:

a) personas con un empleo pero temporalmente ausentes del mismo debido a enfermedad o lesión , vacaciones o licencia anual, licencia por maternidad/paternidad, licencia para estudios o capacitación, ausencia sin autorización, conflictos laborales, mal tiempo, desperfectos mecánicos, etc.;

b) personas que realizaron algún trabajo remunerado o por un beneficio durante el período de referencia pero que estaban sometidas a escolaridad obligatoria, jubiladas y percibían una pensión, inscritas como desempleadas en busca de trabajo en una oficina de empleo o percibiendo indemnizaciones de desempleo;

c) estudiantes de dedicación completa y parcial que trabajaban a tiempo completo o parcial;

d) aprendices y personas en formación remunerados;

e) trabajadores familiares no remunerados que trabajaban o estaban temporalmente ausentes del trabajo;

f) personas ocupadas en la producción de bienes para su propio uso final;

g) trabajadores estacionales que no trabajan durante la temporada inactiva.

Se excluyen los miembros de las fuerzas armadas, así como personas del servicio civil equivalente al servicio militar y personas que realizan un trabajo voluntario social para la comunidad.

Desempleo: Todas las personas de 15 años y más de edad que no trabajaban o que tenían un empleo del que estaban temporalmente ausentes durante la semana de referencia, pero buscaron trabajo de manera activa en las cuatro semanas anteriores a la de la encuesta, y estaban disponibles para trabajar y tenían deseos de hacerlo.

Subempleo:

Subempleo por insuficiencia de horas: La encuesta no abarca este punto.

Situaciones de empleo inadecuado: La encuesta no abarca este punto.

Horas de trabajo: Se calculan tanto las horas trabajadas durante la semana de referencia como las habitualmente trabajadas.

Ingresos relacionados con el empleo:

Ingresos relacionados con el empleo asalariado: Ingresos brutos relacionados con el empleo, incluidas propinas y comisiones antes de cualquier deducción e ingresos relacionados con la inversión (dividendos, ingresos por percepción de alquileres, regalías, pensión alimenticia, etc.). Se refiere tanto a empleos principales como secundarios.

Ingresos relacionados con el empleo independiente: Ingresos de todos los empleos, netos de gastos de explotación.

Sector informal: La encuesta no abarca este punto.

Actividad habitual: La encuesta no abarca este punto.

Clasificaciones:

Rama de actividad económica (industria):

Título de la clasificación utilizada: Clasificación nacional, correspondiente a la CIIU Rev.2 al nivel de división superior.

Grupos de población clasificados por industria: Personas empleadas y desempleadas.

Número de Grupos utilizados para la codificación: Nueve grupos.

Vínculos con la CIIU: CIIU Rev.2.

Ocupación:

Título de la clasificación utilizada: Clasificación nacional, correspondiente a la CIUO -1988.

Grupos de población clasificados por ocupación: Personas empleadas y desempleadas.

Número de Grupos utilizados para la codificación: Nueve grupos principales.

Vínculos con la CIUO: CIUO -1988.

Situación en el empleo:

Título de la clasificación utilizada Clasificación nacional, correspondiente a la CISE-1993.

Grupos de población clasificados por situación en el empleo: Personas empleadas.

Grupos utilizados para la codificación: Empleados (empleados gubernamentales y privados por separado), empleadores, trabajadores independientes, trabajadores familiares no remunerados.

Vínculos con la CISE: CISE -1993.

Educación:

Título de la clasificación utilizada: Clasificación nacional.

Grupos de población clasificados por educación: Personas empleadas y desempleadas.

Grupos utilizados para la codificación: Seis grupos: sin escolaridad, escuela primaria, escuela secundaria, escuela de estudios superiores, escuela técnica/profesional, otro.

Vínculos con la CINE: No.

Tamaño y diseño de la muestra:

Unidad final de muestreo: Hogar.

Tamaño de la muestra (unidades finales de muestreo): 2 700 hogares.

Fracción de muestreo: Varía según la Isla de que se trate.

Marco de la muestra: Censo de Hogares y Población de 1990.

Actualización de la muestra: En base al nuevo Censo.

Rotación

Esquema: Dos tercios (2/3) de los hogares permanecen en la muestra durante tres años consecutivos, mientras que el un tercio (1/3) restante forma parte de la muestra por primera vez.

Porcentaje de unidades que permanecen en la muestra durante dos encuestas consecutivas: 66 por ciento.

Número máximo de entrevistas por unidad de muestreo: Tres veces

Tiempo necesario para renovar completamente la muestra: 10 años.

Levantamiento da la encuesta:

Tipo de entrevista: Entrevistas personales.

Número de unidades finales de muestreo por área de muestra: No se proporcionó información.

Duración del trabajo de campo

Total: Tres semanas en mayo.

Por área de muestra: No se proporcionó información.

Organización de la encuesta: Los empadronadores se contratan para cada encuesta.

Número de personas que trabajan en el campo: Once supervisores y 57 empadronadores.

Substitución de las unidades finales de muestreo que no responden: No.

Estimaciones y ajustes:

Tasa de no-respuesta total: No.

Ajuste por no-respuesta total: No.

Imputación por no respuesta de ítemes: No.

Ajuste por áreas/poblaciones no abarcadas: No.

Ajuste por falta de cobertura: No.

Ajuste por exceso de cobertura: No.

Ajuste por variaciones estacionales: No.

Historia de la encuesta:

Título y fecha de la primera encuesta: Encuesta sobre la Fuerza de Trabajo y de Hogares de 1973 (Labour Force and Household Survey 1973).

Modificaciones y revisiones significativas: Encuestas bianuales hasta 1979. No se realizó ninguna encuesta entre 1979 y 1986.
Documentación y difusión:
Documentación:
Título de las publicaciones con los resultados de la encuesta: (periodicidad)
Labour Force and Household Income Report (anual).
Título de las publicaciones con la metodología de la encuesta: (periodicidad) Labour Force and Household Income Report (anual).
Difusión:
Tiempo necesario para difundir los primeros datos: Casi un año.
Información adelantada acerca de la fecha de la primera difusión pública: No.
Disponibilidad de datos no publicados si se solicitan: En algunos casos.
Disponibilidad de datos por medios informáticos: Sí.

Bangladesh

Título de la encuesta: Encuesta sobre la Fuerza de Trabajo (Labour Force Survey).
Organismo responsable de la encuesta:
Planificar y realizar la encuesta: Oficina de Estadísticas de Bangladesh.
Analizar y publicar los resultados: Oficina de Estadísticas de Bangladesh.
Temas abarcados: Empleo, desempleo, subempleo, horas realmente trabajadas, salarios, ingresos, empleo en el sector informal, duración del empleo, rama de actividad económica (industria), ocupación, situación en el empleo, nivel de educación/calificación, empleos secundarios.
Alcance de la encuesta:
Ámbito geográfico: Todo el país.
Grupos de población: La encuesta abarca los miembros habituales de hogares privados en Bangladesh, que estén presentes en el hogar en el momento de realizarse la encuesta o temporalmente ausentes. Se excluyen las personas que viven en hogares colectivos, poblaciones no asentadas, miembros de las fuerzas armadas, ciudadanos no residentes, extranjeros y personas que residen en el extranjero.
Disponibilidad de estimaciones de otras fuentes para las áreas/grupos excluidos: No corresponde.
Grupos abarcados por la encuesta pero excluidos de los resultados publicados: Ninguno.
Periodicidad:
Recolección de datos: Con irregularidad. Hasta el momento, la encuesta se ha realizado en 1983, 1984, 1985, 1989, 1990, 1995 y 1999.
Publicación de los resultados: Con irregularidad, según la encuesta realizada.
Períodos de referencia:
Empleo: El periodo de referencia se adelanta una semana antes de la fecha de la entrevista.
Búsqueda de trabajo: Periodo de referencia fijo de una semana.
Disponibilidad para trabajo: Periodo de referencia fijo de una semana.
Conceptos y definiciones:
Empleo: Personas de 5 años o más de edad que trabajaban una o más horas durante la semana de referencia por una remuneración o ganancia, o las que trabajaban sin remuneración en una explotación agrícola, empresa u organización familiar.
Se incluyen: a) trabajadores familiares que trabajaban durante la semana de referencia; b) trabajadores a tiempo completo o parcial que buscaban otro trabajo; c) estudiantes de dedicación parcial que trabajaban a tiempo completo; d) aprendices y personas en formación remunerados; y e) personas ocupadas en la producción de bienes para su propio uso final.
Se consideran también empleados a las personas de 5 años o más de edad que no estaban en el trabajo, pero que tenían un empleo o una empresa del que estaban temporalmente ausentes durante la semana de referencia debido a: a) enfermedad o lesión, b) vacaciones o licencia anual, c) licencia por maternidad/paternidad, d) licencia parental, e) licencia para estudios o capacitación, f) ausencia sin autorización, g) conflictos laborales, h) mal tiempo, desperfectos mecánicos, etc., o i) suspendidas de su trabajo temporalmente sin remuneración.
Se excluyen: a) personas que realizaron algún trabajo remunerado o por un beneficio durante la semana de referencia pero que estaban sometidas a escolaridad obligatoria, o jubiladas y percibían una pensión, o inscritas como desempleadas en busca de trabajo en una oficina de empleo, o percibiendo indemnizaciones de desempleo; b) estudiantes de dedicación completa que trabajaban a tiempo completo o parcial; c) aprendices y personas en formación no remunerados; d) personas suspendidas de su trabajo por tiempo indeterminado sin remuneración; y e) personas ocupadas en servicios personales o no remunerados para miembros de su propio hogar.
Desempleo: Personas de 5 años o más de edad que involuntariamente no se encontraban en un empleo remunerado durante la semana de referencia y que habían estado buscando activamente trabajo, o que deseaban trabajar pero no buscaban empleo por enfermedad o porque pensaban que no había ningún empleo disponible.
Se incluyen: a) personas sin empleo y disponibles para trabajar que han tomado disposiciones para comenzar un nuevo empleo en una fecha subsiguiente a la semana de referencia; b) personas sin empleo y disponibles para trabajar, que están procurando establecer su propia empresa; c) personas sin empleo y disponibles para trabajar, pero que no buscan trabajo porque piensan que en ese momento no hay empleos disponibles; d) personas suspendidas de su trabajo por tiempo indeterminado sin remuneración; y e) personas que realizaron algún trabajo remunerado o por un beneficio durante la semana de referencia pero que estaban inscritas como desempleadas en busca de trabajo en una oficina de empleo o percibiendo indemnizaciones de desempleo.
Se excluyen: a) personas sin trabajo que buscaban trabajo y/o estaban disponibles para trabajar, pero estaban sometidas a escolaridad obligatoria, o jubiladas y percibían una pensión; y b) estudiantes de dedicación completa que buscaban trabajo a tiempo completo o parcial.
Subempleo:
Subempleo por insuficiencia de horas: Personas empleadas, que consideraban que el empleo era inadecuado en términos de tiempo trabajado, ingresos percibidos, productividad o uso de sus capacidades, y que estaban buscando un empleo adicional de conformidad con su educación y capacidades.
Situaciones de empleo inadecuado: La encuesta no abarca este punto.
Horas de trabajo: Horas realmente trabajadas durante la semana de referencia. Para las personas con más de un empleo, las horas trabajadas se refieren al número total de horas trabajadas en todos los empleos.
Ingresos relacionados con el empleo:
Ingresos relacionados con el empleo asalariado: Ingresos regulares brutos en efectivo o en especie durante el período de referencia. Para las personas con más de un empleo, los ingresos brutos se refieren al total de todos los empleos.
Ingresos relacionados con el empleo independiente: Ingresos brutos de trabajadores independientes durante el periodo de referencia. Para las personas con más de un empleo, los ingresos brutos se refieren al total de todos los empleos.
Sector informal: Empresas no constituidas en sociedad propiedad de hogares, incluidas industrias familiares.
Actividad habitual: La encuesta no abarca este punto.
Clasificaciones:
Rama de actividad económica (industria):
Título de la clasificación utilizada: Clasificación Industrial Internacional Uniforme de todas las actividades económicas (CIIU, Rev.3).
Grupos de población clasificados por industria: Personas empleadas.
Número de Grupos utilizados para la codificación: Nivel de dos dígitos de la CIIU, Rev.3.
Vínculos con la CIIU: No corresponde.
Ocupación:
Título de la clasificación utilizada: Clasificación Uniforme de Ocupaciones de Bangladesh (Bangladesh Standard Classification of Occupations).
Grupos de población clasificados por ocupación: Personas empleadas.
Número de Grupos utilizados para la codificación: Nivel de dos dígitos.
Vínculos con la CIUO: CIUO-68.
Situación en el empleo:
Título de la clasificación utilizada: Clasificación nacional de situación en el empleo (National classification of status in employment).
Grupos de población clasificados por situación en el empleo: Personas empleadas.

Grupos utilizados para la codificación: a) Trabajadores independiente/por cuenta propia; b) empleadores; c) empleados; d) ayudantes familiares sin remuneración; e) jornaleros.
Vínculos con la CISE: Parcialmente.
Educación:
Título de la clasificación utilizada: Clasificación nacional de niveles de instrucción (National classification of levels of educational attainment).
Grupos de población clasificados por educación: Personas empleadas y personas desempleadas.
Grupos utilizados para la codificación: a) Ninguna instrucción; b) Clase I-V; c) Clase VI-VIII; d) Clase IX-X; e) SSC, HSC o equivalente; f) Diploma; g) Grado; h) Licenciatura; (i) BAg y superior; j) MBBS y superior; k) BSc técnico y superior; l) PhD.
Vínculos con la CINE: No.
Tamaño y diseño de la muestra:
Unidad final de muestreo: Hogar.
Tamaño de la muestra (unidades finales de muestreo): 9 790 hogares.
Fracción de muestreo: No se proporcionó información.
Marco de la muestra: Marco general de 442 unidades primarias de muestreo basado en el área del marco del censo de la población de 1991.
Actualización de la muestra: Antes de la encuesta, se prepara una nueva lista completa de hogares en las áreas de muestreo.
Rotación:
Esquema: No se hace rotación de las muestras. La recopilación de datos se extiende por un periodo de doce meses. Con ese fin, la muestra de la encuesta se divide en doce submuestras mensuales independientes.
Porcentaje de unidades que permanecen en la muestra durante dos encuestas consecutivas: No corresponde.
Número máximo de entrevistas por unidad de muestreo: No corresponde.
Tiempo necesario para renovar completamente la muestra: No corresponde.
Levantamiento da la encuesta:
Tipo de entrevista: La información se obtiene mediante entrevistas personales.
Número de unidades finales de muestreo por área de muestra: 25 hogares en zonas urbanas; 20 hogares en zonas rurales.
Duración del trabajo de campo:
Total: Doce meses (última encuesta: abril de 1999-marzo de 2000).
Por área de muestra: Una semana.
Organización de la encuesta: La organización de la encuesta es permanente.
Número de personas que trabajan en el campo: Ocho supervisores y 20 entrevistadores.
Substitución de las unidades finales de muestreo que no responden: Los hogares de los que no se tiene respuesta se sustituyen por otros.
Estimaciones y ajustes:
Tasa de no-respuesta total: No corresponde.
Ajuste por no-respuesta total: No corresponde.
Imputación por no respuesta de ítemes: No.
Ajuste por áreas/poblaciones no abarcadas: No corresponde.
Ajuste por falta de cobertura: No se proporcionó información.
Ajuste por exceso de cobertura: No se proporcionó información.
Ajuste por variaciones estacionales: No corresponde.
Historia de la encuesta:
Título y fecha de la primera encuesta: La primera Encuesta sobre la Fuerza de Trabajo en Bangladesh se realizó en 1983.
Modificaciones y revisiones significativas: En 1989 se hicieron importantes modificaciones en el cuestionario de la encuesta. A partir de1989, se consideraron como actividades económicas algunas actividades de producción para el consumo propio (tales como trillado, secado, cocimiento, procesamiento y conservación de alimentos, cuidado de la producción ganadera y avícola, recogida de leña y bosta de vaca, pesca, cultivo de legumbres y hortalizas, etc.), gracias a lo cual aumentó substancialmente el porcentaje de actividades femeninas.
Documentación y difusión:
Documentación:
Título de las publicaciones con los resultados de la encuesta: Oficina de Estadísticas de Bangladesh, Report on Labour Force Survey in Bangladesh (periodicidad: irregular).
Título de las publicaciones con la metodología de la encuesta: La publicación antes mencionada incluye información metodológica sobre la encuesta.
Difusión:
Tiempo necesario para difundir los primeros datos: Unos 12 meses después de finalizar la encuesta.
Información adelantada acerca de la fecha de la primera difusión pública: No.
Disponibilidad de datos no publicados si se solicitan: Sí.
Disponibilidad de datos por medios informáticos: Sí.

Barbados

Título de la encuesta: Encuesta Continua por Muestra sobre la Fuerza de Trabajo (Continuous Labour Force Sample Survey (CLFSS)).
Organismo responsable de la encuesta:
Planificar y realizar la encuesta: Servicio de Estadísticas de Barbados (Barbados Statistical Service).
Analizar y publicar los resultados: Servicio de Estadísticas de Barbados (Barbados Statistical Service).
Temas abarcados: Empleo, desempleo, subempleo, horas de trabajo, salarios, ingresos, años de experiencia laboral, duración del desempleo, rama de actividad económica (industria), ocupación, situación en el empleo, nivel de educación/calificación, empleos secundarios.
Alcance de la encuesta:
Ámbito geográfico: Todo el país.
Grupos de población: Población civil que no vive en hogares colectivos de 15 años y más de edad, es decir quienes residen normalmente en hogares privados.
Se excluyen las personas de instituciones u hogares colectivos, tales como hoteles, prisiones, hospitales, cuarteles, etc.
Disponibilidad de estimaciones de otras fuentes para las áreas/grupos excluidos: No se proporcionó información.
Grupos abarcados por la encuesta pero excluidos de los resultados publicados: Ninguno.
Periodicidad:
Recolección de datos: Trimestralmente.
Publicación de los resultados: Trimestralmente.
Períodos de referencia:
Empleo: Una semana antes de la fecha de la entrevista.
Búsqueda de trabajo: Tres meses antes de la fecha de la entrevista.
Disponibilidad para trabajo: Dos semanas después de la fecha de la entrevista.
Conceptos y definiciones:
Empleo: Personas de 15 años y más de edad que:
a) realizaron algún trabajo remunerado o por un beneficio durante la semana de referencia;
b) trabajaban en el empleo o empresa que tenían, pero se encontraban temporalmente ausentes del mismo durante la semana de referencia debido a enfermedad, lesión, conflictos laborales, vacaciones u otra licencia, o a la desorganización temporal del trabajo por razones como mal tiempo o desperfectos mecánicos.
Se incluyen:
a) trabajadores a tiempo completo o parcial que buscaban otro empleo durante la semana de referencia;
b) personas que realizaron algún trabajo remunerado o por un beneficio durante la semana de referencia pero que estaban jubiladas y percibían una pensión, inscritas como desempleadas en busca de trabajo en una oficina de empleo o percibiendo indemnizaciones de desempleo;
c) estudiantes de dedicación completa o parcial que trabajaban a tiempo completo o parcial;
d) miembros de las fuerzas armadas (miembros de carrera, reclutas y voluntarios).
e) aprendices remunerados y no remunerados (personas en formación no remuneradas).
Se excluyen:
a) trabajadores familiares no remunerados que ayudaron al funcionamiento de una empresa o explotación agrícola menos de 15 horas durante la semana de referencia;
b) personas que realizaron algún trabajo remunerado o por un beneficio durante la semana de referencia pero que estaban sometidas a escolaridad obligatoria.
Desempleo: Personas de 15 años y más de edad que estaban:
a) disponibles para trabajar y cuyos contratos de empleo habían llegado a término o se encontraban temporalmente suspendidos y quienes carecían de un empleo y buscaban un trabajo remunerado o por un beneficio durante los tres meses anteriores a la fecha de la entrevista;

b) disponibles para trabajar (salvo indisposición de salud menor) y que habían buscado trabajo remunerado o por un beneficio durante los tres meses anteriores a la fecha de la entrevista, incluidas personas que no habían trabajado previamente o cuya última situación de empleo era otra que la de empleado, es decir antiguos empleadores o personas jubiladas;
c) sin empleo y disponibles para trabajar siempre que hubiesen concertado acuerdos para comenzar un nuevo empleo o para establecer su propia empresa en una fecha posterior a la fecha de la entrevista;
d) suspendidas de su trabajo temporalmente o por tiempo indeterminado sin remuneración o con licencia sin goce de sueldo por iniciativa del empleador;
e) sin empleo y que habían buscado trabajo en algún momento durante los tres meses anteriores a la semana de referencia y que todavía estaban disponibles para trabajar durante la semana de referencia,
f) estudiando (dedicación completa o parcial) y que buscaban trabajo a tiempo completo o parcial y que estaban disponibles para trabajar.
Se excluyen las personas que realizaron algún trabajo remunerado o por un beneficio durante la semana de referencia pero que estaban sometidas a escolaridad obligatoria o quienes buscaban un empleo y/o estaban disponibles para trabajar pero estaban sometidas a escolaridad obligatoria o jubiladas y percibían una pensión.
Subempleo:
Subempleo por insuficiencia de horas: Todas las personas empleadas, que estuvieran o no en el trabajo, que habitualmente trabajaban menos que la duración normal del trabajo determinada para una actividad específica por razones independientes de su voluntad, y que estaban buscado un empleo y estaban disponibles para hacer un trabajo adicional durante la semana de referencia.
Situaciones de empleo inadecuado: No corresponde.
Horas de trabajo: Horas reales y habituales para todos los empleos durante la semana de referencia.
Ingresos relacionados con el empleo:
Ingresos relacionados con el empleo asalariado: Todos los ingresos de todos los empleos durante la semana de referencia, es decir, salarios, sueldos y otros ingresos en efectivo o en especie; remuneración por tiempo no trabajado y pagado por el empleador (se excluyen las indemnizaciones por despido o cese de servicio); bonificaciones, propinas, subsidios de vivienda y familiares pagados por el empleador; beneficios netos corrientes de la seguridad social y planes de seguros para los empleados.
Ingresos relacionados con el empleo asalariado: No corresponde.
Sector informal: No corresponde.
Actividad habitual: No corresponde.
Clasificaciones:
Rama de actividad económica (industria):
Título de la clasificación utilizada: Clasificación Industrial Uniforme de Barbados (Barbados Standard Industrial Classification).
Grupos de población clasificados por industria: Personas empleadas y desempleadas (rama de actividad económica (industria) del último trabajo para el desempleado).
Número de Grupos utilizados para la codificación: 29 grupos.
Vínculos con la CIIU: CIIU Rev. 2.
Ocupación:
Título de la clasificación utilizada: Clasificación Uniforme de Ocupaciones de Barbados (Barbados Standard Occupational Classification (1989)).
Grupos de población clasificados por ocupación: Personas empleadas y desempleadas (ocupación en el último trabajo para el desempleado).
Número de Grupos utilizados para la codificación: Ocho grupos.
Vínculos con la CIUO: CIUO-1968.
Situación en el empleo:
Título de la clasificación utilizada: Clasificación nacional.
Grupos de población clasificados por situación en el empleo: Personas empleadas.
Grupos utilizados para la codificación: Empleadores, empleados (divididos a su vez en empleados gubernamentales y empleados del sector privado, trabajadores independientes, trabajadores familiares no remunerados, aprendices).
Vínculos con la CISE: Sí.
Educación:
Título de la clasificación utilizada: Clasificación nacional.
Grupos de población clasificados por educación: Personas empleadas y desempleadas.
Grupos utilizados para la codificación: Ninguna instrucción, educación primaria, secundaria, universitaria, técnica o profesional, otra, no se menciona.
Vínculos con la CINE: CINE-1976.
Tamaño y diseño de la muestra:
Unidad final de muestreo: Hogar.
Tamaño de la muestra (unidades finales de muestreo): 1 800 hogares por ronda (trimestral).
Fracción de muestreo: 2 por ciento del total de hogares civiles no colectivos.
Marco de la muestra: El Censo de Población y Hogares de 2000. El país está dividido en 538 distritos de enumeración (DE) que abarcan todas las once parroquias. Cada DE abarca unos 300 hogares.
Actualización de la muestra: Cada 10 años basándose en los resultados del censo de la población.
Rotación:
Esquema: No se proporcionó información.
Porcentaje de unidades que permanecen en la muestra durante dos encuestas consecutivas: 50 por ciento. El otro 50 por ciento se entrevista cuatro semanas más tarde.
Número máximo de entrevistas por unidad de muestreo: Dos.
Tiempo necesario para renovar completamente la muestra: Un año.
Levantamiento de la encuesta:
Tipo de entrevista: Entrevistas personales.
Número de unidades finales de muestreo por área de muestra: 45.
Duración del trabajo de campo:
Total: Tres meses.
Por área de muestra: No se proporcionó información.
Organización de la encuesta: Permanente.
Número de personas que trabajan en el campo: 15 funcionarios sobre el terreno y 3 supervisores.
Substitución de las unidades finales de muestreo que no responden: No.
Estimaciones y ajustes:
Tasa de no-respuesta total: No se proporcionó información.
Ajuste por no-respuesta total: No.
Imputación por no respuesta de ítemes: Para ingresos percibidos, horas de trabajo, etc., en base a respuestas similares de los hogares.
Ajuste por áreas/poblaciones no abarcadas: No se proporcionó información.
Ajuste por falta de cobertura: No se proporcionó información.
Ajuste por exceso de cobertura: No se proporcionó información.
Ajuste por variaciones estacionales: No.
Historia de la encuesta:
Título y fecha de la primera encuesta: Encuesta Continua sobre la Fuerza de Trabajo (Continuous Labour Force Survey), octubre de 1975.
Modificaciones y revisiones significativas: No se proporcionó información.
Documentación y difusión:
Documentación:
Título de las publicaciones con los resultados de la encuesta: (periodicidad): Continuous Labour Force Sample Survey Report (anual); Boletín sobre la fuerza de trabajo (Labour Force Bulletin) (trimestralmente).
Título de las publicaciones con la metodología de la encuesta: (periodicidad): Continuous Labour Force Sample Survey Report (anual).
Difusión:
Tiempo necesario para difundir los primeros datos: Dos meses.
Información adelantada acerca de la fecha de la primera difusión pública: No.
Disponibilidad de datos no publicados si se solicitan: Sí.
Disponibilidad de datos por medios informáticos: Sí y en el sitio web:
http://www.bgis.gov.bb/stats/.

Bélgica

Título de la encuesta: Encuesta sobre las Fuerzas de Trabajo (Enquête sur les Forces du Travail).
Organismo responsable de la encuesta:
Planificar y realizar la encuesta: Instituto Nacional de Estadística (Institut National de Statistique).
Analizar y publicar los resultados: Instituto Nacional de Estadística (Institut National de Statistique).

Temas abarcados: Empleo, desempleo, subempleo, duración del empleo, salarios, ingresos, duración del empleo y el desempleo, trabajadores desalentados y ocasionales, rama de actividad económica (industria), ocupación, situación en el empleo, nivel de educación o calificación, empleo secundario, lugar de trabajo, motivos del tiempo parcial, horarios atípicos, último empleo ocupado, nivel de formación, etc.

Alcance de la encuesta:

Ámbito geográfico: Todo el país.

Grupos de población: Personas de 15 años o más de edad. Se excluyen la población que vive en hogares colectivos y las personas que residen en el extranjero.

Disponibilidad de estimaciones de otras fuentes para las áreas/grupos excluidos: No corresponde.

Grupos abarcados por la encuesta pero excluidos de los resultados publicados: No corresponde.

Periodicidad:

Recolección de datos: Encuesta continua.

Publicación de los resultados: Anualmente.

Periodo de referencia:

Empleo: Una semana (variable).

Búsqueda de trabajo: Cuatro semanas (variable).

Disponibilidad para trabajo: Dos semanas (variable).

Conceptos y definiciones:

Empleo: Personas de 15 años o más de edad que estaban, durante la semana de referencia, en una de las siguientes categorías:

1)Empleo asalariado:

a)trabajando, es decir personas que, durante la semana de referencia, realizaron un trabajo (con o sin contrato formal) por un salario o una remuneración en efectivo o en especie;

b)personas con un empleo pero que no estaban en el sitio de trabajo, es decir personas que tenían un empleo pero estaban ausentes durante la semana de referencia (por vacaciones, enfermedad, licencia por maternidad, conflictos sociales, mal tiempo u otro motivo) y mantenían un vínculo formal con su empleo. Los aprendices que reciben una remuneración en efectivo o en especie se consideran como trabajadores asalariados.

2)Empleo no asalariado:

a)trabajando, es decir personas que, durante la semana de referencia, realizaron algún trabajo por un beneficio o una ganancia familiar, en efectivo o en especie (las ayudas familiares no remuneradas se consideran como trabajadores no remunerados);

b)personas con una empresa pero que no estaban en el sitio de trabajo: personas que, durante la semana de referencia, tenían una empresa (industrial, comercial, agrícola o de servicios) pero que temporalmente no estaban en el sitio de trabajo por cualquier motivo.

En la práctica, el trabajo efectuado durante la semana de referencia se refiere al realizado durante una hora como mínimo. Por lo tanto, un trabajador a tiempo muy parcial se considera como una persona con empleo.

Se consideran también empleados:

a)las personas temporalmente ausentes del trabajo, por menos de tres meses, debido a enfermedad o lesión, licencia parental, licencia para estudios o capacitación, ausencia sin autorización, conflictos laborales, mal tiempo o desperfectos mecánicos, así como vacaciones anuales o licencia por maternidad o paternidad;

b)las personas suspendidas de su trabajo, por menos de tres meses;

c)las personas que realizaron algún trabajo, remunerado o por un beneficio, durante la semana de referencia, pero que estaban sometidas a escolaridad obligatoria, jubiladas y recibían una pensión, inscritas como desempleadas en busca de trabajo en una oficina de empleo o percibiendo indemnizaciones de desempleo;

d)los estudiantes de dedicación completa o parcial que trabajan a tiempo completo o parcial;

e)los aprendices y las personas en formación remunerados;

f)los trabajadores familiares no remunerados que trabajaron durante la semana de referencia;

g)los militares de carrera y los voluntarios.

Desempleo: Personas de 15 años o más de edad que, durante la semana de referencia, estaban sin trabajo, disponibles para trabajar y en busca de un empleo.

Subempleo:

Subempleo por insuficiencia de horas: Personas que desean trabajar más en el empleo que tienen actualmente o en otro empleo.

Situaciones de empleo inadecuado: Personas que buscan otras condiciones de trabajo, como salarios, horarios, trayectos, etc.

Horas de trabajo: Horas reales y habituales.

Ingresos relacionados con el empleo:

Ingresos relacionados con el empleo asalariado: Salario mensual neto y los otros ingresos, pagados anualmente, como primas de fin de año, vacaciones, participación en los beneficios, etc.

Ingresos relacionados con el empleo independiente: La encuesta no abarca este punto.

Sector informal: No corresponde.

Actividad habitual: No corresponde.

Clasificaciones:

Rama de actividad económica (industria):

Título de la clasificación utilizada: Nomenclatura de Actividades en las Comunidades Europeas (NACE).

Grupos de población clasificados por industria: Personas empleadas, así como las inactivas desde hace ocho años como máximo.

Número de Grupos utilizados para la codificación: 60 grupos.

Vínculos con la CIIU: CIIU Rev.3.

Ocupación:

Título de la clasificación utilizada: Clasificación nacional basada en la CIUO.

Grupos de población clasificados por ocupación: Personas empleadas, así como las inactivas desde hace ocho años como máximo.

Número de Grupos utilizados para la codificación: Unos 300 grupos.

Vínculos con la CIUO: CIUO-88.

Situación en el empleo:

Título de la clasificación utilizada: Clasificación nacional.

Grupos de población clasificados por situación en el empleo: Personas empleadas, así como las inactivas desde hace ocho años como máximo.

Grupos utilizados para la codificación: Asalariados (obreros, empleados y funcionarios) y trabajadores no asalariados (trabajadores independientes, empleadores y ayudas familiares).

Vínculos con la CISE: No se dispone de información.

Educación:

Título de la clasificación utilizada: No se dispone de información.

Grupos de población clasificados por educación: Personas de 15 años y más de edad.

Grupos utilizados para la codificación: 13 categorías: primaria (o sin diploma); secundaria inferior general; secundaria inferior técnica, artística o profesional; secundaria superior general; secundaria superior técnica; secundaria superior artística; secundaria superior profesional; postsecundaria no superior; superior no universitaria corta o larga; universitaria o ingeniería; segundo grado universitario; doctorado.

Vínculos con la CINE: CINE-1976.

Tamaño y diseño de la muestra:

Unidad final de muestreo: Hogar.

Tamaño de la muestra (unidades finales de muestreo): Unos 47 000 hogares (es decir 11 960 hogares por trimestre).

Fracción de muestreo: Casi el 1,1 por ciento.

Marco de la muestra: Registro nacional de personas físicas, obtenido de los registros de población de los municipios.

Actualización de la muestra: No se dispone de información.

Rotación:

Esquema: Depués de la primera entrevista se realiza, 13 semanas más tarde, una segunda entrevista.

Porcentaje de unidades que permanecen en la muestra durante dos encuestas consecutivas: 50 por ciento.

Número máximo de entrevistas por unidad de muestreo: No se dispone de información.

Tiempo necesario para renovar completamente la muestra: Trece semanas.

Levantamiento de la encuesta:

Tipo de entrevista: Los hogares se interrogan en dos ocasiones: la primera entrevista que realizan los encuestadores es personal y la segunda, tres meses más tarde, se basa en un cuestionario simplificado que se envía por correo o se rellena por teléfono.

Número de unidades finales de muestreo por área de muestra: Unos 2 390 grupos de 20 hogares.

Duración del trabajo de campo:

Total: Un año.

Por área de muestra: No se dispone de información.

Organización de la encuesta: Estructura permanente.

Número de personas que trabajan en el campo: 10 personas en los preparativos y 300 encuestadores.

Substitución de las unidades finales de muestreo que no responden: Sí.

Estimaciones y ajustes:
Tasa de no-respuesta total: Casi el 17 por ciento.
Ajuste por no-respuesta total: Sí.
Imputación por no respuesta de ítemes: No.
Ajuste por áreas/poblaciones no abarcadas: No.
Ajuste por falta de cobertura: Sí.
Ajuste por exceso de cobertura: Sí.
Ajuste por variaciones estacionales: No.
Historia de la encuesta:
Título y fecha de la primera encuesta: Encuesta sobre la población activa, 1968 (Enquête sur la population active).
Modificaciones y revisiones significativas: A partir de enero de 1999, se pasó a un sistema de encuesta continua y se adoptó el criterio de una hora de trabajo en el nuevo cuestionario.
Documentación y difusión:
Documentación:
Título de las publicaciones con los resultados de la encuesta (periodicidad): Emploi et chômage: enquête sur les forces de travail et Statistiques sociales (anualmente).
Título de las publicaciones con la metodología de la encuesta (periodicidad): Emploi et chômage: enquête sur les forces de travail et Statistiques sociales (anualmente).
Difusión:
Tiempo necesario para difundir los primeros datos: Unos cuatro meses después del año de referencia para los primeros resultados y diez meses para los resultados detallados.
Información adelantada acerca de la fecha de la primera difusión pública: No.
Disponibilidad de datos no publicados si se solicitan: Sí.
Disponibilidad de datos por medios informáticos: Sitio web: http://www.statbel.fgov.be

Botswana

Título de la encuesta: Encuesta sobre la Fuerza de Trabajo (Labour Force Survey (LFS)).
Organismo responsable de la encuesta:
Planificar y realizar la encuesta: Oficina Central de Estadísticas (Central Statistics Office (CSO)).
Analizar y publicar los resultados: CSO.
Temas abarcados: Personas corriente y económicamente activas, empleados y desempleados; personas subempleadas, temporalmente ausentes del trabajo y que no están en la fuerza de trabajo; personas habitualmente empleadas con o sin desempleo, personas con algún empleo y personas que por lo general no están activas económicamente; capacitación; ingresos; sector institucional, rama de actividad económica (industria), ocupación, situación en el empleo.
Alcance de la encuesta:
Ámbito geográfico: Todo el país.
Grupos de población: Población que no vive en hogares colectivos de 12 años y más de edad, es decir personas que normalmente residen en hogares privados. Se excluyen visitantes de menos de 14 días y personas que viven en hoteles, prisiones, cuarteles, etc.
Disponibilidad de estimaciones de otras fuentes para las áreas/grupos excluidos: No se dispone de.
Grupos abarcados por la encuesta pero excluidos de los resultados publicados: No se dispone de información.
Periodicidad:
Recolección de datos: Ocasional, es decir en 1995-96 y 1997-98.
Publicación de los resultados: Ocasional.
Periodos de referencia:
Empleo: Una semana antes de la fecha de la entrevista.
Búsqueda de trabajo: Periodo de búsqueda de un mes según la definición estricta. No se requiere de la búsqueda para una definición amplia.
Disponibilidad para trabajo: No se dispone de información.
Conceptos y definiciones:
Empleo: Personas que a) realizaron algún trabajo remunerado o por un beneficio durante la semana de referencia; o b) se encontraban temporalmente ausentes
del trabajo durante la semana de referencia debido a enfermedad o licencia, pero que se reintegrarían al trabajo. Se incluyen trabajadores familiares no remunerados ocupadas en negocios familiares. "Algún trabajo" se puede definir como el realizado durante 1 hora o más durante la semana de referencia.
Desempleo: Definición estricta: personas que estaban sin empleo, disponibles para trabajar y que habían buscado un empleo durante el último mes. Definición amplia: personas que estaban sin empleo y disponibles para trabajar.
Subempleo:
Subempleo por insuficiencia de horas: Personas que trabajaban menos de 35 horas y que decían que estaban disponibles para trabajar más horas.
Situaciones de empleo inadecuado: No se dispone de información.
Horas de trabajo: No se dispone de información.
Ingresos relacionados con el empleo:
Ingresos relacionados con el empleo asalariado: No se dispone de información.
Ingresos relacionados con el empleo independiente: No se dispone de información.
Sector informal: Se excluyen todas las personas que trabajaban por cuenta propia o como trabajadores asalariados en el sector agrícola tradicional, así como las que trabajaban para el gobierno local o central o para empresas con 5 o más empleados asalariados o que estaban en una sociedad constituida legalmente o mantenían una serie completa de registros. Se incluyen, pero se identifican por separado, los trabajadores del servicio doméstico y otros que trabajaban para hogares privados.
Actividad habitual: Económicamente activos por 6 meses o más de los 12 meses de referencia.
Clasificaciones:
Rama de actividad económica (industria):
Título de la clasificación utilizada: Clasificación Industrial de Botswana (Botswana Industrial Classification (BISIC)).
Grupos de población clasificados por industria: No se dispone de información.
Número de Grupos utilizados para la codificación: No se dispone de información.
Vínculos con la CIIU: CIIU-Rev.3 con códigos extraordinarios para identificar actividades informales.
Ocupación:
Título de la clasificación utilizada: Clasificación Uniforme de Ocupaciones de Botswana (Botswana Standard Classification of Occupations (BSCO)).
Grupos de población clasificados por ocupación: No se dispone de información.
Número de Grupos utilizados para la codificación: No se dispone de información.
Vínculos con la CIUO: CIUO-88.
Situación en el empleo:
Título de la clasificación utilizada: Clasificación nacional, no se dan títulos.
Grupos de población clasificados por situación en el empleo: Población empleada.
Grupos utilizados para la codificación: Empleados remunerados; trabajadores independientes en el sector agrícola tradicional; trabajadores independientes fuera del sector agrícola tradicional, divididos a su vez en empleados remunerados, empleados no remunerados y trabajadores familiares no remunerados.
Vínculos con la CISE: Sí.
Educación:
Título de la clasificación utilizada: Clasificación nacional de temas de capacitación.
Grupos de población clasificados por educación: No se dispone de información.
Grupos utilizados para la codificación: No se dispone de información.
Vínculos con la CINE: No se dispone de información.
Tamaño y diseño de la muestra
Unidad final de muestreo: Hogar.
Tamaño de la muestra (unidades finales de muestreo): 11 000.
Fracción de muestreo: No se dispone de información.
Marco de la muestra: Censo de la población de 1991, con 5 estratos urbanos y 9 rurales, con un total de 420 bloques de muestras.
Actualización de la muestra: Ninguna, pero supone un 15 por ciento del crecimiento de la población.
Rotación:
Esquema: No corresponde.
Porcentaje de unidades que permanecen en la muestra durante dos encuestas consecutivas: No corresponde.
Número máximo de entrevistas por unidad de muestreo: No corresponde.
Tiempo necesario para renovar completamente la muestra: No corresponde.
Levantamiento da la encuesta:
Tipo de entrevista: Entrevistas personales.

Número de unidades finales de muestreo por área de muestra: No se dispone de información.
Duración del trabajo de campo:
Total: Trece meses.
Por área de muestra: No se dispone de información.
Organización de la encuesta: No se dispone de información.
Número de personas que trabajan en el campo: No se dispone de información.
Substitución de las unidades finales de muestreo que no responden: No se dispone de información.
Estimaciones y ajustes:
Tasa de no-respuesta total: 2 por ciento.
Ajuste por no-respuesta total: No.
Imputación por no respuesta de ítemes: No.
Ajuste por áreas/poblaciones no abarcadas: No corresponde.
Ajuste por falta de cobertura: No corresponde.
Ajuste por exceso de cobertura: No corresponde.
Ajuste por variaciones estacionales: No corresponde.
Historia de la encuesta:
Título y fecha de la primera encuesta: Encuesta sobre la Fuerza de Trabajo de Botswana (Botswana Labour Force Survey), 1984/5.
Modificaciones y revisiones significativas: No se dispone de información.
Documentación y difusión:
Documentación:
Título de las publicaciones con los resultados de la encuesta: No se dispone de información.
Título de las publicaciones con la metodología de la encuesta: Encuesta sobre la Fuerza de Trabajo de 1995-96: Informe Técnico y Operacional (marzo de 1998).
Difusión:
Tiempo necesario para difundir los primeros datos: No se dispone de información.
Información adelantada acerca de la fecha de la primera difusión pública: No se dispone de información.
Disponibilidad de datos no publicados si se solicitan: No se dispone de información.
Disponibilidad de datos por medios informáticos: No se dispone de información. Sitio web: http://www.cso.gov.bw/cso/.

Brasil

Título de la encuesta: Pesquisa Mensal de Emprego (Encuesta Mensual de Empleo).
Organismo responsable de la encuesta:
Planificar y realizar la encuesta: Instituto Brasileiro de Geografía e Estatística (IBGE).
Analizar y publicar los resultados: Instituto Brasileiro de Geografía e Estatística (IBGE).
Temas abarcados: Empleo, desempleo, horas de trabajo, salarios, ingresos, duración del desempleo, ramas de actividad económica, ocupación, situación en el empleo, nivel de educación, trabajos secundarios.
Alcance de la encuesta:
Ámbito geográfico: desde su inicio en 1980, abarca las regiones metropolitanas de Recife, Salvador, Belo Horizonte, Río de Janeiro, Sao Paulo y Porto Alegre. En marzo de 1999 se añadió la región metropolitana de Curitiba.
Grupos de población: toda la población de 10 años o más residente en la fecha de la entrevista en los hogares seleccionados. Se excluyen a las personas residentes en embajadas, consulados e instituciones extranjeras y a las personas residentes en un domicilio colectivo tales como militares en casernas o instalaciones militares, presos en cárceles o reformatorios, etc., o internos en escuelas, hospitales, asilos, orfelinatos, etc., religiosos en conventos, monasterios, etc.
Disponibilidad de estimaciones de otras fuentes para las áreas/grupos excluidos: Sí.
Grupos abarcados por la encuesta pero excluidos de los resultados publicados: Los indicadores de empleo excluyen a las personas de 10 a 14 años.
Periodicidad:
Recolección de datos: Mensual.
Publicación de los datos: Mensual.
Períodos de referencia:
Empleo: Una semana móvil.
Búsqueda de trabajo: Una semana móvil.
Disponibilidad para trabajo: Una semana móvil.

Conceptos y definiciones:
Empleo: Comprende a las personas que ejercieron una ocupación remunerada en dinero, productos, mercancías o beneficios y a las personas que ejercieron una ocupación no remunerada por al menos 15 horas en la semana, ya sea ayudando a un miembro del hogar en su actividad económica, ayudando a una institución religiosa, de beneficiencia o cooperativa, o como aprendiz. Se incluyeron a todas las personas que trabajaron durante toda o parte de la semana de referencia, y a las que no trabajaron durante la semana de referencia por razones tales como vacaciones, licencias, huelgas, etc.
Desempleo: Comprende a las personas no ocupadas que estaban disponibles para trabajar y que habían tomado pasos concretos para obtener un empleo en la semana de referencia.
Subempleo:
Subempleo por insuficiencia de horas: No información.
Situaciones de empleo inadecuado: No información.
Horas de trabajo: Se obtiene el número de horas efectivamente trabajadas en la semana de referencia en el empleo principal y separadamente en los otros empleos de esa semana. Se registran las horas enteras, considerando treinta minutos o más como una hora entera y despreciando un período inferior a treinta minutos.
Ingresos relacionados con el empleo:
Ingresos relacionados con el empleo asalariado: Se obtiene el ingreso en dinero, o productos o mercaderías en la rama agrícola, que se recibieron efectivamente en el mes de referencia en el trabajo principal y separadamente en los demás trabajos de la semana de referencia. Se registra en reales, despreciando los centavos. Para el asalariado se obtiene la remuneración bruta del trabajo efectivamente recibida durante el mes de referencia, incluyendo el 13er y 14to salario, y otros montos adicionales al salario u otro ingreso del trabajo tales como indemnizaciones, primas, propinas, participaciones en los beneficios, etc. Para el asalariado con indemnizaciones de un instituto de seguridad social federal, estatal o municipal se investiga el ingreso bruto del beneficio efectivamente recibido durante el mes de referencia (indemnización por enfermedad, accidentes del trabajo, etc.). Para el empleado que recibe productos o mercancías se investiga el valor de mercado de los productos o mercaderías efectivamente recibido durante el mes de referencia.
Ingresos relacionados con el empleo independiente: Para el trabajador por cuenta propia o empleador se obtiene el beneficio o ganancia líquida efectivamente recibido durante el mes de referencia, esto es, el ingreso bruto descontando los gastos operativos de la empresa tales como los salarios de los empleados, materias primas, energía eléctrica, teléfono, etc. Para el trabajador por cuenta propia o empleador indemnizado por un instituto de seguridad social federal, estatal o municipal se obtiene el ingreso bruto del beneficio efectivamente recibido durante el mes de referencia (indemnización por enfermedad, accidentes del trabajo, etc.). Para el trabajador por cuenta propia o empleador que recibe productos o mercancías se obtiene el valor de mercado de los productos o mercancías efectivamente recibidos durante el mes de referencia.
Sector informal: No información.
Actividad habitual: No información.
Clasificaciones:
Rama de actividad económica (industria):
Titulo de la clasificación utilizada: No información.
Grupos de población clasificados por industria: Los ocupados se clasifican de acuerdo a la rama de actividad de su empleo principal.
Número de Grupos utilizados para la codificación: 169 para codificación, 5 para divulgación.
Vínculos con la CIIU: CIIU-Rev 2.
Ocupación:
Titulo de la clasificación utilizada: No información.
Grupos de población clasificados por ocupación: Los ocupados se clasifican de acuerdo a la ocupación de su empleo principal; los desocupados e inactivos que buscaron trabajo en los últimos 23 días se clasifican de acuerdo a su último trabajo remunerado.
Número de Grupos utilizados para la codificación: 381.
Vínculos con la CIUO: CIUO-1968.
Situación en el empleo:
Titulo de la clasificación utilizada: No información.
Grupos de población clasificados por situación en el empleo: Los ocupados se clasifican de acuerdo a la situación en el empleo de su empleo principal; los desocupados e inactivos que buscaron trabajo en los últimos 23 días se clasifican de acuerdo a su último trabajo remunerado.
Grupos utilizados para la codificación: Empleador, cuenta propia, empleado y no remunerados

Vínculos con la CISE: CISE-1993.
Educación:
Titulo de la clasificación utilizada: No información.
Grupos de población clasificados por educación: Ocupados
Grupos utilizados para la codificación: Sin instrucción, 1er a 3er año completo de enseñanza fundamental o equivalente, 4to a 7mo año completo de enseñanza fundamental o equivalente; enseñanza fundamental o equivalente completa; enseñanza media o equivalente incompleta; enseñanza media o equivalente completa; superior incompleto; superior completo.
Vínculos con la CINE: No.
Tamaño y diseño de la muestra:
Unidad final de la muestreo: La vivienda particular o la unidad de habitación en los domicilios colectivos.
Tamaño de la muestra (unidades finales de muestreo): 5120 en la región metropolitana de Recife.
Fracción de muestreo: 1/430 para la región metropolitana de Río de Janeiro, 1/6 000 para la región metropolitana de Sao Paulo, 1/170 para las regiones metropolitanas de Recife, Salvador, Belo Horizonte, Curitiba y Porto Alegre.
Marco de la muestra: Marco geográfico y medidas de tamaño para la selección de la muestra basado en el Censo Demográfico de 1991.
Actualización de la muestra: Se actualiza con frecuencia anual llevando a cabo una operación de listado de todos los sectores (que son subdivisiones de los municipios para fines estadísticos) seleccionados en la muestra. Esta operación de listado consiste en relacionar ordenadamente todas las unidades residenciales y no residenciales que existen en el área. Además de la actualización del marco básico se creó un marco complementario de nuevas construcciones, constituido por grupos (tales como conjuntos residenciales, edificios y favelas) con al menos 30 viviendas surgidos después del Censo Demográfico en los sectores (seleccionados o no) de los municipios pertenecientes a la muestra, lo cual sirve para evaluar su crecimiento. Este marco de nuevas construcciones también se actualiza anualmente.
Rotación:
Esquema: Cada mes se sustituye un cuarto de las viviendas seleccionadas en la muestra. Una unidad permanece en la muestra cuatro meses consecutivos, se reitra de la muestra los siguientes ocho meses y se reintegra por la última ves por cuatro meses más. Operacionalmente se distribuyen los sectores aleatoriamente en cuatro grupos, correspondientes a cada una de las semanas del mes. En cada sector se retiran sistemáticamente varias submuestras. Se fijan cuatro semanas de entrevistas y en cada una se entrevista a un cuarto de la muestra del mes. En este esquema 75% de las viviendas seleccionadas para la muestra de un mes son las mismas que las del mes anterior y en el mismo mes de dos años sucesivos alternadamente hay una concordancia del 100% de las unidades seleccionadas en la muestra o ninguna concordancia. En ningún mes es la muestra totalmente nueva.
Porcentaje de unidades que permanecen en la muestra durante dos encuestas consecutivas: 75%.
Número máximo de entrevistas por unidad de muestreo: 8 meses.
Tiempo necesario para renovar completamente la muestra: 1 año y cuatro meses.
Levantamiento da la encuesta:
Tipo de entrevista: Entrevista personal escritas a lápiz en papel.
Número de unidades finales de muestreo por área de muestra: Cada mes, la muestra del conjunto de las siete regiones metropolitanas cubiertas por la encuesta está constituida por 45 267 viviendas.
Duración del trabajo de campo:
Total: 4 semanas
Por área de muestra: No información.
Organización de la encuesta: Personal permanente.
Número de personas que trabajan en el campo: 408 personas.
Substitución de las unidades finales de muestreo que no responden: No.
Estimaciones y ajustes:
Tasa de no-respuesta total: 2.5%.
Ajuste por no-respuesta total: Para la imputación de la no-respuesta se utiliza el método de "hot-deck", excepto para las variables de ingreso para las cuales no se efectúa una imputación.
Imputación por no respuesta de ítemes: No.
Ajuste por áreas/poblaciones no abarcadas: No.
Ajuste por falta de cobertura: No.
Ajuste por exceso de cobertura: No.
Ajuste por variaciones estacionales: Las tasas de desocupación se ajustan por las variaciones estacionales utilizando un método interactivo de medias móviles, implementado con el X-12-ARIMA.
Historia de la encuesta:
Titulo y fecha de la primera encuesta: Encuesta Mensual del Empleo (PME) se inició en enero de 1980 con el objetivo de producir indicadores mensuales sobre la fuerza de trabajo para evaluar las fluctuaciones y la tendencia, a mediano y largo plazo, del mercado de trabajo en las nuevas regiones metropolitanas existentes en la época (Belén, Fortaleza, Salvador, Belo Horizonte, Río de Janeiro, Sao Paulo, Curitiba y Porto Alegre) y en el Distrito Federal.
Modificaciones y revisiones significativas: No información.
Documentación y difusión:
Documentación:
Resultados de la encuesta: No información.
Metodología de la encuesta: No información.
Difusión:
Tiempo necesario para difundir los primeros datos: No información.
Información adelantada acerca de la fecha de la primera difusión pública: No información.
Disponibilidad de datos no publicados si se solicitan: No información.
Disponibilidad de datos por medios informáticos: sitio web: http://www.ibge.gov.br/ .

Bulgaria

Título de la encuesta: Encuesta sobre la Fuerza de Trabajo (Labour Force Survey)
Organismo responsable de la encuesta:
Planificar y realizar la encuesta: Instituto Nacional de Estadísticas
Analizar y publicar los resultados: Instituto Nacional de Estadísticas
Temas abarcados: Empleo, desempleo, subempleo, horas de trabajo, duración del desempleo, trabajadores desalentados, rama de actividad económica (industria), ocupación, situación en el empleo y nivel de educación.
Alcance de la encuesta:
Ámbito geográfico: Todo el país.
Grupos de población: Todos los residentes habituales, de 15 años y más de edad que no viven en hogares colectivos, incluidas las personas que se encuentran temporalmente ausentes.
Disponibilidad de estimaciones de otras fuentes para las áreas/grupos excluidos: No.
Grupos abarcados por la encuesta pero excluidos de los resultados publicados: Ninguno.
Periodicidad:
Recolección de datos: Desde 2000, encuesta trimestral realizada en marzo, junio, septiembre y diciembre. Antes se realizaba tres veces al año.
Publicación de los resultados: Desde 2000: trimestralmente. Antes: cada dos años.
Períodos de referencia:
Empleo: Una semana antes de la fecha de la entrevista.
Búsqueda de trabajo: Cuatro semanas antes de la fecha de entrevista.
Disponibilidad para trabajo: Dos semanas después de la fecha de la entrevista.
Conceptos y definiciones:
Empleo: Empleados son todas las personas de 15 años y más de edad que, durante el periodo de referencia: a) realizaban un trabajo por lo menos de una hora por una remuneración o un beneficio (en efectivo o en especie); b) no trabajaban pero tenían un empleo o una empresa de los que se encontraban temporalmente ausentes debido a licencia, enfermedad, mal tiempo, licencia para capacitación profesional u otra razón similar.
Se consideran empleados todas las personas que tienen un empleo remunerado; tienen en funcionamiento su propia empresa, negocio o explotación agrícola; realizan un trabajo independiente por un beneficio y las personas que trabajan sin remuneración en una empresa propiedad de un familiar, miembro del mismo hogar (por una hora como mínimo) así como los miembros de carrera de las fuerzas armadas. Las personas con licencia por maternidad se consideran como empleadas únicamente durante el tiempo de la licencia totalmente remunerado (135 días de calendario), sino se estima que están fuera de la fuerza laboral.
Desempleo: Desempleadas son todas las personas de 15 años y más de edad que no trabajaban durante la semana de referencia,

estaban buscando activamente trabajo durante las cuatro semanas anteriores a la entrevista y estaban disponibles para comenzar a trabajar dentro de las dos semanas siguientes a la semana de la entrevista. Se incluían también como desempleadas todas las personas que no estaban buscando activamente trabajo porque esperaban reintegrarse a su antiguo empleo del que estaban dispensadas o con licencia sin goce de sueldo (si la duración total de la ausencia es más de un mes), siempre que tuvieran la promesa del empleador y una fecha concreta para reintegrarse al trabajo, así como estudiantes de dedicación a tiempo completo o parcial que buscaban trabajo a tiempo completo o parcial.

Subempleo:

Subempleo por insuficiencia de horas: Personas que generalmente trabajaban a tiempo parcial debido a razones económicas.

Situaciones de empleo inadecuado: No corresponde.

Horas de trabajo: Horas habituales trabajadas en el empleo principal y horas reales trabajadas separadamente en los empleos principal y secundario.

Ingresos relacionados con el empleo:

Ingresos relacionados con el empleo asalariado: No corresponde.

Ingresos relacionados con el empleo independiente: No corresponde.

Sector informal: No corresponde.

Actividad habitual: No corresponde.

Clasificaciones:

Rama de actividad económica (industria):

Título de la clasificación utilizada: Clasificación nacional.

Grupos de población clasificados por industria: Personas empleadas y personas no empleadas con experiencia previa de trabajo durante los últimos 8 años.

Número de Grupos utilizados para la codificación: 503.

Vínculos con la CIIU: CIIU-Rev.3 a nivel de tres dígitos.

Ocupación:

Título de la clasificación utilizada: Clasificación nacional.

Grupos de población clasificados por ocupación: Personas empleadas y personas no empleadas con experiencia previa de trabajo durante los últimos 8 años.

Número de Grupos utilizados para la codificación: 550.

Vínculos con la CIUO: CIUO-88 a nivel de tres dígitos.

Situación en el empleo:

Título de la clasificación utilizada: Clasificación nacional.

Grupos de población clasificados por situación en el empleo: Personas empleadas y personas no empleadas con experiencia previa de trabajo durante los últimos 8 años.

Grupos utilizados para la codificación: 5 grupos (empleados, empleadores, trabajadores por cuenta propia, miembros de cooperativas productivas y trabajadores familiares sin remuneración).

Vínculos con la CISE: CISE-1993.

Educación:

Título de la clasificación utilizada: Clasificación nacional.

Grupos de población clasificados por educación: Toda la población de 15 años y más de edad.

Grupos utilizados para la codificación: 8 grupos (primaria, secundaria inferior, profesional, secundaria general, secundaria profesional, secundaria especializada, superior no completada (estudios superiores), superior (universidad).

Vínculos con la CINE: CINE-97.

Tamaño y diseño de la muestra:

Unidad final de muestreo: Hogar.

Tamaño de la muestra (unidades finales de muestreo): Unos 24 000 hogares.

Fracción de muestreo: 0,8 por ciento.

Marco de la muestra: Censo de la población.

Actualización de la muestra: Anualmente.

Rotación:

Esquema: 2-2-2.

Porcentaje de unidades que permanecen en la muestra durante dos encuestas consecutivas: 50 por ciento

Número máximo de entrevistas por unidad de muestreo: Cuatro.

Tiempo necesario para renovar completamente la muestra: Cuatro años.

Levantamiento da la encuesta:

Tipo de entrevista: Papel y lápiz.

Número de unidades finales de muestreo por área de muestra: 12 hogares por distrito de enumeración.

Duración del trabajo de campo:

Total: Una semana calendario (7 días).

Por área de muestra: Una semana calendario (7 días).

Organización de la encuesta: Encuesta permanente.

Número de personas que trabajan en el campo: Unos 800 entrevistadores y 140 supervisores.

Substitución de las unidades finales de muestreo que no responden: No.

Estimaciones y ajustes:

Tasa de no-respuesta total: del 12 al 15 por ciento.

Ajuste por no-respuesta total: No.

Imputación por no respuesta de ítemes: No.

Ajuste por áreas/poblaciones no abarcadas: No.

Ajuste por falta de cobertura: No.

Ajuste por exceso de cobertura: No.

Ajuste por variaciones estacionales: No.

Historia de la encuesta:

Título y fecha de la primera encuesta: Encuesta sobre la Fuerza de Trabajo (Labour Force Survey), de septiembre de 1993.

Modificaciones y revisiones significativas: En 1994, la encuesta se realizó en dos rondas (junio y octubre). A partir de 1995 hasta 2000, la encuesta se realizaba tres veces al año y el tamaño de la muestra se había reducido de 30 000 a 24 000 hogares. Desde 2000 se realizan encuestas trimestralmente. A partir de 2001, se han hecho importantes modificaciones en el cuestionario.

Documentación y difusión:

Documentación

Título de las publicaciones con los resultados de la encuesta: (periodicidad): Reference Book of the Republic of Bulgaria (anualmente); (Employment and Unemployment (bianual); Anuario de Estadísticas.

Título de las publicaciones con la metodología de la encuesta: (periodicidad): Employment and Unemployment (bianual); Anuario de Estadísticas.

Difusión:

Tiempo necesario para difundir los primeros datos: 52 días después del periodo de referencia de la encuesta.

Información adelantada acerca de la fecha de la primera difusión pública: Sí.

Disponibilidad de datos no publicados si se solicitan: Sí.

Disponibilidad de datos por medios informáticos: En disquetes e Internet (información seleccionada). Sitio web: http://www.nsi.bg.

Canadá

Título de la encuesta: Encuesta sobre la Fuerza de Trabajo (Labour Force Survey).

Organismo responsable de la encuesta:

Planificar y realizar la encuesta: Estadísticas del Canadá (Statistics Canada).

Analizar y publicar los resultados: Estadísticas del Canadá (Statistics Canada).

Temas abarcados: Personas corriente y económicamente activas, empleadas y desempleadas; personas subempleadas por insuficiencia de horas y personas fuera de la fuerza de trabajo; trabajadores desalentados; horas de trabajo; duración del empleo y el desempleo; salarios; empleos secundarios; rama de actividad económica (industria); ocupación; situación en el empleo; nivel de educación/calificación.

Alcance de la encuesta:

Ámbito geográfico: Se excluyen el Yukón (se recopilan datos, pero no se incluyen en las estimaciones nacionales), Territorios del Noroeste, Nunavut y reservas indígenas.

Grupos de población: Población civil que no vive en hogares colectivos, de 15 años y más de edad, excluidos miembros a tiempo completo de las Fuerzas Armadas de Canadá y detenidos en instituciones penitenciarias.

Disponibilidad de estimaciones de otras fuentes para las áreas/grupos excluidos: Estimaciones para el Yukón como media móvil de tres meses.

Grupos abarcados por la encuesta pero excluidos de los resultados publicados: Yukón, véase más arriba.

Periodicidad:

Recolección de datos: Mensualmente

Publicación de los resultados: Mensualmente, el primer o segundo viernes del mes después del mes del periodo de referencia.

Períodos de referencia:

Empleo: Semana que incluye el 15º día del mes.

Búsqueda de trabajo: Las últimas cuatro semanas anteriores a la entrevista.

Disponibilidad para trabajo: La semana de referencia que incluye el 15º día del mes.

Conceptos y definiciones:
Empleo: Son personas empleadas las que tienen 15 años y más de edad que, durante la semana de referencia:
a) efectuaban cualquier clase de trabajo en un empleo o negocio, es decir, un trabajo remunerado en el contexto de una relación empleador-trabajador, o una actividad laboral independiente. Se incluye también a trabajadores familiares no remunerados, cuando contribuyan directamente al funcionamiento de una explotación agrícola, empresa u oficina cuya propiedad y administración corresponde a un familiar que forma parte del mismo hogar; o,
b) tenían un trabajo pero estaban ausentes del mismo debido a enfermedad o incapacidad, responsabilidades familiares o personales, vacaciones, conflicto laboral u otras razones (excluidas las personas suspendidas, entre empleos ocasionales y los que tenían un empleo para comenzar en una fecha futura).
Desempleo: Son desempleadas las personas de 15 años y más de edad que, durante la semana de referencia:
a) estaban suspendidas temporalmente de su trabajo durante la semana de referencia con posibilidad de reintegrarse y estaban disponibles para trabajar, o
b) estaban sin trabajo, habían buscado activamente empleo en las últimas cuatro semanas y estaban disponibles para trabajar, o
c) tenían un nuevo empleo que debían comenzar dentro de las cuatro semanas siguientes a la semana de referencia y estaban disponibles para trabajar.
Subempleo:
Subempleo por insuficiencia de horas: No se proporcionó información.
Situaciones de empleo inadecuado: No se proporcionó información.
Horas de trabajo: Las horas realmente trabajadas incluyen tanto las horas de trabajo remuneradas como no remuneradas. Las horas de trabajo habituales para empleados asalariados se refieren a las que normalmente se pagan u horas de contrato, no se tienen en cuenta las horas extraordinarias, pero para los empleados independientes se refiere al número de horas trabajadas en una semana típica.
Ingresos relacionados con el empleo:
Ingresos relacionados con el empleo asalariado: Los empleados asalariados informan sobre su salario/sueldo antes de las deducciones fiscales y de otro tipo, e incluyen propinas, comisiones y bonificaciones del empleo principal.
Ingresos relacionados con el empleo independiente: No se proporcionó información.
Sector informal: No corresponde.
Actividad habitual: No se proporcionó información.
Clasificaciones:
Rama de actividad económica (industria):
Título de la clasificación utilizada: Sistema de Clasificación Industrial de América del Norte (North American Industry Classification System (NAICS)).
Grupos de población clasificados por industria: Personas empleadas y desempleadas (si trabajaron en los últimos 12 meses).
Número de Grupos utilizados para la codificación: 312.
Vínculos con la CIIU: Vínculos indirectos con la CIIU-Rev.3.
Ocupación:
Título de la clasificación utilizada: Clasificación Normalizada de Ocupaciones de 1991 (Standard Occupational Classification 1991 (SOC-91)).
Grupos de población clasificados por ocupación: Personas empleadas y desempleadas (si trabajaron en los últimos 12 meses).
Número de Grupos utilizados para la codificación: 514.
Vínculos con la CIUO: Vínculos indirectos con la CIUO-88.
Situación en el empleo:
Título de la clasificación utilizada: Clasificación nacional, no se dan títulos.
Grupos de población clasificados por situación en el empleo: Personas empleadas y desempleadas (si trabajaron en los últimos 12 meses).
Grupos utilizados para la codificación: Empleados remunerados (se distingue entre privado y público) y trabajadores independientes (se distingue entre trabajadores de sociedades comerciales constituidas, sociedades comerciales no constituidas y trabajadores familiares no remunerados).
Vínculos con la CISE: CISE-1993.
Educación:
Título de la clasificación utilizada: Clasificación nacional, no se dan títulos.
Grupos de población clasificados por educación: Personas empleadas y desempleadas.
Grupos utilizados para la codificación: No se proporcionó información.
Vínculos con la CINE: Vínculos indirectos con la CINE-1976.
Tamaño y diseño de la muestra:
Unidad final de muestreo: Vivienda y hogar.
Tamaño de la muestra (unidades finales de muestreo): 61 000 viviendas; 53 500 hogares.
Fracción de muestreo: 1/240.
Marco de la muestra: Marco de área estratificado de etapas múltiples. Lista marco de edificios de apartamentos en grandes ciudades.
Actualización de la muestra: Proceso constante para tener en cuenta el crecimiento demográfico. Las principales modificaciones se hacen cada 10 años.
Rotación:
Esquema: Las viviendas permanecen en la muestra durante 6 meses consecutivos y luego se sustituyen.
Porcentaje de unidades que permanecen en la muestra durante dos encuestas consecutivas: 83,3 por ciento.
Número máximo de entrevistas por unidad de muestreo: No se proporcionó información.
Tiempo necesario para renovar completamente la muestra: No se proporcionó información.
Levantamiento de la encuesta:
Tipo de entrevista: Entrevistas asistidas por computadora, realizadas por teléfono y personales.
Número de unidades finales de muestreo por área de muestra: No se proporcionó información.
Duración del trabajo de campo:
Total: Una semana.
Por área de muestra: No se proporcionó información.
Organización de la encuesta: Permanente.
Número de personas que trabajan en el campo: 777 entrevistadores y 79 supervisores.
Substitución de las unidades finales de muestreo que no responden: No.
Estimaciones y ajustes:
Tasa de no-respuesta total: 5 por ciento.
Ajuste por no-respuesta total: Sí.
Imputación por no respuesta de ítemes: Sí, utilizando la respuesta del mes anterior, si se dispone, por un máximo de un mes. Imputación por asignación dinámica (hot deck).
Ajuste por áreas/poblaciones no abarcadas: No.
Ajuste por falta de cobertura: Sí.
Ajuste por exceso de cobertura: Sí.
Ajuste por variaciones estacionales: Sí, utilizando la versión X11-ARIMA de estadísticas del Canadá.
Historia de la encuesta:
Título y fecha de la primera encuesta: Encuesta sobre la Fuerza de Trabajo (Labour Force Survey), noviembre de 1945.
Modificaciones y revisiones significativas: a) En enero de 1997 se cambió la definición de horas de trabajo habituales para empleados asalariados; antes era la misma que para trabajadores independientes y abarcaba tanto las horas remuneradas como no remuneradas; b) las estimaciones se volvieron a calcular después de que tener disponibles las estimaciones del censo de población. Las estimaciones de la LFS se basan en las cifras del último censo de la población. La última revisión se realizó con los resultados de enero de 2000, para las estimaciones incluidas hasta 1976.
Documentación y difusión:
Documentación:
Título de las publicaciones con los resultados de la encuesta: Labour force information (Catálogo número 71-001-PPB) (periodicidad): (mensualmente).
Título de las publicaciones con la metodología de la encuesta: Guide to the Labour Force Survey (71-543-GIE); Methodology of the Canadian Labour Force Survey, diciembre de 1998 (71-526-XPB).
Difusión:
Tiempo necesario para difundir los primeros datos: Un mes.
Información adelantada acerca de la fecha de la primera difusión pública: Sí.
Disponibilidad de datos no publicados si se solicitan: Sí.
Disponibilidad de datos por medios informáticos: CD-ROM: Labour Force Historical Review (Catálogo 71F0004XCB) (anualmente, por lo general en febrero). Sitio web: http://www.statcan.ca/.

Colombia

Título de la encuesta: Encuesta Continua de Hogares

Organismo responsable de la encuesta:

Planificar y realizar la encuesta: Departamento Administrativo Nacional de Estadística (DANE).

Analizar y publicar los resultados: Departamento Administrativo Nacional de Estadística (DANE).

Temas abarcados: Empleo, desempleo, subempleo, horas de trabajo, salarios, ingresos, empleo en el sector informal, duración del empleo, duración del desempleo, trabajadores desalentados y ocasionales, ramas de actividad económica, ocupación, situación en el empleo, nivel de educación, actividad habitual, trabajos secundarios. Se han realizado módulos especiales acerca de los siguientes temas: vivienda, hogar, seguridad social en salud, trabajo voluntario y trabajo para el autoconsumo, actividades productivas del hogar, gastos y consumo de los hogares.

Alcance de la encuesta:

Ámbito geográfico: cobertura nacional con estimaciones separadas por zona urbana y rural, grandes regiones y total por departamento, además de estimaciones para trece ciudades y áreas metropolitanas. Bogotá, Medellín, Cali, Bucaramanga, Manizales, Pasto, Pereira, Cúcuta, Ibagué, Montería, Cartagena y Villavicencio. Excluye la población de los llamados Territorios Nacionales antes de la Constitución de 1991, en los cuales reside aproximadamente el 4% de la población.

Grupos de población: Toda la población residente.

Disponibilidad de estimaciones de otras fuentes para las áreas/grupos excluidos: No.

Grupos abarcados por le encuesta pero excluidos de los resultados publicados: Ninguno.

Periodicidad:

Recolección de datos: Continua y mensual.

Publicación de los resultados: Mensual, bimestral y trimestral.

Períodos de referencia:

Empleo: Una semana móvil.

Búsqueda de trabajo: Una semana, cuatro semanas y un año, móviles.

Disponibilidad para trabajo: Una semana móvil.

Conceptos y definiciones:

Empleo: Son las personas que durante el período de referencia se encontraban en una de las siguientes situaciones: (a) trabajaron por lo menos una hora remunerada en la semana de referencia; (b) no trabajaron la semana de referencia pero tenían un trabajo; (c) los trabajadores familiares sin remuneración que trabajaron en la semana de referencia por lo menos una hora.

Desempleo: Son las personas que en la semana de referencia se encontraban en una de las siguientes situaciones: (a) sin empleo en la semana de referencia pero hicieron alguna diligencia para conseguir trabajo en las últimas cuatro semanas y estaba disponibles para trabajar; (b) no hicieron diligencias en el último mes pero sí en los últimos 12 meses y tienen una razón válida de desaliento (por ejemplo: no hay trabajo disponible en la ciudad, están esperando que los llamen, no saben como buscar trabajo, están cansados de buscar trabajo, no encuentran trabajo apropiado en sus oficios o profesiones, están esperando la temporada alta, carecen de la experiencia necesaria, no tienen recursos para instalar un negocio, los empleadores los consideran muy jóvenes o muy viejos) y están disponibles para trabajar. Esta población se divide en dos grupos: los "cesantes" que son personas que trabajaron antes por lo menos dos semanas consecutivas, y los "aspirantes" que son personas que buscan trabajo por primera vez.

Subempleo:

Subempleo por insuficiencia de horas: Son los ocupados que desean trabajar más horas ya sea en su empleo principal o secundario, están disponibles para hacerlo, y tienen una jornada inferior a 48 horas semanales. Se obtiene también las horas adicionales que desean trabajar.

Situaciones de empleo inadecuado: Son los ocupados que desean cambiar el trabajo que tienen actualmente por razones relacionadas con la mejor utilización de sus capacidades o formación, para mejorar sus ingresos, etc. y están disponibles para hacerlo.

Horas de trabajo: Se obtiene el número de horas que trabaja normalmente la persona en su trabajo principal y las horas efectivamente trabajadas durante la semana de referencia en el empleo principal y separadamente en los otros empleos de esa semana.

Ingresos relacionados con el empleo:

Ingresos relacionados con el empleo asalariado: Están compuestos por el salario en dinero y en especie y los ingresos de empleo secundario.

Ingresos relacionados con el empleo independiente: Son las ganancias e ingresos de empleo secundario.

Sector informal: Son las personas que cumplen con las siguientes características: (a)laboran en establecimientos, negocios o empresas que ocupan hasta diez trabajadores en todas sus agencias y sucursales; (b) trabajan en el servicio doméstico o son trabajadores familiares sin remuneración; (c) trabajan por cuenta propia, excepto si son profesionales; (d) son empleadores con empresas de 10 o menos trabajadores (incluyéndose ellos); (e) no trabajan en el gobierno.

Actividad habitual: Se obtiene información acerca de la actividad en que las personas pasaron la mayor parte del tiempo durante la semana de referencia: trabajaron, buscaron trabajo, estudiaron, oficios del hogar, otra actividad, incapacitado para trabajar.

Clasificaciones:

Rama de actividad económica (industria):

Título de la clasificación utilizada: No información.

Grupos de población clasificados por industria: Ocupados y desocupados

Número de Grupos utilizados para la codificación: 444 clases, 186 grupos, 60 divisiones, 17 secciones.

Vínculos con la CIIU: CIIU-Rev.3.

Ocupación:

Título de la clasificación utilizada: No información.

Grupos de población clasificados por ocupación: Ocupados y desocupados.

Número de Grupos utilizados para la codificación: Se codifica a 2 dígitos pero se presentan los datos para 8 grupos de ocupación.

Vínculos con la CIUO: CIUO-1968.

Situación en el empleo:

Título de la clasificación utilizada: No información.

Grupos de población clasificados por situación en el empleo: Ocupados y desocupados

Grupos utilizados para la codificación: Obrero, empleado particular; obrero, empleado del gobierno; empleado doméstico; trabajador por cuenta propia; patrón o empleador; trabajador familiar sin remuneración.

Vínculos con la ICSE: ICSE-1993.

Educación:

Título de la clasificación utilizada: No información.

Grupos de población clasificados por educación: Ocupados y desocupados

Grupos utilizados para la codificación: Ninguno; preescolar; primaria; secundaria; superior; no informa.

Vínculos con la CINE: CINE-1997.

Tamaño y diseño de la muestra:

Unidad final de muestreo: segmentos de 10 viviendas en promedio cada uno.

Tamaño de la muestra (unidades finales de muestreo): 2497 segmentos para trece ciudades con sus áreas metropolitanas en cada uno de los trimestres del año.

Fracción de muestra: No información.

Marco de la muestra: Muestra Maestra Nacional obtenida de la encuesta de cobertura del Censo de Población y Vivienda de 1993.

Actualización de la muestra: se utiliza cartografía digitalizada.

Rotación:

Esquema: ninguno.

Porcentaje de unidades que permanecen en la muestra durante dos encuestas consecutivas: No se aplica.

Número máximo de entrevistas por unidad de muestreo: No se aplica.

Tiempo necesario para renovar completamente la muestra: No se aplica.

Levantamiento da la encuesta: Tiempo necesario para renovar completamente la muestra

Tipo de entrevista: entrevista personal.

Número de unidades finales de muestreo **Por área de muestra:** 30 000 hogares aproximadamente en cada trimestre del año y 2 500 hogares en la encuesta nacional.

Duración del trabajo de campo:

Total: un trimestre

Por área de muestra: No información..

Organización de la encuesta: personal contratado para cada encuesta.

Número de personas que trabajan en el campo: 3 supervisores con 3 recolectores a cargo en cada una de las 7 principales ciudades; para las 9 ciudades restantes, dos supervisores con dos recolectores a su cargo cada uno.

Substitución de las unidades finales de muestreo que no responden: no.

Estimaciones y ajustes:
Tasa de no-respuesta total: 4% en las 13 principales ciudades y áreas metropolitanas
Ajuste por no-respuesta total: no.
Imputación por no-respuesta de ítemes: no.
Ajuste por áreas/poblaciones no abarcadas: no.
Ajuste por falta de cobertura: no.
Ajuste por exceso de cobertura: no.
Ajuste por variaciones estacionales: no.
Historia de la encuesta:
Título y fecha de la primera encuesta: Sistema de Encuestas de Hogares, de 1970 a 1975.
Modificaciones y revisiones significativas: A partir de 2000 se diseñó la Encuesta Continua de Hogares (ECH) utilizando las definiciones internacionales de la OIT y del Sistema de Cuentas Nacionales.
Documentación y difusión:
Documentación:
Resultados de la encuesta:
Boletín Mensual de Estadística
Boletín de Coyuntura Económica
20 años de la Encuesta Nacional de Hogares
Colombia Estadística
Boletines de Prensa e Informes de Empleo
Tabulados de Cuadros de Salida de Resultados (Bancos de Datos del DANE).
Metodológica de la encuesta: Documento: metodología de Encuesta Nacional de Hogares.
Difusión:
Tiempo necesario para difundir los primeros datos: No información. **Información adelantada acerca de la fecha de la primera difusión pública:** sí
Disponibilidad de datos no publicados si se solicitan: sí.
Disponibilidad de datos por medios informáticas: medio magnético e internet. Sitio web: http://www.dane.gov.co.

República de Corea

Título de la encuesta: Encuesta sobre la Población económicamente activa (Economically Active Population Survey).
Organismo responsable de la encuesta:
Planificar y realizar la encuesta: Oficina Nacional de Estadísticas (National Statistical Office).
Analizar y publicar los resultados: Oficina Nacional de Estadísticas (National Statistical Office).
Temas abarcados: Empleo, desempleo, horas de trabajo, duración del desempleo, rama de actividad económica (industria), ocupación, situación en el empleo, educación.
Alcance de la encuesta:
Ámbito geográfico: Todo el país.
Grupos de población: Personas de 15 años y más de edad que habitualmente residen en hogares privados dentro del territorio de la República de Corea en el momento de la entrevista.
Se excluyen miembros de las fuerzas armadas, prisioneros, población que vive en hogares colectivos, ciudadanos no residentes, extranjeros y personas que residen en el extranjero.
Disponibilidad de estimaciones de otras fuentes para las áreas/grupos excluidos: No.
Grupos abarcados por la encuesta pero excluidos de los resultados publicados: No.
Periodicidad:
Recolección de datos: Mensualmente.
Publicación de los resultados: Mensualmente.
Periodo de referencia:
Empleo: La semana que comprende el día 15 del mes.
Búsqueda de trabajo: La semana que comprende el día 15 del mes.
Disponibilidad para trabajo: La semana que comprende el día 15 del mes.
Conceptos y definiciones:
Empleo: Todas las personas de 15 años y más de edad que realizaron un trabajo remunerado o por un beneficio, por lo menos una hora, durante la semana de referencia y trabajadores familiares no remunerados que trabajaron 18 horas o más durante la semana de referencia.
Se incluyen:
a)personas con empleo por que estaban temporalmente ausentes del mismo debido a enfermedad o lesión, vacaciones o licencia anual, licencia por maternidad, paternidad o parental, licencia para estudios o capacitación, conflictos laborables, mal tiempo o desperfectos mecánicos;
b)trabajadores a tiempo completo o parcial que buscan otro empleo durante la semana de referencia; otras obligaciones familiares, conflictos laborales, desorganización temporal durante la semana de referencia;
c)personas que realizaron algún trabajo remunerado o por un beneficio durante la semana de referencia pero que estaban sometidas a escolaridad obligatoria, jubiladas y percibían una pensión, inscritas como desempleadas en busca de trabajo en una oficina de empleo, percibiendo indemnizaciones de desempleo;
d)estudiantes de dedicación completa o parcial que trabajaban a tiempo completo o parcial;
e)aprendices y personas en formación remunerados.
Se excluyen los miembros de las fuerzas armadas pese a que el servicio militar es obligatorio.
Desempleo: Todas las personas de 15 años y más de edad que no trabajaban pero estaban disponibles para hacerlo y buscaban trabajo activamente durante la semana de referencia. Además, desde 1999, la Oficina Nacional de Estadísticas recopila datos sobre las personas desempleadas que buscan trabajo durante un periodo de cuatro meses que incluye la semana de la encuesta.
"Buscar trabajo activamente" significa haber realizado una o más de las siguientes gestiones durante la semana de referencia: registrarse en una oficina de empleo, enviar los datos personales y profesionales, colocar o responder avisos relativos a empleos, visitar lugares de trabajo, ponerse en contacto con amigos o parientes, tomar disposiciones para establecer su propio negocio, etc.
"Disponibilidad para trabajar" se refiere a la disposición de la persona encuestada para aceptar de inmediato cualquier empleo apropiado que se le pueda proponer.
Se incluyen también las personas que buscaban trabajo y/o estaban disponibles para trabajar pero que estaban sometidas a escolaridad obligatoria, jubiladas y percibían una pensión y estudiantes de dedicación completa o parcial que buscaban trabajo a tiempo completo o parcial si estaban disponibles durante la semana de referencia.
Se excluyen los trabajadores estacionales en espera de la temporada agrícola o de otro trabajo de temporada; además, se les considera inactivos.
Subempleo:
Subempleo por insuficiencia de horas: No corresponde.
Situaciones de empleo inadecuado: No corresponde.
Horas de trabajo: Total de horas realmente trabajadas en el empleo principal durante la semana de referencia, incluidas horas extraordinarias y las dedicadas a la preparación, tales como notas para conferencias, poner en orden las mercancías, etc.
Se excluyen las horas que no están relacionadas con el empleo, como las pausas para comidas, desplazamientos desde el hogar hasta el sitio de trabajo y viceversa o por motivos privados.
Ingresos relacionados con el empleo:
Ingresos relacionados con el empleo asalariado: No corresponde.
Ingresos relacionados con el empleo independiente: No corresponde.
Sector informal: No corresponde.
Actividad habitual: No corresponde.
Clasificaciones:
Rama de actividad económica (industria):
Título de la clasificación utilizada: Clasificación Industrial Uniforme de Actividades Económicas de Corea (KSIC) de 1992
Grupos de población clasificados por industria: Empleados y desempleados.
Número de Grupos utilizados para la codificación: 60 divisiones (nivel de 2º dígito).
Vínculos con la CIIU: CIIU-Rev.3.
Ocupación:
Título de la clasificación utilizada: Clasificación Uniforme de Ocupaciones de Corea (KSOC) de 1993
Grupos de población clasificados por ocupación: Empleados y desempleados.
Número de Grupos utilizados para la codificación: 27 divisiones (nivel de 2º dígito).
Vínculos con la CIUO: CIUO-88.
Situación en el empleo:
Título de la clasificación utilizada: No se dispone de información.
Grupos de población clasificados por situación en el empleo: Empleados.

Grupos utilizados para la codificación: Empleados permanentes, empleados temporeros, jornaleros, empleadores, trabajadores por cuenta propia y trabajadores familiares no remunerados (6 grupos).
Vínculos con la CISE: CISE-1993.
Educación:
Título de la clasificación utilizada: No se dispone de información.
Grupos de población clasificados por educación: Empleados y desempleados.
Grupos utilizados para la codificación: Nunca asistieron a la escuela, escuela primaria, escuela media, escuela secundaria, escuela superior, universidad (6 grupos).
Vínculos con la CINE: CINE-1976.
Tamaño y diseño de la muestra:
Unidad final de muestreo: Hogares.
Tamaño de la muestra (unidades finales de muestreo): Unos 30 000 hogares.
Fracción de muestreo: Cerca de 1/430.
Marco de la muestra: Censo de Población y Hogares de 1995.
Actualización de la muestra: Cada 5 años, según los resultados del Censo.
Rotación:
Esquema: No corresponde.
Porcentaje de unidades que permanecen en la muestra durante dos encuestas consecutivas: No corresponde.
Número máximo de entrevistas por unidad de muestreo: No corresponde.
Tiempo necesario para renovar completamente la muestra: No corresponde.
Levantamiento de la encuesta:
Tipo de entrevista: A partir de 1999: CATI. Antes: CAPI.
Número de unidades finales de muestreo por área de muestra: Unos ocho hogares.
Duración del trabajo de campo:
Total: Dos semanas, incluida la semana de la encuesta.
Por área de muestra: Dos semanas, incluida la semana de la encuesta.
Organización de la encuesta: Enumeradores permanentes que trabajan a tiempo completo para las 47 oficinas regionales.
Número de personas que trabajan en el campo: Unas 530 personas.
Substitución de las unidades finales de muestreo que no responden: No.
Estimaciones y ajustes:
Tasa de no-respuesta total: 0,2 por ciento.
Ajuste por no-respuesta total: No.
Imputación por no respuesta de ítemes: No.
Ajuste por áreas/poblaciones no abarcadas: No.
Ajuste por falta de cobertura: No.
Ajuste por exceso de cobertura: No.
Ajuste por variaciones estacionales: Sí. A partir de enero de 1999, se utiliza el método X12-12 ARIMA.
Historia de la encuesta:
Título y fecha de la primera encuesta: Encuesta de la Población Económicamente Activa, 1963. Desde 1957, las estadísticas sobre la fuerza de trabajo se recopilan a través de la red local administrativa del Ministerio de Asuntos Internos.
Modificaciones y revisiones significativas: En 1998, se revisó el cuestionario de la encuesta para recoger y reflejar los cambios sociales, el patrón de actividad de la fuerza de trabajo e incluir las cuatro semanas de búsqueda de trabajo de las personas desempleadas, a fin de hacer comparaciones con otros países. Además, en junio de 1999, se revisaron las estimaciones de la Encuesta de la Población Económicamente Activa, basándose en el Censo de Población y Hogares de 1995, desde 1991 de forma retrospectiva.
Documentación y difusión:
Documentación:
Título de las publicaciones con los resultados de la encuesta (periodicidad): “Monthly Report on the Economically Active Population” y “Annual Report on the Economically Active Population” (mayo de cada año).
Título de las publicaciones con la metodología de la encuesta (periodicidad): “Monthly Report on the Economically Active Population” y “Annual Report on the Economically Active Population” (mayo de cada año).
Difusión:
Tiempo necesario para difundir los primeros datos: Un mes.
Información adelantada acerca de la fecha de la primera difusión pública: Sí.
Disponibilidad de datos no publicados si se solicitan: Sí.
Disponibilidad de datos por medios informáticos: Disquetes, cintas magnéticas y sitio web en Internet (http://www.nso.go.kr/).

Croacia

Título de la encuesta: Encuesta sobre la Fuerza de Trabajo (Labour Force Survey)
Organismo responsable de la encuesta:
Planificar y realizar la encuesta: Oficina Central de Estadísticas (Central Bureau of Statistics)
Analizar y publicar los resultados: : Oficina Central de Estadísticas (Central Bureau of Statistics)
Temas abarcados: Empleo, desempleo, subempleo, horas de trabajo, duración del empleo, duración del desempleo, trabajadores desalentados, trabajadores ocasionales, rama de actividad económica (industria), ocupación, situación en el empleo, nivel de educación y empleos secundarios.
Alcance de la encuesta:
Ámbito geográfico: Todo el país salvo los territorios ocupados durante la guerra de 1995-1996.
Grupos de población: Todos los residentes habituales, de 15 años y más de edad que no viven en hogares colectivos, incluidos los que estaban temporalmente ausentes. Se excluyen las personas que residen en el extranjero y los ciudadanos no residentes.
Disponibilidad de estimaciones de otras fuentes para las áreas/grupos excluidos: No.
Grupos abarcados por la encuesta pero excluidos de los resultados publicados: Ninguno
Periodicidad:
Recolección de datos: Continua.
Publicación de los resultados: Bianual.
Períodos de referencia:
Empleo: Última semana de cada mes, sin días de fiesta pública u otros días sin trabajar.
Búsqueda de trabajo: Cuatro semanas antes de la fecha de la entrevista.
Disponibilidad para trabajo: Dos semanas después de la fecha de la entrevista.
Conceptos y definiciones:
Empleo: empleados son todas las personas de 15 años y más de edad que, durante el periodo de referencia: a) habían realizado algún trabajo por una hora como mínimo por una remuneración en efectivo o en especie; b) no habían trabajado pero tenían la seguridad de reintegrarse al mismo empleo cuando ya no existiera la razón para estar ausente.
En los totales también se incluyen las personas que durante la semana de referencia:
a)estaban temporalmente ausentes del trabajo debido a licencia, enfermedad, mal tiempo, licencia para capacitación u otra razón similar.
b)trabajaban a tiempo completo o parcial y buscaban otro empleo durante el período de referencia;
c)estudiaban (dedicación completa o parcial) y trabajaban a tiempo completo o parcial;
d)realizaron algún trabajo durante la semana de referencia y estaban jubiladas y percibían una pensión; estaban inscritas como desempleados en busca de trabajo en una oficina de empleo o percibiendo indemnizaciones de desempleo;
f)trabajaban para la familia (trabajadores familiares) remunerados o no remunerados (si trabajaban por lo menos una hora);
g)trabajaban como servicios domésticos privados;
h)eran miembros de carrera de las fuerzas armadas que vivían en hogares;
i)estaban ocupadas en la producción de bienes para su propio uso final.
Desempleo: Son desempleadas todas las personas de 15 años y más de edad que no trabajaron durante la semana de referencia, estaban buscando de forma activa un empleo durante las cuatro semanas anteriores a la entrevista y estaban disponibles para comenzar a trabajar en las dos semanas posteriores a la semana de la encuesta. Se incluyen también como desempleadas las personas que no buscaban activamente un trabajo porque habían encontrado uno para comenzar en el futuro.
Subempleo:
Subempleo por insuficiencia de horas: Personas que, durante la semana de referencia, trabajaron menos horas que las reglamentarias, deseaban trabajar horas adicionales y estaban disponibles para hacerlo.
Situaciones de empleo inadecuado: Personas que, durante la semana de referencia:

a)deseaban cambiar el empleo que tenían y estaban disponibles para hacerlo porque trabajaban contra su voluntad menos horas que las reglamentarias;
b) deseaban cambiar de empleo debido al uso inadecuado de sus capacidades, las condiciones de trabajo no eran satisfactorias o tenían razones personales o de salud, etc.
Horas de trabajo: Horas habituales y reales trabajadas durante la semana de referencia en el empleo principal y horas reales trabajadas durante la semana de referencia en los empleos secundarios.
Ingresos relacionados con el empleo:
Ingresos relacionados con el empleo asalariado: Ingresos netos mensuales de cada persona entrevistada.
Ingresos relacionados con el empleo independiente: Ingresos netos mensuales de cada persona entrevistada.
Sector informal: No corresponde.
Actividad habitual: No corresponde.
Clasificaciones:
Rama de actividad económica (industria):
Título de la clasificación utilizada: Clasificación nacional.
Grupos de población clasificados por industria: Personas empleadas (en el empleo principal y empleos secundarios) y personas desempleadas con experiencia previa de trabajo.
Número de Grupos utilizados para la codificación: 571
Vínculos con la CIIU: CIIU-Rev.3.
Ocupación:
Título de la clasificación utilizada: Clasificación nacional.
Grupos de población clasificados por ocupación: Personas empleadas (en el empleo principal y empleos secundarios) y personas desempleadas con experiencia previa de trabajo.
Número de Grupos utilizados para la codificación: 402
Vínculos con la CIUO: CIUO-98.
Situación en el empleo:
Título de la clasificación utilizada: Clasificación nacional.
Grupos de población clasificados por situación en el empleo: Personas empleadas y desempleadas con experiencia previa en el trabajo.
Grupos utilizados para la codificación: 4 grupos (empleados, empleadores, trabajadores independientes, trabajadores familiares no remunerados).
Vínculos con la CISE: ICSE-1993.
Educación:
Título de la clasificación utilizada: Clasificación nacional.
Grupos de población clasificados por educación: Todas las personas de 15 años y más de edad.
Grupos utilizados para la codificación: 9 grupos (sin escolaridad, 4-7 años de escuela primaria, 1-2 años de escuela secundaria de capacitación, 3er año de escuela secundaria de capacitación, 4º año de escuela secundaria de capacitación, escuela de estudios superiores, universidad, postgrado, doctorado).
Vínculos con la CINE: Sí.
Tamaño y diseño de la muestra:
Unidad final de muestreo: Vivienda.
Tamaño de la muestra (unidades finales de muestreo): Unas 8 500 viviendas que representan 6 900 hogares y abarcan unas 20 000 personas.
Fracción de muestreo: 0,74 por ciento.
Marco de la muestra: A partir de 2002, el marco de la muestra se obtiene a partir de la base de datos del Censo de Población de 2001. Si bien para el periodo 1996-1999, el marco de la muestra principal básica se preparó con los datos del censo de población de 1991, actualizados en 1996, para 2000 y 2001 se basa en la base de datos de la Compañía de Energía Eléctrica de Croacia.
Actualización de la muestra: Actualizada en 2002 con los datos del Censo de Población de 2001.
Rotación:
Esquema: A partir de 2000 no se hace rotación. De 1996 a 1999, en cada una de las rondas de la encuesta (6 meses), se sacaba un tercio de la muestra de viviendas y se sustituía por nuevas viviendas, de manera que dos tercios de unidades se mantenían sin cambiar.
Porcentaje de unidades que permanecen en la muestra durante dos encuestas consecutivas: No corresponde.
Número máximo de entrevistas por unidad de muestreo: No se proporcionó información.
Tiempo necesario para renovar completamente la muestra: No se proporcionó información.
Levantamiento da la encuesta:
Tipo de entrevista: Papel y lápiz.
Número de unidades finales de muestreo por área de muestra: 12 hogares por distrito de enumeración.
Duración del trabajo de campo:
Total: 14 días después del periodo de referencia.
Por área de muestra: 14 días después del periodo de referencia.
Organización de la encuesta: La organización de la encuesta es permanente.
Number of field staff: Unos 203 entrevistadores y 31 supervisores.
Substitución de las unidades finales de muestreo que no responden: No.
Estimaciones y ajustes:
Tasa de no-respuesta total: 10 por ciento para la encuesta del primer semestre de 2001. Por lo general es de casi un 12 por ciento.
Ajuste por no-respuesta total: No.
Imputación por no respuesta de ítemes: No.
Ajuste por áreas/poblaciones no abarcadas: No.
Ajuste por falta de cobertura: No.
Ajuste por exceso de cobertura: No.
Ajuste por variaciones estacionales: No.
Historia de la encuesta:
Título y fecha de la primera encuesta: Encuesta sobre la Fuerza de Trabajo (Anketa o radno snazi), noviembre de 1996.
Modificaciones y revisiones significativas: Mejoras periódicas del cuestionario de la encuesta; actualización del marco de la muestra.
Documentación y difusión:
Documentación:
Título de las publicaciones con los resultados de la encuesta: (periodicidad): Primeras publicaciones: LFS – Labour Force Survey in the Republic of Croatia (bi-anual); LFS Results: comparison with the European Union results (anualmente); Statistical Year Book; Monthly Statistical Report.
Título de las publicaciones con la metodología de la encuesta: En todas las publicaciones antes mencionadas se incluye información metodológica pertinente.
Difusión
Tiempo necesario para difundir los primeros datos: Tres meses.
Información adelantada acerca de la fecha de la primera difusión pública: Sí.
Disponibilidad de datos no publicados si se solicitan: Sí.
Disponibilidad de datos por medios informáticos: Disquetes, CD-Rom e información seleccionada a través de Internet en el sitio web: http://www.dzs.hr/.

República Checa

Título de la encuesta: Encuesta por Muestra sobre la Fuerza de Trabajo (Labour Force Sample Survey)
Organismo responsable de la encuesta:
Planificar y realizar la encuesta: Oficina de Estadísticas (Czech Statistical Office).
Analizar y publicar los resultados: Oficina de Estadísticas (Czech Statistical Office).
Temas abarcados: Empleo, desempleo, subempleo, horas de trabajo, duración del empleo, duración del desempleo, trabajadores desalentados, trabajadores ocasionales, rama de actividad económica (industria), ocupación, situación en el empleo, nivel de educación, situación habitual en el empleo principal, empleos secundarios.
Alcance de la encuesta:
Ámbito geográfico: Todo el país.
Grupos de población: Toda la población de 15 años y más de edad que vive en hogares. Más específicamente, abarca todas las personas que viven en viviendas de manera continua por tres meses como mínimo, independientemente de la situación de su estadía en el mismo (permanente, temporal o no registrada). Se excluyen los reclutas que en la encuesta se incluyen en su lugar de residencia antes de realizar el servicio militar.
La encuesta no abarca las personas que viven en hogares colectivos durante un largo periodo de tiempo, razón por la cual son escasos algunos grupos de población (en particular, extranjeros que viven y trabajan en la el país).
Disponibilidad de estimaciones de otras fuentes para las áreas/grupos excluidos: No.
Grupos abarcados por la encuesta pero excluidos de los resultados publicados: Ninguno.
Periodicidad:
Recolección de datos: Continuamente.
Publicación de los resultados: Trimestralmente.

Períodos de referencia:
Empleo: Una semana (últimos siete días antes de la fecha de la entrevista).
Búsqueda de trabajo: Cuatro semanas antes de la fecha de la entrevista.
Disponibilidad para trabajo: Dos semanas después de la fecha de la entrevista.
Conceptos y definiciones:
Empleo: Todas las personas de 15 años y más de edad que, durante la semana de referencia, trabajaron por lo menos una hora, y estaban incluidas en las siguientes categorías:
a) empleados remunerados:
En el trabajo: personas que realizaron cualquier tipo de trabajo durante la semana de referencia por un salario o sueldo, en efectivo o en especie. El empleo puede ser permanente, temporal, estacional, ocasional o relativo al empleo principal o secundario;
Con un empleo pero no estaban en el lugar de trabajo: personas temporalmente ausentes de su trabajo, durante la semana de referencia, y que tenían un vínculo formal con su empleo, como un contrato de trabajo, etc.;
b) empleados en su propia empresa:
En el trabajo: personas que realizaron cualquier tipo de trabajo, durante la semana de referencia, para obtener beneficios o ingresos para la familia, en efectivo o en especie;
En su empresa pero no en el lugar de trabajo: personas con una empresa que estaban temporalmente ausentes del trabajo durante la semana de referencia por cualquier razón especifica.
En esta definición también se incluyen los miembros de las fuerzas armadas (miembros de carrera y reclutas) así como aprendices, estudiantes, personal doméstico, etc., que perciben un salario, un sueldo o una remuneración.
No obstante, las personas con licencia para ocuparse de sus hijos no se clasifican automáticamente como empleados.
Se excluyen las personas ocupadas en la producción de bienes para su propio hogar, tales como reparaciones, pintura, etc.
Desempleo: Todas las personas de 15 años y más de edad que cumplían con las tres condiciones siguientes durante la semana de referencia:
(i) no tenían empleo;
(ii) estaban buscando trabajo activamente. La búsqueda activa de trabajo incluye la inscripción en una oficina de empleo o de intercambio de empleo privado, la verificación en los sitios de trabajo, explotaciones agrícolas, mercados u otros sitios colectivos, contestar o publicar avisos en los diarios, tomar medidas para establecer su propio negocio, presentar solicitudes de permiso o licencia de trabajo, o buscar un empleo de otra manera, y
(iii) estaban disponibles para trabajar – es decir, estaban disponibles durante el periodo de referencia para realizar un trabajo remunerado o independiente inmediatamente o en las dos semanas después de la fecha de la entrevista.
Si las personas no cumplen una de las condiciones antes mencionadas, se clasifican como empleadas o inactivas. La única excepción se refiere a las personas que no buscaban trabajo, porque ya habían encontrado uno, pero comenzaban a trabajar en una fecha fija posterior. De acuerdo con la definición de Eurostat, esas personas se clasifican como desempleadas.
Subempleo:
Subempleo por insuficiencia de horas: Personas que, durante la semana de referencia, trabajaron involuntariamente menos que las horas normales de trabajo establecidas en un tipo de actividad determinada. Se excluyen las personas que sólo trabajaron cuatro semanas.
Situaciones de empleo inadecuado: No corresponde
Horas de trabajo: Horas habituales y reales trabajadas en el empleo principal. Horas reales trabajadas en empleos secundarios.
Ingresos relacionados con el empleo:
Ingresos relacionados con el empleo asalariado: No corresponde.
Ingresos relacionados con el empleo independiente: No corresponde.
Sector informal: No corresponde.
Actividad habitual: Se interrogan los siguientes grupos de población sobre su situación económica habitual: aprendices, estudiantes de escuelas secundarias, estudiantes universitarios, personas con licencia por maternidad y licencia para ocuparse de sus hijos (licencia parental), amas de casa, personas jubiladas, personas jubiladas por invalidez, desempleados, reclutas, personas ocupadas en servicios a la comunidad, niños menores de 15 años.
Clasificaciones:
Rama de actividad económica (industria):
Título de la clasificación utilizada: CZ-NACE.
Grupos de población clasificados por industria: Personas empleadas y desempleadas con experiencia previa de trabajo.
Número de Grupos utilizados para la codificación: No se proporcionó información.
Vínculos con la CIIU: CIIU-Rev.3 (nivel de 4 dígitos).
Ocupación:
Título de la clasificación utilizada: CZ-CIUO-88.
Grupos de población clasificados por ocupación: Personas empleadas y desempleadas con experiencia previa de trabajo.
Número de Grupos utilizados para la codificación: No se proporcionó información.
Vínculos con la CIUO: CIUO-88 (nivel de 4 dígitos).
Situación en el empleo:
Título de la clasificación utilizada: CZ-CISE.
Grupos de población clasificados por situación en el empleo: Personas empleadas y desempleadas.
Grupos utilizados para la codificación: 5 grupos (empleados, empleadores, trabajadores independientes, miembros de cooperativas de productores, trabajadores familiares.
Vínculos con la CISE: CISE-1993.
Educación:
Título de la clasificación utilizada: Clasificación Nacional de Temas de **Educación:** (National Classification of Education Subjects (KKOV)), 2ª edición, 1991 y CINE-1997.
Grupos de población clasificados por educación: todos los grupos de población.
Grupos utilizados para la codificación: No se proporcionó información.
Vínculos con la CINE: CINE-1997.
Tamaño y diseño de la muestra:
Unidad final de muestreo: Vivienda.
Tamaño de la muestra (unidades finales de muestreo): Unas 25 000 viviendas que abarcan unas 630 000 personas.
Fracción de muestreo: 0,6 por ciento de viviendas ocupadas permanentemente.
Marco de la muestra: El marco de la muestra se preparó basándose en el Censo de Población de 1991.
Actualización de la muestra: Trimestralmente.
Rotation:
Esquema: El grupo de viviendas seleccionadas varía durante la encuesta. Cada trimestre se hace la rotación de una quinta parte del grupo.
Porcentaje de unidades que permanecen en la muestra durante dos encuestas consecutivas: 80 por ciento.
Número máximo de entrevistas por unidad de muestreo: cinco cuartos.
Tiempo necesario para renovar completamente la muestra: cinco trimestres.
Levantamiento da la encuesta:
Tipo de entrevista: Papel y lápiz, teléfono y CAPI/CATI donde sea posible.
Número de unidades finales de muestreo por área de muestra: 300 viviendas por trimestre.
Duración del trabajo de campo:
Total: Continuamente.
Por área de muestra: Cada entrevistador trabaja 4 días por semana, más un día para los suplementos del cuestionario.
Organización de la encuesta: La organización de la encuesta es permanente.
Número de personas que trabajan en el campo: 113 entrevistadores y 14 supervisores.
Substitución de las unidades finales de muestreo que no responden: No.
Estimaciones y ajustes:
Tasa de no-respuesta total: 24 por ciento.
Ajuste por no-respuesta total: Sí.
Imputación por no respuesta de ítemes: No.
Ajuste por áreas/poblaciones no abarcadas: No.
Ajuste por falta de cobertura: No.
Ajuste por exceso de cobertura: No.
Ajuste por variaciones estacionales: No.
Historia de la encuesta:
Título y fecha de la primera encuesta: Encuesta por Muestra sobre la Fuerza de Trabajo (Czech Labour Force Sample Survey), diciembre de 1992.
Modificaciones y revisiones significativas: Desde 1993, la base de datos se ha corregido en el marco de la preparación de datos históricos. Más específicamente cabe señalar los siguientes cambios:

a) eliminación de diferencias en los periodos de referencia: todos los datos de 1993 a 1997, cuando la encuesta se realizaba en trimestres estacionales, se convirtieron a trimestres de calendario;
b) se incluyeron i) reclutas y ii) mujeres con licencia por maternidad o para el cuidado de sus hijos en los resultados de las encuestas de 1992 y 1993;
c) se volvieron a ponderar los datos de 1993 a 1996 de manera retrospectiva en base a los últimos datos demográficos;
d) armonización de todo el cuestionario de la encuesta con los cuestionarios de Eurostat para las rondas de encuesta que comenzaron en enero de 2002.
Documentación y difusión:
Documentación:
Título de las publicaciones con los resultados de la encuesta: (periodicidad) Employment and Unemployment in the Czech Republic as Measured by the Labour Force Survey (trimestralmente); Labour Market in the Czech Republic: Time series LFSS (1993-1999).
Título de las publicaciones con la metodología de la encuesta: Employment and Unemployment in the Czech Republic as Measured by the Labour Force Survey.
Difusión:
Tiempo necesario para difundir los primeros datos: No se proporcionó información.
Información adelantada acerca de la fecha de la primera difusión pública: Sí.
Disponibilidad de datos no publicados si se solicitan: Sí.
Disponibilidad de datos por medios informáticos: Disquetes, internet y correo electrónico. Sitio web: http://www.czso.cz/.

Chile

Título de la encuesta: Encuesta Nacional del Empleo.
Organismo responsable de la encuesta:
Planificar y realizar la encuesta: Departamento de Estadísticas de Hogares, Instituto Nacional de Estadísticas (INE)
Analizar y publicar los resultados: Departamento de Estadísticas de Hogares, Instituto Nacional de Estadísticas (INE)
Temas abracados: Empleo, desempleo, horas de trabajo, ingresos, ramas de actividad económica, ocupación, situación en el empleo, nivel de educación.
Alcance de la encuesta:
Ámbito geográfico: Cobertura nacional: urbano, grandes centros urbanos, resto del área urbana, rural, región, provincia.
Grupos de población: Toda la población del país residente en viviendas particulares, excluyendo a la población que habita en viviendas colectivas como hospitales, cárceles, conventos, cuarteles y otros, pero incluyendo a las personas que habitan en viviendas particulares dentro de dichos centros. Se excluye a los grupos de población residentes en Chile insular (Isla de Pascua e Isla Juan Fernández) y los residentes en las áreas de difícil acceso por razones de orden climático, topográfico o por ausencias de vías y medios de comunicación expeditos (representando el 1% del total de la población).
Disponibilidad de estimaciones de otras fuentes para las áreas/grupos excluidos: No información.
Grupos abarcados por la encuesta pero excluidos de los resultados publicados: No información.
Periodicidad:
Recolección de datos: Continua y mensual.
Publicación de los resultados: Trimestral.
Periodo de referencia:
Empleo: Una semana fija.
Búsqueda de trabajo: Dos meses fijo.
Disponibilidad para trabajo: No información.
Conceptos y definiciones:
Empleo: Comprende a las personas que trabajaron una hora o más como empleado u obrero por remuneración (sea éste sueldo, salario, jornal, comisión, pago en especies, etc.) o como empleador o cuenta propia, por utilidades o ganancias tales como: agricultores, comerciantes o como familiar no remunerado que trabaja 15 horas o más normalmente a la semana.
Desempleo: Comprende a las personas no ocupadas en la semana de referencia porque estaban (a) cesantes, es decir, deseaban trabajar y habían hecho esfuerzos para conseguir trabajo durante los dos meses precedentes a la fecha de la entrevista, habiendo trabajado anteriormente en un empleo regular, o (b) buscaban trabajo por primera vez, es decir, que deseaban trabajar e hicieron esfuerzos para conseguir trabajo durante dos meses anteriores a la fecha de la entrevista, pero que no tienen experiencia laboral. No se consulta por la disponibilidad para trabajar, pero sí por el período de búsqueda de trabajo y las medidas para encontrarlo.
Horas de trabajo:
Horas semanales normales: Son las horas que la persona trabaja normalmente en su empleo o actividad principal. Por lo general estas horas corresponden al horario que por contrato de trabajo, reglamento o convenio debe cumplir en su trabajo.
Horas semanales efectivas trabajadas: son las horas que la persona trabajó realmente en su empleo o actividad principal en la semana de referencia, descontadas las horas no trabajadas (vacaciones, licencias u otros permisos particulares) y sumadas las horas adicionales (horas extraordinarias).
Ingresos relacionados con el empleo:
Ingresos relacionados con el empleo: Se calculan netos y para todos los empleos que realiza la persona e incluye toda la población corriente y activa. Se utiliza un período de referencia de un año.
Ingresos relacionados con el empleo independiente: Se consulta el ingreso de todos los hogares y de las personas en ellos utilizando un período de referencia de un año.
Sector informal: No información.
Actividada habitual: No información.
Clasificaciones:
Rama de actividad económica (industria):
Título de la clasificación utilizada: No información.
Grupos de población clasificados por industria: Empleados y desempleados.
Número de Grupos utilizados para la codificación: 29 alfanuméricos.
Vínculos con la CIIU: CITU Rev. 2 y Rev.3.
Ocupación:
Título de la clasificación utilizada: No información.
Grupos de población clasificados por ocupación: Empleados y desempleados
Número de Grupos utilizados para la codificación: Se codifica utilizando dos dígitos pero se presentan solo para 10 grupos ocupacionales.
Vínculos con la CIUO: CIUO-88; con la COTA 70 revisada para el programa del Censo de Población de Chile, 1982.
Situación en el empleo:
Título de la clasificación utilizada: No información.
Grupos de población clasificados por situación en el empleo: Empleados y desempleados.
Grupos utilizados para la codificación: Empleador o patrón; trabajador por cuenta propia, independiente; asalariado sector privado (empleado, obrero, jornalero); asalariado sector público; personal de servicio doméstico puertas adentro; personal de servicio doméstico puertas afuera; familiar no remunerado.
Vínculos con la CISE: CISE-1993.
Educación:
Título de la clasificación utilizada: No información.
Grupos de población clasificados por educación: Empleados, desempleados e inactivos.
Grupos utilizados para la codificación: Kinder, Básica o primaria, Media común, Media técnico, Profesional, Humanidades, Normal, Centro de formación técnica, Instituto Profesional, Universidad.
Vínculos con la CINE: No.
Tamaño y diseño de la muestra:
Unidad final de muestreo: Vivienda particular ocupada dentro de las secciones. La unidad de información o análisis es la persona de 15 años y más.
Tamaño de la muestra (unidades finales de muestreo): 37 326 viviendas distribuidas en 149 estratos o áreas geográficas en 3 462 secciones.
Fracción de muestreo: 1%.
Marco de la muestra: Información registrada en el Precenso de 1991 y actualizada con los datos del Censo de Población y Vivienda de 1992.
Actualización de la muestra: El proceso es continuo, permitiendo incorporar periódicamente a las personas y hogares que ocupan nuevas viviendas en el período, dándoles una probabilidad positiva de pertenecer a la muestra. También se realiza una actualización por nuevas construcciones que permite mantener el tamaño original de la muestra, dividiendo aquellas secciones que han crecido en más de un 300% asegurando así la validez de la información recogida.
Rotación:
Esquema: La muestra de unidades de primera etapa (secciones) permanecerá fija indefinidamente. Las unidades de segunda etapa

(viviendas) dentro de cada sección solo se mantendrán durante seis períodos de encuesta consecutivos en las áreas urbanas y doce en las áreas rurales.
Porcentaje de unidades que permanecen en la muestra durante dos encuestas consecutivas: 100%.
Número máximo de entrevistas por unidad de muestreo: 6 o 12.
Tiempo necesario para renovar completamente la muestra: 1 año y seis meses (parte urbana) y 3 años (parte rural)
Levantamiento da la encuesta:
Tipo de entrevista: Entrevista personal escritas a lápiz en papel.
Número de unidades finales de muestreo por área de muestra: Permanece en la muestra 1/6 parte de las secciones urbanas y ½ de las secciones rurales cada trimestre.
Duración del trabajo de campo:
Total: Mensual.
Por área de muestra: No información.
Organización de la encuesta: Personal permanente.
Número de personas que trabajan en el campo: 88 encuestadores y 14 supervisores.
Substitución de las unidades finales de muestreo que no responden: No.
Estimaciones y ajustes:
Tasa de no-respuesta total: 10%.
Ajuste por no-respuesta total: No.
Imputación por no repuesta de ítemes: No.
Ajuste por áreas/poblaciones no abarcadas: No.
Ajuste por falta de cobertura: No.
Ajuste por exceso de cobertura: No.
Ajuste por variaciones estacionales: Sí.
Historia de la encuesta:
Título y fecha de la primera encuesta: Encuesta Nacional del Empleo 1966 (basada en una muestra nacional de hogares diseñada con los antecedentes originados en el Censo Nacional de Población y Vivienda de 1960). Una única publicación (julio-diciembre 1966)
Modificaciones y revisiones significativas: En los años 1972 a 1973 no se realizaron encuestas a nivel nacional, por problemas internos del país.
Documentación y difusión:
Documentación:
Título de las publicaciones con los resultados de la encuesta: Indicadores de empleo por sexo y grupos de edad (anual); Total nacional, enero-marzo 1996 a octubre-diciembre 2000; Indicadores de Empleo (mensual).
Título de las publicaciones con la metodología de la encuesta: Metodología de la Encuesta Nacional del Empleo, 1996; Manual del Encuestador, 1998.
Difusión:
Tiempo necesario para difundir los primeros datos: 1 mes.
Información adelantada acerca de la fecha de la primera difusión pública: Sí.
Disponibilidad de datos no publicados si se solicitan: Sí.
Disponibilidad de datos por medios informáticos: Publicación en medios magnéticos de 43 tabulados generados mensualmente, por trimestre móvil (mensual),
disquette, cinta magnética, internet. Sitio web: http://www.ine.cl.

China

Título de la encuesta: Encuesta por Muestra sobre la Fuerza de Trabajo Urbana (Urban Labour Force Sampling Survey)
Organismo responsable de la encuesta:
Planificar y realizar la encuesta: Departamento de Estadísticas de la Población, Sociales y Ciencias y Tecnología de las Estadísticas (Department of Population, Social, Science and Technology Statistics)
Analizar y publicar los resultados: Departamento de Estadísticas de la Población, Sociales y Ciencias y Tecnología de las Estadísticas (Department of Population, Social, Science and Technology Statistics)
Temas abarcados: Empleo, desempleo, horas de trabajo, tipo de permiso de residencia, duración del desempleo, situación en el empleo y nivel de educación.
Alcance de la encuesta:
Ámbito geográfico: Zonas urbanas del país.
Grupos de población: Todas las personas de 16 años y más de edad, excluidos los miembros de las fuerzas armadas y extranjeros.
Disponibilidad de estimaciones de otras fuentes para las áreas/grupos excluidos: Disponible para las fuerzas armadas únicamente.
Grupos abarcados por la encuesta pero excluidos de los resultados publicados: Los desempleados.
Periodicidad:
Recolección de datos: Tres veces al año.
Publicación de los resultados: Anualmente, para algunas variables.
Períodos de referencia:
Empleo: Una semana.
Búsqueda de trabajo: Tres meses antes de la fecha de la entrevista.
Disponibilidad para trabajo: Dos semanas después de la fecha de la entrevista.
Conceptos y definiciones:
Empleo: Todas las personas que viven en zonas urbanas, de una determinada edad y que perciben ingresos al estar ocupadas en actividades económicas, es decir: 1) personas de 16 años y más de edad que trabajaron una hora como mínimo durante la semana de referencia por un ingreso y 2) personas con una unidad de trabajo o un sitio de trabajo pero que estaban temporalmente ausentes del mismo durante la semana de referencia por ser día de fiesta, vacaciones, estudios u otra actividad similar.
Se incluyen:
a) personas con un empleo pero temporalmente ausentes del mismo debido a enfermedad o lesión, vacaciones o licencia anual, licencia de maternidad o paternidad, licencia parental, licencia para estudios o capacitación, mal tiempo, etc.;
b) personas sin empleo, disponibles para trabajar y que habían tomado disposiciones para comenzar en un nuevo empleo en una fecha posterior al periodo de referencia;
c) personas que realizaron algún trabajo remunerado o por un beneficio durante la semana de referencia pero que estaban jubiladas y percibían una pensión, inscritas como desempleadas en busca de trabajo en una oficina de empleo o percibiendo indemnizaciones de desempleo;
d) trabajadores familiares no remunerados en un trabajo durante la semana de referencia;
e) todos los miembros de las fuerzas armadas.
Desempleo: Todas las personas que viven en zonas urbanas, de una determinada edad, disponibles para trabajar, pero sin un empleo durante la semana de referencia, y que buscaban un trabajo de determinadas maneras, es decir personas de 16 años y más de edad: 1) sin empleo por un ingreso durante la semana de referencia y que no pertenecían al segundo grupo de la definición de empleo, 2) que buscaron un empleo mediante medidas específicas en los 3 meses anteriores a la semana de referencia y 3) estaban disponibles para trabajar en dos semanas.
Se incluyen personas sin empleo y disponibles para trabajar que estaban tratando de establecer su propia empresa; personas que estaban buscando un empleo y/o estaban disponibles para trabajar pero estaban jubiladas y percibían una pensión.
Subempleo:
Subempleo por insuficiencia de horas: No corresponde.
Subempleo por insuficiencia de horas: No corresponde.
Horas de trabajo: Horas reales de trabajo en todos los empleos; la unidad de tiempo es la hora.
Ingresos relacionados con el empleo:
Ingresos relacionados con el empleo asalariado: No corresponde.
Ingresos relacionados con el empleo independiente: No corresponde.
Sector informal: No corresponde.
Actividad habitual: No corresponde.
Clasificaciones:
Rama de actividad económica (industria):
Título de la clasificación utilizada: No se dispone de información.
Grupos de población clasificados por industria: No se dispone de información.
Número de Grupos utilizados para la codificación: No se dispone de información.
Ocupación:
Título de la clasificación utilizada: No se dispone de información.
Grupos de población clasificados por ocupación: No se dispone de información.
Número de Grupos utilizados para la codificación: No se dispone de información.
Situación en el empleo:
Título de la clasificación utilizada: No se dispone de información.

Grupos de población clasificados por situación en el empleo: No se dispone de información.
Grupos utilizados para la codificación: Siete grupos: 1. Empleo en unidades urbanas, 2. Empleo en empresas municipales, 3. Empleo en servicios relacionados con la agricultura, pesca, silvicultura y caza, 4. Empleados en unidades individuales privadas, 5. Empleadores en unidades individuales privadas, 6. Trabajadores independientes, 7. Otro.
Vínculos con la CISE: No.
Educación:
Título de la clasificación utilizada: No se dispone de información.
Grupos de población clasificados por educación: No se dispone de información.
Grupos utilizados para la codificación: Cinco grupos: 1. Analfabetos y semianalfabetos, 2. Escuela primaria, 3. Escuela secundaria inferior, 4. Escuela secundaria superior, 5. Escuela de estudios superiores y nivel superior.
Vínculos con la CINE: No.
Tamaño y diseño de la muestra:
Unidad final de muestreo: Grupo de unos 50 a 100 hogares.
Tamaño de la muestra (unidades finales de muestreo): (1,2 millones de hogares en todo el país) unos 0,34 millones en las zonas urbanas.
Fracción de muestreo: 1 por ciento; el diseño de la muestra se combina con la Encuesta anual de la Población que abarca todo el país.
Marco de la muestra: El marco se basa en los datos del último Censo y el Registro del Ministerio de Seguridad Pública. Los enumeradores preparan el marco de la muestra para las unidades finales de muestreo,.
Actualización de la muestra: Normalmente cada año; las unidades finales de muestreo se cambian todos los años en cada una de las provincias.
Rotación: No existe un plan de rotación
Esquema: No corresponde
Porcentaje de unidades que permanecen en la muestra durante dos encuestas consecutivas: No disponible.
Número máximo de entrevistas por unidad de muestreo: No disponible.
Tiempo necesario para renovar completamente la muestra: No disponible.
Levantamiento da la encuesta:
Tipo de entrevista: Entrevistas personales utilizando papel y lápiz.
Número de unidades finales de muestreo por área de muestra: Unas 1 400.
Duración del trabajo de campo
Total: Veinte días
Por área de muestra: No disponible.
Organización de la encuesta: En cada provincia la encuesta se organiza permanentemente. También se contrata personal para cada ronda.
Número de personas que trabajan en el campo: Unas 1 500 personas.
Substitución de las unidades finales de muestreo que no responden: Sí.
Estimaciones y ajustes:
Tasa de no-respuesta total: Casi un 5 por ciento.
Ajuste por no-respuesta total: Sí.
Imputación por no respuesta de ítemes: No.
Ajuste por áreas/poblaciones no abarcadas: Sí.
Ajuste por falta de cobertura: Sí.
Ajuste por exceso de cobertura: Sí.
Ajuste por variaciones estacionales: No.
Historia de la encuesta:
Título y fecha de la primera encuesta: Encuesta sobre la Fuerza de Trabajo del Sistema Urbano (Urban Labour Force Survey System), 1 de octubre de 1996.
Modificaciones y revisiones significativas: Ninguna.
Documentación y difusión:
Documentación
Título de las publicaciones con los resultados de la encuesta: China Statistical Yearbook.
Título de las publicaciones con la metodología de la encuesta: China Statistical Yearbook.
Difusión
Tiempo necesario para difundir los primeros datos: Todavía no se dispone de esta información.
Información adelantada acerca de la fecha de la primera difusión pública: Sí.
Disponibilidad de datos no publicados si se solicitan: No hasta la fecha.
Disponibilidad de datos por medios informáticos: Se pueden obtener tabulaciones en disquetes. Sitio web: http://www.stats.gov.cn .

Chipre

Título de la encuesta: Encuesta sobre la Fuerza de Trabajo (Labour force survey).
Organismo responsable de la encuesta:
Planificar y realizar la encuesta: Servicio de Estadísticas (Statistical Service).
Analizar y publicar los resultados: Servicio de Estadísticas (Statistical Service).
Temas abarcados: Empleo, desempleo, subempleo, horas de trabajo, duración del empleo y el desempleo, rama de actividad económica (industria), ocupación, situación en el empleo, nivel de educación/calificación, empleos secundarios.
Alcance de la encuesta:
Ámbito geográfico: La zona controlada por el Gobierno de Chipre.
Grupos de población: Personas de 15 años y más de edad. Se excluyen las personas que viven en instituciones, ciudadanos no residentes, turistas, personas que residen en el extranjero y estudiantes que estudian en el extranjero.
Disponibilidad de estimaciones de otras fuentes para las áreas/grupos excluidos: No corresponde.
Grupos abarcados por la encuesta pero excluidos de los resultados publicados: No corresponde.
Periodicidad:
Recolección de datos: Anualmente.
Publicación de los resultados: Anualmente.
Períodos de referencia:
Empleo: Una semana en el segundo trimestre.
Búsqueda de trabajo: Cuatro semanas en el segundo trimestre.
Disponibilidad para trabajo: Dos semanas en el segundo trimestre.
Conceptos y definiciones:
Empleo: Personas de 15 años y más de edad que, durante la semana de referencia, trabajaron por lo menos una hora y personas que tenían un empleo del que estaban temporalmente ausentes.
Se incluyen:
a) personas con un empleo pero que estaban temporalmente ausentes del mismo debido a enfermedad o lesión, vacaciones o licencia anual, licencia por maternidad o paternidad, licencia para estudios o capacitación por menos de seis meses, ausencia sin autorización, conflictos laborales, mal tiempo, desperfectos mecánicos, etc.
b) trabajadores a tiempo completo o parcial que buscaban otro empleo durante la semana de referencia;
c) personas que realizaron algún trabajo remunerado o por un beneficio durante la semana de referencia, pese a que estaban sometidas a escolaridad obligatoria, jubiladas y percibían una pensión, inscritas como desempleados en busca de trabajo en una oficina de empleo o percibiendo indemnizaciones de desempleo;
d) estudiantes de dedicación completa o parcial que trabajaban a tiempo completo o parcial;
e) aprendices y personas en formación remunerados;
f) trabajadores familiares no remunerados que trabajaron durante la semana de referencia o estaban temporalmente ausentes del trabajo;
g) voluntarios y miembros de carrera de las fuerzas armadas y personas que trabajaban en un servicio civil equivalente al servicio militar.
Desempleo: Personas de 15 a 64 años de edad que estaban sin trabajo pero disponibles para trabajar durante la semana de referencia y habían buscando trabajo durante las últimas cuatro semanas o que van a trabajar o tratan de establecer su propia empresa en las dos semanas posteriores a la semana de la entrevista. Se incluyen también estudiantes de dedicación parcial en busca de trabajo a tiempo completo y trabajadores estacionales que no trabajan durante la temporada inactiva, si estaban buscando trabajo.
Subempleo:
Subempleo por insuficiencia de horas: No se proporcionó información.
Situaciones de empleo inadecuado: No se proporcionó información.
Horas de trabajo: No se proporcionó información.

Ingresos relacionados con el empleo:
Ingresos relacionados con el empleo asalariado: No están cubiertos.
Ingresos relacionados con el empleo independiente: No están cubiertos.
Sector informal: No está cubierto.
Actividad habitual: No está cubierto.
Clasificaciones:
Rama de actividad económica (industria):
Título de la clasificación utilizada: Nomenclatura de Actividades de la Comunidad Europea (Nomenclature d'Activités de la Communauté Européenne (NACE)).
Grupos de población clasificados por industria: Personas empleadas y desempleadas.
Número de Grupos utilizados para la codificación: No se proporcionó información.
Vínculos con la CIIU: CIIU Rev.3 a nivel de dos dígitos (División).
Ocupación:
Título de la clasificación utilizada: CIUO-1988.
Grupos de población clasificados por ocupación: Personas empleadas y desempleadas.
Número de Grupos utilizados para la codificación: 226 grupos menores (nivel de tres dígitos).
Vínculos con la CIUO: CIUO-1988.
Situación en el empleo:
Título de la clasificación utilizada: No se proporcionó información.
Grupos de población clasificados por situación en el empleo: Personas empleadas y desempleadas.
Grupos utilizados para la codificación: Cuatro grupos: trabajadores independientes con o sin empleados; empleados; trabajadores familiares no remunerados.
Vínculos con la CISE: CISE-1993.
Educación:
Título de la clasificación utilizada: CINE-1997.
Grupos de población clasificados por educación: Personas empleadas y desempleadas.
Grupos utilizados para la codificación:
Vínculos con la CINE: CINE-1997.
Tamaño y diseño de la muestra:
Unidad final de muestreo: Vivienda.
Tamaño de la muestra (unidades finales de muestreo): 4 157 viviendas.
Fracción de muestreo: 1,6 por ciento.
Marco de la muestra: Lista de viviendas derivada del Censo de Población de 1992.
Actualización de la muestra: Las viviendas recientemente construidas se añaden, cada año, al marco.
Rotación:
Esquema: se sustituye un 25 por ciento cada año.
Porcentaje de unidades que permanecen en la muestra durante dos encuestas consecutivas: 75 por ciento.
Número máximo de entrevistas por unidad de muestreo: Cuatro veces.
Tiempo necesario para renovar completamente la muestra: Cuatro años.
Levantamiento da la encuesta:
Tipo de entrevista: CAPI:
Número de unidades finales de muestreo por área de muestra: Unas 250 unidades.
Duración del trabajo de campo:
Total: 13 semanas.
Por área de muestra: Una semana.
Organización de la encuesta: Un grupo básico de tres personas permanentes.
Número de personas que trabajan en el campo: 22 personas.
Substitución de las unidades finales de muestreo que no responden: Sí.
Estimaciones y ajustes:
Tasa de no-respuesta total: Cerca del uno por ciento.
Ajuste por no-respuesta total: Sí.
Imputación por no respuesta de ítemes: No.
Ajuste por áreas/poblaciones no abarcadas: No.
Ajuste por falta de cobertura: Sí.
Ajuste por exceso de cobertura: No corresponde.
Ajuste por variaciones estacionales: No.
Historia de la encuesta:
Título y fecha de la primera encuesta: Encuesta sobre la Fuerza de Trabajo de 1999 (Labour Force Survey 1999).
Modificaciones y revisiones significativas: No corresponde.
Documentación y difusión:
Documentación:
Título de las publicaciones con los resultados de la encuesta: (periodicidad): Todavía no existen publicaciones; está previsto que se harán anualmente.
Título de las publicaciones con la metodología de la encuesta: (periodicidad): Todavía no existen publicaciones; está previsto que se harán anualmente.
Difusión
Tiempo necesario para difundir los primeros datos: No se proporcionó información.
Información adelantada acerca de la fecha de la primera difusión pública: No.
Disponibilidad de datos no publicados si se solicitan: Sí.
Disponibilidad de datos por medios informáticos: Sí. Sitio web: http://www.pio.gov.cy/dsr/.

Dinamarca

Título de la encuesta: Encuesta sobre la Fuerza de Trabajo (Beskaeftigelsesundersökelsen (BU)).
Organismo responsable de la encuesta:
Planificar y realizar la encuesta: Estadísticas de Dinamarca.
Analizar y publicar los resultados: Estadísticas de Dinamarca.
Temas abarcados: Personas corriente, habitual y económicamente activas, empleadas y desempleadas. Personas corrientemente subempleadas por insuficiencia de horas, personas en situaciones de empleo inadecuado y personas corrientemente fuera de la fuerza de trabajo. Trabajadores desalentados. Horas de trabajo. Duración del empleo y el desempleo. Empleos secundarios. Rama de actividad económica (industria), ocupación, situación en el empleo, nivel de educación/calificación.
Alcance de la encuesta:
Ámbito geográfico: Todo el país, excluidos los territorios autónomos de Groenlandia y las Islas Feroe.
Grupos de población: Abarca la población residente registrada de 15 a 66 años de edad (74 a partir de 2001). Se excluyen las personas no residentes y sin domicilio fijo.
Disponibilidad de estimaciones de otras fuentes para las áreas/grupos excluidos: Ninguna.
Grupos abarcados por la encuesta pero excluidos de los resultados publicados: Ninguno.
Periodicidad:
Recolección de datos: Trimestralmente.
Publicación de los resultados: Trimestralmente.
Períodos de referencia:
Empleo: Una semana.
Búsqueda de trabajo: En las últimas cuatro semanas.
Disponibilidad para trabajo: En las dos semanas siguientes.
Conceptos y definiciones:
Empleo: Personas que a) realizaron algún trabajo remunerado, por un beneficio o una ganancia familiar durante la semana de referencia; y b) estaban temporalmente ausentes
del trabajo durante la semana de referencia debido a enfermedad o licencia, pero que seguramente se iban a reintegrar al mismo. "Algún trabajo" significa trabajar 1 hora o más durante la semana de referencia..
Desempleo: Personas que corrientemente no tenían empleo, pero estaban disponibles para trabajar dentro de las dos semanas siguientes y que habían buscado trabajo en cualquier momento durante las últimas cuatro semanas.
Subempleo:
Subempleo por insuficiencia de horas: Personas empleadas que han buscado un empleo adicional durante el periodo de referencia y/o deseaban trabajar en un empleo adicional y estaban disponibles para hacerlo.
Situaciones de empleo inadecuado: Personas empleadas que buscan otro trabajo o empleo porque quieren tener mejores condiciones de trabajo, estar más cerca del sitio de trabajo y/o utilizar mejor sus capacidades.
Horas de trabajo: Normales: según los acuerdos concertados. Habituales: en una semana típica. Reales: horas realmente trabajadas durante la semana de referencia.
Ingresos relacionados con el empleo:
Ingresos relacionados con el empleo asalariado: No corresponde.
Ingresos relacionados con el empleo independiente: No corresponde.
Sector informal: No corresponde.
Actividad habitual: No se dispone de información.

Clasificaciones:
Rama de actividad económica (industria)
Título de la clasificación utilizada: Adaptación danesa de la NACE, Rev.1.
Grupos de población clasificados por industria: Personas empleadas y desempleadas (última rama de actividad económica para el desempleado).
Número de Grupos utilizados para la codificación: A nivel del 3er dígito.
Vínculos con la CIIU: CIIU-Rev. 2 y Rev.3.
Ocupación:
Título de la clasificación utilizada: Dansk erhversnomenklatur (DISCO).
Grupos de población clasificados por ocupación: Personas empleadas y desempleadas (última ocupación para el desempleado).
Número de Grupos utilizados para la codificación: A nivel del 4° dígito.
Vínculos con la CIUO: CIUO-68 y CIUO-88.
Situación en el empleo:
Título de la clasificación utilizada: No se dispone de información.
Grupos de población clasificados por situación en el empleo: Personas empleadas y desempleadas (última situación para el desempleado).
Grupos utilizados para la codificación: Empleados, trabajadores independientes con o sin por lo menos un empleado; trabajadores familiares no remunerados.
Vínculos con la CISE: CISE-1993.
Educación:
Título de la clasificación utilizada: Clasificación nacional.
Grupos de población clasificados por educación: Todas las personas.
Grupos utilizados para la codificación: No se dispone de información.
Vínculos con la CINE: CINE-1997.
Tamaño y diseño de la muestra:
Unidad final de muestreo: Particulares.
Tamaño de la muestra (unidades finales de muestreo): 15 600.
Fracción de muestreo: 0,00428.
Marco de la muestra: Registro Central de la Población (Central Population Register (CPR)).
Actualización de la muestra: Semanalmente.
Rotación:
Esquema: No se dispone de información. Se entrevista a cada persona en dos trimestres consecutivos y luego un año después de la segunda entrevista, es decir que el 66 por ciento de la muestra participa en la ronda previa.
Porcentaje de unidades que permanecen en la muestra durante dos encuestas consecutivas: Se entrevista a cada persona en dos trimestres consecutivos y luego un año después de la segunda entrevista, es decir que el 66 por ciento de la muestra participa en la ronda previa.
Número máximo de entrevistas por unidad de muestreo: No se dispone de información.
Tiempo necesario para renovar completamente la muestra: No se dispone de información.
Levantamiento da la encuesta:
Tipo de entrevista: Entrevistas telefónicas asistidas por computadora, y el cuestionario de la encuesta se envía y recibe por correo en el caso de las personas que no se pueden entrevistar por teléfono.
Número de unidades finales de muestreo por área de muestra: No se dispone de información.
Duración del trabajo de campo:
Total: 6 a 7 semanas.
Por área de muestra: No se dispone de información.
Organización de la encuesta: Permanente.
Número de personas que trabajan en el campo: 40 entrevistadores y supervisores.
Substitución de las unidades finales de muestreo que no responden: No.
Estimaciones y ajustes:
Tasa de no-respuesta total: 27 por ciento.
Ajuste por no-respuesta total: Imputaciones, no se describen.
Imputación por no respuesta de ítemes: No.
Ajuste por áreas/poblaciones no abarcadas: No.
Ajuste por falta de cobertura: No.
Ajuste por exceso de cobertura: No.
Ajuste por variaciones estacionales: No.

Historia de la encuesta:
Título y fecha de la primera encuesta: Encuesta sobre la Fuerza de Trabajo (Labour Force Survey (LFS)), primavera de 1972.
Modificaciones y revisiones significativas: Interrupciones importantes en las series cronológicas en 1984, 1987, 1992, 1994 y 2000.
Documentación y difusión:
Documentación:
Título de las publicaciones con los resultados de la encuesta: Statistiske Efterretninger: Arbejdsmarked.
Título de las publicaciones con la metodología de la encuesta: Idem.
Difusión:
Tiempo necesario para difundir los primeros datos: 3 meses.
Información adelantada acerca de la fecha de la primera difusión pública: Sí.
Información adelantada acerca de la fecha de la primera difusión pública: Sí.
Disponibilidad de datos por medios informáticos: Disquetes o cintas magnéticas. SItio web: http://www.dst.dk/ .

Egipto

Título de la encuesta: Encuesta por Muestra sobre la Fuerza de Trabajo (Labour force sample survey).
Organismo responsable de la encuesta:
Planificar y realizar la encuesta: Organismo Central de Movilización Pública y Estadísticas (Central Agency for Public Mobilisation and Statistics, CAPMAS)
Analizar y publicar los resultados: CAPMAS.
Temas abarcados: Empleo, desempleo, horas de trabajo, duración del empleo, duración del desempleo, trabajadores ocasionales, rama de actividad económica (industria), ocupación actual y anterior, situación en el empleo y nivel de educación.
Alcance de la encuesta:
Ámbito geográfico: Todo el país, incluidas zonas urbanas y rurales.
Grupos de población: Se excluyen miembros de las fuerzas armadas, extranjeros, poblaciones no asentadas y nacionales que residen en el extranjero.
Disponibilidad de estimaciones de otras fuentes para las áreas/grupos excluidos: No se proporcionó información.
Grupos abarcados por la encuesta pero excluidos de los resultados publicados: Ninguno.
Periodicidad:
Recolección de datos: Bianual.
Publicación de los resultados: Anual.
Período de referencia:
Empleo: Semana de referencia fija.
Búsqueda de trabajo: Semana de referencia.
Disponibilidad para trabajo: Semana de referencia.
Conceptos y definiciones:
Empleo: Personas, de 6 años y más de edad, que estaban ocupadas en la producción de bienes o servicios, por una hora o más durante la semana de referencia, o tenían vínculos contractuales con el empleo pero estaban temporalmente ausentes del trabajo durante la semana de referencia debido a enfermedad o lesión, vacaciones o licencia anual, licencia por maternidad o paternidad, licencia parental, licencia para estudios o capacitación, ausencia sin autorización, conflictos laborales, mal tiempo, desperfectos mecánicos.
Se incluyen:
a)personas que realizaron algún trabajo remunerado o por un beneficio durante la semana de referencia pero que estaban sometidas a escolaridad obligatoria, jubiladas y percibían una pensión, inscritas como desempleadas en busca de trabajo en una oficina de empleo o percibiendo indemnizaciones de desempleo;
b)estudiantes de dedicación completa o parcial que trabajan a tiempo completo o parcial;
c)aprendices y personas en formación remunerados y personas que participan en planes de promoción del empleo;
d)personas ocupadas en la producción de bienes para su propio uso final.
Se excluyen:
a)aprendices y personas en formación no remunerados, personas ocupadas en la producción de servicios para su propio hogar;
b)trabajadores familiares no remunerados temporalmente ausentes del trabajo durante la semana de referencia y trabajadores estacionales que no trabajan durante la temporada inactiva;

c)personas suspendidas de su trabajo temporalmente o por tiempo indeterminado sin remuneración y personas con licencia sin goce de sueldo por iniciativa del empleador.

Desempleo: Personas, de 15 años y más de edad, que no estaban empleadas durante la semana de referencia, estaban disponibles para trabajar, deseaban hacerlo y estuvieron buscando un empleo durante la semana de referencia.

Se incluyen:

a)personas sin empleo y corrientemente disponibles para trabajar, que buscaban un empleo y habían tomado disposiciones para comenzar un nuevo empleo en una fecha ulterior a la semana de referencia;

b)personas sin empleo y corrientemente disponibles para trabajar, que buscaban un empleo y estaban procurando establecer su propia empresa;

c)estudiantes de dedicación completa o parcial que buscaban trabajo a tiempo completo o parcial;

d)personas que buscaban trabajo o estaban disponibles para hacerlo, pero estaban sometidas a escolaridad obligatoria o jubiladas y percibían una pensión.

Se excluyen personas sin empleo, disponibles para trabajar, pero que no estaban buscando trabajo durante la semana de referencia.

Clasificaciones:

Rama de actividad económica (industria):

Título de la clasificación utilizada: No se dispone de información.

Grupos de población clasificados por industria: Personas empleadas y desempleadas con experiencia previa de trabajo.

Número de Grupos utilizados para la codificación: 18 categorías.

Vínculos con la CIIU: CIIU-Rev.3.

Ocupación:

Título de la clasificación utilizada: No se dispone de información.

Grupos de población clasificados por ocupación: Personas empleadas y desempleadas con experiencia previa de trabajo.

Número de Grupos utilizados para la codificación: 10 grupos principales.

Vínculos con la CIUO: CIUO-88.

Situación en el empleo:

Título de la clasificación utilizada: No se dispone de información.

Grupos de población clasificados por situación en el empleo: Personas empleadas únicamente.

Grupos utilizados para la codificación: Empleados. Empleadores. Trabajadores por cuenta propia. Trabajadores familiares no remunerados.

Vínculos con la CISE: CISE-1993.

Educación:

Título de la clasificación utilizada: No se dispone de información.

Grupos de población clasificados por educación: Personas empleadas y desempleadas.

Grupos utilizados para la codificación: Analfabetos. Personas que pueden leer y escribir. Inferior a la educación media. **Educación:** media completa. Superior a la educación media. Superior a la escuela secundaria. Universidad y superior.

Vínculos con la CINE: Algunos grupos están vinculados a la CINE.

Tamaño y diseño de la muestra:

Unidad final de muestreo: Hogar (compuesto de uno o más hogares).

Tamaño de la muestra (unidades finales de muestreo): 41 660 hogares divididos por igual entre dos rondas anuales (mayo y noviembre).

Fracción de muestreo: 6 por ciento.

Marco de la muestra: Muestra básica basada en datos de 1995. Muestreo de dos etapas. En la primera etapa, las unidades primarias de muestreo (UPM), que abarcan unos 1 500 hogares, se seleccionan sistemáticamente, 261 UPM en zonas urbanas y 185 en zonas rurales. En la segunda etapa, se seleccionan 95 hogares en cada muestra de las UPM urbana o rural.

Actualización de la muestra: Todavía no se ha hecho ninguna actualización.

Rotación: Ninguna.

Levantamiento da la encuesta:

Tipo de entrevista: Entrevista personal.

Número de unidades finales de muestreo por área de muestra: 95 hogares.

Duración del trabajo de campo:

Total: 28 días para la ronda de mayo (1º a 28 de junio) y 28 días para la ronda de noviembre (1º a 28 de diciembre).

Por área de muestra: No se proporcionó información.

Organización de la encuesta: Permanente.

Número de personas que trabajan en el campo: 210 entrevistadores y 70 supervisores.

Substitución de las unidades finales de muestreo que no responden: No.

Estimaciones y ajustes :

Tasa de no-respuesta total: 1,7 por ciento.

Ajuste por no-respuesta total: Sí.

Imputación por no respuesta de ítemes: No.

Ajuste por áreas/poblaciones no abarcadas: No.

Ajuste por falta de cobertura: No.

Ajuste por exceso de cobertura: No.

Ajuste por variaciones estacionales: No.

Historia de la encuesta:

Título y fecha de la primera encuesta: Encuesta por Muestra sobre la Fuerza de Trabajo, noviembre de 1957 (Labour force sample survey, November 1957).

Modificaciones y revisiones significativas: Las encuestas realizadas entre 1957 y 1964 totalizan 24 rondas con diferentes periodicidades. De 1968 a 1985, la encuesta se realizaba anualmente. De 1987 a 1992, trimestralmente. Desde 1993, se realiza cada dos años. La encuesta no se realiza en los años de censo. Las encuestas efectuadas entre 1987 y 1992 abarcaron dos puntos adicionales: actividad habitual y empleos secundarios.

Documentación y difusión:

Documentación:

Título de las publicaciones con los resultados de la encuesta: (periodicidad): Annual Bulletin of Labour Force Sample Survey of the Arab Republic of Egypt.

Título de las publicaciones con la metodología de la encuesta: (periodicidad): En Annual Bulletin.

Difusión

Tiempo necesario para difundir los primeros datos: Un año. Los últimos datos de 1998 se publicaron el 30 de diciembre de 1999.

Información adelantada acerca de la fecha de la primera difusión pública: No.

Disponibilidad de datos no publicados si se solicitan: No se proporcionó información.

Disponibilidad de datos por medios informáticos: Se pueden obtener datos tabulados en disquetes si se solicitan. Está prevista la difusión futura en internet. Sitio web: http://www.capmas.gov.eg/ .

Eslovaquia

Título de la encuesta: Encuesta sobre la Fuerza de Trabajo (Labour Force Sample Survey).

Organismo responsable de la encuesta:

Planificar y realizar la encuesta: Oficina de Estadísticas de la República de Eslovaquia (Statistical Office of the Slovak Republic).

Analizar y publicar los resultados: Oficina de Estadísticas de la República de Eslovaquia (Statistical Office of the Slovak Republic).

Temas abarcados: Empleo, desempleo, subempleo, horas de trabajo, duración del empleo, duración del desempleo, trabajadores desalentados, trabajadores ocasionales, rama de actividad económica (industria), ocupación, situación en el empleo, nivel de educación, empleo secundario y trabajo atípico.

Alcance de la encuesta:

Ámbito geográfico: Todo el país.

Grupos de población: Todos los residentes permanentes de 15 años y más de edad que viven en el hogar.

Se excluyen:

a)estudiantes que viven en albergues y niños en edad escolar que viven en internados;

b)reclusos de instituciones penales y psiquiátricas;

c)extranjeros que están en el país durante un corto periodo de tiempo, hasta 6 meses.

Disponibilidad de estimaciones de otras fuentes para las áreas/grupos excluidos: No.

Grupos abarcados por la encuesta pero excluidos de los resultados publicados: Ninguno.

Periodicidad:

Recolección de datos: Permanentemente.

Publicación de los resultados: Trimestralmente.

Periodo de referencia:

Empleo: Una semana (últimos siete días antes de la fecha de la entrevista).

Búsqueda de trabajo: Cuatro semanas antes de la fecha de la entrevista.

Disponibilidad para trabajo: Dos semanas después de la fecha de la entrevista.

Conceptos y definiciones:

Empleo: Personas de 15 años y más de edad que en la semana de referencia realizaron algún trabajo por lo menos durante una hora, así como los trabajadores familiares no remunerados y las personas que no estaban en el trabajo pero tenían un empleo o negocio del que se encontraban temporalmente ausentes debido a enfermedad, mal tiempo, vacaciones, conflicto laboral, etc. Se excluyen las personas con licencia por maternidad (parental) prolongada.

También se incluyen en los totales:

a)trabajadores a tiempo completo o parcial que buscaban otro empleo durante el periodo de referencia;

b)estudiantes de dedicación completa o parcial que trabajaban a tiempo completo o parcial;

c)personas que realizaban algún trabajo durante la semana de referencia pero estaban jubiladas y recibían una pensión, o estaban inscritas como desempleadas en busca de trabajo en una oficina de empleo o recibían indemnizaciones de desempleo;

d)servicios domésticos privados;

e)aprendices y personas en formación remunerados.

Se excluyen las personas ocupadas en la producción de bienes para su propio hogar (pintura, reparación, quehaceres domésticos, etc.).

Desempleo: Se consideran desempleadas todas las personas de 15 años y más de edad que, durante la semana de referencia, no trabajaban por una remuneración o ganancia, estaban buscando activamente un empleo durante las cuatro últimas semanas anteriores a la encuesta y estaban disponibles para comenzar a trabajar en las dos semanas ulteriores a la encuesta.

Subempleo:

Subempleo por insuficiencia de horas: Personas que, durante la semana de referencia, trabajaban a tiempo parcial por razones ajenas a su voluntad pero que hubiesen querido trabajar a tiempo completo.

Situaciones de empleo inadecuado: Personas que estaban buscando otro empleo para mejorar sus condiciones de trabajo (mayores ingresos, experiencia profesional, mejor trabajo, etc.).

Horas de trabajo: Horas reales y habituales trabajadas en el empleo principal.

Ingresos relacionados con el empleo:

Ingresos relacionados con el empleo asalariado: No corresponde.

Ingresos relacionados con el empleo independiente: No corresponde.

Sector informal: No corresponde.

Actividad habitual: No corresponde.

Clasificaciones:

Rama de actividad económica (industria):

Título de la clasificación utilizada: Clasificación nacional.

Grupos de población clasificados por industria: Personas empleadas y desempleadas con experiencia previa de trabajo.

Número de Grupos utilizados para la codificación: 16 grupos principales.

Vínculos con la CIIU: CIIU-Rev.3 (nivel de 2 dígitos).

Ocupación:

Título de la clasificación utilizada: Clasificación nacional.

Grupos de población clasificados por ocupación: Personas empleadas y desempleadas con experiencia previa de trabajo.

Número de Grupos utilizados para la codificación: 10 grupos principales.

Vínculos con la CIUO: CIUO-88 (3 dígitos).

Situación en el empleo:

Título de la clasificación utilizada: Clasificación nacional.

Grupos de población clasificados por situación en el empleo: Personas empleadas y desempleadas.

Grupos utilizados para la codificación: 6 grupos (empleados, empleadores, trabajadores por cuenta propia, miembros de cooperativas de productores, trabajadores que contribuyen con la familia, trabajadores no clasificados por situación.

Vínculos con la CISE: CISE-1993.

Educación:

Título de la clasificación utilizada: Clasificación nacional.

Grupos de población clasificados por educación: Todos los grupos de la población.

Grupos utilizados para la codificación: 12 grupos (sin educación escolar, primaria (1a y 2a etapas), aprendizaje, secundaria (sin examen), aprendizaje con examen, escuela secundaria completa, escuela vocacional completa, escuela superior, bachillerato, universidad, investigación.

Vínculos con la CINE: CINE-1976.

Tamaño y diseño de la muestra:

Unidad final de muestreo: Viviendas.

Tamaño de la muestra (unidades finales de muestreo): Unas 10 250.

Fracción de muestreo: 0,6 por ciento.

Marco de la muestra: El marco de la muestra se prepara de acuerdo con los registros municipales de la población y el Censo de población de 1991.

Actualización de la muestra: Anualmente.

Rotación:

Esquema: 20 por ciento de las viviendas de la muestra se sustituye cada trimestre. Se hace la rotación de un quinto del grupo cada trimestre.

Porcentaje de unidades que permanecen en la muestra durante dos encuestas consecutivas: 75 por ciento.

Número máximo de entrevistas por unidad de muestreo: No se proporcionó información.

Tiempo necesario para renovar completamente la muestra: Cinco trimestres.

Levantamiento da la encuesta:

Tipo de entrevista: Papel y lápiz, CAPI o CATI cuando es posible.

Número de unidades finales de muestreo por área de muestra: 250 viviendas permantemente por trimestre.

Duración del trabajo de campo:

Total: 30 minutos por hogar.

Por área de muestra: No se proporcionó información.

Organización de la encuesta: Oficina de Estadísticas de la República de Eslovaquia (Statistical Office of the Slovak Republic).

Número de personas que trabajan en el campo: 45 entrevistadores y 8 supervisores.

Substitución de las unidades finales de muestreo que no responden: No.

Estimaciones y ajustes:

Tasa de no-respuesta total: 6 por ciento.

Ajuste por no-respuesta total: No.

Imputación por no respuesta de ítemes: No.

Ajuste por áreas/poblaciones no abarcadas: No.

Ajuste por falta de cobertura: No.

Ajuste por exceso de cobertura: No.

Ajuste por variaciones estacionales: Sí.

Historia de la encuesta:

Título y fecha de la primera encuesta: Encuesta por muestra sobre la Fuerza de Trabajo (Labour Force Sample Survey), diciembre de 1992.

Modificaciones y revisiones significativas: Desde el primer trimestre de 1997, los reclutas se incluyen en la muestra. Desde el primer trimestre de 1999, se ha utilizado un nuevo diseño de muestra. Desde el primer trimestre de 2000, se pasó de trimestres estacionales a trimestres civiles.

Documentación y difusión:

Documentación:

Título de las publicaciones con los resultados de la encuesta (periodicidad): Labour Force Sample Survey Results (trimestralmente).

Título de las publicaciones con la metodología de la encuesta (periodicidad): Labour Force Sample Survey Results (trimestralmente).

Difusión:

Tiempo necesario para difundir los primeros datos: 80 días.

Información adelantada acerca de la fecha de la primera difusión pública: Sí.

Disponibilidad de datos no publicados si se solicitan: Sí.

Disponibilidad de datos por medios informáticos: Disquetes y correo electrónico. Sitio web: http://www.statistics.sk.

Eslovenia

Título de la encuesta: Encuesta sobre la Fuerza de Trabajo (Labour Force Survey).

Organismo responsable de la encuesta:

Planificar y realizar la encuesta: Oficina de Estadísticas de la República de Eslovenia (Statistical Office of the Republic of Slovenia).

Analizar y publicar los resultados: Oficina de Estadísticas de la República de Eslovenia (Statistical Office of the Republic of Slovenia).

Temas abarcados: Empleo, subempleo, desempleo, horas de trabajo, sector informal, duración del desempleo, trabajadores desalentados, trabajadores ocasionales, rama de actividad económica (industria), ocupación, situación en el empleo, nivel de educación, empleo secundario.

Alcance de la encuesta:
Ámbito geográfico: Todo el país.
Grupos de población: Todas las personas que viven en hogares privados cuyo lugar de residencia se encuentra en el territorio de Eslovenia, incluidas las personas temporalmente ausentes (menos de seis meses). Se excluye la población institucional (por ejemplo, militares que viven en cuarteles) y las personas que viven temporal o permanentemente en el extranjero. A los niños menores de 15 años de edad sólo se les hace unas cuantas preguntas básicas (nombre, sexo, edad, nacionalidad).
Disponibilidad de estimaciones de otras fuentes para las áreas/grupos excluidos: No disponible.
Grupos abarcados por la encuesta pero excluidos de los resultados publicados: No disponible.
Periodicidad:
Recolección de datos: Encuesta trimestral continua.
Publicación de los resultados: Trimestral y anualmente.
Periodo de referencia:
Empleo: Última semana (periodo de referencia móvil) lunes a domingo.
Búsqueda de trabajo: Cuatro últimas semanas.
Disponibilidad para trabajo: Dos semanas.
Conceptos y definiciones:
Empleo: Personas de 15 años y más de edad que durante la semana de referencia realizaron algún trabajo por una remuneración (en efectivo o en especie) o ganancia, incluidos trabajadores familiares no remunerados y personas que no estaban trabajando pero tenían un empleo del cual estaban temporalmente ausentes. Se incluyen también los trabajadores suspendidos (temporalmente o por tiempo indeterminado) y las personas con licencia por maternidad (12 meses).
Se incluyen:
a)personas con un empleo pero temporalmente ausentes del mismo debido a enfermedad o lesión, vacaciones o licencia anual, licencia parental, licencia sin goce de sueldo por iniciativa del empleador, licencia para estudios o capacitación, ausencia sin autorización, huelga o conflicto laboral, interrupción temporal por mal tiempo, desperfectos mecánicos, escasez de materia prima o energía, etc.;
b)trabajadores a tiempo completo o parcial que buscaban otro trabajo;
c)personas que realizaron algún trabajo remunerado o por un beneficio durante la semana de referencia, pero estaban sometidas a escolaridad obligatoria, estaban jubiladas y recibían una pensión, inscritas como desempleadas en busca de trabajo en una oficina de empleo o que recibían indemnizaciones de desempleo;
d)estudiantes de dedicación completa o parcial que trabajaron por lo menos una hora durante la semana de referencia;
e)aprendices y personas en formación remunerados;
f)participantes en planes de promoción del empleo;
g)personas ocupadas en la producción de bienes o servicios para su propio consumo;
h)voluntarios y miembros de carrera de las fuerzas armadas.
Desempleo: Personas de 15 años y más de edad que, durante la semana de referencia, no trabajaron por una remuneración, ganancia o beneficio para la familia, estaban buscando trabajo activamente durante las cuatro últimas semanas y estaban corrientemente disponibles para trabajar en las dos semanas siguientes.
Se incluyen:
a)personas que tomaron medidas concretas para establecer su propio negocio para comenzar en dos semanas;
b)personas que habían tomado las disposiciones necesarias para comenzar un nuevo empleo en dos semanas;
c)estudiantes de dedicación completa o parcial que buscan un empleo a tiempo completo o parcial, niños con escolaridad obligatoria y personas jubiladas.
Subempleo:
Subempleo por insuficiencia de horas: Personas que trabajaban menos de 36 horas por semana, deseaban trabajar más horas por semana (en un empleo adicional o en el empleo que tenían, o en otro empleo haciendo más horas que en el trabajo que tenían) y deseaban comenzar a trabajar más horas en las próximas dos semanas.
Situaciones de empleo inadecuado: No corresponde.
Horas de trabajo: Horas realmente trabajadas (por semana) incluidas las horas extraordinarias periódicas. Las horas realmente trabajadas (por semana) se refieren al empleo principal realizado durante la semana de referencia.

Ingresos relacionados con el empleo:
Ingresos relacionados con el empleo asalariado: No corresponde.
Ingresos relacionados con el empleo independiente: No corresponde.
Sector informal: Se refiere a los trabajadores que reciben "dinero en efectivo" por su actividad económica.
Actividad habitual: No corresponde.
Clasificaciones:
Rama de actividad económica (industria):
Título de la clasificación utilizada: No disponible.
Grupos de población clasificados por industria: Personas empleadas.
Número de Grupos utilizados para la codificación: 16 grupos; codificación a nivel de 2 dígitos.
Vínculos con la CIIU: CIIU-Rev.3.
Ocupación:
Título de la clasificación utilizada: No disponible.
Grupos de población clasificados por ocupación: Personas empleadas.
Número de Grupos utilizados para la codificación: No disponible.
Vínculos con la CIUO: CIUO-88.
Situación en el empleo:
Título de la clasificación utilizada: No disponible.
Grupos de población clasificados por situación en el empleo: Personas empleadas.
Grupos utilizados para la codificación: Doce grupos: empleados en una empresa u organización, empleado-artesano, empleado-independiente, empleado-agricultor, trabajadores en su propio negocio (empleado independiente), artesano, agricultor, independiente, trabajador familiar no remunerado, trabajadores con contrato -tipo 1 y 2, trabajadores que reciben dinero en efectivo (informal).
Vínculos con la CISE: CISE-1993.
Educación:
Título de la clasificación utilizada: No disponible.
Grupos de población clasificados por educación: Personas empleadas y desempleadas.
Grupos utilizados para la codificación: Nueve grupos: No asistió a ninguna escuela, escuela primaria incompleta, escuela primaria, primer y segundo año de escuela secundaria (programa reducido), segundo y tercer año de escuela secundaria, cuarto y quinto año de escuela secundaria, diploma no universitario, diploma univesitario, postgrado.
Vínculos con la CINE: CINE-1997 con cuadros cruzados.
Tamaño y diseño de la muestra:
Unidad final de muestreo: Hogares.
Tamaño de la muestra (unidades finales de muestreo): Unos 7 000 hogares (y 19 000 entrevistados).
Fracción de muestreo: Aproximadamente el 1 por ciento de la población.
Marco de la muestra: La muestra de la LFS se prepara en base al registro de la población, del cual se hace cada trimestre una lista de personas adultas. Se entrevista a los miembros de los hogares que viven en las direcciones de las personas seleccionadas.
Actualización de la muestra: Cada trimestre se seleccionan unos 2 000 nuevos hogares.
Rotación: El grupo de encuesta hace la rotación contantemente durante todo el año civil.
Esquema: La rotación de la muestra sigue el esquema 3-(1)-2. De esta manera, los hogares seleccionados se entrevistan durante tres trimestres consecutivos y se excluyen un trimestre, luego se vuelven a entrevistar durante otros dos trimestres consecutivos antes de sacarlos definitivamente de la muestra.
Porcentaje de unidades que permanecen en la muestra durante dos encuestas consecutivas: 60 por ciento.
Número máximo de entrevistas por unidad de muestreo: Cinco veces.
Tiempo necesario para renovar completamente la muestra: 18 meses.
Levantamiento da la encuesta:
Tipo de entrevista: Se utiliza una combinación de entrevistas personales con lápiz y papel, entrevistas asistidas por computadora (CAPI) con computadoras portátiles y entrevistas por teléfono.
Número de unidades finales de muestreo por área de muestra: Unos 28 000 hogares por año.
Duración del trabajo de campo:
Total: Todo el año.
Por área de muestra: No corresponde.

Organización de la encuesta: La organización de la encuesta es permanente.
Número de personas que trabajan en el campo: 55.
Substitución de las unidades finales de muestreo que no responden: No.
Estimaciones y ajustes:
Tasa de no-respuesta total: 11,2 por ciento (el porcentaje de rechazo es del 7,4 por ciento). En el grupo que forma parte de la muestra, la tasa de no-respuesta total es del 8,9 por ciento; entre los hogares entrevistados por teléfono, el 9,4 por ciento y en entrevistas personales, el 5 por ciento.
Ajuste por no-respuesta total: Sí.
Imputación por no respuesta de ítemes: Sí, se utiliza el método "Hot-deck" (método de asignación dinámica). Se utilizan los datos de entrevistas previas y, si no se dispone de ellos, los datos de personas con características similares (por sexo, edad y educación).
Ajuste por áreas/poblaciones no abarcadas: Sí.
Ajuste por falta de cobertura: Sí.
Ajuste por exceso de cobertura: Sí.
Ajuste por variaciones estacionales: No.
Historia de la encuesta:
Título y fecha de la primera encuesta: Encuesta sobre la Fuerza de Trabajo (Labour Force Survey), 1993.
Modificaciones y revisiones significativas: Ninguna. El cuestionario se modificó en 1995 y 1997 sin interrupciones importantes en las series cronológicas.
Documentación y difusión:
Documentación:
Título de las publicaciones con los resultados de la encuesta (periodicidad): Labour Force Survey: Results; Labour Force Survey: Rapid Results; Statistical Yearbook of the Republic of Slovenia, Monthly Statistical Review; CESTAT Bulletin. (mensual, trimestral y anualmente).
Título de las publicaciones con la metodología de la encuesta (periodicidad): Idem.
Difusión:
Tiempo necesario para difundir los primeros datos: Aproximadamente un trimestre.
Información adelantada acerca de la fecha de la primera difusión pública: Sí.
Disponibilidad de datos no publicados si se solicitan: Sí.
Disponibilidad de datos por medios informáticos: Sí, en disquete y por correo electrónico. Sitio web: http://www.sigov.si/zrs/.

Estados Unidos

Título de la encuesta: Encuesta Continua de Población (Current Population Survey (CPS)).
Organismo responsable de la encuesta:
Planificar y realizar la encuesta: Oficina del Censo de los Estados Unidos de América (U.S. Bureau of the Census).
Analizar y publicar los resultados: Oficina de Estadísticas del Trabajo de los Estados Unidos de América (U.S. Bureau of Labor Statistics).
Temas abarcados:
Población económicamente activa, empleo, desempleo, subempleo (tiempo parcial involutario), horas de trabajo, ingresos medios semanales, ingresos anuales (suplemento de marzo), duración del empleo y el desempleo, trabajadores desalentados y ocasionales, rama de actividad económica (industria), ocupación, situación en el empleo, nivel de educación, actividad habitual (suplemento de marzo) y empleo secundario.
Alcance de la encuesta:
Ámbito geográfico: Todo el país.
Grupos de población: Población civil de 16 años y más de edad que no reside en hogares colectivos. Se excluyen los miembros de las fuerzas armadas, la población que vive en hogares colectivos, los ciudadanos de otros países que viven en embajadas y los ciudadanos estadounidenses que viven en el extranjero.
Disponibilidad de estimaciones de otras fuentes para las áreas/grupos excluidos: No corresponde.
Grupos abarcados por la encuesta pero excluidos de los resultados publicados: Ninguno.
Periodicidad:Recolección de datos: Mensualmente.
Publicación de los resultados: Mensualmente.
Periodo de referencia:
Empleo: Semana civil (domingo a sábado) que comprende el día 12 del mes.
Búsqueda de trabajo: Cuatro semanas.
Disponibilidad para trabajo: Una semana.
Conceptos y definiciones:
Empleo: Son empleadas las que personas que, durante la semana de referencia:
a)realizaron algún trabajo (una hora como mínimo) como empleados asalariados, en su propio negocio, profesión o en su propia explotación agrícola, o que trabajaron 15 horas o más como trabajadores no remunerados en una empresa administrada por un miembro de la familia;
b)no trabajaban pero tenían un empleo o negocio del cual estaban ausentes temporalmente por vacaciones, enfermedad, mal tiempo, problemas de guardería, licencia por maternidad o paternidad, conflictos laborales, formación profesional u otras razones personales o familiares, que hayan sido remunerados o no durante el tiempo de ausencia o que hayan estado en busca de otro empleo.
Se incluyen también como empleados:
a)las personas sin empleo asalariado que procuraban establecer su propia empresa;
b)los trabajadores a tiempo completo o parcial que buscaban otro empleo durante la semana de referencia;
c)las personas que realizaron algún trabajo remunerado o por un beneficio durante la semana de referencia pero que estaban sometidas a escolaridad obligatoria, jubiladas y recibían una pensión, inscritas como desempleadas en busca de trabajo en una oficina de empleo o percibiendo indemnizaciones de desempleo;
d)los estudiantes de dedicación completa o parcial que trabajaban a tiempo completo o parcial;
e)los aprendices y personas en formación remunerados;
f)los ciudadanos de otros países que residen en los Estados Unidos pero no viven en el recito de una embajada;
g)las personas que residen en los Estados Unidos pero que trabajan en México o Canadá.
Se excluyen las personas cuya única actividad se limita a los trabajos de su casa (pintura, reparaciones o quehaceres domésticos) o al trabajo voluntario para instituciones religiosas, caritativas u otras organizaciones.
Desempleo: Se consideran desempleadas todas las personas que no tenían un empleo durante la semana de referencia, estaban disponibles para trabajar, salvo por enfermedad temporal, y que habían tomado disposiciones concretas para encontrar empleo en algún momento durante el periodo de 4 semanas que finalizaba con la semana de referencia. Las personas que esperaban reintegrarse a un empleo del cual estaban suspendidas no necesitan haber estado en busca de un trabajo para clasificarlas como desempleadas.
Se incluyen también como desempleadas:
a)las personas suspendidas de su trabajo temporalmente sin remuneración;
b)las personas que buscaban trabajo y estaban disponibles para hacerlo, pero estaban sometidas a escolaridad obligatoria o jubiladas y recibían una pensión;
c)los estudiantes de dedicación completa o parcial que buscaban un empleo a tiempo completo o parcial.
Subempleo:
Subempleo por insuficiencia de horas: Abarca las personas que trabajan a tiempo parcial por razones económicas.
Situaciones de empleo inadecuado: No corresponde.
Horas de trabajo: Horas reales y habituales trabajadas por semana. Las horas se refieren a todos los empleos.
Ingresos relacionados con el empleo: Los datos sobre los ingresos no se recopilan como parte de la encuesta mensual sino en el suplemento de marzo, del cual se encarga la Oficina del Censo.
Ingresos relacionados con el empleo asalariado: Suplemento de marzo.
Ingresos relacionados con el empleo independiente: Suplemento de marzo.
Sector informal: No se obtienen estimaciones oficiales directamente de la encuesta.
Actividad habitual: Las preguntas sobre la actividad habitual sólo se plantean a quienes no forman parte de la fuerza de trabajo y únicamente en el suplemento anual de ingresos.
Clasificaciones:
Rama de actividad económica (industria):
Título de la clasificación utilizada: Sistema de Clasificación Industrial de 1990 de la Oficina de Censo de los Estados Unidos de América.
Grupos de población clasificados por industria: Empleados y desempleados (rama de actividad económica del último empleo para el desempleado).

Número de Grupos utilizados para la codificación: 13 grupos principales y 236 categorías.
Vínculos con la CIIU: Vínculos indirectos con la CIIU Rev.2.
Ocupación:
Título de la clasificación utilizada: Sistema de Clasificación de Ocupaciones de 1990 de la Oficina de Censo de los Estados Unidos de América.
Grupos de población clasificados por ocupación: Empleados y desempleados (ocupación en el último empleo para el desempleado).
Número de Grupos utilizados para la codificación: 6 grupos resumidos, 13 grupos principales y 501 categorías.
Vínculos con la CIUO: Vínculos indirectos con la CIUO-1968.
Situación en el empleo:
Título de la clasificación utilizada: Categorías de Clases de Trabajadores de la Oficina de Censo de los Estados Unidos de América.
Grupos de población clasificados por situación en el empleo: Empleados y desempleados (situación en el último empleo para el desempleado).
Número de grupos clasificados por situación en el empleo: Tres categorías principales: obreros y empleados asalariados en el sector privado y gubernamental; empledados independientes y trabajadores familiares no remunerados.
Vínculos con la CISE: Vínculos indirectos con la CISE-1993, con algunas categorías similares.
Educación:
Título de la clasificación utilizada: Categorías de educación de la Oficina de Censo de los Estados Unidos de América.
Grupos de población clasificados por educación: Empleados y desempleados.
Grupos utilizados para la codificación: Cuatro grupos principales: grado inferior a la escuela secundaria; escuela secundaria; no profesional; grado inferior a la licenciatura; estudios superiores.
Vínculos con la CINE: Vínculos indirectos con la CINE-1976, con algunas categorías similares.
Tamaño y diseño de la muestra:
Unidad final de muestreo: Hogar.
Tamaño de la muestra (unidades finales de muestreo): Unos 60 000 hogares.
Fracción de muestreo: Uno en 2 000.
Marco de la muestra: Censos decenales. En la actualidad, el Censo de 1990; a comienzos de 2003, el Censo de 2000.
Actualización de la muestra: Durante el decenio, se actualiza la muestra para introducir las nuevas viviendas construidas utilizando los permisos de construcción y las listas periódicas de unidades seleccionadas.
Rotación:
Esquema: El sistema de rotación es 4-8-4, es decir que los hogares permanecen en la muestra durante 4 meses consecutivos, luego de excluyen en los 8 meses siguientes y, por último, se vuelven a introducir en la muestra por 4 meses más.
Porcentaje de unidades que permanecen en la muestra durante dos encuestas consecutivas: 75 por ciento.
Número máximo de entrevistas por unidad de muestreo: Ocho.
Tiempo necesario para renovar completamente la muestra: 17 meses.
Levantamiento de la encuesta:
Tipo de entrevista: Combinación de entrevistas personales y por teléfono, utilizando la CAPI (un 90 por ciento) y la CATI (10 por ciento).
Número de unidades finales de muestreo por área de muestra: Variado.
Duración del trabajo de campo:
Total: Domingo de la semana de referencia hasta el miércoles de la semana siguiente.
Por área de muestra: No se proporcionó información.
Organización de la encuesta: Permanente.
Número de personas que trabajan en el campo: 2 000 entrevistadores y 100 supervisores.
Substitución de las unidades finales de muestreo que no responden: No.
Estimaciones y ajustes:
Tasa de no-respuesta total: 7 por ciento.
Ajuste por no-respuesta total: Sí.
Imputación por no respuesta de ítemes: Sí.
Ajuste por áreas/poblaciones no abarcadas: No.
Ajuste por falta de cobertura: Sí.
Ajuste por exceso de cobertura: No.
Ajuste por variaciones estacionales: Sí.

Historia de la encuesta:
Título y fecha de la primera encuesta: Encuesta por Muestra sobre el Desempleo de 1940 (Sample Survey of Unemployment 1940).
Modificaciones y revisiones significativas: En 1994 se introdujeron las principales modificaciones a la CPS, que incluyen el diseño totalmente nuevo del cuestionario y el uso de entrevistas asistidas por computadora para toda la encuesta. Asimismo, se revisaron algunos conceptos y definiciones de la fuerza de trabajo, entre otros la aplicación de algunos cambios recomendados en 1979 por la Comisión Nacional sobre el Empleo y el Desempleo. Además de la introducción de un cuestionario nuevo y automatizado, algunos de los principales cambios se refieren a los criterios utilizados para definir los trabajadores desalentados y las personas empleadas a tiempo parcial por razones económicas, así como la adición de preguntas directas sobre la suspensión en el trabajo y los empleos secundarios.
Documentación y difusión:
Documentación:
Título de las publicaciones con los resultados de la encuesta (periodicidad): Employment and Earnings (mensualmente); The Employment Situation news release (mensualmente).
Título de las publicaciones con la metodología de la encuesta (periodicidad): Employment and Earnings (mensualmente); BLS Handbook of Methods 1997 and Current Population Survey: Design and Methodology (Documento técnico 63).
Difusión:
Tiempo necesario para difundir los primeros datos: Unas dos semanas.
Información adelantada acerca de la fecha de la primera difusión pública: Sí.
Disponibilidad de datos no publicados si se solicitan: Sí.
Disponibilidad de datos por medios informáticos: Disquetes y cintas magnéticas. Sitio web: http://www.bls.gov/

Estonia

Título de la encuesta: Encuesta Nacional sobre la Fuerza de Trabajo de 2001 (Estonian Labour Force Survey 2001 (ELFS 2001)).
Organismo responsable de la encuesta:
Planificar y realizar la encuesta: Oficina de Estadísticas de Estonia, División de Estadísticas sobre la Fuerza de Trabajo (Statistical Office of Estonia, Labour Force Statistics Division).
Analizar y publicar los resultados: Oficina de Estadísticas de Estonia, División de Estadísticas sobre la Fuerza de Trabajo (Statistical Office of Estonia, Labour Force Statistics Division).
Temas abarcados: Empleo, desempleo, subempleo, horas de trabajo, salarios, ingresos, duración del empleo, duración del desempleo, trabajadores desalentados, trabajadores ocasionales, rama de actividad económica (industria), ocupación, situación en el empleo, nivel de educación, actividad habitual, empleos secundarios.
Alcance de la encuesta:
Ámbito geográfico: Todo el país.
Grupos de población: La ELFS de 2001 abarca los residentes de Estonia en edad de trabajo, es decir, las personas que, al 1 de enero de 2001, habían cumplido entre 15 y 74 años de edad (o sea, los nacidos entre 1926 y 1985). En los totales se incluyen los miembros de carrera y voluntarios de las fuerzas armadas, pero no se publican datos por separado.
Disponibilidad de estimaciones de otras fuentes para las áreas/grupos excluidos: No.
Grupos abarcados por la encuesta pero excluidos de los resultados publicados: Ninguno.
Periodicidad:
Recolección de datos: 2 encuestas continuas.
Publicación de los resultados: Trimestralmente.
Períodos de referencia:
Empleo: Una semana (últimos siete días antes de la fecha de la entrevista).
Búsqueda de trabajo: Cuatro semanas antes de la fecha de la entrevista.
Disponibilidad para trabajo: Dos semanas después de la fecha de la entrevista.
Conceptos y definiciones:
Empleo: Empleadas son todas las personas entre 15 y 74 años de edad que, durante el periodo de referencia, realizaron algún trabajo durante por lo menos una hora y tenían un empleo remunerado o eran trabajadores independientes. Se consideran como no activas

las personas con licencia parental, sea la madre sea el padre, hasta que el niño cumple 3 años de edad. Los reclutas se clasifican como no activos, así como los miembros de carrera y voluntarios de las fuerzas armadas.

En los totales se incluyen las personas que durante el periodo de referencia estaban temporalmente ausentes del trabajo debido a enfermedad, lesión, vacaciones o licencia anual, licencia para estudios, ausencia sin autorización, mal tiempo, conflictos laborales, desperfectos mecánicos, otras reducciones en la actividad económica o suspendidas de su trabajo temporalmente sin remuneración, siempre que el periodo de ausencia sea inferior a 3 meses.

Se incluyen también:

a)mujeres con licencia remunerada prenatal y postnatal cuya duración sea de 70 y 56 días, respectivamente;

b)trabajadores a tiempo completo o parcial que buscaban otro empleo durante el período de referencia;

c)estudiantes de dedicación completa o parcial que trabajan a tiempo completo o parcial;

d)personas que realizaron algún trabajo durante la semana de referencia pero que estaban jubiladas y percibían una pensión, inscritas como desempleadas en busca de trabajo en una oficina de empleo o percibiendo indemnizaciones de desempleo;

e)servicios domésticos privados;

g)aprendices y personas en formación remunerados.

Se excluyen las personas ocupadas en la producción de bienes para sus propios hogares (pintura, reparaciones, quehaceres domésticos, etc.).

Desempleo: Desempleadas son todas las personas entre 15 y 74 años de edad que cumplían las tres condiciones siguientes durante la semana de referencia: i) no tenían trabajo; ii) estaban buscando trabajo activamente; y iii) estaban corrientemente disponibles para trabajar, es decir estaban disponibles para hacer un trabajo remunerado o de manera independiente, de inmediato o dentro de los 14 días después de la semana de referencia.

Subempleo:

Subempleo por insuficiencia de horas: Personas que, durante la semana de referencia, estuvieron obligados a trabajar menos horas que las horas de trabajo normales establecidas para una determinada actividad y que deseaban trabajar horas adicionales y estaban disponibles para hacerlo.

Situaciones de empleo inadecuado: Personas que estaban en busca de otro empleo con mejores condiciones (sueldo, ubicación, etc.).

Horas de trabajo: Horas habituales y reales trabajadas en el empleo principal.

Ingresos relacionados con el empleo:

Ingresos relacionados con el empleo asalariado: Ingresos mensuales del empleo principal, es decir salarios, sueldos y otros ingresos en efectivo o en especie; remuneraciones por tiempo no trabajado y pagado por el empleador; bonificaciones trimestrales y anuales, bonificaciones de Navidad, etc.; todos los tipos de pagos extraordinarios; indemnizaciones por incapacidad temporal o por estar al cuidado personas enfermas.

Ingresos relacionados con el empleo independiente: A los empresarios, agricultores y trabajadores independientes sólo se les pide información sobre los pagos recibidos en forma de salario.

Sector informal: No corresponde.

Actividad habitual: A los siguientes grupos de población se les pide información sobre su situación económica habitual: aprendices, estudiantes de escuela secundaria, estudiantes universitarios, personas con licencia por maternidad o que están al cuidado del niño (licencia parental), amas de casa, personas jubiladas, personas jubiladas por incapacidad, personas jubiladas por incapacidad parcial, desempleados, reclutas.

Clasificaciones:

Rama de actividad económica (industria):

Título de la clasificación utilizada: Clasificación nacional.

Grupos de población clasificados por industria: Personas empleadas y desempleadas con experiencia previa de trabajo.

Número de Grupos utilizados para la codificación: 60 grupos (códigos 01-99).

Vínculos con la CIIU: CIIU- Rev.3.

Ocupación:

Título de la clasificación utilizada: Clasificación nacional.

Grupos de población clasificados por ocupación: Personas empleadas y desempleadas con experiencia previa de trabajo.

Número de Grupos utilizados para la codificación: 400 grupos (grupos de nivel de 4 dígitos).

Vínculos con la CIUO: CIUO-88 a nivel del 4º dígito.

Situación en el empleo:

Título de la clasificación utilizada: Clasificación nacional.

Grupos de población clasificados por situación en el empleo: Personas empleadas y desempleadas.

Grupos utilizados para la codificación: 4 grupos (empleados, empleadores, trabajadores por cuenta propia, trabajadores familiares no remunerados).

Vínculos con la CISE: CISE-1993.

Educación:

Título de la clasificación utilizada: Clasificación nacional.

Grupos de población clasificados por educación: Todos los grupos de población.

Grupos utilizados para la codificación: 10 grupos (educación no primaria, educación primaria, educación básica, educación secundaria, educación no vocacional (especializada o profesional), educación vocacional/técnica, diploma universitario, licenciatura, maestría, doctorado/PhD.)

Vínculos con la CINE: CINE-1997.

Tamaño y diseño de la muestra:

Unidad final de muestreo: Hogar.

Tamaño de la muestra (unidades finales de muestreo): 2 200 hogares por trimestre

Fracción de muestreo: 0,4 por ciento de la población en edad de trabajar por trimestre.

Marco de la muestra: Para preparar el marco de la muestra se utiliza la base de datos de la población de Andmevara Ltd.

Actualización de la muestra: Trimestralmente.

Rotación:

Esquema: 2-2-2. Cada hogar de la muestra se entrevista cuatro veces; durante dos trimestres consecutivos y, después de un periodo de dos trimestres, se vuelven a entrevistar dos veces en los trimestres correspondientes del año siguiente.

Porcentaje de unidades que permanecen en la muestra durante dos encuestas consecutivas: 50 por ciento.

Número máximo de entrevistas por unidad de muestreo: No se proporcionó información.

Tiempo necesario para renovar completamente la muestra: 6 trimestres.

Levantamiento da la encuesta:

Tipo de entrevista: Papel y lápiz.

Número de unidades finales de muestreo por área de muestra: No se proporcionó información.

Duración del trabajo de campo:

Total: No se proporcionó información.

Por área de muestra: No se proporcionó información.

Organización de la encuesta: Permanente.

Número de personas que trabajan en el campo: 179 entrevistadores y 18 supervisores.

Substitución de las unidades finales de muestreo que no responden: No.

Estimaciones y ajustes:

Tasa de no-respuesta total: 9 por ciento.

Ajuste por no-respuesta total: Sí.

Imputación por no respuesta de ítemes: Sí.

Ajuste por áreas/poblaciones no abarcadas: No.

Ajuste por falta de cobertura: Sí.

Ajuste por exceso de cobertura: No.

Ajuste por variaciones estacionales: No.

Historia de la encuesta:

Título y fecha de la primera encuesta: Encuesta Nacional sobre la Fuerza de Trabajo, enero-abril de 1995 (Estonian Labour Force Survey, January-April 1995).

Modificaciones y revisiones significativas: De 1997 a 1999, la encuesta se realizaba durante el segundo trimestre. Desde 2000, la encuesta se realiza continuamente.

Documentación y difusión:

Documentación

Título de las publicaciones con los resultados de la encuesta: (periodicidad)

"Estonian Labour Force Survey, 1995, 1997, 1998, 1999" (anualmente)

Título de las publicaciones con la metodología de la encuesta: (periodicidad) "Estonian Labour Force Survey, 1995, 1997, 1998, 1999. Methodological report" (anualmente).

Difusión

Tiempo necesario para difundir los primeros datos: Desde 2000, dos meses para los resultados trimestrales y tres meses para los resultados anuales (fines de marzo del año siguiente). Los datos están disponibles para todos los usuarios interesados, el

mismo día, en la publicación titulada "Employment and Unemployment".
Información adelantada acerca de la fecha de la primera difusión pública: Sí.
Disponibilidad de datos no publicados si se solicitan: Sí.
Disponibilidad de datos por medios informáticos: Disquetes y correo electrónico. Sitio web: http://www.stat.ee .

Etiopía

Título de la encuesta: Encuesta Nacional sobre la Fuerza de Trabajo. (National Labor Force Survey).
Organismo responsable de la encuesta:
Planificar y realizar la encuesta: Junta Central de Estadística (Central Statistical Authority).
Analizar y publicar los resultados: Junta Central de Estadística (Central Statistical Authority).
Temas abarcados: Empleo, desempleo, subempleo, horas de trabajo, empleo en el sector informal, duración del desempleo, rama de actividad económica (industria), ocupación, situación en el empleo, nivel de educación y actividad habitual. Otros Temas abarcados: variables demográficas sobre migración, grupo étnico/religión, características socioeconómicas y demográficas de niños entre 5 y 14 años, capacitación vocacional/profesional.
Alcance de la encuesta:
Ámbito geográfico: Todo el país. Se entrevistan a las personas de 10 años y más de edad.
Grupos de población: Todas las personas de 10 años y más de edad que normalmente residen en el país. Se excluyen: poblaciones no asentadas, ciudadanos no residentes, extranjeros y personas que residen en el extranjero.
Disponibilidad de estimaciones de otras fuentes para las áreas/grupos excluidos: Ninguna.
Grupos abarcados por la encuesta pero excluidos de los resultados publicados: Ninguno.
Periodicidad:
Recolección de datos: En 1981/82 y 1986/87.
Publicación de los resultados: Irregular.
Períodos de referencia:
Empleo: Una semana (los últimos siete días) antes de la fecha de la entrevista.
Búsqueda de trabajo: Tres meses antes de la fecha de la entrevista.
Disponibilidad para trabajo: Un mes después de la fecha de la entrevista.
Todos los periodos son periodos de referencia móviles.
Conceptos y definiciones:
Empleo: Todas las personas de 10 años y más de edad que tenían un empleo remunerado o independiente durante los últimos 7 días, realizaban algún trabajo (por lo menos durante 4 horas) por un salario o sueldo, en efectivo o en especie, o estaban temporalmente ausentes del trabajo pero tenían vínculos formales con el empleo.
Se incluyen:
a)personas temporalmente ausentes debido a enfermedad o lesión, vacaciones o licencia anual, licencia por maternidad o paternidad, licencia parental, licencia para estudios o capacitación, conflictos laborales, mal tiempo, etc.;
b)personas con licencia sin goce de sueldo por iniciativa del empleador;
c)trabajadores a tiempo completo o parcial que buscan otro empleo;
d)personas que realizaron algún trabajo remunerado o por un beneficio durante la semana de referencia pero que estaban sometidas a escolaridad obligatoria, jubiladas y percibían una pensión, inscritas como desempleadas en busca de trabajo en una oficina de empleo o percibiendo indemnizaciones de desempleo;
e)estudiantes de dedicación completa o parcial que trabajan a tiempo completo o parcial;
f)aprendices y personas en formación remunerados o no remunerados;
g)personas que participan en planes de promoción del empleo, si eran remunerados;
h)personas ocupadas en la producción de bienes para su propio uso final;
i)miembros de las fuerzas armadas (voluntarios, de carrera y reclutas y miembros del servicio civil equivalente al servicio militar);
j)trabajadores familiares no remunerados en el trabajo.
Desempleo: Todas las personas de 10 años y más de edad que no tenían un empleo remunerado o independiente durante los últimos 7 días, que estaban disponibles para realizar un trabajo remunerado o independiente en un periodo de un mes a partir de la fecha de la entrevista, y que habían buscado un empleo de varias maneras (gestiones), en los últimos 3 meses.
Se incluyen:
a)personas suspendidas de su trabajo temporalmente o por tiempo indeterminado y sin remuneración;
b)personas que habían tomado disposiciones para comenzar un nuevo empleo o procuraban establecer su propia empresa;
c)personas jubiladas y que percibían una pensión;
d)estudiantes de dedicación parcial que buscan trabajo a tiempo completo o parcial;
e)trabajadores familiares no remunerados que estaban ausentes temporalmente del trabajo y trabajadores estacionales que no trabajan durante la temporada inactiva, si estaban disponibles para hacer otro trabajo;
f)personas que no buscaban trabajo porque no había ningún empleo disponible en el mercado o uno que se adaptara a sus capacidades;
g)personas que realizaban trabajos voluntarios (servicios no remunerados) o sociales para la comunidad.
Subempleo:
Subempleo por insuficiencia de horas: Personas que, durante la semana de referencia, estaban empleadas pero deseaban trabajar más horas (horas adicionales) y estaban disponibles para hacerlo en el trabajo que realizaban, en otro empleo, o en otro empleo a tiempo completo hasta el número de horas seleccionado.
Situaciones de empleo inadecuado: No corresponde.
Horas de trabajo: Únicamente horas reales trabajadas cada día en todos los empleos durante los últimos 7 días.
Ingresos relacionados con el empleo:
Ingresos relacionados con el empleo asalariado: No corresponde.
Ingresos relacionados con el empleo independiente: No corresponde.
Sector informal: 1. Si el negocio (o empresa para la que trabajan) mantiene una contabilidad regular de sus transacciones; 2. Si el negocio tiene por lo menos 10 trabajadores; 3. Si la empresa tiene licencia o no. Si las personas no cumplen todos los 3 criterios con respecto al empleo principal, se les clasifica en el sector informal.
Actividad habitual: En la encuesta se hacen dos preguntas, una sobre la ocupación en la actividad económica durante los últimos 12 meses; la otra se refiere a las razones por las cuales no se trabajó durante los últimos 12 meses, que sirven para clasificar a las personas como desempleadas o inactivas.
Clasificaciones:
Rama de actividad económica (industria):
Título de la clasificación utilizada: No disponible.
Grupos de población clasificados por industria: Personas empleadas.
Número de Grupos utilizados para la codificación: 14
Vínculos con la CIIU: Si, CIIU.Rev.3.
Ocupación:
Título de la clasificación utilizada: No disponible.
Grupos de población clasificados por ocupación: Personas empleadas.
Número de Grupos utilizados para la codificación: 10
Vínculos con la CIUO: CIUO-1988
Situación en el empleo:
Título de la clasificación utilizada: No disponible.
Grupos de población clasificados por situación en el empleo: Personas empleadas.
Grupos utilizados para la codificación: Empleadores, empleados (gubernamentales, no gubernamentales, privados, organización de desarrollo gubernamental), trabajadores por cuenta propia, trabajadores familiares no remunerados, aprendices, miembros de cooperativas.
Vínculos con la CISE: CISE-1993.
Educación:
Título de la clasificación utilizada: No disponible.
Grupos de población clasificados por educación: Personas empleadas y desempleadas.
Grupos utilizados para la codificación: a) Analfabetos, b) Alfabetizados c) Grado completado La clasificación se expresa en términos del grado más alto completado y se distinguen los siguientes niveles:
1. no saben leer ni escribir,
2. educación no oficial o grados 1 a 3,
3. grados 4 a 6,
4. grados 7 y 8,

5. grados 9 a 11,
6. grado 12,
7. superior al grado 12.

Vínculos con la CINE: Sí, CINE-1997.

Tamaño y diseño de la muestra:

Unidad final de muestreo: Hogar.

Tamaño de la muestra (unidades finales de muestreo): 35 hogares por número de zonas de enumeración; 1 448 zonas de enumeración rurales, más 913 zonas de enumeración urbanas, que totalizan 82 635 hogares.

Fracción de muestreo: No disponible.

Marco de la muestra: Lista de zonas de enumeración preparadas para el censo de 1994; para las zonas urbanas se preparó una nueva lista de hogares, y para las zonas rurales se preparó una lista de hogares 6 meses antes de la fecha de la encuesta.

Actualización de la muestra: Ninguna.

Rotación: No se hace rotación.

Esquema: No corresponde.

Porcentaje de unidades que permanecen en la muestra durante dos encuestas consecutivas: No corresponde.

Número máximo de entrevistas por unidad de muestreo: No corresponde.

Tiempo necesario para renovar completamente la muestra: No corresponde.

Levantamiento de la encuesta:

Tipo de entrevista: Entrevista personal.

Número de unidades finales de muestreo por área de muestra: Variable.

Duración del trabajo de campo:

Total: Del 15 al 26 de marzo de 1999.

Por área de muestra:

Organización de la encuesta: La organización de la encuesta es permanente.

Número de personas que trabajan en el campo: 1 654 entrevistadores, 343 supervisores y 88 instructores. Personal **Total:** 2 085.

Substitución de las unidades finales de muestreo que no responden: Sí.

Estimaciones y ajustes:

Tasa de no-respuesta total: No disponible.

Ajuste por no-respuesta total: Ninguno.

Imputación por no respuesta de ítemes: A los casos de no respuesta se les asignan los códigos 9, 99 o 999 según los dígitos de la columna respectiva.

Ajuste por áreas/poblaciones no abarcadas: Ninguno.

Ajuste por falta de cobertura: Ninguno.

Ajuste por exceso de cobertura: Ninguno.

Ajuste por variaciones estacionales: Ninguno.

Historia de la encuesta:

Título y fecha de la primera encuesta: La Primera Encuesta sobre la Fuerza de Trabajo Rural se realizó durante el periodo de abril de 1981 y abril de 1982. Se realizó otra encuesta en 1987 y 1988. Esta Encuesta Nacional sobre la Fuerza de Trabajo se realizó por primera vez en marzo de 1999.

Modificaciones y revisiones significativas: Las preguntas que se hacen son muy parecidas a las que se plantean en las Encuestas sobre la Fuerza de Trabajo Rural.

Documentación y difusión:

Documentación

Título de las publicaciones con los resultados de la encuesta: No se dispone de información.

Título de las publicaciones con la metodología de la encuesta: No se dispone de información.

Difusión:

Tiempo necesario para difundir los primeros datos: No se dispone de información.

Información adelantada acerca de la fecha de la primera difusión pública: No se dispone de información.

Disponibilidad de datos no publicados si se solicitan: No se dispone de información.

Disponibilidad de datos por medios informáticos: No se dispone de información.

Filipinas

Título de la encuesta: Encuesta sobre la Fuerza de Trabajo (The Labour Force Survey).

Organismo responsable de la encuesta:

Planificar y realizar la encuesta: Oficina Nacional de Estadísticas (National Statistics Office).

Analizar y publicar los resultados: Oficina Nacional de Estadísticas (National Statistics Office).

Temas abarcados: Empleo, desempleo, subempleo, horas de trabajo, duración del empleo, trabajadores desalentados, trabajadores ocasionales, rama de actividad económica (industria), ocupación (empleo principal y secundario), situación en el empleo, nivel de educación, actividad habitual y otros temas como nuevos participantes en el mercado del trabajo, base de pago y salario básico diario, etc.

Alcance de la encuesta:

Ámbito geográfico: Todo el país - nacional, regional, provincial/ciudades clave, zonas urbanas y rurales.

Grupos de población: Todas las personas que viven en hogares privados. No se consideran como miembros del hogar:

a)personas o miembros de la familia que viven en instituciones, como colonias penales/agrícolas, campamentos de detención, hogares de personas mayores, orfanatos, instituciones psiquiátricas, sanatorios antituberculosos, lazaretos, etc., y quienes tienen previsto ausentarse por 30 días o más;

b)miembros de las fuerzas armadas de Filipinas si se encuentran alejados de su lugar habitual de residencia por más de 30 días;

c)filipinos que viven en el extranjero, que han estado o estarán en el país por menos de un año a partir de la fecha de llegada;

d)ciudadanos de países extranjeros y miembros de su familia que se encuentran en el país como turistas, estudiantes, por asuntos de negocio o de empleo si tienen previsto estar en el país por un año o menos a partir de la fecha de llegada;

e)embajadores, ministros, cónsules extranjeros u otros representantes diplomáticos y miembros de su familia, independientemente del tiempo que hayan estado en el país;

f)ciudadanos de países extranjeros que son jefes o funcionarios de organizaciones internacionales, tales como las Naciones Unidas, etc., y miembros de su familia, independientemente del tiempo que hayan estado en el país.

Disponibilidad de estimaciones de otras fuentes para las áreas/grupos excluidos: No disponible.

Grupos abarcados por la encuesta pero excluidos de los resultados publicados: Trabajadores con contrato en el extranjero.

Periodicidad:

Recolección de datos: Trimestralmente.

Publicación de los resultados: Trimestralmente.

Periodo de referencia:

Empleo: Semana anterior (periodo de referencia móvil).

Búsqueda de trabajo: Semana anterior (periodo de referencia móvil).

Disponibilidad para trabajo: Semana anterior (periodo de referencia móvil).

Conceptos y definiciones:

Empleo: Todas las personas que habiendo cumplido 15 años y más de edad que, durante la semana de referencia, realizaron algún trabajo remunerado o por un beneficio, o trabajaban sin remuneración en un negocio o explotación agrícola de un familiar miembro del mismo hogar, durante por lo menos una hora, con la intención de producir bienes o servicios, así como quienes tenían un empleo o negocio pero estaban ausentes del mismo por enfermedad pasajera, vacaciones o licencia, personas suspendidas temporalmente de su trabajo sin remuneración o con licencia sin goce de sueldo por iniciativa del empleador, huelga, reducción de la actividad económica, etc., así como quienes esperaban el resultado de sus gestiones para obtener trabajo o comenzar un negocio o explotación agrícola dentro de las dos semanas contadas a partir de la fecha de la entrevista.

También se incluyen:

a)trabajadores a tiempo completo o parcial que buscaban otro empleo durante la semana de referencia;

b)personas que durante la semana de referencia realizaron algún trabajo remunerado o por un beneficio, pero estaban sometidas a escolaridad obligatoria, jubiladas y recibían una pensión, eran estudiantes de dedicación completa o parcial y trabajaban a tiempo completo o parcial, estaban inscritas como desempleadas en una oficina de empleo o recibían indemnizaciones de desempleo;

c)aprendices con acuerdos previos de trabajo o personas en formación remunerados;

d)trabajadores familiares no remunerados en el trabajo o temporalmente ausentes del mismo;

e)servicios domésticos privados;

f)miembros de cooperativas de productores;

g)miembros del servicio civil equivalente al servicio militar;

h)personas ocupadas en la producción de bienes para la venta o el consumo de la familia (cultivo de hortalizas en 100 metros cuadrados de terreno como mínimo).

Desempleo: Todas las personas que habían cumplido 15 años y más de edad y que no estaban trabajando por una remuneración o ganancia ni como trabajadores familiares no remunerados durante el periodo de referencia, pero que comunicaron que deseaban trabajar y estaban en busca de empleo. Se incluyen asimismo las personas sin empleo o negocio que comunicaron que no buscaban empleo porque consideraban que no había trabajo disponible, o por mal tiempo, enfermedad de poca importancia, esperaban el resultado de una solicitud de trabajo o de reintegro al empleo, esperaban tener una entrevista para un determinado empleo, etc. Se incluyen también las personas suspendidas de su trabajo por tiempo indeterminado sin remuneración, trabajadores estacionales en espera de trabajo de temporada, y las siguientes categorías de personas:

a)quienes habían tomado disposiciones para comenzar un negocio o el ejercicio privado de una profesión;

b)quienes buscaban y/o estaban disponibles para trabajar pero estaban jubiladas y percibían una pensión;

c)estudiantes de dedicación completa o parcial que buscaban trabajo a tiempo completo o parcial;

d)aprendices y personas en formación no remunerados;

e)participantes en planes de promoción del empleo.

Subempleo:

Subempleo por insuficiencia de horas: Personas empleadas que expresaron el deseo de trabajar más horas en el empleo que tenían o en otro adicional, o de tener un nuevo empleo con mayor número de horas de trabajo.

Situaciones de empleo inadecuado: No corresponde.

Horas de trabajo: Número real de horas trabajadas por una persona en todos los empleos que tenía durante la semana de referencia

Ingresos relacionados con el empleo:

Ingresos relacionados con el empleo asalariado: A partir de enero de 2001, después de la introducción del nuevo cuestionario de encuesta: salario básico diario.

Ingresos relacionados con el empleo independiente: No corresponde.

Sector informal: Este punto no está claramente separado. Las personas empleadas se clasifican por "clase de trabajador" (véase " Situación en el empleo"), incluido el sector informal, y sólo se refiere al empleo u ocupación principal.

Actividad habitual: La actividad principal u ocupación habitual se refiere al tipo de empleo o negocio en la que estaban ocupadas las personas la mayor parte del tiempo (más de 6 meses) o en la que habían pasado más tiempo durante los últimos 12 meses.

Clasificaciones:

Rama de actividad económica (industria):

Título de la clasificación utilizada: Clasificación Industrial Normalizada de Filipinas de 1994 (1994 Philippine Standard Industrial Classification (PSIC)).

Grupos de población clasificados por industria: Personas empleadas.

Número de Grupos utilizados para la codificación: 9 divisiones principales y un código para actividades que no están definidas de manera adecuada.

Vínculos con la CIIU: CIIU-Rev. 2, para el nivel de división principal únicamente, salvo para la División 6 que excluye restaurantes y hoteles. Éstos se incluyen en la División 9 (código 98).

Ocupación:

Título de la clasificación utilizada: Clasificación Normalizada de Ocupaciones de Filipinas de 1992 (1992 Philippine Standard Occupational Classification (PSOC)).

Grupos de población clasificados por ocupación: Personas empleadas.

Número de Grupos utilizados para la codificación: 9 grupos principales.

Vínculos con la CIUO: CIUO-68, a nivel de 2 dígitos, salvo para el grupo principal 3 (CIUO código 3.1 - los funcionarios ejecutivos públicos se incluyen en el código 2.0 de la PSOC -funcionarios legislativos, administradores públicos y ejecutivos públicos.)

Situación en el empleo:

Título de la clasificación utilizada: Clase de trabajadores.

Grupos de población clasificados por situación en el empleo: Personas empleadas.

Grupos utilizados para la codificación: Siete grupos: 0. Trabaja para un hogar privado, 1. Trabaja para establecimientos privados, 2. Trabaja para empresas o establecimientos públicos, 3. Independiente sin ningún empleado, 4. Empleador en una explotación agrícola o un negocio familiar, 5. Trabaja con remuneración para una explotación agrícola o un negocio familiar, 6. Trabaja sin remuneración para una explotación agrícola o un negocio familiar.

Vínculos con la CISE: CISE-1993. Los códigos 0, 1 y 2 anteriores se refieren al código 1 de la CISE.

Educación:

Título de la clasificación utilizada: Clasificación Normalizada de **Educación:** de Filipinas (Philippine Standard Classification of Education (PSCED)).

Grupos de población clasificados por educación: Personas empleadas y desempleadas.

Grupos utilizados para la codificación: Siete grupos: 00. No terminaron ningún grado de estudio, 01. Nivel elemental sin terminar, 02. Nivel elemental finalizado, 03. Escuela secundaria sin terminar, 04. Escuela secundaria finalizada, 05. Escuela superior sin terminar, 06. Escuela superior finalizada (especificación del grado más alto terminado y materia de estudio).

Vínculos con la CINE: No disponible.

Tamaño y diseño de la muestra:

Unidad final de muestreo: Hogares.

Tamaño de la muestra (unidades finales de muestreo): El tamaño de la muestra ampliada es de 3 416 barangays/zonas de enumeración (ZE) o 40 992 hogares, para estimaciones fiables a nivel de provincia; el tamaño de la muestra básica es de 2 247 ZE o 26 964 hogares, a nivel regional y nacional. Las muestras ampliadas o básicas se utilizan según el presupuesto disponible.

Fracción de muestreo: Aproximadamente 1/250 para zonas urbanas y 1/400 para zonas rurales.

Marco de la muestra: Se preparó básicamente a partir de los resultados del Censo de Población de 1995 (POPCEN). La lista de barangays sirve como marco para la primera etapa. La lista de ZE en cada barangay seleccionado sirve como marco para la segunda etapa, mientras que la lista de hogares de cada ZE seleccionada sirve como marco de muestra de la tercera etapa.

Actualización de la muestra: La muestra principal de ZE se divide sistemáticamente en 4 submuestras de 25 por ciento, identificadas como submuestras 1, 2, 3 y 4. La lista de hogares (hecha en teoría anualmente o una submuestra cada trimestre) se preparó en la submuestra 4 únicamente por limitaciones presupuestarias. Las nuevas listas reúnen información sobre el nombre del jefe del hogar, el seudónimo del jefe de familia y la dirección.

Rotación:

Esquema: Un 25 por ciento (una submuestra) de la muestra de hogares se saca de cada muestra de ZE cada trimestre y se sustituye por una nueva serie de muestra de hogares de las respectivas áreas de muestra.

Porcentaje de unidades que permanecen en la muestra durante dos encuestas consecutivas: 75 por ciento.

Número máximo de entrevistas por unidad de muestreo: Según el diseño previsto, deben ser 4 veces, pero para adaptarse a las necesidades de las encuestas basadas en los hogares, pueden ser más de 4.

Tiempo necesario para renovar completamente la muestra: En general un año.

Levantamiento da la encuesta:

Tipo de entrevista: Entrevistas personales.

Número de unidades finales de muestreo por área de muestra: Doce hogares por barangay de muestra.

Duración del trabajo de campo:

Total: Tres semanas (para octubre de 2001, del 8 al 31 de octubre).

Por área de muestra: No disponible.

Organización de la encuesta: La Oficina de Coordinación de Estadísticas, con estadígrafos adicionales.

Número de personas que trabajan en el campo: Para octubre de 2001: 569 miembros sobre el terreno y 285 estadígrafos contratados.

Substitución de las unidades finales de muestreo que no responden: Sí, la substitución se hace para grupos recién rotados cuando la unidad de vivienda/hogar no se puede localizar.

Estimaciones y ajustes:

Tasa de no-respuesta total: 4,6 por ciento para octubre de 2001.

Ajuste por no-respuesta total: Sí.

Imputación por no respuesta de ítemes: No.

Ajuste por áreas/poblaciones no abarcadas: No disponible.

Ajuste por falta de cobertura: Sí.

Ajuste por exceso de cobertura: No disponible.

Ajuste por variaciones estacionales: Sí, se utiliza el método X-II Arima para niveles de empleo, desempleo y fuerza laboral por sexo únicamente.

Historia de la encuesta:
Título y fecha de la primera encuesta: Encuesta de Hogares sobre Estadísticas de Filipinas, 1956 (Philippine Statistical Survey of Households).
Modificaciones y revisiones significativas:
1962: Se adoptó un nuevo diseño de muestreo, en función de los resultados del Censo de 1960 (POPCEN), lo que permitió la publicación de la clasificación rural y urbana a nivel nacional, hasta 1969.
1971 (marzo): Nuevo diseño que proporcionó estimaciones del empleo y características de la población a nivel regional. La frecuencia de la encuesta pasó a ser trimestral.
1975: Nueva encuesta, diseño de muestreo revisado y conceptos utilizados para los datos de la fuerza laboral. El mayor cambio se introdujo en el periodo de referencia que pasó de la semana anterior al trimestre anterior.
1976: Se integró la Encuesta Agrícola y la Encuesta sobre la Fuerza de Trabajo a la primera encuesta del plan integrado realizada en noviembre. Todas las estimaciones de las encuestas de hogares realizadas utilizaron la población prevista para controlar las fluctuaciones en los niveles de estimaciones.
1987: El periodo de referencia para las estadísticas de empleo volvió a ser la "semana anterior". La ronda del primer trimestre de 1987 fue la última serie en la que se utilizó el "trimestre anterior" como periodo de referencia.
1996: A partir de julio de 1996, el nuevo diseño de la muestra se basó en los resultados del Censo de Población de 1995.
2000: A partir de octubre de 2000, las estimaciones se basan en la Proyección del Censo de Población de 1995.
2001: A partir de enero, revisiones del cuestionario de la encuesta, con la inclusión de cuestiones sobre otros empleos, nuevos participantes en el mercado del trabajo, base de pago y salario básico diario, así como el uso de las clasificaciones industrial de 1994 y ocupacional de 1992.
Documentación y difusión:
Documentación:
Título de las publicaciones con los resultados de la encuesta (periodicidad): ISH Bulletin (trimestralmente).
Título de las publicaciones con la metodología de la encuesta (periodicidad): ISH Bulletin (trimestralmente).
Difusión:
Tiempo necesario para difundir los primeros datos: Unos dos meses (los resultados de octubre de 2001 se publicaron el 15 de diciembre de ese año).
Información adelantada acerca de la fecha de la primera difusión pública: Sí.
Disponibilidad de datos no publicados si se solicitan: Sí.
Disponibilidad de datos por medios informáticos: Sí. Sitio web: http://www.census.gov.ph.

Finlandia

Título de la encuesta: Encuesta sobre la Fuerza de Trabajo (Labour Force Survey).
Organismo responsable de la encuesta:
Planificar y realizar la encuesta: Oficina de Estadísticas de Finlandia (Statistics Finland).
Analizar y publicar los resultados: Oficina de Estadísticas de Finlandia (Statistics Finland).
Temas abarcados: Empleo, desempleo, subempleo, horas de trabajo, duración del empleo, duración del desempleo, trabajadores desalentados, rama de actividad económica (industria), ocupación, situación en el empleo, nivel de educación – según el Registro de **Educación:** y Grados Completados (Register of Completed Education and Degrees), (actividad habitual, véase más abajo) y empleos secundarios.
Alcance de la encuesta
Ámbito geográfico: Todo el país.
Grupos de población: Todas las personas de 15 a 74 años de edad que residen en el país, incluidos trabajadores extranjeros, ciudadanos que se encuentran temporalmente en el extranjero (menos de un año), miembros de las fuerzas armadas, ciudadanos no residentes, poblaciones no asentadas y quienes viven en hogares colectivos.
Disponibilidad de estimaciones de otras fuentes para las áreas/grupos excluidos: No corresponde.
Grupos abarcados por la encuesta pero excluidos de los resultados publicados: Sí.

Periodicidad:
Recolección de datos: A partir de 2000, encuesta continua. Antes: encuesta mensual.
Publicación de los resultados: Mensual, trimestral y anualmente.
Períodos de referencia:
Empleo: Una semana. Antes de 2000, una semana fija (por lo general, la semana que incluye el día 15 de cada mes).
Búsqueda de trabajo: Cuatro semanas (periodo de referencia móvil).
Disponibilidad para trabajo: Dos semanas (periodo de referencia móvil).
Conceptos y definiciones:
Empleo: Todas las personas que durante la semana de la encuesta realizaron algún trabajo (por lo mínimo de una hora) por una remuneración, un beneficio marginal o una ganancia, o que estaban temporalmente ausentes del trabajo debido a que estaban suspendidas de su trabajo por un determinado periodo de tiempo. Las personas empleadas pueden ser empleados, trabajadores independientes o trabajadores familiares no remunerados.
Se incluyen también:
a) personas que tienen un empleo pero que se encuentran temporalmente ausentes
del mismo debido a enfermedad, lesión, vacaciones, licencia anual, licencia por maternidad o paternidad, ausencia sin autorización, conflictos laborales, mal tiempo, desperfectos mecánicos, etc., o con licencia sin goce de sueldo por iniciativa del empleador;
b)trabajadores a tiempo completo o parcial que buscan otro empleo durante la semana de referencia;
c) personas que realizaron algún trabajo remunerado o por un beneficio durante la semana de referencia pero que estaban sometidas a escolaridad obligatoria, jubiladas y percibían una pensión, inscritas como desempleadas en busca de trabajo en una oficina de empleo o percibiendo indemnizaciones de desempleo;
d)estudiantes de dedicación completa o parcial que trabajaban a tiempo completo o parcial;
e)aprendices y personas en formación remunerados;
f)trabajadores familiares remunerados y no remunerados, temporalmente ausentes del trabajo;
g) servicios domésticos privados;
h)miembros de carrera de las fuerzas armadas.
Desempleo: Personas que, durante toda la semana de la encuesta estaban sin trabajo, habían buscado activamente un empleo durante las últimas cuatro semanas como empleados o trabajadores independientes y podían aceptar un empleo dentro de dos semanas. Se registran también como desempleadas las personas que carecían de un empleo y que esperaban comenzar un nuevo empleo dentro de dos semanas, así como las personas suspendidas de su trabajo por tiempo indeterminado que cumplen con los criterios de búsqueda y aceptación de trabajo.
Se incluyen también, sólo si están disponibles y buscan trabajo:
a)personas que perciben indemnizaciones de desempleo;
b)personas que tratan de establecer sus propias empresas;
c)personas sometidas a escolaridad obligatoria;
d)estudiantes de dedicación completa o parcial que buscan trabajo a tiempo completo o parcial;
e)personas que participan en planes de promoción del empleo;
f)trabajadores estacionales que están a la espera de trabajos agrícolas u otros tipos de trabajos estacionales.
Subempleo:
Subempleo por insuficiencia de horas: Personas que realizaron un trabajo a tiempo parcial porque no había trabajo disponible a tiempo completo, porque los empleadores les habían reducido el tiempo de trabajo semanal, porque no tenían trabajo debido a una reducción de los pedidos de los clientes o porque habían sido suspendidas de su trabajo por un determinado periodo de tiempo.
Situaciones de empleo inadecuado: No corresponde.
Horas de trabajo: Se recopilan las horas reales y habituales. Las horas realmente trabajadas durante la semana de referencia incluyen todas las horas trabajadas, pagadas o no, horas suplementarias y horas trabajadas en empleos secundarios. Las horas habituales se refieren a las horas normales de trabajo semanal de las personas empleadas en el empleo principal únicamente. Si se requiere, es posible presentar esos dos conceptos por separado.
Ingresos relacionados con el empleo:
Ingresos relacionados con el empleo asalariado: No corresponde.
Ingresos relacionados con el empleo independiente: No corresponde.
Sector informal: No corresponde.

Actividad habitual: (A las personas desempleadas, se les pregunta sobre la actividad primaria durante la semana de la encuesta. A las personas empleadas, se les pregunta sobre su principal actividad, pero no da ningún marco temporal especial).
Clasificaciones:
Rama de actividad económica (industria):
Título de la clasificación utilizada: Clasificación Industrial Uniforme (Standard Industrial Classification (SIC-1995)).
Grupos de población clasificados por industria: Personas empleadas y desempleadas.
Número de Grupos utilizados para la codificación: Unos 95 grupos a nivel de 2 y 3 dígitos.
Vínculos con la CIIU: CIIU-Rev.3 a nivel de 2 y 3 dígitos.
Ocupación:
Título de la clasificación utilizada: Clasificación Uniforme de Ocupaciones de Finlandia (CSO-2001), desde 2002, a nivel de cuatro o cinco dígitos.
Grupos de población clasificados por ocupación: Personas empleadas y desempleadas.
Número de Grupos utilizados para la codificación: 489.
Vínculos con la CIUO: CIUO-88.
Situación en el empleo:
Título de la clasificación utilizada: Situación económica de grupos.
Grupos de población clasificados por situación en el empleo: Personas empleadas y desempleadas.
Grupos utilizados para la codificación: Tres grupos: empleados, empleadores/trabajadores por cuenta propia, trabajadores familiares no remunerados.
Vínculos con la CISE: CISE-1993.
Educación:
Título de la clasificación utilizada: Clasificación Finlandesa Normalizada de la **Educación:** de 1997 (FSCED-97).
Grupos de población clasificados por educación: Todas las personas de 15 a 74 años de edad.
Grupos utilizados para la codificación: Los datos se obtienen del Registro de **Educación:** y Grados Completados, a nivel de 6 dígitos.
Vínculos con la CINE: CINE-1997.
Tamaño y diseño de la muestra:
Unidad final de muestreo: Particulares (de 15 a 74 años de edad).
Tamaño de la muestra (unidades finales de muestreo): 12 000 personas por mes.
Fracción de muestreo: Aproximadamente 1/311.
Marco de la muestra: Se obtiene del Registro Central de la Población que mantiene la Oficina de Estadísticas y que abarca toda la población.
Actualización de la muestra: Los datos de la muestra (direcciones, etc.) se actualizan mensualmente utilizando para ello los cambios que se reciben tanto del Registro Central de la Población (que se actualiza continuamente) como de los entrevistadores.
Rotación:
Esquema: La rotación se realiza según un sistema de cinco pasos progresivos: la primera entrevista se realiza en "t", la segunda en "t+3", la tercera en "t+6", la cuarta en "t+12", y la quinta en "t+15".
Porcentaje de unidades que permanecen en la muestra durante dos encuestas consecutivas: 0 por ciento (las muestras se superponen en 3/5 de un trimestre a otro y en 2/5 después de un año).
Número máximo de entrevistas por unidad de muestreo: Cinco.
Tiempo necesario para renovar completamente la muestra: Dieciocho meses.
Levantamiento da la encuesta:
Tipo de entrevista: Entrevistas telefónicas asistidas por computadora (CATI) para el 98 por ciento de las entrevistas y entrevistas personales asistidas por computadora (CAPI) para el 2 por ciento.
Número de unidades finales de muestreo por área de muestra: No corresponde.
Duración del trabajo de campo
Total: 10 a 15 días.
Por área de muestra: 10 a 15 días.
Organización de la encuesta: Permanente.
Número de personas que trabajan en el campo: Unos 160 entrevistadores.
Substitución de las unidades finales de muestreo que no responden: No.
Estimaciones y ajustes:
Tasa de no-respuesta total: 14 por ciento.
Ajuste por no-respuesta total: Sí.
Imputación por no respuesta de ítemes: Horas trabajadas por semana, si no se conocen.
Ajuste por áreas/poblaciones no abarcadas: No corresponde.
Ajuste por falta de cobertura: No.
Ajuste por exceso de cobertura: Sí.
Ajuste por variaciones estacionales: Sí, utilizando una versión ligeramente modificada del método Census X-11 Arima para los niveles de empleo, desempleo, fuerza de trabajo, tasa de empleo y tasa de desempleo.
Historia de la encuesta:
Título y fecha de la primera encuesta: Encuesta Finlandesa por Muestra sobre la Fuerza de Trabajo, 1958.
Modificaciones y revisiones significativas:
1983: La encuesta postal se transformó en encuesta por entrevistas. Se amplió el contenido de los datos.
1997: Se hizo un nuevo diseño de la encuesta para adaptarla más a las recomendaciones de la OIT.
Desde 2000: La encuesta se realiza de manera continua.
Documentación y difusión:
Documentación:
Título de las publicaciones con los resultados de la encuesta: Statistics Finland, Labour Market Series; Employment and Labour Force Bulletin. (periodicidad: mensual).
Título de las publicaciones con la metodología de la encuesta: Statistics Finland, Labour Market Series – Boletín anual.
Difusión:
Tiempo necesario para difundir los primeros datos: Tres semanas.
Información adelantada acerca de la fecha de la primera difusión pública: Sí.
Disponibilidad de datos no publicados si se solicitan: Sí.
Disponibilidad de datos por medios informáticos: Sí. Sitio web: http://tilastokeskus.fi/index_en.html .

Francia

Título de la encuesta: Encuesta anual sobre el empleo (Enquête annuelle Emploi).
Organismo responsable de la encuesta:
Planificar y realizar la encuesta: Instituto Nacional de Estadística y Estudios Económicos (Institut National de la Statistique et des Etudes économiques (INSEE)).
Analizar y publicar los resultados: INSEE.
Temas abarcados: Empleo, desempleo, subempleo, duración del trabajo, salarios, duración del empleo y el desempleo (antigüedad), trabajadores desalentados, rama de actividad económica (industria), ocupación, situación en el empleo, educación/calificación, empleo secundario.
Alcance de la encuesta:
Ámbito geográfico: Francia metropolitana.
Grupos de población: Personas de 15 años y más de edad que viven en residencias principales. Se excluyen las personas que viven en comunidades, salvo las que se mantienen vinculadas a sus hogares porque regresan periódicamente (alumnos de internados, residentes universitarios, etc.).
Disponibilidad de estimaciones de otras fuentes para las áreas/grupos excluidos: No corresponde.
Grupos abarcados por la encuesta pero excluidos de los resultados publicados: No corresponde.
Periodicidad:
Recolección de datos: Anual.
Publicación de los resultados: Anual.
Periodo de referencia:
Empleo: Una semana (variable).
Búsqueda de trabajo: Un mes (variable).
Disponibilidad para trabajo: 15 días (variable).
Conceptos y definiciones:
Empleo: Personas de 15 años y más de edad que se declararon activas o que habían trabajado por lo menos una hora durante la semana de referencia (semana anterior a la encuesta), a condición de que realmente tuviesen una actividad efectiva o, aunque no trabajaron durante la semana de referencia, mantuvieran un vínculo formal con el empleo (vacaciones, licencia por maternidad, etc.), sin emplear el criterio de la remuneración.
Se consideran también empleados:
a)las personas temporalmente ausentes del trabajo debido a enfermedad o lesión por menos de un año, vacaciones anuales, licencia por maternidad o paternidad, ausencia sin autorización, conflictos laborales, mal tiempo o desperfectos mecánicos, etc.;

b)los trabajadores a tiempo completo o parcial en busca de otro empleo durante el periodo de referencia;
c)las personas que realizaron algún trabajo, remunerado o por un beneficio, durante el periodo de referencia, pero que estaban sometidas a escolaridad obligatoria, jubiladas y recibían una pensión, inscritas como desempleadas en busca de trabajo en una oficina de empleo o percibiendo indemnizaciones de desempleo;
d)los estudiantes de dedicación completa o parcial que trabajan a tiempo completo o parcial;
e)los aprendices y las personas en formación remunerados o no, si participan efectivamente en la producción de la empresa;
f)los trabajadores familiares no remunerados que trabajaron durante el periodo de referencia;
g)las fuerzas armadas (voluntarios, militares de carrera y reclutas), así como las personas que realizan un servicio civil equivalente al servicio militar.
Desempleo: Personas de 15 años y más de edad sin empleo durante la semana de referencia, que han buscado empleo desde hace un mes y que están disponibles para trabajar en un plazo inferior a 15 días.
Subempleo:
Subempleo por insuficiencia de horas: Se distinguen dos categorías:
a)las personas que trabajan a tiempo parcial y que buscan un empleo para trabajar más horas (tiempo completo o tiempo parcial más importante) o que no buscan otro empleo pero desean trabajar más tiempo y están disponibles para hacerlo;
b)las personas que trabajan a tiempo completo y que, en contra de su voluntad, han trabajado menos tiempo que el habitual (desempleo parcial, etc.).
Para determinar el subempleo no se tiene en cuenta ningún nivel de duración del trabajo.
Situaciones de empleo inadecuado: Para las personas sin empleo, en la encuesta hay una pregunta sobre el principal motivo para buscar otro empleo (remuneración, calificación, deseos de trabajar más, etc.).
Horas de trabajo: Horas de trabajo realmente efectuadas durante la semana de referencia y número de horas habituales por semana para el empleo principal únicamente.
Ingresos relacionados con el empleo:
Ingresos relacionados con el empleo asalariado: La encuesta no abarca este punto.
Ingresos relacionados con el empleo independiente: La encuesta no abarca este punto.
Sector informal: No corresponde.
Actividad habitual: No corresponde.
Clasificaciones:
Rama de actividad económica (industria):
Título de la clasificación utilizada: Nomenclatura de Actividades Francesas (NAF).
Grupos de población clasificados por industria: Personas empleadas.
Número de Grupos utilizados para la codificación: 696 cargos, de los cuales 334 para la industria.
Vínculos con la CIIU: Relación entre la NAF, la NACE (Nomenclatura de Actividades en las Comunidades Europeas) y la CIIU.
Ocupación:
Título de la clasificación utilizada: Profesiones y Categorías de Ocupación (PCS).
Grupos de población clasificados por ocupación: Personas empleadas.
Número de Grupos utilizados para la codificación: 455 cargos.
Vínculos con la CIUO: CIUO-1988.
Situación en el empleo:
Título de la clasificación utilizada: Clasificación nacional.
Grupos de población clasificados por situación en el empleo: Personas empleadas.
Grupos utilizados para la codificación: Por cuenta propia; asalariado pero jefe de su empresa; asalariado del Estado o de la colectividad local; otro asalariado.
Vínculos con la CISE: No.
Educación:
Título de la clasificación utilizada: Clasificación nacional.
Grupos de población clasificados por educación: No se dispone de información.
Grupos utilizados para la codificación: Nivel alcanzado en la educación general (12 modalidades), la educación técnica (13 modalidades) y la educación superior (10 modalidades).
Vínculos con la CINE: No.

Tamaño y diseño de la muestra:
Unidad final de muestreo: Vivienda.
Tamaño de la muestra (unidades finales de muestreo): 105 000 viviendas.
Fracción de muestreo: 1/300 de viviendas.
Marco de la muestra: Último censo disponible, así como los ficheros SITADEL del Ministerio del Equipamiento para la elaboración de la muestra de los "Grupos Especiales de Empleo" (GSE) que representan las nuevas viviendas construidas, después del último censo de la población, con permiso de construcción para diez viviendas o más.
Actualización de la muestra : Un tercio en cada encuesta.
Rotación:
Esquema: No se dispone de información.
Porcentaje de unidades que permanecen en la muestra durante dos encuestas consecutivas: No se dispone de información.
Número máximo de entrevistas por unidad de muestreo: No se dispone de información.
Tiempo necesario para renovar completamente la muestra : Tres años.
Levantamiento de la encuesta:
Tipo de entrevista: Entrevista personal asistida por computadora.
Número de unidades finales de muestreo por área de muestra: No se dispone de información.
Duración del trabajo de campo:
Total: Cinco semanas a partir de comienzos de marzo.
Por área de muestra: No se dispone de información.
Organización de la encuesta : La gestión de la encuesta está a cargo de la Dirección General y las Direcciones Regionales del INSEE.
Número de personas que trabajan en el campo: 250 personas en el INSEE (pero no a tiempo completo) y 750 encuestadores.
Substitución de las unidades finales de muestreo que no responden: No.
Estimaciones y ajustes:
Tasa de no-respuesta total: 11 por ciento de viviendas.
Ajuste por no-respuesta total: Sí.
Imputación por no respuesta de ítemes: No se dispone de información.
Ajuste por áreas/poblaciones no abarcadas: No se dispone de información.
Ajuste por falta de cobertura: Sí.
Ajuste por exceso de cobertura: Sí.
Ajuste por variaciones estacionales: No.
Historia de la encuesta:
Título y fecha de la primera encuesta: Encuesta sobre el Empleo, 1950 (Enquête sur l'Emploi).
Modificaciones y revisiones significativas: 1982: cambio a la nomenclatura PCS (Profesiones y Categorías de Ocupaciones) para determinar las ocupaciones. 1990: los militares del contingente se consideran activos ocupados.
Documentación y difusión:
Documentación:
Título de las publicaciones con los resultados de la encuesta (periodicidad): INSEE Première et INSEE-Résultats (anualmente).
Título de las publicaciones con la metodología de la encuesta (periodicidad): INSEE-Résultats (anualmente).
Difusión:
Tiempo necesario para difundir los primeros datos: Unos tres meses: los resultados de la Encuesta de marzo de 2000 se publicaron en junio de ese año.
Información adelantada acerca de la fecha de la primera difusión pública: No.
Disponibilidad de datos no publicados si se solicitan: Sí.
Disponibilidad de datos por medios informáticos: CD Rom. Sitio web: http:///www.insee.fr

Gambia

Título de la encuesta: Encuesta sobre la Fuerza de Trabajo en Greater Banjul (Labour Force Survey in Greater Banjul).
Organismo responsable de la encuesta:
Planificar y realizar la encuesta: Departamento Central de Estadísticas (Central Statistics Department).
Analizar y publicar los resultados: Departamento Central de Estadísticas (Central Statistics Department).
Temas abarcados: Empleo, desempleo, subempleo por insuficiencia de horas, horas de trabajo, ingresos, empleo en el sector informal, rama de actividad económica (industria), ocupación, situación en el empleo, nivel de educación, actividad habitual y capacitación.

Alcance de la encuesta:
Ámbito geográfico: Limitado a Banjul y Kombo St. Mary's.
Grupos de población: Población de facto de 10 años y más de edad, es decir incluidos miembros habituales y visitantes que pasan la noche en los hogares de la muestra.
Disponibilidad de estimaciones de otras fuentes para las áreas/grupos excluidos: No disponible.
Grupos abarcados por la encuesta pero excluidos de los resultados publicados: Ninguno.
Periodicidad:
Recolección de datos: Encuesta especial realizada en 1992.
Publicación de los resultados: Agosto de 1995.
Períodos de referencia:
Empleo: Una semana antes de la fecha de la entrevista.
Búsqueda de trabajo: Una semana antes de la fecha de la entrevista.
Disponibilidad para trabajo: Una semana antes de la fecha de la entrevista.
Conceptos y definiciones:
Empleo: Personas que realizaron un trabajo remunerado, por un beneficio o una ganancia para la familia, en efectivo o en especie, durante el periodo de referencia, o que tenían un empleo o una empresa propia del que estaban ausentes debido a enfermedad o lesión, vacaciones, licencia por maternidad, licencia para estudios, conflictos laborales, mal tiempo, desperfectos mecánicos, etc. Se incluyen las personas suspendidas de su trabajo temporalmente sin remuneración, pero no las suspendidas por tiempo indeterminado. Se realizaron pruebas para incluir actividades marginales, la mayoría de las cuales se hacen para el consumo de la familia, como trabajos agrícolas, pesca, actividades de reparación, recogida de leña y fabricación de cestas y prendas de vestir.
Desempleo: Personas que carecían de empleo pero estaban disponibles para trabajar o se preparaban para comenzar a trabajar en su propia empresa durante el periodo de referencia. Se incluyen las personas que habían tomado disposiciones para comenzar un nuevo empleo en una fecha ulterior al periodo de referencia, así como los estudiantes de dedicación completa que estaban disponibles para trabajar. Se pueden identificar por separado las personas que buscaban trabajo durante el periodo de referencia.
Subempleo:
Subempleo por insuficiencia de horas: Personas que, durante la semana de referencia, trabajaban menos de 35 horas y estaban disponibles para trabajar más horas. Es posible identificar los trabajadores que buscaban hacer horas adicionales.
Situaciones de empleo inadecuado: No se dispone de información.
Horas de trabajo: Número total de horas realmente trabajadas en todos los empleos (excluidas las horas de comida y otro tiempo fuera del trabajo) cada día durante el periodo de referencia.
Ingresos relacionados con el empleo:
Ingresos relacionados con el empleo asalariado: Ingresos mensuales habituales del empleo principal remunerado. Se pueden identificar por separado los ingresos en efectivo y en especie.
Ingresos relacionados con el empleo independiente: No se dispone de información.
Sector informal: No se dispone de información.
Actividad habitual: Personas que realizaron un trabajo remunerado o para beneficio de la familia en cualquier momento durante los últimos 12 meses. Se obtiene información sobre el número de semanas trabajadas, así como sobre el número de semanas disponibles para el trabajo durante los últimos 12 meses. En relación con las personas habitualmente empleadas, se solicita información sobre la ocupación habitual, la rama de actividad económica (industria) y la situación en el empleo, mientras que para las personas habitualmente desempleadas la información requerida es sobre la última ocupación, la rama de actividad económica (industria) y la situación en el empleo. Para las personas habitualmente inactivas, se obtiene información sobre su situación como estudiantes, personas encargadas de las labores domésticas, incapacitados o pensionados.
Clasificaciones:
Rama de actividad económica (industria):
Título de la clasificación utilizada: No se dispone de información.
Grupos de población clasificados por industria: Personas empleadas y desempleadas con experiencia previa de trabajo.
Número de Grupos utilizados para la codificación: 10.
Vínculos con la CIIU: CIIU-Rev.2.
Ocupación:
Título de la clasificación utilizada: No se dispone de información.
Grupos de población clasificados por ocupación: Personas empleadas y desempleadas con experiencia previa de trabajo.
Número de Grupos utilizados para la codificación: 7.
Vínculos con la CIUO: CIUO-68.
Situación en el empleo:
Título de la clasificación utilizada: No se dispone de información.
Grupos de población clasificados por situación en el empleo: Personas empleadas y desempleadas con experiencia previa de trabajo.
Grupos utilizados para la codificación: 6 grupos (empleadores, trabajadores por cuenta propia, empleados remunerados, trabajadores familiares no remunerados, aprendices, otros).
Vínculos con la CISE: CISE-1993.
Educación:
Título de la clasificación utilizada: No se dispone de información.
Grupos de población clasificados por educación: Todas las personas de 5 años y más de edad.
Grupos utilizados para la codificación: 9 grupos (sin grado, grados 1 a 3, grados 4 a 6, grado 7, oficial 1 a 4, Nivel O, Nivel A, Primer Grado, Grado Superior y otros).
Vínculos con la CINE: Sí.
Tamaño y diseño de la muestra:
Unidad final de muestreo: Hogares.
Tamaño de la muestra (unidades finales de muestreo): 1 280 hogares seleccionados de 64 zonas de enumeración.
Fracción de muestreo: No disponible.
Marco de la muestra: No disponible.
Actualización de la muestra: No disponible.
Rotación:
Esquema: No corresponde.
Porcentaje de unidades que permanecen en la muestra durante dos encuestas consecutivas: No corresponde.
Número máximo de entrevistas por unidad de muestreo: No disponible.
Tiempo necesario para renovar completamente la muestra: No corresponde.
Levantamiento da la encuesta:
Tipo de entrevista: Entrevista personal.
Número de unidades finales de muestreo por área de muestra: 1 280 hogares.
Duración del trabajo de campo
Total: Un año.
Por área de muestra: Un año.
Organización de la encuesta: Organización especial.
Número de personas que trabajan en el campo: Ocho enumeradores y dos supervisores.
Substitución de las unidades finales de muestreo que no responden: Sí.
Estimaciones y ajustes:
Tasa de no-respuesta total: No disponible.
Ajuste por no-respuesta total: No disponible.
Imputación por no respuesta de ítemes: No disponible.
Ajuste por áreas/poblaciones no abarcadas: No disponible.
Ajuste por falta de cobertura: No disponible.
Ajuste por exceso de cobertura: No disponible.
Ajuste por variaciones estacionales: No disponible.
Historia de la encuesta:
Título y fecha de la primera encuesta: Ésta es la primera encuesta que se realiza.
Modificaciones y revisiones significativas: No corresponde.
Documentación y difusión:
Documentación:
Título de las publicaciones con los resultados de la encuesta: No disponible.
Título de las publicaciones con la metodología de la encuesta: No disponible.
Difusión:
Tiempo necesario para difundir los primeros datos: 3 años.
Información adelantada acerca de la fecha de la primera difusión pública: No.
Disponibilidad de datos no publicados si se solicitan: Sí.
Disponibilidad de datos por medios informáticos: No disponible.

Georgia

1.Título de la encuesta
Labour force sample survey (LFSS) (Encuesta por Muestreo sobre la Mano de Obra).

2.Organización responsable de la encuesta
State Department for Statistics (Servicio Estatal de Estadísticas).
3.Alcance de la encuesta
(a) Ambito geográfico
Todo el país, con excepción de Apkhazeti y Osseti Sur.
(b) Personas comprendidas
Toda la población de 15 y más años de edad.
Están excluidos:
•las personas ausentes del hogar durante doce meses o más;
•el personal militar (reclutas y militares de carrera) que vive en cuarteles;
•las personas internadas en instituciones penales y siquiátricas;
4.Periodicidad de la encuesta
La encuesta, que se lleva a cabo desde enero de 1998, es trimestral.
5.Período de referencia
La semana civil.
6.Temas abarcados
La población económicamente activa y no activa, incluidos los empleos principales y secundarios, clasificados por lugar de residencia, edad, sexo, tipo de actividad económica, nivel de educación, situación en el empleo, horas trabajadas, razones para buscar un nuevo empleo, así como el empleo declarado y el empleo oficioso, el subempleo debido a ausencias prolongadas del trabajo; duración y razones de desempleo.
7.Conceptos y definiciones:
(a) Empleo
Todas las personas de 15 y más años de edad que durante la semana de referencia:
•realizaron algún trabajo remunerado durante por lo menos una hora; y
•todas las personas que no trabajaron, pero que tienen trabajos o negocios de los cuales estuvieron temporalmente ausentes,
Están incluidos en las cifras totales:
•los trabajadores a tiempo completo y a tiempo parcial en busca de otro trabajo durante el período de referencia;
•los estudiantes a tiempo completo y a tiempo parcial que trabajan a tiempo completo o parcial.
•las personas que han realizado ciertos trabajos durante la semana de referencia, a la vez que son jubilados y pensionistas, o están inscriptos en una oficina de empleo como personas que buscan trabajo, o son beneficiarios de indemnizaciones de desempleo;
•los trabajadores familiares remunerados o no (a condición de que hayan trabajado por lo menos 12 horas);
•el personal doméstico privado;
•los miembros de cooperativas de productores;
•los miembros del ejército que viven en hogares.
Están excluidas las personas cuya única actividad es el trabajo en la vivienda (pintura, reparación, tareas domésticas), así como en sus explotaciones agrícolas para su consumo propio. También están excluidas las personas que trabajan benévolamente para organizaciones religiosas, caritativas y similares. Se considera que esas personas no ejercen una actividad económica.
(b) Desempleo:
Todas las personas de 15 y más años de edad que no tenían empleo durante el período de referencia, estaban disponibles para trabajar, salvo por enfermedad momentánea, y habían tomado medidas específicas para encontrar un empleo durante las cuatro semanas previas a la entrevista. También están incluidas las personas que encontraron un trabajo y adoptaron disposiciones para comenzar el nuevo trabajo en una fecha posterior al período de referencia
La búsqueda de trabajo comprende todas las iniciativas tomadas por una persona para encontrar un trabajo o crear una empresa: inscribirse en las oficinas de empleo, publicar y responder a anuncios, buscar la ayuda de familiares y amigos, tomar disposiciones para obtener recursos financieros, etc.
8.Diseño de la muestra
(a) Marco de la muestra
La muestra LFSS se estableció a partir del censo de población efectuado en 1989.
(b) La muestra
La muestra utiliza un plan de muestreo estratificado por zonas en dos fases, en el cual la probabilidad de selección es proporcional a la población. Para la primera fase, se seleccionaron, de un total de 12 000 distritos de enumeración (DE), 282 utilizando el principio del inicio aleatorio. La selección se efectúa de manera de que cada estrato tenga un número de DE múltiplo de 3 (con el objeto de realizar una repartición igual entre los meses de los cuatro trimestres). Cada estrato urbano comprende de 7 a 12 direcciones de muestra, y cada estrato rural de 16 a 24. En la segunda fase, se seleccionan sistemáticamente 3 351 hogares por medio de un inicio aleatorio, lo que representa el 0.3 por ciento del número total de hogares.
(c) Rotación
La muestra se caracteriza por el modelo de rotación siguiente: los distritos de enumeración (DE) seleccionados se dividen por partes iguales en 12 grupos de rotación a nivel de cada estrato. Todos los meses, se renueva el 8.3% de la muestra, lo que significa que a lo largo de un año toda la muestra será renovada. Todo hogar que ingresa en la muestra es entrevistado durante un período de cuatro trimestres consecutivos, y luego abandona la muestra definitivamente.
9.Documentación
Los resultados preliminares de la encuesta por muestreo sobre la mano de obra (LFSS) se publicaron en un comunicado de prensa, preparado por el Servicio de Estadísticas. Los resultados definitivos se publican en el Yearbook of Statistics.

Grecia

Título de la encuesta: Encuesta sobre la Fuerza de Trabajo (Labour Force Survey).
Organismo responsable de la encuesta:
Planificar y realizar la encuesta: Servicio Nacional de Estadísticas de Grecia (National Statistical Service of Greece).
Analizar y publicar los resultados: Servicio Nacional de Estadísticas de Grecia (National Statistical Service of Greece).
Temas abarcados: Empleo, desempleo, subempleo, horas de trabajo, ingresos, duración del empleo y el desempleo, trabajadores desalentados y ocasionales, rama de actividad económica (industria), ocupación, situación en el empleo, nivel de educación/calificación, actividad habitual, empleos secundarios, otros temas tales como información demográfica, condiciones de vida, relaciones sociales, consumo y gastos, etc.
Alcance de la encuesta:
Ámbito geográfico: Todo el país.
Grupos de población: Todas las personas de 15 años y más de edad. Se excluyen:
a)miembros de carrera y reclutas, incluso si viven solos o con su familia en una residencia fuera del campamento;
b)clientes permanentes de hoteles;
c)miembros de hogares colectivos;
d)miembros de hogares extranjeros que trabajan en embajadas, consulados, en misiones comerciales, económicas o militares y miembros de fuerzas armadas extranjeras.
Disponibilidad de estimaciones de otras fuentes para las áreas/grupos excluidos: No se proporcionó información.
Grupos abarcados por la encuesta pero excluidos de los resultados publicados: Algunos datos demográficos se obtienen a partir de personas que han abandonado el hogar, tales como reclutas, personas que viven otros hogares colectivos, ètc. Se prevé hacer una estimación de estas categorías y publicar los datos pertinentes.
Periodicidad:
Recolección de datos: Trimestralmente.
Publicación de los resultados: Anualmente.
Períodos de referencia:
Empleo: Una semana fija.
Búsqueda de trabajo: Cuatro semanas antes de realizarse la entrevista de la encuesta (periodo fijo).
Disponibilidad para trabajo: Dos semanas después de la entrevista (periodo fijo).
Conceptos y definiciones:
Empleo: Personas de 15 años y más de edad que, durante la semana de referencia anterior a la encuesta, habían trabajado por lo menos una hora o más o estaban temporalmente ausentes del trabajo debido a enfermedad, vacaciones, huelgas, mal tiempo, desperfectos mecánicos, etc. Aprendices remunerados y trabajadores familiares no remunerados.
Se incluyen también en la definición de empleo:
a)trabajadores a tiempo completo o parcial que buscan otro empleo durante el período de referencia;
b)personas que realizaron algún trabajo remunerado o por un beneficio durante el período de referencia, pero que estaban sometidas a escolaridad obligatoria, jubiladas y percibían una pensión, inscritas como desempleadas en busca de trabajo en una oficina de empleo o percibiendo indemnizaciones de desempleo;
c)estudiantes de dedicación completa y parcial que trabajan a tiempo completo o parcial;

d)personas que participan en planes de promoción del empleo si trabajan de manera regular;
e)voluntarios y miembros de carrera de las fuerzas armadas.
Desempleo: Todas las personas de 15 años y más de edad, sin empleo, que buscaban un trabajo, habían tomado algunas disposiciones específicas (tales como inscribirse en una oficina privada o pública de empleo, colocar o contestar anuncios, solicitar trabajo a los empleadores, pedir ayuda a amigos o parientes) durante las últimas 4 semanas para encontrar un empleo y estaban disponibles para trabajar en dos semanas.
Subempleo:
Subempleo por insuficiencia de horas: Personas que quieren trabajar más horas en el trabajo actual o en un empleo adicional.
Situaciones de empleo inadecuado: Personas que buscan otro empleo para hacer un mejor uso de sus capacidades.
Horas de trabajo: Horas habituales y reales de trabajo por semana en el empleo principal y en el empleo secundario.
Ingresos relacionados con el empleo:
Ingresos relacionados con el empleo asalariado: Se incluyen: a) los pagos mensuales del empleo principal, netos de cotizaciones a la seguridad social y de impuestos, incluidos pagos extraordinarios al mes, tales como horas extraordinarias, propinas, etc.; b) pagos adicionales netos (total de pagos anuales) como bonificaciones u otros beneficios de la empresa.
Ingresos relacionados con el empleo independiente: No está cubierto.
Sector informal: No corresponde.
Actividad habitual: No está cubierto.
Clasificaciones:
Rama de actividad económica (industria):
Título de la clasificación utilizada: Clasificación nacional basada en la NACE Rev.1.
Grupos de población clasificados por industria: Empleados y desempleados (rama de actividad económica del último empleo para el desempleado).
Número de Grupos utilizados para la codificación: 17 y 60 grupos a nivel de 1 y 2 dígitos, respectivamente.
Vínculos con la CIIU: CIIU-Rev.3.
Ocupación:
Título de la clasificación utilizada: Clasificación nacional basada en la CIUO-88 (COM).
Grupos de población clasificados por ocupación: Empleados y desempleados (ocupación en el último empleo para el desempleado).
Número de Grupos utilizados para la codificación: 10, 46 y 210 a nivel de 1, 2 y 3 dígitos, respectivamente.
Vínculos con la CIUO: CIUO-88.
Situación en el empleo:
Título de la clasificación utilizada: Clasificación nacional.
Grupos de población clasificados por situación en el empleo: Empleados y desempleados (situación en el último empleo para el desempleado).
Grupos utilizados para la codificación: Empleados, empleadores, trabajadores por cuenta propia, trabajadores familiares no remunerados, aprendices remunerados.
Vínculos con la CISE: CISE-1993.
Educación:
Título de la clasificación utilizada: Clasificación nacional
Grupos de población clasificados por educación: Empleados y desempleados.
Grupos utilizados para la codificación: 5 grupos: preprimaria, primaria, secundaria inferior, secundaria superior y educación terciaria posterior, primera y segunda etapas de educación terciaria.
Vínculos con la CINE: CINE-1997.
Tamaño y diseño de la muestra:
Unidad final de muestreo: Hogar.
Tamaño de la muestra (unidades finales de muestreo): Unos 31 000 hogares por trimestre.
Fracción de muestreo: 8,698 por ciento.
Marco de la muestra: Censo de Población y Hogares de 1991.
Actualización de la muestra: Cada trimestre.
Rotación:
Esquema: Cada trimestre se hace la rotación de 1/6 de la muestra de hogares, combinando las dos maneras siguientes: selección de una nueva muestra de hogares a partir de unidades de área y selección de nuevas unidades de área.
Porcentaje de unidades que permanecen en la muestra durante dos encuestas consecutivas: 84 por ciento.
Número máximo de entrevistas por unidad de muestreo: Seis.
Tiempo necesario para renovar completamente la muestra: 13 trimestres.
Levantamiento da la encuesta:
Tipo de entrevista: De puerta en puerta y método de lápiz y papel.
Número de unidades finales de muestreo por área de muestra: No se dispone de información.
Duración del trabajo de campo:
Total: 13 semanas.
Por área de muestra: No se dispone de información.
Organización de la encuesta: Personal permanente y especial.
Número de personas que trabajan en el campo: 200 entrevistadores y 10 supervisores.
Substitución de las unidades finales de muestreo que no responden: No.
Estimaciones y ajustes:
Tasa de no-respuesta total: 8 por ciento.
Ajuste por no-respuesta total: No.
Imputación por no respuesta de ítemes: Sí.
Ajuste por áreas/poblaciones no abarcadas: No.
Ajuste por falta de cobertura: No.
Ajuste por exceso de cobertura: No.
Ajuste por variaciones estacionales: No.
Historia de la encuesta:
Título y fecha de la primera encuesta: Encuesta sobre la Fuerza de Trabajo de 1981 (Labour Force Survey 1981).
Modificaciones y revisiones significativas: De 1981 a 1997, la encuesta se realizaba durante el segundo trimestre de cada año. A partir de 1988, la encuesta se realiza trimestralmente. Revisiones de los cuestionarios en 1992 y 1998.
Documentación y difusión:
Documentación:
Título de las publicaciones con los resultados de la encuesta: Labour Force Survey (Employment); Statistical Yearbook of Greece; Concise Statistical Yearbook of Greece.
Título de las publicaciones con la metodología de la encuesta: Statistical Yearbook of Greece.
Difusión:
Tiempo necesario para difundir los primeros datos: Casi un año.
Información adelantada acerca de la fecha de la primera difusión pública: Sí.
Disponibilidad de datos no publicados si se solicitan: Sí
Disponibilidad de datos por medios informáticos: Sí. Sitio web: http://www.statistics.gr/.

Hong Kong, China

Título de la encuesta: Encuesta General de Hogares (General Household Survey (GHS)).
Organismo responsable de la encuesta:
Planificar y realizar la encuesta: Departamento de Censo y Estadísticas (Census and Statistics Department (C&SD)).
Analizar y publicar los resultados: C&SD.
Temas abarcados: Personas corriente y económicamente activas, empleadas y desempleadas; personas corrientemente subempleadas por insuficiencia de horas; personas corrientemente fuera de la fuerza de trabajo; trabajadores desalentados; horas de trabajo, duración del desempleo; ingresos mensuales del empleo, etc., rama de actividad económica (industria), ocupación, situación en el empleo, nivel de educación.
Alcance de la encuesta:
Ámbito geográfico: Todo el territorio, excluidas las regiones marinas.
Grupos de población: Población civil que no vive en hogares colectivos, de 15 años y más de edad; se excluyen las personas recluidas en instituciones y las que viven en embarcaciones.
Disponibilidad de estimaciones de otras fuentes para las áreas/grupos excluidos: Ninguna.
Grupos abarcados por la encuesta pero excluidos de los resultados publicados: Ninguno.
Periodicidad:
Recolección de datos: Continua.
Publicación de los resultados: Publicación mensual de un promedio móvil de tres meses, centrado en el segundo mes.
Períodos de referencia:
Empleo: Siete días antes de la enumeración.
Búsqueda de trabajo: Ha buscado trabajo durante los 30 días anteriores a la enumeración.
Disponibilidad para trabajo: Los siete días antes de la enumeración.

Conceptos y definiciones:
Empleo: Personas que realizaron algún trabajo (por lo menos una hora) remunerado o por un beneficio durante los siete días anteriores a la enumeración o que tenían un vínculo formal con el empleo durante los siete días anteriores a la enumeración.
Desempleo: Personas sin trabajo, disponibles para trabajar durante los siete días anteriores a la enumeración y que buscaron trabajo durante los 30 días anteriores a la enumeración.
Subempleo:
Subempleo por insuficiencia de horas: Personas que involuntariamente habían trabajado menos de 35 horas durante los siete días anteriores a la enumeración y que habían buscado un empleo adicional durante los 30 días anteriores a la enumeración, o estaban disponibles para trabajar durante los siete días anteriores a la enumeración.
Involuntariamente se refiere a un periodo de poca actividad, escasez de materiales, desperfectos mecánicos e incapacidad para encontrar un empleo a tiempo completo.
Situaciones de empleo inadecuado: No se proporcionó información.
Horas de trabajo: Horas reales trabajadas en todos los empleos durante los siete días anteriores a la enumeración, incluidas horas trabajadas remuneradas o no, tanto en el empleo principal como secundario.
Ingresos relacionados con el empleo:
Ingresos relacionados con el empleo asalariado: ingresos mensuales del empleo: ingresos en efectivo de todos los empleos durante el último mes; para los empleos asalariados se incluyen salarios y sueldos, bonificaciones, comisiones, subsidios de vivienda, así como horas extraordinarias y subsidios de asistencia, pero se excluyen los pagos atrasados y los pagos en especie.
Ingresos relacionados con el empleo independiente: Se pueden utilizar como representativos los ingresos en efectivo relativos a la suma obtenida de su propia empresa para uso personal o del hogar, pero no a los ingresos del negocio.
Sector informal: No corresponde, pero los buhoneros se pueden identificar por separado.
Actividad habitual: No se proporcionó información.
Clasificaciones:
Rama de actividad económica (industria):
Título de la clasificación utilizada: Clasificación Industrial Uniforme de Hong Kong (Standard Industrial Classification (HSIC)).
Grupos de población clasificados por industria: Personas empleadas y desempleadas (rama de actividad económica del último empleo para el desempleado).
Número de Grupos utilizados para la codificación: 96.
Vínculos con la CIIU: CIIU-Rev. 2.
Ocupación:
Título de la clasificación utilizada: Índice de Ocupación del Censo de Población de Hong Kong (2001).
Grupos de población clasificados por ocupación: Personas empleadas y desempleadas (ocupación en el último trabajo para el desempleado).
Número de Grupos utilizados para la codificación: 45.
Vínculos con la CIUO: CIUO-88.
Situación en el empleo:
Título de la clasificación utilizada: Clasificación nacional, no se dan títulos.
Grupos de población clasificados por situación en el empleo: Personas empleadas.
Grupos utilizados para la codificación: Empleados, excluidos buhoneros; trabajadores a domicilio; empleadores, excluidos buhoneros; trabajadores independientes, excluidos buhoneros; buhoneros (se hace la diferencia entre empleado, empleador y trabajador independiente); trabajadores familiares no remunerados.
Vínculos con la CISE: CISE-1993.
Educación:
Título de la clasificación utilizada: Clasificación nacional, no se dan títulos.
Grupos de población clasificados por educación: Personas empleadas y desempleadas.
Grupos utilizados para la codificación: 25.
Vínculos con la CINE: CINE-1997.
Tamaño y diseño de la muestra:
Unidad final de muestreo: Trimestres permanentes en zonas y segmentos edificados.
Tamaño de la muestra (unidades finales de muestreo): 27 000 viviendas por un periodo de 3 meses.
Fracción de muestreo: 1,2 por ciento de la población que se desea abarcar por un periodo de 3 meses.
Marco de la muestra: Registro de Viviendas (RQ) con direcciones de todas las viviendas permanentes construidas en zonas de habitación, y Registro de Segmentos (RS) con segmentos limitados por puntos de referencia como caminos y ríos, que mantiene el Departamento de Censo y Estadísticas.
Actualización de la muestra: El RQ se actualiza continuamente tras la notificación de diversas fuentes de la construcción o demolición de edificios. El RS se actualiza cada 5 años antes de realizarse los censos de población o basándose en los censos.
Rotación:
Esquema: Los hogares permanecen en la muestra dos veces, con un intervalo de 3 meses.
Porcentaje de unidades que permanecen en la muestra durante dos encuestas consecutivas: No se proporcionó información.
Número máximo de entrevistas por unidad de muestreo: No se proporcionó información.
Tiempo necesario para renovar completamente la muestra: No se proporcionó información.
Levantamiento da la encuesta:
Tipo de entrevista: Personal y entrevistas telefónicas asistidas por computadora (CATI).
Número de unidades finales de muestreo por área de muestra: No se proporcionó información.
Duración del trabajo de campo:
Total: Un mes.
Por área de muestra: No se proporcionó información.
Organización de la encuesta: Permanente.
Número de personas que trabajan en el campo: 76 entrevistadores, 14 supervisores y 3 jefes de trabajo sobre el terreno.
Substitución de las unidades finales de muestreo que no responden: No.
Estimaciones y ajustes:
Tasa de no-respuesta total: 10 por ciento.
Ajuste por no-respuesta total: No.
Imputación por no respuesta de ítemes: No.
Ajuste por áreas/poblaciones no abarcadas: No.
Ajuste por falta de cobertura: No corresponde.
Ajuste por exceso de cobertura: No corresponde.
Ajuste por variaciones estacionales: Tasas de desempleo únicamente.
Historia de la encuesta:
Título y fecha de la primera encuesta: Encuesta sobre la Fuerza de Trabajo (Labour Force Survey (LFS)), septiembre de 1975.
Modificaciones y revisiones significativas: Desde septiembre de 1975 hasta septiembre de 1980, la LFS se realizaba a intervalos de seis meses. En agosto de 1981, se sustituyó por la GHS.
Documentación y difusión:
Documentación:
Título de las publicaciones con los resultados de la encuesta: Quarterly Report on General Household Survey.
Título de las publicaciones con la metodología de la encuesta: Quarterly Report on General Household Survey.
Difusión:
Tiempo necesario para difundir los primeros datos: 2 a 3 semanas después de finalizar el trimestre.
Información adelantada acerca de la fecha de la primera difusión pública: Sí.
Disponibilidad de datos no publicados si se solicitan: Sí.
Disponibilidad de datos por medios informáticos: Sí, en el sitio web del C&SD: http://www.info.gov.hk/censtatd .

Hungría

Título de la encuesta: Encuesta sobre la Fuerza de Trabajo (Labour Force Survey).
Organismo responsable de la encuesta:
Planificar y realizar la encuesta: Oficina Central de Estadísticas de Hungría (Hungarian Central Statistical Office).
Analizar y publicar los resultados: Oficina Central de Estadísticas de Hungría (Hungarian Central Statistical Office).
Temas abarcados: Empleo, desempleo, subempleo, horas de trabajo, duración del empleo, duración del desempleo, trabajadores desalentados, trabajadores ocasionales, rama de actividad económica (industria), ocupación, situación en el empleo, nivel de educación, empleo secundario.
Alcance de la encuesta:
Ámbito geográfico: Todo el país.
Grupos de población: Toda la población de 15 a 74 años de edad que vive en hogares privados durante la semana de referencia. Se excluyen la población de hogares colectivos y no asentada, así

como los miembros del hogar temporalmente ausentes y quienes residen en el extranjero, a condición de que tengan un consumo común con el hogar encuestado.
Disponibilidad de estimaciones de otras fuentes para las áreas/grupos excluidos: Sí, parcialmente.
Grupos abarcados por la encuesta pero excluidos de los resultados publicados: Ninguno.
Periodicidad:
Recolección de datos: Trimestralmente.
Publicación de los resultados: Trimestralmente.
Períodos de referencia:
Empleo: Una semana (últimos siete días antes de la fecha de la entrevista).
Búsqueda de trabajo: Cuatro semanas antes de la fecha de la entrevista.
Disponibilidad para trabajo: Dos semanas después de la fecha de la entrevista.
Conceptos y definiciones:
Empleo: Personas de 15 a 74 años de edad que, durante la semana de referencia:
a)realizaron algún trabajo durante una hora como mínimo por una remuneración en efectivo o en especie, o por un beneficio;
b)trabajaron por lo menos una hora sin remuneración en un negocio o explotación agrícola familiar ("trabajadores familiares no remunerados");
c)no trabajaban, aunque tenían un empleo, porque estaban temporalmente ausentes del trabajo por enfermedad, día de fiesta, mal tiempo, conflicto laboral, etc.
Se excluyen de esta definición las personas que durante la semana de la encuesta estaban ocupadas en las siguientes actividades:
a)trabajando sin remuneración por otro hogar o institución (trabajo voluntario);
b)construcción o renovación de su propia casa o apartamento;
c)quehaceres domésticos;
d)cultivaba un jardín privado o un pedazo de terreno para su propio consumo.
Se incluyen también en los totales:
a)miembros de las fuerzas armadas (de carrera y reclutas); el número de reclutas se obtiene de los registros administrativos y se atribuye al final del procesamiento de datos;
b)trabajadores a tiempo completo o parcial que buscaban otro empleo durante el periodo de referencia;
c)estudiantes de dedicación completa o parcial que trabajan a tiempo completo o parcial;
d)Personas que realizaron algún trabajo durante la semana de referencia pero que estaban jubiladas y percibían una pensión; o estaban inscritas como desempleadas en busca de trabajo en una oficina de empleo o percibiendo indemnizaciones de desempleo;
e)servicios domésticos privados;
f)aprendices y personas en formación remunerados.
Desempleo: Desempleadas son todas las personas de 15 a 74 años de edad que no trabajaron durante la semana de referencia, estaban buscando activamente un empleo durante las cuatro semanas anteriores a la entrevista, estaban disponibles para trabajar dentro de las dos semanas después de la semana de la encuesta y estaban esperando comenzar un nuevo trabajo en un periodo de 30 días.
La única excepción son las personas que no buscaban trabajo porque ya habían encontrado uno pero comenzarían en una fecha ulterior al periodo de referencia. Esas personas se clasifican como desempleadas.
Subempleo: Subempleo por insuficiencia de horas: Personas que, durante la semana de referencia, trabajaron involuntariamente menos de 36 horas.
Situaciones de empleo inadecuado: Personas que estaban buscando otro empleo.
Horas de trabajo: Horas habituales y reales trabajadas en el empleo principal y secundario.
Ingresos relacionados con el empleo:
Ingresos relacionados con el empleo asalariado: No corresponde.
Ingresos relacionados con el empleo independiente: No corresponde.
Sector informal: No corresponde.
Actividad habitual: No corresponde.
Clasificaciones:
Rama de actividad económica (industria):
Título de la clasificación utilizada: Clasificación nacional.
Grupos de población clasificados por industria: Personas empleadas y personas desempleadas.
Número de Grupos utilizados para la codificación: No se proporcionó información.
Vínculos con la CIIU: CIIU-Rev.3.
Ocupación:
Título de la clasificación utilizada: Clasificación nacional.
Grupos de población clasificados por ocupación: Personas empleadas y personas desempleadas.
Número de Grupos utilizados para la codificación: No se proporcionó información.
Vínculos con la CIUO: CIUO-88.
Situación en el empleo:
Título de la clasificación utilizada: Clasificación nacional.
Grupos de población clasificados por situación en el empleo: Personas empleadas.
Grupos utilizados para la codificación: 5 grupos (empleados, empleadores, trabajadores por cuenta propia, miembros de cooperativas de productores, trabajadores familiares no remunerados).
Vínculos con la CISE: CISE-1993.
Educación:
Título de la clasificación utilizada: Se utiliza la clasificación nacional.
Grupos de población clasificados por educación: Personas empleadas y desempleadas.
Grupos utilizados para la codificación: No se proporcionó información.
Vínculos con la CINE: Sí.
Tamaño y diseño de la muestra:
Unidad final de muestreo: Vivienda.
Tamaño de la muestra (unidades finales de muestreo): 32 000 hogares o unas 65 000 personas.
Fracción de muestre: 0,8 por ciento.
Marco de la muestra: El marco de la muestra está constituido por 12 775 unidades de muestra que abarcan 751 asentamientos del país y comprenden unas 626 000 direcciones.
Actualización de la muestra: Bianual.
Rotación:
Esquema: Se espera que cualquier hogar que entra a formar parte de la muestra proporcione información sobre el mercado de trabajo en seis trimestres consecutivos, periodo después del cual se retira definitivamente de la muestra.
Porcentaje de unidades que permanecen en la muestra durante dos encuestas consecutivas: 83.
Número máximo de entrevistas por unidad de muestreo: Seis.
Tiempo necesario para renovar completamente la muestra: 18 meses.
Levantamiento da la encuesta:
Tipo de entrevista: Papel y lápiz.
Número de unidades finales de muestreo por área de muestra: No se proporcionó información.
Duración del trabajo de campo:
Total: Una semana.
Por área de muestra: No se proporcionó información.
Organización de la encuesta: Oficina Central de Estadísticas de Hungría.
Número de personas que trabajan en el campo: Unos 700 entrevistadores y supervisores.
Substitución de las unidades finales de muestreo que no responden: No.
Estimaciones y ajustes:
Tasa de no-respuesta total: 12,2 por ciento.
Ajuste por no-respuesta total: No.
Imputación por no respuesta de ítemes: No.
Ajuste por áreas/poblaciones no abarcadas: No.
Ajuste por falta de cobertura: No.
Ajuste por exceso de cobertura: No.
Ajuste por variaciones estacionales: No.
Historia de la encuesta:
Título y fecha de la primera encuesta: Encuesta sobre la Fuerza de Trabajo, enero de 1992.
Modificaciones y revisiones significativas: Ninguna.
Documentación y difusión:
Documentación:
Título de las publicaciones con los resultados de la encuesta: (periodicidad) Monthly Report, LFS Quarterly Bulletin and LFS Time-Series (anual).
Título de las publicaciones con la metodología de la encuesta: (periodicidad) LFS Methodology (en húngaro y parcialmente en inglés).

Difusión:
Tiempo necesario para difundir los primeros datos: No se proporcionó información.
Información adelantada acerca de la fecha de la primera difusión pública: Sí.
Disponibilidad de datos no publicados si se solicitan: Sí.
Disponibilidad de datos por medios informáticos: Sí. Sitio web: http://www.ksh.hu .

India

Título de la encuesta: Encuesta sobre Empleo y Desempleo (Employment and Unemployment Survey).
Organismo responsable de la encuesta:
Planificar y realizar la encuesta: Organización Nacional de Encuestas por Muestra (National Sample Survey Organisation (NSSO))
Analizar y publicar los resultados: SDRD, NSSO
Temas abarcados: Empleo, desempleo, subempleo por insuficiencia de horas, horas de trabajo, salarios, duración del empleo y el desempleo, trabajadores ocasionales, rama de actividad económica (industria), ocupación, situación en el empleo, nivel de educación y actividad habitual.
Alcance de la encuesta:
Ámbito geográfico: Todo el país excepto algunas zonas internas de dos estados y un territorio.
Grupos de población: Personas de 5 años y más de edad, salvo la población sin hogar.
Disponibilidad de estimaciones de otras fuentes para las áreas/grupos excluidos: No.
Grupos abarcados por la encuesta pero excluidos de los resultados publicados: No disponible.
Periodicidad:
Recolección de datos: Se realiza una encuesta anual en una pequeña muestra. La muestra completa se encuesta cada cinco años, la última fue entre julio de 1993 y junio de 1994.
Publicación de los resultados: anualmente para la "pequeña" muestra; cada cinco años para la muestra completa.
Períodos de referencia:
Empleo: Una semana antes de la fecha de la entrevista.
Búsqueda de trabajo: Un día y una semana antes de la fecha de la entrevista.
Disponibilidad para trabajo: Un día y una semana antes de la fecha de la entrevista.
Conceptos y definiciones:
Empleo: Personas ocupadas en una actividad lucrativa por lo menos una hora durante la semana de referencia. Se incluyen los miembros de las fuerzas armadas, pero se excluyen personas jubiladas, personas que perciben una pensión y que también trabajan.
Desempleo: Personas que no estaban ocupadas en una actividad lucrativa pero que habían buscado empleo o estaban disponibles para trabajar (aunque no buscaban empleo) en cualquier momento durante el periodo de referencia. Se excluyen personas jubiladas y personas que perciben una pensión.
Subempleo: Subempleo por insuficiencia de horas: Personas empleadas que, durante la semana de referencia, deseaban trabajar horas adicionales.
Situaciones de empleo inadecuado: No se dispone de información.
Horas de trabajo: No disponible.
Actividad habitual: Se consideran empleadas las personas ocupadas en una actividad lucrativa por un periodo de tiempo más largo durante los últimos 365 días. Se consideran generalmente como desempleadas las personas que buscaban un empleo o estaban disponibles para trabajar por un periodo de tiempo más largo durante los últimos 365 días.
Clasificaciones:
Rama de actividad económica (industria):
Título de la clasificación utilizada: No se dispone de información.
Grupos de población clasificados por industria: Personas empleadas.
Número de Grupos utilizados para la codificación: 9
Vínculos con la CIIU: CIIU-Rev .3.
Ocupación:
Título de la clasificación utilizada: No se dispone de información.
Grupos de población clasificados por ocupación: Personas empleadas.
Número de Grupos utilizados para la codificación: 31
Vínculos con la CIUO: CIUO-88.
Situación en el empleo:
Título de la clasificación utilizada: No se dispone de información.
Grupos de población clasificados por situación en el empleo: Personas empleadas y personas desempleadas con experiencia previa de trabajo.
Grupos utilizados para la codificación: 10 grupos.
Vínculos con la CISE: CISE-1993.
Educación:
Título de la clasificación utilizada: No se dispone de información.
Grupos de población clasificados por educación: Personas empleadas y personas desempleadas.
Grupos utilizados para la codificación: 5 grupos.
Vínculos con la CINE: Sí.
Tamaño y diseño de la muestra:
Unidad final de muestreo: Hogares.
Tamaño de la muestra (unidades finales de muestreo): Unos 40 000 hogares para la encuesta anual, y unos 125 000 hogares para la encuesta quinquenal.
Fracción de muestreo: 1/5 000.
Marco de la muestra: Lista de lugares con caseríos en formación en zonas rurales y bloques urbanos en zonas urbanas.
Actualización de la muestra: Una vez cada diez años en zonas rurales y cada cinco años en zonas urbanas.
Rotación:
Esquema: Se hace la rotación de la mitad de la muestra de la subronda anterior.
Porcentaje de unidades que permanecen en la muestra durante dos encuestas consecutivas: 50 por ciento.
Número máximo de entrevistas por unidad de muestreo: Dos.
Tiempo necesario para renovar completamente la muestra: Tres años.
Levantamiento da la encuesta:
Tipo de entrevista: Entrevista personal.
Número de unidades finales de muestreo por área de muestra: 4 hogares para la encuesta anual y diez para la encuesta quinquenal.
Duración del trabajo de campo
Total: Un año.
Por área de muestra: Un año.
Organización de la encuesta: Permanente.
Número de personas que trabajan en el campo: 1 300 enumeradores y 400 supervisores.
Substitución de las unidades finales de muestreo que no responden: Sí, de hogares.
Estimaciones y ajustes:
Tasa de no-respuesta total: No disponible.
Ajuste por no-respuesta total: Sí.
Imputación por no respuesta de ítemes: Substitución.
Ajuste por áreas/poblaciones no abarcadas: No.
Ajuste por falta de cobertura: No.
Ajuste por exceso de cobertura: No.
Ajuste por variaciones estacionales: No.
Historia de la encuesta:
Título y fecha de la primera encuesta: Encuesta anual desde mayo de 1955-noviembre de 1955; encuesta quinquenal desde 1972-73.
Modificaciones y revisiones significativas: En 1972-73 y en 1977-78 se adoptaron los conceptos de situación habitual y situación corriente. Las últimas encuestas quinquenales no son comparables.
Documentación y difusión:
Documentación:
Título de las publicaciones con los resultados de la encuesta: (periodicidad) Government of India, Department of Statistics, national Sample Survey Organisation: "NSSO Journal (Sarvekshana)" trimestral, New Dehlil. Informes NSS mimeografiados.
Título de las publicaciones con la metodología de la encuesta: Idem.
Difusión:
Tiempo necesario para difundir los primeros datos: 4 años.
Información adelantada acerca de la fecha de la primera difusión pública: No.
Disponibilidad de datos no publicados si se solicitan: Sí.
Disponibilidad de datos por medios informáticos: Sí.

Indonesia

Título de la encuesta: Encuesta Nacional sobre la Fuerza de Trabajo (National Labor Force Survey (NLFS)).

Organismo responsable de la encuesta:
Planificar y realizar la encuesta: Oficina Central de Estadísticas de Indonesia (BPS-Statistics Indonesia).
Analizar y publicar los resultados: Oficina Central de Estadísticas de Indonesia (BPS-Statistics Indonesia).
Temas abarcados: Empleo, desempleo, horas de trabajo, salarios, duración del desempleo, rama de actividad económica (industria), ocupación, situación en el empleo, nivel de educación, empleo secundario. (Los datos del empleo en el sector informal se pueden obtener a partir de los datos sobre la situación en el empleo).
Alcance de la encuesta:
Ámbito geográfico: Todo el país.
Grupos de población: Todas las personas de 15 años y más de edad, excluidas las personas que viven en hogares colectivos y poblaciones no asentadas, así como las personas ausentes durante más de 6 meses.
Disponibilidad de estimaciones de otras fuentes para las áreas/grupos excluidos: No disponible.
Grupos abarcados por la encuesta pero excluidos de los resultados publicados: No disponible.
Periodicidad:
Recolección de datos: Anualmente.
Publicación de los resultados: Anualmente.
Períodos de referencia:
Empleo: Periodo de referencia de una semana móvil.
Búsqueda de trabajo: No se especifica un periodo.
Disponibilidad para trabajo: No se especifica un periodo.
Conceptos y definiciones:
Empleo: Actividad realizada por lo menos una hora en la semana de referencia por una persona (de 15 años y más de edad) para ganar o ayudar a obtener un ingreso/beneficio o por una persona que tiene un cargo pero estaba temporalmente ausente del trabajo, por ejemplo con licencia. Se incluyen también las actividades realizadas por trabajadores familiares no remunerados que ayudan a sus padres a obtener un ingreso/beneficio.
Se incluyen también:
a)personas con un empleo pero temporalmente ausente del mismo debido a enfermedad o lesión, licencia por maternidad o paternidad, licencia parental, licencia para estudios o capacitación, ausencia sin autorización, conflictos laborales, mal tiempo, personas suspendidas de su trabajo temporalmente o por tiempo indeterminado y sin remuneración;
b)trabajadores a tiempo completo o parcial que buscan otro empleo durante el período de referencia;
c)personas que realizaron algún trabajo remunerado o por un beneficio durante la semana de referencia pero que estaban sometidas a escolaridad obligatoria, inscritas como desempleadas en busca de trabajo en una oficina de empleo;
d)estudiantes de dedicación completa o parcial que trabajan a tiempo completo o parcial;
e)trabajadores familiares no remunerados que estaban en el trabajo durante la semana de referencia;
f)todos los miembros de las fuerzas armadas.
Desempleo: Todas las personas de 15 años y más de edad y sin empleo (no tenían ningún trabajo) durante la semana de referencia, y que todavía buscan un empleo.
Se incluyen:
a)personas sin trabajo y corrientemente disponibles para trabajar que habían tomado disposiciones para comenzar un nuevo empleo después de la semana de referencia;
b)personas sometidas a escolaridad obligatoria que estaban buscando un empleo y/o estaban disponibles para trabajar; y estudiantes de dedicación completa o parcial que buscaban un trabajo a tiempo completo o parcial;
c)personas que estaban buscando un empleo y/o estaban disponibles para trabajar pero estaban jubiladas y percibían una pensión.
Subempleo: Subempleo por insuficiencia de horas: No corresponde.
Situaciones de empleo inadecuado: Personas que trabajan menos de 35 horas por semana que siguen buscando otro(s) empleo(s) o que podrían cambiar su(s) trabajo(s) actual(es) si se presenta la oportunidad para hacerlo.
Horas de trabajo: Número real de horas trabajadas en el empleo principal y cualquier empleo adicional por día durante una semana (la de referencia).
Ingresos relacionados con el empleo:
Ingresos relacionados con el empleo asalariado: Todos los ingresos recibidos (incluidos los pagos en especie y en servicios) después de deducir los impuestos sobre la renta. Estos datos se obtienen de la población corrientemente activa.
Ingresos relacionados con el empleo independiente: No corresponde.
Sector informal: Esta información se deriva de los datos sobre la situación en el empleo de los trabajadores; en el sector informal se incluye a quienes trabajan como empleadores y empleados. En el sector informal se incluye también a los trabajadores independientes que no tienen ayuda de ninguna persona, los trabajadores independientes que reciben ayuda de miembros de la familia o ayuda temporal y los trabajadores familiares no remunerados.
Actividad habitual: No corresponde.
Clasificaciones:
Rama de actividad económica (industria):
Título de la clasificación utilizada: Clasificación Uniforme de Industrias de Indonesia (Klui).
Grupos de población clasificados por industria: Personas empleadas.
Número de Grupos utilizados para la codificación: Hasta 1999, grupos codificados a nivel de 2 dígitos; a partir de 2000, hasta el nivel de 3 dígitos.
Vínculos con la CIIU: CIIU-68 hasta 1999 y la CIIU-Rev.3 a partir de 2000.
Ocupación:
Título de la clasificación utilizada: Clasificación Uniforme de Industrias de Indonesia (Kji).
Grupos de población clasificados por ocupación: Personas empleadas.
Número de Grupos utilizados para la codificación: Hasta 1999, grupos codificados a nivel de 2 dígitos; a partir de 2000, hasta el nivel de 3 dígitos.
Vínculos con la CIUO: CIUO-68 hasta 1999 y la CIUO-88 a partir de 2000.
Situación en el empleo:
Título de la clasificación utilizada: No disponible.
Grupos de población clasificados por situación en el empleo: Personas empleadas.
Grupos utilizados para la codificación: Cinco grupos: 1. Empleados independientes, 2. Empleadores asistidos por trabajadores familiares no remunerados, 3. Empleadores con trabajadores remunerados (permanentes), 4. Empleados, 5. Trabajadores familiares no remunerados.
Vínculos con la CISE: Sí, CISE-1993.
Educación:
Título de la clasificación utilizada: No disponible.
Grupos de población clasificados por educación: Personas empleadas y desempleadas.
Grupos utilizados para la codificación: Diez grupos: 1. No escolarizados, 2. Escuela primaria sin terminar, 3. Escuela primaria, 4. Secundaria general de primer ciclo, 5. **Educación:** técnica general de jóvenes, 6. Escuela secundaria general de segundo ciclo, 7. Escuela profesional secundaria de segundo ciclo, 8. Diplomas I/II, 9. Título académico/ Diploma III, 10. Universidad.
Vínculos con la CINE: Sí, CINE-76.
Tamaño y diseño de la muestra:
Unidad final de muestreo: Hogar.
Tamaño de la muestra (unidades finales de muestreo): 49 000 hogares.
Fracción de muestreo: Varía entre provincias y entre zonas urbanas y rurales.
Marco de la muestra: El marco de la muestra se basa en el archivo central de los archivos de aldeas, que consisten en listas de las unidades de área estadísticas más pequeñas (unos 30 hogares) para zonas urbanas y rurales.
Actualización de la muestra: No disponible.
Rotación: No disponible.
Esquema: No disponible.
Porcentaje de unidades que permanecen en la muestra durante dos encuestas consecutivas: No disponible.
Número máximo de entrevistas por unidad de muestreo: No disponible.
Tiempo necesario para renovar completamente la muestra: No disponible.
Levantamiento da la encuesta:
Tipo de entrevista: Entrevista personal.
Número de unidades finales de muestreo por área de muestra: No disponible.
Duración del trabajo de campo
Total: Un mes (en agosto).
Por área de muestra: No disponible.
Organización de la encuesta: Personal permanente de la Oficina de Estadísticas de Indonesia.

Número de personas que trabajan en el campo: No disponible.
Substitución de las unidades finales de muestreo que no responden: No.
Estimaciones y ajustes:
Tasa de no-respuesta total: Uno por ciento.
Ajuste por no-respuesta total: Sí.
Imputación por no respuesta de ítemes: No.
Ajuste por áreas/poblaciones no abarcadas: No.
Ajuste por falta de cobertura: No.
Ajuste por exceso de cobertura: No.
Ajuste por variaciones estacionales: No.
Historia de la encuesta:
Título y fecha de la primera encuesta: Encuesta sobre la Fuerza de Trabajo Nacional, trimestralmente entre 1986 y 1993.
Modificaciones y revisiones significativas: A partir de 1994, la encuesta se realiza anualmente.
Documentación y difusión:
Documentación:
Título de las publicaciones con los resultados de la encuesta: (periodicidad) Labour Force Situation in Indonesia; Labourers/Employees' Situation in Indonesia. (anual).
Título de las publicaciones con la metodología de la encuesta: No disponible.
Difusión:
Tiempo necesario para difundir los primeros datos: Seis meses (los resultados de agosto de 1998 se publicaron en febrero de 1999).
Información adelantada acerca de la fecha de la primera difusión pública: No.
Disponibilidad de datos no publicados si se solicitan: Sí.
Disponibilidad de datos por medios informáticos: Las principales tabulaciones se presentan en Internet: http://www.bps.go.id.

Irán, Rep. Islámica del

Título de la encuesta: Encuesta de las características del empleo y el desempleo en los hogares (Survey of household employment and unemployment characteristics).
Organismo responsable de la encuesta:
Planificar y realizar la encuesta: Centro de Estadísticas del Irán, Ministerio de Planificación (Statistical Centre of Iran, Ministry of Planning).
Analizar y publicar los resultados: Centro de Estadísticas del Irán, Ministerio de Planificación (Statistical Centre of Iran, Ministry of Planning).
Temas abarcados: Empleo, desempleo, horas de trabajo, duración del empleo, duración del desempleo, trabajadores ocasionales, rama de actividad económica (industria), ocupación, situación en el empleo, nivel de educación, empleo secundario.
Alcance de la encuesta:
Ámbito geográfico: Todas las zonas rurales y urbanas del país.
Grupos de población: Toda la población civil, excluidas las poblaciones no asentadas y las personas que viven en hogares colectivos. Se excluyen también los invitados y visitantes y las personas que viven en el extranjero, por ejemplo por motivos de trabajo o estudios.
Disponibilidad de estimaciones de otras fuentes para las áreas/grupos excluidos: Los resultados de la encuesta se limitan a la población que abarca la encuesta. Cuando es necesario, se separan las estimaciones para la población excluida y éstas se añaden a los resultados de la encuesta.
Periodicidad:
Recolección de datos: Anual.
Publicación de los resultados: Anual.
Período de referencia:
Empleo: Semana de referencia fija.
Búsqueda de trabajo: Semana de referencia fija.
Disponibilidad para trabajo: Semana de referencia.
Conceptos y definiciones:
Empleo: Personas, de 10 años y más de edad, en hogares normalmente asentados, que estaban ocupadas en un empleo por lo menos 2 días durante los últimos siete días antes de realizarse la entrevista de la encuesta.
Se incluyen:
a)personas con un trabajo pero temporalmente ausentes del mismo por cualquier razón, y personas suspendidas de su trabajo temporalmente sin remuneración;
b)trabajadores a tiempo completo o parcial que buscaban trabajo durante el periodo de referencia;
c)Personas que realizaron algún trabajo remunerado o por un beneficio durante la semana de referencia pero estaban sometidas a escolaridad obligatoria, jubiladas y percibían una pensión o indemnizaciones de desempleo, inscritas como desempleadas en busca de trabajo en una oficina de empleo o estaban buscando otro trabajo durante la semana de referencia;
d)estudiantes de dedicación completa o parcial que trabajan a tiempo completo o parcial;
e)aprendices y personas en formación remunerados y personas que participan en planes de promoción del empleo;
f)trabajadores familiares no remunerados o temporalmente ausentes del trabajo;
g)trabajadores estacionales que no trabajan durante la temporada inactiva;
h)miembros de las fuerzas armadas, incluidos voluntarios y oficiales de carrera, reclutas y personas del servicio civil equivalente al servicio militar.
Se excluyen:
a)aprendices y personas en formación no remuneradas;
b)personas ocupadas en la producción de bienes o servicios para su propio uso final;
c)personas que realizan un trabajo voluntario social para la comunidad;
d)personas con un empleo pero ausentes sin autorización.
Desempleo: Personas, de 10 años y más de edad, en hogares normalmente asentados, que no estuvieron ocupadas en un empleo por lo menos 2 días y estaban buscando un trabajo durante los últimos siete días antes de realizarse la entrevista de la encuesta.
Se incluyen:
a)personas suspendidas de su trabajo por tiempo indeterminado sin remuneración o con licencia sin goce de sueldo por iniciativa del empleador;
b)personas sin empleo y corrientemente disponibles para trabajar y que buscan trabajo, que habían tomado disposiciones para comenzar un nuevo empleo en una fecha ulterior a la semana de referencia;
c)personas sin empleo y corrientemente disponibles para trabajar y que buscan trabajo, que estaban procurando establecer su propia empresa;
d)estudiantes de dedicación completa o parcial que buscan trabajo a tiempo completo o parcial;
e)personas que estaban buscando trabajo y estaban disponibles para trabajar pero sometidas a escolaridad obligatoria o jubiladas y percibían una pensión.
Se excluyen personas sin trabajo pero que no estaban buscando trabajo durante el periodo de referencia.
Subempleo:
Subempleo por insuficiencia de horas: No se dispone de información.
Situaciones de empleo inadecuado: No se dispone de información.
Horas de trabajo: Número total de horas de trabajo regulares y horas extraordinarias relativas al empleo principal y otros empleos del empleado.
Ingresos relacionados con el empleo:
Ingresos relacionados con el empleo asalariado: No se dispone de información.
Ingresos relacionados con el empleo independiente: No se dispone de información.
Sector informal: No se dispone de información.
Actividad habitual: No se dispone de información.
Clasificaciones:
Rama de actividad económica (industria):
Título de la clasificación utilizada: No se conoce.
Grupos de población clasificados por industria: Personas empleadas y desempleadas con experiencia previa de trabajo.
Número de Grupos utilizados para la codificación: Códigos de 4 dígitos, pero publicados en orden alfabético y en códigos de 1 dígito.
Vínculos con la CIIU: CIIU- Rev.3.
Ocupación:
Título de la clasificación utilizada: No se conoce.
Grupos de población clasificados por ocupación: Personas empleadas y desempleadas con experiencia previa de trabajo.
Número de Grupos utilizados para la codificación: códigos de 4 dígitos, pero publicados a nivel de 1 dígito.
Vínculos con la CIUO: CIUO-88.
Situación en el empleo:
Título de la clasificación utilizada: No se dispone de información.

Grupos de población clasificados por situación en el empleo: Personas empleadas y desempleadas con experiencia previa de trabajo.

Grupos utilizados para la codificación: Empleadores, trabajadores por cuenta propia, salarios y sueldos del sector público, salarios y sueldos del sector privado, salarios y sueldos del sector de cooperativas, trabajadores familiares no remunerados.

Vínculos con la CISE: CISE-1986.

Educación:

Título de la clasificación utilizada: No se dispone de información.

Grupos de población clasificados por educación: Personas empleadas y desempleadas.

Grupos utilizados para la codificación: Educación: no formal, alfabetización, educación informal, ciencias teológicas, escuela primaria, escuela secundaria de primer ciclo, escuela secundaria de segundo ciclo, diploma de escuela secundaria y preuniversiario, educación superior.

Vínculos con la CINE: CINE-1976.

Tamaño y diseño de la muestra:

Unidad final de muestreo: Persona.

Tamaño de la muestra (unidades finales de muestreo): 56 753.

Fracción de muestreo: 0,95 por ciento.

Marco de la muestra: Censo Nacional de Población y Hogares de 1996.

Actualización de la muestra: No disponible.

Rotación: Ninguna.

Levantamiento da la encuesta:

Tipo de entrevista: Entrevista personal realizada por enumeradores.

Número de unidades finales de muestreo por área de muestra: 25 muestras de hogares por grupo. Cada grupo requiere un promedio de 1,5 días de trabajo de un enumerador.

Duración del trabajo de campo: 15 días.

Organización de la encuesta: Permanente.

Número de personas que trabajan en el campo: Se requiere un total de 640 personas para realizar la encuesta.

Substitución de las unidades finales de muestreo que no responden: No.

Estimaciones y ajustes:

Tasa de no-respuesta total: No se proporcionó información.

Ajuste por no-respuesta total: No.

Imputación por no respuesta de ítemes: No.

Ajuste por áreas/poblaciones no abarcadas: No.

Ajuste por falta de cobertura: No.

Ajuste por exceso de cobertura: No.

Ajuste por variaciones estacionales: No.

Historia de la encuesta:

Título y fecha de la primera encuesta: Encuesta de las características del empleo y el desempleo en los hogares (11-26 de diciembre de 1997).

Modificaciones y revisiones significativas: De 1969 a 1972, el Ministerio de Trabajo y Asuntos Sociales realizó las primeras rondas de la encuesta (titulada "Encuesta sobre la Fuerza de Trabajo). En febrero de 1989, el Centro de Estadísticas del Irán efectuó la segunda ronda (titulada "Encuesta de Población y Fuerza de Trabajo").

En febrero de 1994, el Centro de Estadísticas del Irán realizó la tercera ronda (titulada "Encuesta de las características del empleo y el desempleo en los hogares"). Desde diciembre de 1997, el Centro de Estadísticas del Irán realiza anualmente la cuarta ronda (que también se titula "Encuesta de las características del empleo y el desempleo en los hogares").

Está previsto realizar la encuesta dos veces al año. Asimismo, se prevé añadir temas de la encuesta al cuestionario, en particular "ingresos", "nacionalidad" y "tipo de empleo".

Documentación y difusión:

Documentación:

Título de las publicaciones con los resultados de la encuesta: Iran Statistical Yearbook Results of the household employment and unemployment characteristics survey. Collection of statistical instruction manuals for each survey.

Título de las publicaciones con la metodología de la encuesta: Idem.

Difusión:

Tiempo necesario para difundir los primeros datos: Unos 16 meses. Los resultados de la encuesta de 1997 se publicaron en junio de 1998.

Información adelantada acerca de la fecha de la primera difusión pública: Sí.

Disponibilidad de datos no publicados si se solicitan: Sí, a través de la Dependencia de Difusión de Información y la red nacional del Centro de Estadísticas del Irán.

Disponibilidad de datos por medios informáticos: Sí, en disquetes y en el sitio web del Centro de Estadísticas del Irán: http://www.sci.or.ir/.

Irlanda

Título de la encuesta: Encuesta Trimestral Nacional de Hogares (Quarterly National Household Survey (QNHS)).

Organismo responsable de la encuesta:

Planificar y realizar la encuesta: Oficina Central de Estadísticas (Central Statistical Office (CSO)).

Analizar y publicar los resultados: Oficina Central de Estadísticas (Central Statistical Office (CSO)).

Temas abarcados: Personas corriente, habitual y económicamente activas, empleadas y desempleadas; personas corrientemente subempleadas por insuficiencia de horas, personas en situaciones de empleo inadecuado y personas corrientemente fuera de la fuerza de trabajo; trabajadores desalentados; horas de trabajo; duración del empleo y el desempleo; empleo secundario; rama de actividad económica (industria); ocupación; situación en el empleo; nivel de educación/capacitación.

Alcance de la encuesta:

Ámbito geográfico: Todo el país.

Grupos de población: Personas de 15 años y más de edad que no viven en hogares colectivos,

Disponibilidad de estimaciones de otras fuentes para las áreas/grupos excluidos: Ninguna.

Grupos abarcados por la encuesta pero excluidos de los resultados publicados: Ninguno.

Periodicidad:

Recolección de datos: Continua.

Publicación de los resultados: Trimestralmente.

Períodos de referencia:

Empleo: Una semana.

Búsqueda de trabajo: Las cuatro semanas anteriores a la entrevista.

Disponibilidad para trabajo: Las cuatro semanas anteriores a la entrevista.

Conceptos y definiciones:

Empleo: Personas de 15 años y más de edad que: a) realizaron algún trabajo remunerado o por un beneficio, por una hora o más, la semana anterior a la encuesta, incluido el trabajo en una explotación agrícola o negocio familiar; y b) estaban temporalmente ausentes del trabajo durante la semana de referencia por enfermedad, día de fiesta, etc. Los miembros de las fuerzas armadas se incluyen como empleados.

Desempleo: Personas de 15 años y más de edad que estaban corrientemente sin trabajo y disponibles para trabajar en cuatro semanas, y que habían buscado trabajo en algún momento durante las últimas cuatro semanas.

Subempleo:

Subempleo por insuficiencia de horas: Personas empleadas a tiempo parcial con "muy pocas horas", que habían buscado trabajo y estaban disponible para trabajar en otro empleo.

Situaciones de empleo inadecuado: No se publica actualmente, pero se podría hacer un análisis adicional.

Horas de trabajo: Habituales y reales (horas trabajadas) durante la semana de referencia.

Ingresos relacionados con el empleo:

Ingresos relacionados con el empleo asalariado: No corresponde.

Ingresos relacionados con el empleo independiente: No corresponde.

Sector informal: No se indica por separado.

Actividad habitual: No se proporcionó información.

Clasificaciones:

Rama de actividad económica (industria):

Título de la clasificación utilizada: Adaptación irlandesa de la NACE, Rev.1.

Grupos de población clasificados por industria: Personas empleadas y desempleadas (los desempleados se clasifican únicamente si habían tenido un trabajo en los últimos 10 años).

Número de Grupos utilizados para la codificación: nivel de 3 dígitos.

Vínculos con la CIIU: CIIU-Rev.3 (nivel de 2 dígitos).

Ocupación:
Título de la clasificación utilizada: Clasificación Uniforme de Ocupaciones de 1990 (SOC 90).
Grupos de población clasificados por ocupación: Personas empleadas y desempleadas (los desempleados se clasifican únicamente si habían tenido un trabajo en los últimos 10 años).
Número de Grupos utilizados para la codificación: nivel de 3 dígitos.
Vínculos con la CIUO: CIUO-88 (nivel de 3 dígitos).
Situación en el empleo:
Título de la clasificación utilizada: No se proporcionó información.
Grupos de población clasificados por situación en el empleo: Personas empleadas.
Grupos utilizados para la codificación: Empleados; trabajadores independientes sin empleados o por lo menos con uno; parientes que prestan ayuda.
Vínculos con la CISE: CISE-1993.
Educación:
Título de la clasificación utilizada: Clasificación nacional.
Grupos de población clasificados por educación: Todas las personas de 15 años y más de edad.
Grupos utilizados para la codificación: Sin educación formal; preprimaria; primaria; certificado de primer ciclo/grupo/intermedio; programa de año de transición; certificado de terminación de estudios; programa profesional para obtener el certificado de terminación de estudios; certificado de terminación de estudios establecidos; PLC; aprendizaje; certificado agrícola; practicante; certificado/diploma nacional; primer grado; certificado/diploma de postgrado; grado de postgrado; doctorado; otro.
Vínculos con la CINE: CINE-1976 y CINE-1997.
Tamaño y diseño de la muestra:
Unidad final de muestreo: Hogar.
Tamaño de la muestra (unidades finales de muestreo): 39 000 cada trimestre.
Fracción de muestreo: 1/32.
Marco de la muestra: Se basa en el censo de población de 1996. Está diseñado en dos etapas: la primera etapa de muestreo es de 2 600 bloques con unas 75 viviendas cada uno a nivel de municipio para representar 8 estratos de acuerdo con la densidad de la población. En cada bloque se entrevistan 15 viviendas.
Actualización de la muestra: Estaba previsto hacerlo después del censo de población de 2001. Sin embargo, debido a las precauciones tomadas por el brote de fiebre aftosa, el Censo de Población de 2001 se retrasó hasta 2002. El marco de la muestra se actualizó utilizando una combinación del trabajo preliminar hecho para el Censo de 2001, el directorio geográfico y otras fuentes, y se hará otra actualización una vez se disponga de los resultados del Censo de Población de 2002.
Rotación:
Esquema: Los hogares participan en 5 trimestres consecutivos y luego se sustituyen por otros hogares en el bloque.
Porcentaje de unidades que permanecen en la muestra durante dos encuestas consecutivas: 80 por ciento.
Número máximo de entrevistas por unidad de muestreo: No se proporcionó información.
Tiempo necesario para renovar completamente la muestra: Unos 5 años.
Levantamiento da la encuesta:
Tipo de entrevista: Entrevista personal asistida por computadora (CAPI).
Número de unidades finales de muestreo por área de muestra: No se dispone de información.
Duración del trabajo de campo:
Total: Continua.
Por área de muestra: No se dispone de información.
Organización de la encuesta: Permanente.
Número de personas que trabajan en el campo: 150 entrevistadores y 10 coordinadores sobre el terreno.
Substitución de las unidades finales de muestreo que no responden: No.
Estimaciones y ajustes:
Tasa de no-respuesta total: 6,3 por ciento.
Ajuste por no-respuesta total: No.
Imputación por no respuesta de ítemes: No.
Ajuste por áreas/poblaciones no abarcadas: No.
Ajuste por falta de cobertura: No.
Ajuste por exceso de cobertura: No.
Ajuste por variaciones estacionales: Como la Encuesta Trimestral Nacional de Hogares se realiza desde 1997, todavía no se han hecho ajustes estacionales. Con todo, se efectúan algunos trabajos de preparación.
Historia de la encuesta:
Título y fecha de la primera encuesta: La QNHS comenzó en septiembre-noviembre de 1997 y sustituyó la Encuesta Anual sobre la Fuerza de Trabajo que se realizaba entre abril y mayo de cada año.
Modificaciones y revisiones significativas: Ninguna después de 1997.
Documentación y difusión:
Documentación:
Título de las publicaciones con los resultados de la encuesta: Quarterly National Household Survey (ISSN 1393-6875).
Título de las publicaciones con la metodología de la encuesta: Quarterly National Household Survey (ISSN 1393-6875).
Difusión:
Tiempo necesario para difundir los primeros datos: Unos 3 meses.
Información adelantada acerca de la fecha de la primera difusión pública: Sí.
Disponibilidad de datos no publicados si se solicitan: Sí.
Disponibilidad de datos por medios informáticos: Sí, susceptible de cambios. Sitio web: http://www.cso.ie .

Italia

Título de la encuesta: Encuesta Trimestral sobre la Fuerza de Trabajo (Rilevazione Trimestrale sulle Forze di Lavoro).
Organismo responsable de la encuesta:
Planificar y realizar la encuesta: Instituto Nacional de Estadísticas (Istituto Nazionale di Statistica (ISTAT)).
Analizar y publicar los resultados: ISTAT.
Temas abarcados: Empleo, desempleo, subempleo, horas de trabajo, duración del empleo y el desempleo, trabajadores desalentados, rama de actividad económica (industria), ocupación, situación en el empleo, educación/calificación, empleo secundario.
Alcance de la encuesta:
Ámbito geográfico: Todo el país.
Grupos de población: Personas residentes que no viven en hogares colectivos, de 15 años y más de edad, que viven en hogares privados.
Disponibilidad de estimaciones de otras fuentes para las áreas/grupos excluidos: No se dispone de información.
Grupos abarcados por la encuesta pero excluidos de los resultados publicados: No se dispone de información.
Periodicidad:
Recolección de datos: Trimestralmente.
Publicación de los resultados: Trimestralmente.
Períodos de referencia:
Empleo: Una semana fija.
Búsqueda de trabajo: Periodo fijo de cuatro semanas.
Disponibilidad para trabajar: Periodo fijo de dos semanas.
Conceptos y definiciones:
Empleo: Personas de 15 años y más de edad que declaren estar empleadas y quienes declaren no estar empleadas pero que habían trabajado por lo menos una semana durante la semana de referencia.
Se incluyen también en la definición de empleo:
a)trabajadores a tiempo completo o parcial que buscaban otro empleo durante la semana de referencia;
b)personas que realizaron algún trabajo remunerado o por un beneficio durante la semana de referencia pero estaban sometidas a escolaridad obligatoria, jubiladas y percibían una pensión, inscritas como desempleadas en busca de trabajo en una oficina de empleo, percibiendo indemnizaciones de desempleo;
c)estudiantes de dedicación completa o parcial que trabajan a tiempo completo o parcial;
d)trabajadores familiares no remunerados en el trabajo durante la semana de referencia;
e)miembros voluntarios y de carrera de las fuerzas armadas.
Desempleo: Personas de 15 años y más de edad sin empleo durante la semana de referencia y que buscaban trabajo, habían tomado por lo menos una disposición para buscar trabajo durante la semana de referencia (4 semanas) y estaban disponibles para comenzar a trabajar dentro de 2 semanas, así como las personas que no buscan trabajo porque ya habían encontrado uno en el que comenzarían en el futuro.
Subempleo:
Subempleo por insuficiencia de horas: Personas empleadas que hubiesen querido trabajar horas adicionales durante la semana de

referencia y que estaban disponibles para trabajar horas adicionales en la semana de referencia.
Situaciones de empleo inadecuado: No se dispone de una definición específica, pero la encuesta italiana sobre la fuerza de trabajo recopila datos sobre personas empleadas que buscan otro trabajo o sobre las razones que tienen para buscar otro empleo (miedo a perder el empleo actual; empleos a plazo determinado; búsqueda de una segunda actividad; búsqueda de mejores condiciones, etc.).
Horas de trabajo: Horas de trabajo habituales y reales en la segunda actividad durante la semana de referencia, así como las horas realmente trabajadas en la segunda actividad durante la semana de referencia.
Ingresos relacionados con el empleo:
Ingresos relacionados con el empleo asalariado: No corresponde.
Ingresos relacionados con el empleo independiente: No corresponde.
Sector informal: No corresponde.
Actividad habitual: No se dispone de información.
Clasificaciones:
Rama de actividad económica (industria):
Título de la clasificación utilizada: Clasificación nacional.
Grupos de población clasificados por industria: Personas empleadas y desempleadas con experiencia previa de trabajo.
Número de Grupos utilizados para la codificación: 60 a nivel de 2 dígitos.
Vínculos con la CIIU: CIIU-Rev.3.
Ocupación:
Título de la clasificación utilizada: Clasificación nacional.
Grupos de población clasificados por ocupación: Personas empleadas y desempleadas con experiencia previa de trabajo.
Número de Grupos utilizados para la codificación: 35.
Vínculos con la CIUO: CIUO-88.**Situación en el empleo:**
Título de la clasificación utilizada: Clasificación nacional.
Grupos de población clasificados por situación en el empleo: Personas empleadas y desempleadas con experiencia previa de trabajo.
Grupos utilizados para la codificación: Para el empleo: empleados, empleadores, trabajadores por cuenta propia, trabajadores familiares y miembros de una cooperativa; para el des**Empleo:** empleados, empleados independientes con empleados, empleados independientes sin empleados y trabajadores familiares.
Vínculos con la CISE: CISE-1993.
Educación:
Título de la clasificación utilizada: ISCED-97.
Grupos de población clasificados por educación: Todas las personas.
Grupos utilizados para la codificación: Sin instrucción; educación primaria (nivel 1); educación secundaria inferior (nivel 2); educación secundaria superior (nivel 3); educación postsecundaria no terciaria (nivel 4); educación terciaria (nivel 5); educación de postgrado (nivel 6).
Vínculos con la CINE: CINE-97.
Tamaño y diseño de la muestra:
Unidad final de muestreo: Hogar.
Tamaño de la muestra (unidades finales de muestreo): 75 000 hogares cada trimestre.
Fracción de muestreo: 0,35 por ciento de familias residentes cada trimestre.
Marco de la muestra: Registros municipales.
Actualización de la muestra: En abril de cada año.
Rotación:
Esquema: 2-2-2.
Porcentaje de unidades que permanecen en la muestra durante dos encuestas consecutivas: 50 por ciento.
Número máximo de entrevistas por unidad de muestreo: 4.
Tiempo necesario para renovar completamente la muestra: 15 trimestres.
Levantamiento da la encuesta:
Tipo de entrevista: papel y lápiz y entrevista personal.
Número de unidades finales de muestreo por área de muestra:
Duración del trabajo de campo:
Total: No se dispone de información.
Por área de muestra: No se dispone de información.
Organización de la encuesta: Permanente.
Número de personas que trabajan en el campo: 1 351 supervisores y 3 000 entrevistadores.
Substitución de las unidades finales de muestreo que no responden: Sí.
Estimaciones y ajustes:
Tasa de no-respuesta total: 5 por ciento.
Ajuste por no-respuesta total: Sí.
Imputación por no respuesta de ítemes: Sí.
Ajuste por áreas/poblaciones no abarcadas: No.
Ajuste por falta de cobertura: Sí.
Ajuste por exceso de cobertura: Sí.
Ajuste por variaciones estacionales: Sí, para el empleo: por zona geográfica y actividad económica; para el desempleo y las tasas de des**Empleo:** por zonas geográficas, y para la fuerza de trabajo: por zona geográfica.
Historia de la encuesta:
Título y fecha de la primera encuesta: Rilevazione Nazionale delle Forze di Lavoro 1959.
Modificaciones y revisiones significativas: 1977-1984: la muestra se basaba en el Censo de Población de 1981; comienzos del segundo trimestre de 1992: revisión de la metodología y de la edad límite inferior que se refiere a personas de 15 años y más de edad, en lugar de 14 años anteriormente.
Documentación y difusión:
Documentación:
Título de las publicaciones con los resultados de la encuesta: (periodicidad) Comunicados de prensa (trimestralmente); Resultados anuales.
Título de las publicaciones con la metodología de la encuesta: Idem.
Difusión:
Tiempo necesario para difundir los primeros datos: Unos 3 meses. **Información adelantada acerca de la fecha de la primera difusión pública:** Sí.
Disponibilidad de datos no publicados si se solicitan: Sí.
Disponibilidad de datos por medios informáticos: Sí. Sitio web: http://www.istat.it/

Jamaica

Título de la encuesta: Encuesta sobre la Fuerza de Trabajo (Labour Force Survey).
Organismo responsable de la encuesta:
Planificar y realizar la encuesta: Instituto de Estadísticas de Jamaica (Statistical Institute of Jamaica).
Analizar y publicar los resultados: Instituto de Estadísticas de Jamaica (Statistical Institute of Jamaica).
Temas abarcados: Empleo, desempleo, horas de trabajo, salarios, ingresos, duración del empleo, rama de actividad económica (industria), ocupación, situación en el empleo, educación y empleo secundario.
Alcance de la encuesta:
Ámbito geográfico: Todo el país.
Grupos de población: Todas las personas de 14 años y más de edad, salvo las personas que viven en hogares colectivos, ciudadanos no residentes y diplomáticos.
Disponibilidad de estimaciones de otras fuentes para las áreas/grupos excluidos: No se dispone de información.
Grupos abarcados por la encuesta pero excluidos de los resultados publicados: No se dispone de información.
Periodicidad:
Recolección de datos: Encuesta realizada trimestralmente en enero, abril, julio y octubre.
Publicación de los resultados: Anualmente.
Periodo de referencia:
Empleo: Una semana.
Búsqueda de trabajo: Tres meses.
Disponibilidad para trabajo: No se dispone de información.
Conceptos y definiciones:
Empleo: Las personas con empleo comprenden todas las de 14 años y más de edad que, durante la semana de la encuesta, habían trabajado por lo menos una hora y las que tenían un empleo pero estaban temporalmente ausentes del mismo.
En las personas con empleo se incluyen las que:
a)trabajaron por un salario o sueldo, durante un periodo de tiempo determinado, a una escala de precios, por comisiones, propinas, casa o comida o por cualquier otro tipo de pago en especie;
b)trabajaron como personas en formación o aprendices;
c)trabajaron por un beneficio u honorarios en su propio negocio;
d)trabajaron sin remuneración, salario o sueldo en trabajos (otros que no eran los quehaceres o tareas de su propio hogar) que contribuyeron al funcionamiento de una explotación agrícola o negocio propio y explotado por un beneficio, en la mayoría de los casos, por algún miembro de su familia;

e)pasaron un cierto tiempo en la explotación de un negocio o profesión aunque no se realizaran ventas ni se suministraran servicios profesionales, tales como un médico o un abogado que pasa tiempo en su oficina en espera de clientes.
Se incluyen también todas las personas que tenían un empleo, pero que por alguna razón no trabajaron durante la semana de la encuesta. Entre estas personas se incluyen las que:
a)tenían un empleo, pero trabajaron menos de una hora durante la semana de la encuesta;
b)no trabajaron por enfermedad o incapacidad temporal, pero que mantenían sus empleos hasta su regreso al mismo;
c)no pudieron trabajar debido al mal tiempo;
d)no trabajaron porque tenían algún tipo de licencia, incluidas vacaciones, remuneradas o no, durante todo el tiempo que se les mantuviera su empleo hasta su regreso;
e)no trabajaron debido a algún tipo de conflicto laboral, como huelga o cierre patronal;
f)estaban suspendidas de su trabajo temporalmente pero no más de 30 días, y que tenían instrucciones de reincorporarse a su trabajo al finalizar los 30 días.
Desempleo: El desempleo abarca todas las personas de 14 años y más de edad que buscaban un empleo, querían trabajar y estaban disponibles para hacerlo. Las personas que buscan un empleo deben haber tomado alguna medida efectiva para encontrar un trabajo, tales como:
a)inscribirse en una oficina de empleo, gubernamental o privada;
b)visitar sitios de trabajo en busca de un empleo;
c)presentar su candidatura personalmente a probables empleadores;
d)colocar avisos en cualquier periódico o lugar público;
e)enviar su candidatura;
f)pedir a alguien que le ayude a buscar un empleo;
g)hacer las averiguaciones necesarias para comenzar su propia explotación agrícola o negocio.
Subempleo:
Subempleo por insuficiencia de horas: No se dispone de información.
Situaciones de empleo inadecuado: No se dispone de información.
Horas de trabajo: Horas habituales trabajadas por semana en todos los empleos.
Ingresos relacionados con el empleo:
Ingresos relacionados con el empleo asalariado: Promedio de ingresos brutos, del empleo y otras fuentes, en los últimos 12 meses.
Ingresos relacionados con el empleo independiente: Véase más arriba.
Sector informal: No se dispone de información.
Actividad habitual: No se dispone de información.
Clasificaciones:
Rama de actividad económica (industria):
Título de la clasificación utilizada: Clasificación nacional.
Grupos de población clasificados por industria: Empleados y desempleados (rama de actividad económica del último empleo para el desempleado).
Número de Grupos utilizados para la codificación: Nueve.
Vínculos con la CIIU: CIIU-Rev. 2.
Ocupación:
Título de la clasificación utilizada: Clasificación nacional.
Grupos de población clasificados por ocupación: Empleados y desempleados (ocupación en el último empleo para el desempleado).
Número de Grupos utilizados para la codificación: Nueve.
Vínculos con la CIUO: Parcialmente vinculada a la CIUO-88.
Situación en el empleo:
Título de la clasificación utilizada: Clasificación nacional.
Grupos de población clasificados por situación en el empleo: Empleados.
Grupos utilizados para la codificación: Cinco grupos: empleados públicos remunerados, empleados del sector privado, trabajadores familiares no remunerados, empleadores; trabajadores por cuenta propia.
Vínculos con la CISE: CISE-1993.
Educación:
Título de la clasificación utilizada: No corresponde.
Grupos de población clasificados por educación: No corresponde.
Grupos utilizados para la codificación: No corresponde.
Vínculos con la CINE: No corresponde.
Tamaño y diseño de la muestra:
Unidad final de muestreo: Vivienda.
Tamaño de la muestra (unidades finales de muestreo): Muestreo estratificado en dos etapas de 7 648 viviendas basado en el listado de 1997.
Fracción de muestreo: 1,5 por ciento.
Marco de la muestra: Resultados del Censo de Población de 1991.
Actualización de la muestra: Cada 3 años en base a los nuevos listados.
Rotación:
Esquema: Se abarcan cuatro grupos en cada ronda de la encuesta.
Porcentaje de unidades que permanecen en la muestra durante dos encuestas consecutivas: 50 por ciento.
Número máximo de entrevistas por unidad de muestreo: No se dispone de información.
Tiempo necesario para renovar completamente la muestra: Un año.
Levantamiento de la encuesta:
Tipo de entrevista: Entrevista personal con papel y lápiz.
Número de unidades finales de muestreo por área de muestra: No se dispone de información.
Duración del trabajo de campo:
Total: Tres a cuatro semanas.
Por área de muestra: No se dispone de información.
Organización de la encuesta: Permanente.
Número de personas que trabajan en el campo: 3 supervisores principales, 16 supervisores y 65 entrevistadores.
Substitución de las unidades finales de muestreo que no responden: No.
Estimaciones y ajustes:
Tasa de no-respuesta total: No se dispone de información.
Ajuste por no-respuesta total: Sí.
Imputación por no respuesta de ítemes: No.
Ajuste por áreas/poblaciones no abarcadas: Sí.
Ajuste por falta de cobertura: No.
Ajuste por exceso de cobertura: No.
Ajuste por variaciones estacionales: No.
Historia de la encuesta:
Título y fecha de la primera encuesta: Fuerza de Trabajo, 1968.
Modificaciones y revisiones significativas: En 1991, nueva clasificación industrial.
Documentación y difusióin:
Documentación:
Título de las publicaciones con los resultados de la encuesta: (periodicidad): Encuesta sobre la Fuerza de Trabajo (anualmente).
Título de las publicaciones con la metodología de la encuesta: (periodicidad): Encuesta sobre la Fuerza de Trabajo (anualmente).
Difusión:
Tiempo necesario para difundir los primeros datos: 6 meses.
Información adelantada acerca de la fecha de la primera difusión pública: No.
Disponibilidad de datos no publicados si se solicitan: Sí.
Disponibilidad de datos por medios informáticos: Sí. Sitio web: http://www.stainja.com .

Japón

Título de la encuesta: Encuesta sobre la Fuerza de Trabajo (Labour Force Survey).
Organismo responsable de la encuesta:
Planificar y realizar la encuesta: Servicio de Estadísticas, Ministerio de Gestión Pública, Asuntos Internos, Correos y Telecomunicaciones (Statistics Bureau, Home Affairs, Posts and Telecommunications).
Analizar y publicar los resultados: Servicio de Estadísticas, Ministerio de Gestión Pública, Asuntos Internos, Correos y Telecomunicaciones (Statistics Bureau, Home Affairs, Posts and Telecommunications).
Temas abarcados: Empleo, desempleo, horas de trabajo, salarios, duración del empleo, trabajadores desalentados, rama de actividad económica (industria), ocupación, situación en el empleo, nivel de educación/calificación.
Alcance de la encuesta:
Ámbito geográfico: Todo el país, salvo los territorios septentrionales.
Grupos de población: Todo japonés o extranjero de 15 años y más de edad que viva o vaya a vivir en el país por más de tres meses, salvo el cuerpo diplomático extranjero, el personal militar extranjero y sus acompañantes. Las fuerzas de autodefensa y los

internados en reformatorios se enumeran por separado y se incluyen en los resultados.
Las personas temporalmente ausentes de sus hogares por motivos de viaje, las que trabajan en otros sitios o están hospitalizadas se incluyen en sus hogares cuando el periodo de ausencia es menor de tres meses. Si han estado o van a estar ausentes de sus hogares por tres meses o más, se las enumera donde se encuentran.
Disponibilidad de estimaciones de otras fuentes para las áreas/grupos excluidos: No se proporcionó información.
Grupos abarcados por la encuesta pero excluidos de los resultados publicados: No se proporcionó información.
Periodicidad:
Recolección de datos: Mensualmente.
Publicación de los resultados: Mensual y trimestralmente para los "Resultados Detallados" (antes "Encuesta Especial").
Periodo de referencia:
Empleo: Una semana fija.
Búsqueda de trabajo: Una semana fija, incluidas las personas que esperaban los resultados de las gestiones anteriores para conseguir un empleo.
Disponibilidad para trabajo: Un día fijo.
Conceptos y definiciones:
Empleo: Son personas con empleo:
1)"Las que están trabajando", es decir las que lo hacían por una remuneración o ganancia durante una hora por lo menos durante la semana de referencia. Los trabajadores familiares que trabajan por lo menos una hora durante la semana de referencia también se incluyen en esta categoría.
2)"Las personas con empleo, pero ausentes del mismo", es decir quienes teniendo empleo no trabajaron durante la semana de referencia.
También se incluyen:
1)trabajadores a tiempo completo o parcial que buscaban otro empleo durante la semana de referencia;
2)trabajadores a tiempo completo o parcial que trabajan a tiempo completo o parcial;
3)personas que durante la semana de referencia realizaban algún trabajo remunerado o por un beneficio, pero que estaban jubiladas y percibían una pensión, o inscritas como desempleados en busca de trabajo en una oficina de empleo;
4)aprendices y personas en formación remunerados;
5)personas que participan en planes de promoción del empleo;
6)trabajadores familiares remunerados o no, siempre que estos últimos no estuvieran ausentes del trabajo durante la semana de referencia;
7)servicio doméstico privado;
8)fuerzas de autodefensa;
9)personas con empleo pero temporalmente ausentes debido a enfermedad o lesión, vacaciones o licencia anual, licencia por maternidad/paternidad, licencia para estudios o capacitación, ausencia sin autorización, mal tiempo o desperfectos mecánicos, conflictos laborales u otra reducción de la actividad económica;
10)personas temporalmente suspendidas del trabajo (siempre que no hayan sido despedidas y perciban su salario o sueldo habitual). (En Japón no existe un sistema de suspensión propiamente dicho).
Para considerar a una persona como empleada, pese a estar ausente del trabajo, es necesario que reciba o espere recibir su salario o sueldo; si se trata de trabajadores independientes el periodo de ausencia no debe exceder los 30 días.
Se excluyen de la categoría de empleado y se consideran fuera de la fuerza de trabajo las personas dedicadas a los quehaceres domésticos en el propio hogar y las consagradas a labores comunitarias o sociales no remuneradas.
Desempleo: Son desempleadas las personas que no trabajaban durante la semana de referencia, pero estaban disponibles para trabajar y prontas a aceptar de inmediato un empleo, además de buscar de forma activa un empleo o estar en espera de los resultados de las gestiones realizadas con anterioridad en ese sentido.
"Buscar empleo en forma activa" significa haber realizado cualquiera de las siguientes gestiones durante la semana de referencia: inscribirse en una oficina de empleo; colocar o responder avisos; solicitar pruebas de admisión a un empleo; ponerse en contacto con amigos o parientes; concurrir a sitios de contratación de mano de obra; hacer preparativos para comenzar un negocio, obteniendo fondos y materiales, etc.
Se incluyen los estudiantes de dedicación completa o parcial que buscan trabajo a tiempo completo o parcial
Los trabajadores familiares no remunerados que estaban temporalmente ausentes del trabajo durante la semana de referencia están fuera de la fuerza de trabajo, a menos que cumplan las condiciones anteriores.
Los trabajadores estacionales en espera de la temporada agrícola o de cualquier otro trabajo estacional se excluyen de la categoría de desempleado y se consideran fuera de la fuerza de trabajo.
Subempleo:
Subempleo por insuficiencia de horas: La encuesta no abarca este punto.
Situaciones de empleo inadecuado: La encuesta no abarca este punto.
Horas de trabajo: Las "horas de trabajo durante la semana de la encuesta" se refieren al número de horas realmente trabajadas que incluyen las extraordinarias pero no las de trabajos domésticos, trabajos voluntarios sin remuneración, las pausas para comidas, las transferencias, etc. Si una persona trabajó en más de un empleo durante la semana de la encuesta, se suma el total de horas de cada empleo.
Ingresos relacionados con el empleo:
Ingresos relacionados con el empleo asalariado: La encuesta no abarca este punto.
Ingresos relacionados con el empleo independiente: La encuesta no abarca este punto.
Sector informal: La encuesta no abarca este punto.
Actividad habitual: La encuesta no abarca este punto.
Clasificaciones:
Rama de actividad económica (industria):
Título de la clasificación utilizada: Clasificación nacional.
Grupos de población clasificados por industria: Personas empleadas y desempleadas (rama de actividad económica del último empleo para el desempleado).
Número de Grupos utilizados para la codificación: 30 grupos.
Vínculos con la CIIU: CIIU-Rev. 2 a nivel del 3er dígito (grupos principales).
Ocupación:
Título de la clasificación utilizada: Clasificación nacional.
Grupos de población clasificados por ocupación: Personas empleadas y desempleadas (ocupación en el último empleo para el desempleado).
Número de Grupos utilizados para la codificación: 15 grupos.
Vínculos con la CIUO: CIUO-68 a nivel del 1er dígito (grupos principales).
Situación en el empleo:
Título de la clasificación utilizada: Clasificación nacional.
Grupos de población clasificados por situación en el empleo: Personas empleadas y desempleadas. Las personas desempleadas se clasifican según su último empleo, si procede, únicamente en los "Resultados Detallados".
Grupos utilizados para la codificación: 4 grupos: empleados (empleados permanentes, empleados temporeros y jornaleros), trabajadores independientes, trabajadores familiares y trabajadores caseros a destajo.
Vínculos con la CISE: CISE-1993.
Educación:
Título de la clasificación utilizada: Clasificación nacional.
Grupos de población clasificados por educación: Personas empleadas y desempleadas.
Grupos utilizados para la codificación: Sólo en los "Resultados Detallados". Todas las personas se clasifican por "los estudios realizados" para la fecha de la encuesta en: concurre a la escuela, egresado de escuela con título y nunca concurrió a la escuela. Las expresiones "concurrir a la escuela" y "egresado con título de una escuela" comprenden varios niveles de educación completos según la siguiente clasificación: escuela primaria o primer ciclo de secundaria, segundo ciclo de secundaria, preuniversitaria, superior o universitaria, incluidos títulos de facultades.
Vínculos con la CINE: CINE-1976.
Tamaño y diseño de la muestra:
Unidad final de muestreo: Vivienda.
Tamaño de la muestra (unidades finales de muestreo): Unos 2 900 distritos de enumeración (DE) que comprenden 40 000 viviendas.
Fracción de muestreo: No se proporcionó información.
Marco de la muestra: Censo de Población quinquenal. La muestra actual se construyó y actualizó tomando como base el Censo de Población de 1995.
Actualización de la muestra: Todos los años, las prefecturas elaboran listas de nuevos distritos de hogares colectivos que se añaden a los DE.

Rotación:
Esquema: Un DE permanece en la muestra durante cuatro meses consecutivos, queda fuera los ocho meses siguientes y vuelve a ingresar a la muestra durante los mismos meses del año siguiente. Para cada DE se seleccionan dos conjuntos de unidades de vivienda. En el primer año de enumeración de un DE, los hogares de las unidades de vivienda del primer conjunto se encuestan durante los dos primeros meses consecutivos, y luego se sustituyen por los hogares de las unidades de vivienda del otro conjunto. En el segundo año, las unidades de vivienda del primer conjunto vuelven a entrar en la muestra de DE y se sustituyen por las del otro conjunto de la misma forma que el año anterior.
Según este sistema, un cuarto de la muestra de DE y la mitad de la muestra de hogares se sustituyen todos los meses. Tres cuartos de la muestra de DE es común de un mes a otro y la mitad de un año a otro.
Porcentaje de unidades que permanecen en la muestra durante dos encuestas consecutivas: 50 por ciento.
Número máximo de entrevistas por unidad de muestreo: Cuatro.
Tiempo necesario para renovar completamente la muestra: 16 meses.
Levantamiento de la encuesta:
Tipo de entrevista: Papel y lápiz.
Número de unidades finales de muestreo por área de muestra: No se proporcionó información.
Duración del trabajo de campo:
Total: 13 días.
Por área de muestra: No se proporcionó información.
Organización de la encuesta: La organización de la encuesta es permanente (División de Estadísticas de gobiernos prefectorales). Los enumeradores se contratan con carácter temporal para cada ronda.
Número de personas que trabajan en el campo: Unas 3 180 personas.
Substitución de las unidades finales de muestreo que no responden: No.
Estimaciones y ajustes:
Tasa de no-respuesta total: No.
Ajuste por no-respuesta total: No.
Imputación por no respuesta de ítemes: No.
Ajuste por áreas/poblaciones no abarcadas: No.
Ajuste por falta de cobertura: No.
Ajuste por exceso de cobertura: No.
Ajuste por variaciones estacionales: Sí. Método del censo II (X-11).
Historia de la encuesta:
Título y fecha de la primera encuesta: Encuesta sobre la Fuerza de Trabajo, julio de 1947.
Modificaciones y revisiones significativas: En 1953.
Documentación y difusión:
Documentación:
Título de las publicaciones con los resultados de la encuesta: (periodicidad): Monthly Report on the Labour Force Survey; Annual Report on the Labour Force Survey (marzo de cada año).
Título de las publicaciones con la metodología de la encuesta: (periodicidad): No se proporcionó información.
Difusión:
Tiempo necesario para difundir los primeros datos: Un mes.
Información adelantada acerca de la fecha de la primera difusión pública: Sí.
Disponibilidad de datos no publicados si se solicitan: Sí.
Disponibilidad de datos por medios informáticos: Internet. Sitio web: http://www.stat.go.jp.

Jordania

Título de la encuesta: Encuesta sobre Empleo y Desempleo, 2001 (Employment and Unemployment Surveys, 2001).
Organismo responsable de la encuesta:
Planificar y realizar la encuesta: Departamento de Estadísticas, Dirección de Encuestas de Hogares (Department of Statistics, Household Surveys Directorate).
Analizar y publicar los resultados: Departamento de Estadísticas, Dirección de Encuestas de Hogares (Department of Statistics, Household Surveys Directorate).
Temas abarcados: Empleo y desempleo actual. Horas realmente trabajadas en todos los empleos y razones de la ausencia temporal del trabajo. Deseos y razones para cambiar de empleo . Nivel de educación, rama actual de actividad económica (industria), ocupación y situación en el empleo principal. Ingresos mensuales del empleo y trabajadores independientes. Experiencia previa de trabajo , disponibilidad actual para trabajar, búsqueda activa de trabajo, medios utilizados en la búsqueda de trabajo, duración de la búsqueda de trabajo y duración de la última búsqueda de trabajo. Actividad principal de la población fuera de la fuerza de trabajo.
Alcance de la encuesta:
Ámbito geográfico: Toda la nación, salvo zonas de nómadas.
Grupos de población: Toda la población, salvo la que vive en zonas alejadas (sobre todo nómadas) y la que vive en hogares colectivos tales como hoteles, campamentos de trabajo, prisiones, etc.
Disponibilidad de estimaciones de otras fuentes para las áreas/grupos excluidos: No.
Grupos abarcados por la encuesta pero excluidos de los resultados publicados: No jordanos. Los resultados de la encuesta se limitan a la población jordana. No se dispone de estimaciones separadas para los no jordanos.
Periodicidad:
Recolección de datos: Trimestralmente.
Publicación de los resultados: Trimestral y anualmente.
Periodo de referencia:
Empleo: Semana de referencia móvil. Siete días antes de la fecha de la entrevista.
Búsqueda de trabajo: Búsqueda de trabajo de manera activa del desempleado durante las 4 semanas anteriores a la fecha de la entrevista.
Disponibilidad para trabajo: Siete días antes de la fecha de la entrevista o en los 15 días siguientes después de la fecha de la entrevista.
Conceptos y definiciones:
Empleo: Personas de 15 años o más de edad que trabajaron por lo menos una hora durante el periodo de referencia en el sector público o privado. La definición de empleo incluye cualquier trabajo remunerado, actividad remunerada o no en un negocio, parcial o totalmente propio. En el empleo se incluyen también los trabajadores remunerados e independientes que estaban temporalmente ausentes del trabajo durante el periodo de referencia por razones como enfermedad, vacaciones, días de fiesta, reducción de la actividad económica (falta de clientes, disminución de la demanda, etc.), interrupciones temporales en el establecimiento (cierre, escacez de materia prima, falta de combustible, desperfectos eléctricos o mecánicos).
Desempleo: Personas de 15 años y más, sin empleo pero que podían y estaban disponibles para trabajar y buscaban trabajo activamente. Disponibilidad para trabajar significa estar dispuesto o preparado para aceptar un empleo de inmediato, durante los siete días anteriores a la fecha de la entrevista o en los 15 días siguientes a esa fecha. Buscar trabajo activamente significa haber tomado medidas concretas y dedicar parte o todo el tiempo en busca de un empleo durante las cuatro semanas anteriores a la fecha de la entrevista. Como medidas concretas se incluyen: registrar y presentar directamente la candidatura para un empleo a los empleadores, buscar trabajo en reuniones o asambleas especiales de trabajadores, colocar o responder avisos en diarios, buscar ayuda de amigos y parientes, etc. La definición de desempleo incluye personas sin empleo, corrientemente disponibles para trabajar que no buscaban trabajo durante las cuatro semanas anteriores a la fecha de la entrevista porque esperaban reintegrarse a su empleo previo o habían encontrado un trabajo en el que comenzarían más tarde.
Subempleo: Se refiere a personas empleadas que quieren tener un empleo de sustitución o adicional y estaban disponibles para realizar dicho trabajo durante el periodo de referencia. Tres razones para querer un empleo de sustitución o adicional son: el empleo actual es insuficiente en términos de sueldo y bonificaciones, el empleo actual no se adapta al grado de instrucción de la persona y son muy pocas las horas de trabajo en el empleo actual.
Horas de trabajo: Se refiere al número de horas realmente trabajadas durante los siete días anteriores a la fecha de la entrevista y comprende los cinco componentes siguientes: 1) horas realmente trabajadas durante periodos de trabajo regulares; 2) horas extraordinarias; 3) tiempo pasado en el lugar de trabajo durante el cual no se ocupan de la actividad propiamente dicha sino de la preparación, el mantenimiento y la limpieza de herramientas y equipos de trabajo, o en la preparación de recibos, hojas de presencia e informes, etc.; 4) tiempo pasado en el lugar de trabajo en espera de recibir material de trabajo, o por la reparación de daños o desperfectos mecánicos o eléctricos, etc.; y 5) tiempo pasado en el lugar de trabajo durante pausas cortas o periodos de descanso.

Se excluyen las horas pagadas pero no trabajadas, tales como vacaciones anuales pagadas, días de fiesta pública u oficial pagados y licencias por enfermedad pagadas. Asimismo, se excluyen el tiempo de las pausas para comidas que normalmente no exceden tres horas y el tiempo que transcurre en el trayecto entre el hogar y el lugar de trabajo y viceversa.

Ingresos relacionados con el empleo:

Ingresos relacionados con el empleo asalariado: Ingresos mensuales. La suma de dinero y otros beneficios en especie recibidos durante el mes civil anterior a la fecha de la entrevista, como por ejemplo: 1) salarios o sueldos, en efectivo o en especie, recibidos a cambio de un trabajo realizado por un empleado permanente o temporero o una persona en formación. Se incluyen los pagos de horas extraordinarias en efectivo o en especie. En caso de múltiples empleos, se debe registrar el total de ingresos de todos los empleos. Los pagos en especie incluyen el valor real de prendas de vestir, comidas, transporte, vivienda y subsidios similares que proporciona el empleador; 2) ingresos relacionados con el empleo independiente, en efectivo o en especie, obtenidos como empleador o trabajador por cuenta propia, independientemente de la rama de actividad económica.

Ingresos relacionados con el empleo independiente: No se dispone de información.

Sector informal: No se dispone de información.

Actividad habitual: No se dispone de información.

Clasificaciones:

Rama de actividad económica (industria):

Título de la clasificación utilizada: No se dispone de información.

Grupos de población clasificados por industria: Personas empleadas y desempleadas con experiencia previa de trabajo.

Número de Grupos utilizados para la codificación: Nivel de 3 dígitos. Resultados publicados a nivel de 1 dígito con 17 categorías.

Vínculos con la CIIU: CIIU-Rev.3.

Ocupación:

Título de la clasificación utilizada: No se dispone de información.

Grupos de población clasificados por ocupación: Personas empleadas y desempleadas con experiencia previa de trabajo.

Número de Grupos utilizados para la codificación: Nivel de 3 dígitos. Resultados publicados a nivel de 1 dígito con 9 categorías.

Vínculos con la CIUO: CIUO-88.

Situación en el empleo:

Título de la clasificación utilizada: No se dispone de información.

Grupos de población clasificados por situación en el empleo: Personas empleadas y desempleadas con experiencia previa de trabajo.

Lista de grupos: Empleados, empleadores, trabajadores independientes, trabajadores familiares no remunerados, trabajadores no remunerados.

Vínculos con la CISE: CISE-1993.

Educación:

Título de la clasificación utilizada: No se dispone de información.

Grupos de población clasificados por educación: Población de 15 años y más de edad.

Lista de grupos: Analfabetos. Saben leer y escribir. **Educación:** elemental. Preparatoria. **Educación:** básica. Aprendiz vocacional. **Educación:** secundaria. Diploma intermedio. B.S.C. Diploma universitario y superior.

Vínculos con la CINE: CINE-1997.

Tamaño y diseño de la muestra:

Unidad final de muestreo: Hogares.

Tamaño de la muestra trimestral (unidades finales de muestreo): 8 800 hogares en 440 unidades primarias de muestreo (UPM) que son unidades o bloques de área .

Fracción de muestreo: 1 por ciento.

Marco de la muestra: Basado en zonas de enumeración del censo de población y hogares de 1994. Cada una de las 12 gobernaciones en Jordania se consideró como un estrato independiente. En cada gobernación, las localidades se dividieron en urbanas y rurales, salvo en las cinco principales ciudades: Amman, Wadi Essier, Zarqa, Russeifa e Irbid. Las localidades urbanas y rurales se dividieron a su vez en categorías según el número de habitantes de la localidad y se ordenaron en orden geográfico.

Las unidades primarias de muestreo (UPM) en cada estrato se dividieron en cuatro categorías (baja, media baja, media alta y alta) de acuerdo con el puntaje calculado con la información socioeconómica basada en los resultados del Censo de Población y Hogares de 1994. Las UPM así formadas se ordenaron en cada estrato según un procedimiento geográfico para zonas urbanas y rurales, y de acuerdo con las características socioeconómicas de las principales ciudades.

La muestra se seleccionó en dos etapas. En la primera, se seleccionó una muestra de 110 UPM según las probabilidades proporcionales al tamaño con un procedimiento de selección sistemática. En la segunda, después de actualizar el marco de las UPM seleccionadas, se escogió un número constante de unidades finales de muestreo (20 hogares) de cada UPM empleando para ello un procedimiento sistemático de la lista de hogares.

Actualización de la muestra: Las unidades finales de muestreo se actualizan en la etapa de listado de las muestras de las UPM preparadas para cada nueva ronda de la encuesta.

Rotación:

Esquema: A comienzos de 2000, se introdujo un sistema de rotación de muestras según el cual una muestra de hogares inicialmente seleccionada se matiene en la muestra durante dos rondas consecutivas, se saca de la muestra en las próximas dos rondas y se reintegra a la muestra por dos rondas consecutivas más antes de sacarla definitivamente.

Porcentaje de unidades que permanecen en la muestra durante dos encuestas consecutivas: De conformidad con ese sistema, un 75 por ciento de las unidades de muestras se superponen entre dos trimestres consecutivos y un 50 por ciento entre trimestres de un año a otro.

Número máximo de entrevistas por unidad de muestreo: No se dispone de información.

Tiempo necesario para renovar completamente la muestra: Año y medio.

Levantamiento de la encuesta:

Tipo de entrevista: Entrevista personal con papel y lápiz.

Número de unidades finales de muestreo por área de muestra: 20 hogares.

Duración del trabajo de campo:

Total: Un mes, incluida la actualización de las UPM, la selección de muestras de hogares y las entrevistas.

Por área de muestra: No se dispone de información..

Organización de la encuesta: Permanente.

Número de personas que trabajan en el campo: Entre 50 y 60 personas, incluidos entrevistadores y supervisores.

Substitución de las unidades finales de muestreo que no responden: No.

Estimaciones y ajustes:

Tasa de no-respuesta total: 2 por ciento. El número de entrevistas completadas de forma satisfactoria después de tres intentos, en los cuatro trimestres de 2001 fue de 32 540, o sea el 92,4 por ciento del total de muestras de hogares. Algunas de las razones por las cuales no se realizaron algunas entrevistas son: la vivienda estaba cerrada en el momento de la visita (4,0 %), la vivienda estaba vacía (2,5%), no había una persona que respondiera a los entrevistadores y rechazo a responder (0,6%)

Ajuste por no-respuesta total: Sí, por inversión de la tasa de respuesta en cada estrato.

Imputación por no respuesta de ítemes: No.

Ajuste por áreas/poblaciones no abarcadas: No.

Ajuste por falta de cobertura: Sí, por estimación proporcional a las cifras previstas de la población.

Ajuste por falta de cobertura: No.

Ajuste por variaciones estacionales: No.

Historia de la encuesta:

Título y fecha de la primera encuesta: Encuesta sobre Empleo y Desempleo, 1982.

Modificaciones y revisiones significativas: Las encuestas sobre la fuerza de trabajo se realizaron dos veces en 1982 y una vez en 1986 y 1987. Entre 1991 y 1997, las encuestas se efectuaron una o dos veces al año, salvo en 1992 cuando no hubo encuesta. En 1998 y 1999, se llevaron a cabo tres rondas de encuesta al año (mayo-junio, septiembre-octubre y noviembre-diciembre). Desde comienzos de 2000, la encuesta se realiza trimestralmente.

Documentación y difusión:

Documentación:

Título de las publicaciones con los resultados de la encuesta: Annual Report of Employment and Unemployment Survey 2001, publicado en marzo de 2002.

Título de las publicaciones con la metodología de la encuesta: Annual Report of Employment and Unemployment Survey 2001, publicado en marzo de 2002.

Tiempo necesario para difundir los primeros datos: 2 meses.

Información adelantada acerca de la fecha de la primera difusión pública: No.

Disponibilidad de datos no publicados si se solicitan: Sí.

Disponibilidad de datos por medios informáticos: Se pueden obtener, previa solicitud, datos tabulados en medios informáticos. Sitio web: http://www.dos.gov.jo.

Kosovo (Serbia y Montenegro)

Título de la encuesta: Encuesta sobre la Fuerza de Trabajo (Labour Force Survey).

Organismo responsable de la encuesta:

Planificar y realizar la encuesta: Oficina de Estadísticas de Kosovo en cooperación con el Ministerio del Trabajo y Asistencia Social (Statistical Office of Kosovo in cooperation with the Ministry of Labour and Social Welfare).

Analizar y publicar los resultados: Oficina de Estadísticas de Kosovo en cooperación con el Ministerio del Trabajo y Asistencia Social (Statistical Office of Kosovo in cooperation with the Ministry of Labour and Social Welfare).

Temas abarcados: Empleo, desempleo, subempleo, horas de trabajo (horas habituales de trabajo, horas realmente trabajadas), ingresos del empleo, empleo en el sector informal, lugar de trabajo, duración del empleo, duración del desempleo, trabajadores desalentados, trabajadores ocasionales, rama de actividad económica (industria), ocupación, situación en el empleo, nivel de educación o calificación, empleo secundario, fuentes de subsistencia, ingresos del hogar.

Alcance de la encuesta:

Ámbito geográfico: Todo el territorio.

Grupos de población: La encuesta abarca los miembros habituales de hogares privados en Kosovo, independientemente de su origen étnico (albanés, serbio, etc.). No se abarcan las personas que viven en hogares colectivos. Se excluyen los miembros de las tropas de la KFOR, el personal internacional de la UNMIK y otros extranjeros que residen temporalmente en Kosovo.

Disponibilidad de estimaciones de otras fuentes para las áreas/grupos excluidos: No.

Grupos abarcados por la encuesta pero excluidos de los resultados publicados: Ninguno.

Periodicidad:

Recolección de datos: Anualmente (planificada). La primera encuesta se realizó entre diciembre de 2001 y enero de 2002.

Publicación de los resultados: Anualmente (planificada).

Periodo de referencia:

Empleo: Periodo de referencia móvil de una semana antes de la fecha de la entrevista.

Búsqueda de trabajo: Periodo de referencia móvil de cuatro semanas antes de la fecha de la entrevista.

Disponibilidad para trabajo: Periodo de referencia móvil de una semana antes de la fecha de la entrevista.

Conceptos y definiciones:

Empleo: Personas de 15 a 64 años de edad que, durante la semana de referencia, tenían un empleo o una empresa o actividad propia, del cual esas personas, sus hogares o sus familias obtenían un ingreso en efectivo o en especie. Se incluyen las personas que trabajaban como empleados permanentes, empleados ocasionales, empleadores, trabajadores por cuenta propia (empleados independientes), agricultores, miembros de cooperativas de productores, trabajadores familiares no remunerados en el hogar o en una empresa o explotación agrícola propiedad de la familia y miembros del servicio militar y de la policía.

Se incluyen también las personas de 15 a 64 años de edad que, durante la semana de referencia, realizaron algún trabajo remunerado o no (salvo la producción de bienes para su propio uso final y la prestación de servicios no remunerados o personales para su propio hogar) por lo menos una hora, incluso si eran estudiantes de dedicación completa o parcial, desempleados, amas de casa o personas jubiladas y que trabajaron sólo a tiempo parcial u ocasionalmente. Por ejemplo: empleo remunerado como trabajador a tiempo parcial o empleado temporero, ayudante, sustituto, trabajador ocasional, etc.; trabajo no remunerado en el hogar, en una empresa o explotación agrícola familiar; trabajo no remunerado como aprendiz; venta o intercambio de productos agrícolas cultivados en un terreno propio, o producción de esos bienes para la venta; venta de productos alimenticios, bebidas, comidas, prendas de vestir, libros, materiales de oficina, discos de música, cigarrillos, flores, etc., en la calle, mercados o en el hogar; reparaciones de casas, apartamentos, vehículos o bienes de consumo duraderos para otros por un pago; transporte de pasajeros o bienes en vehículo por un pago; consultas pagas o enseñanza privada (idiomas, formación en materia de informática, etc.); limpieza del hogar para otros, lavado de vehículos o cuidado de niños de otros.

Se incluyen además como empleadas las personas de 15 a 64 años de edad que tenían un empleo o una empresa o actividad al que se podían reintegrar, pero en el que no trabajaron durante la semana de referencia por alguna de las siguientes razones: enfermedad, lesión o indisposición temporal; licencia por maternidad; cese de actividades por razones personales; cuidado de un miembro de la familia; licencia anual; otros tipos de licencia; mal tiempo, suspensiones de trabajo por causas técnicas y de otro tipo; educación y capacitación; tiempo flexible o días libres; falta de trabajo, pedidos o clientes; huelga, conflicto laboral o suspensión del trabajo; otras razones. Se incluyen trabajadores familiares no remunerados y temporalmente ausentes del trabajo durante la semana de referencia. Se excluyen las personas que no estaban en el trabajo durante la semana de referencia porque su empresa estaba cerrada debido a catástrofes naturales o a los efectos de la guerra, estaba en quiebra o cerrada, así como los trabajadores estacionales que no trabajan durante la temporada inactiva.

Las personas de 15 a 64 años de edad, que informaron que estaban corrientemente sin trabajo, se clasifican como empleadas si durante la semana de referencia realizaron alguna actividad que les proporcionó algún ingreso, incluso si no consideraban esas actividades como trabajo.

Desempleo: Personas de 15 a 64 años de edad que: i) estaban sin empleo durante la semana de referencia (incluidas las personas cuya empresa estaba cerrada debido a catástrofes naturales o a los efectos de la guerra, en quiebra o cerrada); ii) buscaban un empleo o procuraban establecer su propia empresa o una actividad que genere ingresos, y que durante las últimas cuatro semanas habían realizado una o más gestiones para encontrar un trabajo o establecer su propia empresa o una actividad que genere ingresos; y iii) estaban corrientemente disponibles para trabajar, es decir habrían estado disponibles y prontas para comenzar a trabajar durante la semana de referencia si se les hubiese ofrecido la oportunidad de hacerlo (incluidas personas temporalmente enfermas durante la semana de referencia). Esta definición incluye estudiantes de dedicación completa o parcial, amas de casa o personas jubiladas, que buscaban trabajo y estaban disponibles para trabajar.

Se incluyen también como desempleadas las personas de 15 a 64 años de edad que: i) no estaban empleadas durante la semana de referencia; ii) buscaban empleo o querían trabajar, pero no habían realizado ninguna gestión para encontrar trabajo durante las últimas cuatro semanas; iii) estaban corrientemente disponibles para trabajar; y iv) ya habían encontrado un empleo o habían hecho arreglos para establecer su propia empresa para comenzar posteriormente.

Subempleo:

Subempleo por insuficiencia de horas: Personas empleadas cuyo número total de horas realmente trabajadas durante la semana de referencia en todos sus empleos o actividades era inferior a 40 horas, y que deseaban y estaban disponibles para trabajar más horas durante la semana de referencia.

Situaciones de empleo inadecuado: Personas empleadas que quieren cambiar su situación laboral actual (es decir, personas que quieren cambiar su empleo o actividad actual, encontrar un empleo o actividad adicional o cambiar a otro empleo o actividad) por alguna de las siguientes razones: temen o saben que serán despedidas o que su empresa cerrará; tienen un empleo de duración limitada como empleado por otras razones que les impide tomar un empleo permanente o que no quieren tener un empleo permanente, temporal, estacional u ocasional como empleador, trabajador por cuenta propia (empleado independiente), trabajador familiar no remunerado o miembro de una cooperativa de productores, y quieren tener un empleo más estable; quieren trabajar más horas; razones personales, familiares o relativas a la salud; tienen un total de ingresos inferior a 150 DM al mes de todos sus empleos o actividades y quieren tener un mejor salario o remuneración por hora, quieren mejorar sus condiciones de trabajo (mejores acuerdos sobre las horas de trabajo, un empleo menos difícil); su empleo actual es inferior o superior a sus calificaciones y quieren un trabajo más acorde con sus calificaciones o aptitudes; quieren trabajar menos horas con la correspondiente reducción de sus ingresos; otras razones.

Horas de trabajo: Horas habituales de trabajo por semana; horas suplementarias o extraordinarias durante la semana de referencia; horas no trabajadas durante la semana de referencia; horas realmente trabajadas durante la semana de referencia. La información sobre las horas habituales de trabajo y las horas realmente trabajadas se recopilan por separado para el empleo o actividad principal y para los otros trabajos o actividades, si procede.

Ingresos relacionados con el empleo:
Ingresos relacionados con el empleo asalariado: Salario o sueldo neto habitual por mes. La información se recopila por separado para el empleo o actividad principal y para los otros trabajos o actividades, si procede.
Ingresos relacionados con el empleo independiente: Beneficio neto habitual por mes. La información se recopila por separado para el empleo o actividad principal y para los otros trabajos o actividades, si procede.
Sector informal: Las empresas del sector informal se definen como negocios o actividades de empleadores o trabajadores por cuenta propia (empleados independientes) que reúnen todas las características siguientes: el negocio o actividad es una empresa no constituida en sociedad de capital (propiedad de una sola persona o asociación); tiene menos de 10 personas empleadas y no está registrada en la municipalidad. El empleo en el sector informal se refiere al número total de personas empleadas en empresas del sector informal, incluidos los administradores, socios comerciales, trabajadores familiares no remunerados y empleados de esas empresas.
Actividad habitual: La encuesta no abarca este punto.
Clasificaciones:
Rama de actividad económica (industria):
Título de la clasificación utilizada: Clasificación Industrial General de Actividades Económicas de las Comunidades Europeas (NACE, Rev.1).
Grupos de población clasificados por industria: Personas empleadas; personas desempleadas con experiencia previa de trabajo durante los últimos 12 años; personas económicamente inactivas con experiencia previa de trabajo durante los últimos 12 años, si querían trabajar y estaban disponibles para hacerlo durante la semana de referencia.
Número de Grupos utilizados para la codificación: Grupos a nivel de 4 dígitos.
Vínculos con la CIIU: CIIU-Rev.3.
Ocupación:
Título de la clasificación utilizada: Clasificación Internacional Uniforme de Ocupaciones (CIUO-88).
Grupos de población clasificados por ocupación: Personas empleadas; personas desempleadas con experiencia previa de trabajo durante los últimos 12 años; personas económicamente inactivas con experiencia previa de trabajo durante los últimos 12 años, si querían trabajar y estaban disponibles para hacerlo durante la semana de referencia.
Número de Grupos utilizados para la codificación: CIUO-88 grupos de unidades (nivel de 4 dígitos).
Vínculos con la CIUO: No corresponde.
Situación en el empleo:
Título de la clasificación utilizada: Clasificación nacional sobre la situación en el empleo.
Grupos de población clasificados por situación en el empleo: Personas empleadas; personas desempleadas con experiencia previa de trabajo durante los últimos 12 años; personas económicamente inactivas con experiencia previa de trabajo durante los últimos 12 años, si querían trabajar y estaban disponibles para hacerlo durante la semana de referencia.
Grupos utilizados para la codificación: a) Empleados (empresas, instituciones u organizaciones públicas); b) empleados (sector privado); c) empleadores; d) trabajadores por cuenta propia (empleados independientes), incluidos trabajadores temporeros; e) trabajadores familiares no remunerados; f) miembros de cooperativas de productores.
Vínculos con la CISE: CISE-1993.
Educación:
Título de la clasificación utilizada: Clasificación nacional de niveles de educación.
Grupos de población clasificados por educación: Todas las personas de 15 a 64 años de edad.
Grupos utilizados para la codificación: a) Sin escolaridad; b) 1º-4º grado de escuela elemental; c) 5º-7º grado de escuela elemental; d) escuela elemental completa; e) 1-3 años de escuela secundaria vocacional o escuela para trabajadores especializados; f) escuela secundaria vocacional de 4 años o más de duración; g) escuela secundaria (gimnasio); h) escuela superior no universitaria; i) universidad o academia; j) licenciatura; k) doctorado.
Vínculos con la CINE: Por establecer.
Tamaño y diseño de la muestra:
Unidad final de muestreo: Hogares.
Tamaño de la muestra (unidades finales de muestreo): 3 239 hogares.
Fracción de muestreo: 1,0 por ciento de los hogares.
Marco de la muestra: Listas de direcciones de 180 zonas de enumeración urbanas y 180 aldeas o segmentos de aldeas rurales. Las listas de direcciones se preparó para la Encuesta sobre las Condiciones de Vida de 2000 (Living Standards Measurement Survey 2000). Las zonas de enumeración y las aldeas y segmentos de aldeas se seleccionaron de estratos definidos según la zona militar de la KFOR (Estados Unidos, Reino Unido, Francia, Alemania, Italia), características urbanas y rurales y étnia de las poblaciones (albanés y serbio). Para la Encuesta sobre la Fuerza de Trabajo, se seleccionó una nueva muestra de hogares de las listas de direcciones.
Actualización de la muestra: Se está preparando un nuevo marco de la muestra de hogares.
Rotación:
Esquema: Por determinar.
Porcentaje de unidades que permanecen en la muestra durante dos encuestas consecutivas: Por determinar.
Número máximo de entrevistas por unidad de muestreo: Por determinar.
Tiempo necesario para renovar completamente la muestra: Por determinar.
Levantamiento de la encuesta:
Tipo de entrevista: La información se obtiene mediante entrevistas personales.
Número de unidades finales de muestreo por área de muestra: De 8 a 14 hogares por zona de enumeración urbana; 8 hogares por aldea o segmento de aldea rural.
Duración del trabajo de campo:
Total: Unas seis semanas.
Por área de muestra: Un día con cuatro entrevistadores.
Organización de la encuesta: Todavía no existe una organización permanente para la encuesta.
Número de personas que trabajan en el campo: 18 supervisores y 78 entrevistadores.
Substitución de las unidades finales de muestreo que no responden: Se seleccionó una reserva de hogares por cada zona de enumeración y aldea o segmento de aldea incluidos en la muestra. Los hogares sin respuesta se sustituyeron por hogares de las listas de reserva.
Estimaciones y ajustes:
Tasa de no-respuesta total: No corresponde.
Ajuste por no-respuesta total: No corresponde.
Imputación por no respuesta de ítemes: No corresponde. La no respuesta de ítemes se identifica durante el proceso de edición de los datos. Los hogares de la muestra se vuelven a contactar para obtener la información faltante.
Ajuste por áreas/poblaciones no abarcadas: No corresponde.
Ajuste por falta de cobertura: No.
Ajuste por falta de cobertura: No.
Ajuste por variaciones estacionales: No corresponde.
Historia de la encuesta:
Título y fecha de la primera encuesta: La primera Encuesta sobre la Fuerza de Trabajo se realizó entre diciembre de 2001 y enero de 2002.
Modificaciones y revisiones significativas: No corresponde.
Documentación y difusión:
Documentación:
Título de las publicaciones con los resultados de la encuesta: Oficina de Estadísticas de Kosovo/Ministerio del Trabajo y Asistencia Social: Encuesta sobre la Fuerza de Trabajo (Labour Force Survey).
Título de las publicaciones con la metodología de la encuesta: La publicación antes mencionada incluye información metodológica sobre la encuesta.
Difusión:
Tiempo necesario para difundir los primeros datos: Unos cuatro meses.
Información adelantada acerca de la fecha de la primera difusión pública: No.
Disponibilidad de datos no publicados si se solicitan: Sí.
Disponibilidad de datos por medios informáticos: Sí.

Kuwait

Título de la encuesta: Encuesta por Muestra sobre la Fuerza de Trabajo (The Labour Force Sample Survey).
Organismo responsable de la encuesta:
Planificar y realizar la encuesta: Oficina Central de Estadísticas. Departamento de Censo y Estadísticas de Población (Central Statistical Office. Census & Population Statistics Department).

Analizar y publicar los resultados: Oficina Central de Estadísticas. Departamento de Censo y Estadísticas de Población (Central Statistical Office. Census & Population Statistics Department).
Temas abarcados: Empleo y desempleo actual. Horas realmente trabajadas. Salarios y sueldos de empleados. Nivel de educación. Rama actual de actividad económica (industria), ocupación y situación en el empleo principal. Número de meses en el empleo actual. Duración del desempleo. Empleo en el sector informal. Actividad habitual.
Alcance de la encuesta:
Ámbito geográfico: Toda la nación.
Grupos de población: Toda la población, tanto kuwaities como de otras nacionalidades, y personas que viven en hogares colectivos.
Disponibilidad de estimaciones de otras fuentes para las áreas/grupos excluidos: No disponible.
Grupos abarcados por la encuesta pero excluidos de los resultados publicados: No disponible.
Periodicidad:
Recolección de datos: Irregular, 1973, 1988.
Publicación de los resultados: Después de la encuesta.
Periodo de referencia:
Empleo: Semana de referencia fija.
Búsqueda de trabajo: El mismo periodo de referencia que para el empleo.
Disponibilidad para trabajo: El mismo periodo de referencia que para el empleo.
Conceptos y definiciones:
Empleo: Personas de 15 años y más de edad que formaban parte de la mano de obra disponible para la producción de bienes y servicios y que durante la semana de referencia eran empleadores, trabajadores por cuenta propia, empleados o trabajadores familiares no remunerados. La definición de empleado incluye personas con un empleo pero temporalmente ausentes del trabajo debido a enfermedad, lesión, vacaciones, licencia por maternidad, licencia para estudios o capacitación, conflictos laborales, mal tiempo, desperfectos mecánicos, etc. Incluye también a las personas suspendidas de su trabajo temporalmente o por tiempo indeterminado sin remuneración y personas con licencia sin goce de sueldo por iniciativa del empleador. Se incluyen también los trabajadores a tiempo completo o parcial que buscaban otro empleo durante el periodo de referencia, así como estudiantes de dedicación parcial que trabajaban a tiempo completo o parcial. Se excluyen los estudiantes de dedicación completa que trabajan a tiempo completo o parcial. Se incluyen los trabajadores familiares no remunerados y temporalmente ausentes del trabajo, pero no los aprendices y las personas en formación remunerados o no. Asimismo, se excluyen los trabajadores estacionales que no trabajan durante la temporada inactiva. Se incluyen las personas que participan en planes de promoción del empleo y los miembros de las fuerzas armadas. Se excluyen las personas ocupadas en la producción de bienes o servicios para su propio uso final. Se excluyen también las personas que realizaron algún trabajo durante la semana de referencia pero que estaban sometidas a escolaridad obligatoria o jubiladas y percibían una pensión.
Desempleo: Personas de 15 años y más de edad que, durante la semana de referencia, estaban sin empleo o trabajaban menos de 20 horas, estaban corrientemente disponibles para trabajar y buscaban trabajo. Los desempleados comprenden dos grupos: quienes trabajaron anteriormente en el Estado de Kuwait, pero no tenían empleo y buscaban trabajo durante la semana de referencia; y quienes nunca habían trabajado y buscaban trabajo durante esa semana. La definición de desempleado incluye personas sin empleo y corrientemente disponibles para trabajar que habían tomado disposiciones para comenzar un empleo en una fecha ulterior a la semana de referencia, así como personas sin trabajo y corrientemente disponibles para trabajar y que procuraban establecer su propia empresa. Se incluyen también los estudiantes de dedicación parcial que buscan un empleo a tiempo completo o parcial. Sin embargo, se excluyen los estudiantes de dedicación completa que buscan trabajo a tiempo completo o parcial. Se excluyen igualmente las personas que buscan trabajo y están disponibles para trabajar pero sometidas a escolaridad obligatoria, jubiladas o perciben una pensión. Se excluyen también las personas sin empleo y disponibles para trabajar, que no buscaban trabajo durante la semana de referencia.
Subempleo:
Subempleo por insuficiencia de horas: No se dispone de información.
Situaciones de empleo inadecuado: No se dispone de información.
Horas de trabajo: Se refiere al número de horas realmente trabajadas en el lugar de trabajo durante la semana de referencia. Se incluyen las horas trabajadas durante el periodo normal de trabajo, así como las horas adicionales (extraordinarias).
Ingresos relacionados con el empleo:
Ingresos relacionados con el empleo asalariado: Salarios y sueldos: Se incluyen salarios y sueldos directos, ingresos totales en efectivo, pagos en especie y servicios, pagos relacionados con beneficios, beneficios de la seguridad social relacionados con el empleo, pagos de horas extraordinarias y otros valores imputados de bienes y servicios que otorga el lugar de trabajo como pagos en especie por trabajos realizados.
Ingresos relacionados con el empleo independiente: No se dispone de información.
Sector informal: Empleo en empresas no registradas, empresas o negocios no organizados o pequeños o micro negocios o empresas.
Actividad habitual: No se dispone de información.
Clasificaciones:
Rama de actividad económica (industria):
Título de la clasificación utilizada: No se dispone de información.
Grupos de población clasificados por industria: Personas empleadas y desempleadas con experiencia previa de trabajo.
Número de Grupos utilizados para la codificación: Nivel de 2 dígitos.
Vínculos con la CIIU: CIIU-Rev.3.
Ocupación:
Título de la clasificación utilizada: No se dispone de información.
Grupos de población clasificados por ocupación: Personas empleadas y desempleadas con experiencia previa de trabajo.
Número de Grupos utilizados para la codificación: Nivel de 2 dígitos.
Vínculos con la CIUO: CIUO-68.
Situación en el empleo:
Título de la clasificación utilizada: No se dispone de información.
Grupos de población clasificados por situación en el empleo: Empleados.
Grupos utilizados para la codificación: Empleadores. Empleados independientes. Empleados. Trabajadores familiares no remunerados.
Vínculos con la CISE: No.
Educación:
Título de la clasificación utilizada: No se dispone de información.
Grupos de población clasificados por educación: Población de 15 años y más de edad.
Grupos utilizados para la codificación: Analfabetos. Saben leer y escribir. **Educación:** primaria. **Educación:** media. **Educación:** secundaria. **Educación:** superior a la secundaria pero inferior a la universitaria. **Educación:** universitaria. Estudios de postgrado.
Vínculos con la CINE: CINE-1976.
Tamaño y diseño de la muestra:
Unidad final de muestreo: Hogares privados y particulares en hogares colectivos.
Tamaño de la muestra (unidades finales de muestreo): Unos 11 000 hogares privados y 558 hogares colectivos.
Fracción de muestreo: 0,05 por ciento.
Marco de la muestra: Basado en las zonas de enumeración del Censo de Población de 1985 de Kuwait, estratificado en 54 estratos para los hogares privados de kuwaities y no kuwaities, y 43 estratos para hogares colectivos no kuwaities.
Las 1 729 zonas de enumeración del censo estratificado constituyeron las unidades primarias de muestreo (UPM) de la encuesta. Se seleccionaron unas 345 UPM en la primera etapa de la selección de la muestra. Esas UPM se actualizaron con listas de todos los edificios, viviendas y hogares. En la segunda etapa, se escogieron unos 11 000 hogares de las listas de UPM. En el caso de los hogares colectivos, se seleccionaron unos 558 de las UPM de muestra y dentro de esos hogares seleccionados se muestrearon unos 11 000 particulares.
Actualización de la muestra: Las UPM se actualizaron en la fase de listado de la primera etapa de la selección de muestras.
Rotación: No existe un plan de rotación.
Levantamiento de la encuesta:
Tipo de entrevista: Entrevistas personales realizadas por 60 entrevistadores y 5 supervisores sobre el terreno.
Número de unidades finales de muestreo por área de muestra: 20 hogares.
Duración del trabajo de campo: Un mes.
Organización de la encuesta: Permanente.

Número de personas que trabajan en el campo: Unos 60 entrevistadores, 5 supervisores sobre el terreno, 2 empleados de oficina, 4 operadores de entrada de datos, 1 experto en estadísticas y 1 administrador.
Substitución de las unidades finales de muestreo que no responden: Sí.
Estimaciones y ajustes:
Tasa de no-respuesta total: No disponible.
Ajuste por no-respuesta total: No.
Imputación por no respuesta de ítemes: No.
Ajuste por áreas/poblaciones no abarcadas: No.
Ajuste por falta de cobertura: No.
Ajuste por exceso de cobertura: No.
Ajuste por variaciones estacionales: No.
Historia de la encuesta:
Título y fecha de la primera encuesta: Encuesta por muestra sobre la fuerza de trabajo, 1973.
Modificaciones y revisiones significativas: No disponible.
Documentación y difusión:
Documentación:
Título de las publicaciones con los resultados de la encuesta: (periodicidad): Labour force sample survey, marzo de 1988, Primera Parte, junio de 1990. Ministerio de Planificación, Estado de Kuwait.
Título de las publicaciones con la metodología de la encuesta: (periodicidad): Igual al de la publicación anterior.
Difusión:
Tiempo necesario para difundir los primeros datos: No se dispone de información.
Información adelantada acerca de la fecha de la primera difusión pública: No.
Disponibilidad de datos no publicados si se solicitan: No se dispone de información.
Disponibilidad de datos por medios informáticos: No se dispone de información.

Letonia

Título de la encuesta: Encuesta sobre la Fuerza de Trabajo de Letonia (Latvian Labour Force Survey).
Organismo responsable de la encuesta:
Planificar y realizar la encuesta: Servicio Central de Estadísticas (Central Statistical Bureau).
Analizar y publicar los resultados: Servicio Central de Estadísticas (Central Statistical Bureau).
Temas abarcados: Empleo, desempleo, subempleo, horas de trabajo, salarios, fuente de ingresos, duración del desempleo, trabajadores desalentados, trabajadores ocasionales, rama de actividad económica (industria), ocupación, situación en el empleo, nivel de educación, actividad habitual, empleo secundario y experiencia previa de trabajo.
Alcance de la encuesta:
Ámbito geográfico: Todo el país.
Grupos de población: Todas las personas de 15 años y más de edad que residen en hogares privados durante la semana de referencia. Se excluyen los miembros del hogar ausentes del mismo durante más de 3 meses (como reclutas, estudiantes que viven en albergues, marineros, etc.), así como la población que vive en hogares colectivos (internados en instituciones penales y psiquiátricos, hospitales, prisiones, etc.).
Disponibilidad de estimaciones de otras fuentes para las áreas/grupos excluidos: No.
Grupos abarcados por la encuesta pero excluidos de los resultados publicados: Ninguno.
Periodicidad:
Recolección de datos: Bianual.
Publicación de los resultados: Bianual.
Periodo de referencia:
Empleo: Una semana (últimos siete días antes de la fecha de la entrevista).
Búsqueda de trabajo: Cuatro semanas antes de la fecha de la entrevista.
Disponibilidad para trabajo: Dos semanas después de la fecha de la entrevista.
Conceptos y definiciones:
Empleo: Son empleadas todas las personas de 15 años y más de edad que, durante la semana de referencia, a) realizaron, durante una hora por lo menos, algún trabajo remunerado o por un beneficio (en efectivo o en especie); b) no trabajaban pero tenían un empleo o una empresa del que estaban temporalmente ausentes debido a vacaciones o licencia anual, enfermedad, licencia para capacitación u otra razón similar. Además, se consideran empleadas las personas que realizaban un trabajo social para la comunidad, remunerado o no, así como las mujeres con licencia para cuidar sus hijos hasta que éstos cumplan tres meses de edad.
Se incluyen también en los totales:
a)trabajadores a tiempo completo o parcial que buscaban otro empleo durante el periodo de referencia;
b)estudiantes de dedicación completa o parcial que trabajaban a tiempo completo o parcial;
c)personas que realizaron algún trabajo durante la semana de referencia pero que estaban jubiladas y percibían una pensión, inscritas como desempleadas en busca de trabajo en una oficina de empleo o percibiendo indemnizaciones de desempleo;
d)trabajadores familiares remunerados o no (si trabajaron por lo menos una hora);
e)personas ocupadas en la producción de bienes para su propio uso final.
Desempleo: Son desempleadas todas las personas de 15 años y más de edad, registradas o no en el Servicio Nacional del Empleo, que:
a)no trabajaban durante la semana de referencia ni estaban temporalmente ausentes del trabajo;
b)estaban buscando trabajo activamente durante las cuatro semanas anteriores a la entrevista;
c)estaban disponibles para comenzar a trabajar en las dos semanas siguientes a la semana de la encuesta.
Se incluyen también como desempleadas las personas que no buscaban activamente trabajo porque habían encontrado uno y habían tomado disposiciones para comenzar un empleo remunerado en una fecha ulterior al periodo de referencia.
Subempleo:
Subempleo por insuficiencia de horas: Personas que, durante la semana de referencia, trabajaban menos horas que las horas ordinarias establecidas debido a razones económicas (contra su voluntad).
Situaciones de empleo inadecuado: Personas que buscaban otro empleo con mejores condiciones de trabajo (sueldo, ubicación, experiencia profesional, etc.).
Horas de trabajo: Horales habituales y reales trabajadas en el empleo principal. Horas realmente trabajadas en empleo(s) secundario(s).
Ingresos relacionados con el empleo:
Ingresos relacionados con el empleo asalariado: Salarios brutos incluidos impuestos en el empleo principal para todo el mes civil.
Ingresos relacionados con el empleo independiente: No corresponde.
Sector informal: No corresponde.
Actividad habitual: Sí.
Clasificaciones:
Rama de actividad económica (industria):
Título de la clasificación utilizada: Clasificación Industrial General de Actividades Económicas de las Comunidades Europeas (NACE, Rev.1).
Grupos de población clasificados por industria: Personas empleadas y personas desempleadas con experiencia previa de trabajo (si habían tenido un empleo durante los últimos tres años).
Número de Grupos utilizados para la codificación: 33
Vínculos con la CIIU: CIIU-Rev.3 (nivel de 2 dígitos).
Ocupación:
Título de la clasificación utilizada: Clasificación de Ocupaciones de Letonia.
Grupos de población clasificados por ocupación: Personas empleadas y personas desempleadas con experiencia previa de trabajo (si habían tenido un empleo durante los últimos tres años).
Número de Grupos utilizados para la codificación: Numeroso.
Vínculos con la CIUO: CIUO-88.
Situación en el empleo:
Título de la clasificación utilizada: CISE (Clasificación Internacional de la Situación en el Empleo).
Grupos de población clasificados por situación en el empleo: Personas empleadas y personas desempleadas con experiencia previa de trabajo (si habían tenido un empleo durante los últimos tres años).
Grupos utilizados para la codificación: 4 grupos (empleados, empleadores, trabajadores por cuenta propia, trabajadores familiares no remunerados).
Vínculos con la CISE: CISE-1993.
Educación:
Título de la clasificación utilizada: Clasificación nacional.

Grupos de población clasificados por educación: Toda la población, personas empleadas, desempleadas e inactivas.
Grupos utilizados para la codificación: 8 grupos (sin educación formal, primaria incompleta, primaria, vocacional, secundaria general, secundaria técnica, secundaria especializada, superior).
Vínculos con la CINE: No se puede comparar totalmente con la CINE.
Tamaño y diseño de la muestra:
Unidad final de muestreo: Para las zonas rurales: hogares; para las zonas urbanas: particulares.
Tamaño de la muestra (unidades finales de muestreo): Unos 8 000 hogares.
Fracción de muestreo: Casi el 0,75 por ciento.
Marco de la muestra: El marco de la muestra para las zonas urbanas se obtiene del Registro de la Población. Para las zonas rurales se prepara con la lista completa de hogares.
Actualización de la muestra: La última actualización se efectuó en 1998.
Rotación:
Esquema: Cada hogar se mantiene en la encuesta durante tres rondas consecutivas. Este sistema de rotación permite que un tercio de hogares de cada pueblo seleccionado para la muestra se sustituya en una nueva ronda. Para las zonas rurales, todos los hogares se sustituyen en un tercio de las unidades primarias de muestreo ('pagasts').
Porcentaje de unidades que permanecen en la muestra durante dos encuestas consecutivas: 66,7 por ciento.
Número máximo de entrevistas por unidad de muestreo: 9.
Tiempo necesario para renovar completamente la muestra: 18 meses.
Levantamiento de la encuesta:
Tipo de entrevista: Papel y lápiz (entrevista personal).
Número de unidades finales de muestreo por área de muestra: Siete en unidades primarias de muestreo (UPM) rurales; de 15 a 459 en UPM urbanas.
Duración del trabajo de campo:
Total: Un mes civil.
Por área de muestra: Un mes civil.
Organización de la encuesta: No se proporcionó información.
Número de personas que trabajan en el campo: Unas 631 personas y 31 supervisores.
Substitución de las unidades finales de muestreo que no responden: No.
Estimaciones y ajustes:
Tasa de no-respuesta total: En mayo de 1999: 9,46 por ciento. En mayo de 2000: 10,12 por ciento.
Ajuste por no-respuesta total: Sí.
Imputación por no respuesta de ítemes: No.
Ajuste por áreas/poblaciones no abarcadas: Sí.
Ajuste por falta de cobertura: Sí.
Ajuste por exceso de cobertura: Sí.
Ajuste por variaciones estacionales: No.
Historia de la encuesta:
Título y fecha de la primera encuesta: Encuesta sobre la Fuerza de Trabajo de Letonia, noviembre de 1995.
Modificaciones y revisiones significativas: A partir de mayo de 1997, también se calcularon a nivel regional indicadores como la tasa de actividad, la tasa de participación en el empleo y la tasa de desempleo.
Documentación y difusión:
Documentación:
Título de las publicaciones con los resultados de la encuesta: (periodicidad): "Labour Force in Latvia" (bianual), "Monthly Bulletin of Latvian Statistics" (bianual).
Título de las publicaciones con la metodología de la encuesta: (periodicidad): "Labour Force in Latvia" (bianual).
Difusión:
Tiempo necesario para difundir los primeros datos: Cuatro meses.
Información adelantada acerca de la fecha de la primera difusión pública: Sí.
Disponibilidad de datos no publicados si se solicitan: Sí.
Disponibilidad de datos por medios informáticos: Disquetes. Sitio web: http://www.csb.lv (información seleccionada).

Lituania

Título de la encuesta: Encuesta sobre la Fuerza de Trabajo (Labour Force Survey (LFS)).
Organismo responsable de la encuesta:
Planificar y realizar la encuesta: Servicio de Estadísticas de Lituania (Statistics Lithuania).
Analizar y publicar los resultados: División de Estadísticas del Empleo del Servicio de Estadísticas de Lituania (Employment Statistics Division of Statistics Lithuania).
Temas abarcados: Empleo, desempleo, subempleo, horas de trabajo, salarios, ingresos, empleo en el sector informal, duración del empleo y el desempleo, trabajadores desalentados y ocasionales, rama de actividad económica (industria), ocupación, situación en el empleo, nivel de educación/calificación, empleo secundario.
Alcance de la encuesta:
Ámbito geográfico: Todo el país.
Grupos de población: Población de 15 años y más de edad, que reside en hogares privados (antes de 2000, población civil de 14 años y más de edad), incluidas personas ausentes por periodos cortos por motivos de estudios, así como miembros del hogar temporalmente ausentes.
Se excluyen internados de instituciones penales y psiquiátricos, reclutas que viven en cuarteles y extranjeros.
Disponibilidad de estimaciones de otras fuentes para las áreas/grupos excluidos: No.
Grupos abarcados por la encuesta pero excluidos de los resultados publicados: Ninguno.
Periodicidad:
Recolección de datos: Dos veces al año, en mayo y noviembre.
Publicación de los resultados: Dos veces al año.
Periodo de referencia:
Empleo: Una semana.
Búsqueda de trabajo: Cuatro semanas antes de la fecha de la entrevista.
Disponibilidad para trabajo: Dos semanas después de la semana de la entrevista.
Conceptos y definiciones:
Empleo: Son empleadas todas las personas de 15 años y más de edad que, durante la semana de referencia, estaban en alguna de las siguientes categorías:
a)personas en el trabajo, con un empleo remunerado o independiente, que habían trabajado una hora o más por salarios o sueldos en efectivo o en especie, por un beneficio o ingreso familiar en efectivo o en especie;
b)personas con un empleo pero que no se encontraban en el trabajo, es decir quienes ya trabajaban en su empleo actual (remunerado o independiente) pero que estaban ausentes durante la semana de referencia y tenían un vínculo formal con el empleo.
Se incluyen también como empleadas:
a)personas que tienen un empleo pero que se encuentran temporalmente ausentes del mismo debido a enfermedad o lesión, licencia por maternidad o licencia parental, días de fiesta, licencia para capacitación o interrupción del trabajo debido a razones económicas o técnicas, mal tiempo, desperfectos mecánicos;
b)personas que realizaron algún trabajo remunerado o por un beneficio durante la semana de referencia pero que estaban sometidas a la escolaridad obligatoria, jubiladas y percibían una pensión, inscritas como desempleadas en busca de trabajo en una oficina de empleo o percibiendo indemnizaciones de desempleo;
c)trabajadores a tiempo completo o parcial que buscaban un empleo durante la semana de referencia;
d)estudiantes de dedicación completa o parcial que trabajaban a tiempo completo o parcial;
e)aprendices y personas en formación remunerados;
f)trabajadores familiares remunerados y no remunerados;
g)servicio doméstico privado;
h)personas que participan en planes de promoción del empleo remunerados o que reciben formación en el lugar de trabajo;
i)miembros de carrera y voluntarios remunerados de las fuerzas armadas.
Se excluyen aprendices y personas en formación no remunerados, personas ocupadas en sus propios quehaceres domésticos y quienes realizan un trabajo voluntario no remunerado para la comunidad o social.
Desempleo: Todas las personas de 15 años y más de edad que estaban:
a)sin empleo durante la semana de referencia;
b)disponibles para trabajar en cuatro semanas;
c)buscando trabajo activamente, es decir habían realizado gestiones concretas (como matenerse inscritas en una oficina de empleo, establecer contacto con agencias de trabajo privadas, etc.) en las últimas cuatro semanas, o habían tomado disposiciones para comenzar un nuevo empleo.

Se incluyen también los estudiantes de dedicación completa y parcial que buscaban un empleo a tiempo completo o parcial.
Se excluyen de la definición de desempleo y se clasifican como trabajadores desalentados las personas sin empleo, disponibles para trabajar pero que no buscaban trabajo y que informaron que no había ningún trabajo disponible.
Subempleo:
Subempleo por insuficiencia de horas: Todas las personas empleadas que trabajaban a tiempo parcial porque no habían podido encontrar un trabajo a tiempo completo y estaban buscando otro empleo o personas que trabajaban menos de 40 horas durante la semana de referencia y estaban buscando otro empleo.
Situaciones de empleo inadecuado: Todavía no está disponible.
Horas de trabajo: Horas trabajadas. Se incluyen las horas extraordinarias, pero no las horas pagadas y no trabajadas como el tiempo de trayecto entre el hogar y el lugar de trabajo, las horas perdidas a causa de enfermedad, días de fiesta, desempleo, etc.
Ingresos relacionados con el empleo:
Ingresos relacionados con el empleo asalariado: Total de ingresos en efectivo, incluidas las cotizaciones a la seguridad social relacionadas con el empleo, etc., salvo los pagos en especie (alimentos) recibidos del trabajo en el sector agrícola. Se refiere a todos los empleos.
Ingresos relacionados con el empleo independiente: Beneficios brutos.
Sector informal: Teóricamente la encuesta abarca este punto.
Actividad habitual: No corresponde.
Clasificaciones:
Rama de actividad económica (industria):
Título de la clasificación utilizada: Clasificación nacional.
Grupos de población clasificados por industria: Personas empleadas y desempleadas (rama de actividad económica del último empleo para el desempleado).
Número de Grupos utilizados para la codificación: 59 grupos.
Vínculos con la CIIU: CIIU-Rev.3.
Ocupación:
Título de la clasificación utilizada: Clasificación nacional.
Grupos de población clasificados por ocupación: Personas empleadas y desempleadas (ocupación en el último empleo para el desempleado).
Número de Grupos utilizados para la codificación: 28 grupos subprincipales, 116 grupos menores y 390 grupos de unidades.
Vínculos con la CIUO: CIUO-88.
Situación en el empleo:
Título de la clasificación utilizada: Clasificación nacional.
Grupos de población clasificados por situación en el empleo: Personas empleadas.
Grupos utilizados para la codificación: 5 grupos: empleadores, empleados, trabajadores por cuenta propia, trabajadores que contribuyen con la familia, trabajadores no clasificados por situación.
Vínculos con la CISE: CISE-1993.
Educación:
Título de la clasificación utilizada: Clasificación nacional.
Grupos de población clasificados por educación: Personas empleadas.
Grupos utilizados para la codificación: 6 grupos: sin escolaridad, primaria, básica, secundaria, universitaria, superior.
Vínculos con la CINE: CINE-1997.
Tamaño y diseño de la muestra:
Unidad final de muestreo: Vivienda.
Tamaño de la muestra (unidades finales de muestreo): 8 500 personas que viven en 3 000 viviendas.
Fracción de muestreo: 0,3 por ciento del total de la población.
Marco de la muestra: El Registro de Población abarca la población residente.
Actualización de la muestra: Continuamente.
Rotación:
Esquema: Cada vivienda de la muestra se entrevista tres veces . Después de mantenerla en la muestra durante dos encuestas consecutivas y excluirla en la tercera ronda siguiente, se vuelve a introducir en la muestra y luego se excluye definitivamente.
Porcentaje de unidades que permanecen en la muestra durante dos encuestas consecutivas: 33 por ciento.
Número máximo de entrevistas por unidad de muestreo: Tres.
Tiempo necesario para renovar completamente la muestra: Dos años y medio.
Levantamiento de la encuesta:
Tipo de entrevista: Papel y lápiz. Entrevistas personales para un 75 por ciento de los entrevistados y entrevistas telefónicas para el 25 por ciento restante.
Número de unidades finales de muestreo por área de muestra: No se dispone de información.
Duración del trabajo de campo:
Total: No se dispone de información.
Por área de muestra: No se dispone de información.
Organización de la encuesta: No se dispone de información.
Número de personas que trabajan en el campo: 200 supervisores y 49 entrevistadores.
Substitución de las unidades finales de muestreo que no responden: No.
Estimaciones y ajustes:
Tasa de no-respuesta total: 15 por ciento.
Ajuste por no-respuesta total: Sí.
Imputación por no respuesta de ítemes: No.
Ajuste por áreas/poblaciones no abarcadas: No.
Ajuste por falta de cobertura: Sí.
Ajuste por exceso de cobertura: Sí.
Ajuste por variaciones estacionales: No.
Historia de la encuesta:
Título y fecha de la primera encuesta: Encuesta sobre la Fuerza de Trabajo, 1994.
Modificaciones y revisiones significativas: De 1994 a 1999, personas de 14 años y más de edad. En 1998 y 1999 se utilizaron cuestionarios para la encuesta.
Documentación y difusión:
Documentación:
Título de las publicaciones con los resultados de la encuesta: (periodicidad): Labour force, employment and unemployment (semestralmente); Economic and Social developments in Lithuania.
Título de las publicaciones con la metodología de la encuesta: (periodicidad): Labour force, employment and unemployment (semestralmente); Economic and Social developments in Lithuania.
Difusión:
Tiempo necesario para difundir los primeros datos: Los resultados de mayo se publican durante el 4º trimestre.
Información adelantada acerca de la fecha de la primera difusión pública: No.
Disponibilidad de datos no publicados si se solicitan: No.
Disponibilidad de datos por medios informáticos: Sitio web: http://www.std.lt .

Macao, China

Título de la encuesta: Encuesta sobre el Empleo (Inquérito ao Emprego).
Organismo responsable de la encuesta:
Planificar y realizar la encuesta: Servicio de Estadísticas y Censo (Statistics and Census Service).
Analizar y publicar los resultados: Servicio de Estadísticas y Censo (Statistics Census Service).
Temas abarcados: Empleo, desempleo, subempleo, horas de trabajo, salarios, ingresos, duración del desempleo, trabajadores desalentados, rama de actividad económica (industria), ocupación, situación en el empleo, nivel de educación, empleo secundario.
Alcance de la encuesta:
Ámbito geográfico: Todo el territorio de la Región Administrativa Especial de Macao (RAEM).
Grupos de población: Población no residente de hogares colectivos, de 14 años y más de edad, salvo los miembros de las fuerzas armadas.
Disponibilidad de estimaciones de otras fuentes para las áreas/grupos excluidos: No.
Grupos abarcados por la encuesta pero excluidos de los resultados publicados: No.
Periodicidad:
Recolección de datos: Mensualmente.
Publicación de los resultados: Mensual y trimestralmente.
Periodo de referencia:
Empleo: Periodo de referencia móvil de una semana antes de la fecha de la entrevista.
Búsqueda de trabajo: Periodo de referencia móvil de un mes antes de la fecha de la entrevista.
Disponibilidad para trabajo: Periodo de referencia móvil de una semana antes de la fecha de la entrevista.
Conceptos y definiciones:
Empleo: Todas las personas de 14 años y más de edad que durante la semana de referencia trabajaron, por lo menos una hora, por una remuneración, beneficio o ingresos para la familia, en efectivo o en especie. Se incluyen también las personas que tienen un empleo y que estaban temporalmente ausentes del trabajo, pero

con un vínculo formal con el empleo, por razones tales como enfermedad, licencia por maternidad, días feriados, etc.
Se incluyen también las personas:
a)con un trabajo pero temporalmente ausentes del mismo por motivos como enfermedad o lesión, vacaciones o licencia anual, licencia por maternidad o paternidad, ausencia sin remuneración o debido al mal tiempo, desperfectos mecánicos, etc., así como las personas suspendidas de su trabajo sin remuneración o con licencia sin goce de sueldo por iniciativa del empleador durante 30 días y trabajadores que buscaban otro empleo durante el periodo de referencia;
b)personas que realizaron algún trabajo remunerado o por un beneficio durante el periodo de referencia pero que estaban sometidas a escolaridad obligatoria, jubiladas y percibían una pensión, inscritas en una oficina de empleo o percibían una pensión;
c)estudiantes de dedicación completa o parcial que trabajaban a tiempo completo o parcial, aprendices y personas en formación remunerados, personas que participan en planes subvencionados de promoción del empleo;
d)trabajadores familiares no remunerados.
Desempleo: Son desempleadas todas las personas de 14 años y más de edad que, durante el periodo de referencia, no tienen un empleo o un vínculo formal con el empleo, pero están disponibles para trabajar por una remuneración o establecer un negocio y han buscado empleo durante el último mes. Las gestiones realizadas para buscar un empleo pueden ser: pedir ayuda a parientes o amigos, inscribirse en una oficina de empleo, colocar o contestar anuncios de diarios, presentar directamente su candidatura para un empleo a los empleadores, visitar lugares de trabajo, buscar equipos de fábrica, financiamiento o licencia para comenzar su propio negocio.
Se incluyen también como desempleadas:
a)las personas suspendidas de su trabajo, remuneradas o no, por más de 30 días;
b)los estudiantes de dedicación completa o parcial, disponibles para trabajar, que buscan trabajo a tiempo completo o parcial
Subempleo:
Subempleo por insuficiencia de horas: Personas empleadas que, independientemente de su situación en el empleo, trabajaban por razones ajenas a su voluntad menos de 35 horas durante el periodo de referencia, y buscaban un empleo adicional o estaban dispuestas a trabajar más horas.
Situaciones de empleo inadecuado: No corresponde.
Horas de trabajo: Horas de trabajo normales y reales por semana; se refiere a todos los empleos.
Ingresos relacionados con el empleo:
Ingresos relacionados con el empleo asalariado: Se refiere a los ingresos brutos (antes de hacer cualquier deducción), en efectivo o en especie, pagados al trabajador periódicamente por el tiempo trabajado o el trabajo realizado, así como por el tiempo no trabajado, como días de fiesta u otra licencia pagada.
Ingresos relacionados con el empleo independiente: Se obtiene al deducir de la producción bruta los gastos de explotación y la depreciación de los costos de sustitución de activos productivos. Para cada actividad, la producción bruta se puede definir como el valor de todos los bienes y servicios producidos, incluida cualquier parte que se ha reservado para su propio consumo o se ha proporcionado gratuitamente o a precios reducidos a un trabajador asalariado. Los gastos de explotación incluyen los pagos al personal asalariado, en efectivo y/o en especie, y otros gastos corrientes de la actividad económica, tales como la compra de materia prima, combustible, herramientas y equipos, pago de renta e intereses, gastos de transporte y mercadeo.
Sector informal: No corresponde.
Actividad habitual: No corresponde.
Clasificaciones:
Rama de actividad económica (industria):
Título de la clasificación utilizada: Clasificación nacional.
Grupos de población clasificados por industria: Empleados y desempleados (rama de actividad económica del último empleo para el desempleado).
Número de Grupos utilizados para la codificación: 66 grupos.
Vínculos con la CIIU: CIIU-Rev.3.
Ocupación:
Título de la clasificación utilizada: Clasificación nacional.
Grupos de población clasificados por ocupación: Empleados y desempleados (ocupación en el último empleo para el desempleado).
Número de Grupos utilizados para la codificación: 10 grupos.
Vínculos con la CIUO: CIUO-88.
Situación en el empleo:
Título de la clasificación utilizada: Clasificación nacional.
Grupos de población clasificados por situación en el empleo: Empleados.
Grupos utilizados para la codificación: Cuatro grupos: empleadores, trabajadores por cuenta propia, empleados y trabajadores familiares no remunerados.
Vínculos con la CISE: CISE-1993.
Educación:
Título de la clasificación utilizada: Clasificación nacional.
Grupos de población clasificados por educación: Empleados y desempleados.
Grupos utilizados para la codificación: Seis grupos: sin escolaridad/preescolar; primaria, secundaria inferior; secundaria superior; terciaria pero no equivalente al primer ciclo de universidad y terciaria equivalente al primer ciclo de universidad.
Vínculos con la CINE: CINE-1997.
Tamaño y diseño de la muestra:
Unidad final de muestreo: Vivienda.
Tamaño de la muestra (unidades finales de muestreo): 3 600 viviendas por trimestre.
Fracción de muestreo: 2,25 por ciento.
Marco de la muestra: “Unidades de Estadísticas del Archivo General” del Servicio de Estadísticas y Censo, que contiene todos los datos sobre las viviendas (estructuras permanentes y provisionales) por orden geográfico.
Actualización de la muestra: Registros administrativos de nuevas construcciones y edificios derribados e información sobre los resultados de las encuestas sobre los hogares.
Rotación:
Esquema: 50 por ciento de la muestra en el mes en curso se enumera tres meses más tarde.
Porcentaje de unidades que permanecen en la muestra durante dos encuestas consecutivas: 50 por ciento.
Número máximo de entrevistas por unidad de muestreo: Dos.
Tiempo necesario para renovar completamente la muestra: Seis meses.
Levantamiento de la encuesta:
Tipo de entrevista: Personal.
Número de unidades finales de muestreo por área de muestra: No se proporcionó información.
Duración del trabajo de campo:
Total: 14 días.
Por área de muestra: No se proporcionó información.
Organización de la encuesta: Permanente.
Número de personas que trabajan en el campo: 20 personas.
Substitución de las unidades finales de muestreo que no responden: No.
Estimaciones y ajustes:
Tasa de no-respuesta total: Cerca del 8 por ciento.
Ajuste por no-respuesta total: No.
Imputación por no respuesta de ítemes: No.
Ajuste por áreas/poblaciones no abarcadas: No.
Ajuste por falta de cobertura: No.
Ajuste por exceso de cobertura: No.
Ajuste por variaciones estacionales: No.
Historia de la encuesta:
Título y fecha de la primera encuesta: Encuesta sobre el empleo, mayo de 1989.
Modificaciones y revisiones significativas: Mayo de 1989 - mayo de 1991: encuesta bianual (mayo y noviembre) con una muestra de 2 100 viviendas por cada ronda de la encuesta. Mayo de 1992 - noviembre de 1995: encuestra trimestral (febrero, mayo, agosto y noviembre) con una muestra de 1 290 viviendas por cada ronda de la encuesta. Desde enero de 1996, encuesta mensual con una muestra de 1 200 viviendas por mes.
Documentación y difusión:
Documentación:
Título de las publicaciones con los resultados de la encuesta: (periodicidad): “Employment Survey”: Brief Report (mensualmente); Quarterly Report; Annual Report and Statistical Yearbook.
Título de las publicaciones con la metodología de la encuesta: Anexo de la publicación “Employment Survey”
Difusión:
Tiempo necesario para difundir los primeros datos: Un mes después de la recopilación de datos.
Información adelantada acerca de la fecha de la primera difusión pública: No.
Disponibilidad de datos no publicados si se solicitan: Sí.
Disponibilidad de datos por medios informáticos: Si, sitio web: ttp://www.dsec.gov.mo/.

Macedonia, Ex Rep. Yugoslava de

Título de la encuesta: Encuesta sobre la Fuerza de Trabajo (Labour Force Survey).
Organismo responsable de la encuesta:
Planificar y realizar la encuesta: Oficina de Estadísticas (Statistical Office).
Analizar y publicar los resultados: Oficina de Estadísticas (Statistical Office).
Temas abarcados: Empleo, desempleo, horas de trabajo, salarios, ingresos, empleo en el sector informal, duración del desempleo, trabajadores desalentados, trabajadores ocasionales, rama de actividad económica (industria), ocupación, situación en el empleo, nivel de educación, actividad habitual, empleo secundario.
Alcance de la encuesta:
Ámbito geográfico: Todo el país.
Grupos de población: Todos los residentes permanentes de 15 años y más de edad, incluidos los temporalmente ausentes que se encuentran en el extranjero por un periodo inferior a un año.
Se excluyen todas las personas menores de 15 años y mayores de 80 años de edad, así como las personas de las siguientes categorías:
a)personas en misión en el extranjero a largo plazo (más de un año);
b)estudiantes que residen en albergues y población no asentada;
c)internados en instituciones penales y psiquiátricas;
d)miembros de las fuerzas armadas;
e)ciudadanos extranjeros.
Disponibilidad de estimaciones de otras fuentes para las áreas/grupos excluidos: No.
Grupos abarcados por la encuesta pero excluidos de los resultados publicados: Ninguno.
Periodicidad:
Recolección de datos: Anual.
Publicación de los resultados: Anual.
Periodo de referencia:
Empleo: Una semana antes de la fecha de la entrevista.
Búsqueda de trabajo: Una semana antes de la fecha de la entrevista.
Disponibilidad para trabajo: Una semana después de la fecha de la entrevista.
Conceptos y definiciones:
Empleo: Son empleadas las personas de 15 años y más de edad que, durante la semana de referencia, realizaron algún trabajo como empleados asalariados, en su propio negocio, profesión o en su propia explotación agrícola, o que trabajaron por lo menos una hora o más como trabajadores familiares no remunerados en una empresa administrada por un miembro de la familia. Se incluyen también a quienes no trabajaban pero tenían un empleo o negocio del cual estaban ausentes temporalmente debido a enfermedad, mal tiempo, vacaciones, capacitación con fines de especialización, conflictos laborales, o razones personales, así como por el fin de actividad de la empresa.
Se incluyen también en los totales:
a)trabajadores a tiempo completo o parcial que buscaban otro empleo durante el periodo de referencia;
b)estudiantes de dedicación completa o parcial que trabajaban a tiempo completo o parcial;
c)personas que realizaron algún trabajo durante la semana de referencia pero que estaban jubiladas y percibían una pensión, inscritas como desempleadas en busca de trabajo en una oficina de empleo o percibiendo indemnizaciones de desempleo;
d)servicio doméstico privado;
e)aprendices y personas en formación remunerados;
f)personas ocupadas en la producción de bienes para su propio uso final (por ejemplo, agricultura de subsistencia).
Desempleo: Son desempleadas todas las personas de 15 años y más de edad que no tenían empleo durante la semana de referencia, estaban disponibles para trabajar durante la semana de referencia o una semana después de la semana de referencia y no habían tomado ninguna disposición concreta para encontrar empleo.
Subempleo:
Subempleo por insuficiencia de horas: Personas que trabajan menos horas que las ordinarias y que desean y están disponibles para trabajar horas adicionales.
Situaciones de empleo inadecuado: No se dispone de información.
Horas de trabajo: Horas habituales y reales trabajadas.
Ingresos relacionados con el empleo:
Ingresos relacionados con el empleo asalariado: Ingresos habituales mensuales (ingresos netos) en el empleo principal.
Ingresos relacionados con el empleo independiente: Ingresos habituales mensuales (ingresos netos) en el empleo principal.
Sector informal: No se dispone de información.
Actividad habitual: Situación durante los últimos 12 meses.
Clasificaciones:
Rama de actividad económica (industria):
Título de la clasificación utilizada: Clasificación nacional.
Grupos de población clasificados por industria: Personas empleadas.
Número de Grupos utilizados para la codificación: 14.
Vínculos con la CIIU: No.
Ocupación:
Título de la clasificación utilizada: Clasificación nacional.
Grupos de población clasificados por ocupación: Personas empleadas.
Número de Grupos utilizados para la codificación: 10.
Vínculos con la CIUO: No.
Situación en el empleo:
Título de la clasificación utilizada: Clasificación nacional.
Grupos de población clasificados por situación en el empleo: Personas empleadas.
Grupos utilizados para la codificación: 5 grupos (empleados, empleadores, trabajadores por cuenta propia, trabajadores familiares no remunerados).
Vínculos con la CISE: Sí.
Educación:
Título de la clasificación utilizada: Clasificación nacional.
Grupos de población clasificados por educación: Personas empleadas y desempleadas.
Grupos utilizados para la codificación: 9 grupos (sin educación, educación primaria sin completar, educación primaria, tres años de educación secundaria, cuatro años de educación secundaria, superior, nivel universitario, licenciatura y doctorado)
Vínculos con la CINE: No.
Tamaño y diseño de la muestra:
Unidad final de muestreo: Hogares.
Tamaño de la muestra (unidades finales de muestreo): 7 200 hogares.
Fracción de muestreo: 1,3 por ciento del total de hogares.
Marco de la muestra: El marco de la muestra se preparó en base al Censo de Población y el Registro de Población de 1994.
Actualización de la muestra: Anualmente.
Rotación:
Esquema: No se proporcionó información.
Porcentaje de unidades que permanecen en la muestra durante dos encuestas consecutivas: 34,5 por ciento.
Número máximo de entrevistas por unidad de muestreo: 3.
Tiempo necesario para renovar completamente la muestra: Cuatro años.
Levantamiento de la encuesta:
Tipo de entrevista: Papel y lápiz.
Número de unidades finales de muestreo por área de muestra: 8 hogares.
Duración del trabajo de campo:
Total: No se proporcionó información.
Por área de muestra: No se proporcionó información.
Organización de la encuesta: Permanente.
Número de personas que trabajan en el campo: 117 entrevistadores.
Substitución de las unidades finales de muestreo que no responden: No.
Estimaciones y ajustes:
Tasa de no-respuesta total: No.
Ajuste por no-respuesta total: No.
Imputación por no respuesta de ítemes: No.
Ajuste por áreas/poblaciones no abarcadas: No.
Ajuste por falta de cobertura: No.
Ajuste por exceso de cobertura: No.
Ajuste por variaciones estacionales: No.
Historia de la encuesta:
Título y fecha de la primera encuesta: Encuesta sobre la Fuerza de Trabajo, abril de 1996.
Modificaciones y revisiones significativas: Desde 1996 se introdujeron algunos cambios (en 1997, 1998 y 1999).
Documentación y difusión:
Documentación:
Título de las publicaciones con los resultados de la encuesta: (periodicidad): "Labour Force Survey: Basic definitions, methods and final results" (anualmente).

Título de las publicaciones con la metodología de la encuesta: (periodicidad): "Labour Force Survey: Basic definitions, methods and final results" (anualmente).
Difusión:
Tiempo necesario para difundir los primeros datos: No se proporcionó información.
Información adelantada acerca de la fecha de la primera difusión pública: Sí.
Disponibilidad de datos no publicados si se solicitan: No.
Disponibilidad de datos por medios informáticos: Disquetes, internet y correo electrónico.

Malasia

Título de la encuesta: Encuesta sobre la Fuerza de Trabajo (Labour Force Survey).
Organismo responsable de la encuesta:
Planificar y realizar la encuesta: Departamento de Estadísticas (Department of Statistics).
Analizar y publicar los resultados: Departamento de Estadísticas (Department of Statistics).
Temas abarcados: Empleo, desempleo, subempleo, horas de trabajo, empleo en el sector informal (derivado de la situación en el empleo), rama de actividad económica (industria), ocupación, situación en el empleo, nivel de educación, actividad habitual.
Alcance de la encuesta:
Ámbito geográfico: Todo el país.
Grupos de población: Todas las personas que son residentes habituales (3 meses o más) de viviendas privadas. Se excluyen las personas que residen en hogares colectivos (por ejemplo, hoteles, albergues, cuarteles militares, prisiones, etc.).
Disponibilidad de estimaciones de otras fuentes para las áreas/grupos excluidos: No disponible.
Grupos abarcados por la encuesta pero excluidos de los resultados publicados: No disponible.
Periodicidad:
Recolección de datos: Trimestralmente.
Publicación de los resultados: Trimestral y anualmente.
Periodo de referencia:
Empleo: Una semana.
Búsqueda de trabajo: Un trimestre fijo.
Disponibilidad para trabajo: No disponible.
Conceptos y definiciones:
Empleo: Son empleadas todas las personas de 15 a 64 años de edad que durante la semana de referencia realizaron algún trabajo (por lo menos una hora) por una remuneración, beneficio o ganancia familiar (como empleador, empleado, trabajador por cuenta propia o trabajador familiar no remunerado).Se consideran también como empleadas las personas que no trabajaban durante la semana de referencia debido a enfermedad, lesión, invalidez, mal tiempo, vacaciones, conflictos laborales y razones sociales y religiosas pero tenían un empleo, explotación agrícola, empresa u otra empresa familiar a la que se iban a reintegrar.Se incluyen asimismo quienes estaban suspendidos de su trabajo temporalmente con remuneración y que con toda seguridad se reintegrarían a su empleo.
Se incluyen también:
a)personas con trabajo pero temporalmente ausentes del mismo debido a licencia por maternidad o paternidad, licencia parental, licencia para estudios o capacitación, ausencia sin autorización, conflictos laborales, mal tiempo;
b)trabajadores a tiempo completo o parcial que buscaban otro empleo durante el periodo de referencia;
c)personas que realizaron algún trabajo remunerado o por un beneficio durante la semana de referencia pero que estaban inscritas como desempleadas en busca de trabajo en una oficina de empleo o percibiendo indemnizaciones de desempleo;
d)estudiantes de dedicación parcial que trabajaban a tiempo completo o parcial;
e)aprendices y personas en formación remunerados;
f)trabajadores familiares no remunerados en el trabajo o temporalmente ausentes del mismo durante la semana de referencia;
g)personas ocupadas en actividades de agricultura de subsistencia;
h)todos los miembros de las fuerzas armadas.
Desempleo: Se incluyen las personas activa e inactivamente desempleadas. Se consideran activamente desempleadas todas las personas de 15 a 64 años de edad que no trabajaban durante la semana de referencia, pero que estaban disponibles para hacerlo y buscaban trabajo activamente durante el periodo de referencia.
Son inactivamente desempleadas todas las personas de 15 a 64 años de edad que no buscaban trabajo porque consideraban que no había un empleo disponible o, si lo había, no estaban suficientemente calificadas para dicho empleo; quienes hubieran buscado un empleo si no hubiesen estado temporalmente enfermos o en reclusión, o si no hubiese habido mal tiempo; quienes esperaban una respuesta a la presentación de su candidatura a un empleo y quienes habían buscado empleo antes de la semana de referencia (es decir, en los últimos tres meses antes de la entrevista), y las personas sin empleo y corrientemente disponibles para trabajar que habían tomado disposiciones para comenzar un nuevo empleo 30 días después de la fecha de la entrevista.
Medidas tomadas para buscar un empleo: inscribirse en una oficina de empleo, de intercambio laboral o en un registro profesional; visitar sitios de trabajo o reunirse con posibles empleadores; colocar o responder avisos relativos a empleos; enviar su candidatura para postular a un empleo; visitar sindicatos o asociaciones similares; estudiar las posibilidades profesionales o empresariales; informar a amigos y parientes, etc.
El periodo de búsqueda de trabajo se divide en 5 grupos: menos de 3 meses, de 3 a 6 meses, de 6 a 12 meses, de 1 a 3 años, más de 3 años.
Se incluyen también:
a) personas suspendidas de su trabajo temporalmente o por tiempo indeterminado sin remuneración y con licencia sin goce de sueldo por iniciativa del empleador;
b)estudiantes de dedicación parcial que buscan un empleo a tiempo completo o parcial;
c)personas que estaban buscado un trabajo y/o disponibles para hacerlo, pero estaban jubiladas y percibían una pensión;
d)aprendices y personas en formación no remunerados y trabajadores estacionales que no trabajan durante la temporada inactiva.
Subempleo:
Subempleo por insuficiencia de horas: Quienes trabajaban menos de 30 horas durante la semana de referencia por razones como insuficiencia de trabajo, tipo de empleo u otras, pero que estaban disponibles y deseaban trabajar más horas si se les diese la oportunidad de hacerlo.
Situaciones de empleo inadecuado: No corresponde.
Horas de trabajo: Horas reales trabajadas durante la semana de referencia para todos los empleos.
Ingresos relacionados con el empleo:
Ingresos relacionados con el empleo asalariado: No corresponde.
Ingresos relacionados con el empleo independiente: No corresponde.
Sector informal: No es una cuestión concreta pero se podría deducir parcialmente como una representación de la situación en el empleo de los trabajadores con respecto al empleo principal.
Actividad habitual: La ocupación que el entrevistado tuvo habitualmente durante los últimos 12 meses.
Clasificaciones:
Rama de actividad económica (industria):
Título de la clasificación utilizada: Clasificación Industrial de Malasia.
Grupos de población clasificados por industria: Personas empleadas.
Número de Grupos utilizados para la codificación: 9.
Vínculos con la CIIU-68: Sí, a todos los niveles.
Ocupación:
Título de la clasificación utilizada: Clasificación de Ocupaciones de Malasia.**Grupos de población clasificados por ocupación:** Personas empleadas.
Número de Grupos utilizados para la codificación: 9.
Vínculos con la CIUO-68: Sí, a todos los niveles.
Situación en el empleo:
Título de la clasificación utilizada: No disponible.
Grupos de población clasificados por situación en el empleo: Personas empleadas.
Grupos utilizados para la codificación: Cuatro grupos: 1. empleadores, 2. empleados, 3. trabajadores por cuenta propia, 4. trabajadores familiares no remunerados.
Vínculos con la CISE-1993: Sí.
Educación:
Título de la clasificación utilizada: No disponible.
Grupos de población clasificados por educación: Todos los miembros del hogar.
Grupos utilizados para la codificación: Cuatro grupos: 1. Escuela primaria –desde el grado uno hasta el grado seis (de 6 a 12 años de edad), 2. Secundaria inferior (13 a 15 años de edad), 3. Secun-

daria superior (16 a 17 años de edad), 4. Terciaria (17 años de edad y más).
Vínculos con la CINE: Sí, todos los niveles se ajustan para adaptarlos a la situación local.
Tamaño y diseño de la muestra:
Unidad final de muestreo: Hogares.
Tamaño de la muestra (unidades finales de muestreo): 60 000 hogares.
Fracción de muestreo: No disponible.
Marco de la muestra: El Marco de Muestreo Nacional de Hogares está compuesto por bloques de enumeración (BE) preparados para el Censo de Población y Hogares de 1991. Los BE corresponden a zonas terrestres geográficamente continuas con límites establecidos, en cada uno de los cuales hay unas 600 personas. Para establecer los BE se utilizan los límites administrativos.
Actualización de la muestra: Todos los años, antes de comenzar la enumeración, se actualizan las unidades de muestra de la segunda etapa o viviendas de los BE para incluir nuevas viviendas en el proceso de selección de muestras. Cuando se utiilcen los datos del Censo de 2000 se sustituirá el marco actual. Los BE de zonas en crecimiento (superpobladas) se subdividirán en BE de menor tamaño para mantener una población constante, es decir unas 600 personas.
Rotación: No disponible.
Esquema: No disponible.
Porcentaje de unidades que permanecen en la muestra durante dos encuestas consecutivas: No disponible.
Número máximo de entrevistas por unidad de muestreo: No disponible.
Tiempo necesario para renovar completamente la muestra: No disponible.
Levantamiento de la encuesta:
Tipo de entrevista: Entrevista personal. Si los entrevistados de las viviendas no están disponibles después de tres visitas, la entrevista se hace por teléfono.
Número de unidades finales de muestreo por área de muestra: No disponible.
Duración del trabajo de campo:
Total: Cuatro semanas más una semana para la preparación de cada trimestre del año (cada ronda).
Por área de muestra: No disponible.
Organización de la encuesta: Personal permanente del Departamento de Estadísticas (oficinas públicas).
Número de personas que trabajan en el campo: Un enumerador abarca un BE. Unos 10 enumeradores por cada supervisor.
Substitución de las unidades finales de muestreo que no responden: Sí.
Estimaciones y ajustes:
Tasa de no-respuesta total: 4 por ciento.
Ajuste por no-respuesta total: Sí.
Imputación por no respuesta de ítemes: Sí. La información sobre las personas de la vivienda más cercana que responde se inserta para el caso de no respuesta.
Ajuste por áreas/poblaciones no abarcadas: No.
Ajuste por falta de cobertura: No.
Ajuste por falta de cobertura: No.
Ajuste por variaciones estacionales: No.
Historia de la encuesta:
Título y fecha de la primera encuesta: Encuesta Nacional sobre Empleo, Desempleo y Subempleo, 1962.
Modificaciones y revisiones significativas:
1964-1965: abarcaba sólo los principales centros urbanos de la Peninsula de Malasia.
1967-1968: Encuesta por Muestra de Hogares de Malasia (tres rondas).
1974-2000: se realizó la Encuesta sobre la Fuerza de Trabajo, salvo en 1991 y 1994.
Documentación y difusión:
Documentación:
Título de las publicaciones con los resultados de la encuesta: (periodicidad): The Labour Force Survey (anual).
Título de las publicaciones con la metodología de la encuesta: Idem.
Difusión:
Tiempo necesario para difundir los primeros datos: Los resultados de 1999 se publicaron en diciembre de ese año.
Información adelantada acerca de la fecha de la primera difusión pública: Sí.
Disponibilidad de datos no publicados si se solicitan: Sí.
Disponibilidad de datos por medios informáticos: Sí. Sitio web: http://www.statistics.gov.my/.

Marruecos

Título de la encuesta: Encuesta nacional sobre el empleo (Enquête nationale sur l'emploi).
Organismo responsable de la encuesta:
Planificar y realizar la encuesta: Dirección de Estadísticas (Direction de la Statistique).
Analizar y publicar los resultados: Dirección de Estadísticas (Direction de la Statistique).
Temas abarcados: Empleo, desempleo, subempleo, duración del empleo, salarios, empleo en el sector informal, duración del empleo y el desempleo, trabajadores ocasionales, rama de actividad económica (industria), ocupación, situación en el empleo, nivel de educación, empleo secundario.
Alcance de la encuesta:
Ámbito geográfico: Todo el país.
Grupos de población: Personas de 15 años y más de edad. Se excluyen de la encuesta las personas que viven en hogares colectivos como cuarteles, prisiones, alojamientos de obras públicas, etc.
Disponibilidad de estimaciones de otras fuentes para las áreas/grupos excluidos: No se dispone de información.
Grupos abarcados por la encuesta pero excluidos de los resultados publicados: Ninguno.
Periodicidad:
Recolección de datos: Continua.
Publicación de los resultados: Trimestral y anualmente.
Periodo de referencia:
Empleo: Un día.
Búsqueda de trabajo: Un día.
Disponibilidad para trabajo: Cuatro semanas.
Conceptos y definiciones:
Empleo: La población activa ocupada comprende todas las personas de 15 años y más de edad que participaron en la producción de bienes y servicios, aunque sólo fuese por una hora, durante las 24 horas anteriores a la entrevista, así como las personas que de costumbre tienen un empleo, pero que estaban temporalmente ausentes del sitio de trabajo.
Se consideran también empleados:
a)las personas temporalmente ausentes del trabajo por enfermedad o lesión, vacaciones anuales, licencia por maternidad, paternidad o parental, licencia para estudios o capacitación en el marco de la empresa y por una duración inferior a dos meses con la seguridad de reintegrarse al trabajo, conflictos laborales de menos de dos meses, mal tiempo, desperfectos mecánicos, etc.;
b)las personas suspendidas de su trabajo sin remuneración pero que mantienen un vínculo formal con el empleo;
c)los trabajadores a tiempo completo o parcial en busca de otro empleo durante el periodo de referencia;
d)las personas sometidas a escolaridad obligatoria, jubiladas o que reciben una pensión, inscritas como desempleadas en busca de trabajo o que perciben indemnizaciones de desempleo, que realizaron algún trabajo (remunerado o por un beneficio) durante el periodo de referencia;
e)los estudiantes de dedicación completa o parcial que trabajan a tiempo completo o parcial;
f)los aprendices y las personas en formación remunerados, si participan en la producción, y los aprendices y las personas en formación no remunerados;
g)los trabajadores familiares no remunerados que trabajaron durante el periodo de referencia o temporalmente ausentes por un periodo inferior a dos meses pero que mantienen un vínculo formal con el empleo;
h)las personas ocupadas en la produccion de bienes para su propio uso final;
i)los voluntarios, militares de carrera y reclutas, así como las personas que realizan un servicio civil equivalente al servicio militar.
Desempleo: Personas de 15 años y más de edad, sin empleo, disponibles para trabajar y en busca de un empleo, incluidos los trabajadores desalentados.
Se consideran también desempleados :
a)las personas temporalmente ausentes porque han sido suspendidas del trabajo por tiempo indeterminado sin remuneración o con licencia sin goce de sueldo por iniciativa del empleador;
b)las personas sin empleo y disponibles inmediatamente para trabajar, que han tomado disposiciones para trabajar en un nuevo

empleo en una fecha ulterior o que han tratado de establecer su propia empresa;
c)las personas en busca de un empleo y/o inmediatamente disponibles para trabajar, pero sometidas a escolaridad obligatoria o jubiladas y que reciben una pensión;
d)los estudiantes de dedicación completa o parcial que buscan un empleo a tiempo completo o parcial;
e)los trabajadores estacionales que no trabajan durante la temporada inactiva y no remunerados durante ese periodo.
Subempleo:
Subempleo por insuficiencia de horas: Personas de 15 años y más de edad que trabajaron menos de 48 horas durante la semana de referencia, dispuestas a trabajar horas suplementarias y disponibles para hacerlo.
Situaciones de empleo inadecuado: Personas de 15 años y más de edad que trabajaron más de 48 horas durante la semana de referencia y que declararon estar en busca de otro empleo o dispuestas a cambiar de empleo por una de las dos siguientes razones:
a)el empleo actual no corresponde a su formación o calificación;
b)los ingresos percibidos del trabajo actual son insuficientes.
Horas de trabajo: Horas efectivamente trabajadas durante la semana.
Ingresos relacionados con el empleo:
Ingresos relacionados con el empleo asalariado: Salarios en efectivo y/o en especie, incluidas las cotizaciones a la seguridad social y otros beneficios vinculados al empleo.
Ingresos relacionados con el empleo independiente: La encuesta no abarca este punto.
Sector informal: La encuesta no abarca este punto.
Actividad habitual: No se dispone de información.
Clasificaciones:
Rama de actividad económica (industria):
Título de la clasificación utilizada: Clasificación nacional.
Grupos de población clasificados por industria: Personas empleadas y desempleadas (rama de actividad económica del último empleo para el desempleado).
Número de Grupos utilizados para la codificación: 17 grupos principales.
Vínculos con la CIIU: CIIU-Rev.3.
Ocupación:
Título de la clasificación utilizada: Clasificación nacional.
Grupos de población clasificados por ocupación: Personas empleadas y desempleadas (ocupación en el último empleo para el desempleado).
Número de Grupos utilizados para la codificación: 11 grupos principales.
Vínculos con la CIUO: CIUO-88.
Situación en el empleo:
Título de la clasificación utilizada: Clasificación nacional.
Grupos de población clasificados por situación en el empleo: Personas empleadas y desempleadas (situación en el último empleo para el desempleado).
Grupos utilizados para la codificación: Asalariados, trabajadores independientes, empleadores, ayudas familiares, aprendices, asociados o miembros de cooperativas, personas en formación o inserción, otros.
Vínculos con la CISE: CISE-1993.
Educación:
Título de la clasificación utilizada: Clasificación nacional.
Grupos de población clasificados por educación: Personas empleadas y desempleadas.
Grupos utilizados para la codificación: Preescolar, escuela coránica, fundamental 1, fundamental 2, secundaria, superior, otro.
Vínculos con la CINE: CINE-1976 y CINE-1997.
Tamaño y diseño de la muestra:
Unidad final de muestreo: Hogar.
Tamaño de la muestra (unidades finales de muestreo): 48 000 hogares, de los cuales 17 000 en zona rural.
Fracción de muestreo: 1/100.
Marco de la muestra: Censo General de la Población y de Hogares de 1994 (RGPH 1994). Muestra por áreas estratificada en dos grados : las unidades primarias (UP) son zonas geográficas constituidas de 600 hogares en promedio y establecidas en base a los trabajos cartográficos del RGPH; las UP se dividen en segmentos de 25 hogares.
Actualización de la muestra: La mitad cada año.
Rotación:
Esquema: Actualización parcial de la muestra.
Porcentaje de unidades que permanecen en la muestra durante dos encuestas consecutivas: 50 por ciento.
Número máximo de entrevistas por unidad de muestreo: Dos.
Tiempo necesario para renovar completamente la muestra: Dos años.
Levantamiento de la encuesta:
Tipo de entrevista: Entrevistas directas; cuestionario en papel.
Número de unidades finales de muestreo por área de muestra: No se dispone de información.
Duración del trabajo de campo:
Total: Un año.
Por área de muestra: 45 minutos por hogar.
Organización de la encuesta: No se dispone de información.
Número de personas que trabajan en el campo: 15 supervisores.
Substitución de las unidades finales de muestreo que no responden: No se dispone de información.
Estimaciones y ajustes:
Tasa de no-respuesta total: 12 por ciento.
Ajuste por no-respuesta total: Sí.
Imputación por no respuesta de ítemes: Sí.
Ajuste por áreas/poblaciones no abarcadas: Sí.
Ajuste por falta de cobertura: Sí.
Ajuste por exceso de cobertura: Sí.
Ajuste por variaciones estacionales: No.
Historia de la encuesta:
Título y fecha de la primera encuesta: Encuesta permanente sobre el empleo en zona urbana, 1976 (Enquête permanente sur l'emploi en milieu urbain).
Modificaciones y revisiones significativas: Revisiones realizadas en ocasión de los censos de población de 1982 y 1994: cambio de la base de sondeo, revisión de los cuestionario a la luz de la experiencia adquirida, etc. Esas revisiones no produjeron rupturas importantes en las series históricas.
Documentación y difusión:
Documentación:
Título de las publicaciones con los resultados de la encuesta (periodicidad): Activité, emploi et chômage (trimestral); Activité, emploi et chômage: rapport de synthèse (anual); Activité, emploi et chômage: rapport des résultats détaillés (anual); Annuaire Statistique du Maroc.
Título de las publicaciones con la metodología de la encuesta (periodicidad): Activité, emploi et chômage: rapport des résultats détaillés (anual).
Difusión:
Tiempo necesario para difundir los primeros datos: Antes de finalizar el segundo mes del trimestre siguiente, para los resultados trimestrales. Informe resumido: mayo del año siguiente.
Información adelantada acerca de la fecha de la primera difusión pública: No se dispone de información.
Disponibilidad de datos no publicados si se solicitan: Sí, después de un estudio de factibilidad.
Disponibilidad de datos por medios informáticos: Según el tipo de información solicitada. Sitio web: http://www.statistic.gov.ma

Mauricio

Título de la encuesta: Encuesta por Muestra sobre la Fuerza de Trabajo (Labour Force Survey).
Organismo responsable de la encuesta:
Planificar y realizar la encuesta: Oficina Central de Estadísticas, Ministerio de Planificación Económica y Desarrollo (Central Statistical Office, Ministry of Economic Planning and Development).
Analizar y publicar los resultados: Oficina Central de Estadísticas, Ministerio de Planificación Económica y Desarrollo (Central Statistical Office, Ministry of Economic Planning and Development).
Temas abarcados: Empleo, desempleo, subempleo, horas de trabajo (horas de trabajo normales y habituales, horas realmente trabajadas) , salarios y sueldos, duración del empleo, duración del desempleo, rama de actividad económica (industria), ocupación, situación en el empleo, niveles de educación y calificación, actividad habitual, empleo secundario.
Alcance de la encuesta:
Ámbito geográfico: Todo el país (Islas Mauricio y Rodrigues)
Grupos de población: La encuesta abarca toda la población mauricia residente de la República de Mauricio que vive en hogares privados. No se incluyen quienes viven en hogares colectivos ni extranjeros (por ejemplo, personal de embajadas y extranjeros que trabajan con un contrato en Mauricio).

Disponibilidad de estimaciones de otras fuentes para las áreas/grupos excluidos: No se proporcionó información.

Grupos abarcados por la encuesta pero excluidos de los resultados publicados: No se proporcionó información.

Periodicidad:

Recolección de datos: Cada diez años, durante los años intermedios del censo. La última encuesta se efectuó entre junio y julio de 1995.

Publicación de los resultados: Cada 10 años. Los resultados de la última encuesta se publicaron en enero-marzo de 1997.

Periodo de referencia:

Empleo: Periodo de referencia fijo de una semana.

Búsqueda de trabajo: Periodo de referencia móvil de dos meses antes de la fecha de la entrevista.

Disponibilidad para trabajo: Periodo de referencia móvil de una semana antes de la fecha de la entrevista.

Conceptos y definiciones:

Empleo: Todas las personas de 12 años y más de edad que realizaron algún trabajo (es decir, por lo menos una hora) por un pago, beneficio o ingresos para la familia, durante la semana de referencia . Se incluyen también las personas que estaban temporalmente ausentes de su trabajo durante la semana de referencia debido a enfermedad, vacaciones, falta de trabajo, conflictos laborales, etc.

En el contexto de la encuesta, trabajo implica la producción de bienes o servicios normalmente previstos para la venta en el mercado. Con todo, también se incluyen algunos tipos de producción no prevista para el mercado. En general, se trata de la producción de productos primarios para consumo propio, construcciones por cuenta propia y producción de otros bienes fijos para uso propio.

Se excluyen las actividades domésticas y los servicios voluntarios para la comunidad.

Desempleo: Personas de 12 años y más de edad que no estaban empleadas durante la semana de referencia, estaban disponibles para trabajar durante la semana de referencia y habían tomado medidas concretas para buscar trabajo en cualquier momento durante los dos meses anteriores a la fecha de la entrevista. Buscar trabajo no sólo implica buscar un empleo asalariado sino que también abarca las gestiones realizadas para comenzar su propio negocio (empleo independiente). Se incluyen como personas desempleadas quienes carecían de trabajo y estaban disponibles para trabajar, pero no buscaban empleo porque ya habían tomado disposiciones para comenzar un trabajo en una fecha ulterior a la semana de referencia.

Los trabajadores suspendidos por sus empleadores, así como los empleados independientes ausentes del sitio de empleo por falta de trabajo, se consideran como desempleados si estaban disponibles para trabajar y habían buscado un empleo en cualquier momento durante los dos meses anteriores a la fecha de la entrevista.

Subempleo:

Subempleo por insuficiencia de horas: Personas empleadas que durante la semana de referencia trabajaron, por razones ajenas a su voluntad, menos horas que la duración normal del trabajo en su respectiva actividad y que estaban disponibles para hacer un trabajo adicional.

Situaciones de empleo inadecuado: La encuesta no abarca este punto.

Horas de trabajo: Horas realmente trabajadas durante la semana de referencia y horas de trabajo normales por semana. Para las personas a las que no se aplica el concepto de horas de trabajo normal, se registra el número de horas de trabajo habituales por semana. La información sobre las horas de trabajo se recopila para el empleo principal y para todos los otros empleos, si procede.

Ingresos relacionados con el empleo:

Ingresos relacionados con el empleo asalariado: Promedio de salario o sueldo bruto mensual en rupias (menos de 2 000, 2 001-4 000, 4 001-6 000, 6 001-8 000, 8 001-10 000, 10 001-15 000, 15 001-20 000, 20 001 o más) para el empleo principal de la persona.

Ingresos relacionados con el empleo independiente: La encuesta no abarca este punto.

Sector informal: La encuesta no abarca este punto.

Actividad habitual: La actividad habitual se refiere a la situación de las personas en la ocupación principal durante un periodo de referencia de un año completo. La situación en la ocupación principal (habitualmente activa, no habitualmente activa) se determina a partir del número de semanas que las personas indican que han estado empleadas o buscando trabajo y disponibles para trabajar durante el año de referencia. La población habitualmente activa comprende personas de 12 años y más de edad que estuvieron económicamente activas (empleadas o desempleadas) por un total de 26 o más semanas durante el último año. Las personas habitualmente activas se clasifican como empleadas o desempleadas según el número de semanas de empleo o desempleo durante el último año.

Clasificaciones:

Rama de actividad económica (industria):

Título de la clasificación utilizada: Clasificación Industrial Internacional Uniforme de todas las Actividades Económicas (CIIU, Rev.3).

Grupos de población clasificados por industria: Personas empleadas; personas desempleadas o económicamente inactivas con experiencia previa de trabajo.

Número de Grupos utilizados para la codificación: No se proporcionó información.

Vínculos con la CIIU: CIIU-Rev.3.

Ocupación:

Título de la clasificación utilizada: Clasificación Internacional Uniforme de Ocupaciones (CIUO-88).

Grupos de población clasificados por ocupación: Personas empleadas; personas desempleadas o económicamente inactivas con experiencia previa de trabajo.

Número de Grupos utilizados para la codificación: No se proporcionó información.

Vínculos con la CIUO: CIUO-88.

Situación en el empleo:

Título de la clasificación utilizada: Clasificación nacional sobre la situación en el empleo.

Grupos de población clasificados por situación en el empleo: Personas empleadas; personas desempleadas o económicamente inactivas con experiencia previa de trabajo.

Grupos utilizados para la codificación: a) empleados independientes; a1) empleados independientes con empleados; a2) empleados independientes sin empleados; b) empleados; b1) empleados a tiempo completo; b2) empleados a destajo; b3) desempleados; b4) aprendices (remunerados o no); c) trabajadores familiares no remunerados; d) otros.

Vínculos con la CISE: CISE-1993.

Educación:

Título de la clasificación utilizada: Clasificación nacional de niveles de educación.

Grupos de población clasificados por educación: Todas las personas.

Grupos utilizados para la codificación: a) Sin escolaridad o preprimaria; b) primaria; b1) primaria, Std. I-V; b2) primaria, CPE o equivalente; c) secundaria; c1) secundaria, grados I-IV; c2) secundaria, SC o equivalente; c3) secundaria, HSC o equivalente; d) diploma universitario o equivalente.

Vínculos con la CINE: Sí.

Tamaño y diseño de la muestra:

Unidad final de muestreo: Hogares.

Tamaño de la muestra (unidades finales de muestreo): 9 900 hogares.

Fracción de muestreo: 4,1 por ciento de hogares.

Marco de la muestra: Basándose en el último Censo de Población y Hogares, se selecciona una muestra de 495 zonas de enumeración para la encuesta sobre la fuerza de trabajo. Antes de la encuesta, se prepara una nueva lista completa de hogares en las zonas de enumeración de la muestra.

Actualización de la muestra: No corresponde.

Rotación:

Esquema: No se hace la rotación de la muestra.

Porcentaje de unidades que permanecen en la muestra durante dos encuestas consecutivas: No corresponde.

Número máximo de entrevistas por unidad de muestreo: No corresponde.

Tiempo necesario para renovar completamente la muestra: No corresponde.

Levantamiento de la encuesta:

Tipo de entrevista: La información se obtiene mediante entrevistas personales.

Número de unidades finales de muestreo por área de muestra: 20 hogares.

Duración del trabajo de campo:

Total: Dos meses.

Por área de muestra: No se proporcionó información.

Organización de la encuesta: Si bien la Sección de Estadísticas Laborales tiene una plantilla permanente, la organización de la encuesta no es permanente- El personal sobre el terreno, de edición y codificación se contrata para la encuesta de manera temporal.

Número de personas que trabajan en el campo: Un supervisor jefe, un supervisor jefe asistente, 10 supervisores principales, 50 supervisores y 495 entrevistadores.
Substitución de las unidades finales de muestreo que no responden: No se proporcionó información.
Estimaciones y ajustes:
Tasa de no-respuesta total: No se proporcionó información.
Ajuste por no-respuesta total: No se proporcionó información.
Imputación por no respuesta de ítemes: No se proporcionó información.
Ajuste por áreas/poblaciones no abarcadas: No se proporcionó información.
Ajuste por falta de cobertura: No se proporcionó información.
Ajuste por falta de cobertura: No se proporcionó información.
Ajuste por variaciones estacionales: No corresponde.
Historia de la encuesta:
Título y fecha de la primera encuesta: La primera Encuesta por Muestra sobre la Fuerza de Trabajo se realizó de junio a julio de 1995.
Modificaciones y revisiones significativas: No corresponde.
Documentación y difusión:
Documentación:
Título de las publicaciones con los resultados de la encuesta: Oficina Central de Estadísticas, Ministerio de Planificación Económica y Desarrollo. Labour Force Sample Survey (periodicidad: cada diez años). Antes de su publicación, se dan a conocer los principales resultados de la encuesta en un informe preliminar.
Título de las publicaciones con la metodología de la encuesta: La publicación antes mencionada incluye información metodológica sobre la encuesta.
Difusión:
Tiempo necesario para difundir los primeros datos: 18 meses.
Información adelantada acerca de la fecha de la primera difusión pública: No se proporcionó información.
Disponibilidad de datos no publicados si se solicitan: No se proporcionó información.
Disponibilidad de datos por medios informáticos: No se proporcionó información.

México

Título de la encuesta: Encuesta Nacional de Empleo Urbano (ENEU)
Organismo responsable de la encuesta:
Planificar y realizar la encuesta : Coordinación de Encuestas de Empleo, Dirección de Estadísticas de Corto Plazo, Dirección General de Estadísticas, Instituto Nacional de Estadística, Geografía e Informática (INEGI)
Analizar y publicar los resultados: idem
Temas abarcados: Empleo, desempleo, horas, salarios, ingresos, duración del desempleo, trabajadores desalentados y ocasionales, ramas de actividad económica, ocupación, situación en el empleo, nivel de educación, actividad habitual, trabajos secundarios, prestaciones, sector de propiedad, motivos para dejar el último empleo, fecha en que dejó el último empleo, tipo de contrato laboral, tipo de local, motivo por el que se trabajó menos de 35 horas o más de 48 horas, forma de pago, búsqueda de otro empleo.
Actividades no económicas, condición de inactividad, forma de sostenimiento económico de los inactivos, tipo de trabajo buscado, condición de experiencia laboral.
Características socio-demográficas de los miembros del hogar y características de la vivienda.
Alcance de la encuesta:
Ámbito geográfico: abarca 48 ciudades del país, que corresponde a aproximadamente 95% de las poblaciones de 100 000 habitantes y más. Comprende 28 capitales de estado, 5 ciudades de la frontera con Estados Unidos y 15 ciudades de importancia económica para el país.
Grupos de población : Se excluyen (a) las personas ausentes de la vivienda por más de tres meses por cualquier motivo si residen en otra vivienda particular; (b) las personas ausentes de la vivienda por más de tres meses, por razones diferentes a estudio o trabajo (por ejemplo, por salud, razones legales o porque no tienen la certeza de regresar a la vivienda) y que residen en viviendas colectivas (por ejemplo, cárceles, hospitales, monasterios, etc.); (c) las personas que están de visita en la vivienda por menos de tres meses o que no tienen la certeza de permanecer más tiempo; (d) las personas que han llegado a la vivienda durante la semana de levantamiento pero que no residían durante la semana de referencia (por ejemplo, los recién nacidos).

Disponibilidad de estimaciones de otras fuentes para las áreas/grupos excluidos: no disponible.
Grupos abarcados por le encuesta pero excluidos de los resultados publicados: Ninguno.
Periodicidad:
Recolección de datos: continua.
Publicación de los resultados: mensual y trimestral.
Períodos de referencia:
Empleo: un día móvil.
Búsqueda de trabajo: una semana (fija).
Disponibilidad para trabajo: no disponible.
Conceptos y definiciones:
Empleo: Comprende a las personas de 12 años y más de ambos sexos que durante la semana de referencia (a) trabajaron al menos una hora o un día para producir bienes y servicios a cambio de una remuneración monetaria o en especie; (b) tenían empleo pero no trabajaron por alguna causa sin dejar de percibir su ingreso; (c) tenían empleo pero no trabajaron por alguna causa dejando de percibir su ingreso pero con retorno asegurado a su trabajo en menos de cuatro semanas; (d) no tenían empleo, pero iniciarían con seguridad uno en cuatro semanas o menos; (e) trabajaron al menos una hora o un día en la semana de referencia, sin recibir pago alguno (ni monetario ni en especie) en un negocio propiedad de un familiar o no familiar.
Desempleo: Personas de 12 años y más que no estando ocupadas buscaron activamente incorporarse a alguna actividad económica, en las cuatro semanas previas a la semana de levantamiento o hasta ocho semanas, siempre y cuando estén disponibles a incorporarse de inmediato. La búsqueda debe ser activa, es decir, la persona tiene que haber hecho algo concreto para encontrar empleo como consultar empleadores, hacer solicitudes de empleo, realizar actividades para establecer un negocio, etc.
Subempleo:
Subempleo por insuficiencia de horas: No información.
Situaciones de empleo inadecuado: No información.
Horas de trabajo: Se refiere al número de horas diarias y por semana que las personas ocupadas declararon haber laborado en su trabajo principal, durante la semana de referencia. No incluye las horas utilizadas para el traslado a su centro de trabajo, ni las que empleó en las comidas.
Ingresos relacionados con el empleo:
Ingresos relacionados con el empleo asalariado: Son las percepciones monetarias y en especie que recibieron los ocupados por su participación en el proceso productivo, durante el período de referencia. Se consideran solo los ingresos netos, es decir, lo que realmente perciben los asalariados después de descontar el pago de los impuestos, cuotas a la seguridad social. Se incluyen los pagos en especie, los ingresos monetarios extras como bonos de productividad, siempre y cuando sean recibidos de manera regular. Se calculan para un período mensual y solo para el empleo principal.
Ingresos relacionados con el empleo independiente: Son las percepciones monetarias y en especie que recibieron los ocupados por su participación en el proceso productivo, durante el período de referencia. Se consideran solo los ingresos netos, es decir, lo que realmente perciben los patrones y trabajadores por su cuenta, después de descontar los gastos del negocio, materias primas, reparación y compra de herramientas, pago de rentas del local, pago de salarios, etc. Se incluye el consumo de lo que producen o venden. Se calculan al mes y solo para el empleo principal.
Sector informal: No información.
Actividad habitual: No información.
Clasificaciones:
Rama de actividad económica (industria):
Título de la clasificación utilizada: No información.:
Grupos de población clasificados por industria: Ocupados y desocupados que dejaron su último trabajo menos de un año antes del período de referencia.
Número de Grupos utilizados para la codificación: 74 ramas, 213 grupos y 390 subgrupos
Vínculos con la CIIU: CIU- Rev.3, con ajustes a nivel de división.
Ocupación:
Título de la clasificación utilizada: Clasificación Mexicana de Ocupaciones (CMO).
Grupos de población clasificados por ocupación: Ocupados y desocupados que dejaron su último trabajo menos de un año antes del período de referencia.
Número de Grupos utilizados para la codificación: 19 grupos principales, 137 subgrupos y 465 grupos unitarios.

Vínculos con la CIUO: CIUO-88, a nivel de grandes grupos. Se cuenta con una tabla comparativa entre la CMO y la CIUO-88.
Situación en el empleo:
Título de la clasificación utilizada: No información.
Grupos de población clasificados por situación en el empleo: Ocupados y desocupados que dejaron su último trabajo menos de un año antes del período de referencia.
Grupos utilizados para la codificación: patrón; trabajador por su cuenta; trabajador a destajo, comisión o porcentaje; trabajador a sueldo fijo, salario o jornal; miembro de una cooperativa; trabajador familiar sin pago; trabajador no familiar sin pago; otro.
Vínculos con CISE: no.
Educación:
Título de la clasificación utilizada: No información.
Grupos de población clasificados por educación: Ocupados, desocupados e inactivos.
Grupos utilizados para la codificación: sin instrucción; primaria incompleta; primaria completa; secundaria incompleta; secundaria completa; media superior; superior o profesional y posgrado. Se cuenta con un clasificador para las carreras de nivel técnico profesional, licenciatura y posgrado con 35 grupos, organizados de acuerdo con la disciplina de estudio.
Vínculos con la CINE: no.
Tamaño y diseño de la muestra:
Unidad final de muestreo: vivienda.
Tamaño de la muestra (unidades finales de muestreo): 134,012 viviendas.
Fracción de muestra: 134 012 viviendas seleccionadas / 11 721 325 viviendas totales.
Marco de la muestra : Información censal y cartografía del Conteo de Población y Vivienda 1995, y croquis y listados de viviendas.
Actualización de la muestra: tres tipos de actualización continua. (a) Actualización debido a la rotación de la muestra: cada trimestre se actualiza solo una quinta parte de las viviendas en la muestra, al interior de cada USM para cada área metropolitana; Al término de la primera rotación competa, con base en la actualización del número de viviendas en las USM, se modifica la fracción de muestreo para evitar que se incremente el tamaño de la muestra. (b) Actualización debido al envejecimiento del marco: cuando un área del listado se satura se sustituye por otra de la misma UPM; cuando la UPM se satura se sutstituye por otra de la misma localidad y estrato; se incluyen los nuevos crecimientos en la periferia de las ciudades. (c) Actualización de la cartografía: cuando se fusionan manzanas de una misma AGEB, de diferentes AGEB o cuando hay cambios en los límites de una AGEB; cuando se crean nuevas manzanas, o aparece una subdivisión de manzanas y apertura de calles o cuando cambias los nombres de las calles.
Rotación:
Esquema: se sustituye cada trimestre una quinta parte de las viviendas y se incluyen todas las actualizaciones del área del listado para mantener actualizada la muestra.
Porcentaje de unidades que permanecen en la muestra durante dos encuestas consecutivas: 80%.
Número máximo de entrevistas por unidad de muestreo: 5.
Tiempo necesario para renovar completamente la muestra: 1 año y tres meses.
Levantamiento da la encuesta:
Tipo de entrevista : personal (escritas a lápiz en papel).
Número de unidades finales de muestro por área de muestra : 5 100 viviendas trimestrales en un área metropolitana, 3 000 viviendas en 6 ciudades, 1 800 viviendas en 2 ciudades, 2 100 viviendas en 39 ciudades.
Duración del trabajo de campo:
Total: un año (la encuesta es continua)
Por área de muestra: 3 meses.
Organización de la encuesta : organización permanente.
Número de personas que trabajan en el campo: 850 personas: 425 encuestadores, 191 crítico-codificadores, 143 supervisores, 55 jefes de área, 25 secretarias, y 11 depuradores.
Substitución de las unidades finales de muestreo que no responden: sí.
Estimaciones y ajustes:
Tasa de no-respuesta total: Aproximadamente 12.8%.
Ajuste por no-respuesta total: no.
Imputación por no-respuesta de ítemes: sí.
Ajuste por áreas/poblaciones no abarcadas: sí.
Ajuste por falta de cobertura: sí.
Ajuste por exceso de cobertura: sí.
Ajuste por variaciones estacionales: sí.
Historia de la encuesta:
Título y fecha de la primera encuesta: Encuesta Nacional de Hogares 1972.
Modificaciones y revisiones significativas: En 1972 la parte de empleo correspondía a un módulo. En 1973 se crea la Encuesta Continua sobre Mano de Obra (ECMO). En 1974 se cambia por la Encuesta Continua sobre Ocupación (ECSO), nombre que mantiene hasta 1983. Las modificaciones y/o revisiones a la Encuesta no han ocasionado interrupciones significativas en las series de tiempo.
Documentación y difusión:
Documentación:
Resultados de la encuesta : Estadísticas Económicas INEGI; Indicadores de Empleo y Desempleo; Cuaderno de Información Oportuna; Instituto Nacional de Estadística, Geografía e Informática (INEGI), Aguascalientes, Ags., México.
Metodología de la encuesta: Documento Metodológico de la Encuesta Nacional de Empleo Urbano, Instituto Nacional de Estadística, Geografía e Informática (INEGI), Aguascalientes, Ags., México.
Difusión:
Tiempo necesario para difundir los primeros datos: 1 mes.
Información adelantada acerca de la fecha de la primera difusión pública: sí.
Disponibilidad de datos no publicados si se solicitan : sí.
Disponibilidad de datos por medios informáticos: CD, diskette, cinta magnética, etc.. Sitio web: http://wwww.inegi.gob.mx.

Moldova, Rep. de

Título de la encuesta: Encuesta sobre la Fuerza de Trabajo (Labour Force Survey).
Organismo responsable de la encuesta:
Planificar y realizar la encuesta: Departamento de Estadísticas y Sociología (Department for Statistics and Sociology).
Analizar y publicar los resultados: Departamento de Estadísticas y Sociología (Department for Statistics and Sociology).
Temas abarcados: Empleo, desempleo, subempleo, horas de trabajo, duración del desempleo, trabajadores desalentados, trabajadores ocasionales, rama de actividad económica (industria), ocupación, situación en el empleo, nivel de educación, actividad habitual y empleo secundario.
Alcance de la encuesta:
Ámbito geográfico: Todo el país, salvo la región de Transnistria y el pueblo de Tighina.
Grupos de población: Todos los residentes permanentes de 15 años y más de edad que residen en hogares.
Se excluyen:
a)estudiantes que residen en albergues y niños en edad escolar que viven en internados;
b)ancianos que viven en asilos especiales;
c)internados en instituciones penales y psiquiátricas;
d)extranjeros.
Disponibilidad de estimaciones de otras fuentes para las áreas/grupos excluidos: No.
Grupos abarcados por la encuesta pero excluidos de los resultados publicados: Ninguno.
Periodicidad:
Recolección de datos: Continuamente.
Publicación de los resultados: Trimestralmente.
Periodo de referencia:
Empleo: Una semana (últimos siete días antes de la fecha de la entrevista).
Búsqueda de trabajo: Cuatro semanas antes de la fecha de la entrevista.
Disponibilidad para trabajo: Dos semanas después de la fecha de la entrevista.
Conceptos y definiciones:
Empleo: Son empleadas todas las personas de 15 años y más de edad que durante la semana de referencia realizaron algún trabajo remunerado o no, por lo menos una hora, así como trabajadores familiares no remunerados y quienes no estaban trabajando pero tenían un empleo o negocio del cual estaban temporalmente ausentes debido a enfermedad, mal tiempo, día de fiesta, conflictos laborales, etc.
Se incluyen también en los totales:
a)trabajadores a tiempo completo o parcial que buscaban otro empleo durante el periodo de referencia;
b)estudiantes de dedicación completa o parcial que trabajaban a tiempo completo o parcial;

c)personas que realizaron algún trabajo durante la semana de referencia pero que estaban jubiladas y percibían una pensión, inscritas como desempleadas en busca de trabajo en una oficina de empleo o percibiendo indemnizaciones de desempleo;
d)servicio doméstico privado;
e)aprendices y personas en formación remunerados.
Se excluyen las personas ocupadas en la producción de bienes para su propio hogar (pintura, reparaciones, quehaceres domésticos, etc.).
Desempleo: Se consideran desempleadas todas las personas de 15 años y más de edad que, durante la semana de referencia, no trabajaban por una remuneración o beneficio, estuvieron buscando activamente un empleo durante las últimas cuatro semanas antes de la encuesta y estaban disponibles para comenzar a trabajar dos semanas después de la encuesta.
Subempleo:
Subempleo por insuficiencia de horas: Personas que, durante la semana de referencia, trabajaban, por razones ajenas a su voluntad, menos horas que las establecidas y estaban buscando trabajar más horas y disponibles para hacerlo.
Situaciones de empleo inadecuado: No corresponde.
Horas de trabajo: Horales habituales y reales trabajadas en el empleo principal y empleo(s) secundario(s).
Ingresos relacionados con el empleo:
Ingresos relacionados con el empleo asalariado: No corresponde.
Ingresos relacionados con el empleo independiente: No corresponde.
Sector informal: No corresponde.
Actividad habitual: No corresponde.
Clasificaciones:
Rama de actividad económica (industria):
Título de la clasificación utilizada: Clasificación nacional.
Grupos de población clasificados por industria: Personas empleadas y personas desempleadas con experiencia previa de trabajo.
Número de Grupos utilizados para la codificación: 55 grupos.
Vínculos con la CIIU: CIIU-Rev, 3 (nivel de 4 dígitos).
Ocupación:
Título de la clasificación utilizada: Clasificación nacional.
Grupos de población clasificados por ocupación: Personas empleadas y personas desempleadas con experiencia previa de trabajo.
Número de Grupos utilizados para la codificación: 10 grupos principales.
Vínculos con la CIUO: CIUO-88 (nivel de 3 dígitos).
Situación en el empleo:
Título de la clasificación utilizada: Clasificación nacional.
Grupos de población clasificados por situación en el empleo: Personas empleadas y desempleadas.
Grupos utilizados para la codificación: 5 grupos (empleados, empleadores, trabajadores por cuenta propia, miembros de cooperativas de productores, trabajadores que contribuyen con la familia).
Vínculos con la CISE: CISE-1993.
Educación:
Título de la clasificación utilizada: Clasificación nacional.
Grupos de población clasificados por educación: Todos los grupos de población.
Grupos utilizados para la codificación: 7 grupos (educación preprimaria, primaria, secundaria inferior, secundaria superior, escuela vocacional, educación terciaria, educación superior (universidad)).
Vínculos con la CINE: No.
Tamaño y diseño de la muestra:
Unidad final de muestreo: Vivienda.
Tamaño de la muestra (unidades finales de muestreo): Unas 8 208 viviendas.
Fracción de muestreo: 1/150.
Marco de la muestra: El marco de la muestra se preparó en base a las listas utilizadas para las elecciones presidenciales de 1996.
Actualización de la muestra: Sí.
Rotación:
Esquema: Cada vivienda de la muestra se entrevista en dos trimestres consecutivos, luego se retira durante dos trimestres, después de los cuales se vuelve a entrevistar en dos trimestres consecutivos y luego se retira definitivamente de la muestra.
Porcentaje de unidades que permanecen en la muestra durante dos encuestas consecutivas: 50 por ciento.
Número máximo de entrevistas por unidad de muestreo: 4.
Tiempo necesario para renovar completamente la muestra: Unos 7 años.
Levantamiento de la encuesta:
Tipo de entrevista: Papel y lápiz.
Número de unidades finales de muestreo por área de muestra: 72 viviendas por trimestre.
Duración del trabajo de campo:
Total: No se proporcionó información.
Por área de muestra: No se proporcionó información.
Organización de la encuesta: Departamento de Estadísticas y Sociología.
Número de personas que trabajan en el campo: 114 entrevistadores y 39 supervisores.
Substitución de las unidades finales de muestreo que no responden: No.
Estimaciones y ajustes:
Tasa de no-respuesta total: 11 por ciento.
Ajuste por no-respuesta total: Sí.
Imputación por no respuesta de ítemes: No.
Ajuste por áreas/poblaciones no abarcadas: No.
Ajuste por falta de cobertura: Sí.
Ajuste por exceso de cobertura: Sí.
Ajuste por variaciones estacionales: No.
Historia de la encuesta:
Título y fecha de la primera encuesta: Encuesta sobre la Fuerza de Trabajo, octubre de 1998.
Modificaciones y revisiones significativas: No se han hecho cambios importantes.
Documentación y difusión:
Documentación:
Título de las publicaciones con los resultados de la encuesta: (periodicidad): "Economic active population, employment and unemployment" (anualmente).
Título de las publicaciones con la metodología de la encuesta: (periodicidad): "Economic active population, employment and unemployment" (anualmente).
Difusión:
Tiempo necesario para difundir los primeros datos: Dos meses.
Información adelantada acerca de la fecha de la primera difusión pública: Sí.
Disponibilidad de datos no publicados si se solicitan: Sí.
Disponibilidad de datos por medios informáticos: Disquetes e internet. Sitio web: http://www.moldova.md.

Nepal

Título de la encuesta: Encuesta Nacional sobre la Fuerza de Trabajo (Nepal Labour Force Survey).
Organismo responsable de la encuesta:
Planificar y realizar la encuesta: Servicio Central de Estadísticas (Central Bureau of Statistics).
Analizar y publicar los resultados: Servicio Central de Estadísticas (Central Bureau of Statistics).
Temas abarcados: Empleo, desempleo, subempleo, horas realmente trabajadas, salarios, empleo en el sector informal, duración del empleo, duración del desempleo, rama de actividad económica (industria), ocupación, situación en el empleo, nivel de educación/calificación, actividad habitual, empleo secundario, experiencia profesional.
Alcance de la encuesta:
Ámbito geográfico: Todo el país.
Grupos de población: La encuesta abarca los residentes permanentes del Nepal, incluidos extranjeros. No están cubiertas las personas sin hogar, quienes viven en hogares colectivos (como albergues escolares, prisiones, campamentos militares u hospitales), ni las personas ausentes de sus hogares por seis meses o más. Se excluyen los hogares de misiones diplomáticas.
Disponibilidad de estimaciones de otras fuentes para las áreas/grupos excluidos: No se proporcionó información.
Grupos abarcados por la encuesta pero excluidos de los resultados publicados: No se proporcionó información.
Periodicidad:
Recolección de datos: Irregularmente. La primera Encuesta Nacional sobre la Fuerza de Trabajo se realizó entre mayo de 1998 y abril de 1999.
Publicación de los resultados: Irregularmente, según la realización de la encuesta.
Periodo de referencia:
Empleo: Periodo de referencia móvil de una semana, es decir los últimos siete días antes de la fecha de la entrevista.

Búsqueda de trabajo: Periodo de referencia móvil de un mes, es decir los últimos 30 días antes de la fecha de la entrevista.

Disponibilidad para trabajo: Periodo de referencia móvil de una semana, es decir los últimos siete días antes de la fecha de la entrevista.

Conceptos y definiciones:

Empleo: Personas de 5 años y más de edad que realizaron algún trabajo (es decir, por lo menos una hora) por un pago, beneficio o ingreso para la familia, durante la semana de referencia . Se incluyen: a) trabajadores familiares en el trabajo durante la semana de referencia; b) trabajadores a tiempo completo o parcial que buscan otro empleo; c) personas que realizaron algún trabajo durante la semana de referencia pero que estaban sometidas a escolaridad obligatoria, jubiladas y percibían una pensión, o inscritas como desempleadas en busca de trabajo en una oficina de empleo; d) estudiantes de dedicación completa que buscan trabajo a tiempo completo o parcial; e) estudiantes de dedicación parcial que buscan trabajo a tiempo completo o parcial; f) aprendices y personas en formación remunerados; g) personas ocupadas en la producción de bienes para su propio uso final; h) personas del servicio civil equivalente al servicio militar.

Las personas que estaban temporalmente ausentes del trabajo durante la semana de referencia debido a enfermedad o lesión, vacaciones o licencia anual, licencia por maternidad o paternidad, licencia para estudios o capacitación, se consideran empleadas si: i) tenían un empleo o un negocio propio al que se podrían reintegrar, ii) recibían un pago (en efectivo o en especie) u otros beneficios de un empleo o negocio mientras no se encontraban en el trabajo, o habían estado ausentes del trabajo sin remuneración o beneficios por menos de dos meses.

Se excluyen: a) trabajadores que contribuyen con su familia y que no estaban en el trabajo durante la semana de referencia; b) aprendices y personas en formación no remunerados; c) personas ausentes del trabajo debido a conflictos laborales; d) personas ausentes del trabajo debido a mal tiempo, desperfectos mecánicos, etc.; e) personas suspendidas de su trabajo temporalmente o por tiempo indeterminado sin remuneración; f) personas con licencia sin goce de sueldo por iniciativa del empleador; g) trabajadores estacionales que no trabajan durante la temporada inactiva; h) personas que proporcionan servicios no remunerados o personales a miembros de su propio hogar; i) personas que realizaban un trabajo voluntario social no remunerado para la comunidad.

Desempleo: Personas de 5 años y más de edad que i) no estaban empleadas durante la semana de referencia (incluidos quienes tenían un empleo o su propio negocio al que podían reintegrarse, pero del que habían estado ausentes sin remuneración o beneficios por dos meses o más), ii) estaban disponibles para trabajar durante la semana de referencia, y iii) habían buscado un empleo durante los últimos 30 días, o no habían buscado un empleo durante los últimos 30 días por cualquiera de los siguientes motivos: piensan que no hay empleos disponibles; esperan respuesta de solicitudes de trabajo anteriores; esperan comenzar en un empleo o negocio para el cual se han comprometido; es la temporada inactiva del sector de la pesca o la agricultura; otras razones. Se considera que se puede buscar trabajo de una de las siguientes maneras: presentar su candidatura a posibles empleadores; pedir a amigos o parientes que le busquen un empleo; tomar las medidas necesarias para comenzar su propio negocio; buscar trabajo de otras maneras.

Se incluyen: a) personas sin trabajo y corrientemente disponibles para trabajar, que habían concertado acuerdos para comenzar un nuevo empleo en una fecha ulterior a la semana de referencia; b) personas sin empleo y corrientemente disponibles para trabajar, que procuraban establecer su propia empresa; c) personas sin trabajo y corrientemente disponibles para trabajar, pero que no buscaban empleo por otras razones que no sean las mencionadas en los apartados a) y b) anteriores; d) personas que buscaban empleo y/o estaban disponibles para trabajar pero sometidas a escolaridad obligatoria o jubiladas y percibiendo una pensión; e) estudiantes de dedicación completa y/o disponibles para trabajar a tiempo completo o parcial; f) estudiantes de dedicacion parcial que buscaban empleo y/o están disponibles para trabajar a tiempo completo o parcial; g) personas que participan en planes de promoción de empleo.

Se excluyen las personas sin empleo que no estaban disponibles para trabajar durante la semana de referencia.

Se dispone de estimaciones separadas sobre las personas desempleadas que habían buscado trabajo o no durante los últimos 30 días.

Subempleo:

Subempleo por insuficiencia de horas: Personas empleadas en el trabajo y que trabajaron menos de 40 horas durante la semana de referencia por cualquiera de las siguientes razones (es decir, económicas) ajenas a su voluntad: no pueden encontrar otro empleo o reducción del volumen de trabajo; falta de financiamiento o de materia prima; desperfectos mecánicos, eléctricos o de otro tipo; inactividad durante la temporada inactiva, huelga o suspensión como resultado de un conflicto laboral; otros motivos ajenos a su voluntad. Para las personas con más de un empleo, el límite de 40 horas se refiere al total de horas trabajadas en todos los empleos durante la semana de referencia.

Situaciones de empleo inadecuado: La encuesta no abarca este punto.

Horas de trabajo: Horas realmente trabajadas durante la semana de referencia. La información se recopila sobre el número total de horas trabajadas en todos los empleos y sobre el número de horas trabajadas en el empleo principal.

Ingresos relacionados con el empleo:

Ingresos relacionados con el empleo asalariado: Salarios y sueldos brutos recibidos en efectivo o en especie durante la última semana o el último mes para el principal empleo remunerado, antes de deducir impuestos, cotizaciones a la seguridad social o pagos de pensión. Se incluyen todos los beneficios adicionales, tales como bonificaciones, propinas o incentivos. Se incluyen también otros ingresos ordinarios del empleo remunerado, pero se convierten a una base semanal o mensual según proceda (por ejemplo, se añade 1/12 del 13 pago mensual que reciben los funcionarios públicos). En los ingresos en especie se incluyen el suministro ordinario de alimentos, prendas de vestir, vivienda, agua, electricidad, combustible, transporte, etc., de forma gratuita o como subsidio. Se excluyen los ingresos no ordinarios, como regalos en efectivo o en especie.

Ingresos relacionados con el empleo independiente: La encuesta no abarca este punto.

Sector informal: El empleo en el sector informal incluye los siguientes grupos: a) empleados asalariados que trabajan para empresas privadas no registradas (o para empresas que no son dependencias públicas, asociaciones públicas, ONG/ONGI, o sociedades privadas registradas) con menos de 10 empleados asalariados permanentes; b) trabajadores por cuenta propia (es decir, personas que explotan su propio negocio con empleados asalariados permanentes); c) empleadores (es decir, personas que explotan su propio negocio con empleados asalariados permanentes) que emplean menos de 10 empleados asalariados permanentes; d) miembros que contribuyen con la familia sin remuneración y otros que trabajan en negocios con menos de 10 empleados asalariados permanentes. Se excluyen las personas que trabajan en el sector de la agricultura. La información se refiere al empleo principal únicamente; no están cubiertas las personas que tienen un empleo secundario en el sector informal.

Actividad habitual: La actividad económica habitual se refiere a la actividad laboral durante un periodo de referencia de un año, es decir los 12 meses del año civil anterior a la fecha de la entrevista. Las personas de 5 años de edad o más se consideran habitualmente activas si, durante los 12 meses de referencia, trabajaron o estaban disponibles para trabajar durante un total de 180 días o más. Las personas habitualmente activas se pueden dividir a su vez en personas habitualmente empleadas y personas habitualmente desempleadas. Son personas habitualmente empleadas las que, durante los 12 meses de referencia, tenían un periodo total de empleo igual o superior al total del periodo de desempleo. Son personas habitualmente desempleadas las que, durante los 12 meses de referencia, tenían un periodo total de desempleo igual o superior al total del periodo de empleo.

Clasificaciones:

Rama de actividad económica (industria):

Título de la clasificación utilizada: Clasificación Industrial Internacional Uniforme de todas las Actividades Económicas (CIIU, Rev.3).

Grupos de población clasificados por industria: Personas empleadas.

Número de Grupos utilizados para la codificación: Divisiones (nivel de 2 dígitos).

Vínculos con la CIIU: CIIU-Rev.3.

Ocupación:

Título de la clasificación utilizada: Clasificación Internacional Uniforme de Ocupaciones (CIUO-88).

Grupos de población clasificados por ocupación: Personas empleadas.

Número de Grupos utilizados para la codificación: Grupos menores (nivel de 3 dígitos).

Vínculos con la CIUO: CIUO-88.

Situación en el empleo:
Título de la clasificación utilizada: Clasificación nacional sobre la situación en el empleo.
Grupos de población clasificados por situación en el empleo: Personas empleadas.
Grupos utilizados para la codificación: a) empleados asalariados ; b) personas que tienen su propio negocio o explotación agrícola con empleados permanentes asalariados; c) personas que tienen su propio negocio o explotación agrícola sin empleados permanentes asalariados; d) miembros que contribuyen con su familia sin remuneración; e) otros.
Vínculos con la CISE: CISE-1993.
Educación:
Título de la clasificación utilizada: Clasificación nacional de niveles de educación.
Grupos de población clasificados por educación: Todas las personas de 5 años o más de edad.
Grupos utilizados para la codificación: a) Nunca asistieron a la escuela; b) preescolar/escuela de párvulos; c) Grados 1 a 10; m) educación media si se trata del Grado 11; n) intermedia si se trata Grado 12; o) bachillerato; p) licenciatura; q) diploma profesional; r) otro.
Vínculos con la CINE: CINE-1976 (nivel de 3 dígitos).
Tamaño y diseño de la muestra:
Unidad final de muestreo: Hogares.
Tamaño de la muestra (unidades finales de muestreo): 14 400 hogares (7 200 en zonas urbanas y 7 200 en zonas rurales).
Fracción de muestreo: 0,4 por ciento de los hogares (1,5 por ciento en zonas urbanas y 0,2 por ciento en zonas rurales).
Marco de la muestra: El marco de la muestra se basa en la lista de las zonas de enumeración del Censo de Población de 1991. Las zonas de enumeración de nuevos municipios creados desde 1991 se transfirieron del marco rural al marco urbano. Antes de la encuesta, se prepara una nueva lista completa de hogares de todas las 720 zonas de enumeración de la muestra.
Actualización de la muestra: No corresponde.
Rotación:
Esquema: No existe un plan de rotación de muestras. La recopilación de datos se extiende en un periodo de un año al dividir la muestra de la encuesta en tres submuestras independientes, cada una de las cuales representa cuatro meses del calendario nepalés (estación de lluvias, invierno, estación seca).
Porcentaje de unidades que permanecen en la muestra durante dos encuestas consecutivas: No corresponde.
Número máximo de entrevistas por unidad de muestreo: No corresponde.
Tiempo necesario para renovar completamente la muestra: No corresponde.
Levantamiento de la encuesta:
Tipo de entrevista: La información se obtiene mediante entrevistas personales.
Número de unidades finales de muestreo por área de muestra: 20 hogares por zona de enumeración de muestra.
Duración del trabajo de campo:
Total: Un año.
Por área de muestra: Cinco días por zona de enumeración de muestra.
Organización de la encuesta: La organización de la encuesta es permanente.
Número de personas que trabajan en el campo: 15 supervisores y 46 entrevistadores.
Substitución de las unidades finales de muestreo que no responden: No se hacen sustituciones de los hogares que no responden.
Estimaciones y ajustes:
Tasa de no-respuesta total: 0,3 por ciento de hogares de la muestra.
Ajuste por no-respuesta total: Sí.
Imputación por no respuesta de ítemes: No.
Ajuste por áreas/poblaciones no abarcadas: No.
Ajuste por falta de cobertura: No.
Ajuste por falta de cobertura: No corresponde.
Ajuste por variaciones estacionales: No corresponde.
Historia de la encuesta:
Título y fecha de la primera encuesta: La primera Encuesta Nacional sobre la Fuerza de Trabajo se realizó entre 1998 y 1999.
Modificaciones y revisiones significativas: No corresponde.
Documentación y difusión:
Documentación:
Título de las publicaciones con los resultados de la encuesta: (periodicidad): Servicio Central de Estadísticas, Report on the Nepal Labour Force Survey 1998/99, diciembre de 1999.
Título de las publicaciones con la metodología de la encuesta: (periodicidad): La publicación antes mencionada contiene información metodológica sobre la encuesta.
Difusión:
Tiempo necesario para difundir los primeros datos: Unos ocho meses.
Información adelantada acerca de la fecha de la primera difusión pública: No.
Disponibilidad de datos no publicados si se solicitan: Sí, en forma de cuadros adicionales.
Disponibilidad de datos por medios informáticos: Sí, en disquetes.

Noruega

Título de la encuesta: Encuesta sobre la Fuerza de Trabajo (Labour Force Survey).
Organismo responsable de la encuesta:
Planificar y realizar la encuesta: Estadísticas de Noruega (Statistics Norway).
Analizar y publicar los resultados: Estadísticas de Noruega (Statistics Norway).
Temas abarcados: Empleo, desempleo, subempleo, horas de trabajo, duración del empleo y el desempleo, trabajadores desalentados, trabajadores ocasionales, rama de actividad económica (industria), ocupación, situación en el empleo, nivel de educación/calificación, actividad habitual, empleo secundario, empleo temporal, así como otros temas correspondientes al programa de encuestas sobre la fuerza de trabajo de EUROSTAT.
Alcance de la encuesta:
Ámbito geográfico: Todo el país.
Grupos de población: Todas las personas de 16 a 74 años de edad que residen en el país.
Disponibilidad de estimaciones de otras fuentes para las áreas/grupos excluidos: No corresponde.
Grupos abarcados por la encuesta pero excluidos de los resultados publicados: Ninguno.
Periodicidad:
Recolección de datos: Encuesta continua.
Publicación de los resultados: Trimestralmente.
Periodo de referencia:
Empleo: Una semana fija.
Búsqueda de trabajo: Cuatro semanas.
Disponibilidad para trabajo: Dos semanas.
Conceptos y definiciones:
Empleo: Todas las personas de 16 a 74 años de edad que realizaron un trabajo remunerado o por un beneficio por lo menos una hora en la semana de referencia, o que estaban temporalmente ausentes del trabajo debido a enfermedad, días de fiesta, etc. Se incluyen las personas con licencia remunerada , o no remunerada hasta un año, si tienen un empleo al que pueden reintegrarse, trabajadores familiares no remunerados, reclutas, así como personas ocupadas por medidas gubernamentales a promover el empleo, si son remuneradas.
Se incluyen:
a)personas que tienen un empleo pero que se encuentran temporalmente ausentes del mismo debido a enfermedad o lesión, vacaciones o licencia anual, licencia por maternidad, paternidad o parental hasta un año (a menos que sigan percibiendo una remuneración), licencia para estudios o capacitación hasta un año (a menos que sigan percibiendo una remuneración), ausencia sin autorización si esas personas tienen un empleo y una fecha de reintegro, conflictos laborales, mal tiempo o desperfectos mecánicos, etc.;
b)trabajadores a tiempo completo o parcial que buscaban otro empleo durante la semana de referencia;
c)personas que realizaban algún trabajo remunerado o por un beneficio durante la semana de referencia pero que estaban sometidas a escolaridad obligatoria, jubiladas y percibían una pensión, inscritas como desempleadas en busca de trabajo en una oficina de empleo o que percibían indemnizaciones de desempleo;
d)estudiantes de dedicación completa o parcial que trabajan a tiempo completo o parcial;
e)aprendices y personas en formación remunerados;
f)personas que participan en planes de promoción del empleo y son remuneradas por sus empleadores;

g)trabajadores familiares no remunerados en el trabajo durante la semana de referencia o temporalmente ausentes del mismo, si no se trata de trabajo de temporada;
h)voluntarios y miembros de carrera de las fuerzas armadas, reclutas y personas del servicio civil equivalente al servicio militar.
Desempleo: Todas las personas de 16 a 74 años de edad que no estaban empleadas durante la semana de la encuesta, habían buscado trabajo durante las últimas cuatro semanas y estaban disponibles en las dos semanas siguientes. Antes de 1996, tenían que estar disponibles durante la semana de la encuesta.
Se incluyen también:
a)personas suspendidas de su trabajo temporalmente sin remuneración;
b) personas sin empleo y corrientemente disponibles para trabajar que habían tomado disposiciones para comenzar un nuevo empleo en una fecha ulterior a la semana de referencia o que procuraban establecer su propia empresa;
c)personas sin empleo, disponibles para trabajar pero que no buscaban trabajo durante la semana de referencia y esperaban respuesta del empleador, si habían buscado un empleo entre cinco y ocho semanas antes;
d)personas que buscaban trabajo y estaban disponibles para trabajar pero estaban sometidas a escolaridad obligatoria, jubiladas y percibían una pensión, si habían buscado un empleo entre una y cuatro semanas antes y estaban disponibles para trabajar en las dos semanas siguientes;
e)estudiantes de dedicación parcial o completa que buscan empleo a tiempo completo o parcial, si habían buscado un empleo entre una y cuatro semanas antes y estaban disponibles para trabajar en las dos semanas siguientes.
Subempleo:
Subempleo por insuficiencia de horas: Trabajadores a tiempo parcial que buscaban más horas de trabajo ordinarias (o habituales) por semana y estaban disponibles para comenzar a trabajar más horas en un mes.
Situaciones de empleo inadecuado: Personas que buscan otro empleo debido a:
a)el riesgo o la seguridad de perder o terminar el empleo actual;
b)el empleo actual se considera como un trabajo provisional;
c)buscan un empleo secundario;
d)desean tener mejores condiciones de trabajo (en el trabajo o el tiempo de transporte, calidad del trabajo);
e)desean mayores remuneraciones;
f)otras razones.
Horas de trabajo: Se refieren a las horas realmente trabajadas y las horas ordinarias (o habituales) por semana. Los empleos principal y secundario se abarcan por separado. La distinción entre trabajo a tiempo parcial y completo se hace en base al total de horas de trabajo ordinarias en el empleo principal y secundario.
Ingresos relacionados con el empleo:
Ingresos relacionados con el empleo asalariado: La encuesta no abarca este punto.
Ingresos relacionados con el empleo independiente: La encuesta no abarca este punto.
Sector informal: La encuesta no abarca este punto.
Actividad habitual: La encuesta no abarca este punto.
Clasificaciones:
Rama de actividad económica (industria):
Título de la clasificación utilizada: Clasificación nacional.
Grupos de población clasificados por industria: Personas empleadas y desempleadas (rama de actividad económica del último empleo para el desempleado).
Número de Grupos utilizados para la codificación: 60 grupos.
Vínculos con la CIIU: CIIU-Rev.3 a nivel de 2 dígitos.
Ocupación:
Título de la clasificación utilizada: Clasificación nacional.
Grupos de población clasificados por ocupación: Personas empleadas y desempleadas (ocupación en el último empleo para el desempleado).
Número de Grupos utilizados para la codificación: 353 grupos.
Vínculos con la CIUO: CIUO-88.
Situación en el empleo:
Título de la clasificación utilizada: Clasificación nacional.
Grupos de población clasificados por situación en el empleo: Personas empleadas y desempleadas (situación en el último empleo para el desempleado).
Grupos utilizados para la codificación: Cuatro grupos: empleados, empleadores, trabajadores independientes y trabajadores familiares no remunerados.
Vínculos con la CISE: CISE-1993.
Educación:
Título de la clasificación utilizada: Clasificación nacional.
Grupos de población clasificados por educación: Personas empleadas y desempleadas.
Grupos utilizados para la codificación: Cinco niveles: escuela primaria, nivel 1 de escuela secundaria, nivel 2 de escuela secundaria, niveles universitarios de uno a cuatro años y cinco años y más, respectivamente. Además, hay nueve materias (programas) de estudio.
Vínculos con la CINE: CINE-1976.
Tamaño y diseño de la muestra:
Unidad final de muestreo: Familia.
Tamaño de la muestra (unidades finales de muestreo): 24 000 personas por trimestre.
Fracción de muestreo: 0,8 por ciento.
Marco de la muestra: Registro Central de la Población, que actualizan de manera continua las oficinas locales de registro de la población.
Actualización de la muestra: Cada trimestre se renueva 1/8 de la muestra.
Rotación:
Esquema: Cada hogar participa en la encuesta ocho veces en un periodo de ocho trimestres consecutivos.
Porcentaje de unidades que permanecen en la muestra durante dos encuestas consecutivas: 87,5 por ciento.
Número máximo de entrevistas por unidad de muestreo: Ocho.
Tiempo necesario para renovar completamente la muestra: Ocho trimestres.
Levantamiento de la encuesta:
Tipo de entrevista: La mayoría se realiza por teléfono y algunas son entrevistas personales (CAPI).
Número de unidades finales de muestreo por área de muestra: Entre 800 y 2 500 por condado y hay 19 condados.
Duración del trabajo de campo:
Total: Dos o tres semanas después de la semana de la encuesta.
Por área de muestra: No se proporcionó información.
Organización de la encuesta: Permanente.
Número de personas que trabajan en el campo: Unas 160 personas.
Substitución de las unidades finales de muestreo que no responden: No.
Estimaciones y ajustes:
Tasa de no-respuesta total: Casi el 10 por ciento.
Ajuste por no-respuesta total: Sí (en el proceso de estimación).
Imputación por no respuesta de ítemes: Sí.
Ajuste por áreas/poblaciones no abarcadas: No corresponde.
Ajuste por falta de cobertura: No corresponde.
Ajuste por exceso de cobertura: No corresponde.
Ajuste por variaciones estacionales: Sí (método X-12-ARIMA).
Historia de la encuesta:
Título y fecha de la primera encuesta: Encuesta sobre la Fuerza de Trabajo, primer trimestre de 1972.
Modificaciones y revisiones significativas: En 1988 y 1996 se introdujeron nuevos cuestionarios.
Documentación y difusión:
Documentación:
Título de las publicaciones con los resultados de la encuesta: (periodicidad): Labour Market Statistics (anual).
Título de las publicaciones con la metodología de la encuesta: (periodicidad): Labour Market Statistics (anual).
Difusión:
Tiempo necesario para difundir los primeros datos: Comienzos del mes siguiente del trimestre de la encuesta.
Información adelantada acerca de la fecha de la primera difusión pública: Sí.
Disponibilidad de datos no publicados si se solicitan: Sí.
Disponibilidad de datos por medios informáticos: Disquetes e internet. Sitio web: http://www.ssb.no/.

Nueva Zelandia

Título de la encuesta: Encuesta de Hogares sobre la Fuerza de Trabajo (Household Labour Force Survey (HLFS)).
Organismo responsable de la encuesta:
Planificar y realizar la encuesta: Estadísticas de Nueva Zelandia (Statistics New Zealand (SNZ)).
Analizar y publicar los resultados: SNZ.
Temas abarcados: Personas corriente y económicamente activas, empleadas y desempleadas; personas corrientemente subemplea-

das por insuficiencia de horas y personas corrientemente fuera de la fuerza de trabajo; trabajadores desalentados; horas de trabajo reales y habituales; duración del desempleo; cuestiones étnicas; rama de actividad económica (industria); ocupación, situación en el empleo, nivel de educación/capacitación.

Alcance de la encuesta:

Ámbito geográfico: Todo el país, salvo los territorios externos.

Grupos de población: Población civil que no reside en hogares colectivos, de 15 años y más de edad.

Disponibilidad de estimaciones de otras fuentes para las áreas/grupos excluidos: No.

Grupos abarcados por la encuesta pero excluidos de los resultados publicados: Ninguno.

Periodicidad:

Recolección de datos: Encuesta continua.

Publicación de los resultados: Trimestralmente.

Periodo de referencia:

Empleo: Una semana.

Desempleo: Las últimas cuatro semanas.

Disponibilidad para trabajo: Durante la semana de referencia.

Conceptos y definiciones:

Empleo: Personas que a) realizaron algún trabajo remunerado o por un beneficio durante la semana de referencia; y b) estaban temporalmente ausentes del trabajo durante la semana de referencia debido a enfermedad o licencia remunerada, o tenían un negocio al que, indudablemente, se reintegrarían. Algún trabajo se define como una hora o más durante la semana de referencia.

Desempleo: Personas que estaban corrientemente sin trabajo, disponibles para trabajar durante la semana de referencia y que habían buscado activamente trabajo en algún momento durante las últimas cuatro semanas.

Subempleo:

Subempleo por insuficiencia de horas: Personas empleadas que trabajaban a tiempo parcial, habían buscado un empleo a tiempo completo en las últimas cuatro semanas y/o querían trabajar más horas.

Situaciones de empleo inadecuado: No se proporcionó información.

Horas de trabajo: En las horas 'reales' y 'habituales' se incluyen las horas trabajadas, remuneradas y no remuneradas, en el empleo principal y empleo(s) secundario(s).

Ingresos relacionados con el empleo:

Ingresos relacionados con el empleo asalariado: No se proporcionó información.

Ingresos relacionados con el empleo independiente: No se proporcionó información.

Sector informal: No corresponde.

Actividad habitual: No se proporcionó información.

Clasificaciones:

Rama de actividad económica (industria):

Título de la clasificación utilizada: Clasificación Industrial Uniforme de Australia y Nueva Zelandia (ANZSIC).

Grupos de población clasificados por industria: Empleados y desempleados (rama de actividad económica del último empleo para el desempleado).

Número de Grupos utilizados para la codificación: 158.

Vínculos con la CIIU: CIIU-Rev.3.

Ocupación:

Título de la clasificación utilizada: Clasificación Uniforme de Ocupaciones de Nueva Zelandia (NZSCO).

Grupos de población clasificados por ocupación: Empleados y desempleados (ocupación en el último empleo para el desempleado).

Número de Grupos utilizados para la codificación: 96.

Vínculos con la CIUO: CIUO-88.

Situación en el empleo:

Título de la clasificación utilizada: Situación en el Empleo – Clasificación Uniforme de 1998.

Grupos de población clasificados por situación en el empleo: Empleados y desempleados (ocupación en el último empleo para el desempleado).

Grupos utilizados para la codificación: Trabajadores asalariados; empleadores con empleados en su propio negocio; trabajadores independientes sin empleados; trabajadores no remunerados en un negocio familiar.

Vínculos con la CISE: CISE-1993.

Educación:

Título de la clasificación utilizada: Clasificación de la Encuesta de Hogares sobre la Fuerza de Trabajo (Household Labour Force Survey Qualification Type Classification (HLF.QUALHIG)).

Grupos de población clasificados por educación: Todas las personas.

Grupos utilizados para la codificación: 17.

Vínculos con la CINE: CINE-1997.

Tamaño y diseño de la muestra:

Unidad final de muestreo: Hogares.

Tamaño de la muestra (unidades finales de muestreo): 18 000 hogares.

Fracción de muestreo: 0,01.

Marco de la muestra: Censos quinquenales. Las unidades primarias de muestreo (UPM) son pequeñas zonas geográficas.

Actualización de la muestra: Cada cinco años.

Rotación:

Esquema: Los hogares permanecen en la muestra durante 8 meses consecutivos y luego se retiran.

Porcentaje de unidades que permanecen en la muestra durante dos encuestas consecutivas: 87,5 por ciento permanece en la muestra durante dos meses consecutivos. Cada UPM se asigna a uno de los ocho grupos de rotación, y un grupo de rotación se sustituye cada trimestre con nuevas viviendas de la misma UPM.

Número máximo de entrevistas por unidad de muestreo: No se proporcionó información.

Tiempo necesario para renovar completamente la muestra: No se proporcionó información.

Levantamiento de la encuesta:

Tipo de entrevista: Lápiz y papel, personal (para la primera entrevista) y por teléfono (para el resto de las entrevistas).

Número de unidades finales de muestreo por área de muestra: No se proporcionó información.

Duración del trabajo de campo:

Total: Una semana.

Por área de muestra: No se proporcionó información.

Organización de la encuesta: Permanente.

Número de personas que trabajan en el campo: 135 entrevistadores y 5 supervisores regionales.

Substitución de las unidades finales de muestreo que no responden: No.

Estimaciones y ajustes:

Tasa de no-respuesta total: 10 por ciento.

Ajuste por no-respuesta total: Sí.

Imputación por no respuesta de ítemes: Sí.

Ajuste por áreas/poblaciones no abarcadas: Sí.

Ajuste por falta de cobertura: Sí.

Ajuste por falta de cobertura: No corresponde.

Ajuste por variaciones estacionales: Sí, para el empleo y el desempleo por sexo, total de horas trabajadas y personas que trabajan a tiempo completo y parcial. Se utiliza el método X-12 para el ajuste estacional concurrente.

Historia de la encuesta:

Título y fecha de la primera encuesta: Encuesta de Hogares sobre la Fuerza de Trabajo, diciembre de 1985.

Modificaciones y revisiones significativas: Junio de 1990: Nuevo cuestionario con nuevas variables: subempleo, calificación, ocupación (hasta el nivel de tres dígitos), rama de actividad económica (industria) (hasta nivel de tres dígitos).

Documentación y difusión:

Documentación:

Título de las publicaciones con los resultados de la encuesta: (periodicidad): Hot off the press - Household Labour Force Survey (Cat. no. 05-500); Labour Market (anualmente) Catálogo no. 01.029.0098 ISSN 1171-283X

Título de las publicaciones con la metodología de la encuesta: (periodicidad): Survey Information Manager - Household Labour Force Survey, en el sitio web.

Difusión:

Tiempo necesario para difundir los primeros datos: Seis semanas después de finalizar el periodo de referencia de la encuesta.

Información adelantada acerca de la fecha de la primera difusión pública: Sí.

Disponibilidad de datos no publicados si se solicitan: Sí.

Disponibilidad de datos por medios informáticos: Sí. Sitio web: http://www.stats.govt.nz.

Países Bajos

Título de la encuesta: Encuesta sobre la Fuerza de Trabajo (The Labour Force Survey).

Organismo responsable de la encuesta:

Planificar y realizar la encuesta: Servicio Central de Estadísticas (Central Bureau of Statistics).

Analizar y publicar los resultados: Servicio Central de Estadísticas (Central Bureau of Statistics).
Temas abarcados: Empleo, desempleo, horas de trabajos, empleo en el sector informal, duración del desempleo, rama de actividad económica (industria), ocupación, situación en el empleo, nivel de educación/calificaciones, actividad habitual, otros temas como, por ejemplo, condiciones de trabajo y licencia parental.
Alcance de la encuesta:
Ámbito geográfico: Todo el país.
Grupos de población: Personas de 15 a 64 años de edad que residen en el país, excepto las personas que viven en hogares colectivos.
Disponibilidad de estimaciones de otras fuentes para las áreas/grupos excluidos: No.
Grupos abarcados por la encuesta pero excluidos de los resultados publicados: Menores de 15 años.
Periodicidad:
Recolección de datos: Encuesta continua.
Publicación de los resultados: Anualmente.
Periodo de referencia:
Empleo: Cuando se realiza la entrevista.
Búsqueda de trabajo: Cuando se realiza la entrevista.
Disponibilidad para trabajo: Cuando se realiza la entrevista.
Conceptos y definiciones:
Empleo: Todas las personas de 15 a 64 años de edad que viven en hogares privados encuestados durante la semana de referencia, salvo la población de hogares colectivos.
A partir de 1992, los datos nacionales se basan en la definición de empleo que incluye sólo a quienes trabajaron 12 horas o más por semana. Para fines internacionales, se aplica el criterio de una hora.
Se incluyen también como empleadas:
a)personas con un trabajo pero temporalmente ausentes del mismo debido a enfermedad o lesión, vacaciones o licencia anual, licencia por maternidad o paternidad, licencia parental, licencia para estudios o capacitación, ausencia sin autorización, conflictos laborales, mal tiempo, desperfectos mecánicos, etc., así como las personas suspendidas de su trabajo temporalmente o por tiempo indeterminado sin remuneración o con licencia sin goce de sueldo por iniciativa del empleador y trabajadores a tiempo completo o parcial que buscaban empleo durante el periodo de referencia;
b)personas que realizaban algún trabajo remunerado o por un beneficio durante el periodo de referencia pero que estaban sometidas a escolaridad obligatoria, jubiladas y percibían una pensión, inscritas como desempleadas en busca de trabajo en una oficina de empleo o que percibían indemnizaciones de desempleo;
c)estudiantes de dedicación completa o parcial que trabajaban a tiempo completo o parcial;
d)aprendices y personas en formación remunerados y personas que participan en planes de promoción del empleo;
e)trabajadores familiares no remunerados en el trabajo durante el periodo de referencia o temporalmente ausentes del mismo;
f)voluntarios y miembros de carrera de las fuerzas armadas y personas del servicio civil equivalente al servicio militar.
Desempleo: Los datos nacionales de desempleo incluyen personas que buscan empleo de 12 horas o más por semana. Las personas que trabajan menos de 12 horas ya no se incluyen en la fuerza de trabajo, salvo si buscan trabajar 12 horas o más por semana; en ese caso, se clasifican como desempleados.
Se incluyen también como desempleadas:
a) personas sin empleo y corrientemente disponibles para trabajar que habían tomado disposiciones para comenzar un nuevo empleo en una fecha ulterior al periodo de referencia o que procuraban establecer su propia empresa;
b)personas que buscaban trabajo y/o estaban disponibles para trabajar, pero estaban sometidas a escolaridad obligatoria o jubiladas y percibían una pensión;
c)estudiantes de dedicación completa o parcial que trabajaban a tiempo completo o parcial;
d)aprendices y personas en formación remunerados.
Subempleo:
Subempleo por insuficiencia de horas: No corresponde.
Situaciones de empleo inadecuado: No corresponde.
Horas de trabajo: No disponible.
Ingresos relacionados con el empleo:
Ingresos relacionados con el empleo asalariado: No corresponde.
Ingresos relacionados con el empleo independiente: No corresponde.
Sector informal: No se proporcionó información.
Actividad habitual: No se proporcionó información.
Clasificaciones:
Rama de actividad económica (industria):
Título de la clasificación utilizada: CIIU-Rev.3.
Grupos de población clasificados por industria: Personas empleadas.
Número de Grupos utilizados para la codificación: 18 grupos.
Vínculos con la CIIU: CIIU-Rev. 2 y Rev.3.
Ocupación:
Título de la clasificación utilizada: CIUO-88.
Grupos de población clasificados por ocupación: Personas empleadas.
Número de Grupos utilizados para la codificación: 11 grupos.
Vínculos con la CIUO: CIUO-88.
Situación en el empleo:
Título de la clasificación utilizada: No se dispone de información.
Grupos de población clasificados por situación en el empleo: Empleados.
Grupos utilizados para la codificación: Empleados, empleadores y trabajadores familiares.
Vínculos con la CISE: Vínculos indirectos con la CISE-1993:
Educación:
Título de la clasificación utilizada: CINE-1997.
Grupos de población clasificados por educación: Personas empleadas y desempleadas.
Grupos utilizados para la codificación: 5 grupos.
Vínculos con la CINE: CINE-1997.
Tamaño y diseño de la muestra:
Unidad final de muestreo: Hogares.
Tamaño de la muestra (unidades finales de muestreo): 8 000 hogares cada mes.
Fracción de muestreo: 1 por ciento.
Marco de la muestra: La encuesta se basa en una muestra estratificada en dos etapas. El Registro Geográfico Básico (GBR) constituye el marco de la muestra. El GBR es una lista de todas las direcciones en los Países Bajos establecido por la Oficina de Correos de Holanda. Se prepara una muestra de unas 11 000 direcciones cada mes para la encuesta sobre la fuerza de trabajo.
Actualización de la muestra: No se proporcionó información.
Rotación:
Esquema: No se proporcionó información.
Porcentaje de unidades que permanecen en la muestra durante dos encuestas consecutivas: No se proporcionó información.
Número máximo de entrevistas por unidad de muestreo: Cinco veces.
Tiempo necesario para renovar completamente la muestra: Un año.
Levantamiento de la encuesta:
Tipo de entrevista: CAPI y CATI: entrevistas personales durante la primera etapa y por teléfono durante la segunda, tercera y cuarta etapas. El intervalo de tiempo entre cada etapa es de tres meses.
Número de unidades finales de muestreo por área de muestra: No se proporcionó información.
Duración del trabajo de campo:
Total: Encuesta continua.
Por área de muestra: Encuesta continua.
Organización de la encuesta: Permanente.
Número de personas que trabajan en el campo: Unas 300 personas.
Substitución de las unidades finales de muestreo que no responden: No.
Estimaciones y ajustes:
Tasa de no-respuesta total: 45 por ciento.
Ajuste por no-respuesta total: No.
Imputación por no respuesta de ítemes: No.
Ajuste por áreas/poblaciones no abarcadas: No.
Ajuste por falta de cobertura: Sí.
Ajuste por exceso de cobertura: Sí.
Ajuste por variaciones estacionales: No.
Historia de la encuesta:
Título y fecha de la primera encuesta: Encuesta sobre la Fuerza de Trabajo de 1987.
Modificaciones y revisiones significativas: En 1992 y 2000.
Documentación y difusión:
Documentación:
Título de las publicaciones con los resultados de la encuesta: (periodicidad): No se proporcionó información.
Título de las publicaciones con la metodología de la encuesta: (periodicidad): No se proporcionó información.

Difusión:
Tiempo necesario para difundir los primeros datos: Un año.
Información adelantada acerca de la fecha de la primera difusión pública: No.
Disponibilidad de datos no publicados si se solicitan: Sí.
Disponibilidad de datos por medios informáticos: Hojas de calcular Excell, previa solicitud, y sitio web en Internet (http://www.cbs.nl).

Pakistán

Título de la encuesta: Encuesta sobre la Fuerza de Trabajo (Labour force survey).
Organismo responsable de la encuesta:
Planificar y realizar la encuesta: Servicio Federal de Estadísticas, División de Estadísticas, Ministerio de Finanzas y Asuntos Económicos (Federal Bureau of Statistics, Statistics Division, Ministry of Finance and Economic Affairs).
Analizar y publicar los resultados: Servicio Federal de Estadísticas (Federal Bureau of Statistics).
Temas abarcados: Empleo, desempleo, subempleo, horas de trabajo, salarios, empleo en el sector informal, duración del desempleo, rama de actividad económica (industria), ocupación, situación en el empleo, nivel de educación, empleo secundario.
Alcance de la encuesta:
Ámbito geográfico: Todas las zonas rurales y urbanas de las cuatro provincias de Pakistán y Azad Jammu y Kashmir definidas según el Censo de población de 1981, salvo las áreas tribales bajo administración federal, las zonas militares reservadas, los distritos de Kohistán, Malakand y las regiones protegidas de la provincia fronteriza noroccidental.
Grupos de población: Se excluye la población no asentada, el personal de las fuerzas de defensa, extranjeros y nacionales que viven en el extranjero.
Disponibilidad de estimaciones de otras fuentes para las áreas/grupos excluidos: La población excluida del ámbito geográfico constituye un 4% del total de la población
Grupos abarcados por la encuesta pero excluidos de los resultados publicados: No corresponde.
Periodicidad:
Recolección de datos: Anual.
Publicación de los resultados: Anual.
Periodo de referencia:
Empleo: Semana de referencia móvil.
Búsqueda de trabajo: Semana de referencia.
Disponibilidad para trabajo: Semana de referencia.
Conceptos y definiciones:
Empleo: Personas de 10 años y más de edad que, durante la semana de referencia, trabajaron por lo menos una hora y eran "empleados asalariados" o "empleados independientes". También se consideran como empleadas las personas que pese a tener un empleo con carácter permanente, no trabajaron por algún motivo durante la semana de referencia.
Se incluyen las siguientes categorías:
a)personas que comunicaron que realizaban tareas domésticas u otras actividades conexas, pero que dedicaban cierto tiempo a determinadas actividades agrícolas y no agrícolas;
b)personas con un empleo, pero temporalmente ausentes del mismo por algún motivo, y personas suspendidas del trabajo temporalmente o por tiempo indeterminado y sin remuneración;
c)personas que durante la semana de referencia realizaron algún trabajo remunerado o por un beneficio, pero estaban sometidas a escolaridad obligatoria, jubiladas y recibiendo una pensión, o prestaciones de desempleo, estaban incritas como desempleadas en busca de trabajo en una oficina de empleo o buscaban otro trabajo durante la semana de referencia;
d)estudiantes de dedicación completa o parcial que trabajaban a tiempo completo o parcial;
e)aprendices y personas en formación remunerados, y participantes en sistemas de promoción del empleo;
f)trabajadores familiares no remunerados en su trabajo o temporalmente ausentes del mismo;
g)personas ocupadas en la producción de bienes para su propio uso final;
h)trabajadores estacionales que no trabajan durante la temporada inactiva.
Se excluyen:
a)aprendices y personas en formación no remunerados;
b)personas ocupadas en la producción de servicios para sus propios hogares;
c)personas ocupadas en actividades inmorales tales como la prostitución, la mendicidad, el robo o el contrabando;
d)trabajadores sociales voluntarios que trabajan fuera del negocio familiar.
Desempleo: Personas de 10 años y más de edad, que durante la semana de referencia estaban: i) "sin trabajo", es decir no tenían un empleo remunerado o independiente; ii) "corrientemente disponibles para trabajar", es decir estaban disponibles para realizar un trabajo remunerado o independiente durante la semana de referencia; y iii) "buscaban trabajo", es decir habían tomado medidas concretas en un determinado periodo de tiempo para buscar un empleo remunerado o independiente.
Se incluyen las siguientes categorías:
a)personas sin trabajo, corrientemente disponibles para trabajar, que buscaban trabajo y que habían tomado las disposiciones necesarias para comenzar en un nuevo empleo en una fecha ulterior a la semana de referencia;
b)personas sin trabajo, corrientemente disponibles para trabajar, que buscaban trabajo y que trataban de establecer su propio negocio;
c)personas sin trabajo, disponibles para trabajar, pero que no buscaban trabajo durante un periodo reciente por determinadas razones;
d)estudiantes de dedicación completa o parcial que buscaban empleo a tiempo completo o parcial;
e)personas que buscaban trabajo o estaban disponibles para trabajar, pero estaban sometidas a escolaridad obligatoria o jubiladas y percibían una pensión.
Se excluyen:
a)personas suspendidas de su trabajo temporalmente o por tiempo indeterminado sin remuneración.
Subempleo:
Subempleo por insuficiencia de horas: Personas empleadas que durante el periodo de referencia cumplían simultáneamente los tres criterios siguientes: i) trabajaban menos tiempo que el normalmente establecido (es decir, menos de 35 horas por semana), ii) trabajaban menos tiempo por razones ajenas a su voluntad, y iii) buscaban trabajo adicional o estaban disponibles para hacerlo.
Situaciones de empleo inadecuado: Véase más arriba.
Horas de trabajo: Número de horas trabajadas en la última semana después de la fecha de la entrevista en las ocupaciones principal y secundaria.
Ingresos relacionados con el empleo:
Ingresos relacionados con el empleo asalariado: Ingresos brutos de los empleados en sus ocupaciones principal y secundaria.
Ingresos relacionados con el empleo independiente: No se dispone de información.
Sector informal: Todos los negocios familiares de trabajadores por cuenta propia que son explotados por esos trabajadores, independientemente del tamaño del negocio (negocios informales por cuenta propia) y negocios familiares explotados por empleadores con menos de 10 personas empleadas. Se excluyen todos los negocios familiares dedicados a actividades agrícolas o totalmente ocupados en la producción de artículos no comercializados.
Actividad habitual: No se dispone de información.
Clasificaciones:
Rama de actividad económica (industria):
Título de la clasificación utilizada: Clasificación Industrial Uniforme de Pakistán (Pakistan Standard Industrial Classification PSIC-1970).
Grupos de población clasificados por industria: Personas empleadas y desempleadas con experiencia previa de trabajo.
Número de Grupos utilizados para la codificación: Nivel de códigos de 2 dígitos, pero se publican a nivel de 1 dígito.
Vínculos con la CIIU: CIIU Rev. 2.
Ocupación:
Título de la clasificación utilizada: Clasificación Uniforme de Ocupaciones de Pakistán (Pakistan Standard Classification of Occupations
PSCO-1994).
Grupos de población clasificados por ocupación: : Personas empleadas y desempleadas con experiencia previa de trabajo.
Número de Grupos utilizados para la codificación: : Nivel de códigos de 2 dígitos, pero se publican a nivel de 1 dígito.
Vínculos con la CIUO: CIUO-68.
Situación en el empleo:
Categorías: Empleadores, trabajadores independientes, ayudantes familiares no emunerados y empleados.

Grupos de población clasificados por situación en el empleo: Personas empleadas y desempleadas con experiencia previa de trabajo.
Vínculos con la CISE: CISE-1993.
Educación:
Grupos de población clasificados por situación en el empleo: Personas empleadas y desempleadas.
Lista de grupos: **Educación:** no formal. Primaria inferior. Primaria pero inferior a primaria media. Enseñanza secundaria sin diploma. Diplomado y superior.
Vínculos con la CINE: No se especifica.
Tamaño y diseño de la muestra:
Unidad final de muestreo: Hogares.
Tamaño de la muestra (unidades finales de muestreo): 22 272 hogares (10 368 en zonas urbanas y 11 904 en zonas rurales).
Fracción de muestreo: 1/465 en zonas urbanas y 1/1119 en zonas rurales.
Marco de la muestra: Se utilizan dos tipos de marcos: lista marco y área marco. Los bloques y aldeas de enumeración del Censo de población de 1981 se utilizan como unidades primarias de muestreo.
Actualización de la muestra: La lista de bloques de enumeración se actualizaron en 1995. El marco de área urbana se elaboró a partir de una Encuesta de Registro de Conteo Rápido (Quick Count Record Survey) realizada en 1972, que se actualiza cada cinco años.
Rotación: Ninguna.
Esquema: No corresponde.
Porcentaje de unidades que permanecen en la muestra: No corresponde.
Número máximo de entrevistas por unidad de muestreo: No corresponde.
Tiempo necesario para renovar completamente la muestra: No corresponde.
Levantamiento da la encuesta:
Tipo de entrevista: Entrevista personal.
Número de unidades finales de muestreo por área de muestra: No se proporcionó información.
Duración del trabajo de campo:
Total: Del 1o de julio de 1996 al 30 de junio de 1997.
Por área de muestra: No se proporcionó información.
Organización de la encuesta: Permanente.
Número de personas que trabajan en el campo: Unos 68 enumeradores y 34 supervisores.
Substitución de las unidades finales de muestreo que no responden: No.
Estimaciones y ajustes:
Tasa de no-respuesta total: No se proporcionó información.
Ajuste por no-respuesta total: No.
Imputación por no respuesta de ítemes: No.
Ajuste por áreas/poblaciones no abarcadas: No.
Ajuste por falta de cobertura: No.
Ajuste por exceso de cobertura: No.
Ajuste por variaciones estacionales: No.
Historia de la encuesta:
Título y fecha de la primera encuesta: Encuesta sobre la Fuerza de Trabajo (Labour Force Survey) (julio de 1963 a junio de 1964).
Modificaciones y revisiones significativas: A partir de 1967-1968, se incluyen los hogares ubicados en instituciones (cárceles, asilos, hoteles, etc.), así como los hogares de mendigos con un miembro que trabaja por una remuneración o beneficio.
Desde 1978-1979, los ayudantes familiares no remunerados que trabajan menos de 15 horas por semana son considerados como empleados. Para obtener más información sobre el empleo y el desempleo, se introdujeron varias preguntas de evaluación en el cuestionario sobre a) el deseo de trabajar si se proporciona un empleo, b) razones para no buscar trabajo, y c) cualquier empleo remunerado o por un beneficio para las personas que se identificaron como "amas de casa" o "estudiantes".
En 1990-1991, se introdujeron otras preguntas de evaluación en el cuestionario de conformidad con lo estipulado en la resolución de 1982 de la OIT. En particular, se diseñó una sección de evaluación especial sobre la actividad económica para personas de 10 años y más de edad que comunicaron que realizaban quehaceres domésticos y otras actividades conexas.
En 1995, se introdujeron preguntas sobre la migración y las características del sector formal e informal.
Documentación y difusión:
Documentación
Título de las publicaciones con los resultados de la encuesta: Report of the Labour Force Survey.
Título de las publicaciones con la metodología de la encuesta: Report of the Labour Force Survey.
Difusión:
Tiempo necesario para difundir los primeros datos: Unos 16 meses. Los datos de la encuesta realizada del 1o de julio de 1996 al 30 de junio de 1997 se publicaron en octubre de 1998.
Información adelantada acerca de la fecha de la primera difusión pública: No.
Disponibilidad de datos no publicados si se solicitan: Sí.
Disponibilidad de datos por medios informáticos: Sí.

Panamá

Título de la encuesta: Encuesta Continua de Hogares.
Organismo responsable de la encuesta:
Planificar y realizar la encuesta: Sección de Población y Vivienda, Dirección de Estadística y Censo.
Analizar y publicar los resultados: idem.
Temas abarcados: Empleo, desempleo, subempleo, horas de trabajo, salarios, ingresos, empleo en el sector informal, duración del empleo y del desempleo, trabajadores desalentados y ocasionales, ramas de actividad económica, ocupación, situación en el empleo, nivel de educación, actividad habitual, trabajos secundarios, seguridad social, lugar de trabajo, tamaño de la empresa, características socio-demográficas.
Alcance de la encuesta:
Ámbito geográfico: todo el país. Se proporcionan estimaciones por regiones. A partir del 2001 se proporcionarán estimaciones por provincias, dentro de las provincias, por áreas urbanas y rurales, y estimaciones separadas para los distritos de Panamá, San Miguelito, Arraiján y la Chorrera.
Grupos de población: Se excluyen (a) personas que residen en viviendas colectivas; (b) residentes permanentes en el extranjero; (c) poblaciones no asentadas. Hasta el 2000 se excluía también a la población indígena y la que vivía en lugares de difícil acceso.
Disponibilidad de estimaciones de otras fuentes para las áreas/grupos excluidos: no.
Grupos abarcados por le encuesta pero excluidos de los resultados publicados: no se aplica.
Periodicidad:
Recolección de datos: trimestral.
Publicación de los resultados: trimestral.
Períodos de referencia:
Empleo: la semana anterior a la semana de la entrevista.
Búsqueda de trabajo: una semana, cuatro semanas y tres meses antes de la semana de la entrevista.
Disponibilidad para trabajo: no se aplica.
Conceptos y definiciones:
Empleo: Comprende a las personas que (a) tienen una ocupación o trabajo remunerado en dinero o en especie, durante el período de referencia; (b) trabajan en formal regular en un negocio o empresa de un miembro de su propia familia, durante 15 horas o más, aún cuando no perciban un sueldo o salario (trabajador familiar); (c) tienen una ocupación fija remunerada, pero no la ejercieron ningún día del período de referencia por una circunstancia transitoria: debido a enfermedad o accidente, por conflictos del trabajo; por interrupción transitoria del trabajo o a causa del mal tiempo o averías en la maquinaria; por estar en uso de vacaciones, permiso o de licencia; (d) hacen trabajos ocasionales durante la semana de referencia.
Desempleo: Comprende este grupo a personas que: (a) no tenían ocupación o trabajo durante la semana de referencia de la Encuesta, pero habían trabajado antes y estaban buscando empleo; (b) nunca habían trabajado o buscaban su primer empleo en la semana de referencia; (c) no estaban buscando trabajo en la semana de referencia, pero buscaron trabajo los tres meses anteriores a la encuesta; (d) no estaban buscando trabajo en la semana de referencia porque manifiestan que es imposible encontrar trabajo.
Subempleo:
Subempleo por insuficiencia de horas: Subempleo por insuficiencia de horas: Comprende este grupo a personas que trabajan menos de 40 horas en todos sus empleos en forma involuntaria y desean trabajar más horas de las que trabajaron la semana de referencia
Situaciones de empleo inadecuado: se utilizó el ingreso en base al salario mínimo.
Horas de trabajo: Se refiere al número de horas efectivamente trabajadas en el trabajo principal y secundario durante la semana de referencia.

Ingresos relacionados con el empleo:
Ingresos relacionados con el empleo asalariado: Se refiere al salario bruto (sin deducir impuestos ni contribuciones al Seguro Social). También se obtiene información sobre los ingresos en especie y décimo tercer mes.
Ingresos relacionados con el empleo independiente: Se investiga el ingreso mensual neto (entradas menos gastos en la actividad). También se obtiene información sobre los ingresos en especie, ingresos de actividades informales ("camarones"), ingresos agropecuarios.
Sector informal: se refiere solo al empleo principal y al sector no agrícola y se define con base en el tipo de contratación, la categoría de ocupación, tamaño de la empresa y la ocupación.
Actividad habitual: No información.
Clasificaciones:
Rama de actividad económica (industria):
Título de la clasificación utilizada: No información.
Grupos de población clasificados por industria: Ocupados y desocupados.
Número de Grupos utilizados para la codificación: 165 grupos.
Vínculos con la CIIU: CIU- Rev.3.
Ocupación:
Título de la clasificación utilizada: No información.
Grupos de población clasificados por ocupación : Ocupados y desocupados.
Número de Grupos utilizados para la codificación: 29 subgrupos principales, 412 grupos primarios y 1 653 ocupaciones específicas.
Vínculos con la CIUO: CIUO-88.
Situación en el empleo:
Título de la clasificación utilizada: No información.
Grupos de población clasificados por ocupación: Ocupados y desocupados.
Grupos utilizados para la codificación: empleado; patrono; cuenta propia; servicio doméstico; trabajador familiar; miembro de cooperativa de productores.
Vínculos con CISE: CISE-1993.
Educación:
Título de la clasificación utilizada: No información.
Grupos de población clasificados por educación: Todas las personas de 5 años y más.
Grupos utilizados para la codificación: ningún grado; enseñanza primaria; enseñanza secundaria; enseñanza superior universitaria; vocacional.
Vínculos con la CINE: no disponible.
Tamaño y diseño de la muestra:
Unidad final de muestreo: viviendas particulares ocupadas.
Tamaño de la muestra (unidades finales de muestreo): 13 500 viviendas particulares.
Fracción de muestra : 0.00749 - 0.05256 en el área urbana, 0.01354 - 0.06559 en el área rural.
Marco de la muestra: Segmentos censales o áreas de empadronamiento del Censo del 2000. En el área urbana el segmento censal tiene un promedio de 12 viviendas particulares, en el área rural, 10.
Actualización de la muestra: Se incorporan nuevas construcciones anualmente.
Rotación:
Esquema: la muestra se realiza tres veces al año y se rotan 25% de las UPM en cada ronda.
Porcentaje de unidades que permanecen en la muestra durante dos encuestas consecutivas: 75%.
Número máximo de entrevistas por unidad de muestreo: 4.
Tiempo necesario para renovar completamente la muestra: 4 año y medio.
Levantamiento da la encuesta:
Tipo de entrevista: entrevista personal.
Número de unidades finales de muestro **Por área de muestra:** 2 032 UPMs.
Duración del trabajo de campo:
Total: 1 mes (comenzando el 1 de marzo, 1 de agosto y 16 de noviembre)
Por área de muestra: 1 día.
Organización de la encuesta: se contrata personal para cada encuesta.
Número de personas que trabajan en el campo: 227 personas: 176 empadronadores y 51 supervisores.
Substitución de las unidades finales de muestreo que no responden: no.

Estimaciones y ajustes:
Tasa de no-respuesta total: 3%.
Ajuste por no-respuesta total: no.
Imputación por no-respuesta de ítemes: no.
Ajuste por áreas/poblaciones no abarcadas: no.
Ajuste por falta de cobertura: no.
Ajuste por exceso de cobertura: no.
Ajuste por variaciones estacionales: no.
Historia de la encuesta:
Título y fecha de la primera encuesta: Encuesta de Hogares 1963.
Modificaciones y revisiones significativas: no disponible.
Documentación y difusión:
Documentación:
Resultados de la encuesta: Estadística del Trabajo, volúmen I. Encuesta de Hogares. Estadística Panameña - Cifras Preliminares. Manual del Encuestador y Supervisor (bianual)
Metodología de la encuesta: idem.
Difusión:
Tiempo necesario para difundir los primeros datos: 2 meses.
Información adelantada acerca de la fecha de la primera difusión pública: sí.
Disponibilidad de datos no publicados si se solicitan: sí.
Disponibilidad de datos por medios informáticas: diskette.

Perú

Título de la encuesta: Encuesta Especializada de Niveles de Empleo.
Organismo responsable de la encuesta:
Planificar y realizar la encuesta: Dirección Nacional de Censos y Encuestas (DNCE), Instituto Nacional de Estadística e Informática (INEI).
Analizar y publicar los resultados: Dirección Técnica de Demografía y Estudios Sociales (DTDES), INEI.
Temas abarcados: Empleo, desempleo, subempleo, horas de trabajo, salarios, ingresos, duración del empleo y del desempleo, trabajadores desalentados, ramas de actividad económica, ocupación, situación en el empleo, nivel de educación, actividad habitual, trabajos secundarios, características del trabajo anterior (para los desocupados e inactivos), seguridad social y migración.
Alcance de la encuesta:
Ámbito geográfico: abarca el total del país, áreas urbanas y rurales en los 24 departamentos y la provincia constitucional del Callao.
Grupos de población: Se incluyen a todos los residentes habituales del hogar, que en el momento de la entrevista cumplían con al menos uno de los siguientes requisitos: (a) eran miembros del hogar familiar y se encontraban habitando el hogar familiar independientemente del número de días; (b) se hallaban presentes 30 días o más en el hogar aunque no eran miembros del hogar familiar; (c) eran trabajadores domésticos que dormían en el hogar, independientemente del número de días que se encuentran en el hogar; (d) personas que son miembros del hogar pero que no se encuentran en su residencia habitual durante el periodo de la encuesta. Se excluyen (a) la población no residente, (b) los extranjeros que están de visita, (c) las personas que viajaron al extranjero en busca de trabajo, (d) las personas en tránsito, etc.
Disponibilidad de estimaciones de otras fuentes para las áreas/grupos excluidos: no disponible.
Grupos abarcados por la encuesta pero excluidos de los resultados publicados: ninguno.
Periodicidad:
Recolección de datos: anual.
Publicación de los datos:anual.
Períodos de referencia:
Empleo: una semana.
Búsqueda de trabajo: una semana.
Disponibilidad para trabajo: una semana.
Conceptos y definiciones:
Empleo: Comprende a las personas de 14 años y más de ambos sexos que durante la semana de referencia (a) estuvieron participando en alguna actividad económica; (b) eran trabajadores dependientes con empleo fijo pero que no trabajaron por hallarse de vacaciones, huelga, licencia por enfermedad, licencia pre y post natal, todas ellas pagadas; (c) eran trabajadores independientes pero no trabajaron aunque la empresa o negocio siguió funcionando; (d) no se encontraban en ninguna de las situaciones anteriores pero que después de indagar por actividades económicas, se encontró que trabajaron al menos una hora por pago en dinero y/o

en especie. Los trabajadores familiares auxiliares se incluyen si trabajaron al menos 15 horas durante la semana de referencia.

Desempleo: Personas de 14 años y más que durante el período de referencia estuvieron (a) sin empleo, es decir que no tenían ningún empleo como asalariado o como independiente; (b) actualmente disponible para trabajar, es decir, con disponibilidad para trabajar en un empleo asalariado o independiente; (c) en busca de empleo, es decir, que habían tomado acciones concretas para buscar un empleo asalariado o independiente en un período de referencia especificado.

Subempleo:

Subempleo por insuficiencia de horas: incluye a las personas de 14 años y más que trabajaron menos de la jornada normal y querían y estaban disponibles para trabajar más horas. También se obtiene información acerca de la cantidad de horas que están dispuestas a trabajar.

Situaciones de empleo inadecuado: No información.

Horas de trabajo: Son las horas efectivamente trabajadas por los ocupados, incluyendo las horas extraordinarias y excluyendo los permisos, licencias, tiempo de refrigerio, tiempo de traslado del domicilio al centro de trabajo y viceversa, etc. Se obtienen las horas trabajadas en el empleo principal y en todos los empleos secundarios.

Ingresos relacionados con el empleo:

Ingreso **Total:** son los ingresos monetarios recibidos por trabajos realizados para un empleador o patrono y comprende: sueldos, salarios, ingresos por horas extras, bonificaciones, pago por concepto de refrigerio y movilidad, comisiones, etc. antes de efectuar los descuentos de ley y otros descuentos, siempre que estos ingresos se obtengan de forma regular o permanente.

Ingresos relacionados con el empleo asalariado: ingresos en efectivo regulares, pago en especie, remuneraciones relacionadas con los beneficios, indemnizaciones. Se capta el ingreso total e ingreso líquido después de deducidas las contribuciones a ESSALUD, AFP, sistemas de pensiones y otros descuentos (judiciales, cooperativas, bancos, asociaciones, etc.) Se obtienen datos de ingresos para el empleo principal y empleos secundarios separadamente utilizando varios períodos de referencia: día, semana, quincena y mes anterior a la entrevista.

Ingresos relacionados con el empleo independiente: Son los ingresos monetarios del trabajo por cuenta propia y los ingresos por autoconsumo o autosuministro. Se obtiene información por separado acerca del (a) ingreso bruto, (b) los gastos de materiales y mercaderías (capital fijo), (c) el autconsumo, (d) el autosuministro, (e) las ganancias netas (ingreso deducidos los gastos por materia prima e insumos, materiales, mano de obra y otros gastos de operación y antes de deducir los impuestos); y para el empleo principal y secundarios, utilizando varios períodos de referencia (día, semana, etc.).

Sector informal: No información.

Actividad habitual: se obtiene información acerca de la actividad económica (empleo y desempleo) en los últimos 12 meses. El objetivo es evaluar la movilidad en la condición de actividad de esta población y los flujos de entrada en el mercado laboral.

Clasificaciones:

Rama de actividad económica (industria):

Titulo de la clasificación utilizada: No información.

Grupos de población clasificados por industria: Ocupados y desocupados con experiencia de trabajo.

Número de Grupos utilizados para la codificación: se utiliza CIIU_Rev.3 a tres dígitos.

Vínculos con la CIIU: CIIU-Rev.3.

Ocupación:

Titulo de la clasificación utilizada: No información.

Grupos de población clasificados por ocupación: Ocupados y desocupados con experiencia de trabajo.

Número de Grupos utilizados para la codificación: se utiliza CIUO-88 a tres dígitos.

Vínculos con la CIUO: CIUO-88.

Situación en el empleo:

Titulo de la clasificación utilizada: No información.

Grupos de población clasificados por situación en el empleo: Ocupados, desocupados con experiencia de trabajo e inactivos.

Grupos utilizados para la codificación: empleador o patrono, trabajador independiente, empleado, obrero, trabajador familiar no remunerado, trabajadora del hogar u otro.

Vínculos con la ICSE: ICSE-19993.

Educación:

Titulo de la clasificación utilizada: No información.

Grupos de población clasificados por educación: Ocupados, desocupados e inactivos.

Grupos utilizados para la codificación: sin nivel, inicial, primaria incompleta, primaria completa, secundaria incompleta, secundaria completa, superior no universitaria incompleta, superior no universitaria completa, superior universitaria incompleta, superior universitaria completa.

Vínculos con la CINE: sí

Tamaño y diseño de la muestra:

Unidad final de la muestreo: vivienda particular.

Tamaño de la muestra (unidades finales de muestreo): 11 960 viviendas, 8 610 en el área urbana y 3 350 en el área rural.

Fracción de muestreo: 1/458.

Marco de la muestra: basado en la información del Censo de Población y Vivienda de 1993 y el material cartográfico respectivo.

Actualización de la muestra: La información del marco muestral ha sido actualizada en 1999 en las capitales departamentales. Las unidades secundarias de muestreo seleccionadas tienen un promedio de 100 viviendas y se acutalizan antes de la ejecución de la encuesta.

Rotación:

Esquema: no existe rotación ya que se cuenta con muestras independientes y muestras paneles.

Porcentaje de unidades que permanecen en la muestra durante dos encuestas consecutivas: No información.

Número máximo de entrevistas por unidad de muestreo: 3.

Tiempo necesario para renovar completamente la muestra: 1 año.

Levantamiento da la encuesta:

Tipo de entrevista: entrevista directa o personal.

Número de unidades finales de muestreo por área de muestra: 10 viviendas en cada conglomerado.

Duración del trabajo de campo:

Total: se organiza en 6 períodos de 9 días cada uno por trimestre (5 días de trabajo de campo, 2 días de recuperación de viviendas incompletas, 1 día de trabajo en la oficina y 1 día de descanso).

Por área de muestra: No información.

Organización de la encuesta: se contrata personal especialmente para cada encuesta.

Número de personas que trabajan en el campo: No información.

Substitución de las unidades finales de muestreo que no responden: no.

Estimaciones y ajustes:

Tasa de no-respuesta total: 12%.

Ajuste por no-respuesta total: sí.

Imputación por no respuesta de ítemes: no.

Ajuste por áreas/poblaciones no abarcadas: no.

Ajuste por falta de cobertura: no.

Ajuste por exceso de cobertura: no.

Ajuste por variaciones estacionales: sí.

Historia de la encuesta:

Titulo y fecha de la primera encuesta: Encuesta Especializada de niveles de empleo, III trimestre de 1996.

Modificaciones y revisiones significativas: en el III trimestre de 1997.

Documentación y difusión:

Documentación:

Resultados de la encuesta: Perú: Trabajo Infantil y Adolescente (octubre 1998);

Perú: Mercado Laboral Urbano y Género (octubre 2000); Perú: Condición Socio-Económica de la Población Urbana que Trabaja por Primera Vez (diciembre 2000); Correspondencia del nivel Educativo con la Ocupación Desempeñada (por publicar).

Metodología de la encuesta: idem.

Difusión:

Tiempo necesario para difundir los primeros datos: No información.

Información adelantada acerca de la fecha de la primera difusión pública: no.

Disponibilidad de datos no publicados si se solicitan: sí.

Disponibilidad de datos por medios informáticos: CD, disquette, cinta magnética. Sitio web: http://www.inei.gob.pe.

Polonia

Título de la encuesta: Encuesta sobre la Fuerza de Trabajo (The Labour Force Survey).

Organismo responsable de la encuesta:

Planificar y realizar la encuesta: Oficina Central de Estadísticas, División de Estadísticas del Trabajo (Central Statistical Office, Labour Statistics Division).

Analizar y publicar los resultados: Oficina Central de Estadísticas, División de Estadísticas del Trabajo (Central Statistical Office, Labour Statistics Division).

Temas abarcados: Empleo, desempleo, subempleo, horas de trabajo, salarios, duración del empleo, duración del desempleo, trabajadores desalentados, trabajadores ocasionales, rama de actividad económica (industria), ocupación, situación en el empleo, nivel de educación, empleo secundario.

Alcance de la encuesta:

Ámbito geográfico: Todo el país.

Grupos de población: Todas las personas de 15 años y más de edad que son miembros de hogares privados seleccionados para la encuesta, incluidos miembros ausentes del hogar por menos de dos meses por razones como viaje de negocios, etc., y personas ausentes por más de dos meses, como marineros, pescadores, etc.

Se excluyen:

1.personas que viven en hogares colectivos (por ejemplo, residencias de trabajadores y estudiantes, internados, cuarteles militares, hogares de personas mayores, etc.);

2.reclusos de instituciones penales y psiquiátricas;

3. miembros de hogares privados que residen por más de dos meses en el extranjero;

4.invitados temporeros que permanecen menos de dos meses en un determinado hogar,

5.extranjeros.

Disponibilidad de estimaciones de otras fuentes para las áreas/grupos excluidos: No disponible.

Grupos abarcados por la encuesta pero excluidos de los resultados publicados: No disponible.

Periodicidad:

Recolección de datos: Continua.

Publicación de los resultados: Trimestralmente.

Periodo de referencia:

Empleo: Una semana (periodo de referencia móvil).

Búsqueda de trabajo: Cuatro semanas (la semana de referencia es la 4 a semana).

Disponibilidad para trabajo: Dos semanas (el periodo de referencia más la semana siguiente).

Conceptos y definiciones:

Empleo: Personas de 15 años y más de edad que en la semana de referencia:

-realizaron algún trabajo remunerado o por un beneficio, por lo menos durante una hora, como empleados asalariados, trabajaron en su propia explotación agrícola o negocio no agrícola, ayudaron sin remuneración (trabajadores que contribuyen con la familia) en la explotación de un negocio familiar no agrícola;

-no realizaron ningún trabajo por razones como enfermedad, vacaciones, licencia, suspensión de trabajo en la empresa, huelga, mal tiempo, etc., pero mantenían vínculos oficiales con el trabajo como empleados o empleados independientes (empleador o trabajador por cuenta propia).

Se consideran también como empleados los aprendices en formación profesional remunerados o con contratos previos pagados por su futuro empleador (privado o público) durante el periodo de formación contractual.

También se incluyen:

a)personas suspendidas temporalmente de su trabajo sin remuneración o con licencia sin goce de sueldo por iniciativa del empleador;

b)trabajadores a tiempo completo o parcial que buscaban otro empleo durante la semana de referencia;

c)personas que realizaron algún trabajo remunerado o por un beneficio durante la semana de referencia, pero que estaban sometidas a escolaridad obligatoria o eran estudiantes de dedicación completa o parcial que trabajaban a tiempo completo o parcial; estaban jubiladas y percibían una pensión; estaban inscritas como desempleadas en busca de trabajo en una oficina de empleo o percibían indemnizaciones de desempleo;

d)participantes en planes de promoción del empleo;

e)personas ocupadas en la producción de bienes para su propio uso final;

f)todos los miembros de las fuerzas armadas, incluidos los miembros del servicio civil equivalente al servicio militar.

Desempleo: Personas de 15 años y más de edad que no estaban empleadas según los criterios antes mencionados durante la semana de referencia, estaban disponibles para trabajar durante la semana de referencia o la semana siguiente, y habían buscado activamente un empleo durante cuatro semanas (el periodo de referencia es la cuarta semana) y habían tomado medidas concretas para encontrar un empleo. Se incluyen las personas que no buscaban trabajo porque ya habían encontrado uno y estaban esperando comenzar en un periodo de 30 días.

También se incluyen:

a)personas que estaban procurando instalar su propio negocio o establecerse en el ejercicio privado de una profesión;

b) trabajadores estacionales que esperaban un empleo de temporada;

c)personas jubiladas que recibían una pensión;

d)personas sometidas a escolaridad obligatoria;

e)estudiantes de dedicación completa o parcial que buscaban un empleo a tiempo completo o parcial.

Subempleo:

Subempleo por insuficiencia de horas: Personas que trabajaban a medio tiempo por razones económicas (por ejemplo, suspensión de trabajo, licencia obligatoria, imposibilidad de encontrar un empleo a tiempo completo). (En la actualidad, se trata de cambiar la definición de trabajo para adaptarla a la nueva definición de la OIT).

Situaciones de empleo inadecuado: No corresponde.

Horas de trabajo: Número de horas realmente trabajadas por una persona en todos los empleos (principal y secundario) durante la semana de referencia.

Ingresos relacionados con el empleo:

Ingresos relacionados con el empleo asalariado: Ingresos mensuales netos del empleo asalariado a tiempo completo; se refiere al empleo principal y está relacionado con el mes anterior a la semana de referencia.

Ingresos relacionados con el empleo independiente: No corresponde.

Sector informal: No corresponde.

Actividad habitual: No corresponde.

Clasificaciones:

Rama de actividad económica (industria):

Título de la clasificación utilizada: No disponible.

Grupos de población clasificados por industria: Personas empleadas y desempleadas.

Número de Grupos utilizados para la codificación: 35 grupos.

Vínculos con la CIIU: CIIU-Rev.3.

Ocupación:

Título de la clasificación utilizada: No disponible.

Grupos de población clasificados por ocupación: Personas empleadas y desempleadas.

Número de Grupos utilizados para la codificación: 371 grupos.

Vínculos con la CIUO: CIUO-88.

Situación en el empleo:

Título de la clasificación utilizada: No disponible.

Grupos de población clasificados por situación en el empleo: Personas empleadas y desempleadas.

Grupos utilizados para la codificación: Cuatro grupos: empleados, empleadores, trabajadores por cuenta propia, trabajadores familiares no remunerados.

Vínculos con la CISE: CISE-1993.

Educación:

Título de la clasificación utilizada: No disponible.

Grupos de población clasificados por educación: Personas empleadas y desempleadas.

Grupos utilizados para la codificación: Seis grupos: Escuela primaria y primaria incompleta, escuela básica vocacional, escuela secundaria general, escuela secundaria vocacional, escuela secundaria posterior, escuela terciaria.

Vínculos con la CINE: CINE-76 y CINE-1997.

Tamaño y diseño de la muestra:

Unidad final de muestreo: Vivienda.

Tamaño de la muestra (unidades finales de muestreo): 24 400 viviendas. El total de la muestra elemental trimestral consiste de cuatro muestras elementales (muestras "e", para abreviar) independientes.

Fracción de muestreo: Asignación territorial diferenciada, desproporcionada, aproximadamente 1/2 000 de viviendas registradas para zonas urbanas y 1/1 818 para zonas rurales.

Marco de la muestra: La muestra se deriva de las unidades estadísticas geográficas del Registro de la OCE, distritos de enumeración (DE), grupos de DE o grupos del censo y unidades de viviendas del censo nacional. El registro se actualiza anualmente, teniendo en cuenta la información sobre las viviendas recién construidas, demolidas o convertidas en no residenciales al 1.o de enero.

Actualización de la muestra: Se realiza después de la actualización anual del marco.

Rotación:
Esquema: Cuatro grupos de rotación denominados muestras elementales (muestras "e", para abreviar): en un trimestre determinado, la muestra comprende dos muestras "e" encuestadas en el trimestre anterior, se introduce una nueva muestra "e" en la encuesta por primera vez y una muestra "e" introducida en el trimestre correspondiente del año anterior. Las cuatro muestras "e" trimestrales se hacen rotar de acuerdo al esquema 2-(2)-2, es decir que una unidad de vivienda se mantiene durante dos trimestres consecutivos en una muestra, se saca por dos trimestres y se vuelve a introducir por otros dos trimestres consecutivos antes de sacarla definitivamente de la muestra.
Porcentaje de unidades que permanecen en la muestra durante dos encuestas consecutivas: 50 por ciento.
Número máximo de entrevistas por unidad de muestreo: 4 veces.
Tiempo necesario para renovar completamente la muestra: 5 trimestres.
Levantamiento da la encuesta:
Tipo de entrevista: Entrevistas personales o por teléfono, con papel y lápiz.
Número de unidades finales de muestreo por área de muestra: 1 880 viviendas.
Duración del trabajo de campo:
Total: No disponible.
Por área de muestra: Una semana civil.
Organización de la encuesta: Se ha establecido una plantilla permanente de encuesta para ejecutar la nueva metodología de encuesta continua.
Número de personas que trabajan en el campo: 300.
Substitución de las unidades finales de muestreo que no responden: No.
Estimaciones y ajustes:
Tasa de no-respuesta total: 11,6 por ciento.
Ajuste por no-respuesta total: Sí.
Imputación por no respuesta de ítemes: No.
Ajuste por áreas/poblaciones no abarcadas: Sí.
Ajuste por falta de cobertura: No.
Ajuste por exceso de cobertura: No.
Ajuste por variaciones estacionales: No.
Historia de la encuesta:
Título y fecha de la primera encuesta: Encuesta sobre la Fuerza de Trabajo de 1992 (Labour Force Survey, 1992).
Modificaciones y revisiones significativas: En el 2o y 3er trimestres de 1999 se suspendió la encuesta trimestral que, a partir del 4o trimestre de 1999, pasó de periódica a continua.
En mayo de 1994, las clasificaciones económicas utilizadas se vincularon a las internacionales.
Documentación y difusión:
Documentación:
Título de las publicaciones con los resultados de la encuesta (periodicidad: Statistical Yearbook of the Republic of Poland. Labour Force Survey in Poland, (documentos de información y estadísticas) (en inglés); Quarterly Information on the Labour Market Developments (en polaco e inglés); Quarterly Economic Activity of the Population (en polaco); y Economic Activity and Unemployment in Poland (en polaco) (trimestralmente).
Título de las publicaciones con la metodología de la encuesta: Labour Force Survey in Poland.
Difusión:
Tiempo necesario para difundir los primeros datos: El mismo trimestre.
Información adelantada acerca de la fecha de la primera difusión pública: Sí.
Disponibilidad de datos no publicados si se solicitan: Sí.
Disponibilidad de datos por medios informáticos: Sí, en disquete y por correo electrónico. Sitio web: http://www.stat.gov.pl .

Portugal

Título de la encuesta: Encuesta sobre el empleo (Inquérito ao emprego).
Organismo responsable de la encuesta:
Planificar y realizar la encuesta: Instituto Nacional de Estadística (Instituto Nacional de Estatística (INE)).
Analizar y publicar los resultados: Instituto Nacional de Estadística (Instituto Nacional de Estatística (INE)).
Temas abarcados: Empleo, desempleo, subempleo, horas de trabajo, ingresos, duración del empleo y el desempleo, trabajadores desalentados, trabajadores ocasionales, empleo secundario, rama de actividad económica (industria), ocupación, situación en el empleo, nivel de educación.
Alcance de la encuesta:
Ámbito geográfico: Todo el país.
Grupos de población: Población de 15 años y más de edad que reside en viviendas privadas. Se excluyen las personas que viven en hogares colectivos si no tienen vínculos familiares con miembros de hogares privados y las personas que se alojan en hogares móviles.
Disponibilidad de estimaciones de otras fuentes para las áreas/grupos excluidos: No corresponde.
Grupos abarcados por la encuesta pero excluidos de los resultados publicados: La encuesta no abarca este punto.
Periodicidad:
Recolección de datos: Encuesta continua.
Publicación de los resultados: Trimestralmente.
Periodo de referencia:
Empleo: La semana anterior a la entrevista.
Búsqueda de trabajo: Cuatro semanas antes de la entrevista.
Disponibilidad para trabajo: Dos semanas después de la entrevista.
Conceptos y definiciones:
Empleo: Son empleadas las personas de 15 años y más de edad que, durante la semana de referencia:
a)trabajaron por una remuneración o un beneficio (en efectivo o en especie) por lo menos durante una hora;
b)no trabajaron pero tenían un empleo y un vínculo formal con el empleo;
c)eran propietarias de un negocio pero, por alguna razón, estaban ausentes del lugar de trabajo;
d)estaban en jubilación previa, pero trabajaron durante la semana de referencia.
Se incluyen también como empleados:
a)las personas con empleo pero temporalmente ausentes del mismo debido a enfermedad o lesión por un plazo máximo de 3 meses, licencia anual, licencia por maternidad, paternidad o parental, licencia para estudios o capacitación, conflictos laborales, mal tiempo, desperfectos mecánicos;
b)las personas con licencia sin goce de sueldo por iniciativa del empleador o suspendidas con o sin remuneración por un plazo máximo de 3 meses;
c)los trabajadores a tiempo completo o parcial en busca de otro empleo durante el periodo de referencia;
d)las personas que realizaron algún trabajo remunerado o por un beneficio durante la semana de referencia pero que estaban sometidas a escolaridad obligatoria, jubiladas y recibían una pensión, inscritas como desempleadas en busca de trabajo en una oficina de empleo o que percibían indemnizaciones de desempleo;
e)los estudiantes de dedicación completa o parcial que trabajaban a tiempo completo o parcial;
f)los aprendices y las personas en formación remunerados;
g)las personas que participan en planes de promoción del empleo;
h)los trabajadores familiares no remunerados;
i)los trabajadores estacionales, si la temporada comenzaba en 3 meses;
j)los voluntarios y miembros de carrera de las fuerzas armadas.
Desempleo: Personas de 15 años y más de edad que no trabajaron durante la semana de referencia, estaban disponibles para trabajar en las dos semanas siguientes, estaban buscando trabajo (es decir, habían tomado medidas específicas para buscar empleo) durante las cuatro últimas semanas o las que no estaban trabajando ni buscaban empleo pero habían encontrado un trabajo para comenzar en 3 meses.
Se incluyen también como desempleados:
a)las personas que buscaban trabajo y/o estaban disponibles para trabajar, pero estaban sometidas a escolaridad obligatoria o jubiladas y recibían una pensión;
b)los estudiantes de dedicación completa o parcial que buscaban trabajo a tiempo completo o parcial y estaban disponibles para trabajar inmediatamente.
Tomar medidas específicas para buscar trabajo significa inscribirse en una oficina de empleo pública o en un organismo privado (oficina de trabajo temporal, empresa especializada en la contratación, etc.); solicitar trabajo a empleadores; buscar la ayuda de amigos, parientes, sindicatos, etc.; publicar o responder avisos de trabajo; presentar pruebas o exámenes o tener entrevistas para conseguir a un empleo; tratar de obtener terrenos, inmuebles o equipos; solicitar permisos, licencias o recursos financieros.

Subempleo:
Subempleo por insuficiencia de horas: Personas empleadas de 15 años y más de edad que, durante la semana de referencia, deseaban trabajar horas adicionales (buscaban un empleo adicional además del empleo actual, otro trabajo con más horas que en el empleo actual o más horas en el empleo actual) y estaban disponibles para trabajar horas adicionales.
Situaciones de empleo inadecuado: Condiciones de trabajo, como nivel de enseñanza, remuneración, que, comparadas con otras, pueden llevar a una disminución de la competitividad o productividad de los trabajadores.
Horas de trabajo: Horas reales trabajadas en los empleos principal y secundarios: número de horas realmente trabajadas durante la semana de referencia, incluidas las horas extraordinarias pero se excluyen las horas de ausencia. Horas habituales en el empleo principal: número de horas habitualmente trabajadas por semana, incluidas las horas extraordinarias habituales.
Ingresos relacionados con el empleo:
Ingresos relacionados con el empleo asalariado: Ingresos netos de los empleados: ingresos mensuales de pagos ordinarios y sumas anuales para los otros tipos de pago.
Ingresos relacionados con el empleo independiente: No corresponde.
Sector informal: No corresponde.
Actividad habitual: No se dispone de información.
Clasificaciones:
Rama de actividad económica (industria):
Título de la clasificación utilizada: NACE.
Grupos de población clasificados por industria: Empleados y desempleados (rama de actividad económica del último empleo para el desempleado).
Número de Grupos utilizados para la codificación: No se dispone de información.
Vínculos con la CIIU: CIIU-Rev.3.
Ocupación:
Título de la clasificación utilizada: Clasificación Nacional de Ocupaciones (CNP 1994).
Grupos de población clasificados por ocupación: Empleados y desempleados (ocupación en el último empleo para el desempleado).
Número de Grupos utilizados para la codificación: No se dispone de información.
Vínculos con la CIUO: CIUO-88.
Situación en el empleo:
Título de la clasificación utilizada: No se dispone de información.
Grupos de población clasificados por situación en el empleo: Empleados y desempleados (situación en el último empleo para el desempleado).
Grupos utilizados para la codificación: Empleados; empleadores con empleados; trabajadores por cuenta propia sin empleados; trabajadores familiares no remunerados; otros.
Vínculos con la CISE: CISE-1993.
Educación:
Título de la clasificación utilizada: No se dispone de información.
Grupos de población clasificados por educación: Empleados y desempleados.
Grupos utilizados para la codificación: 10 grupos.
Vínculos con la CINE: No se dispone de información.
Tamaño y diseño de la muestra:
Unidad final de muestreo: Viviendas.
Tamaño de la muestra (unidades finales de muestreo): 20 747 viviendas.
Fracción de muestreo: 0,68 por ciento.
Marco de la muestra: Resultados del Censo Electoral de 1989 y el "Marco Geográfico de Referencia Espacial" utilizado para el Censo de Población y Hogares de 1991.
Actualización de la muestra: No se dispone de información.
Rotación:
Esquema: Las viviendas permanecen en la muestra durante seis trimestres consecutivos. Cada trimestre se sustituye 1/6 de la muestra.
Porcentaje de unidades que permanecen en la muestra durante dos encuestas consecutivas: 83,3 por ciento.
Número máximo de entrevistas por unidad de muestreo: Seis.
Tiempo necesario para renovar completamente la muestra: Seis trimestres.
Levantamiento de la encuesta:
Tipo de entrevista: CAPI (entrevista personal asistida por computadora).
Número de unidades finales de muestreo por área de muestra: No se dispone de información.
Duración del trabajo de campo:
Total: Encuesta continua.
Por área de muestra: No se dispone de información.
Organización de la encuesta: Se contratan entrevistadores para cada encuesta.
Número de personas que trabajan en el campo: No se dispone de información.
Substitución de las unidades finales de muestreo que no responden: No.
Estimaciones y ajustes:
Tasa de no-respuesta total: 10 por ciento.
Ajuste por no-respuesta total: No.
Imputación por no respuesta de ítemes: No.
Ajuste por áreas/poblaciones no abarcadas: No.
Ajuste por falta de cobertura: No.
Ajuste por exceso de cobertura: No.
Ajuste por variaciones estacionales: No.
Historia de la encuesta:
Título y fecha de la primera encuesta: Encuesta sobre el empleo, 1974 (Inquérito ao emprego).
Modificaciones y revisiones significativas: 1983-1997: Encuesta trimestral. Comienzos de 1998: encuesta continua, revisión del diseño de la muestra y modificaciones del cuestionario de la encuesta.
Documentación y difusión:
Documentación:
Título de las publicaciones con los resultados de la encuesta (periodicidad): Boletim Mensal de Estatística (mensualmente); Estatísticas de Emprego (trimestralmente).
Título de las publicaciones con la metodología de la encuesta (periodicidad): Estatísticas de Emprego (trimestralmente).
Difusión:
Tiempo necesario para difundir los primeros datos: Unos dos meses después de finalizar el trimestre.
Información adelantada acerca de la fecha de la primera difusión pública: Sí.
Disponibilidad de datos no publicados si se solicitan: Sí.
Disponibilidad de datos por medios informáticos: Sí. Sitio web: http://www.ine.pt

Qatar

Título de la encuesta: Encuesta por muestra sobre la Fuerza de Trabajo (Labour force sample survey), abril de 2001.
Organismo responsable de la encuesta:
Planificar y realizar la encuesta: Departamento de Estadísticas, Consejo de Planificación (Department of Statistics, Planning Council).
Analizar y publicar los resultados: Departamento de Estadísticas y Departamento de Planificación Social, Consejo de Planificación (Department of Statistics, and Department of Social Planning, Planning Council).
Temas abarcados: Situación actual en el empleo y el desempleo de la población qatari y no qatari en edad de trabajar. Ingresos, horas y patrones de trabajo de la población empleada. Nivel de educación, ocupación actual o último empleo, rama de actividad económica (industria), situación en el empleo, sector de empleo y duración del empleo de personas corrientemente empleadas y desempleadas con experiencia previa de trabajo. Duración y métodos de búsqueda de trabajo corrientemente utilizados por los desempleados para buscar trabajo, y utilizados con anterioridad por los empleados para obtener el empleo actual. Participación en programas de capacitación y razones para no buscar trabajo en el sector privado o mixto para los desempleados qatari. Razones de la inactividad económica de la población que corrientemente no forma parte de la población activa.
Alcance de la encuesta:
Ámbito geográfico: Toda la nación.
Grupos de población: Todas las personas residentes qatari y no qatari que no viven en hogares colectivos. Se incluyen también las personas no qatari que viven en recintos y hogares colectivos.
Disponibilidad de estimaciones de otras fuentes para las áreas/grupos excluidos: No disponible.
Grupos abarcados por la encuesta pero excluidos de los resultados publicados: La encuesta sobre la fuerza de trabajo incluye las personas de 12 años y más de edad, pero debido al pequeño número de trabajadores que tienen entre 12 y 14 años de edad, los resultados publicados se limitan a la población que tiene 15 años y

más de edad. Sin embargo, se pueden obtener los datos omitidos sobre esa población más joven.

Periodicidad:

Recolección de datos: Ocasional.

Publicación de los resultados: Todavía no se han publicado.

Periodo de referencia:

Empleo: Semana de referencia fija: del 24 al 30 de marzo de 2001.

Búsqueda de trabajo: Búsqueda activa de trabajo del desempleado durante el mes anterior. Con todo, la información no se utiliza para clasificar al entrevistado como desempleado.

Disponibilidad para trabajo: La disponibilidad para trabajar no se examina explícitamente en el cuestionario.

Conceptos y definiciones:

Empleo: Personas de 12 años y más de edad que realizaron algún trabajo, durante una hora por lo menos, en cualquier día de la semana de la encuesta, o que tenían un vínculo oficial con un empleo pero estaban temporalmente ausentes del mismo, con o sin licencia, por cualquier motivo durante la semana de la encuesta. La palabra "trabajo" se define ampliamente en términos de trabajo por remuneración, beneficio o ingreso familiar.

Desempleo: Personas de 12 años y más de edad que no trabajaron, ni una hora, durante la semana de la encuesta, no estaban temporalmente ausentes del trabajo ni tenían un vínculo oficial con un empleo y comunicaron que no encontraron un empleo durante la semana de la encuesta.

Subempleo:

Subempleo por insuficiencia de horas: No se define de manera explícita, pero el subempleo por insuficiencia de horas se puede obtener a partir de dos cuestiones: personas empleadas que trabajaron menos de 6 días durante la semana de la encuesta por falta de oportunidades de trabajo en los otros días de la semana.

Situaciones de empleo inadecuado: No corresponde.

Horas de trabajo: Tres conceptos: Número de días realmente trabajados durante la semana de la encuesta. Número de horas reales trabajadas durante la semana de la encuesta, incluidas las horas extraordinarias. Horas normales de trabajo semanal. Las horas reales trabajadas abarcan el total de horas ocupadas en el trabajo, incluidas las horas extraordinarias, tiempo de mantenimiento, tiempo de espera y breves periodos de descanso. Se excluyen las horas pagadas pero no trabajadas, las horas de comida y de transporte.

Ingresos relacionados con el empleo:

Ingresos relacionados con el empleo asalariado: Ingresos totales de empleados durante el último periodo de pago. El periodo de pago puede ser diario, semanal o mensual. El ingreso se define como el sueldo neto total, incluido el pago de horas extraordinarias básicas, bonificaciones, compensaciones especiales en relación con el tipo de trabajo, subsidio de vivienda, subsidio familiar, gastos de transporte, subsidios alimenticios y otros tipos de subsidios.

Ingresos relacionados con el empleo independiente: No corresponde.

Sector informal: No se dispone de información.

Actividad habitual: No se dispone de información.

Clasificaciones:

Las clasificaciones utilizadas en la encuesta de 2001 sobre la fuerza de trabajo en Qatar son las que se prepararon para el Censo de población y hogares de marzo de 1997.

Rama de actividad económica (industria):

Título de la clasificación utilizada: Clasificación Nacional Uniforme de Actividades Económicas (The National Standard Classification of Economic Activities) (mayo de 1996).

Grupos de población clasificados por industria: Personas empleadas y desempleadas con experiencia previa de trabajo.

Número de Grupos utilizados para la codificación: Nivel de 4 dígitos; los resultados se publican a nivel de 1 dígito, 18 categorías.

Vínculos con la CIIU: CIIU-Rev.3.

Ocupación:

Título de la clasificación utilizada: Clasificación Uniforme de Ocupaciones (The Standard Classification of Occupations) (mayo de 1996).

Grupos de población clasificados por ocupación: Personas empleadas y desempleadas con experiencia previa de trabajo.

Número de Grupos utilizados para la codificación: Nivel de 4 dígitos; los resultados se publican a nivel de 1 dígito.

Vínculos con la CIUO: CIUO-88.

Situación en el empleo:

Título de la clasificación utilizada: No se dispone de información.

Grupos de población clasificados por situación en el empleo: Personas empleadas únicamente.

Grupos utilizados para la codificación: Empleadores. Trabajadores por cuenta propia. Empleados. Trabajadores familiares no remunerados. Otro.

Vínculos con la CISE: CISE-1966.

Educación:

Título de la clasificación utilizada: No se dispone de información.

Grupos de población clasificados por educación: Población de 10 años y más de edad.

Grupos utilizados para la codificación: Codificación a nivel de 5 dígitos; los resultados se publican a nivel de 1 dígito para el nivel de educación. La codificación de 5 dígitos se utiliza para la especialización de la población que tiene educación secundaria o superior.

Vínculos con la CINE: CINE 1977.

Tamaño y diseño de la muestra:

Unidad final de muestreo: Hogares.

Tamaño de la muestra (unidades finales de muestreo): 1 956 hogares qatari, 1 892 hogares no qatari y 4 287 hogares colectivos.

Fracción de muestreo: 5 por ciento.

Marco de la muestra: Zonas de enumeración del Censo de población y hogares de 1997. Muestreo de dos etapas: Las unidades primarias de muestreo (UPM) se forman reuniendo grupos contiguos de bloques del censo (zonas de enumeración) de manera que cada UPM contiene por lo menos 25 unidades finales de muestreo (hogares en el caso de hogares qatari y no qatari, y particulares en el caso de hogares colectivos). Para respetar en la mayor medida posible la estructura administrativa de Qatar, se reduce al mínimo el número de UPM que atraviesan zonas administrativas y se evitan las que pasan por límites municipales. Para fines prácticos, las UPM muy grandes de estratos de hogares colectivos se dividen en partes.

Las UPM se muestrean en función del tamaño, medido en términos del número de hogares en el caso de los dos primeros estratos y de particulares en el caso del tercer estrato. El tamaño medido se determina de acuerdo con el censo de 1997. En la segunda etapa, se seleccionan 20 hogares en cada UPM. En el caso de hogares colectivos, las unidades primarias de muestreo se dividen en UPM urbanas o rurales.

En la segunda etapa, en cada UPM se selecciona una muestra de 20 hogares en los dos estratos de hogares qatari y no qatari, de acuerdo con un plan sistemático de muestreo. En el caso de hogares colectivos, se seleccionan sistemáticamente 50 personas de cada lista del UPM muestreado.

Actualización de la muestra: Actualización a nivel de lista de la UPM muestreada.

Rotación: Ninguna.

Levantamiento da la encuesta:

Tipo de entrevista: Entrevista personal.

Número de unidades finales de muestreo por área de muestra: Unos 20 hogares en el caso de hogares qatari y no qatari, y 50 particulares en el caso de hogares colectivos.

Duración del trabajo de campo:

Total: Las listas de UPM se prepararon en febrero de 2001. Las entrevistas se realizaron en abril de 2001.

Por área de muestra: 3 a 4 hogares diarios en el caso de hogares qatari y no qatari, y unas 20 a 24 personas diarias en el caso de hogares colectivos.

Organización de la encuesta: Según las necesidades.

Número de personas que trabajan en el campo: 64 entrevistadores y 15 supervisores.

Substitución de las unidades finales de muestreo que no responden: No.

Estimaciones y ajustes:

Tasa de no-respuesta total: 3,6 por ciento en hogares qatari y 1,3 por ciento en hogares no qatari.

Ajuste por no-respuesta total: Sí, mediante la inversión de la tasa de respuesta en los estratos.

Imputación por no respuesta de ítemes: Sí, principales grupos.

Ajuste por áreas/poblaciones no abarcadas: No.

Ajuste por falta de cobertura: Sí, por estimación de la tasa de la población qatari y no qatari prevista. Asimismo, por mínimos cuadrados generalizados para la distribución por sexo y edad de los resultados del Censo de la población qatari de 1997.

Ajuste por exceso de cobertura: No disponible.

Ajuste por variaciones estacionales: No.

Historia de la encuesta:

Título y fecha de la primera encuesta: Encuesta por muestra de la fuerza de trabajo, 1993 (Labour force sample survey, 1993).

Modificaciones y revisiones significativas: La encuesta de 2001 sobre la fuerza de trabajo de Qatar se realizó después de una serie de encuestas limitadas de hogares realizadas en 1984, 1989 y 1993. Las encuestas de 1984 y 1989 fueron sobre ingresos y gastos de los hogares, con información limitada sobre las características del empleo de la población. La encuesta de 1993 fue sobre la fuerza de trabajo, pero sus resultados no se publicaron.

Documentación y difusión:

Documentación:

Título de las publicaciones con los resultados de la encuesta: En preparación. Diciembre de 2001.

Título de las publicaciones con la metodología de la encuesta: En preparación. Dieciembre de 2001.

Difusión:

Tiempo necesario para difundir los primeros datos: 8 meses.

Información adelantada acerca de la fecha de la primera difusión pública: No.

Disponibilidad de datos no publicados si se solicitan: Sí.

Disponibilidad de datos por medios informáticos: Se pueden obtener en disquestes, previa solicitud, datos tabulados.

Reino Unido

Título de la encuesta: Encuesta sobre la Fuerza de Trabajo (Labour Force Survey).

Organismo responsable de la encuesta:

Planificar y realizar la encuesta: Oficina de Estadísticas Nacionales (Office for National Statistics).

Analizar y publicar los resultados: Oficina de Estadísticas Nacionales (Office for National Statistics).

Temas abarcados: Empleo, desempleo, subempleo, horas de trabajo, salarios, duración del empleo, duración del desempleo, trabajadores desalentados, rama de actividad económica (industria), ocupación, situación en el empleo, nivel de educación, empleo secundario.

Otros temas incluidos: ingresos, discapacidad, enseñanza y capacitación, desplazamientos por razones de trabajo, enfermedad, representación sindical, indemnizaciones y salud.

Alcance de la encuesta:

Ámbito geográfico: Todo el país.

Grupos de población: Todas las personas de 16 años y más de edad que viven en hogares privados, incluido el personal de carrera de las fuerzas armadas, los estudiantes que viven en pensionados (enumerados en la dirección de los padres) y el personal del Servicio Nacional de Salud (NHS) y de hospitales que vive en alojamientos del NHS o consorcios hospitalarios. Se excluye la población que vive en hogares colectivos y bases comunales de las fuerzas armadas. Para las personas menores de 16 años sólo se recopilan datos demográficos. La edad de trabajo en el Reino Unido es de 16 a 59 años para las mujeres y de 16 a 64 para los hombres.

Disponibilidad de estimaciones de otras fuentes para las áreas/grupos excluidos: No disponible.

Grupos abarcados por la encuesta pero excluidos de los resultados publicados: Todos los grupos incluidos en la muestra se incluyen en los resultados.

Periodicidad:

Recolección de datos: La encuesta se realiza de manera continua y los resultados se publican trimestralmente.

Publicación de los resultados: Las medias sucesivas de tres meses se publican mensual, trimestral y anualmente.

Periodo de referencia:

Empleo: Una semana móvil.

Búsqueda de trabajo: Las cuatro últimas semanas (periodo de referencia móvil).

Disponibilidad para trabajo: Dos semanas (periodo de referencia móvil).

Conceptos y definiciones:

Empleo: Personas que realizaron un trabajo remunerado o por un beneficio durante una hora por lo menos por semana, incluidos los trabajadores familiares no remunerados. Las personas temporalmente ausentes del trabajo se consideran empleadas si la ausencia temporal es inferior a seis meses o si siguen recibiendo una remuneración y tienen la garantía de reintegrarse a su labor.

Se incluyen:

a)las personas ausentes por enfermedad, lesión, vacaciones, licencia anual, licencia por maternidad o paternidad, licencia para estudios o capacitación, ausencia sin autorización, conflictos laborales, mal tiempo, desperfectos mecánicos, suspendidas temporalmente o por tiempo indeterminado (6 meses) sin remuneración y con licencia sin goce de sueldo por iniciativa del empleador;

b)los trabajadores a tiempo completo o parcial que buscaban otro empleo durante la semana de referencia;

c)las personas que realizaron algún trabajo remunerado o por un beneficio durante la semana de referencia, pero que estaban jubiladas y recibían una pensión, estaban inscritas como desempleadas en busca de trabajo en una oficina de empleo o percibiendo indemnizaciones de desempleo;

d)los estudiantes de dedicación completa o parcial que trabajaban a tiempo completo o parcial;

e)los aprendices y personas en formación remunerados;

f)las personas que participan en planes de promoción del empleo;

g)los miembros de carrera y voluntarios de las fuerzas armadas.

Desempleo: Personas sin empleo durante la semana de referencia, disponibles para comenzar a trabajar en el plazo de dos semanas y que habían buscado un empleo en las cuatro semanas anteriores o que ya habían encontrado uno para comenzar en el futuro.

Se incluyen:

a)las personas que procuran establecer su propia empresa;

b)las personas jubiladas y que reciben una pensión, los trabajadores familiares no remunerados y temporalmente ausentes del trabajo y los trabajadores estacionales que no trabajan –si están disponibles y buscan empleo;

c)los estudiantes de dedicación completa o parcial que buscaban un empleo a tiempo completo o parcial.

Subempleo:

Subempleo por insuficiencia de horas: La Oficina de Estadísticas Nacionales recopila datos sobre las personas que quieren trabajar horas adicionales y pronto comenzará una evaluación de esos datos; no se publican las estimaciones sobre el subempleo por insuficiencia de horas. En el futuro se utilizará una definición de subempleo conforme a la interpretación 'operacionalizada' de Eurostat de las recomendaciones internacionales.

Situaciones de empleo inadecuado: No corresponde.

Horas de trabajo: Horas habitualmente trabajadas en el empleo principal, número real de horas trabajadas en la semana de referencia en el empleo principal y el empleo secundario, incluidas las horas extraordinarias remuneradas o no; se excluye el tiempo dedicado a las pausas de comida.

Ingresos relacionados con el empleo:

Ingresos relacionados con el empleo asalariado: Todos los ingresos en efectivo, pagos en especie, pagos relacionados con prestaciones y ciertos beneficios (sostenimiento de la renta, subsidios a las personas que buscan empleo) si los entrevistados se refieren a esos pagos. Se puede identificar tanto el pago bruto como el neto, para el empleo principal y secundario. El periodo de referencia es el que figura en la última paga global.

Ingresos relacionados con el empleo independiente: No corresponde.

Empleo en el Sector informal: No corresponde.

Actividad habitual: No corresponde.

Clasificaciones:

Rama de actividad económica (industria):

Título de la clasificación utilizada: Clasificación Industrial Uniforme de 1992 (SIC92).

Grupos de población clasificados por industria: Personas empleadas y desempleadas.

Número de Grupos utilizados para la codificación: 458.

Vínculos con la CIIU: CIIU-Rev.3 a nivel de 4 dígitos; la SIC92 es idéntica.

Ocupación:

Título de la clasificación utilizada: Clasificación Uniforme de Ocupaciones (SOC).

Grupos de población clasificados por ocupación: Personas empleadas y desempleadas.

Número de Grupos utilizados para la codificación: 374.

Vínculos con la CIUO: La SOC se vincula en la medida de lo posible a nivel de agregado. La Oficina de Estadísticas Nacionales y el Instituto de Investigaciones en materia de Empleo (Institute of Employment Research) están examinando la SOC para adptarla más a la CIUO.

Situación en el empleo:

Título de la clasificación utilizada: No disponible.

Grupos de población clasificados por situación en el empleo: Personas empleadas y desempleadas.

Grupos utilizados para la codificación: Cuatro grupos: Empleados, empleados independientes, personas en planes gubernamentales de capacitación, trabajadores familiares no remunerados.

Vínculos con la CISE: CISE-1993.

Educación:

Título de la clasificación utilizada: No disponible.

Grupos de población clasificados por educación: Personas empleadas y desempleadas.

Grupos utilizados para la codificación: Todos los grupos de la CINE.
Vínculos con la CINE: A partir de 1999, la CINE97 se puede derivar de los datos de la Encuesta sobre la Fuerza de Trabajo del Reino Unido.
Tamaño y diseño de la muestra:
Unidad final de muestreo: Dirección.
Tamaño de la muestra (unidades finales de muestreo): 88 740 direcciones.
Fracción de muestreo: Menos del 0,04 por ciento.
Marco de la muestra: El subarchivo de "pequeños usuarios" del Archivo de Direcciones del Servicio de Correos (PAF), más la lista de alojamientos del NHS/hospitales. El PAF es una lista informatizada que prepara la Oficina de Correos de todas las direcciones (puntos de entrega) a las que se expiden envíos postales. "Pequeños usuarios" son puntos de entrega que reciben menos de 25 piezas de correo al día (es sabido que incluye la mayoría de hogares privados).
Actualización de la muestra: La Oficina de Correos actualiza el PAF cada seis meses y la lista de alojamientos del NHS/hospitales se actualiza una vez cada 5 años.
Rotación:
Esquema: La muestra se divide en cinco partes iguales - cada trimestre se introduce una parte y se saca otra . Las unidades de la muestra se entrevistan una vez por trimestre.
Porcentaje de unidades que permanecen en la muestra durante dos encuestas consecutivas: 80 por ciento.
Número máximo de entrevistas por unidad de muestreo: Cinco.
Tiempo necesario para renovar completamente la muestra: Cinco trimestres.
Levantamiento de la encuesta:
Tipo de entrevista: Entrevista personal asistida por computadora (CAPI) y entrevista telefónica asistida por computadora (CATI).
Número de unidades finales de muestreo por área de muestra: (68 250 unidades finales de muestreo).
Duración del trabajo de campo:
Total: Continua durante el año.
Por área de muestra: No disponible.
Organización de la encuesta: Permanente.
Número de personas que trabajan en el campo: 420.
Substitución de las unidades finales de muestreo que no responden: No.
Estimaciones y ajustes:
Tasa de no-respuesta total: 22,3 por ciento (para la primera parte y 5,5 por ciento para las partes 2 a 5).
Ajuste por no-respuesta total: Sí.
Imputación por no respuesta de ítemes: Sí, para no respuestas y rechazos circunstanciales, los datos de la entrevista anterior se utilizan para un periodo únicamente.
Ajuste por áreas/poblaciones no abarcadas: No.
Ajuste por falta de cobertura: Sí.
Ajuste por exceso de cobertura: Sí.
Ajuste por variaciones estacionales: Sí, se utiliza el método del Censo X-11 Arima. Se utiliza un modelo único, uniforme entre series cruzadas. La imputación por no respuesta de ítemes mejora la aditividad de las series ajustadas estacionalmente. La aditividad se emplea para la mayoría de series ajustadas estacionalmente.
Historia de la encuesta:
Título y fecha de la primera encuesta: Encuesta sobre la Fuerza de Trabajo, 1973 (Labour Force Survey).
Modificaciones y revisiones significativas:
1973-1983: La encuesta se realiza en el trimestre de la primavera cada año. (Los resultados de 1973, 1975 y 1977 no se publicaron porque la encuesta tenía carácter experimental en esos años).
1984-1991: La encuesta se realiza en la primavera de cada año; varios cambios en la clasificación de grupos específicos de la actividad económica (por ejemplo, estudiantes, participantes en planes de capacitación, etc., desde inactivos hasta empleados) de conformidad con las recomendaciones internacionales.
A partir de la primavera de 1992: La encuesta se realiza de manera continua; actualización/revisión de las principales clasificaciones económicas utilizadas en la encuesta.
Documentación y difusión:
Documentación:
Título de las publicaciones con los resultados de la encuesta (periodicidad): Labour Force Survey (año) (anual); LFS User Guide, Volumen 1 (a partir de la página 130). Periodicidad: Anual.
Título de las publicaciones con la metodología de la encuesta (periodicidad): LFS User Guide, Volumen 1.
Difusión:
Tiempo necesario para difundir los primeros datos: De uno a dos meses.
Información adelantada acerca de la fecha de la primera difusión pública: Sí.
Disponibilidad de datos no publicados si se solicitan: La Oficina de Estadísticas Nacionales ofrece tabulaciones simples que no se publican a usuarios gubernamentales e instituciones internacionales. Se pueden suministrar otras tabulaciones a través de un agente comercial que exigirá un pago.
Disponibilidad de datos por medios informáticos: Sí. Sitio web: http://www.statistics.gov.uk.

Ribera occidental y Faja de Gaza

Título de la encuesta: Encuesta sobre la Fuerza de Trabajo (Labour Force Survey).
Organismo responsable de la encuesta:
Planificar y realizar la encuesta: Servicio Central de Estadísticas Palestino (Palestinian Central Bureau of Statistics - PCBS).
Analizar y publicar los resultados: Servicio Central de Estadísticas Palestino (Palestinian Central Bureau of Statistics - PCBS).
Temas abarcados: Empleo, desempleo, subempleo, horas de trabajo, salarios, duración del empleo y el desempleo, trabajadores desalentados, rama de actividad económica (industria), ocupación, situación en el empleo, nivel de educación, empleo secundario, exclusión de la población activa, días de trabajo al mes.
Alcance de la encuesta:
Ámbito geográfico: Todo el territorio.
Grupos de población: Todas las personas de 10 años y más de edad, salvo las personas que viven en instituciones y las que residen en el extranjero durante más de un año.
Disponibilidad de estimaciones de otras fuentes para las áreas/grupos excluidos: No se dispone de información.
Grupos abarcados por la encuesta pero excluidos de los resultados publicados: Personas de 10 a 14 años de edad.
Periodicidad:
Recolección de datos: Encuesta continua.
Publicación de los resultados: Trimestral y anualmente.
Periodo de referencia:
Empleo: Semana de referencia móvil. La semana que finaliza el viernes anterior a la visita del entrevistador al hogar.
Búsqueda de trabajo: Semana de referencia móvil. La semana que finaliza el viernes anterior a la visita del entrevistador al hogar.
Disponibilidad para trabajo: Semana de referencia móvil. La semana que finaliza el viernes anterior a la visita del entrevistador al hogar.
Conceptos y definiciones:
Empleo: Personas de 15 años y más de edad que trabajaron por lo menos una hora durante el periodo de referencia, o que no estaban en el trabajo durante la semana de referencia, pero tenían un empleo o eran propietarios de un negocio del que estaban temporalmente ausentes (por enfermedad, vacaciones, suspensión temporal, licencia por maternidad o parental, licencia para estudios o capacitación, o cualquier otro motivo).
Se consideran también empleados:
a)las personas suspendidas de su trabajo temporalmente sin remuneración;
b)los trabajadores a tiempo completo o parcial que buscaban otro empleo durante la semana de referencia;
c)los estudiantes de dedicación completa o parcial que trabajaban a tiempo completo o parcial;
d)los aprendices y las personas en formación remunerados o no;
e)los trabajadores familiares no remunerados (en el trabajo o temporalmente ausentes del mismo durante la semana de referencia);
f)los miembros de las fuerzas armadas (voluntarios, miembros de carrera y reclutas).
Desempleo: Personas de 15 años y más de edad que no trabajaron durante la semana de referencia, no estaban ausentes del trabajo, estaban disponibles para trabajar y buscaban actividamente un empleo durante la semana de referencia. Buscar trabajo se define como tomar medidas concretas, durante la semana de referencia, para encontrar un empleo asalariado o trabajar como empleado independiente. Los desempleados en busca de trabajo se dividen en:
i)disponible para trabajar: persona dispuesta a trabajar si se le ofrece un empleo, y no hay razones para impedirle que acepte ese empleo aunque no hizo nada para obtenerlo;
ii)busca trabajo activamente: persona que desea trabajar y busca trabajo activamente (lee los avisos de trabajo en los periódicos,

pide ayuda a los amigos, se inscribe en las oficinas de intercambio laboral o solicita trabajo a los empleadores).
Se consideran también desempleados:
a)las personas que trabajaban en Israel y estaban ausentes del trabajo debido a la clausura del lugar de trabajo;
b)las personas suspendidas de su trabajo temporalmente o por tiempo indeterminado sin remuneración o con licencia sin goce de sueldo por iniciativa del empleador;
c)las personas sin empleo y corrientemente disponibles para trabajar que habían tomado disposiciones para comenzar un nuevo empleo en una fecha ulterior a la semana de referencia o que procuraban establecer su propia empresa;
d)los estudiantes de dedicación completa o parcial, disponibles para trabajar, que buscan trabajo a tiempo completo o parcial.
Subempleo:
Subempleo por insuficiencia de horas: Personas que trabajaron menos de 35 horas durante la semana de referencia o que trabajaron menos que las horas normales de trabajo en su ocupación.
Situaciones de empleo inadecuado: Uso inadecuado de los recursos laborales o desequilibrio básico entre factores laborales y de otro tipo, tales como ingresos insuficientes, subutilización, malas condiciones en el empleo actual u otras razones económicas.
Horas de trabajo: Número total de horas realmente trabajadas durante la semana de referencia, así como horas extraordinarias y tiempo pasado en el lugar de trabajo en actividades como la preparación del lugar de trabajo. Se excluyen de las horas de trabajo las licencias, las pausas para comidas y los desplazamiento entre el hogar y el trabajo y viceversa.
Ingresos relacionados con el empleo:
Ingresos relacionados con el empleo asalariado: La encuesta no abarca este punto.
Ingresos relacionados con el empleo independiente: La encuesta no abarca este punto.
Sector informal: La encuesta no abarca este punto.
Actividad habitual: La encuesta no abarca este punto.
Clasificaciones:
Rama de actividad económica (industria):
Título de la clasificación utilizada: Clasificación nacional basada en la CIIU-Rev.3.
Grupos de población clasificados por industria: Personas empleadas y desempleadas con experiencia previa de trabajo durante los últimos 12 meses.
Número de Grupos utilizados para la codificación: Nivel de 4 dígitos.
Vínculos con la CIIU: CIIU-Rev.3.
Ocupación:
Título de la clasificación utilizada: Clasificación nacional basada en la CIUO-88.
Grupos de población clasificados por ocupación: Personas empleadas y desempleadas con experiencia previa de trabajo durante los últimos 12 meses.
Número de Grupos utilizados para la codificación: Nivel de 3 dígitos.
Vínculos con la CIUO: CIUO-88.
Situación en el empleo:
Título de la clasificación utilizada: Clasificación nacional.
Grupos de población clasificados por situación en el empleo: Personas empleadas y desempleadas con experiencia previa de trabajo durante los últimos 12 meses.
Grupos utilizados para la codificación: Empleadores, empleados, trabajadores independientes, trabajadores familiares no remunerados, otros.
Vínculos con la CISE: CISE-1993.
Educación:
Título de la clasificación utilizada: Clasificación nacional.
Grupos de población clasificados por educación: Todas las personas de 10 años y más de edad.
Grupos utilizados para la codificación: Analfabetos; saben leer y escribir; educación elemental; preparatorio; educación secundaria; diploma asociado, BA/BS, diploma superior; licenciatura, doctorado.
Vínculos con la CINE: CINE-76.
Tamaño y diseño de la muestra:
Unidad final de muestreo: Hogares.
Tamaño de la muestra (unidades finales de muestreo): Unos 7 600 hogares que abarcan casi 22 000 personas en edad de trabajar.
Fracción de muestreo: 1,7 por ciento.
Marco de la muestra: La muestra principal se basa en el Censo de Hogares y Establecimientos de 1997. La encuesta se basa en un grupo de muestras aleatorias estratificadas en dos etapas.
Actualización de la muestra: En diciembre de 1999, de conformidad con los listados de hogares.
Rotación:
Esquema: Los hogares se mantienen en la muestra durante dos encuestas consecutivas, luego se sacan en las dos encuestas siguientes y se vuelven a incluir en dos encuestas consecutivas antes de sacarlos de la muestra.
Porcentaje de unidades que permanecen en la muestra durante dos encuestas consecutivas: 50 por ciento.
Número máximo de entrevistas por unidad de muestreo: 4.
Tiempo necesario para renovar completamente la muestra: Cinco años.
Levantamiento de la encuesta:
Tipo de entrevista: Entrevista personal con papel y lápiz.
Número de unidades finales de muestreo por área de muestra: 16 hogares.
Duración del trabajo de campo:
Total: Tres meses (trabajo continuo sobre el terreno).
Por área de muestra: Dos días.
Organización de la encuesta: Permanente.
Número de personas que trabajan en el campo: Doce entrevistadores, 4 supervisores, 2 codificadores, 2 editores y 1 coordinador.
Substitución de las unidades finales de muestreo que no responden: No.
Estimaciones y ajustes:
Tasa de no-respuesta total: 9 por ciento.
Ajuste por no-respuesta total: Sí.
Imputación por no respuesta de ítemes: No.
Ajuste por áreas/poblaciones no abarcadas: No corresponde.
Ajuste por falta de cobertura: Sí.
Ajuste por exceso de cobertura: Sí.
Ajuste por variaciones estacionales: No.
Historia de la encuesta:
Título y fecha de la primera encuesta: Encuesta sobre la Fuerza de Trabajo (Labour Force Survey) 1995.
Modificaciones y revisiones significativas: No corresponde.
Documentación y difusión:
Documentación:
Título de las publicaciones con los resultados de la encuesta (periodicidad): Labour Force Survey: Main Findings (trimestralmente); Labour Force Survey: Informe Anual.
Título de las publicaciones con la metodología de la encuesta (periodicidad): Igual al de las publicaciones anteriores.
Difusión:
Tiempo necesario para difundir los primeros datos: Unos 2 meses.
Información adelantada acerca de la fecha de la primera difusión pública: Sí.
Disponibilidad de datos no publicados si se solicitan: Sí.
Disponibilidad de datos por medios informáticos: Se pueden obtener, previa solicitud, datos tabulados en medios informáticos. Sitio web: http://www.pcbs.org.

Rumania

Título de la encuesta: Encuesta de Hogares sobre la Fuerza de Trabajo (Household Labour Force Survey (AMIGO)).
Organismo responsable de la encuesta:
Planificar y realizar la encuesta: Instituto Nacional de Estadísticas (National Institute for Statistics (NIS)).
Analizar y publicar los resultados: Instituo Nacional de Estadísticas (National Institute for Statistics (NIS)).
Temas abarcados: Empleo, desempleo, subempleo, horas de trabajo, duración del empleo, trabajadores desalentados, rama de actividad económica (industria), ocupación, situación en el empleo, nivel de educación, empleo secundario.
Alcance de la encuesta:
Ámbito geográfico: Todo el país.
Grupos de población: Todos los residentes permanentes que viven en hogares seleccionados para la encuesta, incluidos quienes están temporalmente ausentes por un periodo inferior a seis meses si se mantienen en contacto con su familia, como reclutas, estudiantes y niños en edad escolar que estudian lejos de su lugar de residencia permanente, personas que trabajan en otra localidad que no es la de su residencia permanente, reclusos temporales en instituciones penales y psiquiátricas y personas que se encuentran en hospitales, así como quienes siguen un tratamiento de rehabili-

tación. Se excluyen las personas que viven de manera permanente en hogares comunes, como instituciones especializadas, hogares de personas mayores, establecimientos de minusválidos, sanatorios, etc.

Disponibilidad de estimaciones de otras fuentes para las áreas/grupos excluidos: No disponible.

Grupos abarcados por la encuesta pero excluidos de los resultados publicados: No disponible.

Periodicidad:

Recolección de datos: Encuesta permanente trimestral.

Publicación de los resultados: Trimestral y anualmente.

Periodo de referencia:

Empleo: Una semana (periodo de referencia móvil).

Búsqueda de trabajo: Cuatro semanas ulteriores.

Disponibilidad para trabajo: Próximos quince días.

Conceptos y definiciones:

Empleo: Personas de 15 años y más de edad que realizaron una actividad económica o social para producir bienes o servicios durante una hora por lo menos en el periodo de referencia (una semana), a fin de obtener algún ingreso en forma de salario, una remuneración en especie u otro beneficio. Se consideran también empleadas las personas temporalmente ausentes del trabajo pero que mantienen un vínculo oficial con el sitio de trabajo, y los miembros de las fuerzas armadas (miembros de carrera y reclutas). La duración mínima del trabajo durante la semana de referencia es de 15 horas para los empleados independientes y trabajadores familiares no remunerados en el sector de la agricultura.

Se incluyen:

a)personas con un trabajo pero temporalmente ausentes del mismo debido a enfermedad o lesión, vacaciones o licencia anual, licencia por maternidad reglamentaria, licencia parental, licencia por estudios, capacitación profesional y cursos vocacionales, huelga o conflicto laboral, interrupciones temporales debido a mal tiempo, desperfectos mecánicos, escasez de materia prima o energía, incidentes técnicos, etc.;

b)personas suspendidas que siguen recibiendo de su empleador por lo menos el 50 por ciento de su salario o sueldo o que tienen la seguridad de reincorporarse al trabajo en un periodo de tres meses;

c)personas ausentes del trabajo durante un largo periodo de tiempo (más de tres meses) si siguen recibiendo de su empleador por lo menos el 50 por ciento de su salario o sueldo;

d)trabajadores a tiempo completo o parcial que buscaban otro empleo;

e)personas que realizaron algún trabajo remunerado o por un beneficio durante la semana de referencia, pero estaban sometidas a escolaridad obligatoria, jubiladas y percibían una pensión, incluso si estaban inscritas como desempleadas en busca de trabajo en una oficina de empleo o recibían indemnizaciones de desempleo;

f)estudiantes de dedicación completa o parcial que buscaban un empleo a tiempo completo o parcial;

g)aprendices y personas en formación remunerados;

h)trabajadores familiares no remunerados temporalmente ausentes del trabajo durante la semana de referencia y trabajadores estacionales que no trabajan durante la temporada inactiva (a menos que busquen activamente un trabajo y estén disponibles para hacerlo, en cuyo caso se consideran desempleados).

Desempleo: Personas de 15 años y más de edad que durante el periodo de referencia no tenían trabajo (no tenían un empleo y no realizaban ninguna actividad para obtener un ingreso), estaban disponibles para comenzar un trabajo en los 15 días ulteriores y buscaban activamente un empleo de diversas maneras durante las cuatro últimas semanas.

Se incluyen:

a)personas que encontraron un trabajo y que comenzarían en un periodo de por lo menos tres meses;

b)personas suspendidas que no recibían de su empleador ningún salario o sueldo importante (menos del 50 por ciento) y que estaban corrientemente disponibles para trabajar y buscaban activamente un trabajo;

c)trabajadores estacionales durante la temporada inactiva si estaban corrientemente disponibles para trabajar y buscaban activamente un trabajo.

Subempleo:

Subempleo por insuficiencia de horas: Personas con un empleo que trabajaban menos que el tiempo de trabajo habitual por razones ajenas a su voluntad, deseaban tener una actividad a tiempo completo o un empleo complementario y estaban disponibles para trabajar en los próximos 15 días.

Situaciones de empleo inadecuado: No corresponde.

Horas de trabajo:

Las horas habituales de trabajo se refieren a la duración de una semana de trabajo típica, incluidas horas suplementarias, si se trabajan sistemáticamente, a diferencia de las horas establecidas por un contrato colectivo de trabajo o por otras convenciones o acuerdos.

Las horas realmente trabajadas corresponden a las horas del empleo principal durante la semana de referencia, incluidas las horas suplementarias no trabajadas sistemáticamente y cuyo número puede ser superior, igual o inferior al de las horas habituales.

Ingresos relacionados con el empleo:

Ingresos relacionados con el empleo asalariado: No corresponde.

Ingresos relacionados con el empleo independiente: No corresponde.

Sector informal: No corresponde.

Actividad habitual: La situación de la actividad principal se refiere a la apreciación individual que tiene cada persona sobre su actividad durante los tres últimos meses.

Clasificaciones:

Rama de actividad económica (industria):

Título de la clasificación utilizada: Clasificación de todas las Actividades Económicas Nacionales (Classification of All Activities of National Economy - CANE).

Grupos de población clasificados por industria: Personas empleadas y desempleadas (rama de actividad del último empleo para el desempleado).

Número de Grupos utilizados para la codificación: 17 grupos.

Vínculos con la CIIU: CIIU-Rev.3.

Ocupación:

Título de la clasificación utilizada: Clasificación de Ocupaciones en Rumania (Classification of Occupations in Romania - CORE).

Grupos de población clasificados por ocupación: Personas empleadas y desempleadas (ocupación en el último empleo para el desempleado).

Número de Grupos utilizados para la codificación: 10 grupos.

Vínculos con la CIUO: CIUO-88.

Situación en el empleo:

Título de la clasificación utilizada: No disponible.

Grupos de población clasificados por situación en el empleo: Personas empleadas y desempleadas (situación en el último empleo para el desempleado).

Grupos utilizados para la codificación: Cinco grupos: Empleado, empleado independiente con empleados (empleador), empleado independiente sin empleados (trabajador por cuenta propia), trabajador familiar no remunerado, miembro de una explotación o cooperativa agrícola.

Vínculos con la CISE: CISE-1993.

Educación:

Título de la clasificación utilizada: No disponible.

Grupos de población clasificados por educación: Personas empleadas y desempleadas.

Grupos utilizados para la codificación: Cinco grupos: Sin educación, educación primaria (2 subgrupos), educación vocacional (2 subgrupos), educación secundaria (2 subgrupos), educación universitaria (2 subgrupos).

Vínculos con la CINE: CINE-1997.

Tamaño y diseño de la muestra:

Unidad final de muestreo: Vivienda (con todos los hogares componentes).

Tamaño de la muestra (unidades finales de muestreo): 18 036 viviendas ubicadas en las zonas geográficas seleccionadas.

Fracción de muestreo: En la primera etapa del muestreo: 0,0331 para zonas rurales y 0,0325 para zonas urbanas.

Marco de la muestra: Se elaboró entre 1992 y 1993 en base a los resultados del Censo de Población y Hogares de enero de 1992 como muestra principal (EMZOT) de 501 zonas geográficas (unas 250 000 viviendas). Esas zonas se consideran como unidades primarias de muestreo (UPM) en la primera etapa del diseño de muestreo para todas las encuestas de hogares; 259 UPM en zonas urbanas y 242 en zonas rurales. En la segunda etapa, las unidades Hogares se seleccionan sistemáticamente de cada UPM.

Actualización de la muestra: La muestra principal EMZOT se actualiza periódicamente.

Rotación:

Esquema: La rotación de la muestra se realiza según el esquema 2-(2)-2. De esta manera, se identifican cuatro grupos o submuestras de rotación. Una vivienda se incluye en la muestra por dos trimestres consecutivos, se saca durante dos trimestres y se vuelve

a introducir durante otros dos trimestres antes de sacarla definitivamente.
Porcentaje de unidades que permanecen en la muestra durante dos encuestas consecutivas: 50 por ciento.
Número máximo de entrevistas por unidad de muestreo: Cuatro por unidad final de muestreo.
Tiempo necesario para renovar completamente la muestra: Una vivienda se utiliza durante 6 trimestres.
Levantamiento da la encuesta:
Tipo de entrevista: Personal, con papel y lápiz.
Número de unidades finales de muestreo por área de muestra: 36 viviendas por trimestre.
Duración del trabajo de campo:
Total: Las semanas de referencia se distribuyen de manera uniforme durante todo el año (52 semanas). La entrevista se realiza la semana siguiente a la semana de referencia.
Por área de muestra: Una semana civil.
Organización de la encuesta: La encuesta se organiza de manera permanente.
Número de personas que trabajan en el campo: 501 entrevistadores, 140 supervisores y 47 funcionarios.
Substitución de las unidades finales de muestreo que no responden: No.
Estimaciones y ajustes:
Tasa de no-respuesta total: 6,2 por ciento (en el tercer trimestre de 2001, por ejemplo).
Ajuste por no-respuesta total: Sí.
Imputación por no respuesta de ítemes: Sí, utilizando el método "Hot-deck, Cold-deck".
Ajuste por áreas/poblaciones no abarcadas: No disponible.
Ajuste por falta de cobertura: Sí.
Ajuste por exceso de cobertura: Sí.
Ajuste por exceso de cobertura: No.
Historia de la encuesta:
Título y fecha de la primera encuesta: Encuesta de Hogares sobre la Fuerza de Trabajo (Household Labour Force Survey (AMIGO)) - Marzo de 1992.
Modificaciones y revisiones significativas: Hasta 1996, la encuesta era anual e incluía las personas de 14 años y más de edad. A partir del primer trimestre de 1999, el concepto de subempleo se ajustó a las disposiciones de la 16a Conferencia Internacional de Estadígrafos del Trabajo (1998). A partir del primer trimestre de 2002, los conceptos de empleo, desempleo y situación de la actividad principal se ajustaron a las disposiciones aprobadas por la Comisión de Reglamentación (EC) N° 1897/2000 y N° 1575/2000.
Documentación y difusión:
Documentación:
Título de las publicaciones con los resultados de la encuesta (periodicidad): Household Labour Force Survey (AMIGO) - informe detallado, informe rápido; Statistical Yearbook (NIS); Boletín trimestral (NIS).
Título de las publicaciones con la metodología de la encuesta (periodicidad): Idem.
Difusión:
Tiempo necesario para difundir los primeros datos: Aproximadamente un trimestre.
Información adelantada acerca de la fecha de la primera difusión pública: No.
Disponibilidad de datos no publicados si se solicitan: Sí.
Disponibilidad de datos por medios informáticos: Sí, en disquete. Sitio web: http://www.insse.ro/.

Rusia, Federación de

Título de la encuesta: Encuesta por Muestra de la Población sobre el Empleo (Population Sample Survey of Employment).
Organismo responsable de la encuesta:
Planificar y realizar la encuesta: Comité Estatal de la Federación de Rusia sobre Estadísticas (State Committee of the Russian Federation on Statistics).
Analizar y publicar los resultados: Comité Estatal de la Federación de Rusia sobre Estadísticas (State Committee of the Russian Federation on Statistics).
Temas abarcados: Empleo, desempleo, subempleo, horas de trabajo, empleo en el sector informal, duración del desempleo, trabajadores desalentados, trabajadores ocasionales, rama de actividad económica (industria), ocupación, situación en el empleo, nivel de educación, empleo secundario y personas ocupadas en la producción de productos y bienes en parcelas agrícolas individuales subsidiarias.
Alcance de la encuesta:
Ámbito geográfico: Todo el país, salvo la República Chechena (durante las operaciones militares).
Grupos de población: Toda la población de 15 a 72 años de edad que reside en hogares privados. Se excluye la población que vive en hogares colectivos y las personas ausentes del hogar por seis meses o más.
Disponibilidad de estimaciones de otras fuentes para las áreas/grupos excluidos: Ninguna.
Grupos abarcados por la encuesta pero excluidos de los resultados publicados: Ninguno.
Periodicidad:
Recolección de datos: Trimestralmente.
Publicación de los resultados: Trimestralmente.
Periodo de referencia:
Empleo: Una semana (semana fija – última semana del segundo mes de cada trimestre, es decir la de febrero, mayo, agosto y noviembre).
Búsqueda de trabajo: Cuatro semanas antes de la semana de referencia.
Disponibilidad para trabajo: Dos semanas después de la semana de referencia.
Conceptos y definiciones:
Empleo: Personas de 15 a 72 años de edad que, durante la semana de referencia, realizaron algún trabajo como empleados asalariados, en su propio negocio, profesión o en su propia explotación agrícola, o que trabajaron por lo menos una hora o más como trabajadores familiares no remunerados en una empresa explotada por un miembro de la familia, y quienes no trabajaron pero tenían un empleo o negocio del que se encontraban temporalmente ausentes por enfermedad, mal tiempo, vacaciones, capacitación con fines de especialización, conflictos laborales o razones personales, que hayan sido remunerados durante el tiempo de ausencia o que estuviesen buscando otro empleo.
Se incluyen también en los totales:
a)trabajadores a tiempo completo o parcial que buscaban otro empleo durante el periodo de referencia;
b)estudiantes de dedicación completa o parcial que trabajaban a tiempo completo o parcial;
c)personas que realizaron algún trabajo durante la semana de referencia, pero que estaban jubiladas y percibían una pensión, estaban inscritas como desempleadas en busca de trabajo en una oficina de empleo o percibiendo indemnizaciones de desempleo;
d)trabajadores familiares remunerados o no (si trabajaron por lo menos una hora);
e)servicio doméstico privado;
f)miembros de cooperativas de productores;
g)miembros de las fuerzas armadas que viven en el hogar.
Cada persona empleada se cuenta una sola vez. Quienes tienen más de un empleo se cuentan en el que consideran el empleo principal.
Se excluyen las personas cuya única actividad se limita a los trabajos de la casa (pintura, reparaciones o quehaceres domésticos), los miembros voluntarios de instituciones religiosas, caritativas y similares, así como los aprendices y las personas en formación no remunerados. Estas personas se consideran como desempleadas o económicamente inactivas.
Desempleo: Se consideran desempleadas todas las personas civiles que no tenían empleo durante la semana de referencia, estaban disponibles para trabajar, salvo por enfermedad temporal, y que habían tomado disposiciones concretas para encontrar empleo.
Nota: Los trabajadores familiares remunerados o no y que temporalmente no trabajaban se consideran desempleados o económicamente inactivos, en función de si buscaron o no empleo durante la semana de referencia.
También se incluyen en el desempleo los estudiantes de dedicación completa o parcial, los jubilados y discapacitados siempre y cuando busquen trabajo y estén corrientemente disponibles para hacerlo (si buscan trabajo para una fecha futura, como los meses de verano, se consideran inactivos). Las personas con licencia administrativa no remunerada por 6 meses o más se clasifican como desempleadas o económicamente inactivas.
Subempleo:
Subempleo por insuficiencia de horas: Personas que, durante la semana de referencia, trabajaron menos horas que las establecidas para una determinada categoría de ocupación o trabajo, siempre y cuando estuviesen buscando un trabajo adicional y disponibles para hacerlo.
Situaciones de empleo inadecuado: No corresponde.

Horas de trabajo: Horas habituales y reales trabajadas en el empleo principal y empleo(s) secundario(s).
Ingresos relacionados con el empleo:
Ingresos relacionados con el empleo asalariado: No corresponde.
Ingresos relacionados con el empleo independiente: No corresponde.
Sector informal: Se dispone de información sobre el sector informal en la medida en que los entrevistados en la encuesta informan sobre sus actividades.
Actividad habitual: No corresponde.
Clasificaciones:
Rama de actividad económica (industria):
Título de la clasificación utilizada: Clasificación nacional compatible con la CIIU Rev.3.
Grupos de población clasificados por industria: Personas empleadas y personas desempleadas con experiencia previa de trabajo.
Número de Grupos utilizados para la codificación: 17.
Vínculos con la CIIU: CIIU-Rev.3 (nivel de 4 dígitos).
Ocupación:
Título de la clasificación utilizada: Clasificación nacional compatible con la CIUO-88.
Grupos de población clasificados por ocupación: Personas empleadas y personas desempleadas con experiencia previa de trabajo.
Número de Grupos utilizados para la codificación: 31 (primer y segundo niveles).
Vínculos con la CIUO: CIUO-88 (nivel de 4 dígitos).
Situación en el empleo:
Título de la clasificación utilizada: Se utiliza la CISE-1993.
Grupos de población clasificados por situación en el empleo: Personas empleadas (empleos principal y secundario).
Grupos utilizados para la codificación: 6 grupos (empleados, empleadores, trabajadores por cuenta propia, miembros de cooperativas de productores, trabajadores familiares no remunerados).
Vínculos con la CISE: CISE-1993.
Educación:
Título de la clasificación utilizada: Clasificación nacional.
Grupos de población clasificados por educación: Todos los grupos de población.
Grupos utilizados para la codificación: 8 grupos (sin primaria general, primaria general, secundaria, secundaria general, primaria vocacional, secundaria vocacional, superior no completada; superior (universidad)).
Vínculos con la CINE: No.
Tamaño y diseño de la muestra:
Unidad final de muestreo: Hogares.
Tamaño de la muestra (unidades finales de muestreo): Casi 65 000 personas por trimestre y unas 240 000 personas anualmente.
Fracción de muestreo: 0,24 por ciento.
Marco de la muestra: La muestra se prepara automáticamente a nivel federal basándose en la lista de hogares del microcenso de 1994.
Actualización de la muestra: Anualmente.
Rotación:
Esquema: Rotación del 100 por ciento de un trimestre a otro. Un hogar se puede volver a incluir en la muestra y entrevistarse por segunda vez dos años más tarde.
Levantamiento de la encuesta:
Tipo de entrevista: Papel y lápiz.
Número de unidades finales de muestreo por área de muestra: 60 personas por distrito de enumeración.
Duración del trabajo de campo:
Total: Dos semanas civiles después de la semana de referencia (14 días).
Por área de muestra: No se proporcionó información.
Organización de la encuesta: Entrevistas personales. Los entrevistadores se contratan temporalmente por el tiempo que dura la encuesta. La entrada y el control lógico de los datos se realizan a nivel regional (oblast) después de lo cual los datos primarios se transfieren al nivel federal (Comité Estatal de Estadísticas). A este nivel se crea la base de microdatos, se procesan los datos, se ajustan las ponderaciones y se preparan las variables pertinentes para clasificar la población por situación en la actividad económica.
Número de personas que trabajan en el campo: 1 100 entrevistadores y 130 supervisores.
Substitución de las unidades finales de muestreo que no responden: Sí.
Estimaciones y ajustes:
Tasa de no-respuesta total: 4,5 por ciento.
Ajuste por no-respuesta total: No.
Imputación por no respuesta de ítemes: No.
Ajuste por áreas/poblaciones no abarcadas: No.
Ajuste por falta de cobertura: No.
Ajuste por exceso de cobertura: No.
Ajuste por variaciones estacionales: Sí.
Historia de la encuesta:
Título y fecha de la primera encuesta: Encuesta por Muestra de la Población sobre el Empleo (Population Sample Survey of Employment), octubre de 1992.
Modificaciones y revisiones significativas: La encuesta se realiza trimestralmente desde 1999.
Documentación y difusión:
Documentación:
Título de las publicaciones con los resultados de la encuesta: (periodicidad): “Obsliedovaniye naseleniya po problemam zaniytosty” (Encuesta por Muestra de la Población sobre el Empleo) - trimestralmente, “Rossijsky statistichesky yezhegodnik” (Anuario Estadístico de Rusia) – anual, “Trud I zanis tost v Rossijskoj Federatsii” (Trabajo y Empleo en la Federación de Rusia) – cada 2 años, “Statisticheskoye obozrieniye” (Estudio Estadísticos) – trimestralmente.
Título de las publicaciones con la metodología de la encuesta: (periodicidad): “Obsliedovaniye naseleniya po problemam zaniytosty” (Encuesta por Muestra de la Población sobre el Empleo) - trimestralmente, “Metodologichskiye poplozheniya, No. 3” (Descripciones metodológicas).
Difusión:
Tiempo necesario para difundir los primeros datos: Tres meses después de la semana de referencia.
Información adelantada acerca de la fecha de la primera difusión pública: Sí.
Disponibilidad de datos no publicados si se solicitan: Sí.
Disponibilidad de datos por medios informáticos: Disquetes e internet (datos seleccionados). Sitio web: http://www.gks.ru

Seychelles

Título de la encuesta: Encuesta sobre la Fuerza de Trabajo (Labour Force Survey (LFS)).
Organismo responsable de la encuesta:
Planificar y realizar la encuesta: División de Sistemas de Gestión e Información (Management and Information Systems Division (MISD)), Ministerio de la Tecnología de la Información y la Comunicación (Ministry of Information Technology & Communication).
Analizar y publicar los resultados: MISD.
Temas abarcados: Personas corriente y habitualmente activas económicamente, empleadas y desempleadas; personas corrientemente subempleadas por insuficiencia de horas o en situación de empleo inadecuado y personas corrientemente fuera de la población activa. Personas habitualmente empleadas con o sin desempleo, personas habitualmente desempleadas con algún empleo y personas habitualmente no activas económicamente (se hace la diferencia entre estudiantes, personas ocupadas de los quehaceres domésticos, personas muy mayores, enfermas o minusválidas). Horas de trabajo. Empleo en sector informal. Duración del empleo y el desempleo. Trabajadores desalentados. Empleo secundario. Rama de actividad económica (industria), ocupación, situación en el empleo, nivel de educación y capacitación.
Alcance de la encuesta:
Ámbito geográfico: Las tres islas principales, a saber: Mahé, Praslin y La Digue.
Grupos de población: Población de 15 años y más de edad que reside en hogares.
Disponibilidad de estimaciones de otras fuentes para las áreas/grupos excluidos: No corresponde.
Grupos abarcados por la encuesta pero excluidos de los resultados publicados: Ninguno.
Periodicidad:
Recolección de datos: Ocasional, del 18 de agosto al 17 de septiembre de 1992.
Publicación de los resultados: Ocasional, no se dispone de información sobre la fecha de publicación de los primeros resultados.
Periodo de referencia:
Empleo: Una semana antes de la fecha de la entrevista.
Búsqueda de trabajo: Cuatro semanas.
Disponibilidad para trabajo: Cuatro semanas.

Conceptos y definiciones:

Empleo: Personas que a) realizaban algún trabajo remunerado o por un beneficio durante la semana de referencia; b) estaban temporalmente ausentes del trabajo durante la semana de referencia por enfermedad o con licencia, pero con toda seguridad se iban a reintegrar a su empleo (se incluyen los trabajadores estacionales después de finalizar la temporada inactiva), o c) estaban ocupadas en la producción de bienes para su propio uso final. Se excluyen los trabajadores familiares no remunerados en negocios familiares. Algún trabajo se refiere a la labor realizada durante 1 hora o más en la semana de referencia.

Desempleo: Personas que estaban corrientemente sin trabajo, disponibles para trabajar y que buscaron trabajo durante las cuatro últimas semanas, así como las personas que no buscaban trabajo porque pensaban que no había ningún empleo disponible, esperaban la respuesta de solicitudes previas o esperaban comenzar un trabajo.

Subempleo:

Subempleo por insuficiencia de horas: Personas que trabajaban menos de 35 horas y comunicaron que estaban disponibles para trabajar más horas y que no lo hacían por razones económicas.

Situaciones de empleo inadecuado: No se proporcionó información.

Horas de trabajo: No se proporcionó información.

Ingresos relacionados con el empleo:

Ingresos relacionados con el empleo asalariado: No corresponde.

Ingresos relacionados con el empleo independiente: No corresponde.

Sector informal: Negocios no registrados (se determinan por el nombre del negocio) en el sector privado (incluidas cooperativas) con menos de cinco personas empleadas y que se explotan desde la vivienda del entrevistado, un puesto de mercado o una ubicación temporal.

Actividad habitual: Económicamente activo por 6 meses o más durante los 12 meses del periodo de referencia y empleado durante la mayor parte de ese periodo.

Clasificaciones:

Rama de actividad económica (industria):

Título de la clasificación utilizada: No se proporcionó ningún nombre.

Grupos de población clasificados por industria: Personas empleadas y desempleadas (rama de actividad del último empleo para el desempleado).

Número de Grupos utilizados para la codificación: 26.

Vínculos con la CIIU: CIIU- Rev.3.

Ocupación:

Título de la clasificación utilizada: No se proporcionó ningún nombre.

Grupos de población clasificados por ocupación: Personas empleadas y desempleadas (ocupación en el último empleo para el desempleado).

Número de Grupos utilizados para la codificación: 35.

Vínculos con la CIUO: CIUO-88.

Situación en el empleo:

Título de la clasificación utilizada: Clasificación nacional.

Grupos de población clasificados por situación en el empleo: Personas empleadas y desempleadas (situación en el último empleo para el desempleado).

Grupos utilizados para la codificación: Empleados públicos; empleados paraestatales, empleados del sector privado; empleados de cooperativas; empleados independientes; empleadores y trabajadores familiares no remunerados.

Vínculos con la CISE: CISE-1993.

Educación:

Título de la clasificación utilizada: Clasificación nacional.

Grupos de población clasificados por educación: Personas empleadas y desempleadas.

Grupos utilizados para la codificación: Sin instrucción; P1-P6; FI-FII, P7-P8, S1-S2; FIII, P9, S3; FIV, S4, NYS; Vocacional; Poly1-2, TTC; Poly3-4, FVI; estudios preuniversitarios, universidad.

Vínculos con la CINE: CINE-1976.

Tamaño y diseño de la muestra:

Unidad final de muestreo: Hogares.

Tamaño de la muestra (unidades finales de muestreo): 800.

Fracción de muestreo: 6 por ciento.

Marco de la muestra: Censo de población de 1987.

Actualización de la muestra: 1991.

Rotación:

Esquema: No corresponde.

Porcentaje de unidades que permanecen en la muestra durante dos encuestas consecutivas: No corresponde.

Número máximo de entrevistas por unidad de muestreo: No corresponde.

Tiempo necesario para renovar completamente la muestra: No corresponde.

Levantamiento da la encuesta:

Tipo de entrevista: Entrevistas personales, con papel y lápiz.

Número de unidades finales de muestreo por área de muestra: No se dispone de información.

Duración del trabajo de campo:

Total: Un mes, con dos semanas más para las sustituciones.

Por área de muestra: No se dispone de información.

Organización de la encuesta: Permanente.

Número de personas que trabajan en el campo: 6 entrevistadores y 3 supervisores.

Substitución de las unidades finales de muestreo que no responden: Se sustituyen algunos rechazos, personas que no responden o que se han mudado.

Estimaciones y ajustes:

Tasa de no-respuesta total: 15 por ciento.

Ajuste por no-respuesta total: Sí.

Imputación por no respuesta de ítemes: No.

Ajuste por áreas/poblaciones no abarcadas: No.

Ajuste por falta de cobertura: No.

Ajuste por exceso de cobertura: No.

Ajuste por variaciones estacionales: No corresponde.

Historia de la encuesta:

Título y fecha de la primera encuesta: Encuesta sobre la Fuerza de Trabajo (Labour Force Survey), 1979/80.

Modificaciones y revisiones significativas: No se dispone de información.

Documentación y difusión:

Documentación:

Título de las publicaciones con los resultados de la encuesta: No se dispone de información.

Título de las publicaciones con la metodología de la encuesta: No se dispone de información.

Difusión:

Tiempo necesario para difundir los primeros datos: No se dispone de información.

Información adelantada acerca de la fecha de la primera difusión pública: No.

Disponibilidad de datos no publicados si se solicitan: Sí.

Disponibilidad de datos por medios informáticos: Sí. Sitio web: http://www.seychelles.net/misd/.

Singapur

Título de la encuesta: Encuesta sobre la Fuerza de Trabajo (Labour Force Survey (LFS)).

Organismo responsable de la encuesta:

Planificar y realizar la encuesta: Departamento de Investigación y Estadísticas de Recursos Humanos (Manpower Research and Statistics Department (MRSD)), Ministerio de Recursos Humanos (Ministry of Manpower).

Analizar y publicar los resultados: Departamento de Investigación y Estadísticas de Recursos Humanos (Manpower Research and Statistics Department (MRSD)), Ministerio de Recursos Humanos (Ministry of Manpower).

Temas abarcados: Personas corriente y económicamente activas, empleadas y desempleadas; personas corrientemetne subempleadas por insuficiencia de horas y personas corrientemente fuera de la población activa; trabajadores desalentados, horas de trabajo y empleo a tiempo completo o parcial; duración del empleo y el desempleo, salarios e ingresos, empleo secundario; rama de actividad económica (industria), ocupación, situación en el empleo, nivel de educación/capacitación.

Alcance de la encuesta:

Ámbito geográfico: La gran isla de Singapur, salvo las islas extraterritoriales.

Grupos de población: Personas de 15 años y más de edad que viven en hogares privados. Se excluyen los viandantes y visitantes que viven en tierra, hoteles o embarcaciones, botes y personas a bordo de trasatlánticos, así como obreros de la construcción que viven en los sitios de trabajo y quienes se desplazaban entre Singapur y el extranjero.

Disponibilidad de estimaciones de otras fuentes para las áreas/grupos excluidos: Ninguna.

Grupos abarcados por la encuesta pero excluidos de los resultados publicados: Ninguno.
Periodicidad:
Recolección de datos: Trimestralmente.
Publicación de los resultados: Trimestralmente.
Periodo de referencia:
Empleo: Una semana.
Búsqueda de trabajo: Las cuatro últimas semanas.
Disponibilidad para trabajo: En dos semanas.
Conceptos y definiciones:
Empleo: Personas que a) realizaron algún trabajo por una remuneración, un beneficio o una ganancia familiar durante la semana de referencia; y b) estaban temporalmente ausentes del trabajo durante la semana de referencia por enfermedad o licencia, pero que con toda seguridad se iban a reintegrar. Algún trabajo se define como la labor realizada en una hora o más durante la semana de referencia.
Desempleo: Personas que estaban corrientemente sin trabajo, disponibles para trabajar en dos semanas y habían buscado trabajo en algún momento durante las cuatro últimas semanas.
Subempleo:
Subempleo por insuficiencia de horas: Personas que trabajaban menos de 30 horas durante el periodo de referencia, deseaban realizar un trabajo adicional y estaban disponibles para hacerlo.
Situaciones de empleo inadecuado: No se proporcionó información.
Horas de trabajo: Horas habituales trabajadas en una semana típica.
Ingresos relacionados con el empleo:
Ingresos relacionados con el empleo asalariado: Monto total de ingresos del empleo durante todo el mes anterior. Para los empleados asalariados se incluyen salarios y sueldos, bonificaciones, subsidios, comisiones, pago de horas extraordinarias, propinas y gratificaciones, así como las cotizaciones de los empleados al "Central Provident Fund", pero no la parte del empleador.
Ingresos relacionados con el empleo independiente: Ingresos totales de ventas y servicios menos los gastos de explotación.
Sector informal: No corresponde.
Actividad habitual: No se proporcionó información.
Clasificaciones:
Rama de actividad económica (industria):
Título de la clasificación utilizada: Clasificación Industrial Normalizada de Singapur (Singapore Standard Industrial Classification), de 1996.
Grupos de población clasificados por industria: Personas empleadas y desempleadas.
Número de Grupos utilizados para la codificación: 9.
Vínculos con la CIIU: CIIU-Rev.3 (categorías de tabulación condensadas).
Ocupación:
Título de la clasificación utilizada: Clasificación Normalizada de Ocupaciones de Singapur (Singapore Standard Occupational Classification), de 1990.
Grupos de población clasificados por ocupación: Personas empleadas y desempleadas.
Número de Grupos utilizados para la codificación: 8.
Vínculos con la CIUO: CIUO-88.
Situación en el empleo:
Título de la clasificación utilizada: No se proporcionó información.
Grupos de población clasificados por situación en el empleo: Personas empleadas.
Grupos utilizados para la codificación: Empleados, empleadores, trabajadores por cuenta propia, trabajadores que contribuyen con la familia.
Vínculos con la CISE: CISE-1993.
Educación:
Título de la clasificación utilizada: Clasificación Normalizada de la **Educación:** de Singapur (Singapore Standard Educational Classification).
Grupos de población clasificados por educación: Personas empleadas y desempleadas.
Grupos utilizados para la codificación: Nunca fue a la escuela/primaria inferior; primaria; secundaria inferior; secundaria; postsecundaria; diploma politécnico, grado.
Vínculos con la CINE: CINE-1997
Tamaño y diseño de la muestra:
Unidad final de muestreo: Casas.
Tamaño de la muestra (unidades finales de muestreo): 25 000 casas para la encuesta principal de junio.
Fracción de muestreo: 3 por ciento para la encuesta principal de junio.
Marco de la muestra: Base de datos nacional de viviendas, de cuyo mantenimiento se encarga el Departamento de Estadísticas de Singapur.
Actualización de la muestra: No se proporcionó información.
Rotación:
Esquema: No corresponde.
Porcentaje de unidades que permanecen en la muestra durante dos encuestas consecutivas: No corresponde.
Número máximo de entrevistas por unidad de muestreo: No corresponde.
Tiempo necesario para renovar completamente la muestra: No corresponde.
Levantamiento da la encuesta:
Tipo de entrevista: Entrevistas por teléfono asistidas por computadora (CATI) y entrevistas personales.
Número de unidades finales de muestreo por área de muestra: No se proporcionó información.
Duración del trabajo de campo:
Total: 7 a 8 semanas.
Por área de muestra: No se proporcionó información.
Organización de la encuesta: Permanente.
Número de personas que trabajan en el campo: 140 entrevistadores y supervisores.
Substitución de las unidades finales de muestreo que no responden: No.
Estimaciones y ajustes:
Tasa de no-respuesta total: 2 por ciento.
Ajuste por no-respuesta total: No.
Imputación por no respuesta de ítemes: No.
Ajuste por áreas/poblaciones no abarcadas: No.
Ajuste por falta de cobertura: No.
Ajuste por exceso de cobertura: No.
Ajuste por variaciones estacionales: Para el porcentaje de desempleo trimestral se utiliza el método X-11 ARIMA.
Historia de la encuesta:
Título y fecha de la primera encuesta: Encuesta sobre la Fuerza de Trabajo (Labour Force Survey (LFS)), junio de 1974.
Modificaciones y revisiones significativas: Ninguna.
Documentación y difusión:
Documentación:
Título de las publicaciones con los resultados de la encuesta: "Quarterly Labour Market Reports" para cifras sobre el desempleo.
Título de las publicaciones con la metodología de la encuesta (periodicidad): Report on the Labour Force Survey of Singapore (anualmente), salvo en los años del censo y en la mitad del periodo entre dos censos.
Difusión:
Tiempo necesario para difundir los primeros datos: Menos de seis meses después de finalizar el trabajo sobre el terreno.
Información adelantada acerca de la fecha de la primera difusión pública: Sí.
Disponibilidad de datos no publicados si se solicitan: Sí.
Disponibilidad de datos por medios informáticos: Sí. Sitio web: http://www.singstat.gov.sg.

Sri Lanka

Título de la encuesta: Encuesta sobre la Fuerza de Trabajo de Sri Lanka (Sri Lanka Labour Force Survey).
Organismo responsable de la encuesta:
Planificar y realizar la encuesta: Departamento de Censo y Estadísticas (Department of Census and Statistics).
Analizar y publicar los resultados: Departamento de Censo y Estadísticas (Department of Census and Statistics).
Temas abarcados: Empleo, desempleo, subempleo por insuficiencia de horas, horas de trabajo, ingresos, duración del empleo y el desempleo, razones para no buscar trabajo, tipo de trabajo solicitado, rama de actividad económica (industria), ocupación, situación en el empleo, trabajo por turnos, nivel de educación, capacitación vocacional, actividad habitual y empleo secundario.
Alcance de la encuesta:
Ámbito geográfico: Todo el país salvo las provincias septentrionales y orientales.
Grupos de población: Personas de 10 años y más de edad, excepto la población institucional, las fuerzas armadas y los miembros de la familia que no viven en el hogar.
Disponibilidad de estimaciones de otras fuentes para las áreas/grupos excluidos: No.

Grupos abarcados por la encuesta pero excluidos de los resultados publicados: Ninguno.
Periodicidad:
Recolección de datos: Trimestralmente.
Publicación de los resultados: Trimestralmente.
Periodo de referencia:
Empleo: Semana anterior (fija).
Búsqueda de trabajo: Semana anterior (fija).
Disponibilidad para trabajo: Semana anterior (fija).
Conceptos y definiciones:
Empleo: Miembros del hogar que durante el periodo de referencia trabajaron por lo menos una hora como empleados asalariados, empleadores, trabajadores por cuenta propia (empleados independientes) o trabajadores familiares no remunerados, en empresas familiares. Se incluyen también las personas que tenían un empleo pero que estaban temporalmente ausentes del mismo por razones tales como vacaciones, enfermedad, mal tiempo, conflictos laborales, etc. Se incluyen aprendices y personas en formación remunerados.
Desempleo: Personas que durante el periodo de referencia estaban disponibles y/o buscaban un empleo asalariado o independiente, y no tenían empleo.
Subempleo:
Subempleo por insuficiencia de horas: Personas empleadas que durante el periodo de referencia no tenían un empleo secundario y estaban disponibles para hacer un trabajo adicional. Se puede obtener información por separado sobre las personas que buscan este tipo de trabajo .
Situaciones de empleo inadecuado: No se proporcionó información.
Horas de trabajo: Horas realmente trabajadas durante la semana.
Ingresos relacionados con el empleo:
Ingresos relacionados con el empleo asalariado: Ingresos en efectivo únicamente.
Ingresos relacionados con el empleo independiente: No se proporcionó información.
Sector informal: No se proporcionó información.
Actividad habitual: Personas que en los últimos 12 meses estuvieron empleadas y/o desempleadas durante 26 semanas o más.
Clasificaciones:
Rama de actividad económica (industria):
Título de la clasificación utilizada: Clasificación nacional.
Grupos de población clasificados por industria: Personas empleadas.
Número de Grupos utilizados para la codificación: 10.
Vínculos con la CIIU: CIIU-Rev. 2.
Ocupación:
Título de la clasificación utilizada: Clasificación nacional.
Grupos de población clasificados por ocupación: Personas empleadas.
Número de Grupos utilizados para la codificación: 10.
Vínculos con la CIUO: CIUO-88.
Situación en el empleo:
Título de la clasificación utilizada: Clasificación nacional.
Grupos de población clasificados por situación en el empleo: Personas empleadas.
Grupos utilizados para la codificación: empleados, empleadores, trabajadores por cuenta propia, trabajadores familiares no remunerados.
Vínculos con la CISE: CISE-1993.
Educación:
Título de la clasificación utilizada: Clasificación nacional.
Grupos de población clasificados por educación: Personas empleadas y desempleadas.
Grupos utilizados para la codificación: Sin escolaridad, grados 1 a 5, grados 6 a 10, nivel GCE (O/L), nivel GCE (A/L) y superior.
Vínculos con la CINE: No.
Tamaño y diseño de la muestra:
Unidad final de muestreo: Unidades de vivienda.
Tamaño de la muestra (unidades finales de muestreo): El tamaño de la muestra anual es de 16 000 unidades de vivienda.
Fracción de muestreo: No disponible.
Marco de la muestra: El marco de la muestra principal (lista de unidades de vivienda) se preparó para la Encuesta Demográfica de 1994. A partir de 2002, el Censo de Población y Viviendas de 2001 se utiliza como marco de la muestra.
Actualización de la muestra: Hasta 2001, la lista de unidades de vivienda de las UPM seleccionadas se actualizaba antes de realizar la enumeración de la encuesta; a partir de 2002, la lista de los bloques del Censo se actualiza antes de hacer la enumeración de la encuesta.
Rotación: No corresponde.
Esquema: No corresponde.
Porcentaje de unidades que permanecen en la muestra durante dos encuestas consecutivas: No corresponde.
Número máximo de entrevistas por unidad de muestreo: No se proporcionó información.
Tiempo necesario para renovar completamente la muestra: No se proporcionó información.
Levantamiento de la encuesta:
Tipo de entrevista: Personal.
Número de unidades finales de muestreo por área de muestra: No disponible.
Duración del trabajo de campo:
Total: Dos semanas.
Por área de muestra: Una semana.
Organización de la encuesta: Plantilla permanente.
Número de personas que trabajan en el campo: 300 enumeradores y supervisores.
Substitución de las unidades finales de muestreo que no responden: No.
Estimaciones y ajustes:
Tasa de no-respuesta total: 5 por ciento.
Ajuste por no-respuesta total: Sí.
Imputación por no respuesta de ítemes: No.
Ajuste por áreas/poblaciones no abarcadas: No.
Ajuste por falta de cobertura: Sí.
Ajuste por exceso de cobertura: Sí.
Ajuste por variaciones estacionales: No.
Historia de la encuesta:
Título y fecha de la primera encuesta: Encuesta sobre la Fuerza de Trabajo de Sri Lanka (Sri Lanka Labour Force Survey), 1990.
Modificaciones y revisiones significativas: Se añadieron nuevas preguntas en el primer trimestre de 1996.
Documentación y difusión:
Documentación:
Título de las publicaciones con los resultados de la encuesta (periodicidad): Quarterly Report of the Sri Lanka Labour force Survey; Bulletin of Labour Force (trimestralmente); Annual Bulletin of Labour Force-Provincial Profile.
Título de las publicaciones con la metodología de la encuesta (periodicidad): Idem.
Difusión:
Tiempo necesario para difundir los primeros datos: Unos tres meses.
Información adelantada acerca de la fecha de la primera difusión pública: No.
Disponibilidad de datos no publicados si se solicitan: Sí.
Disponibilidad de datos por medios informáticos: Disquetes y cintas magnéticas. Sitio web: http://www.statistics.gov.lk/

Sudáfrica

Título de la encuesta: Encuesta sobre la Fuerza de Trabajo (Labour Force Survey).
Organismo responsable de la encuesta:
Planificar y realizar la encuesta: Servicio de Estadísticas de Sudáfrica (Statistics South Africa (Stats SA)).
Analizar y publicar los resultados: Servicio de Estadísticas de Sudáfrica (Statistics South Africa (Stats SA)).
Temas abarcados: Empleo, desempleo, subempleo, horas de trabajo, salarios, ingresos, empleo en el sector informal, duración del empleo y el desempleo, trabajadores desalentados, rama de actividad económica (industria), ocupación, situación en el empleo, nivel de educación/calificación.
Alcance de la encuesta:
Ámbito geográfico: Todo el país.
Grupos de población: La encuesta incluye todos los grupos de la población (hogares privados y residentes en albergues para trabajadores), pero las preguntas sobre empleo y desempleo sólo se hacen a personas de 15 años y más de edad. Se excluyen las personas que residen en hogares colectivos (residencias de estudiantes, hogares de ancianos, hospitales, prisiones y cuarteles militares).
Disponibilidad de estimaciones de otras fuentes para las áreas/grupos excluidos: Ninguna.
Grupos abarcados por la encuesta pero excluidos de los resultados publicados: Ninguno.

Periodicidad:
Recolección de datos: Bianual.
Publicación de los resultados: Bianual.
Periodo de referencia:
Empleo: La semana anterior a la entrevista, en febrero y septiembre de cada año.
Búsqueda de trabajo: Cuatro semanas antes de la entrevista, en febrero y septiembre de cada año.
Disponibilidad para trabajo: Una semana después de la entrevista, en febrero y septiembre de cada año.
Conceptos y definiciones:
Empleo: Todas las personas de 15 a 65 años de edad que han realizado cualesquiera de las siguientes actividades, salvo la mendicidad:
a)explotar o administrar cualquier tipo de negocio, grande o pequeño, por cuenta propia o con uno o más asociados;
b)realizar cualquier tipo de trabajo por un salario, sueldo, comisión o el pago en especie (excluido el trabajo doméstico);
c)hacer cualquier trabajo como trabajador doméstico por un salario, sueldo o el pago en especie;
d)ayudar sin remuneración en un negocio familiar de cualquier tipo;
e)efectuar cualquier trabajo en su propia parcela o la de la familia, explotación agrícola, huerto familiar, establo o kraal; ayudar en la producción agrícola o en el cuidado de los animales del hogar;
f)realizar cualquier construcción o trabajo de reparación principal en su propio hogar, parcela, establo o negocio o los del hogar; capturar cualquier tipo de peces, mariscos, moluscos, animales silvestres o recoger alimentos para la venta o el consumo del hogar.
Se clasifican como empleadas las personas que no realizaban ningún trabajo durante la semana de referencia, pero tenían un empleo al que se podían reincorporar. La temporada inactiva en el sector de la agricultura no se considera como ausencia temporal.
Se consideran también como empleados los estudiantes de dedicación completa o parcial que trabajaban a tiempo completo o parcial durante los siete días anteriores a la entrevista, así como los aprendices y personas en formación remunerados o no.
Desempleo: Se utilizan dos definiciones: la "oficial" y la "amplia". La definición "oficial" se refiere a las personas de 15 a 65 años de edad que:
a)no realizaron ningún trabajo durante los siete días anteriores a la entrevista;
b)querían trabajar y estaban disponibles para comenzar un empleo una semana después de la entrevista;
c)habían tomado medidas para buscar un trabajo o comenzar alguna forma de empleo independiente cuatro semanas antes de la entrevista.
La "definición amplia" excluye el criterio c).
Subempleo:
Subempleo por insuficiencia de horas: Abarca las personas que:
a)trabajan menos horas que las normalmente trabajadas en una determinada actividad;
b)no tienen otra posibilidad que la de trabajar menos horas (el número de horas de trabajo que realizan no lo hacen de manera voluntaria);
c)desean trabajar más horas;
d)tomaron disposiciones para buscar un trabajo adicional cuatro semanas antes de la entrevista.
Situaciones de empleo inadecuado: No está cubierto.
Horas de trabajo: La encuesta abarca las horas real y habitualmente trabajadas. En ambos casos, los datos se presentan por separado para el empleo principal, otras actividades laborales y el total de horas.
Ingresos relacionados con el empleo:
Ingresos relacionados con el empleo asalariado: Se refiere a los ingresos regulares o totales en efectivo, incluidos horas extraordinarias, subsidios y bonificaciones antes de las deducciones impositivas o de otro tipo. Se refiere únicamente al empleo principal.
Ingresos relacionados con el empleo independiente: Igual que para el empleo asalariado si se trata de la actividad principal.
Sector informal: Se pregunta a los entrevistados sobre su lugar de trabajo, que sea en el sector formal o informal. El empleo en el sector informal se refiere al empleador (institución, negocio o empleador privado) que no está registrado para ejercer su actividad.
Actividad habitual: La encuesta no abarca este punto.
Clasificaciones:
Rama de actividad económica (industria):
Título de la clasificación utilizada: Clasificación internacional.
Grupos de población clasificados por industria: Empleados y desempleados (rama de actividad económica del último empleo para el desempleado).
Número de Grupos utilizados para la codificación: 190.
Vínculos con la CIIU: CIIU-Rev.3 (1988).
Ocupación:
Título de la clasificación utilizada: Clasificación internacional.
Grupos de población clasificados por ocupación: Empleados y desempleados (ocupación en el último empleo para el desempleado).
Número de Grupos utilizados para la codificación: 369.
Vínculos con la CIUO: CIUO-88.
Situación en el empleo:
Título de la clasificación utilizada: Clasificación nacional.
Grupos de población clasificados por situación en el empleo: Empleados.
Grupos utilizados para la codificación: Empleados asalariados y empleados independientes.
Vínculos con la CISE: No se dispone de información.
Educación:
Título de la clasificación utilizada: Clasificación nacional.
Grupos de población clasificados por educación: Personas empleadas y desempleadas, así como la población inactiva (todas las edades).
Grupos utilizados para la codificación: Sin escolaridad; grado 0 a grado 12; NTC I a NTC III; diploma/certificado inferior al grado 12; diploma/certificado con grado 12; grado, postgrado o diploma.
Vínculos con la CINE: CINE-1997.
Tamaño y diseño de la muestra:
Unidad final de muestreo: Vivienda.
Tamaño de la muestra (unidades finales de muestreo): 30 000 viviendas.
Fracción de muestreo: No se dispone de información.
Marco de la muestra: La base de datos de zonas de enumeración (ZE), establecida durante la fase de delimitación del Censo de 1996, constituyó el marco de la muestra de las ZE seleccionadas para la Encuesta sobre la Fuerza de Trabajo.
Actualización de la muestra: Anualmente.
Rotación:
Esquema: Las mismas viviendas se visitan, a lo sumo, en cinco ocasiones diferentes, lo que significa una rotación del 20 por ciento de las viviendas en cada ocasión.
Porcentaje de unidades que permanecen en la muestra durante dos encuestas consecutivas: 80 por ciento.
Número máximo de entrevistas por unidad de muestreo: Cinco.
Tiempo necesario para renovar completamente la muestra: Cinco rondas.
Levantamiento de la encuesta:
Tipo de entrevista: Personal.
Número de unidades finales de muestreo por área de muestra: Diez.
Duración del trabajo de campo:
Total: 21 días (por ejemplo, del 2 al 22 de septiembre de 2001).
Por área de muestra: Unas 14 horas.
Organización de la encuesta: Organización permanente y ocasional.
Número de personas que trabajan en el campo: 936 personas (miembros de plantilla y contratados).
Substitución de las unidades finales de muestreo que no responden: No.
Estimaciones y ajustes:
Tasa de no-respuesta total: Casi el 10 por ciento.
Ajuste por no-respuesta total: Sí.
Imputación por no respuesta de ítemes: No.
Ajuste por áreas/poblaciones no abarcadas: No.
Ajuste por falta de cobertura: Sí.
Ajuste por exceso de cobertura: Sí.
Ajuste por variaciones estacionales: No.
Historia de la encuesta:
Título y fecha de la primera encuesta: Encuesta sobre la Fuerza de Trabajo, 2000 (Labour Force Survey 2000).
Modificaciones y revisiones significativas: No corresponde.
Documentación y difusión:
Documentación:
Título de las publicaciones con los resultados de la encuesta (periodicidad): Labour Force Survey (bi-anual); Statistical Releases (P0210).
Título de las publicaciones con la metodología de la encuesta (periodicidad): "Labour Force Survey" (bianual).

Difusión:
Tiempo necesario para difundir los primeros datos: Unos 6 meses después de realizarse el trabajo de campo (26 de marzo de 2002 para los resultados de septiembre de 2001).
Información adelantada acerca de la fecha de la primera difusión pública: Sí.
Disponibilidad de datos no publicados si se solicitan: No.
Disponibilidad de datos por medios informáticos: Sí. Sitio web: http://www.statssa.gov.za/

Sudán

Título de la encuesta: Encuesta de Hogares.
Organismo responsable de la encuesta:
Planificar y realizar la encuesta: Ministerio del Trabajo (Ministry of Manpower).
Analizar y publicar los resultados: Ministerio del Trabajo (Ministry of Manpower).
Temas abarcados: Empleo y desempleo actuales. Horas de trabajo. Salarios. Ingresos del hogar. Empleo en el sector informal. Duración del desempleo. Nivel de educación. Rama actual de actividad económica (industria), ocupación y situación en el empleo principal. Empleo secundario. Actividad habitual.
Alcance de la encuesta:
Ámbito geográfico: Zonas urbanas y rurales en 16 estados del Norte de Sudán. Se excluyen 9 estados del Sur del país.
Grupos de población: Todos los residentes permanentes del hogar, incluidos extranjeros y personas ausentes por menos de 3 meses.
Disponibilidad de estimaciones de otras fuentes para las áreas/grupos excluidos: Se dispone de estimaciones basadas en los resultados del censo de población para las zonas y los grupos de población excluidos.
Grupos abarcados por la encuesta pero excluidos de los resultados publicados: Niños menores de 10 años de edad.
Periodicidad:
Recolección de datos: Desde 1990 se han realizado tres encuestas de hogares (1990, 1994 y 1996).
Publicación de los resultados: Después de cada encuesta.
Periodo de referencia:
Empleo: Semana de referencia fija para la ocupación actual y año de referencia para la ocupación habitual.
Búsqueda de trabajo: El mismo periodo de referencia que para el empleo.
Disponibilidad para trabajo: No disponible.
Conceptos y definiciones:
Empleo actual: Personas de 10 años y más de edad que trabajaron por lo menos 2 días durante la semana anterior a la encuesta. [Empleo habitual: Personas de 10 años y más de edad que trabajaron tres meses o más durante el año de referencia]. La definición de empleado incluye las personas con un empleo pero temporalmente ausentes del mismo por enfermedad, lesión, vacaciones, licencia por maternidad, licencia para estudios o capacitación, conflictos laborales, mal tiempo, desperfectos mecánicos, etc. Se incluyen también las personas suspendidas de su trabajo por tiempo indeterminado sin remuneración y las personas sin trabajo y corrientemente disponibles para trabajar que han tomado disposiciones para comenzar en un empleo en una fecha posterior al periodo de referencia. Se excluyen las personas ausentes sin autorización. Se incluyen los aprendices remunerados y participantes en planes de promoción del empleo. Se incluyen los estudiantes de dedicación completa y parcial que trabajan a tiempo completo, pero se excluyen los que trabajan a tiempo parcial. Se excluyen los aprendices y las personas en formación no remunerados, así como los trabajadores familiares no remunerados y temporalmente ausentes del trabajo. Se incluyen las personas ocupadas en la producción de bienes por cuenta propia, pero no las que prestan servicios personales o no remunerados para su propio hogar. Se incluyen los reclutas y miembros del servicio civil equivalente al servicio militar, pero se excluyen las personas que realizan un trabajo voluntario social para la comunidad. Se excluyen también las personas que realizaron algún trabajo remunerado o por un beneficio durante el periodo de referencia pero que estaban sometidas a escolaridad obligatoria, jubiladas y recibían una pensión, estaban inscritas como desempleadas en busca de trabajo en una oficina de empleo o percibiendo indemnizaciones de desempleo.
Desempleo: Personas de 10 años y más de edad que, durante la semana de referencia, estaban sin empleo o trabajaron menos de 2 días, pero estaban disponibles para trabajar, deseaban hacerlo y buscaban trabajo, que hayan trabajado antes o no. [Desempleo habitual: Personas de 10 años y más de edad que trabajaron menos de 3 meses durante el año de referencia, pero estaban disponibles para trabajar, deseaban hacerlo y buscaron trabajo durante el año]. La definición de desempleo incluye las personas suspendidas de su trabajo temporalmente y sin remuneración, así como las personas con licencia sin goce de sueldo por iniciativa del empleador. Se incluyen también los trabajadores familiares no remunerados y temporalmente ausentes del trabajo, así como aprendices y personas en formación no remunerados. Se excluyen los estudiantes de dedicación completa y parcial que buscaban trabajo a tiempo parcial, pero se incluyen los estudiantes de dedicación parcial que buscaban trabajo a tiempo completo. Se excluyen las personas que buscaban trabajo pero que estaban sometidas a escolaridad obligatoria o jubiladas y percibían una pensión. Se excluyen también las personas sin empleo y disponibles para trabajar, que no buscaban trabajo durante el periodo de referencia.
Horas de trabajo: Se refiere al número de horas realmente trabajadas en la actividad principal y las horas dedicadas al empleo secundario.
Salarios y sueldos: Incluye los salarios y sueldos ordinarios, en efectivo y en especie, después de deducir las cotizaciones a la seguridad social, para el trabajo principal y los otros empleos ocupados durante el periodo de referencia. Se miden también los ingresos del empleo independiente en función del valor de producción de actividades agrícolas y ganaderas, tierras arrendadas y capital de todos los trabajos realizados durante el año de referencia.
Empleo en el Sector informal: Empleo en una unidad económica que no tiene un lugar fijo de operaciones, no está registrada en el sistema de registro comercial o no paga impuestos por sus actividades.
Clasificaciones:
Rama de actividad económica (industria):
Grupos de población clasificados por industria: No disponible.
Número de Grupos utilizados para la codificación: No disponible.
Vínculos con la CIIU Rev.3, 1988.
Ocupación:
Grupos de población clasificados por ocupación: No disponible.
Número de Grupos utilizados para la codificación: No disponible.
Vínculos con la CIUO-1988.
Situación en el empleo:
Grupos de población clasificados por situación en el empleo: No disponible.
Lista de grupos: Empleados. Empleadores. Trabajadores por cuenta propia. Trabajadores familiares y personas en formación.
No está vinculada a la CISE-1993.
Educación:
Grupos de población clasificados por educación: No disponible.
Lista de grupos: Analfabetos. Saben leer y escribir. **Educación:** primaria. **Educación:** intermedia. **Educación:** secundaria. **Educación:** universitaria. Estudios de postgrado.
Tamaño y diseño de la muestra:
Unidad final de muestreo: Hogares privados y particulares en hogares colectivos.
Tamaño de la muestra (unidades finales de muestreo): Unos 3 390 hogares privados en zonas urbanas y rurales.
Fracción de muestreo: 0,1 por ciento de la población total.
Marco de la muestra: Basado en zonas de enumeración del censo de población de 1993 y el Censo Nacional Agrícola de 1996. La selección de la muestra se basa en un diseño estratificado en múltiples etapas.
Actualización de la muestra: Se hacen nuevas listas de las UPM de la muestra.
Rotación: Los hogares se entrevistan tres veces, cada trimestre, durante el año de la encuesta.
Levantamiento de la encuesta:
Tipo de entrevista: Entrevista personal con papel y lápiz.
Duración del trabajo de campo Por área de muestra: 2 días.
Duración del trabajo de campo: 15 días.
Organización de la encuesta: Se contrata personal para cada ronda de la encuesta.
Número de personas que trabajan en el campo: Un total de 155 entrevistadores, supervisores y otro personal sobre el terreno.
Substitución de las unidades finales de muestreo que no responden: No.
Estimaciones y ajustes:
Tasa de no-respuesta total: No disponible.

Ajustes: No se hicieron ajustes por posible falta o exceso de cobertura ni por no respuesta.

Imputación por no respuesta de ítemes: No.

Alcance de la encuesta:

Título y fecha de la primera encuesta: Encuesta sobre Migración y Fuerza de Trabajo, 1990 (Migration and Labour force survey, 1990).

Modificaciones y revisiones significativas: No disponible.

Documentación y difusión:

Documentación:

Los resultados se publicaron en volúmenes separados sobre: 1. características de la población; 2. tasas de participación económica; 3. tasas de desempleo; estado civil; 5. migración interna; 6. migracion internacional; y 7. migración de retorno.

Tiempo necesario para difundir los primeros datos: 12 meses. Periodo de encuesta: abril de 1995. Publicación de los primeros datos de la encuesta: abril de 1996.

Información adelantada acerca de la fecha de la primera difusión pública: Sí.

Disponibilidad de datos no publicados si se solicitan: En base de datos y disquetes, previa solicitud.

Suecia

Título de la encuesta: Encuesta sobre la Fuerza de Trabajo (Labour Force Survey (LFS)).

Organismo responsable de la encuesta:

Planificar y realizar la encuesta: Servicio de Estadísticas de Suecia (Statistics Sweden).

Analizar y publicar los resultados: Servicio de Estadísticas de Suecia (Statistics Sweden).

Temas abarcados: Empleo, desempleo, subempleo, horas de trabajo, duración del desempleo, trabajadores desalentados, trabajadores ocasionales, rama de actividad económica (industria), ocupación, situación en el empleo, nivel de educación/calificación, actividad habitual, empleo secundario y familia.

Alcance de la encuesta:

Ámbito geográfico: Todo el país.

Grupos de población: Todos los habitantes de 15 a 74 años de edad comprendidos en el registro civil, incluidos voluntarios y miembros de carrera de las fuerzas armadas.

Disponibilidad de estimaciones de otras fuentes para las áreas/grupos excluidos: No se proporcionó información.

Grupos abarcados por la encuesta pero excluidos de los resultados publicados: Se pueden obtener estimaciones separadas sobre personas de 15 años y de 65 a 74 años de edad.

Periodicidad:

Recolección de datos: Mensualmente.

Publicación de los resultados: Mensualmente.

Periodo de referencia:

Empleo: Una semana.

Búsqueda de trabajo: Una semana.

Disponibilidad para trabajo: Una semana.

Conceptos y definiciones:

Empleo: Todas las personas de 16 a 64 años de edad, que:

1)durante la semana de medida habían trabajado durante una hora por lo menos como empleados asalariados, empresarios, empleados independientes o ayudantes no remunerados en negocios pertenecientes al cónyuge u otro miembro de la familia del mismo hogar (empleado y en el trabajo);

2)no realizaron ningún trabajo de acuerdo con la definición anterior, pero tenían empleo o trabajaban como trabajadores familiares no remunerados, empresarios o empleados independientes y habían estado temporalmente ausentes durante toda la semana de medida por enfermedad, vacaciones, otros motivos (cuidado de los hijos, estudios, servicio militar, otros permisos o conflictos laborales), independientemente de que la ausencia fuera o no remunerada (= empleados, temporalmente ausentes).

Se incluyen también:

a)trabajadores a tiempo completo o parcial que buscaban otro empleo durante la semana de medida;

b)estudiantes de dedicación completa o parcial que trabajaban a tiempo completo o parcial;

c)personas suspendidas temporalmente con remuneración (la suspensión sin remuneración no existe en Suecia);

d)personas que realizaron algún trabajo remunerado o por un beneficio durante la semana de medida pero que estaban sometidas a escolaridad obligatoria, jubiladas y percibían una pensión, inscritas como desempleadas en busca de trabajo en una oficina de empleo o recibiendo indemnizaciones de desempleo;

e)aprendices y personas en formación remunerados;

f)participantes en sistemas de promoción del empleo (talleres protegidos, obras de socorro, equipos juveniles o empleados en virtud de sistemas especiales de subsidios o becas públicas);

g)trabajadores familiares remunerados o no, incluidos los temporalmente ausentes del trabajo durante la semana de medida;

h)servicio doméstico privado;

i)miembros de cooperativas de productores;

j)miembros de carrera y voluntarios de las fuerzas armadas;

k)reclutas y personas que cumplen un servicio civil equivalente al servicio militar, siempre que hayan tenido empleo antes del servicio y obtenido una licencia (es decir, temporalmente ausentes) para ausentarse de su empleo civil durante el cumplimiento del servicio civil o militar.

Las personas con licencia para estudios o capacitación pagadas por el empleador (durante las horas de trabajo pagadas o ausencia autorizada y remunerada) se clasifican como personas con empleo “trabajando”. Las personas con licencia para estudios no remuneradas (licencia para estudios) se clasifican como personas con empleo “no trabajando”.

Se excluyen de la fuerza de trabajo sueca las personas que trabajan en el extranjero y no tienen un empleo en Suecia, que crucen la frontera para ir a trabajar en el exterior o que vivan y trabajen en un país extranjero.

Desempleo: Personas de 16 a 64 años de edad que, durante la semana de medida, no tenían empleo, pero querían y podían aceptar un trabajo y estaban en busca del mismo, o lo hubiesen hecho de no estar temporalmente incapacitadas para hacerlo o en espera de los resultados de alguna gestión para conseguir trabajo, realizada durante las cuatro últimas semanas. Se incluyen también las personas que esperaban comenzar un nuevo empleo en un periodo de cuatro semanas.

Los estudiantes de dedicación parcial que buscan trabajo a tiempo completo o parcial se clasifican también como desempleados.

Los estudiantes de dedicación completa que buscan trabajo a tiempo completo o parcial se excluyen de los desempleados y se consideran como inactivos; sin embargo, se recopilan datos sobre el tamaño de este grupo.

Los trabajadores estacionales en espera de la cosecha o de otra ocupación de temporada se clasifican como desempleados, siempre que se ajusten a la definición de desempleo; de lo contrario, se consideran fuera de la fuerza de trabajo.

“Buscar trabajo activamente” significa haber realizado una o más de las siguientes gestiones durante las cuatro semanas anteriores a la entrevista: ponerse en contacto con oficinas de empleo o con empleadores en forma directa; leer o colocar anuncios; ponerse en contacto con amigos o parientes, etc.

Subempleo:

Subempleo por insuficiencia de horas: Son subempleadas las personas que trabajan menos tiempo del que desean por motivos relacionados con el mercado de trabajo.

Situaciones de empleo inadecuado: No corresponde.

Horas de trabajo: Se recopilan tanto las horas realmente trabajadas (incluidas las horas extraordinarias) durante la semana de medida, como las horas habituales (contractuales). Ambas variables se miden por separado para el empleo principal y secundario.

Ingresos relacionados con el empleo:

Ingresos relacionados con el empleo asalariado: La encuesta no abarca este punto.

Ingresos relacionados con el empleo independiente: La encuesta no abarca este punto.

Sector informal: La encuesta no abarca este punto.

Actividad habitual: A las personas sin empleo asalariado y a los trabajadores ocasionales se les pregunta sobre cuál es la actividad principal que tienen habitualmente.

Clasificaciones:

Rama de actividad económica (industria):

Título de la clasificación utilizada: Clasificación Industrial Uniforme de Suecia (SE-SIC 92) de 1992

Grupos de población clasificados por industria: Empleados y desempleados (rama de actividad económica del último empleo para el desempleado).

Número de Grupos utilizados para la codificación: Los datos se recopilan y clasifican en 64 grupos, pero se presentan en 48 grupos.

Vínculos con la CIIU: CIIU-Rev.3 a nivel de 2 dígitos.

Ocupación:

Título de la clasificación utilizada: Clasificación Uniforme de Ocupaciones de Suecia (SSYK96) de 1996.

Grupos de población clasificados por ocupación: Empleados y desempleados (ocupación en el último empleo para el desempleado).
Número de Grupos utilizados para la codificación: Los datos se recopilan y clasifican en 381 grupos (nivel de 4 dígitos), pero se presentan en 68 grupos.
Vínculos con la CIUO: CIUO-88.
Situación en el empleo:
Título de la clasificación utilizada: Clasificación nacional.
Grupos de población clasificados por situación en el empleo: Empleados y desempleados (situación en el último empleo para el desempleado).
Grupos utilizados para la codificación: Empleadores, empresarios/empleados independientes (con y sin empleados), trabajadores familiares.
Vínculos con la CISE: CISE-1993.
Educación:
Título de la clasificación utilizada: Clasificación Uniforme de Enseñanza de Suecia (SUN 2000).
Grupos de población clasificados por educación: Todos los entrevistados se clasifican según el nivel más alto de educación que hayan alcanzado y el ámbito de conocimientos más elevado que hayan completado. Esta información no se pide en la encuesta, sino que se obtiene del Registro Sueco de Enseñanza.
Grupos utilizados para la codificación: El 'nivel-código' comprende 47 códigos (3 dígitos) pero los datos se presentan en 7 grupos. El 'ámbito-código' comprende un código de 4 dígitos pero los datos se presentan en 9 grupos.
Vínculos con la CINE: CINE-1997.
Tamaño y diseño de la muestra:
Unidad final de muestreo: Particulares.
Tamaño de la muestra (unidades finales de muestreo): 22 000 particulares de una población de casi 6,5 millones (de 15 a 74 años de edad) y 21 000 de 5,6 millones (de 16 a 64 años de edad).
Fracción de muestreo: No se dispone de información.
Marco de la muestra: El registro de población del SCB (Servicio de Estadísticas de Suecia) que se actualiza más o menos de manera constante.
Actualización de la muestra: Se elaboran muestras para cada ronda del año a fin de cumplir las exigencias del año siguiente (abril-marzo). De esta forma la muestra se actualiza cada mes con respecto a las migraciones, los fallecimientos y las modificaciones del estado civil. La muestra se complementa con información sobre los inmigrantes una vez por trimestre.
Rotación:
Esquema: Las personas de la muestra se entrevistan una vez por trimestre, es decir un total de 8 veces en dos años antes de ser sustituidas. Cada mes se renueva 1/8 de la muestra.
Porcentaje de unidades que permanecen en la muestra durante dos encuestas consecutivas: 87,5 por ciento permanece en la misma muestra por dos trimestres consecutivos.
Número máximo de entrevistas por unidad de muestreo: No se dispone de información.
Tiempo necesario para renovar completamente la muestra: Dos años.
Levantamiento de la encuesta:
Tipo de entrevista: Entrevistas por teléfono (CATI) que se completan con una visita personal (0,2 por ciento de los entrevistados) cuando no se puede establecer contacto con la persona de la muestra.
Número de unidades finales de muestreo por área de muestra: No se dispone de información.
Duración del trabajo de campo:
Total: De 5 a 6 semanas.
Por área de muestra: No se dispone de información.
Organización de la encuesta: Permanente.
Número de personas que trabajan en el campo: 200.
Substitución de las unidades finales de muestreo que no responden: No.
Estimaciones y ajustes:
Tasa de no-respuesta total: Casi el 15 por ciento en febrero de 2002.
Ajuste por no-respuesta total: Sí.
Imputación por no respuesta de ítemes: No.
Ajuste por áreas/poblaciones no abarcadas: No se dispone de información.
Ajuste por falta de cobertura: No.
Ajuste por exceso de cobertura: No.
Ajuste por variaciones estacionales: Sí.

Historia de la encuesta:
Título y fecha de la primera encuesta: La Junta Nacional de Mercado del Trabajo realizó la primera Encuesta sobre la Fuerza de Trabajo de Suecia en mayo de 1959.
Modificaciones y revisiones significativas: La encuesta era trimestral (desde agosto de 1961 a 1979) y luego pasó a ser mensual. 1987: Revisión de conceptos y definiciones. 1981: introducción de entrevistas por teléfono (CATI). 1995: nueva clasificación industrial. 1997: nueva clasificación por ocupación. 2000: nueva clasificación en la enseñanza. 2003: los principales cambios previstos se ajustarán a las normas de la UE.
Documentación y difusión:
Documentación:
Título de las publicaciones con los resultados de la encuesta (periodicidad): Statistical Messages (SM): SM Am 10 (mensualmente), SM Am 11 (trimestralmente), SM Am 12 (anualmente).
Título de las publicaciones con la metodología de la encuesta (periodicidad): 2001:5 Urvals- och estimationsförfarandet i de svenska arbetskraftsundersökningarna (AKU (Diseño y estimaciones de la LFS9. Se traducirá al inglés).
Difusión:
Tiempo necesario para difundir los primeros datos: Dos semanas después de finalizar el mes.
Información adelantada acerca de la fecha de la primera difusión pública: Sí.
Disponibilidad de datos no publicados si se solicitan: Sí.
Disponibilidad de datos por medios informáticos: Sí. Sitio web: http://www.scb.se/

Suiza

Título de la encuesta : Encuesta suiza sobre la población activa (Enquête suisse sur la population active).
Organismo responsable de la encuesta:
Planificar y realizar la encuesta: Oficina Federal de Estadísticas (Office fédéral de statistique).
Analizar y publicar los resultados: Oficina Federal de Estadísticas (Office fédéral de statistique).
Temas abarcados: Empleo, desempleo, subempleo, duración del empleo, salarios, ingresos, duración del empleo y el desempleo, trabajadores ocasionales, rama de actividad económica (industria), ocupación, situación en el empleo, empleo secundario.
Alcance de la encuesta :
Ámbito geográfico: Todo el país.
Grupos de población : Personas de 15 años y más de edad. Se excluyen las personas que no están domiciliadas en el país todo el año, tales como los trabajadores estacionales, trabajadores fronterizos, solicitantes de asilo y las personas que residen en el territorio nacional por un breve periodo de tiempo.
Disponibilidad de estimaciones de otras fuentes para las áreas/grupos excluidos: No corresponde.
Grupos abarcados por la encuesta pero excluidos de los resultados publicados: No corresponde.
Periodicidad:
Recolección de datos: Anualmente.
Publicación de los resultados: Anualmente.
Periodo de referencia:
Empleo: Una semana durante el segundo trimestre.
Búsqueda de trabajo: Cuatro semanas durante el segundo trimestre.
Disponibilidad para trabajo: Dos semanas durante el segundo trimestre.
Conceptos y definiciones:
Empleo: Personas de 15 años o más de edad, asalariadas o independientes, que trabajaron por lo menos una hora, por una remuneración, durante la semana de referencia (semana anterior a la entrevista), así como las personas temporalmente ausentes de su trabajo, y quienes trabajaron durante la semana de referencia, sin remuneración, en la empresa familiar.
Se consideran también empleados:
a)las personas ausentes de su trabajo, durante un periodo inferior a tres meses, debido a enfermedad o lesión, vacaciones o licencia anual, licencia por maternidad o paternidad, licencia para estudios o capacitación, ausencia sin autorización, conflictos laborales, mal tiempo o desperfectos mecánicos, etc., así como las personas suspendidas de su trabajo temporalmente sin remuneración (menos de tres meses);
b)las personas que realizaron algún trabajo, remunerado o por un beneficio, durante la semana de referencia, pero que estaban sometidas a escolaridad obligatoria, jubiladas y recibían una pen-

sión, inscritas como desempleadas en busca de trabajo en una oficina de empleo o percibiendo indemnizaciones de desempleo;
c)los estudiantes de dedicación completa o parcial que trabajaban a tiempo completo o parcial;
d)los aprendices y las personas en formación remunerados o no, las personas que participan en planes de promoción del empleo, como los programas de empleo temporal, formación profesional, etc.;
e)los trabajadores familiares no remunerados que trabajaron durante el periodo de referencia;
f)los miembros de las fuerzas armadas: militares de carrera y reclutas, así como las personas que efectúan un servicio civil equivalente al servicio militar de 12 semanas o que ocupan un empleo durante el tiempo que cumplen su servicio militar.
Desempleo: Personas de 15 años y más de edad que no realizaron ninguna actividad remunerada durante la semana anterior a la entrevista, buscaron un empleo durante las cuatro últimas semanas, tomaron durante ese periodo una o varias medidas específicas para encontrar un empleo y que podrían comenzar a trabajar en un plazo de cuatro semanas.
Las personas que ya encontraron un empleo se consideran desempleadas si deben comenzar a trabajar en un plazo de tres meses.
Se consideran también desempleados:
a)las personas sin empleo e inmediatamente disponibles para trabajar, que trataron de establecer su propia empresa;
b)las personas en busca de un empleo y/o inmediatamente disponibles para trabajar, pero que estaban sometidas a escolaridad obligatoria o jubiladas y recibían una pensión;
c)los estudiantes de dedicación completa o parcial en busca de un empleo a tiempo completo o parcial.
Subempleo:
Subempleo por insuficiencia de horas: Se aplican tres criterios: disposición a trabajar más horas, disponibilidad para trabajar más horas y duración del trabajo inferior a un nivel específico, por determinar.
Situaciones de empleo inadecuado: La encuesta no abarca este punto.
Horas de trabajo: Horas realmente trabajadas y horas habituales por semana en todas las actividades. Las horas realmente efectuadas se refieren al empleo principal y al último empleo.
Ingresos relacionados con el empleo:
Ingresos relacionados con el empleo asalariado: Ingresos profesionales (brutos y netos) para todas las actividades.
Ingresos relacionados con el empleo independiente: La encuesta no abarca este punto.
Sector informal: La encuesta no abarca este punto.
Actividad habitual: La encuesta no abarca este punto.
Clasificaciones:
Rama de actividad económica (industria):
Título de la clasificación utilizada: Clasificación nacional.
Grupos de población clasificados por industria: Personas empleadas y desempleadas (rama de actividad económica del último empleo para el desempleado).
Número de Grupos utilizados para la codificación: 222 grupos.
Vínculos con la CIIU: CIIU-Rev.3.
Ocupación:
Título de la clasificación utilizada: Clasificación nacional.
Grupos de población clasificados por ocupación: Personas empleadas y desempleadas (ocupación en el último empleo para el desempleado).
Número de Grupos utilizados para la codificación: 87 grupos, 388 clases y unas 16 000 ocupaciones.
Vínculos con la CIUO: CIUO-88.
Situación en el empleo:
Título de la clasificación utilizada: Clasificación nacional.
Grupos de población clasificados por situación en el empleo: Personas empleadas y desempleadas (situación en el último empleo para el desempleado).
Grupos utilizados para la codificación: Independientes, asalariados, ayudas familiares. Las dos primeras categorías se subdividen en subgrupos.
Vínculos con la CISE: CISE-1993.
Educación:
Título de la clasificación utilizada: Clasificación nacional.
Grupos de población clasificados por educación: Personas empleadas y desempleadas.
Grupos utilizados para la codificación: Escolaridad obligatoria; formación elemental; manualidades; cultura general; aprendizaje; escuela a tiempo completo; bachillerato; formación profesional superior; escuela técnica o profesional; escuela profesional superior; universidad o escuela superior; formación sin finalizar.
Vínculos con la CINE: CINE-1997.
Tamaño y diseño de la muestra:
Unidad final de muestreo: Personas.
Tamaño de la muestra (unidades finales de muestreo): Entre 16 000 y 18 000 personas. A partir de 2002, unas 35 000 personas.
Fracción de muestreo: 0,3 por ciento de la población residente permanente.
Marco de la muestra: Guía de teléfonos en la que figuran todas las personas conectadas a la red de teléfonos. El plan de selección de direcciones se basa en el principio de muestras al azar, estratificado por cantón. El número de direcciones que se selecciona al azar es proporcional al número de habitantes y a la tasa de respuesta de los diferentes cantones.
Actualización de la muestra : No se dispone de información.
Rotación:
Esquema: La muestra se compone de un quinto de las personas interrogadas por primera vez y de cuatro quintos del número de personas que ya se han interrogado por lo menos una vez.
Porcentaje de unidades que permanecen en la muestra durante dos encuestas consecutivas: 80 por ciento.
Número máximo de entrevistas por unidad de muestreo: Cinco veces.
Tiempo necesario para renovar completamente la muestra : Cinco años.
Levantamiento de la encuesta:
Tipo de entrevista: Entrevista por teléfono asistida por computadora (CATI).
Número de unidades finales de muestreo por área de muestra: No se dispone de información.
Duración del trabajo de campo:
Total: 3 meses.
Por área de muestra: No se dispone de información.
Organización de la encuesta : Estructura permanente.
Número de personas que trabajan en el campo: Cinco personas a nivel federal y unos 250 encuestadores de una empresa privada.
Substitución de las unidades finales de muestreo que no responden: No.
Estimaciones y ajustes:
Tasa de no-respuesta total: 20 por ciento.
Ajuste por no-respuesta total: No.
Imputación por no respuesta de ítemes: No.
Ajuste por áreas/poblaciones no abarcadas: No.
Ajuste por falta de cobertura: Sí.
Ajuste por exceso de cobertura: Sí.
Ajuste por variaciones estacionales: No.
Historia de la encuesta:
Título y fecha de la primera encuesta: Encuesta suiza sobre la población activa, 1991 (Enquête suisse sur la population active).
Modificaciones y revisiones significativas : 1996: preguntas relativas al volumen de trabajo. 2001: adaptación a las recomendaciones internacionales y nuevas preguntas sobre el trabajo atípico.
Documentación y difusión:
Documentación:
Título de las publicaciones con los resultados de la encuesta (periodicidad): Enquête suisse sur la population active (ESPA): resultados comentados y cuadros (publicación anual).
Título de las publicaciones con la metodología de la encuesta (periodicidad): Enquête suisse sur la population active (ESPA): conceptos, bases metodológicas, consideraciones prácticas (1996).
Difusión:
Tiempo necesario para difundir los primeros datos: Noviembre del año de referencia de la encuesta.
Información adelantada acerca de la fecha de la primera difusión pública: Sí.
Disponibilidad de datos no publicados si se solicitan: Sí.
Disponibilidad de datos por medios informáticos: Sí. Sitio web: http://www.statistik.admin.ch

Tailandia

Título de la encuesta: Encuesta sobre la Fuerza de Trabajo (Labour Force Survey).
Organismo responsable de la encuesta:
Planificar y realizar la encuesta: Oficina Nacional de Estadísticas (National Statistical Office (NSO)).
Analizar y publicar los resultados: Oficina Nacional de Estadísticas (National Statistical Office (NSO)).

Temas abarcados: Empleo, desempleo, subempleo, horas de trabajo, salarios, ingresos, empleo en el sector informal, duración del desempleo, rama de actividad económica (industria), ocupación, situación en el empleo, nivel de educación, actividad habitual.
Alcance de la encuesta:
Ámbito geográfico: Todo el país.
Grupos de población: Personas de 13 años y más de edad, salvo quienes viven en hogares colectivos (incluidas las fuerzas armadas).
Disponibilidad de estimaciones de otras fuentes para las áreas/grupos excluidos: No corresponde.
Grupos abarcados por la encuesta pero excluidos de los resultados publicados: Ninguno.
Periodicidad:
Recolección de datos: Trimestralmente.
Publicación de los resultados: Trimestralmente.
Periodo de referencia:
Empleo: Una semana (fija).
Búsqueda de trabajo: Un mes (fijo).
Disponibilidad para trabajo: Una semana (fija).
Conceptos y definiciones:
Empleo: Personas de 13 años y más de edad que, durante la semana de referencia: a) trabajaron por lo menos una hora por un sueldo, beneficio, dividendos o cualquier pago en especie; b) no trabajaron pero tenían un empleo regular, empresa comercial o agrícola y estaban temporalmente ausentes por enfermedad o lesión, vacaciones o día de fiesta, huelga o cierre patronal, mal tiempo, fin de temporada u otras razones, como la clausura temporal del lugar de trabajo, independientemente de estar remunerados o no por sus empleadores durante el periodo de ausencia y, si se trata de una clausura temporal del sitio de trabajo, se suponga que volverá a abrir sus puertas en un plazo de 30 días contados a partir de la fecha de clausura y que las personas podrán reintegrarse a su trabajo anterior; o c) trabajaron por lo menos una hora sin remuneración en una empresa comercial o agrícola de propiedad o administración del jefe del hogar o miembros del mismo.
Desempleo: Personas de 13 años o más de edad que, durante la semana de referencia, no trabajaron ni siquiera una hora, no tenían empleo ni empresa comercial o agrícola de su propiedad, no estaban temporalmente ausentes del trabajo pero si disponibles para trabajar. Se incluyen las personas que habían estado en busca de trabajo durante los últimos 30 días y quienes no habían estado en busca de trabajo por enfermedad o por creer que no encontrarían un trabajo adecuado, o porque esperaban comenzar un nuevo empleo o el inicio de la temporada agrícola o por otras razones. Se incluyen las personas suspendidas de su trabajo temporalmente o por tiempo indeterminado sin remuneración.
Subempleo:
Subempleo por insuficiencia de horas: Personas de 13 años y más de edad que trabajaban menos de 35 horas por semana, estaban disponibles y deseaban trabajar horas adicionales.
Situaciones de empleo inadecuado: No se dispone de información.
Horas de trabajo: Horas realmente trabajadas durante la semana de referencia en todos los empleos. Se refiere a las horas normales de trabajo para las personas ausentes del trabajo durante la semana de referencia.
Ingresos relacionados con el empleo:
Ingresos relacionados con el empleo asalariado: Se refiere al empleo principal en la semana de referencia e incluye pagos en efectivo, en especie o servicios.
Ingresos relacionados con el empleo independiente: Se refiere a la producción menos los gastos de explotación de los trabajadores por cuenta propia y trabajadores familiares no remunerados.
Sector informal: Trabajadores por cuenta propia, empleadores de empleados privados y trabajadores familiares no remunerados en establecimientos comerciales con menos de 10 personas.
Actividad habitual: Se mide en un periodo de referencia de un año.
Clasificaciones:
Rama de actividad económica (industria):
Título de la clasificación utilizada: Clasificación Industrial Uniforme de Tailandia (TSIC).
Grupos de población clasificados por industria: Personas empleadas y personas desempleadas con experiencia previa de trabajo.
Número de Grupos utilizados para la codificación: 10 grupos principales.
Vínculos con la CIIU: CIIU-Rev. 2.
Ocupación:
Título de la clasificación utilizada: No se dispone de información.
Grupos de población clasificados por ocupación: Personas empleadas y personas desempleadas con experiencia previa de trabajo.
Número de Grupos utilizados para la codificación: 10 grupos principales.
Vínculos con la CIUO: CIUO-68.
Situación en el empleo:
Título de la clasificación utilizada: No se dispone de información.
Grupos de población clasificados por situación en el empleo: Personas empleadas y personas desempleadas con experiencia previa de trabajo.
Grupos utilizados para la codificación: Empleador, empleado gubernamental, empleado privado.
Vínculos con la CISE: CISE-93, salvo para los miembros de cooperativas de productores que no existen en la clasificación nacional.
Educación:
Título de la clasificación utilizada: No se dispone de información.
Grupos de población clasificados por educación: Personas empleadas y desempleadas.
Grupos utilizados para la codificación: Sin escolaridad, menos que la escuela elemental inferior, escuela elemental inferior.
Vínculos con la CINE: CINE-76 y CINE-97.
Tamaño y diseño de la muestra:
Unidad final de muestreo: Hogar.
Tamaño de la muestra (unidades finales de muestreo): Unos 60 500 hogares.
Fracción de muestreo: Casi el 6 por ciento (5 610/94 955 bloques de viviendas y aldeas).
Marco de la muestra: Basado en bloques de viviendas y aldeas del Censo de Población y Hogares de 1990.
Actualización de la muestra: Anualmente.
Rotación:
Esquema: No corresponde.
Porcentaje de unidades que permanecen en la muestra durante dos encuestas consecutivas: No corresponde.
Número máximo de entrevistas por unidad de muestreo: No corresponde.
Tiempo necesario para renovar completamente la muestra: No corresponde.
Levantamiento de la encuesta:
Tipo de entrevista: Personal.
Número de unidades finales de muestreo por área de muestra: 12 hogares para zonas municipales, 9 hogares para zonas no municipales.
Duración del trabajo de campo:
Total: Un mes.
Por área de muestra: No disponible.
Organización de la encuesta: No disponible.
Número de personas que trabajan en el campo: 800 personas.
Substitución de las unidades finales de muestreo que no responden: No.
Estimaciones y ajustes:
Tasa de no-respuesta total: 10 por ciento.
Ajuste por no-respuesta total: No.
Imputación por no respuesta de ítemes: No.
Ajuste por áreas/poblaciones no abarcadas: No.
Ajuste por falta de cobertura: No.
Ajuste por exceso de cobertura: No.
Ajuste por variaciones estacionales: No.
Historia de la encuesta:
Título y fecha de la primera encuesta: Encuesta sobre la Fuerza de Trabajo, 1963 (Labour Force Survey).
Modificaciones y revisiones significativas: Los conceptos y definiciones actuales se utilizan desde 1983 y la edad mínima de 13 años, desde 1989.
Documentación y difusión:
Documentación:
Título de las publicaciones con los resultados de la encuesta (periodicidad): Report of the Labour Force survey (trimestralmente).
Título de las publicaciones con la metodología de la encuesta (periodicidad): Idem.
Difusión:
Tiempo necesario para difundir los primeros datos: Unos 5 meses.
Información adelantada acerca de la fecha de la primera difusión pública: No.
Disponibilidad de datos no publicados si se solicitan: Sí.
Disponibilidad de datos por medios informáticos: Disquetes e internet; sitio web: http://www.nso.go.th/

Tanzanía, Rep. Unida de

Título de la encuesta: Encuesta sobre la Fuerza de Trabajo (Labour Force Survey).
Organismo responsable de la encuesta:
Planificar y realizar la encuesta: Oficina Nacional de Estadísticas en cooperación con el Departamento de Trabajo (National Bureau of Statistics in cooperation with the Labour Department).
Analizar y publicar los resultados: Oficina Nacional de Estadísticas en cooperación con el Departamento de Trabajo (National Bureau of Statistics in cooperation with the Labour Department).
Temas abarcados: Empleo, desempleo, subempleo, horas de trabajo (horas habituales de trabajo, horas realmente trabajadas), ingresos del empleo, empleo en el sector informal, lugar de trabajo, duración del empleo, duración del desempleo, trabajadores desalentados, rama de actividad económica (industria), ocupación, situación en el empleo, nivel de educación o calificación, actividad habitual, empleo secundario.
Alcance de la encuesta:
Ámbito geográfico: Tierra firme de Tanzanía. No se abarcan las islas de Zanzibar.
Grupos de población: La encuesta abarca los miembros habituales de hogares privados en la tierra firme de Tanzanía, independientemente de su nacionalidad. No se abarcan las personas que viven en hogares colectivos. Se excluyen los diplomáticos extranjeros que residen en el país.
Disponibilidad de estimaciones de otras fuentes para las áreas/grupos excluidos: Sí, de otras encuestas similares realizadas en Zanzibar y de censos de población.
Grupos abarcados por la encuesta pero excluidos de los resultados publicados: Ninguno.
Periodicidad:
Recolección de datos: Cada 10 años. Los datos se recopilan durante un periodo de 12 meses divididos en cuatro trimestres. La última encuesta se realizó durante el periodo de abril de 2000 a marzo de 2001. La presente descripción se refiere a la Encuesta sobre la Fuerza de Trabajo de 1990 a 1991, que se efectuó durante el periodo comprendido entre octubre de 1990 y septiembre de 1991.
Publicación de los resultados: Cada 10 años.
Periodo de referencia:
Empleo: Periodo de referencia móvil de una semana, es decir la última semana civil completa (lunes a domingo) antes de la fecha de la entrevista.
Búsqueda de trabajo: Periodo de referencia móvil de cuatro semanas antes de la fecha de la entrevista.
Disponibilidad para trabajo: Periodo de referencia móvil de una semana, es decir la última semana civil completa (lunes a domingo) antes de la fecha de la entrevista.
Conceptos y definiciones:
Empleo: Todas las personas de 10 años o más de edad que realizaron algún trabajo (es decir, por lo menos una hora) durante la semana de referencia, como empleados por un pago, en efectivo o en especie, o como trabajadores independientes (incluidos agricultores) por un beneficio o ingreso para la familia. Se incluyen: a) trabajadores que contribuyen con la familia en el lugar de trabajo durante la semana de referencia; b) trabajadores a tiempo completo o parcial que buscaban otro empleo; c) personas que realizaron algún trabajo remunerado o por un beneficio durante la semana de referencia pero que estaban sometidas a escolaridad obligatoria, o estaban jubiladas y recibían una pensión; d) estudiantes de dedicación completa que trabajaban a tiempo parcial; e) estudiantes de dedicación parcial que trabajaban a tiempo completo o parcial; f) aprendices y personas en formación remunerados o no; y g) personas ocupadas en la producción de bienes para su propio uso final.
Se incluyen también las personas con empleo o un negocio del que estaban temporalmente ausentes durante la semana de referencia, pero al que sin duda se reintegrarían, debido a: a) enfermedad o lesión; b) vacaciones o licencia anual; c) licencia por maternidad o paternidad; d) licencia para estudios o capacitación; e) conflictos laborales; f) mal tiempo, desperfectos mecánicos, etc., o g) estaban suspendidas temporalmente sin remuneración. La duración de la ausencia está limitada a cuatro meses para los empleados y a un mes para los trabajadores independientes.
Se excluyen: a) trabajadores que contribuyen con la familia que no estaban en el trabajo durante la semana de referencia; b) trabajadores ocasionales que no estaban en el trabajo durante la semana de referencia; c) empleados ausentes del trabajo durante más de cuatro meses; d) trabajadores independientes ausentes del trabajo por más de un mes; e) personas suspendidas por tiempo indeterminado sin remuneración; y f) personas que prestan servicios no remunerados o personales a los miembros de su propio hogar.
Desempleo: Se utilizan dos definiciones: 1) personas de 10 años o más de edad que no estaban empleadas durante la semana de referencia, estaban disponibles para trabajar durante esa semana y habían tomado medidas activas para encontrar trabajo durante las cuatro últimas semanas; y 2) personas de 10 años o más de edad que no estaban empleadas durante la semana de referencia y estaban disponibles para trabajar durante esa semana. Se consideran medidas activas para encontrar trabajo: pedir trabajo a posibles empleadores; examinar las posibilidades de empleo en explotaciones agrícolas, fábricas o lugares de trabajo; pedir información sobre trabajo a amigos y parientes; hacer las gestiones necesarias para comenzar un negocio; tomar las medidas necesarias para establecer una explotación agrícola; otras.
Se incluyen: a) personas sin trabajo y disponibles para trabajar, que habían tomado disposiciones para comenzar un nuevo empleo en una fecha ulterior a la semana de referencia (definiciones 1 y 2); b) personas sin empleo y disponibles para trabajar, que procuraban establecer su propio negocio (definiciones 1 y 2); c) personas sin trabajo y disponibles para trabajar, pero que no buscaban empleo por otras razones que no sean las mencionadas en los apartados a) y b) anteriores (definición 2); d) personas que buscaban empleo y/o estaban disponibles para trabajar pero sometidas a escolaridad obligatoria o jubiladas y percibiendo una pensión (definiciones 1 y 2); e) estudiantes de dedicación completa que buscaban trabajo y /o estaban disponibles para hacerlo a tiempo completo o parcial (definiciones 1 y 2); y f) estudiantes de dedicacion parcial que buscaban empleo y/o están disponibles para trabajar a tiempo completo o parcial (definiciones 1 y 2).
Se excluyen las personas sin trabajo y disponibles para trabajar que no estaban buscando trabajo por otras razones que no sean las mencionadas en los apartados a) y b) anteriores (definición 1), y las personas sin trabajo que no estaban disponibles para trabajar (definiciones 1 y 2).
Subempleo:
Subempleo por insuficiencia de horas: Personas empleadas que trabajaron menos de 40 horas durante la semana de referencia por razones económicas y que estaban disponibles para trabajar más horas.
Situaciones de empleo inadecuado: La encuesta no abarca este punto.
Horas de trabajo: Horas habituales de trabajo por semana y horas realmente trabajadas durante la semana de referencia. La información sobre las horas habituales de trabajo y las horas realmente trabajadas se recopilan por separado para la principal actividad económica y para cualquier otra actividad económica.
Ingresos relacionados con el empleo:
Ingresos relacionados con el empleo asalariado: Salarios o sueldos brutos recibidos en efectivo durante el último mes en todos los empleos remunerados. Se excluyen los salarios o sueldos en especie.
Ingresos relacionados con el empleo independiente: Beneficio neto obtenido del negocio durante la última semana o mes. Para los trabajadores independientes ocupados en actividades no agrícolas, el beneficio neto se deduce de las preguntas sobre los ingresos brutos y los gastos de explotación; para los trabajadores independientes ocupados en el sector agrícola, la información sobre los beneficios netos se obtiene directamente.
Sector informal: Personas que trabajan en empresas que i) no son dependencias gubernamentales, paraestatales, organizaciones del partido CCM ni cooperativas formalmente establecidas; ii) emplean menos de seis empleados asalariados, y iii) están ubicadas en una estructura temporal, en un camino o una calle, o no tienen ubicación fija. Se excluyen las actividades tradicionales de la agricultura, la ganadería, la pesca, así como los servicios profesionales o prestados a las empresas y otros negocios con características formales bien definidas. Se incluyen los trabajadores domésticos remunerados empleados en el hogar.
Actividad habitual: La actividad económica habitual se refiere a la situación en la actividad principal durante un periodo de referencia de un año, es decir todos los 12 meses del año civil anterior a la fecha de la entrevista. Las personas de 10 años o más de edad se consideran habitualmente activas si trabajaron o estaban disponibles para trabajar seis meses o más de los 12 meses de referencia. Las personas habitualmente activas se subdividen en personas habitualmente empleadas y personas habitualmente desempleadas. Las personas habitualmente empleadas son las que han trabajado durante la mitad o más de los meses económicamente activos. Las personas habitualmente desempleadas son las que

han pasado más de la mitad de los meses económicamente activos sin trabajar y disponibles para hacerlo.
Clasificaciones:
Rama de actividad económica (industria):
Título de la clasificación utilizada: Adaptación de la clasificación de Tanzanía a la Clasificación Industrial Internacional Uniforme de todas las Actividades Económicas (CIIU, Rev. 2); se han creado códigos adicionales para describir las actividades del sector informal.
Grupos de población clasificados por industria: Personas empleadas.
Número de Grupos utilizados para la codificación: Grupos a nivel de 4 dígitos.
Vínculos con la CIIU: CIIU-Rev. 2.
Ocupación:
Título de la clasificación utilizada: Clasificación Uniforme de Ocupaciones de Tanzanía (TASCO).
Grupos de población clasificados por ocupación: Personas empleadas y personas desempleadas.
Número de Grupos utilizados para la codificación: Grupos a nivel de 4 dígitos.
Vínculos con la CIUO: CIUO-88.
Situación en el empleo:
Título de la clasificación utilizada: Clasificación nacional sobre la situación en el empleo.
Grupos de población clasificados por situación en el empleo: Personas empleadas.
Grupos utilizados para la codificación: a) empleados asalariados; b) trabajadores independientes (actividades no agrícolas) con empleados; c) trabajadores independientes (actividades no agrícolas) sin empleados; d) trabajadores que ayudan a la familia (actividades no agrícolas); e) personas que trabajan por cuenta propia o en explotaciones agrícolas familiares o shambas.
Vínculos con la CISE: Parcialmente.
Educación:
Título de la clasificación utilizada: Clasificación nacional de niveles de educación obtenidos.
Grupos de población clasificados por educación: Todas las personas de 10 años o más de edad.
Grupos utilizados para la codificación: a) sin escolaridad; b) primaria sin completar; c) primaria completa; d) secundaria hasta el nivel 2; e) secundaria hasta el nivel 4; f) secundaria hasta el nivel 6; g) universidad.
Vínculos con la CINE: No se proporcionó información.
Tamaño y diseño de la muestra:
Unidad final de muestreo: Hogar.
Tamaño de la muestra (unidades finales de muestreo): 7 762 hogares.
Fracción de muestreo: Un 0, 2 por ciento de hogares.
Marco de la muestra: La Muestra Principal Nacional (NMS), que comprende 122 zonas de enumeración urbanas y 150 aldeas rurales, se utiliza como marco de muestra de la encuesta. Antes de la encuesta se hace una lista de hogares en todas las zonas de enumeración y aldeas incluidas en la NMS.
Actualización de la muestra: La muestra se actualizará después de que se haya completado el trabajo cartográfico para el Censo de Población de 2002.
Rotación:
Esquema: No existe un plan de rotación de muestras. La muestra de la encuesta se divide en cuatro submuestras independientes trimestralmente.
Porcentaje de unidades que permanecen en la muestra durante dos encuestas consecutivas: No corresponde.
Número máximo de entrevistas por unidad de muestreo: No corresponde.
Tiempo necesario para renovar completamente la muestra: No corresponde.
Levantamiento de la encuesta:
Tipo de entrevista: La información se obtiene mediante entrevistas personales.
Número de unidades finales de muestreo por área de muestra: De 30 a 35 hogares por zona de enumeración urbana; 80 hogares por aldea rural.
Duración del trabajo de campo:
Total: Un año.
Por área de muestra: 14 días para las zonas de enumeración urbanas y 27 para aldeas rurales.
Organización de la encuesta: Se contrata personal para trabajar sobre el terreno para cada ronda de la encuesta.
Número de personas que trabajan en el campo: No se proporcionó información.
Substitución de las unidades finales de muestreo que no responden: No se hacen sustituciones de los hogares que no responden.
Estimaciones y ajustes:
Tasa de no-respuesta total: 2,4 por ciento de hogares de la muestra.
Ajuste por no-respuesta total: Sí.
Imputación por no respuesta de ítemes: No.
Ajuste por áreas/poblaciones no abarcadas: No corresponde.
Ajuste por falta de cobertura: Sí.
Ajuste por exceso de cobertura: No corresponde.
Ajuste por variaciones estacionales: No corresponde.
Historia de la encuesta:
Título y fecha de la primera encuesta: La primera Encuesta sobre la Fuerza de Trabajo de Tanzanía se realizó en 1965.
Modificaciones y revisiones significativas: No se realizó ninguna encuesta sobre la fuerza de trabajo desde 1966 hasta 1989. Las Encuestas sobre la Fuerza de Trabajo de 1990-1991 y 2000-2001 se basaron en las recomendaciones aprobadas por la Decimotercera Conferencia Internacional de Estadígrafos del Trabajo. Se añadieron módulos sobre el trabajo infantil y el sector informal a la Encuesta sobre la Fuerza de Trabajo de 2000-2001.
Documentación y difusión:
Documentación:
Título de las publicaciones con los resultados de la encuesta (periodicidad): Oficina Nacional de Estadísticas y Departamento de Trabajo, Tanzanía (tierra firme), Encuesta sobre la Fuerza de Trabajo de 1990-1991, junio de 1993 (Labour Force Survey 1990/91).
Título de las publicaciones con la metodología de la encuesta (periodicidad): Oficina Nacional de Estadísticas y Departamento de Trabajo, Tanzanía (tierra firme), Encuesta sobre la Fuerza de Trabajo de 1990-1991 (Labour Force Survey 1990/91), Informe Técnico, junio de 1993.
Difusión:
Tiempo necesario para difundir los primeros datos: Unos 21 meses.
Información adelantada acerca de la fecha de la primera difusión pública: Sí.
Disponibilidad de datos no publicados si se solicitan: Sí.
Disponibilidad de datos por medios informáticos: Se pueden obtener tabulaciones de los datos de la encuesta en disquetes.

Turquía

Título de la encuesta: Encuesta de Hogares sobre la Fuerza de Trabajo (Household Labour Force Survey).
Organismo responsable de la encuesta:
Planificar y realizar la encuesta: Instituto Oficial de Estadísticas (State Institute of Statistics).
Analizar y publicar los resultados: Instituto Oficial de Estadísticas (State Institute of Statistics).
Temas abarcados: Empleo, desempleo, subempleo, horas de trabajo, lugar de trabajo, empleo en el sector informal, duración del desempleo, trabajadores desalentados, rama de actividad económica (industria), ocupación, situación en el empleo, nivel de educación y empleo secundario.
Alcance de la encuesta:
Ámbito geográfico: Todo el país.
Grupos de población: Personas en hogares privados cuyos miembros son nacionales turcos, excluidos los residentes de escuelas, internados, escuelas de párvulos, hogares de ancianos, hospitales especializados, cuarteles militares y alojamientos de recreación para oficiales. A partir de 2000, la población económicamente activa se refiere a personas de 15 años y más de edad.
Disponibilidad de estimaciones de otras fuentes para las áreas/grupos excluidos: No corresponde.
Grupos abarcados por la encuesta pero excluidos de los resultados publicados: Ninguno.
Periodicidad:
Recolección de datos: Mensualmente.
Publicación de los resultados: Trimestralmente.
Periodo de referencia:
Empleo: Una semana (últimos siete días antes de la fecha de la entrevista).
Búsqueda de trabajo: Tres meses antes de la fecha de la entrevista.

Disponibilidad para trabajo: 15 días después de la fecha de la entrevista.
Conceptos y definiciones:
Empleo: Personas de 15 años o más de edad que, durante la semana de referencia, trabajaron por lo menos una hora como empleados regulares u ocasionales, empleadores, trabajadores independientes o trabajadores familiares no remunerados (personas en el trabajo), y personas con un empleo pero que no trabajaron durante la semana de referencia por varias razones pero que tenían un vínculo con el empleo (personas que no estaban en el trabajo).
Se incluyen:
a)personas con trabajo pero temporalmente ausentes debido a enfermedad o lesión, vacaciones o licencia anual, licencia por maternidad o paternidad, licencia parental, licencia para estudios o capacitación, ausencia sin autorización, conflictos laborales, mal tiempo, etc.;
b)trabajadores a tiempo completo o parcial que buscaban otro empleo;
c)personas que realizaban algún trabajo remunerado o por un beneficio durante la semana de referencia pero que estaban sometidas a escolaridad obligatoria, jubiladas y percibían una pensión o estaban inscritas como desempleadas en busca de trabajo en una oficina de empleo;
d)estudiantes de dedicación completa o parcial que trabajaban a tiempo completo o parcial;
e)aprendices y personas en formación remunerados o no;
f)participantes en planes de promoción del empleo;
g)personas ocupadas en la producción de bienes para su propio uso final;
h)miembros del servicio civil equivalente al servicio militar.
Se excluyen los miembros de las fuerzas armadas (voluntarios, miembros de carrera, reclutas).
Desempleo: Personas de 15 años o más de edad (incluidas las personas sometidas a escolaridad obligatoria o jubiladas y recibiendo una pensión) que, durante la semana de referencia, no estaban empleadas, pero habían tomado medidas concretas para buscar un empleo en los últimos tres meses y estaban disponibles para comenzar a trabajar en un plazo de 15 días.
Se consideran también como desempleadas las personas que habían encontrado un empleo o habían establecido su propio negocio pero que esperaban completar algunos documentos para comenzar a trabajar o estaban disponibles para hacerlo en un plazo de 15 días, así como los estudiantes de dedicación completa o parcial que buscaban empleo a tiempo completo o parcial y estaban disponibles para trabajar en un plazo de 15 días.
Subempleo:
Subempleo por insuficiencia de horas: Personas que, durante la semana de referencia, trabajaron menos de 40 horas por razones económicas y estaban disponibles para trabajar más horas en el empleo que tenían o en otro con la misma escala de salarios. Las razones pueden ser: periodo de poca actividad por razones económicas o técnicas, no hay trabajo, imposibilidad de encontrar un trabajo a tiempo completo o que se acababa de comenzar y/o finalizar en el trabajo durante la semana de referencia.
Situaciones de empleo inadecuado: Personas (excluidos los subempleados por insuficiencia de horas) que estaban en busca de otro trabajo porque no tenían suficientes ingresos o una ocupación adecuada.
Horas de trabajo: Horas habituales y reales trabajadas en el empleo principal y empleo(s) secundario(s). Se pide información sobre las horas reales para cada día de la semana de referencia.
Ingresos relacionados con el empleo:
Ingresos relacionados con el empleo asalariado: No corresponde.
Ingresos relacionados con el empleo independiente: No corresponde.
Sector informal: Todas las unidades económicas no agrícolas que no están constituidas en sociedad (situación jurídica: propiedad particular o sociedad simple), pagan un impuesto global o no pagan ningún tipo de impuesto, y trabajan con menos de 10 personas contratadas.
Actividad habitual: No corresponde.
Clasificaciones:
Rama de actividad económica (industria):
Título de la clasificación utilizada: Clasificación Industrial Internacional Uniforme de todas las Actividades Económicas (CIIU Rev.3).
Grupos de población clasificados por industria: Personas empleadas y personas desempleadas con experiencia previa de trabajo.
Número de Grupos utilizados para la codificación: Todas las 292 clases de la CIIU (nivel de 4 dígitos).
Vínculos con la CIIU: CIIU-Rev.3.
Ocupación:
Título de la clasificación utilizada: Clasificación Internacional Uniforme de Ocupaciones (CIUO-88).
Grupos de población clasificados por ocupación: Personas empleadas y personas desempleadas con experiencia previa de trabajo.
Número de Grupos utilizados para la codificación: Todos los 390 grupos de unidades de la CIUO (nivel de 4 dígitos).
Vínculos con la CIUO: CIUO-88.
Situación en el empleo:
Título de la clasificación utilizada: No se dispone de información.
Grupos de población clasificados por situación en el empleo: Personas empleadas y personas desempleadas con experiencia previa de trabajo.
Grupos utilizados para la codificación: 6 grupos (empleados regulares, empleados ocasionales, trabajadores domésticos remunerados, empleadores, trabajadores independientes, trabajadores familiares no remunerados).
Vínculos con la CISE: CISE-1993.
Educación:
Título de la clasificación utilizada: No se dispone de información.
Grupos de población clasificados por educación: Todas las personas de 6 años y más de edad.
Grupos utilizados para la codificación: 11 grupos (sin escolaridad, escuela primaria, educación primaria, escuela secundaria general de primer ciclo, escuela secundaria vocacional de primer ciclo, escuela secundaria general, escuela secundaria nacional, dos años de escuela de capacitación vocacional, tres años de escuela de capacitación vocacional, universidad, licenciatura o postgrado, etc.).
Vínculos con la CINE: Sí.
Tamaño y diseño de la muestra:
Unidad final de muestreo: Hogares.
Tamaño de la muestra (unidades finales de muestreo): Unos 23 000 hogares por trimestre (18 000 de zonas urbanas y 5 000 de zonas rurales).
Fracción de muestreo: 0,388 por ciento.
Marco de la muestra: A partir de la encuesta de 2000, el marco de la muestra se basa en Censo de Población de 1997. Anteriormente, se basó en los resultados de los Censos de Población de 1980, 1985 y 1990.
Actualización de la muestra: Anualmente.
Rotación: Ninguna.
Esquema: No corresponde.
Porcentaje de unidades que permanecen en la muestra durante dos encuestas consecutivas: No corresponde.
Número máximo de entrevistas por unidad de muestreo: No corresponde.**Tiempo necesario para renovar completamente la muestra:** No corresponde.
Levantamiento de la encuesta:
Tipo de entrevista: CAPI (entrevista personal asistida por computadora).
Número de unidades finales de muestreo por área de muestra: Variable.
Duración del trabajo de campo:
Total: Dos semanas.
Por área de muestra: Dos semanas.
Organización de la encuesta: La encuesta se organiza de manera permanente.
Número de personas que trabajan en el campo: 150 entrevistadores, 30 supervisores y 23 personas encargadas de organizar la encuesta.
Substitución de las unidades finales de muestreo que no responden: No.
Estimaciones y ajustes:
Tasa de no-respuesta total: Casi el 10 por ciento.
Ajuste por no-respuesta total: Sí.
Imputación por no respuesta de ítemes: No.
Ajuste por áreas/poblaciones no abarcadas: No.
Ajuste por falta de cobertura: No.
Ajuste por exceso de cobertura: No.
Ajuste por variaciones estacionales: No.

Historia de la encuesta:
Título y fecha de la primera encuesta: Encuesta de Hogares sobre la Fuerza de Trabajo de 1966 (Household Labour Force Survey 1966).
Modificaciones y revisiones significativas: Se han introducido varias modificaciones en el diseño del cuestionario (sobre todo en 1988, 1990 y 2000), el ámbito geográfico, el tamaño o el diseño de la muestra.
Documentación y difusión:
Documentación:
Título de las publicaciones con los resultados de la encuesta (periodicidad): Household Labour Force Results (bianual).
Título de las publicaciones con la metodología de la encuesta (periodicidad): Household Labour Force Survey Results (bianual).
Difusión:
Tiempo necesario para difundir los primeros datos: Unos 4 meses.
Información adelantada acerca de la fecha de la primera difusión pública: No.
Disponibilidad de datos no publicados si se solicitan: Sí.
Disponibilidad de datos por medios informáticos: Disquetes e internet; sitio web: http://www.die.gov.tr/

Ucrania

Título de la encuesta: Encuesta por muestra sobre las Actividades Económicas de la Población (Population Economic Activity Sample Survey (PEASS)).
Organismo responsable de la encuesta:
Planificar y realizar la encuesta: Comité Estatal de Estadísticas de Ucrania (State Statistics Committee of Ukraine).
Analizar y publicar los resultados: Comité Estatal de Estadísticas de Ucrania (State Statistics Committee of Ukraine).
Temas abarcados: Empleo (principal y secundario), desempleo, horas de trabajo, duración del empleo, duración del desempleo, trabajadores desalentados, trabajadores ocasionales, rama de actividad económica (industria), ocupación, situación en el empleo, nivel de educación, así como el empleo en la economía informal.
Alcance de la encuesta:
Ámbito geográfico: Todo el país, excluidas la primera y la segunda zonas de contaminación nuclear debido al accidente de la central nuclear de Chernobil (zona de reubicación forzosa).
Grupos de población: Toda la población de 15 a 70 años de edad que reside en hogares privados durante la semana de referencia. Se excluye la población que vive en hogares colectivos y no asentada, miembros de las fuerzas armadas (reclutas y miembros de carrera) que viven en cuarteles, estudiantes que viven en albergues y niños en edad escolar que viven en internados, así como los miembros del hogar que se encuentran en misiones a largo plazo (seis meses y más) y quienes residen en el extranjero.
Disponibilidad de estimaciones de otras fuentes para las áreas/grupos excluidos: Sí.
Grupos abarcados por la encuesta pero excluidos de los resultados publicados: Ninguno.
Periodicidad:
Recolección de datos: Trimestralmente.
Publicación de los resultados: Trimestralmente.
Periodo de referencia:
Empleo: Una semana (últimos siete días antes de la fecha de la entrevista).
Búsqueda de trabajo: Cuatro semanas antes de la fecha de la entrevista.
Disponibilidad para trabajo: Dos semanas después de la fecha de la entrevista.
Conceptos y definiciones:
Empleo: Personas de 15 a 70 años de edad que, en la semana de referencia:
a)realizaron algún trabajo durante por lo menos una hora por una remuneración en efectivo o en especie, o por un beneficio;
b)trabajaron por lo menos 30 horas en explotaciones agrícolas subsidiarias particulares o en un negocio o explotación agrícola familiar sin remuneración ("trabajadores que contribuyen con la familia no remunerados");
c)no trabajaron, pero tenían un empleo del que estaban temporalmente ausentes debido a enfermedad, día de fiesta, mal tiempo, conflicto laboral, etc.
Se excluyen del empleo las personas que durante la semana de la encuesta estaban ocupadas en las siguientes actividades:
a)trabajar en explotaciones agrícolas subsidiarias particulares para su propio consumo;
b)trabajar como voluntario en instituciones religiosas, caritativas o públicas;
c)efectuar la construcción o renovación de su propia casa o apartamento;
d)hacer los quehaceres domésticos.
Se incluyen también en los totales:
a)miembros de las fuerzas armadas que viven en el hogar;
b)trabajadores a tiempo completo o parcial;
c)estudiantes de dedicación completa o parcial que trabajan a tiempo completo o parcial;
d)personas que realizaron algún trabajo durante la semana de referencia pero que estaban jubiladas y percibían una pensión, inscritas como desempleadas en busca de trabajo en una oficina de empleo o percibiendo indemnizaciones de desempleo;
e)servicio doméstico privado;
f)aprendices y personas en formación remunerados;
g)miembros de cooperativas de productores.
Desempleo: Son desempleadas todas las personas de 15 a 70 años de edad que no trabajaron durante la semana de referencia, estuvieron buscando activamente un empleo durante las últimas cuatro semanas antes de la encuesta, estaban disponibles para comenzar a trabajar dos semanas después de la encuesta o esperaban comenzar en un nuevo empleo en un plazo de 30 días.
La única excepción son las personas que no buscaban trabajo porque ya habían encontrado uno pero en el que comenzarían en una fecha ulterior al periodo de referencia. Estas personas se clasifican como desempleadas.
Subempleo:
Subempleo por insuficiencia de horas: Personas que, durante la semana de referencia, trabajaban menos horas que las establecidas para una categoría de ocupación o trabajo determinado, siempre y cuando estuviesen buscando un trabajo adicional y disponibles para hacerlo.
Situaciones de empleo inadecuado: No corresponde.
Horas de trabajo: Horas habituales y reales trabajadas en el empleo principal y empleo(s) secundario(s).
Ingresos relacionados con el empleo:
Ingresos relacionados con el empleo asalariado: No corresponde.
Ingresos relacionados con el empleo independiente: No corresponde.
Sector informal: Personas ocupadas en cualquier actividad (principal o secundaria) económica no registrada y remunerada en efectivo o en especie.
Actividad habitual: No corresponde.
Clasificaciones:
Rama de actividad económica (industria):
Título de la clasificación utilizada: Clasificación nacional compatible con la CIIU Rev.3.
Grupos de población clasificados por industria: Personas empleadas y personas desempleadas con experiencia previa de trabajo.
Número de Grupos utilizados para la codificación: 159 grupos.
Vínculos con la CIIU: CIIU-Rev.3, a nivel del tercer dígito.
Ocupación:
Título de la clasificación utilizada: Clasificación nacional compatible con la CIUO-88.
Grupos de población clasificados por ocupación: Personas empleadas y personas desempleadas con experiencia previa de trabajo.
Número de Grupos utilizados para la codificación: 390 grupos.
Vínculos con la CIUO: CIUO-88, a nivel del cuarto dígito.
Situación en el empleo:
Título de la clasificación utilizada: CISE-1993.
Grupos de población clasificados por situación en el empleo: Personas empleadas (empleos principal y secundario).
Grupos utilizados para la codificación: 5 grupos (empleados, empleadores, trabajadores por cuenta propia, miembros de cooperativas de productores, trabajadores familiares no remunerados).
Vínculos con la CISE: CISE-1993.
Educación:
Título de la clasificación utilizada: Clasificación nacional.
Grupos de población clasificados por educación: Todos los grupos de población.
Grupos utilizados para la codificación: 8 grupos (sin educación primaria general, primaria general, secundaria, secundaria general, primaria vocacional, secundaria vocacional, superior no completada; superior (universidad)).
Vínculos con la CINE: No.

Tamaño y diseño de la muestra:
Unidad final de muestreo: Hogares.
Tamaño de la muestra (unidades finales de muestreo): Unos 31 000 hogares por trimestre y casi 150 000 personas anualmente.
Fracción de muestreo: 0,12 por ciento.
Marco de la muestra: La muestra se prepara automáticamente a nivel nacional basándose en la muestra principal de 1992 (5%) preparada para una serie de encuestas por muestra especiales, tales como la encuesta sociodemográfica, etc. En 2004, se preparará una nueva muestra basada en el Censo de Población de 2001.
Actualización de la muestra: Anualmente.
Rotación:
Esquema: Se prevé que cualquier hogar que forma parte de la muestra proporcione, en cualquier momento, información sobre el mercado de trabajo durante cuatro trimestres consecutivos, después de lo cual se retira de la muestra definitivamente. En 2004 se introducirá un nuevo plan de **Rotación:** 2-(2)-2. De esa manera, un hogar estará incluido en la muestra durante dos trimestres consecutivos, se sacará por dos trimestres y se volverá a introducir durante otros dos trimestres consecutivos antes de sacarlo definitivamente de la muestra.
Porcentaje de unidades que permanecen en la muestra durante dos encuestas consecutivas: 75 por ciento.
Número máximo de entrevistas por unidad de muestreo: Cuatro.
Tiempo necesario para renovar completamente la muestra: 18 meses.
Levantamiento de la encuesta:
Tipo de entrevista: Papel y lápiz.
Número de unidades finales de muestreo por área de muestra: No se proporcionó información.
Duración del trabajo de campo:
Total: Un mes.
Por área de muestra: No se proporcionó información.
Organización de la encuesta: Comité Estatal de Estadísticas de Ucrania (State Statistics Committee of Ukraine).
Número de personas que trabajan en el campo: 510 enumeradores y supervisores.
Substitución de las unidades finales de muestreo que no responden: No.
Estimaciones y ajustes:
Tasa de no-respuesta total: 12 por ciento.
Ajuste por no-respuesta total: No.
Imputación por no respuesta de ítemes: Parcial.
Ajuste por áreas/poblaciones no abarcadas: No.
Ajuste por falta de cobertura: No.
Ajuste por exceso de cobertura: No.
Ajuste por variaciones estacionales: No.
Historia de la encuesta:
Título y fecha de la primera encuesta: Encuesta por muestra sobre las Actividades Económicas de la Población, octubre de 1995 (Population Economic Activity Sample Survey, October 1995) (anual).
Modificaciones y revisiones significativas: Desde 1999, la encuesta se realiza trimestralmente.
Documentación y difusión:
Documentación:
Título de las publicaciones con los resultados de la encuesta (periodicidad): "Economic Activity of the Population" (anual), "Economic Activity of the Population: quarterly report", "Labour in Ukraine, 2002 (anual)".
Título de las publicaciones con la metodología de la encuesta (periodicidad): "LFS Methodology" (en ucranio y parcialmente en inglés).
Difusión:
Tiempo necesario para difundir los primeros datos: No se proporcionó información.
Información adelantada acerca de la fecha de la primera difusión pública: Sí.
Disponibilidad de datos no publicados si se solicitan: Sí.
Disponibilidad de datos por medios informáticos: Sí. Sitio web: http://www.ukrstat.gov.ua

Uganda

Título de la encuesta: Encuesta Nacional de Hogares de 1996-1997 (Uganda National Household Survey 1996-97). Encuesta Piloto sobre la Fuerza de Trabajo (Pilot Labour Force Survey).
Organismo responsable de la encuesta:
Planificar y realizar la encuesta: Oficina de Estadísticas de Uganda (Uganda Bureau of Statistics).
Analizar y publicar los resultados: Oficina de Estadísticas de Uganda (Uganda Bureau of Statistics).
Temas abarcados: Personas corriente y habitualmente activas económicamente, empleadas y desempleadas. Personas corrientemente subempleadas por insuficiencia de horas y personas corrientemente fuera de la fuerza de trabajo. Personas habitualmente empleadas, personas habitualmente desempleadas y personas habitualmente no activas económicamente (se hace la diferencia entre estudiantes, personas que realizan quehaceres domésticos, personas muy mayores, enfermas e impedidas). Horas de trabajo (para personas corrientemente empleadas). Días trabajados (para personas habitualmente empleadas). Duración del desempleo. Empleo secundario. Rama de actividad económica (industria), ocupación, situación en el empleo, nivel de educación/capacitación.
Alcance de la encuesta:
Ámbito geográfico: 36 de los 39 distritos del país. Los otros 3 distritos se excluyen por razones de seguridad.
Grupos de población: Población de 7 años y más de edad que reside habitualmente en los hogares seleccionados. Se excluyen los miembros irregulares presentes o ausentes, así como los visitantes.
Disponibilidad de estimaciones de otras fuentes para las áreas/grupos excluidos: No disponible.
Grupos abarcados por la encuesta pero excluidos de los resultados publicados: Ninguno.
Periodicidad:
Recolección de datos: Ocasional, es decir de marzo a noviembre de 1997.
Publicación de los resultados: Ocasional, los primeros resultados se publicaron en diciembre de 1998.
Periodo de referencia:
Empleo: Una semana antes de la fecha de la entrevista para las personas corrientemente empleadas y los últimos 12 meses, por evaluación propia, para las personas habitualmente empleadas.
Búsqueda de trabajo: La semana de la encuesta para las personas corrientemente desempleadas y los últimos 12 meses, por evaluación propia, para las personas habitualmente desempleadas.
Disponibilidad para trabajo: La semana de la encuesta para las personas corrientemente desempleadas y los últimos 12 meses, por evaluación propia, para las personas habitualmente desempleadas.
Conceptos y definiciones:
Empleo: Personas que: a) realizaron algún trabajo remunerado o por un beneficio durante la semana de referencia; b) estaban temporalmente ausentes del trabajo durante la semana de referencia por enfermedad o licencia, pero que, con toda seguridad, se reintegrarían a su trabajo; y c) estaban ocupadas en la producción de bienes para su propio uso final.
Se excluyen las personas sometidas a escolaridad obligatoria o que estaban jubiladas y percibían una pensión. Algún trabajo se define como el realizado en una hora o más durante la semana de referencia.
Desempleo: Personas que estaban corrientemente sin trabajo, disponibles para hacerlo y que buscaban empleo.
Subempleo:
Subempleo por insuficiencia de horas: No se dispone de información.
Situaciones de empleo inadecuado: No se dispone de información.
Horas de trabajo: Horas reales trabajadas, medidas por separado para cada uno de los 7 días utilizados para medir el empleo actual.
Ingresos relacionados con el empleo:
Ingresos relacionados con el empleo asalariado: No corresponde.
Ingresos relacionados con el empleo independiente: No corresponde.
Sector informal: No corresponde.
Actividad habitual: No se dispone de información.
Clasificaciones:
Rama de actividad económica (industria):
Título de la clasificación utilizada: No se dispone de información.
Grupos de población clasificados por industria: Personas empleadas.
Número de Grupos utilizados para la codificación: 58.
Vínculos con la CIIU: CIIU-Rev.3.
Ocupación:
Título de la clasificación utilizada: No se dispone de información.

Grupos de población clasificados por ocupación: Personas empleadas.
Número de Grupos utilizados para la codificación: 87.
Vínculos con la CIUO: CIUO-88.
Situación en el empleo:
Título de la clasificación utilizada: Clasificación nacional.
Grupos de población clasificados por situación en el empleo: Personas empleadas.
Grupos utilizados para la codificación: Empleados asalariados (se hace la diferencia entre gubernamentales permanentes, gubernamentales temporeros, gubernamentales ocasionales, privados permanentes, privados temporeros y privados ocasionales) y empleados independientes (se hace la diferencia entre empleadores, trabajadores por cuenta propia y trabajadores familiares no remunerados).
Vínculos con la CISE: CISE-1993.
Educación:
Título de la clasificación utilizada: Clasificación nacional.
Grupos de población clasificados por educación: Todas las personas.
Grupos utilizados para la codificación: 24.
Vínculos con la CINE: CINE-1976.
Tamaño y diseño de la muestra:
Unidad final de muestreo: Hogares.
Tamaño de la muestra (unidades finales de muestreo): 6 656.
Fracción de muestreo: 0,0017.
Marco de la muestra: Censo de Población de 1991.
Actualización de la muestra: Se tiene una muestra para cada encuesta.
Rotación:
Esquema: No corresponde.
Porcentaje de unidades que permanecen en la muestra durante dos encuestas consecutivas: No corresponde.
Número máximo de entrevistas por unidad de muestreo: No corresponde.
Tiempo necesario para renovar completamente la muestra: No corresponde.
Levantamiento de la encuesta:
Tipo de entrevista: Entrevista personal, con papel y lápiz.
Número de unidades finales de muestreo por área de muestra: No se dispone de información.
Duración del trabajo de campo:
Total: De marzo a noviembre de 1997.
Por área de muestra: No se dispone de información.
Organización de la encuesta: Permanente.
Número de personas que trabajan en el campo: 48 entrevistadores y 12 supervisores.
Substitución de las unidades finales de muestreo que no responden: Sí.
Estimaciones y ajustes:
Tasa de no-respuesta total: 0,0006.
Ajuste por no-respuesta total: Sí.
Imputación por no respuesta de ítemes: Sí, se utilizan multiplicadores por diez hogares entrevistados en cada zona de enumeración muestreada a fin de hacer ajustes según el número de hogares entrevistados.
Ajuste por áreas/poblaciones no abarcadas: No.
Ajuste por falta de cobertura: No.
Ajuste por exceso de cobertura: No.
Ajuste por variaciones estacionales: No.
Historia de la encuesta:
Título y fecha de la primera encuesta: Encuesta Nacional de Hogares de 1996-1997 (Uganda National Household Survey 1996-97).
Modificaciones y revisiones significativas: No corresponde.
Documentación y difusión:
Documentación:
Título de las publicaciones con los resultados de la encuesta: 1997 Pilot Labour Force Survey. No se dispone de otra información bibliográfica.
Título de las publicaciones con la metodología de la encuesta: Idem.
Difusión:
Tiempo necesario para difundir los primeros datos: No se dispone de información.
Información adelantada acerca de la fecha de la primera difusión pública: No.
Disponibilidad de datos no publicados si se solicitan: Sí.
Disponibilidad de datos por medios informáticos: Sí.

Yemen, Rep. del

Título de la encuesta: Encuesta por muestra sobre la fuerza de trabajo de 1999 (Labour force sample survey for the year 1999).
Organismo responsable de la encuesta:
Planificar y realizar la encuesta: Organización Central de Estadísticas, Ministerio del Trabajo y Capacitación Vocacional.
Analizar y publicar los resultados: Organismo Central de Estadísticas (Central Statistical Organizacion).
Temas abarcados: Empleo, desempleo, horas de trabajo, salarios, duración del empleo, duración del desempleo, trabajadores desalentados, trabajadores ocasionales, rama de actividad económica (industria), ocupación actual y anterior, situación en el empleo, nivel de educación.
Alcance de la encuesta:
Ámbito geográfico: Todo el país, salvo las islas de Soqotra y Kamarán y las zonas desérticas alejadas de Hadhramout y Al-Jouf. El costo para realizar la encuesta en esas zonas es elevado y la proporción de la población insignificante.
Grupos de población: Se excluyen las personas que viven en hospitales, campamentos, hoteles, moteles, residencias de estudiantes y otros hogares colectivos, nómadas y personas que residían en el extranjero durante el periodo de la encuesta, así como las personas sin hogar y sin un sitio permanente para vivir.
Disponibilidad de estimaciones de otras fuentes para las áreas/grupos excluidos: Existen estimaciones basadas en el censo de 1994 relativas a la población de las islas y zonas alejadas (Muderias), la población nómada y las personas que viven en hogares colectivos.
Grupos abarcados por la encuesta pero excluidos de los resultados publicados: Extranjeros.
Periodicidad:Recolección de datos: Ocasional.
Publicación de los resultados: Después de cada encuesta.
Periodo de referencia:
Empleo: Semana de referencia fija.
Búsqueda de trabajo: Un mes.
Disponibilidad para trabajo: Dos semanas.
Conceptos y definiciones:
Empleo: Personas de 15 años y más de edad, que trabajaron por lo menos una hora durante la semana de referencia por una remuneración, salario o ingreso familiar, o que estaban temporalmente ausentes del trabajo por licencia o enfermedad. [No obstante, las preguntas sobre las características económicas se hacen a todas las personas de 6 años y más de edad].
Se incluyen:
a)las personas que realizaron algún trabajo remunerado o por un beneficio durante la semana de referencia pero que estaban sometidas a escolaridad obligatoria, jubiladas y percibían una pensión, inscritas como desempleadas en busca de trabajo en una oficina de empleo o que recibían indemnizaciones de desempleo;
b)los estudiantes de dedicación completa o parcial que trabajaban a tiempo completo o parcial;
c)los aprendices y las personas en formación remunerados o no, si estaban asociados al trabajo;
d)las personas ocupadas en la producción de bienes para su propio uso final;
e)los trabajadores familiares no remunerados en el trabajo o temporalmente ausentes del mismo durante la semana de referencia;
f)los miembros de las fuerzas armadas, incluidos reclutas, voluntarios y miembros de carrera, y las personas del servicio civil equivalente al servicio militar.
Se excluyen:
a)las personas ocupadas en la producción de servicios para sus hogares;
b)las personas suspendidas de su trabajo temporalmente o por tiempo indeterminado sin remuneración y las personas con licencia sin goce de sueldo por iniciativa del empleador.
Desempleo: Personas de 15 años y más de edad que no estaban empleadas durante la semana de referencia, podían y estaban disponibles para trabajar dos semanas después de la fecha de la entrevista, y habían tomado medidas para buscar trabajo durante el mes anterior al periodo de la encuesta.
Se incluyen:
a)las personas suspendidas de su trabajo temporalmente o por tiempo indeterminado sin remuneración;
b) las personas sin empleo, corrientemente disponibles para trabajar y en busca de trabajo, que habían tomado medidas para comenzar un nuevo empleo en una fecha ulterior a la semana de referencia;

c)las personas sin trabajo, corrientemente disponibles para trabajar y en busca de trabajo, que procuraban establecer su propio negocio;
d)las personas sin empleo, disponibles para trabajar, pero que por razones específicas no buscaron trabajo durante el mes anterior al periodo de la encuesta;
e)los estudiantes de dedicación completa o parcial que buscaban trabajo a tiempo completo o parcial;
f)las personas que buscaban trabajo o estaban disponibles para trabajar, pero estaban sometidas a escolaridad obligatoria o jubiladas y recibían una pensión.

Subempleo:

Subempleo por insuficiencia de horas: No se dispone de información.

Situaciones de empleo inadecuado: No se dispone de información.

Horas de trabajo: Número total de horas realmente trabajadas en el empleo principal durante la semana de referencia. Número total de horas realmente trabajadas en el empleo secundario durante la semana de referencia.

Ingresos relacionados con el empleo:

Ingresos relacionados con el empleo asalariado: Salarios y sueldos totales de empleados asalariados antes de deducir los impuestos sobre la renta y otras deducciones, en efectivo o en especie, obtenidos diaria, semanal, quincenal o mensualmente, incluidos los subsidios e incentivos por vacaciones y pagos similares. Los sueldos se refieren al último pago recibido. Los datos se recopilan por separado para el empleo principal y secundario.

Ingresos relacionados con el empleo independiente: No se dispone de información.

Clasificaciones:

Rama de actividad económica (industria):

Título de la clasificación utilizada: No se dispone de información.

Grupos de población clasificados por industria: Personas empleadas y desempleadas con experiencia previa de trabajo.

Número de Grupos utilizados para la codificación: Al tercer nivel de la clasificación.

Vínculos con la CIIU: CIIU-Rev.3 a nivel del tercer dígito.

Ocupación:

Título de la clasificación utilizada: No se dispone de información.

Grupos de población clasificados por ocupación: Personas empleadas y desempleadas con experiencia previa de trabajo.

Número de Grupos utilizados para la codificación: Al cuarto nivel de la clasificación.

Vínculos con la CIUO: CIUO-1988 a nivel del cuarto dígito.

Situación en el empleo:

Título de la clasificación utilizada: No se dispone de información.

Grupos de población clasificados por situación en el empleo: Personas empleadas únicamente.

Grupos utilizados para la codificación: Empleado asalariado. Trabajador por cuenta propia. Trabajador independiente. Trabajador familiar sin remuneración. Trabajador para otros sin remuneración.

Vínculos con la CISE: CISE-1993.

Educación:

Título de la clasificación utilizada: No se dispone de información.

Grupos de población clasificados por educación: Todas las personas de 10 años y más de edad.

Grupos utilizados para la codificación: Analfabetos. Saben leer y escribir; escuela primaria, unificada. Escuela elemental/básica; instituto y centro de capacitación vocacional; escuela secundaria técnica y vocacional; escuela secundaria general; diploma posterior a la escuela secundaria; universidad; estudios superiores (postgrado).

Vínculos con la CINE: Algunos grupos están vinculados a la CINE-1997.

Tamaño y diseño de la muestra:

Unidad final de muestreo: Hogares.

Tamaño de la muestra (unidades finales de muestreo): 19 955 hogares.

Fracción de muestreo: 0,92 por ciento.

Marco de la muestra: El marco de la muestra principal se preparó para la Encuesta Nacional sobre la Pobreza de 1999, basándose en la lista de Zonas de Enumeración del Censo de Población de 1994. Este marco se dividió en 20 prefecturas y cada una de ellas, en zonas rurales y urbanas. Se seleccionó una submuestra de la Encuesta Nacional sobre la Pobreza de 1999 para la Encuesta sobre la Fuerza de Trabajo de ese año.

Actualización de la muestra: La actualización de la muestra se realizó mediante el proceso de preparación de listas de hogares en cada zona de enumeración seleccionada.

Rotación: Ninguna.

Levantamiento de la encuesta:

Tipo de entrevista: Personal.

Número de unidades finales de muestreo por área de muestra: 15 hogares en zonas rurales y 20 en zonas urbanas.

Duración del trabajo de campo:

Total: 20 días, del 13 de noviembre al 2 de diciembre de 1999.

Por área de muestra: Un día por equipo de tres entrevistadores que abarcan 15 hogares rurales o 20 urbanos.

Organización de la encuesta: Especial.

Número de personas que trabajan en el campo: 253 entrevistadores, 81 jefes de equipo y 20 supervisores.

Substitución de las unidades finales de muestreo que no responden: No se proporcionó información.

Estimaciones y ajustes:

Tasa de no-respuesta total: 4,4 por ciento.

Ajuste por no-respuesta total: No se proporcionó información.

Imputación por no respuesta de ítemes: No.

Ajuste por áreas/poblaciones no abarcadas: Sí.

Ajuste por falta de cobertura: No se proporcionó información.

Ajuste por exceso de cobertura: No se proporcionó información.

Ajuste por variaciones estacionales: No.

Historia de la encuesta:

Título y fecha de la primera encuesta: Encuesta por muestra sobre la fuerza de trabajo (Labour force sample survey), 6 de diciembre de1991 .

Modificaciones y revisiones significativas: No corresponde.

Documentación y difusión:

Documentación:

Título de las publicaciones con los resultados de la encuesta (periodicidad): Final Report. 1999 Labour Force Survey Results

Título de las publicaciones con la metodología de la encuesta (periodicidad): Final Report.

Difusión:

Tiempo necesario para difundir los primeros datos: Un año. Los datos de 1999 se publicaron en noviembre de 2000.

Información adelantada acerca de la fecha de la primera difusión pública: No se proporcionó información.

Disponibilidad de datos no publicados si se solicitan: No se proporcionó información.

Disponibilidad de datos por medios informáticos: Se pueden obtener, previa solicitud, datos tabulados en disquetes y por intermedio del Sistema de Información del Mercado del Trabajo.

Zimbabwe

Título de la encuesta: Control de Indicadores - Encuesta sobre la Fuerza de Trabajo (Indicator Monitoring - The Labour Force Survey).

Organismo responsable de la encuesta:

Planificar y realizar la encuesta: Oficina Central de Estadísticas (Central Statistical Office).

Analizar y publicar los resultados: Oficina Central de Estadísticas (Central Statistical Office).

Temas abarcados: Empleo, desempleo, horas de trabajo, ingresos del empleo, empleo en el sector informal, trabajadores ocasionales, rama de actividad económica (industria), ocupación, situación en el empleo, nivel de educación y calificaciones (capacidades), actividades principal y secundaria en los últimos doce meses.

Alcance de la encuesta:

Ámbito geográfico: Todo el país.

Grupos de población: No se proporcionó información.

Disponibilidad de estimaciones de otras fuentes para las áreas/grupos excluidos: No corresponde.

Grupos abarcados por la encuesta pero excluidos de los resultados publicados: Ninguno.

Periodicidad:

Recolección de datos: Cada cinco años. La última encuesta se realizó en junio de 1999.

Publicación de los resultados: Cada cinco años.

Periodo de referencia:

Empleo: Periodo de referencia móvil de siete días antes de la fecha de la entrevista.

Búsqueda de trabajo: Periodo de referencia móvil de siete días antes de la fecha de la entrevista.

Disponibilidad para trabajo: Perido de referencia móvil de siete días antes de la fecha de la entrevista.

Conceptos y definiciones:

Empleo: Personas de 15 años y más de edad cuya principal actividad durante la semana de referencia fue el empleo y que trabajaron por lo menos una hora durante esa semana. Se incluyen: a) trabajadores en el lugar de trabajo que contribuyeron con la familia durante la semana de referencia; b) trabajadores a tiempo completo o parcial que buscaban otro empleo; c) personas que realizaron algún trabajo remunerado o por un beneficio durante la semana de referencia pero que estaban inscritas como desempleadas en busca de trabajo en una oficina de empleo o recibiendo indemnizaciones de desempleo; d) estudiantes de dedicación completa que trabajaban a tiempo completo o parcial; e) estudiantes de dedicación parcial que buscaban trabajo a tiempo completo o parcial; f) aprendices y personas en formación remunerados o no; g) personas que participaban en planes de promoción del empleo; h) personas ocupadas en la producción de bienes para su propio uso final.

Se incluyen también los empleados asalariados y trabajadores independientes que estaban temporalmente ausentes del trabajo durante la semana de referencia por: a) enfermedad o lesión; b) vacaciones o licencia anual; c) licencia por maternidad o paternidad; d) licencia parental, e) licencia para estudios o capacitación; f) ausencia sin autorización, g) conflictos laborales; h) mal tiempo, desperfectos mecánicos, etc., i) estaban suspendidos temporalmente sin remuneración; j) con licencia sin goce de sueldo por iniciativa del empleador.

Asimismo, se incluyen los trabajadores que contribuyen con la familia temporalmente ausentes del trabajo durante la semana de referencia, así como los trabajadores estacionales que no trabajan durante la temporada inactiva.

Se excluyen: a) personas que realizaron algún trabajo remunerado o por un beneficio durante la semana de referencia pero que estaban sometidas a escolaridad obligatoria o jubiladas y percibían una pensión; b) personas suspendidas de su trabajo por tiempo indeterminado sin remuneración; c) personas que prestaban servicios no remunerados o personales a miembros de su propio hogar.

Desempleo: Personas de 15 años y más de edad cuya principal actividad durante la semana de referencia fue el desempleo, estaban disponibles para trabajar durante esa semana y buscaron activamente un trabajo durante la semana de referencia. Se incluyen: a) personas sin trabajo y corrientemente disponibles para trabajar, que habían concertado acuerdos para comenzar un nuevo empleo en una fecha ulterior a la semana de referencia; b) personas sin empleo y corrientemente disponibles para trabajar, que procuraban establecer su propia empresa; c) personas que buscaban empleo y estaban disponibles para trabajar pero sometidas a escolaridad obligatoria o jubiladas y percibiendo una pensión; d) estudiantes de dedicación parcial que buscaban empleo a tiempo completo o parcial.

Se excluyen los estudiantes de dedicación completa que buscaban empleo a tiempo completo o parcial, a menos que su actividad principal durante la semana de referencia fuese el desempleo.

Se excluyen de la definición restringida de desempleo las personas sin empleo y disponibles para trabajar durante la semana de referencia que no buscaban trabajo. Sin embargo, esas personas se incluyen en una definición más amplia de desempleo.

Subempleo:

Subempleo por insuficiencia de horas: La encuesta no abarca este punto. Con todo, se pregunta a las personas empleadas si hubiesen querido o no trabajar más horas durante la semana de referencia sin que se les pagasen las horas extraordinarias, y cuántas horas adicionales hubiesen preferido trabajar durante la semana de referencia sin que se les pagasen las horas extraordinarias.

Situaciones de empleo inadecuado: La encuesta no abarca este punto.

Horas de trabajo: Horas trabajadas durante la semana de referencia, incluidas las horas extraordinarias y el tiempo aprobado para ausentarse del empleo. Esta información se refiere al empleo principal.

Ingresos relacionados con el empleo:

Ingresos del empleo asalariado: Ingresos en efectivo recibidos del empleo en el último mes (menos de 500 dólares de Zimbabwe (Z$), de Z$ 500 a Z$ 749, de Z$ 750 a Z$ 999, de Z$ 1 000 a Z$ 1 499, de Z$ 1 500 a Z$ 1 999, de Z$ 2 000 a Z$ 2 499, de Z$ 2 500 a Z$ 2 999, Z$ 3 000 o más).

Ingresos relacionados con el empleo independiente: Ingresos en efectivo recibidos del empleo en el último mes (menos de Z$ 500, de Z$ 500 a Z$ 749, de Z$ 750 a Z$ 999, de Z$ 1 000 a Z$ 1 499, de Z$ 1 500 a Z$ 1 999, de Z$ 2 000 a Z$ 2 499, de Z$ 2 500 a Z$ 2 999, Z$ 3 000 o más).

Sector informal: Se hacen preguntas sobre el sector al que pertenece el establecimiento (privado, gobierno central, gobierno local, paraestatal, cooperativa, otro), el número de personas que trabajan en el establecimiento (menos de 10, 10 o más) y el registro/licencia del establecimiento (sólo registrado, licencia con local, licencia sin local, registrado y con licencia, ninguno).

Actividad habitual: La encuesta no abarca este punto. Sin embargo, las preguntas formuladas se refieren a las actividades principal y secundaria de las personas durante los últimos doce meses.

Clasificaciones:

Rama de actividad económica (industria):

Título de la clasificación utilizada: No se proporcionó información.

Grupos de población clasificados por industria: Personas empleadas.

Número de Grupos utilizados para la codificación: 13.

Vínculos con la CIIU: CIIU-Rev. 2.

Ocupación:

Título de la clasificación utilizada: No se proporcionó información.

Grupos de población clasificados por ocupación: Personas empleadas.

Número de Grupos utilizados para la codificación: 23.

Vínculos con la CIUO: CIUO-88.

Situación en el empleo:

Título de la clasificación: Clasificación nacional sobre la situación en el empleo.

Grupos de población clasificados por situación en el empleo: Personas empleadas.

Grupos utilizados para la codificación: a) empleados asalariados-permanentes; b) empleados asalariados-ocasionales, temporales, con contrato o estacionales; c) empleadores; d) trabajadores por cuenta propia-comunales o granjeros reasentados; e) trabajadores por cuenta propia-otros; f) trabajadores familiares no remunerados.

Vínculos con la CISE: Vínculos parciales con la CISE-1993.

Educación:

Título de la clasificación utilizada: Clasificación nacional de niveles de educación.

Grupos de población clasificados por educación: Todas las personas de 5 años o más de edad.

Grupos utilizados para la codificación: a) Grado 1 no completado; b) Grado 1; c) Grado 2; d) Grado 3; e) Grado 4; f) Grado 5; g) Grado 6; h) Grado 7; i) Nivel 1; j) Nivel 2; k) Nivel 3; l) Nivel 4; m) Nivel 5; n) Nivel 6; o) Diploma/certificado posterior a la primaria; p) Diploma/certificado posterior a la secundaria; q) grado o postgrado.

Vínculos con la CINE: No se proporcionó información.

Tamaño y diseño de la muestra:

Unidad final de muestreo: Hogares.

Tamaño de la muestra (unidades finales de muestreo): 14 000 hogares.

Fracción de muestreo: No se proporcionó información. La tasa de muestreo varía según la provincia.

Marco de la muestra: Se utiliza la Muestra Principal de Zimbabwe de 1992 (ZMS 92) como marco de muestreo para la encuesta; la ZMS se preparó después del Censo de Población de 1992.

Actualización de la muestra: Antes de la encuesta, se vuelve a hacer una lista de hogares en todas las zonas de enumeración (ZE) y se actualizan los mapas de las ZE.

Rotación:

Esquema: Los hogares incluidos en la muestra principal se rotan cada tres años.

Porcentaje de unidades que permanecen en la muestra durante dos encuestas consecutivas: 0 por ciento.

Número máximo de entrevistas por unidad de muestreo: Uno.

Tiempo necesario para renovar completamente la muestra: Tres años.

Levantamiento de la encuesta:

Tipo de entrevista: La información se obtiene mediante entrevistas personales.

Número de unidades finales de muestreo por área de muestra: No se proporcionó información.

Duración del trabajo de campo:

Total: Dos semanas.

Por área de muestra: No se proporcionó información.

Organización de la encuesta: La organización de la encuesta es permanente.

Número de personas que trabajan en el campo: 160.

Substitución de las unidades finales de muestreo que no responden: No se hacen sustituciones de los hogares que no responden. Sin embargo, basándose en la experiencia adquirida, el tamaño de la muestra inicial se aumenta para tener en cuenta las no respuestas. El exceso de muestras en zonas urbanas es superior al de zonas rurales.

Estimaciones y ajustes:

Tasa de no-respuesta total: 25 por ciento.

Ajuste por no-respuesta total: Sí.

Imputación por no respuesta de ítemes: No.

Ajuste por áreas/poblaciones no abarcadas: No.

Ajuste por falta de cobertura: No.

Ajuste por exceso de cobertura: No.

Ajuste por variaciones estacionales: No corresponde.

Historia de la encuesta:

Título y fecha de la primera encuesta: La primera Encuesta sobre la Fuerza de Trabajo se realizó en febrero de 1986.

Modificaciones y revisiones significativas: No se proporcionó información.

Documentación y difusión:

Documentación:

Título de las publicaciones con los resultados de la encuesta: Central Statistical Office, Indicator Monitoring – Labour Force Survey Report (periodicidad: cada cinco años).

Survey methodology: La publicación antes mencionada contiene información metodológica sobre la encuesta.

Difusión:

Tiempo necesario para difundir los primeros datos: Unos dos años.

Información adelantada acerca de la fecha de la primera difusión pública: No se proporcionó información.

Disponibilidad de datos no publicados si se solicitan: Se pueden obtener los datos no publicados, previa solicitud escrita dirigida al Director de la Oficina Central de Estadísticas.

Disponibilidad de datos por medios informáticos: Sí.

Publications of the International Labour Office

Yearbook of Labour Statistics, 2003

The sixty-second edition of this unique reference work brings together in statistical form worldwide data on labour conditions of work in some 190 countries and territories. It provides the background information essentiai to a proper understanding of trends and developments in labour and related matters influencing ail aspects of modern society.

The *Yearbook* covers the following main topics: Economically active population, Employment, Unemployment, Hours of work, Wages, Labour cost, Consumer prices, Occupational injuries and Strikes and lockouts.

XVI + 1664 pp., hard cover ISBN 92-2-014184-1 210 Sw. frs.

Publications du Bureau international du Travail

Annuaire des statistiques du travail, 2003

Soixante deuxième édition de cet important ouvrage de référence, qui rassemble des données statistiques provenant du monde entier et portant sur la main-d'œuvre et les conditions de travail dans quelque cent quatre-vingt-dix pays et territoires. L'*Annuaire* contient des informations de base indispensables à qui veut suivre les questions de main-d'œuvre et les problèmes connexes dont l'influence s'exerce dans tous les domaines de la société moderne.

L'*Annuaire* porte sur les principaux sujets suivants: Population active, Emploi, Chômage, Durée du travail, Salaires, Coût de la main-d'œuvre, Prix à la consommation, Lésions professionnelles et Grèves et lock-out.

XVI + 1664 pp., relié ISBN 92-2-014184-1 210 fr. suisses

Publicaciones de la Oficina Internacional del Trabajo

Anuario de Estadísticas del Trabajo, 2003

Sexagésima segunda edición de esta importante obra de referencia, en la que se reúnen datos estadísticos procedentes de todo el mundo relativos a la mano de obra y a las condiciones de trabajo en unos ciento noventa países y territorios. El *Anuario* comprende informaciones básicas indispensables para todo el que se ocupe de cuestiones sociales y del trabajo y de los problemas conexos cuya influencia se deja sentir en todos los campos de la sociedad moderna.

El *Anuario* abarca los principales temas siguientes: Población económicamente activa, Empleo, Desempleo, Horas de trabajo, Salarios, Costo de la mano de obra, Precios al consumidor, Lesiones profesionales y Huelgas y cierres patronales.

XVI + 1664 pp., empastado ISBN 92-2-014184-1 210 francos suizos

Just published

Vient de paraître

Acaba de aparecer

STATISTICS ON OCCUPATIONAL WAGES AND HOURS OF WORK AND ON FOOD PRICES

OCTOBER INQUIRY RESULTS, 2001 AND 2002

STATISTIQUES DES SALAIRES ET DE LA DURÉE DU TRAVAIL PAR PROFESSION ET DES PRIX DES PRODUITS ALIMENTAIRES

RÉSULTATS DE L'ENQUÊTE D'OCTOBRE, 2001 ET 2002

ESTADISTICAS SOBRE SALARIOS Y HORAS DE TRABAJO POR OCUPACION Y PRECIOS DE ARTICULOS ALIMENTICIOS

RESULTADOS DE LA ENCUESTA DE OCTUBRE, 2001 Y 2002

2003

Special supplement to the *Bulletin of Labour Statistics*

Supplément spécial au *Bulletin des statistiques du travail*

Suplemento especial al *Boletín de Estadísticas del Trabajo*

Price: 35 Swiss francs
Prix: 35 francs suisses
Precio: 35 francos suizos

ISSN 1020-0134
ISBN 92-2-014185-X